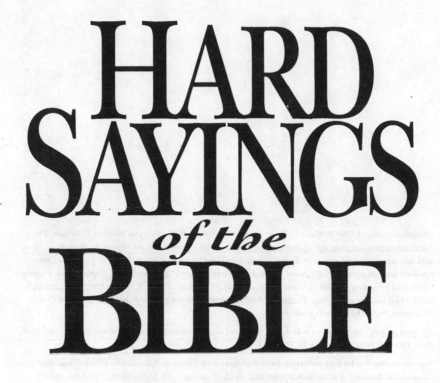

HARD SAYINGS *of the* BIBLE

Walter C. Kaiser Jr.
Peter H. Davids
F. F. Bruce
Manfred T. Brauch

InterVarsity Press
Downers Grove, Illinois

InterVarsity Press® is the book-publishing division of InterVarsity Christian Fellowship®, a student movement active on campus at hundreds of universities, colleges and schools of nursing in the United States of America, and a member movement of the International Fellowship of Evangelical Students. For information about local and regional activities, write Public Relations Dept., InterVarsity Christian Fellowship, 6400 Schroeder Rd., P.O. Box 7895, Madison, WI 53707-7895.

ISBN 0-8308-1423-X
Printed in the United States of America ♾

Old Testament

New Testament

Publisher's Preface

WITH OVER A QUARTER million copies in print, the Hard Sayings series has proved itself among readers as a helpful guide to Bible difficulties. The series was launched with the publication of F. F. Bruce's *The Hard Sayings of Jesus* in 1983, with subsequent volumes appearing in 1988, 1989, 1991 and 1992. Those volumes included *Hard Sayings of the Old Testament* and *More Hard Sayings of the Old Testament,* by Walter C. Kaiser Jr., and *Hard Sayings of Paul* and *More Hard Sayings of the New Testament,* by Manfred T. Brauch and Peter H. Davids, respectively. This edition combines the five earlier versions with new material from Walter Kaiser and Peter Davids. Over one hundred new verses have been added to the list of texts explained, as well as a dozen introductory articles addressing common questions that recur throughout the Bible. The result is that all of the Old Testament texts have been addressed by Walter Kaiser; F. F. Bruce's work is confined to the Synoptic Gospels, with one addition to the Gospel of John; Manfred Brauch's work is confined to Paul's epistles; and Peter Davids's contribution ranges throughout the whole of the New Testament. The general introduction that follows distills the key introductory remarks from the various authors of the separate pieces.

The authors share the conviction that the Bible is God's inspired and authoritative word to the church, but careful readers will observe that they do not all agree on the best solutions to certain Bible difficulties. This is as it should be. If everyone agreed on the best solutions to these questions, they wouldn't be hard sayings.

What F. F. Bruce wrote in his introduction to *The Hard Sayings of Jesus* can likely be said of nearly all the difficult texts in this collection: they may be hard for two different reasons. First are those that, because of differences in culture and time, are hard to understand without having their social and historical backgrounds explained. Second are those that are all too easily understood but that challenge the ways we think and act. As Mark Twain reportedly once remarked, it wasn't the parts of the Bible that he didn't understand that bothered him but those parts that were perfectly clear.

This volume is published with the hope that the former kinds of difficulties may have some helpful light shined on them. We hope, however, in the name of explanation, never to blunt the force of latter kinds of difficulties, where God's Word confronts us to change and conform us into the image of Jesus Christ.

How to Use This Book

FOLLOWING THE GENERAL introduction and a group of twelve introductory essays addressing common questions from throughout the Bible, the hard sayings of the Bible are organized canonically by chapter and verse, running from Genesis to Revelation. Cross-references point readers to comments on other Bible passages or to introductory essays which touch on the same or similar issues. Thus in the comment on Genesis 2:17 on the death of Adam and Eve, readers are referred to the discussion on Romans 5:12. Or readers looking up Mark 5:11-13 to find a discussion of the destruction of the pigs will find themselves referred to the parallel passage in Matthew 8:31-32 for an explanation.

In some cases where there are two or more separate comments on similar Bible passages, readers may discover that different points of view are put forward. This is due to the multiple authorship of this book and the fact that the authors do not always agree on the best solution to certain difficulties. The publisher has felt that readers will be best served by knowing that a variety of solutions have been proposed and by being able to think through for themselves which solutions best satisfy their questions.

The Scripture index at the back of the book will help readers find comments on any Bible passage that is mentioned in the book, whether it is listed as a hard saying or not. The subject index will help readers find comments on issues that they might not otherwise be able to locate or which have not been cross-referenced because of concern for space. For example, *the fear of the LORD* is mentioned so often in Scripture that we have not cross-referenced the many verses where the phrase occurs. The page reference for Proverbs 1:7, where the issue is specifically addressed, will be found in the subject index.

Abbreviations

AB	Anchor Bible
ASV	American Standard Version
AV	Authorized Version
ERV	English Revised Version
JB	Jerusalem Bible
KJV	King James Version
LB	Living Bible
NAB	New American Bible
NASB	New American Standard Bible
NEB	New English Bible
NIV	New International Version
NRSV	New Revised Standard Version
RSV	Revised Standard Version
TEV	Today's English Version

General Introduction

IN ONE SENSE THE TITLE of this book is incorrect. Very little of what is included in this work, outside of the Gospels, is a "saying" of anyone. The title, in fact, is taken from John's Gospel, where Jesus' ministry was recorded as a series of sayings. In John 6:60, responding to one such saying, his disciples observe, "This is a hard teaching ["hard saying" KJV]. Who can accept it?" From this verse came the title of the original work in this series, F. F. Bruce's *The Hard Sayings of Jesus.* Even though the literature under consideration in this volume lies mostly outside the Gospels, the title is still applicable.

Hard Sayings of the Old Testament

All too often people tell me (Walter Kaiser) they have tried to read through the Old Testament but find too much of it hard to understand. Despite their good intentions, many have abandoned the project out of sheer frustration, discouragement or puzzlement. It is not surprising that so many people find the Bible difficult, for our culture has lost contact with the Old Testament. Thus the book remains a closed document and often is treated as an artifact of our primitive origins.

Nothing, of course, could be further from the truth! The Old Testament contains some of the most fascinating and dramatic portions of the entire Bible. Furthermore, if we decide its message is irrelevant to our generation, we are misled by our own false assumptions.

Following our Lord's example, we should take up the Old Testament once again, confident that not even one passage will pass away until all have been fulfilled (Mt 5:18). In fact, the Old Testament is so relevant that our Lord warned that anyone who breaks the least Old Testament commandment, or teaches others to do so, will be called the least in the kingdom of heaven! That ought to give us pause!

The discussion here of Old Testament passages is a response to the cries of thousands of laity (and "tell it not in Gath," clergy as well!). I have tried to answer some of the more difficult sayings which fall into two categories: sayings for which no explanation appears to be given and sayings which seem to contradict other portions of Scripture. Admittedly, the choice of particular hard sayings is somewhat arbitrary and reflects my own experience addressing students' questions for the past thirty years.

Why should we contemplate hard sayings at all? The obvious answer is that scores of serious readers want to understand the difficult issues in Scripture. Besides this, by wrestling with Scripture, we can sharpen our attention to the details in all of our Lord's Word. Thus the more intently and patiently we examine the text, the more handsome the dividends to our spiritual growth.

It was the famous Bishop Whately who commented,

> The seeming contradictions in scripture are too numerous not to be the result of design; and doubtless were designed, not as mere difficulties to try our faith and patience, but as furnishing the most suitable mode of introduction that could have been devised by mutually explaining and modifying and limiting or extending one another's meaning. (*On Difficulties in the Writings of St. Paul,* Essay VII, sec. 4)

He continued:

> Instructions thus conveyed are evidently more striking and more likely to arouse attention; and thus, from the very circumstance that they call for careful reflection, more likely to make a lasting impression.

Others may debate the deliberate design of the difficulties (for often the problem results from our distance from the idiom of that day), but there can be no debate over the therapeutic effect that they produce through our increased efforts to understand and obey God's Word.

Disagreements within Scripture also supply strong incidental proof that there was no collusion among the sacred writers. The variations, instead, go a long way toward establishing the credibility of both the writers and their texts.

These hard sayings also may be viewed as a test of our commitment to Christ. Difficult passages can be handy excuses for begging off and following the Savior no longer. Our Lord spoke in parables for just this reason: so that some who thought they saw, perceived and heard would actually miss seeing, perceiving and hearing (Mk 4:12). Indeed, the apparent harshness and obscurity of some of our Lord's sayings rid him of followers who were unwilling to be taught or were halfhearted in their search (Jn 6:66). They were not willing to look beyond the surface of the issues.

The matter remains where Butler in his famous *Analogy* left it: These hard sayings afford "opportunity to an unfair mind for explaining away and deceitfully hiding from itself that evidence which it might see" (*Analogy,* Part II, ch. vi). For those who seek an occasion to cavil at difficulties, the opportunity is hereby offered in these hard sayings.

There is nothing wrong or unspiritual, of course, about doubting—so long as one continues to search for a resolution. But there are some who, as John W. Haley put it so well,

> cherish a cavilling spirit, who are bent upon misapprehending the truth, and urging captious and frivolous objections [and who] find in the inspired volume difficulties and disagreements which would seem to have been designed as stumbling-stones for those which "stumble at the word, being disobedient: whereunto also they were appointed" [1 Pet 2:8]. Upon the wilful votaries of error God sends "strong delusion, that they should believe a lie" [2 Thess 2:11], that they might work out their own condemnation and ruin. (*An Examination of the Alleged Discrepancies of the Bible,* Andover, Mass., 1874, p. 40)

That is strong medicine for our more urbane and tame ways of disagreeing with objectors today; nevertheless, the matters Haley's quote raises are highly relevant to the discussion of hard sayings.

Before we launch into the hard sayings, perhaps it would be helpful to review some of the background studies on the nature, origin and reasons for biblical discrepancies.

Any observant Bible reader who compares statements of the Old Testament with those of the New Testament, statements of different writers within either Testament, or even at times different passages within the same book will notice that there are apparent discrepancies. These statements, taken at face value, seem to contradict one another.

The Christian church has held over the centuries that there is an essential unity of the Holy Scriptures, that they form a divine library that is consistent and unified in its approach and teaching. Alas, however, as the scope of lay readership and the depth of scholarship have increased, an ever-increasing supply of alleged discrepancies and hard sayings has demanded attention.

Why are there so many discrepancies and difficulties? There are a great number of sources to which we can trace them: errors of copyists in the manuscripts that have been handed down to us; the practice of using multiple names for the same person or place; the practice of using different methods for calculating official years, lengths of regencies and events; the special scope and purpose of individual authors, which sometimes led them to arrange their material topically rather than chronologically; and differences in the position from which an event or object was described and employed by the various writers.

All of these factors, and more, have had a profound influence on the material. Of course, to those who participated in the events and times these factors were less of a barrier than they are to us. Our distance from the times and culture exacerbates the difficulty. Specific issues might be mentioned here as illustrations of the wider field of difficulties. For example, the present Hebrew text of 1 Samuel 13:1 is a classic illustration of an early copyist's error that has continued to be unsolved to the present day. Literally, the Hebrew text reads: "Saul was a year old ['son of a year' in Hebrew] when he began to reign and two years he reigned over Israel." It is clear that the writer is following the custom of recording the monarch's age when he took office, along with the total number of years that he reigned. But it is also clear that the numbers have been lost and that this omission is older than the Greek Septuagint translation, made in the third century B.C. So far the Dead Sea Scrolls and all other ancient manuscripts have left us without a clue as to what the text should read.

The selectivity of the writers, in accord with their purposes in writing, can be illustrated from the genealogy that appears in Exodus 6:13-27. Instead of listing all twelve sons of Jacob, the writer is content to treat Reuben (v. 14), Simeon (v. 15) and Levi (vv. 16-25). Here he stops, even though he has listed only the first three sons of Jacob, because the sons of Levi, and particularly his descendants Moses and Aaron, are his special interest. So he does not proceed further.

In treating some of these issues, I have chosen not to focus on points of tension that arise from such factual elements as time, history, culture and science. Instead, I have listened for points of tension in doctrine and ethics within the books or between authors of the Bible. I have included a few illustrations of difficulties having to do with facts, but my main emphasis is on theological and ethical questions.

Hard Sayings of Jesus

Many of those who listened to Jesus during his public ministry found some of his sayings "hard" and said so. Many of those who read his sayings today, or hear them read in church, also find them hard, but do not always think it fitting to say so.

Our Lord's sayings were all of a piece with his actions and with his way of life in general. The fewer preconceptions we bring from outside to the reading of the Gospels, the more clearly shall we see him as he really was. It is all too easy to believe in a Jesus who is largely a construction of our own imagination—an inoffensive person whom no one would really trouble to crucify. But the Jesus whom we meet in the Gospels, far from being an inoffensive person, gave offense right and left. Even his loyal followers found him, at times, thoroughly disconcerting. He upset all established notions of religious propriety. He spoke of God in terms of intimacy which sounded like blasphemy. He seemed to enjoy the most questionable company. He set out with open eyes on a road which, in the view of "sensible" people, was bound to lead to disaster.

But in those who were not put off by him he created a passionate love and allegiance which death could not destroy. They knew that in him they had found the way of acceptance, peace of conscience, life that was life indeed. More than that: in him they came to know God himself in a new way; here was the life of God being lived out in a real human life and communicating itself through him to them. And there are many people today who meet Jesus, not in Galilee and Judaea but in the Gospel record, and become similarly aware of his powerful attractiveness, entering into the same experience as those who made a positive response to him when he was on earth.

One reason for the complaint that Jesus' sayings were hard was that he made his hearers think. For some people, thinking is a difficult and uncomfortable exercise, especially when it involves the critical reappraisal of firmly held prejudices and convictions, or the challenging of the current consensus of opinion. Any utterance, therefore, which invites them to engage in this kind of thinking is a hard saying. Many of Jesus' sayings were hard in this sense. They suggested that it would be good to reconsider things that every reasonable person accepted. In a world where the race was to the swift and the battle to the strong, where the prizes of life went to the pushers and the go-getters, it was preposterous to congratulate the unassertive types and tell them that they would inherit the earth or, better still, possess the kingdom of heaven. Perhaps the Beatitudes were, and are, the hardest of Jesus' sayings.

For the Western world today the hardness of many of Jesus' sayings is all the greater because we live in a different culture from that in which they were uttered and speak a different language from his. He appears to have spoken Aramaic for the most part, but with few exceptions his Aramaic words have not been preserved. His words have come down to us in a translation, and that translation—the Greek of the Gospels—has to be retranslated into our own language. But when the linguistic problems have been resolved as far as possible and we are confronted by his words in what is called a "dynamically equivalent" version—that is, a version which aims at producing the same effect in us as the original words produced in their first hearers—the removal of one sort of difficulty may result in the raising of another.

For to us there are two kinds of hard saying: there are some which are hard to understand, and there are some which are only too easy to understand. When sayings of Jesus which are hard in the former sense are explained in dynamically equivalent terms, then they are likely to become hard in the latter sense. Mark Twain spoke for many when he said that the things in the Bible that bothered him were not those that he did not understand but those that he did understand. This is particularly true of the sayings of Jesus. The better we understand them, the harder they are to take. (Perhaps, similarly, this is why some religious people show such hostility to modern versions of the Bible: these versions make the meaning plain, and the plain meaning is unacceptable.)

If in the following pages I (F. F. Bruce) explain the hard sayings of Jesus in such a way as to make them more acceptable, less challenging, then the probability is that the explanation is wrong. Jesus did not go about mouthing pious platitudes; had he done so, he would not have made as many enemies as he did. "The common people heard him gladly," we are told—more gladly, at any rate, than members of the religious establishment did—but even among the common people many were disillusioned when he turned out not to be the kind of leader they hoped he would be.

The view of the interrelatedness of the Synoptic Gospels taken in this work does not greatly affect the exposition of the hard sayings, but it will be as well to state briefly here what that view is. It is that the Gospel of Mark provided Matthew and Luke with one of their major sources; that Matthew and Luke shared another common source, an arrangement of sayings of Jesus set in a brief narrative framework (not unlike the arrangement of the prophetic books of the Old Testament); and that each of the Synoptic Evangelists had access also to sources of information not used by the others. (The material common to Matthew and Luke but not found in Mark is conventionally labeled Q. The teaching peculiar to Matthew is labeled M; that peculiar to Luke is labeled L.) It helps at times to see how one Evangelist understood his predecessor by recasting or amplifying his wording.

Some of the sayings appear in different contexts in different Gospels. On this it is often said that Jesus must not be thought incapable of repeating himself. This is freely conceded: he may well have used a pithy saying on a variety of occasions. There is no reason to suppose that he said "He who has ears to hear, let him hear" or "Many are called, but few are chosen" once only. But there are occasions when a saying, indicated by comparative study to have been spoken in one particular set of circumstances, is assigned to different contexts by different Evangelists or different sources. There are other principles of arrangement than the purely chronological: one writer may group a number of sayings together because they deal with the same subject matter or have the same literary form; another, because they have a common keyword (like the sayings about fire and salt in Mark 9:43-50).

Where there is reason to think that an Evangelist has placed a saying in a topical rather than a chronological setting, it can be interesting to try to decide what its chronological setting in the ministry of Jesus probably was. For example, it has been suggested that the saying "You are Peter," which Matthew (alone of the Synoptic Evangelists) includes in the report of Jesus' interchange with the disciples at Caesarea Philippi (see comment on Mt 16:18-19), may have belonged chronologically to another occasion, such as Jesus' appearance to Peter in resurrection. Even more speculative is the interpretation of some of the sayings as words of Jesus spoken not during his public ministry but later, through the mouth of a prophet in the early church. It has been thought best in this work not to engage in such speculation but to treat the sayings primarily in the contexts provided for them by the Evangelists.

Again, this does not seem to be the place for an enquiry into the question whether the sayings examined are authentic sayings of Jesus or not. To help students in answering such a question some scholars have formulated "criteria of authenticity" for application to the sayings recorded in the Gospels. One scholar, who attached great importance to these criteria, told me a few years ago that he had concluded that among all the sayings ascribed to Jesus in the Gospels, only six, or at most eight, could be accepted as undoubtedly his. The reader of this work will realize that it is written from a less skeptical viewpoint than that. Let this be said, however: the fact that a saying is hard is no ground for suspecting that Jesus did not say it. On the contrary, the harder it is, the more likely it is to be genuine.

The second volume of the *Encyclopaedia Biblica,* published in 1901, contained a long and important entry on "Gospels" by a Swiss scholar, P. W. Schmiedel. In the course of this he listed a number of sayings of Jesus and other passages which, to his mind, ran so much counter to the conception of Jesus which quickly became conventional in the church that no one could be thought to have invented them. He therefore regarded their authenticity as beyond dispute and proposed to treat them as "the foundation-pillars for a truly scientific life of Jesus." Several of them will come up for inspection in the following pages, for whether in Schmiedel's sense or otherwise, they are certainly hard sayings.

In the interpretation of the sayings quoted I am, of course, indebted to many other interpreters. Some acknowledgment of my indebtedness is made in the following pages. There is one interpreter, however, to whom I am conscious of a special debt: that is the late Professor T. W. Manson, particularly in respect of his two works *The Teaching of Jesus* and *The Sayings of Jesus*. From the latter of these works I take leave to borrow words which will supply a fitting conclusion to my introductory remarks:

> It will simplify the discussion if we admit the truth at the outset: that the teaching of Jesus is difficult and unacceptable because it runs counter to those elements in human nature which the twentieth century has in common with the first—such things as laziness, greed, the love of pleasure, the instinct to hit back and the like. The teaching as a whole shows that Jesus was well aware of this and recognized that here and nowhere else lay the obstacle that had to be surmounted.

Hard Sayings of Paul

The theme for my (Manfred Brauch) contribution to this book is contained in 2 Peter 3:15-16. Here we are told that the apostle Paul's writings, which speak everywhere of our Lord's gracious and patient work leading to our salvation, have in them "some things that are hard to understand, which ignorant and unstable people distort, as they do the other Scriptures, to their own destruction." Several basic insights emerge from this text which provide an important starting point for my explanations.

First, it is clear that Paul's writings, which come roughly from the period A.D. 50-65, had already begun to circulate rather widely. Second Peter 3:16 refers to "all his letters." Since Paul wrote to churches and individuals across the Greco-Roman empire—from Rome in the West to Galatia in the East—some years must have elapsed for Paul's letters to have become known, distributed and read throughout the churches. Perhaps several decades had elapsed since Paul penned his epistles.

Second, Paul's letters had already attained quite a measure of authority. Though it is doubtful that Paul's writings were at this time already seen on a par with sacred Scriptures (that is, our Old Testament, which was early Christianity's Bible), the reference to "the other Scriptures" certainly indicates that the writings of Christ's apostle to the Gentiles are seen as an extension of the authoritative Word both of the Lord who meets us in the

Old Testament and of Christ, the Lord of the church.

Third, Peter's reference to "hard sayings" in Paul's letters shows that, as early as sometime in the second half of the first century, Christians in the churches had a difficult time accepting or understanding or properly applying certain of Paul's sayings. Now if this was true within the first few decades subsequent to the writing of Paul's letters, how much more is that likely the case for us, who are removed from Paul's time not only by the passing of about two thousand years, but also by such important aspects of human experience as history and culture and language. If it was possible back then to misunderstand or even twist the meaning of certain of Paul's sayings, it is very likely that this possibility is even greater for us.

A leading continental scholar of the last century, Adolf von Harnack, once said that the only one who ever really understood Paul was the second-century heretic Marcion, but that even he misunderstood Paul. Harnack's point was that Marcion clearly grasped the radical nature of Paul's gospel—namely, that salvation comes by God's grace, not by obedience to the Law—but that Marcion's rejection of the Old Testament on the basis of Paul's gospel represented a misunderstanding of Paul.

Thus, from the very early years of Christians' use of Paul's letters, the possibility of either understanding or misunderstanding, of either proper or improper use, have been ever-present realities. For us Christians today, this fact ought to give both humility and hope. There may be times when, after careful and thorough study of a text, we should in all humility acknowledge that we simply cannot grasp the meaning or know definitely what the writer intends the reader to grasp. But there is always also the hope that careful study—always under the guidance of the Spirit—will lead us to a hearing of the hard sayings in such a way that God's Word can do its work in our lives.

The selection of hard sayings of Paul emerges from my experience as a Christian, a student and a teacher. In personal study, in work with college and seminary students, and in countless discussions with Christians in churches and non-Christians in the academy, these texts have again and again emerged as "problem texts." Some thoroughly confuse readers or create unresolved tension between the meaning of one text and another. Others seem obscure or unclear. Still others lead to different misunderstandings. And a few appear to be so out of character with the overall meaning and intention of the gospel that they meet with opposition or outright rejection, even by some who are deeply committed to the authority of the Bible for Christian faith and life.

It is my hope to make a positive contribution in the continuing effort to provide a clearer understanding of some of the hard sayings of the epistle literature.

Understanding and Interpreting Paul's Epistles

The reading and study of any writing, if it is to be faithful to the author's purpose, must take seriously at least three things: (1) the nature of the writing itself, (2) the purpose for which it was written and (3) the situation or context out of which it was written. Failure to observe these matters is more likely than not to lead to misunderstanding or misinterpretation.

In this section I (Manfred Brauch) will discuss the matters of nature, purpose and situation, giving particular attention to principles of biblical interpretation which will assist in the study of Paul's epistles.

But before we begin we must also recognize that every interpreter of Scripture, including me, comes to the text with certain assumptions about the material to be studied. I want you to know before we begin what my assumptions are.

In approaching the hard sayings of Paul, I write self-consciously from within the evangelical tradition of theology, personal faith and commitment. I write from a perspective that cherishes this heritage's deep and central commitment to the Bible as the ultimate criterion for our understanding and application of God's self-revelation, which finds its ultimate expression in the Incarnation. The fundamental affirmation of evangelical faith with regard to the Bible is that we have in this word of God's gracious self-disclosure an authentic, reliable record of God's truth and purposes which, when responded to in faith, leads to restored relationships with God and our fellow human beings. Scripture—including these hard sayings—is our authoritative, infallible guide for faith and life.

Having stated this presupposition, which is at its core an affirmation of faith, I must immediately admit that such a commitment does not in and of itself determine the interpretation of any scriptural text. What it does do is set a tone and provide limits. It means that if you share that assumption with me, we approach the texts, recognizing that they are more than the result of human thought and theological reflection—that they emerge from the ministry and teaching of Christ's commissioned apostles, who were led and inspired by the Spirit of Christ in their ministry of writing.

This assumption about the Bible also means that we cannot simply bypass, ignore or reject texts which may be difficult to reconcile with other aspects of Scripture or whose meaning or instruction we find difficult to accept. Our starting point obligates us to take such sayings with utmost seriousness, seeking to understand what they mean, why they were written, and what implications for our faith and life they have.

Such an obligation brings us directly into the arena of biblical hermeneutics, or interpretation, where persons who are equally committed to the assumptions about the inspiration and authority of the Bible stated above often come to different conclusions. The extent of such differences can be greatly reduced when we come to the hermeneutical task with equal commitment to take seriously the three items mentioned above: the nature of the writings, the situations out of which they were written, and the purposes for which they were written. To these matters we shall now turn.

The Nature and Purpose of Scripture. When we are concerned with the nature and purpose of the biblical text, we are immediately confronted with the issue of its authority, with its character as the Word of God. How are we to understand this authoritative character in light of the fact that the biblical record consists of the writings of a great variety of persons in different historical periods in response to a host of events and situations and experiences?

To answer this question we need to be faithful to the intention of Scripture and take with utmost seriousness the fact that God's final, ultimate form of self-disclosure is the Incarnation.

In 2 Timothy 3:15-17 Paul speaks clearly about the nature of Scripture and its purpose: "You have known the holy Scriptures, which are able to make you wise for salvation through faith in Christ Jesus. All Scripture is God-breathed and is useful for teaching, rebuking, correcting and training in righteousness, so that the man of God may be thoroughly equipped for every good work."

It is divine inspiration that gives to the Bible its authoritative character. And that inspiration, while clearly enunciated in 2 Timothy, is implicitly affirmed throughout the New and Old Testaments by the use of such formulas as "God has said" or "the Holy Spirit spoke" (2 Cor 6:16; Acts 1:16). God and Scripture were so intimately linked that "what Scripture says" and "what God says" could be equated (Rom 9:17; Gal 3:8). Jesus' use of and attitude toward the Old Testament strongly confirms this sense of Scripture's divine origin and content (see, for example, Mt 5:17-18; Jn 10:35). It is also clear from the New Testament that the words of Jesus and the witness of Jesus' apostles share the same inspiration and authority of the Old Testament (see, for example, Jn 10:25; 12:49; 1 Cor 2:13; 1 Thess 2:13; Heb 3:7).

That the Bible claims inspiration is evident then. But what is its intention? What is God's purpose for it? To make us wise for salvation, says Paul, and for teaching, rebuking, correcting and training in righteousness (2 Tim 3:15-16).

The biblical writings were written "to teach us, so that through endurance and the encouragement of the Scriptures we might have hope" (Rom 15:4). This redemptive purpose of inspired Scripture is also the point of John 20:31: "These are written that you may believe that Jesus is the Christ, the Son of God, and that by believing you may have life in his name."

The Acts 8 story of Philip's encounter with the Ethiopian is also instructive here. The understanding and interpretation of the Isaiah passage have one purpose: "Philip began with that very passage of Scripture and told him the good news about Jesus" (v. 35). That is the "what for," the purpose. Jesus did not recommend the Bible as a book of divinely given facts about things in general (science, history, anthropology, cosmology). Rather, he pointed to the Old Testament and said: "These are the Scriptures that testify about me" (Jn 5:39). If our study of Scripture is isolated from these explicit purposes, our attempts to understand the hard sayings may prove futile.

The fact that the writers of our biblical documents were inspired does not mean that they were stripped of their limitations in knowledge, memory or language as specific human beings in certain periods of history. The presence of this human reality in Scripture has been acknowledged throughout the church's history. From Origen through Augustine to the Reformers and beyond, the reality of God's accommodation in Scripture to human weakness and limitation has been affirmed. The condescension of a nurse or a schoolmaster to the limitation of children has been used as an analogy. God stooped down to us and spoke the language of the recipients so that we might hear and understand him.

And we must recognize that it is precisely some of these accommodations to human limitations which make some of Paul's and other biblical writers' words difficult for us to understand, even while we continue to recognize the full authority of their words. Just as Jesus was fully human and yet fully divine—subject to human limitations and yet without sin—so Scripture, while manifesting many of the limitations of its human character, is yet fully God's authoritative Word to us.

While the paradoxical mystery of this juxtaposition of both the human and the divine—in the Incarnation of the living Word and in the written Word—defies final explication, the Gospel of Luke provides us with a key toward understanding. Luke presents Jesus as "conceived by the Spirit" and endowed with the Spirit at his baptism; as the one who, "full of the Spirit," is "led by the Spirit" into the wilderness; as the one who inaugurates his ministry "in the power of the Spirit" (Lk 1—4). For Luke the presence and power of the Spirit mediate the divine reality of Jesus in and through the human limitations. It is the Spirit who makes the incarnate Jesus' human words and actions effective. In his words and actions, God speaks and acts. Such an understanding of the Incarnation, when applied to Scripture, underlines its full humanity (with all that this implies regarding the presence of limitation) and its full divinity (with all that this implies about its authority). The hearing and believing of the divine authority, in and through the fully human, is made possible by the Spirit.

Recognizing both (1) the purpose for which the writers were inspired and (2) the limiting human form and context within which their inspiration took place is frequently an important key in understanding Paul's hard sayings.

The Context of Biblical Texts. Beyond this general understanding of the nature and purpose of the Bible, the specific situations of particular biblical documents have an important bearing on our interpretation and understanding. Though it is necessary to keep this fact in mind regarding each biblical book, the "situational nature" of the Epistles is especially noteworthy.

The Epistles are occasional documents, that is, they were written for specific occasions in the life of Christian congregations or individuals. They respond to questions which have been communicated to the writer (1 and 2 Thess), deal with problems in the church (1 Cor), carry on a debate with a false understanding of the gospel (Gal), nurture hope in a time of persecution (1 Pet) and seek to provide guidance for a pastor in a situation where false teachings and speculative mythology are threatening the integrity of the gospel and the stability of Christian community (1 and 2 Tim).

In addition to these unique needs which called forth the writing of the Epistles, the historical and cultural contexts of the recipients must also be recognized as factors which bear on our interpretation. Thus, when Paul addresses himself to the place of women in the worship of the church in Corinth and calls for certain restrictions, it is important to ask "Why does he give those instructions?" and to recognize that the cultural-religious environment in Corinth may have made these restrictions necessary in that particular situation, whereas in other situations such restrictions were not called for. Or when we read in 1 Timothy 2:11-12 that women are to "learn in quietness" and that they are not permitted "to teach or to have authority over a man," it is of critical importance to recognize that one of the major problems in Timothy's pastoral context was the presence of heretical teachings and mystical speculations, most likely perpetuated by leading women in that particular congregation. For in other early church settings, women were clearly involved in leadership, as well as in teaching and preaching functions.

The consideration of context probably introduces the most difficult issue in the whole task of interpretation: How can we discern between that which is culturally or historically conditioned and that which is transcultural or transhistorical? When is an apostolic instruction an inspired, authoritative word for a particular context in an early church setting and applicable only to that situation, and when is an inspired, authoritative instruction an absolute norm for any and all situations and contexts from the early church to this present day?

The effort to discern between those things which are culturally and historically relative and those which are transcendent is in actuality engaged in by all Christians, in one way or another. At issue is only whether such discernment results from our likes and dislikes, our own cultural conditioning and prejudices, or whether it is the application of a clear principle that emerges from a proper understanding of the nature and purpose of Scripture.

Take, for example, the issue of head coverings. Most Christians have concluded that the "head covering" enjoined upon women during worship in the church in Corinth (1 Cor 11) is culturally relative, and its inspired authority is limited to that historical situation. Many of these same Christians have concluded, at the same time, that Paul's instruction to these women to be silent in worship (1 Cor 14) is not culturally relative and is an authoritative word for all Christian women in all contexts of worship, both then and now.

On what basis is this distinction made? Arbitrariness in this critical and necessary area of biblical interpretation can to some extent be avoided when we recognize that there are different types of texts, and that these differences provide us with clues to discerning that which is relative to the situation and that which is authoritative for all time.

In an article in *Essays on New Testament Christianity,* S. Scott Bartchy gathers texts which deal directly or indirectly with the place and role of women in the ministry of Jesus and the early church into three broad categories: (1) normative (or instructive) texts, (2) descriptive texts and (3) problematic (or corrective) texts. These categories are extremely helpful for purposes of our discussion.

Instructive texts are those which declare the way things ought to be among the followers of Christ. They declare the vision or intention of the gospel without reference to particular problem situations. As such they transcend the contexts in which they are uttered and are normative for both individual and corporate Christian existence. The citation of Joel 2:28-32 in Peter's Pentecost speech (Acts 2:17-21), stating that the Spirit of God was given to both men and women for proclaiming the good news, is such a text.

Descriptive texts describe practices or actions in the early churches without any commentary. The sense conveyed in such texts is that what is described is perfectly acceptable or normal. The writer does not question the practice but rather seems to assume it as appropriate. Thus Luke, in Acts 18:24-26, tells us that both Priscilla and Aquila instructed the learned Apollos in the Christian faith, and in Acts 21:9 mentions that the evangelist Philip had four daughters who were engaged in the prophetic ministry of the church. Women's participation in ministry seems not to have been unusual.

Corrective texts are those which clearly deal with special situations or problems or misunderstandings in the Christian communities which are addressed. Here it is particularly important to understand as much as possible the situation which made the corrective, authoritative, apostolic word necessary for that situation. The problem of heretical teaching, addressed in 1 Timothy, is such a situation. Paul's instruction about the silence of women must be seen in this light. What we must guard against is the temptation to universalize instructions whose primary or exclusive focus was on the situation addressed.

An important dimension of this threefold classification for the interpretation and understanding of a good number of our hard sayings is the matter of their interrelationships. If a corrective text's admonition reflects the vision of the gospel articulated in instructive texts and is further confirmed by descriptive texts, then the particular teaching would undoubtedly be authoritative for the whole church in all times. On the other hand, if an apostolic word addressed to a particular setting does not conform to the way things ought to be (as revealed in instructive texts) and the way things normally are (as revealed in descriptive texts), then the inspired, authoritative word may very well be intended to deal exclusively with a specific problem and thus be limited to that and similar problems.

The foregoing reflections on the nature, purpose and context of biblical texts provide the parameters within which we will explore the hard sayings of Paul. For readers interested in further and more comprehensive study of the issues in biblical interpretation, I highly recommend the book *How to Read the Bible for All Its Worth* (Grand Rapids, Mich.: Zondervan, 1982) by Gordon D. Fee and Douglas Stuart.

Other Hard Sayings of the New Testament

Though not all the texts for which I (Peter Davids) will offer explanations are in the strict sense "sayings," they are "hard" for three different reasons. Some of them are hard because we do not understand them. In many cases they can be clarified simply by adding some background information. In other cases (such as some of the material in Revelation), scholars are unsure of the author's real meaning, so we can only make the best informed guess possible. In such situations dogmatism is ruled out. But any way we look at it both of these categories are the easiest of the hard sayings. Either they can be figured out or they cannot. When they are explained, no problem remains. Those that remain unexplained should serve to increase our humility about interpreting Scripture. We do not yet know all that those writers did. If we accept this proposition, we can set aside these problems.

Another group of hard sayings is doctrinally hard. That is, the saying appears to contradict some other teaching of Scripture or clashes with doctrine that Christians have held for years. The disciples' comment in John 6:60 was made about a saying such as this. Since we as Christians hold our beliefs about the teaching of Scripture deeply and sincerely, we struggle with anything that appears to threaten them. At times it is possible to explain such Scriptures and leave the doctrines intact. Perhaps we are just misunderstanding the scriptural author, and when we understand what he really meant, we can see that there is no conflict. I suspect that the explanation of James 2:24 fits this category. But at other times a real conflict exists between what the author meant and our own doctrinal understanding. This is the real test. Will Scripture be allowed to correct our doctrine, or is our doctrine the grid through which we will insist on understanding Scripture? Either Scripture or our doctrinal understanding is the Word of God. When they conflict, we find out which one we have actually accepted as our final authority.

The hard sayings in the third category are not actually hard to understand. Rather, they are hard because we do not like what they say. They are hard to obey, and we would rather they meant something else than they do. James 4:4 and 1 John 2:15 may be in this category for some people. This book will be of relatively little help with this type, except to assure each reader that the scriptural author does mean exactly what was feared. The issue remains as to whether or not the reader will obey the Scripture. When it comes to obedience, a book cannot help. Each individual reader must decide. Thus, such sayings are in one sense the hardest of all, for we struggle with them most on the personal level.

What, then, is the goal of my writing? It is to understand Scripture, especially some of the more obscure passages. By this I mean understanding what the original author intended to communicate when he wrote the words. That is, the author of each book of Scripture had something in mind when he selected the words to use in writing. My assumption is that these words, when understood within his cultural context, accurately represent what he wanted to communicate. In fact, it is a good working assumption that what an average Christian reader in the first-century context in which that book of Scripture was written would have understood by the words fairly represents what the author intended to communicate. And this is what the church has accepted as the Word of God.

The problem is that we are not first-century readers. None of us speaks Koine Greek (the language of the New Testament) fluently. Unlike most of the authors we are discussing, few of us are Jews. None of us are first-century Jews from the eastern Mediterranean world. We have not read the same books or had the same cultural experiences as the authors of Scripture had. We speak a different language.

Even our experience of the church is different. We know a world in which most churches are buildings with rows of pews and a platform of some type in the front upon which ministers of some description stand to lead worship. The authors of Scripture knew a church that met in groups of no more than sixty or so in private homes, usually at night. They sat around a table for a common meal something like a potluck supper, although for them it was the Lord's Supper. There was no such thing as ordination in our modern sense nor a difference between clergy and people. Leadership was quite fluid. Those who could lead were leaders. Furthermore, we know a church that is split into many different denominations and traditions. In the early period there was only one church, although it contained a lot of variety, even among the house churches in a given city.

We carry our Bibles into church, or take them out of the pews. The Scriptures in the early church (the Old Testament, if they could afford it, and perhaps late in the New Testament period some copies of a Gospel or two or some letters of Paul) were stored in a chest in someone's house and read aloud during meetings by one of the few members who could read. Finally, we know a church that looks back on 2000 years of history and stresses the fact that God has spoken in the Scriptures. They knew a church whose only history was the Old Testament and stories (even eyewitness accounts) about Jesus. What animated them was a common experience of the Holy Spirit and through him the living presence of Jesus in their midst. There was a dynamism (and often a risk) that even the liveliest of our groups has probably not fully captured.

With all of these differences, interpreting Scripture becomes the job of getting back into that ancient world and then understanding how it correlates with our world. To do so we will have to listen to the Old Testament and the sayings of Jesus that the authors we are dealing with certainly knew. We will also have to consult some of the works written by Jews in the period between 400 B.C. and A.D. 100, the intertestamental literature (much of it strange to our ears), which will show what first-century Jews, including the authors of Scripture, thought about various topics. In fact, one of our hard sayings, that in Jude, comes up precisely because Jude quotes some of this literature. Finally we will have to attempt to understand the culture and historical situation, for that, too, will be part of the author's understanding and something that he shares with his readers. This will enable us to translate not just the words but also the ideas of Scripture into our language.

The last stage of interpretation, however, is that of moving from the world of the New Testament into our modern world. Here we will have to be cautious. Some of the discussions and arguments Christians have had over the centuries were not issues in the first century. The New Testament authors will have nothing to say about such concerns. They may refuse to answer our questions. In other cases we may have to discover the principle that informs the author's reasoning and apply it to our modern situation. But in most of the cases the real danger is in jumping too quickly into the modern situation. If we have not taken the time to grasp fully what the author of Scripture was trying to say, we will distort his message when we move into our modern period. But if we fully grasp it, we will be able to see where it applies, although it may apply in a different place than we thought at first.

The study of Scripture is an adventure, for the God who spoke still speaks. One of his ways of speaking to us is through Scripture as we take the time and trouble to study, understand and meditate on it. It is my hope that as we explore these passages each reader will discover the power of the Scripture again as the Holy Spirit makes it alive within him or her.

The History of Hard Sayings

What has been written in this volume on the various discrepancies in the Bible stands in a long tradition of discussion on this topic. Among the early church fathers, Eusebius, Chrysostom, Augustine and Theodoret devoted whole treatises, or parts thereof, to this subject.

The subject apparently dropped out of favor from the latter part of the fifth to the beginning of the sixteenth century A.D. There are almost no extant works that can be cited on this subject for that period of time. However, the Reformation gave a whole new impetus to the study of the Bible, as well as to this subject. John W. Haley, in his magisterial 1874 work entitled *An Examination of the Alleged Discrepancies of the Bible,* was able to cite forty-two works from the Reformation or post-Reformation era dealing with this topic (pp. 437-42).

For example, a 1527 Latin work by Andreas Althamer went through sixteen editions and dealt with some 160 alleged discrepancies. Joannes Thaddaeus and Thomas Man put out a 1662 London publication with the title *The Reconciler of the Bible Inlarged* [sic], in which more than three thousand contradictions throughout the Old and New Testaments were fully and plainly reconciled. This work counted each discrepancy twice, for their earlier editions only had 1,050 cases. Furthermore, complained Haley, he included "a multitude of trivial discrepancies, and omit[ted] many of the more important [ones]."

Oliver St. John Cooper's *Four Hundred Texts of Holy Scripture with their corresponding passages explained* included only fifty-seven instances of disagreement in this 1791 London publication.

Coming to relatively more recent times, Samuel Davidson's *Sacred Hermeneutics, Developed and Applied* included 115 apparent contradictions from pages 516-611 in the 1843 Edinburgh text. In the last forty years, the most notable contributions to this subject have been the following. In 1950, George W. DeHoff wrote *Alleged Bible Contradictions* (Grand Rapids, Mich.: Baker). He dealt with the subject by taking pairs of apparently opposing texts, which he grouped under the topics of systematic theology, ethics and historical facts. This work was followed in 1951 by the reissue of John W. Haley's 1874 text *An Examination of the Alleged Discrepancies of the Bible* (Nashville: B. C. Goodpasture). This was perhaps the most complete array of brief explanations of discrepancies; they were arranged under the divisions of doctrinal, ethical and historical discrepancies. A detailed first section treated the origin, design and results of the difficulties alleged to be found in the Bible.

In 1952 Martin Ralph De Haan published his *508 Answers to Bible Questions* (Grand Rapids, Mich.: Zondervan). It included a mixture of doctrinal, factual and interpretive questions.

J. Carter Swaim contributed *Answers to Your Questions About the Bible* in 1965 (New York: Vanguard). Most of his text dealt with questions of fact rather than interpretation. Later, in 1972, F. F. Bruce published a volume entitled *Answers to Questions* (Grand Rapids, Mich.: Zondervan). With only thirty-eight pages dealing with questions from the Old Testament, this work was divided into questions about Scripture passages and other matters related to the faith. In 1979, Robert H. Mounce contributed a book with a similar title, *Answers to Questions About the Bible* (Grand Rapids, Mich.: Baker). His book had an unusually complete table of contents and dealt with a rather large number of difficulties for such a fairly brief work.

Paul R. Van Gorder added a text in 1980 called *Since You Asked* (Grand

Rapids, Mich.: Radio Bible Class). He organized his book alphabetically by topic and included a scriptural and topical index that gave a quick overview of the areas covered.

Gleason L. Archer produced a large tome in 1982 entitled *Encyclopedia of Bible Difficulties* (Grand Rapids, Mich.: Zondervan). His arrangement followed the order of the biblical books as they appear in the canon. It included a mixture of issues such as authorship of the biblical books, critical objections to some of the books and alleged contradictions and problematical interpretations.

The first in the Hard Sayings series appeared in 1983. F. F. Bruce wrote *The Hard Sayings of Jesus* (Downers Grove, Ill.: InterVarsity Press). He took up seventy sayings of Jesus that were considered "hard" either because we cannot handily interpret them or because they seem so easy to interpret that their application is puzzling.

In 1987 David C. Downing published *What You Know Might Not Be So: 220 Misinterpretations of Bible Texts Explained* (Grand Rapids, Mich.: Baker). Downing concentrated mainly on the confusion that exists between biblical passages and extrabiblical literature, myths and popular religions.

The history of this discussion is filled with the names of the great biblical scholars. Our generation, and the next, must also continue to grapple with these texts for the very reasons already outlined: to understand the Scriptures better and to increase our commitment to Christ.

1

How Do We Know Who Wrote the Bible?

THE ISSUE OF AUTHORSHIP is a difficult one. First, it covers sixty-six biblical books, and it would take a book of its own to discuss the issue properly for each of them. In fact, New Testament introductions and Old Testament introductions are books devoted to this and related issues. Second, there are a number of problems involved in defining exactly what we mean by authorship. I will tackle this second question and then give a brief answer to the first.

First, there are many books in the Bible that do not indicate who their author is. For example, only one of the four Gospels (John) gives any information about the author. Even in that case, the only information we are given is that "the disciple whom Jesus loved" is the witness whose testimony is being reported. It is not at all clear from John 21:20-25 whether "the disciple whom Jesus loved" actually wrote the Gospel (or part of the Gospel) or whether the Evangelist is telling us, "I got my stories from this man." Even if this beloved disciple actually wrote the Gospel, his name is not given. We can therefore safely say that none of the Gospels gives us the name of its author. Other books which do not give us the name of their authors include Acts, Hebrews, 1 John and all of the Old Testament historical books.

There are other instances where scholars do not agree if a particular phrase actually indicates authorship. Many of the Psalms are labeled in English "of David," and Song of Songs is labeled "of Solomon," but scholars debate whether the Hebrew means that the work is by the person named or whether it is in the style or character of that person's tradition. Commentaries make us aware of these discussions, which is one reason to read good exegetical commentaries before jumping to a conclusion about authorship. The issue in this case is not whether the attribution of authorship is inaccurate, but whether the person who put the books together (since Psalms, for example, consists of the work of several authors) intended to indicate authorship at all. It would be silly to say, "You are wrong; David did not write this or that psalm," when the compiler of Psalms would reply (if he were alive), "I never said that he did."

There is another set of books more like the Gospel of John. These works do refer to authorship, and they even give some indication of who the author is, but they do not give a name. For example, 2-3 John were written by "the elder." There is no identification of who "the elder" is. A different situation occurs in the case of Revelation, where the author is named "John," but there is no further indication of who this John is (John was a reasonably common name in some communities at that time).

Naturally, church tradition has added specific identifications in many of these books. Various church fathers stated that Mark was written by John Mark, who was recording the preaching of Peter. The "beloved disciple" and "the elder" and the "John" of Revelation were all identified with John the son of Zebedee, a member of the Twelve. Hebrews was attributed to Paul (although as early as A.D. 250 some church fathers recognized that this attribution was unlikely). However, it is important to understand that tradition may be right or it may be wrong, but *tradition is not Scripture.* In other words, we personally may find it easy to accept the idea that tradition was correct about Mark, but if someone else decides that the work was written by someone other than Mark, we are not discussing whether *Scripture* is right or wrong, but whether *tradition* is right or wrong. Such discussions have nothing to do with the accuracy of the biblical text.

Second, the fact that some biblical books have the name of an author does not mean that the author personally wrote every word in the book. Normally ancient authors used secretaries to write their works. Sometimes we know the names of these secretaries. For example, Tertius wrote Romans (Rom 16:22) and Silas (or Silvanus) probably wrote 1 Peter (1 Pet 5:12); Jeremiah's scribe was Baruch. In some cases these secretaries appear to have been given a lot of independent authority. That may account for stylistic changes among letters (for example, whoever wrote the Greek of 1 Peter did not create the much worse Greek of 2 Peter).

Authorship also does not mean that a work remained untouched for all time. Presumably someone other than Moses added the account of his death to the end of Deuteronomy. There are also notes in the Pentateuch to indicate that the names of places have been updated (for example, Gen

23:2, 19; 35:19). It is possible that other parts of the documents were also updated, but it is only in place names that one finds clear indications of this, because there the later editor includes both the original name and the updated one.

Likewise, it is probable that some works in the Bible are edited works. The book of James may well have been put together from sayings and sermons of James by an unknown editor. Daniel includes both visions of Daniel and stories about him. It would not be surprising to discover that it was a long time after Daniel before the stories and the visions were brought together and put into one book. Psalms is obviously an edited collection, as is Proverbs. We do not know what shape Moses left his works in. Did someone simply have to add an ending to Deuteronomy, or was there a need to put a number of pieces together? Probably we will never know the complete story.

The point is that a work is still an author's work even if it has been edited, revised, updated or otherwise added to. I own a commentary on James by Martin Dibelius. I still refer to it as by Martin Dibelius although I know that Heinrich Greeven revised and edited it (and then Michael A. Williams translated it into English). Dibelius died before the Dead Sea Scrolls were found, so the commentary now refers to things that Dibelius knew nothing about. Yet it is still accurate to refer to it as by Dibelius (and to put his name on the cover) because the basic work is by him.

We have also received letters from various executives with a note "signed in his (or her) absence" at the bottom after the signature. The executive in question probably told his or her secretary to reply to our letter along thus and so lines and then left the rest to be completed and mailed while they were away. It still carries the executive's authority, even if the exact wording is that of the secretary.

Therefore, when the Bible says that a certain work is by a given individual, it need not mean that the author is always responsible for every word or even for the general style. The author is considered responsible for the basic content.

Third, even understanding that a work might have been updated or edited at some time, can we trust the statements that Scripture (rather than tradition) makes about authorship? I am talking about those instances in which a work clearly indicates that Paul or whoever wrote it. The question is whether all of these books are basically by the people whom the Bible claims wrote them.

Scholars would divide on this question. Even evangelical scholars are not totally unified about how much of Isaiah was written by Isaiah son of Amoz or whether Paul actually wrote Ephesians. Yet it is also fair to say that a good case can be made for saying, "Yes, each of the works is basically by the person whom the text claims wrote it." In order to argue this in detail I would have to repeat the work of R. K. Harrison in his massive *Introduction to the Old Testament* or Donald Guthrie in his *New Testament Introduction.* Naturally, other scholars have done equally thorough jobs. In a book like this I cannot repeat that work.

However, it is worthwhile asking if authorship questions are important and why. Basically, two issues are involved. On the one hand, there is the issue of whether the Bible is accurate in what it teaches. So long as the author of Revelation was John, it does not affect the accuracy of the Bible one little bit which John the author turns out to be. All the Bible claims is that he was some John. Yet if we claim that Paul did not write Romans, it would certainly reflect on the accuracy of the Bible, for Romans clearly intends to claim that it was written by Paul of Tarsus, the apostle to the Gentiles.

Some scholars believe that pseudepigraphy (attributing one's work to another person) was accepted in the ancient world and that it would not have been considered deception. Certainly some forms of pseudepigraphy were practiced in the ancient world, yet with some possible exceptions (which would be cases in which a person in a vision thought he or she was actually experiencing something from the point of view of another person or receiving a message from them) the evidence is that pseudepigraphy was not accepted practice. That is, the person who wrote a pseudepigraphical work normally was trying to deceive others to get an authority for his or her work that it would not otherwise have had. Also, when such letters or acts were exposed they were quickly rejected and, in some cases, the author was punished. Thus the evidence does not support the idea that an author could use the name of another and expect others in the church to understand that he or she was not trying to deceive them. It does appear that the accuracy and nondeceptive character of the biblical books is at stake on this point.

On the other hand, there is the issue of the proper setting of a work. For example, if Paul wrote 1 and 2 Timothy, then they were written before the mid-60s (when Paul was executed). We know who the Caesar was and something of what was going on in the world at that time. We also know a lot about Paul's history up to that point. If we argue that Paul did not write them, we have lost a definite historical context. Even when authorship does not matter from the point of view of biblical accuracy (for example, Hebrews does not mention who wrote it), we still discuss authorship, trying to determine all that we can about it because this information helps us give a date and context to the work.

In summary, we can trust what the Bible says about authorship, but we must be careful to be sure that it is saying what we believe it to be saying. If we argue that the Bible is saying more than it actually claims, then we may end up trying to defend a position that even the biblical authors would not agree with! At the same time, accurate information on authorship assists us with interpretation by giving the work a setting in history, a context which is the background of interpretation.

2

Can We Believe in Bible Miracles?

IN THE NEW TESTAMENT we read about numerous miracles. Did these really happen, or are they simply legends or perhaps the way ancient people described what they could not explain?

First we need to look at what is at stake in this question. Both Old Testament and New Testament belief are based on miracles. In the Old Testament the basic event is that of the exodus, including the miracles of the Passover and the parting of the Red Sea. These were miracles of deliverance for Israel and judgment for her enemies. Without them the faith of the Old Testament has little meaning. In the New Testament the resurrection of Jesus is the basic miracle. Every author in the New Testament believed that Jesus of Nazareth had been crucified and on the third day had returned to life. Without this miracle there is no Christian faith; as Paul points out, "If Christ has not been raised, your faith is futile; you are still in your sins" (1 Cor 15:17). Thus in both Old and New Testaments, without miracles, biblical faith is meaningless.

The fact that miracles are at the root of biblical faith, however, does not mean that they happened. Thus we need to ask if it is possible that they did occur. Some people take a philosophical position that miracles cannot happen in that the "laws of nature" are fixed and that God, if he exists, either cannot or will not "violate" them. While this is an honestly held position, it is also outdated. The idea of firmly fixed "laws of nature" belongs to Newtonian physics, not the world of relativity, which views laws as generalities covering observations to date. The issue for us, then, is whether there is evidence that there is a force (a spiritual force) which creates those irregularities in our observations of events that we term miracles.

The response of the Bible in general and the New Testament in particular is that there is. The basic spiritual force is that of God. He, Scripture asserts, is the only fully adequate explanation for the existence of the world. His personality is the only adequate explanation for the existence of personality in human beings. What is more, because he is personal he has remained engaged with this world. Some of his engagement we see in the regular events of "nature" (Col 1:16-17; Heb 1:3), while at other times he reveals his presence by doing something differently. It is those events that we call miracles.

A miracle has two parts: event and explanation. The event is an unusual occurrence, often one which cannot be explained by the normally occurring forces which we know of. Sometimes the event itself is not unique, but its timing is, as is the case in the Old Testament with the parting of the Jordan River and at least some of the plagues of Egypt. At other times, as in the resurrection of the dead, the event itself is unique.

The explanation part of the miracle points out who stands behind the event and why he did it. If a sick person suddenly recovers, we might say, "Boy, that was odd. I wonder what happened?" Or we might say, "Since I've never seen such a thing happen, perhaps he or she was not really sick." We might even say, "This is witchcraft, the operation of a negative spiritual power." Yet if the event happens when a person is praying to God the Father in the name of Jesus, the context explains the event. So we correctly say, "God worked a miracle." Thus in the New Testament we discover that the resurrection of Jesus is explained as an act of God vindicating the claims of Jesus and exalting him to God's throne.

How do we know that such a miracle happened? It is clear that we cannot ever know for certain. On the one hand, I cannot be totally sure even of what I experience. I could be hallucinating that I am now typing this chapter on this computer keyboard. I certainly have had dreams about doing such things. Yet generally I trust (or have faith in) my senses, even though I cannot be 100 percent sure of their accuracy. On the other hand, we did not directly experience biblical miracles, although it is not unknown for Christians (including us) to have analogous experiences now, including experiences of meeting the resurrected Jesus. Still, none of us were present when the *biblical* events happened. Therefore we cannot believe on the basis of direct observation; we have to trust credible witnesses.

When it comes to the resurrection, we have more documents from closer to the time of the event than we have for virtually any other ancient event. The witnesses in those New Testament documents subscribe to the highest standards of truthfulness. Furthermore, most of them died on behalf of their witness, hardly the actions of people who were lying. They claim to have had multiple personal experiences that convinced them that Jesus had indeed risen from the dead (see 1 Cor 15:1-11). None of this *absolutely* proves that this central miracle happened. There could have been some type of a grand illusion. Yet it makes the resurrection believable enough for it to be a credible basis for faith. We see enough evidence for us to commit ourselves to, which is something that we do in everyday life constantly when we commit ourselves to something that someone has told us.

If the central miracle of the New Testament actually happened, then we have much less of a problem with any of the other miracles. Some of those same witnesses are claiming to have observed them, or to have known others who did. After the resurrection of a dead person, a healing or even the calming of a storm appear to be relatively minor. After all, if God is showing himself in one way, it would not be surprising for him to show himself in many other ways.

Miracles in the Bible have several functions. First, they accredit the messengers God sends, whether that person be Moses or a prophet or Jesus or an apostle or an ordinary Christian. Miracles are how God gives evidence that this person who claims to be from him really is from him. He "backs up their act" with his spiritual power.

Second, miracles show the nature of God and his reign. They may work God's justice, but more often they show his character as full of mercy and forgiveness. Jesus proclaimed that the kingdom of God had come. The people might rightly ask what that rule of God looked like. Jesus worked miracles which showed the nature of that reign. The blind see, the lame walk, the outcasts are brought into community, and the wild forces of nature are tamed. That is what the kingdom of God is like.

Third, miracles actually do the work of the kingdom. When one reads Luke 18, he or she discovers that it is impossible for a rich person to be saved, although with God all things are possible. Then in Luke 19:1-10 Zacchaeus, a rich man, is parted from his wealth and is saved. Clearly a miracle has happened, and the kingdom of God has come even to a rich man. The same is true of the demons being driven out, for each time this happens the borders of Satan's kingdom are driven back. Similarly, many other miracles also have this function.

So, did miracles really happen? The answer is that, yes, a historical case can be made for their happening. Furthermore, we have seen that it is important to establish that they happened. A miracle is central to Christian belief. And miracles serve important functions in certifying, explaining and doing the work of the kingdom of God.

Miracles are not simply nice stories for Sunday school. They are a demonstration of the character of God, not only in the past but also in the present.

3

Why Does God Seem So Angry in the Old Testament & Loving in the New?

WHEN MANY PEOPLE READ the Old Testament they get the impression that God is a God of wrath and judgment, but in the New Testament they find a God of love. Why is there this difference in Scripture?

This question has bothered Christians for a number of years. In the period of the church fathers Marcion pointed out this problem and suggested that the Creator God of the Old Testament was an inferior being to the God and Father of Jesus. He then set about to remove from the New Testament any influences from this "Jewish" Creator God (for example, in Gospels like Matthew), for the Creator was evil. He ended up with a shortened version of Luke as the only Gospel we should use. The church's response was to reject Marcion's teaching as heresy, to list all of the books it accepted as part of the canon and to assert that all of these were inspired by the one and same God. Still, Marcion's question remains with us.

The reality is that there is no difference between the images of God presented in the Old and New Testaments. John points this truth out when he states that "No one has ever seen God, but God the One and Only, who is at the Father's side, has made him known" (Jn 1:18). What John is pointing out is that what one sees in Jesus is precisely the character of the Father, the God of the Old Testament. There is no difference among them in character; to meet one of them is to meet them both. Thus Jesus is no more loving than his Father. The Father is no more judging than Jesus. All New Testament writers see a similar continuity between the Old Testament God and the God they experience through Jesus.

There are three points that we can make to expand on this statement: (1) there is love in the Old Testament; (2) there is judgment in the New Testament; and (3) the main difference is a difference between judgment within history and judgment at the end of history.

First, there is love in the Old Testament. God does not present himself first and foremost as a God of judgment, but as a God of love. For example, look at Exodus 34:6-7:

> And he passed in front of Moses, proclaiming, "The LORD, the LORD, the compassionate and gracious God, slow to anger, abounding in love and faithfulness, maintaining love to thousands, and forgiving wickedness, rebellion and sin. Yet he does not leave the guilty unpunished; he punishes the children and their children for the sin of the fathers to the third and fourth generation."

This is God's fundamental presentation of himself to Moses. This is who he is. Notice how he first states his compassion, grace, love, faithfulness and forgiveness. He then notes that this is not to be taken advantage of, for those who do not respond to his love will not escape. He is loving, but he is not an indulgent parent. He will bring justice.

Throughout the Old Testament God continually tells people that he chose Israel out of love, not because they were particularly deserving. When Israel rebels, he reaches out through prophets. When they continue to rebel he threatens (and then sends) judgment, but in the middle of it we find verses like Hosea 11:8, "How can I give you up?" God is anguished over the situation. On the one hand, justice demands that he act in judgment. On the other hand, his loving heart is broken over his people, and he cannot bear to see them hurting and destroyed. As he portrays in Hosea, he is the husband of an adulterous wife. What he wants to do is to gather her into his arms, but he cannot ignore her behavior. His plan is not ultimate judgment but a judgment that will turn her heart back to him so he can restore his "family."

This is not God's attitude toward Israel only. In Jonah 4:2 we read:

> He prayed to the LORD, "O LORD, is this not what I said when I was still at home? That is why I was so quick to flee to Tarshish. I knew that you are a gracious and compassionate God, slow to anger and abounding in love, a God who relents from sending calamity."

Jonah is unhappy about God's grace toward Nineveh. He was apparently quite happy about announcing that in forty days Nineveh would be destroyed, but when they repent and God forgives them, he is upset. This is not a new revelation to him, for he says, "Is this not what I said?" He seems to have hoped that if he did not deliver the warning, the people of Nineveh would not repent and would be destroyed. But God made him deliver the warning so that they would repent and he could forgive them. Jonah's complaint is, "You are too nice, too loving, too forgiving." That is the way God is portrayed with respect to a violent pagan nation, Assyria.

Jonah and Hosea are also clues to reading all of the judgment passages in the Old Testament. God is not in the judgment business but in the forgiveness business. Yet he cannot forgive those who will not repent. So he sends prophets to warn people about the judgment that will inevitably come, his hope being that the people will repent and he will not have to send the judgment. When his prophets are killed and rejected, he often sends more of them. It can take decades or even hundreds of years before he comes to the point when he knows that if justice is to mean anything at all, he must send judgment, even though he does not enjoy doing so. And even then he often sends with the judgment a promise of restoration. Every good parent knows that they must eventually punish an erring child, but no such parent enjoys doing it.

Second, there is judgment in the New Testament. A word count on *judge* or *judgment* in the New Testament in the NIV comes up with 108 verses. Even more significant is the fact that Jesus is the one who warns most about judgment. He is the one who said,

> If your right eye causes you to sin, gouge it out and throw it away. It is better for you to lose one part of your body than for your whole body to be thrown into hell. And if your right hand causes you to sin, cut it off and throw it away. It is better for you to lose one part of your body than for your whole body to go into hell. (Mt 5:29-30)

He is the one who spoke the warnings in Matthew 7:13-29 and 24:45—25:46. Indeed, Jesus talks about judgment more than anyone else in the New Testament, especially when we realize that Revelation is "the revelation of Jesus Christ" (that is, a message from Jesus).

There are several types of judgment in the New Testament. There is self-judgment (Jn 9:39; 12:47-49), the judgment of God (Jn 8:50), judgments on individuals (Acts 12:23) and final judgment (Jn 5:22, 27). There are simple statements that people doing certain things will not inherit the kingdom of God (1 Cor 6:9-10; Gal 5:19-21) and elaborate pictures of judgment scenes (Rev 20:11-15). The point is that all of these involve judgment and many of them involve Jesus. He is indeed just like his Father.

The New Testament preaches grace and love, but grace and love can be rejected. The New Testament also preaches final judgment. Everyone, according to the New Testament, is worthy of final judgment, but God is now offering grace to those who repent. Yet if people refuse this grace, there is one fearful fate awaiting them. Thus it becomes apparent how like the Old Testament the New Testament is. In the Old Testament God sent the prophets with solemn warnings of judgment and also revelations of the heart of God, who was even then ready to receive repentant people. In the New Testament God sends apostles and prophets preaching the gospel, calling people to repentance in the light of the coming judgment of God. In this respect the two Testaments are in complete unity.

Third, there is a difference between the Testaments in their portrayal of judgment. In the Old Testament judgment normally happens within history. When Israel sins, they are not told that they will go to hell when they are raised from the dead, but that they will be punished by the Midianites or the Assyrians. Therefore there are many judgments in the Old Testament. In Judges the Canaanites, Moabites, Midianites, Ammonites and Philistines are all used to punish Israel. Later on it is the Arameans, Egyptians, Assyrians and Babylonians. In other words, Israel "graduates" from being judged by the use of relatively local groups of people to being judged by the use of great empires. Yet in each case the judgment happens within history. It does not happen at the end of time but is already written about in our history books. Even with respect to Daniel most of what he predicts takes place in recorded history in the story of the conflicts of the Seleucid and Ptolemaic dynasties between 300 and 164 B.C.

Because of this difference from the New Testament, Old Testament judgment generally does not talk about eschatological scenes like lakes of fire and the dissolving of the heavens and the earth or the falling of stars or eternal chains. Instead it gives vivid pictures of fearful events that the people living then knew all too well, such as famine, plague, marauding armies and the like. It is unpleasant for us to read the prophets spelling out the details of such events, but they were the realities of life then (and for much of the world, also today). Furthermore, God is spelling them out so that people can repent and avoid them, not because he enjoys them.

Related to these descriptions is the fact that in the Old Testament the idea of an afterlife was only partially revealed and even that revelation comes toward the end of the Old Testament period. Most of the time the people thought of death as going down to the shadow world of Sheol where there was no praise of God and at best only a semilife. What they hoped for was to die at a ripe old age with a good name, having seen their children and grandchildren, who would carry on their name. Therefore the judgments in the Old Testament are those which speak to such hopes: warning of whole families being wiped out or of people dying when they are still young.

By the New Testament period God has revealed a lot more about the future life. Therefore the judgments spoken of there are the judgments related to the end of history and the resurrection of the dead: eternal life or being thrown into hell, seeing all that one worked for being burned up or receiving a crown of life. All of these take place beyond history, when Christ returns, and thus when history as we have known it has come to an end.

So, does the Old Testament reveal a God of judgment and the New Testament a God of love? Emphatically no. Both of the Testaments reveal a God of love who is also a God of justice. God offers men and women his love and forgiveness, urging us to repent and escape the terrible and eternal judgments of the end of history.

4

Why Don't Bible Genealogies Always Match Up?

It is often asked if the numbers of the genealogies of Genesis 5:3-32 and Genesis 11:10-32 can be used to calculate when Adam was born. The most important fact to notice is that the biblical writers never used these numbers for this purpose, although they did provide other numerical summaries. For instance, in Exodus 12:40 they note that Israel was in Egypt for 430 years, in 1 Kings 6:1 that it was 480 years from the exodus until the beginning of the construction of the temple under King Solomon, and in Judges 11:26 that it was 300 years from the entry into the land until the time of Jephthah, a judge who lived around 1100 B.C.

Therefore to add up the numbers of the ten antediluvians in Genesis 5 and the ten postdiluvians in Genesis 11 in order to determine the date for the creation of the world and the creation of Adam and Eve is to do exactly what the text does not encourage us to do!

What, then, is the significance of these numbers that are so carefully recorded in these texts? If they are not to be added up, of what importance could their inclusion be? First, they were given to show us that human beings were originally meant to be immortals and to live forever. If one charts the twenty life spans on a line graph, it is clear that there is a general but determined downward trend from a figure that at first bounces just short of one thousand years to a figure that approximates the life expectancy of persons living today, around seventy years. Second, the figures also show that the effects of sin and death in the human body meant that individuals became unable to have children in as elderly a state as once was possible.

Bishops Lightfoot and Usher were grossly mistaken to advocate that the human race was created on October 24, 4004 B.C., at 9:30 a.m., 45 Meridian time. The data does not allow for this conclusion! Abridgment is the general rule in biblical genealogies. Thus, for example, Matthew 1:8 omits three names between King Joram and Ozias (Uzziah), Ahaziah (2 Kings 8:25), Joash (2 Kings 12:1) and Amaziah (2 Kings 14:1). In Matthew 1:11 Matthew omits Jehoiakim (2 Kings 23:34). Matthew's goal is to reduce the genealogies to a memorable three sets of fourteen individuals, for fourteen is the number of "David," *D* = 4, *V* or Hebrew *waw* = 6 and the last *D* = 4, for a total of 14.

But even more typical of the genealogies is Matthew 1:1, where "Jesus Christ" is said to be the "son of David," who in turn is "the son of Abraham." David lived about 1000 B.C. and Abraham about 2000 B.C. Similar huge leaps over intervening generations are also taking place in Genesis 5 and Genesis 11. If one turns Matthew 1:1 around and puts it in the style of the prepatriarchal genealogies, it could read as follows: "And Abraham was 100 years old [at the time that he begat Isaac through whom his line continued to David], and he begat David. And David was 40 years old [an approximate date for when Solomon was born, through whom Jesus would come], and he begat Jesus Christ." Thus the numbers of when these ancients had their firstborn function as the times when the line that was to come was given to them.

It is as if my father were one of these Very Important Persons (VIPs), and he had four sons, born when he was 100, 120, 140 and 160. Now let us suppose that it was my line, as the eldest in the family, that was the line through which Messiah was to come, and I was born when my father was 100. The Messiah would not come for another 1000 years, but it would be just as accurate, biblically speaking, to say that my father begat Messiah when he was 100.

Furthermore, there are some warnings in the biblical text that if we add up these numbers, there will be distortions and errors. Take, for example, the last one in the series of twenty VIPs: Terah. It would appear that he lived 70 years and then had triplets born to him (Gen 11:26). His total life span was 205 years (Gen 11:32). However, something does not add up, for Abram left Haran after his father died (Gen 12:4; Acts 7:4), but he was only 75 years old at time and not 135, which he should have been had the figures been intended in a way that current usage would approve! Hence, had we added up the numbers in this part of the genealogy, we would already be 60 years in error, for the text must have meant that Terah "began having children when he was 70 years old," but that Abram was actually born when his father was 130 and not when he was 70. He was not the eldest son, but his name is given first because he was the most significant figure.

No one has studied this phenomenon more closely than the late William Henry Green in his April 1890 article in *Bibliotheca Sacra* entitled "Primeval Chronology."[1] For example, Green demonstrates that the same high priestly line of Aaron appears in 1 Chronicles 6:3-14 and Ezra 7:1-15, but it has twenty-two generations and names in Chronicles, while Ezra only has sixteen names. When the two lists are placed side by side, it is clear that Ezra deliberately skipped from the eighth name to the fifteenth name, thereby abridging his list, but in a way that was legitimate within the traditions of Scripture. This is exactly what is illustrated in the lists in Matthew. In fact, Ezra 8:1-2 abridges the list even further, seemingly implying that a great-grandson and a grandson of Aaron, along with a son of David, came up with Ezra from Babylon after the captivity! Now that is abridgment! Of course, Ezra was only indicating the most important persons for the sake of this shorter list.

In our discussion of some of these genealogies and lineages in the corpus of this work, further examples will be found. However, it must be acknowledged that the phenomenon is a major one, and interpreters will disregard it to the damage of their own understanding of the text.

Note

[1]This article was reprinted in Walter C. Kaiser Jr., ed., *Classical Evangelical Essays in Old Testament Interpretation* (Grand Rapids, Mich.: Baker, 1972), pp. 13-28.

5

Aren't Many Old Testament Numbers Wrong?

AMONG THE PARTICULARLY hard sayings of the Bible are those portions that record large numbers, such as those in census lists in the early periods of Israel's history or in numbers coming from the battles of that nation in her latter years.

The transmission of numbers in ancient documents was especially susceptible to textual error due to the fact that the systems were so diverse and with little standardization between cultures or periods of history in the same nation or culture.

In the Old Testament documents now available to us, all the numbers are spelled out phonetically. This is not to say, however, that a more direct numeral system or cipher notation was not also in use originally for at least some of these numbers. While no biblical texts with such a system have been found, mason's marks and examples of what may well be simple tallies have been attested in excavations in Israel. The only numbers that we have found in epigraphical materials uncovered by the archaeologists are those that appear on the earliest inscriptions known as the Gezer Calendar, the Moabite Stone, the Ostraca from Samaria and the Siloam Inscription of Hezekiah. There the numbers are either very small in magnitude, from 1 through 3, or they are written out phonetically.

Some numbers should never have been introduced into the discussion whatsoever, for they come from modern additions not found in the text themselves. Thus, one thinks first of all of the 1,656 years that allegedly elapsed from the creation to the flood according to the Hebrew manuscripts, while the Greek Septuagint has 2,242 years and the Samaritan texts have 1,307 years.

The fact that the Samaritan text has deleted one hundred years from Jared and Methuselah, and one hundred plus another twenty-nine years from Lamech's age, at the time of the birth of their firstborn, is consistent enough to signal perhaps a transcriptional problem in copying from one text to another. Meanwhile, the Septuagint adds another one hundred years to the ages of Adam, Seth, Enosh, Kenan, Mahalalel and Enoch at the birth of their firstborn, while with Lamech they add only six more years. In giving the tally for the rest of the lives of these same six antediluvians, they deduct the same one hundred years. The Hebrew and Greek texts agree on the figures for total years lived (if one were to do what the text never does, that is, add them up), except for a four-year difference in the life of Lamech. The Samaritan text, however, only gives a total of 720 years to Methuselah, while the Hebrew text would add up to 969 years total. The differences between the three texts are so regular that the mistakes are more easily explained if the copyist was working from some direct numeral cipher system that used a system of marks rather than phonetically spelling out these numbers.

Similar problems occur elsewhere. For example, some texts say that the number of persons that were on board with Paul when he was shipwrecked was 276, but a few manuscripts read 76. Likewise, the famous 666 number of Revelation 13:18 is found in a few manuscripts as 616. In the Old Testament the death of 50,070 male inhabitants of Beth-shemesh for irreverent treatment of the ark of God (1 Sam 6:19) is better put, as some manuscripts have it, at 70, since the town hardly even came close to having 50,000 inhabitants at this time.

Not all the large numbers in the Bible are as easily handled as the ones just surveyed. The number of warriors in Israel twenty years and older would seem to imply that the population that came out of Egypt and wandered in the wilderness for forty years exceeded two million people. This has given rise to a number of attempts to reduce this number and to serve as a model for treating similar claims in the Bible. One of the most famous is to take the Hebrew word *'elep̄,* usually translated "thousand," and to translate it instead as "family," "clan" or "tent-group."[1] If the word were so rendered in Numbers 1 and Numbers 26, it would yield a total of only 5,000 or 6,000 men of fighting age, instead of 603,550.

It is true, of course, that the word can be used that way, for Judges 6:15 reads, "my clan *('elep̄)* is the weakest in Manasseh." But the problem with this attempted reduction is that it only creates more problems elsewhere in the text. For example, in Exodus 38:25-26, where a half shekel was to be given for each of the 603,550 warriors above the age of twenty years old, the amount given was 100 talents and 1,775 shekels. There are 3,000 shekels to a talent, therefore 3,000 times 100 equals 300,000, plus 1,775 equals 301,775. Given the fact that each male over twenty was to be valued at a half shekel, 301,775 times 2 equals 603,550, a number matching that of Numbers 1:46, or similar to the number at the end of the march in Numbers 26:51 (601,730 men). Therefore, if the problem is solved at one end as "family units," it is only made worse elsewhere—in this case in the list of materials for the tabernacle; therefore, 603,550 warriors is the correct number and the nation probably numbered around two million.

Some of the most notorious discrepancies in biblical numbers are to be found in the postexilic era, particularly in Chronicles. Most nonevangelical interpreters feel the Chronicler's numbers are impossibly high. It is this fact, more than any other, that has made the Chronicler's work so suspect in the eyes of many modern exegetes. There are some 629 specific numbers that occur in 1 and 2 Chronicles.[2]

A typical example would be the number of Jehoshaphat's army. Second Chronicles 17:14-18 details the fighting personnel in five groups of 300,000, 280,000, 200,000, 200,000 and 180,000, which add up to give an army of 1,160,000 men. This many scholars thought to be excessive. But there are no other comparative figures with which to judge the authenticity of this number except what moderns regard as "excessive."

More serious are those texts where we do have parallel figures. Some noteworthy examples include: 1 Chronicles 19:18 has "7,000 chariots" whereas 2 Samuel 10:18 has "700"; 1 Kings 4:26 has "40,000 stalls," but 2 Chronicles 9:25 has "4,000"; 2 Kings 24:8 declares "Jehoiachin was eighteen years old," while 2 Chronicles 36:9 assures us "Jehoiachin was eight years old."[3] It is clear in each of these examples that there is a transcriptional error that represents a primitive error in one or more of the families of manuscripts of the Hebrew texts.

The conclusion of J. Barton Payne is that "in the eleven cases of disagreement over numbers that have arisen between the MTs of Chronicles and of Samuel/Kings because of copyists' errors, Chronicles is found to be correct in five cases, incorrect in five, and one remains uncertain."[4]

One more outstanding example of some unreconciled numbers in parallel lists can be seen in Nehemiah 7 and Ezra 2.[5] Thirty-three family units appear in both lists with 153 numbers, 29 of which are not the same in Ezra and Nehemiah. Once again, it may be said that if a cipher notation was used with something like vertical strokes for units, horizontal strokes for tens, and stylized *mems* (the initial letter in the Hebrew word *mē'âh*—"hundred") for hundreds, then the scribe miscopied a single stroke. Most of the differences, on this supposition, would involve a single stroke.

There is also the real possibility that the different circumstances under which the count was taken affected the numbers. Ezra's list was made up when the people were assembling in Babylon, while Nehemiah's was drawn up in Judea after the walls of Jerusalem had been built. Thus many could have changed their minds while others may have died in the meantime. In the end the matter is as Allrik stated it: "while at first glance these textual-numerical differences may seem detrimental, actually they greatly enhance the value of the lists, as they bring out much of their real nature and age."[6]

Notes

[1]The first one to have suggested this is Sir W. M. Flinders Petrie, *Egypt and Israel* (London: SPCK, 1911), p. 42. It was picked up and recycled by G. E. Mendenhall, "The Census Lists of Numbers 1 and 26," *Journal of Biblical Literature* 77 (1958): 52-66.

[2]The most recent work on the numbers of these passages from a conservative side was by J. Barton Payne, "The Validity of the Numbers in Chronicles," *Bibliotheca Sacra* 136 (1979): 109-28, 206-20; Payne, "The Validity of the Numbers in Chronicles," *Near East Archaeological Society Bulletin* New Series 11 (1978): 5-58.

[3]Note the important study by John W. Wenham, "Large Numbers in the Old Testament," *Tyndale Bulletin* 18 (1967): 19-53.

[4]J. Barton Payne, "1, 2 Chronicles," in *The Expositor's Bible Commentary,* vol. 4, ed. Frank E. Gaebelein (Grand Rapids, Mich.: Zondervan, 1988), p. 311. Note especially his Appendix A on p. 561, "Numbers in Chronicles That Disagree with Their Old Testament Parallels," and Appendix B on p. 562, "Numbers over 1,000 Unique to Chronicles." See also Payne, "Validity in Numbers," *Bibliotheca Sacra,* p. 126. Payne opined that out of the 629 numbers in 1 and 2 Chronicles, only the figures in 1 Chronicles 22:14 and 29:4, 7, listing the precious metals offered for Solomon's temple, might one need to resort to an explanation of special providence.

[5]See H. L. Allrik, "The Lists of Zerubbabel (Nehemiah 7 and Ezra 2) and the Hebrew Numerical Notation," *Bulletin of the American Schools of Oriental Research* 136 (1954): 21-27.

[6]Ibid, p. 27.

6

Do the Dates of the Old Testament Kings Fit Secular History?

IF CHRONOLOGY, AS THEY SAY, is the backbone of history, it would seem that a major attempt ought to be made to reconcile the plethora of chronological notations about the kings of Israel and Judah in the Bible. The astonishing fact is that the book of Kings is filled with chronological material concerning the Hebrew kings: when their reigns began, when a king came to the throne in the parallel kingdom of Israel or Judah, the total number of years that each king reigned and an occasional correlation of events in biblical history with those in the other nations of the ancient Near East.

But the tangle of dates and systems is so complex that the remark attributed to Jerome in the fourth century appears correct:

> Read all the books of the Old Testament, and you will find such discord as to the number of the years of the kings of Judah and Israel, that to attempt to clear up this question will appear rather the occupation of a man of leisure than of a scholar.[1]

Modern scholars are even more vehement in their denunciations of unwieldy material. But one such scholar who gave most of his life to untangle this Gordian knot was Edwin R. Thiele. He was finally able to make sense out of all the data and to show it all was accurate, as a part of his doctoral program at the University of Chicago. Despite the fact that neither Thiele's system nor anyone else's has achieved anything approaching universal acceptance, the evidence Thiele has amassed has never been completely refuted. The main complaint is only that he has taken the biblical data too seriously and has harmonized it perfectly. However, the word *harmonized* is not seen as a positive concept, but a negative one. Nevertheless, I think his case has stood now for well over forty years and will follow here, though there are numerous other efforts to supply other solutions that do not take all the biblical data as seriously as did Thiele.

Thiele began by first establishing some basic dates. Most important in accomplishing this first step was the archaeological find of the Assyrian eponym list that covered every year in order from 892 to 648 B.C. These lists named a "man of the year" as the eponym, but they often noted principle events that took place as well.

For the year of Bur-Sagale, governor of Guzana, it noted that there was a "revolt in the city of Assur." In the month of Simanu an eclipse of the sun took place. Now this event we can locate on our Julian calendar as June 15, 763 B.C. by astronomical computation. Since we can establish every year with an absolute date on either side of this solar eclipse on June 15, 763 B.C., in the eponym list, it is significant that in the eponymy of Daian-Assur, 853 B.C., the sixth year of Shalmaneser II, the battle of Qarqar was fought, in which the Israelite king Ahab opposed him. Twelve years later, in the eponymy of Adad-rimani, 841 B.C., Shalmaneser received tribute from a king "Ia-a-u," a ruler of Israel. This could be none other than King Jehu.

Now it so happens that there were twelve years between the death of King Ahab and the accession of King Jehu (two official years, but one actual for King Ahaziah, 1 Kings 22:51) and twelve official, but eleven actual, years for Joram, 2 Kings 3:1). Thus 853 is the year of Ahab's death and 841 is the year for Jehu's accession. This gives us a toehold on linking Israel's and Judah's history with absolute time and world events.

Another such linkage is to be found in the Assyrian chronology that puts the third campaign of Sennacherib in 701 B.C., when he came against Hezekiah. The Assyrian sources put 152 years from the sixth year of Shalmaneser III's battle against Ahab at Qarqar in 853 B.C. But according to the reconstructed history of the Hebrews, it was also 152 years from the death of Ahab to the fourteenth year of Hezekiah, 701 B.C. Thus there is a second main tie-in with world history and chronology.

As Thiele worked with these two main linkages with world history, he noted three important chronological procedures in ancient Israel and Judah. The first involved the distinctions in the calendar years of Judah and Israel: Israel began its year from the month of Nisan in the spring, while Judah reckoned its year as beginning in Tishri in the fall. This meant that in terms of an absolute January calendar year, a Nisan year began in the spring and extended into the next spring, thus bridging parts of two of our calendar years. The same would be true of a Tishri year lapsing over into two falls. But even more complicated is the fact that a regnal year in Israel would also overlap two regnal years in Judah.

A second feature was the use of accession year and nonaccession year reckoning. Ever since the division of the country after Solomon's day, the northern and southern kingdoms mostly used the opposite method of counting up regnal years that their neighbor was using. Thus, on the non-accession year principle, the first year counted as year number one, while the accession year principle did not count regnal year one until the month starting the calendar (Nisan or Tishri) was passed and one year after that was completed. Judah used the accession year principle from Rehoboam until Jehoshaphat, while Israel used the nonaccession year principle from Jeroboam to Ahab. However, the relations between the two nations thawed during the days of Ahab and Jehoshaphat, as it was sealed with the marriage of Athaliah, daughter of Ahab and Jezebel, to prince Jehoram, son of Jehoshaphat. Clearly, as 2 Kings 8:18 notices, Jehoram "walked in the way of the kings of Israel, as the house of Ahab had done, for he married a daughter of Ahab." Jehoram and Athaliah introduced the nonaccession year system into Judah, which remained until the snub of King Jehoash of Israel to King Amaziah of Judah over the proposal of marriage of the royal daughter to Amaziah's son (2 Kings 14:8-10). However, prior to this rupture in diplomatic relations, both nations had already resorted to the accession year principle, which for some reason they continued to maintain to the end of their respective histories.

A third principle Thiele sets forth was that each nation used its own system in reckoning the years of a ruler in the other nation. Thus Rehoboam of Judah had a seventeen-year reign according to Judah's accession year system, but according to Israel's nonaccession year principle it was eighteen years. These three basic principles of chronological reckoning in the two nations of Israel and Judah are foundational to grasping the meaning of the numbers used to describe the reigns of the kings.

The date Thiele projected for the division of the kingdom after the death of Solomon was 931/930 B.C. This date, however, is generally rejected by the larger academic community. The fashion had been (until just a decade or two ago) to accept William Foxwell Albright's date of 922 B.C., but his date involved an almost outright rejection of some of the biblical data. Albright argued that in view of the data found in 2 Chronicles 15:19 and 2 Chronicles 16:1, it was necessary to "reduce the reign of Rehoboam by at least eight, probably nine years"[2] from that required by the biblical text. Such a reduction is not necessary when the details are correctly understood, as Thiele sorted them out. More recently, the figure of 927/926 B.C. has been proposed as the first regnal year of Rehoboam in Judah and Jeroboam I in the northern ten tribes of Israel by John Hayes and Paul Hooker.[3] This date is arrived at by denying all three principles of Thiele and readjusting the biblical dates when they are not felt to be accurate for one reason or another.

But Thiele's date of 931/930 B.C. can be demonstrated to be accurate. One need only consult the following diagram to demonstrate this claim.

Judah		**Israel**		
	Official Years		*Official Yrs.*	*Actual Yrs.*
Rehoboam	17	Jeroboam	22	21
Abijam	3	Nadab	2	1
Asa	41	Baasha	24	23
Jehoshaphat	18	Elah	2	1
	79	Omri	12	11
		Ahab	22	21
		Ahaziah	2	1
			86	79

This chart from Thiele demonstrates two important points: (1) the eighty-six years of Israel on the nonaccession year reckoning is only seventy-nine actual calendar years, fully in accord with Judah's accession year system; and (2) from Ahab's death in 853 B.C., as established from the astronomical observations in the eponym lists and the twelve years separating Jehu from Ahab, to the beginning of the divided monarchy was 78 years. Therefore, 78 plus 853 equals 931/930 B.C. for the division of the kingdom.

During the time of the Hebrew kingdoms there were nine overlapping reigns or coregencies. This fact makes the fourth important principle that must be recognized and factored in when using the numbers of the reigns and coregencies of the kings of Israel and Judah. The first overlapping reign was that of Tibni and Omri in Israel. First Kings 16:21 reads, "Then the people of Israel were split into two factions [or, parts]; half supported Tibni son of Ginath for [or, to make him] king, and the other half supported Omri." Accordingly, there were *three* kingdoms at this time: two in the north under Tibni and Omri and one in the south, Judah.

The same three-kingdom phenomenon happened later on, for Menahem ruled one kingdom in the north and Pekah ruled the other, probably from Gilead. Hosea 5:5 witnessed to this fact as it warned, "Therefore Israel and Ephraim *[they]* will stumble [or, fall] in *their* iniquity, Judah also will stumble [or, fall] with *them*" (my own translation, emphasis added). Note the three Hebrew plurals, for again there were two kingdoms in the north.

A third overlapping involved a coregency of twelve years between Jehoash and Jeroboam II in Israel according to 2 Kings 13:10 and 2 Kings 14:23. Thus the sixteen years of Jehoash and the forty-one years of Jeroboam II would add up to fifty-seven, but with the coregency, it was actually only forty-five years.

In another coregency, twenty-four years of Azariah's fifty-two years overlapped with the twenty-nine years of Amaziah. Again, this reduced the total from eighty-one years to fifty-seven actual years.

A fifth overlapping reign came in the coregency of Jotham and Azariah, as mentioned in 2 Kings 15:5. Azariah became a leper, so his son governed the land in his stead. Likewise a sixth overlap took place between Ahaz and Jotham in Judah, for the attack of Pekah and Rezin were not solely against Ahaz (2 Kings 16:5-9), but it is also against Jotham as well (2 Kings 15:37).

King Jehoram was coregent with his father Jehoshaphat, as alluded to in 2 Kings 8:16: "In the fifth year of Joram son of Ahab king of Israel, when Jehoshaphat was king of Judah, Jehoram son of Jehoshaphat began his reign as king of Judah." Further confirmation comes from the synchronism given in 2 Kings 3:1, where Joram began in "the eighteenth year of Jehoshaphat king of Judah," but according to 2 Kings 1:17, he began "in the second year of Jehoram son of Jehoshaphat." Thus, the eighteenth year of Jehoshaphat was the second year of Jehoram's coregency. That would mean that Jehoram became coregent with his father in the seventeenth year of his father's reign, the year in which, it turns out, Judah joined forces with Israel against Syria. Prudence dictated that Jehoshaphat place Jehoram on the throne prior to his undertaking this joint venture—a venture in which Ahab of Israel lost his life (1 Kings 22:29-37), and Jehoshaphat narrowly escaped losing his own life.

The eighth coregency was between Jehoshaphat and his elderly father Asa. In the thirty-ninth year of Asa's reign, he became seriously ill with a disease in his feet. This led him, at the close of his forty-one-year reign, to make Jehoshaphat regent with him to help govern the people (2 Chron 16:12).

The final coregency was between Manasseh and Hezekiah. Here again illness was the factor (2 Kings 20:1, 6). Knowing that he, Hezekiah, had only fifteen years to live, it is only to be expected that he would place his son Manasseh on the throne early enough to train him in the ways of government.

Such is the nature of dual dating in reckoning the reigns, coregencies and synchronisms of the kings of Israel and Judah.

Notes

[1]As cited by Edwin R. Thiele, *A Chronology of the Hebrew Kings* (Grand Rapids, Mich.: Zondervan, 1977), p. 12. No citation given there as to its source.
[2]William Foxwell Albright, "The Chronology of the Divided Monarchy of Israel," *Bulletin of the American Schools of Oriental Research* 100 (December 1945): 20, note 14.
[3]John H. Hayes and Paul K. Hooker, *A New Chronology for the Kings of Israel and Judah and Its Implications for Biblical History and Literature* (Atlanta: John Knox, 1988), p. 18.

7

Does Archaeology Support Bible History?

TO CELEBRATE THE TWENTIETH anniversary of the *Biblical Archaeology Review,* the editors invited Michael D. Coogan to list the "10 Great Finds" or discoveries from the years of modern archaeological exploration in the ancient Near East.[1] His selections included: (1) the Gilgamesh Epic tablet XI from Nineveh, a parallel with the biblical flood story; (2) the Beni Hasan mural from nineteenth-century Egypt, showing 37 Asiatics coming to trade and depicting what the patriarchs may have looked like; (3) the Gezer High Place near Tel Aviv from 1600 B.C.; (4) the carved ivory knife handle from Megiddo in the thirteenth or twelfth century B.C.; (5) the fertility goddess pendant from Ras Shamra, Syria, from the fourteenth or twelfth century B.C.; (6) the Gibeon Pool, six miles north of Jerusalem, from the eleventh century B.C., where David's forces probably fought under Joab against the forces of Saul's son Ishbosheth under Abner (2 Sam 2:12-17); (7) the Beersheba Altar in southern Israel from the eighth century B.C.; (8) the seventh-century B.C. silver scroll amulet from Ketef Hinnom, near Jerusalem, with the name Yahweh on it; (9) Masada on the southwestern shore of the Dead Sea from the second century B.C.; and (10) the sixth-century B.C. mosaic map from Madaba, Jordan. Each of these was indeed a sensational find, illustrating some aspect of the biblical text.

The harvest from archaeological discoveries has truly been amazing. Among some of the most startling finds that have been uncovered in recent years are (1) the 1993 discovery by Avraham Biran of an Aramaic inscription from Tel Dan of a mid-ninth-century mention of the "House of David"; (2) the inscription from Aphrodisias in southwestern Turkey published in 1987, mentioning for the first time indirect evidence for Luke's references to "God-fearers"; (3) the first external evidence for Pontius Pilate, discovered at Caesarea in 1961; (4) a plaster text at Deir Alla in Jordan from the mid-eighth century, recording a vision of Balaam, son of Beor, apparently the same Balaam of Numbers 22—24; (5) the 1990 discovery of twelve ossuaries, or bone chests, including two bearing the name of "Joseph, son of Caiaphas,"[2] probably the same high priest who tried Jesus; and (6) the 1995 location of Bethsaida on the northeastern shores of Galilee from where several of Jesus' disciples came. The list could go on and on.

But not all of the finds have occasioned an advance in our understanding of the biblical world and the Bible. Some have presented us with enormous problems of interpretation and have resulted in hotly contested opposing positions. The most outstanding of these dilemmas is that neither the Egyptian nor the Israelite data have been able to settle the issue of the date, route and nature of the exodus. This is most disappointing, for it covers almost everything from the exodus from Egypt and the wilderness wanderings to the conquest and settlement of Canaan. Today the field is in more disarray than ever before on these questions.

For example, several issues have prevented scholars from accepting the traditional biblical evidence of a 1450 exodus and a 1410 B.C. entry into the land. Since the middle of this century, there has been a tendency to favor what has become known as the Generally Accepted Date (GAD) of 1230-1220 B.C. for entry into the land of Canaan. But even that is breaking down now as six of the sites that the Bible says were conquered by the Israelites (namely, Jericho, Ai, Gibeon, Hebron, Hormah/Zephath and Arad) have yielded no occupation evidence from the thirteenth century. The same story could be repeated for the cities of Debir and Lachish.

This poor "fit" between the archaeological evidence and the biblical tradition of the conquest has led scholars, who had downdated the entry into the land already by nearly 200 years from the date that the biblical evidence implied of 1410 B.C. to the revised date of 1230 or 1220 B.C., to look for different solutions. Several new theories have now gained considerable support. Among them are the *peaceful infiltration theory* (a view long favored by German scholars) or the more recent *peasant revolt* theory of George Mendenhall and Norman K. Gottwald. Both of these theories drop the necessity of a conquest altogether and substitute for it instead a revolt of local peasants against urban centers or a peaceful takeover.

But 1 Kings 6:1 claimed that the exodus was 480 years before Solomon began to build the temple in 967 B.C., which would again place it in 1447 B.C. Judges 11:26 also claimed that the Israelites had been settled for 300 years prior to Jephthah's day, who lived about 1100 B.C., again yielding approximately 1400 B.C. for the entry into the land.

Recently John J. Bimson and David Livingston have offered major strides forward in solving the archaeological problems and in harmonizing these results with the Bible.[3] They accomplish this mainly by moving the dates for the end of the Middle Bronze down 100 years or so from 1550 B.C. to around 1420 B.C. When this shift is made, there is almost a perfect correlation between the archaeological evidence and the biblical account of the conquest of Canaan. It will be interesting to watch what will happen on this issue in the future.

There are other examples of a present incongruity between archaeology and the Bible. One case is that of Genesis 14. If ever there was a chapter that promised to link the patriarchs with the outside world of that day, it is Genesis 14. Alas, we have not been able to identify with certainty any one of the four kings from Mesopotamia. Some think that "Arioch king of Ellasar" (Gen 14:1) might be the Arriyuk mentioned in the eighteenth-century Mari tablets, but that too is not certain. Years ago some thought Hammurabi (allegedly the Amraphel of Gen 14:1) was one of the four, but that proved to be incorrect both on philological grounds and the grounds that Hammurabi came much later in time (c. 1792-1750 B.C.) than the setting given in Genesis 14.

In Genesis 14:13 there is the first occurrence of an ethnic name in the Bible, "Abram the Hebrew." In the Mari tablets and in the Tell el-Amarna letters of the fourteenth and thirteenth centuries B.C., there is frequent mention of a mysterious ethnic group of people who at times also served as mercenaries called the Hapiru, Habiru, Hapiri or Apirim—all variants on what might be a group of people who were associated in one way or another with the Hebrews. Etymologically, the name *Hebrew* comes from the name *Eber*, one of Shem's descendants. Still, it is thought that the Hebrews may have been one group that made up the Hapiru.

The reference to the "trained men" in Genesis 14:14 is a technical term that is a loan word from Egyptian texts dating about 2000 B.C. for "retainers" of Palestinian chieftains.

Finally the title for God found in Genesis 14:19, "God Most High," *'ēl-'elyôn,* "Creator of heaven and earth," occurs in a Phoenician inscription found in Karatepe, dating about the eighth century B.C. Thus, even though we have not found the main characters in any of the external epigraphic materials from archaeology, there are already a number of other points in the chapter that prompt us to continue to look for the evidence that this chapter is an authentic report of actual events.

Scholars have tended to become extremely skeptical, as we have already illustrated in the exodus and conquest debates, about almost all events prior to the days of Omri and Ahab in the middle of the ninth century B.C., when it is felt that the history of Israel, in the technical sense, actually begins. Thus even such figures as David and Solomon are thought by some to be Persian time creations retrojected back onto the eleven and tenth centuries in order to glorify Israel. But the recent find of an inscription from Tel Dan reading "House of David" may have assuaged some of this skepticism and given promise of more evidence to come.

Another sort of archaeological evidence from the Near East is The Instruction of Amen-em-opet, which many believe bears a strong resemblance to Proverbs 22:17—24:22. Papyrus 10474 in the British Museum, or The Instruction of Amen-em-opet, consists of thirty somewhat brief chapters and is of uncertain date, though usually assigned somewhere between the tenth and sixth centuries B.C.

What is most startling about this connection with the Bible is that Proverbs 22:20-21 reads, "Have I not written thirty sayings for you, . . . so that you may give sound answers to him who sent you?" The parallel to these two verses is found in the Egyptian document at xxvi.15, "See thou these thirty chapters: They entertain; they instruct . . . to know how to return an answer to him who said it." The similarity is striking. There are several other close, but not exact, parallels to this short section in the book of Proverbs.

Biblical scholars differ over whether there is a direct or indirect literary dependence of Proverbs on Egyptian wisdom. Since the dating is lower for the Egyptian proverbs than those traditionally assigned as coming from Solomon (971-931 B.C.), there is just as strong a question as to whether there is a direct or indirect dependence of The Instruction of Amen-em-opet on Proverbs. Even if some kind of dependence could be proved, the book of Proverbs remains free of all allusions and senses that are distinctive to the cultural, political and religious environment of Egypt. It would only be an example of common grace of the created order in which all persons are made in the image of God and therefore reflect his truth in bits and pieces all over the world.

Archaeology will continue to produce many exciting moments since it has been estimated that less than one percent of the available material on the tells of Israel have been excavated, not to mention those in the rest of the ancient Near East. Moreover, there are still great quantities of tablets and manuscripts in the basements of many universities that have conducted excavations over the years that still need decipherment and publication. In that sense, the future for this discipline could hardly be brighter.

Notes

[1]Michael D. Coogan, "10 Great Finds," *Biblical Archaeology Review* 21, no. 3 (1995): 36-47.
[2]See Zvi Greenhut, "Burial Cave of the Caiphas Family," *Biblical Archaeology Review* 18, no. 5 (1992): 28-36, 76; and Ronny Reich, "Caiphas Name Inscribed on Bone Boxes," *Biblical Archaeology Review* 18, no. 5 (1992): 38-44, 76.
[3]John J. Bimson and David Livingston, "Redating the Exodus," *Biblical Archaeology Review* 13, no. 5 (1987): 40-53, 66-68.

8

When the Prophets Say, "The Word of the LORD Came to Me," What Do They Mean?

ONE OF THE MOST COMMON introductory sets of words in the prophets is the formula "thus says Yahweh/the LORD." Obviously, what was intended by these messengers of God was to indicate that it was not really the prophet who was speaking, but Yahweh. It was stated explicitly that Yahweh was speaking "through" the prophet (Is 20:3; Jer 37:2; 50:1; Hag 1:1, 3; 2:1; Zech 7:7; Mal 1:1).

The content of some prophetic oracles was so weighted with negative words of judgment at times that it was known as a *maśśā'*, "a burden" (for example, Jer 23:33; Zech 9:1; 12:1; Mal 1:1). Modern translations tend to translate this word as "an oracle," but the heavy, somber, burdensome aspect of this word would seem to demand otherwise.[1] Thus the prophets brought words of comfort, encouragement and judgment.

It was said that the word of the Lord "came" to the prophets. By saying this, the stress was on the action coming from the prompting divine source and not from the prophet who was the recipient. In that setting, Yahweh was said to speak through the prophets. The characteristic technical formula of the prophets that appeared over and over again was *n^{e}'um Yahweh,* "the utterance of the LORD," or simply, as a frequently repeated refrain, "says Yahweh."

Such formulas emphasized the importance and the reliability of what the prophet had just said or was about to say. The chief mission of the prophets was to carry Yahweh's words to the people of Israel and to the nations at large. They had a charge to keep: it was simply that they were to speak God's word. Even when the prophets received nothing but scorn for their efforts, as Jeremiah frequently experienced (Jer 20:8), they were, nevertheless, to carry on with an indefatigable spirit.

Jeremiah, for example, knew that the word spoken to him was veritably "the voice *(qôl)* of the LORD (Yahweh)" (Jer 38:20 RSV). The people also understood it to be the same, for when they responded to what the prophet had said, they obeyed "the voice of the LORD (Yahweh)" their God (Jer 42:6 RSV). Thus the refrain rang out throughout Scripture, from the time of the exodus until the last prophet, "Listen to my voice," said the Lord through his prophets (Jer 11:7; Hag 1:12). Thus there was no essential difference between Yahweh's word as heard through the prophet and Yahweh's own voice.

Even more metaphorical was the expression that "the mouth" of Yahweh had spoken what the prophet just said (Ezek 3:17). Thus the true prophet said what the mouth of the Lord directed him to say, but the false prophet pronounced what came from his own heart, rather than what came from the mouth of the Lord (Jer 23:16).

When a king wanted to know "a word from the LORD," he sent to the prophet to ask him to inquire on his behalf, "Is there any word from the LORD?" (Jer 37:17). It was like asking it from Yahweh's own "mouth" (Is 30:2). When one asked for an oracle from God, one asked, "What has the LORD answered?" or, "What has the LORD spoken?" (Jer 23:35, 37). That is how intimately connected the prophet's word was with the very heart and mind of God.

God would "put [his] words in [the] mouth [of the prophet]" (Jer 1:9, Ezek 3:17), and those words would, at times, be like "a fire and these people the wood it consumes" (Jer 5:14). Those words from God were so certain that they would "overtake" those who thought that they were outside the pale of their effectiveness (Deut 28:15, 45; Zech 1:4-6). It was as if the words themselves were like policemen in their cruisers, with a blinking light on top of them, pulling the law breaker over to the curb for violating the word of God.

The relation between Yahweh and the authors of the divine word is very clearly illustrated in the relation between God, Moses and Aaron (Ex 4:15-16). Moses would be instructed by God what he was to say to Aaron, and Aaron would be his prophet, who would speak the same words to Pharaoh. Therefore, what Aaron is to Moses here, every prophet was in relation to Yahweh. The analogy could not be any clearer or the connection any more direct.

God used many means to communicate with his prophets. There was

God's "mouth," his "voice," his "vision," his "dream" and his "appearance," among a host of other means of communicating, that were used to give the message to individual prophets at one time or another.

It is often asked if the prophets became unconscious and wrote or spoke like automatons, as if in a trance or on drugs. There is no evidence whatsoever for that suggestion, for the prophets were never so fully alert as they were when they were receiving revelation. When they did not understand, they would say so, whether the revelation came in a dream or in a word. Daniel and Zechariah often asked for an interpretation if they did not understand the vision or dream given to them. This would then be followed with another divine word or a word from an interpreting angel. God wanted his prophets to understand what they wrote and spoke, for after all, this was supposed to be a "revelation," a "disclosure," a "making bare or naked" what God wanted to say (1 Pet 1:10-12). The only things the prophets did not understand were "the time" and "the circumstances" surrounding the time. But they did know that they were speaking of the Messiah, his sufferings, his return in glory, the order of the previous two affirmations, and that their words were not simply for their own day, but for the days when Peter was speaking to the church as well!

But did they hear an audible voice? some will ask. Apparently they did at times, for was not the baptism of Jesus accompanied by just such a phenomenon when the Holy Spirit came upon him? Was there not a voice from heaven that said, "This is my Son, whom I love. Listen to him!"? And Paul too heard a voice when he was converted as he was on the road to capture more Christians, even though those around him said it merely thundered. So we can assume that the same audible voice may at times have been the experience of the prophets.

It is curious that the prophets not only are said to have heard the word of God, but they often say they saw it as well. The prophetic revelations are treated as visions even when nothing is "seen" in our sense of the word. Thus Amos tells us about the "words" he "saw" (Amos 1:1). Likewise, Isaiah tells us in his second chapter how he saw the word of God on the mountain of the Lord. It is probably for this reason that the prophets were at first called "seers" (1 Sam 9:9) before they were given the name of "prophets" *(n*^{e}*ḇî'îm).*

But 1 Corinthians 2:13 is the most definitive statement that we have on the nature of inspiration and how it took place on most occasions. Paul argued there that just as no one knows the thoughts of a person except that person, so no one knows the thoughts of God except the Holy Spirit. Now it is this same Holy Spirit who takes the inner thinking of God and makes it known to his prophets. He does this by "expressing spiritual truths in spiritual words." Thus, it is not a mechanical symbiosis between the divine and the human, but instead a living assimilation between the skills and personality of the writers and the mind of God takes place. Accordingly, all that has gone into the preparation of that writer, the vocabulary, the metaphors of life, the occupation entered prior to the call of God, all play a real part in the "teaching" experience of preparing the speakers for their roles as prophets.

What, then, was the process of this communication from God and the actual writing of Scripture? The best description of this process is to be found in Jeremiah 36. There Jeremiah informs us that he was in the habit of dictating "all the words the LORD had spoken to him" to his secretary, Baruch (v. 4). Baruch would then write them down on a scroll. The fact that less than a century later, when Daniel was reading "the Scriptures, according to the word of the LORD given to Jeremiah the prophet," Jeremiah's prophecies were already being read by those as far away as in Babylon and treated as "Scripture" and as being from God is remarkable. This predates any councils by either the Jewish community or the church in the matter of what was canonical and what was inspired.

God is the God who spoke his word to his people and who made it clear to his prophets. Of this fact, the prophets bear consistent and constant witness.

Note

[1]See further evidence for this assertion in Walter C. Kaiser Jr., "Massā'," in *Theological Wordbook of the Old Testament,* ed. R. Laird Harris, Gleason Archer Jr. and Bruce Waltke (Chicago: Moody, 1980), pp. 601-22.

9

Are Old Testament Prophecies Really Accurate?

THE ARGUMENT FROM FULFILLED prophecies of the Bible is essentially an argument from omniscience—that God is able to both know and foretell the future. That, indeed, is the claim that Isaiah 41:22-23 makes:

> Bring in your idols to tell us what is going to happen. Tell us what the former things were, so that we may consider them and know their final outcome. Or declare to us the things to come, tell us what the future holds, so we may know that you are gods. Do something, whether good or bad, so that we will be dismayed and filled with fear.

That is why the test for a prophet in Deuteronomy 18:22 was:

> If what a prophet proclaims in the name of the LORD does not take place or come true, that is a message the LORD has not spoken. That prophet has spoken presumptuously. Do not be afraid of him.

Nevertheless, the arguments against prophecies in the Bible have continued unabated down to the present era. The complaints have been that the language is often too vague, the prophecies are artificially fulfilled, the prophecies were written after the events they were alleged to have predicted, their fulfillments are all a matter of misinterpretation and the same phenomenon occurs in other religions.

But all of these complaints are without justification. For example, what is termed "vague" is certainly sharpened in the progress of revelation and fully by the time of its fulfillment. And to claim that it was an artificial fulfillment takes more faith to believe in than to trust the claims themselves, for how can one prophet arrange events as complex as that of a Babylonian captivity? How can one person, or even a group of persons, arrange for a child to be born in Bethlehem, in the line of Judah, of the house of David, to be announced by a John the Baptist, to do the works that Jesus performed in accordance with the predictions of Scripture, and to die on the cross and rise again on the third day?

Likewise, to claim that these prophecies were *vaticinium ex eventu,* "prophecy after the event," means that the one complaining must be very confident in his or her own ability to date events such as the prophecies of Isaiah 40—66, Daniel or the Olivet Discourse of Matthew 24—25!

But there is something else that is at work here, illustrated by the recent commentary by W. S. Towner on Daniel 8:

> We need to assume that the vision as a whole is a prophecy after the fact. Why? Because human beings are unable accurately to predict future events centuries in advance and to say that Daniel could do so, even on the basis of a symbolic revelation vouchsafed to him by God and interpreted by an angel, is to fly in the face of the *certainties of human nature.* So what we have here is in fact not a road map of the future laid down in the sixth century B.C. but an interpretation of the events of the author's own time, 167—164 B.C.[1]

Towner's distrust of Daniel's prophecy is based in his "certainties of human nature." This is a clear discounting of the power of God and his ability to communicate his word to his servants the prophets, while trusting in "human nature" as being more "certain"! There could not be a clearer example of the way one's presuppositions and hermeneutical circle strongly affect the outcome of any work in predictive prophecy.

Others resort to a misinterpretation thesis, claiming that what is called fulfilled prophecy is often a mere coincidence of language. True, there are some allusions made to the Old Testament by the New Testament precisely because the language is the vehicle they wish to use to carry the freight of their meaning. But these cases are rare and never in a claim about fulfilled prophecy. Those who would cite Hosea 11:1, "Out of Egypt I called my son," as a case of misinterpretation in Matthew 2:15 fail to notice that it is quoted when Jesus and his parents *entered* Egypt, not when they exited it. The reason Matthew quoted this text from Hosea was not the often stressed "out of" Egypt, but because of the corporate solidarity of "my Son" with those who crossed over the Red Sea.[2] Thus God's marvelous deliverance on one occasion was used to serve as a reminder of another deliverance—this time not from Pharaoh's hand, but from Herod's hand!

Finally, to claim that the same phenomenon occurs in other religions is to ask, "Where?" While the histories of pagan nations abound in stories of auguries, oracles and detached predictions, the distance between the dignity and credibility of the prophecies in the Bible and those in the sacred books of other religions is enormous. They form little or no part in any enduring divine plan that embraces the history and redemption of the world; instead, they function as mere curiosities that satisfy particular inquiries or aid the designs of a military or political leader in an immediate and personal predicament. Absent are all global, universal and salvific linkages.

Since the nineteenth century it has been popular to point to the following examples of prophecies that were not fulfilled in Scripture:

1. The prophecy of the ruin of Tyre by Nebuchadnezzar (Ezek 26:7-14; 29:17-20).

2. Jonah's prophecy of the destruction of Nineveh (Jonah 3:4).

3. Elijah's prophecy against King Ahab for murdering Naboth (1 Kings 21:17-29).

4. Isaiah's prophecy of the destruction of Damascus (Is 17:1).

The so-called nonfulfillment of prophecies is to be explained on the basis of the threefold classification of biblical prophecy; that is, prophecy may be unconditionally fulfilled, conditionally fulfilled or sequentially fulfilled.[3] All three types are commonly used by the prophets and are accompanied by textual indicators that aid the reader and interpreter in distinguishing them.

The list of unconditional prophecies is not long, but they are central, for they concern, for the most part, our salvation. They are called unconditional because they are made unilaterally by God without any requirements on the part of mortals to maintain their side of the bargain. Just as God alone passed through the pieces in Genesis 15, implying that an oath of self-imprecation would fall on him if he did not accomplish what he promised Abraham in the Abrahamic covenant, so it follows that the same one-sided obligation rests with the other covenants that fall in this same category. They are God's covenant with the seasons (Gen 8:21-22), his promise to Abraham (Gen 12:2-3; 15:9-21), his promise to David (2 Sam 7:8-16), his promise of the new covenant (Jer 31:31-34) and his promise of a new heavens and a new earth (Is 65:17-19; 66:22-24).

The majority of the prophecies, however, were of the conditional type. They contain a suppressed "unless" or "if you keep my commandments" type of conditionality. Leviticus 26 and Deuteronomy 28, with the alternative prospects for obedience or disobedience, were quoted or alluded to by the sixteen writing prophets literally hundreds of times. It is this provisional nature to the threat or promise delivered by the prophet that explains such a famous case as that of the prophet Jonah. While it is true that he was only to warn the people that in forty days destruction would come from the

Almighty, the people extrapolated, apparently, from Jonah's own case of deliverance (Did not Jesus say that Jonah himself was a "sign" to the Ninevites? A sign of what? Mercy?) that God might be merciful and relent from his announced judgment. They presumed that such a God must have a suppressed "unless" or "if" in the threat of absolute disaster. They were correct, much to Jonah's deep chagrin. This principle received formal articulation in Jer 18:7-10:

> If at any time I announce that a nation or kingdom is to be uprooted, torn down and destroyed, and if that nation I warned repents of its evil, then I will relent and not inflict on it the disaster I had planned. And if at another time I announce that a nation or kingdom is to be built up and planted, and if it does evil in my sight and does not obey me, then I will reconsider the good I had intended to do for it.

This relenting from an announced judgment (or deliverance) by God based on the condition of repentance and change was effective not only in dealing with whole nations but in dealing with individuals as well. That is exactly what took place with regard to Ahab in 1 Kings 21:25-29 after he "humbled himself" before the Lord for what he and Jezebel had done in arranging the murder of Naboth. After noting that "there was never a man like Ahab who sold himself to do evil in the eyes of the LORD" (1 Kings 21:25), the Lord instructed the prophet Elijah to reverse the threat he had just delivered against Ahab, saying, "Because he has humbled himself, I will not bring this disaster in his day, but I will bring it on his house in the days of his son" (1 Kings 21:29). This is a classic example of conditionality in prophecies working at the level of individuals. Presumably if his son also repented, the threatened judgment would likewise be removed from his son and that generation because of the same merciful provision of God.

But there are some prophecies that do not fit comfortably in either the unconditional or conditional category. These are the sequentially fulfilled prophecies, a subcategory of the conditional type. The prophecy in Ezekiel 26:7-14 falls into this third category:

> For this is what the Sovereign LORD says: From the north I am going to bring against Tyre Nebuchadnezzar king of Babylon. . . . He will ravage your settlements on the mainland; . . . he will set up siege works against you. . . . He will direct the blows of his battering rams against your walls and demolish your towers with his weapons. His horses will be so many that they will cover you with dust. . . . He will kill your people with the sword, and your strong pillars will fall to the ground. *They* will plunder your wealth and loot your merchandise; *they* will break down your walls and demolish your fine houses and throw your stones, timber

> and rubble into the sea. (emphasis mine)

According to many critics of biblical prophecy, Ezekiel in 29:18-20 admits that his prophecy was not fulfilled:

> Son of man, Nebuchadnezzar king of Babylon drove his army in a hard campaign against Tyre. . . . Yet he and his army got no reward from the campaign he led against Tyre. . . . I have given him Egypt as a reward for his efforts because he and his army did it for me, declares the Sovereign LORD.

Is this, indeed, an example of nonfulfillment? What has usually gone unnoticed is the shift in pronouns from the third person singular pronouns pointing to Nebuchadnezzar to the third person plural, "they," pointing to some other force beside that of Nebuchadnezzar. Nebuchadnezzar did indeed take the mainland city of Tyre after a long siege, only to have the Tyrians slip through his grasp as they simply moved out to the island a half mile out in the Mediterranean Sea. It was Alexander the Great, some two hundred years later, who came and attempted to capture the island fortress of Tyre. Frustrated in his attempts at first to float a navy that could compete with these masters of the sea, Alexander finally resorted to scraping up the dust, timbers, stones and rubble of the former mainland city, and dumping it into the Mediterranean Sea to form a causeway out to the island. Thus in the 330s B.C. Alexander took the city that Nebuchadnezzar had failed to take in the 570s B.C.

In this manner the prophecy was fulfilled. There was an indicated sequencing of events denoted by the sudden shift in the middle of the prophecy from the repeated references to the third person singular pronoun to the third person plural.

In like manner, Elijah's prophecy about Ahab's punishment for murdering Naboth and stealing his property was fulfilled. The threatened doom was carried out, after Ahab's sudden repentance, on his son a decade later in 2 Kings 9:25-26. Joram's corpse was cast onto Naboth's ground; indeed, the very spot that had been predicted in 1 Kings 21:19.

Isaiah 17:1 has also been used as an example of nonfulfillment: "An oracle concerning Damascus: 'See, Damascus will no longer be a city but will become a heap of ruins.' " But what is missed here is that Damascus, as the capital of the nation, stands for the whole Syrian nation. Furthermore, there is a play on the similar sounding words of "city" and "ruin" (*mē'îr* and *m*^{e}*'î*). A careful reading of the rest of the prophecy will indicate that Damascus is not facing a permanent and full eradication of its existence from off the face of the earth. The other thing to note is that this prophecy is put in the final eschaton, "in that day" (Is 17:4, 7, 9).

Thus we conclude that the prophecies of the Bible were fulfilled just as they were predicted. When one considers the enormous amount of predictive material in the Bible and that it involves some 27 percent of the Bible,[4] it is truly a marvel that it remains so accurate.

Notes

[1]W. S. Towner. *Daniel: Interpretation* (Atlanta: John Knox, 1984), p. 115. Emphasis mine.

[2]For a more detailed defense of this position, see Walter C. Kaiser Jr., *The Uses of the Old Testament in the New* (Chicago: Moody, 1985), pp. 43-53.

[3]All of these options are given in greater detail in Walter C. Kaiser Jr., *Back Toward the Future: Hints for Interpreting Biblical Prophecy* (Grand Rapids, Mich.: Baker, 1989).

[4]J. Barton Payne estimated that there are 8,352 verses (out of a total for the whole Bible of 31,124 verses) with predictive material in them. Out of the Old Testament's 23,210 verses, 6,641 (or 28.5 percent) contain predictive material, while the numbers for the New Testament are 1,711 out of 7,914 verses (for 21.5 percent). See Payne's *Encyclopedia of Biblical Prophecy: The Complete Guide to Scriptural Predictions and Their Fulfillment* (New York: Harper & Row, 1973), pp. 631-82.

10

Why Doesn't the New Testament Always Quote the Old Testament Accurately?

IN MANY PLACES THE NEW TESTAMENT quotations of the Old Testament do not match up with what we have in our English Old Testaments. There are a number of reasons why this is so.

First, our Old Testaments are generally translated from the Masoretic text, the traditional Jewish text, the earliest manuscripts of which are from around A.D. 900. Naturally, none of the New Testament writers had this text. If they knew Hebrew (as Paul did), they cited an earlier version of the Hebrew text, translating it into Greek themselves. This text was not necessarily identical with the text that we have.

Second, we have tried to get our printed Hebrew Bibles as close to the original as possible by comparing the Masoretic Text with manuscripts found among the Dead Sea Scrolls at Qumran and the early translations of the Hebrew text into Aramaic and Greek. None of the New Testament writers had this luxury. They simply accepted whatever Hebrew text they had. In fact, it is unlikely that many of them owned any parts of the Scripture personally, so they were happy whenever they managed to get their hands on a copy of some part of the Scriptures.

Third, even when a New Testament writer knew Hebrew, he did not necessarily use that text. He often used the text that his readers would be familiar with. For example, Paul sometimes quotes the Greek version of the Old Testament, the Septuagint, even though he knew Hebrew and had probably memorized the Old Testament in that language.

Fourth, not all New Testament writers knew Hebrew. The writer of Hebrews, for example, never quotes from the Hebrew text, so if he knew Hebrew, he has kept the fact well hidden. Thus when we come to Hebrews 1:6, which quotes Deuteronomy 32:43, we discover that the New Testament quotation does not agree with our English Old Testaments (translated from the Hebrew), but it does agree with the Septuagint. In many cases the Septuagint is so close to the Hebrew that we cannot tell if an author was using it or translating the Hebrew himself into Greek, but in this passage there is enough difference that we can tell that our author must have been using the Septuagint.

Fifth, sometimes New Testament writers chose a particular version because it made the point they wanted to make, much as preachers today sometimes choose to quote from translations which put a passage in such a way that it supports the point they want to make. For example, when we read Ephesians 4:8 we discover that it reads differently than Psalm 68:18 in English. This is not because Paul used the Septuagint, for in this case that translation agrees with our English Bibles. Instead, Paul appears to have used one of the Aramaic translations (called a Targum). In many Jewish synagogues the Scriptures were first read in Hebrew and then translated into Aramaic, for that is the language the people actually spoke. Paul would have been familiar with both versions, and in this case he chose to translate not the Hebrew but the Aramaic into Greek. The Hebrew text would not have made his point.

Sixth, we must remember that New Testament writers rarely if ever had the luxury of looking up passages they wanted to quote. Normally they quoted from memory. They were satisfied that they had the general sense of the Old Testament text but would not know if they were not exact in their quotation.

Seventh, in quoting the Old Testament an author at times combines more than one passage in a general paraphrase. For example, Paul in 1 Corinthians 2:9 is probably making a loose paraphrase of both Isaiah 64:4 and 65:17. In James 2:23 the author joins Genesis 15:6 with the general sense of either 2 Chronicles 20:7 or Isaiah 41:8. When one is moving along full speed in dictation and is concerned about some issue in the church, a general paraphrase of the Old Testament often did the job without stopping to remember just how the text went.

Finally, we must remember that there are some cases in which the New Testament author did not intend to quote the Old Testament, but his mind was so filled with it that it flowed out almost as if it were his own words. In these cases no quotation formula ("it is written") occurs, but we may think that our author is quoting because it is so close to the Old Testament text.

So what are we saying? We are noticing that New Testament authors were people just like us, but lacking the scholarly tools which we have. They sometimes quoted their favorite version or the version that fit what they were saying, just as we do. They sometimes paraphrased and quoted from memory, just as we do. They sometimes had limited resources available to them, just as is the case with some modern Bible readers. Finally, many of them did not know Hebrew and so had to be satisfied with whatever translation of the Hebrew they could read, just as is the case with many of us. In this we see that God used quite normal human individuals to write the New Testament. They did not have supernatural knowledge of the Old Testament text but lived within the limitations of their own culture and abilities.

Yet it is the New Testament documents they wrote that the church has held to be inspired. The teachings of the New Testament are not inspired because they can prove from the Old Testament that what they say accords with that Scripture; they are inspired because the Spirit inspired what they themselves wrote. None of them are giving their readers lectures on the proper text of the Old Testament. In fact, they are not even giving teaching on Old Testament theology. What they are doing is teaching New Testament truth and showing that the Old Testament supports the point that they are making. In general this is true, even though they did not have the relatively accurate and carefully researched texts of the Old Testament that we have today. When they appear to be "wrong" (allowing that they interpreted the Old Testament differently then than we do now), we must remember (1) that it could be that they may indeed have a better reading for the text in question than we have in our Bibles and (2) that the Spirit of God who inspired the Old Testament text has every right to expand on its meaning.

The point is that while we may understand why the New Testament writers cite the Old Testament as they do, it is the New Testament point that they are trying to make that is inspired in the New Testament document. Thus, while we may enjoy understanding what is happening and why our Old Testament quotations differ from what we expect, the real issue is whether we are obeying the New Testament teaching.

11

Are the New Testament Accounts of Demons True?

CLEARLY THE NEW TESTAMENT refers to demons. According to the Gospels Jesus "cast out" many of them, and they appear to be personal beings who make requests, react in fear and take other actions that characterize personal beings. But are they real? Are demons not a prescientific way of talking about what we would now call psychoses (or some other mental problem)? Are there really spiritual beings in this world that can affect human beings?

It is true that in the Middle Ages and even today in some Christian circles much, if not all, of what we call psychological dysfunction was and is attributed to demons. The results of this misdiagnosis in the Middle Ages were often grotesque and rightly deserve the censure of Christians committed to expressing the love of Christ. Also, demons are rarely mentioned in the Old Testament, and most of the Old Testament texts in which they are mentioned are controversial. They certainly are not called "demons," for that is a Greek word. And it is true that many of the symptoms attributed to demons in the New Testament could also be indications of such dysfunction as hysteria or epilepsy. This in itself makes one want to question the reality of demons. Yet this is not the whole story.

First, the belief in demons is part of a development in doctrine within Scripture. In the Old Testament there is very little said about any spiritual being other than God until after the exile. There is the enigmatic figure of "the serpent" in Genesis 3, but it has no other name and does not appear again in the Old Testament text. There are also indications that at least some of the Old Testament people believed in the reality of the gods of the nations around them, even though they were themselves true worshipers of

Yahweh. Still, that is not the official teaching of the Old Testament. The thrust of the Old Testament is that the gods of the nations were helpless idols, simply wood or stone (Is 44:9-20). To whatever extent they existed, they were helpless before Yahweh, the living God of Israel. This, of course, is in keeping with God's persistent emphasis up to the exile that he is One and that he will not accept both/and worship (such as worshiping both Yahweh and the Baals). It is therefore only late in the Old Testament period that we get references to Satan (and even then "Satan" may be more a name for a heavenly prosecutor than for an evil being) and only in the intertestamental period that we get significant references to demons (see, for example, Tobit). The New Testament is in line with this development of doctrine. The simplicity of the Old Testament view of the universe gives way to a greater complexity in the New. Thus it is not surprising to find references to demons in the New Testament where there are none in the Old.

Second, the Bible as a whole and the New Testament in particular witness to the existence of nonphysical beings and a spiritual realm. Besides God the Father, there is Jesus, who according to John once existed completely in this realm and then became flesh (Jn 1:14). The ascension refers to his return to the spiritual realm, but as a physical being (that is, he remains a human being with a body). Then there are angels, which are referred to 176 times in the New Testament, mostly in the Gospels and Revelation. These holy beings point to the existence of a spiritual realm, which, the New Testament says, also contains a dark side. This dark side includes Satan (or the devil), referred to in the New Testament more than 65 times, spiritual forces that Paul calls "powers and authorities" (Rom 8:38; Eph 3:10; 6:12; Col 1:16; 2:15), and of course demons, mentioned 52 times (and "demon" is only one of the terms used for them; they are also called "unclean spirits" some 23 times). In other words, demons fit into a New Testament picture of a nonphysical or spiritual world surrounding human beings. In this context they are not strange but part of a normal biblical worldview. If one were to deny the possibility of the existence of such beings, the logical extension would be to deny the existence of all spiritual beings, most likely including God.

Third, while demons do cause symptoms which we might at first interpret as psychological dysfunction, it is not true that such problems are all that they cause. Such diseases as epilepsy (Mt 17:14-18), paralysis similar to that caused by some forms of malaria (Lk 13:10-13) and probably fever (Lk 4:38-39) are all attributed to demons. Therefore, many forms of physical disease were attributed to demons, although not all physical disease was attributed to them, for the Gospels differentiate between healing diseases and casting out demons. The key is whether those physical diseases attributed to demons really disappeared when Jesus cast out the demon. If so, his claim that a demon was causing the problem and that it took casting out rather than a healing word would be confirmed.

Fourth, there is a good reason for the emphasis on demons in the New Testament and especially in the Gospels (which is the only place that they receive emphasis). Jesus came announcing the reign or kingdom of God. When that "kingdom" came in a more physical form in the Old Testament, there was a conflict between God (Yahweh) and the gods of Canaan (and before that of Egypt). This ended with God's demonstrating his power over these gods and often with the destruction of the idols. Now in the New Testament the kingdom comes and it is opposed by Satan, as seen in the temptation narratives and other references to Satan throughout the Gospels. Lesser powers associated with Satan (the exact relationship between Satan and the various other dark spiritual forces is never described in detail) would naturally be involved in this opposition. If the kingdom of God is going to come to individuals, the power of the kingdom of darkness is going to be broken and the demons may end up being destroyed (see Mk 1:24; 5:7-8). Thus the demons are part of the cosmic or spiritual conflict going on behind the outward actions of preaching, teaching and healing. Demons fit into the New Testament picture of what the reign of God means and the fact that salvation is not simply deliverance from physical sickness or political oppression or poverty, but at root a deliverance from final judgment, from spiritual sin and from the oppression by evil spiritual forces connected to these things.

Therefore, if one believes that the New Testament picture of the world and the human situation is accurate, it is quite normal and logical to believe in demons as real personal beings. It would also be quite normal to believe that where the kingdom of God is expanding one might run into such beings. However, only spiritual discernment can reveal when words of comfort and counsel, when healing and when a command to expel a demon are needed. Where such discernment is present, the results will be good, as in the case of Jesus and the apostles. Where it is lacking, we will see either the rejection of the existence of demons (with the result that a certain number of people who could be healed will not be healed) or a fascination with them in which people either withdraw in fear or else try to "cast out" what is really a disease and by so doing violate other human beings.

The New Testament teaches us about the reality of demons. It also teaches us not to fear them or to go looking for them, but to recognize that if and when they are encountered, there is more than sufficient power in Christ to expel them.

12

Why Are There Four Different Gospels?

It is clear to any reader of the Gospels that they are different. Sometimes the events are in a different order (John has the cleansing of the temple at the beginning of Jesus' ministry and Mark has it at the end). Sometimes they differ in their details (such as the names of the apostles or the names in the genealogies in Mt 1 and Lk 3). Sometimes there are differences in what they cover (so many of the events in John are not in any of the other three). Why is this the case?

Our tendency in approaching the Gospels is to think of them as modern biography. We want them to give us all of the facts about Jesus and especially to get the chronology of his life right. We in our culture have a tremendous interest in order and detail. Judged by these standards, the Gospels fare poorly indeed.

Yet the Gospel writers did not set out to write modern biography. They did not even know about it or realize that people would be interested in such issues in hundreds of years. What they did know about was ancient biography. The point of such works was not to give a chronology of a life but to present selected facts so as to bring out the significance of the person's life and the moral points that the reader should draw from it. One would see this quickly if one read, for example, Plutarch's *Lives*. Each life is so presented as to bring out a moral for the reader. This ancient literature is closer to what the Gospel writers were doing than what we now call biographies. The way the Gospel writers wrote was quite understandable to the readers of their time.

Thus the Evangelists set about to present selected events from the life of Jesus with a purpose. John makes his purpose quite plain: "Jesus did many other miraculous signs in the presence of his disciples, which are not recorded in this book. But these are written that you may believe that Jesus is the Christ, the Son of God, and that by believing you may have life in his name" (Jn 20:30-31). Of the other Gospels, Mark and Luke have a similar purpose of evangelism. Matthew, as part of his purpose, also appears to include church instruction, for he arranges the sayings of Jesus into five large discourses on topics useful for the church.

Each Gospel was aimed at a different audience. If tradition is correct, Mark records the preaching of Peter in Rome. That is, it is directed to a largely Gentile audience. Luke addresses his Gospel to a person who appears to be a Gentile official (Lk 1:1-4). Nobody knows who this person was (or whether Theophilus [lover of God] is a generic name for any God-loving person who would read the book), yet the two-volume Luke-Acts appears to have as part of its purpose the defense of the Christian faith before Gentile leaders (perhaps even the defense of Paul). This is not the same type of general audience that Mark addresses. Matthew, on the other hand, appears to have a Jewish-Christian or Jewish audience in view. John speaks to yet another audience. Naturally, even the same preacher does not use the same "sermon" for different audiences.

Furthermore, the writers of the various Gospels were different people. The writer of John takes a Judean perspective on Jesus and mentions only a few events that took place in Galilee, while the other Gospels focus far more on Galilee and other non-Judean locations. The writers also had different interests. Luke is very much concerned about issues such as the use of money and possessions, the acceptance of women by Jesus, and prayer. Matthew, on the other hand, is quite interested in Jesus' relationship to the Jewish law. Mark includes very little teaching of Jesus, so his focus is more on what Jesus did. Some of these were personal interests of the author, and some of these were concerns they had because of their intended audiences.

It is also important to look at the length of the Gospels. Matthew, Luke and John are long enough that if they were any longer they would have to go to two volumes. Scrolls only came in certain lengths, and they are at the maximum length. Thus when they use material from Mark they must at times abbreviate if they are not going to have to leave other material of their own out.

The rules of biography writing at that time did not dictate that one had to put everything in chronological order. Mark may have a rough chronology, but the others feel free to group things together by other rules of organization. Luke puts much of the teaching of Jesus within the context of a trip from Galilee to Jerusalem (Lk 9:51—19:10, the so-called "travel narrative"). Yet he also has the Sermon on the Plain in Luke 6. Matthew groups much of this same teaching into his Sermon on the Mount in Matthew 5—7, including both material found in the Sermon on the Plain and material found in Luke's "travel narrative." These two Gospels have two different frameworks for presenting some of the same material. They are shaped by concerns of the respective authors. Luke is quite interested in geographical movement, Galilee to Jerusalem (and then in Acts, Jerusalem to Rome), while Matthew is more interested in Jesus' fulfillment of Moses imagery. Interestingly enough, both Matthew and Luke use Mark, but they tend to use Mark in blocks. Luke edits Mark more than Matthew (partially because Luke is more concerned with Greek style and Mark is fairly rough in that regard).

John is different. He does not tell so many stories about Jesus. Instead he selects seven signs to present, seven specific miracles (although he knows that Jesus worked many other miracles). He does not give a lot of short sayings of Jesus, but groups what Jesus said into longer discourses in which it is difficult to tell where Jesus leaves off speaking and where John begins speaking (in the original manuscripts there were no quotation marks or other punctuation or even word divisions).

The point is that, as was the case in ancient biography, the Gospels are not photographs of Jesus but portraits. In a portrait it is important to bring out an accurate likeness, but the painter can also put in other things he or she sees in the person: perhaps some feature of their character will be brought out or some deed they did or office they held. Perhaps the person sat for the portrait in a bare studio, and then the painter painted a scene surrounding them that would bring out this feature of the person. We do not say that the portrait is inaccurate. We know that that is what a portrait is supposed to do. In fact, in some ways it is more accurate than the photograph, for it allows us to see things that could never be shown in a photograph (such as character), but are very much part of the person.

In the Gospels, then, we have four portraits of Jesus. Each of the four writers is concerned with different aspects of his life and person. This was symbolized early in church history when the Gospels were identified with different images. John was identified with the eagle, while Luke was identified with a human being. Mark was identified with an ox, and Matthew with a lion (for royalty). (The images are drawn from Rev 4:7.) We are therefore not limited to one perspective on Jesus, but have the richness of four.

This is why it is important to read each Gospel for itself rather than combine them into a harmony. A harmony tries to put all of the four Gospels together to make one story, but in doing this it loses the perspective of the Gospels. It is like taking bits and pieces out of four portraits and trying to make one collective portrait from them. The harmony satisfies our desire to get everything in order, but in doing this it often distorts the Gospels. In the end, the harmony is not what God chose to inspire. God chose to inspire four Gospels, not one single authorized biography. In other words, God appears to have *wanted* four pictures of Jesus, not one, four messages for the church, not just a single message.

It is not that the four portraits are contradictory. They are just different. If four painters sat and painted the same sunset, each would have a different picture. Each would leave out or put in different details. Each would have a different perspective and perhaps select a different phase of the setting sun to emphasize. None of them would be "wrong," for each was portraying the same sunset.

Thus when we come to the Gospels the differences are important. When we find a difference we need to ask why this Gospel is different. Some differences are quite insignificant. For example, Mark 6:39 mentions that the grass was green and none of the other Gospels have this detail. They could leave out such a detail and save space. Others are significant. When Matthew reports Jesus' word on divorce (Mt 19:9), he only speaks of a man divorcing a woman, for in Jewish law only men could divorce. When Mark speaks of this (Mk 10:11-12), he speaks of both men divorcing women and women men, for in Rome either sex could divorce. Each reflects the same truth Jesus was saying (probably in Aramaic, not Greek) in tune with the legal system their audience lives under. Each accurately portrays Jesus' concern for the permanence of marriage. Likewise Matthew reports the order of the temptations so that they end up on a mountain, in accordance with his interest in Jesus as the new Moses (Mt 4:1-11), and Luke puts them in an order so Jesus would end up in Jerusalem, in harmony with his Galilee to Jerusalem interest (Lk 4:1-13). Neither claims to have their material in chronological order, so maintaining such an order is not an issue.

Each of the Gospels is trying to deliver a particular message to us. The important issue for us as readers is not that we get the life of Jesus figured out with each event in order, but that we get the message the Gospels are trying to communicate, that we hear their call to faith, that we submit to the teaching of Jesus, and that we live in the discipleship that they are trying to call us to. In the end, we are not called to be art critics, but to fill our homes with the "glow" that comes from these four portraits.

GENESIS

1—2 Elohim or Yahweh?

Why does Genesis 1 refer to God exclusively by the Hebrew title Elohim, "God," while the second chapter of Genesis, beginning in the second half of Genesis 2:4, speaks exclusively of Yahweh Elohim, that is, "the LORD God"? So striking is this divergence of the divine names that it has been common in critical circles of biblical scholarship to conclude that the writer, or, as those in the critical school prefer, the redactor (a sort of copyeditor) used basically two different sources for the two creation accounts found in the two chapters.

The person who paved the way for this theory of dual sources was Jean Astruc (1684-1766), the personal physician to Louis XV and a professor on the medical faculty of the University of Paris. While he still held to the Mosaic authorship of all of the Pentateuch, his volume on the book of Genesis published in 1753 offered the major clue that the names Elohim and Yahweh were the telltale traces that Moses used two sources to compose this material—material that obviously recorded events occurring before his time.

This explanation as to how Moses had access to material far beyond his own lifetime and the reason for the use of the dual names, however, was too facile; it failed to note that the variation in the employment of these two divine names in the book of Genesis was subject to certain rules that could be described rather precisely. First of all, the name Yahweh, "LORD," (notice the English translation convention of rendering this name in large and small capital letters, as opposed to "Lord," which renders another word meaning something like "master") is a proper noun used exclusively of the God of Israel. Elohim, on the other hand, is a generic term for "God" or "gods" that only subsequently became a proper name.

Yahweh is used wherever the Bible stresses God's personal relationship with his people and the ethical aspect of his nature. Elohim, on the other hand, refers to God as the Creator of the whole universe of people and things, and especially of the material world: he was the ruler of nature, the source of all life. This variation of divine names can be seen most dramatically in texts like Psalm 19. In this psalm Elohim is used in the first part, which describes God's work in creation and his relationship to the material world. But in the middle of the psalm the psalmist switches to the topic of the law of the LORD and the relationship the LORD has with those who know him; there the name Yahweh appears.

A further complication occurs because Exodus 6:3 notes that God says, "I appeared to Abraham, to Isaac and to Jacob as God Almighty, but by my name the LORD I did not make myself known to them." The resolution to this apparent contradiction to some 150 uses of the name Yahweh during the patriarchal period is to be found in a technical point of Hebrew grammar, known as *beth essentiae,* in the phrase "by my name." This phrase meant that while Abraham, Isaac and Jacob heard and used the name Yahweh, it was only in Moses' day that the realization of the character, nature and essence of what that name meant became clear. "By the name" is better translated "in the character [or nature] of Yahweh [was I not known]."

Thus the name Yahweh is used when the Bible wishes to present the personal character of God and his direct relationship with those human beings who have a special association with him. Contrariwise, Elohim occurs when the Scriptures are referring to God as a transcendent Being who is the author of the material world, yet One who stands above it. Elohim conveys the more philosophically oriented concept that connects deity with the existence of the world and humanity. But for those who seek the more direct, personal and ethically oriented view of God, the term Yahweh was more appropriate.

Accordingly, Genesis 1 correctly used the name Elohim, for God's role as Creator of the whole universe and of all living things and all mortals is what the chapter teaches. The subject narrows immediately in Genesis 2—3, however; there it describes God's very intimate and personal relationship with the first human pair, Adam and Eve. God is depicted as walking and talking with Adam in the Garden of Eden. Therefore Yahweh is appropriately joined to Elohim to indicate that the Elohim of all creation is now the Yahweh who is intimately concerned to maintain a personal relationship with those who will walk and talk with him.

1—2 Poetic? Figurative? Historical?

Is the creation account in Genesis 1 and 2 in the mythic, poetical style of most ancient Near Eastern stories of the origin of the world, or is it of some other type of literary genre? What are we to make of the repetitious nature of a number of its phrases and of what appears to be a certain stereotyped form to each of the creative acts of God? What is more, look at the way God is depicted with hands, nostrils and the like. Isn't that enough to convince any thinking person that this is not a straightforward natural account of what happened in the creation?

There can be no debate on the fact that there are a large number of figures of speech in these chapters. In fact, one major work, *Figures of Speech in the Bible* by E. W. Bullinger, lists over 150 examples of such in Genesis 1:1—11:32. That is not the issue, for all speech of all literary types will include some, if not many, forms of figurative language. Speaking of God as having human body parts is just one such figure of speech, anthropomorphism.

But the issue of literary types is a separate matter. To declare that since figurative language is present we can assume that the material of Genesis 1—3 is less than a straightforward presentation of real events is to jump to conclusions. Certain other categories can, however, be ruled out because they fail to meet the fairly uniform criteria that are normative in such decisions.

First of all, the biblical account of creation does not exhibit the forms or substance of myth. All attempts to see an allusion to the goddess Tiamat in the Hebrew word *tᵉhôm,* "the deep" (Gen 1:2) were marked with failure from the beginning since such an equation violated the rules of morphology and equivalency in cognate languages. No reputable scholar today appeals to this as evidence that the Bible once was in the form of a myth. Neither is the reference to the Spirit of God "hovering over the waters" in that same verse seen as being a covert allusion to the Phoenician myth of the world being hatched from some type of cosmic egg. In short, nothing has been found in the biblical narrative of creation to tie it to the mythical ancient Near Eastern cosmogonies.

Neither can we say that Genesis 1 or 2 is poetic in form. The Hebrew form of the verb is exactly the same as is routinely used for Hebrew narratives. Furthermore, Hebrew poetry seldom if ever uses the Hebrew indicator for the direct object, whereas Genesis 1 and 2 do. There are additional grammatical and syntactical forms in Genesis 1 and 2 that can only be found in prose literary genre, not in poetry. Thus these accounts may not be listed under poetry.

What we do find, however, is a carefully and closely reasoned narration of events that in Genesis 1 are set in almost a dry didactic form. Emphasis is laid on definition, naming, evaluating and a general ordering of events. As such, the accounts have more in common with narrative prose than anything else.

While the Genesis narrative cannot be called "historical" in the usual sense of the word, in that most use the term to indicate facts independently verifiable by two or more sources or witnesses, it certainly appears to be claiming to record actual events in the stream of happenings in our kind of space-time world.

1:28 Exploiting Nature?

Does the blessing pronounced by God in Genesis 1 encourage us, the human race, to treat the environment in any way we choose? Is the present ecological imbalance observed in so many parts of the world the result of our orthodox Christian arrogance toward nature, as Lynn White Jr. charged in his famous article, "The Historical Roots of Our Ecological Crisis" (*Science* 155 [1967]: 1203-7)?

At long last, it is generally accepted that Western scientific and technological leadership must find its roots in the biblical revelation of the reality of the visible world and the fact that the world had a beginning. (The idea of a beginning was impossible within the framework of the previous cyclical notions of time.) Moreover, the Judeo-Christian heritage fosters such science-advancing concepts as *uniformitarianism,* a concept that was instrumental in the Scientific Revolution of the seventeenth century and the Industrial Revolution of the eighteenth century. But the academic community has given this recent recognition very grudgingly.

No sooner had this battle been won than an accompanying charge was leveled, which is to say that the Bible taught that "it was God's will that man exploit nature for his own proper ends" (White, "The Historical Roots," p. 1205). What we had lost, ecologically, according to White, was the spirit of pagan animism that says that every tree, spring, stream and hill possesses a guardian spirit which has to be placated should any intrusion be made into the environment by cutting down trees, mining mountains or damming brooks. Christianity overcame primitive animism, so White argued, and made it possible to exploit nature with an attitude of indifference for all natural objects. Genesis 1:28 could be cited as the Christian's license to do just that.

However, this schema is a distortion not only of this verse but of Scripture as a whole. Indeed all things are equally the result of God's creative hand; therefore nature is real and has great worth and value. The only difference between humanity and all the rest of creation is that God placed his image in men and women and thus gave them extra value and worth and set the whole creative order before them for their stewardship.

The gift of "dominion" over nature was not intended to be a license to use or abuse selfishly the created order in any way men and women saw fit. In no sense were humans to be bullies and laws to themselves; Adam and Eve were to be responsible to God and accountable for all the ways in which they did or did not cultivate the natural world about them.

True, the words *subdue* and *rule over* do imply that nature will not yield easily and that some type of coercion will be necessary. Because the created order has been affected by sin just as dramatically as the first human pair were, the natural created order will not do our bidding gladly or easily. We must exert a good deal of our strength and energy into our efforts to use nature.

But such an admission does not constitute a case for the rape of the land. It is a twisted use of this authorization to perform such a task with a fierce and perverted delight. Only when our iniquities are subdued by God are we able to exercise this function properly.

God is still the owner of the natural world (Ps 24:1), and all the beasts of the forest and the cattle on a thousand hills are his (Ps 50:10-12). Mortals are mere stewards under God. Under no condition may we abuse and run roughshod over the natural order for the sake of quick profits or for the sheer fun of doing so. Indeed, even Job was aware that the land would cry out against him if, in God's eyes, Job abused it (Job 31:37-40).

Not even in the renovation of the new heavens and the new earth is there a total break and a complete disregard for the present heavens and earth. Instead, the final fire of judgment will only have the effect of *purifying* because "the elements will be destroyed by fire, and the earth and everything in it will be laid bare" (2 Pet 3:10). Even so, the earth will not be burned up!

Lynn White felt we would be better off if we asserted, as did St. Francis of Assisi, the equality of all creatures, including human beings. This would take away from human beings any idea of a limitless rule over creation.

But such an equity fails to comprehend the concept of the image of God in persons. Trees, ants, birds and wildlife are God's creatures, but they are not endowed with his image; neither are they responsible to God for the conduct and use of the creation. What limits humanity is the fact that each must answer to God for one's use or abuse of the whole created order.

Should you ask, "What, then, happened to the cultural mandate given to the human race in Genesis?" we will respond by noting that the mandate is intact. However, it is found not here in Genesis 1:28 but rather in Genesis 2:15. There Adam is given the task to "work" the Garden of Eden and to "take care of it." That is the cultural mandate.

2:16-17 An Unfair Test?

Why would God test Adam by placing the tree of the knowledge of good and evil in the garden and then urging him not to eat of it—especially when, according to his divine foreknowledge, he knew he would do just that? What is the point of this whole exercise? What would it prove in the end?

The Creator saw fit to set a special test of obedience for the man (and eventually the woman) he had formed. Since Adam and Eve were formed perfect from the hand of their Maker, they were bound by the very laws of their natures to love, honor and obey the One who so endowed them. However, this love, honor and obedience were an untested set of gifts. Therefore, it was necessary to make a trial or test of their obedience if they were to be free moral agents.

The test, however, could not be a violation of a moral obligation like those in the Decalogue; it had to be an easy prohibition that would be a suitable test of their fidelity. When free indulgence had been given to them to eat the fruit of all the other trees, the infringement of this injunction would be an act of direct rebellion against a command given by God. The method God chose had to be one of violating what is known as a Positive Law (that is, one that was true merely because God said it was true), or one that appeared to be an arbitrary enactment. The advantage of using a test of such modest means and methods was that, if the mortals had stood some greater test and come out steadfast, they might have expected rewards proportioned to the conflict and have argued that they had earned their own salvation. But the test was simply one of heeding a command from God. It would vindicate God's subsequent actions as well as demonstrate that mortals from the hand of God did possess a certain freedom, for which they would also be responsible.

As such, there is nothing absurd or derogatory to the Supreme Being in this test. The perfections of God demand the same from his creatures. But when those perfections are provisionally granted by right of creation, this goodness of God must be further tested before it can be said to exist permanently from that point on.

2:17 Why Didn't Adam and Eve Die at Once?

Why did not Adam and Eve drop dead the same day that they disobeyed God and ate of the forbidden fruit? Adam lived to be 930 years old according to Genesis 5:5. Was Satan's word in Genesis 3:4—"You will not surely die"—a more accurate assessment of the real state of affairs than what God had said in Genesis 2:17—"When you eat of it you will surely die"? Is Satan more scrupulously honest than God himself?

This hard saying calls for an examination of at least three different concepts embraced within the quotation from Genesis 2:17—(1) the tree of the knowledge of good and evil; (2) the meaning of the phrase "when [more literally, in the day] you eat of it"; and (3) the meaning of the phrase "you will surely die."

First the tree. There are no grounds whatsoever for believing that the tree was a magical symbol or that it contained a secret enzyme which would automatically induce a wide body of knowledge that embraced the whole gamut of good and evil. Instead it is safer to assume that the tree functioned much as the New Testament ordinance or sacrament of the Lord's Supper or Eucharist does. The tree was a symbol embodied in an actual tree, just as the bread and wine of the Eucharist are symbols embodied in real bread and wine. In a similar way the tree of life was also a real tree, yet it symbolized the fact that life was a special gift given to individuals from God. That is also why participants are warned not to partake of the elements of the Lord's Supper in an unworthy manner, for when the elements are eaten and drunk in a flippant manner and when a person has not truly confessed Christ as Savior, the unworthy partaking of these rather ordinary elements (ordinary at least from all outward appearances) will cause illness and, in some cases, death (1 Cor 11:30).

In the same way, the tree was a symbol to test the first human couple's actions. Would they obey God or would they assert their own wills in opposition to God's clear command? To argue that the tree had magical power to confer knowledge of good and evil would be to miss the divine point: the tree was a test of the couple's intention to obey God. That men and women can attain the knowledge of good and evil is not in itself either undesirable or blameworthy; knowledge per se was not what was being forbidden here. The tree only represents the possibility that creatures made in God's image could refuse to obey him. The tree served as the concrete expression of that rebellion.

It is just as naive to insist that the phrase "in the day" means that on that very day death would occur. A little knowledge of the Hebrew idiom will relieve the tension here as well. For example, in 1 Kings 2:37 King Solomon warned a seditious Shimei, "The day you leave [Jerusalem] and cross the Kidron Valley [which is immediately outside the city walls on the east side of the city], you can be sure you will die." Neither the 1 Kings nor the Genesis text implies *immediacy of action* on that very same day; instead they point to the *certainty of the predicted consequence* that would be set in motion by the act initiated on that day. Alternate wordings include *at the time when, at that time, now when* and *the day [when]* (see Gen 5:1; Ex 6:28; 10:28; 32:34).

The final concern is over the definition of death. Scripture refers to three different types of death. Often only the context helps distinguish which is intended. There are physical death, spiritual death (the kind that forces guilty persons to hide from the presence of God, as this couple did when it was time for fellowship in the Garden, Gen 3:8) and the "second death" (to which Rev 20:14 refers, when a person is finally, totally and eternally separated from God without hope of reversal, after a lifetime of rejecting God).

In this case, spiritual death was the immediate outcome of disobedience demonstrated by a deliberate snatching of real fruit from a real tree in a real garden. Death ensued immediately: They became "dead in . . . transgressions and sins" (Eph 2:1). But such separation and isolation from God eventually resulted in physical death as well. This, however, was more a byproduct than a direct result of their sin. Spiritual death was the real killer!

See also comment on ROMANS 5:12.

2:18 A Helper for Man?

Are women inferior to men, merely designed to be their helpers? Is it consistent with the biblical text to view men as the initiators and women as their assistants? Is this what makes women suitable matches for men?

The Creator regarded Adam's situation as incomplete and deficient while he was living without community or a proper counterpart. The Creator judged Adam's situation quite negatively: "It is not good."

Ecclesiastes 4:9-12 expresses this same opinion about aloneness. The wise writer Solomon advised:

Two are better than one. . . . If one

> falls down, his friend can help him up. . . . Also, if two lie down together, they will keep warm. But how can one keep warm alone? Though one may be overpowered, two can defend themselves.

True, in Jeremiah 16:1-9 the prophet Jeremiah is commanded by God to remain alone, but this is meant to be a sign that God's judgment on the people is so near that it will not be worthwhile to get married. Nevertheless, the full life is a life that finds its fulfillment in community with another person or group of persons.

In the Genesis story we find that God created a woman after he had created the man. This would end Adam's loneliness and the state that God judged to be "not good." She was to be his "helper"—at least that is how most of the translations have interpreted this word. A sample of the translations reads as follows: "I shall make a helper fit for him" (RSV); "I will make a fitting helper for him" (New Jewish Publication Society); "I will make an aid fit for him" (AB); "I will make him a helpmate" (JB); "I will make a suitable partner for him" (NAB); "I will make him a helper comparable to him" (NKJV).

However, the customary translation of the two words *'ēzer kᵉnegdô* as "helper fitting him" is almost certainly wrong. Recently R. David Freedman has pointed out that the Hebrew word *'ēzer* is a combination of two roots: *'-z-r*, meaning "to rescue, to save," and *ǵ-z-r*, meaning "to be strong." The difference between the two is the first letter in Hebrew. Today that letter is silent in Hebrew, but in ancient times it was a guttural sound formed in the back of the throat. The *ǵ* was a *ghayyin,* and it came to use the same Hebrew symbol as the other sound, *'ayin.* But the fact that they were pronounced differently is clear from such place names which preserve the *g* sound, such as *Gaza* or *Gomorrah.* Some Semitic languages distinguished between these two signs and others did not; for example, Ugaritic did make a distinction between the *'ayin* and the *ghayyin;* Hebrew did not (R. David Freedman, "Woman, a Power Equal to a Man," *Biblical Archaeology Review* 9 [1983]: 56-58).

It would appear that sometime around 1500 B.C. these two signs began to be represented by one sign in Phoenician. Consequently the two phonemes merged into one grapheme and what had been two different roots merged into one, much as in English the one word *fast* can refer to a person's speed, abstinence from food, his or her slyness in a "fast deal" or the adamant way in which someone holds "fast" to positions. The noun *'ēzer* occurs twenty-one times in the Old Testament. In many of the passages it is used in parallelism to words that clearly denote strength or power. Some examples are:

> There is none like the God of Jeshurun, The Rider of the Heavens in your strength *('-z-r),* and on the clouds in his majesty. (Deut 33:26, my translation)
>
> Blessed are you, O Israel! Who is like you, a people saved by the Lord? He is the shield of your strength *('-z-r)* and the sword of your majesty. (Deut 33:29, my translation)

The case that begins to build is that we can be sure that *'ezer* means "strength" or "power" whenever it is used in parallelism with words for majesty or other words for power such as *'oz* or *'uzzo.* In fact, the presence of two names for one king, Azariah and Uzziah (both referring to God's strength), makes it abundantly clear that the root *'ēzer* meaning "strength" was known in Hebrew.

Therefore I suggest that we translate Genesis 2:18 as "I will make a power [or strength] corresponding to man." Freedman even suggests on the basis of later Hebrew that the second word in the Hebrew expression found in this verse should be rendered *equal to him.* If this is so, then God makes for the man a woman fully his equal and fully his match. In this way, the man's loneliness will be assuaged.

The same line of reasoning occurs in the apostle Paul. He urged in 1 Corinthians 11:10, "For this reason, a woman must have power [or authority] on her head [that is to say, invested in her]."

This line of reasoning which stresses full equality is continued in Genesis 2:23, where Adam says of Eve, "This is now bone of my bones and flesh of my flesh; she shall be called 'woman,' for she was taken out of man." The idiomatic sense of this phrase "bone of my bones" is a "very close relative," "one of us" or in effect "our equal."

The woman was never meant to be an assistant or "helpmate" to the man. The word *mate* slipped into English since it was so close to Old English *meet,* which means "fit to" or "corresponding to" the man. That all comes from the phrase that I have suggested likely means "equal to."

What God had intended then was to make a "power" or "strength" for the man who would in every way "correspond to him" or even "be his equal."

See also comment on GENESIS 2:20-23; 1 CORINTHIANS 11:7; EPHESIANS 5:22; 1 TIMOTHY 2:11-12.

2:20-23 Why from a Rib?

Whereas Adam was formed "from the dust of the ground" (Gen 2:7), the text describes Eve as being formed from "one of the man's ribs." Why this difference? Is there any significance to these two separate materials being used by God in the formation of the first human pair? If so, what is it? If not, why the distinction?

It has become customary for many in recent years to point to the Sumerian "Dilmun poem" as being the best way to explain this association of Eve with a rib. The Sumerian name for "rib" is *tì* (pronounced *tee*). But the Sumerian word *ti* also means "to make alive." These two facts are necessary background information to understand the myth that was told in Sumer.

It happened that the Sumerian water-god, Enki, fell sick, with eight of his organs or bodily parts being affected. A fox promised, if properly rewarded, to bring back the great mother-goddess Ninhursag, who had disappeared after an argument with Enki. Upon her reappearance she brought into existence eight corresponding healing deities, and Enki was restored in time. In order to heal Enki's rib the goddess created Ninti, "the lady of the rib," which may also be translated as "the lady who makes alive."

Now it is true that Adam called the woman that God had formed from his rib "Eve, because she would become the mother of all the living" (Gen 3:20). Samuel Noah Kramer commented, "It was this, one of the most ancient of literary puns, which was carried over and perpetuated in the biblical paradise story, although here, of course, it loses its validity, since the Hebrew word for 'rib' *[tsēlā']* and that for 'who makes alive' *[hoveh]* have nothing in common."[1]

The association of Eve with a "rib" and the "living" appear to be the common features in both the Sumerian and the biblical accounts. In that regard, the Sumerian myth may well be a garbled record of the same oral tradition about the inception of the human race. But the explanation in Sumer, of course, is set in an account with numerous deities and with petty quarrels and misadventures.

But no real explanation has been achieved as yet. It is not necessary to assume that the Hebrew wanted to promote the same pun that the Sumerian Dilmun poem did. The point of the Hebrew story actually takes off in another direction. In fact, Genesis 2:19 had just noted the animals had also been formed "out of the ground." This only emphasized the fact that Adam lacked the kind of companion he needed.

In order to teach the close connection that woman has with man, the text does not say that God also created her from "the ground" or "the dust of the ground"; instead, she came from one of Adam's ribs. Thus the phrase "bone of my bones and flesh of my flesh" pointed not only to the woman's origin, but also to the closeness of her marriage relationship and the partnership she was to share with her mate.

It is not without significance that the Hebrew word for "rib" appears nowhere else with this meaning in the Hebrew Bible; its usual meaning is "side." Thus, as some of the Reformers put it, woman was not taken from man's feet, as if she were beneath him, or from his head, as if she were over him, but from his side, as an equal with him.

Some have tried to relate "rib" to the space or cavity of the body of Adam on the strange assumption that man was originally bisexual. The attempt is then made to substitute the word for female sex organs in place of "rib." But this attempt is foiled from the start, for what will we make of "*one of* the man's ribs"?

The point is that man and woman together share a commonality and partnership observed nowhere else in the created order. To emphasize this closeness, God actually took a real part from the side of the man as he brought to life for the first time this new creation called woman.

See also comment on GENESIS 2:18; EPHESIANS 5:22.

Note

[1]Samuel Noah Kramer, *From the Tablets of Sumer* (Indian Hills, Colo.: Falcon's Wings Press, 1957), pp. 170-72.

3:5 Become like God?

Was the serpent more honest with Adam and Eve than God was? The serpent had explained God's prohibition against eating from the fruit of the tree from the motive of divine envy: "you will be like God, knowing good and evil." What knowledge did the man and woman attain?

Some have seen parallels in this passage to the Babylonian flood story, called the Gilgamesh Epic, in which the wild man Enkidu, who is finally civilized by spending six days and seven nights with a prostitute, sees the animals flee from him, and the woman congratulates him: "You are wise, Enkidu. You have become as a god." But the two sentences from Genesis 3:15 and Gilgamesh are totally different, and Enkidu sheds no light on this passage, contrary to undemonstrated assurances from a number of leading scholars.

There are five passages in which the antithetical pair *good and evil* and the verb *to know* occur: Deuteronomy 1:39; 2 Samuel 14:17; 19:35; 1 Kings 3:9; and Isaiah 7:15. These passages help to dismiss certain theories that have been proposed. Certainly we cannot say that Adam and Eve attained premature sexual union due to the aphrodisiac qualities of the fruit on these trees. The only argument in favor of this dubious interpretation is the awakening of shame (Gen 3:7) and the punishment on the woman, which was placed in what some construe as the area of her sexuality (Gen 3:16). However, even while the disturbance affected the sexual aspect of personhood, the text makes it clear that the knowledge of good and evil is a divine prerogative (Gen 3:5, 22). The extension of a sexual interpretation to God is obviously grotesque and unwarranted.

This would mean that humankind could become like God either by attaining total knowledge or by having autonomy, particularly moral freedom. Such wisdom "to know good and evil" can be seen in 2 Samuel 19:35, where Barzillai as an eighty-year-old man doubts his ability to exhibit the knowledge between good and evil needed from the king's counselor. Likewise, the woman from Tekoa likened David to an angel who was able to discern good and evil (2 Sam 14:17). Solomon asked that God would also give him "a discerning heart to govern your people and to distinguish between right and wrong" (1 Kings 3:9).

The lure of the serpent, then, did not imply that humanity would have infinite knowledge like God's knowledge or even that there was some aphrodisiac in the fruit that would open up sexual or carnal relations as an option until then unknown. Instead, the lure of the serpent was an invitation to experience that perpetual quest of human autonomy and freedom. Unfortunately for all, that autonomy turned out to be illusory and actually ended up in a sense of alienation, which has been studied so often since Freud introduced the concept to the modern world.

3:16 Is Childbearing a Curse or a Blessing?

If bearing children was declared a blessing from God in Genesis 1:28, why did God totally reverse this blessing as a result of the Fall? Indeed, the "pains," a word which reappears in verse 17 in the curse on man as well, are said to have increased. But no pain had been mentioned previously; only a blessing.

There is no doubt that this term refers to physical pain. Its root lies in a verb that means "to injure, cause pain or grief." Whether the pain would lie in the agony of childbirth or in the related grief that accompanies raising that child cannot be finally determined; the text would seem to allow for both ideas.

Katherine C. Bushnell, in *God's Word to Woman,* suggests that verse 16 be translated differently since the Hebrew text could support such a reading. She noted that some ancient versions attached the meaning of "lying in wait," "an ambush" or "a snare" to the word generally read as "multiply." This idea of a snare or a lying in wait, however, may have been moved back to Genesis 3:15 from its more normal position in Genesis 3:16. Bushnell would render the opening words of verse 16 this way: "Unto the woman he said, 'A snare has increased your sorrow and sighing.' "

This translation is not all that different in meaning from the more traditional "I will greatly multiply . . ." The difference between the two readings is found wholly in the interlinear Hebrew vowel signs which came as late as the eighth century of the Christian era. The difference is this (using capital letters to show the original Hebrew consonantal text and lowercase to show the late addition of the vowel letters): *HaRBah AaRBeh,* "I will greatly multiply," and *HiRBah AoReB,* "has caused to multiply (or made great) a lying-in-wait." The participial form *ARB* appears some fourteen times in Joshua and is translated as "ambush" or "a lying in wait."

If this reading is correct (and some ancient versions read such a word just a few words back in verse 15, probably by misplacement), then that "lier-in-wait" would undoubtedly be that subtle serpent, the devil. He it was who would increase the sorrow of raising children. This is the only way we can explain why the idea of "a snare" or "lying-in-wait" still clings to this context.

But another matter demands our attention in verse 16, the word for *conception.* This translation is difficult because the Hebrew word *HRN* is not the correct way to spell *conception.* It is spelled correctly as *HRJWN* in Ruth 4:13 and Hosea 9:11. But this spelling in Genesis 3:16 is two letters short, and its vowels are also unusual. The form is regarded by lexical authorities such as Brown, Driver and Briggs as a contraction or even an error. The early Greek translation (made in the third or second century before Christ) read instead *HGN,* meaning "sighing." The resultant meaning for this clause would be "A snare has increased your sorrow and sighing."

What difference does such a rendering make? The point is simply that this curse cannot be read to mean that the right to determine when a woman will become a mother is placed totally outside her will or that this function has been placed entirely and necessarily in the hands and will of her husband.

Furthermore, it must be remembered that this statement, no matter how we shall finally interpret it, is from a curse passage. In no case should it be made normative. And if the Evil One and not God is the source of the sorrow and sighing, then it is all the more necessary for us to refuse to place any degree of normativity to such statements and describe either the ordeal of giving birth to a child, or the challenge of raising that child, as an evil originating in God. God is never the source of evil; he would rather bless women. Instead, it is Satan who has set this trap.

The next clause strengthens the one we have been discussing by adding "in sorrow [or pain] you will bring forth children." Once again note that bearing children in itself was a blessing described in the so-called orders of creation of Genesis 1:28. The grief lies not so much in the conception or in the act of childbirth itself, but in the whole process of bringing children into the world and raising them up to be whole persons before God.

3:16 How Was the Woman Punished?

The meaning of the second part of the woman's penalty centers around two very important words that have a most amazing translation history, "desire" and "will rule." Seldom has so much mischief been caused by a translation error that became institutionalized.

Is it true that due to the Fall women naturally exhibit overpowering sexual desires for their husbands? And if this is so, did God simultaneously order husbands to exercise authority over their wives? In one form or another, most conservative interpreters answer both of these questions emphatically yes and point to Genesis 3:16 as the grounds for their answer. But will the text itself bear the weight of such important claims?

The Hebrew word *t^e^šûqâh,* now almost universally translated as "desire," was previously rendered as "turning." The word appears in the Hebrew Old Testament only three times: here in Genesis 3:16, in Genesis 4:7 and in Song of Songs 7:10. Of the twelve known ancient versions (the Greek Septuagint, the Syriac Peshitta, the Samaritan Pentateuch, the Old Latin, the Sahidic, the Bohairic, the Ethiopic, the Arabic, Aquila's Greek, Symmachus's Greek, Theodotion's Greek and the Latin Vulgate), almost every one (twenty-one out of twenty-eight times) renders these three instances of *t^e^šûqâh* as "turning," not "desire."

Likewise, the church fathers (Clement of Rome, Irenaeus, Tertullian, Origen, Epiphanius and Jerome, along with Philo, a Jew who died about A.D. 50) seem to be ignorant of any other sense for this word *t^e^šûqâh* than the translation of "turning." Furthermore, the Latin rendering was *conversio* and the Greek was *apostrophē* or *epistrophē,* words all meaning "a turning."

With such strong and universal testimony in favor of "turning," how did the idea of *desire* ever intrude into the translator's agenda? Again, it was Katherine C. Bushnell who did the pioneer research on this problem. She traced its genesis to an Italian Dominican monk named Pagnino who translated the Hebrew Bible. Pagnino, according to the infamous biblical critic Richard Simon, "too much neglected the ancient versions of Scripture to attach himself to the teachings of the rabbis." Pagnino's version was published in Lyons in 1528, seven years before Coverdale's English Bible. Now except for Wycliffe's 1380 English version and the Douay Bible of 1609, both of which were made from the Latin Vulgate, every English version from the time of Pagnino up to the present day has adopted Pagnino's rendering for Genesis 3:16.

The older English Bibles, following Pagnino, rendered this verse as "Thy lust [or lusts] shall pertayne [pertain] to thy husband." Clearly, then, the sense given to the word by Pagnino and his followers was that of libido or sensual desire. The only place that Bushnell could locate such a concept was in the "Ten Curses of Eve" in the Talmud.

It is time the church returned to the real meaning of this word. The sense of Genesis 3:16 is simply this: As a result of her sin, Eve would turn away from her sole dependence on God and turn now to her husband. The results would not at all be pleasant, warned God, as he announced this curse.

Nowhere does this text teach, nor does nature confirm by our observations, that there would now be a tendency for a woman to be driven by a desire for sexual relationships with her husband or with other men. This is both a misrepresentation of the text and a male fantasy born out of some other source than the Bible or human nature. Even if the word is tamed down to mean just an inclination or a tendency, we would be no further ahead. These renderings would still miss the point of the Hebrew. The Hebrew reads, "You are turning away [from God!] to your husband, and [as a result] he will rule over you [take advantage of you]."

Though this text only predicts how some husbands will take advantage of their wives when the wives turn to their husbands after turning away from God, some argue that this second verb should be rendered "he shall rule over you." This would make the statement mandatory with the force of a command addressed to all husbands to rule over their wives.

The Hebrew grammar once again will not allow this construction. The verb contains a simple statement of futurity; there is not one hint of obligation or normativity in this verb. To argue differently would be as logical as demanding that a verb in verse 18 be rendered "It *shall produce* thorns and thistles." Thereafter, all Christian farmers who used weed killer would be condemned as disobedient to the God who demanded that the ground have such thorns and thistles.

The often-repeated rejoinder to this *will rule/shall rule* argument is to go to Genesis 4:7: "Sin is crouching at the door; unto you is its turning, but you will [or *shall* in the sense of *must*] rule over it." There is no doubt that both the word *t^e^šûqâh* ("turning") and the verb *to rule* are found in both contexts. But what is debated is the best way to render the Hebrew.

Several suggestions avoid the traditional interpretation that insists on an obligatory sense to the verb *to rule.* One way predicts that Cain, now governed by sin and pictured as a crouching beast at his door, will rule over him (his brother, Abel). This, however, does not appear to be what the author meant.

A preferred way of handling this phrase would be to treat it as a question. (The absence of the particle introducing questions is a phenomenon witnessed in about half of Hebrew questions.) Hence we would render it "But you, will you rule over it?" or "Will you be its master?" (This interpretation is also favored by H. Ewald, G. R. Castellino and, to some extent, Claus Westermann.)

Even though many hold to the belief that 1 Corinthians 14:34 refers to Genesis 3:16 when it records, "Women should remain silent in the churches. They are not allowed to speak, but must be in submission, as the Law says," I cannot agree. When the Corinthians referred to the law (it seems that Paul is answering a previous question they wrote to him), it was to the Jewish law found in the Talmud and Mishnah that they referred. There it was taught that a woman should not speak and that she must be silent, but that is not taught in the Old Testament!

The only conceivable way a person could link up Genesis 3:16 with 1 Corinthians 14:34-35 would be if the Genesis passage said husbands must rule over their wives. Since such a wording of the verse has been proven impossible, this reference should be surrendered. We should lay no stronger burden on God's people than what is warranted in God's Word.

Later on in God's revelation, our Lord will affirm a job subordination within the marriage relationship, and the husband will be answerable to God for the well-being of his wife and family. However, Genesis 3:16 does not carry any of those meanings.

We may conclude, then, that *t^{e}šûqâh* does not refer to the lust or sexual appetite of a woman for a man. Neither does the verb *to rule* over her express God's order for husbands in their relationships to their wives.

See also comment on EPHESIANS 5:22; 1 PETER 3:6; 3:7.

4:3-4 Did God Favor Abel over Cain?

Does God have favorites? Does he show partiality for one over another—in this case, Abel over Cain? And does God prefer shepherds to farmers? If not, what was the essential difference between these first two sacrifices in the Bible?

The traditional interpretation says that the difference between Cain and Abel is that one offered a bloody sacrifice and the other did not. If this understanding is correct, why are neither we nor they given any specific instructions to that effect? Up to this point, that distinction had not been made. And even if a distinction between the use and absence of blood was in vogue at this early date, why are both sacrifices referred to throughout this whole narrative with the Hebrew term *minḥāh,* a "gift" or "meal offering"?

The answers to these questions are not as difficult as they may appear. There is only one point on which there can be legitimate puzzlement: nothing in this episode indicates that this is the inauguration of the sacrificial system. While it does appear that this is the first time anyone ever sacrificed anything, the text does not specifically say so. That will remain, at best, only an inference.

Actually, the supposition that Cain and Abel's father, Adam, originated sacrifices may be closer to the truth, since no command authorizing or requesting sacrifices appears in these first chapters of Genesis. The whole subject of the origins of sacrifice is one that scholars have debated long and hard, but the subject remains a mystery.

Even with this much caution, we must be careful about importing back into the times of Adam and Eve the instructions that Moses was later given on sacrifices. The word used to describe "sacrifice" throughout this episode of Cain and Abel is the word used in the broadest sense, *minḥâh.* It covers any type of gift that any person might bring. Consequently, the merit one gift might have over another does not lie in the content or type of gift—including the presence or absence of blood.

Of course, there was a problem with Cain's "gift"—*he* was the problem. Genesis 4:3 describes how Cain merely brought "some" of the fruits of the field. Nothing can be said about the fact that he, as an agriculturalist, naturally brought what farmers have to give. But when his offering is contrasted with Abel's, a flaw immediately shows up.

Abel gave what cost him dearly, the "fat pieces"—in that culture considered the choicest parts—of "the firstborn" of his flock. Abel could very well have rationalized, as we might have done, that he would wait until some of those firstborn animals had matured and had one, two or three lambs of their own. Certainly at that point it would have been possible to give an even larger gift to God, and Abel would have been further ahead as well. But he gave instead what cost him most, the "firstborn."

The telltale signs that we are dealing here with a contrast between formalistic worship and true worship are the emphasis that the text gives to the men and the verb it uses with both of them. In Genesis 4:4-5 there are four emphatic marks used with reference to the two brothers.

Literally, the Hebrew of verses 4 and 5 says, "And Abel, he brought, indeed, even he, some of the firstlings of his flock and some of the fat portions belonging to him. And the Lord regarded with favor Abel and [then] his offering. But unto Cain and [then] unto his offering, he did not have regard."

Clearly the focus of this passage is on the men. There are four emphatic elements in the text that mark this emphasis: first, the man's name; then the verb for "bringing" with the pronominal suffix; then the emphasizing particle *gam;* and finally the personal independent pronoun. It is difficult to see how the writer could have made it any more pointed that it was the men, and their hearts' condition, that was the determinative factor in God's deciding whose sacrifice was to be accepted. The text almost stutters: "And Abel, he, he also, he brought."

The verb *shāʿâh* means "to gaze," but when it is used with the preposition *'el* ("unto" or "toward"), as it is here, it means "to regard with favor." Ever since Luther, commentators have noticed that God's favor was pointedly directed toward the person first and then, and only then, toward the offering that person brought. Accordingly, this became the determinative factor in all worship: the heart attitude of the individual. If the heart was not found acceptable, the gift was likewise unacceptable.

It is true that an old Greek translation of this text rendered *shāʿâh* in Greek as *enepyrisen,* "he kindled." Apparently the translator wanted to say that on some occasions God did kindle acceptable sacrifices. But since there is a double object for this verb, namely, Abel and his sacrifice, this translation is unacceptable, for it would set the man on fire as well as the sacrifice!

That Cain's heart and not his offering was the real problem here can be seen from the last part of verse 5: "So Cain was very angry, and his face was downcast"—literally, "it burned Cain greatly [or, to the core] and his face dropped."

God's displeasure with Cain revealed the sad state of affairs in Cain's heart. Instead of moving to rectify his attitude, Cain let it harden into murder. For the moment, however, anger hid itself in Cain's eyes—he avoided looking anyone in the eye. Averting his own gaze, he kept others from seeing (through the eye gate) what was in his heart.

Hermann Gunkel—who unwisely called this episode a myth—was truly unjustified in claiming this story taught that God loved shepherds but not farmers. Despite others who have followed Gunkel's lead, there is no proven connection between this narrative and any parallel stories in the ancient Near East of rivalries between shepherds and farmers.

Sacrifice in the Old Testament is not a "preapproved" way of earning divine credit. The principle behind it remains the same as it does for all acts of service and ritual in the Christian faith today: God always inspects the giver and the worshiper before he inspects the gift, service or worship.

See also comment on 1 SAMUEL 15:22; PSALM 51:16-17, 19.

4:17 Where Did Cain Get His Wife?

Up to this point in Genesis we only know about Adam and Eve, and Cain and Abel. But the most obvious answer to this common question must be that Adam and Eve had other children, including daughters. Indeed, Genesis 5:4 plainly says as much, "[Adam] had other sons and daughters."

Cain must have married his sister. But to admit this is to raise a further difficulty: was he thereby guilty of incest?

At least two things can be said in response to this reproach. First, if the human race was propagated from a single pair, as we believe the evidence indicates, such closely related marriages were unavoidable. The demand for some other way of getting the race started is an unfair expectation.

In the second place, the notion of incest must be probed more closely. At first the sin of incest was connected with sexual relationships between parents and children. Only afterward was the notion of incest extended to sibling relationships.

By Moses' time there were laws governing all forms of incest (Lev 18:7-17; 20:11-12, 14, 17, 20-21; Deut 22:30; 27:20, 22, 23). These laws clearly state that sexual relations or marriage is forbidden with a mother, father, stepmother, sister, brother, half brother, half sister, granddaughter, daughter-in-law, son-in-law, aunt, uncle or brother's wife.

The Bible, in the meantime, notes that Abraham married his half sister (Gen 20:12). Therefore, the phenomenon is not unknown in Scripture. Prior to Moses' time, incest in many of the forms later proscribed were not thought to be wrong. Thus, even Moses' own father, Amram, married an aunt, his father's sister, Jochebed (Ex 6:20). In Egypt, the routine marriage of brothers and sisters among the Pharaohs all the way up to the second century made the Mosaic law all the more a radical break with their Egyptian past.

The genetic reasons for forbidding incest were not always an issue. Close inbreeding in ancient times was without serious or any genetic damage. Today, the risk of genetic damage is extremely high. Since the genetic possibilities of Adam and Eve were very good, there were no biological reasons for restricting marriages to the degree that it became necessary to do later.

5:3-5 How Could Adam Live 930 Years?

Everyone who reads the list of the ten

antediluvians in Genesis 5 and the list of ten postdiluvians in Genesis 11 is immediately struck by the longevity of these patriarchs. How is it possible that these people were able to live so long?

Moreover, we are awed by the ages at which they were still able to father children. Noah became a proud father at a mere 500 years (Gen 5:32)!

The question of the possible reconciliation of the results of scientific inquiry and the claims of Scripture could not be more challenging. The claims for the long lives and the ages at which these men were able to sire children is enough to lead to a distrust of the Scriptures almost from the very first chapters of the Bible.

In fact, so notoriously difficult are the problems presented by the genealogies of Genesis 5 and 11 that they have been paraded for centuries as prime examples of chronological impossibilities in the Bible. A resolution for the kinds of issues raised here are found, however, in an understanding of the writer's method.

In April 1890, William Henry Green of the Princeton faculty wrote an article in *Bibliotheca Sacra* pointing to some clear principles used by the writers of Scripture in the construction of genealogies. Those principles include the following:

1. Abridgment is the general rule because the sacred writers did not want to encumber their pages with more names than necessary.

2. Omissions in genealogies are fairly routine. For example, Matthew 1:8 omits three names between Joram and Ozias (Uzziah); namely, Ahaziah (2 Kings 8:25), Joash (2 Kings 12:1) and Amaziah (2 Kings 14:1). In verse 11, Matthew omits Jehoiakim (2 Kings 23:34). In fact, in Matthew 1:1 the whole of two millennia are summed up in two giant steps: "Jesus Christ, the son of David [about 1000 B.C.], the son of Abraham [about 2000 B.C.]."

3. The span of a biblical "generation" is more than our twenty to thirty years. In Syriac it equals eighty years. Often in the Exodus account a generation is 100 to 120 years.

4. The meanings of *begat, son of, father of* and even *bore a son* often have special nuances, as the context often indicates. To *beget* often means no more than "to become the ancestor of." To be *the father of* often means being a grandfather or great-grandfather. The point is that the next key person was descended from that male named "father" in the text.

The most instructive lesson of all can be gleaned from Kohath's descent into Egypt (Gen 46:6-11) some 430 years (Ex 12:40) before the exodus. Now if Moses (one in the Kohath line) was 80 years old at the time of the exodus (Ex 7:7), and no gaps (such as are suggested by the above-mentioned principles) are understood (as we believe the evidence above now forces us to concede), then the "grandfather" of Moses had in Moses' lifetime 8,600 descendants. Amazing as that might seem, here is the real shocker: 2,750 of those 8,600 descendants were males between the ages of 30 and 50 (Num 3:19, 27-28, 34; 4:36)! It is difficult to believe that the writers of Scripture were that naive.

The form that Genesis 5 and 11 use, with few exceptions, is a stereotypic formula giving the age of the patriarch at the birth of his son, the number of years that he lived after the birth of that son, and then the total number of years that he lived until he died. It is the question of the function of these numbers that attracts our attention here.

Since Zilpah is credited with "bearing" *(yālaḏ)* her grandchildren (Gen 46:18) and Bilhah is said to "bear" *(yālaḏ)* her grandchildren as well (Gen 46:25), it is clear that a legitimate usage of these numbers in the genealogies might well mean that B was a distant relative of A. In this case, the age of A is the age at the birth of that (unnamed) child from whom B (eventually) descended.

The ages given for the "father" when the "son" was born must be actual years, as we shall presently see. The conflation takes place not at the point of supplying the actual years at which the father had a child; it is instead at the point where the name of the next noteworthy descendant is given instead of the immediate son. The ages given function as an indicator of the fact that the effects of the Fall into sin had not yet affected human generative powers as seriously as they have more recently. The same point, of course, is to be made with regard to human longevity. The fact that the record wishes to stress is the sad mortality of men and women as a result of the sin in the Garden of Eden. The repeated litany "and he died" echoes from the pages like the solemn toll of a funeral bell.

Attempts to make the numbers more palatable have been crushed by the internal weight of their own argumentation or from a failure to care for all the data in a single theory. One abortive attempt was to treat the names as names of tribes rather than as names of individuals. This would seem to work until we meet up with Enoch, who was taken to heaven. It hardly seems fair to imply that the whole Enoch tribe was taken to heaven, so we are left with the idea that these really are meant to represent individuals.

Another, equally unsuccessful, rationalization was that the "years" here represented a system of counting months, or something of that sort. In this view, the years would be reduced by a factor of 10 or 12. Accordingly, Adam's total of 930 years could be reduced to the more manageable and believable 93 or 77 years. This theory runs into trouble when Nahor becomes the father of Terah at 29 years of age in Genesis 11:24. This would mean that he actually had a child when he was 2.9 or 2.4 years old! In that case we jump from the pan into the fire. Unfortunately for this theory, there are no known biblical examples of the word *year* meaning anything less than the solar year we are accustomed to in general speech.

One final warning might be in order: do not add up the years of these patriarchs in Genesis 5 and 11 and expect to come up with the Bible's date for the birth of the human race. The reason for this warning is clear: the Bible never adds up these numbers. It is not as though the Bible never gives us sums of years—there are the 430 years of Egyptian bondage in Exodus 12:40 and the 480 years of 1 Kings 6:1. But in Genesis 5 and 11 the writer does not employ his numbers for this purpose; neither should we.

Some who have violated this simple observation have seriously argued that the human race was created on October 24, 4004 B.C., at 9:30 a.m., 45th Meridian time. Being careful scholars from Cambridge, the cynic William Brewster quipped, they did not dare say with any more precision when humankind was born!

The earliest definite date we can fix for any biblical person is around 2100 B.C. for the birth of Abram. The Julian calendar dates for anything before that are impossible to set with the present sets of data at our disposal.

The creation of the universe is dated in Genesis 1:1 as being "in the beginning." Of that we can be as certain as we are of revelation itself. The creation of Adam came six "days" later, but one must be warned that right there in the first chapters of Genesis the Bible uses the word *day* with three different meanings: (1) daylight (Gen 1:5), (2) a twenty-four-hour day (Gen 1:14) and (3) an epoch or era, as we use the word in speaking of the "day" of the horse and buggy or Abraham Lincoln's "day" (Gen 2:4; compare the RSV's "In the day" with the NIV's "When"). I would opt for the day-age theory, given all that must take place on the sixth "day" according to the Genesis record. Incidentally, this day-age view has been the majority view of the church since the fourth century, mainly through the influence of Saint Augustine.

So Adam did live a real 930 years. The sons attributed to him may have been his direct sons or they may have been from two to six generations away, but in the same line.

See also articles on "Why Don't Bible Genealogies Always Match Up?" and "Aren't Many Old Testament Numbers Wrong?"

5:4 Where Did the Wives of the Antediluvians Come From?

See comment on GENESIS 4:17.

5:23-24 What Happened to Enoch?

Too many people assume that there is no uniform and sure doctrine on the subject of life after death in the Old Testament. Only one reference in the Old Testament is counted as a clear and undisputed reference to the resurrection of the dead by most Old Testament scholars, Daniel 12:2: "Multitudes who sleep in the dust of the earth will awake: some to everlasting life, others to shame and everlasting contempt." Unhappily, however, even those who concede this point incorrectly place Daniel in the second century B.C.

A few scholars are willing to add Isaiah 26:19 to the Daniel 12:2 passage and count it as a second passage supporting the idea of resurrection of the dead in the Old Testament. It reads, "But your dead will live; their bodies will rise. You who dwell in the dust, wake up and shout for joy. Your dew is like the dew of the morning; the earth will give birth to her dead."

Nevertheless, it is amazing to see how many learned men and women will deny even these two texts and argue that the Old Testament teaches virtually nothing about resurrection or life after death.

The truth of the matter is that ancient peoples were more attuned to the subject of life after death than moderns suspect. The peoples of the ancient Near East wrote at length about what life was like after one left this earth. One need only consult such representative pieces as the Gilgamesh Epic, The Descent of Ishtar into the Netherworld, the Book of the Dead and the Pyramid Texts. Indeed, the whole economy of Egypt was geared to the cult of the dead, for all who wished a part in the next life had to be buried around the pyramid of the Pharaoh. What these Egyptians could expect in that afterlife was depicted in the scenes on the walls of their mortuaries: eating, drinking, singing and all the joys of this life. Each joy, of course, would be magnified and still enjoyed through a body.

By the time Abraham arrived in Egypt, such concepts had been emblazoned on their walls in hieroglyphics, murals and models made of clay, to make sure no one missed the point. Life after death was not a modern doctrine developed by an educated society that began to think more abstractly about itself and its times. Instead it was an ancient hunger that existed in the hearts of humanity long before the patriarchs, prophets and kings of the Old Testament began to function. Why should we attribute this idea to the second and third centuries B.C. if already in the third and second millennium B.C. there is strong evidence to support it?

The earliest biblical mention of the possibility of a mortal's inhabiting the immortal realms of deity can be found in Genesis 5:24. There we are told that a man named Enoch lived 365 years, all the while "walking with God." Suddenly, "he was no more, because God took him away."

Enoch, whose name means "beginner," must have been unusually godly—not that he achieved this distinction by removing himself from the world and contemplating only the presence of God. In fact, he fathered the famous Methuselah (the man who lived the longest that we know about on planet Earth, 969 years!). And he had other sons and daughters. This man was hardly removed from the daily grind and the problems of life. Nevertheless, he was able to walk with God.

Since this quality of "walking with God" is ascribed only to Enoch and Noah (Gen 6:9), it is significant that Malachi 2:6 shows that the concept involved having a most intimate communion with God. What a tribute to a mortal who is also a sinner! On the other hand, since Exodus 33:20 teaches that "no one may see [God] and live," the possibility of an outward, physical meeting with God is ruled out.

Many think that only since New Testament times have such nearness and inner communion with God become possible. But here was one who found such uninterrupted consciousness of the living God that it appears to match what we in the post-New Testament era experience.

After 365 years of intimacy with the Almighty, suddenly the Lord "took" Enoch. What can it mean that he "took" him?

The Hebrew root for the verb *to take* is used over a thousand times in the Old Testament. However, in two contexts—this Genesis 5 passage and the account of Elijah's assumption into heaven in 2 Kings 2:3, 10-11—it refers to a snatching of a person's body up to heaven.

In light of these two cases of physical assumption, are there other cases where the verb is used in the Old Testament with a similar meaning?

There are two additional contexts in which more is intended than a mere rescue from dying or distress. Psalm 49 presents a stark contrast between the end of the lives of the wicked and the end of the lives of the righteous. The wicked are like "the beasts that perish" (Ps 49:12, 20) without any hope that they "should live on forever" (Ps 49:9). However, the righteous have the triumphant expectation that "God will redeem [them] from the grave [Hebrew *Sheol*]; he will surely take [them] to himself" (Ps 49:15). The idea is the same as that of Genesis 5:24: God will snatch, take or receive us to himself when we die. If the psalmist had in mind the fact that he would be rescued from death for a few years, though he knows he still must eventually die like the beasts, then the psalm has very little, or no, point.

Psalm 73:23-25 makes a similar contrast between the wicked and the righteous. Once again there is faith that reaches beyond this life, and it centers on this verb *to take* (Hebrew *lāqaḥ*). Says the psalmist, "You guide me with your counsel, and afterward you will take me into glory" (Ps 73:24).

Accordingly, it can be argued on very strong linguistic and conceptual grounds that the "taking" of a person from this earth implies that mortals are capable of inhabiting immortal realms. For the believer in Yahweh in Old Testament times, death did not end it all. There was life after death, and that life was to be in the presence of the living God.

While Enoch did not experience "resurrection," he did experience glorification. He did, along with Elijah, transcend this mortal life and go in his body to be with God. Since Enoch had not died, he could not be resurrected.

Such a view of an immediate access into the presence of God would also close down all speculation on any kind of intermediate state, receptacle or location as unscriptural. To say that Old Testament believers stayed in a separate compartment in Sheol or in a kind of purgatory runs directly counter to the fact that God snatched Enoch and Elijah away "to himself."

To say that the Old Testament offers the hope of personal fellowship with God beyond the grave with a real body is not outlandish or incorrect. That hope is a teaching of the text itself.

See also comment on GENESIS 25:8; JOB 19:25-27; PSALM 49:12, 20; ECCLESIASTES 3:19-21.

6:1-4 Who Married the Daughters of Men?

Few texts in the history of interpretation have aroused more curiosity and divergence of opinion than Genesis 6:1-4. It is at once tantalizing and deeply puzzling.

What is most difficult is the identification of the main participants in this short narrative—the "sons of God," the "daughters of men" and the "Nephilim" (or "giants"). An impressive array of scholars has lined up for each of the three major positions taken on the identification of these three groups of participants. The three positions may be labeled "the cosmologically mixed races view" (angels and humans), "the religiously mixed races view" (godly Sethites and worldly Cainites) and "the sociologically mixed races view" (despotic male aristocrats and beautiful female commoners).

By all odds, the view that may perhaps claim the greatest antiquity is the cosmologically mixed races, or the angel theory, view. The pseudepigraphal and noncanonical 1 Enoch, dating from around 200 B.C., claims in 6:1—7:6 that two hundred angels in heaven, under the leadership of Semayaz, noticed that the humans had unusually beautiful daughters. These they desired for themselves, so they took a mutual oath to go down to earth together, and each took a wife. They taught these wives magical medicine, incantations, the cutting of roots and the care of plants. When the women became pregnant, they gave birth to giants that reached three hundred cubits. The giants in turn consumed all the food, thereby arousing the deep hatred of the earthlings. The giants turned to devouring the people along with the birds, wild beasts, reptiles and fish. Then it was that the earth, having had enough of these huge bullies, brought an accusation against them.

The famous Jewish historian Josephus (born 37 B.C.) also appears to follow this angel theory. He wrote, "Many angels accompanied with women, and begat sons that proved unjust" (*Antiquities* 1.3.1). Likewise, the Greek translation of the Bible of the third century B.C. reads "angels of God" for the phrase "sons of God" in Genesis 6:2. In spite of the antiquity of the cosmologically mixed races view, there are such overwhelming problems with it that it is not recommended as the solution to this problem. While it is true, of course, that the term "sons of God" does occur in Job 1:6, 2:1 and 38:7 with the meaning "angels" (and that the phrase "sons of the mighty" appears in Ps 29:1 and 89:7 with the meaning "angels"), it does not fit well here for several reasons.

Nowhere else in Scripture are we told that angels married humans. In fact, our Lord specifically stated that angels do not marry (Mk 12:25). And though the Septuagint translated the expression as being equivalent to "angels," it is in fact only the Alexandrian manuscript that does so. The critical edition by Alfred Rahlfs does not reflect the angelic interpretation.

Even more serious is the problem of why judgment should fall on the humans and on the earth if the angels of heaven were the cause of the trouble. God should have flooded heaven, not earth. The culprits came from above; the women seem to have been doing nothing except being beautiful!

Some, however, will appeal to the New Testament passages of 1 Peter 3:18-20, 2 Peter 2:4 and Jude 6-7 for further support of the angel theory. But these passages do not say anything about angelic marriages. To argue from the phrase "in a similar way" in Jude 7 that the sin of Sodom and Gomorrah is the same as the sin of Genesis 6:1-4 claims too much, for the sin of sodomy is not the same thing as marrying a wife from another part of the universe! In fact, "in a similar way" does not compare the sin of the angels with the sin of the men of Sodom and Gomorrah; instead, it compares the sin of Sodom and Gomorrah with the sins of "the cities about them" (that is, Admah and Zeboiim; see Deut 29:23 and Hos 11:8). Thus the sins of Jude's angels (Jude 6) and the sins of the five cities of the plain (Jude 7) are held up as warnings of the judgment that could come to others. The fall of the angels that Jude mentions is that which took place when Lucifer fell. To connect this fall with the time of the flood because of the proximity of the references in Jude 4-7 would demand that we connect the flood with the overthrow of the five cities of the plain. But the events listed in Jude are successive, not simultaneous: (1) the fall in eternity of Satan (Jude 4), (2) the preaching of Noah prior to the flood (Jude 5) and (3) the overthrow of Sodom and Gomorrah (Jude 6).

To allege that "giants" were the results of such sexual unions is once again to go beyond any data we possess in Scripture. Did the angels procreate without the use of natural bodies? Or did they already possess natural bodies? Or did they create for themselves natural bodies by the use of some mysterious, intrinsic, but rebellious power? Any and all answers to such questions would be purely speculative. To use extracanonical evidence such as 1 Enoch as a witness against or even for Scripture would be unprecedented.

The religiously mixed races view identifies the "sons of God" as the godly line of Seth. Given the sin they committed, they are generally looked on as the apostate line of Seth. "The daughters of men" are equated with the ungodly line of Cain. The sin condemned, then, would be the sin of being "unequally yoked"—that is, the marriage of believers to unbelievers.

This view also fails to meet the test of consistency with the biblical data and context. It uses the term *men* in verses 1 and 2 in two different senses: in verse 1 "men" is used to indicate humanity generically, while in verse 2 it is understood to refer to the Cainite line specifically. Suggesting such an abrupt change in meaning without any indication in the text is unwarranted.

But even more alarming is the problem of the offspring. Why would religiously mixed marriages produce *n^e^pilîm-gibbôrîm* (or, as some translate this Hebrew expression, "giants")? Does the mixture of pagan and godly genes assure that the offspring's DNA will be wild and grotesque?

This religiously mixed view should be abandoned as well as the cosmologically mixed view. Neither one can stand the weight of the evidence of the passage.

The preferable interpretation of this passage is the sociologically mixed view. "Sons of God" is an early, but typical, reference to the titularies for kings, nobles and aristocrats in the ancient Near Eastern setting. These power-hungry despots not only lusted after power but also were powerfully driven to become "men of a name" (or "men of renown"—Gen 6:4).

In their thirst for recognition and reputation, they despotically usurped control of the states they governed as if they were accountable to no one but themselves. Thus they perverted the whole concept of the state and the provision that God had made for some immediate amelioration of earth's injustices and inequities (Gen 6:5-6; see also Gen 10:8-12). They also became polygamous, taking and marrying "any of [the women] they chose" (Gen 6:2).

What evidence can be produced for the correctness of this view? There are five lines of evidence. (1) The ancient Aramaic Targums render "sons of God" as "sons of nobles" (Targums of Onkelos), and the Greek translation of Symmachus reads "the sons of the kings or lords." (2) The word *gods* (Hebrew *ᵉlōhîm*) is used in Scripture for men who served as magistrates or judges ("Then his master must take him before the judges *[ᵉlōhîm],*" Ex 21:6; see also Ex 22:8; Ps 82:1, 6). (3) Structurally, the account of the Cainite Lamech (Gen 4:19-24) and that of the "sons of God" in Genesis 6:1-4 are very much alike. In each there is the taking of wives, the bearing of children and the dynastic exploits. The former passage ends with a boast of judgment by Lamech, and the other ends with God's decree of judgment. Lamech practiced bigamy (Gen 4:19), and he enforced his policies by using tyranny. The portraits are parallel and depict states of tyranny, corruption and polygamy. (4) Near Eastern discoveries have validated the pagan use of all sorts of gods' and goddesses' names in order to give more clout and prestige to the governments of Egypt and Mesopotamia—hence the title "sons of God."

The fifth and final line of evidence concerns the *nᵉpilîm/gibbôrîm* of Genesis 6:4. The word *nᵉpilîm* occurs only here and in Numbers 13:33, where it refers to the Anakim, who were people of great stature. The root meaning of the word *nᵉpilîm* is "to fall." However in Genesis 6:4 the *nᵉpilîm* are associated with the term *gibbôrîm.* The word *gibbôrîm* comes from *gibbôr*, meaning "a mighty man of valor, strength, wealth or power." Nimrod, in Genesis 10:8, was such a *gibbôr.* He also was clearly a king in the land of Shinar. Hence the meaning of *nᵉpilîm/gibbôrîm* is not "giants," but something more like "princes," "aristocrats" or "great men."

Genesis 6:1-4, therefore, is best understood as depicting ambitious, despotic and autocratic rulers seizing both women and power in an attempt to gain all the authority and notoriety they could from those within their reach. Their progeny were, not surprisingly, adversely affected, and so it was that God was grieved over the increased wickedness on planet Earth. Every inclination of the hearts and thoughts of humanity was evil. Thus the flood had to come to judge humankind for the perversion of authority, the state, justice and human sexuality.

6:6 Does God Change His Mind?

In Malachi 3:6 God affirms, "I the LORD do not change." This is why Christian doctrine teaches that God is immutable—that is, unchangeable. The promise of this constancy and permanence in the nature and character of God has been deeply reassuring to many believers down through the ages. When everything else changes, we can remember the living God never fails or vacillates from anything that he is or that he has promised.

For this reason many are legitimately startled when they read that the Lord "was grieved" or "repented" that he had ever made man and woman upon the earth (Gen 6:6). How can both the immutability and the changeableness of God be taught in the same canon of Scripture?

Scriptures frequently use the phrase "God repented." For example, Exodus 32:14 says, "Then [after Moses' intercession for the Israelites] the LORD relented and did not bring on his people the disaster he had threatened." Or again in 1 Samuel 15:11, "I am *grieved* that I have made Saul king, because he has turned away from me and has not carried out my instructions." Again in Jeremiah 26:3, "Perhaps they will listen and each will turn from his evil way. Then I will *relent* and not bring on them the disaster I was planning because of the evil they have done." (See also Jer 26:13, 19; Jon 3:10.)

The Hebrew root behind all the words variously translated as "relent," "repent," "be sorry" and "grieve" is *nḥm.* In its origins the root may well have reflected the idea of breathing or sighing deeply. It suggests a physical display of one's feelings—sorrow, compassion or comfort. The root is reflected in such proper names as Nehemiah, Nahum and Menehem.

When God's repentance is mentioned, the point is not that he has changed in his character or in what he stands for. Instead, what we have is a human term being used to refer—rather inadequately—to a perfectly good and necessary divine action. Such a term is called an *anthropomorphism.*

When the Bible says that God repented, the idea is that his feelings toward some person or group of persons changed in response to some change on the part of the objects of his action or some mediator who intervened (often by God's own direction and plan). Often in the very same passages that announce God's repentance there is a firm denial of any alteration in God's plan, purpose or character. Thus 1 Samuel 15:29 reminds us that "he who is the Glory of Israel does not lie or change his mind; for he is not a man, that he should change his mind." Yet Samuel made that statement the day after the Lord told him that he was *grieved* he had made Saul king (1 Sam 15:11).

From our human perspective, then, it appears that the use of this word indicates that God changed his purpose. But the expression "to repent," when used of God, is anthropopathic (that is, a description of our Lord in terms of human emotions and passions).

In Genesis 6:6 the repentance of God is his proper reaction to continued and unrequited sin and evil in the world. The parallel clause says that sin filled his heart with pain. This denotes no change in his purpose or character. It only demonstrates that God has emotions and passions and that he can and does respond to us for good or ill when we deserve it.

The point is that unchangeableness must not be thought of as if it were some type of frozen immobility. God is not some impervious being who cannot respond when circumstances or individuals change. Rather, he is a living person, and as such he can and does change when the occasion demands it. He does not change in his character, person or plan. But he can and does respond to our changes.

See also comment on 1 SAMUEL 15:29; JONAH 4:1-2.

6:9 Was Noah Perfect?

Genesis 6:9 is a hard saying because it

appears to imply that Noah attained moral and spiritual perfection. How could Noah have achieved such an elevated status of perfection when he came after the Fall? Did he not partake of the sinful nature and the bent toward depravity that all the race had inherited? If he did, as most will affirm, in what sense could it be said that he was "righteous" and "blameless"?

Noah, Daniel and Job are remembered for their righteous lives (Ezek 14:14, 20). But they did not as humans set the standard for others. The standard they shared is still the same today: it is the Lord himself who sets the standard. His nature and will compose the ethical and moral measuring stick for all others to follow.

The Hebrew word *ṣadîq* (which shares the same root as the Hebrew word *ṣeḏeq*) basically connotes conformity to the standard. The original idea may well have been "to be straight." From this came the idea of a "norm" and of being "in the right." The bureau of standards for what was morally and ethically right was to be found only in God himself. "The Lord is righteous *[ṣadîq]* in all his ways and loving toward all he has made" (Ps 145:17). Therefore, the standards and judgments set out in his Word are righteous (Ps 119:144, 160, 172).

Some of the earlier usages of the word occur in connection with the Israelite judges' carrying out of their functions and decisions. They were warned, "Do not pervert justice; do not show partiality to the poor or favoritism to the great, but judge your neighbor fairly *[ṣeḏeq]*" (Lev 19:15). This same type of "righteousness" applied to scales and weights: "Use *honest [ṣeḏeq]* scales and *honest* weights, an *honest* ephah and an *honest* hin" (Lev 19:36). Thus, the righteousness of God opposed commercial or judicial fraud and deception.

Righteousness applied to three areas of personal relationships: the ethical, the forensic and the theological. None of these three areas depended on current norms or practices; the righteousness that God wanted could be found only in the standards set forth in his Word. The ethical area dealt with the conduct of persons with one another. The forensic aspect required equality before the law for small and great, rich and poor. The theological aspect demanded that God's covenant people live a life of holiness, following the path laid out by God's righteousness.

In the case of Noah, he conformed to the standard set by God. When all the people around him were immersing themselves in evil and earning the wrath and judgment of God, Noah set his heart to follow the path found in the person and character of God. He stood his ground and remained uninfluenced by all that was happening around him.

The word *righteous* simply meant that he accepted and used the righteous standard for his living and acting. It does not imply perfection. The term does not in itself establish total approbation of his actions, any more than it does in connection with Tamar in Genesis 38:26. The text expresses an estimate of the comparative rightness of Tamar and Judah. When Judah was exposed as the adulterer by whom Tamar had become pregnant, he said, "She is more righteous than I"—that is, she was more within her rights to act as she did than Judah was in what he did. This can hardly be a complete endorsement of Tamar or her actions. Neither is the use of the same term a total endorsement of Noah.

Noah met the basic requirement set by the norm God had erected, and his conduct proved it. This can also be seen from the parallel clause "and he walked with God"—the same wording that was used of Enoch (Gen 5:24).

But this still leaves the problem of Noah's being called "blameless" or "perfect." Scripture has one preeminent example of the "perfect" man: Job. It is said that he was "blameless" (Job 1:1). He too claimed that he was "blameless" or "perfect" in Job 9:21-22, 12:4 and 31:6. Even under heavy assault to the contrary, he held fast to his "integrity" (same root—Job 27:5). And he was not alone in this opinion, for his wife ascribed "integrity" to him (Job 2:9). Even Yahweh in heaven agreed that Job was indeed "blameless" or "perfect" (Job 1:8; 2:3).

In spite of all these high accolades for Job, he knew that he was a sinner, for he queried, "How can a mortal be righteous before God?" (Job 9:2). He further acknowledged his sin (Job 10:6; 14:16-17). Accordingly, the use of the word *blameless* or *perfect* does not imply that one has attained perfection or a state in which one no longer sins. Even the creature in Eden (probably Lucifer) that was created "perfect" was found to be capable of sin (Ezek 28:13-15).

The Hebrew root of the word *perfect* involves the idea of completeness. Thus we conclude that Noah conformed to the standard set by God and that his life was "complete," with no essential quality missing.

The modifying phrase "among the people of his time" indicates all the more clearly that Noah's righteousness and blamelessness stood out against his contemporaries' sinfulness.

Just as Job had to admit his sin, so the same Scripture that tells us that Noah was righteous and blameless also tells us that he became drunk from the fruit of the vine (Gen 9:21). Clearly then there is no case for perfection and sinlessness in these words *righteous* and *blameless.* Instead, this is a case of someone who walked with God and delighted in following what he had said and living by the standards he had established.

6:19-20; 7:2-3 How Many Animals Went into the Ark?

During the last century and a half, the prevailing nonevangelical interpretation of the Noah story has been that this is not one story but at least two separate stories poorly patched together in an attempt to make them one unified whole. Evidence offered for the existence of two original stories is the fact that Noah is first told to take two of each kind of animal on board the ark and then to take seven of each clean kind.

In the final analysis, according to one eminent critical scholar, there is only one piece of evidence for the disunity of the Noah story, and that is repetition or repeated occurrence. The repetition, he reasoned, makes no sense unless two or more narratives have been conflated.

Repetition can sometimes be a sign of divergent traditions and of an editor having welded together several versions of the same story, or even different stories. But there are other explanations for this same phenomenon. Repetition is one of the most fundamental tools of the literary artist. Its presence does not necessarily indicate that the literary piece is a composite hodgepodge reflecting heterogeneous elements of mixed sources, oral or written.

To claim, as many have done, that Genesis 6:19-20 came from a priestly source around 450 B.C. and that Genesis 7:2-3 came from an earlier Yahwistic source around 850 B.C. is to say that the editor of the material let the contradiction stand. There is no need for such extravagant theories of origins, especially since we have a second-millennium flood story from Mesopotamia, the Gilgamesh Epic, with many of the same details. The Gilgamesh Epic, only unearthed in this century, could hardly have incorporated the so-called priestly and Yahwistic sources from the fifth and ninth centuries B.C., having been written and buried long before then. Why then must we suppose that Genesis incorporates such allegedly later sources?

The truth is that there is no inherent incompatibility between the two texts as they presently stand. Genesis 7:2-3 is just more precise than 6:19-20 on the question of the types and numbers of animals and birds that would board the ark.

Noah's first instruction was to admit pairs of all kinds of creatures on the ark to preserve their lives (Gen 6:19-20). That was the basic formula. Then he was given more specific instructions about admitting seven pairs of each of the clean animals and seven pairs of each kind of bird. The purpose of this measure was to become clear only after the flood. Birds would be needed to reconnoiter the earth (Gen 8:7-12), and the clean animals and birds would be offered in sacrifice to the Lord (Gen 8:20). If Noah had taken only one pair of each and then offered each of these pairs in sacrifice, these species would have become completely extinct.

The simplest and most adequate explanation is that chapter 6 of Genesis contains general summary directions—take two of each. After Noah had understood these general instructions, God spoke more specifically about the role the clean beasts and birds were to play.

Scripture does not indicate how the distinction between "clean" and "unclean" arose. Later on the Mosaic law would sanction this distinction and formally define it. But we are left without any indication of the origin of the distinction, just as we are left in the dark regarding how and when the whole idea of sacrifices started. Cain and Abel both sacrificed, but a formal declaration inaugurating this ritual is not recorded.

If some analysts still wish to excise the clean animals from the so-called priestly account of the Genesis flood story, they only introduce into what they are calling the Yahwistic account the very sort of repetition that they had earlier taken as a sign of divergent sources. This is too high a price to pay just to avoid admitting that perhaps the accounts of the boarding of pairs of unclean animals are connected with the boarding of seven pairs of clean animals. Genesis 7:6-15 does not support a Yahwistic-and-priestly-source explanation; indeed, it causes unusual trouble for such an analysis of the material.

7:19 A Worldwide Flood?

How widespread was this flood geographically? If it covered all the high mountains under the entire heavens, then it must, on present-day topographies, have amounted to some six miles of water clinging to all sides of the globe for the better part of a year. Is this possible without some real permanent effects such as observable disturbances in the realm of astrophysics and the pollution of the freshwater systems around the world?

If, however, the final judgment of the whole earth with fire is likened to the Noachian flood in 2 Peter 3:3-7, is that not final proof that Noah's flood was also universal in its geographical extent? The flood was extensive enough to wipe all living humans on earth except the eight persons who were on board the ark (Gen 7:23; 1 Pet 3:20). That is the main point of the biblical narrative and the one nonnegotiable argument in the whole discussion. Scripture is adamant on this point. Genesis 6:17 clearly says that the flood destroyed *all* life under the heavens—except, of course, the fish and the eight who were on the ark. Moreover, it lasted 371 days, something a whole lot worse than some local flood!

It is clear that we must proceed carefully in order to give due weight to all the evidence from all sides. All of that cannot be listed here, for some have taken full volumes to do it—with much still left unsaid. Nevertheless, here are some of the salient facts that help place this question into perspective.

First, the word translated "earth" is also rendered equally well at times as "land" or "country." The common word for "world," *tēḇel,* does not occur anywhere in the flood narrative. Elsewhere in Genesis, even the word "earth" (Hebrew *'ereṣ*) has the same ambiguity, for "the famine was severe in all the world *['ereṣ]*" (Gen 41:57), but it is not necessary to conclude that this was a seven-year *global* famine. This manner of speaking is similar to Luke 2:1, where "all the world" (Gk) went to be taxed, when it meant only the Roman world (see NIV), or Colossians 1:23, where Paul rejoices that the gospel "has been proclaimed to every creature under heaven." Thus it is possible that some of the phrases used in the flood account may be conscious exaggerations, that is, hyperboles, in order to make the point that indeed this was no ordinary flood, for it wiped out all human life except for the eight persons on board the ark.

But if the flood may not have reached geographically around the entire globe, how then were all persons except eight wiped out by the flood? The answer to that question depends on how far mortals had migrated at that time and what was the exact date for the flood. Both of these questions are unknowns. However, one may legitimately posit one of the pluvial phases (melting periods) from the glaciers, which would have had the effect of driving those on the Euro-African-Asian continents down into the Mediterranean climes and south. But when it comes to answering the question about those from the Americas or from Australia and related areas, we simply do not know enough to state anything with any confidence.

The fact that the waters rose above all the high mountains to a depth of at least twenty feet (Gen 7:19-20) is probably taken from the draft or the waterline that was seen on the ark by those who emerged and saw it after the waters had receded. And the fact that the ark had drifted perhaps some five hundred miles from the place where it had been built (as judged from parallel accounts of the flood in the ancient Near East) and that it had landed high up on the side of Mount Ararat legitimately gave rise to this way of presenting the enormity of this flood.

Our conclusion is that the jury is still out on this question. The strongest arguments for a worldwide flood ("all" life destroyed, 6:17; waters rise to over twenty feet above the high mountains, 7:19-20; flood lasts 371 days; and the fiery final judgment affecting all the earth just as Noah's flood did, 2 Pet 3:3-7) can all be met with (1) comparison with other similar biblical expressions and (2) the fact that this judgment of God did involve all mortals except the eight on the ark. But the fact that all these expressions can be explained this way does not necessitate that the writer of this text meant to use them in a hyperbolic way.

Similar questions can be raised for those who hold to a local flood. If the flood was merely a local phenomenon, why did the ark land somewhere on Mount Ararat (Gen 8:4)? Why was it necessary to bring a pair from each of the unclean animals on board the ark and seven of each of the clean animals (for use in sacrifices) if they could have been obtained by going just beyond the confines of the flood after they emerged from the ark?

Some believe that the flood was spread over the whole earth, while others insist that it was limited to the Mesopotamian basin or some other defined geographical area in the Near East. The point is that Scripture is anxious only to teach that it was God's judgment on all mortals living on earth except the eight on the ark. On the other matters we must await more information.

9:6 Capital Punishment Mandated by God?

Can Genesis 9:6 properly be used to answer modern questions about capital punishment? The debate is one of no small proportions, and the consequences both for the condemned murderer and for society are great indeed.

Genesis 9:5-6 is the simplest statement mandating society to punish their fellow beings for murder. However, its very simplicity and lack of any development allow opponents of capital punishment to question the passage's relevance. Missing, they claim, are all references to civil government, due process, exceptions and distinctions between various degrees of murder.

Genesis 9:5-6 is part of the covenant God established with Noah following the flood. Involved in this covenant were the animals' fear of people, permission to eat meat that did not contain the lifeblood and the delegation of the death penalty for murder into the hands of men and women. But more than this was involved, and this tends to demonstrate the enduring nature of the provisions of this covenant. Seasons were instituted as part of the enduring natural order (Gen 8:22), the rainbow would serve as a continuing pledge that the earth would not be flooded again (Gen 9:13) and the image of God provided the rationale for exacting the extreme penalty (Gen 9:6). The covenant established with Noah is therefore one that involves his representing "every living creature" (Gen 6:18-19; 9:10-11, 12, 15-17).

The text has a clear statement on capital punishment. God requires a "reckoning" of both the person and the beast who shed anyone's blood. But since both are held responsible, even though the beasts cannot make moral discriminations or act intentionally, how can advocates of capital punishment use this text to sort out the issue?

One could argue that Exodus 21:28-36 supplies the principle of animal liability while the Mosaic law makes a distinction between manslaughter and murder, or between first, second and third degree murder. Opponents would contend, however, that the Mosaic law was made between God and Israel while the Noachian covenant was between God and every living creature.

This distinction, however, is most curious, because it makes a sharper dichotomy between law and grace than what Scripture intends. For even when the civil code of the Mosaic law demonstrates a particularistic and distinctively cultural relevancy, which is limited to the period for which they were written, these same laws have behind them eternal principles as enduring as the character of God. That is the point so clearly made by the recent discovery that the Ten Commandments, with their moral code, set the agenda for both the Covenant Code of Exodus 21—23 and the specifications of Deuteronomy 6—26. I have argued this case in some detail in *Toward Old Testament Ethics* (Grand Rapids, Mich.: Zondervan, 1983).

But let us settle the matter on the textual grounds of Genesis 9:6 itself. First, it is clear that the text is giving us a command and not just a suggestion or permission. Verse 5 states that God demands a punishment: "I [God] will demand an accounting for the life of his fellow man." Moreover, the reason given for this action is one that remains in force for as long as men and women are made in the image of God.

This matter of the image of God brings us to the heart of the issue: "for [because] in the image of God has God made man." The word *for* cannot be rendered "although" here, as in Genesis 8:21 or Joshua 17:13—as if the fact that a person was made in the image of God was no impediment to the sentence of death. The clearest reading is that the murderer had to suffer for his or her actions because it was a fundamental denial of the image of God in the harmed individual. The person who destroyed another being made in God's image in fact did violence to God himself—so sacred and so permanent was the worth and value that God had invested in the slain victim.

Some interpreters connect the causal conjunction not with the shedding of blood, but with everything that preceded it—verses 1, 2 and 7. On these grounds, the reason given in the last part of verse 6 is instead the reason that God saved a remnant of the human race through Noah and why he protects people from the threats of wild animals.

But all of this is too distantly related. Furthermore, it is based on the alleged excuse that verse 6 has a peculiar structure (chiastic). This seems more like special pleading than solid exegesis. Ordinarily, one takes the nearest expression when seeking the expression or word that the *for* or *because* clause modifies. More indicators are needed to prove that a chiastic word order is unusual in this situation. This happens in poetry regularly.

Others object to transferring this demand for capital punishment in Genesis 9:6 to the law books as a universally binding law without including Genesis 9:4-5—"You must not eat meat that has its lifeblood still in it" and "I will demand an accounting from every animal." This can be partially answered by recognizing that the New Testament forbids Gentiles from eating blood or things that have not been properly bled (Acts 15:20, 29; compare with Lev 3:17; 17:14; Deut 12:16, 23). And Exodus 21:28-36 does enforce the principle of animal liability.

It is likewise too much to assert that "the shedding of blood" be taken merely as a metaphor for death. Most frequently the concept of pouring was a physical act; its metaphoric usages were reserved for such ideas as the pouring out of the wrath of God or the pouring out of one's heart or soul. But when blood was poured out in a violent way, that outpouring was said to pollute the land (Num 35:33; 2 Kings 24:4; Ezek 22:3-4). It is this pouring out of blood that constitutes the single most frequent use of this verb. It is hardly a metaphoric usage. No picture of violent death could be more graphically depicted.

Later in the sixth commandment, one word is chosen to depict first degree murder out of the seven possible verbs in Hebrew for *kill. Rāṣaḥ* became restricted to deliberate and premeditated murder (Ps 94:6; Prov 22:13; Is 1:21; Jer 7:9; Hos 4:2; 6:9). This verb was not used for killing beasts for food (Gen 9:3), defending oneself in a nighttime attack (Ex 22:2), accidental killings (Deut 19:5) or even manslaughter (Num 35:16, 25). What joins murder with manslaughter is that both incur blood guilt and both pollute the land. What differentiates the two is that there is no substitute allowed for death which comes by the hand of a murderer (that is to say, for one who premeditates his act), but the text implies that for every other of the sixteen to twenty death penalty crimes in the Old Testament a substitute is permitted (Num 35:31). It is with this concept that the shedding of blood would appear to be linked.

Nowhere does the text introduce the political state as the one that demands that life from the murderer. While this is true, it is only another evidence of the phenomenon of progressive revelation.

No one passage supplies all the details. Even the statement in Romans 13 on the state does not include the caveat raised in Acts 4:19-20 that circumscribes the authority of the state over a Christian when obeying human government would exclude obeying God.

Jesus himself seems to have accepted the principle of capital punishment when he reminded Pilate that government was divinely conferred (Jn 19:11). The same position is elsewhere supported in the New Testament by Romans 13:4 and Acts 25:11. However, the major argument for capital punishment still rests in the image-of-God argument given in Genesis 9:6. This can hardly be bypassed by any who take Scripture seriously.

But if a society persists in refusing to take the life of those conclusively proven to have deliberately and violently taken others' lives, then that society will stand under God's judgment and the value, worth, dignity and respect for persons in that society and nation will diminish accordingly. It is self-defeating to argue on the one hand for civil and women's rights and to turn around on the other and deny them to the one struck down by a murderous blow.

Of course this principle must be applied with such reluctance that where "reasonable doubt" exists, we err on the side of mercy and waive the death penalty. In an imperfect judicial system not all defendants will be treated equally or fairly because economic status, social standing, race or political and legal connections will place some "above the law." However, we will warn that such cheating does not escape God's notice, nor does it change his laws. It only becomes another divine indictment on that society that dares to exercise unevenly the divinely ordained demand for justice. That nation is going to be judged for such a cavalier attitude toward God's mission.

See also comment on EXODUS 20:13; LEVITICUS 20:1-7; NUMBERS 35:31.

9:24-25 What Was the Curse on Canaan?

One of the saddest moments in the history of interpretation was when advocates of slavery decided to use this text as a justification for their inhuman treatment of dark-skinned people. It was asserted that this divine prophecy given by Noah after the flood legitimized slavery for a group of people who had been cursed perpetually. Supporters of slavery argued that the Arabic version of Genesis 9:25 reads "Cursed be the father of Canaan" instead of "Cursed be Canaan." A vehement allegiance to the misapplication of this text has continued among some groups to the present day.

But the oppression of blacks by whites cannot be justified from this story. What happened is that Noah, a righteous and blameless man, had been drinking wine (Gen 9:21). That in itself was not the issue here, for in Scripture wine is viewed as one of God's gifts to humankind (Ps 104:15). Every burnt offering and peace offering was accompanied by a libation of wine (Num 15:5-10), and the drinking of wine at festivals was acknowledged (Deut 14:26). One of the symbols for Israel was the vine (Is 5:1-7; Mk 12:1-11).

But the Bible also warns about the dangers of wine. Nazirites were to abstain from all alcohol and wine (Num 6:3-4), and priests were forbidden to drink prior to officiating in the sanctuary lest they die (Lev 10:9). The laity were also warned that drinking too much wine was dangerous to people and offensive to God (Prov 21:17; 23:20-21, 29-35; Is 5:22). Drunkenness was especially reprehensible when it led to self-exposure (Hab 2:15; Lam 4:21). The exposure of one's nakedness was not only publicly demeaning but also incompatible with the presence of the living God (Ex 20:26; Deut 23:12-14).

Because Noah drank to excess, he became drunk. The heat generated by the alcohol in his bloodstream led the patriarch to thrust off his covering involuntarily as he lay in his tent. The reflexive form of the verb makes it clear that he uncovered himself (Gen 9:21).

Noah's youngest son, Ham, entered the tent, and there he was confronted with the situation I have just described (Gen 9:22). Apparently his gaze was not a mere harmless notice or an accidental glance. The verb used here has such force that some say it means "he gazed with satisfaction."

What exactly Ham did has been the subject of much speculation. The most bizarre of all suggestions is that Ham castrated his father in a struggle for family power. But there is no evidence to support this idea other than the precedent of some Greek and Semitic stories with the motif of paternal castration. A second suggestion is that the expression "to see a man's nakedness" is an idiomatic phrase for sexual intercourse with that man's wife. But this expression is quite different from the idiom "to uncover the nakedness" of Leviticus 18 and 20. Leviticus 20:17 is the only place where the verb "to see" is used, but it is not in a parallel construction with "uncover." The view that Ham had an incestuous relationship with his mother is an impossible explanation. Even if Ham had committed incest with his mother, he would hardly have told his brothers!

Thus, Ham could be faulted simply for this: he failed to cover up his father's nakedness and chose rather to make fun of his father to his brothers. Such an act was serious enough to prompt Noah to utter his curse on Ham's descendants, who would be guilty of the kinds of sexual perversions that many suspected Ham of carrying out. To lie exposed meant that one was unprotected, dishonored and at risk of exploitation. Ham had transgressed a natural and sacred barrier. His disgusting ridicule of his father before his brothers aggravated the act and perhaps betrayed a moral weakness that had established itself in his personality.

Who, then, was Canaan? And why was he cursed if Ham was the culprit? Since the law of God insists that God deals with all people justly, this curse of Canaan is all the more puzzling.

Genesis 10:6 lists the sons of Ham as Cush (basically Ethiopia), Mizraim (Egypt), Put (generally taken to be one of the North African countries) and Canaan (of the country of Palestine/Canaan). We are not talking about Africans or blacks here, but the Canaanite peoples who inhabited ancient Palestine.

Canaan was not singled out for the curse because he was the youngest son of Ham, nor was it a random selection. Apparently Noah saw in the youngest son of Ham the same tendencies and perversions that had been evidenced in Ham. When Noah had fully recovered from the effects of his drunkenness, he uttered this curse against Canaan. Noah could not have cursed his son, for he and his brothers, along with Noah, had been the objects of a blessing in Genesis 9:1. Neither Noah nor anyone else could reverse such a blessing with a curse. Balaam the son of Beor learned this the hard way in Numbers 22—24.

Still, there may well have been an element of "mirroring" punishment here, especially if Canaan was to exhibit the outworkings of the tendencies already present in Ham's failure to cover Noah's nakedness. Finally, it is a matter of historical record that the Canaanites were notoriously deviant in their sexual behavior. Almost everywhere the archaeologist's spade has dug in that part of the world there have been fertility symbols accompanying texts explicit enough to make many a modern pornographic dealer seem a mere beginner in the trade of deviant sexuality. Sodom left its name for the vice these people practiced. Even the Romans, so depraved in their own practices, were shocked by the behavior of the Phoenicians at the colony of Carthage (the last vestige of the Canaanite race).

Why was this story included in the biblical narrative? It tells the reader that unless there was some moral change in the Canaanites, they were slated for removal from their land. That God is longsuffering and slow to anger is attested by the fact that this judgment did not fall on that group of descendants until the time of Joshua's conquest of Canaan. It is impossible to date Noah's times, but it is known that Joshua lived around 1400 B.C. At a minimum this would mean that the grace of God was extended to the Canaanites for several millennia. Surely God was most generous with these people, giving more than adequate time for sinners to repent.

See also comment on EXODUS 21:2-11; 1 SAMUEL 15:18; EPHESIANS 6:5-8.

11:1-9 One Language Before Babel?

Genesis 11:1-9 is the record of the departure from one language and common speech to a plurality of tongues in the human race. This event took place at the tower of Babel, where mortals had decided that they would "make a name for [them]selves [lest they be] scattered over the face of the whole earth" (Gen 11:4). A recently discovered Sumerian tablet also tells for the first time from an extrabiblical perspective the story of a time when all languages were one on the earth.[1]

The problem therefore is this: why does Genesis 10:5, 20, 31 describe each of the descendants of Noah's three sons as having differing languages when this was not supposed to have happened until the next chapter? Isn't this a mistake (called by scholars an anachronism) on the part of the writer of Scripture, in that it is a misplacement in time and space?

The Bible does not represent itself as always desiring to present its material in a strictly chronological sequence. Often it prefers to present it in a topical sequence. For example, the three temptations of Jesus in the Gospels are found in three different arrangements because the aim of the author was to present them so as to make the preaching and teaching point of theology that each had in mind. Likewise, the writer of Genesis jumps ahead of himself for the moment to describe what happened to the descendants of Noah's three sons, even though it outdistanced the story that he would resume in chapter 11. This technique is typical of the writer of Genesis.

There is another clue in the text itself that demonstrates that this is so. In Genesis 10:25 it mentions "one [who] was named Peleg, because in his time the earth was divided." Here is a clear allusion to the confusion of languages at the tower of Babel that will be described in the next chapter (Gen 11: 8-9). Since *Peleg* in Hebrew means "to divide" or "to split," it is more than likely that he received his name in memory of this event.

[1]Samuel Noah Kramer, "The Babel of Tongues: A Sumerian Version," *Journal of the American Oriental Society* 88 (1968): 108-111. See also Nahum M. Sarna, *Understanding Genesis* (New York: McGraw Hill, 1966), pp. 63-80.

12:11-13 Sarai Is My Sister?

This incident is puzzling not only because of the subterfuge involved but also because the same kind of episode occurs three times (here and in Gen 20:1-3;

26:7-11). In all three episodes the plot is essentially the same. A patriarch visits a foreign land, accompanied by his wife. Fearing that his wife's beauty will become a source of danger to himself, he resorts to the subterfuge of pretending that his wife is his sister.

The recurrent wife-sister theme in Genesis has provoked an unusual number of comments and speculative solutions. Interpreters have been puzzled about why father and son should have fallen back on this ploy so frequently.

The old explanation, the documentary source hypothesis, was that there was a single story told in different parts of the country at different times with different heroes. When these various traditions were welded together, the rough edges of the original sources were left for more intelligent moderns to detect. Hence Genesis 12:10-20 came from the Yahwistic writer of the "J" document, offering a Judean or southern viewpoint, and a written source coming from around 850 B.C. The Isaac parallel likewise came from the "J" document, but it featured another protagonist, Isaac. Genesis 20:1-18 was attributed to the "E" document, since it favored a northern or Ephraimite viewpoint and was committed to writing about a century later than "J."

Even though critical scholars concerned themselves with determining which story was the original and how the others developed from it, there is no compelling reason to doubt that all three incidents occurred. But why did the writer find it necessary to include all three stories?

Such an attitude betrays a lack of feeling for Hebrew rhetoric, in which repetition was a favorite device. Yet more is at work here. The two protagonists of these stories, Abram—or as he was later renamed, Abraham—and Isaac, were at the center of the promise-plan by which God was going to bless the very nations they were coming in contact with. Moreover, the means by which God was going to bless these Gentile nations was to be carried in the womb of the very woman to whom these potentates were being attracted. Each of these stories, then, sets up a moment of real suspense for divine providence and for the patriarchs, who, in spite of all their blundering, lying and mismanagement, were still the means through whom God was going to bless the world.

It must be stated clearly that Abraham and Isaac both practiced deception. The Bible merely reports that they did so, without approving of it. God preserved the purity of Sarai and Rebekah in spite of all the maneuverings of their husbands. No one can make a case for lying based on these passages. It will always be wrong to lie, since God is truth.

What about half lies? Wasn't it true that Sarai was Abraham's half sister? Was it not also true that the Hurrian society, in such centers as Haran, where Abraham had stayed on his way to Canaan, had a special legal fiction in which the bonds of marriage were strengthened when the groom adopted his wife as his "sister" in a legal document parallel to the marriage contract?

Yes, both are true. Sarai was Abraham's half sister (Gen 11:29). And there was the Hurrian legal form of sister-marriage. However, most scholars have now concluded that there is very little basis for assuming that Abraham had such a document in mind, since the details of patriarchal and Hurrian marriage documents are quite different.

What, then, was Abraham's motivation? Was he willing to sacrifice his wife's honor and allow her to marry any suitor in order to save his own skin and possibly get some financial gain? Though Genesis 12:13 might appear to support such an interpretation, subsequent events (Gen 12:15-16) provide a basis for questioning its correctness. Oriental attitudes toward adultery were much more sensitive than ours (Gen 20:2-9). It is doubtful that Abraham would have allowed his wife to bear that sin on her conscience, much less allow himself to be an accomplice in it.

The medieval commentators suggested that what Abraham hoped to get out of his "brother" status was the right to receive and deny all suitors' requests to be Sarai's husband. This suggestion works in those stories where brothers attempt to delay their sister's marriage (Laban and Rebekah in Gen 24:55, and Dinah and her brothers in Gen 34:13-17).

Abraham and Isaac are to be condemned for their complicity in lying, no matter how noble a motive they may have had, or how much truth the lie contained. Still, God was not to be deterred in his plan to bring life and blessing to the nations through the offspring of Sarai and Rebekah.

See also comment on EXODUS 1:15-21; 3:18.

14:18-19 Who Was Melchizedek?

Melchizedek was a Canaanite, but he is called a "priest of God Most High." In addition to his office of priest, he also is described as the king of Salem, apparently a reference to the shortened name for Jerusalem, which at that time was occupied by the Canaanites.

This Gentile, about whom we have had no previous notice, either in the text or anywhere else for that matter, comes forward to pay homage to Abram. He brings with him bread and wine as he goes out to meet Abram on his return from the amazing victory by the 318 servants of the patriarch over four Mesopotamian kings. In so doing, the priest-king pays respect to Abram, yet he acknowledges that what has been accomplished could only be attributed to God Most High.

This is a most unexpected turn of events, for out of the grossly pagan world of the Canaanites emerges not only one who shares belief and worship in the same God as the Semitic Abram but one who pronounces the blessing on the patriarch whom God had already blessed. Abram also acknowledges the priestly dignity of this Canaanite priest-king by giving him a tithe.

This situation is very similar to that of Jethro in Exodus 18. He too was a priest who worshiped the same God Moses did, yet he too was a Gentile Midianite (Ex 2:16; 3:1; 18:12). Evidently God was also calling out a people for his own name from among the Gentiles even though the text rarely pauses in its pursuit of the promise-plan of God through the Hebrew people to reflect on this phenomenon.

Who then was Melchizedek? Was he an early preincarnate appearance of Christ or, as theologians label this type of happening, a christophany? Or was he a type of Christ, since Psalm 110:4 and Hebrews 6:20—7:21 link Christ's priesthood not to Aaron and the famous Levitical priestly line in Israel, but to Melchizedek?

The sudden and almost mysterious appearance of Melchizedek is what gives him that quality of timelessness and uniqueness. There can be little doubt that the text treats him as if he were a real historical character who touched the life of the biblical patriarch at a very crucial time in his service for God.

But Melchizedek also has a typological aspect to his character, not in all aspects of his person and character, but most significantly in the fact that we know absolutely nothing about his parentage or his age. This fact sets him apart from all other priests we are told about in the biblical narrative. Thus the author of Hebrews likens Melchizedek to Jesus: "Without father or mother, without genealogy, without beginning of days or end of life, like the Son of God he remains a priest forever" (Heb 7:3).

What is intended, of course, is that the biblical record does not mention Melchizedek's parents, his ancestry, his birth or his death. In that sense he was different from any other individual found in the biblical narrative. This fact uniquely fits him to be a type of Christ. As such, he functions as a symbol of eternity. His unique priesthood offers a picture of the eternal and universal priesthood of Jesus Christ.

This explains how the Messiah could come from the promise line of Abram and eventually from the tribe of Judah and could also be a priest as well as a prophet and a king. Messiah could not come from two tribes at once, both from Judah (as king) and from Levi (as priest). But he solved the dilemma by becoming a priest "not on the basis of a regulation as to his ancestry [that is, a legal requirement concerning bodily descent] but on the basis of the power of an indestructible life" (Heb 7:16).

One more point needs to be made: Abram gave a tenth to this priest-king, not the other way around. The "everything" of which Abram gave a tithe was the spoils Abram had taken in battle. This was Abram's response to Melchizedek's offer of bread and wine and the blessing which Melchizedek had offered—a blessing which normally comes from the greater person to the lesser. Strangely enough, as the author of Hebrews points out (Heb 7:10), in this sense Levi paid tithes and recognized a priesthood which would supersede his own line even before he was born, because "Levi was still in the body of his ancestor" when Abram offered the tithe to Melchizedek.

16:1-4 Was It Right for Abraham to Sleep with Hagar?

Why would a wife ever urge her husband to have an affair with another woman who was living and serving in their home? Is this action approved by the Bible and suggested as normative for us—at least under certain kinds of conditions? Is this the biblical basis for some kind of open marriage?

What Sarai did was in accord with the practice and culture of the day. This can be seen from numerous clay tablets that come from this period of time. Thus, for example, the Code of Hammurabi, the Nuzi Tablets, the Alalakh Tablets and the Mari Tablets (all derived from approximately the larger Near Eastern area and a period of two to three centuries around the time of the patriarchs) provide for exactly the very eventuality listed here in this text. A barren wife could be credited with children that her maidservant bore to the wife's husband. A similar instance arose in Genesis 30:3, 9 concerning Rachel, and in part in Ruth 4:11. Sarai's motivation for so acting is clearly stated: "Perhaps I can build a family through her." The idea was that a family could be built with children from a concubine similar to the way a building was built with blocks.

But did it accord with the morality and ethics given by God? Abram was wrong to go along with his wife's proposal, for now it appeared that he thought he could help God to fulfill the divine promise given to him about a "seed" by indulging in polygamy. This seems to be an ancient variant on the saying "God helps those who help themselves!"

At the creation of the first couple, God had stated a strong case for monogamous relationships as being the norm for marriage. The first departure from this standard came with Lamech in Genesis 4:19, when he took two wives. But the exceptions to this rule of one wife for each man are not so numerous as first impressions may seem. Apart from the kings of Judah and Israel (wherein other considerations were also operating, such as the possibility of using the foreign wife as a hostage in order to assure compliance with treaties), there are hardly more than a dozen and a half examples of polygamous marriages in the entire Old Testament.

In the meantime, the model of the monogamous marriage was held forth throughout the Old Testament as the norm. For example, Proverbs 5:15-23 taught the same truth by means of the allegory of drinking water from one's own well (a delicate but clear figure of speech for the coital act within a monogamous marriage). Moreover, a whole book of the Old Testament was dedicated to celebrating the joys and desirability of reserving oneself for only one other person of a different sex, even if the one trying to interrupt that commitment was a wealthy king like Solomon—the book of Song of Songs.

While the Bible does not stop to moralize on Abram's cohabitation with Hagar, it nevertheless expects each reader to realize that what was taking place was contrary to the will and morality that God approved.

See also comment on GENESIS 29:25-28; 2 SAMUEL 20:3; PROVERBS 5:15-21.

16:7-12 Who Is the Angel of the Lord?

See comment on JUDGES 6:22-23.

17:17; 18:12-15 Discriminatory Treatment of Abraham and Sarah?

It is clear that both Abraham and Sarah laughed at the news that they would have a son so late in life. The question, then, is this: Why was Sarah the only one who was rebuked? Is this a case where male chauvinism shines through the text of the older testament?

Some have tried to explain the difference between the two laughters as arising from two different states of mind: Abraham's from a state of surprise and ecstasy; Sarah's from a state of unbelief. But the text will not let Abraham off that easily. There is no reason to connect Abraham's laughter with that of Psalm 126:2 (when the Lord brought back the captives from Babylon, "our mouths were filled with laughter") or even that of Job 8:21 ("he will yet fill your mouth with laughter"). Both the Jerusalem Targum and Calvin were too hasty in getting Abraham off the hook here by equating his laughter with joyous amazement.

The fact that Abraham immediately posed the issue of Ishmael and how he would fit into the promised seed if another son were born shows that he too spoke out of unbelief, just as much as did Sarah. The issue was not just Ishmael's person, but his posterity as well. The promise of another son, Abraham feared, would destroy all hope that he had placed in the one already given. So Abraham was equally guilty of unbelief. So why the rebuke on Sarah?

It is true that Sarah only laughed to herself; but so did Abraham. Nevertheless, the Lord saw what transpired in her inner being and openly spoke of his displeasure of the same. And since the principle from which both of their inward laughing sprang was the same (that is, unbelief, and not that one was a laugh of admiration and joy whereas the other was a laugh of disbelief and distrust), the unbelief of both of them was the main basis for the rebuke.

The question "Why did Sarah laugh?" was not addressed to her, but to Abraham. But Sarah felt the sting of inquiry most pointedly, for she felt that she had been trapped in her unbelief. Thus it was that she blurted out, "I did not laugh." This foolish and untruthful reaction was also rebuked when the Lord said, "Yes, you did laugh."

Does this mean that Abraham's unbelief was without blame, but Sarah's was? No, for the condemnation of one was equally a condemnation of the other. The text focuses on Sarah's unbelief because she went on to deny it (thereby making the issue memorable and newsworthy) and because when the whole matter was ended, it also became the basis for the naming of Isaac, which is associated with the word "he laughs" or "laughter" (Gen 21:3, 6).

18:19 Covenant Blessings Conditional or Unconditional?

See comment on GENESIS 26:3-5.

18:20; 19:1-29 Homosexuality Condemned?

See comment on ROMANS 1:27.

20:1-3 Sarah Is My Sister?

See comment on GENESIS 12:11-13.

21:14 Was It Wrong for Abraham to Send Hagar Away?

Was it not wrong and heartless of Abraham to turn out Hagar, whom he had taken as a wife? In fact, was it not even contrary to the social conventions of the day to refuse food and lodging in his own dwelling to a woman who had honored him by bearing him a son? And was it not all the more reprehensible since the boy was so young that he had to be carried on the shoulders of Hagar as they left?

A number of commentators have insisted on the fact that Ishmael was placed on the shoulders of Hagar when she left. This would imply that at the time the boy was a mere infant who needed to be carried by his mother. Then in Genesis 21:15 he is spoken of as being cast or placed under a bush. Now after these interpreters have reached these conclusions about Ishmael being a mere infant, they go on to declare that this assessment is in conflict with Genesis 16:16, 17:25 and 21:5, where the boy seems to be at least thirteen or fourteen years old, and that this is the mark of multiple sources, for the texts were not edited as carefully as they should have been.

The solution to the question of the boy's age is rather straightforward. There is no basis for the translation of the Septuagint or the Peshitta: "and laid the boy on her shoulder." If this were the correct reading, there would be no way to explain the present Hebrew text, which does not make "the boy" the object of the verb "lay" or "set"; instead, it is the object of the verb "gave." The literal rendering of the Hebrew is: "And Abraham rose up early in the morning and he took bread and a skin of water, and he gave [them] unto Hagar putting [them] on her shoulder, and he gave [her] the boy, and he sent her away, and she went and she wandered in the wilderness of Beersheba."

Since Abraham was living at the time in Gerar between Kadesh and Shur, Hagar wandered in the desert far to the north of Abraham, rather than heading south to Egypt, as she had done when she fled from Sarah on a previous occasion (Gen 16:7). There is no basis for insisting, as some have, that Abraham was at Hebron at the time, and therefore Hagar was on her way to Egypt when her location was given at Beersheba.

But what of Abraham's action? Can it be justified?

It is clear that God instructed Abraham to follow Sarah's wishes (Gen 21:12-13), even though it grieved Abraham greatly (Gen 21:11). But as George

Bush commented, "God does not require Abraham to acquiesce in Sarah's proposal because he approved the spirit which prompted it, but because it accorded with his counsel and his repeated declarations that all the blessings of the covenant were to belong pre-eminently to Isaac."[1]

Accordingly, there is more here than a mere domestic scuffle. Surely it demonstrates how much evil can come from a polygamous marriage. But it also demonstrates that the promise made to Abraham in the covenant could not be abandoned, even when it was due to the unwise actions of the one to whom the promise had been made.

God requires that Abraham deny his natural feelings, based on the promise that he would also make the son of the maidservant the ancestor of a nation because he came from Abraham and because God would perform his word. And from what follows, it appears that Hagar met with no great difficulty in providing for herself or her son, whether it came indirectly from Abraham or from some other means that God had provided.

Thus Sarah sinned in recommending that Abraham take Hagar as his wife and sinned again in the attitude that prompted her to urge Abraham to send her away. But just as in the case of Joseph, where his brothers intended him harm, God meant it for good—the good of both Isaac and Ishmael.

See also comment on GENESIS 29:25-28; 50:19-21.

[1]George Bush, *Notes on Genesis,* vol. 1 (1860; reprint, Minneapolis, Minn.: James and Klock, 1976), p. 352.

22:1 Why Did God Test Abraham?

Even though the writer carefully couches his description of God's command to Abraham as a "test," many people have puzzled over God's being involved in what many view as entrapment. How then shall we view this test from God?

The term used here for "to test" is used in eight other Old Testament passages where God is said to be the "tester." In six of these (Ex 15:22-26; 16:4; 20:18-20; Deut 8:2, 16; Judg 2:21-22; 3:1-4), Israel is tested. In 2 Chronicles 32:31 King Hezekiah was tested, and in Psalm 26:2 David appealed to God to test him. In five of the six cases where Israel was tested, the context shows the testing stemmed from concern over the nation's obedience to God's commands, laws or ways. That same concern is implied in Exodus 20:18-20, where the issue is the fear of the Lord, just as it is here in Genesis 22:1, 12. Likewise the passages in Psalm 26 and 2 Chronicles 32:31 focus on the matter of obedience and invite God to prove whether David and Hezekiah are not willing to obey God with all their hearts and souls.

Therefore, based on these eight passages where God is the subject and author of the testing, we may conclude that God wanted to test Abraham to know his heart and to see if he would obey and fear the Lord who gave him the son he loved so dearly. Just as the queen of Sheba came to "test" Solomon's wisdom (1 Kings 10:1), so God also tests without any sinister connotations.

When the word "test" is used as a term in which man tests or tries God, the meaning is altogether different (Ex 17:2, 7; Num 14:22; Is 7:12). Such a test flows from an attitude of doubt and a sinful heart on man's part. In this situation, man wants to determine whether God's power will be adequate, the effect of which is to "tempt" God.

But when used of God, there is no connotation of doubt or a desire to trick or deceive the one placed under the test. His testing was only concerned with obedience or with the fear of God, that is to say, an attitude which expressed that same spirit of obedience to God. Deuteronomy 8:2 describes the wilderness wanderings with its particularly harsh experiences along the way as a testing by God—"Remember how the LORD your God led you . . . in the desert these forty years, to humble you and to test you in order to know what was in your heart."

Such a test demonstrated in action what Abraham claimed: he was willing to trust the God who had provided this son born so late in the patriarch's life.

The old English word for test was *prove.* In the context of this passage it does not have the sense of exciting to sin or provoking someone to commit an evil. Indeed, James 1:13 states, "God cannot be tempted by evil, nor does he tempt anyone." Temptation or testing in the bad sense always proceeds from the malice of Satan working on the corruptions of our own hearts. God, however, may bring his creatures into circumstances of special testing, not for the purpose of supplying information for himself, but in order to manifest to individuals and others the dispositions of their hearts. In this context, all forms of divine testing, putting to the proof and trying individuals are used in such a way as to leave God's attributes unimpeachable.

But if it is asked, "How could a holy God put his servant through such an ordeal as this?" the answer rests in the special relationship that Abraham and the Lord enjoyed. The relationship of father and son that existed between Abraham and Isaac was exactly the same relationship that existed between God and Abraham. Abraham's test was indeed a qualifying test that had as much evidential value for Abraham as it had for the Lord who issued the test.

The point is that the test was not a temptation to do evil or a test that was meant to trap the hapless patriarch. Instead, it had the opposite purpose: it was intended to strengthen him and to build him up, as did the numerous tests in the desert. As used here, the ideas of tempting, testing or trying are religious concepts. It is God's testing the partner of the covenant to see if he is keeping his side of the agreement. God never tests the heathen; he tests his own people exclusively. Thus the test is ever a test of God's own in order to know whether they will love, fear, obey, worship and serve him.

Testing, finally, is one of the means by which God carries out his saving purposes. Often people do not know why they were tested until after the test is over. Only after they have been preserved, proved, purified, disciplined and taught can they move beyond the situation, strong in faith and strengthened for the more difficult tasks ahead.

See also comment on GENESIS 2:16-17; JAMES 1:13.

22:2 Sacrifice Your Son?

What can be said of such an astonishing demand? Does God really demand or approve of human sacrifice?

This chapter has been linked with the blind obedience operative in the tragedy at Jonestown, Guyana. But God did not command Abraham to commit murder. This incident is not to be classed with the foolish sacrifice of Jephthah's daughter (Judg 11:30-40); Gibeon's demands (2 Sam 21:8, 9, 14); or the practices of Ahaz or Manasseh (2 Kings 16:3; 21:6, 2 Chron 33:6). It was this practice of human sacrifice that Josiah abolished (2 Kings 23:10) and the prophets condemned (Jer 19:5; Ezek 20:30-31; 23:36-39). Indeed, the law clearly prohibited the sacrifice of individuals and spoke scornfully of those who offered their eldest sons to Molech as human sacrifices (Lev 18:21; 20:2).

In the abstract, human sacrifice cannot be condemned on principle. The truth is that God owns all life and has a right to give or take it as he wills. To reject on all grounds God's legitimate right to ask for life under any conditions would be to remove his sovereignty and question his justice in providing his own sacrifice as the central work of redemption.

However, our God has chosen to prohibit human sacrifice. It is this dilemma of the forthrightness of the command to Abraham versus the clear prohibition against human sacrifice that must be solved. From the chapter, it seems clear that God never intended that this command be executed. The proof of this is that God restrained Abraham's hand just as he was about to take his son's life. " 'Do not lay a hand on the boy,' he said. 'Do not do anything to him. Now I know that you fear God, because you have not withheld from me your son, your only son' " (Gen 22:12). God's purpose was simply to test Abraham's faith. Since the deed was not carried out, there is nothing unworthy of divine goodness in having instituted the trial of his faith.

The testing may have been of greater benefit to Abraham than we often suppose. Some, such as the ancient Bishop Warburton, supposed that Abraham wanted to know how it was that God would bless all the families of the earth through his seed as promised in Genesis 12:3. On this supposition, it is conjectured that our Lord designed a way to teach him through an experience what he had already communicated to him in words. He was given a prefiguration, or a type, of the sacrifice that the last in the line of the seed, even Christ, would accomplish.

John 8:56 substantiates this claim when Jesus said, "Your father Abraham rejoiced at the thought of seeing my day; he saw it and was glad." The reply of the Jewish audience, "You are not yet fifty years old, . . . and you have seen Abraham!" (Jn 8:57), indicates that they understood the verb *to see* in a most literal way. Our Lord does not correct them in this notion. But it must be noticed that it was not he himself that Christ asserted that Abraham rejoiced to see, but his day, by which he meant the circumstance of his life which was of the greatest importance.

That the term *day* will permit this interpretation is clear from the parallel words *hour* and *time.* Throughout the Gospels we read, "his time has not yet come" (Jn 7:30); "he . . . prayed that if possible the hour might pass from him" (Mk 14:35); or "the hour has come for the Son of Man to be glorified" (Jn 12:23). In all of these instances it is not merely a portion of time that is being referred to but some particular life circumstance unique to Christ and his mission.

But if *day* functions in the same manner as *hour,* and the peculiar circumstance referred to is the one in which Jesus became the Savior of the world, where is it recorded in the Old Testament that Abraham saw anything pertaining to the death of Christ?

Nothing in the Old Testament says in so many words that Abraham saw the death of Messiah as the Savior of the world. It is possible, however, that what our Lord is referring to is the transaction in Genesis 22 when Abraham was asked to sacrifice his only son on Mount Moriah. In offering his son, Abraham would have had a lively figure of the future offering of the Son of God as a sacrifice for the sins of the world.

Several factors point to this conclusion: (1) the place where the binding of Isaac took place was "the region of Moriah" (a land which included the site of Jerusalem and a well-known mountain by the same name); (2) the distance to which Abraham is asked to go is most unusual if the purpose was simply to test his faith (a test which could have been accomplished many miles closer to home than the Jerusalem area where he was sent by God); and (3) the fact that Isaac was the promised seed who bore in his person and in his life the promise of all that God was going to do in the future.

There were two kinds of child or human sacrifice known in the Old Testament. First there were those sacrifices of children or older individuals offered as a building sacrifice at the laying of the cornerstone of a city and its gates (1 Kings 16:34) or in a particular time of crisis, such as when a city was under siege or in imminent prospect of being captured (2 Kings 3:27; Mic 6:7). Probably this category should also include sacrifices of individuals as a gift to the pagan gods for granting victory (Judg 11) and the taking of prisoners of war for sacrifice.

But this is separate from the sacrifice required in the Old Testament of all the firstborn (Ex 13:12-13; 34:19-20; Num 3:44-51). Of course it must be hastily added that nowhere in Scripture did God require the sacrifice of persons as he did of animals and the produce of the field; instead he took one Levite for service at the temple for the eldest son in each household as a substitute for the life which was owed to God.

As stated earlier, God has the right to require human sacrifice. All biblical sacrifice rests on the idea that the gift of life to God, either in consecration or in expiation, is necessary to restore the broken fellowship with God caused by sin. What passes from man to God is not regarded as property belonging to us but only what is symbolically regarded as property and thus is the gift of life of the offerer.

However, the offerer is in no shape, because of sin, to make such a gift. Thus the principle of vicariousness is brought into play: one life takes the place of another. Accordingly, Abraham is asked by God to offer life, the life that is dearest to him, his only son's. But in the provision of God, a ram caught in the thicket is interposed by the angel of the Lord, thus pointing out that the substitution of one life for another is indeed acceptable to God. But this in no way gives comfort to the devotees of nature-worship systems whose alleged deities were subject to life and death and who therefore wrongly required their worshipers to immolate themselves or their children to achieve fellowship with these nonbeings.

25:8 What Does "Gathered to His People" Imply?

What was the Old Testament saints' concept of life after death? Did they have a clear belief in life after death? If so, what did it involve? For example, was it a ghostly existence? Did it involve personal, conscious awareness? Did they expect the spirit to be joined with a body? At what point? All of these questions are relevant to understanding this text about Abraham.

The expression "to be gathered to one's people" is similar to another expression, "to go to one's fathers," found in Genesis 15:15. The former phrase is found frequently—for example, here in Genesis 25:8, 17; 49:29, 33; Deuteronomy 32:50; and 2 Kings 22:20.

Do these phrases simply mean, as many scholars claim, that the Old Testament individual was laid to rest in the family grave? Is it true that there was no thought of an afterlife?

By Abraham's time, the human life span had been so curtailed, due to the physical effects of the Fall, that 175 years was regarded as a "good old age." What happened after Abraham died? Was he simply buried with his ancestors, end of story? Unfortunately, too many carelessly conclude that this is precisely the case.

Actually, the expression "he was gathered to his people" or "he went to his fathers" cannot mean that he was buried with his relatives and ancestors. In Genesis 25:8-9 such an analysis is impossible, because we know that none of Abraham's kin, except his wife, was buried at the cave of Machpelah.

In the Old Testament, those who have already died are regarded as still existing. The event of being "gathered to one's people" is always distinguished from the act of burial, which is described separately (Gen 25:8-9; 35:29; 49:29, 31, 33). In many cases only one ancestor was in the tomb (1 Kings 11:43; 22:40) or none at all (Deut 31:16; 1 Kings 2:10; 16:28; 2 Kings 21:18), so that being "gathered to one's people" could not mean being laid in the family sepulcher.

Readers of the text should not infer something special from the use of *Sheol* in some of these texts. In every one of the sixty-five instances of *Sheol* in the Old Testament, it refers simply to "the grave," not to the shadowy region of the netherworld. The writer of the book of Hebrews in the New Testament supports the notion that the patriarchs expected an afterlife:

> All these people [from Abel to Abraham] were still living by faith when they died. They did not receive the things promised; they only saw them and welcomed them from a distance. And they admitted that they were aliens and strangers on earth. People who say such things show that they are looking for a country of their own. If they had been thinking of the country they had left, they would have had opportunity to return. Instead, they were longing for a better country—a heavenly one. Therefore God is not ashamed to be called their God, for he has prepared a city for them. (Heb 11:13-16)

Here is a clear testimony that through faith these early participants in the promises of God were fully expecting to enjoy life after death. While the full revelation of the life hereafter and the resurrection of the body awaited a later unveiling in the Old and New Testaments, the common assertion that the Old Testament saint knew nothing at all about such a possibility is an error caused by preconceptions.

In Genesis 17:8 Abraham was given a promise by God: "The whole land of Canaan, where you are now an alien, I will give as an everlasting possession *to you* and your descendants after you." The rabbis reasoned that since Abraham never actually enjoyed the fulfillment of this promise, he would be raised from the dead to possess the land.

While this reasoning is curious, it is not all that far off. It is no more fanciful than the reasoning of our Lord in reminding the Sadducees—who did not believe in the resurrection—that the God of Abraham, Isaac and Jacob was not the God of the dead but of the living. Thus the patriarchs were not to be counted out of the hope of resurrection (Mt 22:23-32). The believer's relationship to God carries with it life in the body now and immortality in the future.

If some object that such concepts are too "developed" for the primitive times and minds of Old Testament people, we need only remind each other that life after death was already the overriding passion of the Egyptian culture. It was to be a life of material things, with real bodies, real wine, women and song. That concept had been imaged in the pyramid monuments for a thousand years before Abraham arrived in Egypt. How, then, could the afterlife be an impossible concept for him?

Other evidences of the belief of a real life after death are afforded by the stern warnings from Mosaic times about any dabbling in necromancy, the cult of contacting the dead. What harm would there have been in fooling around with something that had no reality? Already in the middle of the second millennium B.C., the Israelites knew the afterlife was real, and thus they were warned not to be involved in any contacting of individuals who had passed beyond this world.

Abraham died and was buried. But he also joined a community of believers who had gone on before. No details of the nature of that community are given at this point. But these expressions, "to be gathered to one's people" and "to go to one's fathers," are not a mere euphemism for death without any clear theological import. The evidence argues to the contrary.

See also comment on GENESIS 5:23-24; JOB 19:23-27; PSALM 49:12, 20; ECCLESIASTES 3:19-21; DANIEL 12:1-2.

26:3-5 Obedience the Way to Blessing?

Did God grant his gracious gifts to Abraham on the basis of works? Are we to surmise that Old Testament men and women got salvation the old-fashioned Smith-Barney way: "They earned it"?

It is the word *because* in Genesis 26:3-5 that causes us to raise our eyebrows and see this as a hard saying. There does appear to be a tension here between the free and unconditional offer of the promise to Abraham and the promise conditioned on Abraham's keeping all God's commands, decrees and laws. Surely law and grace are on a theological collision course.

There are five key passages that are cited as demonstrating that the patriarch Abraham performed the requirements of God and in return God offered to him the everlasting covenant as a gift for his obedience: Genesis 12:1; 17:1, 9-14; 22:16; 26:3-5. Some have added additional commands to this list, but generally these are not as directly related to the promise-plan as the five already cited.

The difficulty of this argument for conditionality and earning the promise is the stress the text makes on God's actively conferring this covenant on Abraham. In one of the most dramatic scenes in the patriarch's life, Genesis 15:12-21 depicts Abraham as being only a passive party to the formalization of the covenant, while the Lord, appearing as a "smoking firepot with a blazing torch," passes between the pieces of the animals in the act of making a covenant with Abraham. It is well worth noting that only God passed between the pieces and therefore obligated himself. Had this been a bilateral covenant in which the covenant depended equally on both parties fulfilling their sides of the bargain, then both God and Abraham would have had to move between the pieces of the animals divided in half and thus say in effect, "May it happen to me what has happened to these animals if I do not uphold my side of the covenant."

So how shall we explain the disparity that now seems to intrude, requiring obedience from Abraham if the covenant is to be maintained?

The answer will be this: promise and blessing still precede the command to obey and to keep the commands of God. Obedience is no more a condition for Abraham than it is for the church living under the command "If you obey my commands, you will remain in my love" (Jn 15:10) or "If you love me, you will obey what I command" (Jn 14:15).

The promise does not oppose God's law, either in Abraham's gift of the promise or in our gift of eternal life. The promise-giver who initiated the covenant with the patriarchs is the same one who gave the commandments, laws and statutes. Obedience, then, was not a condition for receiving the promise-blessing of God but was instead the evidence of real participation in that same promise. Because God was faithful, it was possible for these patriarchs to receive the promised blessings even if they themselves did not participate in them through their own belief. Even those who were not personal participants in the benefits of the covenant still had to pass on these benefits to those who followed in the line of the seed of the patriarchs. That belief was most easily demonstrated by the way in which individuals obeyed God—just as John puts it in his Gospel for the believing community of the New Testament.

Therefore, the alleged conditional elements in the Abrahamic (and Davidic) covenant never threatened the constituent elements of the promise, nor did they add any stipulations to them. The matter of duty or obedience, which indeed is intimately bound up with the promise, is a matter of outcome and sequel rather than a prior condition to being a participant in its benefits by faith.

The most remarkable text expressing the unconditional nature of the promise is Leviticus 26:44-45—"Yet in spite of this [the sins of disobedience], . . . I will not reject them or abhor them so as to destroy them completely, breaking my covenant with them. But for their sake I will remember the covenant with their ancestors." Surely that sounds as if it is indeed an unconditional covenant!

See also comment on LEVITICUS 18:5; MICAH 6:6-8; JAMES 2:24.

26:7-11 Rebekah Is My Sister?

See comment on GENESIS 12:11-13.

29:25-28 Is Polygamy Approved by God?

Is this episode a case of polygamy? Or did the special circumstances excuse Jacob, Laban or both? If it is polygamy, what is the case for or against polygamy?

Polygamy was never lawful for any of the persons in the Bible. There never existed an express biblical permission for such a deviation from the ordinance of God made at the institution of marriage in the Garden of Eden (Gen 2:21-24).

There are at least four passages that conceivably could be construed as giving temporary permission from God to override the general law of marriage found in Genesis 2:24. They are Exodus 21:7-11, Leviticus 18:18, Deuteronomy 21:15-17 and 2 Samuel 12:7-8.[1] But each one falls far short of proving that anything like divine permission was being granted in these passages.

Scripture does not always pause to state the obvious. In many cases there is no need for the reader to imagine what God thinks of such states of affairs, for the misfortune and strife that come into the domestic lives of these polygamists cannot be read as a sign of divine approval.

It is true that Jacob was deceived by Laban on Jacob's wedding night, but that did not justify Jacob in agreeing to Laban's crafty plan to get him to stay around for another seven years to ensure continued prosperity. Two wrongs in this case did not make a right.

See also comment on GENESIS 16:1-4; 2 SAMUEL 20:3.

---

[1]For a full discussion of these passages see Walter Kaiser Jr., *Toward Old Testament Ethics* (Grand Rapids, Mich.: Zondervan, 1983), pp. 182-90.

31:11-13 Who Is the Angel of God?

See comment on JUDGES 6:22-23.

31:34 Why Did Rachel Have Household Gods?

Why did Rachel steal the household

gods of her father Laban? Does the text thereby indicate that she put some sort of trust or belief in them?

It is clear that what was involved here was nothing less than images of Laban's gods, for his angry accusation against his son-in-law was "Why did you steal my gods?" (Gen 31:30). These images must have been small, portable figurines, for this is the only way that Rachel could have managed to conceal them in her camel saddle or cushion.

The significance of these images has been debated for the last three decades. Ever since the Nuzi documents with an adoption contract were found, it has been popular to link them with rights to the family inheritance or the will. The text from Nuzi stipulates, "If Nashwi has a son of his own, he shall divide [the estate] equally with Wullu, but the son of Nashwi shall take the gods of Nashwi. However, if Nashwi does not have a son of his own, then Wullu shall take the gods of Nashwi."[1] The thought that possession of the household gods somehow was connected with a legal claim to the inheritance has had general acceptance previously, but now is not as firmly held as it once was.[2]

Thus, while we do not know for certain what the significance of these gods was, we know that they normally would belong to the father of the family. Did Rachel steal them in order to assure that she would have the leverage when it came time to assessing the inheritance, or were these deities in some way attached to her own religious feelings and commitments at the time? It is impossible to say which, if either of these options, is correct.

The fact that the Nuzi Tablets come from North Mesopotamia several centuries removed in time from the patriarchs makes it uncertain whether the same cultural coloration is shared by the two ends of this comparison.

However, a clue may be gleaned from Genesis 35:2, where Jacob must be commanded by God later on to "get rid of the foreign gods you have with you, and purify yourselves." Could some of these gods be the ones that Rachel had stolen? It seems more than likely. Thus Rachel may well have been attached religiously to these false gods as she left her father's house.

See also comment on 1 SAMUEL 19:13.

[1]James B. Pritchard, *Ancient Near Eastern Texts Relating to the Old Testament* (Princeton, N.J.: Princeton University Press, 1955), pp. 219-20.

[2]See Cyrus H. Gordon, "Biblical Customs and the Nuzi Tablets," *Biblical Archaeologist* 3 (1940): 6. Gordon was the strongest advocate of this position.

32:20 Is Bribery Permitted?

See comment on PROVERBS 21:14.

32:23-33 With Whom Did Jacob Wrestle?

According to Martin Luther, "Every man holds that this text is one of the most obscure in the Old Testament." The principal issue is the identity of the man who wrestled with Jacob at the Jabbok ford all night until the dawn of the next day. Was he a mere mortal, or was he an angel? Or, still more startling, was this individual actually a preincarnate form of the Son of God, the second person of the Trinity?

Some have attempted to solve the interpretive problem by making the whole sequence a dream narrative. Josephus understood it as a dream wherein the apparition made use of words and voices (*Antiquities* 1.20.2). Others have been content to allegorize the story, viewing it as the fight of the soul against the passions and vices hidden within oneself (for example, Philo *Legum Allegoriae* 3.190). Clement of Alexandria did equate the wrestler with the Logos of John's Gospel, but he argues that the

Logos remained unknown by name to Jacob because Jesus had not yet appeared in the flesh (*Paedagogus* 1.7.57).

Jewish literature, recognizing that there was an actual fight at the heart of the story, says that the struggle was with the prince or angel of Esau, named Samael, rather than with any theophany, much less a christophany.

Others, like Jerome, have tried to make the episode a portrayal of long and earnest prayer. Such prayer involved meditation on the divine presence, confession of sin and a deep yearning for communication with the divine.

Modern interpreters, chary of assuming any real contact of mortals with the immortal or supernatural, prefer to identify the story with the types of myth that have gods fighting with heroes. Of course this point of view would devalue the narrative into pure fiction and attribute its source not to revelation, but to literary borrowing from other polytheistic mythologies. Such a solution stands condemned under the weight of its own assertions when lined up against the claims of the biblical text itself.

The best commentary ever written on this passage is to be found in Hosea 12:3-4:

> As a man [Jacob] struggled with God. He struggled with the angel and overcame him; he wept and begged for his favor. He found him at Bethel and there [God] talked with *us*. (my translation)

Hosea 12:4 describes the antagonist, then, as an "angel." But since Old Testament appearances of God, or theophanies, are routinely described as involving the "angel of the Lord," it should not surprise us that the Lord of glory took the guise or form of an angel. In fact, that is exactly what God would do later on in his enfleshment, or incarnation. He would take on flesh; in his coming as a babe to Bethlehem, however, he took on human flesh forever.

But what really clinches the argument for this identification is the fact that in verse 3 of Hosea 12, the parallel clause equates this "angel" with God himself. Jacob struggled with an "angel," yes, but he also "struggled with God."

What makes this identification difficult to conceive is the fact that the encounter involved wrestling. How is it possible for the second person of the Trinity—for that is the person connected with the "angel of the Lord" so frequently—to grapple in such a physical way with a mortal?

Clearly there is a sort of punning wordplay in this story with Jacob *(ya'ᵃqōḇ)*, Jabbok *(yabbo̱q)* and the action of wrestling *(yē'āḇēq)*. These similar-sounding words attract hearers' and readers' attention to the linking of the story's key ideas. The wrestling took place at the threshold of the Promised Land. Ever since Jacob's flight from his disaffected brother Esau, Jacob had been outside the land God had deeded to him in his promise.

As a result of this wrestling, Jacob was renamed Israel and prepared for his part in fathering the nation that God had promised. In order to preserve Jacob's memory of this spiritual crisis, God left a permanent mark on his body. God touched Jacob's thigh and dislocated it; so he limped from that point onward.

Unfortunately, we cannot identify the exact nature of the wrestling. It is clear, however, that it involved more than a battle in the spiritual realm. It left Jacob with a real physical impairment. And although the narrative says only that Jacob wrestled with a "man," he was told by this individual that he had wrestled "with God" and had "overcome" (Gen 32:28); similarly, Hosea says that Jacob "overcame" an angel (Hos 12:4).

Incidentally, the touch on Jacob's

thigh became the basis in postexilic times for a food taboo in the Jewish community. Jews may not eat the sinew of the nerve along the thigh joint, called the *nervus ischiadicus* or sciatic nerve.

It thus appears that the "man" or "angel" with whom Jacob wrestled was Jesus himself, in a temporary incarnate form prior to his permanent enfleshment when he would come to earth as a human baby. This is consistent with other places in the Old Testament where the "angel of the Lord" can be identified as the second person of the Trinity.

See also comment on JUDGES 6:22-23; EXODUS 33:18-23.

35:29 Gathered to His People?

See comment on GENESIS 25:8.

38:26 Was Tamar Righteous?

See comment on GENESIS 6:9.

42:7 Was Joseph Cruel to His Brothers?

Why does Joseph pretend that he does not know his brothers and proceed to speak to them so harshly? Is this in character with how he is portrayed elsewhere in Scripture?

While Joseph recognized his brothers, they did not at first link this high Egyptian official with their younger brother whom they had sold into slavery over a decade and a half ago. Thus Joseph had the advantage of learning some answers to questions that had been on his mind over the past years.

It does not appear that Joseph spoke to his brothers out of a revengeful spirit. There is no indication that he ever dealt unfairly, unkindly or unjustly with those who treated him in that way. Even after his heart had been made tender by the distress of his brethren, he continued to speak roughly with them.

What, then, could his motives have been for assuming such a stern demeanor? In part it was, no doubt, to obtain the much-desired information about his father and mother's family without revealing who he was. But there was another motive for his strange actions: it was to bring them to a sense of the real evil it was to deal with others in an unjust or harsh manner. By this means also, he could determine if there was any evidence of remorse for the wrong the brothers had done to him and to their father. It was a case of kindness putting on a stern or angry appearance in order to bring the guilty parties to a realization of the dreadful wrong in which they had been involved.

46:27 How Many Went to Egypt?

See comment on ACTS 7:14-15.

48:20 How Many Tribes?

When Jacob blessed Joseph's two sons and made them part of the twelve-tribe confederacy in place of Joseph, why is it that the number of tribes does not now add up to thirteen?

The answer to this question will be worked out in the history of Israel. But in general it involved the curse of Simeon and Levi being dispersed among the tribes of Judah and Israel (Gen 48:5-7) for their savagery when they killed all the inhabitants of the small town of Shechem as revenge for the rape of their sister Dinah (Gen 34), even after the men of the town had agreed to be circumcised.

Depending on the period of history, Simeon tended to be absorbed into Judah both in territory and name, while Levi, which never was assigned any landed territory, turned the curse into a means of ministering to all twelve tribes. Thus Joseph's two sons, Ephraim and Manasseh, take not only Joseph's place in the list of the twelve, but also either that of Levi, or at other times, when Levi is also listed, the place of Simeon.

49:10 Who or What Is Shiloh?

Rarely, if ever, has one word had as many possible meanings or emendations attached to it with no general agreement being reached as the word *Shiloh* here. The clause in the NIV rendered "until he comes to whom it belongs" is more literally "until Shiloh comes."

What did the patriarch Jacob have in mind as he spoke his blessing to his fourth son, Judah, and predicted the arrival of "Shiloh"? It is clear from a postexilic text (1 Chron 5:1-2) that Joseph and Judah shared what would have been the blessings normally inherited by the firstborn, Reuben. Joseph received the double portion, and through Judah the line of the "ruler" was to come. This helps us understand the way later generations were taught under inspiration to regard the role Judah played, but what are we to make of Jacob's understanding of the blessing he pronounced on Judah in Genesis 49?

Did Jacob intend to point to a future city where the ark of the covenant would rest until that city came to an end? Why then did Jacob speak of "*his* feet" and the obedience that would be *his?* The antecedent of the pronouns seems to be a person, not an object like the city Shiloh.

If Jacob did not intend to point to a city named Shiloh, did he have a specific person in mind? And if he did, did the name mean "Rest" or "Peace-giver?" Or are we to take the alleged Akkadian cognate word and conclude that the name means "Ruler"?

Perhaps this name is only a title meaning something like "His Peace." Or perhaps we are to accept one or another of the numerous emendations (changes in spelling of the Hebrew *shîlōh,* all of which have particular nuances of meaning).

Most startling of all is the statement that someone from the tribe of Judah would own the obedience not just of the tribe or even of all Israel, but of all the nations. This suggests a kingship that would extend well beyond the boundaries of the ancient land of Israel.

The problem, then, is clear; the solution is more difficult. Let us note first of all that the scepter symbolizes the rule and dominion exercised by a ruler. The "ruler's staff" or "commander's staff" may be a parallel synonym to "scepter." But since its verbal root means "to inscribe" or "to cut," as in setting forth a decree, the term may refer to the concept of a lawgiver, one who proclaims the law or rules and governs on the basis of law. Given the context of Judah as the person in view, it would seem better to take "ruler's staff" as a correlative term with "scepter." It would then mean one who wields the scepter with power and authority on the basis of the decree or law given to him.

Now comes the more difficult phrase, "until Shiloh comes." The *until* is used not in an *exclusive* but in an *inclusive* sense. That is, the coming of Shiloh does not mark the limits of Judah's domination over the nation of Israel, for if it did it would constitute a threat and not a blessing. Instead, the idea is that the sovereignty of Judah is brought to its highest point under the arrival and rule of Shiloh.

Who or what, then, is Shiloh? It cannot refer to the place where the tabernacle would be pitched centuries later. If it did, Jacob would be prophesying about a place that was unknown at the time of prediction, and one that was rarely if ever mentioned in the literature of later years except as a symbol of judgment. This interpretation would also involve changing the verb "comes" to "comes to an end," a meaning that adds more than the text says and only raises another question: What end and why?

Martin Luther connected "Shiloh" with the Hebrew *shilyâh,* which he translated "womb." This would suggest the son of the womb, the Messiah. John Calvin had a similar idea. He connected Shiloh with the Hebrew *shîl,* plus the third-person suffix, giving the meaning "his son." But Luther and Calvin failed to realize that these were two different words. *Shîl* does not mean "son." In modern Hebrew *shîl* or *shilîl* means "embryo." The closest biblical Hebrew comes to the form Calvin was thinking of is *shilyâh,* "afterbirth."

Others have looked for a verbal root rather than a nominal one. One connects it to *shālâh,* "to be peaceful"—hence "rest," or perhaps "Man of Peace." Another suggests the verb *shālal,* "to draw out or plunder," with the pronoun "his"—hence "his drawn-out one" or "his child to be born." One other view connects the word with *shālaḥ,* "to send." This would yield "until he who is sent comes."

Since the second half of the poetic line begins with "and to him" in the emphatic position, it is proper to assume that we are dealing with a coming person. Moreover, since "the obedience of the nations is his," he will be a ruler who will emanate from the line of Judah.

The rabbis were convinced that Ezekiel 21:27 (v. 32 in the Hebrew) provided the proper clue for the meaning of Shiloh. They suggested that behind this word lies *shel,* meaning "which," and *lōh,* meaning "belongs to him." Thus understood, the meaning of Shiloh accords with Ezekiel 21:27, "until he comes to whom it rightfully belongs."

It was the tribe of Judah that led the march through the wilderness (Num 10:14). When the Israelites reached the Promised Land, Judah's inheritance was allotted first (Josh 15:1). Later, Judah would emerge as the leader of the tribes in a totally new way. Thus Jacob referred as much to Judah as he did to the successor who would come through his line.

The verses that follow this passage, Genesis 49:11-12, have a lush rural setting. They describe the rich blessings in store for Judah and this ruling successor, the Messiah himself. There would be great prosperity for the coming royal one, but there would also be pain and bloodshed (perhaps the references to wine and the treading of the winepress imply this struggle).

Shiloh, we conclude, is the royal Messiah who comes through the line of Judah and who will take the throne that rightfully belongs to him.

49:29, 33 What Does "Gathered to His People" Imply?

See comment on GENESIS 25:8.

50:19-20 Human Intentions Versus God's Intentions

How can God be God if individuals are truly free to make their own choices? It would appear that sooner or later these two free agents would collide and one would need to give way to the other.

This passage has comforted many and helped them better understand how the principles of divine sovereignty, human freedom and individual responsibility relate to each other. It affirms that divine sovereignty and human freedom operate in ways that are sometimes surprising.

God hates all sin with a perfect and unremitting hatred. However, it is his prerogative to allow good to come out of the evil others devise. Indeed, no sin can be committed without his knowledge or against his holy will. In this sense, sinners are often just as much the ministers of his providential workings as are his saints.

When because of jealousy and deep hatred Joseph's half brothers sold Joseph into slavery, God by his own mysterious working sent him to Egypt, not only to save that pagan nation (proof of common grace available to all by virtue of the decrees of creation) but to save the very people who had sold him into those horrible circumstances. By so doing, Joseph attained the position his brothers were attempting to undermine. And ultimately God was glorified.

Accordingly, Joseph was taught to acknowledge and revere God's providence in his circumstances. He taught his brothers to share these same truths. They and we are to view God's hand not only in his goodness and mercy to us, but in our afflictions and trials as well.

Sinners cannot undo their actions or prevent the natural consequences of sin from producing its usual miserable effects, but there are innumerable occasions to thank a gracious Lord for counteracting and mitigating the otherwise devastating effects of such evil. God can and does work all things for good to those who love him and who are called according to his purposes to be transformed into his Son's image (Rom 8:28-29).

This does not mean that the nature of sin is altered and that believers never experience pain caused by sin. Poison does not cease to be poison just because it can sometimes be used medicinally.

However, this text claims that God need not worry that his purposes will be countermandated by society's sinful actions. Nor will God have to limit the freedoms which all individuals have, both believers and unbelievers, in order to preserve his sovereignty. He can cope with it, and he does succeed. The result is that God remains God and individuals remain responsible, blameworthy and culpable for all their acts.

There is both a directive will and a permissive will in the divine purpose. Men and women may be culpable and blameworthy for an act such as crucifying the Lord of glory, but as a permitted act it can still come under the total plan of God. As Acts 2:23 states, "This man [Jesus] was handed over to you by God's set purpose and foreknowledge; and you, with the help of wicked men, put him to death by nailing him to the cross." If that is true for Christ's crucifixion, then it is no less true in the case of Joseph and all similarly besieged men and women today.

EXODUS

1:5 How Many Went to Egypt?

See comment on ACTS 7:14-15.

1:15-21 Were the Midwives Right to Lie?

The ethical issue of lying arises with regard to the midwives Shiphrah and Puah's report to Pharaoh. When asked by the Egyptian king if they had been carrying out his order that all Hebrew male babies must be killed as they were being delivered by the midwives, they lied by telling Pharaoh that they had not been able to be fast enough to make it to any male deliveries lately (Ex 1:19).

Surely they were lying, but the Scripture, as usual, does not stop to moralize on the point. Nevertheless, it does expect us to evaluate what is going on against the message of the whole of Scripture.

It has been argued that God blessed these women for their act of lying, but the approval of a character in one area is not an approval in all areas. For example, God declared David to be a man after his own heart, but there was also the matter of Uriah and Bathsheba. Solomon was called Jedidiah, meaning "loved of the Lord"; but I can think of a thousand things wrong with him! Exodus 1:21 specifically says that Shiphrah and Puah were blessed of the Lord because they "feared God," not because they lied. Thus their respect and awe of God took precedence over their allegiance to Pharaoh. They trusted the Lord and feared falling into his hands to give an account for murdering the babies more than they feared falling into the hands of Pharaoh. But this is not to say that the women were right in everything they did or said.

The midwives had no more right to lie, even when there seemed to be such conflicting absolutes as telling the truth and protecting life, than we do. Instead, they were obligated both to sustain and save life and to honor the truth.

See also comment on EXODUS 3:18; JOSHUA 2:4-6; 1 SAMUEL 16:1-3.

3:2-6 Who Is the Angel of the Lord?

See comment on JUDGES 6:22-23.

3:13-15 Elohim or Yahweh?

See comment on GENESIS 1—2.

3:18 Is Deception Ever Justifiable?

Is this an example of a half-truth or a ruse intended to deceive Pharaoh? In other words, is Israel's request for a three-day wilderness trip to worship God only an excuse to leave Egypt in order to make a break for Palestine before Pharaoh's troops could easily follow?

Since this pagan king would never submit his will to God's, would Moses and the Hebrew elders have been justified in tricking him as long as they got the children of Israel out of town? After all, does not the end justify the means? Or if that appears to be too casuistic for believers, should not Moses and the elders have chosen the lesser evil or perhaps even the greater good?

Each of these options has been offered in ethical theory. But each raises a different set of problems for the Christian. Even the appeal to Psalm 18:26 by Rabbi Rashi misses the point: "With the crooked [some interpreted to mean with Pharaoh] you [God] are crafty." But we object that divine judgment never came until Pharaoh had rejected all divine appeals to acquiesce to God's plan.

Instead, the best solution was proposed long ago by the fourth-century church father Augustine and the fifteenth-century Spanish exegete Abarbanel. In their view, God deliberately graded his requests of Pharaoh by first placing before him a fairly simple plea that the people of Israel be allowed a three-day journey into the wilderness after which they would return. True, this first plea would lead to requests increasingly more difficult for Pharaoh to grant; however, they would each prepare Pharaoh to do what he might otherwise be unprepared to do.

Had Pharaoh complied with this request, the Israelites could not have exceeded the bounds of this permission. After returning to Egypt they would have needed to present a series of such pleas leading to the final request for full release. Here we can see God's tender love and concern for Pharaoh. This king is more than just a pawn in the plan of God. And Israel was responsible to honor the "powers that be."

Remarkably, God warns Moses that the king of Egypt will deny the request. Thus God knows both what actually takes place and what could have taken place. This warning confirms Amos 3:7: "Surely the Sovereign LORD does nothing without revealing his plan to his servants the prophets." Not even God's "mighty hand" of miracles, evidenced in the plagues, will budge Pharaoh's obduracy and recalcitrance.

One further question might be posed here: Did not Moses, under the instigation of Yahweh, deliberately mislead Pharaoh when he concealed his real intention? If Moses ultimately intended to ask Pharaoh to release the Israelites, did not this concealment constitute a half-truth? In other words, is not the essence of falsehood the intention to deceive? If Pharaoh received the impression that Moses wanted only to journey far enough away to sacrifice without offending the Egyptians (they would sacrifice animals sacred in Egypt), are not Moses and God telling lies?

No! There is a vast difference between telling a lie and concealing information that others have forfeited a right to know because of their hostile attitude toward God or his moral standards. King Saul, for example, forfeited his right to know all the reasons for the prophet Samuel's visit, which was actually to anoint David the next king (1 Sam 16:1-2). We must sharpen our definition of lying to mean the intentional deception of an individual who has the right to know the truth from us, and under circumstances in which he or she has a claim to such knowledge. The point is that lying is more than an intentional deception. Such deception may be a moral evil, but one cannot tell this until it is determined if such individuals have a claim to all or even part of the truth. Therefore, all men and women always have an obligation to speak only the truth, but they do not have an obligation always to speak up or tell everything they know just because they are asked—especially when some have forfeited their right to know the truth by flouting the truth they already possess.

See also comment on EXODUS 9:12; JOSHUA 2:4-6; 1 SAMUEL 16:1-3; 1 KINGS 22:20-22; 2 KINGS 6:19.

4:21 The Lord Hardened Pharaoh's Heart?

See comment on EXODUS 9:12.

4:24-26 Why Was the Lord About to Kill Moses?

What surprises and puzzles us about this text is its brevity, the abruptness of its introduction, the enigmatic nature of its cryptic statements and the difficulty of establishing the correct antecedents for several of its pronouns. But most troubling of all is the bald statement that the Lord wanted to kill the leader he had worked to prepare for eighty years.

These verses are some of the most difficult in the book of Exodus. Why did the Lord wish to kill Moses? What had he done—or failed to do? Why did his Midianite wife, Zipporah, pick up a flint knife without being told to do so and immediately circumcise her son? What is the significance of her taking her son's excised prepuce and touching Moses' feet while complaining, "Surely you are a bridegroom of blood to me"? Why did the Lord then let Moses go? (It would seem that Moses is the one to whom the pronoun "him" refers.)

The narrative begins with an adverb meaning "at that time." This immediately solves one problem: this text is not an etiological story (that is, an attempt to explain why certain things function or have the meaning they do—usually based on a made-up story). Nowhere in the Old Testament is such an adverb used to introduce etiological material. The writer wanted us to place the episode in the setting of the real world.

The link between verses 24-26 and the material before and after it is important. It is not that God is seeking Moses' life, as Pharaoh had. There are two key themes. First, there is the matter of the sons. Pharaoh's "firstborn" (Ex 4:23) and Moses' son (perhaps his firstborn) are involved in a crucial contest that involves God's call to Israel, his "firstborn" (Ex 4:22). The contrasts are deliberate, and they manifest the grace of God and a call for response to the word of God.

The second issue is the preparation of God's commissioned servant. God had prepared the nation of Israel, by virtue of their groaning, and he had prepared Moses in leadership skills; yet there was still the small but important matter of the preparation of the family. Moses had failed to have his son circumcised, either as a concession to his wife's scruples or because of his own relaxation of standards. As a result, he almost lost the opportunity to do what he had been prepared all his life to do—and he almost lost his life as well.

Obviously, Zipporah was moved to act quickly on her own. Without a word of instruction, she suddenly seized a flint knife (or stone) and circumcised her son. Usually this would be a ceremony performed by the head of the house. Zipporah's action shows that she instinctively connected her husband's malady with the failure to place their son under God's covenant through circumcision (Gen 17:10-14). Moses may well have been too ill to act on his own; therefore Zipporah took the initiative.

When Zipporah had excised the prepuce, she touched her husband's feet with it and said, with what must have been a tone of disgust and scorn, "Surely you are a bridegroom of blood to me." These words cannot be understood as communicating anything but derision and revulsion for the rite of circumcision.

There may well have been a long debate in this household over whether their son would be circumcised or not. Perhaps Zipporah argued that the operation struck her as repulsive. Moses may have countered, "But God commanded that we must circumcise all of our male children." In order to keep the peace, however, Moses may have let the matter drop and risked disobeying the command of God.

Just as he was preparing to return to Egypt and take up the mantle of leadership after a forty-year absence, however, Moses was suddenly struck down, faced with a peril that was clearly life-threatening. Zipporah knew immediately wherein the problem lay, so she acted with haste. Yet she was still unpersuaded about the rightness of the act. She complied under duress, not with a willing heart.

Moses plays no active part in this narrative at all. Some have attempted to argue that he had neglected his own circumcision, since he had spent all those years in Pharaoh's palace and then in Midian. But there is nothing in the text to confirm this idea. It is true, of course, that the Egyptians practiced a form of adult circumcision, but some contend that it was a partial circumcision only. In any case, Scripture does not make an issue of Moses' own circumcision.

If the scenario I have offered is reasonably close to what did indeed take place, then how can we defend God's intent to kill Moses? Even putting it mildly, this sounds most bizarre and extreme.

The syntax of Old Testament Hebrew tends to be unconcerned with secondary causes; thus, what God permitted is often said in the Old Testament to be done directly *by* him. So if, as I believe, God permitted Moses to be afflicted with a severe sickness or some other danger, the proper way to express that in Hebrew language patterns would be to say that God wanted to kill him. It was not simply that Moses was sick and near death; it was a case of the sovereignty of God, who controls all events and happenings on the earth. Thus the secondary causes were not important. The ultimate cause took precedence as a means of explanation.

6:3 Elohim or Yahweh?

See comment on GENESIS 1—2.

6:16-20 How Many Generations in Egypt?

The list of four generations in this text presents no problems on its face until one reads in Exodus 12:40 that the time period is 430 years. Such genealogical lists in the Old Testament have been a source of special delight and enormous difficulty. In a positive sense, they express a sense of order and attachment to history. These were real people who lived in real times with real family connections.

The difficulty, however, is that all too many interpreters have been tempted to assume that these genealogies are complete lists of names and figures and that we can therefore add up all the ages and obtain absolute dates for a number of prepatriarchal events for which we otherwise would have no data. Unfortunately the assumption is faulty. These are not complete genealogical records, and it was not the writers' intention to provide this material for readers who might wish to add up numbers. Usually what the text is reluctant to do, we must be reluctant to do as well.

So we must ask, Is there evidence that these genealogies were condensed through the omission of less important names? In particular, can we determine whether there were only four generations from Levi to Moses during the 430 years of bondage in Egypt? Were Amram and Jochebed Aaron and Moses' immediate parents? If not, why does the text say Jochebed "bore him [Amram] Aaron and Moses?" (Ex 6:20). On the other hand, why does Exodus 2:1 remain noncommittal about the names of Moses' parents—"Now a man of the house of Levi married a Levite woman, and she became pregnant and gave birth to a son [Moses]"?

A parallel genealogy for the same period of time—from the days just before Jacob went to Egypt until his descendants came out 430 years later—is preserved in the line of Joshua, a younger contemporary of Moses, given in 1 Chronicles 7:23-27; there are eleven generations listed between Jacob and Joshua.

The logical conclusion is that Moses' genealogy is condensed. It is inconceivable that there should be eleven links between Jacob and Joshua and only four or five between Jacob and Moses.

But if more proof is needed, we have it. An altogether overwhelming set of data can be seen in Numbers 3:19, 27-28. If no abridgment is understood in the four generations of Moses' ancestry, what results is this unbelievable set of numbers: the grandfather of Moses had, during Moses' lifetime, 8,600 male descendants (forget, for the moment, the females!), 2,750 of whom were between the ages of thirty and fifty (Num 4:36)! Now, all of us know that those were times of large families, but is it possible to make sense of what has been reported in these texts—unless there is considerable condensing and compression of the record to get at just the key characters?

Another piece of evidence is to be found in the fact that Levi's son Kohath was born before Jacob and his twelve sons went down to Egypt (Gen 46:11), where the emerging nation of Israel lived for 430 years (Ex 12:40). Now if Moses was 80 years old at the exodus (Ex 7:7), he must have been born 350 years after Kohath, who, as a consequence, could not have been his grandfather. In fact, Kohath is said to have lived a total of 133 years, and his son Amram lived 137 years. These two numbers do not add up to the 350 years needed to account for the 430 years in Egypt minus Moses' 80 years at the time of the exodus. What has happened, then, to Moses' genealogy? Unquestionably Levi was Jacob's son. Likewise, Kohath was born to Levi before they went down to Egypt. There is also a strong possibility that Amram was the immediate descendant of Kohath. The missing links do not appear to come between Jacob and Levi, Levi and Kohath, or even Kohath and Amram.

But if the gaps come after Amram, why does Exodus 6:20 specifically say that Jochebed "bore" Moses to Amram? In the genealogies, such expressions are routinely used to say that individuals were descended from grandparents or even great-great-grandparents. A case in point is Genesis 46:18, where the sons of Zilpah, her grandsons and her great-grandsons are listed as "children *born* to Jacob *by Zilpah* . . . sixteen in all." Genesis 46:25 makes the same type of reckoning for the descendants of Bilhah. Therefore, the phrases "son of," "bore to," "born to" and "father of" have a wider range of meaning in Scripture than they have in contemporary Western usage. If we are to understand Scripture, we must accept the usage of the Hebrew writers of that time.

Some will point to Leviticus 10:4 and note that Uzziel, Amram's brother, is called "Aaron's uncle." The Hebrew word translated "uncle," though applicable to a definite degree of relationship, has a wider scope of meaning, both etymologically and in its usage. A great-great-great-granduncle is still an uncle in the biblical usage of the term.

It is fair to conclude, then, that this is why Exodus 2:1 does not supply us with the names of the Levitical couple who were the parents of Aaron and Moses. This example should alert us not to use genealogical lists in an attempt to obtain absolute dates for events and persons. Amram and Jochebed were not the immediate parents of Aaron and Moses. How many generations intervened we cannot tell. All that must be known for the purposes of revelation, however, has been disclosed.

There is selection and arrangement in the list that appears in Exodus 6:14-25. It includes only three of Jacob's twelve sons—Reuben, Simeon and Levi. It is framed by the near-verbatim repetition of Exodus 6:10-13 in Exodus 6:26-30, and the first part of Exodus 6:14 in the last part of Exodus 6:25. Clearly its purposes are theological, not chronological or numerical.

See also comment on "Why Don't Bible Genealogies Always Match Up?"

7:3, 13 The Lord Hardened Pharaoh's Heart?

See comment on EXODUS 9:12.

7:11, 22; 8:7 Did the Egyptian Magicians Perform Magic?

Did the Egyptian magicians actually perform magic of a miraculous kind, or were they fakes and tricksters?

The "wise men" of Egypt were the learned and schooled men of that time. The "magicians" or "sorcerers" (from the intensive form of the Hebrew verb meaning "to pray, to offer prayers") is used in the Old Testament only in the sense of sorcery. This word for "magicians" is derived from the Egyptian loan-word *hry-hbt,* later shortened to *hry-tp,* "the chief of the priests."

The use of magic in Egypt is best seen in the Westcar Papyrus, where magicians are credited with changing wax crocodiles into live ones and back to wax again after seizing them by their tails. However, the relation between Aaron's miracles and those done by the magicians, whom the apostle Paul named as Jannes and Jambres in 2 Timothy 3:8, is difficult to describe. It could well be that the magicians cast spells over serpents that were rendered immobile by catalepsy, due to pressure on the nape of their necks. However, it is just as likely that by means of demonic power they were able to keep up with Aaron and Moses by using supernatural powers from a realm other than God's for the first two plagues. But when they came to the third plague, they bowed out with the declaration to Pharaoh that "this is the finger of God" (Ex 8:19).

9:12 The Lord Hardened Pharaoh's Heart?

The theme of "hardening" occurs twenty times between Exodus 4 and 14. But the most troublesome aspect of these verses is that in ten out of the twenty occurrences God himself is said to have hardened Pharaoh's heart. This fact troubles many readers of the Scriptures, for it appears God authors evil and then holds someone else responsible. Did God make it impossible for Pharaoh to respond and then find Pharaoh guilty for this behavior?

God twice predicts he will harden

Pharaoh's heart. These two prophetic notices were given to Moses before the whole contest began (Ex 4:21; 7:3). However, if these two occurrences appear to cast the die against Pharaoh, it must be remembered that all God's prophecies to his prophets have a suppressed "unless you repent" attached to them. Few prophecies are unconditional; these few include God's covenant with the seasons in Genesis 8:22; his covenant with Abraham, Isaac, Jacob and David; his new covenant; and his covenant with the new heavens and the new earth in Isaiah 65—66.

In general, only the promises connected with nature and our salvation have no dependence on us; all others are much like Jonah's message to Nineveh. Even though Jonah never even hinted at the fact that Nineveh's imminent destruction (only forty days away) could be avoided by repentance, the king assumed such was the case, and Jonah's worst fears were realized: the nation repented and the barbarous Assyrians did not get what was coming to them!

In Pharaoh's case, Pharaoh initiated the whole process by hardening his own heart ten times during the first five plagues (Ex 7:13, 14, 22; 8:15, 19, 32; 9:7, 34, 35; and 13:15). It was always and only Pharaoh who hardened his heart during these plagues! Rather than letting the work of God soften his heart during these plagues and concluding that Yahweh is the only true God, Pharaoh made this evidence the basis for hardening his heart. Meanwhile, the plagues must have had some impact on the general population of Egypt, for when the Israelites left Egypt, they were accompanied by "many other people" (Ex 12:38). Even Pharaoh's own magicians confessed, "This is the finger [the work] of God" (Ex 8:19), and they bowed out of the competition with the living God.

It appears that Pharaoh reached the limits of his circumscribed freedom during the fifth plague, for after that time, during the last five plagues, God consistently initiated the hardening (Ex 9:12; 10:1, 20, 27; 11:10; 14:4, 8, 17).

God is not the author of evil. There is no suggestion that he violated the freedom of Pharaoh's will or that he manipulated Pharaoh in order to heap further vengeance on the Egyptian people. God is not opposed to the cooperation of pagan monarchs. Pharaoh could have cooperated with God just as Cyrus did in the Babylonian exile; God was still glorified when that king decided on his own to let Israel return from Babylon. If Pharaoh had acted as King Cyrus would later do, the results of the exodus would have been the same. It is Pharaoh, not God, who is to be blamed for the hardening of his own heart.

Note that the same topic is raised again in Deuteronomy 2:30, Joshua 11:20 and 1 Samuel 6:6. While these allusions are briefer, one can be sure that the process of accountability and human responsibility was just as fair as in the case of Pharaoh.

See also comment on 1 SAMUEL 2:25; ISAIAH 63:17.

10:1, 20, 27 The Lord Hardened Pharaoh's Heart?

See comment on EXODUS 9:12.

11:10 The Lord Hardened Pharaoh's Heart?

See comment on EXODUS 9:12.

12:35-36 Plundering the Egyptians?

Three separate passages in Exodus record the narrative generally referred to as the spoiling of the Egyptians (Ex 3:21-22; 11:2-3; 12:35-36). The problems associated with the passages are partly a modern translation problem, which existed in most translations until just recently, and partly the question of whether Israel deceived the Egyptians by borrowing clothing and jewelry they would never return. How could God have commanded them to borrow items when he knew the Israelites would never return with them?

Let us first address the verb sometimes translated "to borrow." This verb can as easily be rendered "to ask for something [with no thought of return]" (Judg 8:24; 1 Sam 1:28). Accordingly, the third-century B.C. Greek translation of the Septuagint and the Latin Vulgate translated it "to ask." This same Hebrew word is occasionally translated "to borrow," as in Exodus 22:14 or 2 Kings 4:3 and 6:5. In these instances, context determines its rendering.

In this case, the context also contains the verb *to plunder.* Here the meaning is clear, as it is in 2 Chronicles 20:25. It is a military metaphor which could, in some contexts, imply taking things by force, but never by fraud, deceit or any kind of a ruse or cunning device. It is not, however, the usual term for plundering the enemy.

The background for this thrice-recorded incident is the ancient promise God had given to Abraham in Genesis 15:14 that the Hebrews would leave Egypt "with great possessions." God repeated this promise to Moses: Israel would "not go empty-handed" (Ex 3:20-21) away from Egypt.

God himself favorably disposed the hearts of the Egyptians toward Israel (Ps 106:46 says, "He caused them to be pitied"). Also Moses was "highly regarded" (Ex 11:3) by the Egyptians. However, such esteem was not solely attributable to Moses' personal qualifications, though he had garnered quite a reputation with the magicians (Ex 8:18-19), the court officials (Ex 9:20; 10:7) and Pharaoh himself (Ex 9:27; 10:16). The general populace of Egypt recognized that God was with this man and his people. Therefore a great outpouring of generosity ensued, and that is what these three texts record. All the Israelites had to do was ask. The people were so ready to acknowledge that Israel indeed had been mistreated and that God had been remarkably present with the Jewish leadership that they gave openhandedly.

Notice that the women did not ask for such objects as weapons, armor, cattle, food supplies or goods for their homes, tables or job occupations. To avoid all suggestions in this direction, the author of Psalm 105:37 may have dropped the word *articles* before the words *silver and gold* so as not to imply that the Israelites asked for a third group of things besides the jewels and clothing.

This type of spoiling is not the usual term used of plundering someone who has fallen in battle. When one adds that the Egyptians willingly surrendered their jewels and articles of silver and gold, the apparent moral problem is resolved. One can guess that the Egyptians viewed their gifts as partial compensation for the grief and toil the Hebrews endured during their centuries of slavery in that land.

No legitimate moral questions remain once the situation is understood as a straightforward request which the Egyptians answered only too gladly, for by now almost everyone sympathized with their cause.

12:40 430 Years for Four Generations?

See comment on EXODUS 6:16-20.

14:4, 8, 17 The Lord Hardened Pharaoh's Heart?

See comment on EXODUS 9:12.

14:21 What Happened to the Red Sea?

Did the Red Sea actually divide in two,

leaving a path for the Israelites to cross over on dry land? Or did the Israelites cross over a tidal basin during low tide, assisted by the drying effect of a strong east wind?

The sea that the Israelites crossed is called the "Red" or "Reed Sea." The name probably comes from the Egyptian *ṯwf,* hence Hebrew *sûp̄,* meaning "reeds." These "reeds" appear as the same word that was used in Exodus 2:3, where Miriam hid among the "reeds" to see what would happen to her brother Moses in the small ark.

But there is no indication in the association of reeds with the place where the Israelites crossed that it was just a marshy set of wetlands or a tidal swamp. In fact, the name "Red" or "Reed" Sea is used in Deuteronomy 1:1 and 1 Kings 9:26 of the saltwater areas of the Red Sea and the Gulf of Aqabah that surround the Sinai peninsula.

The actual crossing was either at the southern end of the Bitter Lakes or the northern end of the Red Sea rather than Lakes Ballah, Timsah, Menzaleh or even the radical suggestion that it was at the sandy strip of land that separates Lake Sirbonis from the Mediterranean Sea.

The fact that the waters formed a "wall" (Ex 14:22) on the right and the left and were piled up in a "heap" (Ex 15:8; Ps 78:13) surely gives the picture of a corridor formed by the rolling back of the waters that normally would be located there.

Some may object, of course, that Exodus 15 and Psalm 78 are poetic in form, and therefore the language may also be merely poetic. With that we can agree. But Exodus 14 is straight prose, and thus the attempt to explain its Exodus 14:22 with a "wall of water on their right and on their left" as a metaphor for God's protection and nothing more is unconvincing.

God used the secondary means of "a strong east wind" (Ex 14:21) blowing all night to accomplish what the poetic version in Exodus 15:8 called in poetry "the blast of [God's] nostrils" and the "breath" of his mouth (Ex 15:10).

20:4-6 Is Art Forbidden?

Was this second of the Ten Commandments intended to stifle any or all forms of artistic expression in Israel and even in our own day? Is the depiction of any of God's creatures or any aspect of his creation strictly forbidden, whether it be by means of oil painting or sculpting in wood, stone, clay, silver or gold?

Does this text also teach that children may be expected to pay for the sins of their evil parents, regardless of their own lifestyle or personal ethics and practices? And are some children shown great love and kindness simply because one of their relatives loved God and kept his commandments?

Exodus 20:3, generally regarded as the first commandment, deals with the internal worship of God. The third commandment, Exodus 20:7, deals with the spoken worship of God and the proper use of the tongue. Exodus 20:4-6 has to do with the external worship of God. Covered in this second commandment are both the mode of worshiping God (Ex 20:4-5) and the penalty for failing to do so (Ex 20:5-6). The prohibition is clearly aimed at the sin of idolatry.

The Old Testament is replete with synonyms and words for idols; in fact, it has fourteen such words. The word *idol* used here refers to an actual statue, while the word *form* or *resemblance* applies to real or imagined pictorial representations of any sort.

But neither term is used in this context to speak to the question of what is or is not legitimate artistic expression. The context addresses the matter of worship—and only that. It is wrong to use the second commandment to forbid or curtail the visual or plastic arts.

The commandment speaks instead to the issue of using images that would, in effect, rival God. The actual proscription is "You shall not bow down to them or worship them." Here two expressions (*bow down* and *worship*), in a figure of speech called *hendiadys,* are used to convey a single idea: do not use images to offer religious worship to the living God. The worshiper must not compromise that worship by having a concrete center for that worship. Such a practice would be too close to what the heathen were doing.

This prohibition must be viewed against the background of Egyptian religion, for Israel had just emerged from its bondage in Egypt. Egyptian worship was directed toward the heavenly bodies, especially the sun, and such creatures as birds, cows, frogs and fish. Thus what is forbidden is not the making of images of fish, birds, bulls or the like. Instead, it is forbidden to make an image of God with a view to using it as part of one's worship. Such substitutes would only steal hearts and minds away from the true worship of God.

Should further support be needed for this interpretation, one need only remember what the Lord commanded with regard to the tabernacle. Under divine direction, all sorts of representations of the created order were included in this structure and its accouterments. Had all such representations been wrong, this would not have been commanded.

No, this commandment does not prohibit artistic representations of the created world. It does, however, prohibit the use of images that call our hearts and minds away from focusing on the one true and living God, who is spirit and not like any of the shapes and forms that he created.

The penalty or sanction that follows the second commandment's proscription begins with the magisterial reminder that "I, the Lord your God, am a jealous God." God's jealousy does not involve being suspicious or wrongfully envious of the success of others, or even mistrusting. When used of God, the word *jealous* refers to that quality of his character that demands exclusive devotion to all that is just, right and fair. Jealousy is the anger that God directs against all that opposes him. It is also the energy he expends in vindicating those who believe in the rightness of this quality and of his name.

God's jealousy, or his zeal, is that emotion by which he is stirred up against whatever hinders the enjoyment of what he loves and desires. Therefore, the greatest insult against God's love for us is to slight that love and to choose instead a lesser or baser love. That is idolatry. It is a spiritual form of adultery that results in neglect, substitution and finally contempt for the public and private worship of God.

20:5 Should Children Die for Their Fathers' Sins?

See comment on DEUTERONOMY 24:16.

20:7 Do Not Take God's Name in Vain?

See comment on MATTHEW 5:34.

20:8-11 Should We "Remember the Sabbath Day"?

There are a number of questions connected with the fourth commandment. It is not the meaning of the words of this commandment that makes it a hard saying, but the application of its meaning to today.

Do the origins of a sabbath day lie in the Babylonian concept of such a sabbath on the seventh, fourteenth, twenty-first and twenty-eighth days? Does the name "sabbath" come from the Babylonian *shabatu,* the fifteenth day of the Babylonian month? Were these days of rest in Babylon, or did they have some other meaning?

In our day, how seriously must we take the command to reserve one day each week, and on that day to avoid all forms of work done on the other six days? Is this command purely ceremonial in its origins, or does it have moral force? Further, does this command represent the law of Moses from which the Christian is freed, since it reflects forms and ceremonies that were done away with when Christ died on the cross? And what relation, if any, does the seventh-day injunction have with the new first day of worship set up by several New Testament texts?

Since this command begins with the word *remember,* it is clear that the sabbath day already existed prior to this Mosaic legislation. Exodus 20:11 connects it with the work pattern of the Creator, who took six "days" to create the world and then rested on the seventh day. His example is meant to be normative and therefore transcends all local custom, cultures and ceremonies of Mosaic legislation.

As for the claim that the whole concept comes from the Babylonians, it needs to be pointed out that they did not call their seventh, fourteenth, twenty-first and twenty-eighth days "days of rest." Actually, these were "evil" or "unlucky" days when it was best not to do anything so as to avoid harm. Superstitious fear can hardly be equated with a theology of rest.

Likewise, the name "sabbath" did not originate with the Babylonians, for its Hebrew etymology is related to the semantic field of *shāḇāt,* meaning "to rest" or "to cease." In the Old Testament the sabbath was a day of cessation, for religious reasons, from the normal routine of life. In the Babylonian culture there was a midmonth day—unrelated to the pattern of seven—called *shabatu,* meaning "the day of the stilling of the heart," that is, the heart of the gods. The Babylonians themselves made no connection between the pattern of the seventh, fourteenth, twenty-first and twenty-eighth days and this fifteenth day.

Now if this ordinance goes back to creation and has as its purpose the imitation of the Lord himself, what of its continuing relevance for us? Was there any indication, even in the Old Testament itself, that the day set apart to the Lord might be changed from the seventh to the first, as many Christians say today?

To take the latter question first, yes, there is such evidence. In Leviticus 23:15, during the Feast of Weeks, the day after the sabbath had significance along with the sabbath itself. Israel was to count off fifty days, up to the day of the seventh sabbath; then, on "the day after the seventh Sabbath," they were to present an offering of new grain to the Lord (Lev 23:15-16). Again on this "eighth day" Israel was to hold another "sacred assembly and present an offering made to the LORD by fire" (Lev 23:36). "The first day is a sacred assembly; do no regular work," the Lord said (Lev 23:35), and on the eighth day, when the closing assembly was held, they were again to do no work. "The first day is a day of rest, and the eighth day also is a day of rest" (Lev 23:39). Since the Feast of Booths or Tabernacles cannot be properly celebrated until the time of Israel's kingdom rest—after they have once again been regathered in their land from all over the world—it is clear that this passage looks forward to the eternal state and the rest of all, when the tabernacle of God is once again with humanity (Rev 21:3).

These arguments, along with the fact

that the early church worshiped on the first day of the week, fit the prediction of an eighth-day (that is, first-day-of-the-week) sabbath very well (Acts 20:7; 1 Cor 16:2; Rev 1:10). Justin Martyr (c. A.D. 150) indicates in his *Apology* 1.67-68 that in his day offerings were being brought to the church on Sunday—the first day of the week.

Many will still argue, "Isn't this law a ceremonial piece of legislation from which we as believers are exempt?"

Actually, the fourth commandment is both ceremonial and moral. It is ceremonial in that it specifies the seventh day. It is moral because there is a sanctity of time; it sets aside a portion of time for the worship and service of God as well as for the refreshment and recuperation of human beings.

God is the Lord of time. As such, he has a legitimate right to claim a proportion of our time, just as he has a claim on a proportion of our money and our talents.

The fourth commandment's prohibition of any forms of normal work on the seventh day was so seriously regarded that it affected not only all members of the Israelite household but also all aliens residing in the land and even the country's cattle.

The book of Hebrews, of course, continues to argue on the basis of the relevance of the sabbath rest for the people of God. This sabbath still remains. It is a "stop" day, picturing the millennial rest of God that is to come when Christ returns the second time to rule and reign with his saints.

This commandment must not be lightly regarded as a piece of antique history or as conventional wisdom that may be used as one sees fit. Rather, it calls for an imitation of God's own action, and it carries a blessing for all who will observe it.

See also comment on MARK 2:27-28.

20:13 You Shall Not Take Life?

Is the sixth commandment a prohibition against the taking of all forms of life in any manner whatsoever? Or is it limited to the taking of human life, as the NIV translation suggests? And if it is limited to the taking of human life, is that a prohibition under all circumstances, by all methods, for all causes and in all times?

The Hebrew language possesses seven words related to killing, and the word used in this sixth commandment appears only forty-seven times in the Old Testament. This Hebrew verb, *rāṣaḥ,* refers only to the killing of a person, never to killing animals, and not even to killing persons in a war. It carries no implications of the means of killing.

If any one of the seven words for killing in the Old Testament signifies what we refer to as "murder," this is the verb. It implies premeditation and intentionality. Without exception, especially in the later Old Testament periods, it refers to intentional, violent murder (Ps 94:6; Prov 22:13; Is 1:21; Jer 7:9; Hos 4:2; 6:9). In each instance, the act was conceived in the mind first and the victim was chosen deliberately.

Thus the Old Testament would never use this verb to denote the killing of beasts for food (Gen 9:6) or the nation's involvement in a war commanded by God. It would, however, use this verb in reference to self-murder (suicide) and in reference to the actions of accessories to a murder (2 Sam 12:9).

Note that Numbers 35:31 specifically distinguishes the capital offense of murder from the almost twenty other offenses punishable by death. Jewish and modern interpreters have long held that since this verse prohibited taking a "ransom for the life of a murderer"—a substitute of some kind—in all the other cases a substitution could be made for the death penalty. But so serious was murder that the death penalty was to be enforced.

In cases of nighttime invasion of a household by burglars, the prohibition in this verse did not apply, and *rāṣaḥ* is not the verb used (Ex 22:2). Nor does this commandment apply to accidental killings—that is, cases of manslaughter (Deut 19:5)—or to the execution of murderers by the recognized arm of the state (Gen 9:6).

Life was so sacred to God that all violent forms of taking human life caused guilt to fall upon the land. This was true of both manslaughter and premeditated murder. Both forms of killing demanded some type of atonement.

The reason life was so valuable was that men and women are made in the image of God. That is why the life of the murderer was owed to God, not to the bereaved relatives of the victim or to society. Capital punishment for first-degree murder was, and continues to be, mandated because God honors his image in all humanity. To fail to carry out this mandate is ultimately to attack the value, worth and dignity of all. It undermines other struggles as well, including those for racial equality, women's rights, civil rights and human embryo rights—all are equally based on the fact that persons are made in the "image of God."

Life was and remains sacred to the Giver of life. Under no circumstances was one to take one's own life or lie in wait to take someone else's life. So valuable was life, however fallen, that the only way to cleanse the evil caused by killing was atonement before God. Each murder placed blood-guilt on the land until it was solved and atoned for.

See also comment on NUMBERS 35:31; JUDGES 5:24-27.

21:2-11 Does God Approve of Slavery?

Does God approve of slavery? If not, why do we find so much legislation in the Old Testament on how to treat slaves?

There were basically two types of slaves in the Old Testament: the fellow Hebrew who sold himself in order to raise capital (Lev 25:39-55; Deut 15:12-18) and the foreign prisoner of war. In the postexilic days, during the days of Ezra and Nehemiah, there was a third type known as the *n*[e]*ṯînîm*. Their origins were probably the same as those Gibeonites of Joshua's day who became cutters of woods and carriers of water rather than risk losing their lives in further miliary opposition to Israel.

Never, however, did Israel ever enter into the capture and sale of human life as did the Phoenician and Philistine traders and later the European nations. The third class of slaves called the *n*[e]*ṯînîm* never were real serfs, but instead formed a clerical order attached to the temple with positions ranking just below that of the Levites, who also assisted in the services at the temple.

A fellow Israelite who needed to raise money to pay for debts or the like could not borrow against his property (for that was owned by the Lord according to Leviticus 25:23) but had to sell the only asset he possessed: his labor power. However, there were strict rules that governed his or her treatment during the maximum of six years that such a relationship could be entered into with another Israelite. Should any master mistreat his slave with a rod, leaving an injury, the owner forfeited his whole investment (Ex 21:20-21, 26) and the slave was immediately released, or if the master caused the slave's death, the master was subject to capital punishment.

What about the status of non-Hebrew slaves? These captives were permanent slaves to the Israelites, but that did not mean that they could treat them as if they were mere chattel. The same rules of Exodus 21:20-21, 26 applied to them as well. One evidence of a mistreatment and they too went free. The foreign slave, along with the Hebrew household, had a day of rest each week (Ex 20:10; Deut 5:14).

A female slave who was married to her captor could not be sold again as a slave. If her master, now her husband, grew to hate her, she had to be liberated and was declared a free person (Deut 21:14).

The laws concerning slavery in the Old Testament appear to function to moderate a practice that worked as a means of loaning money for Jewish people to one another or for handling the problem of the prisoners of war. Nowhere was the institution of slavery as such condemned; but then, neither did it have anything like the connotations it grew to have during the days of those who traded human life as if it were a mere commodity for sale. This type of slavery was voluntary for the Hebrew and the *n*[e]*ṯînîm;* only the war prisoner was shackled involuntarily. But in all cases the institution was closely watched and divine judgment was declared by the prophets and others for all abuses they spotted.

See also comment on EPHESIANS 6:5-8.

21:7-11 Is Polygamy Approved by God?

See comment on GENESIS 29:25-28; 2 SAMUEL 20:3.

21:23-25 Eye for Eye, Tooth for Tooth?

Lex talionis, "law of the tooth," or the so-called law of retaliation, is found here in Exodus 21:23-25 in its fullest form. It is preserved in a shorter form in Leviticus 24:19-20 and Deuteronomy 19:21. It raises the issue of whether the Israelites were allowed to practice private vendettas and to retaliate every time they were personally wronged.

This legislation was never intended to allow individuals to avenge their own injuries. It is included in the section of Exodus addressed to the judges (Ex 21:1—22:17). These laws functioned, then, as precedents for the civil and criminal magistrates in settling disputes and administering justice, but they were not to be applied in a wooden or literalistic way.

Simply stated, the *talion* principle was "life for life." But in actuality this rule functioned as a stereotyped expression for the judges who had to assign compensations and amounts of restitution in damage cases. If the law were pressed too literally, it would become an unmanageable concept conjuring up images of the most gross and barbarous infliction of recriminating justice on a society gone mad!

One must not conclude that the Bible authorized physical mutilation, because the biblical rejection and proscription against any such personal vendetta is clearly set forth in Exodus 21:26-27, the very next verses of the passage we're looking at.

The expression "eye for eye and tooth for tooth" simply meant that the compensations paid were to match the damages inflicted—no more and no less. The modern version would be "bumper for bumper, fender for fender"—don't try to get two years' free tuition added on to the insurance claim by some phony story about whiplash!

In modern law, such terms as *damages* or *compensation* usually replace the term *restitution.* In modern law an offense is seen as against the state or one's neighbor; in biblical law the offense was seen as against God as well.

Even in those cases where life was literally required as the punishment for the offense, a substitution was available, as Numbers 35:31 implies. This text specifies that no ransom is available for murder, implying that a commensurate compensation might be possible in cases other than first-degree murder. The Hebrew verb for *to give* appears in Exodus 21:23; in the surrounding verses, this verb refers to monetary compensation (see Ex 21:19, 22, 30, 32). The ordinary verb that is used for restoring in kind, or paying the exact equivalent, is the verb *to make whole* or repay.

The earlier stages of biblical law did not distinguish as sharply as present legislators do between criminal law (determining punishment) and civil law (determining commensurate compensation). If this is so, then Exodus 21:23-25 is not a *lex talionis,* a law of retaliation, but a formula for compensation. Moreover, the principle of equivalence also applies. It appears at this point because it applies not only to the laws preceding it (theft), but also to the laws following it (assault); indeed, it applies even to third parties who were drawn involuntarily into a clash.

A literal interpretation of "hand for hand" may not be a fair and equivalent compensation if one man was a singer and the other a pianist. The formula must be understood conceptually to mean "the means of livelihood for the means of livelihood."

Interpreters must be careful not to fall into the ditch on either side of this issue: (1) the danger of transferring to the private sector what these verses assigned solely and properly to the judges; or (2) an overliteralizing tendency that fails to see that this principle comes under the heading of restitution and not retaliation, that the compensation was to fit the damages—no more and no less. In fact, while some have thought that this text condoned excessive retribution, it actually curbed all retribution and any personal retaliation among Israel's citizens.

See also comment on MATTHEW 5:39.

21:28-36 Capital Punishment Mandated by God?

See comment on GENESIS 9:6.

22:25 Is Charging Interest Permitted?

Discussion about money divides friends, and when it comes to talking about interest on money from a biblical point of view, it divides interpreters! To be sure, the one "who lends his [or her] money without usury [interest]," according to Psalm 15:5, is a godly man who also "does not accept a bribe against the innocent." But what is not immediately noticed is that the borrower is usually described as one who is in need and who is unable to support himself or herself. That point is made in two of the three main teaching passages on this topic, namely Exodus 22:25 and Leviticus 25:35-37. (The third passage is Deut 23:19-20.)

The reason for such a stern prohibition against charging interest was that all too many in Israel used this method to avoid helping the poor and their own fellow citizens. Deuteronomy 23:20 did say, "You may charge a foreigner interest." Apparently this was the same as charging interest for a business loan or an investment. The foreigner fell under the category of the "resident alien" who had taken up permanent residence among the Israelites. But where the law protected a "resident alien" with the same privileges granted a native Israelite, we may expect the same prohibitions against loaning at interest to the poor (see Lev 25:35).

Of course, all morality condemned excessive rates of interest. Proverbs 28:8 warned, "He who increases his wealth by exorbitant interest amasses it for another, who will be kind to the poor." The prophet Ezekiel also described the "righteous person" as one who "does not lend at usury or take excessive interest" (Ezek 18:8, see also 18:13, 17; 22:12).

What has changed the sentiment in modern times on legitimate forms of interest-taking is an altered perception of the nature and use of money. In the first place, loans today are mostly needed for quite different purposes. In that day it was only a matter of extreme and dire need that would force a person into the position of needing to borrow. In these cases what was owed to one another was compassion. People were to help one another, not use their neighbor's calamity as the opportunity to realize quick and illegitimate profits.

In modern times loans are required principally as a means of increasing the capital with which one works. Unless one has the increased capital, one may not be capable of bringing in the increased revenue. But in ancient times such concerns were not as large as they have become. Loans then were almost exclusively for the purpose of relieving destitution and extreme poverty.

While Hebrew uses two different terms for interest, it is doubtful one can distinguish between them, such as between a long-term and short-term loan, or an exorbitant rate of interest versus a fair rate of return for the use of one's money. Neither can it be said that one relates to the substance loaned and the other to the method by which the loan was computed.

It is a reasonable conclusion that interest was and is still approved for those ventures not attempting to circumvent one's obligation to the poor. This thesis is reinforced by Jesus' allusion to and apparent approval of taking interest for commercial ventures in Matthew 25:27 and Luke 19:23.

The appropriateness of loaning money to a church or a Christian nonprofit agency at interest is also greatly debated. Some counsel that ministries that invite "investments" with the offer to pay back the principal with interest may well end up paying the interest out of the tithes, thus robbing God.

If the reason for the prohibition on all church loans is that believers are not to be charged interest, then I must demur, since that is not the biblical reason. Scripture is concerned about our dodging our responsibilities to the poor in our midst. The absolute prohibition of lending at interest to believers will not stand scriptural scrutiny. This is not to say that there are no other traps in this whole discussion. There are. The abuse of the tithe would be a most serious matter. However, because ministries seem to grow in proportion to their facilities, a group may choose to build ahead in order to expand both their ministry and their base of supporters. Such an expansion is not only warranted but may be a legitimate and responsible exercise of good Christian stewardship.

The Bible is anxious mainly about a profiteer's loan which should have been a charity loan at no interest. Once that demand has been met, other principles in Christian morality must be met as well, but the pressure will no longer be to decry all forms of interest-taking as such.

23:20-23 Who Is the Angel of the Lord?

See comment on JUDGES 6:22-23.

24:9-11 Did Moses and the Elders See God?

The claim that Moses and his company "saw the God of Israel" appears to contradict the flat denials of such a possibility in texts such as Exodus 33:20. John 1:18 affirms that "no one has ever seen God, but God the One and Only [the only Son], who is at the Father's side, has made him known." Similarly, 1 Timothy 6:16 teaches that God is the one "who alone is immortal and who lives in unapproachable light, whom no one has seen or can see."

What are we to believe? Did some see God who is spirit and without form, or did they not? These passages surely look as if they contradict each other.

The translators who compiled the Greek version of the Old Testament, the Septuagint, were so concerned about any wrong connotations in Exodus 24:9 that they added "in the place where he stood" to the words "they saw the God of Israel." There is no basis for such an addition, however, except the tendency of this translation to avoid any descriptions of God in terms that are used of human beings (the so-called antianthropomorphic trend of the LXX).

Even though verse 10 clearly says that the leaders "saw the God of Israel," the text does not go on to describe him, any more than did Isaiah when he saw Adonai exalted in the (heavenly) temple (Is 6). The verb used in verse 10 is used of seeing with one's eyes. Only when we get to verse 11 is there a qualification, for it uses another verb that means "to see in a vision."

Moreover, despite the assertion that Moses and the leaders saw God, the description of what they saw is of what was at his feet, not the appearance of God himself. It could well be that the group was not given permission to lift their faces toward God, but saw only the pavement beneath his feet. Maybe that is what the Greek translators were attempting to get at when they added the abovementioned phrase.

When Moses asked to be shown the glory of God, he was refused on the grounds that humans cannot see the face of God and live (Ex 33:18-20). In the earlier text, since no request to see God's glory is cited, we must assume that what Moses and his companions experienced was a theophany of the presence of God.

Even what little they saw of the setting of God's presence so humbled and awed them that they apparently flung themselves down in an act of obeisance. Hence, what they saw and reported was no higher than the level of the pavement. In spite of the uniqueness and unnaturalness of this experience, Moses and his companions were not harmed or disciplined by God; he "did not raise his hand" against them (Ex 24:11). But they did experience a special nearness to God as they partook together of a covenantal meal.

We conclude that no one has ever seen God except the Son. What Moses, Aaron, Nadab, Abihu and the seventy elders experienced was the real presence of God and the place where he stood. When God is said to have shown his "back" or his "face" to anyone, it is an anthropomorphic usage—a description of God in terms used of humans so as to point to a definite reality, but only in ways that approximate that reality. God's "back" suggests his disapproval, and his "face" suggests his blessing and smile of approval. In no sense can these terms be used to denote any shape or form of God. God remains unseen but mightily able to manifest the reality and majesty of his presence.

See also comment on EXODUS 33:18-23; JOHN 1:18.

31:18 How Were the Tablets Inscribed with the Finger of God?

Readers of the New Testament know that "God is spirit, and his worshipers must worship in spirit and in truth" (Jn 4:24). But this same incorporeal argument for God is in the Old Testament: "But the Egyptians are men and not God; their horses are flesh and not spirit" (Is 31:3). Clearly God and spirit are balancing concepts in the Hebrew poetic device called synonymous parallelism. How, then, can Moses describe God as having fingers to write on the tablets of stone?

Since God is not corporeal in the sense that he has bodily form (Is 31:3; Jn 4:24), all references to parts of the body such as fingers are what we call anthropomorphisms—something about the divine person more graphically told in human terms.

The finger of God is also a figure of speech known as *synecdoche,* wherein a portion of the divine person is used to denote some larger aspect of his person or characteristics. In this case God's power is being indicated by his finger.

In a similar way, when the magicians bowed out after the third plague, they stated, "This is the finger of God [or of a god]" (Ex 8:19). Clearly, by their use of the word *finger* they meant they had been outmaneuvered by a supernatural power that was at work, not by some kind of cheap trickery or quackery.

Some have argued, on the alleged bases of Egyptian parallels such as chapter 153 in the Egyptian Book of the Dead, that "finger of God" refers to Aaron's staff. This theory also presupposes an artificial distinction between the singular and plural forms for *finger* and cannot be supported. The statement of these Egyptian magicians, therefore, attributes to God the power they had just observed in the third plague.

God's power is again symbolized as the "work of [his] fingers" in creating the world, according to the psalmist (Ps 8:3). What is more, it was by the same "finger of God" that Jesus claimed to have cast demons out of individuals in Luke 11:20. We may be confident, then, that the term *finger of God* refers to his power.

The use of this expression in connection with the writing of the Ten Commandments on the two tablets of stone is most interesting, for while we do not believe in a mechanical view of dictation for the Bible, nevertheless this passage certainly indicates that here is one passage that is in some ways markedly different from the other portions of Scripture, which are nonetheless just as inspired. It must mean that this passage came, in some way, through the direct intervening power of God. Perhaps we are to envision something approximating the handwriting on the wall at Belshazzar's Babylonian feast in Daniel 5:5. Some have likened it to a bolt of lightning which engraved the stones by a supernatural power.

The truth is that no one knows the method for sure, but we do know it is as much a product of the direct power of God as Jesus' miracles or his creation of the world. This part of the law known as the "Two Tablets of the Testimony" was the result of the direct intervention of God, most graphically described as the "finger of God."

See also comment on EXODUS 24:9-11; 33:18-23.

33:18-23 Did Moses See God's Back?

Is it possible to see God? On the one hand some texts indicate that God was seen. Genesis 32:30 says, "So Jacob called the place Peniel, saying, 'It is because I saw God face to face.' " Exodus 24:9-10 likewise teaches that "Moses and Aaron, Nadab and Abihu, and the seventy elders of Israel . . . saw the God of Israel." Exodus 33:11 strikes another intimate note: "The LORD would speak to Moses face to face, as a man speaks with his friend." Judges 13:22 states that Manoah said to his wife, "We are doomed to die! . . . We have seen God!" Again, in Isaiah 6:1, "In the year that King Uzziah died, I saw the Lord seated on a throne, high and exalted." Finally, Daniel 7:9 affirms, "As I looked, thrones were set in place, and the Ancient of

Days took his seat. His clothing was as white as snow; the hair of his head was white like wool. His throne was flaming with fire." All these texts appear to claim that at times God can be seen and was seen.

However, there are other passages that appear to argue that it is impossible to see God. Foremost among them is Exodus 33:20. Likewise, Deuteronomy 4:15 warns, "You saw no form of any kind the day the LORD spoke to you at Horeb out of the fire." Even more to the point is John 1:18, "No one has ever seen God, but God the One and Only, who is at the Father's side, has made him known." And again in John 5:37, "You have never heard his voice nor seen his form." Indeed, God is described in 1 Timothy 1:17 as "the King eternal, immortal, invisible," the one "whom no one has seen or can see" (1 Tim 6:16).

To resolve this dilemma, note first that some of these sightings are visions, such as the cases of Isaiah and Daniel. In others the terms for sight stress the directness of access. For instance, in Exodus 24:9-11, Moses, Aaron, Nadab, Abihu and the seventy elders eat and drink in God's presence, but they describe only his feet and what he stood on. They were apparently not permitted to look on God's face. In another instance, Jacob's access to God is described as being "face to face," similar to Moses' later friendship with God. (The difference may arise from the way the term *face of God* was used in various contexts. In one, it expressed familiarity beyond previous visions or divine appearances; in others, it referred to knowledge of God which exceeds our abilities and hopes.) Others, such as Manoah and his wife, experienced a christophany or a theophany, which means an appearance of Christ or God through a vision or a preincarnate appearance.

What Moses requests in Exodus 33:18, "Now show me your glory," was more than the Lord would grant for Moses' own good. Even so, God allowed his "goodness" to pass in front of Moses and proclaimed his "name" in Moses' presence.

Thus, instead of showing Moses his person or describing his appearance, the Lord gave Moses a description of who he is. The "name" of God included his nature, character (Ps 20:1; Lk 24:47; Jn 1:12), doctrine (Ps 22:22; Jn 17:6, 26) and standards for living righteously (Mic 4:5). Romans 9:15 quotes Exodus 33:19 and applies it to God's sovereignty.

After God proclaims his name and sovereignty, he promises Moses a look at certain of his divine aspects. What these aspects were is still debated—needlessly, when one considers the range of meaning for the word *back* or the context in which it is used.

God placed Moses in a cleft in the rock, apparently a cavelike crevice, and he then caused his glory to pass by. The glory of God refers first and foremost to the sheer weight of the reality of his presence. The presence of God would come near Moses in spatial terms.

But Moses would not be able to endure the spectacular purity, luminosity and reality of staring at the raw glory of God himself. Instead, God would protect Moses from accidental (and apparently fatal) sight of that glory. Therefore, in a striking anthropomorphism (a description of the reality of God in terms or analogies understandable to mortals), God would protect Moses from the full effects of looking directly at the glory of God by placing his hand over Moses' face until all his glory had passed by.

That this is a figure of speech is clear from the double effect of God passing by while simultaneously protecting Moses with the divine "hand." Only after his glory, or presence, had passed by would God remove his gracious, protecting "hand." Then Moses would view what God had permitted.

But what was left for Moses to see? The translators say God's "back." But since God is spirit (Is 31:3; Jn 4:24) and formless, what would this refer to? The word *back* can as easily be rendered the "aftereffects" of the glory that had passed by.

This would fit the context as well as the range of meanings for the Hebrew word used. Moses did not see the glory of God directly, but once it had gone past, God did allow him to view the results, the afterglow, that his presence had produced.

See also comment on EXODUS 24:9-11; JOHN 1:18.

34:7 Should Children Be Punished for Their Parents' Sins?

See comment on DEUTERONOMY 24:16.

LEVITICUS

1:2 Are Animal Sacrifices Repulsive?

In a culture where we are accustomed to buying meat packaged in plastic wrap, the whole description of slaughtering animals seems repulsive and unbelievable. What was intended by such inordinate waste (for so it would seem) of such valuable animals that could otherwise have served Israel in so many other ways?

The whole idea of sacrifice is so foreign to our day that we tend to think of a sacrifice as a loss we have suffered or something we have deprived ourselves of. But that negative concept was not how the Israelites regarded a sacrifice. It was not a matter of giving up something for some greater good; it was, rather, a joyous dedication of something valuable to one's Lord.

The word *sacrifice* comes from the Latin "to make something holy." It also implied something brought near to the altar or presence of God. Nowhere does the Bible tell us how sacrifices originated; instead, we find Cain and Abel already offering sacrifices in Genesis 4.

But there was more to it. Animal sacrifices were used mainly in connection with the human problem of sin. So serious was the problem of sin that life itself was forfeited. To indicate this forfeiture, an animal was substituted for the person's life. However, this animal's life could never be compared to a person's life; hence the act had to be repeated constantly, for sin was ever with Israel. But the impact of the sacrifice was enormous: the individual was declared forgiven and set free of the debt and the guilt that would have hung over his head from there on out had he or she not been delivered or ransomed by a substitute. Just as the blood symbolized the death of a life (Lev 17:11), so the life of the animal was given in exchange for the life of the sinner. Anything less than such a payment would devalue sin in the eyes of the people. What the worshiper offered to God, therefore, had to be the best, the most perfect of its kind, and it had to cost the presenter something.[1]

Sacrifices are not as gross as our culture sometimes makes them out to be,

since we are so far removed from the slaughter process by which our meat is made available for us. While we are shocked by the presence of blood and the scene of death, the Old Testament offerer concentrated on freedom from the debt of his or her sin and found new life in exchange for a forfeited life.
See also comment on GENESIS 4:3-4.

---

[1]For a more detailed discussion of the seven major sacrifices in Leviticus 1—7, see Walter Kaiser Jr., "The Book of Leviticus: Introduction, Commentary, and Reflections," in *The New Interpreter's Bible,* ed. Leander E. Keck (Nashville: Abingdon, 1994), pp. 1005-55.

10:1-3 Why Did God Destroy Nadab and Abihu?

See comment on 2 SAMUEL 6:6-7.

11:3-6 Do the Camel, the Coney and the Rabbit Chew the Cud?

Do the animals listed in Leviticus 11:3-6 actually "chew the cud" in the scientific sense of having a gastronomical system wherein several stomachs are used for processing food?

True ruminants generally have four stomachs. As the stomachs work, the food is regurgitated into the mouth, where it is chewed up again. Do the camel, coney and rabbit qualify as ruminants? If not, how do we explain the presence of this classification here?

Cows, sheep and goats "chew the cud." They swallow their food without chewing it especially fine and store it in one of their stomach compartments. Later, at leisure, they bring it up and rechew it more thoroughly, again swallowing it. Clearly, the Hebrews were not working with this definition of "chewing the cud." The camel, coney and rabbit are also said to "chew the cud," but these animals only appear to chew their food as the true ruminants do. In the technical sense neither the hyrax syriacus (Hebrew *šāpān*) of Leviticus 11:5—which is called the "coney" in the KJV and NIV and the "rock badger" in the NASB—nor the rabbit in Leviticus 11:6 chews the cud.

The Hebrew expression for "chew the cud" is literally "raising up what has been swallowed." But what does this raising up of what has been swallowed refer to? Surely there is the appearance of a cud-chewing process in these animals. In fact, so convincing was this appearance that Carolus Linnaeus (1707-1778), to whom we owe the modern system of biological classification, at first classified the coney and the hare as ruminants.

We believe the rule in Leviticus should be understood not according to later scientific refinements of classification; instead, it was based on simple observation. The fact that the camel, the coney and the rabbit go through motions similar to those of cows, sheep and goats must take precedence over the fact that we later limited the cud-chewing category to just animals that have four stomachs. The modern definition of terms does not take away from Moses' ability, or even his right, to use words as he sees fit to use them. To question his use of a term to which Linnaeus eventually gave a more restrictive meaning is anachronistic argumentation.

Interestingly, resting hares and rabbits do go through a process that is very similar to what we moderns call chewing the cud. The process is called refection. As the hare rests, it passes droppings of different composition, which it once again eats. Thus the hare is chewing without taking fresh greens into its mouth. During this second passage of the food through its stomach, that which had been indigestible can be better assimilated through the action of bacteria.

The case of the three animals that chewed the cud in Moses' day but no longer do so can be solved. Moses' classification had a solid observational basis that was accessible to all. In modern times, the phrase "chewing the cud" has been given a more restrictive meaning. Later generations, having forgotten which came first, have tended to freeze the meaning to the most recent definition and then accuse Moses of not using the term in this later sense.

16:7-10 What Was the Purpose of the Scapegoat?

What is the scapegoat of the Day of Atonement in Leviticus 16? Why do some scholars say that this goat was offered to Azazel, a desert demon that was capable of feeding on an animal laden with the sins of the entire nation of Israel? Does the Old Testament actually give aid and comfort to such views and teach that demons inhabit the desert?

And if the demon view is true, why does Leviticus 17:7 expressly forbid making offerings or sacrifices to demons? Also, what is the meaning of the Hebrew name used in connection with the scapegoat, *azazel?* Is this name to be connected with other demons named in Scripture, such as Lilith, "the night creature" (Is 34:14), or the Shedim, "demons" (Lev 17:7; 2 Chron 11:15; Is 13:21; 34:14), literally "the hairy ones," "satyrs" or "goat idols"?

No day was, or is, as sacred to the Jewish community as Yom Kippur, the Day of Atonement. After the high priest had made atonement for his own sins and those of his household, he proceeded with the rites of atonement for the whole community. The community brought two male goats as a single sin offering and a ram as a burnt offering. Both goats were for atonement: one dealt with the fact of atonement and the other with the effect of atonement in removing sin. The first goat had to be slain in order to picture the atonement proffered; the other goat was presented alive and then released into the wilderness, symbolizing the removal of the forgiven sins (on the basis of the slain substitute).

Thus far all interpreters tend to agree, but after this point disagreement breaks out. First of all, it has been pointed out that the name for the goats is not the standard term, but the expression that is used always in connection with the sin offering (*šᵉʿîr ʿizzîm*—Lev 4:23-24, 28; 5:6; 9:3; 23:19).

But the most difficult specification to deal with is that as the two goats are placed at the entrance to the Tent of Meeting—the tabernacle—and the lots are drawn, one goat is said to be "for the *Lord*," and the other lot falls "for azazel" (Lev 16:8—*layhwâh; laʿᵃzāʾzēl*).

The Greek translators did not regard *azazel* as a proper name, but connected it with *ʾāzal,* a verb that does not appear in the Old Testament. The meaning they gave it was "to send away." Hence the full meaning of the Hebrew expression would be "in order to send away." The Latin translation followed this same understanding. But, it is objected, this meaning will not easily fit the contexts of the last part of verse 10 and the first part of verse 26.

In later Jewish theology, the apocryphal book of Enoch uses Azazel as the name for one of the fallen angels. But there is no evidence for the existence of a demon by that name in Moses' day. Enoch's elaborate demonology is admittedly late (c. 200 B.C.) and often uses the late Aramaic forms for these names. It is clear that they are all of postbiblical invention.

The most adequate explanation is to view the term *ʿᵃzāʾzēl* as being composed of two words: the first part, *ʿēz,* meaning "goat," and the second part, *ʾāzēl,* meaning "to go away." With recent evidence from the Ugaritic (the language of ancient Canaan from which Hebrew is derived), compound names such as this one are turning up more frequently than what we had expected based on evidence from the Hebrew alone. This is how the rendering "scapegoat" came to be. Today, however, we would need to call it the "escape-goat," for by "scapegoat" we mean the one who always gets blamed or gets stuck with a task that is distasteful. Originally, however, the King James translators meant "the goat that was led away."

Since this ceremony is part of one sin offering, in no sense is the second goat an offering to the devil or his demons. The arguments that are brought in to support the view that the second goat is for the devil or his demons are unconvincing. One says that since the first clause of verse 8 indicates that the goat is designated for a person—the Lord—the second clause also must refer to the goat's being designated for a person—Azazel. While this is a grammatical possibility, it is not required by the text, and the specific prohibition of making such offerings to demons, found in Leviticus 17:7, is decisive in ruling out this possibility.

According to another argument, the words in 16:10 cannot mean that atonement is being made *with* azazel (that is, azazel as the scapegoat) to propitiate the Lord, but rather that atonement is being made to propitiate Azazel (that is, Azazel as a wilderness demon). The reply is that the same Hebrew expression for atonement is used throughout the chapter. Moreover, in Exodus 30:10 the same expression is translated "to atone over or upon." Here the high priest was to make atonement "over" the scapegoat by putting Israel's guilt on it and then sending it away. If the expression appears strange, the answer is that the act described is itself unusual, and no other word could fit it better.

The high priest did not atone for sin by making an offering to Satan or to his demons. There is evidence that the Old Testament teaches the existence of demons, for Deuteronomy 32:17 and Psalm 106:37 speak of such beings. But in no sense were the Israelites ever told to sacrifice to them; as we have seen, Leviticus 17:7 specifically warns against such sacrifices.

See also comment on JONAH 1:4-5, 7.

18:5 The One Who Obeys My Laws Will Live?

This saying's importance is assured by its appearance in such later contexts as Ezekiel 20:11, Luke 10:28, Romans 10:5 and Galatians 3:12. But it is also a hard saying. The text appears to offer an alternate method of gaining eternal life, even if only theoretically. Is it true, in either the Old Testament or the New, that a person could have eternal life by perfectly keeping the law of God? In other words, can we read this saying as "Do this and you will have [eternal] life"?

Unfortunately, all too many teachers of the Scriptures have uncritically assumed that the words *live in them* meant that "eternal life was to be had by observing the laws of God." Accordingly, if a person were to keep these commandments perfectly, the very keeping would be eternal life.

But this claim misses a major amount of contrary evidence, foremost that the benefits of God's promise-plan to the Old Testament believers were not conditioned on anything, much less on obedience. Such a position would reverse the unconditional word of blessing God gave to Abraham, Isaac, Jacob and David.

But what about the "if you obey me fully" statements of Exodus 19:5, Leviticus 26:3-13 and Deuteronomy 11:13-15 and 28:1? Do not these texts flatly declare that without obedience salvation is impossible?

The *if* is admittedly conditional, but conditional to what? It was conditional only to enjoyment of the full benefits of a relationship begun by faith and given freely by God. Israel must obey God's voice and heed his covenant and commandments, not "in order to" establish their new life in God, but "so that" (Deut 5:33) they might experience completely this new life begun in faith.

The very context of this verse speaks against a works salvation. First, Leviticus 18 begins and ends with the theological assumption that the hearers have the Lord as their God. Thus, this instruction deals with sanctification rather than justification.

Second, "those things" which they were not to do were the customs and ordinances; in short, the pagan idolatries of the Egyptians and Canaanites. This is a whole world apart from the question of salvation.

Third, never in the Old or New Testaments has pleasing God constituted the external performance of acts; these acts carried with them the evidence of a prior attitude of the heart. For instance, circumcision of the flesh without the circumcision of the heart was wasted effort.

In fact, our Lord coupled the act and the heart when the people pledged, "All that the Lord says, we will do." Imperiously, some call such a pledge rash, judging the people foolish for falling for an offer they would never be able to live up to.

But our Lord did not see it that way. Rather, he said in so many words, "Oh that there were such a heart in them that they would always fear me and keep my commandments." Our Lord connects their doing with the heart. He never reproved them by saying, "Oh, what deluded people! Given your previous track record, how on earth do you ever expect to enter my heaven by keeping any of my laws?" There is not a word about this. Therefore, this verse cannot be said to teach a hypothetical offer of salvation by works.

Some may argue that the words *live by them,* quoted in Romans 10:5 and Galatians 3:12, surely means in those contexts that salvation was "by means of" works (an instrumental use of the preposition). I respond that this expression should be translated live "in the sphere of them" (a locative use of the preposition).

Moses, therefore, was not describing the means of attaining salvation but only the horizon within which an earthly, godly life should be lived.

See also comment on GENESIS 26:3-5; MICAH 6:6-8; PHILIPPIANS 2:12-13; JAMES 2:24.

18:18 Was Polygamy Permitted in the Old Testament?

See comment on 2 SAMUEL 20:3.

18:22 Homosexuality Condemned?

See comment on ROMANS 1:27.

20:1-27; 24:10-23 Is the Death Penalty Justified for All the Crimes Listed?

Are all the crimes listed in Leviticus 20 and 24 worthy of being punished by death? Surely there is a difference between burning babies to honor the god Molech and marrying a close relative. What explanation can be given for what appears to be such harsh penalties?

Leviticus 20 is mainly a penal code. It can be divided into two main sections: the penalty for worshiping Molech with child sacrifices and going to mediums and spiritists (Lev 20:1-8, 27), and the penalties for sinning against the family (Lev 20:9-26). And whereas the laws in Leviticus 18—19 were apodictic in form (that is, similar to the form of the Ten Commandments: "you shall . . ."), the laws of chapter 20 are casuistic (that is, in the form of case laws, with "If a person . . . then . . .").

The horror of taking healthy babies and placing them on the arms of the god Molech and letting the baby roll down the arms into the interior of the idol where a burning fire would consume the live baby is clear enough. To demand the death penalty for such a violation of the rights, dignity and image of God in those children ought to present its own rationale for all thinking persons who ought also to be outraged at such a violation of innocence and the destruction of the lives of these children.

Not so clear to us, but likewise just as deadly, was the habit of consulting mediums and spiritists in the hopes that they possessed supernatural powers. These practices involved consulting the dead and other dangerous forms of yielding one's body to the realm of the demonic in order to obtain information or power over someone or something else. More than we moderns can appreciate, this too led to some very deadly practices.

What about such a severe penalty for sins against the family, especially since all the verses in this section (Lev 20:9-21) deal with sexual sins, except verse 9? At the very minimum this section shows that the family was extremely important. Violations of the family that called for the death penalty included cursing one's parents (Lev 20:9), adultery (Lev 20:10), incest with one's mother, stepdaughter, daughter-in-law or mother-in-law (Lev 20:11-12, 14), homosexual behavior or sodomy (Lev 20:13), bestiality (Lev 20:15-16), incest with one's half sister or full sister (Lev 20:17), and relations with a woman in her monthly period (Lev 20:18).

Many of the penalties listed here prescribe a "cutting off," in contrast to a judicial execution as in Leviticus 20:2-5. Could this signify something different from capital punishment? Some have rather convincingly argued that the expression to "cut off" in many of these lists of penalties meant to excommunicate that person from the community of God. The case, however, is not altogether clear, for in some of these situations, the threat of punishment from God in some form of premature death appears to fit the meaning best.

It must be noted that the death penalty might also indicate the seriousness of the crime without calling for the actual implementation of it in every case. In fact, there is little evidence that many of these sanctions were ever actually carried out in ancient Israel. Only in the case of premeditated murder was there the added stricture of "Do not accept a ransom for the life of a murderer, who deserves to die" (Num 35:31). The word "ransom" is the Hebrew *kōper,* meaning a "deliverance or a ransom by means of a substitute." Traditional wisdom, both in the Jewish and Christian communities, interpreted this verse in Numbers 35:31 to mean that out of the almost twenty cases calling for capital punishment in the Old Testament, every one of them could have the sanction commuted by an appropriate substitute of money or anything that showed the seriousness of the crime; but in the case of what we today call first-degree murder, there was never to be offered or accepted any substitute or bargaining of any kind: the offender had to pay with his or her life.

The case of the blasphemer in Leviticus 24:10-23 is similar. In one of the rare narrative passages in Leviticus, the blasphemer was incarcerated in jail until God revealed what should be done with him. The blasphemer had cursed "the Name" of God in the heat of passion. The penalty for blasphemy against God, or, as it will also be stated later in the New Testament, against the Holy Spirit, is death. This was an affront against the holiness of God and had to be dealt with by the whole community lest the guilt fall on all the community. This incident of blasphemy provides, then, further occasion for spelling out six more laws (Lev 24:16-22) that had previously had been announced in Genesis 9:6; Exodus 21:12-14, 18-25, 35-36, and later in Deuteronomy 19:21. The reason for their repetition is to show that these laws apply equally to the resident aliens as to the Israelites. Of course, whenever the lose of life was the result of accidental manslaughter (Num 35:9-34), no capital punishment was required.

See also comment on GENESIS 9:6.

24:19-20 Eye for Eye, Tooth for Tooth?

See comment on EXODUS 21:23-25.

25:35-38 Is Charging Interest Permitted?

See comment on EXODUS 22:25.

25:39-55 Does God Approve of Slavery?

See comment on EXODUS 21:2-11.

NUMBERS

4:3; 8:24 Why the Discrepancy in Ages for Levitical Service?

Why does the Bible give varying ages as the qualification for the Levites to perform the work of the service of the tabernacle or temple? Was the minimum twenty, twenty-five or thirty years of age? And was there a maximum age of fifty, or was it left open?

A Levite must not be younger than thirty or older than fifty years old according to Numbers 4:3, 23, 30, 35, 39, 43, 47. But in Numbers 8:24-25 the age limit was set at twenty-five and fifty. The Greek Septuagint text for Numbers 4 also reads "from twenty-five to fifty."

But the author of Chronicles set an even lower age limit of twenty, but he does not give an upper age limit (1 Chron 23:24, 27; 2 Chron 31:17; Ezra 3:8). We can probably assume that it remained at fifty. But even the chronicler recognized some change, for in the same chapter he gave the qualifying age as thirty in 1 Chronicles 23:3 and twenty in 1 Chronicles 23:24.

What can account for this vacillation from twenty, twenty-five to thirty years old as the minimum age to work in the sanctuary? No doubt the qualifying age varied from era to era depending on the needs of the sanctuary and the availability of persons. The change, except for the textual variant in the Septuagint of Numbers 4:3 (which raises the question as to what was the best and original reading of this text), occurs in the days following David's era. Apparently this reflects a change necessitated by the additional duties in the temple after it became a royal sanctuary.

11:31-34 Why the Punishment of God After This Complaint?

Why did God punish the children of Israel for grumbling about the food and asking for meat in the second year of wandering in the wilderness, recorded in Numbers 11, but not the previous year when they had made the same request (Ex 16:11-18)? What so distinguishes the two events that it would demand the judgment of God in the second instance but not in the first?

When Israel complained, they were doing more than objecting to a monotonous diet; they were challenging the goodness of God and his ability to provide for them. The affair in Numbers 11:4 began when the "rabble" of the foreign element that had joined the Israelites in their exodus from Egypt (Ex 12:38) began wailing about the lack of meat and vegetables in their diet. The rest of the people of Israel joined in, and the pressure was on for Moses and the leadership of the nation.

In answer to the people's request, God drove a quail migration, which regularly takes place each spring from the winter habitat in Africa, in from across the Red Sea by a strong wind. So the quails, exhausted from their long journey and from the force of the wind, flew as low as three feet above the ground over the Sinai peninsula, where Israel was now journeying.

So many were the quails that they covered an area about a day's walk in either direction of the camp. The people greedily gathered no less than "ten homers" each, that is, about sixty bushels full! Given the hot climate and the lack of refrigeration, this was going to spell trouble for a selfish and ecologically insensitive people.

It appears that an epidemic of food poisoning broke out among the people as a result of their wanton craving and disobedience. Israel's oft-expressed complaining came to a head here in a way it had not in the Exodus 16 passage, where God had patiently put up with the same thing as a mark of his grace. This time he gave the people what they wanted, but they did themselves in with their own greed and their unwillingness to listen. The number of people who died is not given, but the place was named "graves of craving," Kibroth Hattaavah, as a result of the large number that perished.

12:3 Moses Was More Humble than Anyone Else?

Numbers 12:3 is the most difficult text in the whole book of Numbers. Critical scholars (and others) have correctly observed that it is rather unlikely that a truly humble person would write in such a manner about himself, even if he actually felt the statement was true. Many critical scholars are so convinced of the inappropriateness of recording such a note about oneself that they have used this as a strong mark against the Mosaic authorship of the whole book.

One scholar has suggested recently that the word translated "humble" or "meek" should instead be translated "miserable." The idea of "miserable" certainly would fit the context of this chapter very well. To be sure, Moses had a most unmanageable task. He had just said in Numbers 11:14, "The burden is too heavy for me." With all the attacks on his family, he may have passed into a deep depression. Thus, a very good translation possibility is "Now Moses was exceedingly miserable, more than anyone on the face of the earth"!

Those who retain the meaning "humble" usually cite this passage, along with other passages such as the Deuteronomy 34 announcement of Moses' death and burial site, as evidence for post-Mosaic additions authorized by the Spirit of God to the inspired text. Normally Joshua is credited with contributing these comments. Joshua 24:26 says, "And Joshua recorded these things in the Book of the Law of God"—a clear reference to the five books of the Law, whose authorship is usually ascribed to Moses. This is the view that I favor, though the idea of translating the word as "miserable" is also a possible solution.

Moses, of course, was not a naturally humble man. If he became so, he learned it through the trials he had to experience as the leader of a very stubborn group of people.

Some have argued for Moses' authorship of the verse, reminding us that the apostle Paul was compelled by challenges to his apostleship to point out his own excellence of character in 2 Corinthians 11:5; 12:11-12. But it does not seem that Moses was facing exactly the same set of circumstances.

Biblical writers speak of themselves with an objectivity that is rarely matched in other pieces of literature. Their self-references usually lay bare their sins and failures. It is rare for them to praise themselves.

The translators of the NIV were no doubt justified in placing this verse in parentheses. The note is a later parenthetical remark made under the direction of the Holy Spirit by Joshua.

See also comment on DEUTERONOMY 34:5-8.

13:3 Where Did the Spies Start Out?

Why does Numbers 13:3 say that the spies left from the desert of Paran while Numbers 32:8 says it was from Kadesh Barnea? Were these two different sites or is there some way of explaining how both may be correct?

The desert of Paran is a poorly defined area in the east-central portion of the Sinai peninsula, bordered on the northwest by the wilderness of Shur, on the northeast by the wilderness of Zin and by the Sinai desert on the south. For most of the forty years of their wandering the Israelites were camped at Kadesh Barnea (Num 14:34; Deut 1:19-20).

Topographically, the site of Kadesh Barnea was a part of the wilderness of Paran. In fact, the Greek Septuagint of Numbers 33:36 had a gloss, that is, an explanatory appositional note, that read "in the desert of Paran, this is Kadesh."

From Genesis 14:5-7 we learn that El-paran was located south of Kadesh, therefore one could properly describe Kadesh as being located on the border of the Paran wilderness.

14:18 Should Children Be Punished for Their Parents' Sins?

See comment on DEUTERONOMY 24:16.

20:24 Gathered to His People?

See comment on GENESIS 25:8.

20:28 Where Did Aaron Die?

Numbers 20:28, as well as Numbers 33:38-39, indicates that Aaron died on Mount Hor. Deuteronomy 10:6, however, seems to locate Aaron's death at Moserah. Furthermore, if we follow the sequence of places in Numbers 33:30-33, it does not fit the journey schedule listed just before the death of Aaron given in Deuteronomy 10:6 or Numbers 20:28 and 33:38-39. Which is correct, and how did the error, if that is what it is, creep into the text?

The sequence of the camping sites on the wilderness journey in Numbers 33:30-33 is different from the sequence of Deuteronomy 10:6-9. Numbers 33:31-33 has Moseroth and Bene Jaakan, Haggidgad and Jotbathah. But this was an earlier journey than the later journey back to Kadesh mentioned in Numbers 33:37. It would appear that Israel left Kadesh and traveled toward Edom and then returned to Kadesh before starting on their last trip around Edom up into the plains of Moab.

The best solution that can be posed to this problem so far is that Moserah is probably a larger area that included Mount Hor. Thus it would be quite correct to declare that Aaron's death was either on Mount Hor (Num 20:22-29; 33:38-39; Deut 32:50) or Moserah (Deut 10:6).

22:20-22 God Said Go but Was Very Angry Because He Went

Was Balaam permitted to travel to the

plains of Moab to curse Israel, courtesy of Balak, king of Moab, or was he not? At first this appears to be a case where God gave his permission and then turned back on what he had said.

This narrative has several surprising aspects. First of all, we are shocked to learn a prophet of Yahweh was living in Upper Mesopotamia, in the region where Abraham had stopped off at Haran on his way from Ur of the Chaldees to the land of promise.

In fact, it is so amazing and unexpected that God would have a non-Jewish prophet, it is widely supposed that Balaam was a baru, a priest-diviner, who used the usual tricks of the trade, such as dreams and omens, to forecast the future. But the Bible does not seem to support this, for Balaam used the name Yahweh, a name that implies a personal relationship ("He will be [there]"). Though Balak commissions him to curse the Israelites, it must be remembered that properly pronounced blessings and curses were also extremely effective in biblical teaching (Gen 48:14-20; Judg 17:1-2; Mt 21:18-22).

Was Balaam the embodiment of evil, or was he basically a good man? Perhaps as is true of many others, he was a mixture of good and evil. He really knew the true, personal God of Israel, and like so many other believing Gentiles who receive only a passing reference in Scripture (such as Melchizedek, Jethro, Rahab), he too really believed to the saving of his soul. As a matter of fact, God not only used him to protect Israel from a curse, he was also the instrument of the great Messianic prophecies concerning the "Star out of Jacob," a guiding light for the Eastern wise men who later searched out the new king of the Jews.

How, then, shall we deal with the apparent contradiction in this passage? The solution lies in the text itself, not in suppositions or harmonizations.

Balaam had already received one royal delegation in Numbers 22:7-14. Balaam rightly replies that the Lord refused him permission to go with the princes of Moab to curse Israel. What Balaam had artfully neglected to mention was God's reason for refusing: "Because [Israel is] blessed" (Num 22:12). Mentioning this probably would have ended the Moabites' attempts to curse a people God blessed. Balaam apparently was playing both sides of the street on this one; he deliberately left the door open, perhaps hoping that he could somehow benefit from such a highly visible ministry.

As if anticipated, a second delegation returned to Balaam with an offer that amounted to a blank check. Now some have attempted to relieve the tension observed here by distinguishing between God and Yahweh. Balaam's pretensions of having Yahweh as his God (as in Num 22:18-19) are exposed as phony, for it is not Yahweh who comes to him, but Elohim (Num 22:20). This solution is artificial, for Numbers 22:22 reports that it was Elohim who got angry. Champions of this theory note that the Samaritan Pentateuch and several important manuscripts of the Septuagint read "Yahweh" instead of "Elohim" here.

This may be true, but it still fails to see that the text itself does not make such a sharp distinction between God and Yahweh. Instead, the text stresses that the permission of Balaam was conditional. The KJV phrases it, "If the men come to call thee, rise up, and go with them; yet the word which I shall say unto thee, that shalt thou do" (Num 22:20). Balaam, however, was all too anxious to go and did not wait for the men to call him; rather, he saddled his donkey and sought them out. The KJV rendering of verse 20 is to be preferred to both the NIV's "Since these men have come" and the RSV's "If the men have come" because the very next verse, Numbers 22:21, makes it clear that Balaam initiated the action and did not wait for the test that God proposed to take effect. It says, "Balaam got up in the morning, saddled his donkey and went with the princes of Moab." He "loved the wages of wickedness" (2 Pet 2:15).

Most commentators acknowledge that the proper force of the Hebrew *'im* is "if"; however, they incorrectly reason that the men from Moab had already called and invited Balaam to go, thus there was no reason to suppose that any additional call was anticipated. Consequently, many treat the word *if* as a concessive particle with the meaning "since." What these scholars fail to realize is that Balaam had asked these men to spend the night while he made further investigations from the Lord.

This brief respite gave Balaam one more opportunity to sense God's will through his providential working—in this case, the disgust of the Moabite delegation, which would have packed up and left in the morning had not Balaam been so desirous of taking the job. Instead Balaam took the very initiative God had left in the hands of the Moabites ("*If* the men come") and thus evidenced his own disobedient inclinations.

Despite Balaam's strong declaration in verse 18 that "even if Balak gave me his palace filled with silver and gold, I could not do anything great or small to go beyond the command of the Lord my God," his mentioning both money and going beyond the will of God raises the question that this is exactly what he not only did, but planned to do if possible.

This passage, like many others, teaches us to differentiate between the directive and permissive will of God. God's directive will was clearly seen in the words "Do not go with them . . . because they are blessed." This is so clear that it will admit no exceptions. But when Balaam continued to press God, God tested his willingness to obey (if it needed to be demonstrated that he had trouble knowing God's will). The test was a condition that depended on the discouraged princes' returning one last time before leaving for home. However, Balaam could not wait, perhaps fearing they would not return. Only then was the anger of God excited.

The love of God did not cease at this point but was demonstrated in three more warnings from God that he was headed into trouble. Even though this was enough to straighten out Balaam for the immediate mission, it did not insulate him from future difficulties that God must have wished to spare Balaam.

The end of Balaam's ministry was tragic, for after he had served God by repeatedly blessing Israel, he became the instrument of both Israel's downfall and his own (Num 31:7-8, 15-16). But for this he had only himself to blame and not God, for he had been sternly warned. Sometimes God gives us the desires of our hearts after we have begged and begged for a reversal of his will, but the result often is leanness for our spiritual lives.

23:19 God Does Not Change His Mind?

See comment on GENESIS 6:6; 1 SAMUEL 15:29; JONAH 4:1-2.

25:7-13 Why Was Phinehas Praised?

Several questions are generally raised in connection with this most unusual story of Phinehas. The first involves the action of Cozbi and Zimri. What were they doing that so stirred the holy indignation of Phinehas that he impaled both of them with one thrust of his spear?

We will need to understand what was

involved in the worship of Baal of Peor (Num 25:1-5). And was Israel's lapse into this sin in any way connected with the advice or at the instigation of Balaam, the son of Beor?

Finally, we wish to know how the death of the couple, Zimri and Cozbi, could effect an atonement and assuage the wrath of God. All of these questions arise from one of the most bizarre episodes in Israel's long wilderness wanderings.

At this point, Israel was encamped at Shittim, or Acacia. It was a site east of the Jordan and six miles north of the Dead Sea, if this name is to be connected with modern Tel el-Kefrein.

It appears that the Israelite men began to have sexual relations with the Moabite and Midianite women (Num 25:1, 6). How such liaisons began we can only guess, but they seem to be connected with the bad advice given to the Moabites by the prophet Balaam, son of Beor. Prior to this event, the king of Moab had hired Balaam to curse the people of Israel; because of the strong hand of God on his life, however, Balaam had only been able to bless them. Apparently still bent on helping the Moabite king, Balaam had stayed on in the land of Moab and Midian. Numbers 31:16 informs us that "[the Midianite women] were the ones who followed Balaam's advice and were the means of turning the Israelites away from the LORD in what happened at Peor, so that a plague struck the LORD's people." (Apparently the Midianites were in Moab giving military advice to the Moabites at this time.)

The Moabites worshiped the war god Chemosh, but they must have also indulged in the fertility religion of Baal. This cult was marked by some of the most depraved religious practices in Canaan. In lurid and orgiastic rites, the worshipers would emulate the sacred prostitution of their gods and goddesses, often also participating in a ceremonial meal. In the case of Baal of Peor, we suspect that the cult also involved veneration for the dead. *Peor* may be the Hebrew and Phoenician spelling for the Luwian Pahura. This word in Hittite means "fire" and may derive from some form of the root that underlies the Greek *pyr,* "fire."

Among the Israelites, then, the Midianite and Moabite women continued to prostrate themselves in Baal worship, imitating fertility rituals. And one day, as all the Israelites were gathered in front of the tabernacle confessing their sin, the son of one of the leaders in the tribe of Simeon paraded before them with a Moabite woman, headed for his tent.

Reading the situation clearly, Phinehas swung into action. By the time he reached them in the back (bedroom) part of the tent, the couple were already involved in sexual intercourse. With a single thrust, Phinehas speared both of them. His action stopped the plague that had broken out among the Israelites.

Israel's wholesale embracing of the immorality and idolatry of pagan ritualistic sex had aroused the anger of God. While God had saved Israel from the curses of Balaam, the Israelites could not save themselves from sinning against God.

Phinehas was no vigilante. He was heir apparent to the priesthood; thus he, no doubt, was one of the appointed judges whom Moses had ordered to slay all known offenders. This story does not justify the actions of private persons who, under the guise of zeal for expediting God's purposes, take matters into their own hands when they see wrongdoing rather than contacting the appropriate authorities.

Because of the Israelites' apostasy and sin, atonement was required before divine forgiveness could be proffered.

The atonement that Phinehas offered was that of two human offenders.

Normally in the Old Testament, atonement is mentioned in connection with sacrifices, such as the sin offering. But in twenty-two passages, atonement was effected by means other than ceremonial offerings (for example, Ex 32:30-32; Deut 21:1-9; 2 Sam 21:3-9). Therefore, just as the life of the animal was a substitute, the means of ransoming the life of the guilty party, so the holiness of God was defended in this case through the substitution of the lives of the sinning couple. With atonement made, God could pardon his people and halt the spread of the plague.

The reward given to Phinehas was that his descendants would enjoy eternal possession of the priesthood. That priesthood continued, except for the interval of the priesthood of Eli, without interruption until the collapse of the nation in 586 B.C.

25:9 Twenty-three Thousand or Twenty-four Thousand?

See comment on 1 CORINTHIANS 10:8.

27:13; 31:2 Gathered to His People?

See comment on GENESIS 25:8.

32:8 Where Did the Spies Start Out?

See comment on NUMBERS 13:3

33:30, 38-39 Where Did Aaron Die?

See comment on NUMBERS 20:28

35:21 No Ransom for a Murderer?

Of the crimes punishable by death under Old Testament law, was it possible to obtain compensation for damages through some type of substitutionary restitution in every case except first-degree, premeditated murder? If so, why was this crime singled out for special treatment? Were not the other crimes as serious? If they were not, why did they carry such a stiff sanction—the death penalty?

The key text in this discussion must be Numbers 35:31, "Do not accept a ransom [substitute] for the life of a murderer, who deserves to die. He must surely be put to death."

There are sixteen crimes that called for the death penalty in the Old Testament: kidnapping, adultery, homosexuality, incest, bestiality, incorrigible delinquency in a child, striking or cursing parents, offering a human sacrifice, false prophecy, blasphemy, profaning the sabbath, sacrificing to false gods, magic and divination, unchastity, the rape of a betrothed virgin, and premeditated murder. In each case, where the evidence was clear and beyond a reasonable doubt, the death penalty was demanded.

One major distinction was drawn, however, between the penalty for premeditated murder and penalties for the other fifteen crimes on this list. Only in the case where someone had lain in wait to kill with malice and forethought does Scripture specify that the officials were forbidden to take a ransom.

The word *ransom* comes from a root meaning "substitute." The only fair inference from Number 35:31, then, is that perpetrators of any of the other fifteen capital crimes could escape death by offering a proper ransom or substitute. In those fifteen cases, the death penalty served to mark the seriousness of the crime. It is important, however, to note that only God could say which crimes might have their sanctions lessened.

Some have contended that this argument is an argument from silence, and therefore fallacious. But the alternative to this argument from silence (which has venerable precedent in rabbinic and Protestant commentary) would require upholding the death penalty for all sixteen crimes as valid to our present day. And if death is the only proper punishment for these crimes even in the present day, why did the apostle Paul not make any reference to it, especially when he had specific occasion to do so when he dealt with the case of incest in 1 Corinthians 5? Why did Paul recommend church discipline rather than capital punishment for the offending mother and son?

I am not arguing here that the penalties of the Old Testament are too severe or that the New Testament is more "urbane" and "cultured." Some have properly noted that even Hebrews 2:2 says that "every violation and disobedience received its just [or appropriate] punishment." In fact, too many people misunderstand the *talion* ("tooth-for-a-tooth") principle (Ex 21:23-25). It is simply a "life-for-life" stereotype expression that worked out in actual practice to this: Make the punishment fit the crime; don't try to profit from or trade on calamity.

Since the taking of life involved deep disregard for God and for the creatures made in his image, Genesis 9:6 makes it clear that the only way the state and society could preserve the rights, dignity and worth of all humanity was to offer the life of the proven first-degree murderer back to God. That is why this one capital offense remained when the others were allowed the option of a "ransom" or "substitute."

See also comment on GENESIS 9:6; EXODUS 20:13; 21:23-25; LEVITICUS 20:1-7; DEUTERONOMY 21:18-21.

33:38-39 Where Did Aaron Die?

See comment on NUMBERS 20:28.

DEUTERONOMY

2:30 God Made His Spirit Stubborn?

See comment on EXODUS 9:12.

2:34; 3:6 Completely Destroy Them!

See comment on 1 SAMUEL 15:18.

5:12-15 Should We "Remember the Sabbath Day"?

See comment on EXODUS 20:8-11.

5:12-16, 21 A Different Ten Commandments?

Given the fact that the wording for the fourth and tenth commandments differs here in Deuteronomy, how shall we explain this if these words were written directly by God while Moses was on the mount? One would expect the wording to agree perfectly with that of Exodus 20:8-12, 17.

The major differences between the two accounts of the Ten Commandments are these: (1) "Remember the Sabbath day" of Exodus 20:8 is replaced in Deuteronomy 5:12 with "Observe the Sabbath day"; (2) Deuteronomy twice adds to the fifth commandment "as the LORD your God has commanded you" in keeping with the exhortation characteristic of this book; (3) Deuteronomy 5:14 expands "nor your animals" with "so that your manservant and maidservant may rest, as you do"; (4) the grounding of the sabbath command in creation in Exodus 20:11 is absent here, for Deuteronomy appeals to Israel's deliverance from the bondage in Egypt; (5) "so that you may live long" has added to it in Deuteronomy "and that it may go well with you"; (6) the ninth commandment had "false" in the Deuteronomy law instead of the (literally) "mendacious testimony" of Exodus 20:16; (7) the tenth commandment of Deuteronomy places "your neighbor's wife" first while Exodus 20:17 has "your neighbor's house" first; (8) the word "covet," which appears twice in Exodus 20:17, is replaced the second time with a different verb in Deuteronomy 5:21, "set your desire on"; and (9) Deuteronomy adds "or land" to the tenth commandment in keeping with its more elaborate style and anticipation of entering into the land of Canaan.

The fact that the two accounts differ is an indication that one of the two is not a verbatim presentation of the Decalogue as it was written by "the finger of God" on Mount Sinai. There is nothing in a high view of inspiration that would require that both accounts adhere to a verbatim report, but given the fact that the Decalogue is said to have come in some direct manner from the hand of God, one would assume that at least one of them was a faithful record of that transaction. The most reasonable assumption is that the text of Exodus is the original one and that Moses' restatement in Deuteronomy is somewhat free. This allowed Moses to present the commandments with some modifications and updating of the situation in light of their pending entrance into the land of Canaan, while still adhering rather closely to the original form. In fact, these differences are very slight and of very little consequence except as viewed against the challenges that present themselves in entering into the land. Deuteronomy also had more of an exhortation character to it along with special attention given to women as taking priority over property.

7:1-2 Completely Destroy Them!

See comment on 1 SAMUEL 15:18.

10:6 Where Did Aaron Die?

See comment on NUMBERS 20:28.

10:12 How to Obtain Salvation?

See comment on MICAH 6:6-8.

10:22 How Many Went to Egypt?

See comment on ACTS 7:14-15.

15:4, 7, 11 Will the Poor Always Be Present?

At first glance there certainly does seem to be an outright conflict here. First we are told that the Lord will so richly bless Israel that there will be no poor people in the land. Then provisions are made for the eventuality that there should be some poor in the land. Finally we are advised that the poor will always be with us. Which statement is true? Or if they are all true, how do we reconcile the discrepancies?

If Deuteronomy 15:4 is taken in isolation, it certainly does look like a flat contradiction of Deuteronomy 15:11. But verse 4 begins with a "however." This introduces a correction or a limitation on what has preceded it in Deuteronomy 15:1-3 about the cancellation of debts due to loans that have now been paid off. That is, it should not be necessary to cancel any debts if the people are fully experiencing the blessing of the Lord as he promised in verse 4. There was a stated condition, however, for the nonexistence of the poor in the land mentioned in Deuteronomy 15:5: Israel must "fully obey" and be "careful to follow all these commands I am giving you today."

But if Israel was to refuse to fully obey (which they did), then the eventuality of Deuteronomy 15:7 is provided for, and the general assessment of Deuteronomy 15:11 is that "there will always be poor people in the land."

The situation in these verses is very much like that in 1 John 2:1, "I write this to you so that you will not sin. But if anybody does sin . . ." Thus the ideal is set forth while an alternative is also graciously provided in the way that poor people must be dealt with in an open, generous and magnanimous way.

15:12-18 Does God Approve of Slavery?

See comment on EXODUS 21:2-11.

19:21 Eye for Eye, Tooth for Tooth?

See comment on EXODUS 21:23-25.

21:15-17 Was Polygamy Permitted in the Old Testament?

See comment on GENESIS 29:25-28; 2 SAMUEL 20:3.

21:18-21 Stone a Stubborn and Rebellious Son?

At first glance this law seems pitiless in its demands both of a society with incorrigibly delinquent children and of the emotionally torn parents of such ruffians. But a second glance would question if our pity is well placed. Shall we pity the criminal or the community? Does Scripture side with the offender or the offended? The issue is not abstract or antiquated. It haunts modern society as well as the Christian community.

The case represented here particularizes the fifth of the Ten Commandments. The sanctity of the family is at the heart of this command to honor one's parents. Accordingly, God's plan for the family in its origin, function and perpetuity was not to be measured by humanistic or societal conventions but by the counsel of God.

Children were to honor their parents as God's earthly representatives. To rebel against these representatives was equal to rebelling against God. In practice, obedience to parents (a command strictly qualified by "in the Lord") could then be transferred as obedience to God, for the parents taught the children the law of God. Parents were to impress the commandments of God on their children's hearts while sitting together at home, walking along the road or getting up (Deut 6:6-7).

What happened when a serious case of juvenile delinquency appeared in the community? Should the family strike out in wrath to rid themselves of this embarrassment?

Deuteronomy 21:19-21 limits the power of the family. Parents were restricted to chastening and disciplining their children. They were never given power to kill or to abort life. Only under Roman law, as R. J. Rushdoony points out, was the parent the source and lord of life. In Scripture God is the source and Lord over life.

Thus, when anyone in the extended family rebelled and refused to obey his or her parents (*son* does not restrict this law to sons, for it also included daughters and, by extension, all relatives), the rest of the family was to align themselves with God's law and not with the recalcitrant family member.

In fact, the family order was so sacred to the fabric of society and the plan of God that the accusing family members were not considered the complaining witnesses as in other cases. Ordinarily witnesses were required to participate in the execution by throwing the first stones (Deut 17:7). In this case, however, "all the men of his town" were required to participate, for the complaint was a complaint by the community against one of its members.

What disrupted one family in the community attacked the whole community. Moreover, if the parents had refused to bring the guilty and incorrigible individual to the elders, they would have been guilty of condoning and, in a sense, participating in the defiant son's crimes.

Did the town actually kill one of its own members just for being rebellious? Such behavior came under the curse of God himself, so serious was the charge of parental abuse by children or their defiant refusal to listen to them (Deut 27:16).

However, for each crime demanding capital punishment (except premeditated murder) there was a substitution or ransom that could be offered (Num 35:31). Thus, while the penalty marked the seriousness of the crime, the offer of a ransom would mitigate some of the severity in the actual sentencing. Scripture suggests no proper ransom or substitute in this case, but it likely was similar to contemporary sentences that require community service for a specified time.

Could pity play any part in the sentencing of these crimes? Not if that pity were directed toward the violator rather than the violated or the word of God. Pity could distract people from serving God and honoring his word. There was to be no pity, for example, for the idolatrous worshipers of Canaan (Deut 7:16), the subverter of the faith (Deut 13:6-9) or the coldblooded murderer (Deut 19:11-13). Instead, our affection ought to be toward the living God and what he has spoken. Any love, loyalty or pity which preempts that love is itself a lawless and faithless love.

See also comment on GENESIS 9:6; NUMBERS 35:31.

23:19-20 Is Charging Interest Permitted?

See comment on EXODUS 22:25.

24:1-4 Is Divorce Permitted?

Does Deuteronomy 24:1-4 assert that a man must give a certificate of divorce to his wife if she displeases him? If not, why do the AV (the King James), the ASV of 1901 and the ERV say, "He shall write a bill of divorcement"?

Was divorce an intrinsic "right" or prerogative that had divine approval and legitimation in Old Testament times? What becomes then of the teachings of Jesus in Mark 10:2-12 and the apostle Paul in 1 Corinthians 7:10-16? All these questions continue to make Deuteronomy 24:1-4 a hard saying that demands some solid answers.

First of all, Deuteronomy 24:1-4 does not bestow any divine approval, or even an implied approval, on divorce as such. It sought, rather, to soften some of the hardships and injustices that divorce caused for women in a society that persisted in this practice.

Unfortunately, the translators of the three above-mentioned English versions of this text failed to notice that Deuteronomy 24:1-3 constitutes a protasis (or conditional clause) whose apodosis (or resolution) comes only in Deuteronomy 24:4. The significance of this syntax is that Moses did not make divorce mandatory. This passage does not authorize husbands to divorce their wives.

Rightly understood, the rule simply prohibits a husband from returning to a wife whom he had divorced after she has married a second time—even if her second husband has died in the interim.

The most difficult part of this Deuteronomy passage is the phrase "something indecent." Literally it means "nakedness of a thing."

The offensive act of the wife against her husband, which he is using as his grounds for a divorce, can hardly be adultery. The Mosaic law prescribed death for adultery (Lev 20:10; Deut 22:22). And when adultery was only suspected, but not proved, there were specified ways to handle such situations (Num 5:11-31). And this phrase cannot refer to a case where the wife was charged with previous sexual promiscuity, for that too had been anticipated (Deut 22:13-21). In none of these other cases does the phrase "something indecent" appear, nor is divorce set forth as the appropriate punishment for any of them.

The rabbis held vastly different opinions on the meaning of "something indecent." Rabbi Hillel taught that it referred to something repulsive—a physical defect, or even ruining a meal!

Rabbi Akiba interpreted it even more liberally: divorce could be "for any and every reason" (Mt 19:3), such as a man's finding another woman more attractive than his own wife. Others have believed that the phrase refers to some type of illness, for example, a skin disease.

Whatever the indecency was, it is clear that the common law allowed considerable latitude. The conclusion we are left with is that "something indecent" refers to some kind of improper behavior, short of illicit sexual intercourse.

But the precise definition actually matters little, since the law is not prescribing divorce as a punishment here, only assuming that some divorces were being carried out on the basis of common law. The reason for divorce is not the point that this legislation aims to address. Deuteronomy 24:4 is more concerned about protecting the woman from exposure to the whims of a fickle or vindictive husband, who, without putting his declaration of divorce in writing, could resume or drop his married state—depending on what his sexual needs, laundry pile or desires for a good meal were!

What is taught here is not God's final word, even in the Old Testament, about divorce. Malachi 2:16 condemns divorce in the strongest of terms. Many have tried to say that God didn't actually "hate" divorce, but that is what the text says. The New Testament texts (Mt 5:31-32; 19:7-9; Mk 10:4-12; Lk 16:18; 1 Cor 7:10-11) make the same point, permitting divorce only in the cases of irreconcilable adultery and unalterable abandonment.

When Jesus was questioned about this passage (Mk 10:2-12; Mt 19:1-9), he explained to the Pharisees that Moses had recorded this word "because your hearts were hard," but that the principles of Genesis 2:24 were still normative for all marriages. The two were to become one flesh. What God had joined together, no person was to separate.

Deuteronomy 24:1-4, however, deals only with the situation in which a former partner wishes to return to a previous marriage partner after one or the other has been married to a different person in the meantime and then divorced. There are three reasons the first husband, then, could not take back his wife after she had married another: (1) "she has been defiled," (2) remarriage "would be detestable in the eyes of the LORD," and (3) it would "bring sin upon the land." The logic here is the same as that found in the incest laws of Leviticus 18 and 20. Remarrying a woman one had divorced would be like marrying one's closest relative, for that is what she had become by virtue of being of one flesh. Because the husband and wife are "one flesh" (Gen 2:24), to be physically intimate with one partner was equivalent to exposing the other half of that marriage team who was not present in the illicit sexual relationships (Lev 18:6-20).

In Hebrew thinking, marriage made the bride not just a daughter-in-law, but a daughter of her husband's parents (see Ruth 1:11; 3:1). She became a sister to her husband's brother.

The results of our investigation are the following. The main clause and actual prohibition are found in verse 4 of Deuteronomy 24. The certificate or bill of divorce was for the woman's protection (against an on-again, off-again marriage) rather than the salving of the divorcing husband's conscience. And what the "something indecent" means matters little, since it was based not on Scripture and divine principle, but on common law and the custom of the day. For example, the most recent attempt to define "something indecent" views it as a euphemism for menstrual irregularities that would render a woman perpetually unclean and thus prohibit her from intercourse (Lev 15:14). Such a condition created a convenient excuse for the first husband to get out of a marriage not to his liking.[1]

See also comment on MALACHI 2:16; MARK 10:11-12.

[1]See John Walton, *Hebrew Studies* 32 (1991): 7-17.

24:16 Should Children Be Punished for Their Parents' Sins?

The principle governing Israelite courts was that human governments must not impute to children or grandchildren the guilt that their fathers or forebears accumulated. In Scripture each person stands before God as accountable for his or her own sin.

While this principle is acknowledged in Deuteronomy 24:16, there seem to be cases where it was not put in practice. For example, the child born to David and Bathsheba died because of their sin (2 Sam 12:14-18). And Saul's seven grandchildren were put to death because of Saul's sin (2 Sam 21:5-9). How are we to reconcile these contradictory sets of facts?

Some will also bring up the fact that the sins of the fathers have an ill effect on the children to the third and fourth generations (Ex 20:5; Deut 5:9). Surely this is a direct contradiction of the principle in Deuteronomy 24:16.

But Deuteronomy 24:16 is dealing with normal criminal law. It explicitly forbids blaming the children for the sin and guilt earned by the parent. If the son deserves the death penalty, the father must not be put to death in his place, or vice versa. This point is repeated in a number of texts, such as 2 Kings 14:6, 2 Chronicles 25:4, Jeremiah 31:30 and Ezekiel 18:20.

The legal principle of dealing with each individual according to individual guilt is one side of the equation. The other side is that God has reserved for himself the right to render all final decisions. Not all situations can, or are, resolved in human courts. Some must await the verdict that God will give.

There is a third element that must be accounted for as well. This notion is difficult for Westerners to appreciate, since we place such a high premium on the individual. But Scripture warns us that there is such a thing as corporate responsibility. None of us functions in complete isolation from the society and neighborhood to which we are attached. Lines of affinity reach beyond our home and church groups to whole communities and eventually to our nation and the world in which we live.

There are three factors involved in communal responsibility in the Old Testament. First is unity. Often the whole group is treated as a single unit. In 1 Samuel 5:10-11, for example, the ark of God came to Ekron of the Philistines. Because the bubonic plague had broken out in the previous Philistine cities where the ark had been taken, the Ekronites cried out, "They have brought the ark of the god of Israel around to us to kill us and our people." The whole group sensed that they would share in the guilt of what their leaders had done in capturing the ark of God.

Second, sometimes a single figure *represents* the whole group. Rather than someone who embodies the psychology of the group, this is a case of one, such as the suffering Servant of the Lord, standing in for many others.

The third factor is *oscillation* from the individual to the group, and vice versa. The classic example appears in Joshua 7:11, where the Lord affirms, "Israel has sinned," even though Achan confesses, "I have sinned" (Josh 7:20).

Each situation must be evaluated to see whether it is a principle of a human court that is involved, a divine prerogative of final judgment or a case of corporate solidarity. We in the West still understand that one traitor can imperil a whole army, but we do not always understand how individual actions carry over into the divine arena or have widespread implications. Scripture works with all three simultaneously.

In the case of David and Bathsheba, it is clear that the loss of the baby was linked to the fact that David committed adultery with Uriah's wife, though Uriah remained determined to serve David faithfully in battle. This did not involve a human court but was a matter of divine prerogative.

The story about Saul's seven grandchildren takes us into the area of national guilt. Saul violated a treaty made with the Gibeonites in the name of the Lord (Josh 9:3-15). The whole nation was bound by this treaty made in Joshua's day. Thus when Saul, as head of the nation, committed this atrocity against the Gibeonites, it was an act against God and an act that involved the whole nation. A divinely initiated famine devastated the land until the demands of justice were met. When David inquired into the reason for the famine, God answered, "It is on account of Saul and his blood-stained house; it is because he put the Gibeonites to death" (2 Sam 21:1).

Saul and his sons had already fallen in the battle at Mount Gilboa, but his household shared in the stigma. Only God knew why the seven grandchildren shared in the guilt; it is not spelled out in the text. Apparently they had had some degree of complicity in the matter. Because only God knew, it was up to God, not a human court, to settle such cases.

As for the commandment that has the sins of the fathers visiting the children to the third and fourth generations, we can only observe that the text clearly teaches that this happens when the children repeat the motivating cause of their parents' sin—that is, they too hate God. But when the children love God, the effect is lovingkindness for thousands of generations!

Both individual responsibility and group or communal responsibility are taught in Scripture. We must carefully define and distinguish these types of responsibility. But in no case should the principle of courts be to blame children for the wrongful deeds of their forebears. And if God demanded that principle as a basis for fairness in human governments, should we think he would do any less in the running of his own government?

No one will ever be denied eternal life because of what his or her forebears did or did not do. Each will live eternally or suffer everlasting judgment for his or her own actions (Ezek 18). Our standard of what constitutes fairness and justice, after all, is rooted in the character of God himself.

The graciousness of God and his swift move to forgive and to forget every sin that we call upon him to cleanse is seen in Exodus 34:6-7. The theme of these verses is essentially repeated in Numbers 14:18, 2 Chronicles 30:9, Nehemiah 9:17, Psalm 86:15, 103:8, 111:4, 116:5, 145:8, Joel 2:13, Jonah 4:2 and Nahum 1:3.

But God's grace is balanced by the last part of Exodus 34:7, which warns that "[God] does not leave the guilty unpunished." The reverse side of the same coin that declares God's mercy and his love speaks of his justice and righteousness. For the wicked persons who by their actions tend to second their father's previous motions by continuing to sin boldly against God as their fathers did, with no repentance, this text again warns that the chastisement of God will be felt down to the "third and fourth generation." However, note carefully that the full formula includes the important qualifier "of those who hate me." But wherever there is love, the effect is extended to thousands of generations!

In this connection, it is important to note that 2 Samuel 12:14 likewise declares about David's sin with Bathsheba, "But because by doing this you have made the enemies of the LORD show utter contempt, the son born to you will die." While it true that David was thoroughly forgiven of his sin of adultery and complicity in murder (see Psalms 32 and 51), there were consequences to his sin that could not be halted, for they followed as inexorably as day follows night. To put it in another way, just because God knows that a mugger will accept him as Savior a number of years after a mugging, God does not, thereby, turn the molecular structure of the bat used in the mugging, and which is now descending on the head of an innocent victim, into limp spaghetti; it leaves permanent damage on the skull of its poor unsuspecting target. The case of David and Bathsheba is similar: the consequences of sin are as real as the creation of a new life that comes out of a sexual affair. This in turn gave occasion for the enemies of God to vaunt themselves and demonstrate even further contempt for God, his people, and their alleged different style of life. It was for this reason that God brought immediate judgment on David: "the son born to [him would] die."

See also comment on JOSHUA 7:1, 10-11; 2 SAMUEL 21:1-9; EZEKIEL 21:4; ROMANS 5:12.

29:4 The Lord Is Responsible?

See comment on ISAIAH 63:17; 2 CORINTHIANS 3:14.

31:16 What Does "Rest with Your Fathers" Imply?

See comment on GENESIS 25:8.

32:50 Gathered to Your People?

See comment on GENESIS 25:8.

34:5-8 Prewritten Posthumous Writing?

If Moses wrote the book of Deuteronomy, indeed even the Pentateuch itself, how could he have written of his own death? What is more, he would have needed to describe not only his own death, but also the general location of his burial plot, with the added knowledge that no one knew where it was "to this day," whatever that would mean from the standpoint of Moses having written it, along with the mourning process that took place after that. How was all of this possible?

Few will be willing to debate the thesis that Moses was not the author of this last chapter of Deuteronomy. There are just too many expressions that make little or no sense if placed in Moses' mouth. For example, the phrases "to this day" (Deut 34:6), "since then, no prophet has risen" (Deut 34:10) and "for no one has ever shown the mighty power or performed the awesome deeds that Moses did in the sight of all Israel" (Deut 34:12) just do not seem naturally attributed to Moses. On the contrary, such expressions must be put along with the other "post-Mosaica" such as Numbers 12:3 and treated as additions which were added by a later writer under the inspiration of the Spirit of God or as early glosses that were brought into the text under divine approval.

Ancient Jews held that Joshua was the one whom the Spirit of God authorized to add statements such as appear in Deuteronomy 34 to the book Moses had left. The evidence generally cited for this view, which is also shared by a number of evangelical believers, is found in Joshua 24:26: "And Joshua recorded these things in the Book of the Law of God" (a reference that many of us take to be pointing to the Pentateuch).

If this is a correct assessment of the situation, then Moses did not write Deuteronomy 34 as a prognostication of his death and the events that would surround it. Instead, it was his understudy, Joshua, who undertook the task at the prompting of the Holy Spirit.

See also comment on NUMBERS 12:3.

JOSHUA

2:4-6 Was Rahab Right to Lie?

Does God approve of dubious actions to accomplish his will in certain perilous situations? Can strong faith go hand in hand with the employment of methods which are alien to the integrity of God's character and word? Are Rahab's treason and lying in any way justifiable, perhaps as a "white lie"?

The Bible is unhesitating in its praise of Rahab. Hebrews 11:31 praises her faith in God, while James 2:25 praises her for lodging and then sending off the spies in a different direction from those seeking them. But approval of Rahab in these areas does not mean that she enjoyed God's approval in every area of her life. The areas of Rahab's faith must be strictly observed.

She won recognition by biblical writers because she trusted in the God of Israel more than she trusted her own king of Jericho. She had heard what God had done for Israel at the Red Sea and in defeating the two kings of the trans-Jordan (Josh 2:8-12). And she demonstrated her faith by receiving the spies and sending them out another way. Even Joshua 6:25 notes her actions and contrasts her response with that of Achan.

No guilt should be assigned, therefore, to her treason in abandoning her people, who like herself had great reason for trusting the God of the Hebrews. When it comes to choosing between serving God or a local king, the answer must always be to serve the higher power, God (Acts 4:19).

Rahab's lie, on the other hand, cannot be so easily dismissed. She said, "I don't know which way they went." That was palpably false. Romans 3:8 warns us not to say, "Let us do evil that good may result." Neither should we argue, especially from a descriptive or a narrative passage, that a text validates deceit under certain conditions.

The so-called dutiful lie ignores how precious the truth is in God's sight. Even lies told for very good purposes are not free from divine disapproval. Moreover, even if in the de facto providence of God, Rahab's untruth allowed the two spies to escape harm, this does not therefore justify such a method. God is not reduced to unholy acts to fulfill his will. At most God allowed his purposes to be fulfilled in this most unusual manner, because his grace can operate in spite of the sinful maneuverings of men and women. Untruth cannot be vindicated simply because it is closely tied to the total result.

To argue for lying in this manner would be not only poor exegesis and theology but worse theodicy. Any other conclusion would eventually validate David's adultery because the next heir in the Messianic line, Solomon, resulted from David's union with Bathsheba. We are specifically told that David's sin was abhorrent to God. It happens we are not told the same about Rahab's sin. This is no reason to vote differently in the two cases; each violates a clear commandment of God.

We cannot say that protecting innocent lives is a greater good than the demand always to tell the truth. Scripture nowhere advocates or allows for such hierarchy. To do so would pit part of God's nature against other parts of his nature. To say that lying is a lesser evil than being involuntarily implicated in murder is again an artificial and subjective construct. We need to follow all of God's Word, and that Word involves respect for both life and truth, as difficult as that is in a world that often pits one moral absolute against another.

Truth-telling is not only a covenantal responsibility (that is, a responsibility to those who are part of the family of God), but a universal responsibility for all times, all peoples, in all places. We must not form our own subjective hierarchies or personal priorities in assigning what we believe is the greater good or lesser evil.

On the other hand, we may not surrender innocent lives just because an army or police force demands it. Rahab should have hidden the spies well and then refused to answer the question whether she was hiding them. She could, for instance, have volunteered, "Come in and have a look around," while simultaneously praying that God would make the searchers especially obtuse.

It is possible to maintain a position of nonconflicting absolutes. God will provide a way to avoid the conflicts (1 Cor 10:13).

See also comment on EXODUS 1:15-21; 3:18; 1 SAMUEL 16:1-3; 1 KINGS 22:20-22.

6:20 Did Jericho's Walls Really Collapse?

Is the description of the capture of Jericho a real event or does it belong to the literary genre of fiction or myth? Is there any corroboration from archaeological sources, or any other external data, that this event actually took place? As one academician recently quipped, "All the shouting and trumpet blowing in the world will not cause fifteen-foot-thick walls to collapse. The whole Joshua/Jericho account is just a religious legend." The archaeologist Kathleen Kenyon affirmed right up to her death in 1978 that the evidence for a conquest of this city during the days of Joshua was plain missing.

However, Kenyon based her conclusion on a very limited excavation area (two 26-foot squares), and her dating was based solely on the fact that she failed to find any expensive, imported pottery from Cyprus, which was common to the Late Bronze I period (that is, the days of Joshua). But she grounded this conclusion on a small excavation area in an impoverished part of the city, a city obviously situated far away from the major trade routes.

However, an evangelical archaeologist, Bryant G. Wood,[1] argues just the reverse. In his judgment the ceramic evidence does validate a date around 1450 to 1400 B.C. Furthermore, Jericho is one of the oldest cities in the world and one of the best fortified. The outer wall surrounded the city with stone about twelve feet high. In back of that there was an inner mud-brick wall about eighteen feet high. Behind that wall there was a sloping earthen embankment going around the inside of the entire city. At the top of the embankment was another mud-brick wall approximately fifteen feet high, below which the houses of Jericho's outcasts were placed. This is where the harlot Rahab no doubt lived. Archaeologists found the base of the outer wall had collapsed into piles of bricks.

So how did the Israelites get over these walls? If an earthquake was responsible for stopping up the Jordan River as the Israelites crossed over in the days just prior to the siege of Jericho (Josh 3:16), it is reasonable to assume that the same earthquake left cracks and serious fissures in the walls of Jericho. Some think there is evidence for an earthquake of the magnitude of 8.0 on the Richter scale (a quake, if that estimate is correct, that would match the 1906 earthquake in San Francisco).

When a further quake at the time of the Israelites' seventh circling of the city on the seventh day hit (or, alternatively, as a result of aftershocks on the already weakened walls from the previous earthquake), the mud-brick walls collapsed over the outer stone wall, forming a ramp for the Israelites to go up and enter the city and set it on fire.

All archaeologists attest that there were great quantities of grain found within the city, indicating both that it was a very short siege and that the normal looting and plundering of whatever grain remained was not carried out since the Israelites were under an interdict that nothing should be taken; it was dedicated to the Lord for destruction *(ḥerem)*.

The earlier excavator of the city, John Garstang, at the beginning of this century, was confident that the city fell in the times of Joshua, around 1400 B.C. To demonstrate this, he produced a series of scarabs, small Egyptian amulets shaped like the scarab beetle, often with the name of a Pharaoh on the bottom of them. These scarabs represented the line of the Pharaohs right up to the time of the Pharaoh who died in 1349 B.C. Added evidence came from a recent carbon-14 sample from material from the Jericho site that dated to 1410 B.C., plus or minus forty years.

Accordingly, the evidence is mounting that Jericho was captured as Israel claimed around 1400 B.C. The city, indeed, was heavily fortified (Josh 2:5, 7, 15; 6:5, 20). The attack did come just after the harvest time in the late spring (Josh 2:6; 3:15; 5:10). The siege was short (Josh 6:15) and the walls were breached, possibly by an earthquake (Josh 6:20).

---

[1]Bryant G. Wood, "Did the Israelites Conquer Jericho?" *Biblical Archaeology Review* 16 (1990): 44-59.

5:13—6:5 Whom Did Joshua See?

See comment on JUDGES 6:22-23.

7:1, 10-11 Was It Achan or All Israel That Sinned?

It is not clear from the first verse of Joshua 7 whether the whole nation was unfaithful or just one man, Achan. But if it was only one man who sinned, as the story later discloses, why was the transgression imputed to the whole nation? It would appear that Achan alone should have been punished on the principle that "the soul who sins is the one who will die" (Ezek 18:4).

Another troubling feature in this text is the identification of the "devoted things." What were they, and why should their possession jeopardize the Israelites' mission of attacking Ai?

The best way to begin is to start with the question of the "devoted things." This is a very distinctive concept in the Old Testament. The word used, *ḥerem,* means the "curse" or, more accurately, the "thing dedicated for destruction." This word comes from the verb "to separate"; hence the Arabic word *harem,* an enclosed living area set aside for women. In many ways, the act of dedicating *ḥerem* is the reverse of the voluntary dedication spoken of in Romans 12:1-2. Both are acts of separating oneself or something unto God. But in the case of *ḥerem,* the placing of an item under "the ban," or its dedication "to destruction," is an involuntary act, whereas what is "holy" to the Lord is separated unto him as a voluntary act.

Behind this concept lies the fact that all the earth and all that is in it belongs to the Lord. After mortals had tried the patience of God to the limit, he finally stepped in and required that what he owned should come back to him. The judgment of fire and death meant that all life and all gifts returned to the Lord, their owner. Items that could not burn, such as silver, gold and certain metals, were declared to belong to the Lord. They were to be placed in the tabernacle or temple of God. They had been set apart for destruction and hence were sacred.

Under no circumstances could these items be sold, collected or redeemed by substituting something else for them. There was a compulsory dedication connected with them. Jericho was one of the few places to be placed under this curse or ban in the Old Testament (Josh 6:21). Other such cities included Ai (Josh 8:26), Makkedah (Josh 10:28) and Hazor (Josh 11:11).

Interestingly, the word *ḥerem* is the last word in the Old Testament canon (in English order). Malachi 4:6 warns that God might come and take a "forced dedication" if men and women persist in refusing to give a voluntary one.

Perhaps it will be seen, now, why Achan's sin was viewed with such severity. He had done more than take several battle mementos; he had robbed God of items that specifically indicated that he was the Lord of the whole earth and should have received praise and honor from the Canaanites of Jericho.

Make no mistake: Achan was responsible for his own sin. Whether other members of his family were participants in the crime cannot be determined for certain, though it seems likely. Joshua 7:24 tells us that "his sons and daughters, his cattle, donkeys and sheep, his tent and all that he had" were brought to the Valley of Achor ("trouble"), and there "all Israel stoned him" (Josh 7:25). While the text begins by focusing on Achan, saying they "stoned *him,*" it continues noting that "they stoned *the rest*" and "they burned *them.*" Thus it would appear that the children were accomplices to the crime.

Since Achan had violated the ban and brought the goods from Jericho into his tent, he in essence made his tent, its contents and whatever was under the aegis of that tent part of the destruction and judgment that was on Jericho.

Finally, we must ask why the whole nation was viewed by God as an organic unity. Can the sin of one member of the nation or group defile everyone?

That is exactly the point made by this text. It is not difficult to see how the goodness of one person can bring blessing on the whole group. God blessed the whole world through Abraham (Gen 12:3). And we rarely complain when we enjoy the blessing and accumulated goodness of God on our nation as a result of the godly lives of our ancestors.

In a real sense, our acts do have ramifications beyond our own fortunes and future. The act of one traitor can imperil a battalion of soldiers, a nation or a multinational corporation. In the same way, one thoughtless act of a member of a community can have enormous consequences for the whole group.

This in no way bears on the ultimate destiny and salvation of any one of the persons in that group, but it can have enormous implications for the temporal and material well-being of each member.

When an individual Israelite violated a specific command of God, it brought sin on the whole group. In that case, the sin ignited the anger of God against the whole group. Achan was not acting merely on his own behalf when he sinned. As a leader among the clans of the important tribe of Judah, he had committed sacrilege; he had stolen what God had declared to be both sacred and separated from ordinary objects. Such a crime was aimed directly at God and at his covenant. It impinged on his right to be Lord and infringed on his rights of ownership. It had to be dealt with immediately and severely, just as did the sin of Ananias and Sapphira in the New Testament (Acts 5).

God holds each person individually responsible for his or her own sin; that is clear. But some, by virtue of their position or office, their offense against that which is sacred to God, or the implications that their acts have for their group, can also bring the wrath of God on their nation, community, institution or group. There are times where we are our nation's keepers. When we deny or ignore this reality, Western individualism runs amuck and biblical truth is neglected.

See also comment on DEUTERONOMY 24:16; 1 SAMUEL 15:18; EZEKIEL 21:4; ROMANS 5:12.

9:8-9, 16, 18-19 Why Did Joshua Spare the Gibeonites?

The story of the ruse pulled by the Gibeonites presents several moral and ethical dilemmas. Is a person required to keep his or her word when the means used to obtain that promise is obviously false? Can the end justify the means in cases such as the one before us? Do wartime conditions lessen the requirements for keeping one's word?

Why did Joshua feel that he was obligated to maintain the terms of a treaty into which he had been tricked? Could he not have legitimately said that he was involved in a war and the enemy remained just that, regardless of the agreement they had reached? Why did Joshua act so faintheartedly for a military general?

The Gibeonites were worried after they had witnessed the sudden fall of Jericho and Ai. The citizens of Gibeon and its associated cities, seized with alarm, decided that they would approach the invading armies of Joshua and pretend that they had come from a distant country and wanted to make a treaty. The delegation dressed themselves in torn clothing and sandals and carried awkwardly mended wineskins. Even their bread was crumbly and dry. They played their parts to perfection; Joshua and the leadership of Israel were indeed completely deceived.

Three days after the treaty had been ratified by oath, it was learned that these were men from Gibeon and its environs. That city was only six miles northwest of Jerusalem. Humiliated by the deception, the Israelite people grumbled about the way the leadership had mishandled this matter.

Why the Gibeonites had chosen to risk so much on the Israelites' commitment to honoring their promise is difficult to explain. Had they gotten an initial indication that the God of this people required truthfulness and integrity from his own? Or did the Gibeonites share a common Semitic concept of the effect of the word—that once a word had gone forth, there was no way to stop it, for it had a mission to fulfill? But that concept seems rather lofty for the Canaanites, given what we know about their ethics and morals.

Speculation will not help fill the gaps in our knowledge. What we do know is that for Joshua the matter was now a sacred trust, since the Israelite leaders had given their oath by the name of the God of Israel. To go back on that word would be to tarnish the high name of God. For the moment, the Gibeonites had succeeded. Eventually, they would be put under a perpetual servanthood as woodcutters and water carriers for the house of God. They would appear in this role as late as the postexilic times of Nehemiah.

It is true that the leaders should have sought God's guidance in their uncertainty. But they did not.

This story is particularly difficult for moderns to understand, for we do not generally have the same concept of the effect of one's words. In Old Testament times, giving one's word was not taken lightly. Once a word was uttered, it could not be flippantly recalled or canceled. God saw to it that each word had the effect for which it was intended. This is not to say that a magical view of words is taught in the Old Testament, or that there is an independent power in words. The health-wealth-and-prosperity gospel that would urge us to simply "name it [our desire] and claim it" has been exploded as being nonbiblical.

There was, however, a sacredness to the word uttered in the Lord's name. Integrity demanded that such a word be kept, for it had been sealed with an oath.

Truth-telling and integrity in keeping one's word were serious matters for all who loved and obeyed the God of truth. And to make a covenant in God's name was binding, for it meant that God's reputation was involved. True, the grounds and means the Gibeonites used to obtain this treaty or covenant were less than honorable, but that in no way nullified the terms of the agreement, once it had been agreed to in the great name of the God of heaven and earth.

See also comment on EXODUS 3:18; 21:2-11; JOSHUA 2:4-6; 1 KINGS 22:20-22.

10:12-14 The Sun Stood Still?

Among the many miracles recorded in the Bible, this one is perhaps the most notable. Did the Lord actually halt the earth's rotation for a period of approximately twenty-four hours so that the sun stood still in the sky and the moon failed to come up at its appointed time? And if God did halt the earth's normal rotation for a full day, would this not have led to an inconceivable catastrophe for the entire planet and everything that is held on its surface by the force of gravity? The implications of some of these questions are, indeed, cosmic.

Or is there some other meaning to the natural force of the words used in this account? For example, can the words in verse 13 (literally rendered, "The sun did not hasten to go down for about a whole day") point to a retardation of the earth's movement, so that it took forty-eight hours rather than twenty-four hours for the earth to make its circuit around the sun? Or could the Hebrew word *dōm,* "stand still" (much like our onomatopoeic word "be dumb") signify that the sun was to remain hidden—hence "silent"—during the violent thunderstorm that accompanied the troops as they fled before the Israelites down the Valley of Aijalon? These are some of the reasons this passage is listed among the hard sayings.

Of course, the God who made the universe can momentarily stop it without the catastrophes that most of us would envisage according to the laws known to us at this time. Surely he is capable of holding in abeyance those physical laws that might have countermanded his actions with regard to the sun and the moon. But the question is, *Would* he have done so? This is like saying that God is omnipotent, yet God will not do contradictory things like making ropes with only one end or squares in the form of circles; and he will never sin. There are some things that he will not do because they are contradictory to his very nature. The question then is, Would stopping the planet be such a contradiction? Most would say that it is.

Alleged stories about a long day in Egyptian, Chinese and Hindu sources are difficult to validate. Similarly, the reports that some astronomers, and more recently some space scientists, have uncovered evidence for a missing day are difficult to vouch for. The claim by Edward Charles Pickering of the Harvard Observatory and Professor Totten of Yale that they had discovered a day missing from the annals of the heavens has never been substantiated, since no records exist to support it. It has been said in defense of this omission that the university officials preferred not to keep records of that sort in their archives. But that has not been demonstrated either. Some other explanation is needed.

What happened on that day when Joshua was pursuing the Amorites after a long night's forced march from Gilgal, a city near Jericho? That day the army covered more than thirty miles over some pretty rough terrain. The enemy fled westward to Beth Horon and then turned south into the Valley of Aijalon ("Deerfield"). At that point, the men, having made an all-night uphill climb from Gilgal, were exhausted. The heat of the July day was sapping what little energy they had left. But to their great relief, God sent a hailstorm that kept pace with the forward ranks of the fleeing Amorites. More were dying that day from the Lord's hailstones than from the Israelites' arrows and spears. The Lord had heard the prayer of his leader Joshua and answered in a most dramatic way.

Given the presence of a hailstorm (Josh 10:11), it is difficult to see how the sun could have been seen as stopped in the sky. There was light under the cloud cover, of course, but there would have been no actual view of the sun during a hailstorm so violent that it was killing the Amorites by the scores.

We can conclude that *dōm* in verse 13 should be translated "was dumb" or "silent." The sun did not "stop" in the middle of the sky, but its burning heat was "silenced." The presence of the hailstorm lends more than a little credence to this view. In a sense, then, this is not "Joshua's long day" but rather "Joshua's long night," for the coolness brought by the storm relieved the men and permitted them to go on fighting and marching for a total of more than eighteen hours. This seems to be the preferable interpretation.

Some have suggested that there was a prolongation of the day merely in the sense that the men did in one day what should have taken them two. But this suggestion fails to account for some of the special vocabulary used in this text.

Others have argued that God produced an optical prolongation of the sunshine, continuing its effect far beyond the normal time of sunset. Perhaps there was an unusual refraction of the sun's rays, or perhaps a comet or meteorite appeared in the heavens just about this time. Both of these ideas, however, do not account for enough time, for usually these types of astronomical events are of short duration.

The best solution is this. Joshua prayed early in the morning, while the moon was in the western sky and the sun was in the east, that God would intervene on their behalf. God answered Joshua and sent a hailstorm. This had the effect of prolonging the darkness and shielding the men from the searing rays of the summer sun. The sun, therefore, was "silenced" in the middle of the sky, and the moon "did not hasten" to come.

What a day to remember, for on it God went out and personally fought for Israel—and more died from the hailstones than from the weapons of the army of Israel!

11:20 God Hardened Their Hearts?

See comment on EXODUS 9:12.

18:8 Casting Lots Encouraged?

See comment on JONAH 1:4-5, 7.

JUDGES

5:24-27 A Murderer Praised?

Why is Jael praised for murdering Sisera, the commander of the army of Jabin, king of Canaan, especially when it was a gross violation of Middle Eastern customs of protecting one's guest? Was she not being deceptive in the way she at first extended lavish hospitality and then tricked him into sleeping while she carried out her gruesome murder? And how, then, can she be praised and eulogized as being the "most blessed of women"?

Once again Israel had been sold into the hands of an oppressor—this time it was Jabin, the king of Canaan, who ruled from the city of Hazor (Judg 4:2). Deborah, the prophetess and judge that God had raised up at that time to deliver Israel, summoned Barak to rid the country of this new oppressor, but Barak insisted that he would go into battle only if Deborah went with him. Deborah's prophecy was that God would therefore hand Sisera, the commander of Jabin's army, over into the hands of a woman (Judg 4:9). Here may be one of the most important hints that the forthcoming action of Jael was divinely initiated.

In the meantime a Kenite (related to Moses through his wife Zipporah) named Heber had taken up residence among the people of Israel, apparently signaling something important about what his beliefs were, for residence in that day had more attached to it than mere location. After the battle on Mount Tabor in which Sisera and his troops were routed, Sisera abandoned his chariot and fled on foot, while Barak finished off the entire chariot division of Sisera. Because Jabin and the clan of Heber had a history of friendly relations, Sisera entered the tent of Heber's wife, Jael (Judg 4:17-18), a most unusual act in itself, for no one went into a woman's quarters when her husband was not around. After she had refreshed him with a skin of milk and was instructed to stand watch while he slept, she took a tent peg and hammer and drove the peg through his temple while he slept.

Jael is usually charged with six faults: (1) disobedience to her husband, who had friendly relations with Jabin; (2) breaking a treaty (Judg 4:17); (3) deception in entertaining Sisera, giving no hint of her hostile intentions as she assuaged his thirst by giving him a kind of buttermilk or yogurt when all he asked for was water; (4) lying, saying, "Fear not," when Sisera had much to fear; (5) violating the conventions of hospitality by murdering one that she had agreed to accept as a guest; (6) murder (Judg 4:21).

How many of these charges are true? Jael should not have lied, no matter how grave her circumstances. But, as for the other charges, remember that this was a time of war. Some had already shirked their potential for assisting Israel during a desperate time of need, namely the city of Meroz (Judg 5:23). But here was Jael, related only through marriage to Moses and Israel, who had chosen to dwell in the midst of the people of God. When involuntarily thrust into the vicinity of the war by virtue of the location of her tent, she did not hesitate to act by killing the man who stood against the people of God with whom she had come to identify herself. It is for this that she is so lavishly praised.

Some have argued that Sisera's entering Jael's tent also had sexual overtones. The first phrase in Judges 5:27 may be a graphic description of a rape: "At her feet he sank, he fell; there he lay." Not only may the word "feet" be a euphemism for one's sexual parts, as it is in other parts of Scripture at times, but especially significant are the verbs "lay" (Hebrew *šāḵaḇ*), meaning "to sleep" or "to have sexual intercourse" (for example, Gen 19:32; Deut 22:23, 25, 28; 2 Sam 13:14), and "to bow" (Hebrew *kāra'*), meaning "to bend the knee," "kneel," or in Job 31:10 to "crouch" over a woman. If this understanding of the delicately put poetry is correct, then Jael is more than justified in her actions of self-defense of her person as well. For years Canaanite men had been raping Hebrew women in just this fashion.

There is no clear evidence that Jael disobeyed her husband. Nor is there clear evidence that there actually was a treaty in force. But even if there were, it is doubtful that it could be legitimately enforced during wartime, which very act was a violation of the peace, since Heber had the same relations with Israel and Jabin.

Jael did violate the conventions of hospitality, but this is at the level of custom and social mores and not at the level of ethics. After all, this was a war zone, and a war was going on.

What is clear is that Jael lied to Sisera and she killed him. Is her lying justifiable? No! To say, as one commentator did, that "deception and lying are authorized in Scripture any time God's kingdom is under attack" is unsupported by the Bible. This same writer went on to affirm that "since Satan made his initial assault on the woman by means of a lie (Gen 3:1-5), it is fitting that the woman defeat him by means of a lie, . . . lie for lie."[1]

I would agree with the conclusions reached over a century ago by Edward L. Curtis:

> But from a moral standpoint, . . . at first glance it appears like the condemnation of a base assassination, especially when one reads Judges 4:18-21. [Shall we suppose] that in good faith she received Sisera and pledged him protection, but afterwards, while she saw him sleeping, God moved her to break her word and slay him? . . . The numerous manifestations of God, his frequent communications at that time to his agents, might suggest that Jael received [just such] a divine communication, but to consider her act otherwise morally wrong and to use this as

> a ground for its justification, is impossible. Right and wrong are as fixed and eternal as God, for they are of God, and for him to make moral wrong right is to deny himself.[2]

Jael's loyalty to Yahweh and his people is her justification. It was part of the old command to exterminate the Canaanite (Deut 20:16). Jael came to the assistance of the people of God, and for this she is declared blessed.

See also comment on NUMBERS 25:7-13; JOSHUA 2:4-6.

---

[1]James B. Jordan, *Judges: God's War Against Humanism* (Tyler, Tex.: Geneva Ministries, 1985), p. 89. Jordan's whole discussion of this problem (to which I am indebted at many points in this discussion) is, however, one of the most extensive and suggestive that I found anywhere.

[2]Edward L. Curtis, "The Blessing of Jael," *The Old Testament Student* 4 (1884-1885): 12-14.

6:22-23 Who Is the Angel of the Lord?

If Gideon only saw an angel, why did he fear that he might die? Many interpreters believe that an angel takes God's place and acts as his representative. However, others do not feel this explanation fits all the data. Who, then, is this "angel of the LORD"?

The angel of the Lord first appears in Genesis 16:7 and then intermittently throughout the early Old Testament books. In other passages an individual manifesting himself in human form is frequently called "the LORD" (Gen 12:7; 17:1; 18:1). If this angel actually were God, why is he called an angel? Since the root meaning of *angel* is "messenger" or "one who is sent," we must determine from context whether the word refers to the *office* of the sent one or to the *nature* of created angels as finite beings.

Initially, some contexts of the term "angel of the LORD" appear to refer to nothing more than any other angel (as in Judg 6:11). But as the narrative progresses, that angel soon transcends the angelic category and is described in terms suited only to a member of the Trinity. Thus in the Judges 6 episode, we are startled when verse 14 has the Lord speaking to Gideon, when previously only the angel of the Lord had been talking.

Many Old Testament passages state that this angel is God. Thus, after being told that Hagar had been speaking with the angel of the Lord (four times in Gen 16:7, 9-11), Genesis 16:13 informs us that Hagar "gave this name to the LORD who spoke to her: 'You are the God who sees me.' " Jacob's testimony in Genesis 48:15-16 is even more striking. He identifies the God in whose presence his fathers Abraham and Isaac had lived as "the God who has been my shepherd all my life to this day, the Angel who has delivered me from all harm."

This angel spoke to Jacob earlier in a dream and identified himself by saying, "I am the God of Bethel, where you anointed a pillar and where you made a vow to me" (Gen 31:11, 13).

Likewise in Exodus 3:2-6 the phrase "the angel of the LORD" is used interchangeably with "the LORD." In fact the angel claims, "I am the God of your father, the God of Abraham, the God of Isaac and the God of Jacob" (Ex 3:6).

The passage, however, that really clinches this remarkable identification is Exodus 23:20-23. There God promises to send his angel ahead of the children of Israel as they go through the desert. The Israelites were warned that they must obey and not rebel against this angel. The reason was a stunning one: "Since my Name is in him." God would never share his memorial name with anyone else, for Isaiah 42:8 advised that he would never share his glory with another. Thus the name of God stands for himself. And when a person is said to have the name of God in him, that person is God!

This angel has divine qualities, prerogatives and authority. He has the power to give life (Gen 16:10) and to see and know all (Gen 16:13; Ex 3:7). Only God can forgive sin, yet this angel did the same in Exodus 23:21. The angel performed miracles such as keeping a burning bush from being consumed (Ex 3:2), smiting Egypt with plagues (Ex 3:20), calling forth fire on the rock to consume the meal set for him (Judg 6:21) and ascending the flame of the altar (Judg 13:20).

Finally, this angel commanded and received worship from Moses (Ex 3:5) and Joshua (Josh 5:14). Angels were not to receive worship. When John attempted to worship an angel in Revelation 19:10; 22:8-9, he was corrected quickly and told not to do it.

It is clear from this abundance of evidence that the angel of the Lord in the Old Testament was a preincarnate form of our Lord Jesus Christ, who would later permanently take on flesh when he came as a babe in Bethlehem. But mark it well: the one who came after John had already been before—he was that angel of the Lord. His full deity was always observed and yet he presented the same mystery of the Trinity that would later be observed in "I and the Father are one" (Jn 10:30) and "my other witness is the Father, who sent me" (Jn 8:18). It is that word *sent* that ties together the angel, messenger or sent one into an Old Testament theology of christophanies, appearances of God in human form.

See also comment on GENESIS 32:23-33; EXODUS 24:9-11; 33:18-23.

6:36-40 Was Gideon Right to Test God?

Was Gideon wrong in asking God for reassurance by means of a wet or dry fleece? Had not God made his will clear to Gideon already at the time of his call (Judg 6:14-16)? While it is understandable that Gideon was apprehensive over his impending conflict with Midian, given the disparity in the number of weapons and men and the morale of the soldiers, he was still wrong in doubting God. Or, at least, that is what some contend.

Did Gideon use a proper type of test? Supposing a test is permissible, isn't it wrong to ask God to accommodate our weakness, to assure us through physical signs or miracles of a word he has already spoken?

One further objection focuses on the fact that Gideon did not keep his word. Gideon promised that he would know God was going to use him to deliver Israel if God made the fleece wet and left the ground dry. Though God complied, Gideon insisted on running the same experiment in reverse fashion before he would believe. So what can we say, not only for Gideon but also for modern believers who wish to use similar tactics in order to validate the will of the Lord for them?

Some who object to Gideon's method for discerning God's will feel that he was not really desiring to know the will of God. Instead, they say, Gideon was angling to have that will *changed!*

This does not appear to be the case, based on what we are told in the text itself. Such an assertion tends to psychologize Gideon. How can we penetrate into his heart and mind and say what it was that Gideon was feeling or hoping?

Clearly, Gideon struggled. But he wanted God to provide his overwhelmed mind with more evidence for the words "as [God had] said" (Judg 6:37). He *was* responding to God's call (Judg 6:14-16). Thus he was hesitant, but not unbelieving.

What about the matter of asking for

signs? When we do so, are we acting like the scribes and Pharisees of Jesus' day, who always wanted a sign? And how specific is the will of God in our ordinary life? Granted, in revelation God often gave specific, detailed instructions for particular actions. But is Judges 6 an invitation for all believers to demand similar specificity? Must the will of God be a dot with a fixed point and nothing else?

Gideon's boldness can be seen both in his asking for a sign and in his specifying what that sign should be. The sign, though simple, involved a miracle. He would place the fleece on the leveled ground where the people threshed their grain (probably in the entrance to the city gate). If the dew was on the fleece alone while all the ground was dry, then he would know that God really would use him to deliver Israel from the hand of the Midianites.

The next night, using rather deferential language, he asked that the sign be reversed, with the fleece being dry and the ground soaked with the dew of the night. In both instances Gideon's request was granted, confirming what God had promised—that his strength comes to peak performance and full throttle in our weakness (2 Cor 12:9).

Thus Gideon's faith was supported. The phantom fears that had haunted his countrymen about the Midianites no longer afflicted him. Before setting out to overthrow the Midianites, he had approached God in prayer, and there he had found his courage renewed and fortified. His importunity was not wrong. And actually he provides a model for us: when we are beset by internal struggles and when challenges seem too great for us to handle, we must go to God in prayer.

Nevertheless, this passage does not give encouragement to those who assume they can expect God to attend each of his instructions with whatever signs we may request! God could just as well have refused Gideon's request. The fact that he didn't does not set a precedent to which any and all believers may appeal in their moment of distress. God may be pleased to repeat such an act of mercy, but he is not bound to satisfy our desire for visual, physical miracles to confirm his will. Whether he does so rests in his hand alone.

9:23 God Sent an Evil Spirit?

See comment on 1 SAMUEL 16:14; 1 KINGS 22:20-22.

11:30-39 Jephthah Sacrificed His Daughter?

The story of Jephthah and his famous vow has caused heated debates among interpreters. The question dividing interpreters is simply, Did Jephthah sacrifice his own daughter or did he not? If he did, did God condone such an unspeakable act?

Almost all early writers portrayed Jephthah as actually offering up his own daughter. It was not until the Middle Ages that commentators began to look for ways to soften Jephthah's act. Indeed, sane men and women would naturally be incensed and shocked by Jephthah's autocratic and nonbiblical ways of thinking and acting.

But the reader must remember the theme of Judges: Everyone was doing what was right in his or her own eyes. Jephthah was no different. As a matter of fact, the people at first had hesitated to call him as judge over the tribes on the east bank because his mother was a prostitute and his own brothers had driven him from the family inheritance.

There are three main questions to answer here: (1) Exactly what did Jephthah mean by his vow? (2) How did he carry it out? (3) Did God condone his actions?

Before Jephthah marched out of Mizpah, he solemnly vowed to give God whoever came out the door of his house if he returned victorious over the Ammonites. This raises the issue of vows and the problem of translating *whoever*.

Vows are not unbiblical, but there are some dangers to avoid in making them. First, it is best to avoid making vows that will afterward prove difficult for one's conscience or for carrying out (Prov 20:25; Eccles 5:2-6). Second, vows should never be used to purchase favor with God—as if we could work for God's grace or influence God to do for us what he would not otherwise do. Instead our vows should express gratitude to him for his unmerited favor.

When a vow has been made, the promise ought to be fulfilled (Num 36:2-13; Ps 15:4; 66:14; 76:11; Acts 5:1-4). Oaths or vows that violate a moral law of God, however, should not be kept. Therefore the rash promise of Herod, which resulted in the request for John the Baptist's head, should never have been kept. Unfortunately it was (Mk 6:23-27). Herod should have retreated from his vow and sought pardon from all involved for making it at all. Only vows and oaths made in faith need never be regretted. Others will be the occasion of lament or shock.

What then did Jephthah vow? Some have tried to soften the vow by translating what was vowed as "whatever comes out." However, if the Hebrew text intended this neuter idea (which would have allowed for anything, including Jephthah's animals), it should have used a different gender here (neuter in the Hebrew would have been signaled by the feminine form of the word). Since the masculine form is used, and the verb is *to come out*, it must refer (as it does in every other context) only to persons and not to animals or anything else.

Jephthah promised that whoever first came out to meet him on his victorious return would belong to the Lord and be sacrificed to the Lord. Did he mean this literally? If he did not, then why did he use these words? And if he did, then how could a judge, with his unusual anointing of the Holy Spirit for the task of leadership in battle, be guilty of such a gross violation of an explicit law of God (Lev 18:21; Deut 12:31)—the injunction against human sacrifice?

Such irrational behavior can only be explained in this manner: God's approval of a person in one area is no guarantee of approval in all areas of life. For example, David was also Spirit-led and a man after God's own heart, but not everything David did should be imitated by believers.

Some interpreters have attempted to translate the word "and" between "will be the Lord's" and "I will sacrifice" with a disjunctive meaning, "or." Unfortunately for this ingenious solution, this translation of the Hebrew particle is never permitted anywhere else in the Old Testament. The only other case where it has been tried (2 Kings 18:27) also appears to be very questionable.

Jephthah was acquainted with the law of Moses that forbade human sacrifice. Judges 11:12-28 shows he knew the history of Israel and could recite it at will. But this, of course, is no proof that what he knew he always did, any more than our knowing what is right guarantees we will always do it.

That Jephthah actually sacrificed his daughter, tragic as that would be, seems the most natural reading of the text. If Jephthah's "sacrifice" of his daughter meant relegating her to a life of perpetual virginity and service at the temple, not one word in the text says so. The only possible support is the comment that whoever comes out of the house "will be the LORD's" (Judg 11:31). But the statement immediately after this proves he had a whole burnt offering in mind—"sacrifice . . . as a burnt offering."

There is one other problem with the dedication to the temple view. Why didn't Jephthah pay the monetary substitute set forth in Leviticus 27:1-8 in order to gain the release of his daughter? After all, it bothered him that she would be childless and his line and name would fall out of the rosters of Israel. A woman could be redeemed for thirty shekels of silver (Lev 27:4).

Some, like James Jordan, attempt to answer this critically important question by quoting Leviticus 27:28-29, which demands that any person who has been "devoted" to the Lord may not be ransomed. This is true, but the term used there for *devoted* is a very technical term. It is the opposite of a voluntary offering, which is the essence of a vow. In the conquest, Jericho was such a "devoted" place to the Lord, and therefore everything in that town belonged to God. What could not be burned, such as silver, gold or iron, had to be collected and placed in the tabernacle. Thus when Achan took some of the loot of Jericho for himself, he stole from God.

But that is not what we are talking about here. Jephthah was not forced to "devote" his daughter for destruction in return for God's victory over the Ammonites. He did it voluntarily, and thus these verses do not apply. Furthermore, persons devoted under that "ban" *(ḥerem)* were slain, not as a sacrifice or a burnt offering, but as required by the command of God (Num 21:2-3; Deut 13:12-18; 1 Sam 15:33). The irony of this whole situation is, as Micah warns us, that a person cannot offer the "fruit of [his or her] body [in exchange] for the sin of [his or her] soul" (Mic 6:7).

Why does Judges 11:39 note that "she was a virgin" if Jephthah actually sacrificed her? The answer is that the Hebrew is best translated as a pluperfect, "She had never known a man." This point is added to emphasize the tragedy and grief of the events described.

If Jephthah's daughter was immolated, in contradiction to the Mosaic law, why would her decease be the occasion for an annual celebration or memorial in Holy Writ? Would not the people in revulsion have silently tried to forget it as best they could?

The fact that the "young women of Israel go out for four days to commemorate the daughter of Jephthah the Gileadite" (Judg 11:40) is not a biblical endorsement of this event. Nor does it say this event was observed throughout all Israel. But even if it were a national holiday, it came about by local or national custom and not by the word of God from his prophets or inspired leaders.

The tragedy of Jephthah's foolish and autocratic vow stands as a reminder to the perverseness of human wisdom when we fail to depend on the living God. In no way should we make Jephthah's action normative for believers who also have made foolish vows in the past and feel that now they must stick to their guns, as it were, because the Bible says Jephthah stuck to his vow. Just because something is described in Scripture does not mean God wants us to follow it. Only a direct word from God based in his character or authority can have that claim over our lives.

13:21-22 Who Is the Angel of the Lord?

See comment on JUDGES 6:22-23.

13:21-22 Seeing God?

See comment on EXODUS 33:18-23.

14:2-4 Samson's Marriage Was from the Lord?

God had clearly forbidden the Israelites to intermarry with the Canaanites (Ex 34:11-16; Deut 7:1-4). The Philistines, not technically listed as Canaanites, were actually cousins to the Egyptians (Gen 10:14). Nevertheless, it would seem that the principle of avoiding intermarriage would apply to the Philistines as well as to the Canaanites, since the rule was based not on race but on religion. Believers were not to marry unbelievers.

Furthermore, there is an ambiguity in verse 4. Who sought the occasion against the Philistines: God or Samson? The Hebrew text simply says "he." Some commentators, such as George Bush, J. K. F. Keil and Andrew Robert Fausset, take Samson as the intended reference; others, such as Dale Ralph Davis, Leon Wood and Luke Wiseman, make God the antecedent.

The story of Samson serves as the thematic climax to the book of Judges. The refrain of the book is "everyone did as he saw fit" or "everyone did what was right in his own eyes" (Judg 17:6; 21:25). The narrator of Judges uses the same refrain to describe Samson in chapter 14. A literal translation of verse 3 would render his demand as "Get her for me, for she is right in my eyes." Again, Judges 14:7 comments, "She was right in Samson's eyes" (NIV "he liked her"). In this respect, Samson was typical of his period of Israelite history—it was the day for doing one's own thing.

It is probably best to assume that the antecedent of *who* or *he* in Judges 14:4 is meant to be Yahweh, since to think otherwise would strain grammatical construction. Samson appears to be governed more by his glands than by any secret purpose on behalf of his nation. He was doing his own thing. The purpose was not his but God's.

But that will only seem to make the difficulty of this passage worse. How could the Lord go back on his own rules in order to accomplish some other goal, even a high purpose?

James Jordan argues that God was guiding Samson to move toward marriage, even though Samson was doing his own thing. The purpose of such a marriage, in Jordan's view, was evangelism. Had the nation of Philistia accepted the olive branch symbolized by this marriage and recognized that they were occupying Israel's land, the war would have ended. But instead, the riddle Samson put forth at the banquet (14:10-20) allowed the Philistines' true colors to show. Most of the Israelites had failed to see the domination of the Philistines for what it was; they needed to be stirred up. Since the Philistines were cousins to the Egyptians, the captivity of Israel to the Philistines was equivalent to captivity in Egypt. The lionlike Sphinx is the guardian of Egypt, and it was a lion that attacked Samson as he went down to Philistia.

But Jordan's argument seems obscure and depends too much on symbolism—especially since a particularly difficult theological issue has been raised. His solution seems contrived when judged from the standpoint of an outsider.

Better is the approach of Dale Ralph Davis. For him, the one who was seeking an occasion against the Philistines was Yahweh. But that does not mean God condoned everything Samson did or the way he did it. Says Davis, "Many Christian parents have stood in the sandals of Manoah and his wife. They have, though realizing their own sinful inadequacies, faithfully taught, prayed for, disciplined, and loved a son or a daughter only to see that child willfully turn from the way of the Lord. No one can deny it is anything but devastating. Yet one should not forget verse 4: 'But his father and mother did not realize it was from Yahweh.' What we don't know may yet prove to be our deepest comfort."[1]

The sin of Samson must not be attributed to the Lord, but the deliverance of the Israelites by Samson was from the

Lord. Remember, scriptural language frequently attributes directly to God what he merely permits.

Samson surely was directed by God to seek an occasion against the Philistines and to lead the Israelites in breaking out from under their yoke. But Samson did not take the time to inquire of the Lord how, or in what legitimate ways, he might do this. We do not find him asking, as his successor Samuel did, "Speak, Lord, for your servant is listening." Nor did he seek divine guidance when his parents questioned his seeking a bride among the Philistines. All that mattered was whether he was pleased—whether his choice was "right in his own eyes." Little wonder, then, that he would only begin to deliver Israel from the Philistines. Perhaps his potential for greatness was truncated by his vices, his partaking too deeply of the cultural appetites of his day.

My conclusion is that Samson was neither directed nor tempted by God to do what God had specifically prohibited in his Word. God wanted the defeat of the Philistines, but that did not give Samson carte blanche. Moreover, God's blessing on one or more aspects of a person's life is no indication that everything that person does is approved. Samson was plain bullheaded about this decision, and he refused to listen to his parents or to God. But neither Samson's foolishness nor his stubbornness would prevent the design of God from being fulfilled.

See also comment on GENESIS 50:19-21.

---

[1]Dale Ralph Davis, *Such a Great Salvation* (Grand Rapids, Mich.: Baker, 1990), p. 172.

17:1-2 A Thief Cursed and Then Blessed?

Here is a story that seems so mixed up and crazy that it easily raises as much embarrassment as anything else. What is happening in this densely packed exchange between mother and son?

One wonders where the writer's—or even God's—evaluation of things appears in this bizarre narrative. How can a mother curse a thief and then turn around and bless him when she finds out the culprit was her own son? Isn't thievery still wrong for all the Bible and its people? And how can God suddenly bless what was just cursed? What did the woman expect to happen? Why did she utter such a strange response upon learning that her money was in the hands of one of her own children?

The writer of the book of Judges wanted us to see that everything was out of control in Israel. Almost every aspect of this story discloses a violation of the will of God as he had revealed it to Israel.

Clearly the narrative is compressed and in a tightly woven form. Micah's mother, realizing that she had been swindled out of eleven hundred shekels of silver, responded with an oath. The effect of such an oath was not taken lightly in that culture, for once the word was uttered, it was as if it were an accomplished fact. It was not, as it often is in our culture, where someone might say something off the cuff and then quickly, or even later, retrieve it: "Aw, forget I said that; I didn't mean anything by it." The Israelites of Old Testament times believed that God monitored all speech and saw to it that vows, oaths and even idle words fulfilled their mission. Theirs was not a magical view of words, but they did know that talk is not cheap and words often carry consequences.

When Micah heard his mother cut loose with this oath, he immediately confessed that he was the thief. He obviously feared the consequences of the oath. It is doubtful that his mother had suspected her son and spoken her curse in his hearing deliberately. Probably she had been unaware of her son's presence. Curses were taken too seriously in those days for us to think otherwise.

Delighted to have the money back, the mother was not immediately concerned to ask Micah why he had stolen. On the contrary, she was now worried about reversing the effect of the curse she had invoked over her son's head. That is why she said, "The LORD bless you, my son." She hoped that this blessing would mitigate, if not nullify, the negative effect of the curse placed on Micah.

Now it must be made clear that the Bible only reports what happened here; it does not teach that any of this is normative or worth emulating. The narrative must be read in the context of the revelation of God up to this point.

At least six sins can be discovered in this story. First, the eighth commandment (Ex 20:15) is clear: "You shall not steal." Micah stole from his mother, and later the tribe of Dan stole his religious articles from his private sanctuary.

In the second place, Micah and his mother, wishing to buy some insurance, as it were, against God's carrying out her original oath, gave part of the money for the making of several images. This ran counter to the second commandment. But notice how dulled their theological senses were. How could they have expected God's blessing when they had substituted graven and molten images for the sovereign Lord of the universe?

Third, Micah established a private sanctuary in his home. God had said there was to be only one sanctuary for all the people, and that was at the tabernacle in Shiloh (Deut 12:4-14). God had promised to dwell there and place his name in a central sanctuary, not in individual tents or homes throughout Israel.

Then Micah made one of his sons his private priest, though God had said that only members of the family of Aaron in the tribe of Levi were to represent the people before the altar. Apparently that arrangement did not work out, and Micah then hired a Levite who had been wandering the countryside looking for work. Here again, Micah (and later the tribe of Dan) was still in violation of God's directive, for Aaron and his family were the sole legitimate priests.

When the tribe of Dan decided to leave the coastal plain, they committed the fifth sin in this narrative by moving from their allotted inheritance. They should have conquered the territory assigned to them rather than capitulating to the Philistines and moving north to the exposed city of Laish.

Finally, the movement of the Levite from his assigned city to work for Micah and then for the tribe of Dan shows that he was an opportunist. As a Levite, he would have had an assigned place to work. Instead of remaining there, he determined to make his own way in the world; as a result a number of people were impacted by his sin.

Neither the story nor the times are pretty; but this account is entirely realistic, and its implied warning is instructive. We should not doubt in the darkness what God has already told us in the light.

RUTH

3:7-9 What Happened on the Threshing Floor?

Some commentators on this text have suggested that Ruth's bold move that night on the threshing floor went beyond the normal boundaries of propriety and included sexual relations with Boaz. Their argument is that harvest time the world over is a time of celebration of the rites of fertility. At these times the ancients allowed themselves more license than usual. During this harvest celebration, then, after Boaz had imbibed enough wine to make himself drunk, Ruth approached him in order to force him into marriage.

Others have interpreted Boaz's "feet" as a sexual euphemism for the male reproductive organ. If this were the meaning, then the story would be making a discreet reference to fleshly indulgence.

But these suggestions are unnecessary; it seems that the author chose his words carefully so as to avoid any possible innuendo.

To begin with, it is extremely unlikely that Boaz was drunk after the good meal he had eaten. The text simply says that he "was in good spirits." His mood was mellow, and his demeanor was upbeat. And why not? He had the results of all his hard labor right there on the threshing floor with him. But his feasting brought on drowsiness, so he retired to one side of the pile of grain that had been threshed. It is doubtful that he would have guarded this pile of grain by himself, that there would have been no other workers present who would awaken at the crack of dawn to get back to work alongside him.

Later, after Boaz had fallen asleep, Ruth went and carefully uncovered his feet and apparently crawled under his cover, lying perpendicular to his feet. There are no sexual overtones in the reference to his feet, for Boaz was startled at midnight when his feet suddenly touched the woman's body.

Ruth immediately made her objective clear when she requested, "Spread the corner of your garment over me." She was using the accepted idiom meaning "Marry me"—other passages in which the same expression is used are Ezekiel 16:8, Deuteronomy 22:30 and 27:20, and Malachi 2:16. No doubt the idiom reflected the custom, still practiced by some Arabs, of a man's throwing a garment over the woman he has decided to take as his wife. The gesture is a symbol of protection as well as a declaration that the man is willing to enter into sexual consummation with his chosen partner.

Boaz had prayed in Ruth 2:12 that Ruth might be rewarded by the Lord under whose wings she had taken refuge. Ruth now essentially asked Boaz to answer his own prayer, for "garment-cover" and "wing" are from a similar root in Hebrew.

Ruth's reason for this action is expressed in her appeal to Boaz as a "kinsman-redeemer." That is a legal status. Under Jewish law, then, her request was not particularly unusual.

That Boaz handled himself honorably can be seen in his revelation that there was someone who actually had prior claim over Ruth and her inheritance, since he was a closer relative. However, if he should prove unwilling to take responsibility in the matter (and he was), then Boaz would marry Ruth.

Remarkably, Ruth seems willing to marry even this other relative sight unseen, again subordinating her own happiness to her duty of raising up an heir to her deceased husband and to Naomi. In doing so she demonstrates again why this book singles her out as a most worthy example of what Proverbs 31 refers to as a "virtuous woman" or a person "of noble character."

The charges against Ruth and Boaz are false and without foundation. While the couple's encounter did occur in the context of darkness and sleep, the text does not present their behavior as morally questionable or even particularly abnormal within the social and moral conventions of the godly remnant of those days.

1 SAMUEL

1:1 Was Samuel a Levite or an Ephraimite?

See comment on 1 CHRONICLES 6:16.

1:11 Was Hannah Right to Bargain with God?

Is the desperate prayer of Hannah for a son a legitimate way to approach God, or is it a bad example of trying to bargain with God?

Hannah's prayer has no more the ill sense of bargaining with God than many of our prayers. While it is true that we can abuse the privilege that we have of direct access to the throne of God to make our requests known, it is God who will judge the propriety and motivation of each prayer, not any mortal.

What is surprising is to notice the same directness of access and the simplicity with which this woman, who is part of the fellowship of the many barren women in the Bible, makes her request known to God. There is no demanding or threatening here. Her prayer is not formal, contrived or ritualistic. It is as direct as any might wish it to be. If only God would look, if only he would remember her and if only he would give her a son, she vowed that she would not grow proud, forgetful or ungrateful; on the contrary, she would give this son (she never considered that it might be a girl) back to God.

God was not obligated to answer her. But the fact that he did indicates that he judged her motives to be right and her request appropriate.

2:25 Did God Prevent Eli's Sons from Repenting?

In what way was it God's will to put Eli's sons to death? Does this mean that God actually intervened in some way to make sure that Hophni and Phinehas never repented and were therefore condemned to die? How free were the wills of these two priestly sons of the high priest, Eli, in this regard?

The Lord can both reverse the fortunes of the poor and rich (1 Sam 2:6) and confirm the hardness of heart of the rebellious and reprobate (1 Sam 2:25).

The hapless Eli, now in his advanced

years, had more than he could contend with in his two strong-willed sons. To their earlier callous treatment of the Israelites who came bringing offerings to the house of God (1 Sam 2:13-16) the men now added sexual promiscuity (1 Sam 2:22; compare Ex 38:8). Such ritual prostitution, as practiced among their Canaanite neighbors, was strictly forbidden in Israel (Num 25:1-5; Deut 23:17; Amos 2:7-8).

Eli finally challenged the riotous and autocratic conduct of his two sons, but the rebuke fell on deaf ears: the men were determined to do what they were determined to do (1 Sam 2:25). What followed, then, was another instance of divine judicial hardening. Just as the Pharaoh of Israel's oppression in Egypt defiantly refused any invitations to repent, even though God mercifully sent him one plague after another as a sign to that same effect, so God had finally decided in this case that he would end Eli's sons' lives: the decision was irrevocable.

Was this unfair or sudden? Hardly. God must have been calling these men to change for many years, but they, like Pharaoh, squandered these times of mercy and opportunities for change until time was no longer available. Moreover, the double jeopardy rule was in vogue here, for those who serve in the ministry of the things of God are doubly accountable, both for themselves and for those who look up to them for teaching and example (Jas 3:1). They had thereby sinned against the Lord. If the case seems to draw more judgment more swiftly, then let the fact that these men were under the double jeopardy rule be factored in and the appropriateness of the action will be more than vindicated.

See also comment on EXODUS 9:12.

6:19 Death for Just Looking into the Ark?

See comment on 2 SAMUEL 6:6-7.

8—12 Did God Want Israel to Have a King?

What makes this section a hard saying is not the fact that it contains what some have unfairly labeled the ramblings of a disappointed prophet. Instead, it is the fact that up until very recent times, most nonevangelical Old Testament scholars strongly believed that they detected an ambivalent attitude toward kingship in the narratives of 1 Samuel 8—12, in light of the covenantal tone of 1 Samuel 11:14—12:25.

It has been fairly common to find 1 Samuel 8—12 characterized as a collection of independent story units or tradition complexes, some being promonarchial and others antimonarchial. This division was supposedly evidenced in different attitudes and responses to the idea of a monarchy and kingship in Israel. Generally an antimonarchial orientation was attributed to 1 Samuel 8:1-21, 10:17-27 and 12:1-25, while a promonarchial stance was seen in 1 Samuel 9:1—10:16 and 11:1-15. Endorsing this analysis of the material would leave us with a dilemma: how could Scripture both approve and reprove the concept of a monarchy?

A second problem in the debate surrounding 1 Samuel 8—12 is the sequencing of events presented in the book. It has been widely alleged that the present sequence is an artificial device imposed by a late editor as a result of the growth of tradition.

Finally, many scholars have said that the antimonarchial sections show indications of editorial revisions arising from Deuteronomic influence; this argument is based on a late dating of Deuteronomy in the postexilic period of the fifth or fourth century B.C.

Each of these three allegations must be answered. There is no doubt that a tension of sorts does exist in the narratives of 1 Samuel 8—12. The prospect of establishing a kingship in Israel elicited numerous reservations, and these are fairly aired in 1 Samuel 8:1-21, 10:17-27 and 12:1-25.

Yet it cannot be forgotten that kingship was also within the direct plan and permission of God. God had divulged that part of his plan as far back as the days of Moses (Deut 17:14-20). Accordingly, when Samuel presented Saul to the people, it was as the one whom the Lord had chosen (1 Sam 10:24). Saul's appointment was the outcome of the twice-repeated guidance that Samuel received: "Listen to all that the people are saying" (1 Sam 8:7, 22). In fact, 1 Samuel 12:13 specifically says, "See, the LORD has set a king over you."

But here is the important point. These five chapters of 1 Samuel cannot be neatly divided into two contrasting sets of narratives; the ambivalence is present even within the units that have been labeled as corresponding to one side or the other! The problem, in fact, is to explain this ambivalence at all. What is the cause for this love-hate attitude toward kingship in Israel?

My answer is the same as Robert Vannoy's.[1] It is the covenantal relationship expressed in 1 Samuel 11:14—12:25 that explains this ambivalence. The issue, then, is not the presence of kingship so much as it is the *kind* of kingship and the *reasons* for wanting a monarchy.

There is no question but that the presence of a king in Israel was fully compatible with Yahweh's covenant with Israel. What hurt Samuel and the Lord was the people's improper motive for requesting a king in the first place: they wanted to "be like all the other nations" (8:20) and have a king to lead them when they went out to fight. This was tantamount to breaking the covenant and rejecting Yahweh as their Sovereign (8:7; 10:19). To act in this manner was to forget God's provision for them in the past. Hadn't he protected them and gone before them in battle many times?

Since the people were so unfaithful in their motivation for desiring a king, it was necessary to warn them about "the manner of the king" (literal translation of *mišpaṭ hammelek*—8:11). If what the people wanted was a contemporary form of monarchy, then they had better get used to all the abuses and problems of kingship as well as its splendor.

Five serious problems with the contemporary forms of kingship are cited in 1 Samuel 8:11-18. That these issues were real can be attested by roughly contemporaneous documents from Alalakh and Ugarit.[2] The problems they would experience would include a military draft, the servitude of the populace, widespread royal confiscation of private property, taxation and loss of personal liberty.

This delineation of "the manner of the king" served to define the function of kings in the ancient Near East. But over against this was the gathering that took place at Mizpah (1 Sam 10:17-27). Here Samuel described "the manner of the kingdom" (literal translation of *mišpaṭ hammᵉlukâh*—10:25). In so doing Samuel began to resolve the tension between Israel's improper reasons for desiring a king, their misconceptions of the king's role and function, and Yahweh's purpose in saying that he also desired Israel to have a king. Samuel's definition of "the manner of the kingdom" clearly distinguished Israelite kingship from the kingship that was practiced in the surrounding nations of that day.

In Israel, the king's role was to be compatible with Yahweh's sovereignty over the nation and also with all the laws, prescriptions and obligations of the covenant given to the people under Moses' leadership. Thus "the manner of the kingdom" was to be normative for the nation of Israel rather than "the manner of the king."

The issue of the sequencing of the narratives is less difficult. Given the tensions of the time—the various attitudes toward kingship and the legitimacy of establishing it—one can easily see how the text does reflect the back-and-forth unfolding of the process at various geographic locations and on different days. Each phase of the negotiations dramatized the seesaw nature of this battle between those holding out for the sovereignty of Yahweh and those wanting a more visible and contemporaneous model of kingship.

The most critical problem in connection with the sequencing of the events is the relationship between 1 Samuel 11:14-15 and 1 Samuel 10:17-27, particularly in connection with the statement in 1 Samuel 11:14, "Come, let us go to Gilgal and there *reaffirm* the kingship."

This phrase constitutes the most compelling evidence for the argument that several accounts have been put together in these chapters. The simplest, and best, explanation for the meaning of this debated phrase, however, is that the reference is not to Saul, but to a renewal of allegiance to Yahweh and his covenant. It is a call for the renewal ceremony that is described in greater detail in 1 Samuel 12. This explanation makes the most sense and makes possible the best harmonization of the parallel accounts of Saul's accession to the throne in 1 Samuel 10:17-27 and 11:15.

The third and final objection concerns the alleged Deuteronomic influence on the so-called antimonarchial sections. Bear in mind that those who raise this objection also date Deuteronomy to the fifth or fourth century B.C. rather than attributing it to Moses as it properly should be.

Their argument runs into several problems of its own. Long ago Julius Wellhausen (1844-1918) noted its basic flaw: for all of Deuteronomy's alleged antimonarchial views, it had put forth a positive "law of the king" (Deut 17:14-20) long before any of the Israelites thought of having a king! Furthermore, the pictures of David, Hezekiah and Josiah in 1 and 2 Kings (other books often alleged to be Deuteronomic in viewpoint and influence) were likewise promonarchial.

There is no doubt that Deuteronomy had a profound influence on the events described in 1 Samuel 8—12, but none of them can be shown to have resulted from a late editorializing based on an exilic or postexilic revisionist view of how kingship had come about in Israel.

Thus we conclude that none of these three problems can be used as evidence for a lack of unity, coherence or singularity of viewpoint. Most important of all, the covenantal perspective of 1 Samuel 11:14—12:25 provides the best basis for the unity and historical trustworthiness of these accounts as they are know today.

[1]Robert Vannoy, *Covenant Renewal at Gilgal* (Cherry Hill, N.J.: Mack Publishing, 1978), p. 228.

[2]I. Mendelson, "Samuel's Denunciation of Kingship in Light of Akkadian Documents from Ugarit," *Bulletin of the American Schools of Oriental Research* 143 (1956): 17.

13:13-14 Would God Have Established Saul's Kingdom?

How was it possible for Samuel to say that Saul's house could have had perpetuity over Israel when Genesis 49:10 had promised it to the tribe of Judah (not Benjamin, from which Saul hailed) long before Saul's reign or downfall? Of course, the Lord had planned to place a king over Israel, as Deuteronomy 17:14 had clearly taught. But if the family that was to wield the scepter was from Judah, how could God—in retrospect, to Saul's disappointment—say that Saul could indeed have been that king?

The solution to this problem is not to be found in Samuel's vacillating attitudes toward Saul, for it is clear that Saul was also God's choice from the very beginning (1 Sam 9:16; 10:1, 24; 12:13).

The Lord had allowed the choice of the people to fall on one whose external attributes made an immediate positive impression on people. Saul's was strictly an earthly kingdom, with all the pageantry and showmanship that impress mortals.

Unfortunately, Saul was not disposed to rule in humble submission to the laws, ordinances and commandments that came from above. As one final evidence of his attitude, he had refused to wait for the appointment he had made with Samuel. As he went ahead and took over the duties of a priest, in violation of his kingly position, God decided that he would not keep his appointment with him as king.

The type of kingship Samuel had instituted under the direction of God was distinctive. It was a theocracy; the Israelite monarchy was to function under the authority and sovereignty of Yahweh himself. When this covenantal context was violated, the whole "manner of the kingdom" (1 Sam 10:25) was undermined.

While this explanation may suffice for what happened in the "short haul," how shall we address the issue of God's having promised the kingship to the family of Judah, rather than to the Benjamite family of Kish? Would God have actually given Saul's family a portion or all of the nation, had Saul listened and kept the commandments of God? Or did the writer, and hence God also, regard the two southern tribes of Judah and Benjamin as one? In that case, perhaps what had been promised to Judah could have gone to Saul just as easily as to David.

There is evidence from Scripture itself that the tribes of Benjamin and Judah were regarded as one tribe: 1 Kings 11:36 says, "I will give one tribe to [Solomon's] son so that David my servant may always have a lamp before me in Jerusalem." If these two could later be regarded as "one," no objection can be made to doing so earlier.

Ultimately, this is one of those questions that are impossible to resolve fully, since we are asking for information that belongs to the mind of God. However, it seems important that we be able to offer several possible solutions.

Another possible solution is that it may well have been that God fully intended that Judah, and eventually the house of David, would rule over Israel and Judah. But it is also possible that Saul's family would have been given the northern ten tribes of Israel after the division of the kingdom, which God in his omniscience of course could anticipate. That would resolve the question just as easily.

The best suggestion, however, is that God had agreed to appoint Saul king in deference to the people's deep wishes. Though the Lord had consented, this was not his directive will; he merely permitted it to happen. Eventually, what the Lord knew all along was proved true: Saul had a character flaw that precipitated his demise. Nevertheless, it is possible to describe Saul in terms of what he could have been, barring that flaw, in the kingdom of God and the kingdom of the Israelites.

A combination of these last two views is possible—that in his permissive will God would have given Saul the northern ten tribes in perpetuity without denying to the house of Judah the two southern tribes, according to his promise in Genesis 49:10. An interesting confirmation of this possibility can be seen in 1 Kings 11:38, where King Jeroboam is promised an enduring dynasty, in a parallel to the promise God had made to King David.

Since the promise to Jeroboam in no way replaced the long-standing promise to the tribe of Judah and the house of David, it is similar to God's "might-have-been" to Saul. God offered the ten northern tribes to Jeroboam just as he had offered them to Saul.

One final possibility is that Saul was given a genuine, though hypothetical, promise of a perpetual dynasty over (northern) Israel. However, the Lord surely knew that Saul would not measure up to the challenge set before him. God had chosen Saul because he wanted him to serve as a negative example in contrast to David, whose behavior was so different. This, then, set the stage for the introduction of the legitimate kingship as God had always intended it.

See also comment on 1 SAMUEL 8—12.

15:11 Does God Change His Mind?

See comment on GENESIS 6:6; 1 SAMUEL 15:29.

15:18 Completely Destroy Them!

A chief objection to the view that the God of the Old Testament is a God of love and mercy is the divine command to exterminate all the men, women and children belonging to the seven or eight Canaanite nations. How could God approve of blanket destruction, of the genocide of an entire group of people?

Attempts to tone down the command or to mitigate its stark reality fail from the start. God's instructions are too clear, and too many texts speak of consigning whole populations to destruction: Exodus 23:32-33; 34:11-16; and Deuteronomy 7:1-5; 20:16-18.

In most of these situations, a distinctive Old Testament concept known as *ḥerem* is present. It means "curse," "that which stood under the ban" or "that which was dedicated to destruction." The root idea of this term was "separation"; however, this situation was not the positive concept of sanctification in which someone or something was set aside for the service and glory of God. This was the opposite side of the same coin: to set aside or separate for destruction.

God dedicated these things or persons to destruction because they violently and steadfastly impeded or opposed his work over a long period of time. This "dedication to destruction" was not used frequently in the Old Testament. It was reserved for the spoils of southern Canaan (Num 21:2-3), Jericho (Josh 6:21), Ai (Josh 8:26), Makedah (Josh 10:28) and Hazor (Josh 11:11).

In a most amazing prediction, Abraham was told that his descendants would be exiled and mistreated for four hundred years (in round numbers for 430 years) before God would lead them out of that country. The reason for so long a delay, Genesis 15:13-16 explains, was that "the sin of the Amorites [the Canaanites] has not yet reached its full measure." Thus, God waited for centuries while the Amalekites and those other Canaanite groups slowly filled up their own cups of condemnation by their sinful behavior. God never acted precipitously against them; his grace and mercy waited to see if they would repent and turn from their headlong plummet into self-destruction.

Not that the conquering Israelites were without sin. Deuteronomy 9:5 makes that clear to the Israelites: "It is not because of your righteousness or your integrity that you are going in to take possession of their land; but on account of the wickedness of these nations."

These nations were cut off to prevent the corruption of Israel and the rest of the world (Deut 20:16-18). When a nation starts burning children as a gift to the gods (Lev 18:21) and practices sodomy, bestiality and all sorts of loathsome vices (Lev 18:25, 27-30), the day of God's grace and mercy has begun to run out.

Just as surgeons do not hesitate to amputate a gangrenous limb, even if they cannot help cutting off some healthy flesh, so God must do the same. This is not doing evil that good may come; it is removing the cancer that could infect all of society and eventually destroy the remaining good.

God could have used pestilence, hurricanes, famine, diseases or anything else he wanted. In this case he chose to use Israel to reveal his power, but the charge of cruelty against God is no more deserved in this case than it is in the general order of things in the world where all of these same calamities happen.

In the providential acts of life, it is understood that individuals share in the life of their families and nations. As a result we as individuals participate both in our families' and nations' rewards and in their punishments. Naturally this will involve some so-called innocent people; however, even that argument involves us in a claim to omniscience which we do not possess. If the women and children had been spared in those profane Canaanite nations, how long would it have been before a fresh crop of adults would emerge just like their pagan predecessors?

Why was God so opposed to the Amalekites? When the Israelites were struggling through the desert toward Canaan, the Amalekites picked off the weak, sick and elderly at the end of the line of marchers and brutally murdered these stragglers. Warned Moses, "Remember what the Amalekites did to you along the way when you came out of Egypt. When you were weary and worn out, they met you on your journey and cut off all who were lagging behind; they had no fear of God" (Deut 25:17-18).

Some commentators note that the Amalekites were not merely plundering or disputing who owned what territories; they were attacking God's chosen people to discredit the living God. Some trace the Amalekites' adamant hostility all through the Old Testament, including the most savage butchery of all in Haman's proclamation that all Jews throughout the Persian Empire could be massacred on a certain day (Esther 3:8-11). Many make a case that Haman was an Amalekite. His actions then would ultimately reveal this nation's deep hatred for God, manifested toward the people through whom God had chosen to bless the whole world.

In Numbers 25:16-18 and 31:1-18 Israel was also told to conduct a war of extermination against all in Midian, with the exception of the prepubescent girls, because the Midianites had led them into idolatry and immorality. It was not contact with foreigners per se that was the problem, but the threat to Israel's relationship with the Lord. The divine command, therefore, was to break Midian's strength by killing all the male children and also the women who had slept with a man and who could still become mothers.

The texts of Deuteronomy 2:34; 3:6; 7:1-2 and Psalm 106:34 are further examples of the principle of *ḥerem,* dedicating the residents of Canaan to total destruction as an involuntary offering to God.

See also comment on NUMBERS 25:7-13; 2 KINGS 6:21-23.

15:22 Does the Lord Delight in Sacrifices?

Though some texts call for burnt offerings or daily offerings to God (for example, Ex 29:18, 36; Lev 1—7), others appear to disparage any sacrifices, just as 1 Samuel 15:22 seems to do. How do we reconcile this seeming contradiction?

God derives very little satisfaction from the external act of sacrificing. In fact, he complains, "I have no need of a bull from your stall or of goats from your pens. . . . If I were hungry I would not tell you, for the world is mine, and all that is in it" (Ps 50:9, 12).

Indeed, David learned this same lesson the hard way. After his sin with Bathsheba and the rebuke of Nathan the prophet, David confessed, "The sacrifices of God are a broken spirit; a broken and contrite heart, O God, you will not despise" (Ps 51:17). After the priority of the heart attitude had been corrected, it was possible for David to say, "Then there will be righteous sacrifices, whole burnt offerings to delight you; then bulls will be offered on your altar" (Ps 51:19).

Samuel's harangue seconds the message of the writing prophets: Perfunctory acts of worship and ritual, apart from diligent obedience, were basically worthless both to God and to the individual.

This is why the prophet Isaiah rebuked his nation for their empty ritualism. What good, he lamented, were all the sacrifices, New Moon festivals, sabbaths, convocations and filing into the temple of God? So worthless was all this feverish activity that God said he was fed up with it all (Is 1:11-15). What was needed, instead, was a whole new heart attitude as the proper preparation for meeting God. Warned Isaiah, " 'Wash and make yourselves clean. . . . Come now, let us reason together,' says the LORD. 'Though your sins are like scarlet, they shall be as white as snow; though they are red as crimson, they shall be like wool' " (Is 1:16, 18). Then real sacrifices could be offered to God.

Jeremiah records the same complaint: "Your burnt offerings are not acceptable; your sacrifices do not please me" (Jer 6:20). So deceptive was the nation's trust in this hollow worship that Jeremiah later announced that God had wanted more than sacrifices when he brought Israel out of Egypt (Jer 7:22). He had wanted the people to trust him. It was always tempting to substitute attendance at God's house, heartless worship or possessing God's Word for active response to that Word (Jer 7:9-15, 21-26; 8:8-12).

No less definitive were the messages of Hosea (Hos 6:6) and Micah (Mic 6:6-8). The temptation to externalize religion and to use it only in emergency situations was altogether too familiar.

Samuel's rebuke belongs to the same class of complaints. It was couched in poetry, as some of those listed above were, and it also had a proverbial form. The moral truth it conveys must be understood comparatively. Often a proverb was stated in terms that call for setting priorities. Accordingly one must read an implied "this first and then that." These "better" wisdom sayings, of course, directly point to such a priority. What does not follow is that what is denied, or not called "better," is thereby rejected by God. Arguing on those grounds would ignore the statement's proverbial structure.

God does approve of sacrificing, but he does not wish to have it at the expense of full obedience to his Word or as a substitute for a personal relationship of love and trust. Sacrifices, however, were under the Old Testament economy. Animal sacrifices are no longer necessary today, because Christ was our sacrifice, once for all (Heb 10:1-18). Nevertheless, the principle remains the same: What is the use of performing outward acts of religion if that religious activity is not grounded in an obedient heart of faith? True religious affection for God begins with the heart and not in acts of worship or the accompanying vestments and ritual!

See also comment on PSALM 51:16-17, 19.

15:29 God Does Not Change His Mind?

Here in 1 Samuel 15 we have a clear statement about God's truthfulness and unchanging character. But elsewhere in the Old Testament we read of God repenting or changing his mind. Does God change his mind? If so, does that discredit his truthfulness or his unchanging character? If not, what do these other Old Testament texts mean?

It can be affirmed from the start that God's essence and character, his resolute determination to punish sin and to reward virtue, are unchanging (see Mal 3:6). These are absolute and unconditional affirmations that Scripture everywhere teaches. But this does not mean that all his promises and warnings are unconditional. Many turn on either an expressed or an implied condition.

The classic example of this conditional teaching is Jeremiah 18:7-10: "If at any time I announce that a nation or kingdom is to be uprooted, torn down and destroyed, and if that nation I warned repents of its evil, then I will relent and not inflict on it the disaster I had planned. And if at another time I announce that a nation or kingdom is to be built up and planted, and if it does evil in my sight and does not obey me, then I will reconsider the good I had intended to do for it."

This principle clearly states the condition underlying most of God's promises and threats, even when it is not made explicit, as in the case of Jonah. Therefore, whenever God does not fulfill a promise or execute a threat that he has made, the explanation is obvious: in all of these cases, the change has not come in God, but in the individual or nation.

Of course some of God's promises are unconditional for they rest solely on his mercy and grace. These would be: his covenant with the seasons after Noah's flood (Gen 8:22); his promise of salvation in the oft-repeated covenant to Abraham, Isaac, Jacob and David; his promise of the new covenant; and his promise of the new heaven and the new earth.

So what, then, was the nature of the change in God that 1 Samuel 15:11 refers to when he says, "I am grieved that I have made Saul king, because he has turned away from me and has not carried out my instructions"? If God is unchangeable, why did he "repent" or "grieve over" the fact that he had made Saul king?

God is not a frozen automaton who cannot respond to persons; he is a living person who can and does react to others as much, and more genuinely, than we do to each other. Thus the same word *repent* is used for two different concepts both in this passage and elsewhere in the Bible. One shows God's responsiveness to individuals and the other shows his steadfastness to himself and to his thoughts and designs.

Thus the text affirms that God changed his actions toward Saul in order to remain true to his own character or essence. Repentance in God is not, as it is in us, an evidence of indecisiveness. It is rather a change in his method of responding to another person based on some change in the other individual. The change, then, was in Saul. The problem was with Saul's partial obedience, his wayward heart and covetousness.

To assert that God is unchanging does not mean he cannot experience regret, grief and repentance. If unchangeableness meant transcendent detachment from people and events, God would pay an awful price for immutability. Instead, God enters into a relationship with mortal beings that demonstrates his willingness to respond to each person's action within the ethical sphere of their obedience to his will.

When our sin or repentance changes our relationship with God, his changing responses to us no more affect his essential happiness or blessedness than Christ's deity affected his ability to genuinely suffer on the cross for our sin.

See also comment on GENESIS 6:6; JONAH 4:1-2.

16:1-3 Does God Authorize Deception?

On the face of it, God appears to be telling Samuel to lie or, at the very least, to be deceptive. Is this an indication that under certain circumstances God approves of lying in order to accomplish some higher good?

It is always wrong to tell a lie. Never does the Scripture give us grounds for telling either a lie or a half-truth. The reason for this is because God is true and his nature is truth itself. Anything less than this is a denial of him as God.

But what about the divine advice given to Samuel in this text when he objects to anointing David when Saul was already so jealous that he would kill the prophet Samuel should he be so presumptuous as to anoint someone else in his place? Is God's advice a mere "pretext" as some commentators conclude? Or is it tacit approval for persons in a tight spot to lie?

The most important word in this connection is the word *how.* Samuel did not question whether he should go or even if he should anoint the one God had in mind; he just wanted to know how such a feat could be carried out. The divine answer was that he was to take a sacrifice and that would serve as a legitimate answer to Saul, or any other inquirer, as to what he was doing in those parts, so obviously out of his regular circuit of places to minister. He was there to offer a sacrifice. Should Saul have encountered Samuel and asked him what he was doing in those parts at that time, Samuel could correctly answer, "I have come to sacrifice to the LORD."

Some will complain that this is a half-truth. And isn't a half-truth the same as speaking or acting out a lie? It is at this point where the discussion of John Murray[1] is so helpful. Murray observed that Saul had forfeited his right to know *all* the truth, but that did not mean that Samuel, or anyone else for that matter, ever had, or has, the right to tell a lie. Everything that Samuel spoke had to be the truth. But Samuel was under no moral obligation in this situation to come forth with everything that he knew. Only when there are those who have a right to know and we deliberately withhold part or all of the information does it qualify as a lie or does the half-truth become the living or telling of a lie.

We use this principle in life when a young child prematurely asks us for the facts of life or a sick or elderly person inquires of a medical doctor what is wrong with them and if they will get well. The answer in all these cases is to answer truthfully without elaborating on those details which the person is not ready for by reason of their age or the possible impact it might have on their desire to rally and get well.

Some may complain that this seems to be saying that we cannot deceive anyone in our *words,* but that we have the right to deceive them through our *actions.* This is not what I am saying. It was God's right to give Samuel a second mission, the offering of a sacrifice, which was not a deception, but a routine act he performed. Saul did not have the right to know all the other actions Samuel would perform while carrying out that mission—God does not "deceive" us when he does not choose to disclose all that he knows!

The only exceptions to this rule against deception are to be found in war zones or in playing sports. For example, nations that engage in war count on the fact that some of the movements of the enemy will be carried out to deliberately mislead and throw their opposition off balance. Likewise, if I go into a football huddle and the team captain says, "Now, Kaiser, I want you to run a fake pattern around right end pretending you have the ball," I do not object by saying, "Oh, no you don't; give me the ball or nothing. I'm an evangelical and I have a reputation for honesty to protect." It is part of the sport that there will be accepted types of dissimulation that take place.

Truth is always required in every other situation. Only when someone forfeits that right to know everything may I withhold information; but under no circumstances may I speak an untruth. Thus when the Nazis of the Third Reich in Germany during World War II were asking if someone was hiding Jews, the correct procedure would have been to say as little as possible, all of which had to be true, while carefully hiding those Jews as best as one could.

See also comment on EXODUS 1:15-21; 3:18; JOSHUA 2:4-6.

---

[1]John Murray, *Principles of Conduct: Aspects of Biblical Ethics* (Grand Rapids, Mich.: Eerdmans, 1957), pp. 139-41.

16:10-11 Did Jesse Have Seven or Eight Sons?

See comment on 1 CHRONICLES 2:13-15.

16:14 An Evil Spirit from the Lord?

Just as the prophet Samuel anointed David as the next king, King Saul became bereft of the Spirit of God and fell into ugly bouts of melancholia, which were attributed to an evil spirit sent from the Lord.

The Spirit of God had overwhelmed Saul when he had assumed the role of king over the land (1 Sam 10:6, 10; 11:6). Exactly what the Spirit's presence with Saul entailed is not explained, but it seems to have included the gift of government, the gift of wisdom and prudence in civil matters, and a spirit of fortitude and courage. These gifts can be extrapolated from the evidence that after Saul was anointed king, he immediately shed his previous shyness and reticence to be in the public eye. It is obvious that Saul did not have a natural aptitude for governing, for if he had, why did he hide among the baggage when he knew already what the outcome would be? But when the Spirit of God came upon him in connection with the threatened mutilation of the citizens of Jabesh Gilead (1 Sam 11), and Saul sent out word that all able-bodied men were to report immediately for battle, the citizens of Israel were so startled that this had come from the likes of Saul that they showed up in force. God had suddenly gifted him with the "Spirit of God" (1 Sam 11:6), and Saul was a great leader for twenty years (1 Sam 14:47-48).

But all of this was lost as suddenly as it had been gained—the Spirit had removed his gift of government.

But what was the evil spirit mentioned here and in 1 Samuel 18:10 and 19:9? The ancient historian Josephus explained it as follows: "But as for Saul, some strange and demonical disorders came upon him, and brought upon him such suffocations as were ready to choke him" (*Antiquities* 6.8.2). Keil and Delitzsch likewise attributed Saul's problem to demon possession. They specified that this

> was not merely an inward feeling of depression at the rejection announced to him, . . . but a higher evil power, which took possession of him, and not only deprived him of his peace of mind, but stirred up the feelings, ideas, imagination, and thoughts of his soul to such an extent that at

times it drove him even into madness. This demon is called "an evil spirit [coming] from Jehovah" because Jehovah sent it as a punishment.[1]

A second suggestion is that this evil spirit was a messenger, by analogy with the situation in 1 Kings 22:20-23. This unspecified messenger did his work by the permission of God.

A third suggestion is that this evil spirit was a "spirit of discontent" created in Saul's heart by God because of his continued disobedience.

Whatever the malady was, and whatever its source, one of the temporary cures for its torments was music. David's harp-playing would soothe Saul's frenzied condition, so that he would once again gain control of his emotions and actions (1 Sam 16:14-23).

All this happened by the permission of God rather than as a result of his directive will, for God cannot be the author of anything evil. But the exact source of Saul's torment cannot be determined with any degree of certitude. The Lord may well have used a messenger, or even just an annoying sense of disquietude and discontent. Yet if Saul really was a believer—and I think there are enough evidences to affirm that he was—then it is difficult to see how he could have been possessed by a demon. Whether believers can be possessed by demons, however, is still being debated by theologians.

[1]Johann Karl Friedrich Keil and Franz Delitzsch, *Biblical Commentary on the Books of Samuel* (Grand Rapids, Mich.: Eerdmans, 1950), p. 170.

17:12-14 Did Jesse Have Seven or Eight Sons?

See comment on 1 CHRONICLES 2:13-15.

17:49 Who Killed Goliath?

In 1 Samuel 17 and 21:9 it is claimed that David is the one who killed Goliath; however, in 2 Samuel 21:19 it says that Elhanan killed him. Both cannot be right, can they? And who was Lahmi, mentioned in 1 Chronicles 20:5?

While some have tried to resolve the contradiction by suggesting that Elhanan may be a throne name for David, a reference to David, under any name, in a summary of exploits by David's mighty men appears most peculiar.

The bottom line on this whole dispute is that David is the one who slew Goliath and Elhanan slew the brother of Goliath, as it says in 1 Chronicles 20:5. The problem, then, is with the 2 Samuel 21:19 text. Fortunately, however, we can trace what the original wording for that text was through the correctly preserved text in 1 Chronicles 20:5.

The copyist of the 2 Samuel 21:19 text made three mistakes: (1) He read the direct object sign that comes just before the name of the giant that Elhanan killed, namely Lahmi, as if it were the word "Beth," thereby getting "the Bethlehemite," when the "Beth" was put with "Lahmi." (2) He also misread the word for "brother" (Hebrew *'āḥ*) as the direct object sign (Hebrew *'eṯ*) before Goliath, thereby making Goliath the one who was killed, since he was now the direct object of the verb, instead, as it should have been, "the brother of Goliath." (3) He misplaced the word "Oregim," meaning "weavers," so that it yielded "Elhanan son of Jaare-Oregim," a most improbable reading for anyone: "Elhanan the son of the forests of weavers." The word for "weavers" should come as it does in 1 Chronicles 20:5 about the spear being "a beam/shaft like a weaver's rod."[1]

Elhanan gets the credit for killing Lahmi, the brother of Goliath; but David remains the hero who killed Goliath.

[1]See J. Barton Payne, "1 Chronicles," in *The Expositor's Bible Commentary*, vol. 4, ed. Frank E. Gaebelein (Grand Rapids, Mich.: Zondervan, 1988), pp. 403-4;

Gleason L. Archer, *Encyclopedia of Bible Difficulties* (Grand Rapids, Mich.: Zondervan, 1982), pp. 178-79.

17:55-58 Why Did Saul Ask David's Identity?

Saul's questions about the identity of David in 1 Samuel 17 create a rather difficult problem in light of 1 Samuel 16, especially 1 Samuel 16:14-23. It would appear from chapter 16 that by the time of David's slaying of Goliath Saul had already been introduced to David and knew him quite well.

The traditional way of resolving this dilemma in nonevangelical circles is to suppose that these two accounts stem from independent traditions. Thus the confusion over whether David's debut at court preceded his conquest of the Philistine is unnecessary, since the stories come from different sources and do not intend to reflect what really happened so much as teach a truth. However, this resolution of the matter is not attractive to most who take the claims of the Bible more straightforwardly. The difficulty continues: how could Saul—and Abner too—be ignorant about this lad who had been Saul's armor bearer and musician?

Some have blamed Saul's diseased and failing mental state. On this view, the evil spirit from God had brought on a type of mental malady that affected his memory. Persons suffering from certain types of mania or insanity often forget the closest of their friends.

Others have argued that the hustle and bustle of court life, with its multiplicity of servants and attendants, meant that Saul could have easily forgotten David, especially if the time was long between David's service through music and his slaying of Goliath. Yet a long period of time does not appear to have separated these events. Furthermore, David was a regular member of Saul's retinue (1 Sam 16:21).

A third option is to suggest that Saul was not asking for David's identity, which he knew well enough. Instead he was attempting to learn what his father's social position and worth were, for he was concerned what type of stock his future son-in-law might come from. (Remember, whoever was successful in killing Goliath would win the hand of Saul's daughter, according to the terms of Saul's challenge.) While this might explain Saul's motives, does it explain Abner's lack of knowledge? Or must we posit that he also knew who David was but had no idea what his social status and lineage were? Possibly!

The most plausible explanation, and the one favored by most older commentators, is that the four events in the history of Saul and David in 1 Samuel 16—18 are not given in chronological order. Instead, they are transposed by a figure of speech known as hysterologia, in which something is put last that according to the usual order should be put first. For example, the Genesis 10 account of the dispersion of the nations comes before the cause of it—the confusion of languages at the tower of Babel in Genesis 11.

The fact that the order has been rearranged for special purposes in 1 Samuel 16—18 can be seen from the fact that the Vaticanus manuscript of the Septuagint deletes twenty-nine verses in all (1 Sam 17:12-31 and 17:55—18:5).

E. W. Bullinger suggested that the text was rearranged in order to bring together certain facts, especially those about the Spirit of God.[1] Thus in 1 Samuel 16:1-13 David is anointed and the Spirit of God comes upon him. Then, in order to contrast this impartation of the Spirit of God with the removal of the Spirit from Saul, 1 Samuel 16:14-23 is brought forward from later history. In the straightforward order of events, Bullinger suggests, it should follow 18:9.

First Samuel 17:1—18:9 records an event earlier in the life of David, which is introduced here in a parenthetical way as an illustration of 1 Samuel 14:52. This section is just an instance of what 14:52 claims.

The whole section, therefore, has this construction:

A	16:1-13	David anointed. The Spirit comes on him.
B	16:14-23	Saul rejected. The Spirit departs from him. An evil spirit torments him.
A	17:1—18:9	David. An earlier incident in his life.
B	18:10-30	Saul. The Spirit departs and an evil spirit troubles him.

Thus the narration alternates between David and Saul, creating a didactic contrast between the Spirit of God and the evil spirit that tormented Saul. The focus is on the spiritual state of the two men, not the historical order of events.

All too frequently, the books of Joshua, Judges, Samuel and Kings are given the label "Historical Books" rather than the more correct label "Earlier Prophets." They aim at teaching lessons from the prophetic eye of inspiration rather than simply providing a chronicle of how events occurred in time and history.

That these texts appear in topical, rather than chronological, order is the best explanation, especially when we note how the theology of the text is embedded in it.

See also comment on GENESIS 11:1-9; 1 SAMUEL 8—12.

---

[1]E. W. Bullinger, *Figures of Speech* (1898; reprint ed., Grand Rapids, Mich.: Baker, 1968), pp. 706-7.

18:10; 19:9 An Evil Spirit from the Lord?

See comment on 1 SAMUEL 16:14.

19:13 David's House Has an Idol?

What is an idol doing in the house of David, a monotheist and the one through whom the line of Christ is to come? Where did his wife Michal lay her hands on such an item, no matter what good intentions she had of protecting her husband from her jealous father?

Michal's ruse gave David time to flee from the soldiers who were sent to capture David, but that is not the point. Michal's dummy is described as being one of the *tᵉrāp̱îm,* "idols" or "household gods." The word is always found in the plural form, and the idols were sometimes small enough to be tucked away in a camel's saddle (Gen 31:19, 34-35), but here the idol seems to be man-sized, since Michal used it to simulate David's presence in bed.

The fact that household gods or idols were part of Michal's belongings, if not David's as well, probably reflects a pagan inclination or ignorant use of the surrounding culture. It would appear that the narrator made a deliberate connection between Michal and Rachel, who hid the teraphim in her camel saddle in Genesis 31. Each woman deceived her father in the use of the teraphim and thereby demonstrated more love and attachment to her husband than to her father. If our estimate of Rachel was that the teraphim may not have been symbols of the person who held the will, that is, the rights to the inheritance, but were idols that would later have to be gotten rid of (Gen 35), then Michal, and David by implication, would be guilty of the same sin and in need of repentance and God's forgiveness.

See also comment on GENESIS 31:34.

19:19-24 How Did Saul Prophesy?

Seeking a naturalistic explanation for

the phenomenon of prophecy in the Old Testament, some have theorized that such powers derived from ecstatic experiences in which the prophet wandered outside his own consciousness during a period of artistic creation. One of the passages used to sustain such a thesis is 1 Samuel 19:19-24.

Quite apart from the issue of ecstasy in prophecy are two other matters. Could a king also be a prophet? And did the king really strip off all his clothes as a result of this powerful experience of prophesying?

The story told here is clear enough. In a jealous rage over David's popularity and success, Saul was bent on capturing David. No doubt rumors were now spreading that Samuel had anointed David as king in place of the then-reigning Saul.

Saul sent three different groups of messengers to apprehend David, who had fled from Saul to join Samuel at his prophetic school at Ramah. All three groups encountered Samuel's band of prophets prophesying. And each of the groups of messengers began to prophesy as well.

At last Saul had had enough and decided to go in search of David himself. While he was still on the way, however, the "Spirit of God" came on him; so he too prophesied. Later, after coming to where the others were, he removed some of his clothing and lay in an apparent stupor the rest of that day and the following night.

Each of the three problems raised by this text deserves some response based on the meaning of certain words used in this context and other similar contexts.

It has been claimed that the Greeks thought artistic genius was always accompanied by a degree of madness; thus, those who prophesied must have similarly experienced "ecstasy"—a word literally meaning "to stand apart from or outside oneself." Furthermore, it was argued that the behavior of the Canaanite prophets of Baal on Mount Carmel was just like that of earlier Israelite prophets.

But the verb *to prophesy,* as used in this context, does not mean "to act violently" or "to be mad." The Old Testament makes a clear distinction between the prophets of Canaan and those under the inspiration of God.

Only three Old Testament passages have been used as evidence that prophesying entailed a temporary madness and standing apart from oneself. These three passages, however, record the estimates of others rather than God's estimates of prophets and the source of their inspiration. In 2 Kings 9:11, a young prophet sent by Elisha to anoint Jehu as king is called a "madman" *(m^{e}šugāʿ)* by the soldiers who are sitting in Jehu's barracks. Their label is hardly a statement from God or a source of normative teaching. The Bible simply records that that is what these men thought of prophets—an attitude not altogether dissimilar from that held today by some about the clergy. A second text, Jeremiah 29:26, quotes a certain Shemaiah, then captive in Babylon, from a letter where he too opines: "Every man that is mad *[m^{e}šugāʿ]* makes himself a prophet" (my translation). In the final text, Hosea 9:7, Hosea characterizes a point in Israel's thinking by saying, "The prophet is considered a fool, the inspired man a maniac *[m^{e}šugāʿ]*."

None of these three texts demonstrates that the verb *to prophesy* legitimately carries the connotation of madness. Instead, they simply show that many associated prophecy with madness in an attempt to stigmatize the work of real prophets. It was the ancient equivalent of the Elmer Gantry image of Christian ministers today!

As for Saul's being "naked" all day

and night, the term used might just as well refer to his being partially disrobed. It seems to be used with the latter meaning in Job 22:6, 24:7, Isaiah 58:7 and probably Isaiah 20:2-3, where Isaiah is said to have walked "stripped and barefoot for three years." Saul probably stripped off his outer garment, leaving only the long tunic beneath. The figure of speech involved here is synecdoche, in which the whole stands for a part. Thus, *naked* or *stripped* is used to mean "scantily clad" or "poorly clothed."

In an attempt to shore up the failing theory of ecstasy, some have pointed to 1 Samuel 19:24 as evidence that Saul was "beside himself"—again, the etymology of our word *ecstasy*. However, this will not work since the verb in verse 24 simply means "to put off" a garment (by opening it and unfolding it; the verb's other meaning is "to expand, to spread out, to extend"). There is no evidence that it means "to stand beside oneself" or anything like that.

What about the apparent stupor? Did Saul momentarily lose his sanity? While the three groups of messengers experienced a strong influence of the Spirit of God, it was Saul, we may rightfully conclude, who fell under the strongest work of the Spirit.

The Spirit fell more powerfully on Saul than on the messengers because Saul had more stubbornly resisted the will of God. In this manner, God graciously warned Saul that he was kicking against the very will of God, not just against a shepherd-boy rival. The overmastering influence that came on Saul was to convince him that his struggle was with God and not with David. His action in sending the three groups to capture David had been in defiance of God himself, so he had to be graphically warned. As a result, the king also, but unexpectedly, prophesied. So surprised were all around them that a proverb subsequently arose to characterize events that ran against ordinary expectations: "Is Saul also among the prophets?" (1 Sam 19:24). Kings normally did not expect to receive the gift of prophecy. But here God did the extraordinary in order to move a recalcitrant king's heart to see the error of his ways.

The noun *prophecy* and verb *to prophesy* appear more than three hundred times in the Old Testament. Often outbursts of exuberant praise or of deep grief were connected with prophesying. But there seems to be no evidence for ecstasy as wild, uncontrollable enthusiasm that forced the individual to go temporarily mad or insane. And if we dilute the meaning of *ecstasy* so as to take away the negative implications—like those attached to the Greek's theory that artists only drew, composed or wrote when temporarily overcome with madness—the term becomes so bland that it loses its significance. In that case we all might qualify to join the band of the prophets. Certainly nothing in this text suggests the dancing, raving and loss of consciousness sometimes seen in contemporary extrabiblical phenomena.

See also comment on "When the Prophets Say, 'The Word of the LORD Came to Me,' What Do They Mean?" and DANIEL 12:8-10.

24:5 Why Was David Upset That He Had Cut Saul's Clothing?

Why was David so upset with himself for merely cutting off a corner of King Saul's robe? This does not sound as if it is any big deal.

David had a high regard for the fact that Saul was God's anointed person holding the office of king. Saul's anointing signified the election of God. Therefore, David vowed that he would do nothing to intervene to vindicate himself or to remove Saul from that office unless God did so.

The best explanation of David's sudden pang of conscience was that he viewed the violation of Saul's robe as equivalent to violating Saul's very person. Since David held that the office that Saul occupied was something sacrosanct and from the Lord, even this small token—taken as evidence that even though they had occupied the same cave together he had not tried to take Saul's life—was itself blameworthy.

28:7-8, 14-16 What Did the Witch of Endor Do?

The problems raised by the account of Saul's encounter with the witch of Endor in 1 Samuel 28 are legion! To begin with, spiritism, witches, mediums and necromancers (those who communicate with the dead) are not approved in Scripture. In fact, a number of stern passages warn against any involvement with or practice of these satanic arts. For example, Deuteronomy 18:9-12 includes these practices in a list of nine abominations that stand in opposition to revelation from God through his prophets. Exodus 22:18 denies sorceresses the right to live. Leviticus 19:26, 31 and 20:6, 27 likewise sternly caution against consulting a medium, a sorceress or anyone who practices divination. Those cultivating these arts were to be put to death—the community was not to tolerate them, for what they did was so heinous that it was the very antithesis of the revelation that came from God (see Jer 27:9-10).

But there are other issues as well. Did the witch of Endor really have supernatural powers from Satan, which enabled her to bring Samuel up from the dead? Or was Samuel's appearance not literal, merely the product of psychological impressions? Perhaps it was a demon or Satan himself that impersonated Samuel. Or perhaps the whole thing was a trick played on Saul. Which is the correct view? And how does such a view fit in with the rest of biblical revelation?

The most prevalent view among orthodox commentators is that there was a genuine appearance of Samuel brought about by God himself. The main piece of evidence favoring this interpretation is 1 Chronicles 10:13-14: "Saul died because he was unfaithful to the LORD; he did not keep the word of the LORD and even consulted a medium for guidance, and did not inquire of the LORD." The Septuagint reading of this text adds: "Saul asked counsel of her that had a familiar spirit to inquire of her, and Samuel made answer to him." Moreover, the medium must not have been accustomed to having her necromancies work, for when she saw Samuel, she cried out in a scream that let Saul know that something new and different was happening. That night her so-called arts were working beyond her usual expectations.

Then, too, the fact that Saul bowed in obeisance indicates that this probably was a real appearance of Samuel. What seems to have convinced Saul was the witch's description of Samuel's appearance. She reported that Samuel was wearing the characteristic "robe" *(m^{e}'îl)*. That was the very robe Saul had seized and ripped as Samuel declared that the kingdom had been ripped out of his hand (1 Sam 15:27-28).

Is Samuel's statement to Saul in 1 Samuel 28:15 proof that the witch had brought Samuel back from the dead? The message delivered by this shade or apparition sounds as if it could well have been from Samuel and from God. Therefore, it is entirely possible that this was a real apparition of Samuel. As to whether Samuel appeared physically, in a body, we conclude that the text does not suggest that he did, nor does Christian theology accord with such a view. But there can be little doubt that there was an appearance of Samuel's spirit or ghost. The witch herself, in her startled condition, claimed that what she saw was a "god" (*ᵉlōhîm*, 1 Sam 28:13) coming up out of the earth. The most probable interpretation of this term *ᵉlōhîm* is the "spirit" of a deceased person. This implies an authentic appearance of the dead, but one that did not result from her witchcraft. Instead, it was God's final means of bringing a word to a king who insisted on going his own way.

Those who have argued for a psychological impression face two objections. The first is the woman's shriek of horror in 1 Samuel 28:12. She would not have screamed if the spirit had been merely Saul's hallucination, produced by psychological excitement. The second objection is that the text implies that both the woman and Saul talked with Samuel. Even more convincing is the fact that what Samuel is purported to have said turned out to be true!

As for the demon impersonation theory, some of the same objections apply. The text represents this as a real happening, not an impersonation. Of course Satan does appear as "an angel of light" (2 Cor 11:14), but there is no reason to suppose that this is what is going on here.

Our conclusion is that God allowed Samuel's spirit to appear to give Saul one more warning about the evil of his ways.

One of the reasons believers are warned to stay away from spiritists, mediums and necromancers is that some do have powers supplied to them from the netherworld. Whether the witch accomplished her feat by the power of Satan or under the mighty hand of God we may never know in this life. Of course, all that happens must be allowed or directed by God. Thus the question is finally whether it was his directive or permissive will that brought up Samuel. If it were the latter, did the witch apply for satanic powers, or was she a total fraud who was taught a lesson about the overwhelming power of God through this experience? It is difficult to make a firm choice between these two possibilities.

31:4 How Did Saul Die?

Who is telling the truth? The narrator of 1 Samuel 31 or the Amalekite of 2 Samuel 1:6-10? Or to put the question in another way: Did Saul commit suicide, or was he killed by this Amalekite, as he claimed, at Saul's own request?

Although there have been attempts at harmonizing the two accounts, the effort always seems to fall short of being convincing. For example, as early as the first Christian century, Josephus tried to make the accounts fit each other. Josephus claimed (*Antiquities* 6, 370-72 [xiv.7]) that after Saul's armor-bearer refused to kill Saul, Saul tried to fall on his own sword, but he was too weak to do so. Saul turned and saw this Amalekite, who, upon the king's request, complied and killed him, having found the king leaning on his sword. Afterward the Amalekite took the king's crown and armband and fled, whereupon Saul's armor-bearer killed himself.

While everything seems to fit in this harmonization, there is one fact that is out of line: the armor-bearer. The armor-bearer was sufficiently convinced of Saul's death to follow his example (1 Sam 31:5). Thus, Josephus's greatest mistake was in trusting the Amalekite. Also, it is most improbable that the Amalekite found Saul leaning on his sword, an unlikely sequel of a botched attempt at suicide.

It is my conclusion that Saul did commit suicide, a violation of the law of God, and that the Amalekite was lying in order to obtain favor with the new administration.

2 SAMUEL

1:6-10 How Did Saul Die?

See comment on 1 SAMUEL 31:4.

6:6-7 Why Did God Destroy Uzzah?

Over the years, many have complained that God was unfair to kill Uzzah when he tried to protect the ark of God from damage or shame when the oxen stumbled and the ark slipped. Should not Uzzah have been praised for lunging forward to protect the ark of God?

There is no doubt that David's intentions in bringing the ark to Jerusalem were noble and good. Now that his kingdom was established, he did not forget his earlier vow to return the ark to its rightful place of prominence. But what began as a joyful day quickly became a day of national grief and shame. Why?

A significant omission in 2 Samuel 6:1-3 sets the scene for failure. Previously when David needed counsel, for example when he was attacked by the Philistines, the text records that David "inquired of the Lord" (2 Sam 5:19, 23). But those words are sadly missing in 2 Samuel 6:1-3. Instead, we are told in the parallel account in 1 Chronicles 13:1-14 that David "conferred with each of his officers."

There was no need to consult these men. God had already given clear instructions in Numbers 4:5-6 as to how to move the ark. It should be covered with a veil, to shield the holiness of God from any kind of rash intrusion, and then carried on poles on the shoulders of the Levites (Num 7:9).

God had plainly revealed his will, but David had a better idea—one he had learned from the pagan Philistines. He would put it on a "new cart" (2 Sam 6:3). However, God had never said anything about using a new cart. This was a human invention contrary to the will and law of God.

Thus David did things in the wrong way, following his own ideas or those of others instead of God's ways. Surely this passage warns that it is not enough to have a worthy purpose and a proper spirit when we enter into the service of God; God's work must also be performed in God's way. Pursuing the right end does not automatically imply using the right means.

But why did God's anger break out against Uzzah if David was at fault? The Lord had plainly taught that even the Kohathites, the Levite family designated to carry the ark, "must not touch the holy things or they will die" (Num 4:15). Even if Uzzah were not a Kohathite or even a Levite, he still would know what the law taught in Numbers 4 and 7. God not only keeps his promises, but also fulfills his threats!

When the Philistines, who had no access to the special revelation of God, sinned by touching the ark and using a new cart to transport it, God's anger did not burn against them (1 Sam 6). God is more merciful toward those less knowledgeable of his will than toward those who are more knowledgeable. This is why it will be more tolerable for Sodom and Gomorrah in the day of judgment than it will be for those who personally witnessed the great acts of the Savior in Capernaum (Mt 11:23-24).

Uzzah's motive, like David's, was pure, but he disregarded the written Word of God, just as David did. Thus one sin led to another. Consulting one's peers is no substitute for obeying God when he has spoken. Good intentions, with unsanctified minds, interfere with the kingdom of God. This is especially true of the worship of God and the concept of his holiness.

Because God is holy, he is free of all moral imperfections. To help mortals understand this better, a sharp line of demarcation was drawn between holy things and the common or profane. Our word *profane* means "before" or "forth from the temple." Thus all that was apart from the temple, where the holiness of God was linked, was by definition profane. However, Uzzah's act made the holiness associated with the ark also profane and thereby brought disrepute to God as well.

It is unthinkable that God could condone a confusion or a diffusion of the sacred and the profane. To take something holy and inject into it the realm of the profane was to confuse the orders of God. Thus in 1 Samuel 6:19 seventy men of Beth Shemesh were killed for peering into the ark.

The situation with Uzzah can be contrasted with that of the Philistines in 1 Samuel 6:9. These uncircumcised Gentiles also handled the ark of God as they carted it from city to city in what is now called the Gaza Strip, as they did when they prepared to send the ark back home to Israel on a cart. But where the knowledge of holy things had not been taught, the responsibility to act differently was not as high as it was for Uzzah, who should have known better.

In fact, in order to determine if the calamities that had struck each of the cities where the ark had gone (a calamity that was almost certainly an outbreak of the bubonic plague) was merely a chance happening unrelated to any divine wrath from the God of Israel, the Philistines rigged up an experiment that was totally against the grain of nature. They took two cows that had just borne calves, penned up the calves, and hitched these cows, who had never previously been hitched to a cart, to a new cart, and watched to see if against every maternal instinct in the animal kingdom the cows would be directed back to the territory of the Philistines. They were. The Philistines were convinced that what happened to them in the outbreak in each city during the seven months when the ark of God was in their midst was no chance or freak accident at all: it was the hand of God! And they had better not harden their hearts as the Egyptians did years ago (1 Sam 6:6).

The Philistines had enough sense for

the holiness of God to use a new cart and to send back offerings of reparation, to the degree that they had any knowledge, but they were not judged for what they did not know about the distinction between the sacred and the common.

Another case of trivializing that which is holy can be seen in the brief reference to Nadab and Abihu offering strange fire on the altar of God (Lev 10:1-3). It is impossible to say whether the two sons of Aaron, the high priest, erred in the manner in which they lighted their fire-pans, the timing, or in the place of the offering. The connection with strong drink and the possibility of intoxication cannot be ruled out, given the proximity and discussion of that matter in the same context (Lev 10:8-11). If that was the problem, then the drink may have impeded the sons' ability to think and to act responsibly in a task that called for the highest degree of alertness, caution and sensitivity.

The offense, however, was no trivial matter. Nor was it accidental. There was some reversal of everything that had been taught, and what had been intended to be most holy and sacred was suddenly trivialized so as to make it common, trite and secular. Exodus 30:9 had warned that there was to be no "other incense" offered on the altar to the Lord. From the phrase at the end of Leviticus 10:1, "which he did not command them" (literal translation), what was done was a clear violation of God's command.

As a result fire comes from the presence of the Lord and consumed Nadab and Abihu. Again, the fact that they are ministers of God makes them doubly accountable and responsible. Moses then used this as an occasion to teach a powerful lesson on the holiness and worship of God (Lev 10:3).

See also comment on 1 SAMUEL 2:25.

6:20 Was David's Public Dancing Indecent?

Was Michal correct in her estimate of David's dancing in front of the ark of God as it was being brought to the tent David had prepared for it in his city? Or did she misinterpret David's actions and purpose?

If David had expected his wife Michal, the daughter of Saul, to rejoice with him in the arrival of the ark of God in the capital city, he had a long wait coming. It is a real question if this ever was a happy marriage, for as Alter notes, "Until the final meeting between Michal and David, at no point is there any dialogue between them—an avoidance of verbal exchange particularly noticeable in the Bible, where such a large part of the burden of narration is taken up by dialogue. When the exchange finally comes, it is an explosion."[1]

In one sentence Michal's sarcastic words tell us what she thinks of David's actions. To her way of thinking, the king had demeaned himself by divesting himself of his royal robes and dressing only in a "linen ephod" (2 Sam 6:14). With abandoned joy David danced before the Lord as the ark, properly borne this time on the shoulders of the Levites, went up to Jerusalem.

Michal did not even deign to go out on the streets to be part of the festivities, but she watched from a window (2 Sam 6:16). Obviously, there was more bothering Michal than David's undignified public jubilation. Her words about David "distinguish[ing] himself" are further punctuated by her disdainfully emphasizing the fact three times over that the king had "disrob[ed]" (the final clause of 2 Sam 6:20 literally reads, "as any vulgar fellow, disrobing, would disrobe"). Was David's dress, or lack thereof, as scandalous as Michal made it out to be? Though some have thought that they detected overtones of orgiastic rituals in preparation for sacred marriage rites (in, for example, the presence of slave girls), such suggestions are overdrawn if we are to take seriously David's rejoinders to Michal in 2 Samuel 6:21-22. David speaks of his election and appointment to the office of king by God. He does rub in the fact that God chose him over her father Saul. But as far as David was concerned, it was not an issue of public nudity or scandalous dress, but a matter of humiliating himself before the Lord. Furthermore, he danced not for the "slave girls," but for the Lord. The "linen ephod" consisted probably of a linen robe used normally by the Levites.

[1]See Robert Alter, *The Art of Biblical Narrative* (New York: Basic Books, 1981), p. 123.

10:18 How Many Charioteers?

See comment on 1 CHRONICLES 19:18.

12:7-8 Was David Right to Take Concubines?

See comment on 2 SAMUEL 20:3.

12:14-18 Should Children Die for Their Parents' Sins?

See comment on DEUTERONOMY 24:16.

12:21-23 What Happened to David and Bathsheba's Son?

What are the prospects of the dead in the Old Testament? And what shall we say about those who die in infancy and thus have never heard about the wonderful grace of our Lord? Is their future gloomy and dark, without hope? These are some of the questions raised by this passage on the child born to David and Bathsheba as a result of their adulterous act.

Several passages in the Old Testament show that death is not the absolute end of all life. For example, 1 Samuel 28:15-19 says that upon the death of Saul and his sons in battle the next day, they would join Samuel, who was already dead, yet who here was conscious and able to speak.

Likewise, David affirmed his confidence that he would one day go to meet his deceased son; in the meantime, it was impossible for his son to come and join him back on earth. Surely this implies that the child still consciously and actually existed, even though it was impossible for him to transcend the boundaries set by death.

If David's expectation was to see God and to be with God after death, he believed that his son would also be in the presence of God, even though that son never had the opportunity to hear about the gospel or to respond to its offer of grace. Apparently, the grace of God has made provisions that go beyond those that apply to all who can hear or read about God's revelation of his grace in his Son Jesus.

Those psalms of David in which the dead are said to lack any knowledge or remembrance of God are highly poetical and figurative expressions of how unnatural and violent death is. Death will continue to separate the living from each other and from the use of their bodies until Christ returns to restore what has been lost. Psalms 6:5 and 30:9 indicate how central the act of praising God was to the total life of the individual and the congregation. But death would seem, according to the views expressed by the psalmists in these texts, to interrupt that flow of praise to God. Isn't it better, David continues, for people to be alive so that they can praise God? "Who praises you from the grave?" The dead are without the ability to lift praises to God. That seems to be David's burden.

Neither can Ecclesiastes 9:5-6 count against the position we have taken here. To claim that "the dead know nothing" is not to deny any hope beyond the grave. The point of Ecclesiastes is limited to what can be observed from a strictly human point of view, "under the sun." Its statement that the dead "have no further reward" is reminiscent of Jesus' words, "As long as it is day [while we are still alive], we must do the work of him who sent me. Night is coming, when no one can work" (Jn 9:4).

In 2 Samuel 12:23 David does not take the perspective of this life—as some of these other passages do—but the perspective of an eternity with God. And from that perspective, there is much to hope for.

David took comfort in the hope that God would take this little one to himself. He left the child, therefore, to the grace of God, expressing his hope of rejoining that child in the future. There is life after death, even for infants who die before they have seen any, or many, days.

14:27; 18:18 Did Absalom Have Three Sons or None?

Some scholars find an irresolvable conflict between 14:27 and 18:18, usually taking the latter to be the authentic, original and earlier text. Is this resolution of the problem the correct one?

The most reasonable supposition is that the three sons are left unnamed, while contrary to usual convention their sister Tamar's name is given, because the three boys died in childhood. There is nothing in the text or from external records that would support this thesis at this time, but this is the only explanation that will satisfy all the evidence.

It may have been this sorrowful event that later motivated Absalom to build a monument for himself, so that his own name would be remembered. Absalom observed that he had no sons, therefore the need for the monument.

20:3 Was David Right to Take Concubines?

The institution of concubinage seems to many of us as wrong and as evil as the institution of slavery. And so it was from an Old Testament point of view as well.

Genesis 2:21-24 presents us with God's normative instructions for marriage: one man was to be joined to one woman so as to become one flesh.

Polygamy appears for the first time in Genesis 4:19, when Lamech became the first bigamist, marrying two wives, Adah and Zillah. No other recorded instances of polygamy exist from Shem to Terah, the father of Abraham (except for the episode in Gen 6:1-7).

Was polygamy (with its correlative concubinage) ever a lawful practice in the Old Testament? No permission can be recited from the text for any such institution or practice. To support it, one could appeal only to illustrations in the lives of a rather select number of persons. None of these examples has the force of normative theology. The Bible merely describes what some did; it never condones their polygamy, nor does it make their practices normative for that time or later times.

From the beginning of time up to 931 B.C., when the kingdom was divided after Solomon's day, there are only fifteen examples of polygamy in the Old Testament: Lamech, the "sons of God" in Genesis 6:1-7, Abraham's brother Nahor, Abraham, Esau, Jacob, Gideon, Jair, Ibzan, Abdon, Samson, Elkanah, Saul, David and Solomon. In the divided monarchy, Rehoboam, Abijah, Ahab and Jehoram all were bigamists, and possibly Joash (depending on how we interpret "for him" or "for himself" in 2 Chron 24:2-3). This gives us a total of nineteen instances, and among them thirteen were persons of absolute power whom no one could call into judgment except God.

The despotic way in which the rulers of Genesis 6:1-7 took as many wives as they pleased is censured by Scripture, as are those who indulged in adulterous and polygamous behavior prior to the flood. The law of Moses also censures those who violate God's prescription of monogamous marriage. Scripture does not, however, always pause to state the obvious or to moralize on the events that it records.

Those who say the Old Testament gave direct or implied permission for polygamy usually point to four passages: Exodus 21:7-11, Leviticus 18:18, Deuteronomy 21:15-17 and 2 Samuel 12:7-8. Each of these texts has had a history of incorrect interpretation.[1]

There is no suggestion of a second marriage with "marital rights" in Exodus 21:10, for the word translated "marital rights" should be rendered "oil" or "ointments." The text says that a man who has purchased a female servant (perhaps to fulfill a debt) must continue to provide for her if he proposes marriage and then decides not to consummate it. Leviticus 18:18 does not imply that a man may marry a second wife so long as she is not a sister to the one he already has. Instead, it prohibits his marrying his wife's sister during the lifetime of his wife, since having her sister as a rival would vex her. Likewise, Deuteronomy 21:15-17 legislates the rights of the firstborn, regardless of whether that child is the son of the preferred wife or of the wife who is not loved. To contend, as some do, that legislation on rights within polygamy tacitly condones polygamy makes about as much sense as saying that Deuteronomy 23:18 approves of harlotry since it prohibits bringing the wages earned by harlotry into the house of the Lord for any vow!

Finally, 2 Samuel 12:7-8 supplies no encouragement to polygamy when it says that all that Saul had, including his wives, were to be David's possessions. Nowhere in all the lists of David's wives are Saul's two wives listed; hence the expression must be a stereotypic formula signifying that everything in principle was turned over for David's disposition.

Malachi 2:14 says that God is a witness to all weddings and contends for the "wife of [our] youth," who is all too frequently left at the altar in tears because of the violence caused by divorce (or any of marriage's other perversions). Jeremiah had to rebuke the men of his own generation who were "neighing for another man's wife" (Jer 5:8). Had polygamy been customarily or even tacitly approved, this text of Jeremiah would have had to record "another man's wives." Furthermore, these men's sin would have had a ready solution: they should look around and acquire several new wives on their own, instead of seeking those who were already taken! No, polygamy never was God's order for marriage in the Old Testament. David sinned, therefore, in having a plurality of wives. But what of his putting the ten concubines under guard after his son Absalom had violated them in a palace coup?

The answer this time is one of political expediency of that day. If David had had relations with any one of them and she conceived, it would be difficult to know whether the son was his or Absalom's. And he dare not turn these women out in the streets, for that would have violated the rules of compassion and could have produced another contender to the throne, since all who had any contact with the king, even as a concubine, could lay some claim to the throne in the future.

Thus, David took the only course he could under such circumstances. There is no doubt about it: he had sown to the wind and now he must reap the whirlwind. God had never changed his mind about the appropriateness of one wife for one husband to become one flesh.

See also comment on GENESIS 6:1-4; PROVERBS 5:15-21.

[1]For more details, see Walter C. Kaiser Jr., *Toward Old Testament Ethics* (Grand Rapids, Mich.: Zondervan, 1983), pp. 184-90.

21:1-9 Why Were Saul's Descendants Killed?

The background for this episode goes all the way back to the days of Joshua. Under the pretense of being from afar, the inhabitants of the town of Gibeon in Canaan, known variously as Hivites (Josh 9:7) and Amorites (2 Sam 21:2), precipitously won a treaty from Joshua and the elders, who later discovered that these people were not from a great distance, but in fact lived right in the path of the ongoing conquest. Reluctantly Joshua and the elders conceded that they had sworn an oath before Yahweh that they would do these people no harm. So the Gibeonites remained untouched in Israel, though they were required to serve as hewers of wood and drawers of water for the house of God (see Josh 9 for details).

Psalm 15:4 makes it a point of honor to keep one's oath, even when it hurts. But in his zeal for Israel Saul had violated Joshua's ancient oath and brought "blood-guiltiness" on the whole land. Apparently, some dissatisfaction with the Gibeonites had provided Saul with a pretext to vent his prejudices against these non-Israelites who lived in their midst. And the Lord, who inspects all that is said and done on earth, required justice to be done. Thus it was that even as late as David's reign a famine fell on all the land for three successive years. Having asked the Lord why they were experiencing this continual drought, David was told of the injustice that had been done to the Gibeonites. Whether David had known about this wrongdoing previously is not told.

When David consulted with the Gibeonites, asking what they wished by way of compensation for Saul's attack on them, they demanded that seven of Saul's sons be killed and displayed in Saul's hometown and capital city, Gibeah. David agreed to their request.

What made David agree to such a hideous retribution, and how could that compensate the Gibeonites? And why did it satisfy divine justice (since the rains came after the act had been completed)? Does God favor human sacrifice?

The Mosaic law clearly prohibits human sacrifice (Lev 18:21; 20:2). But the text we are considering does not depict the killing of Saul's descendants as an offering to anyone, so this is not a case of sacrifice.

Neither does the Old Testament deny the principle of individualism, so dear to (and so abused by) Westerners. Deuteronomy 24:16 teaches that "fathers shall not be put to death for their children, nor children put to death for their fathers; each is to die for his own sin." Yet sometimes factors beyond individual responsibility are at work in a world of sin.

The Old Testament also reminds us of our corporate involvement, through which a member of a group can be held fully responsible for an action of the group, even though he or she personally may have had nothing to do with that act. Thus the whole group may be treated as a unit or through a representative. This is not to argue for a type of collectivism or a rejection of individual responsibility. Ten righteous men could have preserved Sodom and Gomorrah (Gen 18). A righteous man blesses his children after him (Prov 11:21). On the flip side, however, the sin of the few can bring judgment on the many, as in the story of the Korah, Dathan and Abiram incident in Numbers 16.

Certainly, there was to be collective

punishment in Israel when a whole city was drawn into idolatrous worship at the incitement of a few good-for-nothing fellows (Deut 13:12-16). Complicity in the crime perpetrated against Naboth, in the taking of his land and life by the throne, led to judgment against the royal house, since there was no repentance in the interim (1 Kings 21; 2 Kings 10:1-11).

David granted the Gibeonites' request because, according to the law of Moses, "bloodshed pollutes the land, and atonement cannot be made for the land on which blood has been shed, except by the blood of the one who shed it" (Num 35:33). This being so, the members of Saul's house had to be delivered over to the Gibeonites. Hope of the land's deliverance from the judgment of God did not lie in any other avenue. In fact, 2 Samuel 21:3 specifically mentions "making expiation" or "atonement" *(kipper)*. (The NIV translates it as "make amends"!) The Gibeonites insisted that it was not possible for them to accept a substitute such as "silver or gold." The seriousness of the crime demanded something more, as Numbers 35:31, 33 teaches.

David was careful to spare Mephibosheth, the recently discovered son of Jonathan, because of the covenant he had made with Jonathan (1 Sam 18:3; 20:8, 16). But he delivered to the Gibeonites two sons of Rizpah, a concubine of Saul, and five sons of Saul's eldest daughter, Merab.

After killing them, the Gibeonites impaled the bodies on stakes and left them hanging in Saul's hometown of Gibeah as a rebuke to all who would attempt genocide, as Saul apparently had. According to Deuteronomy 21:22-23, persons who were executed were not to remain hanging through the night on a stake, but were to be buried before evening. This law, however, did not appear to have any application to this case, where expiation of guilt for the whole land was concerned, and where non-Israelite Gibeonites were involved. It seems that the bodies remained on display until the famine actually ended; they were taken down as the rains began to fall.

Though David complied with the Gibeonite request, there is nothing in the text that suggests that he engineered the situation so as to get rid of any potential rivals from Saul's line. Rather, the text stresses how important it is to honor covenants made before God. In the so-called second plague prayer given by the Hittite king Mursilis II (fourteenth century B.C.), he similarly blames a twenty-year famine in his land on a previous ruler's breach of a treaty between the Hittites and the Egyptians. How much more accountable would Israel be for a similar violation before Yahweh!

One traitor can affect the outcome of a whole battle and the lives of a whole army. So, too, the acts of those who rule on behalf of a whole nation can affect all either for good or for ill. Blood-guiltiness left on the land, whether through the betrayal of a covenant made before God or through a failure to put to death those who deliberately took the lives of innocent victims, must be avenged on those who caused the guilt. Otherwise, the land will languish under the hand of God's judgment.

See also comment on GENESIS 9:6; NUMBERS 35:31; DEUTERONOMY 24:16; JOSHUA 7:1, 10-11.

24:1 Why Was the Census a Sin?

See comment on 1 CHRONICLES 21:1-2, 8.

24:9 What Was Israel's Population?

The problem is this: 2 Samuel 24:9 has 300,000 less fighting men in northern Israel than 1 Chronicles 21:5. And 2 Samuel has 500,000 fighting men from Judah while 1 Chronicles states there were only 470,000. What is the explanation for these statistical inconsistencies?

As if this were not enough to deal with, both Josephus and the Lucianic texts (a recension of the Greek Septuagint) of Samuel record the number as 900,000 for Israel and 400,000 for Judah.

The solution proposed by J. Barton Payne[1] seems best. He proposed that 2 Samuel 24:9 refers simply to "Israel" (that is, the northern ten tribes), but that 1 Chronicles 21:5 covers "all Israel," including the regular army of 288,000 (1 Chron 27:1-15), a figure when rounded out comes to 300,000.

The difference between 470,000 of Chronicles and 500,000 of 2 Samuel can be explained much the same way: it is a rounding off of the numbers.

But what about the problem of such huge numbers? If taken at face value, this would imply that Israel and Judah had a combined population at this time of something like three to six million people. However, all attempts to size down these numbers runs into the further problem of creating new dilemmas. For example, to say that the word for "thousand" (Hebrew *'elep̄*) here means "tribal unit, contingent," as it sometimes does in other contexts, or even that *'elep̄* had other vowels put with the constant consonants to read *'allûp̄*, "specially trained warriors," leaves us with pondering the question as to why it took three hundred days to conduct a census of 1,570 outstanding military figures. Either someone was unusually slow in math, lazy, or the numbers are what they present themselves to be.

See also essay on "Aren't Many Old Testament Numbers Wrong?"

---

[1]J. Barton Payne, "The Validity of Numbers in Chronicles," *Near Eastern Archaeological Society Bulletin* 11 (1978): 5-58.

24:24 How Many Shekels for the Altar Site?

See comment on 1 CHRONICLES 21:25.

1 KINGS

2:10 What Does "Rested with His Fathers" Imply?

See comment on GENESIS 25:8.

2:23-25 What Was So Wrong with Adonijah's Request?

Why was Solomon so upset at Adonijah's request to marry Abishag? Was this a serious enough breach of custom that it merited his being executed? Or was Solomon totally wrong to demand Adonijah's death?

Possession of one or all of the wives of a reigning king was a virtual title to the throne. This custom can be seen not only in 2 Samuel 12:8, where the wives of Saul were said to have been passed on to David, but also in Absalom's coup, where he took possession of David's harem to indicate that he was now king (2 Sam 16:21-22). According to Herodotus (3:68), the Persians had the same custom, as did the Arabs.

It is doubtful that Adonijah had any romantic aspirations whatsoever. He just thought he could play Solomon's mother, Bathsheba, for all she was worth. Since Adonijah had lost out to Solomon as king through Bathsheba and Nathan's quick actions, Adonijah thought there was one last chance that he might get the power of the throne: he would innocently ask Bathsheba, and she might just naively grant his request, or work on Solomon to do so.

Bathsheba, while realizing that Abishag has been close to King David during his final ailing days, apparently saw no harm in the request. But Solomon saw through the whole scheme immediately and did not wait around until he had a palace coup or a national revolution on his hands. He acted swiftly and deftly.

So things are not always what they seem on the surface. What looked like a polite question from a good sport, who had just lost the race for king, turns out to have the potential for a deadly challenge to the throne. It was for this reason that Solomon acted so swiftly. If he hadn't, things might have turned out very differently in the history of Israel.

11:1-2 Why Did Solomon Take So Many Foreign Wives?

How could Solomon take so many foreign wives when it was clearly forbidden? It is almost unbelievable. Is there any explanation that might serve to mitigate some of the blatant disobedience that such action seems to imply—especially for a man who was endowed with wisdom as a gift from God?

There is no question but that Moses stipulated that the kings God was going to give to Israel must not imitate the ways of the nations around them by taking many wives, for the wives would lead their hearts astray (Deut 17:17).

Particularly noticeable in Scripture is the extreme moral degeneracy of the Canaanites (Gen 19; Lev 18:24-30; Deut 9:5; 12:29-31). It was for this reason that the Israelites were warned that intermarriage would result in their tolerating Canaanite religious practices (Ex 34:12-17; Deut 7:1-5).

Even though one would expect a higher standard from a king who should set the example for the nation, Solomon began to regard himself as beyond the need for such warnings. It is true, of course, that the text specifically noted that the seven hundred wives were of royal birth, for it was customary in that day to employ marriages with a foreign king's daughters as a way of cementing diplomatic alliances. In case of nonperformance of a treaty, Solomon had only to imply that the dissident king's daughter was most anxious to hear that her father had done what he had promised to do—so that her health might be enjoyed for more years. The reverse side of that coin, however, was that a daughter might write home to her father complaining that Solomon cared not at all for her religion in that he never went to her idol's services. Thus the trap was sprung against Solomon, no matter how politically savvy he might have thought that such marriages were. Spiritual disaster resulted.

See also comment on GENESIS 29:25-28; 2 SAMUEL 20:3.

12:24 This Is the Lord's Doing?

See comment on 2 CHRONICLES 11:2-4.

18:40 Why Did Elijah Kill All 450 Prophets of Baal?

Why was it necessary to kill the prophets of Baal once it had been shown that they could not call down fire from heaven as Elijah had? Wasn't it enough to prove that they were false prophets without any power? And if some of the prophets of Baal had to die, why all 450?

Elijah stepped forward after the prophets of Baal had been asking Baal to send down fire from six o'clock in the morning to three o'clock in the afternoon with no results. In less than a minute's petition to Almighty God, the fire of God fell from heaven. The crowd was impressed and fell facedown, crying, "The LORD—he is God! The LORD—he is God" (1 Kings 18:39).

The fire of God could just as well have consumed the 450 prophets of Baal right then and there (and the 400 prophets of Asherah, for that matter). But the divine fire was not the fire of judgment this time, but the fire that signified that the bull Elijah had placed on the altar was accepted. After three and a half years in which the weather forecast was "sunny, clear and warmer" each day, you would have thought that the God that answered by rain would prove he was Lord. But no, before the mercies of God could come, there must first be the sacrifice that prepared the way for those mercies and graces.

Immediately Elijah commanded that all the prophets of Baal were to be rounded up and taken down to the Kishon Valley to be slaughtered there. There was no hesitation on the part of the people; the Lord's command now came to a crowd that had been startled into responding positively and quickly. Once they had collected all the prophets of Baal, the actual killing may have been done by the people, for on linguistic grounds it is possible to read the fact that Elijah "killed" the prophets of Baal in the sense that he ordered them to be put to death (as in NIV). Here again is another case where secondary causes were passed over as being unnecessary to state, for to attribute the action to the primary or ultimate cause could also involve secondary causes as well.

Why Elijah chose the Kishon Valley instead of using Mount Carmel we may only guess. Perhaps he did not wish to defile the place of sacrifice where the Lord had sanctified himself in a miracle.

The wicked crimes of these prophets of Baal demanded the death penalty (Deut 13:13-15; 17:2-5). Modern thought might consider this to be an overreaction and quite unnecessary, yet when one considers that because of these prophets many persons went into eternity forever cast away from the presence of God, the sanction is completely justified.

Seen in this light, not only are the reaction of the people and the command of Elijah understandable; they are also according to the law of God. It is a serious matter to fool with the holiness of God and his truth.

See also comment on NUMBERS 25:7-13.

22:20-22 Is God the Author of Falsehood?

Could the God of truth be guilty of sponsoring or condoning falsehood? Some have charged just that. The passages that are raised to back this charge are 1 Kings 22:20-23, 2 Chronicles 18:18-22, Jeremiah 4:10, 20:7 and Ezekiel 14:9.

Such a charge is possible only if one forgets that many biblical writers dismiss secondary causes and attribute all that happens directly to God, since he is over all things. Therefore, statements expressed in the imperative form of the verb often represent only what is permitted to happen. Accordingly, when the devils begged Jesus to let them enter the swine, he said, "Go" (Mt 8:31). This did not make him the active sponsor of evil; he merely permitted the demons to do what they wanted to do. In a similar manner, Jesus commanded Judas, "What you are about to do, do quickly" (Jn 13:27). But Jesus did not become the author of the evil perpetrated on himself.

God can be described as deceiving Ahab only because the biblical writer does not discriminate between what someone does and what he permits. It is true, of course, that in 1 Kings 22 God seems to do more than permit the deception. Without saying that God does evil that good may come, we can say that God overrules the full tendencies of preexisting evil so that the evil promotes God's eternal plan, contrary to its own tendency and goals.

Because Ahab had abandoned the Lord his God and hardened his own heart, God allowed his ruin by the very instrument Ahab had sought to prostitute for his own purposes, namely, prophecy. God used the false declarations of the false prophets that Ahab was so enamored with as his instruments of judgment.

That God was able to overrule the evil does not excuse the guilty prophets or their gullible listener. Even though the lying spirit had the Lord's permission, this did not excuse the prophets who misused their gifts. They fed the king exactly what he wanted to hear. Their words were nothing less than echoes of the king's desires. Thus the lying prophets, the king and Israel were equally culpable before God. The responsibility had to be shared. These prophets spoke "out of their own minds."

This principle is further confirmed when we note that the passage in question is a vision that Micaiah reveals to Ahab. God is telling Ahab, "Wise up. I am allowing your prophets to lie to you." In a sense, God is revealing further truth to Ahab rather than lying to him. If God were truly trying to entrap Ahab into a life-threatening situation, he would not have revealed the plan to him! Even so, Ahab refuses to heed God's truth, and he follows his prophets' advice.

The other two passages used to charge God with falsehood are easier to understand. In Ezekiel 14:9 we have another case of God allowing spiritual blindness to take its course. The biblical writer merely attributes the whole process of hardening of heart followed by judgment as falling within God's sovereignty. The strong statement of Jeremiah 20:7 is a complaint by the prophet, who had mistaken the promise of God's presence for the insurance that no evil or derision would come on him or his ministry. However, these verses cannot be cited as the basis for giving any credence to the charge that God is deceptive.

Another instance where God sent an evil spirit was in Judges 9:23. There, one of Gideon's sons, Abimelech, acted as king for three years over the city of Shechem. But after those three years, God sent an evil spirit between Abimelech and the citizens of Shechem so that they "acted treacherously against Abimelech."

In this case, the "evil spirit" was the breaking out of discord and treachery against Abimelech. Once again, under the direction of his providence, but not in any positive agency, God allowed jealousies to arise, which produced factions and in turn became insurrections, civil discontent and ultimately bloodshed. God remained sovereign in the midst of all the evil that ensued—much of it deservedly happening to those who deliberately refused the truth and preferred their own version of reality.

See also comment on 1 SAMUEL 16:14; JOB 1:6-12.

2 KINGS

2:11 What Happened to Elijah?

See comment on GENESIS 5:23-24.

2:23-24 A Cruel Punishment for Childhood Pranks?

The way many read this text, a mild personal offense by some innocent little children was turned into a federal case by a crotchety old prophet as short on hair as he was on humor. Put in its sharpest form, the complaint goes: How can I believe in a God who would send bears to devour little children for innocently teasing an old man whose appearance probably was unusual even for that day?

At first reading, it appears the prophet chanced on guileless children merrily playing on the outskirts of Bethel. Seeing this strange-looking man, they began to chant in merriment, "Go on up, you baldhead! Go on up, you baldhead!" Instead of viewing the situation for what it was, the old prophet became enraged (as some would tell the story), whirled around and, with eyes flashing anger, shouted a curse in the name of the Lord.

But this is a false reconstruction of the event. The problem begins with the two Hebrew words for "little children," as many older translations term the youths. If we are to untangle this puzzling incident, the age and accountability level of these children must take first priority. "Little children" is an unfortunate translation. The Hebrew expression *n^{e}'ûrîm q^{e}ṭannîm* is best rendered "young lads" or "young men." From numerous examples where ages are specified in the Old Testament, we know that these were boys from twelve to thirty years old. One of these words described Isaac at his sacrifice in Genesis 22:12, when he was easily in his early twenties. It described Joseph in Genesis 37:2 when he was seventeen years old. In fact, the same word described army men in 1 Kings 20:14-15.

If someone objects, yes, but the word *q^{e}ṭannîm* (which is translated "little" in some versions) makes the difference in this context, I will answer that it is best translated "young," not "little." Furthermore, these words have a good deal of elasticity to them. For example, Samuel asked Jesse, "Are these all your children *[nᵉʿûrîm]*?" But Jesse replied, "There is still the youngest *[qāṭān]*." But David was old enough to keep sheep and fight a giant soon after (1 Sam 16:11-12).

"Little children," then, does not mean toddlers or even elementary-school-aged youngsters; these are young men aged between twelve and thirty!

But was Elisha an old man short on patience and a sense of humor? This charge is also distorted, for Elisha can hardly have been more than twenty-five when this incident happened. He lived nearly sixty years after this, since it seems to have taken place shortly after Elijah's translation into heaven. Some would place Elijah's translation around 860 B.C. and Elisha's death around 795 B.C. While Elijah's ministry had lasted less than a decade, Elisha's extended at least fifty-five years, through the reigns of Jehoram, Jehu, Jehoahaz and Joash.

Did Elisha lose his temper? What was so wrong in calling him a "baldhead," even if he might not have been bald, being less than thirty?

The word *baldhead* was a term of scorn in the Old Testament (Is 3:17, 24). Natural baldness was very rare in the ancient Near East. So scarce was baldness that it carried with it a suspicion of leprosy.

Whether Elisha was prematurely bald or not, it is clear that the epithet was used in utter contempt, as a word of insult marking him as despicable.

But since it is highly improbable that Elisha was prematurely bald, the insult was aimed not so much at the prophet as at the God who had sent him. The point is clear from the other phrase. "Go on up," they clamored. "Go on up!" These were not topographical references to the uphill grade of the Bethel road. Instead, the youths were alluding to Elijah's translation to heaven. This they did not believe or acknowledge as God's work in their midst. To put it in modern terms, they jeered, "Blast off! Blast off! You go too. Get out of here. We are tired of both of you." These Bethel ruffians used the same Hebrew verb used at the beginning of the second chapter of 2 Kings to describe the taking up of Elijah into heaven. The connection cannot be missed.

Apparently, news of Elijah's ascension to glory traveled near and far but was greeted with contemptuous disbelief by many, including this youthful mob. The attack was on God, not his prophet.

Elisha uses no profanity in placing a curse on these young men. He merely cited the law of God, which the inhabitants of Bethel knew well. Moses had taught, "If you remain hostile toward me and refuse to listen to me, . . . I will send wild animals against you, and they will rob you of your children" (Lev 26:21-22).

Elisha did not abuse these young men, nor did he revile them; he was content to leave the work of judging to God. He pronounced a judgment on them and asked God to carry out the action which he had promised when his name, his cause and his word were under attack. No doubt these young men only reflected what they heard at the dinner table each evening as the population went further and further away from God.

The savagery of wild animals was brutal enough, but it was mild compared to the legendary cruelty of the Assyrians who would appear to complete God's judgment in 722 B.C. The disastrous fall of Samaria would have been avoided had the people repented after the bear attack and the increasingly severe divine judgments that followed it. But instead of turning back to God, Israel, as would Judah in a later day, "mocked God's messengers, despised his words and scoffed at his prophets until the wrath of the LORD was aroused against his people and there was no remedy" (2 Chron 36:16).

Instead of demonstrating unleashed cruelty, the bear attack shows God trying repeatedly to bring his people back to himself through smaller judgments until the people's sin is too great and judgment must come full force.

See also comment on MARK 10:35.

3:27 Human Sacrifice Worked?

Did not the sacrifice of the king of Moab's son, the heir apparent to the throne, work in that Israel broke off the siege of the city of Kir Hareseth in Moab? Does this count as evidence that the god of the Moabites intervened on their behalf?

When Mesha, king of Moab, refused to send the required annual tribute of wool to Israel, King Jehoram mobilized his forces, in addition to successfully enlisting King Jehoshaphat of Judah, to go to Moab to enforce this tribute.

The whole campaign almost ended in a disaster for both Israel and Judah as they chose to attack from the desert side of that nation, but the prophet Elisha happened to be along to give divine counsel and direction. Miraculously the fortunes of the two armies were reversed, and very quickly the soldiers of Moab turned in full retreat to the city of Kir Hareseth.

King Mesha, seeing that the battle had gone against him, in desperation took his oldest son and offered him on the city wall, apparently hoping that this would appease their god and he would act in delivering them. The Israelites did break off their siege and return home.

Does this mean that their god delivered them? Hardly, given his nonexistence. There was no need to continue the hostilities any further, for the object of the campaign had been achieved: Moab's power was broken and the rebellion suppressed. The country was once again under the jurisdiction of Israel. What more could be achieved? That, along with the revolting spectacle, was enough for all the troops of Israel and Judah.

This is not the only time such a desperate action has been taken in the ancient Near East. Nor is the mention of "fury" to be attributed to God's fury against Israel because of the lengths to which they had pressed the king of Moab, as C. F. Keil thought. Instead, the "fury" was Israel's indignation and revulsion over so gruesome an act and so senseless a waste of life. The guilt was solely on the shoulders of the king of Moab, for as Psalm 106:38 warned:

> They shed innocent blood,
> the blood of their sons and daughters,
> whom they sacrificed to the idols of Canaan,
> and the land was desecrated by their blood.

The sacrifice was so disgusting and revolting to the Israelites because they understood that it rendered the whole land impure, accursed and covered with blood-guilt.

See also comment on GENESIS 22:2; 2 SAMUEL 21:1-9.

6:19 Did Elisha Lie to the Syrians?

Was Elisha truthful when he told the temporarily blinded Syrians who had been sent to capture him that they were not on the right road or in the right city? Or is this to be explained as an example of Elisha's choosing the "greater good" or "lesser evil"?

Some commentators, like Keil and Delitzsch, comment on this verse by saying that Elisha makes an untruthful declaration when he says this is not the way. They judge this to be a statement like every other military stratagem that attempts to deceive the enemy. But W. G. Sumner thought differently. He announced: "There is not untruth in the words of Elisha, for his home was not in Dothan, where he was temporarily residing, but in Samaria; and the words '[I will lead you] to the man' may well mean: to his house." He went on to say that

> Josephus understood the passage correctly; he says: "Elisha asked them whom they had come to seek. When they answered: 'the prophet Elisha,' . . . where he is to be found, . . . [h]e certainly used a form of speech which the Syrians might understand otherwise than as he meant it, but he did not pretend in the least to be anything else than what he was. That they did not know him was a divine dispensation, not the result of an untruth uttered by him. How could the 'man of God,' after repeated prayers to Jehovah, straightway permit himself a falsehood, and try, by this means, to save himself from danger? If he saw, as his companion did, horses and chariots of fire round about him, and if he was thus assured of the divine protection, then he needed for his deliverance neither a falsehood nor a stratagem."[1]

See also comment on EXODUS 1:15-21; 3:18; JOSHUA 2:4-6; 1 SAMUEL 16:1-3.

[1]W. G. Sumner, *The Book of Kings,* Lange Commentary, Book II (New York: Scribner, Armstrong & Co., 1872), p. 69.

6:21-23 Why Were the Syrians Spared?

Why did Elisha spare the lives of this reconnaissance group when most say that the Old Testament elsewhere is marked by a ruthless treatment of Israel's enemies? Does this point to an inconsistent policy in the nation and the testament?

The problem here is that it is wrong to universalize the provision of Deuteronomy 20:13, with its principle of *ḥerem,* the involuntary dedication for total destruction of all those so marked out by God. The conditions of total destruction of all living things and possessions (except what could not burn, such as gold, silver or iron, which was to be put into the tabernacle or temple) applied only to the nation of Canaan. The only other peoples to be involved in the *ḥerem* were the Amalekites, for the reasons announced in the Bible (1 Sam 15:2-3).

All other nations were to be treated differently, even when God had authorized Israel or Judah to proceed against them. The divine permission did not give Israel the right to run roughshod over the population and abuse their human rights and dignity. To do so would be to earn the wrath of God.

Instead of exterminating them, they were to be offered terms of peace. Thus, Elisha prepared a table in the presence of his enemies. Moreover, the Syrian raids ceased operating, for who can fight against a God who knows even the secrets of one's bedroom? Nothing could be concealed from him and nothing could compete with him. No wonder the prophet Elisha was not intimidated in the least by all Syria's power and might. Why should he be?

See also comment on 1 SAMUEL 15:18.

9:6-10 Jehu Punished for Doing As He Was Commanded?

Why is Jehu at first told to carry out the destruction of the house of Ahab and then later on threatened with punishment by the prophet Hosea for doing as he was told (Hos 1:4)?

Jehu was given a twofold divine commission: (1) he was to annihilate all the wicked and apostate house of Ahab, and (2) he was to avenge the blood that Jezebel had shed of the prophets of Yahweh. God's instrument of choice was the army captain, Jehu. These tasks Jehu carried out to the full.

Why then was God displeased with Jehu, as Hosea seems to imply? Because it is one thing to be the instrument God has chosen to punish another person (or group of persons or even a nation) and another to find automatic approval at the completion of the act for the manner in which this task was carried out. For example, Assyria was ordered to move against Israel, but God disapproved of the brutal way Assyria carried out the warfare (Is 10:5-19). Babylon was likewise authorized to move against Judah but was excoriated for cruelty in that war (Hab 1:6; 3:13-16).

Therefore, although Jehu was obedient to God's directive (2 Kings 9:7), he erred grievously in that he killed more people than God had directed and did so with a savagery that did not earn God's approval. It seems clear from Jehu's conduct that he was motivated not by a desire to be obedient to God but by sheer personal ambition—thereby making his act of obedience wicked. It was this same spirit that was transmitted to his descendants, in a heightened degree if anything.

Jehu showed unnecessary cruelty when he slew not only the house of Ahab at Jezreel, but also the visiting monarch from Judah, Ahaziah, and almost all the members of the Davidic family (2 Kings 9:27; 10:13-14). Jehu, furthermore, extended this massacre to all the friends of the ruling family (2 Kings 10:11).

The point is most evident that divine approval for an act does not thereby carry with it indifference as to how that act is accomplished and how many others it may involve.

14:6 Should Children Die for Their Parents' Sins?

See comment on DEUTERONOMY 24:16.

22:20 Gathered to His People?

See comment on GENESIS 25:8.

23:26 Why Did the Lord Not Turn from His Anger?

Is it possible to overcome the effects of years of wickedness and evil by a time of unprecedented reform and revival? Can a godly grandson's thirty-year reign make up for his ruthless grandfather and father, who provoked God to the limit for sixty years? In other words, does evil have a corporate and cumulative effect on society, or, as the saying goes, does "every tub always stand on its own bottom"?

In spite of the probability that Manasseh of Judah became king, or coregent, about ten years before his father, Hezekiah, died, his godly father had no influence on his fifty-year reign. This is especially shocking after the great revival under Hezekiah.

Manasseh illustrates the old saying "God may have children, but he has no grandchildren." In his case a godly home was no guarantee that he would follow the Lord.

For half a century Manasseh duplicated all the depravity of the Canaanites. He murdered so many righteous men that there were too few to defend Jerusalem when the need arose (2 Kings 21:10-15); all of which the people tolerated. This ruthless monarch ordered Isaiah "sawed in two" (Heb 11:37). Manasseh's idolatry and unrighteousness brought Judah and Jerusalem to unavoidable rejection by God (2 Kings 24:3; Jer 15:4).

Manasseh did have what is today called a deathbed conversion experience. For offending the Assyrian king Ashurbanipal, Manasseh was hauled off to prison where "in his distress he sought the favor of the LORD his God and humbled himself greatly before the God of his fathers. And when he prayed to him, the LORD was moved by his entreaty and listened to his plea. . . . Then Manasseh knew that the LORD is God" (2 Chron 33:12-13). This came at the end of his reign.

But it was too late to reverse the trends in society and his own household. Manasseh was succeeded by his wicked son Amon, who himself was assassinated by other ruffians. Second Chronicles 33:23 pointedly informs us that King Amon "did not humble himself before the LORD."

Mercifully God prepared Amon's eight-year-old son, Josiah, to take over as king. From the very beginning, Josiah walked in David's ways and not in the ways of his grandfather Manasseh or his father Amon. He deserves the credit for initiating one of the most intensive periods of reformation and revival known in Judah's history. But it seems this revival never deeply penetrated the culture, for it carried no lasting effects and had insufficient strength to overcome the years of compounded evil accumulated under Manasseh. Josiah's work was insufficient to offset the evil done by his father and grandfather before him.

Though Josiah ended outward and gross forms of idolatry in his sincere desire to dedicate himself and his people to the Lord, the people themselves did not turn back to the Lord. They followed their religious king out of fear, but their hearts and minds, apparently, were affected very little.

If the early chapters of Jeremiah reflect the conditions under King Josiah, then they describe the people's deep inner apostasy, not only before Josiah's reform and discovery of the Book of the Law, but also during and following it.

The Holy One of Israel could no longer forgive and extend mercy; he at last was obligated to bring the judgment foretold to Manasseh in 2 Kings 21:12-15. Thus, even though God is patient and long-suffering in his mercy, judgment will and must eventually come, even though someone arrives on the scene who seemingly cancels the debt standing against all the people (2 Kings 22:15-20).

24:6 A Failed Prophecy?

See comment on JEREMIAH 36:30.

1 CHRONICLES

1:1—9:44 Why So Many Long Genealogies?
It seems pointless, if not boring, to occupy so many chapters of the Bible with what is tantamount to a telephone directory list of names. Why is so much space devoted to what does not seem to be of any spiritual profit or usefulness to subsequent generations?

Chronicles begins with nine chapters of genealogies. The purpose of this exercise is quite complex. Naturally, if one's own family were involved, it would have a lot more direct personal interest, for you can be sure you would look to see if the name of your relative was listed. But given the whole history of the plan of redemption, our individual interests are not far removed from that at all—in fact, if anything, all the more increased. For it was through this family of Adam, Eve, Shem and Abraham that all the families of the earth would be blessed.

First of all, 1 Chronicles 1—9 proposes to present a historical review of Israel in outline form. Second, it provides a literary connection with the death of Saul (described in 1 Chron 10) and a list of the returning exiles (1 Chron 9). Some of the names, no doubt, are included merely for the sake of completeness, or at least to help bridge the centuries. But the most important purpose of these genealogies, in the third place, is to demonstrate that there is movement in history toward a divinely predetermined goal. Even though the Israelites throughout the ages are marshaled here from the famous and the infamous, the north and the south, the rich and the poor, the underlying factor common to them all is the fact that the God of Israel is the one who has preserved and guided his people thus far to that goal and end that God has planned; he, therefore, will be the one who will complete that very same process.

Thus the chronicler moved from Adam (1 Chron 1:1) to the decree of Cyrus allowing the people to return to rebuild the temple (2 Chron 36:22-23). It was all part of one plan, with the tapestry being woven principally with just ordinary people in Israel whom God had called.

See also comment on "Why Don't Bible Genealogies Always Match Up?"

2:13-15 Did Jesse Have Seven or Eight Sons?

Did Jesse father seven or eight sons? Chronicles says it was seven, but Samuel says it was eight (1 Sam 16:10-11; 17:12-14). Which one is accurate?

First Samuel 16 only names four of Jesse's sons: Eliab, Abinadab, Shammah, who is called Shimea in 1 Chronicles, and David. First Chronicles gives the names of three other sons, Nethanel, Raddai and Ozem, but specifies that David is the seventh. What happened to the other unnamed son, that 1 Chronicles 2 totally ignores, is unknown. Some commentators suggest that this unnamed son may have died without any posterity, and therefore his name was not included in the list in Chronicles.

The reading of the Syriac lists an Elihu as the seventh son in 1 Chronicles 2:15 and then lists David as the eighth, thereby bringing the two lists in Samuel and Chronicles into harmony with each other. The Syriac reading is based on the Hebrew reading of 1 Chronicles 27:18, where the Septuagint has Eliab instead of Elihu (apparently going with the known name from the list in 1 Samuel). If the Syriac and Hebrew preserve accurate traditions, then Elihu is the son missing from the list of 1 Chronicles 2:15.

3:1-9 Why So Many Wives?

See comment on 2 SAMUEL 20:3; 1 KINGS 11:1-2.

6:16, 22-23, 25-26 Was Samuel a Levite or an Ephraimite?

Which tribe did Samuel come from? Why does 1 Samuel 1:1 list him as being from Ephraim, while Chronicles declares he was a Levite?

Critical commentators suppose that Samuel's father, Elkanah, was depicted as a Levite, even though there was nothing in the Samuel narrative that said as much, because the chronicler noted that there was an Elkanah in the line of Kohath and the line of Samuel. Therefore, he mistakenly, or deliberately, attached Samuel's name to the line of Kohath.

But there is an indication in the Samuel narrative that he was from a Levitical line: the fact that he was accepted by the high priest Eli to be an apprentice. Later, when Samuel reached maturity, he functioned as a priest and conducted sacrifices at various centers in Israel.

But what about 1 Samuel 1:1? It simply states that Elkanah was "from" Ramathaim-zophim, or "Ramathaim, a Zuphite," on Mount Ephraim, or the hill country of Ephraim. Typically the Levites would be assigned to "Levitical cities" throughout Israel. Numbers 35:6 knows of forty-eight cities so designated, but we do not know if Ramathaim was one of them.

Our conclusion is that Elkanah was a Levite assigned to, or living in, Ephraim. Even the ancestry listed in Samuel accords with that given in Chronicles. No contradiction, therefore, need be assumed.

13:9-10 Why Did God Destroy Uzzah?

See comment on 2 SAMUEL 6:6-7.

15:29 Was David's Public Dancing Indecent?

See comment on 2 SAMUEL 6:20.

19:18 How Many Charioteers?

The Chronicles account says that David killed seven thousand charioteers, but 2 Samuel 10:18 gives the number as seven hundred. Some claim that this illustrates a tendency for the chronicler to somewhat magnify David's stature and character. Is this an accurate assessment of the habits of the chronicler, or is there some adequate explanation for this discrepancy?

First Chronicles 18:4-5 is the fullest and best statement of what took place at this encounter. If this is true, the Chronicles figure of seven thousand charioteers, or horsemen, is no doubt the correct figure and the one that lies behind the transcriptional error of seven hundred in 2 Samuel 10:18. Note that some Septuagintal texts of 2 Samuel 10:18 agree with Chronicles. Furthermore, the forty thousand "foot soldiers" of Chronicles is the correct reading, not "horsemen" as in Samuel, for the figure matches closely, as a rounded number, the twenty thousand plus twenty-two thousand foot soldiers given in 1 Chronicles 18:4-5. This seems to be the best solution to the problem.

The present Hebrew manuscripts for the books of 1 and 2 Samuel have more transcriptional errors in them than any other book or combination of books in the Old Testament. From the preliminary checks seen in the Dead Sea Scroll manuscripts of Samuel, the Greek translation of the Septuagint appears to reflect a much better Hebrew manuscript.[1]

Another attempt to resolve this problem suggests that when Samuel talked about the "[men of] chariots" or "[men of the] chariot divisions" (to which the seven hundred presumably belonged), he was speaking of a separate group of personnel from the (seven thousand) "charioteers," but no evidence exists to support this distinction.

The discrepancy is a problem of the correct text of Samuel and does not support the thesis that the chronicler had a tendency to magnify numbers in order to glorify David.

[1]Some preliminary but as yet unpublished reports from the Dead Sea Scrolls of Qumran do indicate that at least some readings of the Dead Sea Scroll copies of Samuel are in agreement with readings previously found only in Chronicles. See Frank M. Cross Jr., *The Ancient Library of Qumran*, rev. ed. (Garden City, N.Y.: Anchor Books, 1961), pp. 188-91, and Ralph W. Klein, *Textual Criticism of the Old Testament* (Philadelphia: Fortress, 1974), pp. 42-50.

21:1-2, 8 Why Was the Census a Sin?

God had commanded Moses twice to take a census in Numbers 1 and 26, yet in 2 Samuel David numbers Israel because God, angry with Israel, incites him to it; 1 Chronicles attributes the result to the influence of Satan on David. Are these contradictory passages an instance where error has crept into Scripture?

Let us first establish why census-taking could be sinful. In effect, the census acted as a draft notice or a mustering of the troops. Some conclude, based on 1 Chronicles 27:23-24, that David sinned by numbering those people under twenty years of age—an illegal act. Others see the numbering as doubting God's promise that David's descendants would be as measureless as the sand and stars. The best solution is that it was motivated by presumption. God had given David no objective or reaon to go out to battle. Only David's pride and ambition could have brought on such an act.

The *and* at the beginning of 1 Chronicles 21:1 in some translations seems to invite us to look at the conclusion of the previous chapter. First Chronicles 20:8 mentions that the giant's descendants were among those whom David and his men vanquished. The connection could be that David, flushed with his successes, grew too big in his own eyes and opened the door for Satan to successfully tempt him.

This brings us to the second difficulty of this hard saying: Was it God or Satan who tempted David to sin? Satan is mentioned infrequently in the Old Testament. He was introduced in Job 1—2 and in the postexilic period in Zechariah 3:1. However, in both of these latter cases, the definite article is used; 1 Chronicles 21:1 does not use it. Even though the doctrine of the supernatural being named Satan was not well developed in the Old Testament, the appearance of Satan cannot be reduced to Persian dualism or one's adversary in general. Even in the Garden of Eden there exists a hostile presence called "the serpent." What is new in this passage is the formalizing of his name as "the adversary" or "opposer." But the activities of the serpent and Satan make it clear that they are the same person.

How then does this relatively unidentified but never-absent personage play a key role in one version of David's sin when God receives the dubious credit in another?

The thought that God instigates or impels sinners to do evil is incorrect. In no sense could God author what he disapproves of and makes his whole kingdom stand against. How then shall we understand 2 Samuel 24:1, where God seems to instigate something which he will immediately label as sin?

God may and does occasionally impel sinners to reveal the wickedness of their hearts in deeds. God merely presents the opportunity and occasion for letting the evil desires of the heart manifest themselves outwardly. In this manner, sinners may see more quickly the evil which lies dormant in their hearts and motivates them to act counter to God's will.

It is also true, according to Hebrew thinking, that whatever God permits he commits. By allowing this census-taking, God is viewed as having brought about the act. The Hebrews were not very concerned with determining secondary causes and properly attributing them to the exact cause. Under the idea of divine providence everything ultimately was attributed to God; why not say he did it in the first place?

Since the number of variations here between Samuel and Chronicles are greater than usual and point to no clear rationale for emphasizing one set of facts over another, scholars suggest that Chronicles may represent the better and more dependable text tradition of the original Hebrew rather than that reflected in English versions of Samuel.

Although we should not overestimate the textual variants between Samuel and Chronicles in this chapter, some of the texts from Qumran's Dead Sea Scrolls indicate that some of its Samuel readings agree with readings previously found only in Chronicles. This would bring more harmony to the differences among texts.

Almost all students of Scripture judge that Chronicles was composed during the exile or just after it. Therefore it likely was based on an earlier form of the Samuel narrative no doubt well known and widely used. Note the way that the writer of Chronicles linked his materials; it reflects a linkage explicitly made in 2 Samuel 24:1. There the writer of 2 Samuel 24:1 noted, "Again the anger of the LORD burned," a reference to 2 Samuel 21:1-14, which also had to do with atonement for guilt. Accordingly, even though the chronicler omitted the material in 2 Samuel 23—24, he had a literary precedent for linking the materials in 2 Samuel 21 and 24. The selection of a site for the temple in Jerusalem marked a fitting climax to this phase of David's activity.

Having shown that David did indeed sin and that Satan, not God, was to blame, that still leaves all Israel the victims of the plague God sent to punish the sin. But David's subjects were as guilty as their king, according to 2 Samuel 24:1. Thus God dealt with all Israel through the act of the king who exemplified the national spirit of pride.

21:5 What Was Israel's Population?

See comment on 2 SAMUEL 24:9.

21:25 How Many Shekels for the Altar Site?

This is another of the alleged cases of the chronicler's exaggeration, this time to magnify the temple by increasing the sale price for David's altar (and eventually the site of the temple) from 50 shekels of silver (2 Sam 24:24) to 600 shekels of gold.

But the Chronicles text clearly and explicitly says that David bought "the site" (Hebrew *hammāqôm*), which included the whole area of Mount Moriah. Using the standard of one ounce of gold equal to $400 in modern currency, David paid approximately $100,000 for the site. Samuel, however, stated the price for the oxen and the threshing floor, a very small portion of the entire area. For that David paid a mere 50 shekels of *silver*. Some have noted that 600 is 12 times 50, a fact that might have been intended to imply national significance. The purchase of this larger area may have come later, after the initial purchase of the threshing floor and oxen used by David in the original sacrifice.

The distinction between the two purchases also helps explain why Araunah offered, at first, to donate to David the threshing floor. It is difficult to conceive that he would have been in a position to donate all of Mount Moriah, but he might well offer just the threshing floor.

22:14 Too Much Gold and Silver?

The figures stated for gold and silver raised by David to build the temple seem so high as to be beyond being credible. Furthermore, they stand in poor relationship to other figures given in 1 Chronicles 29:4, 7 and 2 Chronicles 9:13. What is the best explanation of this matter?

The total amount of gold and silver adds up to over forty thousand tons—a sum that boggles the mind even for one of the Caesars or Pharaohs.

Yet C. F. Keil supported these figures by saying that "in the capitals of the Asiatic kingdoms of antiquity, enormous quantities of the precious metals were accumulated," for he quotes from ancient documents to show that Cyrus obtained 500,000 talents of silver in his Asiatic campaigns alone.[1] He concluded his discussion of these amounts by saying, "We cannot therefore regard the sums mentioned in our verse either as incredible or very much exaggerated, nor hold the round sums which correspond to the rhetorical character of the passage with certainty to be mistakes."[2]

We cannot use the figures given in 1 Chronicles 29:4, 7 as a means to determine the accuracy of those in the text we are examining. In 1 Chronicles 22 David makes the lead donation for the work of the temple, to which he then invited others to add in supporting the same project. These, then, are supplemental contributions beyond the major gift already promised by David.

The fact that Solomon received yearly only 666 talents of gold, or about 25 tons, has a bearing on this problem, of course. But that amount in 2 Chronicles 9:13 did not include the money brought in by the merchants and traders and the kings of Arabia and governors of the land (2 Chron 9:14). Therefore assuming something much in excess of 25 tons of gold per year, David could have collected in almost 40 years a considerable amount of gold, since he was capturing and looting all the neighboring kingdoms, while Solomon could only depend on the revenue that came from taxes and trade.

Therefore, it is quite possible that this is another error in textual transmission, for which numbers were especially susceptible in antiquity. But so far there is no way to prove the case either one way or the other. The jury is still out on this problem.

---

[1]C. F. Keil, *The Books of Chronicles* (Grand Rapids, Mich.: Eerdmans, 1950), pp. 247-48.

[2]Ibid., pp. 248-49. See also Alan R. Millard, "Does the Bible Exaggerate King Solomon's Golden Wealth?" *Biblical Archaeology Review* 15, no. 3 (1989): 21-29, 31, 34, and Kenneth A. Kitchen, "Where Did Solomon's Wealth Go?" *Biblical Archaeology Review* 15, no. 3 (1989): 30, 32-33.

2 CHRONICLES

11:2-4 This Is the Lord's Doing? After the ten northern tribes had renounced their allegiance to King Rehoboam, the son of Solomon, Rehoboam decided that he would force these renegades to submit to his sovereignty and to pay the taxes which were their reason for leaving. This would have pitted brother against brother in open civil war.

But God sent his prophet Shemaiah to intervene. Rehoboam was commanded in the Lord's name to abandon his attempt at a military solution. Shemaiah's surprising announcement seemed to oppose all God's previous promises. The prophet's assurance that God had permitted the incident sealed the revolt but left us with a dilemma: How could the division of a nation be God's doing if he had previously promised otherwise?

Having David's glorious kingdom divided into ten northern tribes and two southern tribes seemed contrary to every provision that God had so graciously given from the time of the patriarchs on. How could God apparently aid a cause that contravened his plan for Israel?

The Lord approved the revolt not as the author of evil or as the instigator of the rebellion but as the one who must chastise the house of David which had refused to walk in his ways. Solomon had flouted the will and law of God by taking scores of foreign wives. These wives had turned him from the Lord and exposed him to divine anger.

Rehoboam had only increased the guilt of the house of David. The tribes were already overwhelmed by taxation and unsatisfying treatment of their complaints. They had demanded that the burdens Solomon had placed on them be lightened, not increased. Instead, Rehoboam exacerbated the situation by deciding to tax them further.

The ten northern tribes already disliked and resisted the theocratic rule of the house of David. While they correctly detected Rehoboam's wrong attitudes toward his responsibilities as king, Rehoboam's treatment did not justify their actions. They chiefly rebelled against the God who had selected the dynasty of

David and the tribe of Judah as the royal tribe. Apparently they felt such rule did not represent enough of their northern interests; the taxation issue was as good a reason as any for seceding (see 1 Kings 12:19-24).

Here we meet another passage where human freedom and divine sovereignty seem opposed. This phenomenon is especially prevalent in Chronicles. Once again we must note that the biblical writers did not always take time to spell out secondary causes; for what God permits, he is often said to do directly since he is ultimately in charge. What the North intended as a revolt against the South, and thereby against the plan of God, God used first to punish the house of David for its sin and second to reveal the North's sinful tendencies and spiritual bankruptcy. This latter fact is underscored by the number of northern priests and Levites who abandoned their pasturelands and property to come to Judah and Jerusalem. The northern king, Jeroboam, had rejected their priesthood! With them came all those who "set their hearts on seeking the LORD, the God of Israel" (2 Chron 11:16).

See also comment on GENESIS 50:19-21.

11:20 Who Was Absalom's Daughter?

In 2 Samuel 14:27 Tamar is spoken of as the only daughter of Absalom. Why, then, is Maacah also called Absalom's daughter?

Tamar was named after Absalom's sister, whom Absalom's half brother, Amnon, had raped, but whom Absalom avenged by killing him. Later Tamar married Uriel of Gibeah. Their daughter was Maacah, who married King Rehoboam, and was the mother of the next king, Abijam. Thus Rehoboam's wife Maacah was actually the granddaughter of Absalom, through Absalom's immediate daughter Tamar.

The use of the word *daughter* to fit the concept of granddaughter is a phenomenon not unknown in Hebrew. See the similar usage in Genesis 46:15, where the "sons" of Leah includes grandsons.

18:18-22 Is God the Author of Falsehood?

See comment on 1 KINGS 22:20-22.

35:22 Pharaoh Neco Spoke at God's Command?

Few incidents in the life of Israel and Judah are as sad as this episode. Rarely had one of the nation's monarchs so genuinely desired to serve God. Even as Josiah began his reign at the tender age of eight, he had purposed to walk in the ways of David and not in the ways of his evil father, Amon, and grandfather, Manasseh.

It was Josiah who had started the great reforms in Judah. These were followed by the discovery of the Book of the Law when the temple was cleaned in the eighteenth year of his reign, 621 B.C. When at age twenty-six Josiah first had the law of God read to him, he tore his robes in grief and true repentance before God. Here was one of history's great men. His heart was responsive to God, and he did not hesitate to humble himself before God (2 Chron 34:27).

But in 609 B.C., when this king with all his potential for furthering the kingdom of God was only thirty-nine, he was struck down by one giant act of foolish disobedience.

In 2 Kings 23:25-38 the catastrophe is partially explained: Even though Josiah had followed the Lord with all his heart, soul and strength and had obeyed the law of Moses so that there was no king like him, yet God did not turn from his great wrath against Judah. God would still destroy Judah because of King Manasseh's sins and the superficial repentance of the people. Such an explanation softens the blow of the pending tragedy.

In the Chronicles account, however, no such didactic connection was included. Instead, Josiah's godly obedience alone introduces the tragic episode: "After all this, when Josiah had set the temple in order" (2 Chron 35:20). This would seem to stress that Josiah was devoted to the temple right up to the end of his life.

The scene for Josiah's end was now set. The Assyrian king Asshur-uballit had established a new capital at Carchemish in 610 B.C. The Egyptians were interested in helping the Assyrians, for they feared that the emerging fortunes of the Babylonians would upset the balance of power in the Near East. Thus in the summer of 609 B.C. a great Egyptian army moved up the Palestinian coast to join the Assyrians in a great counteroffensive.

A phrase in 2 Kings 23:29 sometimes translated "Neco went up against the king of Assyria" is better translated as "Neco went up *on behalf of* the king of Assyria, to the river Euphrates." When translated accurately, this verse illuminates Josiah's reason for fighting Neco.

Josiah viewed Neco's advance as a menace to his own designs for a reunited Hebrew state. Josiah thought that any friend of the hated Assyrians must be his enemy. Therefore he boldly disregarded all prophetic warnings to the contrary and directly intervened, trying to block the Egyptian army from joining the Assyrians.

Amazingly enough, in this case the prophetic warnings do not come from one of Israel's traditional prophets but from a pagan Pharaoh who warns Josiah to halt his attempt to meddle with his mission. Neco claimed that "God has told me to hurry; so stop opposing God, who is with me, or he will destroy you" (2 Chron 35:21).

Then follow the mournful yet amazing words of the inspired writer: "Josiah, however, would not turn away from him, but disguised himself to engage him in battle. He would not listen to what Neco had said at God's command, but went to fight him on the plain of Megiddo. Archers shot King Josiah, and . . . he died" (2 Chron 35:22-24).

This is indeed one of the strangest statements in Scripture, which we would dismiss as Egyptian propaganda had not the inspired writer confirmed that God did use a pagan monarch to warn Josiah and assist the Assyrians.

God had spoken to pagan kings previously without implying that they had become prophets of Israel or converted to worshiping the one true God (see Gen 12:17-20; 20:3-7; and Dan 4:1-3). The instrument was not the focal point of the prophecy; its content was. God had also previously spoken through the mouth of an ass (Num 22:28-31) and would later speak through a profane high priest (Jn 11:51). But King Josiah did not perceive that God could use such an instrument as a Pharaoh.

In an act reminiscent of King Ahab, Josiah disguised himself and went into a battle he was not supposed to be in. The archer's arrow found its mark, and Josiah was carried away to die.

But the plan of God was still operating. Josiah, it had been prophesied by Huldah, would be gathered to his fathers and "buried in peace" (2 Chron 34:28). His "eyes [would] not see all the disaster [God was] going to bring on [that] place and on those who live[d] [there]."

The event was so tragic that Jeremiah the prophet composed lamentations for Josiah. But in spite of these laments, the people marched relentlessly toward the destruction that would take place within twenty-three years of Josiah's death. In fact, not more than three years after his death, in 606 B.C., the Babylonians, whom Josiah seemed to favor, took the first Hebrew captives, including the prophet Daniel and his three friends. In 597 B.C. Ezekiel was taken into exile. Finally the city fell and was burned down, temple included, in 586 B.C.

For one major blunder, a leader's whole career ended. Yet graciously the record did not dwell on this one sin. Instead it attributed most of the cause to his grandfather Manasseh. Furthermore, the account of Josiah's life magnanimously ends not by underscoring the king's final weakness and disobedience, but by recalling Josiah's "acts of devotion" or "his goodness" (2 Chron 35:26). God's commendation was "Well done, good and faithful servant." Thus out of tragedy, God was still working his purposes. What seemed a horrible end for God's faithful servant-king was in fact a reward. He was spared the horror of viewing the demise of everything the nation and God had built in Judah during the preceding millennium and a half.

36:22-23 Did the Pagan King Cyrus Believe in the God of Israel?

See comment on EZRA 1:1-2.

EZRA

1:1-2 Did the Pagan King Cyrus Believe in the God of Israel?

Does the text of Ezra 1:1 imply that Cyrus was using these titles for Yahweh, engaging in the task of building the temple in Jerusalem and releasing those who wished to return from their exile to Israel, because he was a convert to the Lord God of Israel?

The oral proclamation (which was also recorded in writing) referred to here is the famous "Edict of Cyrus." A similar inscription from the same king was found by Hormuzd Rassam's excavations of Babylon in 1879-82, called the "Cyrus Cylinder." This clay, barrel-shaped artifact demonstrates that Cyrus made similar proclamations concerning other people's gods, so very little can be gained from his use of such terms as "Yahweh" (here translated "LORD"), "the God [or god] of heaven," or even that God "moved on his heart," other than the fact that this king had a knack for being politically correct long before this term ever came into vogue.

From the writer's point of view, it was Yahweh who had moved the heart of Cyrus to adopt a policy of repatriating and erecting the houses of worship of those peoples whom he helped to repatriate. The heart of the king, regardless of his own religious proclivities, is in the hand of the Lord (Prov 21:1).

Jeremiah had predicted that Judah would be seventy years in Babylonian captivity (Jer 25:1-12; 29:10). Some two hundred years prior to Cyrus's day, Isaiah had foretold that a man named Cyrus would both enact the policy of repatriation and aid in the reconstruction of the temple; indeed, Cyrus would be the Lord's "shepherd" (Is 44:28; 45:1).

Judah was not the only nation to benefit from Cyrus's enlightened policies; his generosity went to all his subjects alike, to judge from those archaeological records that are left to us. Cyrus probably, like the other Achaemenidian kings, was influenced by Zoroastrianism. No evidence exists that he ever became a believer in the Lord God who revealed himself in Israel and Judah.

3:8 Why the Discrepancy in Ages for Levitical Service?

See comment on NUMBERS 4:3.

4:2 Why Refuse Help to Build the Temple?

Why would the returned exiles refuse a sincere offer to help with the construction of the temple of God, especially from those who also claimed to be worshipers of the true God? It seems a bit extreme and peculiar to just flatly refuse any kind of assistance. What was the reason for their firm denial?

The persons who offered help were probably from the area of Samaria, though it is not explicitly stated. The Assyrians had imported large numbers of newcomers from all over the empire into Samaria and northern Israel after the fall of the capital in 722 B.C., in a policy of fragmenting the cultures so that a chance for a coordinated insurrection was minimal. This infusion of peoples further diluted the already watered-down faith of the northern kingdom, as the various ethnic and religious groups brought their own gods and religions with them. Where isolationism did not exist for a displaced ethnic group, religious syncretism was the order of the day.

Now the offer of these people to help build the temple was not as innocent as it appeared on the surface. They did not have the same convictions, share the same allegiance to the Word of God, or worship Yahweh alone. Though they claimed to worship the same God as the Jews did, their acknowledgment of him was in name only, for they simultaneously worshiped other gods (2 Kings 17:33). Such syncretism was not compatible with the exclusive demands that Yahweh made on his people.

Zerubbabel's refusal to accept help, then, must not be viewed as being sinfully separatistic or just plain mistaken. No doubt the leaders of the province of Samaria viewed the emergence of a new, aggressive presence in Judah, one that enjoyed the favor of the imperial government of Persia, as a threat. Hence their offer to help in sharing the costs and labor in building the temple would have entailed a certain amount of control in the temple itself. It would appear that the offer had more of the overtones of political power than of pure neighborliness. It was for this reason that Zerubbabel refused help from these who usually were their enemies.

10:2-3 Let Us Send Away All These Women and Their Children!

The issue of divorce is never a pleasant topic, for those who are affected by it or for those who must interpret what the Scriptures say about it. This text arouses the question of whether divorce is a morally proper corrective for apostasy. If so, how can this be squared with the outright statement in Malachi 2:16 that God hates divorce?

The marriage problems in Ezra 9—10 began in this way. In the seventh year of Artaxerxes (458 B.C.), Ezra led a second group of Jewish exiles from Babylon to Jerusalem, only to learn that a serious problem existed in the community that had developed under Zerubbabel. Influenced by leaders of this new community, the priests and Levites, along with others in Jerusalem, had intermarried with the pagan population they had found living in the land. When Ezra learned this, he ripped his garments and pulled out his hair in horror and grief. He was dumbfounded as to what to do.

At the evening sacrifice, Ezra fell on his knees in prayer before God, confessing his shame and guilt on behalf of his nation. As he prayed, others joined him in weeping and prayer. Suddenly, Shecaniah, one of the sons of Elam, proposed a solution: the people would acknowledge their sin and make a covenant with God that all pagan wives be put away. Ezra apparently agreed that this was the mind of the Lord, and so an announcement was made that in three days the putting away would take place.

On that third day, the people stood in the rain as Ezra intoned these words: "You have been unfaithful; you have married foreign women, adding to Israel's guilt. Now make confession to the LORD, the God of your fathers, and do his will. Separate yourselves from the peoples around you and from your foreign wives" (Ezra 10:10-11).

Now according to the list in Ezra 10, only 113 had taken foreign wives (17 priests, 6 Levites, 1 singer, 3 porters and 86 laity). Since the total number of families was something like 29,000, the size of the problem shrinks under closer scrutiny to about 0.4 percent. Nevertheless, the issue was not size but the severing of Israel's marriage covenant with God, which forbade God's people marrying persons outside the covenant.

Even before Israel had entered into the land, they had been warned not to intermarry with the inhabitants (Ex 34:11-16; Deut 7:1-5). Such intermarriage would inevitably result in idolatry. Though there were many intermarriages throughout Israel's history, apparently many of these involved proselytes. The outstanding examples, of course, are Ruth, Rahab and Moses' Cushite wife. But many others cannot be explained as converts; they often appear to be tolerated and left in the midst of God's people. Ultimately, this was one of the factors that led to God's judgment and the Babylonian captivity.

What did Ezra do with these wives? The word translated "to send away" or "to cause to go out" in Ezra 10:3 is not the usual word for divorce. Nevertheless, that is what appears to have happened. Even more surprising, their solution is said to agree with the law!

Divorce was permitted under certain circumstances in Deuteronomy 24:1-4. Could it be that Ezra unlocked the meaning of that mysterious phrase "for something unseemly, shameful" or, as the NIV translates it, "he finds something indecent about her"? This could not refer to adultery, as the law provided the death penalty in that case (Deut 22:22). Thus it had to be something else that brought shame on God's people. What could bring greater shame than the breaking of the covenant relationship and the ultimate judgment of God on all the people? Perhaps Ezra had this passage in mind when he provided for the divorce of these unbelieving wives.

There are many questions that remain. Were the ostracized children and wives provided for? Were any attempts made to win them to faith in the one true God? No direct answers are given to these and similar questions, perhaps because these matters were not germane to the main point of revelation.

Those attempting to show that Ezra rendered a questionable decision say he lost his prestige and influence in the community as a result of this decision. However, when the chronology of Ezra and Nehemiah is restored to its proper sequence, according to the textual claims and the most recent historical studies, Ezra was once again before the public during the revival of Nehemiah recorded in Nehemiah 8.

Are we left then with an argument for divorcing unbelieving spouses today? No! In fact, 1 Corinthians 7:12-16 says that if the unbeliever is willing to continue living with the believer, then they must not divorce, for the unbelieving partner is sanctified by the believer! However, should the unbeliever finally and irremediably desert the believer, the believer "is not bound in such circumstances; God has called us to live in peace" (1 Cor 7:15). The object is to win the unbelieving spouse to Christ. But when an unbeliever chooses to desert his or her partner and marriage vows, then reluctantly the believer may let that one go, that is, sadly accept the divorce, with the right to be married to another.

See also comment on DEUTERONOMY 24:1-4; MALACHI 2:16; MARK 10:11-12.

NEHEMIAH

8:8 Making Clear the Book of the Law?

The issue in this verse concerns the word here translated as "making it clear" (*mᵉpōrāš*). Some render it "to translate." This would mean that the exiles who had returned from seventy years of captivity in Babylon had become fluent in Aramaic but had lost their ability to understand the text of the Law as it was read in Hebrew.

But if these Jews really had lost their knowledge of Hebrew, then why were such postexilic books as 1 and 2 Chronicles, Ezra, Nehemiah, Esther, Haggai, Zechariah and Malachi written in Hebrew? If the writers of these texts wanted to reach the Jewish audience of the fifth and fourth centuries B.C., why would they have chosen to use an archaic language that the people no longer grasped?

Approximately one week after the returnees had completed the walls of Jerusalem (Neh 6:15; 7:1), the people assembled in the square in front of the famous Water Gate (Neh 3:26). There Ezra, the scribe, began a public reading of the Torah of Moses (Neh 8:1).

Although Ezra is not recorded as having had a major part in the fifty-two-day rebuilding of the walls of Jerusalem, he now appeared on the scene as a spiritual leader and as the reader of the Law of God. Ezra had led an earlier return of some fifty thousand Jews from Babylon in 458 B.C. Nehemiah had come later, in 445 B.C., as a civil leader leading an aroused populace to quickly rebuild the walls of the holy city.

It was the first day of the month of Tishri, the day designated as the Feast of Trumpets (Lev 23:24; Num 29:1). As specified by the law, this was a day of rest and worship. It was a time of preparation for the most significant day in Israel's religious calendar, the Day of Atonement, celebrated on the tenth of Tishri (approximately our September/October).

The assembly included all men, women and children who could understand (Neh 8:2). The meeting began early in the morning, at the break of day, and

Ezra read until midday—approximately six hours! He spoke from a wooden platform that accommodated not only his pulpit but also the thirteen Levites who helped him in this work. Just how these thirteen men functioned is not altogether clear. Did they assist him in the reading of the Law, or did they split the people up into small groups from time to time to assist them in their comprehension of what was being read?

As the Book of the Law was opened, the people stood to show their respect for the Word of God. Prior to the reading, however, Ezra led the people in a prayer of praise to the Lord their God. The people responded with "Amen! Amen!" as they lifted their hands and bowed down in worship to the Lord (Neh 8:6).

At this point the problematic verse appears. What does *m*^{e}*pōrāš* mean? Does it mean "to translate"—in this case, from Hebrew into the cognate tongue of Aramaic—or does it mean to give an exposition of the passage and make the sense clear?

The root from which this word comes, *pāraš,* has the basic meaning "to make distinct or separate." It could refer to the way the words were distinctly articulated, or better still, to the Law's being read and expounded section by section. The word *pārāšā,* a cognate of the term we are considering, was used by the Hebrew Masoretic scribes to speak of dividing the Pentateuch into paragraphs or sections for each reading. Therefore, we cannot agree that the Levites were mere translators for the people. They "broke out" the standard Pentateuchal sections and followed the readings with exposition, "giving the meaning so the people could understand what was being read."

The motive for observing this Feast of Trumpets (or Rosh Hashanah, the Jewish New Year's Day) was the people's thanksgiving for God's gracious assistance in rebuilding the wall. This goodness of God led them instinctively to want to hear more of God's Word. They stood by the hour to listen intently to that Word and to have it explained to them.

There is no need to wonder why so many postexilic books of the Old Testament were written in Hebrew. The only alleged evidence that the Jewish returnees could not speak Hebrew is this one word in Nehemiah 8:8, and there are no linguistic grounds for thinking that it means "translating."

ESTHER

4:13-14 Esther—For Such a Time as This

Why does the book of Esther, which so wonderfully illustrates the doctrine of the providence of God, never once use the name of God? And what does this strange saying in Esther 4:14 mean? The sentence contains a figure of speech known as aposiopesis—a sudden breaking off of what was being said or written so that the mind is more impressed by what is left unsaid, it being too wonderful, solemn or awful to verbalize. In English this figure is sometimes called the "sudden silence."

Taking the last problem first, it must be noted that the last clause in Esther 4:14 is usually understood to mean "Who knows whether you have not for a time like this attained royalty?" This makes very good sense, but it cannot be justified linguistically. The sentence contains an aposiopesis, since the object of "who knows" is unexpressed. It is incorrect to translate the verse with a conditional "whether . . . not" (as in the RSV, for example) rather than "but that." The omitted clause in the aposiopesis would be "what might not have been done." The resulting translation, with the suppressed clause now included, would be "Who knows what might not have been done but that you attained to royalty for such a time as this?"

"Who knows" can also be translated "perhaps." On that rendering, Mordecai would have said, "Perhaps you have attained to royalty [to the dignity of being queen] for a time like this [to use your position to deliver your people]." Thus Mordecai's speech contains an urgent appeal to Esther to use her high position to preserve her fellow Jews from destruction.

The absence of God's name from the book must also be faced. Many interpreters rightly focus on the phrase "another place" in Esther 4:14 ("if you remain silent at this time, relief and deliverance for the Jews will arise from another place"). This particular phrase is one of the most debated yet most crucial in the book of Esther.

Did Mordecai have another individual in mind? Or did he think that some other world power would arise to deliver the Jews out of this empire?

Surely the Greek "A" text, Josephus, and 1 and 2 Targums are correct in seeing in "another place" a veiled reference to God, just as the New Testament uses "kingdom of heaven" as a circumlocution for "the kingdom of God" and as 1 Maccabees 16:3 uses "mercy" as a veiled allusion to God. Often in later Talmudic literature, the word "place" *(māqôm)* would be used in place of the name of God.

Furthermore, the fact that Esther asked the community of Jews to fast on her behalf (Esther 4:16) indicates that she and they sought divine help. Moreover, faith in the providence of God and his hand in history is illustrated throughout the book. In Esther, the wonderful works of God declare his name; there is no need to spell out that name when his hand and presence can be detected everywhere.

8:11 Approval of Slaughter?

Some object to this part of the Esther story, stating that no ruler would issue such an arbitrary decree sanctioning the slaughter of vast numbers of his subjects, including many unoffending citizens. But surely this appeal is not based on history; these objectors have not read much about the extent or excesses of despotic power.

The real point is not the apparent injustice the Jews called for. Rather, it was the enormous unfairness of the king's original agreement with Haman to annihilate a total race of people. Therefore, if blame must be laid at someone's feet, it must be at those of King Xerxes'.

Some have attempted to build a case for the fact that Haman was a descendant of the Amalekites whom Saul had been instructed to annihilate under the divine decree of the "ban." No certain evidence exists to certify this connection, however.

Whatever his motivation, Haman weaseled out of the king this foolish decree: "Dispatches were sent by couriers to all the king's provinces with the order to destroy, kill and annihilate all the Jews—young and old, women and little children—on a single day, the thirteenth day of the twelfth month, the month of Adar, and to plunder their goods" (Esther 3:13). Apparently, according to the laws of the Medes and the Persians, once a royal decree had been signed and issued it could not be retracted.

The only recourse that Xerxes had left was to countermand his previous decree with one extending the same privilege to the Jews. In fact, most have noted that Esther 8:11 is almost an exact duplicate of the original decree in Esther 3:13.

The posture of the Jews was one of self-defense. Their enemies attacked them with a vengeance, as can be seen in the death of five hundred in the citadel of Susa alone. While this is not an incredibly large number if the population of Susa was about half a million, it surely speaks of the danger the Jews faced as a result of the hatred Haman had fanned into existence. Had self-defense been denied the Jews, they would have been in deep trouble indeed.

The text consistently shows the Jews as morally superior to their oppressors. It records three times that the Jews did not take advantage of the royal provision to plunder (Esther 9:10, 15-16). Presumably, they also were allowed to put to death women and little children as well as the armed forces that came against them (Esther 3:13). This the Jews refused to do, in accordance with God's law. Instead, the text expressly says that they put to death only men (Esther 9:6,

12, 15). As defenders, the Jews did not attack nonmilitary targets. They themselves were the subjects of the attack.

In all the provinces, with an estimated population of one hundred million, seventy-five thousand of the enemy were slain. No mention is made of even one Jew being killed. (The Greek version of this same text puts the number at fifteen thousand slain.)

If some object that Esther was bloodthirsty in asking the king for a second day of such atrocities and killings (Esther 9:13), the response is found in Esther 9:12, where Xerxes himself was concerned that the Jews needed to do more to protect themselves from oppression.

True, Esther is made of stern stuff, but her character is not one easily described as vindictive. Her request was only for an added day of self-defense, not additional days to carry the battle to their enemy's doorstep.

See also comment on 2 SAMUEL 15:18.

JOB

1:1 Was Job Perfect?

See comment on GENESIS 6:9.

1:6-12 Satan in Heaven?

Several points arrest our attention as we read this well-known story about the trials of Job. Who are these angels ("sons of God") who come to present themselves before God in Job 1:6? And who is "Satan"? Can he be the same being the New Testament calls by that name? If he is, what is he doing appearing before God? Finally, why does God permit Job to be tested, since the New Testament book of James makes it clear that God tempts no one?

This passage gives us a glimpse of a most extraordinary scene in the invisible world. Its most surprising feature is the presence of Satan, whom we otherwise know as the Prince of Darkness. This seems such an astonishing and unusual event that we are led to think that the Satan of the book of Job cannot be the Satan of later Scriptures. How could he have anything to do with light and the presence of God?

A moment's reflection, however, will show that there is no dichotomy between the Satan of the Old Testament and the Satan of the New Testament. There is profound meaning in representing Satan as appearing before God, for he is thereby designated as subordinate and in subjection to divine control. He cannot act on his own discretion or without any boundaries. He must receive permission from the Sovereign Lord.

It used to be fashionable in scholarship to regard Satan in the book of Job as a creation of the author's fancy, due to the paucity of references to Satan in the Old Testament. Others attributed the origin of a concept of a personage of evil to Persia, perhaps the character Ahriman. But there are no striking similarities between Satan and Ahriman, nor bases for conjecturing a link between them.

Satan is not the phantom of some author's imagination or an import from an ancient Near Eastern culture. Neither is he an impartial executor of judgment and overseer of morality, for he denies everything that God affirms. He has no love toward God and is bent on destroying whatever love he observes, except self-love. He is more than a cosmic spy. He is the accuser of God's people, the destroyer of all that is good, just, moral and right. And he is similarly described in the New Testament.

Who, then, are the "sons of God," referred to as "angels" in the NIV and other translations? This same phrase is used in Genesis 6:2 (though with a different meaning), Psalm 29:1, Psalm 89:6 and Daniel 3:25.

They are called "sons"—thus they are beings that came forth from God and are in the likeness of God. They appear to serve as God's attendants or servants to do his will. One of these creatures withdrew himself from God's love and became the enemy of God and of everything that is holy, righteous and good. This one is now called Satan, because he "opposes," "resists" or "acts as an adversary" to the will of God.

This agrees with 1 Kings 22:19-22, Zechariah 3:1-2 and Revelation 12:7-8, where Satan is pictured as appearing among the good angels. Thus the whole course of redemption as described in the Bible covers the same time in which Satan manifests his enmity to God and during which his damnation is completed. The other "sons of God" are God's angels who do his bidding and thus stand for everything opposite to Satan and his practices.

As for the testings of Job, of course it can be said that God tempts no one. But the tempter, Satan, must receive permission from God to carry out even his work of harassment.

The book of Job is as much about God being on trial as it is about Job being tested. It was God who called Job to Satan's attention. But Satan scoffed, suggesting that Job had his reasons for serving God so faithfully. Job was a special focus of God's love and attention—that's why he served God, charged the accuser.

Though the Lord gave Satan opportunity to do his worst, Job refused to curse God as Satan had anticipated. On that score, Satan lost badly and God was vindicated.

Job did fear and worship God "for nothing." He had not been bribed or promised a certain amount of health, wealth and prosperity if he would serve God completely, as Satan had charged. It is possible for men and women to love and fear God apart from any special benefits, or even when their circumstances are not conducive to faith. Job demonstrated that point marvelously well.

2:1-6 Does God Put People into Satan's Hands?

Does God really put people into the hands of Satan merely to prove that he is right? And what about the suffering of the person in the meantime?

What God permits or allows is sometimes directly attributed to him. This is not to say that God is the author or sponsor of evil. The evil that came to Job could not be laid at the feet of the Lord just because he gave the go-ahead sign to Satan. Satan must take full responsibility for all that happened to Job. There were boundaries that were set by God, thus proving he still was sovereign and in control of the situation.

Satan had a cause or a reason for what he did; it was to discredit God and to ruin Job. But God had other purposes in mind. He wanted Job to grow through this experience. God was not at fault because Satan did not believe what he said about Job or about his relationship with him; Satan was the one at fault. God needed no proof for himself that he was in the right, nor did Job need proof from God; it was the Evil One himself

who was deficient.
See also comment on ISAIAH 45:7; LAMENTATIONS 3:38-39.

13:15 Job—Defiant or Trusting?

The King James rendering of this verse is one of the most famous lines from the Old Testament: "Though he slay me, yet will I trust in him." However, this beautiful affirmation of trust, though retained by the NIV, has largely been abandoned by modern translators. The RSV has "Behold, he will slay me; I have no hope." This turns Job's determination to defend himself into what one writer called "a futile gesture of defiance, which he knows will be fatal."

This response by Job comes at the end of the first round of speeches and sets the scene for Job's second round with Eliphaz, Bildad and Zophar. This hard saying comes in the midst of a speech (Job 12—14) exceeded in length only by Job's final speech in Job 29—31. The verses surrounding the text exude trust that Job will be vindicated (Job 13:18). He is prepared to defend himself and his ways, if need be, to God's face (Job 13:15). His principle is stated in Job 13:16: "No godless man would dare come before him!" But that is just what Job claims he is not, "a godless man."

With Job's protests ringing in our ears, we may now attempt to understand Job 13:15. Job is not saying, as many moderns claim, that he is going to stand up for his rights and have his say—even if it kills him! This view assumes Job cares less about life than about ending his suffering and having his prosperity back.

But the view violates the flow of the context. Job does expect, at least at this point, to be vindicated. The pessimism of moderns and the RSV just does not fit.

The chief translation problem is the verb, which can be translated "trust," "wait," "hesitate" or "tremble." But the mood of the context should help us decide which it is. Whether Job's confidence is expressed as one of waiting, hoping or trusting is not half as important as the fact that he is confident and expects full vindication.

How then shall we translate the apparently negative statement in the RSV's "I have no hope"? It is probably best handled as an assertative *lōʾ,* which would be "certainly," in place of the usual emphatic Hebrew *lᵉ*. We conclude that the KJV's rendering is the one to retain. To agree with the RSV would have Job staging a type of bravado similar to what his wife had advised: "Curse God and die."

What does Job mean by the expression "Though he slay me"? It figuratively means "No matter what happens to me, I still remain confident that I will be vindicated, for I know I am innocent and I know the character of God."

14:7-14 Bodily Resurrection?

See comment on JOB 19:23-27.

19:23-27 Bodily Resurrection?

Here is a passage notoriously difficult to translate yet celebrated worldwide for its strong affirmation of faith in a bodily resurrection. Much depends on the authenticity and meaning of the central declaration, "my Redeemer lives."

One point on which everyone can agree is that Job expected to "see God," for he made the point three times. Nor did Job expect this visual experience to occur to a disembodied shade or ghost. His references to his skin, flesh and eyes make that abundantly plain. He even used the emphatic pronoun *I* three times in Job 19:27. It is clear that he expected personally to see God. But when?

Job was willing to stake his reputation on a future vindication of a permanent written record of his claims that he was innocent. Job wanted that record chiseled onto the hardest rock and then filled in with lead to lessen the chance that time or defacers would blot out the text.

One thing was sure, Job "knew that his Redeemer lives." The one who would stand up to defend Job was called his *gō'ēl*, his "kinsman-redeemer" or "vindicator." This kinsman-redeemer basically functioned as the avenger of the blood of someone unjustly killed (2 Sam 14:11). He had the right to preempt all others in redeeming property left by a kinsman (Ruth 4:4-6). He also recovered stolen items (Num 5:8) or vindicated the rights of the oppressed (Prov 23:10-11). He was one who redeemed, delivered and liberated.

In the Psalms, God was cast into this role of kinsman-redeemer (see Ps 19:14). God was that vindicator or redeemer for Job as well.

But when did Job hope to be cleared by God—before or after death? Apparently, as Job debated with his friends, he progressively lost hope in being cleared in this life (Job 17:1, 11-16). But vindication would come one day. Hence the need for a written testimony of his complaint. Job believed that even if a person were cut down in life just as a tree was, the tree and the person would share the same hope—that a "shoot" would sprout out of the stump (Job 14:14). Even though it might take time (see "after" in Job 19:25-26), he hoped in the end for God's vindication.

In what state would Job be when that took place? Would he have a body or only a spirit, or would he be merely a memory? Job believed he would have a body, for only from inside that body (Job 19:26) and with his own eyes (Job 19:27) would he see God. He made the point that the experience would have a direct impact on his own eyeballs, and not on someone else's eyes. Thus Job was expecting a resurrection of his body! It was this which lay at the heart of his hope in God and in his vindication.

If some complain, as they surely will, that this is too advanced a doctrine for such primitive times (probably patriarchal), I would respond that long before this, Enoch had been bodily translated into heaven (Gen 5:24). The fact that this mortal body could inhabit immortal realms should have settled the abstract question forever. Indeed, the whole economy of Egypt was tied to the expectation that bodily resurrection was not only possible but also probable. That expectation had functioned a full millennium and a half before Abraham went down into Egypt. Thus our modern complaints about bodily resurrections say more about modern problems than about ancient culture.

See also comment on GENESIS 5:23-24; 25:8; PSALM 49:12, 20; ECCLESIASTES 3:19-21.

25:4-6 Man Is But a Maggot?

The words sting: "Man, who is but a maggot—a son of man, who is only a worm!" The words, however, come from Bildad, not the inspired writer of the book of Job. But Bildad was not all that original, especially in this final round of speeches by Job's three "friends." Many of Bildad's best lines were pirated either from Job or from Eliphaz.

The first issue here is whether anything in this speech expresses God's point of view. Is it revelation or only an accurate description of what took place, of no normative or prescriptive value? Second, one must ask if Bildad's extreme position runs counter to the truth that humans are made in God's image.

To the first question, most commentators answer that what is recorded is a true description or report of what Bildad said, but not normative teaching. This is acceptable until what Bildad says involves concepts that the author of Job or God reinforces in the book itself. Then we may be sure that those concepts too are normative for believers.

Bildad contrasted the imperfection of humanity with the majesty of God. In order to make his point, he modified the arguments of Eliphaz in Job 4:17-19 and Job 15:14-16. Indeed, the clause "How can a mortal be righteous before God?" (Job 25:4) reproduced verbatim Job's question in Job 9:2. The second part of the line in verse 4 again borrowed from Job in Job 15:14: "What is man, that he could be pure, or one born of woman, that he could be righteous?" Thus the question was an authoritative one, placing the allusion to humans as being compared to maggots or worms in its proper perspective.

This text must not be used to devalue the dignity or worth that God has placed in men and women. They truly are made in God's image. But nothing can better portray the relative position of mortals when compared to God's majesty than these references to individuals as grubs or crawling earthworms. The statement is not an absolute one but one of comparison. Nothing more vividly demonstrates the misery of man than Bildad's statement. The psalmist shared this sentiment when he bemoaned on behalf of the Suffering Servant, "But I am a worm and not a man" (Ps 22:6).

In Bildad's thought, as in Job 4:19 and 15:16, the emphasis falls on the fragility and the corruptibility of mortal beings. This is further emphasized by Bildad's word choices for humans that stress weakness and their link to the soil.

The contrast is more striking after the soaring thought that God is on high, reigning above. The same sentiment is even found in an ancient Mesopotamian wisdom text which also wrestled with theodicy. It asked, "Was ever sinless mortal born?"

Job answered that question with divine authority, "No, especially when you place mortal man next to the brilliant majesty and the purity of the living God!"

31:1 New Testament Morality or Old?

It is commonly said that Jesus expanded or deepened the morality of the Old Testament. One example from the Sermon on the Mount is "You have heard that it was said, 'Do not commit adultery.' But I tell you that anyone who looks at a woman lustfully has already committed adultery with her in his heart" (Mt 5:27-28).

But how can that understanding of Jesus' statement be accurate, given Job's claim in Job 31:1? Note that Jesus did not in fact contrast what he said with what the Old Testament taught. If one carefully notes the language of Matthew 5, it contrasts what "you have heard" with what Jesus said.

Since our Lord is the author of the Old Testament as well as the New, it can hardly be appropriate to see the two in opposition to each other, unless we assume that God can contradict himself. Instead, what is being contrasted is the oral tradition of the Jewish community of that day with the written and personal revelation of Jesus Christ. Thus, for example, Matthew 5:43 says that conventional wisdom dictated, "Love your neighbor and hate your enemy." Nowhere in the Old Testament can one find a verse supporting the second half of that bit of advice. This confirms that the opposition Jesus set up was between what passed for truth in the public mind (some of that being correct and some of it being plain wrong) and what God wants us to know and do.

But what of Job's claim? Some contend, with a great deal of persuasive evidence, that he lived during the patriarchal age. But could a man living between 2000 and 1750 B.C. have made as high an ethical statement as Job makes here?

Job clearly was concerned about more than external behaviors. He offered daily sacrifices on behalf of all his children, for he feared that they might have sinned inwardly (Job 1:5). Here, then, was a man who thought about his own internal intentions and those of others. Can we be all that surprised to learn that he had decided to shun not only all acts of adultery but also the wrong desires that form in the eye and the heart?

Desires arising from greed, deceit and lust were taboo in this man's life. Coveting a woman was just as much a sin as the act of adultery itself. Both the desire and the act were culpable before God and renounced by this Old Testament man who "feared God and shunned evil" (Job 1:1, 8; 2:3).

The point made in Job 31:1 is repeated in Job 31:9-12. There Job once again denies that he has been guilty of adultery; he has committed no sinful acts and has in fact restrained all the drives that could lead to such acts. He rejected all inducements to adultery.

The obligation Job laid on his eyes is consistent with warnings in other wisdom literature in which "the eye" is seen as the source of evil impulses (Prov 6:17; 10:10; 30:17). The eye also is viewed as the seat of pride (Prov 30:13) and, in the Apocryphal wisdom books, as the source of sexual desire (Sirach 9:8; 26:9).

Job's claim to have made a covenant with his eyes and a determination not to look upon or turn his thoughts toward an unmarried girl or another man's wife corresponds well with Ben Sirach's teaching (Sirach 9:5). Moreover, Job 31:3-4 makes it clear that he expected divine retribution if he failed, and that he would have to answer to God, not society, for any lapses in morality.

His covenant was no manifestation of moral heroism on his part, but a decision that was in accord with the Word of God. In fact, according to Job 31:4, Job realized that God saw everything; all of a person's ways were open before the Lord. Again, this concept of God's awareness of all a person does and thinks is echoed in other wisdom teaching (for example, Ps 33:13-15; 69:5; 94:11; 119:168; 139; Prov 5:21).

On these points there is very little difference between the moral expectations of the New Testament and those of the Old. The teaching of our Lord through Job's book and the teaching of Jesus in the Sermon on the Mount are harmonious.

See also comment on MATTHEW 5:28.

40:15; 41:1 Mythological Creatures?

Are these two monsters mere animals such as the hippopotamus and the crocodile, or are they mythological creatures? If they are mythological, what are they doing in a sober biblical account?

All who regard these two creatures as being literal animals, such as the Egyptian hippopotamus and crocodile, must admit that the description of them given in Job verges far on the side of hyperbole and is an exaggeration of their appearances and power. The name *behemoth* is a feminine plural Hebrew noun commonly used for animals or cattle. Even though it is a feminine plural word, all the verbs describing it here are masculine singular, thereby forcing us to treat *behemoth* with intensive force, meaning "the beast par excellence."

But is the alternative to regard them as pure mythology that has crept into the biblical text? No, it is quite conceivable that the text uses mythological terminology to present graphically the powers of evil. Similar mythopoetic language is used in Psalm 74:13-14, which refers to the breaking of the "heads" of the monster *tannînîm* and the "heads" of Leviathan; here both monsters refer to the power of Egypt that was smashed when Israel crossed the Red Sea.

In Job 41:1 Leviathan is declared to be too powerful for mortals to handle; God alone can handle him. Neither can anyone capture behemoth (Job 40:24). Some scholars have guessed that Behemoth was the largest of all land animals, a mighty dinosaur, while Leviathan was the largest and fiercest of all the aquatic dinosaurs. Such animals may well have lain behind the spiritual applications.[1]

When the Lord tells Job of his dominion over Behemoth and Leviathan, he merely illustrates what he has already said in Job 40:8-14. He is the one who has triumphed over the forces of evil. Satan has been proven wrong, though Job does not know about it. The forces of moral disorder, though veiled under mythopoetic language about ferocious and untamable creatures, are used here as a symbol of those who can only be handled by God behind the scenes on behalf of all who must suffer in ignorance of what is ultimately going on.

Therefore, the Bible does not give even tacit credence or approval to any pagan mythology; but it will borrow some of its terms and language to depict exotic aspects of the titanic struggle against evil and unrighteousness that goes on behind the scenes. That is what is illustrated here in Job.

See also comment on PSALM 74:13-14.

---

[1]Henry M. Morris, *The Remarkable Record of Job* (Grand Rapids, Mich.: Baker, 1988), pp. 111-25.

PSALMS

5:5 The Lord Hates All Who Do Wrong?

How can a God of love and mercy be categorized as one who hates? Yet this verse (as well as Psalm 11:5) clearly affirms that God does hate wrongdoers, the wicked and all who love violence. What makes such a strong contrast possible?

Scriptural talk about God's hatred involves an idiom that does not suggest a desire of revenge. Why would God feel any need for getting even, when he is God?

Our problem with any description of God's displeasure with sin, unrighteousness or wickedness is that we define all anger as Aristotle defined it: "the desire for retaliation." With such a definition of anger goes the concept of anger and hatred of sin as a "brief madness" or "an uneasiness or discomposure of the mind, upon receipt of an injury, with the purpose of revenge." All such notions of hatred, anger and displeasure in the divine being are wide of the mark and fail to address the issues involved. Better is the definition of the third-century church father Lactantius: anger is "a motion of the soul rousing itself to curb sin."

The problem is that anger can be dangerously close to evil when it is left unchecked and without control. Who could charge God with any of these common human faults? Thus we often object upon being told that God is angry with our sin and that he absolutely hates wrongdoing, violence and sin. Our concept of anger and our experiences with it have all too frequently involved loss of control, impulsiveness and sometimes temporary derangement. No wonder no one wants to link those kinds of thoughts with God!

But God's anger toward sin is never explosive, unreasonable or unexplainable. It is never a force that controls him or a ruling passion; rather, it always remains an instrument of his will. His anger has not, therefore, shut off his compassion (Ps 77:9).

Instead, God's anger marks the end of indifference. He cannot and will not remain neutral and impassive in the presence of injustice, violence or any other sin. While God delights in doing good to his creatures (Jer 32:41) rather than expressing evil, he will unleash his anger and wrath against all sin. Yet Scripture pictures his anger as lasting only for a moment, in contrast to his love, which is much more enduring (Ps 30:5). His love remains (Jer 31:3; Hos 2:19), while his anger passes quickly (Is 26:20; 54:7-8; 57:16-19).

Passions are not in themselves evil. Kept under control, they are avenues of virtue. And our Lord is not without emotions just because he is God. In fact, divine anger *(ira Dei)* has been sharply debated in the history of the church as the question of divine passibility (that is, God's capacity to feel, suffer or become angry) versus his impassibility (imperviousness to emotion). Teachings issuing from Gnosticism (a philosophy that combined Greek and Eastern ideas with Christian teaching) forced the church to develop a doctrine of divine passibility—that God could indeed experience feelings, suffer, and be angry.

One Gnostic best known for his view that God never took offense, was never angry and remained entirely apathetic was Marcion. Marcion was expelled from the church and his doctrines were anathematized in A.D. 144. Tertullian, one of the church fathers, tried to answer Marcion on this point in his work *Against Marcion,* but he unfortunately concluded that God the Father was impassible while the Son was passible and irascible—that is, able to exercise anger. Tertullian, at this point, was more Platonic than scriptural. In the last half of the third century Lactantius wrote *De Ira Dei (The Anger of God),* arguing that passions and emotions were not bad in and of themselves. What was evil was *not* being angry in the presence of sin! Nonetheless, other church fathers, Thomas Aquinas and the Protestant Reformers all taught impassibility. Only in the last two centuries has impassibility been challenged again on biblical grounds.

God's hatred of evil is not some arbitrary force, striking where and when it wishes without any rhyme or reason. Instead, his anger against sin is measured and controlled by his love and his justice. Expressions of his outrage against the evil perpetrated on earth are actually signals that he continues to care deeply about us mortals and about our good.

See also comment on NAHUM 1:2-3; MALACHI 1:2-3.

8:3 Poetic? Figurative? Historical?

See comment on GENESIS 1—2.

8:6-8 Exploiting Nature?

See comment on GENESIS 1:28.

11:5 The Lord Hates All Who Do Wrong?

See comment on PSALM 5:5.

15:5 Is Charging Interest Permitted?

See comment on EXODUS 22:25.

16:8-10 Who Is "Your Holy One"?

Few psalms give rise to as many important methodological and theological questions as does Psalm 16. And few passages from the Old Testament are given a more prominent place in the New Testament witness about Jesus as the Messiah. In fact, on the Day of Pentecost, Peter made Psalm 16 the showpiece in his arsenal of arguments to prove that Jesus was the expected Messiah (Acts 2:25-33).

This opinion has not, however, been shared among all Bible scholars. Some protest that in Jewish exegesis Psalm 16 is not traditionally understood to refer to the Messiah. It does not support the contentions the apostles built on it, argue many scholars; in particular, it does not predict the resurrection of Christ. These arguments are serious enough to warrant our considering this psalm among the hard sayings of the Old Testament.

According to its ancient title, Psalm 16 came from the hand of David. The particular events in David's life that occasioned the writing of this psalm are not known, but three principal suggestions have been made: (1) a severe sickness, (2) a time when he was tempted to worship idols during his stay at Ziklag (2 Sam 30) and (3) his response to Nathan's prophecy about the future of his kingdom (2 Sam 7). My preference lies with the third option, since it fits best with the messianic content of the psalm.

The psalmist has experienced a time of unbounded joy and happiness, knowing that he is secure under the sovereignty of Yahweh (Ps 16:1). The Lord himself is David's "portion" (Ps 16:5) and his "inheritance" (Ps 16:6). There is no good beside the Lord.

The psalmist reverts to the Hebrew imperfect tense as he begins to think and talk about his future and the future of the kingdom God has given him (Ps 16:9). David will rest secure, for neither he nor God's everlasting "seed" (here called "Holy One," *ḥāsîḏ*) will be left in the grave. God has made a promise that his "seed" or "Holy One" will experience fullness of joy and pleasure in God's presence forever.

One of the most frequently asked questions is whether this reference to not being abandoned in the grave expresses the psalmist's hope for a future resurrection or his faith that God will watch over his body and spirit and preserve him from all harm on this earth.

The answer hangs on the meaning and significance of the word *ḥāsîḏ*, "Holy [or Favored] One." *Ḥāsîḏ* occurs thirty-two times in the Old Testament, all in poetic texts; seventeen times it is in the plural and eleven times in the singular, and four times there are variant readings. The best way to render it is with the passive, "one to whom God is loyal, gracious or merciful," or better, "one in whom God manifests his grace and favor."

In Psalm 4:4[5] David claims that he is Yahweh's *ḥāsîḏ*. Likewise, Psalm 89:19-20 connects David with this term: "Of all you spoke to your *ḥāsîḏ* in a vision and said: 'I have set the crown on a hero, I have exalted from the people a choice person. I have found David my servant [another messianic term] with my holy oil, and I have anointed him [a cognate term for Messiah]' " (my translation).

What else can we conclude but that David and Yahweh's "Holy One" are one and the same?

As early as Moses' era, there is a reference to "the man of your *ḥāsîḏ* whom you [Israel] tested at Massah" (Deut 33:8; see Ex 17, where water came out of the rock at Massah as Moses struck it). The only "man" who was tested in Exodus 17:2, 7 was the Lord. Thus, *ḥāsîḏ* seems to be identified with the Lord. Hannah also spoke of the coming *ḥāsîḏ* in the phrase "the horn of his anointed" (1 Sam 2:9-10)—a concept confirmed as being messianic by Psalm 89:17-21.

The seventeen plural usages should not present any problems to this interpretation. The oscillation between the One and the many is exactly what is presented when all Israel is called the "seed" of Abraham, yet Christ is that "Seed" par excellence. The same phenomenon occurs with the words "anointed one," "servant" and "firstborn." Each is used in the plural as well as the singular.

Thus the apostle Peter was fully within the proper bounds of scriptural interpretation in his treatment of Psalm 16. The man David did indeed die, but the *ḥāsîḏ* was eternal. David himself was *an* anointed one, but *the* Anointed One was eternal and thus the guarantee of David's confidence about the future.

David the individual went to his grave and experienced decay, but the ultimate fulfillment of Yahweh's eternal promise did not cease to exist. He experienced resurrection from the grave, just as David foresaw under the inspiration of the Spirit as he wrote Psalm 16.

18:26 Does God Practice Deception?

See comment on EXODUS 3:18.

22:1 A Prophecy of Christ's Passion?

Psalm 22 is one of the best-known psalms because the Passion narratives in the Gospels refer to it quite frequently. In fact, Psalm 22 was the principal resource employed by the New Testament evangelists as they attempted to portray the life, death and resurrection of Jesus to show that he was the Messiah.

Of the thirteen (some count seventeen) major Old Testament texts that are quoted in the Gospel narratives, nine come from the Psalms, and five of those from Psalm 22. The best known of them all is the cry of dereliction, "Eloi, eloi, lama sabachthani" (Mt 27:46; Mk 15:34).

The problem is this: how do we move from the context of the psalmist to that of our Lord? In what sense were the psalmist's words appropriately applied to Jesus as well as to their original speaker (who probably was David, according to the psalm's ancient title)?

The psalm does not immediately appear to have been written as a direct prediction. In fact some claim that the psalm actually contains nothing that its human author or its original readers would have recognized as pertaining to the Messiah.

The psalm begins by expressing grief and suffering in what is known as the "lament" form. In Psalm 22:22, however, the lament turns into a psalm of thanksgiving and praise for the deliverance that has been experienced. Structural divisions are clearly marked by the emphatic use of certain words: "my God" and "yet you" (Ps 22:1, 3), "but I" (Ps 22:6), "yet you" (Ps 22:9) and "but you" (Ps 22:19).

What in this text forces us to look beyond David to a messianic interpretation, as the church has done for two millennia? One of the first clues is the strong adversative that comes in verse 3 with its reference to the "Holy." This adjective may function as an attribute ("Yet you are holy") or as a reference to the divine person himself, as in the NIV's "Yet you are enthroned as the Holy One."

If the second option, "Holy One" *(qāḏôš)*, is the correct rendering, as I believe it is, then it is interesting that this Holy One is further linked with the coming Man of Promise "in [whom the] fathers [Abraham, Isaac, Jacob and others] put their trust" (Ps 22:4). From Genesis 15:1-6 it is clear that the patriarchs did not merely put their trust in God (as simple theists); they rested their faith in the "seed" promised to Abraham (in lieu of Abraham's offer to adopt his Arab servant Eliezer). To this same Lord the psalmist turned for deliverance when he was beset by some unspecified suffering and anguish.

Yet the psalmist's suffering was merely illustrative of the suffering that would come to the Messiah. What happened to David in his position as head of the kingdom over which the Lord himself would one day reign was not without significance for the kingdom of God. To attack David's person or realm, given that he was the carrier and the earnest of the promise to be fulfilled in Christ's first and second comings, was ultimately to attack God's Son and his kingdom.

Small wonder, then, that this psalm was on Jesus' mind as he hung on the cross. The so-called fourth word from the cross, "My God, my God, why have you forsaken me?" and the sixth word, "It is finished," come from the first and last verses of this psalm. Not only is the first verse quoted in two Gospels, but Psalm 22:7-8 is clearly alluded to in Matthew 27:39, 43; Psalm 22:18 is quoted directly in John 19:24 and in part in Matthew 27:35, Mark 15:24 and Luke 23:34; and Psalm 22:22 is quoted directly in Hebrews 2:12. The final verse, Psalm 22:31, is cited, in part, in John 19:30. No wonder this psalm has been called "the Fifth Gospel."

I conclude that the God in whom David's forefathers trusted—the Man of Promise, the Messiah—is the same one to whom David now entrusts his life as he experiences savage attacks. And those attacks were only a foreshadowing of what the Messiah himself would one day face.

But there is really no despair here. Triumph was certain; the dominion of the coming One would be realized (Ps 22:28). Just as God sat down and rested at the conclusion of creation, there would be a day when the Lord would cry, "It is finished!" as redemption was completed. Yet even this would be only a foretaste of the final shout of triumph in Revelation 21:6 over the fulfillment of the new heavens and new earth: "It is done."

John Calvin observed, "From the tenor of the whole [psalm], it appears that David does not here refer merely to one persecution, but comprehends all the persecutions which he suffered under Saul."[1] Though that is doubtless true, under the inspiration of the Holy Spirit David went beyond the boundaries of all his own sufferings as he pictured the one who would suffer an even greater agony.

Yes, David did see the sufferings of that final one who would come in his life; but he also saw that the Messiah would emerge victorious, with a kingdom that would never fail.

---

[1]John Calvin, *Commentary on Psalms* (Edinburgh: T & T Clark, 1845), 1:357.

37:25-26 The Psalmist Has Never Seen the Righteous Forsaken?

One wonders where the psalmist has been all his life if he has never seen the righteous forsaken or their children begging bread. David must surely have seen good people in great difficulties!

But this misses the psalmist's point. He did not question that the righteous may be temporarily forsaken, needy and poor. Rather, he observed that nowhere can it be shown that the righteous have experienced continued desertion and destitution.

David himself had plenty of opportunity to complain that God had forgotten him. For example, he had to beg rich Nabal for bread. Therefore, it is important to note that David carefully sets his statement in the context of life's long haul, for he had been young and now he was much older.

Thus, what looks like desertion to those taking a short view of life is actually only a passing phase. A full trust in God will prove the reverse when life has been viewed from his perspective.

This acrostic psalm was designed to meet the very temptation assailing anyone in such dire circumstances. It contrasts what ultimately endures with the transitory. However, this does not mean God has not also provided, in some measure, relief even in this present life. As our Lord would later teach, those who seek first the kingdom of God will have all other things given to them according to their needs.

In fact, our Lord taught us to ask for our daily bread. Thus what is a command is also a promise. He invites us to pray for that which he wishes to give to us.

God does not abandon his people; he cares for them and provides for them. For those who have lived long enough in this world to see that God does finally right wrongs and avenge gross injustice, the psalmist's declarations ring true even if the short term offers many temporary exceptions.

If we are sure that God's watch-care includes his concern for even the small sparrows, should we think he will allow his children to go unloved and uncared for in this present age? While some may experience a temporary sense of being forsaken, that cannot and will not be their *continued* experience.

If it be objected, as I have already conceded, that some wrongs and deprivations never appear to be righted in this life, two further points must be made. First, the truth expressed here is proverbial in form. Proverbs gather up the largest amount of experience that fits the case without pausing to speak to the exceptions or to nuance the general teaching with the fewer, but real, objections. Such is the very nature of proverbs and the way we must understand them. If we press contemporary or biblical proverbs into being exhaustive treatments of every topic they comment on, our teaching and practice will become simplistic and reductionistic.

Second, the psalmist deliberately mentions the second generation as being the recipients of God's blessing. Thus, while some Third World peoples struggle with poverty, famine and starvation, out of the ashes of such real sorrow and pain often comes a whole new opportunity for the children who survive. The point is this: in the long haul, God does not forsake his own whether they have little or much; their children will be blessed!

44:23-26 Does God Sleep?

How strange is this accusation that the Lord may be sleeping and need to be aroused! Other psalms, including Psalms 7, 35, 59, 73 and 74, also speak of God as sleeping or arising from sleep, just as other Near Eastern deities are said to do. But Psalm 121:4 asserts just the opposite: "Indeed, he who watches over Israel will neither slumber nor sleep."

Bernard Batto[1] has attempted to argue that in Near Eastern mythology to sleep undisturbed was a symbol of the supreme deity's unchallenged authority. He further argued that the motif as applied to Yahweh expressed Israel's belief in Yahweh's absolute kingship. He could be counted on to "awaken" and to maintain justice and order.

Batto's explanation of Psalm 121:4 is not satisfactory; the sleeping deity image here, he counters, is turned around as an image of one who is ever vigilant, allowing not the slightest evil to be tolerated. Exactly; but which is correct? Or are we to have it both ways: Yahweh sleeps but he never slumbers? Furthermore, why is Elijah's taunt effective when he mockingly suggests that the prophets of Baal should call louder to awaken him, for he is known to sleep at times? Surely Elijah is not reciting their theology approvingly.

Batto believes that the motif of divine rest is connected with the theme of sleeping. In this association of ideas, he may well be on to something important. Scripture does declare that as God concludes his work in creation he rests. Is it from this moment of leisure that he is now called to "awake" and act on behalf of the one in trouble? It is to be noted that Psalms 7, 35 and 59 are all laments of an individual who is in dire straits. But in each case they are confident that God will "arise" in time to vindicate them. Thus there is an element of poetic license and the use of an anthropomorphism to describe God's action.

Psalm 44 represents the believing community's search for answers after suffering military defeats of national proportion. The problem raised was this: if the king and the people have been faithful to the covenant (Ps 44:18-22), then why was God unfaithful to his promise to deliver and defend?

There is no attempt here to give either a theological or a practical solution. In fact, this psalm is one of the clearest examples of a search for some cause or reason for national disasters besides deserved punishment by God for sin and guilt. The psalmist exclaims in exasperation, "Yet for your sake we face death all day long" (Ps 44:22). The wrath they experienced on this occasion had little to do with their sin but more to do with the spiritual battle between their enemies and the Lord they served. Theirs was a faith that went beyond any available evidences or handy theologies, but they continued to believe, to trust and to pray.

Accordingly, the psalm contrasts the glorious past (Ps 44:1-8) with some present disaster (Ps 44:9-16). God seemed not to have been with the army when they had gone out to battle (Ps 44:9). Israel's defeat had made them a reproach and the scorn of their enemies (Ps 44:13-14). All this had happened even though Israel had not forgotten God (Ps 44:17-18); nevertheless, God had crushed them with a humiliating defeat (Ps 44:19).

In spite of all of this ignominy and shame, their prayer and hope still centered on the Lord (Ps 44:23-26). This prayer is phrased in military terms. The call for God to awake and to arouse himself here does not refer to sleep but to a military action similar to that in the Song of Deborah in Judges 5:12: "Wake up, wake up, Deborah! Wake up, wake up, break out in song! Arise, O Barak! Take captive your captives." The same battle chant was used time and time again when the ark of the covenant was raised at the head of the procession as Israel went forth into battle: "Whenever the ark set out, Moses said, 'Rise up, O LORD! May your enemies be scattered; may your foes flee before you' " (Num 10:35).

The prayer is for divine help in the crisis that may have continued even though the battle had been lost. Perhaps the same war continued. "Rise up and help us" (Ps 44:26), they cried in the psalm. But the final word of the psalm is the confidence that God would yet help them because of his *unfailing love*—that word of grace which occurs in the Old Testament over two hundred and fifty times and speaks of God's unmerited lovingkindness, mercy and grace (Ps 44:26).

Therefore, this psalm does not contradict the psalm which assures us that our God never slumbers or sleeps. He does not! That God sometimes defers his punishments and extends apparently unwarranted tolerance to the wicked and their evil indicates to the superficial observer that God sleeps and needs rousing. But such divine long-suffering and mercy must not be confused with indifference or unawareness on his part. Furthermore, the language is not the language of weariness or slumber, but the language of a call for God to march forth to defend his holy name and his kingdom.

---

[1]Bernard Batto, "When God Sleeps," *Bible Review* 3 (1987): 16-23, and "The Sleeping God: An Ancient Near Eastern Motif of Divine Sovereignty," *Biblica* 68 (1987): 153-77.

45:6 The Throne of God or Man?

How are the words "Your throne, O God" to be understood? In what sense could any mortal's throne be connected with deity? And if it is a statement that applies to divinity, then in what sense can it apply to any earthly throne?

Not a few scholars, daunted by what they consider to be insuperable difficulties with the text as it stands, have suggested a long list of emendations, yet without any manuscripts to warrant such revisions and with no consensus of opinion as to which is correct.

It is clear that the ancient versions uniformly treat *ᵓᵉlōhîm*, "God," as a vocative (that is, as a noun of address—"O God," as found in the NIV), even though it has no article attached to the divine name. *'Elōhîm* appears as a vocative with the presence of the article only once (Judg 16:28), but in fifty other cases there is no article present in the Hebrew.

Translators have been forced to concede that they must deal with the words that are before us in the Hebrew text. But since this phrase appears in such a succinct form of Hebrew poetry, at least five different ways of interpreting this phrase have been set forth.[1]

The RSV adopts a genitival relationship, suggesting possession or source: "Your throne of God," that is, "the throne God has given you" or "the throne established and protected by God." Yet this will not work, since the word *throne* has two different kinds of genitives or possessives—a construction without parallel in the rest of the Old Testament.

R. A. Knox's rendering, "God is the support of your throne," is grammatically possible (as it uses *ᵓᵉlōhîm* either as a subject or as a predicate, with the idea that God is the creator or sustainer of the king's rule), but it runs into conceptual problems. Even in a book where bold metaphors are used, the concepts of God and of a throne are much too dissimilar to permit their easy linkage. How could any human throne belong to the category of divine beings ("is God")? Furthermore, it is unlikely that words like "is founded by," "is protected by," "is the support of" or "has divine qualities" can be extracted from the single Hebrew word *ᵓᵉlōhîm*.

A third rendition adds the word *throne* a second time: "Your throne is God's throne," or "Your throne will be a divine throne." There is nothing wrong with the concept that a royal throne could belong to God, for that is expressed in 1 Chronicles 29:23 (see also 28:5; 1 Kings 3:28), where Solomon is described as sitting "on the throne of Yahweh." But in those instances generally cited in support of this translation, such as "its walls [were walls of] wood" (Ezek 41:22), there is an implied identity between the subject and the predicate. The second noun denotes the material of which the object was made or a characteristic it possessed. But God is neither the material of which the throne is made nor a characteristic it possesses.

The NEB renders this phrase "Your throne is like God's throne." But such a translation must assume the conflation of two idioms in Psalm 45:6, which are otherwise unattested anywhere else in the Old Testament. There are just too many words added to the text without foundation.

The best translation, and the one that has been supported by all the ancient versions, is "Your throne, O God." The KJV, the ERV, the RSV margin, the NASB, the NAB, the JB, the NIV, Knox and the Berkeley translation all translate the Hebrew in this way, as do many modern commentators.

To whom, then, does *ᵓᵉlōhîm* refer? The king was not regarded as the incarnation of deity. Rather, he was "Yahweh's anointed" and served as the Lord's deputy on earth. This was particularly true of David, who stood in the promised line of the Messiah. He had been adopted as God's "son" in 2 Samuel 7:14 (see also Ps 2:7; 89:26).

Yet he was more than merely elected by God. Since he was endowed with the Spirit of Yahweh, he exhibited certain characteristics that foreshadowed the coming divine rule and reign of the greater David, Christ Jesus. While allowance must be made for hyperbolic language in some of these psalms and in the ancient Near Eastern court, the court and throne given to David and his descendants are described in terms that suggest they exceed anything known previously or since.

However, lest we start attributing qualities of deity to mere mortals and not to the office, dynasty and kingdom that they represented, Psalm 45:7 reminds us that the extraordinary use of *ᵓᵉlōhîm* in the preceding verse is not without qualification. Yahweh was the king's God; the king was not his own God! "Therefore God, your God, has set you above your companions by anointing you with the oil of joy," declares the psalmist with care.

The rendering "Your throne, O God" is the most defensible and most satisfactory solution of all. King David is addressed as *ᵓᵉlōhîm,* but it was because of the promise he carried in his person from God, because of his office, his dynasty and the kingdom he had received as an inauguration of the final kingdom of God to which the Messiah would one day lay total claim.

---

[1]See Murray Harris, "Elohim in Psalm 45," *Tyndale Bulletin* 35 (1984): 65-89, for a detailed discussion of these alternatives.

49:12-20 Man Is Like the Beasts That Perish?

This twice repeated refrain (with similar, but not identical, words) not only divides the psalm into two major parts (introduction—Ps 49:1-4; first section—Ps 49:5-12; second section—Ps 49:13-20), but also introduces what appears to be an unexpectedly pessimistic statement comparing human death to that of the beasts! Thus the "riddle" (Ps 49:4) that the psalm introduces is not the Samson type of riddle, but the riddle of life itself. What is the relationship of life to death? And is human life (and death) different in any significant way from that of animals?

Apparently, the psalmist was in the midst of some grave situation. In such times of despair, it was and still is all too easy to compare one's own desperate situation with the wicked's luxurious successes. These proud despisers of religion boasted of their riches and flaunted their wealth in the faces of the godly.

But did such success also ensure, as these arrogant sinners seemed to infer, that their wealth and privilege would carry over into the world after death? It was on that point that the psalmist began to get some perspective on the fears haunting him. Indeed, a person's wealth could not redeem his or her person, family or goods; mortals could not pay their own ransoms (Ps 49:7-8). When the wealthy sinner died, everything was left behind.

Therefore, in that sense death was the great leveler of all life, whether it was animal or human life. For everyone, the grave was the prospect, unless something else intervened. If money had been the criterion for gaining eternal life, then the rich should have achieved everlasting life. But that is patently incorrect, for neither one's position nor wealth has yet to buy an escape from the grim reaper, death.

It is against this background, and only on this comparative basis, that we are warned that "man . . . does not endure"

(Ps 49:12), that is to say, literally, "lodge overnight." Hence the text is ironic, for in searching for permanency through position or wealth, the realities of life assured no such guarantee. Death would cut down all beings, human and animal, without respect to influence, wealth or power.

To trust in one's self or wealth, consequently, was highest folly. Old Testament wisdom literature expresses the opposite value, namely, the fear of the Lord. Not only was the fear of the Lord the beginning of knowledge (Prov 1:7), it was also that which made possible the elimination of two possible fears found in this psalm: the fear of one's enemies in times of affliction (Ps 49:5) and the fear of the advantage of wealth in the face of death (Ps 49:16-19).

But Psalm 49:15 gives the reassuring truth that "God will redeem my life [literally, *my soul*] from the grave; he will surely take me to himself." In spite of the psalmist's somewhat embarrassing position in the areas of power, position or finances, he had a confidence that money could not purchase. He knew the grave would not seal his doom and end his hope of any more life; it could only be the place from which God would rescue him and redeem him. There is no doubt that the word *soul* in this passage functions, as it does in so many, as the expression for the personal pronoun *me.*

If all men, women and beasts are led like sheep to the grave so that death feeds on them (Ps 49:14), doubtless a strong contrast has begun to set in already in the second half of verse 14. This contrast is completed in verse 15. God himself will step in and ransom those who fear him from the power of death and the grave.

There is more. God will "take" or "receive" those who so believe in him "to himself." This word *to take* or *receive* is more positive than it might first sound. It is an allusion to God's "taking" Enoch to heaven in Genesis 5:24. Enoch no longer walked this earth after God suddenly came and took him to be with him. This clearly says that all believers will be resurrected and defeat death. This is a hope which exceeds any that even the rich and the mighty possess.

Psalm 73:24 expresses similar confidence: "You guide me with your counsel, and afterward you will take me into glory." The hope being held out here is the hope of the resurrection, just as it is offered in Psalm 49:15. Why, you ask, are the rich compared to the beasts if the text only contrasts the believer who fears God and the unbeliever who fears nothing since he or she has all the power money can buy?

In answer, those in positions of honor and wealth can be so brutish in their thinking and living that they may as well be animals. They are "without understanding" (Ps 49:20). It is for this reason that the psalm calls for "all . . . peoples" to "listen" (Ps 49:1) and to find "understanding" (Ps 49:3) unless, of course, they wish to be like the beasts and brutes without understanding. In their death they too will be like the beasts: they will perish.

The lesson of the "riddle" is clear: Do not trust in yourself or your riches to save you or to give eternal life; only God can ransom you from the grave and take you to himself!

See also comment on ECCLESIASTES 3:19-21.

49:15 Life After Death in the Old Testament?

See comment on GENESIS 5:23-24; 25:8; 2 SAMUEL 12:21-23; JOB 19:23-27.

51:5 A Sinner at Birth?

What does David mean by his being sinful at the time of his birth, indeed, from the time that his mother conceived him? Does he mean he was born out of wedlock, or that matrimony is evil, or is he teaching something else? How could David sin in the womb or at the time of his birth?

There is no hint here that David was born out of wedlock or that he had committed a particular sin as he was being born. His confession is that he is a sinner not only in act or deed, as his affair with Bathsheba painfully pointed out, but also by virtue of his nature. Original sin was present even before he was born and ever did even one act. David confesses that he had a sinful nature that must be confronted by God's righteousness and holiness.

See also comment on ROMANS 5:12.

51:11-12 Who Is the Old Testament Holy Spirit?

Are we to suppose that the Holy Spirit of Psalm 51 is the same Holy Spirit to which the New Testament refers? Or is an understanding of the Holy Spirit too advanced for the state of revelation under the older covenant?

Few doctrines suffer more from neglect of the Old Testament data than the doctrine of the Holy Spirit. Even those scholars who do consider some of the Old Testament evidence quickly summarize it and use it merely as a jumping-off point to address the main pieces of evidence, which are assumed to be in the New Testament.

However, if that is so, why is it that Jesus expected Nicodemus, in John 3, to know about the person and work of the Holy Spirit? Where could this "teacher of the Jews" have gained such a doctrine if the Old Testament has such a paucity of teaching on this theme? There are only three uses of the complete expression "Holy Spirit" in the Old Testament: Psalm 51:11 and Isaiah 63:10 and 11. The most common Hebrew term is *rûaḥ,* appearing 378 times and translated variously as "wind," "spirit," "direction," "side" and some half-dozen other words.

It is the three major prophets who use the word "spirit" most often. The term *rûaḥ* appears fifty-two times in Ezekiel, fifty-one times in Isaiah and eighteen in Jeremiah. Particularly important is Ezekiel 37:1-14, which portrays the life-giving power of God's Spirit in the Valley of Dry Bones. Only the Spirit of God can put life and spirit back into a nation, such as Israel, that has passed out of existence.

What, then, was the operation of the Holy Spirit in the Old Testament? Did the Spirit in the old covenant come upon persons for a short period of time for a special task, while in the New Testament he indwelt the believer, as some have argued? If so, this assumes that the saints of the older covenant became members of the family of God merely by observing the rules and regulations of the Torah. But how could that be true in light of Jesus's stern rebuke to Nicodemus before the cross, a rebuke that demanded a knowledge of the Spirit from the Old Testament alone? And how can that be made to square with the Old Testament's demand for a heart religion—Jeremiah's "circumcision of the heart" rather than a mere circumcision of the flesh?

What did Ezekiel mean when, in Ezekiel 36:24-28, he pressed the necessity of a new heart and a new spirit, which was probably the passage that Jesus held Nicodemus responsible for? The Old Testament does teach of a personal Holy Spirit who brought people to faith in the Man of Promise who was to come in the line of Abraham and David—and the Spirit indwelt those saints just as surely as he indwelt believers in the New Testament.

In Psalm 51:11 David confessed his sin with Bathsheba. His desire was to have a clean heart and spirit before God. He feared that God might withdraw the indwelling presence and work of his Holy Spirit from him. What David desired was a "steadfast spirit" (Ps 51:10) to be renewed within him. He feared the removal of God's Holy Spirit because he had drifted away from God as a result of his sin and decision to ride it out while Bathsheba's pregnancy was in progress. At last he had confessed his sin, and now he found himself in deep spiritual hunger and desiring to be reconciled with God.

Some will object, "If the Old Testament believer already possessed the Holy Spirit, why was Pentecost necessary?" George Smeaton gave the best answer to that question when he affirmed, "[The Holy Spirit] must have a coming in state, in a solemn and visible manner, accompanied with visible effects as well as Christ had and whereof all the Jews should be, and were, witnesses."[1] Pentecost signaled a visible and mightier-than-ever manifestation of the person and work of the Holy Spirit. (See Joel 2:28; it was a "downpour" of the Spirit compared to the previous showers.) This was the inception of the *full* experience of the Holy Spirit. After all, the Holy Spirit, like the Father and Son, had existed from all eternity. He did not remain bound and without assignment in the older era. But Pentecost did mark a fuller realization of what had been already in progress.

But certain New Testament texts do seem to imply that the Holy Spirit's coming to indwell the believer is a brand-new feature of the gospel era. Especially relevant are John 7:37-39, 14:16-17 and 16:7.[2] However, most will agree that in John 3:5-10, Jesus himself suggested that the Holy Spirit was operating in bringing salvation prior to Christ's death on the cross. When Jesus taught his disciples how to pray, he said, "If you . . . know how to give good gifts to your children, how much more will your Father in heaven give the Holy Spirit to those who ask him!" (Lk 11:13). Apparently, that gift was already available, even before Pentecost.

Of all the texts cited in this debate, the most important is John 14:17: "You know him, for he lives with *[para]* you and *is* in you." There is a strong manuscript tradition for reading the present tense of the verb *to be* ("is") rather than the future tense ("will be"). The two forms, *estai* and *esti,* are very easily confused, but the present tense appears, as B. F. Westcott concludes, to be less like a correction and probably represents the more difficult reading. (Textual critics adhere to the principle of choosing the "more difficult" reading, since copiers of the text tended to "correct" the text to the simpler or more expected reading.) Thus the Holy Spirit already was with the Old Testament believer and present in all who believed.

The Holy Spirit did bring new life to those who believed under the old covenant and personally indwelt them. But just as Calvary was necessary even though Jesus' life and work were anticipated in the Old Testament, Pentecost was necessary even though the benefits of the Holy Spirit's work were already present in the Old Testament.

That is why David feared the possible loss of the Holy Spirit. Even if one of the ministries of the Holy Spirit was the gift of government—a gift that had been given to and then taken away from his predecessor King Saul—David appears to have been worried about more than the loss of his ability to govern in Jerusalem. He feared losing the indwelling comfort and help of the Paraclete himself. That would be tantamount to standing outside the presence of God.

See also comment on ISAIAH 63:10-11.

---

[1]George Smeaton, *The Doctrine of the Holy Spirit,* 2nd ed. (Edinburgh: T & T Clark, 1889), p. 49.

[2]For a fuller discussion of this point, see Walter C. Kaiser Jr., *Toward Rediscovering the Old Testament* (Grand Rapids, Mich.: Zondervan, 1987), pp. 135-41.

51:16-17, 19 Does God Desire Sacrifices?

It is startling to read in Psalm 51 that God does not wish worshipers to bring any sacrifices. When one considers the extensive instructions to the contrary in the book of Leviticus, what could the psalmist have had in mind except what appears to be a flat-out contradiction? Hadn't God issued a command that sacrifices were to be brought to his house?

This text is not alone in posing this problem. A number of other texts appear to teach the same disavowal of sacrifices and other ritual acts, such as fasting. Some of them are 1 Samuel 15:14-22, Jeremiah 7:21-23, Hosea 6:6, Micah 6:6-8 and Zechariah 7:4-7. In each of these texts God appears to be spurning the external acts and rituals of worship, usually as expressed in sacrifices. But we will be mistaken if we assume that this is an absolute rejection of the acts of worship he had previously required under the Mosaic covenant.

Some have sought to relieve the tension produced by texts such as this one by saying that the instructions for the sacrifices came later; they were not, as a first reading of the text would suggest and as most conservative scholars have assumed, from the hand of Moses. However, this solution is too high a price to pay for a quick harmonization of the data. If the law had come later (in the fifth century B.C.), surely the writers, or even their editors and redactors (if such were involved), would not have been careless enough to ignore the fact that they had created a problem in the text. There must have been some other solution that was apparent to and understood by those earlier audiences.

Such a solution is to be found in the Old Testament writers' constant pleading for the worshiper's heart attitude to be set right. That is the precise point of these verses from Psalm 51 as well. What was the use of piling on sacrifices if they were not expressions of a spirit of contrition and genuine piety of life? God always inspects the giver, even in the Old Testament, before he inspects the gift, offering or praise. How can one who is unclean offer a clean sacrifice?

Psalm 51:16's statement of denial is qualified by what follows in verse 17. The sacrifices of a broken and contrite spirit are the gifts God seeks as a prelude to any sacrifices of sheep, goats or bulls. One whose heart is repentant is never despised by God. Consequently, the sacrifices from such a one are prized, as Psalm 51:19 says, "Then you will be pleased with the sacrifices of the righteous and whole burnt offerings, then they will offer on your altar bulls" (my literal translation).

The difficulty of these verses is not to be solved in the manner once fashionable (by dating the law to the fifth or fourth century B.C.), but by noticing the constant urging of God's servants that the people give their hearts and their lives in deep contrition and brokenness of spirit before they observe feasts, fasts, sabbaths or sacrifices.

Isaiah, for example, demanded that the people stop their sacrifices, convocations, appointed feast days and prayers (Is 1:11-15); instead, he said, they must begin by coming before God with clean hands and a clean heart. If only the Israelites would first come and reason with the Lord, even if their sins were as red as crimson, they could be as white as wool; they had only to be obedient and willing (Is 1:16-18). Then God could accept their sacrifices, just as he accepted David's sacrifices for his sin with Bathsheba *after* David repented. Rote religion can never substitute for purity of heart.

See also comment on GENESIS 4:3-4; 1 SAMUEL 15:22; ECCLESIASTES 7:16-18.

55:15 Hate Your Enemies?

See comment on PSALMS 137:8-9; 139:20.

59:5, 10-13 Hate Your Enemies?

See comment on PSALMS 137:8-9; 139:20.

68:11 Who Proclaimed the Word?

Perhaps many will remember the great chorus from Handel's *Messiah* based on this psalm. The loud acclamation rings out: "The Lord gave the word! Great was the company of the preachers." What may not be so obvious is that this is a hard saying for those who believe all of Scripture restricts women from preaching. Two major issues have been associated with this text: (1) What was the word that was announced? and (2) Were the announcers women?

The first problem is the less difficult one. "The word" *('ōmer)* in this context hardly means mere news of the victory that had just been won. It is a divine word, either a promise (Ps 77:8) or a command with accompanying divine power (Hab 3:9), or else it is the word of God that is likened elsewhere to mighty thunder or a trumpet blast (Ps 68:33; Is 30:30; Zech 9:14).

The older commentators found in this *word* a reference to gospel preaching, probably because they linked this text directly with Isaiah 40:9. That meaning fits well the Isaiah context, but no direct reference to preaching the good news or gospel appears in this context.

It would be too reductionistic, however, to limit this word, as many unfortunately do, to a watchword in war. Now it is true that women were leaders of the songs of victory, and the feminine gender is used for *announcers.* It will be remembered that when Israel defeated Pharaoh, Deborah and Barak overthrew Sisera, Jephthah routed the Ammonites and David beat Goliath, the women went forth with a song of victory.

But a song of victory from God does not appear to cover all that this psalm talks about. It is used of the word of promise as well, and this is what opens this text up for a larger sphere of reference. Therefore, everything included in that word of promise was being communicated to a great host who would announce that word.

As mentioned before, the announcers of the good news *(hamᵉḇaśśᵉrôṯ)* appear to be women, for the Hebrew participle is in the feminine plural form. God placed his word in the mouths of his announcers; the word of promise and power in the face of a hostile world. As such, this word is very close to that of Isaiah 40:9 and especially Joel 2:28-29. These heralders comprised a great host of individuals. Surely this foreshadows what God would do at Pentecost and what he has since done all over the world through the great missionary force which has included so many women.

69:22-28 Hate Your Enemies?

See comment on PSALMS 137:8-9; 139:20.

73:2-12 Do the Wicked Prosper?

Psalm 73 deals with a problem that has often perplexed God's people. Actually, it is a twofold problem whose parts are interrelated: why must the godly suffer so frequently, and why do the ungodly seem to be so prosperous?

Psalm 73 is one of the classic statements of this two-pronged question. In fact, so open is the psalmist about his own doubts that he allows us to penetrate deep into his inner being as he leads us to the very brink of despair over this most grievous problem. But he recovers just in the nick of time; he reorders his thinking about this problem and thus saves himself, and those of us who read his psalm, from falling over the precipice of despair. Like a number of other psalms, this one begins with the conclusion. The resolution of the problem ultimately comes not from a particular apologetic approach, but from the contemplation of the goodness of God (Ps 73:1).

The steps by which the psalmist, Asaph, arrived at his conclusion are also important. Having started out right, he went astray as he looked around, but then he came back to God again. The difficulty is in how he came back. His journey almost led him into disaster.

Asaph has given us a most memorable picture of what the world calls successful people: their position in life ("they have no struggles"), their health ("their bodies are healthy and strong"), their responsibilities ("they are free from the burdens common to man"), their arrogance ("pride is their necklace; they clothe themselves with violence") and their insensitivity to evil ("from their callous hearts comes iniquity").

As if all of this were not enough, the psalmist heard these proud, wealthy, healthy people boast, "How can God know? Does the Most High have knowledge?" (Ps 73:11). Such blasphemy! "We don't care what you say about God," these folks boast. "We are doing just fine without him or his help! Nothing goes wrong for us; look at some of you who claim God exists. If he does, then why are you not being helped? Why aren't you doing at least as well as we are?"

Such taunts are galling and hard to swallow. But let it be said that being perplexed or having doubts over this problem is not a sin; what is a sin is to forget God's goodness and what we have learned in God's house about the end of all such boasters. That would be to take the short view of a problem that must be considered over the long haul, and it leads to envy (Ps 73:3) and depression (Ps 73:16).

In order to get understanding, Asaph went into the sanctuary of God. Religion is not the opiate of the people; it is supposed to bring understanding (Ps 73:17). Such understanding can help us gain our footing once again.

What the prosperous, healthy, arrogant people do not realize is that they are standing "on slippery ground" (Ps 73:18). They are not as free as they think themselves to be. And all that they have is temporary, on loan from God.

Over against this precarious position rests the steadfast goodness of God, who holds his own by the hand (Ps 73:23) and guides them (Ps 73:24). "Afterward [he] will take [us] into glory" (Ps 73:24).

The problem of the prosperity of the wicked and the suffering of believers is to be resolved in the goodness of the God who personally walks and talks with his own and who will ultimately bring us to be with him in glory. Contrariwise, the prosperity of the wicked is very short-lived when judged from God's perspective. It is their feet that are on a slippery slope, not the believers'. Those who believe are gaining understanding of God's goodness as they approach God's house.

The wicked often do prosper, at least for the moment; but the righteous shall endure forever. And the righteous will always experience the goodness of God.

See also comment on PSALM 37:25-26.

73:20 Does God Sleep?

See comment on PSALM 44:23-26.

73:24 Life After Death in the Old Testament?

See comment on GENESIS 5:23-24; 25:8; JOB 19:23-27; PSALM 49:12, 20; ECCLESIASTES 3:19-21.

74:13-14 Mythological Cosmic Conflicts?

It is not unusual, of course, to find imagery used in the Bible, especially in biblical poetry. But when that imagery seems to make use of mythological allusions, as does Psalm 74, we may wonder what it means. Is the Bible implying the reality of the mythological world? Or perhaps the imagery was already remote in time and function from its original connotations, so that the psalmist used it as casually as we use mythological names for the days of the week and for certain holidays, such as Easter.

In Psalm 74 the psalmist is attempting to convince God that he should intervene on behalf of his city Jerusalem, just as he had done in his victory over evil—perhaps, as some think, at the creation of the universe.

As he makes his appeal, the poet adopts language parallel to that used in mythical texts from Ugarit (a Canaanite language whose vocabulary and spelling are similar to those of Hebrew). Heavily influenced by the Ugaritic mythological parallels, many modern scholars assume that the allusion to splitting (or "dividing") the sea refers to some primordial powers. But actually it could well refer to the division of the Red Sea (or better, "Reed Sea") at the exodus. The name for "sea" is *yām* in Hebrew and Ugaritic, and thus the real and the mythological share the same word. Only context and usage can determine the difference.

Given the context of Psalm 74, with its references to multiple heads and to Leviathan, it may well be that the poet has borrowed the terms from their Canaanite and mythological background without in any way endorsing the myth. If God could part the waters at the exodus, think of what he could do for Israel in this time of need! This is the psalmist's point.

In verse 13, God also is said to have "broke[n] the heads of Tannim," another name for "sea[monster]" *(yām)*. According to the Ugaritic text 67:3 (approximately 1400 B.C.), this monster had seven heads. Earlier Mesopotamian cylinder seals depict seven-headed dragons being attacked by the gods of that land.

God also "crushed the heads of Leviathan" (Ps 74:14). Leviathan appears only six times in the Old Testament, often as a figure for Egypt. In Ugaritic this monster was known under the name of Lotan, but it appears here in Psalm 74:13-14 with other beasts such as Yam and Tannin (Tannim).

If Leviathan must be made to correspond with a known creature, then the large aquatic animal known as the crocodile (Job 41) would probably be correct. Leviathan swims in God's great and wide sea (Ps 104:25-26). He has a scaly hide (Job 41:7, 15-17) and fearsome teeth (Job 41:14). But whether the multiheaded Leviathan of Psalm 74 is one of the mythological creatures or a name from old myths for the contemporary crocodile is difficult to say. If the imagery is not from pagan sources, then the references to the "heads of Leviathan" may well be a historical allusion, an image for the corpses of the Egyptian troops that washed ashore after the Reed Sea closed over them.

I lean toward the view that these are words that originally had mythological associations but in their biblical context have been purged of all such overtones. They now function as words of hyperbolic force to suggest the kinds of powers that God is capable of dealing with, and they particularly remind us of God's marvelous deliverance at the exodus and the Reed Sea. The Bible makes reference to these images from the dead world of myth without giving the slightest hint of approval to this mythology, and without implying that the authors believed in it.[1]

See also comment on JOB 40:15; 41:1.

[1]For more examples of the biblical use of such imagery, see Elmer B. Smick, "Mythology and the Book of Job," *Journal of the Evangelical Theological Society* 13 (1970): 101-8.

78:13 What Happened to the Red Sea?

See comment on EXODUS 14:21.

78:18-31 Punishment for Requesting Food?

See comment on NUMBERS 11:31-34.

78:58 A Jealous God?

See comment on NAHUM 1:2-3.

79:6, 12 A Prayer for Vengeance?

See comment on PSALMS 137:8-9; 139:20.

82:1 God Presides Among the Gods?

It is surprising to find a biblical text appearing to acknowledge the tacit existence of gods rivaling Yahweh. The singer Asaph beholds Elohim presiding over a great congregation and rendering judgments before what the text refers to as "gods." Does this perhaps unexpurgated passage confirm polytheism?

Before us is a courtroom. The matter before the court is the ever-present, nettlesome problem of the wicked and the injustices that seem to sweep along in their path.

In addressing the "gods" (in Hebrew, *ᵓᵉlōhîm*), God is not acknowledging pagan deities or recognizing the existence of other supernatural beings like himself; rather, he is addressing the earthly judges and administrators of his law whom he has set up to represent him. Our Lord depends on these administrators, functioning as magistrates in the divinely ordained state, to bring a measure of immediate relief from the injustices and brutalities of life.

This usage of the word *ᵓᵉlōhîm* is not as unusual as it might appear at first. Other passages refer to this class of Israelite rulers and judges as God's representatives on earth. Exodus 21:6, using the same word, orders the slave who voluntarily wishes to be indentured for life to be taken "before the judges." Likewise, Exodus 22:8 advises the owner who complains of a theft, even when no thief has been found, to "appear before the judges." Using the same word, the psalmist affirmed in Psalm 138:1, "I will praise you, O LORD, with all my heart; before the 'gods' [better rendered "rulers" or "judges"] I will sing your praise."

Therefore, it should not be altogether surprising that Psalm 82:1 should use this same word to refer to the executive or judicial branches of government—or that scholars have translated the word as "gods" in the past. In fact, Psalm 82:6 makes the case crystal clear by making all believers who "are sons of the Most High" to be "gods."

In John 10:34, when accused of blasphemy, our Lord appealed to Psalm 82:6 by saying, "Is it not written in your Law, 'I have said you are gods'?" In so doing, Jesus was demonstrating that the title could be attached to certain men "to whom the word of God came" (Jn 10:35), and therefore there could not be any prima facie objections lodged against his claim to be divine. There was a legitimate attachment of the word *ᵓᵉlōhîm* to those people who had been specially prepared by God to administer his law and word to the people.

Ever since Genesis 9:6, God had transferred to humankind the execution of his personal prerogative of determining life and death and had instituted among them an office that bore the sword. God had transferred the exercise of his power to these subordinate "gods" without thereby divesting himself of ultimate say.

God now sits in judgment of these magistrates, for all they do goes on before his eyes. The question from on high is "How long will you defend the unjust and show partiality to the wicked?" This is the great assembly over which our Lord presides and the ones he now questions for their shabby handling of the complaints of the oppressed. But there is no hint of a belief in many gods or goddesses. Nor does God thereby imply they have the divine nature exclusive to the Trinity. It is simply a case where one term, *ᵉlōhîm*, must do double duty, referring not only to God but also to his special servants appointed for the unique tasks described in these contexts.

102:25 Poetic? Figurative? Historical?

See comment on GENESIS 1—2.

105:23-25 Is God the Author of Evil?

See comment on EXODUS 9:12.

106:28-31 Why Was Phinehas Praised?

See comment on NUMBERS 25:7-13.

106:34 Completely Destroy Them!

See comment on 1 SAMUEL 15:18.

109:6-12 A Prayer for Vengeance?

See comment on PSALMS 137:8-9; 139:20.

137:8-9 A Call for Revenge?

Many tenderhearted believers have read these words with shock and chagrin. They are frankly at a loss to explain how one could speak with what appears to be such malice, vindictiveness and delight of the sufferings of others, especially children. How can the gentleness of the opening verses of this psalm be harmonized with the call for such brutal revenge in the last verses?

In all, there are only eighteen psalms that have any element of imprecation or cursing about them. These eighteen psalms contain 368 verses, of which only 65 of those verses have an element of cursing. This psalm is just one of six psalms that are generally classified as imprecatory psalms. These are Psalms 55, 59, 69, 79, 109 and 137. There is no author or title to Psalm 137; however, the scene is pictured as taking place "by the rivers of Babylon." Psalm 79 is ascribed to Asaph; the remaining four are from David's pen, according to the ancient titles. The label *imprecatory* may be misleading if it is not understood as the invocation of judgment, calamity or curse in an appeal to God who alone is the just judge of all beings.

But how can it ever be right to wish or pray for the destruction or doom of others, as is done in at least portions of these psalms? Could a Christian ever indulge in such a prayer?

These invocations are not mere outbursts of a vengeful spirit; they are, instead, prayers addressed to God. These earnest pleadings to God ask that he step in and right some matters so grossly distorted that if his help does not come, all hope for justice is lost.

These hard sayings are legitimate expressions of the longings of Old Testament saints for the vindication that only God's righteousness can bring. They are not statements of personal vendetta, but utterances of zeal for the kingdom of God and his glory. The attacks that provoked these prayers were not just from personal enemies; rather, they were rightfully seen as attacks against God and especially his representatives in the promised line of the Messiah. Thus, David and his office bore the brunt of most of these attacks, and this was tantamount to an attack on God and his kingdom!

It is frightening to realize that a righteous person may, from time to time, be in the presence of evil and have little or no reaction to it. But in these psalms we have the reverse of that situation. These prayers express a fierce abhorrence of sin and a desire to see God's name and cause triumph. Therefore, those whom the saints opposed in these prayers were the fearful embodiments of wickedness.

Since David was the author of far more imprecatory psalms than anyone else, let it also be noted that David exhibited just the opposite of a vindictive or revengeful spirit in his own life. He was personally assaulted time and time again by people like Shimei, Doeg, Saul and his own son Absalom. Never once did he attempt to effect his own vindication or lift his hand to exercise what many may have regarded as his royal prerogative.

In fact, in some of these very psalms where he prays for God to vindicate his own honor and name, David protests that he has kind thoughts toward these same evildoers. Thus in Psalm 35:12-14 David mourns, "They repay me evil for good and leave my soul forlorn. Yet when they were ill, I put on sackcloth and humbled myself with fasting. When my prayers returned to me unanswered, I went about mourning as though for my friend or brother. I bowed my head in grief as though weeping for my mother."

Finally, these imprecations only repeat in prayer what God had already stated elsewhere would be the fate of those who were impenitent and who were persistently opposing God and his kingdom. In almost every instance, each expression used in one of these prayers of malediction may be found in plain prose statements of what will happen to those sinners who persist in opposing God. Compare, for example, such expressions in Psalms 37:2, 9-10, 15, 35-36, 38; 55:23; 63:9-11; and 64:7-9.

But let us apply these principles to the special problems of Psalm 137:8-9, which many regard as the most difficult of all the imprecatory psalms. First, the word *happy* is used twenty-six times in the book of Psalms. It is used only of individuals who trust God. It is not an expression of a sadistic joy in the ruin or destruction of others.

The words "dashes [your infants] against the rocks" are usually regarded as being so contrary to the teachings of the New Testament that here is little need to discuss the matter any further. Curiously enough, these very same words are repeated in the New Testament by no one less than our Lord (Lk 19:44). In fact, the verb in its Greek form is found only in Psalm 137:9 (in the Septuagint, the Greek translation of the Hebrew text) and in the lament of our Lord over Jerusalem in Luke 19:44. This is the clearest proof possible that our Lord was intentionally referring to this psalm. Moreover, our Lord found no more difficulty in quoting this psalm than he did in quoting the other two psalms most filled with prayers of imprecation, namely, Psalms 69 and 109.

God "shattered the enemy" at the Red Sea (Ex 15:6) and will continue to do so through the triumph of his Son as he "will rule them with an iron scepter" and "dash them to pieces like pottery" (Rev 2:26-27; 12:5; 19:15).

The word translated "infant" is somewhat misleading. The Hebrew word does not specify age, for it may mean a very young or a grown child. The word focuses on a relationship and not on age; as such, it points to the fact that the sins of the fathers were being repeated in the next generation.

That the psalmist has located the site of God's judgment in Babylon appears to denote this psalm as being composed while Judah was in exile in Babylon and also that there are figurative elements included in the psalm. One thing Babylon was devoid of was rocks or rocky cliffs against which anything could be dashed. In fact there were not any stones available for building, contrary to the rocky terrain of most of Palestine. All building had to depend on the production of sun-dried mud bricks and the use of bituminous pitch for mortar. Therefore when the psalmist speaks of "dashing [infants] against the rocks," he is speaking figuratively and metaphorically. Close to this metaphorical use of the same phrase is that of Psalm 141:6, "Their rulers will be thrown down from the cliffs." But that same psalm adds, "And the wicked will learn that my words were well spoken [the literal rendering is "sweet"]." If the rulers had literally been tossed over a cliff, they surely would have had a hard time hearing anything!

What, then, does "Happy is he who repays you for what you have done to us—he who seizes your infants and dashes them against the rocks" mean? It means that God will destroy Babylon and her progeny for her proud assault against God and his kingdom. But those who trust in God will be blessed and happy. For those who groaned under the terrifying hand of their captors in Babylon there was the prospect of a sweet, divine victory that they would share in as sons and daughters of the living God. As such, this is a prayer Christians may also pray, so long as it is realized that what is at stake is not our own reputation or our personal enemies, but the cause of our Lord's great name and kingdom.

See also comment on PSALM 139:20.

138:1 Before the Gods?

See comment on PSALM 82:1.

139:20 Are We to Hate Our Enemies?

Are we to actually hate certain people at certain times? Especially if they are hating the Lord and rising up against him?

Just as a cry goes out from the martyrs in heaven for God's vengeance for what has been done against them (Rev 6:10), so we too may cry out for God's action against all the workers of iniquity. In fact, that is what the return of the Lord will signal: a time when God's vindication of all his people will take place. To see evil and not be alarmed by it is a sign that there is something terribly wrong with us.

But indiscriminate hatred is also wrong. The concern must be for God's character and name, not personal vendetta. The hatred, then, is aimed at the evil deeds that are done, not primarily at the persons who do them.

But this distinction is an arbitrary one, claimed C. S. Lewis at one time. Later, however, he noticed one day that that is how he treats himself: he hated what he did at times while affirming himself as a person. Said Lewis, if I can make this distinction, why do I object to the saying that God loves the sinner but hates his sin? God does—just like I do, but on a much different scale!

Even though these workers of iniquity are regarded as one's enemies and as the objects of one's hatred, yet this kind of ultimate causation must be mitigated by the same psalmist's statements elsewhere. For David, the author of Psalm 139, as he was of almost all of the psalms of imprecation or cursing, showed how reluctant he was to take things into his own hands when his enemy Saul was pursuing him and falsely charging him with things that just were not true. The whole conclusion to the book of 1 Samuel contains one illustration after another of how David treated his enemy. Note, for example, the touching "Song of the Bow" that David composed at the death of Saul and Jonathan. He did not express glee that his former enemy was killed. In fact, he executed the Amalekite for rejoicing over Saul's death and lying about killing him (2 Sam 1).

But that did not mean that David did not hate evil and its workers with a dedicated passion. That is where the difference was. Love for one's enemies was an obligation in the Old Testament (Ex 23:4-5; Lev 19:17-18). Moreover, the so-called high ethical stance of the New Testament found in Romans 12:20, about feeding one's enemy when he is hungry, is actually a citation from Proverbs 25:21. Incidentally, it should be noted that there are imprecations in the New Testament as well—Galatians 5:12, 2 Timothy 4:14 and Revelation 6:10.

Thus while some room must be left for Eastern poetry that loves hyperbole (as when David moans, groans, yea does weep so much that he makes his bed to float!), nevertheless, these impassioned utterances are longings of the Old Testament believers for God's righteousness to be vindicated. They are utterances of zeal for God and his kingdom. They are expressions of an abhorrence for sin, for sinners who practice such deeds are God's enemies (Ps 5:10; 10:15; 139:19-22).

Finally, it must be realized that there is hardly a single expression of imprecation which cannot be found elsewhere in the Bible as a simple statement of the fate of the wicked (for example, Ps 5:10 = 5:6 and 9:5; 28:4 = 9:16; 10:15 = 37:17 and 72:4). That is why the people of God were required to say "amen" to the curses of God on evildoers, just as they were to say "amen" to his blessings (Deut 27:15-26). And if these psalms of imprecation seem to be somewhat off the main track of New Testament spirituality, then let it be remembered that no other psalms are quoted more frequently in the New Testament, with the exception of Psalms 1, 22, 110 and 118. Thus, Psalm 69 is quoted in five New Testament passages.

See also comment on PSALMS 5:5; 137:8-9.

PROVERBS

1:7 Love God or Fear Him?

Wouldn't it be better if the author just said that we are to love God rather than commending our fear of him? Why is fearing God mentioned so frequently in the Bible? The phrase is used so frequently that cross-referencing all the instances here has been avoided in the interests of space.

The term *to fear* can describe everything from dread (Deut 1:29) or being terrified (Jon 1:10) to standing in awe (1 Kings 3:28) and having reverence (Lev 19:3). When used of the Lord, it encapsulates both aspects of the term, a shrinking back in recognition of the difference or holiness of God and the drawing close in awe and worship. To fear the Lord is not to experience a dread that paralyzes all action, but neither is it just a polite respect. It is an attitude of both reluctance and adoration that results in a willingness to do what God says. The fear of the Lord, then, is absolutely necessary if we are even to begin on the right foot in learning, living or worshiping.

The problem with saying that loving God is enough is that this informs us as to what the proper emotion should be, but it says nothing, in and of itself, as to what we should do about expressing that love. It also leaves the important aspect of the holiness and difference of God's nature and character untouched and without a response.

But with the fear of the Lord there is a foundation for wisdom, discipline, learning and life. It expresses itself in a hatred of evil (Prov 8:13) and demonstrates its presence by its willingness to be obedient (Gen 22:12).

5:15-21 Drink Water from Your Own Cistern?

Proverbs 5:15-21 is usually classified as an allegory. As such, it bears the same relationship to a metaphor as a parable does to a simile. Parables use words in their natural sense, while allegories use words metaphorically. The temptation in interpreting allegories is to overinterpret, finding too many minute meanings by making all the details of the imagery significant in and of themselves.

Proverbs 5 appears to be talking about the conservation of water. But then we are baffled by verse 17's assertion that water should be for oneself, not shared with strangers. Why would the writer suddenly express such a selfish attitude about sharing water from his well?

When Proverbs 5:18 interjects "and may you rejoice in the wife of your youth," it is our first real clue that this may be an allegory whose point is not the conservation of water.

One of the rules for interpreting allegories is to note the context. The entire first part of this chapter is a warning against the loose woman. Given that context, along with this reference to rejoicing in the wife of one's youth, it slowly dawns on us that what is being extolled in this allegory is the enjoyment and fidelity of marital love over against illicit intercourse. That teaching is strikingly brought out in Proverbs 5:19, where one's own marriage partner is described as "a loving doe, a graceful deer"—a most appropriate pair of metaphors for the beauty found in one's own wife as opposed to the adulterous woman depicted in the earlier part of the chapter.

But what about the particulars in the interpretation of this beautiful allegory (which was probably written by Solomon and serves as an introduction to the themes of the Song of Songs)? Five different words or phrases are used here for the source of water: *cistern, well, springs, streams of water* and *fountain.* Attempts to isolate some special metaphorical meaning in each and every one of these terms would prove fruitless. Remember, we must not try to make everything in the allegory a symbol of something else. In any case, the form of Hebrew parallelism used with these terms assures us that different meanings are not intended; these are synonymous terms used for the sake of variety and effect.

The wife is a cistern, well, spring, stream or fountain because she is able to satisfy the desire of her husband. In the ancient Near East, a spring on one's property was regarded as very valuable and significant.

The idea, then, is this: be content with marital relations with your own wife. Find your delight and satisfaction in her rather than going elsewhere to taste the wells and springs of others. Faithfulness to your own wife is so natural and so pleasant that the question must be asked, Why would you ever be attracted to anyone else? What is more, remember that all of your life is directly viewed by God—and that includes the bedroom!

Some confusion has existed over whether Proverbs 5:16 should be translated in the affirmative ("Your springs will overflow in the streets"), the imperative ("Let your springs overflow in the streets") or the interrogative ("Should your springs overflow in the streets?"). Some, believing that the affirmative and imperative renderings made the writer contradict himself, inserted a negative particle in the text, but this was without any warrant from preserved Hebrew texts. Those who adopted the affirmative and imperative renderings understood them to indicate numerous progeny. But this concept of the passage breaks the unity of the image of marital fidelity and does not fit with Proverbs 5:17.

All these difficulties are avoided if we take it as an interrogative. The meaning, then, would be "Why would you let your wife go about the streets as a harlot? On the contrary, let her be for yourself only, and not for strangers. Likewise, the husband should drink from his own well. His wife should be the only person to satisfy him."

The Scriptures do much to foster marital fidelity and to lift high this loyalty as the best road to fulfillment and happiness. In fact, the Lord continues to inspect all of a person's ways, for everything is open and plain before the God who has called us to be holy to him and faithful to our marriage vows.
See also comment on 1 CORINTHIANS 7:1.

16:33 Casting Lots Encouraged?
See comment on JONAH 1:4-5, 7.

17:8 Is Bribery Permitted?
See comment on PROVERBS 21:14.

21:14 Is Bribery Permitted?
At first blush, this proverb appears to commend bribery. It reads as if bribery is God's approved way of dealing with certain, or even most, adverse circumstances. But this first reading cannot be sustained, for the proverb does not commend bribery but, rather, good sense. The point is this: when someone is angry with you, sue for peace as quickly as possible. At that time, genuine peace is more important than how it is cloaked or the form it comes in. Pacifying the angry person is often one's first duty, and the price of peace is much smaller than the cost of anger and constant strife.

This is borne out in everyday life. Often, logical arguments are not half as effective in winning the day as some token of esteem or appreciation. Consider the person who has quarreled with his or her spouse and decides to give up arguing about who was right and who was wrong in favor of offering a gift of appreciation. At times this strategy wins the peace and effects more harmony than acting like a collegiate debater.

In the same way Jesus in the Sermon on the Mount encouraged his followers to give a cloak or an additional mile of service when coerced to give the first. Certainly such acts could well be interpreted as offering a gift to assuage the wrath of those with jurisdiction over them. This kind of gift is not what we would call a bribe. It is a gift given in good conscience to achieve a righteous end.

Of course we are dealing with a proverb. Therefore, this statement must not be absolutized, for if it were, it could be made to teach the false conclusion that we must sue for peace at any price and under any conditions. The book of Proverbs, instead, picks up the largest number of cases and puts its teaching in the broadest perspective possible. However, we would be scandalized to hear a pastor from an American pulpit urging believers to bribe state officials under certain circumstances.

How, then, can we resolve this apparent conflict of interests? Some suggest that the Bible condemns only the taking of bribes, since it is assumed that the godly person will carry out God's law without needing to be prodded by payoffs. This argument would disallow accepting bribes for one's own personal profit, especially for perverting justice or administering justice that the public already deserves. With that part of the argument we can agree.

But some may further claim that the Bible nowhere condemns giving bribes to impede the progress of apostate governments. Here we must proceed with caution. If this type of bribery is grouped with treason, or spying under conditions of war or enemy occupation of one's native land, it should be treated separately from a general statement on bribery for personal ends. It could be wrong or it could be permissible, depending on whether it is being used as a weapon against evil or against righteousness. The most basic teaching of bribe-taking is found in Exodus 23:8, "Do not accept a bribe, for a bribe blinds those who see and twists the words of the righteous." That same warning is repeated for rulers in Deuteronomy 16:18-19: "Appoint judges and officials . . . [who] do not pervert justice or show partiality [or who] do not accept a bribe, for a bribe blinds the eyes of the wise and twists the words of the righteous." The point is clear: bribery perverts justice for the sake of personal gain.

Solomon made the same point in Proverbs 17:8, "A bribe is a charm to the one who gives it; wherever he turns, he succeeds." Again in Proverbs 17:23 it warns, "A wicked man accepts a bribe in secret to pervert the course of justice."

This perversion is well illustrated in the lives of Samuel's sons in 1 Samuel 8:3: "But his sons did not walk in his ways. They turned aside after dishonest gain and accepted bribes and perverted justice." And that was the sin mentioned by Isaiah (Is 1:23), Amos (Amos 5:12) and the psalmist (Ps 26:10). The evil side of bribery lies in the perversion of justice—taking gifts for personal gain when justice and leadership should be granted without them. When Jehoshaphat warned the newly appointed judges to "judge carefully, for with the LORD our God there is no injustice or partiality or bribery ['taking of gifts']" (2 Chron 19:7), he was not excluding all gift-giving, as 2 Chronicles 32:23 shows. He was condemning gifts meant to pervert judgment.

Thus gifts, like all gain from this world, can carry with them great danger when they threaten to rearrange a person's general scale of values and purposes for doing things. But they are highly acceptable when they are used in a responsible way and given without any implied or explicit demand for a favor in return. They even are commended when used to cool down the wrath of an enemy, a foe or a relative who may be temporarily out of control. These gifts could avoid great wrath, yet they would also be called bribes in Scripture.

22:6 Train a Child

What makes this text a hard saying is not the meaning of the words as they stand; they are plain and easy to translate. Instead, the problem centers in the differing views of the central phrase, "the way he should go," and in the fact that the verse doesn't always "come true."

Readers often assume this verse is a promise given to all godly parents: Raise your children as moral, God-fearing believers, and they will turn out all right in the end. But what about children raised in just such Christian homes who appear to abandon their faith or lapse into immorality?

To answer this extremely important question it is best to start with an analysis of the text itself. The verb translated "train" means to dedicate something or someone for the service of God. The verb is found in Deuteronomy 20:5 and in the parallel passages on the temple dedication in 1 Kings 8:63 and 2 Chronicles 7:5. In its noun form it is the name of the Jewish feast of Hanukkah.

The resulting range of meanings for this act of dedication includes: to prepare a child for service, to dedicate a child to God or to train a child for adulthood. Parents are urged to dedicate and begin training each child as an act of dedication to the living God.

But interpretation problems emerge as soon as we look for an antecedent for the pronoun in the phrase "according to his way," translated above as "in the way he should go." Literally, the phrase is "according to the mouth of," which has led some to suggest "in accordance with the training he received at his 'beginning.' " However, the use of the word *mouth* for this concept instead of the word *beginning* would be strange indeed. Or it could be rendered more generally as "after the measure of, conformably to" or "according to his way."

What is the "way"? It could mean the way that the child ought to go according to God's law; the proper way in light of God's revelation. It could also mean the way best fitting the child's own personality and particular traits.

Which is correct? There is no doubt that the first presents the highest standard and more traditional meaning. However, it has the least support from the Hebrew idiom and seems to be a cryptic way of stating what other proverbial expressions would have done much more explicitly.

Therefore we conclude that this enigmatic phrase means that instruction ought to be conformed to the nature of the youth. It ought to regulate itself according to the stage of life, evidence of God's unique calling of the child and the manner of life for which God is singling out that child. This does not give the child carte blanche to pick and choose what he or she wishes to learn. It does, however, recognize that the training children receive must be as unique as the number of children God has given to us.

The result will be, as the second line of the proverb underscores, that even "when he gets old he will not turn from it." The "from it" refers to the training of youth which was conformed to God's work in the child's very nature and being. This training was so imbued, inbred and accustomed that it became almost second nature.

As with many other moral proverbs of this sort, the question often comes from a distraught parent: "Does this proverb have any exceptions to it, or will it always work out that if we train our children as this verse advises, we can be sure they won't turn from the Lord?"

No, this verse is no more an ironclad guarantee than is any other proverb. Like many other universal or indefinite moral prescriptions (proverbs), it tells us only what generally takes place, without implying there are no exceptions to the rule. The statement is called a proverb, not a promise. Many godly parents have raised their children in ways that were genuinely considerate of the children's own individuality and the high calling of God, yet the children have become rebellious and wicked.

There is, however, the general principle which sets the standard for the majority. This principle urges parents to give special and detailed care in the awesome task of rearing children so that the children may continue in that path long after the lessons have ceased.

24:11-12 Whom Are We to Rescue?

This text had remained largely unnoticed until it came into national prominence as a theme verse to ground Operation Rescue's project of blocking access to abortion clinics. The question we must pose, then, is this: Does this text provide grounds for actively opposing those who are involved in evil?

These two verses belong to a section of Proverbs (Prov 22:17—24:22) that shares many similarities with the Egyptian wisdom piece known as Instruction of Amenemope. Whether the Egyptian book is dependent on the biblical book of Proverbs, as Robert Oliver Kevin has argued,[1] or the book of Proverbs is dependent to some degree on the Egyptian work, as Adolf Erman argued in 1924 in a German work, or both Proverbs and the Egyptian piece are dependent on a third unknown Semitic source, as argued by W. O. E. Oesterley,[2] is too difficult to say from the evidence at hand. The Egyptian work had some thirty "chapters" or sayings. Given that the Hebrew text of Proverbs does not organize its collection according to this scheme, it is difficult to avoid the question of Proverbs 22:20, "Have I not written thirty sayings for you?" Following such a scheme, on purely hypothetical and internal grounds some have divided these verses into twenty-five sayings.

It would appear that this text warns against negligence and a general lack of concern for those of our neighbors who are threatened with danger. Since the particular danger is not defined in this passage, we must infer that the warning applies to all cases when our neighbor is in danger.

Two literal demands are made here: rescue the person who is in prison awaiting death, and also rescue the person on the way to execution. This presumes that those whose lives are threatened are innocent and have been condemned unjustly.

Some take the words *death* and *slaughter* to be metaphors for the oppression of the poor. Nothing in the text, however, supports a metaphorical interpretation.

According to Proverbs 24:12, to claim that one was unaware of the issues or the consequences is not adequate to negate one's responsibility to help. In fact, this verse strengthens the religious character of the call to action in Proverbs 24:11. Disclaimers and feigned ignorance will not divert from us the eye and gaze of God. Surely he knows what is right and wrong, and what we could and could not have done. To whine that it was no business of ours, when we were in the presence of wrong, will not satisfy the Judge of the universe. God will weigh our hearts—not like the Egyptian god of wisdom, Thot, who allegedly placed the heart of an individual on one side of a scale and a feather of truth on the other side to see whether the hearts of Egyptians were true or false—but with the righteousness of his own divine character and the witness of his all-seeing eyes.

These texts do call for an active involvement where we might have wished to excuse ourselves. Whether it authorizes all "rescue" actions is a question that goes beyond our purview here. It certainly does not mean that believers should become vigilantes, taking the law into their own hands, or opposing the state because they think it is evil. But there will come times when we must take a stand and do all that is rightfully within our power to rescue the one who has been left bereft of scriptural justice.

---

[1]Robert Oliver Kevin, "The Wisdom of Amen-em-apt and Its Possible Dependence upon the Book of Proverbs," *Journal of the Society for Oriental Research* 14 (1930): 115-57.

[2]W. O. E. Oesterley, "The 'Teaching of Amen-em-Ope' and the Old Testament," *Zeitschrift für alttestamentliche Wissenschaft* 45 (1927): 9-24.

25:21-22 Burning Coals?

See comment on ROMANS 12:20.

29:18 What Vision?

For many years this proverb has been misinterpreted, probably because the KJV translates it "Where there is no vision, the people perish." One can infer from that translation that wise groups must have a five-, ten- or twenty-year plan for the future if they do not wish to become defunct as an organization. And many have taken just that meaning from this text.

However, the word *vision* does not refer to one's ability to formulate future goals and plans. Instead, it is a synonym for the prophetic word itself. It is what a prophet does. It refers to the prophetic vision, revelation which comes as the word of God.

Israel endured times when the prophetic word was silent. When Samuel was a young boy, "in those days the word of the LORD was rare" (1 Sam 3:1).

For all the times Israel rejected the word, God sent a famine on the earth; not a famine of food and water, but an even more damaging famine: a famine of the word of God (Amos 8:12; see also 2 Chron 15:3; Ps 74:9).

Besides *vision,* a second key word has been misunderstood in this verse: the word *perish.* This does not refer to the perishing of churches with inactive planning committees (a fact which may be true on grounds other than those presented here in this text). Nor does it mean the perishing of the unevangelized heathen who will die in their sin if someone does not reach them quickly (a fact which is also true on other grounds).

The word translated in the KJV as "perish" has a very impressive background to it. It means "to cast off all restraint." It clearly warns that where the word of God is silenced so that it no longer comments on the local situation, the results are terrifying. The populace becomes ungovernable as they cast aside all that is decent and civil for whatever their own baser appetites wish to indulge in.

The best picture of how this takes place can be found in Exodus 32:25. While Moses was absent for a mere forty days on Mount Sinai receiving the law of God, the people began to fear that he would never return. Without the input of the prophetic word, the people began to get out of control. They cast off all restraint and began to dance about a newly made golden calf. They ate and drank and indulged in open immorality, apparently recalling what they had seen in Egypt.

Without the announcement of the word of God, teaches this text, the people will become unrestrained, disorderly and grossly obscene in their manner of life. The verb means to "let loose," that is, "to let one's hair down," whether literally or figuratively (see also Lev 13:45 and Num 5:18).

On the other hand, this proverb continues, "Blessed is he who keeps the law." Thus, on the one hand, people are in an untenable position when the voice of the preacher ceases, because they let loose and nothing is left to restrain them; but, on the other hand, they are only truly happy when they have the good fortune of possessing the word of God and then place themselves under the hearing and doing of that word.

31:6-7 Give Them Beer?

Some have been startled by these two verses and have had trouble fitting them in with the rest of scriptural teaching. The problem here is to determine who are those who are "perishing" and "in anguish." And why do they need a drink to lessen the pain of their misery and to help them forget their poverty? The reference is cryptic, to say the least.

If we are to construct a response, Proverbs 31:6-7 must be set in its larger context. At the very minimum, the section comprises Proverbs 31:4-7. A contrast is set up between kings, who are advised against drinking lest they be incapable of responding justly when the oppressed come to them for legal relief, and those who are perishing and who carry no responsibilities such as the king carries.

Thus this proverb begins by warning us that wine and beer could cause the king to compromise his integrity. If the king were to become addicted to alcohol to escape the rigors of his office and the burdens of his responsibilities, he would be expressing cowardice, a loss of nerve for the tasks set before him (Prov 31:4-5). A drinking sovereign would have his vitality sapped; his mind would not be clear, but unpredictable, irresponsible and inconsistent.

On the other hand, the king is urged

to give wine and beer to those who need respite from the intolerable weight of their burdens. Whether these individuals were only criminals who had been condemned to die or whether a much larger group is meant cannot be determined from this text.

It is true that condemned convicts were given a potion just prior to their execution. Perhaps it was on the grounds of this proverb that the noblewomen of Jerusalem prepared a sop for Jesus as he hung on the cross, but Jesus rejected it, apparently because he wished to be sensitive to the pain for which he was giving his life (Mk 15:23; also note the Talmud: Sanhedrin 43a).

All who have read the Bible carefully are quite aware that it makes a case for moderation, not total abstinence. It is only because of the failure of many to control their drinking that many believers have advocated total abstinence; they are objecting to the large numbers of people who are abused, injured or killed each year as a result of drunkenness. Alcohol abuse has become a major moral problem in our day, and more than Mothers Against Drunk Driving should be protesting the carnage that takes place on our highways.

Yet there is the other side of the coin for those who are able to be moderate in their alcoholic intake: wine can make the heart happy (Ps 104:15) and lift one's spirits above sorrow and poverty. But lest Proverbs 31:6-7 be viewed as emphatically endorsing the use of alcohol by those who are poor and miserable, it must be remembered that the proverb aims at making a comparative judgment, not an absolute one. Ordinary men and women may drink sometimes to forget their poverty and their perplexities; the king, on the other hand, would be in danger of forgetting the law and cheating those who needed help if he adopted a similar lifestyle. The proverb is more concerned about drunken kings than it is about giving instructions for the general populace.

Furthermore, it must be kept in mind that those who are contrasted with the king may well be prisoners on death row who need something to assuage their terror in the final moments before the state takes their lives in punishment for their crimes.

See also comment on 1 TIMOTHY 5:23.

ECCLESIASTES

1:1 Is "the Teacher" Solomon?

Even though the heading for this book of Ecclesiastes does not name the author of this book, can we assume from the fact that he is the "son of David" and a "king in Jerusalem" that he is Solomon? Or is there a certain genre of writing that allows for such attributions without intending them to be taken literally?

The main speaker in this book of Ecclesiastes is called *qōheleṯ*, meaning "teacher" or "preacher," a feminine participle from a verbal root meaning "to assemble." But at that point the agreement ceases.

The well-known conservative scholar of the nineteenth century, Franz Delitzsch, declared in a much-quoted opinion, "If the book of Koheleth were of old Solomonic origin, then there is no history to the Hebrew language."[1] However, Fredericks devoted a careful inspection of all the linguistic arguments for dating the book late and concluded that they were unpersuasive.[2] The other approach to show that the book is late is to try to show affinities in thought between Hellenistic thought and Ecclesiastes. This would mean that the book originated in the Greek period, but this method also has been beset by problems. These so-called affinities can be shown to be just as easily related to far earlier thought and literary forms than the late Greek period.

So this leaves us with deciding if indeed the text could have come from Solomon. Evangelical scholars such as Moses Stuart, Hengstenberg, Delitzsch, Young and Kidner have all challenged the view that Solomon wrote the book. But much of that was on the strength of the allegedly late language and concepts. Now that that obstacle has fallen, at least since Fredericks's study in 1988, it is worth looking at the idea of Solomonic authorship one more time.

The only *immediate* son of David who was also king over Israel in Jerusalem would be Solomon. But against his authorship it is argued that in Ecclesiastes 1:12 the king is represented as saying, "I . . . *was* king over Israel in Jerusalem." But far from declaring that he was no longer king, Solomon is saying "I *have been* king," for the action of the Hebrew verb begins in the past and continues up to the present. The argument shifts to Ecclesiastes 1:16, where the writer compares himself advantageously to "anyone who has ruled over Jerusalem before me." Since David was the only Hebrew ruler to precede him in Jerusalem, the words hardly seem appropriate in Solomon's mouth. The reference could very well be to the line of Canaanite kings who preceded Solomon in Jerusalem, such as Melchizedek (Gen 14:18) and Adonizedek (Josh 10:1).

But the most convincing telltale signs that Solomon is "the Teacher" are the allusions to circumstances that fit only Solomon's life and experience: (1) his unrivaled wisdom (Eccles 1:16; compare 1 Kings 3:12); (2) his unsurpassed wealth (Eccles 2:4-10, compare 1 Kings 7:1-8); (3) his huge retinue of servants (Eccles 2:7-8, compare 1 Kings 9:17-19); (4) "there is no man that does not sin" (Eccles 7:20, compare 1 Kings 8:46); (5) not a god-fearing woman in a thousand (Eccles 7:28, compare 1 Kings 11:1-8); and (6) his weighing, studying and arranging proverbs (Eccles 12:9, compare 1 Kings 4:32). This forms a very convincing case that Solomon is "the Teacher."

[1]Franz Delitzsch, *Commentary on Song of Songs and Ecclesiastes* (1872; Grand Rapids, Mich.: Eerdmans, 1950), p. 190. Earlier a similar type of argument had been mounted by the Catholic scholar Mitchell Dahood, "Canaanite-Phoenician Influence in Qoheleth," *Biblica* 33 (1952): 201-2 and Gleason L. Archer Jr., "The Linguistic Evidence for the Date of Ecclesiastes," *Journal of the Evangelical Theological Society* 12 (1969): 171.

[2]D. C. Fredericks, *Qoheleth's Language: Re-evaluating Its Nature and Date,* ANETS 3 (Lewiston, N.Y.: Edwin Mellen, 1988).

2:24-26 Eat, Drink and Be Merry?

All too often the writer of Ecclesiastes has been blamed for all too much. For example, with regard to the text before us, it is not uncommon to hear charges of Epicureanism, the philosophy that advises us to eat, drink and be merry for we only go around once and then we die!

But this charge is false on several counts. For one thing, the text has not been translated correctly. For another, it misses the point that death is not the natural sequel to eating and drinking. Instead, the text insists that even such mundane experiences as eating and drinking are gifts from the hand of a gracious God.

But let us begin with the translation issue. Literally rendered, the text here affirms, "There is not a good [inherent?] in a person that he [or she] should be able to eat, drink or get satisfaction from his [or her] work. Even this, I realized, was from the hand [or 'the power'] of God." This translation avoids the phrase "there is nothing better." Even though such a comparative form does exist in a somewhat similar formula in Ecclesiastes 3:12 and 8:15, it does not appear in this context.

Scholars uniformly assume that the word for *better* has dropped out of this context, but there is no evidence to back up that assumption. Furthermore, the writer is not saying at this point that no other options exist for the race other than to try calmly to enjoy the present. This indeed would be a hedonistic and materialistic philosophy of life that would effectively cut God off from any kind of consideration.

The Preacher's point is not one of despair—"There's nothing left for us to do than the basically physical acts of feeding one's face and trying to get as many kicks out of life as we can." Rather, his point is that whatever good or value is to be found, its worth cannot be determined merely by being part of the human race.

We mortals must realize that if we are to achieve satisfaction and pleasure from anything in life, even things as base and mundane as eating and drinking, we must realize that it all comes from the hand of God. The source of pleasure, joy and goodness does not reside in the human person, as humanism or idealism would want us to believe.

Ecclesiastes 2:25 is more adamant on this point. Who will be able to find any enjoyment unless they first find the living God who is the only true source of all joy, satisfaction and pleasure? The text assures us that "without him" such satisfaction is a lost search.

The ground for the distribution of this joy is carefully set forth in Ecclesiastes 2:26: it is a matter of pleasing God first. The opposite of pleasing God is "one who continues to live in sin." This same contrast between pleasing God and being a sinner is found in Ecclesiastes 7:26 and 8:12-13. Another way to define the one continually choosing sin is "one who does not fear God."

Such a call to please God as a basis for realizing joy, pleasure and satisfaction is not, as some claim, too cheery a note for such a pessimistic book. The truth of the matter is that all too many have missed the positive note that is deeply rooted in the repeated refrains in Ecclesiastes.

God will grant three gifts to those who please him: wisdom, knowledge and joy. But to the sinner who persists in trying to remake God's world, there is also an outcome: "a chasing after the wind." This reference to the chasing of wind is to the frustrating activity in which the sinner works night and day to heap things up only to find in the end that he must, and as a matter of fact does, turn them over to the one who pleases God.

If only the sinner would come to know God and please him, then he too would receive the ability to find joy in all of life just as the one who fears God has found it.

3:19-21 Man's Fate Like the Animals?

If ever there were a hard saying in the Scriptures, this would surely be among the most difficult! It is bad enough that death seems to unfairly level all humans—young or old, good or bad. But this saying casts a grim shadow that appears to say that all hope is lost after death as well—a startling statement indeed! Is it true that men and beasts have about the same hope for any kind of life after death? Is it really only a matter of "fate"? These are some of the questions this text raises.

First, the word *fate* is an overtranslation. The word that appears here is merely the word *happening*. Thus, no references are made to chance, luck or ill fortune. It is solely the fact that one happening, one event—namely, death—overtakes all things that share mortality.

The text then affirms that "all go to the same place." But the place that is intended here is not oblivion or nonexistence; it is the grave. Both men and beasts are made out of dust, and therefore it is to the dust that they will return. In that sense, as one dies, so dies the other. Death is no respecter of persons or animals!

But most disturbing about those who insist on this hopeless view of death in the Old Testament is the way they translate some texts in order to substantiate their own views. In the clearest tones possible in the Hebrew, Ecclesiastes 3:21 states that "the spirit of man rises upward, and the spirit of the animal goes down into the earth." The verbs *to go upward* and *to go downward* are active participles with the sign of the article. There is no need to say that Hebrew has confused the article with a slightly different reading for the interrogative.

Furthermore, had not Solomon already argued in this very context that the unjust judges would face the living God at the last judgment (Eccles 3:17)? How could they do this if it was all over when they died? And did not Solomon warn just as forcibly that the final judgment of God would bring every earthly deed into the light of his justice (Eccles 12:7, 14)? But if it were the end of existence, who would care about such idle threats that warned about a later judgment?

The concept that people could and did live after death is as old as Enoch himself. That man, it is recorded in Genesis 5:24, entered into the eternal state with his body! Likewise, the patriarch Job knew that a person would live again if he died, just as a tree would sprout shoots after it had been cut down (Job 14:7, 14).

Nor should we stress too much the words "Who knows," as if the text gives us a question for which there is no answer. In the nine places where this expression occurs in Scripture, only three are actually questions (Esther 4:14; Eccles 2:19; 6:12). In the two passages that are similar to this text, it is followed by a direct object. The statement is a rhetorical remark that calls for us to remember that it is God who knows the difference between persons and beasts, and that the spirit or soulish nature of one is immortal (and hence "goes up" to God) while the spirit of the other is not immortal (and hence "goes down" to the grave just as the flesh disintegrates into dust).

The final verse of the chapter reiterates this same rhetorical question. "Who can bring him to see what will happen after him?" From the context the answer is abundantly clear, even if the answer is not immediately verbalized: it is God who will make the final evaluation on life in its totality. Men and women should not live as if God were not to be faced in eternity and as if there were nothing more to mortal humans than their flesh, which will turn to dust in the grave just as the flesh of animals will. There is more. The undertaker cannot and does not get everything when he calls for the remains. The spirit has gone already to be with God in the case of those men and women who fear him and who wish to please him.

Therefore, I would translate Ecclesiastes 3:19-21 as follows:

> For what happens to humanity also happens to the beast; one and the same thing happens to both of them; as the one dies, so the other dies: the same breath is in both of them; there is no advantage [based on this one event of death] of the man over the beast. Both go to one place, that is, the grave. Both are [made out] of the dust and both return to the dust. Who knows the spirit of an individual? He [or she] is the one that goes upward [to God], but the spirit of the beast is the one that goes downward to the earth.

See also comment on PSALM 49:12, 20.

7:16-18 Don't Be Too Righteous or Too Wise?

Too many people have seen Solomon's advice as the golden mean. It is as if he had said, "Don't be too holy and don't be an outright criminal; just sin moderately!"

But this reading of these verses is indefensible. The Preacher (as the writer calls himself) is not cautioning against people being "Goody Two Shoes" or possessing too much religion or consistency in their faith. There was an altogether different danger occupying his mind. It was the danger not of how men and women are perceived by others, but of how men and women perceive themselves. The danger was that individuals might delude themselves through the multiplicity of their pseudoreligious acts that were nothing more in reality than ostentatious pieces of showmanship.

The real clue to this passage is to be found in the second verb of Ecclesiastes 7:16, *to be wise.* This form must be rendered reflexively according to the Hebrew verb form: to think oneself to be furnished with wisdom. As such, it makes the same point as the famous text in Proverbs 3:7 does, "Be not wise in your own eyes" (RSV). Thus it was not the case of having too much righteousness or wisdom; rather, it was the problem of self-delusion and the problem of having a superego that needed to have large doses of humility added. When people become too holy, too righteous and too wise in their own eyes, then they become too holy and too wise for everyone—not in reality, of course, but in their own estimation!

Since Ecclesiastes 7:17 follows the pattern of verse 16, and since the two verses are part of the same thought, the resulting translation would be:

> Do not multiply [your] righteousness and do not play the part of the wise [in your own eyes]—why destroy yourself? Do not multiply [your] wickedness and do not be a [downright] fool—why die before your time?

The fact that this interpretation is the correct one can now be tested by its contextual compatibility with Ecclesiastes 7:18. It is good, urged Solomon, that women and men take hold of "the one" (namely, true wisdom that comes from the fear of God and not that which comes from braggadocio), rather than grasping "the other" (that is, the folly of fools). In the end, it is the person who fears God who will be delivered from all these extremes. That is what protects God's people from absurdity. Neither folly nor conceited righteousness will serve well as a guide or as a guise to mask the real need of the heart. True wisdom can only be found in coming to fear God.

But no one is ever going to be able to stand before a just and holy God based on a so-called middle way of the golden mean which attempts to counterbalance opposites in moderate doses. Such self-imposed estimates of what God desires are fruitless and of no spiritual benefit. It is impossible to claim to have arrived morally while maintaining a middle path based on acting sometimes virtuously and sometimes viciously.

The Preacher, then, is not suggesting something that is immoral; he is, on the contrary, an enemy of false righteousness as well as an exposer of false pretensions to wisdom.

12:13-14 What Does Ecclesiastes Teach?

Many modern readers of the book of Ecclesiastes cannot believe that the book originally ended on such a high ethical and theological note. Therefore, the conventional wisdom of many scholars is to attribute these final verses of the book to a late manuscript addition intended to ensure that the book would be adopted into the canon of Scriptures.

Could a book that could very well have come from the hand of Solomon have been capable of such elevated theology as to conclude that fearing God was the main task of men and women and that obeying God was the most excellent way? Could it argue that one day each person would give an account of all he or she had done in life before God, from whom it was impossible to hide anything? First, we must note that there is no manuscript evidence to suggest that this alleged pious ending was dropped into place by some late redactor wanting to make sure Ecclesiastes remained in the scriptural canon. All available manuscripts reflect the present ending, so the supposition of its being an addition must remain just that: a supposition.

On the other hand, this brief text might well supply one of the keys for understanding the book, for it purports to be the summary of the whole book.

The warning that everything done on earth is reviewable in the final day was not meant to scare people, but to put a holy restraint in them. If God will judge all these acts, then it would follow that those being judged are capable of being resurrected, or at least able to appear personally and consciously before the living Lord for his verdict. The implication is that death is not a final end for the author of this book—though many who have studied Ecclesiastes have assumed that it is.

Injustice in this world is so objectionable that God has provided avenues for immediate amelioration of wrongdoing through human courts of law. However, final relief must come in the future, when the ultimate Judge, the Lord himself, comes to rectify all wrong. This theme of the need for a final judgment is raised several times in the course of the book (Eccles 3:17; 9:1; 11:9), as well as in the conclusion in Ecclesiastes 12:14. Obviously, the Preacher believes in a judgment after death and expects that all that has not been set right on earth will be set right in that day by God.

This interpretation of the last two verses is in harmony with the rest of the epilogue (Eccles 12:8-14). The writer concludes by restating the theme he had announced in Ecclesiastes 1:2: " 'Meaningless! Meaningless!' says the Teacher. 'Everything is meaningless.' " In other words, how futile it is to have lived life without having known the key to life.

But that is not the end of the matter; the writer has a solution. He quickly adds his qualifications for giving such heady advice in Ecclesiastes 12:9-10. He laid claim, by virtue of revelation, to being "wise"; therefore, he "imparted knowledge to the people" with a caring attitude and a deliberateness that elicited his audience's serious attention.

His words were "pleasant" ones or "words of grace." His was not a haphazard spouting of negativisms, nihilisms or an eat-drink-and-be-merry philosophy. Rather, he taught "right words . . . upright and true." Any interpreter of this book who fails to take these claims seriously is not listening patiently enough to what is being said. So useful are the words of this whole book that they can be used as goads to proper action or as nails on which you can hang your hat (Eccles 12:11). These teachings are not experiential or autobiographical; they come from "the one Shepherd." This can be no one but the Shepherd of Israel (Ps 80:1), the Shepherd of Psalm 23:1. The ideas in Ecclesiastes do not come from cynicism, skepticism or worldly wisdom, but from the Shepherd.

The grand conclusion to this book is that we are to fear the living God and heed his Word. This is no legalistic formula, but a path for happiness. In coming to know God we come to know ourselves, for believing faith opens us up to the riches of the treasures of God, humankind and the world.

Since God is a living being and since men and women live forever, every deed, even what has been secret, is reviewable in that final day by the Lord who knows us so well. The apostle Paul echoes this teaching in 2 Corinthians 5:10. Humans are responsible beings, and one day each will personally face the Lord to give an account of the deeds done in the flesh.

SONG OF SONGS

8:6-7 Love Is As Strong As Death?

Song of Songs has long been a closed book to many people because of the difficulty they have had in interpreting it. If the book is teaching on what true marital love is all about from a divine perspective, which is certainly what it seems to be, why is the chief character Solomon? Most of us hardly consider Solomon a paragon of monogamous marriage!

Furthermore, where do we find the proper key to make a good entry into the book? Is there any place where the narrative, play, drama or poem (whichever it really is) comes to some kind of focus and gives the reader a clue as to its interpretation?

The answer, I believe, is to be found in Song of Songs 8:6-7. The pronominal suffixes of the Hebrew text here are all clearly masculine; hence the speaker is the Shulamite maiden. She is addressing her beloved one, the man to whom she has sung praises and whom she has courted with affection.

Not all scholars are agreed on who this man is. Most, in recent times, take him to be the same one who composed Song of Songs under the inspiration of God—Solomon. But I believe a better case can be made for the presence of a third character to whom this young woman had pledged her love some months before. In the interim, Solomon had seen her and had attempted to woo her to be a part of his growing harem. The Shulamite maiden refused, in spite of the persistent urging of the other women of the court. They thought she would "have it made" if only she would give in to the king's offers of love.

But the maiden could not forget the shepherd boy to whom she had been pledged and for whom she had great love. It is to him she addresses these lines. And the love the two of them had for each other was the means by which Solomon learned, with the help of the Spirit of God, about true marital love. He who had loved and lost so much was now the recipient of God's normative pattern for love, sex and marriage.

These verses mark the conclusion of the book and thus indicate to us the purpose for which it was written. Addressing her beloved as the one she had met under the apple tree and who had awakened love in her for the first time, she requests to be placed as a seal on a cord about his neck and as a signet ring on his arm, to be his wife forever. The signet ring was worn either on the hand (Gen 41:42; Esther 3:12; Jer 22:24) or around the neck with a string through it (Gen 38:18). The seal was a mark of ownership and authority. The typical Israelite name seal was made out of stone, often pierced with a hole and worn about the neck on a cord, or occasionally on the finger as a ring. A few personal seals have been found in Israel inscribed with the words "wife of . . ." Thus the Shulamite woman pleads for a unique relationship, to be chosen by him and to belong to him forever.

The love she describes has five elements that make it distinctive. First, it is as strong as death. Its power is as unbreakable and as irresistible as death itself. One cannot withstand it or deny it, so that it can be compared only with death—who has ever successfully withstood that power?

Second, its jealousy is as unyielding and as obdurate as the grave. The word *jealousy* has both positive and negative meanings in the Bible. When used positively, in reference to God (Ex 20:5; 34:14; Deut 5:9), it suggests an undivided devotion to its object, an ardent love that brooks no rival and demands undivided attention in return. It is used in this sense in Song of Songs, pointing to a love that is jealous *for* someone, not *of* someone. Thus it is a manifestation of genuine love and protective concern. It is "cruel" or "hard" too—unyielding and resolute in its desire to be with the loved one. In the lengths to which this love will go, it is as deep, inexorable and hard as the grave.

Third, this love burns flames of fire given by the Lord himself. The word "flames" has, in Hebrew, the suffix *yâh*, which must be understood as the shortened form of the name of Yahweh, the Lord (which is why I have followed the NIV marginal reading in the translation above). This love, then, does not originate solely from some carnal instinct; it emanates from the Lord himself! He is the true source of marital love. The flames of love in the heart of a man or a woman are lit by the Lord who made them. Within the bounds of marriage, the flame of love comes from the Lord.

Fourth, it is impossible to drown out this love with much water or even with a flood. Solomon had to forget trying to woo the Shulamite maiden, for all his promises of position, jewels, wealth and leisure could not drown her love for that shepherd boy back home.

Finally, such love is beyond any purchase price offered anywhere. This is the victorious side of love, and it comes from God; it cannot be bought or sold. This was not intended to condemn the custom of paying a "bride price." Such a payment was never construed as a payment "for love," nor was it used to gain love. The point, instead, was that true love from God for a man or a woman was beyond any kind of price.

Thus this text celebrates physical love within the bounds of marriage for its strength, its unquenchable nature and its source—the Lord himself.

ISAIAH

1:11-15 Does God Desire Sacrifices?

See comment on PSALM 51:16-17, 19.

6:1, 5 Did Isaiah See God?

See comment on EXODUS 33:18-23.

6:9-10 Is God the Author of Evil?

See comment on EXODUS 9:12; ISAIAH 45:7; LAMENTATIONS 3:38-39; MARK 4:11-12; 2 CORINTHIANS 3:14.

7:14 A Virgin Shall Conceive?

Why do many claim that "virgin" in Isaiah 7:14 should be rendered "young woman," "damsel" or "maiden"? Would not these renderings effectively negate the force of this word as being a prophecy about Jesus' miraculous birth?

It is important to capture the occasion for which this prophecy was given in order to understand it. The setting begins with Ahaz, king of Judah, refusing to join Rezin, the king of Aram (Syria) in Damascus, and Pekah, the king of the northern ten tribes of Israel in Samaria, against the Assyrians, who had subjugated most of the Near East. For Ahaz's resistance to their overtures, Pekah and Rezin marched against Judah with the intent of overthrowing the Davidic dynasty and placing the son of Tabeel (Is 7:6; Tabeel is probably a distortion from a name meaning "God is good" to something like "Good for nothing!") on the throne in Jerusalem.

In order to reassure Ahaz that nothing like this was going to happen, God sent the prophet Isaiah to join King Ahaz as he was out inspecting the water reserves for the city of Jerusalem, apparently calculating how long he could hold out against these two firebrands from the north. Isaiah's instructions from God were to invite king Ahaz to request from God any "sign" (that is, miracle) that he wished, for that miracle would be God's promise to the king that Pekah and Rezin would not have their way. God's word to Ahaz was "If you do not stand firm in your faith, you will not stand at all" (Is 7:9).

Ahaz refused, protesting that Scripture (presumably Deut 6:16) did not allow him to tempt/test God. But, Isaiah explained, this was not the same as testing God, for God himself invited the request. It appears, however, that Ahaz had in the meantime sent off a secret message with financial encouragements to the king of Assyria with the request that he attack either or both Rezin and Pekah, thereby forcing them to withdraw from Ahaz's doorstep.

Despite Ahaz's reluctance to cooperate, Isaiah proceeded to give a "sign" from the Lord himself that would be for all the house of David. Isaiah 7:14 begins with a *therefore,* indicating that what precedes is the reason for what follows. So the divine word is not unattached to all that we have just described. Isaiah began: "The Lord ['ᵃdōnāy, the name signifying that he is the one who is master over everything] himself will give you [plural, thereby referring to the whole Davidic house] a sign" (even though Ahaz had refused to request such in his unbelief). "Behold [untranslated in the NIV, but a term that calls special attention to a particular fact] the virgin *[hā'almâh]* will be with child and will give birth to a son, and will call him Immanuel [that is, 'God with us']."

The word *hā'almâh* has caused much debate. The Septuagint translated it by the Greek noun *parthenos,* a word that has the specific meaning of "virgin." But what does the Hebrew mean? When all the passages in the Old Testament are investigated, the only conclusion one can come to is that the word means "virgin." To date, no one has produced a clear context, either in Hebrew or in the closely related Canaanite language from Ugarit (which uses the cognate noun *ǵlmt*), where *'almâh* can be applied to a married woman. Moreover, the definite article with this word must be rendered "*the* virgin"—a special one God had in mind. Added to this is the question of what would be so miraculous ("sign") about a "young woman" having a baby?

Nevertheless, this message must have some significance for Ahaz and the people of his day, rather than it being only for an event that turns out to be more than seven centuries away! What significance could it hold for Ahaz and his generation if this event pointed solely to something over seven hundred years away? There was simultaneously a near as well as a distant fulfillment, and the prophecy simultaneously pointed to both a near and a distant future. Rather than a son of Tabeel taking over the throne of David, through whom God had promised to send his Messiah, a son was born to Ahaz: Hezekiah. It may well have been that the prophet pointed to a "young woman" standing nearby, who at the time was unmarried and a virgin (the two were assumed to go together). The son born to them, then, would be Ahaz's son, Hezekiah.

But this interpretation raises at least two major problems: (1) Hezekiah's birth was not the result of a miraculous conception, and (2) Hezekiah, according to most chronologies, was about ten years of age at the time. To the first objection, we respond that this misunderstands the connection between the near and the distant fulfillments in prophecy. Rarely does the "now," or near fulfillment, meet most, much less all, the details and expectations that the ultimate event completes. For example, John the Baptist came in the "spirit and power" of Elijah (Lk 1:17), and he was in that regard Elijah who was to come; but Elijah would still come again before the great and notable day of the Lord (Mal 4:5). Likewise, many antichrists have already come, but they are a small kettle of fish compared to the person and powers of the final antichrist (1 Jn 2:18). Again, five prophets in four centuries declared in five different crises that they were undergoing the "day of the LORD," yet they in no way experienced what the final day of the Lord would be like. Similarly, "*now* we are the children of God, and what we will be has *not yet* been made known" (1 Jn 3:2; emphasis mine). Here is that same tension between the "now" and the "not yet." So Hezekiah did not fulfill all that the prophet had in mind, especially since he spoke of "you" as a plurality of the house of David.

What about the chronological problem? There is one remaining synchronism in the kings of Israel and Judah that has not been resolved: it is a ten-year problem in the years of Hezekiah. A reexamination of the date of the Syro-Ephraimite War, I believe, will show that the prophecy is properly aligned for the announcement of the pending birth of the next resident on the throne of David, thereby providing an unbroken string of occupants leading up to the grandest of them all.[1]

Therefore, the word *'almâh* was deliberately used because it always referred to a young woman who was a virgin. God promised that there would be something miraculous about the birth, and if that promise was not completed in the near fulfillment, then it would be in the final fulfillment. That One would be Immanuel, "God with us."

[1]For a more elaborate discussion of this point and passage, see my article "The Promise of Isaiah 7:14 and the Single-Meaning Hermeneutic," *Evangelical Journal* 6 (1988): 55-70.

10:5-6 Assyria Punished for Obedience?

See comment on 2 KINGS 9:6-10.

14:12-14 Lucifer: Satan or the King of Babylon?

In a prophecy of Isaiah addressed to the king of Babylon, there is a sudden shift from this world to a realm outside it. It describes a being with a hubris that will brook no rival who wishes to challenge God himself for position, authority and power.

Some of the early church fathers, such as Tertullian, along with Gregory the Great and scholastic commentators, linked this prophecy in Isaiah with Luke 10:18 and Revelation 12:8. As a result, they applied the passage to the fall of Satan or Lucifer. The expositors of the Reformation era, however, would have no part of this exegesis, which they regarded as a popular perversion. The passage, in their minds, discussed human pride, not angelic—even though the pride was monumental, to be sure. Which interpretation, then, is correct? Is this passage a record of the time when Satan fell like lightning from heaven? Or is it a description of the Babylonian king only?

The key word for resolving this problem is *hêlēl,* rendered at first as an imperative of the verb signifying "howl" ("Howl, son of the morning, for your fall"). Then it was connected with the verb *to shine* and made a derivative denoting "bright one," or more specifically "bright star," the harbinger of daybreak. The Latin term for it became *Lucifer.*

In Canaanite mythology from Ugarit, the god Athtar seems to be connected with the morning star. At one point, the gods attempted to replace Baal with Athtar, but he declined, as he found that he was unsuited for the position. The throne was too large for him. Athtar was the son of the Ugaritic god El and his wife Asherah. Athtar was the chief god in the South Arabic pantheon, known there as an astral deity, the planet Venus. In the Ugaritic world he was known as "the terrible, awesome one" or as "the lion." Some have translated the first epithet as "a flash [of lightning]." The Ugaritic text 49, column 1, tells how his greed for power caused him to ascend the vacant throne of Baal, who had been dealt a death blow by the god of death, Mot. Assisted by his mother, he attempted to fill the vacuum left by Baal, but he was unable to do so. His feet did not reach the footstool, and his head did not clear the top of the throne. So he descended from the throne of Baal, stepping down so that "he might rule over the grand earth." Like Isaiah's Lucifer, he had aspired to ascend to a throne above the heavens but suffered a fall.

While there are a number of similarities between the Ugaritic myth and Isaiah's account, no great interpretive advantage seems to be gained by following this lead. "The mount of assembly" is parallel with Mount Zaphon or Mount Cassius in North Syria, where the gods assembled. Whether the story Isaiah tells came first or the Ugaritic myth cannot be decided from this text. Normally one would expect the real event to have been told before the mythmakers took up the tale and made secondary applications of it.

So is the story referring to the king of Babylon in hyperbolic terms, or does it refer to Satan? Normally the rules of sound interpretation demand that we assign only one interpretation to every passage; otherwise the text just fosters confusion.

In this situation, however, the prophet uses a device that is found often in prophetic texts: he links near and distant prophecies together under a single sense, or meaning, since the two entities, though separated in space and time, are actually part and parcel of each other.

Isaiah saw the king of Babylon as possessing an enormous amount of disgusting pride and arrogance. In cultivating aspirations that exceeded his stature and ability, he paralleled the ultimate ruler with an exaggerated sense of his own accomplishments: Satan.

Just as there was a long messianic line in the Old Testament, and everyone who belonged to that line was a partial manifestation of the One to come and yet not that One, so there was an antimessianic line of kings in the line of antichrist and Satan. The king of Babylon was one in a long line of earthly kings who stood opposed to God and all that he stood for.

This would explain the hyperbolic language, which while true in a limited sense of the king of Babylon, applied ultimately to the one who would culminate this line of evil, arrogant kings. In this sense, the meaning of the passage is single, not multiple or even double. Since the parts belonged to the whole and shared the marks of the whole, they were all of one piece.

Just as the king of Babylon wanted equality with God, Satan's desire to match God's authority had precipitated his fall. All this served as a model for the antichrist, who would imitate Satan, and this most recent dupe in history, the king of Babylon, in the craving for power.

A similar linking of the near and the distant occurs in Ezekiel 28, where a prophecy against the king of Tyre uses the same hyperbolic language (Ezek 28:11-19). In a similar fashion the prophet Daniel predicted the coming of Antiochus Epiphanes (Dan 11:29-35); in the midst of the passage, however, he leaps over the centuries in verse 35 to link Antiochus Epiphanes to the antichrist of the final day, since they shared so much as members of the line of the antimessiah. Thus this prophetic device is well attested in the Old Testament and should not cause us special concern.

See also comment on EZEKIEL 28:11-19.

24:21-23 Millennium in the Old Testament?

This prophecy belongs to the section in

Isaiah's collection of messages known as the "Little Apocalypse" or "Little Book of Revelation" (Is 24—27). Here the prophet tells of a time designated as "that day." This "day" is probably the same as the "day of the Lord," referred to so frequently in the Old Testament. The "day of the Lord" is a period of time that is to close our present age; it is the time of the Second Coming of Christ, in judgment for all who have refused to accept him and in deliverance for all who have believed in him.

In what ways, if any, does Isaiah 24:21-23 accord with what we know from other texts about our Lord's Second Coming—especially from the New Testament? What is meant by the "prison" into which the celestial powers and the kings of the earth are to be herded? And why would they be "punished," or "released," after "many days"?

The vision of this chapter, which has already included the whole earth, is here enlarged further still to encompass the powers of heaven and earth. The term translated "powers" is sometimes used merely of heavenly bodies (Is 34:4; 40:26; 45:12), but at other times it is used of armies of angels (1 Kings 22:19; 2 Chron 18:18). In this case it seems to refer to the fallen angels who rebelled along with Satan and were thrown out of heaven.

Isaiah 14 depicted the king of Babylon descending to Sheol itself in an act of rebellion. Here, both the heavenly and the earthly potentates have rebelled against God, and as a result they are to be confined to a prison (see also 2 Pet 2:4; Jude 6; Rev 20:1-3).

The time of shutting out Satan and his hosts from access to the heavenly regions is also mentioned in Revelation 12:7-17, where the dragon, in great rage, makes war with the woman and "the rest of her offspring—those who obey God's commandments and hold to the testimony of Jesus."

It has been argued that "after many days" in Isaiah 24:22 refers to the same period of time that Revelation 20:1-7 labels the "thousand years." According to John in the book of Revelation, Satan will be released from his prison at the end or conclusion of the thousand years, but just for a brief season. This would seem to correspond to the "punishing" or "releasing" of Isaiah 24:22. The word has the basic idea of "visiting," but it is a visitation for judgment; the word is used in the same way in Jeremiah 27:22. Thus, the loosing of Satan is only a prelude to his total destruction (Rev 20:10).

In this chapter Isaiah shows four judgments: (1) the judgment on the earth and the plagues that will come on humankind in the end time (parallel to the opening of the sixth seal in the book of Revelation); (2) the judgment on the world-city, or Babylon of the future; (3) the final judgment on Jerusalem and all who have dealt treacherously with Israel's remnant; and (4) the judgment that God will hold "in that day" of his Second Coming for all the powers of heaven and earth that have opposed him. It is this fourth judgment that is dealt with in the verses selected here (Is 24:21-23).

The heavenly and earthly powers that have deceived mortals into apostasy will be visited with punishment in one and the same "day." They will be cast into the pit, only to be "visited" once more "after many days"—the millennium. Their release will not last long, for after a brief conflict, the eternal kingdom of God will come in its full glory. The millennium that has preceded this kingdom will only have prepared men and women for its majesty and glory.

25:8; 26:19 Life After Death in the Old Testament?

See comment on GENESIS 5:23-24; 25:8; 2 SAMUEL 12:21-23; JOB 19:23-27; HOSEA 13:14.

28:13 Do and Do, Rule on Rule?

This translation appears to be little more than nonsense. What is the prophet really saying, and what is the meaning of "Do and do, do and do, rule on rule, rule on rule; a little here, a little there"?

The problem here is with the translations of the Hebrew. They fail to take into account that what follows in this meaningless chatter are the impressions and mocking representations of those drunken listeners of the prophet. The words are no doubt slurred by virtue of their inebriated states, mockingly going back to their childhood rubrics for memorizing the alphabet. But they also are represented in the Hebrew by means of an abbreviation, where the first letter is the letter for the alphabet and the second consonant is the letter *waw,* here used as a sign for an abbreviation. The Masoretes added an unnecessary "a" class vowel to make it appear that it was some type of Hebrew word, but no exact fit for such a word is usually identified.

The words rendered in the NIV as "do" and "rule," or in the older versions as "precept upon precept," "line upon line," misunderstand the fact that the Hebrew is representing letters of the alphabet: "*ṣādê* upon *ṣādê, ṣādê* upon *ṣādê, qôp̄* upon *qôp̄, qôp̄* upon *qôp̄,*" approximately where *p* and *q* come in the English alphabet.[1] They are mocking the prophet's preaching by sneering, "The word of the LORD amounts to 'Watch your p's and watch your q's; watch your p's and watch your q's.' That's all it is—one rule after another." With that, they stagger and reel, and then vomit on the tables where they are drinking (Is 28:7-8), laughing over the words with which the prophet has wounded them, but without any evidence of change.

Our expression "mind your p's and q's," of course, comes from the similar saying that one must watch his "pints and quarts" of liquor. But these rascals had turned it around and aimed it at the prophet for having what they deemed too many rules and injunctions against sin.

The result, however, is that they themselves fall backward, are injured, snared and finally captured, both figuratively and actually in the Assyrian invasion that was to come.

---

[1]This interpretation was first proposed in 1753 by Houbigant in *Biblical Hebrew* IV (1753): 73-74. See now W. W. Hallo, "Isaiah 28:9-13 and the Ugaritic Abecedaries," *Journal of Biblical Literature* 77 (1958): 324-38. The translation "do" or "command" supposes that *ṣaw* is a deliberately shortened form of *miṣwâh,* meaning "commandment," and *qaw,* "line," represents a measuring line, which with a plumb line determines if a building is in line or not. But a rubric from a line that was used to teach the alphabet, given in a singsong manner by drunken men, would fit best the stupor the listeners were in and their regard for the words that came from the prophet.

45:1 Did the Pagan King Cyrus Believe in the God of Israel?

See comment on EZRA 1:1-2.

45:7 Is God the Author of Evil?

The assertion in this passage is so bold that Marcion, an early Christian heretic, used this text to prove that the God of the Old Testament was a different being from the God of the New. Thus the nature of this hard saying is simply this: Is God the author of evil?

Numerous texts flatly declare that God is not, and could not be, the author of evil. For example, Deuteronomy 32:4 declares that "his works are perfect, and all his ways are just. [He is] a faithful God who does no wrong, upright and just is he." Similarly, Psalm 5:4 notes, "You are not a God who takes pleasure in evil." If we read the Bible in its total canonical setting, it would seem that God is without evil or any pretense of evil.

The text in question refers to physical evil. As does Lamentations 3:38, it contrasts prosperity and adversity. Thus the good is physical goodness and happiness, while the evil is physical distress, misfortune, calamity and natural evil, such as storms, earthquakes and other disasters.

Even though much of the physical evil often comes through the hand of wicked men and women, ultimately God permits it. Thus, according to the Hebrew way of speaking, which ignores secondary causation in a way Western thought would never do, whatever God permits may be directly attributed to him, often without noting that secondary and sinful parties were the immediate causes of the disaster.

The evil spoken of in this text and similar passages (such as Jer 18:11; Lam 3:38 and Amos 3:6) refers to natural evil and not moral evil. Natural evil is seen in a volcanic eruption, plague, earthquake and destructive fire. It is God who must allow (and that is the proper term) these calamities to come. But, one could ask, isn't a God who allows natural disasters thereby morally evil?

To pose the question in this manner is to ask for the origins of evil. Christianity has more than answered the problem of the presence of evil (for that is the whole message of the cross) and the problem of the outcome of evil (for Christ's resurrection demonstrates that God can beat out even the last enemy and greatest evil, death itself). But Christianity's most difficult question is the origin of evil. Why did God ever allow "that stuff" in the first place?

Augustine taught that evil is not a substance. It is, as it were, a byproduct of our freedom, and especially of our sin. The effects of that sin did not fall solely on the world of humans. Its debilitating effects hit the whole natural world as well. Nevertheless, it is not as if God can do nothing or that he is just as surprised as we are by natural evil. Any disaster must fall within the sovereign will of God, even though God is not the sponsor or author of that evil. When we attempt to harmonize these statements we begin to invade the realms of divine mystery.

What we can be sure of, however, is the fact that God is never, ever, the originator and author of evil. It would be contrary to his whole nature and being as consistently revealed in Scripture.

See also comment on EXODUS 9:12; LAMENTATIONS 3:38-39.

45:17 Israel Will Be Saved?

See comment on ROMANS 11:26.

63:10-11 The Indwelling Holy Spirit?

We are startled to find two explicit references to the Holy Spirit in this Old Testament text. Why would he be mentioned here when the New Testament seems to place his coming after the Son returned to his Father in heaven?

All too frequently interpreters have repeated the traditional adage that the Holy Spirit came on certain Old Testament leaders temporarily, but he did not dwell permanently in people until the New Testament period. But here an Old Testament text clearly teaches that the general class of people "rebelled" and "grieved" the Holy Spirit. The text does not refer only to the leaders; all the people were involved in an act which reminds us of the New Testament warning "Do not grieve the Holy Spirit of God" (Eph 4:30).

Even more amazing, this text appears to contain a reference to all three persons of the Trinity. Isaiah 63:9 refers to the Father who shared Israel's distress in Egypt, the wilderness and Canaan. But it was "the angel of his presence" (or "his face") that delivered them (Is 63:9). This is the One in whom the Father had put his name (Ex 23:20-21). That is tantamount to saying that he had the same nature, essence and authority as the Father. That surely was no ordinary angel. It had to be the second person of the Trinity, the Messiah.

Having referred to the Father and the Son, the passage then mentions the Holy Spirit (Is 63:10-11). Yahweh, the angel of his presence (that is to say, Jesus, the Messiah) and the Holy Spirit are distinguished as three persons, but not so that the latter two are altogether different from the first. They in fact derive their existence, as we learn from other texts, from the first, and they are one God, forming a single unity. The Holy Spirit was known to the individual believers in the Old Testament, and they could and did rebel against the Holy Spirit individually just as New Testament believers often did, and as we do today. *See also comment on* PSALM 51:11.

63:17 God Hardens Israel's Heart?

Such modes of expression seem rough and harsh. Why would God harden the hearts of Israel? Would he still hold the Israelites responsible for what happened as a result of this hardening?

Some have thought that unbelievers were being introduced here, since the words are so harsh and rough. But the connection of the words will not allow such an interpretation, for the prophet will affirm that as a result of their infirmities, they were made ashamed and acknowledged their faults.

But why then do they blame God? John Calvin put it just right. He said:

> And indeed when they trace their sins to the wrath of God, they do not intend to free themselves from blame, or to set aside their guilt. But the prophet employs a mode of expression which is of frequent occurrence; for in the Scriptures it is frequently said that God drives men into error (2 Thess ii. 11); "gives them up to a reprobate mind," (Rom i. 28); and "hardens them." (Rom ix. 18). When believers speak in this manner, they do not intend to make God the author of error or of sin, as if they were innocent, or to free themselves from blame; but they look higher, and rather acknowledge that it is by their own fault that they are estranged from God and deprived of his Spirit, and that this is the reason why they are plunged into every kind of evil.
>
> Those who say that God leads us into error by privation, that is, by depriving us of his Spirit, do not perceive the actual design; for God himself is said to harden and to blind, when he gives up men to be blinded by Satan, who is the minister and executioner of his wrath. Without this, we would be exposed to the rage of Satan; but, since he can do nothing without the command of God, to whose dominion he is subject, there is no impropriety in saying that God is the author of blinding and hardening, as Scripture also affirms in many passages (Rom ix. 18). And yet it cannot be said or declared that God is the author of sin, because he punishes the ingratitude of men by blinding them in this manner.[1]

See also comment on EXODUS 9:12; 2 CORINTHIANS 3:14.

[1]John Calvin, *Calvin's Commentaries,* vol. 3, *Isaiah* (Grand Rapids, Mich.: Associated Publishers and Authors Inc., n.d.), pp. 843-44.

65:20 Death in the New Earth?

This strange verse is found within one

of the two Old Testament passages speaking of "the new heavens and the new earth," Isaiah 65:17-25. (The other passage is Is 66:22-24.) Both Peter (2 Pet 3:13) and John (Rev 21:1) must have had the first Isaiah passage in mind, for they borrowed its wording.

The problem comes when we examine Isaiah 65:20-25 in light of what John had to say in the Apocalypse about the new heavens and the new earth. In Isaiah 65:20 death is possible, but in Revelation 21:4 death is no longer a feature of that new estate. John assures us that God "will wipe every tear from their eyes. There will be no more death or mourning or crying or pain, for the old order of things has passed away."

John depicts the new order of things in the new heavens and the new earth as conditions in which absolute perfection has been reached and where sin, death and sorrow are no more. Jesus mentioned that there would be no begetting of children at that time (Lk 20:36). Why then does Isaiah depict what appears to be the same period of time as one in which death, begetting of children (Is 65:23) and "sinners" are present? True, the power of death may be limited, but the very fact that it is at all present is the embarrassing issue in this text.

The only suggestion that seems to make sense treats Isaiah 65:20-25 as a distinct subparagraph within the topic of the new heavens and the new earth. Verses 17-19 may be paraphrased in this manner: "I will make new heavens and a new earth in which the former troubles will be forgotten, but Jerusalem will not be forgotten. Jerusalem will be completely free of any blemish. Sin may be forgotten, but God's people and the city of Jerusalem will not be forgotten."

Within this subparagraph form, the Jerusalem of Isaiah 65:17-19 pertains to the new Jerusalem of the new heavens and the new earth. The Jerusalem of Isaiah 65:20-25, however, is the Jerusalem of the millennial kingdom of Christ. Such an interpretation recognizes that the writers of Scripture often arranged their materials in a topical rather than a chronological order.

In the eternal state, when the new heavens and the new earth will have arrived, there will be no sin, sorrow and death. But when Christ reigns on earth, just prior to this eternal state, some of these burdens will remain, even if only in limited forms. So unexpected will death be that if people die after only living one hundred years, they will be regarded as having died as infants. Isaiah 65:20-25 breaks the chronological order expected in the chapter and interjects a related note about Jerusalem during the millennium.

Almost universally the early church believed Revelation 20:1-6 to represent a period of time, roughly corresponding to a thousand years, which would begin and conclude with two resurrections (the first of the righteous dead in Christ and the second of all the dead) and would be the time when, at the end of this period, Satan would be loosed for one last fling at opposing God before being finally and forever vanquished. It is to this same time period, then, that we would assign the strange collection of facts stated by Isaiah 65:20-25.

Since the millennium is part of the eternal state it introduces, "this age" could be expected to overlap with "the coming age." Thirty times the New Testament uses the dual expressions "this age" and "the coming age." "This age" is the current historical process. But with our Lord's casting out of the demons (Lk 11:20), and especially with the resurrection of Christ from the dead, "the powers of the coming age" (Heb 6:5) had already begun and overlapped this present age's historical process. Thus in the "now" believers were already experiencing some of the evidences and powers to be experienced in the "not yet" inbursting of Christ into history at his Second Coming.

In Isaiah 65:25 the prophet repeats the word from Isaiah 11:6-9. The description of that age to come again closes with a description of peace in the world of nature. In the new age the patriarchal measure of life will return, death will be the anomaly and then no more, and the hostility between man and undomesticated animals will be exchanged for peace.

Some may argue that the prophet could not have handled such a sharp distinction between the two periods in the age to come. I concede that the prophet may not yet have distinguished and separated these into two separate periods. In the foreshortening of horizons, which was so typical in prophecy, this indeed may have happened. But the resolution here mapped out would have been needed, since death could not have been abolished and continued to exist at one and the same time. That alone would have been enough to suggest that a subplot had developed within the main theme of God's new age to come.

JEREMIAH

6:20; 7:21-23 Does God Desire Sacrifices?

See comment on 1 SAMUEL 15:22; PSALM 51:16-17, 19.

20:7 Is God the Author of Falsehood?

See comment on 1 KINGS 22:20-22.

22:24, 30 None of Jehoiachin's Line to Rule?

Did Jesus the Messiah come from Jehoiachin's line? If so, how could he claim the throne of David through a line cursed by God?

According to 1 Chronicles 3:16-17, Jehoiachin had seven descendants. These, however, were hauled off into Babylon and there, according to an archaeological finding on a Babylonian tablet in the famous Ishtar Gate, all seven were made eunuchs. In this manner, Jehoiachin became "as if childless," as no man of his seed prospered, nor did any sit on David's throne.

David's line through his son Solomon abruptly ended. However, the line of David did continue through one of Solomon's brothers, Nathan (not to be confused with Nathan the prophet).

By the best reconstructions possible from the evidence on hand, Jehoiachin adopted the seven sons of Neri, a descendant of David through Nathan. Neri's son Shealtiel died childless and so his brother Pedaiah performed the duty of levirate marriage (Deut 25:5-10), and as a result Zerubbabel was born.

Accordingly, Zerubbabel, the postexilic governor of Judah during the days of Haggai and Zechariah, was the legal son of Shealtiel, the actual son of Pedaiah, and thus the descendant of David on two counts. First Chronicles 3:19 informs us that Zerubbabel was the son of Pedaiah, brother of Shealtiel. Luke's genealogy states that Shealtiel was a descendant of Neri (Lk 3:27).

We conclude, therefore, that Jehoiachin's line did come to an end and that God in his wisdom provided for another branch of David's line to continue the promise made to David which led to the coming of Christ the Messiah.

23:6 Israel Will Be Saved?

See comment on ROMANS 11:26.

31:29-30 Children Pay for Their Parents' Sins?

See comment on DEUTERONOMY 24:16; JOSHUA 7:1, 10-11; 2 SAMUEL 21:1-9.

36:30 A Failed Prophecy?

King Jehoiakim had personally taken his knife and cut off the scroll with the words of the Lord from Jeremiah the prophet, section by section, as it was being read. Each piece was then tossed into the fire. For this, Jeremiah had a new oracle of doom when he rewrote the scroll: No descendant of Jehoiakim would sit on the throne of David.

Was this prediction fulfilled? As it turned out, when Jehoiakim died in 597 B.C., his son Jehoiachin took over for a mere three months, apparently without any official coronation ceremony, for Jerusalem was under siege from the king of Babylon. Jehoiachin was not allowed to remain on the throne; instead, his uncle Zedekiah was installed by the Babylonians in his place, as Jehoiachin and his sons were carted off to exile, where he remained until he died (see 2 Kings 24:6 and 2 Chron 36:9).

The Hebrew verb *yāšaḇ* "to sit [on the throne]," when used of a king, carries with it a certain sense of permanence and stability, which a short reign of approximately ninety days hardly appears to properly signify. Jehoiakim's son was not allowed to remain on the throne, if he ever could properly be said to occupy it: he was unceremoniously removed.

Thus the king who "cast" the Word of God into the fire that was burning in the palace on that cold day would himself be "cast" (the same Hebrew word) out so that his dead body would be exposed to the heat by day and the frost by night. *See also comment on* "Are Old Testament Prophecies Really Accurate?"

LAMENTATIONS

3:38-39 Calamities Come from God?

This text involves the problem of evil being linked with God as its sponsor or author. Judah faced the destruction of every clear evidence it had ever had that God's promise to the patriarchs and David was valid. Jerusalem and God's own dwelling place, the temple, had been destroyed. Was not God the author of these events?

An alphabetic acrostic (a means of presenting ideas by beginning each line or group of lines with successive letters of the alphabet) marks Lamentations 3:37-39 as the strophe unit (that is to say, poetic paragraph) in which this hard saying occurs.

The preceding strophe, Lamentations 3:34-36, forms one long sentence. Each of its three members opens with an infinitive that depends on the main verb, which comes last, in verse 36. Thus the sentence asks the question, Has not the Lord seen the three injustices mentioned in the three infinitives? Indeed, he had! He knew about the cruel treatment of war prisoners (Lam 3:34), the disregard of basic human rights (Lam 3:35) and the malpractice in the halls of justice (Lam 3:36).

Abuse of prisoners outrages God, as we are also told in Psalms 68:6, 69:33 and 107:10-16. Likewise, God is offended when a person receives no justice in the halls of government (Ex 23:6; Deut 16:19; 24:17; Prov 17:23; 18:5). God never approves of such distortions, and he has noted the sources of our grief (Lam 3:36). This is the context of the strophe in Lamentations 3:37-39. Whatever successes evil persons may have are only temporarily permitted by God for his wise purposes.

Lamentations 3:37 appears to have Psalm 33:9 in mind: "He spoke, and it came to be; he commanded, and it stood firm." Everything must be permitted by the hand of God. However, woe betide the individual, the institution or the group by which evil comes! Though God may permit temporary success of such evil and even use it for his glory, that does not negate the responsibility of wicked people for what they do and how they do it.

Accordingly, God used Assyria as the rod of his anger against Israel (Is 10), as he later used the Babylonians to chastise Judah (Hab 1—2), but he also heaped harsh words on both these foreign nations for the way they did the task. God judged them with a series of woes (see, for example, the end of Hab 2).

Note that Lamentations 3:38 does not contrast moral good and evil but calamity and good. Furthermore, it does not ascribe these calamities directly to God but says that they cannot occur without God's permission. Those claiming that this is unfair should look at Lamentations 3:39, "Why should any living man complain when punished for his sins?" As the theme of this section declares, "Because of the LORD's great love we are not consumed, for his compassions never fail" (Lam 3:22). Thus, the Israelites' very existence bore evidence that God still cared for them.

God, however, is angry with mortals for their sin. This whole question of divine anger has been sharply debated over the centuries. It became known as the debate over divine passibility (the quality or aptness in God to feel, suffer or be angry).

Marcion, a second-century Gnostic heretic, demanded that his God be impassible, incapable of taking offense, never angry, entirely apathetic and free of all affections. Though the early church expelled Marcion and anathematized his doctrines in A.D. 144, the struggle continued over whether God could be angered by sin and unrighteousness.

The cause of anger, according to Aristotle, is our desire to avenge harm done to us. Thus anger came to have a connotation of a "brief madness" and lack of self-control. This definition did not fit our Lord's anger or any righteous anger, and it was rejected by the church.

Late in the third Christian century the church father Lactantius wrote a classic book entitled *De Ira Dei,* "The Anger of God." For Lactantius, emotions and passions were not inherently evil if they were controlled. But it *was* evil for someone to be in the presence of evil and not to dislike it or be angered by it. To love the good was by definition to hate the evil. Contrariwise, not to hate the evil was not to love the good.

That is why we affirm that God's anger is never explosive, unreasonable or unexplainable. It is, instead, a firm expression of displeasure with all wickedness and sin. In God, anger is never a ruling force or passion; it is merely the instrument of his will—an instrument he handles with deftness and care. But however he may use his anger to punish or teach, he will never shut off his compassion from us (Ps 77:9).

See also comment on 2 KINGS 9:6-10; PSALMS 5:5; 11:5; ISAIAH 45:7.

EZEKIEL

14:9 Is God the Author of Falsehood?

See comment on 1 KINGS 22:20-22.

18:1-20 Should Children Die for Their Fathers' Sins?

See comment on DEUTERONOMY 24:16; EZEKIEL 21:4.

20:25 Statutes That Were Not Good?

How could a law of God issued to give life to its followers instead cause their deaths? And why would God deliberately admit, as this text appears to make him say, that he gave Israel laws that were not good for them and impossible to live by?

Some attempt to explain this text by saying Ezekiel 20:25-26 are the blasphemous words of the people. However, the Lord is clearly the speaker in these verses, not the people. Neither is Ezekiel 20:25 a reference to Ezekiel 20:11, as many have thought in both ancient and modern times. Nor is it an allusion to some aspect of the Mosaic law. Some may attempt to argue that this verse foreshadows Paul's recognition of the intrinsic deadliness of the law, which he explains in Romans 5:20, 7:13 and Galatians 3:19. But in fact Paul holds the opposite point of view: he denies that the law, which was inherently good, became evil for some through their disobedience (Rom 7:13). Furthermore, in Ezekiel 20 there is the clear echoing of the sentiment in Leviticus 18:5, "Keep my decrees and laws, for the man who obeys them will live by them. I am the LORD." That same thought is repeated in Ezekiel 20:11, 13 and 21. God's statues were such that men and women were expected to "live in them," not die from them.

Therefore the statutes mentioned in Ezekiel 20:25 cannot be statutes from the Mosaic code, some part of that law, such as the ceremonial law, or even the threats contained there. Certainly God's ceremonial commandments were good and came with promises. And the threats were never called "statutes" or "judgments" by Moses.

Ezekiel 20:26 makes clear what these statutes were. Israel had been defiled by adopting the Canaanite practice of sacrificing their firstborn children to the god Molech. Indeed, there is a quasi-allusion to the commandment given in Exodus 13:12: "You are to give over to the LORD the first offspring of every womb." However, the Israelites perverted the practice by offering the children to Molech instead of dedicating them to the Lord as he had prescribed. Israel also confused their perversions with another law of God, Exodus 22:29: "You must give me the firstborn of your sons."

In this manner, God sent them "a powerful delusion" (2 Thess 2:11) and "gave them over to the worship of the heavenly bodies" (Acts 7:42). In a sense, all this was a type of hardening in which all who did not renounce idolatry were given up to its power and control. That is why we find the verse concludes with the dreadful note "that I might fill them with horror so they would know that I am the LORD."

Isaiah 63:17 asks, "Why, O LORD, do you make us wander from your ways and harden our hearts so we do not revere you?" In the same way, God is said here to have given death-bringing statutes to the Israelites when he saw their perverse behavior toward his ordinances and commandments. To punish their unfaithfulness, he subjected them to influences that accelerated their already clear departure from the truth. They wrongfully thought they were observing the law of God. However, they had so distorted their thinking that they could no longer discern God's law from the law of the pagan land.

Likewise, when Ezekiel 20:26 says, "I polluted them in their gifts," or as the NIV has it, "I let them become defiled through their gifts," this text also speaks as if God himself polluted them so he might return them more quickly to their spiritual senses. Thus in both cases God's participation is dramatically stated to jar the consciences of a blinded populace. God identifies himself with the instruments of his wrath and of his providential chastisements as an answer to Israel's sin. Sin became its own punishment (Ps 81:12; Ezek 14:9; Rom 1:24-25).

Without stopping to acknowledge the presence of secondary, and culpable, causes, what God permitted and allowed is directly attributed to him. But on no account was there the least hint that the Mosaic law was to be faulted or judged beyond anyone's ability to live by.

21:4 Judgment for Both the Righteous and the Wicked?

How could the Lord indiscriminately send judgment on both the righteous and the wicked when in Ezekiel 18:1-20 he had stated that each person would be responsible for his or her own sin? Isn't this a reversal of policy?

Ezekiel 18 focuses on the responsibility of the individual for individual guilt. That is one side of the coin. But the Bible also recognizes the reality of the concept of corporate responsibility when it comes to accounting for the effect of some individual sins. The case of Achan in Joshua 7:1-26 is the best example of corporate solidarity, for when Achan sinned, it was said that all Israel had sinned as well.

We can understand how one traitor can sell a whole army into major trouble, but we forget how the effects of some sins fall on whole communities, nations or assemblies of persons. In the case in Ezekiel 21, the sword would cut both the righteous and the wicked. That is because in war often both the good and the bad fall. But that was not to say that everyone was individually guilty; no, it was the effect that reached and impacted all.

Ezekiel's main purpose here was to

alarm sinners, who were boasting of their security; but the distinction between the righteous and the wicked must not be thought of as being no longer in existence. It was. The fact remained, however, that the sword would not be put back into the scabbard until everything that had been predicted had been accomplished. The wicked were guilty, but many people, including some righteous, would suffer because of the sins of the wicked.

See also comment on JOSHUA 7:1, 10-11.

28:11-19 The King of Tyre or Satan?

Is this simply bold, exaggerated, metaphorical language describing the king of Tyre, or is it an allegory or a straightforward statement about Satan? If it is the latter, then why is it addressed to the king of Tyre?

The historic fall of Satan, otherwise not directly described in the Bible but alluded to in a number of passages, supplied the background terminology and metaphor for this text, just as it did for Isaiah 14. His fall from heaven back, apparently, before time began will supply the model for the fall of the king of Tyre, as it had for the king of Babylon.

But in keeping with the concept of inaugurated eschatology, in which both the near and the distant future are brought together in one horizon, the fall of the king of Tyre will be but a small indication of what the fall of Satan will be like in the final day.

The king of Tyre was compared to the Evil One himself, who was in the Garden of Eden, the garden of God. But this exalted one became corrupt and lost his position in heaven. Similarly, the king of Tyre is about to lose his position for the same reasons: he exalted himself above God. Thus the description seems to shift back and forth from the king of Tyre to Satan himself, but that fluidity of language can be seen elsewhere as the near fulfillments of many prophecies do not embrace the totality of the language as the final fulfillment does.

Thus, the mastermind behind God's enemies is not always recognized, but here it is clearly the devil himself. He is the one that finally must suffer a fiery judgment, thereby appalling the nations who knew him, just as the nation of Tyre will suffer a fiery judgment from God, prior to God's dealing with their sponsor.

See also comment on ISAIAH 14:12-14.

37:1-14 Who Is the Old Testament Holy Spirit?

See comment on PSALM 51:11.

38:1 Who Are Gog and Magog?

Who is Gog? And where is the land of Magog? Where is Meshech and Tubal? Do any of these places or person(s) have anything to do with the events that are to take place in the end times? If so, what are these events?

Gog is called the prince of Meshech and Tubal, provinces of Asia Minor. However, the geographical area that these would have embraced would be comparable to what we today would label as parts of Iran, all of Turkey and the southern provinces of the C.I.S. (formerly the U.S.S.R.).

But who is Gog? The locations of Gog's allies do not help us to identify who Gog is. One interesting suggestion is that Gog is a cryptogram for Babel or Babylon,[1] since Babylon was omitted from the nations mentioned in the prophecies against the nations in Ezekiel 25:1—32:35. That fact is strange, in that it omits the one nation that was at that time holding Judah captive. Why omit the nation that is most on their minds at that time? So Babylon as Gog or Magog is one good guess.

When does this all take place? Nothing described in these chapters has ever taken place in history. All views that would place the events of Ezekiel 33—48 in an allegorical or spiritual type of interpretation fall significantly short of explaining the plethora of detail that is found in these chapters. The setting for these chapters is in the end times, where a conflict between God and evil is consummated and the wickedness of this present age is replaced by peace, righteousness and the divine presence, such as has previously been unknown to mortals.

There are seven messages about what Gog, the enemy of Israel, is destined to face: (1) The Lord will bring Gog and his allies against Israel (Ezek 38:1-9; compare Rev 16:13-14; 20:7-8); (2) Gog will invade Israel (Ezek 38:10-13); (3) Gog will invade Israel from the north (Ezek 38:14-16); (4) God will unleash tremendous judgment against Gog (Ezek 38:17-23); (5) it will take seven years to gather up the spoils and seven months to bury the dead from Gog's army (Ezek 39:1-16); (6) Gog will be eaten by the birds of the air and the beasts of the field in a great supper (Ezek 39:17-24); and (7) this will conclude the salvation of God and the restoration of Israel (Ezek 39:25-29).

Ezekiel 38—39 describe one of the most devastating conflicts in the prophecies of the end times. It sees an inevitable judgment of God coming at the climax of history with the forces of evil completely decimated. The older guesses that this was a picture of the U.S.S.R. have never been sustained by adequate lexicographical work, but at least the southern part of the republics that make up the new C.I.S. may still be involved. The real identities of most of the participants remain unknown.

History is the final interpreter of prophecy, for as Jesus said, "I am telling you now before it happens, so that when it does happen you will believe that I am He" (Jn 13:19). And prophecy ultimately points to the fact that Christ was right, not we or our charts!

---

[1]I suppose this would have to be a strange variation of an "atbash" formation, where, instead of folding the alphabet in half on itself and using the corresponding letter on the other half as the one really intended, it folds the alphabet in half, but in the case of "Magog," it uses the letter to the left of it on the bottom half and the letter to the right of it on the top half. m=l, g [gimel]=b, g=b. Then the word must be turned around to read Bbl, that is, Babel. It is possible, but strange.

DANIEL

1:17—2:23 Is Astrology Biblical?
See comment on MATTHEW 2:1-2.

7:9 Did Daniel See God?
See comment on EXODUS 33:18-23.

9:24-27 A Prophecy of Christ?
Was Daniel's prophecy about the coming "Anointed One," that is, the Messiah, accurate? Or has the text been wrongly interpreted and is there a Messiah who comes at the end of the first set of seven sevens, that is, at the end of 49 years, and another Messiah who comes at the end of the sixty-two sevens, that is, after another 434 years? If there are two Messiahs spoken of in this text, then the text has been doctored to make it seem that there was only one who came at the end of the sixty-nine weeks, or 483 years after the decree went forth to rebuild and restore Jerusalem. And in that case, it cannot be a prophecy about Jesus.

Originally the 1611 edition of the KJV of the Bible rendered it this way:

> Know therefore and vnderstand, *that* from the going foorth of the commandement to restore and to build Ierusalem, vnto the Messiah the Prince, *shall be* seuven weekes; and threescore and two weekes, the street shall be built againe, and the wall euen in troublous times. And after threescore and two weekes, shall Messiah be cut off, but not for himselfe, and the people of the Prince that shall come, shall destroy the citie, and the Sanctuarie, and the ende thereof *shall be* with a flood. (Dan 9:25-26)

The reason the 1611 edition put "Messiah the Prince" (Hebrew: *māšîaḥ nāḡîḏ*) at the end of the "seven sevens" was because the Hebrew text has an *athnach* at the end of this clause, which sometimes indicates a break in the thought. But neither a comma nor an *athnach* is sufficient in and of itself to require the conclusion that Daniel intended a break in thought at this point and a radical separation of the seven sevens from the sixty-two sevens, thus making two appearances of Messiah, one at the end of 49 years and the other at the end of 434 years. Of course there is always the possibility that the sixth-century Jewish scholars, the Masoretes, who supplied the vowel points to the original consonantal text as well as the accents that serve as a form of punctuation at times, were in error. But if the Masoretic *athnach* be retained, it may serve not to indicate a principal division of the text, as the 1611 edition of the KJV took it (which translation was in vogue up until 1885), but to indicate that one was not to confuse or to absorb the seven sevens into the sixty-two sevens. The point is that a violent separation of the two periods with a projection of two Messiahs is out of harmony with the context. Therefore, we contend that only one Anointed One is being addressed in this passage.

But what led Daniel to start talking about groups of sevens anyway? Daniel had been having devotions in the recent writings of Jeremiah (Dan 9:2) when he realized that Jeremiah's predicted seventy years of captivity in Babylon had almost expired. Thus it happened that while he was praying, confessing his sin and the sin of his people, God answered his inquiry as to what was going to happen in the future. There would be an additional seventy sevens for Daniel's people and for the holy city in order to do six things: (1) "to finish transgression," (2) "to put an end to sin," (3) "to atone for wickedness," (4) "to bring in everlasting righteousness," (5) "to seal up vision and prophecy" and (6) "to anoint the most holy [place?]" (Dan 9:24). That would embrace everything from Daniel's day up to the introduction of the eternal state. What an omnibus plan!

But first the seventy sevens must take place. Now the Hebrew people were accustomed to reckoning time in terms of sevens, for the whole sabbatical cycle was laid out that way; accordingly, to equate the "sevens" with years was not a major problem for Jewish listeners. But these seventy sevens were divided up into three segments: (1) the first seven sevens were for the rebuilding of Jerusalem, which was consummated forty-nine years after the decree to rebuild the city was announced; (2) sixty-two additional sevens bring us to the time when Messiah the Prince will come; and (3) a remaining seven concludes the full seventy sevens as they were given to Daniel.

While the first two segments appear to be continuous, making up the first sixty-nine (7 + 62 = 69), Daniel 9:26 describes a gap after the first sixty-nine sevens. In this gap, Messiah will "be cut off," a reference to the death of Messiah around A.D. 30, and the city and sanctuary of Jerusalem will be destroyed, a prediction of the Roman destruction of Jerusalem in A.D. 70. Given the forty-year spread between these two events, it is enough to indicate that the final seven in the seventy will not come in sequence with the other sixty-nine.

When was this "decree" or "word" to restore and rebuild Jerusalem issued? This constituted the *terminus a quo,* or the beginning point for this prophecy. One of three points has been variously adopted by interpreters for this *terminus a quo,* with a slight edge going to the third one. First, the decree was the one Cyrus issued in 538/37 B.C. (Ezra 1:2-4; 6:3-5). Second, the decree was the one Artaxerxes announced in 458 B.C., when Ezra returned to Jerusalem (Ezra 7:11-26). Third, it was the decree that the same Artaxerxes proclaimed in 445 B.C., when Nehemiah returned. Since it was Nehemiah who rebuilt the walls, while Cyrus's decree focused on rebuilding the temple and Ezra focused on reestablishing proper services at the temple, 445 B.C. is favored as the *terminus a quo.*

The *terminus ad quem* (ending point)

of the first sixty-nine sevens is usually put during the life of the Messiah; some preferring his birth (5/4 B.C.), others the beginning of his ministry at his baptism (A.D. 26/27) and some his triumphal entry into Jerusalem (A.D. 30).

So is this prophecy accurate in what it said about the coming Messiah, given in the sixth century B.C. to Daniel? Yes it was. It correctly said that Messiah the Prince would come and that he would die. Some have argued that it was possible to give the exact date for the announcement of Messiah's kingdom by supposing that a "prophetic year" consists of 360 days (instead of 365¼ days of the solar year). This is based on the fact that during Noah's flood, the 150 days equaled five months. There is no need, however, to make such an extrapolation. It is enough to know that there are some 483 years (69 × 7 = 483 years) from 445 B.C. to A.D. 30-33, when Christ was crucified.

11:29-35 Antiochus or Antichrist?

See comment on ISAIAH 14:12-14.

12:8-10 Clarity of Prophecy?

It has been argued that the prophets who wrote Scripture often did not understand what they wrote. Daniel's plain assertion, "I heard, but I did not understand," is used to prove that prophets often "spoke better than they knew."

But this conclusion is too simplistic. It fails to ask the question, What was it that Daniel did not understand? Was it the meaning of his scriptural writings?

Not at all! The incomprehensible words were not his own, but those of the angel who had been speaking to him (Dan 12:7). Moreover, the angel's words were never clarified. They were to be "closed up and sealed until the time of the end." This expression echoes Isaiah 8:16, "Bind up the testimony and seal up the law." In both of these texts, the "sealing" of the testimonies referred to the *certainty* of their predictions, not their mysteriousness to the prophet to whom they had been disclosed or unveiled (as the word *revelation* means).

In this case, Daniel's question was a temporal one, "What will the outcome of all this be?" Daniel wanted to know the state of affairs at the close of the "time, times and half a time" (Dan 12:7). But to this question, as with most temporal questions arising from prophecy, God gives no further disclosure. Even the Son of Man did not know the time of his own Second Coming.

Failure to know the temporal details of prophecy is hardly a basis for asserting that "the prophets wrote better than they knew." Unfortunately this dubious principle has gained widespread popularity. The obvious rejoinder is "Better than what?" What could be meant by the term *better?* Since our Lord has disclosed all that can be classified as Scripture, how then could he know less than he recorded? And if it is argued that this phrase means that the writers sometimes wrote things down but had little or no knowledge of what they had said or meant, then I will counter that a case for automatic or mechanical writing must be proven. The only biblical cases for mechanical writing are the Ten Commandments and the writing on the wall during Belshazzar's feast in the book of Daniel. But these cases hardly set the pattern for all the other texts.

Because the "sealing up" of the prophecy indicated its certainty, not its hiddenness, Daniel was at times overcome by the meaning of his prophecies. On one occasion he lay sick for days (Dan 8:27).

I conclude, then, that Daniel knew all but two aspects of the prophecies revealed to him: (1) the temporal aspects (an exclusion we share even today, as noted in 1 Pet 1:10-12) and (2) additional information beyond that revealed to him. No prophet claimed omniscience, only an adequate, God-given knowledge of a limited topic of importance.

Let us acknowledge, of course, that we often are better able than the prophets themselves to understand the *implications* of prophecies because we can now see many different streams of history and prophecy coming together. This is similar to one person's accurately describing a country he or she has never visited versus another person's not only reading this author's account but visiting that country as well. Nevertheless, our historical advantages cannot diminish the value of the original contributions by God's earthly spokesmen.

HOSEA

1:2-3 Marry an Adulteress?

If we were to take this narrative at face value, we would assume God was commanding something he had forbidden. Exodus 20:14 had clearly prohibited adultery. Moreover, God had forbidden priests to marry harlots in Leviticus 21:7. If that was God's will for priests, his will for prophets could hardly be less demanding.

So we are shocked to hear the Almighty commanding Hosea to "go, take to yourself an adulterous wife." Was this meant literally?

Several matters must be carefully observed. First is the matter of Hosea's writing style, which was very pointed, concise and laconic. In fact, Hosea is so brief and elliptical at times that he borders on obscuring several points, since many allusions escape readers unfamiliar with the ancient context.

In the second place, Hosea obviously wrote this text many years after the fact. The phrase "In the beginning when Yahweh spoke" or, as the NIV has it, "When the Lord began to speak through Hosea," refers back to the time when the prophet began his work. This cryptic notice suggests the story has been foreshortened and the author may leap ahead to tell us what this woman would become, a fact unknown to Hosea but which God, in his foreknowledge and omniscience, could see. This assertion is not as arbitrary as it may first appear, as we will attempt to show.

Let me emphasize that the events described here really took place and are not merely an internal vision or an allegory, as a long list of interpreters have argued. Placing these events in a dream world or making them purely illustrative would not overcome the implied moral problem on God's part.

I assert that Hosea was told by God to marry Gomer, but that she was not a harlot at that time. The telltale signal of this is the figure of speech known as zeugma, which occurs whenever one verb is joined to two objects but grammatically refers only to one of them. In this case the zeugma involves the double verbs *Go, take to yourself,* a Hebrew idiom for "get married" (Gen 4:19; 6:2; 19:14; Ex 21:10; 34:16; 1 Sam 25:43). However, though these verbs apply only to Gomer, the text links them to the children as well. There is an ellipsis (that is to say, a dropping out) of a third verb which normally would have been inserted before the noun to read "and *beget* children." Thus the children are given the same odious name (that is, "children of harlotry"—"children of unfaithfulness" [NIV]), even though two were males—apparently being stigmatized because of their mother's unsavory reputation.

The very fact that Gomer "bore *to him* a son" proves that the eldest child was not born out of wedlock of an unknown father through Gomer's loose living (Hos 1:3). It is not stated, as it was of the first child, that Gomer bore her next two children "to him." However, since Hosea named them, a function normally left for the father, there is a strong implication that these children are his as well. Thus the evidence would show that the secondary label "children of adulteries" or "unfaithfulness" is given to the children not because they are products of adultery but because of their mother's subsequent activity.

But what about the label put on Gomer? Must we regard her as a soliciting prostitute? No, the term used in the Hebrew text is too restricted to mean that. The Hebrew text does not say *zônâh,* as if it were the intensive form. Instead it uses the plural abstract form of the same word, *z^{e}nûnîm,* thus referring to a personal quality and not to an activity.

So distinctive is this abstract plural that it could describe a personal trait that might have been recognizable prior to the marriage, even though it had not shown itself in actual acts of unfaithfulness. According to this interpretation, the Lord directed Hosea to marry a woman who was imbued with a propensity for sexual liaisons. Gomer, of course, represented Israel, who was frequently depicted as being pure when God first met her, though filled with a desire to go off into spiritual whoredoms. This interpretation would explain the "children of whoredoms" as well. The term would refer to Israel's apostasy, not her sexual activity.

This type of construction, where the result is put for what appears to be the purpose, is common in other writings from Israel. For example, in Isaiah 6:9-12, it first appears that Isaiah must preach in order to blind the eyes of the people and to stop their ears, but this is actually the result rather than the purpose of his preaching, as Jesus and the apostles later clarified.

I conclude, then, that Hosea's children were not born out of wedlock from adulterous unions and that Hosea was initially unaware of what God discerned in the heart of Gomer, that she had an adulterous predisposition and a bent toward sexual promiscuity.

Speaking of this same woman, the Lord told Hosea to "go, show your love to your wife again" (in Hebrew the word *again* goes with the verb *go,* according to the ancient suggested punctuation of the Hebrew Masoretes, and not with the verb *The Lord said*) in Hosea 3:1. It is for this reason that the book of Hosea has been called the Gospel of John of the Old Testament and the book that shows the heart and holiness of God. The apostatizing Israelites were just as undeserving as Gomer was.

In conclusion, this hard saying must be understood to be a combination statement. It contains both the original command and additions reflecting a later perspective. To sort out the two parts of the verse, I will place square brackets around the additions to show they were not technically part of the original command but were later revealed as the divine reason God chose this wife for Hosea and allowed him to go through such a trying experience. The verse then reads: "Go, take to yourself a[n adulterous] wife and (beget) children [of unfaithfulness, because the land is guilty of the vilest adultery in departing from the LORD.]" Thus the earlier divine command was combined with the subsequent realization of his wife's moral lapses. When fitted together, both word and deed, they constituted the total claim and call of God on Hosea's life.

1:4 Jehu Punished for Doing as He Was Commanded?

See comment on 2 KINGS 9:6-10.

6:6 Does God Desire Sacrifices?

See comment on PSALM 51:16-17, 19.

11:8-9 Ephraim Pitied

The surprise in this passage is the fact that God is reluctant to give up on the northern ten tribes. While judgment had been exercised by God in the past (as in the destruction of the five cities of the plain—Sodom, Gomorrah, Admah, Zeboiim and Zobah), he definitely would not act with such fierceness here. The question is why. What made God change?—for that is exactly what he had done in choosing not to impose the judgment that was richly deserved by Ephraim.

A number of texts in the Pentateuch reiterate that death and destruction will be the results of all continued disobedience. Leviticus 26:38 warns, "You will perish among the nations; the land of your enemies will devour you," and the next verse adds, "Those of you who are left will waste away." "You will quickly perish from the land" (Deut 4:26). The people would "come to sudden ruin" until they were "destroyed . . . from the land" and had "perish[ed]" (Deut 28:20-22). The perpetually disobedient could expect death (Deut 30:19), and God would "blot out their memory from mankind" (Deut 32:26).

In light of such serious threats, the gracious words of Hosea 11:8-9 are totally unexpected. How are we to reconcile the two?

The sudden shift in Hosea 11:8-9 signals new hope for Israel. The main reasons for the shift from a message of judgment to one of hope are to be found in two facts: (1) Israel would suffer a full punishment for disloyalty and would go into exile under the Assyrian conquest, and (2) the character of God, like the faces of a coin, has two sides: judgment and compassion.

In the freedom of God, he chose to deal with Israel after its exile under his attribute of grace and compassion. God is not like any human being whose emotions swing back and forth arbitrarily and whose wrath might suddenly turn vindictive rather than be equitable. He is God, not a man. He is the Holy One and therefore is set apart from all that is fallible, unpredictable, vacillating and arbitrary. It is his holiness that determines his difference from humans, especially in his qualities of thinking and in his moral behavior.

The passage sets up a contrast between Ephraim's stubborn, selfish rebellion and Yahweh's sovereign holiness and grace. Since God had exercised the necessary judgment for Israel's sin, he chose now to exercise his compassion and protection and to spare the people of Israel rather than obliterating them. Even though they deserved the fate of Admah and Zeboiim, he would bring them back home from captivity, just as he had promised the patriarchs in times past. God's ways are above the ways of Israel. Grace is able to overcome the shameful effects of sin. God would rescue the Israelites in spite of themselves.

The threats of Deuteronomy 4 and 30,

with their parallels in Leviticus 26, were always two-sided. Judgment must come when sin has dominated, but since the covenant was a unilateral, one-sided agreement, in which only God obligated himself to fulfill its terms while humans were not asked to take on a similar obligation, God can restore the erring party back into the agreement. Since the sin of those who had been disobedient had been dealt with, God could now deal in mercy with the new generation.

This is one of the biblical passages that most clearly reveal the character and motives of God. God's heart was stirred within him (Hos 11:8; 12:6) when he thought of how lonely, desperate and needy his people were in their exiled state. Thus he would reverse his judgment for his own name's sake.

This revelation makes this passage one of the great texts on the mercy, love and compassion of our Lord. Where sin abounded, God's grace abounded much more vigorously, overcoming even the unattractiveness and unworthiness of the recipients of that grace.

12:3-4 With Whom Did Jacob Wrestle?

See comment on GENESIS 32:23-33.

13:14 Is Death Conquered?

Either this text is one of the greatest notes of triumph over death in the Old Testament, or it surrenders the helpless to all the weapons of death. Which is true: the first view with its long history of translations going all the way back to the Greek Septuagint, or the second view, which shows up in such modern translations as the RSV ("Shall I redeem them from Death? O Death, where are your plagues?"), NEB ("Shall I ransom him from death? Oh, for your plagues, O death!") and TEV ("Bring on your plagues, death!")?

The first part of this verse has no sign of an interrogative, and therefore I understand it as one of the most beautiful gospel promises in the Old Testament. The Lord, who spoke in Hosea 13:4-11, is the speaker, not Hosea. Our Lord affirms that he will ransom and redeem Israel from the grip of death and the grave. To ransom means to buy the freedom of a person by paying the stipulated price for deliverance. The opening couplet gives a ringing challenge that makes it a straightforward promise. Our God will deliver mankind by fulfilling the law (Mt 3:15), removing the guilt (Jn 1:29) and personally suffering the penalties due to mankind for their sin (Jn 3:16).

How then shall we translate it? "*Where,* O death . . . ?" and "*Where,* O grave . . . ?" or "*I will be* your plagues, O death" and "*I will be* your destruction, O grave"? Normally the translation which denotes permission, as in "I will be," is restricted to the second- and third-person pronouns *(you* and *he/she)* forms; however, the first-person Hebrew jussive form does occur in some exceptional cases.

But Hosea 13:10 of this chapter had just translated this same Hebrew word as "where." That would seem to settle the matter, even though that has an added Hebrew adverb in this same expression. The form probably reflects Hosea's special northern dialect.

But some protest that a promise of redemption is incompatible with the threats pronounced in Hosea 13:7-13 and repeated in Hosea 13:15-16. The complaint charges that this promise is surrounded contextually with curses and judgments.

The answer, of course, is that the same situation is found in Genesis 3:15. It too is surrounded with the curses on the woman, the serpent, the man and the ground (Gen 3:8-14; 16-19). Often God will interject this note of hope right in the midst of humanity's darkest moments and most deserved judgments.

Therefore, the taunt song to death and the grave is the most appropriate rendering of the last part of Hosea 13:14. It is this same paean that the apostle Paul will raise in 1 Corinthians 15:55. It only asks in mocking tones what the first part of the verse had clearly affirmed as a statement: God can and will ransom them from the power of the grave. He can deliver them even after death has done its worst. No wonder the prophet cries out with such triumphant glee and says (after a manner of speaking), "Come on, death, let's see your stuff now! Come on, grave, put up your fists and fight!"

So certain is this affirmation that even God himself can see no cause or condition for changing his mind or intentions. He will have no repentance, says the end of verse 14. There will be no regrets or remorse over this decision in the divine mind, for God has spoken and that will be that.

See also comment on GENESIS 5:23-24; 25:8; 2 SAMUEL 12:21-23; JOB 19:23-27; ECCLESIASTES 3:19-21; DANIEL 12:1-2.

JOEL

1:15 The Day of the Lord

What will this day of the Lord be like? And how can Joel say it is near or imminent when five different prophets in four different centuries (the latter ones aware of the earlier ones) declared that it was just that—near? If it were so near, why hadn't it happened in over four hundred years?

Ten times the prophets warned that that day was near (Joel 1:15; 2:1; 3:14; Obad 15; Is 13:6; Zeph 1:7, 14 [twice]; Ezek 30:3 [twice]). But these prophets ministered in the ninth century B.C. (probably, but not with total certainty, Joel and Obadiah), the eighth century (Isaiah), the seventh century (Zephaniah) and the sixth century (Ezekiel). Yet each repeatedly warned that the day of the Lord was imminent and certain to come. They even gave their contemporaries instances of what impact it would have on people and the nations. But they always reserved the worst and final fulfillment for the future.

The day of the Lord is much too complex a subject to be contained in a brief discussion, for the prophets found it a most engaging topic in their ministries and writings. But it does not completely defy description. It will be a time when God judges the wicked as never before and simultaneously completes the salvation and deliverance of the redeemed.

The Lord will come to "judge the world" (Ps 9:8; 96:13; 98:9). In that day, "The LORD will be king over the whole earth. On that day there will be one LORD, and his name the only name" (Zech 14:9).

It will also be a day of theophany or the appearance of God. He will appear on the Mount of Olives, just where the Son of God told the men from Galilee that he would come again in like manner as they had seen him go (Zech 14:3-4). When he appears, Jerusalem will be attacked and he personally will lead his people against the nations that have gathered there to settle the Jewish question once and for all (Zech 14:3-12; Joel 3).

Because of this insurrection against the Lord and his cause, Amos describes this day as one of darkness and mourning (Amos 5:18-20) for those who had only the popular concept that the Messiah would return to magically right all wrongs for everyone, regardless of the person's personal belief in him. Amos went on to show how false this hope was.

In the New Testament this day is still being discussed. It is known as *that day* (Mt 7:22; 1 Thess 5:4), the *day of God* (2 Pet 3:12), the *day of wrath* (Rom 2:5-6) and the *day of our Lord Jesus Christ* (2 Cor 1:14; Phil 1:6, 10). It had the same foreboding aspect of horrors for the unbeliever, yet it was a bright day of release and joy for all who looked forward to Christ's coming.

But this day always had an impending nature to it. Though it found partial fulfillment in such events as Joel's locust plagues, the destruction of Jerusalem and the threat of national invasions, its final and climactic fulfillment always remained in Christ's future return.

Therefore, the *day of the Lord* was a term rich in content. It marked off a divinely inaugurated future period, which already had in some sense begun with the ongoing history of the kingdom of God. In such a blend of history and prophecy, the prophet's promise that that day was coming in the eschatological (last days) setting was reinforced by God's present-day foreshadowings of what was to come. This would induce men and women to repent and to prepare for that day. Its blessings would extend to a new Jerusalem, the endowment of the Holy Spirit in a unique way and the cleansing and purification of all that needed it.

When this came, the kingdom would be the Lord's and all other rivalries would cease—forever!

AMOS

3:6 Is God the Author of Evil?

See comment on EXODUS 9:12; LAMENTATIONS 3:38-39; ISAIAH 45:7.

4:4 Does God Encourage Sinning?

Is the invitation to go up to Bethel or Gilgal and get a special offer on sinning· perhaps four sins for the price of two today (to be just as cynical)? Nowhere else in Scripture does God encourage sin; why here, or so it would appear?

The prophet Amos speaks with real irony and sarcasm to an audience that has grown somewhat deaf and tired of hearing his calls for repentance. In an attempt to startle an otherwise recalcitrant nation, Amos spoke in a dissimulating way to see if that would bring any reaction.

To be sure, the people zealously went on their pilgrimages to Bethel, Gilgal and Beersheba, all places with religious connotations and associations. At Bethel, of course, the ten northern tribes had set up for themselves a rival altar to the one in Jerusalem, so that worshipers would not need to travel there and one's politics and potential allegiances would not get confused. But this was in contradiction to the will of God, for God had prescribed that his name would dwell only in Jerusalem. King Jeroboam, amazingly enough, set up a golden calf at Bethel and one at Dan, saying: "Here are your gods, O Israel, who brought you up out of Egypt" (1 Kings 12:28). Amos wasn't the only one who was contemptuous of the site of Bethel; the prophet Hosea changed the name Bethel, meaning "house of God," into Beth Aven, meaning "house of wickedness" (Hos 4:15), while he too castigated Gilgal as an improper place to worship God.

The irony of this invitation to go and sin at Bethel and Gilgal comes out in the word for "sin," for it also could mean to "fall away" from God. The Israelites would even prefer to do too much than do too little in their false worship. Thus, they burnt on the altar a portion of the leavened loaves of their praise-offerings, which were intended to be eaten at the sacrificial meals, even though only the unleavened bread was allowed to be offered (Amos 4:5). They were really proud of the fact that they offered freewill offerings in addition to all the rest of the religious acts that they were doing.

But why mention Gilgal along with Bethel as a place of idolatrous worship? This was not the Gilgal in the Jordan Valley, where Israel had camped after crossing over the river Jordan. It was northern Gilgal upon the mountains, to the southwest of Silo or Seilun, where there had been a school of the prophets in the days of Elijah and Elisha (2 Kings 2:1; 4:38). Now in the eighth century B.C. it had been chosen as the seat of idolatrous worship (Hos 4:15; 9:15; 12:11; Amos 5:5).

No, God does not encourage sin. The prophet was merely using ironic and graphic words in hopes of getting the attention of those whose moral quotients had sunk to new lows.

JONAH

1:4-5, 7 Casting Lots Encouraged?

The use of "lots," or the throwing of dice, in order to discover what is unknown seems more at home in the world of divination and enchantment than in the biblical world of the will of God. It is not surprising, I suppose, that these sailors would have resorted to this means of discovery in such terrifying circumstances. But it is surprising to learn that this method did uncover the real culprit—that it worked. How can this fact be explained and reconciled with the rest of Scripture?

The sailors' use of divination in order to learn the source of their problem was altogether fitting to the culture of those times. As far as they were concerned, a storm of this intensity and ferocity must have represented some sort of divine punishment. Someone on their ship must have angered his god in some way, they reasoned. If they were to come out of the experience alive, they had to find out who the offender was and what he had done.

As best we can tell, lots were very similar to our dice, usually with alternating light and dark sides. Some think the mysterious Urim (possibly "lights") and Thummim (possibly "darks") may have been lots used by the high priest and kept in his ephod for discerning the will of God (Ex 28:30).

The casting of lots was probably interpreted along these lines: two dark sides up meant no, while two light sides up meant yes. A combination of a light and a dark side might have meant that one should throw again. On this system, the sailors probably asked the lots "yes" or "no," taking each sailor in turn until it came Jonah's turn and the lots both came up light.

The use of lots was not altogether foreign among the people of God. At several key points in the history of Israel, lots had been used with the apparent approval and blessing of God. This may be one more case where it was not the use but the abuse of a cultural tool that made it objectionable. Lots were used to determine which of the two goats would be sacrificed on the Day of Atonement (Lev 16). Joshua used lots to ferret out Achan as the guilty party after the defeat at Ai (Josh 7:14). Lots were used in the allocation of land (Josh 18—19; Ps 16:6) and in the assignment of temple duties (1 Chron 24:5). In the New Testament, our Lord's clothes were gambled for by the casting of the dice (Mt 27:35). In fact, the whole church decided between two men to fill the position left by Judas's death by the use of lots (Acts 1:15-26). True, here the casting of lots was accompanied with prayer, but my point is that lots were used. Some are fond of pointing out that all these examples were prior to Pentecost, but there seems to be no scriptural significance to such an observation.

The best way to explain the use of lots is by noting the mild endorsement expressed in Proverbs 16:33: "The lot is cast into the lap, but its every decision is from the LORD." Though this proverb is quite brief, its point seems to be that the Lord, not fate, is the reason for success, if there is any. It also seems to warn that the casting of lots does not carry with it an automatic validity, for in every case the freedom to answer lies with God, who is not at the beck and call of the thrower.

It may please God to use this means to give further confidence that one's decision, when it does not conflict with Scripture or with one's best discernment, is indeed his will. But in no sense should the casting of lots be used or viewed as a means of bypassing what can be known of God and his will through Scripture, prayer and the inner testimony of the Holy Spirit.

Accordingly, what might appear to be no more than raw superstition to a twentieth-century Westerner was an evidence of divine intervention and providence. Even the casting of lots came under the controlling eye of God.

1:17 Myth or History?

Could Jonah really have been swallowed by a great fish, survive for three days inside that creature and live to tell about it? Is this a myth, a parable, an allegory or real history?

The Bible, of course, does not speak of Jonah being swallowed by a "whale"; it specifically mentions a "great fish" (Jon 1:17). Some English versions of Matthew 12:40 use the word "whale," but the Greek original is *kētos,* a general word meaning a huge sea-monster. Taken as such, there are several sea-monsters that would be able to swallow a full-grown man easily enough, but the true whale, which has its home in the Arctic seas and is not found in the Mediterranean Sea, has a narrow throat that would generally prevent such a swallowing. There is another species of the same order in the Mediterranean Sea, however, which could swallow a man.

Ambrose John Wilson in the *Princeton Theological Review* for 1927 mentions a case of a sailor on a whaling ship near the Falkland Islands who was swallowed by a large sperm whale. The whale was later harpooned, and when it was opened up on deck the surprised crew found their lost shipmate unconscious inside its belly. Though bleached from the whale's gastric juices, he recovered, even though he never lost the deadly whiteness left on his face, neck and hands.[1]

The problem with claiming that this text is a parable, allegory or myth is that each "solution" presents its own problems of literary genre. For example, parables are simple; they treat one subject. But the book of Jonah has at least two distinct parts: his flight and his preaching. Neither does Jonah fit the category of allegory, for there is no agreement on what the values are for each of the characters and events. The very diversity of answers is enough to state that allegory is not the solution. The same judgment would hold for suggesting that Jonah is a myth.

The book of Jonah, up until modern times, was everywhere treated as an historical record of the repentance of the city of Nineveh under the preaching of a man named Jonah. The apocryphal book Tobit has Tobit commanding his son Tobias to go to Media, for Tobit believes the word of God spoken about Nineveh. The Greek Septuagint text says that the preacher who predicted judgment on Nineveh was Jonah. In New Testament times, Jesus and the early believers took Jonah to be a real character. Thus, the objections to the book come down to this: it has too many miracles! But that is hardly an adequate basis on which to reject the internal claims of the book itself. Jonah is a believable account of a harrowing sea experience and of an unprecedented Gentile response to an ever-so-brief exposure to preaching about the need for repentance. But it happened!

[1]A. J. Wilson, "The Sign of the Prophet Jonah," *Princeton Theological Review* 25 (1927): 636. For more examples, see R. K. Harrison, *Introduction of the Old Testament* (Grand Rapids, Mich.: Eerdmans, 1969), pp. 907-8. See also the interesting article by G. Macloskie, "How to Test the Story of Jonah," *Bibliotheca Sacra* 72 (1915): 336-37, and, more recently, G. Ch. Aalders, *The Problem of the Book of Jonah* (London: Tyndale, 1948).

3:10; 4:1-2 A God Who Relents?

So sharp is the contrast between what God had said would happen to Nineveh and what actually took place that we are left to wonder whether divine words are always fulfilled or whether God is presented in the Old Testament as a rather fickle person. Even though from the start Jonah had suspected, because of God's gracious character, that he would not carry out his threats against Nineveh, we are still left in doubt over God's ability to predict the future or his constancy of character.

Some have attempted to rescue the situation by distinguishing between God's secret will and his declared will. The former, so this line of argumentation goes, is his real intention, which remains fixed and unchangeable, while the latter varies depending on conditions. But this representation of God's will does not accord with Scripture elsewhere, for it still conveys the appearance of insincerity on the part of God—as if God were deceptive, representing his thoughts differently from what they really were, and representing future events differently from what he knew would eventually happen!

The language of this verse, which represents our Lord as "relent[ing]" or "repent[ing]," is undoubtedly an anthropomorphism—a depiction of God in human terms. Certainly the infinite, eternal God can be known to us only through human imagery, and thus he is represented as thinking and acting in a human manner. Without anthropomorphisms, we could never speak *positively* of God; to try would be to entangle ourselves in deism, which makes God so transcendent that he is never identified with us in our world. When we rush to get rid of the human forms in our talk about God, we sink into meaningless blandness.

Nevertheless, when it comes to the eternal principles of righteousness, Scripture is just as insistent about the impossibility of change in God. Consider, for example, the declaration made to Balaam: "God is not a man, that he should lie, nor a son of man, that he should change his mind" (Num 23:19). Similarly in 1 Samuel 15:29 Samuel informs Saul, "He who is the Glory of Israel does not lie or change his mind; for he is not a man, that he should change his mind."

The descriptions of God that have to do with his inherent and immutable righteousness allow no room for change in the character of deity or in his external administrations. His righteousness calls for consistency and unchangeableness.

But such representations argue nothing against the possibility, or even the moral necessity, of a change in God's carrying out of his declarations in cases where the people against whom the judgment was issued have changed, so that the grounds for the threatened judgment have disappeared. For God *not* to change in such cases would go against his essential quality of justice and his responsiveness to any change that he had planned to bring about.

If this is the case, some wonder why the announcement made by Jonah took such an absolute form: "Forty more days and Nineveh will be overturned" (Jon 3:4). Why not plainly include "if the people do not repent"?

This objection assumes that the form given to the message was not the best suited to elicit the desired result. Actually, as the record shows, this message indeed awakened the proper response, and so the people were spared. As delivered, it was a proper account of how God felt and the danger to which Nineveh was exposed.

Of course God's warnings always carried with them the reverse side of the coin, the promises. This element of alternatives within one prophecy can be seen best in Jeremiah 18:9-11 and Ezekiel 18:24 (see, too, Rom 11:22). The good things promised in these prophecies cannot be attributed to any works righteousness or to any merited favor, but are always found in connection with the principles of holiness and obedience to God's Word.

Does this imply that all the predictions from the prophets' lips were operating under this same rule, that nothing was absolute or certain in the revealed predictive realm? Far from it! There are portions that may be regarded in the strictest sense as absolute, because their fulfillment depended on nothing but the faithfulness and power of God. Such were the declarations of Daniel about the four successive world empires. All the statements about the appearance of Christ, in his first and second advents, are included here, along with predictions about the progress of the kingdom of God and promises connected with our salvation.

But when the prophecy depicts judgment or promises good things to come, the prophetic word is not the first and determining element; it is secondary and dependent on the spiritual response of those to whom the words are delivered.

God changed, but his character and nature as the altogether true and righteous One has never changed. As a living person, he changed only in response to a required change in the Ninevites to whom Jonah's word was delivered. Thus he exhibits no fickleness or instability. He remains the unchanging God who will withdraw his threatened judgment as soon as the human responses justify his doing so.

See also comment on GENESIS 6:6; 1 SAMUEL 13:13-14; 15:29; ACTS 1:26.

MICAH

5:2 A Ruler from Bethlehem?

The difficulty attached to this verse is whether the "ruler" who is depicted here is claimed to be both human and divine. Furthermore, is he the promised Messiah? And if he is, why does the text not link him more directly with David and his family? And what is the significance of adding the word *Ephrathah* to Bethlehem?

To answer the questions in reverse order, Ephrathah is not to be explained as the name for the environs of the village of Bethlehem. In Genesis 35:19, Ephrathah is exactly equivalent with Bethlehem. It was the older name for the same town.

But that was not the only reason for introducing the name Ephrathah; the prophet wanted to call attention to the theology of the passage where these two names were first associated: Genesis 35:16-19. As in that passage, which tells of the birth of Benjamin, a new birth is about to happen. The old name Ephrathah (coming from a verb meaning "to be fruitful") is not meant to suggest the inferior things and persons in that city; instead, this town is to be most blessed, the source of fruitfulness on a grand scale for all the earth.

Bethlehem is referred to here in a masculine rather than its usual feminine form, for the prophet is viewing the city in the image of its ideal representative or personification. The city and the person are thus identified with each other.

Had the prophet intended to indicate the Bethlehem that was in Judah, not the one in Zebulun (Josh 19:15), he normally would have said "Bethlehem Judah." Obviously he had more in mind than that, and thus the allusion to Genesis 35 seems certain.

Bethlehem's smallness in size and significance is evidenced by its omission from the list of the cities of Judah in Joshua 15 (even though some later copyists tried to amend this presumed oversight by adding it to their manuscripts).

Here is the marvel: out of a place too small to merit mention goes forth one who is to be head over Israel! But he is not called "the ruler," only "*a* ruler." He will be unknown and unheralded at first—merely *a* ruler. But for the moment the focus is on the idea of dominion, not on the individual.

"Out of you will come *for me*" does not refer to the prophet, but *to God.* The contrast is between human meanness and the greatness of God. Now it must be seen that it is God who is able to exalt what is small, low and inferior.

The ruler was, in the first instance, David. He sprang from these lowly roots in Bethlehem, but that was not the end of it. The promise he carried went far beyond his days and his humble origins. The soil from which Messiah sprang began in ancient times, the days of Abraham, Isaac and Jacob. Boaz, who took Ruth the Moabitess as is wife, was from Bethlehem (Ruth 2:4). David, the great-grandson of Boaz, was born in Bethlehem as well (1 Sam 16:1; 17:12).

But the conclusion of the matter will be the "days of eternity." Two Hebrew phrases, in parallel position, speak of "from ancient times" and "from days of eternity." The first refers to the distant past, the second to the actions that God initiated from before time began and that will last into eternity future. The sending of the Messiah was not an afterthought; it had been planned from eternity. In other words, Messiah existed before his temporal birth in Bethlehem. His eternity is thus contrasted with all the days of the Bethlehem families through which line he eventually came, as regards his human flesh.

The Hebrew *'ôlām,* "eternity," is used in connection with either God himself or the created order. While it can just mean "ancient times" within history, given the contrast here with the early beginnings of David in olden days, the meaning that best fits the context would be a reference to Christ's preexistence. Thus, our Lord came in the line of David (2 Sam 7:8-16; Ps 89:35-37), yet he was one with the Father from all eternity.

6:6-8 Salvation Through Righteousness?

Two different and opposing kinds of false claims are made about this text. Some readers see the text as refuting all external, ceremonial religion in favor of a totally internalized faith response to God. Others, reacting against more conservative theologies of the atonement, argue that essential religious acts focus solely on issues of justice, mercy and humility; all else is beyond what God expects of even the most devout.

Unfortunately, both positions are extremes that fail to grasp the prophet Micah's point. His answer to the question "With what [things] shall I come before the Lord?" certainly went beyond the people's appalling response. They were convinced that they could earn God's favor by deeds and various types of religious and even pagan acts, such as the human sacrifice of their oldest child. They were ready to bargain with God and to bid high if need be. But their attempts to earn righteousness availed them nothing in God's sight.

The prophet's answer, on behalf of his Lord, was very different from theirs, though it was hardly novel. They had already known what was good and pleasing to God, because God had revealed it time and time again. Each time they had refused to acknowledge it as God's way.

Three items are mentioned: justice, mercy and humility before God. The norm of justice had been set by the character and person of the living God, not by human standards. God's norm of justice, announced in his law, demanded perfect righteousness available only by faith in the God who had promised to send the seed of promise.

Mercy, the second demand, should be

patterned after God's mercy as defined in his Word—an unselfish love toward God and one's neighbor.

The third was a call for the people to remember that any good found in them was due to the Lord's enabling. Those claiming the Lord as their God were to prove it by a godly lifestyle. Pride was the antithesis of what was required here: faith. To walk humbly was to live by faith. Such faith sought to give God first place instead of usurping it for oneself. In our Lord's use of this passage in Matthew 23:23, he listed the three requisites for pleasing God as "justice, mercy and faithfulness."

Thus, this passage is more than just an ethical or cultic substitute for all inventions of religion posed by mortals. It is duty, indeed, but duty grounded in the character and grace of God. The question asked in Micah 6:6 is very similar to the question posed in Deuteronomy 10:12: "And now, O Israel, what does the LORD your God ask of you?" The background for both questions is the same, for in Deuteronomy 10, as in Micah 6, God had announced himself ready to destroy Israel, in that case for their disobedience in the golden-calf episode.

Thus this saying is not an invitation, in lieu of the gospel, to save oneself by kindly acts of equity and fairness. Nor is it an attack on the forms of sacrifices and cultic acts mentioned in the tabernacle and temple instructions. It is instead a call for the natural consequence of truly forgiven men and women to demonstrate the reality of their faith by living it out in the marketplace. Such living would be accompanied with acts and deeds of mercy, justice and giving of oneself for the orphan, the widow and the poor.

See also comment on GENESIS 26:3-5; PSALM 51:16-17, 19.

NAHUM

1:2-3 A Jealous God?

The declaration of Exodus 34:6, which appears to assure us that God is not jealous, is repeated ten times in the Old Testament: "The LORD, the LORD, the compassionate and gracious God, slow to anger, abounding in love and faithfulness, maintaining love to thousands, and forgiving wickedness, rebellion and sin."

Other texts, however, appear to assert that God is indeed jealous. Exodus 20:5 clearly states, "I, the LORD your God, am a jealous God." Deuteronomy 29:20 reiterates, "The LORD will never be willing to forgive [the person who invokes God's blessing on himself and goes his own way thinking it is safe to do as he pleases]; his wrath and zeal [jealousy] will burn against that man." Psalm 78:58 asserts, "They angered him with their high places; they aroused his jealousy with their idols." Ezekiel 36:5 confirms, "This is what the Sovereign LORD says: In my burning zeal [or jealousy] I have spoken against the rest of the nations and against all Edom, for with glee and with malice in their hearts they made my land their own possession so that they might plunder its pastureland." So how are we to understand God?

The anthropopathic descriptions of God (which describe God's emotions in human terms) help us understand that God is not just an abstract idea but a living and active person. He does have emotions similar to our human emotions of jealousy, vengeance, anger, patience and goodness—with the exception that none of these are tainted with sin.

Certainly God has many agreeable traits, as Nahum 1:7 goes on to affirm: "The Lord is good. . . . He cares for those who trust in him." In Nahum 1:3 God is also described as being "slow to anger and great in power." But what of his seemingly less attractive emotions?

God's jealousy is often linked in Scripture with his anger. As such, it is an expression of his holiness: "I will be zealous [or jealous] for my holy name" (Ezek 39:25). But in no sense is his jealousy or zeal explosive or irrational. Those depicting the God of the Old Testament as having a mysterious if not primal force, which could break out against any of his creatures at any time for any or no reason, have an overly active imagination. Never does God's zeal or wrath border on caprice or the demonic.

God's wrath is indeed a terrible reality

in both Testaments, but it always reflects a totally consistent personality which cannot abide the presence of sin. God's anger never causes him to avenge himself or retaliate, as if he were briefly insane. In our Lord, anger may be defined as his arousing himself to act against sin.

The same could be said about the word translated "vengeance" in the hard saying at hand. Divine vengeance can only be understood in the light of the Old Testament's teaching on the holiness and justice of God. Of the seventy-eight times this word is used in the Old Testament, fifty-one involve situations where God is the perpetrator. The classical text is Deuteronomy 32:35, "It is mine to avenge; I will repay." God cannot be God if he allows sin and rebellion to go unpunished. His very character cries out for the opposite.

Basically, there are two ways in which God takes vengeance: (1) he becomes the champion of those oppressed by the enemy (Ps 94) and (2) he punishes those who break covenant with him (Lev 26:24-25).

If the book of Nahum appears to exhibit savage joy over the crushing defeat of the Assyrian capital, Nineveh, the question must arise: When is one justified in rejoicing over the downfall of a despotic and tyrannical nation? If the answer is that one must wait until the rejoicing nation has been purged of their own sins, then we should be careful in our smugness over the destruction of Nazi Germany. Our own purging may lie ahead.

Contrary to the popular criticism of the book of Nahum, Nahum's condemnation of Nineveh grows out of a moral and ethical concept of God. In the prophet's thought, God is sovereign Lord over the whole creation, including all the nations. As a holy God, he abhors any form of unrighteousness, but all the more when it is committed on an international scale.

There are three basic reasons why God decreed the end of the Assyrian empire. First, the Assyrians not only opposed Israel, they opposed God (Nahum 1:9, 11, 14). Second, they flouted the law and moral order of God. Not only did Assyria draw her own citizens into the dragnet of idolatry, but she also lured many other nations into her practices, just as a harlot lures her prey to destruction (Nahum 2:13; 3:4). Finally, Assyria's imperial greed provoked robberies and wrongs of every sort.

God, therefore, does not indifferently and helplessly watch the sins of the nations multiply. Instead, he is a warm-hearted, understanding, but thoroughly just and righteous God who will act against those who persist in flouting everything he is and stands for. The fact that God expresses jealousy, vengeance or wrath is a sign that he cares for his people and champions their cause. He can and he will administer justice with equity among the nations.

The words *jealousy*—or, as it is more accurately rendered when referring to God, *zeal*—and *vengeance* may both be used in a good and a bad sense. When applied to God, they denote that God is intensely concerned for his own character and reputation. Thus, everything that ultimately threatens his honor, esteem and reverence may be regarded as the object of his jealousy and vengeance. The metaphor best depicting this emotion is that of the jealous husband, which God is said to be when false gods and false allegiances play the parts of suitors and potential paramours. He cannot and will not tolerate rivalry of any kind—our spiritual lives depend on his tenacious hold on us.

See also comment on EXODUS 20:4-6; PSALMS 5:5; 11:5.

HABAKKUK

1:5-6 Why Does God Use Pagan Nations to Judge His People?

See comment on 2 KINGS 9:6-10; ISAIAH 45:7; LAMENTATIONS 3:38-39; HOSEA 11:8-9.

3:16-18 Joy in All Circumstances?

The prophet Habakkuk had been given a vision that left him deeply agitated. He was so shaken by the terrifying news that God would bring the Babylonian hordes down on Judah that his body seemed to collapse. There can be no doubt that the prophet experienced real fear with pronounced physical and psychological effects.

The amazing aspect of this saying, and the fact that makes it so noteworthy, is that in spite of all the trauma, Habakkuk received the gift of joy. This was not merely resignation about things over which he had no control. The prophet wasn't saying, "Let's make the best of it; one thing is for sure: you can't fight city hall."

Instead, this text teaches us to rejoice in God even when every instinct in our bodies is crying out with grief. Though fully alarmed at the outrage that would take place, Habakkuk experienced a holy joy, a divine enabling to rejoice in the Lord.

The object of his joy was the God of his salvation. Some things are just more abiding and important than this temporal world. Sometimes it seems as if history is out of control and no one knows where it all will end. Since God is ultimately behind the course of history, he is in control and he knows where it will end.

Thus, all the symbols of prosperity (the fig tree, the vine, the olive, the fields, the flocks and the herds of cattle) could be removed, but none of these compared with the joy that came from the living God himself. Even though that joy did not in itself mitigate the depth of the physical pain felt in the body, it did transcend it in worth, reality and depth.

This text has enormous relevance for a Christian view of history and for those who are oppressed and experiencing the reality of the conqueror's or enemy's wrath.

See also comment on JAMES 1:2.

HAGGAI

2:6-7 The Desired of All Nations?

The translation "desire of all nations" in Haggai 2:7 has taken such deep root, through its use in sermons, Christmas hymns and a long history of Jewish and Christian commentary, that it is difficult to handle this text objectively.

The King James rendering, "The Desire of all nations shall come," has been challenged by almost every modern translation in English. The 1901 ASV changed "desire" to "precious things," while the NASB now reads, "They will come with the wealth of all nations." The NEB has "The treasure of all nations shall come hither," and the NAB uses the word "treasures." Clearly, the trend is away from giving the word *desire* a messianic connotation, favoring instead the impersonal idea of "valuables" or "desired things."

All the controversy stems from the use of the singular feminine noun *desire* with a plural verb, *[they] come.* As soon as this is pointed out, modern commentators drop any further search or references to a person and assume that the noun must be plural in meaning.

Actually, both the singular and plural forms of this Hebrew noun, *ḥemdâh,* are used in the Old Testament to refer to persons. Saul was described as being "the desire of Israel" in 1 Samuel 9:20. Likewise Daniel 11:37 speaks of "the one desired by women." The plural form of the same word appears three times to refer to Daniel himself in Daniel 9:23 and 10:11, 19. In these cases, the word is usually translated as "highly esteemed" and a "man of high esteem" *('îš-ḥ^{a}mudôt).*

This same word is also used to describe valuable possessions, especially silver and gold. In this construction the emphasis usually falls on the preciousness of the items.

Did Haggai intend to talk about the valuables that the Gentiles would bring, or did he intend to refer to the Messiah himself, as most of the ancient commentaries and the Vulgate had it?

Those opting for a reference to precious gifts believe this rendering makes contextual sense. The precious gifts would compensate for the temple's lack of adornment. Accordingly, the Gentiles would come laden down with gifts for the temple out of homage to the Lord of the earth, a foretaste of the good things to come in the New Covenant. This interpretation is said to square with the plural verb and the feminine singular subject.

However, the earliest Jewish interpretation and the majority of early Christian interpreters referred this passage to the Messiah. Since the word *desire* is used to refer to a person in several key passages, and since there is a longing of all the nations for a deliverer, acknowledged or not, it seems fair to understand this passage as a reference to the Messiah, our Lord Jesus Christ.

Hebrew often places the concrete word for an abstract noun. Nor should we be thrown off balance by the presence of a plural verb, for often when one verb is controlled by two nouns, the verb agrees with the second noun even if the verb actually belongs with the former.

Although some are reluctant to adopt a messianic interpretation, the word *desire* can be treated as an accusative—a construction which is frequently adopted with verbs of motion: "And they will come to the desire of all nations [namely, Christ]." This rendering avoids the problem of the plural verb *come,* as was first suggested by Cocceius.

In accordance with a messianic interpretation, just as the first temple was filled with the glory of God, so this temple will yet be filled with the divine glory in Christ (Jn 1:14), a glory which shall be revealed at his Second Coming (Mal 3:1).

ZECHARIAH

3:1-2 Satan in Heaven?

See comment on JOB 1:6-12.

6:12-13 Who Is This Branch?

Who is this one who is called the Branch and who seems to possess the office and authority of both priest and king? Is this a messianic passage, or does it refer to a postexilic prophet?

When the Babylonian captives heard the temple was being rebuilt, they sent a delegation of three men with a gift for the temple. The Lord, pleased with the exiles' response, instructed the prophet to make the gift of silver and gold into a crown and to place it on the head of Joshua, the high priest. Although the action was merely symbolic, such transference of the royal crown from the tribe of Judah to the tribe of Levi must have met with surprise. Had God not promised in Genesis 49:10-12 that the privilege of reigning would be vested in the tribe of Judah? And would not the coming Messiah King come from David's line (2 Sam 7:12-20)?

Many unbelieving modern scholars attempt to harmonize these facts by substituting the name Zerubbabel (the Davidic descendant and governor of Judah at the time) for the name Joshua. But the Lord himself reveals the interpretation of this symbolic act in verses 12-15.

It is clear that the term *Branch* is a messianic term, for under this title four different aspects of his character are presented in four major teaching passages: he is the king (Jer 23:5-6), the servant (Zech 3:8), the man (Zech 6:12) and the Branch of Yahweh (Is 4:2). Indeed, many have noted how this fourfold picture of the Messiah corresponds to the fourfold picture of the historical Christ in the four Gospels of the New Testament.

This prophecy promises four particulars regarding the Messiah's character and rule: (1) "He will be a priest on his throne"; (2) "He . . . will build the temple of the LORD"; (3) "He will be clothed with majesty and will sit and rule on his throne"; and (4) "Those who are far away [Gentiles] will come and help to build the temple of the Lord."

It is easy to identify these features with the character and the program of Jesus of Nazareth. He is represented as the High Priest and King in the New Testament. It is also true that Gentiles, those who were "far off" (Acts 2:39; Eph 2:13), will come in the end time and acknowledge his dignity.

Accordingly, there is perfect harmony and accord between the two offices of priest and king in the Messiah—"harmony between the two" (Zech 6:13). The Messiah as Priest-King will produce peace because he will personally hold both the administrative and judicial functions: the ecclesiastical and spiritual ones combined! He becomes our peace.

The crowning of the high priest in the temple of the Lord was to be a reminder concerning the coming union of the king and priest in one person, the Messiah. Such princely gifts coming from the far-off Babylonian exiles were but a harbinger and precursor of the wealth of the nations that would pour into Jerusalem when Messiah the Branch would be received as King of kings and Lord of lords.

See also comment on GENESIS 14:18-19; 49:10; PSALM 45:6; MICAH 5:2.

11:12-13 Thirty Pieces of Silver—A Confused Prophecy?

Two difficulties appear when Zechariah's prophetic actions are compared with their fulfillment recorded in Matthew 27:7-10. First, certain details of Zechariah's prophetic symbolism do not seem to fit the historical account. Second, Matthew ascribes these words to Jeremiah, but he clearly is quoting Zechariah.

Zechariah's prophetic parable followed his prophecy of the Good Shepherd's relations to the flock. In Zechariah 11:11 the people reacted to Zechariah's breaking his staff. They realized that God was annulling the covenant of protection over them. Some terrible acts of judgment were ahead!

In Zechariah 11:12 the prophet requested payment for his services and for alerting the people. He posed his request delicately, assuming that they might not wish to pay him because they had treated their Shepherd so contemptibly. In effect, he said, "If you don't care to pay me, fine; don't bother!" However, the people did not realize that Zechariah's abrupt termination of his pastoral role reflected more their own abandonment of their Shepherd than his choice to end his service.

Their reply insulted him and the cause he represented. They paid him thirty pieces of silver, the same price fetched by a slave gored by an ox (Ex 21:32). Zechariah, here impersonating the Messiah, was then advised to take this most "handsome" (surely said in irony and sarcasm) price and cast it to the potter in the house of the Lord. The expression "to cast it to the potter" usually was an idiomatic proverb approximately meaning "Throw it to the dogs" or "Get rid of it." But its connection with the house of the Lord makes that solution unlikely. Moreover, it is doubtful that the potter would have been in the house of the Lord. Rather, this phrase could be a cryptic description of his casting the money into the temple where it was taken up and used to purchase a field of the potter, since tainted money was unwelcome in the temple (Deut 23:18).

But what of Matthew's use of this acted-out parable? Matthew probably attributed the text to Jeremiah because Jeremiah, in many Hebrew manuscripts, headed up the collection of the prophets and his name was used to designate all in the collection. Our book titles with their chapter and verse divisions are a fairly recent innovation. Also Matthew may have attributed this quotation to Jeremiah because this text was paired with Jeremiah 18:1-4, 32:6-9. Thus he cited the name of the better-known and more prominent prophet. In fact, in not one of the four other places where the New Testament quotes from Zechariah does it mention his name (Mt 21:4-5; 26:31; Jn 12:14; 19:37).

On the second problem, Matthew's use of this text, we counter by arguing that the New Testament citings of the Old very much agree with the meaning found in the Old Testament. Judas did receive thirty pieces of silver for betraying Jesus of Nazareth. Because these wages represented blood money, with stricken conscience Judas took the money and threw it into the temple. However, because this money was unfit for temple service, it was used to buy a potter's field as a burial place for strangers (Mt 27:6-10).

Certainly these actions follow the pattern set by the prophet, even though there are a few slight differences, such as "I threw" being rendered in the Gospel as "and they used them" (Mt 27:10), and "I took the thirty pieces of silver" becoming "they took the thirty silver coins" (Mt 27:9), and "at which they priced me" becoming "the price set on him by the people of Israel" (Mt 27:9). But these changes are required by the position of the narrator, his use of his own tenses and the place where he introduced this text into his story.

Zechariah, we may conclude, accurately saw the tragic events connected with the betrayal of our Lord and warned Judah long before the events took place. What a fantastic prophecy!

12:10 They Will Look on Me, the One They Have Pierced?

Does this text teach, or even imply, that there will be two comings of Messiah to earth? Few texts have been cited in Jewish-evangelical discussions more than this one. And if one were to search the Old Testament for evidence that Christ would come twice, this is probably the only text that could be used.

At the heart of debate over this verse are the following questions. Is the subject of the verb *look* the same as the subject of *pierced?* Is *me* to be equated with *him* in Zechariah 12:10? Are those who participated in the piercing the same ones who in the eschatological day will look on him and grieve bitterly? One final problem is this: is it possible to pierce God, who is spirit?

That God is spirit and not corporeal flesh is taught not only in John 4:24 but also in Isaiah 31:3. The mystery of this Zechariah passage is that the speaker is Yahweh himself. He is the One who will pour out grace and supplication on the house of Israel and David. Moreover, the first person occurs over and over again in this chapter (Zech 12:2, 3, 4, 6, 9 and 10), but in every case it refers to the Messiah, the one who is pictured as one with God himself. In fact, Zechariah 11 says that Yahweh's representative, the Good Shepherd, will be rejected. Thus, one can only conclude that it is the Messiah who is divine and who will be rejected and pierced. However, he will be deeply mourned at some time in the future and then finally appreciated by all those who had previously rejected him.

"On that day" (Zech 12:11), when Messiah is restored to rightful recognition by all those who formerly rejected his person and work, he will return to restore paradisiacal conditions. Most Jewish interpreters will concede that there will indeed be such a coming of Messiah—when there will be peace. They insist, however, that he could not have come previously.

That is precisely where this text comes into play. If it is agreed that the context has to do with Messiah's coming when there is peace, then it must be recognized that he has at some previous time been pierced. When did this happen? And by whom? And for what? Only the Christian claims for Jesus of Nazareth can fit the details of this passage.

Others have seen the irresistible force of this argument and therefore have sought to show a switch in pronoun antecedents in the middle of the verse. This interpretation makes the people of Israel the ones looking, but the nations are the ones piercing. Since the two occurrences of *they* are separated in the text solely by the prepositional phrase *on me* and the pronominal expression *whom* (*the one* in NIV), it would be most unnatural to assume that the antecedent has changed. The only reason for doing so would be to avoid the obvious force of the statement.

The New Jewish Publication Society's translation Tanakh: The Holy Scriptures (1988) has rendered this verse a bit more smoothly: "But I will fill the House of David and the inhabitants of Jerusalem with a spirit of pity and compassion; and *they shall lament to Me about those who are slain,* wailing over them as over a favorite son and showing bitter grief as over a first-born" (emphasis mine—to point out the section where the problem occurs).

The problem with this translation is that it breaks the rules of Hebrew grammar to avoid the obvious implications of this Hebrew verse. It turns the active form of *pierce* into passive, and the subjects into objects; and this the Hebrew will not allow! It is a heroic effort to bypass the logical implication that the one who speaks is the one who was pierced by those who now stare in amazement in the eschatological, or future, day.

Other Jewish interpreters have given up and have instead found here a case for two Messiahs: Messiah son of Joseph, who did in fact suffer, and Messiah son of David, who did not suffer, but who is to come in glory and power to rule at a time when peace comes on earth. This is a late invention, created in response to the claims of the Christian movement.

Messiah has already come once. He suffered on the cross for our sin. He will come again in power and with glory.

MALACHI

1:2-3 I Have Hated Esau?

If God is depicted as being good to all (Ps 145:9), how can he hate Esau? Surely this runs counter to all we know about the God and Father of our Lord Jesus Christ.

With his usual abruptness, Malachi announces his message succinctly enough to please even the most impatient listener. It is simply this: "I have loved you."

Typical for this crowd, as Malachi reported, they answered back in that incredulous tone of unbelief, "Who? Us? God has loved us? Since when?" This, then, became the basis for the contrast which now had to be drawn between Jacob and Esau, two brothers who represented two different ways that God works.

God's election love illustrates how God can claim to love Jacob. Both Esau and Jacob were the sons of that man of promise, Isaac. However, even though Esau was the firstborn, God chose Jacob, emphasizing that his grace had nothing to do with natural rights or works. From Esau came the nation of Edom, and from Jacob came the nation of Israel. It is said that God hates Edom and loves Israel. Why?

When Scripture talks about God's hatred, it uses a distinctly biblical idiom which does not imply that Yahweh exhibits disgust, disdain or a desire for revenge. There are clear objects meriting God's hatred, including the seven evils of Proverbs 6:16-19, all forms of hypocritical worship (Is 1:14; Amos 5:21) and even death itself, as Jesus demonstrated at the grave of Lazarus in John 11:33, 38 (see also Mk 3:5; 10:14; and Jn 2:17). Hate can be a proper emotion for disavowing and for expressing antipathy for all that stands against God and his righteous standards. Only one who has truly loved can experience burning anger against all that is wrong and evil.

But in this antonymic pair of *love* and *hate,* as used in Scripture, there is a specialized meaning. A close parallel to the emotions expressed for Jacob and Esau is Jacob's response to his wives, Rachel and Leah, in Genesis 29:30-33. While

Genesis 29:31, 33 says that Jacob hated Leah, Genesis 29:30 clarifies this usage by stating in the same context that he loved Rachel *more than* Leah. A similar situation is found in Deuteronomy 21:15-17.

To summarize, the hated one is the one *loved less*. The New Testament uses the same terminology in Matthew 6:24 and Luke 16:13. There are two parallel lists which use the formula even more dramatically. Matthew 10:37 says, "Anyone who loves . . . more than me," while Luke 14:26 states the same concept as, "If anyone comes to me and does not hate . . ."

God does not experience psychological hatred with all its negative and sinful connotations. In this text, he merely affirms that Jacob had had a distinctive call, for when he had been blessed, all the nations of the world would eventually, if not immediately, profit from his blessing. Thus there came a ranking and a preference, in order to carry out God's plan and to bring the very grace that Esau would also need.

God's love and hate (in his deciding to prefer one person for a certain blessed task) were bestowed apart from anything these men were or did. God's choice of Jacob took place before Jacob's birth (Gen 25:23; Rom 9:11). Thus it is unfair to interpret these verses as evidence of favoritism or of partiality on the part of God. They express a different set of realities from what English words generally signify.

See also comment on PSALMS 5:5; 11:5.

1:11 The Worship of Gentiles?

Malachi has the ability to startle and shock both his audience and his readers as few prophets can. In Malachi 1:11, in the midst of an otherwise dull recital of the priests' sins, Malachi suddenly announced that God would indeed triumph with or without the obedience of those entrusted with the nation's spiritual care. But Malachi's outburst of good news was so shocking that many have found this passage a hard saying indeed.

Malachi meant his words to startle, for he began them in verse 11 with a Hebrew word that is almost a shout of joy like "Yes, indeed!" This truth would be so unexpected, transcending as it did the paltry service and heartless attitudes of the priesthood, that it was necessary for Malachi to awaken the reader before introducing a whole new concept.

The new wave of excitement heightened when Malachi foretold that God's name would be exalted by Gentiles worldwide. Though Israel's spiritual leaders despised and demeaned the Lord's great name, that did not mean God was stuck with these worshipers or his cause was at an impasse. God could, and would, raise up true worshipers to his name from all the nations of the world. His cause and his great name would succeed. God was not saddled with Israel, just as he is not saddled with any contemporary group of Christians.

The geographical, political and ethnic scope of this promise is set forth in even more startling tones. The text affirms that it will be from "the rising to the setting of the sun." The sweep of God's success from east to west reaffirmed the state of affairs noted in 1:5, "Great is the LORD—even beyond the borders of Israel!"

Furthermore, incense and offerings, in fact "pure" offerings, will be offered up "in every place." That must have shaken all those who remembered that only in Jerusalem were they to offer sacrifices and burn incense before God. In the terms of Leviticus 11 and Deuteronomy 14:3-19, an offering was *pure* when an unblemished animal was offered as the law prescribed. But the word for "without blemish" was not used here; it was the word that involved one's moral and physical purity as well as ceremonial purity.

That raised the question of how the Gentile nations could offer a pure offering in places other than Jerusalem. This could only be possible in a day yet unseen when the good news would reach beyond the borders known to Malachi's audience.

The term *incense* referred, no doubt, to the altar of incense with its symbolic sweet aroma of the saints' prayers constantly rising to God. But this incense would no longer emanate from the temple alone; it would be offered "in every place."

Some try to say this verse refers only to the Jews of the Dispersion or to Gentile proselytes. This is only partially true, for it hardly embraces all the terms and conditions of Malachi's text. The Jewish Diaspora and the Gentile proselytes signaled just the first fruits of the harvest that was to come in the messianic age. Moreover, the fact that offerings would be offered worldwide indicated something bigger and newer than what Israel had ever seen or imagined. No wonder Malachi exclaimed, "My name will be great among the nations." The middle wall of partition had been destroyed (Eph 2:14) and God's kingdom had been announced over all the earth.

2:16 God Hates Divorce

In all Scripture, Malachi 2:16 is at once one of the most succinct and most contested statements on the permanence of marriage. The difficulty comes, in part, from the Hebrew text, which some have pronounced the most obscure in the Old Testament. Further problems come from trying to fathom the Old Testament's position on marriage and divorce. Many have (wrongly) assumed that Malachi voiced an opinion that contradicts earlier statements in Scripture.

The section opens with a double question that amounts to a double premise: (1) all Israel has one Father—God, and (2) God created that nation (Mal 2:10). Sadly, however, the population was dealing treacherously with each other and thereby profaning the covenant God had made with their fathers. Malachi 2:10-16 discusses Israel's disloyalty to their national family (Mal 2:10), spiritual family (Mal 2:11-12) and marriage partners (Mal 2:13-16), evidenced by spiritual harlotry, mixed marriages with unbelieving partners, adultery and, finally, divorce.

In Malachi 2:11-12, Israelites are charged with unashamedly marrying women who worshiped other gods. Such religiously mixed marriages flew right in the face of warnings to the contrary (Ex 34:12-16; Num 25:1-3; Deut 7:3-4; 1 Kings 11:1-13). But there were more accusations: "Another thing you do" (Mal 2:13). They had caused the Lord's altar to be flooded with such tears and mourning that the Lord refused to accept further sacrifices. The tears resulted from broken marriage vows to which the Lord was a party, being a witness at every wedding. Put very simply, God said, "I hate divorce" (Mal 2:16).

Two key words dominate this text: the word *one* (which occurs four times in Mal 2:10, 15) and the word *breaking/broken faith* (which appears five times in Mal 2:10, 11, 14, 15, 16).

The identity of the "one" in Malachi 2:10 is not "Abraham, your father" (Is 51:2), as Jerome and Calvin thought, or the patriarch Jacob, whom Malachi did mention elsewhere very frequently (Mal 1:2; 2:12; 3:6). Instead, it is God, who created Israel (Is 43:1). Thus those who have the same Father should not be dealing so treacherously with each other.

But who is the "one" in Malachi 2:15? Again it is not Abraham (as if the sentence read: "Did not one, that is to say, Abraham, do so [take a pagan Egyptian named Hagar to wife]?" with the prophet conceding the point and replying, "Yes, he did!" But Abraham is never called the "one," nor could his conduct in "putting away" Hagar be the issue here, since the divorced wives in Malachi's context were covenant wives, not pagan wives.

The subject of Malachi 2:15 must be God, and "the one" must be the object of the sentence, not its subject. As such, the "one" would parallel the "one flesh" of Genesis 2:24, for returning to God's original instructions would be a natural way to dispute covenant-breaking divorces. In a similar manner, our Lord referred to Genesis in Matthew 19:4-6: " 'Haven't you read,' he replied, 'that at the beginning the Creator "made them male and female," and said, "For this reason a man will leave his father and mother and be united to his wife, and the two will become one flesh"?' " (see also Mk 10:7-9).

Even though the Hebrew does not explicitly indicate that the first clause of Malachi 2:15 is an interrogative or that *he* refers to God, both possibilities fit the context, previous Scripture and normative Hebrew grammar and syntax observed in other passages.

The resulting thought would be as follows: Why did God make Adam and Eve only one flesh when he could have given to Adam many wives or to Eve many husbands? Certainly God had more than enough creative power to furnish multiple sex partners! So why only "one"? Because God was seeking a godly offspring, a process incompatible with multiple partners.

The two examples of faithlessness this passage raises are divorce and being unequally married to unbelievers. Both violate God's holy law. Marriage's covenant status is seen in other Old Testament passages, such as Genesis 31:50, Proverbs 2:17, Ezekiel 16:8 and Hosea 1—2. Genesis 2:24 most clearly defines marriage: It consists of "leaving" one's parents and "cleaving" to one's wife. The leaving and cleaving go together and in that order. Marriage, then, is a public act (leaving), in order to establish a permanent relationship (cleaving), and is sexually consummated (becoming one flesh). Any violation of this covenant is a breach of promise made in the presence of God and each other.

So fundamental and inviolable is the union created by this marriage covenant that nothing less than a rupture in sexual fidelity can begin to affect its durability (note Mt 5:31-32; 19:3-12). That such a rift may lead to one of the two grounds for breaking the marriage covenant (1 Cor 7 treats the other one) is hinted at in Jeremiah 3:8, where God "gave faithless Israel her certificate of divorce and sent her away because of all her adulteries." In effect, God divorced Israel. But note the grounds!

Accordingly, the Bible is not silent, either on divorce or on the reasons it may be granted. But when God still says that he hates divorce, we gather how strongly he desires to see marriage covenants succeed.

The Mosaic legislation never encouraged, enjoined or approved of divorce in Deuteronomy 24:1-4. Instead, it merely prescribed certain procedures if and when divorce tragically took place. The main teaching of Deuteronomy 24:1-4 forbids a man to remarry his first wife after he had divorced her and either he or she had remarried in the meantime. Unfortunately, the AV (King James), the ERV, the ASV and some others have adopted a translation of Deuteronomy 24:1-4 that adds to the confusion. On their incorrect rendering, divorce is not just permitted or tolerated, it is commanded when some "uncleanness" is present! But in fact the conditional *if* which begins in Deuteronomy 24:1 continues through verse 3 with the consequence of the conditional sentence coming in verse 4 (contrary to all the incorrect renderings noted above). No Old Testament law instituted divorce; Hebrew law simply tolerated the practice while condemning it theologically.

Those objecting that the absolute statement of Malachi 2:16 precludes all arguments for a biblically permissible divorce do not take Scripture holistically. God is certainly able to qualify his own teaching with further revelation in other contexts. For instance, in Romans 13:1-7 God states that citizens must obey the civil powers that be, yet he qualifies that absolute in Acts 5:29: Citizens should obey God rather than any sinful civil law.

God's hatred of divorce is further expressed in the statement "one who covers his garment with violence." The "garment" refers to the ancient custom of spreading a garment over a woman, as Ruth asked Boaz to do to claim her as his wife (Ruth 3:9; see also Deut 22:30; Ezek 16:8). Thus to cover one's bed with violence was to be unfaithful to the marital bed and one's nuptial obligations. The symbol of wedded trust, much like our wedding ring, became the agent of violence toward these wives.

See also comment on DEUTERONOMY 24:1-4.

3:6 I the Lord Do Not Change?

See comment on GENESIS 6:6; 1 SAMUEL 13:13-14; 15:29; JONAH 4:1-2.

3:10 Does Tithing Always Pay Off?

If we faithfully give to God a tithe, that is, a tenth of all our income, will that mean that we will automatically receive a blessing every time? What is the meaning of the promise in Malachi 3:10? And is the "storehouse" to which we bring the tithe solely the local church?

God had no other recourse than to show the people one example of their failure of turning back to him: their failure to tithe and make offerings to him. This is not to imply that this was the only area where the nation had failed, but it would serve well enough for those who were unconvinced that they had turned their backs on God. They were robbing God of the tenth that belonged to him.

The tithe was generally considered to be a tenth of what a person earned, for that is what the priest of Salem (Jerusalem), Melchizedek (Gen 14:20), gave to Abraham even before the law of Moses gave similar instructions (Lev 27:30). From this tithe, a tenth of it went to the priests, while others who benefited were widows, orphans and resident aliens (Deut 14:28-29).

The offerings, however, were those portions of the animal sacrifices designated for the priests (Ex 29:27-28; Lev 9:22; Num 5:9) or those gifts that were voluntarily given for a special purpose (Ex 25:2-7).

But are Christians governed by any law that requires us to give a tithe? No, there is no such direct statement; however, it must be noticed that the practice of tithing antedates the law of Moses, therefore it cannot be said to be a legal or ceremonial legislation, limited to the Mosaic covenant. It must also be noticed that, if it was appropriate under the law to give a tenth, Christian believers would not want to do less, seeing how much more we have received and know today. No one robs God without badly cheating themselves in the bargain.

But can we count on an automatic blessing—the tithe goes in here and the blessing comes out here? No, we cannot. The motivation for doing something so poorly ought to be its own best rebuke. Why would we wish to give only to get more? The reason for giving would be so selfish and so sinful that it could hardly command the attention and respect of the God it purported to serve.

One other matter: some have argued that this text requires that all tithing be done through the local church, the "storehouse." But this text will not bear that weight. The storehouse is best viewed as God's storehouse, not simply or exclusively the local church. In the eighty times this word appears in the Old Testament, the storehouse is either the treasury of the temple (for example, 1 Kings 7:51) or, in a more figurative sense, the place from which all of God's blessings proceed (for example, in Deut 28:12, and obliquely in Jer 50:25, God's treasury house is in the heavens).

MATTHEW

2:1-2 Is Astrology Biblical?

The term *magi* was used in Greek to refer to "a wide range of astronomers, fortune tellers, priestly augurers, and magicians."[1] The reference to the star makes it most likely that, unlike Simon Magus in Acts 8:9, these men were astrologers. The text is not clear about where they came from, for "the east" could refer to Persia, where the people to whom the term was originally applied lived, to Babylonia, which was said to be full of astrology, or to the desert areas east of Palestine, where the types of gifts the magi brought were often found. What is clear is that these men saw some type of astronomical phenomenon ("star" could refer to any one of a variety of such phenomena), quite possibly a particular planetary conjunction, and interpreted it to mean that a king had been born in Judea.

Even as early as A.D. 110 Christians struggled with the account of these magi. Ignatius (*Ephesians* 19:3), followed by many other ancient writers, argued that by means of this event these occult sciences ended. However, we do not read that evaluation in Matthew. The fact is that the Bible is quite unapologetic not only about these magi, but also about Daniel, who was more learned than all of the magi of Babylon (Dan 1:17, 20), having been trained as a Chaldean or astrologer-priest (Dan 1:4, compare Dan 2:2). Likewise, a Jewish contemporary of Matthew viewed Balaam as a magi who had received true revelation from God (Philo *On the Life of Moses* I, 50 [I, 276-77]). However, neither Philo writing about Balaam nor the writer of Daniel believed that *divine revelation* came to their respective subjects through astrology, but that the fact that the person was an astrologer did not seem to hinder God from giving them his prophetic Spirit. In the case of Matthew it is different, for the revelation of the birth of Jesus comes to them through their astrological observations.

The truth is that the Old Testament does speak against a large number of occult arts (e.g., Ex 22:18; Deut 18:10), but astrology is not among them. The Hebrew term for astrologer appears only in Daniel 1:20 and 2:10. Even in the Greek

Old Testament it is only in Daniel that the term *magi* appears. Unlike the case with other occult arts, the Old Testament is more concerned with the weakness or inability of the astrologers when compared with the Spirit of God in Daniel than with their evil nature. This does not mean that the Old Testament *approves* of astrology, but simply that it does not contain a specific condemnation of it.

All of this, however, does not explain what Matthew is trying to say. Who are these magi (whether there were two or ten of them, for the text only indicates that there was more than one)? There were many Jewish magi in the ancient world, but since these men ask for "the king of the Jews" (rather than "our king" or something like that), they are being presented as pagan magi. They come to Herod, the reigning king of the Jews (although he was an Idumean by race), who gathers the Jewish leaders. What is more, the city of Jerusalem hears about this and is "frightened" or "disturbed" just like Herod is. None of these Jewish people (for Herod practiced Judaism, at least when living in Judea) makes any move to seek Jesus, let alone to worship him. It is the pagan astrologers who have come to worship him and who go on to fulfill their purpose. Now Matthew is known as a very Jewish Gospel, but there is also a clear theme in Matthew about Jesus' rejection by the Jewish people and the gospel reaching out to the Gentiles. Of course this outreach of the gospel is clear in Matthew 28:19-20, but the dual theme is even clear as early as Matthew 8:10-12 (and John the Baptist in Mt 3 indicates the rejection of the Jewish leaders). Thus throughout Matthew we learn about Jews rejecting Jesus and pagans showing faith.

Now the meaning of the story becomes clear. God speaks to some pagan astrologers by means of natural revelation through the language that they would understand (either a planetary conjunction or a comet or some other astronomical phenomenon). They respond in faith and travel a long distance seeking the king to honor and worship. Their revelation is imperfect, for Jerusalem appears to have been a guess (Would not a king be born in the capital city?); and it is only after getting information from Scripture that their trip to Bethlehem is confirmed by the reappearance of the "star" (the apparent disappearance and reappearance is what makes some scholars believe this to be a planetary conjunction in which the planets came together, then parted, then reconverged). Meanwhile the Jewish people have the Scriptures that clearly indicate the birthplace of the Messiah, yet far from carefully watching that town, even when confronted by the magi they respond with upset and anger rather than faith.

Can God speak through astrology? Yes, for he did it once. Is it then a normal means of his revelation? By no means! God has given us his Word, a far more accurate and fuller means of revelation. Yet when his people are ignoring his Word, it may well be that God will speak to some pagan through the stars and that pagan will respond with a faith that shames the indifference of the people who claim to be God's and who are custodians of his revelatory book.

---

[1]Raymond E. Brown, *The Birth of the Messiah* (Garden City, N.Y.: Doubleday, 1977), p. 167.

4:5-10 Order of the Temptations?

See comment on LUKE 4:1-13.

4:5-10 Tempted in Every Way Like Us?

See comment on HEBREWS 4:15.

5:11-12 Rejoice in Persecution?

See comment on JAMES 1:2.

5:13 Saltless Salt?

See comment on MARK 9:50.

5:17-20 Eternal Law?

Here is surely an uncompromising affirmation of the eternal validity of the law of Moses. Not the smallest part of it is to be abrogated—"not the smallest letter, not the least stroke of a pen." The "jot" (KJV) is the smallest letter of the Hebrew alphabet; the "iota" (RSV) is the smallest letter of the Greek alphabet. The "tittle" (KJV) or "dot" (RSV) was a very small mark attached to a letter, perhaps to distinguish it from another which resembled it, as in our alphabet *G* is distinguished from *C*, or *Q* from *O*.

What is hard about this uncompromising affirmation? For some readers the hardness lies in the difficulty of recognizing in this speaker the Christ who, according to Paul, "is the end of the law, so that there may be righteousness for everyone who believes" (Rom 10:4).

Others find no difficulty in supposing that Paul's conception of Jesus differed radically from the presentation of his character and teaching in the Gospels. The view has indeed been expressed (not so frequently nowadays as at an earlier time) that Paul is pointed to as the man who "breaks one of the least of these commandments and teaches others to do the same." This implies that the saying does not come from Jesus, but from a group in the early church that did not like Paul. Even where the reference to Paul would not be entertained, it is held by many that these words come from a group in the early church that wished to maintain the full authority of the law for Christians. The saying, according to Rudolf Bultmann, "records the attitude of the conservative Palestinian community in contrast to that of the Hellenists."[1]

There were probably several selections of sayings of Jesus in circulation before the Gospels proper began to be produced, and one of these, which was preferred by stricter Jewish Christians, seems to have been used, along with others, by Matthew. Such a selection of sayings could be drawn up in accordance with the outlook of those who compiled it; sayings which in themselves appeared to support that outlook would be included, while others which appeared to go contrary to it would be omitted. The teaching of Jesus was much more diversified than any partisan selection of his sayings would indicate. By not confining himself to any one selection Matthew gives an all-around picture of the teaching. A saying such as has just been quoted had three successive life-settings: its life-setting in the historical ministry of Jesus, its setting in a restricted selection of Jesus' sayings, and its setting in the Gospel of Matthew. It is only its setting in the Gospel of Matthew that is immediately accessible to us. (In addition to these three settings, of course, it may have acquired subsequent life-settings in the history of the church and in the course of interpretation. The statement "I have not come to abolish them but to fulfill them" has been used, for example, to present the gospel as the crown of fulfillment of Hinduism,[2] but such a use of it is irrelevant to the intention of Jesus or of the Evangelist.)

To the remark that it is only in its setting in the Gospel of Matthew that the saying is immediately accessible to us there is a partial exception. Part of it occurs in a different context in the Gospel of Luke. In Luke 16:16-17 Jesus says, "The Law and the Prophets were proclaimed until John. Since that time, the good news of the kingdom of God is being preached, and everyone is forcing his way into it. It is easier for heaven and earth to disappear than for the least stroke of a pen to drop out of the Law." The second of these two sentences is parallel to (but not identical with) Matthew 5:18.

The selection of sayings which is supposed to have been drawn up in a more legally minded Christian circle, and which Matthew is widely considered to have used as one of his sources, is often labeled M (because it is represented in Matthew's Gospel only). Another, more comprehensive, selection on which both Matthew and Luke are widely considered to have drawn is commonly labeled Q. It may be, then, that the form of the "jot and tittle" saying found in Matthew 5:18 is the M form, while that found in Luke 16:17 is the Q form. T. W. Manson was one scholar who believed that this was so, and he invited his readers to bear two possibilities in mind. The first possibility was that Luke's form of the saying is closer to the original wording and that the form in Matthew "is a revision of it to bring it explicitly into line with Rabbinical doctrine." The other possibility, which follows on from this one, was "that the saying in its original form asserts not the perpetuity of the Law but the unbending conservatism of the scribes," that it is not intended to be "sound Rabbinical dogma but bitter irony." Jesus, that is to say, addresses the scribes and says, "The world will come to an end before you give up the tiniest part of your traditional interpretation of the law."[3]

It is plain that Jesus did not accept the rabbinical interpretation of the law. Indeed, he charged the scribes, the acknowledged students and teachers of the law, with "break[ing] the command of God for the sake of your tradition" (so the wording runs in Mt 15:3, in a passage based on Mk 7:9). He said that by their application of the law "they tie up heavy loads and put them on men's shoulders" (Mt 23:4); by contrast, he issued the invitation "Take my yoke upon you and learn from me, for . . . my yoke is easy, and my burden is light" (Mt 11:29-30).

But he did not relax the requirements of God's law as such, nor did he recommend a lower standard of righteousness than the "Pharisees and the teachers of the law" required. On the contrary, he insisted that admittance to the kingdom of heaven called for righteousness exceeding that of the scribes and Pharisees. This last statement, found in Matthew 5:20, serves as an introduction to the paragraphs which follow, in which Jesus' account of what obedience to the law involves is given in a succession of hard sayings, at which we shall look one by one. But at the moment we may mention two principles by which he interpreted and applied the law.

First, he maintained that the proper way to keep any commandment was to fulfill the purpose for which it was given. He did this with regard to the law of marriage; he did it also with regard to the sabbath law. On the sabbath day, said the fourth commandment, "you shall not do any work." In the eyes of some custodians of the law, this called for a careful definition of what constituted "work," so that people might know precisely what might or might not be done on that day. Circumstances could alter cases: an act of healing, for example, was permissible if it was a matter of life and death, but if the treatment could be put off to the following day without any danger or detriment to the patient, that would be better. It was precisely on this issue that Jesus collided repeatedly with the scribes and their associates. His criterion for the keeping of this law was to inquire for what purpose the sabbath was instituted. It was instituted, he held, to provide rest and relief for human beings: they were not made for the sake of the sabbath, but the sabbath was given for their sake. Therefore, any action which promoted their rest, relief and general well-being was permissible on the sabbath. It was not merely permissible on the sabbath: the sabbath was the most appropriate day for its performance, because its performance so signally promoted God's purpose in instituting the sabbath. Jesus appears to have cured people by preference on the sabbath day, because such an action honored the day.

He did not abrogate the fourth commandment; he interpreted it in a different way from the current interpretation. Did his principle of interpretation "surpass the righteousness of the Pharisees and the teachers of the law"? Perhaps it did. There are some people who find it easier to have a set of rules. When a practical problem arises, they can consult the rules and know what to do. But they have to decide which action best fulfills the purpose of the law. That involves thought, and thought of this kind, with the personal responsibility that accompanies it, is a difficult exercise for them.

Second, Jesus maintained that obedience or disobedience to the law began inwardly, in the human heart. It was not sufficient to conform one's outward actions and words to what the law required; the thought-life must be conformed to it first of all. One of the Old Testament psalmists voiced his feelings thus: "I desire to do your will, O my God; your law is within my heart" (Ps 40:8). This Psalm is not quoted by Jesus in the Gospels, but in another place in the New Testament its language is applied to him (Heb 10:7, 9). It does indeed express very well the attitude of Jesus himself and the attitude which he recommended to his hearers. Where the mind and will are set to do the will of God, the speaking and acting will not deviate from it.

Besides, where this is so, there will be an emphasis on the inward spiritual aspects of ethics and religion, rather than on outward and material aspects. The idea that a religious obligation could be given precedence over one's duty to one's parents was one with which Jesus had no sympathy (see Mk 7:10-13). This idea was approved by some exponents of the law in his day, but in general Jewish teaching has agreed with him here. Again, Jesus set very little store by details of ritual purification or food regulations, because these had no ethical content. Mark goes so far as to say that by his pronouncements on these last matters he "declared all foods 'clean' " (Mk 7:19). If Matthew does not reproduce these words of Mark, he does reproduce the pronouncements of Jesus which Mark so interprets (Mt 15:17-20).

But did the ritual washings and food restrictions not belong to the jots and tittles of the law? Should they not be reckoned, at the lowest estimate, among "the least of these commandments"? Perhaps so, but in Jesus' eyes "justice, mercy and faithfulness" were of much greater importance (Mt 23:23). And what about the sacrificial ceremonies? They were included in the law, to be sure, but Jesus' attitude to such things is summed up in his quotation from a great Old Testament prophet: "I desire mercy, not sacrifice" (Hos 6:6). It is Matthew, and Matthew alone among the Evangelists, who records Jesus as quoting these words, and he records him as using them twice (Mt 9:13; 12:7). The law is fulfilled ethically rather than ceremonially. Jesus confirmed the insistence of the great prophets that punctiliousness in ceremonial observances is worse than useless where people neglect "to act justly and to love mercy and to walk humbly with . . . God" (Mic 6:8). It is human beings, and not inanimate things, that matter.

The law for Jesus was the expression of God's will. The will of God is eternal and unchangeable. Jesus did not come to modify the will of God; he fulfilled it. The standard of obedience to that will which he set, by his example and his teaching alike, is more exacting than the standard set by the written law. He insisted that the will of God should be done from the heart. But, in so insisting, he provided the means by which the doing of God's will from the heart should not be an unattainable ideal. If Paul may be brought in to interpret the teaching of Jesus here, the apostle who maintained that men and women are justified before God through faith in Jesus and not through keeping the law also maintained that those who have faith in Jesus receive his Spirit so that "the righteous requirements of the law might be fully met in us, who do not live according to the sinful nature but according to the Spirit" (Rom 8:4). The gospel demands more than the law, but supplies the power to do it. Someone has put it in doggerel but telling lines:

To run and work the law commands,
Yet gives me neither feet nor hands;
But better news the gospel brings:
It bids me fly, and gives me wings.

See also comment on ROMANS 10:4.

[1]Rudolf Bultmann, *The History of the Synoptic Tradition* (Oxford: Oxford University Press, 1963), p. 138.
[2]For example, by J. N. Farquhar, *The Crown of Hinduism* (Oxford: Oxford University Press, 1913); compare E. J. Sharpe, *Not to Destroy But to Fulfil* (Lund: Gleerup, 1965).
[3]T. W. Manson, *The Sayings of Jesus* (reprint; Grand Rapids, Mich.: Eerdmans, 1979), p. 135.

5:22 "You Fool!" Merits Hell?

This is the first of a series of statements in which Jesus makes the requirements of the law more radical than the strict letter might indicate. Quoting the sixth commandment, Jesus says, "You have heard that it was said to the people long ago, 'Do not murder, and anyone who murders will be subject to judgment.' But I say to you . . ." and then comes the hard saying under discussion.

Murder was a capital offense under Israelite law; the death penalty could not be commuted to a monetary fine, such as was payable for the killing of someone's domestic animal. Where it could be proved that the killing was accidental—as when a man's axe-head flew off the handle and struck his fellow workman on the head—it did not count as murder, but even so the owner of the axe-head had to take prudent measures to escape the vengeance of the dead man's next of kin. Otherwise, the killer was brought before the village elders and on the testimony of two or three witnesses was sentenced to death. The death penalty was carried out by stoning: the witnesses threw the first stones, and then the community joined in, thus dissociating themselves from bloodguiltiness and expiating the pollution which it brought on the place.

Jesus points out that the murderous act springs from the angry thought. It is in the mind that the crime is first committed and judgment is incurred. The earthly court cannot take action against the angry thought, but the heavenly court can—and does. This in itself is a hard saying. According to the KJV, "whosoever is angry with his brother without a cause shall be in danger of the judgment," but the phrase "without a cause" is a later addition to the Greek text, designed to make Jesus' words more tolerable. The other man's anger may be sheer bad temper, but mine is righteous indignation—anger with a cause. But Jesus' words, in the original form of the text, make no distinction between righteous and unrighteous anger: anyone who is angry with his brother exposes himself to judgment. There is no saying where unchecked anger may end. "Be angry but do not sin," we are told in Ephesians 4:26 (RSV); that is, "If you are angry, do not let your anger lead you into sin; let sunset put an end to your anger, for otherwise it will provide the devil with an opportunity which he will not be slow to seize."

There seems to be an ascending scale of seriousness as Jesus goes on: "subject to judgment . . . answerable to the Sanhedrin . . . in danger of the fire of hell." "The Sanhedrin" is apparently a reference to the supreme court of the nation in contrast to a local court. Evidently, then, to insult one's brother is more serious than to be angry with him. This is clearly so: the angry thought can be checked, but the insult once spoken cannot be recalled and may cause violent resentment. The person insulted may retaliate with a fatal blow, for which in fact if not in law the victim of the blow may be as much to blame as the one who strikes it. The actual insult mentioned by Jesus is the word "Raca" as it stands in the KJV. The precise meaning of "Raca" is disputed; it is probably an Aramaic word meaning something like "imbecile" but was plainly regarded as a deadly insult. (Words of abuse are above all others to be avoided by speakers of a foreign language; they can have an unimagined effect on a native speaker of the language.)

But "anyone who says, 'You fool!' will be in danger of the fire of hell." From this we might gather that "You fool!" is a deadlier insult than "Raca," whatever "Raca" may mean. For "the hell of fire" (RSV) or "hell fire" (KJV) is the most severe penalty of all. The "hell of fire" is the fiery Gehenna. Gehenna is the valley on the south side of Jerusalem which, after the return from the Babylonian exile, served as the city's rubbish dump and public incinerator. In earlier days it had been the site of the worship of Molech, and so it was thought fit that it should be degraded in this way. In due course it came to be used as a symbol of the destruction of the wicked after death, just as the Garden of Eden became a symbol of the blissful paradise to be enjoyed by the righteous.

But was "You fool!" actually regarded as being such a deadly insult? In this same Gospel of Matthew the cognate adjective is used of the man who built his house on the sand (Mt 7:26) and of the five girls who forgot to take a supply of oil to keep their torches alight (Mt 25:2-3), and Jesus himself is reported as calling certain religious teachers "blind fools" (Mt 23:17). It is more probable that, just as "Raca" is a non-Greek word, so is the word *mōre* that Jesus used here. If so, then it is a word which to a Jewish ear meant "rebel (against God)" or "apostate"; it was the word which Moses in exasperation used to the disaffected Israelites in the wilderness of Zin: "Listen, you rebels; must we bring you water out of this rock?" (Num 20:10). For these rash words, uttered under intense provocation, Moses was excluded from the Promised Land.

Whether this was the word Jesus had in mind or not, he certainly had in mind the kind of language that is bound to produce a murderous quarrel: chief responsibility for the ensuing bloodshed, he insisted, lies with the person who spoke the offending word. But behind the offending word lies the hostile thought. It is there that the guilty process starts; and if the hostile thought is not killed off as soon as the thinker becomes aware of it, then, although no earthly court may be in a position to take cognisance of it, that is what will be the first count in the indictment before the judgment-bar of God.

5:28 Adultery in the Heart?

This is another instance of Jesus' making the law more stringent by carrying its application back from the outward act to the inward thought and desire. The seventh commandment says, "You shall not commit adultery" (Ex 20:14). In the cultural context of the original Decalogue, this commandment forbade a man to have sexual relations with someone else's wife. To infringe this commandment was a capital offense; the penalty was stoning to death (as it still is in some parts of the Near and Middle East). Another commandment seems to carry the prohibition back beyond the overt act: the second clause of the tenth commandment says, "You shall not covet your neighbor's wife" (Ex 20:17), where his wife is mentioned among several items of his property. In a property context one might covet someone else's wife not by way of a sexual urge but because of the social or financial advantages of being linked with her family.

However that may be, Jesus traces the adulterous act back to the lustful glance and thought, and says that it is there that the rot starts and it is there that the check must be immediately applied. Otherwise, if the thought is cherished or fed by fantasy, the commandment has already been broken. There may be significance in the fact that Jesus does not speak of someone else's wife but of "a woman" in general. Parallels to this saying can be found in rabbinical literature.

Pope John Paul II excited some comment in 1981 by saying that a man could commit adultery in this sense with his own wife. Emil Brunner, in fact, had said something to very much the same effect over forty years before.[1] But there is nothing outrageous about such a suggestion. To treat any woman as a sex object, and not as a person in her own right, is sinful; all the more so when that woman is one's own wife.

See also comment on JOB 31:1.

[1]Emil Brunner, *The Divine Imperative* (London: Lutterworth Press, 1937), p. 350.

5:29 Gouge Out Your Right Eye?

This saying is not so hard in the NIV form as it is in some older versions. The KJV says, "If thy right eye offend thee . . . ," which is generally meaningless to readers today; the verb *offend* no longer means "trip up" or anything like that, which in literary usage it still did in 1611. Less excusable is the ERV rendering, "If thy right eye causeth thee to stumble . . . ," because this introduced an archaism which in 1881 was long since obsolete.

The NIV rendering, however, is more intelligible. It means, in effect: "Don't let your eye lead you into sin." How could it do that? By resting too long on an object of temptation. Matthew places this saying immediately after Jesus' words about adultery in the heart, and that is probably the original context, for it provides a ready example of how a man's eye could lead him into sin. In the most notable case of adultery in the Old Testament—King David's adultery with the wife of Uriah the Hittite—the trouble began when, late one afternoon, David from his palace roof *saw* the woman bathing (2 Sam 11:2). Jesus says, "Better pluck out your eye—even your right eye (as being presumably the more precious of the two)—than allow it to lead you into sin; it is better to enter into eternal life with one eye than to be thrown into Gehenna (as a result of that sin) with two."

Matthew follows up this saying about the right eye with a similar one about the right hand. This strong assertion seems to have stayed with the hearers; it is repeated in Matthew 18:8-9 (in dependence on Mk 9:43-48), where the foot is mentioned in addition to the eye and the hand.

Shortly after the publication of William Tyndale's English New Testament, the attempt to restrict its circulation was defended on the ground that the simple reader might mistakenly take such language literally and "pluck out his eyes, and so the whole realm will be full of blind men, to the great decay of the nation and the manifest loss of the King's grace; and thus by reading of the Holy Scriptures will the whole realm come into confusion." So a preaching friar is said to have declared in a Cambridge sermon; but he met his match in Hugh Latimer, who, in a sermon preached the following Sunday, said that simple people were well able to distinguish between literal and figurative terms. "For example," Latimer went on, "if we paint a fox preaching in a friar's hood, nobody imagines that a fox is meant, but that craft and hypocrisy are described, which so often are found disguised in that garb."[1]

In fact, it is not recorded that anyone ever mutilated himself because of these words in the Gospels. There is indeed the case of Origen, but if the story is true that he made himself a eunuch "for the kingdom of heaven's sake," that was in response to another saying, at which we shall look later.

[1]Hugh Latimer, Sermon preached in St. Edward's Church, Cambridge, in 1529, quoted in J. P. Smyth, *How We Got Our Bible* (1885; London: Religious Tract Society, 1938), p. 102.

5:34 Do Not Swear at All?

Perjury is a serious offence in any law code. It was so in the law of Moses and is forbidden in the third commandment: "You shall not take the name of the Lord your God in vain; for the Lord will not hold him guiltless who takes his name in vain" (Ex 20:7 RSV). To swear an oath falsely in the name of God was a sin not only against the name but against the very person of God. Later the scope of the commandment was broadened to include any light or thoughtless use of the divine name, to the point where it was judged safest not to use it at all. That is why the name of the God of Israel, commonly spelt Yahweh, came to be called the ineffable name, because it was forbidden to pronounce it. The public reader in the synagogue, coming on this name in the Scripture lesson, put some other form in its place, lest he should "take the name of the Lord [his] God in vain" by saying "Yahweh" aloud. But originally it was perjury that was in view in the commandment, and in other injunctions to the same effect from Exodus to Deuteronomy. Summing up the sense of those injunctions, Jesus said, "You have heard that it was said to the people long ago, 'Do not break your oaths, but keep the oaths you have made to the Lord' " (Mt 5:33).

Realizing the seriousness of swearing by God if the truth of the statement was not absolutely sure, people tended to replace the name of God by something else—by heaven, for example—with the idea that a slight deviation from the truth would then be less unpardonable. From another passage in this Gospel (Mt 23:16-22) it may be gathered that there were some casuists who ruled that vows were more binding or less binding according to the precise wording of the oath by which they were sworn. This, of course, would be ethical trifling.

It was necessary that people should be forbidden to swear falsely, whether in the name of God or by any other form of words. "Fulfill your vow," says the Preacher whose practical maxims enrich the Old Testament Wisdom literature; "It is better not to vow than to make a vow and not fulfill it" (Eccles 5:4-5). But Jesus recommends a higher standard to his disciples. "Do not swear at all," he says; "Simply let your 'Yes' be 'Yes,' and your 'No,' 'No'; anything beyond this comes from the evil one" (Mt 5:37). An echo of these words is heard in a later book of the New Testament: "Above all, my brothers, do not swear—not by heaven or by earth or by anything else. Let your 'Yes' be yes, and your 'No,' no, or you will be condemned" (Jas 5:12).

The followers of Jesus should be known as men and women of their word. If they are known to have a scrupulous regard for truth, then what they say will be accepted without the support of any oath. This is not mere theory; it is well established in experience. One body of Jesus' followers, the Society of Friends, has persisted in applying these words of his literally. And such is their reputation for probity that most people would more readily trust the bare word of a Friend than the sworn oath of many another person. "Anything beyond this," said Jesus, "comes from the evil one"; that is to say, the idea that a man or woman can be trusted to speak the truth only when under oath (if then) springs from dishonesty and suspicion, and tends to weaken mutual confidence in the exchanges of everyday life. No one demands an oath from those whose word is known to be their bond; even a solemn oath on the lips of others tends to be taken with a grain of salt.

5:39 Turn the Other Cheek?

This is a hard saying in the sense that it prescribes a course of action which does not come naturally to us. Unprovoked assault prompts resentment and retaliation. If one wants to be painfully literal, the assault is particularly vicious, for if the striker is right-handed, it is with the back of his hand that he hits the other on the right cheek.

This is one of a number of examples by which Jesus shows that the lifestyle of the kingdom of God is more demanding than what the law of Moses laid down. "You have heard that it was said, 'Eye for eye, and tooth for tooth' " (Mt 5:38). This was indeed laid down in Israel's earliest law code (Ex 21:24), and when it was first said it marked a great step forward, for it imposed a strict limitation on the taking of vengeance. It replaced an earlier system of justice according to which if a member of tribe X injured a member of tribe Y, tribe Y was under an obligation to take vengeance on tribe X. This quickly led to a blood feud between the two tribes and resulted in suffering which far exceeded the original injury. But incorporated into Israel's law code was the principle of exact retaliation: one eye, and no more, for an eye; one life, and no more, for a life. When wounded honor was satisfied with such precisely proportionate amends, life was much less fraught with hazards. The acceptance of this principle made it easier to regard monetary compensation as being, in many cases, a reasonable replacement for the infliction of an equal and opposite injury on the offending party.

But now Jesus takes a further step. "Don't retaliate at all," he says to his disciples. "Don't harbor a spirit of resentment; if someone does you an injury or puts you to inconvenience, show yourself master of the situation by doing something to his advantage. If he gets some pleasure out of hitting you, let him hit you again." (It should not be necessary to say that this saying is no more to be pressed literally than the saying about plucking out one's right eye and throwing it away—it is not difficult to envisage the other cheek being turned in a very provocative manner.) If a soldier or other government official conscripts your services to carry a load for him so far, you are under compulsion; you are forced to do it. But, when you have reached the end of the stipulated distance, you are a free person again; then you can say to him, "If you'd like it carried farther, I will gladly carry it for you." The initiative has now become yours, and you can take it not by voicing a sense of grievance at having been put to such inconvenience but by performing an act of grace. This way of reacting to violence and compulsion is the way of Christ.

To have one's services conscripted to carry a soldier's pack for him is not an everyday experience in the Western world. How, in our situation, could this particular injunction of Jesus be applied? Perhaps when a citizen is directed by a policeman to assist him in the execution of his duty. But if (say) it is a matter of helping him to arrest a larger number of suspicious characters than he can cope with single-handed, would they not also come within the scope of duty to one's neighbor? This simply reminds us that Jesus' injunctions are not usually of the kind that can be carried out automatically; they often require careful thought. Whatever sacrifices he expects his followers to make, he does not ask them to sacrifice their minds. What they are urged to do is to have their minds conformed to his, and when careful thought is exercised in accordance with the mind of Christ, the resulting action will be in accordance with the way of Christ.

Another parallel might be the Christian's reaction to his income tax demand. The tax demanded must be paid; no choice can be exercised there. But suppose the Christian taxpayer, as an act of grace, pays double the amount demanded, or at least adds a substantial amount to it; what then? The computer would probably record it as tax overpaid, and the surplus would come back to him as a rebate. Perhaps it would be wisest if he were to send it to the government anonymously—not only so as not to let his left hand know what his right hand was doing, but to forestall unworthy suspicions and enquiries. Once again, the carrying out of the simple injunctions of Jesus in a complex society like ours is not so easy. But where the spirit which he recommended is present, the performance should not go too far astray.

The admonition to turn the other cheek is given by Jesus to his disciples. It belongs to the sphere of personal behavior. There are many Christians, however, who hold that this teaching should be put into practice by communities and nations as well as by individuals. Where Christian communities are concerned, we may well agree. The spectacle of the church enlisting the aid of the "secular arm" to promote its interests is rarely an edifying one. "It belongs to the church of God," someone once said, "to receive blows rather than to inflict them—but," he added "she is an anvil that has worn out many hammers."[1] But what about a political community?

The situation did not arise in New Testament times. The first disciples of Jesus did not occupy positions of authority. Joseph of Arimathea might be an exception: he was a member of the Sanhedrin, the supreme court of the Jewish nation, and according to Luke (Lk 23:50-51), he did not go along with his colleagues' adverse verdict on Jesus. As the gospel spread into the Gentile world, some local churches included in their membership men who occupied positions of municipal responsibility, like Erastus, the city treasurer of Corinth (Rom 16:23); but neither Paul nor any other New Testament writer finds it necessary to give special instructions to Christian rulers corresponding to those given to Christian subjects. But what was to happen when Christians became rulers, as in due course some did? Should the Christian magistrate practice nonretaliation toward the criminal who comes up before him for judgment? Should the Christian king practice nonretaliation toward a neighboring king who declared war against him?

Paul, who repeats and underlines Jesus' teaching of nonretaliation, regards retaliation as part of the duty of the civil ruler. "Would you have no fear of him who is in authority?" he asks. "Then do what is good, and you will receive his approval, for he is God's servant for your good. But if you do wrong, be afraid, for he does not bear the sword in vain; he is the servant of God to execute his wrath on the wrongdoer" (Rom 13:3-4 RSV). For Paul, the ruler in question was the Roman emperor or someone who held executive or judicial authority under him. But his words were relevant to their chronological setting. The time had not yet come (although it did come in less than ten years after those words were written) when the empire was openly hostile to the church. Still less had the time come when the empire capitulated to the church and emperors began to profess and call themselves Christians. When they inherited the "sword" which their pagan predecessors had not borne "in vain," how were they to use it? The answer to that question cannot be read easily off the pages of the New Testament. It is still being asked, and it is right that it should; but no single answer can claim to be the truly Christian one.

See also comment on EXODUS 21:23-25.

---

[1]Theodore Beza to King Charles IX of France at the Abbey of Poissy, near Paris, in 1561.

5:44 Love Your Enemies?

We agree that we should resist the impulse to pay someone who harms us back in his own coin, but does that involve *loving* him? Can we be expected to love to order?

Jesus' command to his disciples to love their enemies follows immediately on his words "You have heard that it was said, 'Love your neighbor and hate your enemy' " (Mt 5:43). "You shall love your neighbor" is a quotation from the Old Testament law; it is part of what Jesus elsewhere referred to as the second of the two great commandments: "Love your neighbor as yourself" (Lev 19:18). On this commandment, with its companion "Love the Lord your God" (Deut 6:5), which he called "the greatest and first commandment," Jesus said that all the law and the prophets depend (Mt 22:36-40). But the commandment does not in fact go on to say "hate your enemy." However, if it is only our neighbors that we are to love, and the word *neighbors* be defined fairly narrowly, then it might be argued that we are free to hate those who are not our neighbors. But Jesus said, "No; love your enemies as well as your neighbors."

One difficulty lies in the sentimental associations that the word *love* has for many of us. The love of which the law and the gospel alike speak is a very practical attitude: "Let us not love with word or tongue [only] but with actions and in truth" (1 Jn 3:18). Love to one's neighbor is expressed in lending him a helping hand when that is what he needs: "Right," says Jesus, "lend your *enemy* a helping hand when that is what *he* needs. Your feelings toward him are not the important thing."

But if we think we should develop more Christian feelings toward an enemy, Jesus points the way when he says, "Pray for those who persecute you" (or, as it is rendered in Lk 6:28, "Pray for those who mistreat you"). Those who have put this injunction into practice assure us that persistence in prayer for someone whom we don't like, however much it goes against the grain to begin with, brings about a remarkable change in attitude. Alexander Whyte quotes from an old diary the confessions of a man who had to share the same house and the same table with someone whom he found unendurable. He betook himself to prayer, until he was able to write, "Next morning I found it easy to be civil and even benevolent to my neighbour. And I felt at the Lord's Table today as if I would yet live to love that man. I feel sure I will."[1]

The best way to destroy an enemy is to turn him into a friend. Paul, who in this regard (as in so many others) reproduces the teaching of Jesus, sums it up by saying, "Do not be overcome by evil, but overcome evil with good" (Rom 12:21). He reinforces it by quoting from Proverbs 25:21-22: "If your enemy is hungry, give him food to eat; if he is thirsty, give him water to drink. In doing this, you will heap burning coals on his head." Whatever that proverb originally meant, Paul adapts it to his purpose by omitting the self-regarding clause which follows those he quotes: "and the Lord will reward you." In this new context the "burning coals" may mean the sense of shame which will be produced in the enemy, leading to a change of heart on his side too. But first do him a good turn; the feelings can be left to their own good time.

See also comment on PSALMS 137:8-9; 139:20; MATTHEW 5:39; 5:48; ROMANS 12:20.

---

[1]Alexander Whyte, *Lord, Teach Us to Pray,* 2nd ed. (London: Oliphants, 1948), pp. 33-35.

5:48 You Must Be Perfect?

Some students of Christian ethics make a distinction between the general standards of Christian conduct and what are called "counsels of perfection," as though the former were prescribed for the rank and file of Christians while the latter could be attained only by real saints.

Such a distinction was not made by Jesus himself. He did make a distinction between the ordinary standards of morality observed in the world and the standard at which his disciples should aim; but the latter was something which should characterize all his disciples and not just a select few. For example, the principle that one good turn deserves another was observed by quite irreligious people and even by pagans. For anyone to repay a good turn with a bad one would be regarded as outrageous. But Jesus' followers were not to remain content with conventional standards of decent behavior. According to conventional standards one good turn might deserve another, but according to the standards which he laid down for his disciples, one bad turn deserves a good one—except that "deserves" is not the right word. One bad turn may deserve a bad one in revenge, but one bad turn done to his disciples should be repaid by them with a good one. They must "go the second mile"; they must do more than others do if they are to be known as followers of Jesus. If you confine your good deeds to your own kith and kin, he said to them, "what are you doing more than others? Do not even pagans do that?" (Mt 5:47). It is immediately after that that the words come: "Be perfect, therefore, as your heavenly Father is perfect."

This indeed sounds like a "counsel of perfection" in the most literal sense. "Be perfect like God." Who can attain perfection like his? Is it worthwhile even to begin to try? But the context helps us to understand the force of these words. Why should the disciples of Jesus, the heirs of the kingdom of God, repay evil with good? The ancient law might say, "Love your neighbor as yourself" (Lev 19:18), but the fulfillment of that commandment depends on the answer given to the question "Who is my neighbor?" (Lk 10:29). When Jesus was asked that question, he told the story of the good Samaritan to show that my "neighbor" in the sense intended by the commandment is anyone who needs my help, anyone to whom I can render a "neighborly" service. But those Israelites to whom the commandment was first given might not have thought of a Canaanite as being a "neighbor" within the meaning of the act, and their descendants in New Testament times might not have thought of a Roman in this way.

Most systems of ethics emphasize one's duty to one's neighbor, but progress in ethics is marked by the broadening scope indicated in the answer to the question "Who is my neighbor?" Why should I be neighborly to someone who is unneighborly to me? If someone does me a bad turn, why should I not pay him back in his own coin? Because, said Jesus, God himself sets us an example in this regard. "Your Father in heaven . . . causes his sun to rise on the evil and the good, and sends rain on the righteous and the unrighteous" (Mt 5:45). He bestows his blessings without discrimination. The followers of Jesus are children of God, and they should manifest the family likeness by doing good to all, even to those who deserve the opposite. So, said Jesus—go the whole way in doing good, just as God does.

The same injunction appears in a similar context, but in slightly different words, in Luke 6:36: "Be merciful, even as your Father is merciful" (RSV). When we find one and the same saying preserved in different forms by two Evangelists, as we do here, the reason often is that Jesus' Aramaic words have been translated into Greek in two different ways. We do not know the precise Aramaic words that Jesus used on this occasion, but they probably meant, "You must be perfect (that is, all-embracing, without any restriction) in your acts of mercy or kindness, for that is what God is like."

When the books of the law were read in synagogue from the original Hebrew, the reading was accompanied by an oral paraphrase (called a *targum*) in Aramaic, the popular vernacular. There is a passage in the law (Lev 22:26-28) which prescribes kindness to animals. In one of the Aramaic paraphrases, this passage ended with the words "As our Father is merciful in heaven, so you must be merciful on earth." Perhaps, then, some of Jesus' hearers recognized a familiar turn of phrase when this hard saying fell from his lips. It is not, after all, hard to understand; it is sometimes hard to practice it.

See also comment on MATTHEW 5:44; HEBREWS 10:14.

6:13 Lead Us Not into Temptation?

The traditional rendering of the Lord's Prayer in English contains as its second-last petition, "And lead us not into temptation." It is a petition that has puzzled successive generations of Christians for whom the word *temptation* ordinarily means temptation to sin. Why should we ask God not to lead us into this? As if God would do any such thing! "God cannot be tempted by evil, nor does he tempt anyone" (Jas 1:13).

Perhaps this was absolutely the last petition in the original form of the Lord's Prayer, as it is to this day in the authentic text of Luke's version. The petition which follows it in the traditional rendering, "but deliver us from evil," found in Matthew's version, was perhaps added to help explain the preceding one—whether the added petition means "Deliver us from what is evil" or "Deliver us from the evil one." Is God asked to deliver his children from evil by preserving them *from* temptation or by preserving them *in* temptation? By preserving them *in* temptation, probably. It is appropriate to be reminded of a very similar petition which occurs in the Jewish service of morning and evening prayer: "Do not bring us into *the power of* temptation." That seems to mean, "When we find ourselves surrounded by temptation, may we not be overpowered by it."

Temptation, when the word occurs in the older versions of the Bible, means more than temptation to sin; it has the wider sense of testing. God tempts no one, according to James 1:13; yet the same writer says, according to the KJV, "Count it all joy when ye fall into divers temptations" and "Blessed is the man that endureth temptation" (Jas 1:2, 12). What he means is brought out by the RSV: "Count it all joy . . . when you meet various trials, for you know that the testing of your faith produces steadfastness" and "Blessed is the man who endures trial, for when he has stood the test he will receive the crown of life which God has promised to those who love him." To the same effect other Christians are assured in 1 Peter 1:6-7 that the purpose of their being called to undergo various trials—"manifold temptations" in the KJV—is "so that your faith . . . may be proved genuine and may result in praise, glory and honor when Jesus Christ is revealed." That is to say, when faith is tested it is strengthened, and the outcome is reinforced stability of character.

It was so in Old Testament times. When the KJV of Genesis 22:1 says that "God did tempt Abraham," the meaning is that he *tested* him—tested his faith, that is to say. An untested faith is a weak faith, compared with one that has passed through a searching test and emerged victorious.

Jesus himself was led into "temptation." So Matthew implies when he says (Mt 4:1) that "Jesus was led by the Spirit into the desert to be tempted by the devil." Mark (Mk 1:12) uses an even stronger verb: after Jesus's baptism, he says, "the Spirit immediately drove him out into the wilderness" (RSV). What was the nature of his "temptation"? It was the testing of his faith in God, the testing of his resolution to accept the path which he knew to be his Father's will for him in preference to others which might have seemed more immediately attractive. It was from that testing that he returned—"in the power of the Spirit," says Luke (Lk 4:14)—to undertake his public ministry.

So, whatever is meant by the petition "Lead us not into temptation," it is highly unlikely that it means "Do not let our faith be tested" or, as the NEB puts it, "Do not bring us to the test." "Do not bring us to the test" is at least as obscure as "Lead us not into temptation." It invites the question "What test?"

Perhaps Paul had this petition in his mind when he says to his friends in Corinth, "No temptation has seized you except what is common to man. And God is faithful; he will not let you be tempted beyond what you can bear. But when you are tempted, he will also provide a way out so that you can stand up under it" (1 Cor 10:13). This could well be regarded as an expansion of this problem petition, which unpacks its concentrated meaning. It was evidently so regarded by those whose thought lies behind the fifth-century Eastern *Liturgy of St. James*. In this liturgy the celebrant, after reciting the Lord's Prayer, goes on:

> Yes, O Lord our God, lead us not into temptation which we are not able to bear, but with the temptation grant also the way out, so that we may be able to remain steadfast; and deliver us from evil.

This implies something like the following as the intention of our petition. We know that our faith needs to be tested if it is to grow strong; indeed, the conditions of life in this world make it inevitable that our faith must be tested. But some tests are so severe that our faith could not stand up to the strain; therefore we pray not to be brought into tests of such severity. If our faith gave way under the strain, that might involve us in moral disaster; it would also bring discredit on the name of the God whom we call our Father.

When we use the prayer, we may generalize this petition along these lines. But in the context of Jesus' ministry and his disciples' association with him, the petition may have had a more specific reference. What that reference was may be inferred from his admonition to some of his disciples in Gethsemane just before his arrest: "Watch and pray so that you will not fall into temptation" (Mk 14:38). When some regard is paid to the Aramaic wording which probably lies behind the Evangelist's Greek rendering of the admonition, there is much to be said for the view of some scholars that it meant, "Keep awake, and pray not to fail in the test!" The disciples had no idea how crucial was the test which was almost upon them. It was the supreme test for him; what about them? Would they, who had continued with their Master in his trials thus far, stand by him in the imminent hour of ultimate trial, or would they fail in the test? We know what happened: they failed—temporarily, at least. Mercifully (for the world's salvation was at stake), he did not fail. When the Shepherd was struck down, the sheep were scattered. But he endured the ordeal of suffering and death and, when he came back to life, he gathered his scattered followers together again, giving them a new start—and this time they did not fail in the test.

Our perspective on the events of Gethsemane and Calvary, even when our lives are caught up into those events and revolutionized by them, is necessarily different from theirs at that time. Jesus was prepared for the winding up of the old age and the breaking in of the new—the powerful coming of the kingdom of God. The transition from the old to the new would involve unprecedented tribulation, the birthpangs of the new creation, which would be a test too severe even for the faith of the elect, unless God intervened and cut it short. This tribulation would fall preeminently on the Son of Man, and on his endurance of it the bringing in of the new age depended. He was ready to absorb it in his own person, but would he find one or two others willing to share it with him? James and John had professed their ability to drink his cup and share his baptism, but in the moment of crisis they, with their companions, proved unequal to the challenge.

Going back, then, from our Lord's admonition in Gethsemane to the problem petition we are considering, we may conclude that in the context of Jesus' ministry its meaning was "Grant that we may not fail in the test"—"Grant that the test may not prove too severe for our faith to sustain." The test in that context was the crucial test of the ages to which Jesus' ministry was the immediate prelude. If we adopt the rendering of the petition followed in the Series 3 Anglican Order for Holy Communion, "Do not bring us to the time of trial," or the variant proposed by the International Consultation on English Texts, "Save us from the time of trial," then the "time of trial" originally intended was one against which the disciples who were taught to use the petition needed to be forearmed. But the force of the petition would be better expressed by rendering it, "May our faith stand firm in the time of trial" or "Save us *in* the time of trial." Through *that* trial we can no longer pass; the Son of Man passed through it as our representative. But the time of trial which will show whether we are truly his followers or not may come upon any Christian at any time. Those who have confidence in their ability to stand such a test may feel no need of the petition. But those who know that their faith is no more reliable than that of Peter and James and John may well pray to be saved from a trial with which their faith cannot cope or, if the trial is inescapable, to be supplied with the heavenly grace necessary to endure it: "Grant that we may not fail in the test."

See also comment on GENESIS 22:1; JAMES 1:13.

6:14-15 No Forgiveness for the Unforgiving?

See comment on MATTHEW 18:35.

6:24 You Cannot Serve Both God and Mammon?

Mammon (NIV "money") is a term that Jesus sometimes used to denote wealth. He was not the only teacher in Israel to use it, and whenever it is used it seems to indicate some unworthy aspect of wealth—not so much, perhaps, the unworthiness of wealth itself as the unworthiness of many people's attitudes to it. The derivation of the word is uncertain. Some think that it originally meant that in which men and women put their trust; others, that it originally meant "accumulation," "piling up." But the derivation is not very important; it is the use of a word, not its derivation, that determines its meaning.

Since the service of mammon is presented in this saying as an alternative to the service of God, mammon seems to be a rival to God. Service of mammon and service of God are mutually exclusive. The servant of mammon, in other words, is an idol worshiper: mammon, wealth, money has become an idol, the object of worship.

The man who depended on finding enough work today to buy the next day's food for his family could pray with feeling, "Give us today our daily bread" (Mt 6:11) or, as Moffat rendered it, "give us to-day our bread for the morrow." But the man who knew he had enough laid by to maintain his family and himself, whether he worked or not, whether he kept well or fell ill, would not put the same urgency into the prayer. The more material resources he had, the less wholehearted his reliance on God would tend to become. The children of the kingdom, in Jesus' teaching, are marked by their instant and constant trust in God; that trust will be weakened if they have something else to trust in.

In the Western world today we are cushioned, by social security and the like, against the uncertainties and hardships of life in a way that was not contemplated in New Testament times. It was in a society that did not provide widows' pensions that the words of 1 Timothy 5:5 were written: "She who is a real widow, and is left all alone, has set her hope on God and continues in supplications and prayers night and day" (RSV). This is not a criticism of social security (for which God be thanked); it is a reminder of the difficulty we find in applying the sayings of Jesus and his apostles to our own condition. But when we hear of victims of famine or refugees fleeing war, we can try to imagine what it must be like to be in their situation and consider what claim they have on our resources. This will not get us into the kingdom of God, but at least it may teach us to use material property more worthily than by treating it as something to lay our hearts on or rest our confidence in.

A covetous person, says Paul, is an idolater (Eph 5:5), and in saying so he expressed the same idea as Jesus did when he spoke about mammon. "Watch out!" said Jesus on another occasion. "Be on your guard against all kinds of greed; a man's life does not consist in the abundance of his possessions" (Lk 12:15). That should teach us not to say "How much is So-and-so worth?" when we really mean "How much does he possess?" Luke follows this last saying with the parable of the rich fool, the man who had so much property that he reckoned he could take life easy for a long time to come. He went to bed with this comforting thought, but by morning he was a pauper—he was dead, and had to leave his property behind. He had treated it as mammon, the object of his ultimate concern, and in his hour of greatest need it proved useless to him. If he had put his trust in God and accumulated the true and lasting riches, he would not have found himself destitute after death.

See also comment on JAMES 4:4; 5:1.

7:6 Pearls Before Swine?

The construction of this saying seems to be chiastic. It is the swine that will trample the pearls beneath their feet and the dogs that will turn and bite the hand that fed them, even if it fed them with "holy" flesh.

The general sense of the saying is clear: objects of value, special privileges, participation in sacred things should not be offered to those who are incapable of appreciating them. Pearls are things of beauty and value to many people—Jesus himself in one of his parables compared the kingdom of God to a "pearl of great value" (Mt 13:45-46)—but pigs will despise them because they cannot eat them. Holy flesh—the flesh of sacrificial animals—has a religious value over and above its nutritive value for worshipers who share in a "peace offering," but pariah dogs will make no difference between it and scraps of offal for which they battle in the street; they will not feel specially grateful to anyone who gives it to them.

But has the saying a more specific application? One could imagine its being quoted by some more restrictive brethren in the Jerusalem church as an argument against presenting the gospel to Gentiles, certainly against receiving them into full Christian fellowship. At a slightly later date it was used as an argument against admitting unbelievers to the Lord's Supper; thus the *Didache (Teaching of the Twelve Apostles),* a manual of Syrian Christianity dated around A.D. 100, says, "Let none eat or drink of your Eucharist except those who have been baptized in the name of the Lord. It was concerning this that the Lord said, 'Do not give dogs what is holy' " (9.5).

It would be anachronistic to read this interpretation back into the ministry of Jesus. It is better to read the saying in the context given it by Matthew (the only Gospel writer to report it). It comes immediately after the injunction "Do not judge, or you too will be judged" (Mt 7:1), with two amplifications of that injunction: you will be judged by the standard you apply in the judgment of others (Mt 7:2), and you should not try to remove a speck of sawdust from someone else's eye when you have a whole plank in your own (Mt 7:3-5). Then comes this saying, which is a further amplification of the principle, or rather a corrective of it: you must not sit in judgment on others and pass censorious sentences on them, but you ought to exercise discrimination. *Judgment* is an ambiguous word. In Greek as in English, it may mean sitting in judgment on people (or even condemning them), or it may mean exercising a proper discrimination. In the former sense judgment is deprecated; in the latter sense it is recommended. Jesus himself knew that it was useless to impart his message to some people: he had no answer for Herod Antipas when Herod "plied him with many questions" (Lk 23:9).

7:23 I Never Knew You?

See comment on MATTHEW 25:11-12.

8:5 Did the Centurion Come to Meet Jesus?

See comment on LUKE 7:6.

8:13 How Much Faith Do We Need?

See comment on MARK 5:34.

8:22 Let the Dead Bury Their Dead?

See comment on LUKE 9:60.

8:28-34 Two Demoniacs or One?

When we compare Matthew 8:28 with Mark 5:2 and Luke 8:27, there is one major difference: Mark and Luke refer to one demonized man while Matthew refers to two. This is not the only place in which Matthew has this difference in number. In Matthew 9:27, which may be parallel to Mark 8:22-23, there are two blind men, in Matthew 20:30 there are also two blind men, although Mark 10:46 has only one, whom he names as Bartimaeus, and in Matthew 21:1-11 there are two animals that are brought to Jesus. What are we to make of these Matthean doublets, as they have been called? We will deal with the issue of the two animals in a later chapter; here we will deal only with the problem of the two people being healed.

Several explanations have been given. First, it is quite possible that there were two men in each instance and that Mark has left one out. While this might be understandable in Mark 10:46, since he might know the name of only one of them or perhaps only one of them continued as a follower of Jesus, this is more of a problem in this passage. What reason could Mark have had for leaving one person out? Is it not more frightening and more dangerous and therefore a more significant miracle to be confronted by two demonized men than one? It is difficult to understand why Mark (and Luke, who, of course, may never have read Matthew and only copied Mark) would be so *consistently* different without any motive.

Second, some scholars have argued that it is simply the nature of miracle stories to grow in the telling. Thus, like a fish story, where originally there was one man, now there are two. This explanation is far too simplistic. If the stories were just being exaggerated, why would the number always be two? Why would not some of the stories have had two and others three or perhaps five or six? This explanation gives no reason for the consistency. Also, if this were true, there would be no analogy between these stories about healing and the two animals in the triumphal entry.

Third, other scholars have argued that Matthew has deliberately increased the number to two to make a theological point. They point out that the Gospels were not written as biographies and certainly not as modern biographies. In modern biographies we want to present something like a photograph of the person, while in ancient biographies, and even more so in the Gospels, the authors wanted to paint an interpretive portrait of the person. An interpretive portrait could paint a king with both a prime minister from the first part of his reign and one from the last part of his reign, even though the two men never met and never served the king at the same time. We would not fault the portrait for that, for it is trying to express a truth: both of these men served the king (or perhaps, each of these men represents one theme of the king's reign). This interpretive character is the nature of ancient historical writing: the important thing was not to get the details right but to present the main character so that his or her true nature and character was evident.

What, then, could be Matthew's point? First, Matthew may be indicating that he has left out a story about a demonized person which he found in Mark (Mk 1:23-28); he also omits one story of healing a blind man (Mk 8:22-26, assuming that Mt 9:27 is too different to be a version of this story). On this view he is playing "catch-up" and indicating that Jesus did this sort of thing more than once. Yet, we may ask, why would he not be content with the single instance? Would it not be enough to show that Jesus could do these things?

We need to remember, second, that it is Matthew who, ever conscious of the law, in Matthew 18:16 quotes Deuteronomy 19:15 to the effect that "every matter may be established by the testimony of two or three witnesses." Furthermore, each of these passages has an important confession of Christ. In Matthew 8:29 it is "Son of God." In Matthew 9:27-28 and 20:30-31 it is "Lord, Son of David." Thus without having to tell two or more stories he gets his two witnesses to the title of Christ by including more than one demonized person and more than one blind man in the respective stories. While this might not be our idea of accurate reporting (for we, unlike Matthew, can simply add a few more pages to a book to fit in whatever we feel we need to), it would certainly fit the ancient concept, for Matthew has brought out the truth of the matter (for example, that Jesus did heal more than one demonized person and than many of them gave witness to him as the Son of God) in how he paints his picture.[1]

Even if one chooses to accept that it is easier to believe that Mark left one of the persons out in each case (for we can never know for sure that this was not the case), the explanation above would certainly be a factor in why Matthew felt that having two was so important and Mark, lacking his concern about the law, would not have felt that it mattered.

[1]For further discussion see Donald A. Hagner, *Matthew 1—13,* Word Biblical Commentary 33A (Dallas: Word, 1993), p. 227.

8:31-32 Why No Concern for the Pigs?

In the age of Greenpeace and animal rights the idea that Jesus of Nazareth sentenced two thousand pigs, one of the more intelligent mammals, to death by drowning by allowing demons to invade and terrorize them raises problems for most readers. Didn't Jesus care about animals? In the Old Testament God does (for example, Prov 12:10). And even if Jesus did not care about pigs, shouldn't he have cared about the livelihood of the swineherds and the owners? He certainly did not ask anyone's permission.

The story in Matthew 8:28-34 and Luke 8:26-39 is drawn from Mark 5:1-20. In these accounts Jesus, confronted by a severely demonized man, does not immediately drive the demons out, but instead ends up in a short discussion with them. The demons request that Jesus send them into a large herd of pigs feeding nearby. When he consents, the demons do enter the pigs. The herd stampedes, rushes into the Sea of Galilee and is drowned.

Before we turn to the main issues, we need to deal with two less important ones. First, the name of the place where this story occurs differs among the Gospels and their translations, which points to a very difficult textual situation. In the best Greek text Matthew has Gadarenes, Mark has Gerasenes, and Luke agrees with Mark. Most modern versions translate the terms accordingly, but the King James has Gergasenes in Matthew and

Gadarenes in the two other Gospels, for it is following a later, probably corrupt, Greek text. But to what town do these names refer?

One possibility is Gerasa, modern Jerash, about thirty miles southeast of the Sea of Galilee. Although it was a very prosperous town in the first two centuries A.D., it is unlikely that its lands reached the lake. The second possibility is Gadara, a site now called Um Qeia, five miles southeast of the sea. Its lands certainly reached the lake, for Josephus mentions the fact and its coins show a ship. The final possibility is that the reference is to a lakeside town. The site of modern Khersa has been suggested, but it probably gave rise to the corrupt reading Gergasenes after Origen's suggestion in the third century. Whatever the actual town (we will never know the names of all of the towns and villages on the east coast of the Sea of Galilee), Mark uses "Gerasene" to refer to its people, and Luke follows him. Matthew (who likely wrote his Gospel in Syria, thereby closer to the site) prefers to refer to the town he knows, in the region he believed the place was located. Later scribes, not knowing any of the places, confused the matter. One thing is certain: all of the places named are in the Decapolis, Gentile territory of the ten independent cities to the east of the Sea of Galilee.

The second preliminary issue is that Matthew mentions two demonized men, while Mark and Luke mention only one. This is a common problem in Matthew. For example, in Matthew 9:27 and Matthew 20:30 he mentions two blind men where the other Gospels mention only one, and in Matthew 21:2, 6 he says that two donkeys were brought to Jesus while the other Gospels mention only one. In each case it is not at all unlikely that two (or more) were present. Blind beggars (and other types as well) would group at city gates, a donkey young enough not to have been used for work would likely be with its mother, and more than one demonized person might find refuge in the same groups of tombs. But even if there is no necessity of seeing a historical problem, we may wonder why Matthew would mention two when one seems to do for the others. While other answers also may suffice, one reason is that Matthew's interest in the miracles is due to his Christology. That is, the miracles show the power of Christ. By mentioning two he heightens that power. The healing of one may have been a coincidence, but not the healing of two. Similarly, if two donkeys are brought to Jesus, the significance of his fulfillment of the Scriptures is underlined.

Concerning the major issues in this passage, it becomes clear that the Gospel writers were interested in quite different issues than those with which modern readers have struggled. We tend to romanticize the role of animals, while in the first century animals were raised for food or for other useful purposes. Everyone was familiar with animal sacrifice, whether for a secular marketplace or in the temple. We also see the economics of the story, while the Gospel writers were far more concerned with God's present provision (Mk 6:7-13) and future treasure in heaven than in preserving economic security now. Furthermore, we see the violence done to animals, while the Gospel writers were concerned with the violent destructive behavior of demons and their effects upon human beings (which they knew from firsthand observation). Therefore, the Gospel writers saw the whole story from another perspective.

In Mark, for example, Jesus comes into the land of the Gerasenes. Mark later notes that this is part of the Decapolis, underlining the fact that it is Gentile country, even if it once belonged to Israel. In other words, Jesus is in an unclean land. The demonized man even uses a title for God ("God Most High") normally used by Gentiles. He lives in the tombs, an unclean place, the place of the dead. He is controlled by "an unclean spirit" [RSV] (Matthew and Luke simply say he is "demonized"). The pigs, of course, are unclean animals (Lev 11:7; Deut 14:8), which Jews were not even to raise for others (so runs the rabbinic rule in Mishnah, Baba Kamma 7:7). So the unclean spirits go into the unclean pigs and drive them to their deaths, while the man who was in the place of the dead (and surely would soon enough die) is delivered and reenters life (returns to his own house). From this perspective the pigs are not the issue—they are unclean—and the townsfolk miss the point when they see only their loss of pigs and fail to see the delivered man. Indeed, the pigs plunging into the sea may suggest that the unclean land had been freed of the unclean spirits with the removal of the unclean animals; but the people do not want salvation, preferring pigs.

Another set of issues is also present in this passage. This is the only exorcism in the Gospels in which the demons answer back to Jesus. In fact, they do so after Jesus commands them to leave the man (a detail not mentioned in Matthew). Their concern is that they not be tormented, that is, sent to hell (Matthew specifically adds "before the time," meaning before the final judgment). Why would they say this? First, Jewish teaching was that demons were free to torment people until the last judgment (see *Jubilees* 10:5-9 and *1 Enoch* 15—16). Second, Jesus' appearance and power to expel them looked to them as if he were beginning the final judgment too early. Therefore, the permission to enter the pigs is an admission that the last judgment is not yet taking place. The demons are still free to do their destructive work. Nevertheless, wherever the King is present he brings the kingdom and frees people from the power of evil.

There is no suggestion in this story that Jesus was not in control or that he was tricked. He had just stilled a destructive (perhaps even demonically inspired) storm (Mt 8:23-27; Mk 4:35-41; Lk 8:22-25). He remains the sovereign "Son of God" in the deliverance of the demonized man. But the account gives the Gospel writers a chance to point out that while the kingdom of God does come in Jesus, it is not yet the time of final judgment when evil will finally and totally be put down. Demons remain and act like demons, tormenting and killing what they inhabit, but they are limited in that Jesus could and still can free people by his power.

We moderns may not like the idea that demons do have this destructive nature, that of their master (see Jn 10:10, where the "thief" is an image for Satan). Jesus, of course, did not tell them to kill the pigs; the demons just did to them what they wished to do to the man in the long run. Nor do we like the idea that God is limited in his options here, choosing in his mercy to delay the final judgment, which would have been brought about had he removed the evil forces totally. But both of these facts underline the most important issue, the value of a person. So precious is human life that, when necessary, a whole herd of animals may be sacrificed for one or two people.

See also comment on MATTHEW 8:28-34.

9:22 How Much Faith Do We Need?

See comment on MARK 5:34.

9:24 Not Dead but Sleeping?

See comment on MARK 5:39.

10:5-6 Not to the Gentiles?

These words occur in Matthew's account of Jesus' sending out the twelve apostles two by two at a fairly early stage in his Galilean ministry, in order that the proclamation of the kingdom of God might be carried on more extensively and more quickly than if he had done it by himself alone. The message they were to preach was the same as he preached: "The kingdom of heaven is near." The works of healing that were to accompany their preaching were of the same kind as accompanied his.

Mark (Mk 6:7-13) and Luke (Lk 9:l) also report the sending out of the Twelve, but more briefly than Matthew does. Matthew is the only Evangelist to include these "exclusive" words in his account. "The lost sheep of Israel" is an expression peculiar to his Gospel (although it is not dissimilar to "sheep without a shepherd" in Mk 6:34); it occurs again in his account of the healing of the Canaanite woman's daughter (Mt 15:24).

Since Matthew is the only Evangelist to report these words, it might be argued that they were not originally spoken by Jesus but were ascribed to him by the Evangelist or his source. We cannot make Matthew responsible for inventing them; there is no reason to think that Matthew had an anti-Gentile bias or entertained a particularist view of the gospel. At the beginning of his record he brings the Gentiles in by telling how the wise men came from the east to pay homage to the infant king of the Jews—the occasion traditionally referred to as the "epiphany" or "manifestation" of Christ to the Gentiles. In the course of his report of Jesus' teaching he quotes him as saying that, before the end comes, "this gospel of the kingdom will be preached throughout the whole world, as a testimony to all nations" (Mt 24:14). At the end of the book (Mt 28:19) he tells how the risen Christ commissioned the apostles to "go . . . and make disciples of all nations" (that is, among all the Gentiles). And in the course of his record he tells of Jesus' praise for the Roman centurion of Capernaum, in whom he found greater faith than he had found in any Israelite (Lk 7:2-10), and of his following assertion that "many will come from the east and the west, and will takes their places at the feast with Abraham, Isaac and Jacob in the kingdom of heaven," while some of the descendants of Abraham, Isaac and Jacob would find themselves excluded from the feast (Mt 8:5-13; compare Lk 13:28-29). Those last words would certainly be a hard saying for Jewish hearers, just as hard as "Do not go among the Gentiles" might be for Gentile readers.

Matthew probably did derive some of the material peculiar to his Gospel from a source marked by a Jewish emphasis—perhaps a compilation of sayings of Jesus preserved by a rather strict Jewish-Christian community. "Do not go among the Gentiles" may well have been found in this source.[1] But the source in question probably selected those sayings of Jesus which chimed in with its own outlook; that is no argument against their genuineness.

When Jesus sent out the Twelve, the time at their disposal was short, and it was necessary to concentrate on the people who had been specially prepared for the message of the kingdom. Even if the Twelve did confine themselves to the "lost sheep of Israel," they would not have time to cover all of these. This has sometimes been thought to be the point of the cryptic words "you will not have gone through all the towns of Israel, before the Son of man comes" (Mt 10:23 RSV).

Moreover, it is taught in the prophetic writings of the Old Testament, and nowhere more clearly than in Isaiah 40—55, that when Israel grasps the true knowledge of God, it will be its privilege to share that knowledge with other nations. Nearly thirty years later, Paul, apostle to the Gentiles though he was, lays down the order of gospel presentation as being "first for the Jew, then for the Gentile" (Rom 1:16). This statement of primitive evangelistic policy was evidently founded on Jesus' own practice. Even so, there are hints here and there in the Synoptic Gospels that the Gentiles' interests were not forgotten. The incident of the Roman centurion of Capernaum has been mentioned; the healing of the Canaanite woman's daughter will receive separate treatment (see comment on Mk 7:27). Such occasions, isolated and exceptional as they were during Jesus' ministry, foreshadowed the mission to the Gentiles which was launched a few years after his death. The Fourth Gospel emphasizes this by relating an incident that took place in Jerusalem during Holy Week, only two or three days before Jesus' arrest and crucifixion. Some Greeks who were visiting the city approached one of the disciples and asked for an interview with Jesus. His reply, when he was told of their request, was in effect "Not yet, but after my death"—"when I am lifted up from the earth, I will draw all men to myself," all without distinction, Gentiles and Jews alike (Jn 12:20-32). That is exactly what happened.

The ban on entering any town of the Samaritans is to be understood in the same way. Samaritans were not Jews, but neither were they Gentiles. Jesus did not share his people's anti-Samaritan bias (although the evidence for this is supplied by Luke and John, not by Matthew), and after his death and resurrection his message of salvation was effectively presented to Samaritans even before it was presented to Gentiles (Acts 8:5-25).

See also comment on MARK 7:27; 10:31.

[1]To this source (commonly labeled M) may also be assigned Matthew 18:17, with its direction that the insubordinate brother should be treated "as a Gentile and a tax collector" (RSV).

10:9-10 Were the Twelve to Take a Staff?

See comment on MARK 6:8.

10:23 Unfulfilled Expectation?

This saying, found in Matthew's Gospel only, comes at the end of Jesus' commission to the twelve apostles when he sent them out two by two. It was brought to public attention early in the twentieth century when the great Albert Schweitzer made it the foundation of his interpretation of the ministry of Jesus. Jesus, he believed, expected the kingdom of God to dawn with power and glory at harvest time that year, before the Twelve had completed their mission. "He tells them in plain words . . . that He does not expect to see them back in the present age."[1] Jesus would be supernaturally revealed as the Son of Man, in a manner involving his own transformation, as well as the transformation of his followers, into a state of being suited to the conditions of the resurrection age. But the new age did not come in; the Twelve returned from their mission. Jesus then tried to force its arrival. He "lays hold of the wheel of the world to set it moving on that last revolution which is to bring all ordinary history to a close. It refuses to turn, and He throws Himself upon it. Then it does turn; and crushes Him."[2] Yet in the hour of his failure he released a liberating power in the world which is beyond description.

The teaching of the Sermon on the Mount and related passages in the Gospels was understood by Schweitzer to be an "interim ethic" to guide the lives of Jesus' disciples in the short interval before the manifestation of the Son of Man in power and glory. When, on Schweitzer's reading of the evidence, the hope of that manifestation was disappointed, what happened to the interim ethic? Logically, it should have been forgotten when its basis was removed. Actually, the interim ethic survived in its own right, as is magnificently evident from Schweitzer's own career. It was the driving force behind his life of service to others in West Africa. What, on his understanding, was but the prologue to the expected drama "has become the whole drama . . . the ministry of Jesus is not a prelude to the Kingdom of God: it *is* the Kingdom of God."[3]

The commission to the Twelve, as given in Matthew 10:5-23, has two parts, each with its own perspective. The first part (Mt 10:5-18) deals with the immediate situation, within the context of Jesus' own Galilean ministry. The second part (Mt 10:19-23) envisages a later period, when the apostles will be engaged in a wider ministry—the kind of ministry in which they were in fact engaged in the period *following* the resurrection of Jesus and the coming of the Spirit. Think of the warning "Be on your guard against men; they will hand you over to the local councils and flog you in their synagogues. On my account you will be brought before governors and kings as witnesses to them and to the Gentiles" (Mt 10:17-18). This reference to the Gentiles presents a contrast with the reference to them in Matthew 10:5, where they are excluded from the scope of the earlier preaching tour. The warning just quoted has a close parallel in Mark 13:9-10, where the situation is that leading up to the destruction of Jerusalem in A.D. 70. And in both places the warning is followed by an assurance that, when the disciples are put on trial and required to bear witness to their faith, the Holy Spirit will put the right words into their mouths. It is this second part of the commission in Matthew 10 that is rounded off with the hard saying "You will not finish going through the cities of Israel before the Son of Man comes."

What, then, does the saying mean in this context? It means, simply, that the evangelization of Israel will not be completed before the end of the present age, which comes with the advent of the Son of Man. The parallel passage in Mark has a similar statement, which, however, takes more explicit account of Gentile as well as Jewish evangelization: before the end time, "the gospel must first be preached to all nations" (Mk 13:10). (This statement is reproduced in slightly amplified form in Mt 24:14: "And this gospel of the kingdom will be preached in the whole world, as a testimony to all nations, and then the end will come.") Paul, from his own perspective, expresses much the same hope when he foresees the salvation of "all Israel," the sequel to the ingathering of the full sum of Gentile believers, being consummated at the time when "the deliverer will come from Zion" (Rom 11:25-27).

The wording of Matthew 10:23 is earlier in its reference than that of the other passages just mentioned: here witness-bearing to the Gentiles receives a brief mention, but all the emphasis lies on the mission to the Jews. This mission, as we know from Galatians 2:6-9, was taken seriously by the leaders of the Jerusalem church in the early apostolic age, and they carried it out with some sense of urgency. For anything they knew to the contrary, the Son of Man might come within their own generation. We must not allow our understanding of their perspective to be influenced by our own very different perspective. We know that their mission, in the form in which they pursued it, was brought to an end by the Judean rebellion against Rome in A.D. 66, but it would be unwise to say that *that,* with the fall of Jerusalem four years later, was the coming of the Son of Man of which Jesus spoke.

---

[1]Albert Schweitzer, *The Quest of the Historical Jesus* (London: A. and C. Black, 1910), p. 357.
[2]Ibid., p. 369.
[3]T. W. Manson, *Studies in the Gospels and Epistles* (Manchester: Manchester University Press, 1962). pp. 9-10.

10:28 Whom Should We Fear?

See comment on LUKE 12:4-5.

10:34 Not Peace but a Sword?

This is a hard saying for all who recall the message of the angels on the night of Jesus' birth: "Glory to God in high heaven, and peace on earth among human beings, the objects of God's favor" (as the message seems to mean). True, the angels' message appears only in Luke (Lk 2:14) and the hard saying comes from Matthew. But Luke records the same hard saying, except that he replaces the metaphorical "sword" by the nonmetaphorical "division" (Lk 12:51). Both Evangelists then go on to report Jesus as saying, "For I have come to turn 'a man against his father, a daughter against her mother, a daughter-in-law against her mother-in-law' " (Mt 10:35; Lk 12:53), while Matthew rounds the saying off with a quotation from the Old Testament: "a man's enemies will be the members of his own household" (Mic 7:6).

One thing is certain: Jesus did not advocate conflict. He taught his followers to offer no resistance or retaliation when they were attacked or ill-treated. "Blessed are the peacemakers," he said, "for they will be called sons of God" (Mt 5:9), meaning that God is the God of peace, so that those who seek peace and pursue it reflect his character. When he paid his last visit to Jerusalem, the message which he brought it concerned "what would bring you peace," and he wept because the city refused his message and was bent on a course that was bound to lead to destruction (Lk 19:41-44). The message that his followers proclaimed in his name after his departure was called the "gospel of peace" (Eph 6:15) or the "message of reconciliation" (2 Cor 5:19 RSV). It was called this not merely as a matter of doctrine but as a fact of experience. Individuals and groups formerly estranged from one another found themselves reconciled through their common devotion to Christ. Something of this sort must have been experienced even earlier, in the course of the Galilean ministry: if Simon the Zealot and Matthew the tax collector were able to live together as two of the twelve apostles, the rest of the company must have looked on this as a miracle of grace.

But when Jesus spoke of tension and conflict within a family, he probably spoke from personal experience. There are indications in the gospel story that some members of his own family had no sympathy with his ministry; the people who on one occasion tried to restrain him by force because people were saying, "He is out of his mind" are called "his friends" in the KJV but more accurately "his family" in the NIV (Mk 3:21). "Even his own brothers did not believe in him," we are told in John 7:5. (If it is asked why, in that case, they attained positions of leadership alongside the apostles in the early church, the answer is no doubt to be found in the statement of 1 Cor 15:7 that Jesus, risen from the dead, appeared to his brother James.)

So, when Jesus said that he had come to bring "not peace but a sword" he meant that this would be the *effect* of his coming, not that it was the *purpose* of his coming. His words came true in the life of the early church, and they have verified themselves subsequently in the history of Christian missions. Where one or two members of a family or other social group have accepted the Christian faith, this has repeatedly provoked opposition from other members. Paul, who seems to have experienced such opposition in his own family circle as a result of his conversion, makes provision for similar situations in the family life of his converts. He knew that tension could arise when a husband or a wife became a Christian and the other spouse remained a pagan. If the pagan spouse was happy to go on living with the Christian, that was fine; the whole family might become Christian before long. But if the pagan partner insisted on walking out and terminating the marriage, the Christian should not use force or legal action, because "God has called us to peace" (1 Cor 7:12-16 RSV).

In these words, then, Jesus was warning his followers that their allegiance to him might cause conflict at home and even expulsion from the family circle. It was well that they should be forewarned, for then they could not say, "We never expected that we should have to pay this price for following him!"

11:11 Who Is Greater Than John the Baptist?

See comment on LUKE 7:28.

11:12 Violently into the Kingdom?

See comment on LUKE 16:16.

11:27 The Father and the Son

No one would have been surprised had this saying appeared somewhere in the Gospel of John. The language is characteristically Johannine; the saying has been called "an aerolite from the Johannine heaven" or "a boulder from the Johannine moraine." For all its Johannine appearance, it does not come in the Gospel of John but in the non-Mark material common to the Gospels of Matthew and Luke, drawn (it is widely supposed) from the Q collection of sayings of Jesus, which may have been in circulation not long after A.D. 50. The nearest thing to it in the Synoptic Gospels is the utterance of the risen Christ at the end of Matthew's Gospel: "All authority in heaven and on earth has been given to me" (Mt 28:18).

In both Matthew and Luke (and therefore presumably also in the source on which they drew), the saying follows on immediately from words in which Jesus thanks God that things hidden from the wise and understanding have been revealed to "babes"—that is, apparently, to the disciples. The one who has revealed those things is Jesus himself; indeed, he is not only the revealer of truth; he is the Son who reveals the Father. In this context the "all things" that have been delivered to him by the Father would naturally be understood to refer to the content of his teaching or revelation. But the content of this teaching or revelation is not an abstract body of divinity; it is personal, it is God the Father himself. Jesus claims a unique personal knowledge of God, and this personal knowledge he undertakes to impart to others. Unless it is imparted by him, it is inaccessible. He is the one who at his baptism heard the Father acclaim him as his Son, his beloved, his chosen one (Mk 1:11). He enjoys a special relation and fellowship with the Father, but that relation and fellowship is open to those who learn from him. As he calls God "Abba, Father," they may know him and call him by the same name. All the other gifts which the Father has to bestow on his children come with this personal knowledge, which is mediated by Jesus.

Matthew and Luke give the saying two different literary contexts; if we look for a historical context, we might think of some occasion when the disciples showed that they had grasped the heart of his teaching to which the minds of others remained closed, as at Caesarea Philippi.

There is nothing hard in this except to those who cannot accept the claim to uniqueness, the "scandal of particularity," implicit in the gospel. But to those who accept the presuppositions current in a plural society this can be hard enough.

But what of the statement that "no one knows the Son except the Father"? One line of traditional interpretation takes this to mean that the union of the divine and human natures in the one person of the Son of God is a mystery known only to the Father. But it is anachronistic to impart later christological teaching into the context of Jesus' ministry. More probably the two clauses "no one knows the Son except the Father" and "no one knows the Father except the Son" constitute a fuller way of saying "no one except the Father and the Son know each other." It has been suggested, indeed, that there is an argument from the general to the particular here—that a saying to the effect that "only a father and a son know each other" (and therefore only the son can reveal the father) is applied to the special relation of Jesus and God: "only the Father and the Son know each other" (and therefore only the Son can reveal the Father). Whatever substance there may be in this suggestion, it is clear that a reciprocity of personal knowledge between the Son of God and his Father is affirmed. As none but the Father knows the Son, so none but the Son knows the Father, but the Son shares this knowledge with those whom he chooses, and in the present context that means his disciples.

There is a fascinating collection of variant readings in the textual transmission of this saying; they bear witness to difficulties which early scribes and editors found in it. The only variation at which we need to look is that between Matthew's wording and Luke's: whereas Matthew says "knows the Son . . . knows the Father," Luke says "knows who the Son is . . . or who the Father is." Luke's wording might appear to weaken the emphasis on direct personal knowledge expressed by Matthew's wording, but this was probably not Luke's intention. If consideration be given to the Semitic construction behind the Greek of the two Gospels, Matthew's wording can claim to be closer to what Jesus actually said.

12:30 For or Against Christ?

See comment on LUKE 11:23.

12:31-32 An Unpardonable Sin?

See comment on MARK 3:28-29.

12:39 No Sign?

See comment on LUKE 11:29-30.

12:40 How Long Was Jesus in the Tomb?

While referring to the example of Jonah (Jon 1:17) Jesus uses a phrase which appears only here, in Jonah and in 1 Samuel 30:12. Yet it is clear even in Matthew that Jesus was raised "on the third day" (Mt 16:21; 17:23; 20:19; compare Mt 27:63 "after three days"), and this agrees with the narrative (Mt 27:57—28:1). What are we to make of this?

First, we know what we would mean by the phrase in Matthew 12:40: we would mean a seventy-two-hour period or at least most of that period. Second, we know that Jesus was not in the tomb more than thirty-six to thirty-eight hours, since he was buried at evening (which began at about 6 p.m.) on Friday and rose by morning (about 6 a.m.) on Sunday. Third, we know that the phrase "three days and three nights" was not a problem for Matthew, for he can use both that and "on the third day" and include no explanation, which he does in other cases where he senses a problem.

Having seen what we know, we now need to look at what we may be assuming erroneously. First, we may be assuming that first-century Jews thought about time in the same way that we do. In fact they did not. Any part of a day could be counted as if it were a full day, much as in Canada and the U.S.A. a child is deductible for income-tax purposes at the full year rate even if he or she was born at 11 p.m. on December 31. The "three days and three nights," then, may simply refer to three twenty-four-hour days (sunset to sunset periods), and Jesus was in fact in the tomb parts of three different days.

Second, we may be assuming that Jesus was simply making a statement, when, given the unusual nature of this phrase, he was actually quoting Jonah. The sign of Jonah was that the prophet was "buried" for three days and then "rose again," so to speak, to announce judgment (and, implicitly, salvation). In quoting the scriptural phrase Jesus probably did not mean that he would be buried the exact length of time as Jonah was in the fish, but that he would like Jonah be "buried" for that approximate time and then be "raised." The phrase is used to remind the hearers of the familiar Scripture. This is much like a modern person saying, "I laid a 'fleece' before God." They do not mean to indicate that they put out wool before God, but that, like Gideon in the Bible, they asked God for a particular sign to see if something was or was not his will. Thus, when he wants to remind people of Jonah, Jesus uses the phrase found there, but when he is not citing Jonah and simply intends to describe how long he would be in the tomb, he uses the more accurate "on the third day."

While either of these explanations above resolves the apparent problem, the second is more likely the central reason for the phrase. Together they remind us that there are a number of ways of using language. We must be certain we understand how a phrase is being used before jumping to conclusions; the fact that ancient scripts did not have quotation marks does not make this job any easier. The main clue for us is that Matthew does not indicate that he feels a problem, so either he did not see the two phrases as meaning anything different or else he realized that what Jesus intended was simply a citation of Jonah. *See also comment on* LUKE 11:29-30.

13:13 Why in Parables?

See comment on MARK 4:11-12.

13:32 How Small Is a Mustard Seed?

There is no doubt but that the mustard seed is a small seed. All the same, even the naked eye can tell that there are smaller seeds. While the round mustard seed is smaller than wheat, millet, barley, caraway and dill, it is debatable whether it is smaller than the sesame seed (a flat seed, which is larger in one dimension but about the same volume as the mustard seed), and it is several times the size of a poppy seed. How then could Jesus in Matthew make the statement in Matthew 13:32 (which literally reads, "the smallest of seeds"; the NIV has added an interpretive "all your" based upon Mk 4:31, "It is like a mustard seed, which is the smallest seed you plant in the ground")?

First, we notice that the purpose of the passage is not to teach about botany, but to make a natural comparison to the kingdom of God. Jesus is pointing out something as an illustration, not trying to give an absolute truth. Holding Jesus responsible for something he had no intention of teaching or implying shows the inability of the accuser to understand language, not a failure of Jesus or the Gospel writers.

Second, the context of Jesus' point is found in the version in Mark: "the smallest seed you plant in the ground." Which seeds did Palestinian Jews plant? The mustard seed is smaller than any other they commonly planted. In fact, it is quite possible that the original setting of the saying was near some garden toward which Jesus motioned as he taught. (This assumes that he was intending the cultivated or black mustard, *brassica nigra;* there is a wild mustard, *brassica arvensis,* which he might have pointed out had he been teaching in some rural setting.)

Third, the focus of Jesus' saying is to make a contrast between the smallness of the seed planted and the size of the resulting shrub. It does not grow into a thin grass or weak-stemmed flower, unable to support the weight of anything more than insects, but into a sturdy shrub perhaps three feet high with stems strong enough to support the weight of small birds. Here is a seed which is as tiny as a large grain of sand. A person plants it in the garden. A shrub sprouts that grows large enough to support the weight of birds. The kingdom of heaven is like that. It begins with Jesus and his small band of followers, hardly noticeable in the towns and cities of Palestine, let alone the Roman Empire (Roman historians do not even mention him). Yet, he predicts, that kingdom will grow until it becomes something large and strong.

What was this supposed to mean for the listener? The smallness of this nucleus of the kingdom of heaven was easy to ignore. One could listen to Jesus and say, "That was interesting," and turn aside to one's business. Yet the kingdom is not going to go away. It will become something large and strong. It is even possible that the reference to the birds implies that the Gentiles would find shelter in the kingdom (birds are sometimes used in that symbolic way in rabbinic teaching). Jesus is not something for the people to ignore. Now is the time for decision, for the future will prove their foolishness if they ignore the small beginning they see in the present.

15:21-28 The Children First?

See comment on MARK 7:27

16:4 No Sign?

See comment on LUKE 11:29-30.

16:18-19 Peter the Rock?

Why should this be reckoned a hard saying? It does, to be sure, contain some figures of speech which require to be explained—"the gates of Hades" (which RSV has interpreted for us as "the powers of death"), "the keys of the kingdom," "binding" and "loosing." But it is not because of these figures of speech that the saying is widely reckoned to be hard—so hard, indeed, that some interpreters have tried not only to explain it but to explain it away.

One reason for regarding it as a hard saying is that Peter in the Gospels is too unstable a character to serve as the foundation for any enterprise or to be given such authority as is conveyed in these words. But the main reason for finding a difficulty in the text is strictly irrelevant to its straightforward reading and interpretation. Few Protestants, asked to name their favorite text, would think of quoting this one. It has been invoked to support the supremacy of the Roman Church over other churches—more precisely, to support the supremacy of the bishop of Rome over other bishops—and those who do not acknowledge this use of it as valid have sometimes reacted by trying to make it mean something much less positive than it appears to mean. Some have suggested, with no manuscript evidence to justify the suggestion, that the text has been corrupted from an original "you have said" (instead of "you are Peter"); others have argued that the Greek wording is not an accurate translation of the Aramaic form in which the saying was cast by Jesus—that what he said was, "I tell you, Peter, that on this rock I will build my church." But this too is conjecture. If we can get rid of the idea that the text has any reference to the Roman Church or to the papacy, we shall lose interest in such attempts to remove what has been felt to be its awkwardness.

Certainly there is nothing in the context to suggest Rome or the papacy. But the context of the saying presents us with a problem of a different kind. All three Synoptic Evangelists record the incident in the neighborhood of Caesarea. All of them tell how Jesus, after asking his disciples what account people were giving of him, next asked them what account they themselves gave: "Who do you say that I am?" To this question Peter, acting as their spokesman, replied, "You are the Christ" (that is the form of his answer in Mk 8:29; the other Gospels have variations in wording). All three Evangelists add that Jesus strictly forbade them to repeat this to anyone. But Matthew inserts, between Peter's answer and Jesus' charge to the disciples not to repeat it, a personal response by Jesus to Peter.

How are we to account for the fact that this response, with its introductory benediction, does not appear in Mark's or Luke's record of the occasion? If Matthew were the source on which Mark and Luke depended, then we could say that they abridged his record for purposes of their own, and we should try to determine what those purposes were. If, however, we are right in thinking that Mark was one of the sources on which Matthew drew, then we have to say that Matthew has amplified Mark's record by incorporating material derived from elsewhere. This is not the only place where Matthew expands Mark's record by the inclusion of material about Peter not found in the other Gospels. We may think, for example, of the episode of Peter's getting out of the boat and beginning to sink when he tried to walk to Jesus on the water (Mt 14:28-31).

It has been argued that the passage we are considering belongs to a later period in Christian history rather than that to which Matthew assigns it. Some have seen in it the report of words spoken by Jesus to Peter when he appeared to him in resurrection—words which Matthew transferred to the Caesarea Philippi context because of the aptness of the subject matter. Others would date them later still. Is it likely, they ask, that the historical Jesus would speak of his "church"? Certainly it is not likely that he used the word in the sense which it usually bears for us, but it is not unlikely that he used an Aramaic word which was represented in Greek by *ekklēsia,* the term regularly rendered "church" in the New Testament. And if he did, what did he mean by it? He meant the new community which he aimed to bring into being, the new Israel in which the twelve apostles were to be the leaders, leading by service and not by dictation.

A helpful analogy to Jesus' words to Peter is provided by an allegory found in rabbinical tradition setting forth God's dealings with humanity from the beginning to the time of Abraham. The written documents in which this allegory is found are later than our Gospels, but behind the written form lies a period of oral transmission. In Isaiah 51:1 Abraham is called "the rock from which you were cut," and the allegory undertakes to explain why Abraham should be called a "rock." It tells how a certain king wished to build a palace and set his servants to dig to find a foundation. They dug for a long time and took soundings twice, but they found nothing but morass. (The soundings were taken first in the generation of Enosh, Adam's grandson, and then in the generation of Noah.) After further digging they took soundings again, and this time they struck rock *(petra)*. "Now," said the king, "at last I can begin to build."[1]

In the allegory the king, of course, is God; the palace which he planned to build is the nation of Israel, and he knew that he could make a beginning with the project when he found Abraham, a man ready to respond to his call with implicit faith and obedience. It would be precarious to envisage any direct relation between this allegory and Jesus' words to Peter as recorded by Matthew, but there is a notable resemblance.

According to John's account of the call of the first disciples, it was during John the Baptist's ministry in Transjordan that Peter heard his brother Andrew say, with reference to Jesus, "We have found the Messiah" (Jn 1:41). Evidently Peter then believed Andrew's testimony, but that would have been an instance of what Jesus now described as "flesh and blood" (a human being) telling him. There were various ideas abroad in the popular mind at that time regarding the kind of person the Messiah was and the kind of things he would do, but Jesus' character and activity, as his disciples had come to know them, probably corresponded to none of those ideas. If Peter believed Jesus to be the Messiah when he first received his call, and now confessed him to be the Messiah a year or more later, the concept "Messiah" must have begun to change its meaning for him. Not long before, he had seen his Master repel the attempt of a band of eager militants, five thousand strong, to make him their king so that he might lead them against the occupying forces of Rome and their creature, Herod Antipas (Jn 6:15). The Messiah as popularly conceived ought surely to have grasped such an opportunity. Some at least of the disciples were disappointed that he refused to do so.

The fact that Peter, even so, was prepared to confess Jesus as the Messiah was evidence that a change had at least begun to take place in his thinking—that he was now coming to understand the term *Messiah* in the light of what Jesus actually was and did, rather than to understand Jesus in the light of ideas traditionally associated with the term *Messiah*. Hence the pleasure with which Jesus greeted his response; hence the blessing which he pronounced on him. For, like the king in the Jewish parable, Jesus said in effect, "Now at last I can begin to build!"

It is well known that "You are Peter, and on this rock I will build my church" involves a play on words. In Greek "Peter" is *petros* and "rock" is *petra* (the difference being simply that between the masculine termination *-os*, necessary in a man's name, and the feminine termination *-a*). In the Aramaic which Jesus probably spoke, there was not even such a minor grammatical distinction between the two forms: "You are *kēphā*," he said, "and on this *kēphā* I will build my church." The form *kēphā*, as applied to Peter, appears in many New Testament versions as Cephas (for example, in Jn 1:42; 1 Cor 1:12), an alternative form of his name. As a common noun, the Aramaic *kēphā* means "rock"; the Hebrew equivalent *kēp̄* is used in this sense in Job 30:6 and Jeremiah 4:29. In some modern languages the play on words can be exactly reproduced: thus in most editions of the French New Testament Jesus says to Peter, "Tu es *Pierre,* et sur cette *pierre* je bâtirai mon église." But this cannot be done in English; if the play on words is to be brought out, a rendering like that of the NEB has to be adopted: "You are Peter, the Rock; and on this rock I will build my church." Now that someone has been found who is prepared to confess Jesus as what he really is, and not try to fit him into some inherited framework, a start can be made with forming the community of true disciples who will carry on Jesus' mission after his departure.

Peter personally might be thought too unstable to provide such a foundation, but it is not Peter for what he is in himself but Peter the confessor of Jesus who provides it. In that building every other confessor of Jesus finds a place. What matters is not the stature of the confessor but the truth of the confession. Where Jesus is confessed as the Messiah or (as Matthew amplifies the wording) as "the Christ, the Son of the God," there his church exists. It is in the one who is thus confessed, and not in any durable quality of its own, that the church's security and survival rest. While it maintains that confession, the gates of the prison-house of Hades (that is, death) will never close on it.

And what about the "keys of the kingdom"? The keys of a royal or noble establishment were entrusted to the chief steward or major domo; he carried them on his shoulder in earlier times, and there they served as a badge of the authority entrusted to him. About 700 B.C. an oracle from God announced that this authority in the royal palace in Jerusalem was to be conferred on a man called Eliakim: "I will place on his shoulder the key to the house of David; what he opens no one can shut, and what he shuts no one can open" (Is 22:22). So in the new community that Jesus was about to build, Peter would be, so to speak, chief steward. In the early chapters of Acts Peter is seen exercising this responsibility in the primitive church. He acts as chairman of the group of disciples in Jerusalem even before the coming of the Spirit at the first Christian Pentecost (Acts 1:15-26); on the day of Pentecost it is he who preaches the gospel so effectively that three thousand hearers believe the message and are incorporated in the church (Acts 2:41); some time later it is he who first preaches the gospel to a Gentile audience and thus "opens a door of faith" to Gentiles as well as Jews (Acts 10:34-38). Both in Jerusalem at Pentecost and in the house of Cornelius at Caesarea, what Peter does on earth is ratified in heaven by the bestowal of the Holy Spirit on his converts. This divine confirmation was specially important in his approach to Gentiles. As Peter put it himself, "God, who knows the heart, showed that he accepted them by giving the Holy Spirit to them, just as he did to us. He made no distinction between us and them, for he purified their hearts by faith" (Acts 15:8-9).

"Binding" and "loosing" were idiomatic expressions in rabbinical Judaism to denote the promulgation of rulings either forbidding or authorizing various kinds of activity. The authority to bind or loose given to Peter in the present context is given to the disciples as a body in Matthew 18:18, in a saying of Jesus similarly preserved by this Evangelist only. Again, the record of Acts provides an illustration. Where church discipline is in view, Peter's verbal rebuke of Ananias and Sapphira received drastic ratification from heaven (Acts 5:1-11). And Paul for his part, though he was not one of the disciples present when Jesus pronounced these words of authorization, expects that when judgment is pronounced by the church of Corinth on a man who has brought the Christian name into public disrepute, "and I am with you in spirit, and the power of our Lord Jesus is present," the judgment will be given practical effect by God (1 Cor 5:3-5). Again, when "the apostles and the elders" came together in Jerusalem to consider the conditions on which Gentile believers might be recognized as fellow members of the church, their decision was issued as something which "seemed good to the Holy Spirit and to us" (Acts 15:28). Here, then, Luke may be held to provide a commentary on Matthew's record by showing how, in pursuance of Jesus' words, the keys of the kingdom were used and the power of binding and loosing was exercised in the primitive church in preaching, discipline and legislation.

This may be added. The words in which Peter is singled out for special commendation and authority were probably handed down in a community where Peter's name was specially esteemed. The church of Antioch in Syria was one such community. There are other reasons for envisaging a fairly close association between the church of Antioch and the Gospel of Matthew, and it may well have been from material about Peter preserved at Antioch that Matthew derived these words which he incorporates into his account of what Jesus said at Caesarea Philippi.

---

[1]*Yalqut Shim'ni* (medieval compilation) 1.766.

16:28 What Is This Coming?

See comment on MARK 9:1.

17:20 Faith Moves Mountains?

See comment on MARK 11:23.

18:8-9 Pluck Out Your Eye?

See comment on MATTHEW 5:29.

18:10 Guardian Angels?

See comment on ACTS 12:15.

18:35 No Forgiveness for the Unforgiving?

This is a very hard saying. The *so* which introduces it refers to the severe punishment which the king in a parable inflicted on an unforgiving servant of his. The parable arises out of a conversation between Jesus and Peter. Jesus repeatedly impressed on his disciples the necessity of forgiveness; they were not to harbor resentment, but to freely forgive those who injured them. "Yes, but how often?" Peter asked. "Seven times?"—and probably he thought that that was about the limit of reasonable forbearance. "Not seven times," said Jesus, "but seventy times seven" [RSV] (or in NIV, "seventy-seven times"). Perhaps by the time one had forgiven for the seventy-times-seventh time, forgiveness would have become second nature!

Some commentators have seen an allusion here to the war song of Lamech in Genesis 4:24. Lamech was a descendant of Cain, who (surprisingly, it may be thought) was taken under God's protection. "If any one slays Cain," said God, "vengeance shall be taken on him sevenfold" (RSV). Lamech boasted in his war song that no one would injure him and get away with it: "If Cain is avenged sevenfold, truly Lamech seventy-sevenfold" [RSV] (or perhaps "seventy times sevenfold"). Over against seventy-times-sevenfold vengeance Jesus sets, as the target for his followers, seventy-times-sevenfold forgiveness.

The gospel is a message of forgiveness. It could not be otherwise, because it is the gospel of God, and God is a forgiving God. "Who is a God like you, who pardons sin?" said one Hebrew prophet (Mic 7:18). "I knew," said another (protesting against God's proneness to forgive those who, he thought, did not deserve forgiveness), "that you are a gracious and compassionate God, slow to anger and abounding in love"

(Jon 4:2). It is to be expected, then, that those who receive the forgiveness that God holds out in the gospel, those who call him their Father, will display something of his character and show a forgiving attitude to others. If they do not, what then?

What then? Jesus answers this question in the parable of the unforgiving servant, which he told to confirm his words to Peter about repeated forgiveness "until seventy times seven." A king, said Jesus, decided to settle accounts with his servants, and found that one of them (who must have been a very high officer of state) had incurred debts to the royal exchequer which ran into millions. The king was about to deal with him as an Eastern potentate might be expected to do, when the man fell at his feet, begged for mercy and promised that, if the king would be patient with him, he would make full repayment. The king knew perfectly well that he could never repay such a debt, but he felt sorry for him and remitted the debt. Then the man found someone else in the royal service who was in debt to him personally—a debt that was minute by comparison. He demanded prompt repayment, and when this debtor asked for time to pay he refused and had him consigned to the debtors' prison. The king got to hear of it, summoned the man whom he had pardoned back into his presence, revoked the pardon and treated him as he had treated the other: "In anger his master turned him over to the jailers to be tortured, until he should pay back all he owed." "So," said Jesus, "in this way my heavenly Father will deal with any one of you if you do not forgive your brother (or sister) from your heart." Revoke a pardon once granted? God would not do a thing like that, surely? Jesus said he would. A hard saying indeed!

That this emphasis on the necessity of having a forgiving spirit had a central place in the teaching of Jesus is evident from the fact that it is enshrined in both versions of the Lord's Prayer. In Luke 11:4 the disciples are told to pray, "Forgive us our sins, for we ourselves forgive every one who is indebted to us" (RSV). It is difficult to believe that anyone could utter this prayer deliberately, knowing at the same time that he or she cherished an unforgiving spirit toward someone else. In the Aramaic language which Jesus spoke the word for "sin" is the same as the word for "debt"; hence "every one who is indebted to us" means "everyone who has sinned against us" (NIV). In the parallel petition of Matthew 6:12 this use of "debt" in the sense of "sin" occurs twice: "Forgive us our debts, as we also have forgiven our debtors" (RSV) means "Forgive us our sins, as we for our part have forgiven those who have sinned against us." This wording implies that the person praying has already forgiven any injury received; otherwise it would be impossible honestly to ask God's forgiveness for one's own sins. Immediately after Matthew's version of the prayer this is emphasized again: "For if you forgive men their trespasses, your heavenly Father also will forgive you; but if you do not forgive men their trespasses, neither will your Father forgive your trespasses" (Mt 6:14-15).

The meaning is unambiguous, and it is unwise to try to avoid its uncomfortable challenge. One well-known annotated edition of the Bible had a comment on the clause "as we forgive our debtors" that ran as follows: "This is legal ground. Cf. Eph. 4.32, which is grace. Under law forgiveness is conditioned upon the spirit in us; under grace we are forgiven for Christ's sake and exhorted to forgive because we have been forgiven."[1] But forgiveness is neither given nor received on "legal ground"; it is always a matter of grace. What Paul says in Ephesians 4:32 is this: "Be kind and compassionate to one another, forgiving each other, just as in Christ God forgave you." But if some of those to whom this admonition was addressed (and it is addressed to all Christians at all times) should persist in an unforgiving attitude toward others, could they even so enjoy the assurance of God's forgiveness? If Jesus' teaching means what it says, they could not.

Jesus told another parable about two debtors to illustrate another aspect of forgiveness. This was in the house of Simon the Pharisee, who neglected to pay him the courtesies normally shown to a guest, whereas the woman who ventured in from the street lavished her grateful affection on him by wetting his feet with her tears (Lk 7:36-50). The point of the parable was that one who has been forgiven a great debt will respond with great love, whereas no great response will be made by one whose sense of having been forgiven is minimal. (It might be objected that the man who had been forgiven a colossal debt in the parable in Mt 18:23-35 showed little love in return, but the two parables are addressed to two different situations, and forgiveness and love are not subject to cast-iron rules of inevitable necessity.) Where there is a genuine response of love, there will be a forgiving spirit, and where there is a forgiving spirit, there will be a still greater appreciation of God's forgiving mercy, and still greater love in consequence. Some commentators find difficulty with Jesus' words about the woman: "Her sins, which are many, are forgiven; for she loved much" (RSV); the logic of the parable would suggest "She loves much, for her sins have been forgiven." But if that had been the meaning, that is what would have been said. Love and forgiveness set up a chain reaction: the more forgiveness, the more love; the more love, the more forgiveness.

See also comment on LUKE 7:47.

[1] *The Scofield Reference Bible,* 2nd ed. (Oxford: Oxford University Press, 1917), p. 1002. The sharpness of the antithesis is modified in *The New Scofield Reference Bible* (Oxford: Oxford University Press, 1967), p. 1000.

19:9 No Divorce and Remarriage?

See comment on MARK 10:11-12.

19:12 Eunuchs for the Kingdom's Sake?

This saying occurs in Matthew's Gospel only; it comes immediately after his version of the saying about marriage and divorce. When their Master ruled out the possibility of their getting rid of their wives by divorce, the disciples suggested that, in that case, it was better not to marry. To this he replied, "Not all men can receive this precept, but only those to whom it is given" (Mt 19:11 RSV). This means that the only ones who can successfully live a celibate life are those who have received the gift of celibacy. This context shown how the following reference to eunuchs is to be understood; it certainly shows how Matthew understood it.

The saying, as reproduced by Matthew, consists of three parts. The first two present no problem. Some men are born eunuchs, and as for being "made eunuchs by men," that was no unfamiliar practice in the ancient Near East. The hard saying is the third part: what is meant by making oneself a eunuch "for the sake of the kingdom of heaven" (RSV)?

It is reported that one eminent scholar in the early church, Origen of Alexandria (A.D. 185-254), took these words with literal seriousness in the impetuousness of youth, and performed the appropriate operation on himself.[1] In later life he knew better; in his commentary on Matthew's Gospel he rejects the literal interpretation of the words, while acknowledging that he once accepted it, and says that they should be understood spiritually and not "according to the flesh and the letter."

What then did Jesus mean? These words are no more to be taken literally than his words about cutting off the hand or foot or gouging out the eye that leads one into sin. In the Jewish culture in which he lived and taught, marriage was the accepted norm and celibacy was not held in the high esteem which it later came to enjoy in many parts of the church. That men such as John the Baptist and Christ himself should deny themselves the comforts of marriage and family life may well have aroused comment, and here is Jesus' answer to unspoken questions. Some men and women have abstained from marriage in order to devote themselves more wholeheartedly to the cause of the kingdom of heaven. The man who marries and brings up a family incurs special responsibilities for his wife and children; they have a major claim on his attention. Jesus indicated his attitude toward the ties of the family into which he was born when he said that anyone who did the will of God was his brother, sister or mother (Mk 3:35). It was people like these—those who had taken on themselves the yoke of the kingdom he proclaimed—who constituted his true family. To incur the more restricted obligations that marriage and the rearing of children involved would have limited his dediction to the ministry to which he knew himself called.

At the same time, Jesus made it plain that only a minority among his followers could "receive" this course: for most of them marriage and family life should be the norm.

Twenty-five years later the same teaching was repeated in different language by Paul. Paul himself found the celibate way of life congenial, but he knew that the consequences would be disastrous if those who were not called to it tried to follow it. Hence his advice for the majority of his converts was that "each man should have his own wife, and each woman her own husband"—for, as he went on to say, "each man has his own gift from God; one has this gift, another has that" (1 Cor 7:2, 7). Those whom God called to the celibate life would receive from him the "gift" of celibacy—of making themselves "eunuchs for the sake of the kingdom of heaven" (RSV).

---

[1]Eusebius *Ecclesiastical History* 6.8.2.

19:17 Why Do You Ask Me About What Is Good?

See comment on MARK 10:18.

19:21 Sell Your Possessions?

See comment on MARK 10:21.

19:24 Easier for a Camel?

See comment on MARK 10:25.

19:30 The First Will Be Last?

See comment on MARK 10:31.

20:14-15 The Rate for the Job?

One of the complaints that right-living and religious people made about Jesus arose from his treatment of the more disreputable members of society. They might have agreed that such persons should not be entirely excluded from the mercy of the all-loving God. Even for them there was hope, if they showed by practical repentance and unquestionable amendment of life that they were not beyond redemption. But not until such evidence had been given could they begin to be accepted as friends and neighbors.

Jesus, however, accepted them immediately; he did not wait to see the outcome before he committed himself to them. This was disturbing; it was even more disturbing that he seemed to think more highly of them than of those who had never blotted their public copybook. He gave the impression that he actually preferred the company of the rejects of society; he not only made them feel at home in his company, so that they felt free to take liberties with him that they would never have thought of taking with an ordinary rabbi, but even accepted invitations to share a meal with them and appeared genuinely to enjoy such an occasion. When he was challenged for this unconventional behavior, his reply was that this was how God treated sinners; and he told several parables to reinforce this lesson.

One of these parables tells of the man who hired a number of casual laborers to gather the grapes in his vineyard when the appropriate time of year came round. It is a disconcerting parable on more levels than one because it seems to defend the unacceptable principle of equal pay for unequal work.

There are certain seasons when a farmer or a vinegrower requires a large supply of labor for a short period. In the economic depression from which most of Palestine suffered in the time of Jesus, anyone who wanted such a short-term supply of labor was sure of finding it. The vinegrower in the parable had only to go to the village marketplace and there he would find a number of unemployed men hanging around in hope that someone would come and offer them a job.

At daybreak, then, this vinegrower went to the marketplace and hired several men to do a day's work for him gathering grapes. The agreed rate for such a day's work was a denarius, which was evidently sufficient to keep a laborer and family at subsistence level for a day. Apparently the vinegrower wanted the job completed within one day. As he considered the amount of work to be done and the speed at which the men were working, he decided that he would need more hands, so at three-hour intervals he went and hired more. He did not bargain with them for a denarius or part of a denarius: he promised to give them what was proper. Then, just an hour before sunset, in order to ensure that the work would not be left unfinished, he went back and found a few men still unemployed, so he sent them to join the others working in the vineyard.

An hour later the work was finished, and the workers lined up to receive their pay, the last-hired being at the front of the line. They had no idea what they would get for an hour's work; in fact, each of them received a denarius. So did the men who had worked three hours, six hours and nine hours. At last came those who had been hired at daybreak and had done twelve hours' work. What would they get? Each of them similarly got a denarius. They complained, "Why should these others get as much as we have done? Why should not we get more after a hard day's work?" But the vinegrower told them that they had no cause for complaint. They had agreed to do a day's work for a denarius, and he had kept his promise to give them that. It was no business of theirs what he gave to others who had entered into no agreement with him for a fixed sum. He might have said, "They and their families have to live." But he did not; he simply said, "Can't I do what I like with my own money?"

The law-abiding people whom Jesus knew tended to feel that they had made a bargain with God: if they kept his commandments, he would give them the blessings promised to those who did so. They would have no reason to complain if God treated them fairly and kept his promises. But what about those others who had broken his commandments, who had started to do his will late in the day after their encounter with Jesus and the way of the kingdom? They were in no position to strike a bargain with God; they could do nothing but cast themselves on his grace, like the tax collector in another parable who could only say, "God, have mercy on me, a sinner" (Lk 18:13). What could they expect? The lesson of the parable seems to be this: when people make a bargain with God, he will honor his promise and give them no cause for complaint; but there is no limit to what his grace will do for those who have no claim at all on him but trust entirely to his goodness. If it be said that this gives them an unfair advantage, let it be considered that they were terribly disadvantaged to begin with. If it be urged that their rehabilitation should involve some payment for their past misdeeds, the truth may be that they have paid enough already. Should those who have turned to God at the eleventh hour and given him only the last twelfth of life get as much of heaven as those who have given him a whole lifetime? If God is pleased to give them as much, who will tell him that he should not? If God did not delight in mercy, it would go hard with the best of us.

> Though justice by thy plea,
> consider this,
> That, in the course of justice,
> none of us
> Should see salvation.[1]

The first arrivals might not have complained if the last comers had been paid only a small fraction of what they themselves received. There was in fact, as T. W. Manson points out in his treatment of this parable, a coin worth one-twelfth of a denarius: "It was called a *pondion.* But there is no such thing as a twelfth part of the love of God."[2]

---

[1]Shakespeare, *The Merchant of Venice,* IV, i.

[2]T. W. Manson, *The Sayings of Jesus* (reprint; Grand Rapids, Mich.: Eerdmans, 1979), p. 220.

20:16 The First Will Be Last?

See comment on MARK 10:31.

20:20 Who Asked for the Seats of Honor?

See comment on MARK 10:35.

20:30 Two Blind Men or One?

See comment on MATTHEW 8:28-34.

21:2 How Many Donkeys?

See comment on LUKE 19:30.

21:19 Why Was the Fig Tree Cursed?

See comment on MARK 11:14.

21:21 Faith Moves Mountains?

See comment on MARK 11:23.

21:27 Neither Will I Tell You?

See comment on LUKE 20:8.

22:12 What Is the Wedding Garment?

The incident of the man who had no wedding garment is attached in Matthew's Gospel to the parable of the wedding feast (Mt 22:1-14). The parable of the wedding feast has a parallel in the parable of the great banquet in Luke 14:16-24. There are differences of detail between the two parables, but the main outline of the story is the same: the host (a king, in Matthew's version) invites many guests, but on the day of the feast they excuse themselves for various reasons. But all the preparations have been made: the food (and plenty of it) is waiting to be eaten. The host therefore sends his servants out into the streets and lanes to round up those whom they find there and bring them to the banqueting hall. All the empty places are filled, and filled by people who are only too glad to be given a square meal. They do full justice to what has been provided, even if those who were originally invited are not interested.

This is readily understood as a parable of Jesus' proclamation of the kingdom of God. The religious people, those who attended synagogue regularly, were not really interested in what he had to say and despised the good news which he brought. But the outcasts of society recognized his message as just what they had been waiting for. The blessings of the gospel, the Father's loving forgiveness, exactly suited their need, and they eagerly seized what Jesus had to give.

But the wedding garment presents a problem. How could people who had been swept in from the streets be expected to have suitable clothes for a festive occasion? One man was asked how he got in without a wedding garment, but they might all have been expected to be similarly unprovided with suitable attire. It would have been more surprising if one of them had come in actually wearing a wedding garment. It may be suggested that the royal host thoughtfully provided them with suitable clothes, but this is not said in the parable, and the implication is that the man who was improperly dressed could have come properly clad. When taxed with his failure he had no excuse: he was "speechless."

It is most probable that this was originally a separate parable. If the host was a king, he would expect those whom he invited to a banquet to honor him by coming appropriately dressed; failure in this respect would be a studied insult to him. The culprit in this case might count himself fortunate if nothing worse befell him than to be trussed up and thrown out into the darkness, to grind his teeth in annoyance with himself for having been so foolish. The requirement of a wedding garment, unsuitable for people peremptorily conscripted from the streets to come and enjoy a free supper, was eminently suitable for the guests whom a king or magnate would normally invite to dine with him. What then is the point of the garment in the parable, if it was originally a parable on its own? Clothes are not infrequently used in the Bible as a symbol of personal character, and it is possibly implied that some might think themselves entitled to be counted among the "children of the kingdom" or the followers of Jesus whose character was out of keeping with such a profession. If so, then the parable of the wedding garment would be a warning against false discipleship; it is not saying "Lord, Lord" that admits one to the kingdom, but doing the heavenly Father's will (Mt 7:21).

22:14 Many Are Called, But Few Are Chosen?

In the original text of the Gospels, these words appear once—as a comment on Matthew's parable of the marriage feast. In the course of transmission of the text it came to be attached to the parable of the laborers in the vineyard also (Mt 20:16), where it appears, for example, in the KJV, but it is not really relevant there.

In form this seems to be a proverbial saying; other sayings with the same construction are found elsewhere in ancient literature. Plato quotes one with reference to the mystery religions: "Many are the wand-bearers, but few are the initiates"[1]; that is to say, there are many who walk in the procession to the cult-center carrying sacred wands, but only a few are admitted to the knowledge of the innermost secret (which confers the prize of immortality). Two sayings with this construction are ascribed to Jesus or his disciples in the second-century *Gospel of Thomas.* In Saying 74 one of the disciples says to him, "Lord, there are many around the opening but no one in the well." (The well is the well of truth; many approach it without getting into it. In this form the saying has a Gnostic flavor; in fact, Celsus, an anti-Christian writer of the second century, quotes it from a Gnostic treatise called the *Heavenly Dialogue.*)[2] Jesus' reply to the disciple is given in Saying 75: "Many stand outside at the door, but it is only the single ones who enter the bridal chamber." (In Gnostic terminology the bridal chamber is the place where the soul is reunited with its proper element, and the "single ones" are those who have transcended the distinctions of age and sex. Hence Saying 49 makes Jesus say, "Happy are the single and the chosen ones, for you will find the kingdom.")

The Gnostic ideas of the *Gospel of Thomas* will give us no help in understanding the saying as it appears at the end of the parable of the wedding feast. There the "called" are those who were invited to the wedding feast; the "chosen" are those who accepted the invitation. The king invited many guests to the feast, but only a few, if any, of those who were invited actually came to it. The feast is a parable of the gospel and the blessings which it holds out to believers. The invitation to believe the gospel and enjoy its blessings goes out to all who hear it. But if all receive the call, not all respond to it. Those who do respond show by that very fact they are "chosen." Protestant theologians used to distinguish between the "common call," addressed to all who hear the gospel, and the "effectual call," received by those who actually respond. In part two of Bunyan's *Pilgrim's Progress* Christiana and her family are taught this lesson in the Interpreter's house by means of a hen and her chickens: "She had a common call, and that she hath all day long. She had a special call, and that she had but sometimes." The only way in which the effectual call can be distinguished from the common call is that those who hear it respond to it. "Effectual calling is the work of God's Spirit, whereby, convincing us of our sin and misery, enlightening our minds in the knowledge of Christ, and renewing our wills, he doth persuade and enable us to embrace Jesus Christ, freely offered to us in the gospel."[3]

Paul insists that "it is not the hearers of the law who are righteous before God, but the doers of the law who will be justified" (Rom 2:13 RSV), and it is those who live "according to the Spirit" in whom "the just requirement of the law" is fulfilled. James, to the same effect, urges his readers to "be doers of the word, and not hearers only" (Jas 1:22 RSV).

The Gnostic teachers whose ideas are reflected in the *Gospel of Thomas* rather liked the idea that "the single and the chosen ones" were a small minority, provided they themselves were included in that elite number. On one occasion the disciples tried to make Jesus commit himself on the relative number of the called and the chosen, asking, "Lord, are only a few people going to be saved?" (Lk 13:23). But he refused to gratify their curiosity; he simply told them to make sure that they themselves entered in through the narrow gate, "for many, I tell you, will try to enter and will not be able to" (RSV).

It has frequently been taken for granted that Jesus' words about the relative fewness of the saved had reference not only to the period of his ministry but to all time. Enoch Powell has interpreted Jesus' words "few are chosen" as an assertion "that his salvation will not be for all, not even for the majority," and has insisted that "ignorance, incapacity, perversity, the sheer human propensity to error are sufficient to ensure a high failure rate."[4] They are sufficient, indeed, to ensure a 100-percent failure rate, but for the grace of God. But when divine grace begins to operate, the situation is transformed.

It may well be that Jesus was speaking more particularly of the situation during his ministry when he spoke of the few and the many. Even the casual reader of the New Testament gathers that there was a great and rapid increase in the number of his followers after his death and resurrection. Within a few months from his crucifixion, the number of his followers in Palestine was ten times as great as it had been during his ministry. And Paul, the greatest theologian of primitive Christianity, speaks of those who receive the saving benefit of the work of Jesus as "the many" (Rom 5:15, 19). No reasonable interpretation can make "the many" mean a minority, for, as John Calvin put it in his commentary on those words of Paul, "if Adam's fall had the effect of producing the ruin of many, the grace of God is much more efficacious in benefiting many, since admittedly Christ is much more powerful to save than Adam was to ruin."[5]

---

[1]Plato *Phaedo* 69 c.

[2]Origen *Against Celsus* 8.16.

[3]*Westminster Shorter Catechism,* Answer to Question 31.

[4]J. E. Powell, "Quicunque Vult," in *Sermons from Great St. Mary's,* ed. H. W. Montefiore (London: Fontana, 1968), p. 96.

[5]J. Calvin, *Romans and Thessalonians,* English translation (Edinburgh: St. Andrew's, 1961), pp. 114-15.

22:21 Render to Caesar?

See comment on MARK 12:17.

23:9 Call No Man Father?

In his criticism of the scribes, contained in the discourse of Matthew 23, Jesus speaks disapprovingly of their liking for honorary titles: "They love to be greeted in the marketplaces, and to have men call them 'Rabbi' " (Mt 23:7). Then he turns to his disciples and tells them not to be like that: "You are not to be called 'Rabbi,' for you have only one Master and you are all brothers" (Mt 23:8). "Rabbi" was a term of respect given by a Jewish disciple to his teacher, and a well-known teacher would be known to the public as Rabbi So-and-so. Jesus was called "rabbi" by his disciples and by others; it was given to him as a mark of courtesy or respect. For Matthew, however, the word "rabbi" has a dubious connotation: in his Gospel the only disciple who calls Jesus "rabbi" is Judas Iscariot, and he does so twice: once at the supper table, when he responds to Jesus' announcement of the presence of a traitor in the company with "Surely not I, rabbi?" (Mt 26:25), and once in Gethsemane, where the "Greetings, rabbi!" which accompanies his kiss is the sign to the temple police that Jesus is the person to arrest (Mt 26:49). This attitude to the term "rabbi" may throw some light on the setting in which Matthew worked and the polemics in which he was engaged.

So, said Jesus to his disciples, refuse all courtesy titles: you have one teacher, and you are all members of one family. Members of a family do not address one another by formal titles, even if some of them indicate high distinction. When John Smith is knighted, his brothers, who have hitherto called him "John," do not begin to address him to his face as "Sir John," although others may properly do so. To them he is still John.

But what about calling no man father? Did Jesus mean that his followers ought not to address their fathers in a way that acknowledged their special relationship? It could be thought that he did mean just that, in view of the fact that he is never recorded as calling Mary "mother." But this is unlikely; he is speaking of the use of honorific titles among his disciples. It is equally unlikely that he meant "Call no man 'Abba' but God alone." For one thing, Matthew's Greek-speaking readers would not naturally take the saying to mean this; for another thing, the whole point of calling God "Abba" was that this was the ordinary domestic word by which the father was called in the family, and to reserve "Abba" as a designation for God alone would do away with its significance (see comment on Mt 11:27). But Jesus' meaning could very well have been: In the spiritual sense God alone is your Father; do not give to others the designation which, in that sense, belongs exclusively to him. Jesus was his disciples' teacher, and they called him "Teacher," but they never called him "Father"; that was his designation for God.

But did not Paul speak of himself as his converts' father, since, as he said, he had become their "father in Christ Jesus through the gospel" (1 Cor 4:15 RSV)? He did, but he was using a spiritual analogy, not claiming a title. Well, in insisting on his authority as an "apostle of Christ Jesus," was he not infringing at least the spirit of Jesus' admonition? No, for again he was not claiming a title but stating a fact; he was indeed commissioned and sent by the risen Lord, and from that was derived the authority with which he spoke. Similarly, if someone is doing the work of a bishop (say) or pastor, then to call him "Bishop So-and-so" or "Pastor So-and-so" simply recognizes the ministry which he is discharging.

Some Christians have interpreted these words of Jesus so literally that they would refrain from the use even of the very democratic "Mister," perhaps because of its derivation from "Master," either using no handle at all or preferring something reciprocal like "Friend" or "Brother." Others, considering (probably rightly) that it is the use of honorific titles in religious life that is deprecated by Jesus, would refuse the designation "The Reverend" to a minister, replacing it by "Mister" (which is perfectly proper) or (in writing) putting it between brackets (which is foolish) or even between quotation marks (which is offensive). But, as with so many of Jesus' injunctions, this one can be carried out in a stilted or pettifogging way which destroys the spirit of his teaching. If the local Catholic priest is known throughout the community as Father Jones, I am simply being silly if I persist in calling him something else. If I stop to think what is meant by my calling him Father Jones, I shall probably conclude that he is not my father in any sense but that he is no doubt a real father in God to his own congregation. "Father" in this sense is synonymous with "Pastor"; the former views the congregation as a family, the latter as a flock of sheep.

When a new bishop arrived in a certain English diocese a few years ago, he quickly let it be known that he did not wish to be addressed as "my lord." That, it may be suggested, was a genuine compliance with the spirit of these words of Jesus.

23:33 You Brood of Vipers!

The chapter in Matthew's Gospel from which this saying is quoted presents a series of woes pronounced against the scribes and Pharisees—or perhaps we should say laments uttered over them. The series may be regarded as an expansion of Mark 12:38-40, where the people who listened to Jesus as he taught in the temple precincts in Jerusalem during Holy Week were warned against "the teachers of the law [who] like to walk around in flowing robes and to be greeted in the marketplaces, and have the most important seats in the synagogues and the places of honor at banquets. They devour widows' houses and for a show make lengthy prayers. Such men will be punished most severely."

Most of the scribes (NIV "teachers of the law")—certainly most of those who appear in the Gospels—belonged to the party of the Pharisees. The Pharisees traced their spiritual lineage back to the pious groups which, in the days of the Maccabees, resisted all temptations to assimilate their faith and practice to pagan ways, and suffered martyrdom rather than betray their religious heritage. In the first century A.D. they are reckoned to have numbered about six thousand. They banded themselves together in fellowships or brotherhoods, encouraging one another in the defense and practice of the law. The law included not only the written precepts of the Old Testament but the interpretation and application of those precepts—what Mark describes as "the tradition of the elders" (Mk 7:3). They were greatly concerned about ceremonial purity. This concern forbade them to have social contact with Gentiles, or even with fellow Jews who were not so particular about the laws of purity as they themselves were. They attached high importance to the tithing of crops (that is, paying 10 percent of the proceeds of harvest into the temple treasury)—not only of grain, wine and olive oil but of garden herbs as well. They would not willingly eat food, whether in their own houses or in other people's, unless they could be sure that the tithe had been paid on it.

From their viewpoint, they could not help looking on Jesus as dangerously lax, whether in the sovereign freedom with which he disposed of the sabbath law and the food laws or in his readiness to consort with the most questionable persons and actually sit down to a meal with them. It was inevitable that he and they should clash; their conflict, indeed, illustrates the saying about the second-best being the worst enemy of the best.

The Pharisaic way of life lent itself to imitation by people who had no worthier motive than the gaining of a popular reputation for piety. The rabbinical traditions illustrate this fact: seven types of Pharisee are enumerated, and only one of these, the Pharisee who is one for the love of God, receives unqualified commendation.[1] The New Testament picture of the Pharisees is generally an unfavorable one, but more so in the Gospels than in Acts. In Acts they are depicted as not unfriendly to the observant Jewish Christians of Jerusalem; the two groups had this in common (by contrast with the Sadducees): they believed in the resurrection of the dead.

The gathering together of the woes or laments regarding the Pharisees in Matthew 23 probably reflects the situation in which this Gospel was written, later in the first century, when the Pharisees and the Jewish Christians were engaged in polemical controversy with one another. That provided an opportunity to collect from all quarters criticisms Jesus had voiced against the Pharisees and to weave them together into a continuous speech, with its refrain (as commonly translated) "Woe to you, teachers of the law and Pharisees, you hypocrites!" Pharisees as such were not hypocrites, and Jesus did not say that they were; he was not the one to bear false witness against his neighbor. *Hypocrite* in New Testament usage means "play-actor"; it denotes the sort of person who plays a part which is simply assumed for the occasion and does not express his real self. The "hypocrites" in this repeated denunciation, then, are those who play at being scribes and Pharisees, who "preach but do not practice" (Mt 23:3 RSV), who assume the actions and words characteristic of scribes and Pharisees without being motivated by true love of God. The genuine Pharisee might disapprove of much that Jesus said and did, but if he was a genuine Pharisee, he was no play-actor. So we might render the recurring refrain of Matthew 23 as "Alas for you, hypocritical scribes and Pharisees!"—alas for you, because you are incurring a fearful judgment on yourselves.

But what about the "brood of vipers"? This expression was used by John the Baptist as he saw the crowds coming to listen to his proclamation of judgment and his call to repentance: "You brood of vipers! Who warned you to flee from the coming wrath?" (Lk 3:7). He compared them to snakes making their way as quickly as possible out of range of an oncoming grass fire. In Matthew 3:7 John directs these words to Pharisees and Sadducees among his hearers. Jesus' use of the same figure may convey a warning that those who pay no heed to impending doom cannot escape "the judgment of Gehenna" (to render it literally). And if it is asked how they had incurred this judgment without being aware of it, the answer suggested by Matthew's context would be that by their unreality they were hindering, not helping, others in following the way of righteousness. (In Mt 12:34 those who charged Jesus with casting out demons by the power of Beelzebul—see comment on Mk 3:28-29—are similarly addressed as "You brood of vipers!")

Finally, Matthew himself apparently indicates that this hard saying, with its context, should be understood as lamentation rather than unmitigated denunciation. For at the end of the discourse, after the statement that the martyr-blood of all generations would be required from that generation (see comment on Mk 13:30), Matthew places the lament over Jerusalem ("O Jerusalem, Jerusalem . . .") which Luke introduces at an earlier point in Jesus' ministry. It is easy to see why Luke introduces it where he does: Jesus has been warned in Galilee that Herod Antipas wants to kill him, and he replies that that cannot be, since Jerusalem is the proper place for a prophet to be put to death (Lk 13:31-33). Then comes "O Jerusalem, Jerusalem, killing the prophets . . ." (Lk 13:34-35 RSV). Actually, the lament would be chronologically appropriate if it were uttered at the end of Jesus' last visit to Jerusalem before the final one, for it ends with the words "You will not see me again until you say, 'Blessed is he who comes in the name of the Lord' " (Lk 13:35; Mt 23:39). This may simply mean, "You will not see me until festival time." (T. W. Manson compares two people parting today and saying, "Next time we meet we shall be singing 'O come, all ye faithful,' " that is, "Next time we meet will be Christmas.")[2] But Luke and Matthew place the lament in contexts where it is topically appropriate; Matthew in particular, by placing it where he does (Mt 23:37-39), communicates something of the sorrow with which Jesus found it necessary to speak as he did about those who should have been trustworthy guides but in fact were leading their followers to disaster.

[1]Palestinian Talmud, tractate *Berakot*, 9.7.

[2]T. W. Manson, "The Cleansing of the Temple," *Bulletin of the John Rylands Library* 33 (1950-51), p. 279, n. 1. (He, however, accepted the setting of Lk 13:55 as original and supposed that Jesus was bidding temporary farewell to the people of Galilee, saying that they would next see him in Jerusalem.)

24:28 There the Eagles Will Be Gathered Together?

See comment on LUKE 17:37.

24:34 This Generation Will Not Pass Away?

See comment on MARK 13:30.

25:11-12 Why Were the Virgins Shut Out?

The picture of people arriving after the door has been shut and finding it impossible to gain entrance appears elsewhere in the teaching of Jesus. In Luke 13:25-28 Jesus speaks of such people who, seeing themselves shut out, protest to the master of the house, "We ate and drank with you, and you taught in our streets." But even so they are refused admittance; they are excluded from the kingdom of God. Matthew's version of the Sermon on the Mount contains a parallel to that passage in Luke; in Matthew's account those who are shut out produce what might be regarded as even stronger credentials entitling them to admittance: "Did we not prophesy in your name, and in your name drive out demons and perform many miracles?" (Mt 7:22)—but all to no avail.

The memorable setting of the picture, however, is in the parable of the ten virgins, as it is traditionally called. The haunting pathos of the latecomers finding the door closed in their faces was caught and expressed by Tennyson in the song "Late, late, so late! and dark the night and chill!" which was sung to Guinevere by the little maid in the nunnery where the queen had sought sanctuary. True, in the scene from real life depicted in the parable the maidens' disappointment was keen, but they suffered no irreparable loss; they had missed the wedding feast, indeed, but there would be other wedding feasts, and they would remember to take an adequate supply of oil another time. But in the application of the parable the loss is more serious.

The parable is one of three which Matthew appends to his version of Jesus' Olivet discourse—the discourse which has its climax in the glorious coming of the Son of Man.

There was a wedding in the village. A wedding story with no mention of the bride seems very odd to us, but different times and different lands have different customs. Just possibly she does receive a mention, but if so, only in passing; some authorities for the text of Matthew 25:1 say that the ten maidens "went to meet the bridegroom *and the bride.*" The ten maidens do not appear to have been bridesmaids, or even specially invited guests; they were girls of the village who had decided to form a torchlight procession and escort the bridegroom and his party to the house where the wedding feast was to be held. They knew that, if they did so, there would be a place at the feast for them, so that they could share in the good cheer. To this day there are parts of the world where a wedding feast is a public occasion for the neighborhood, and all who come find a welcome and something to eat and drink.

No time was announced for the bridegroom to set out for the feast, and the day wore on. That was all right; a torchlight procession is more impressive in the dark. The "torches" were long poles with oil-lamps tied to the top, and the more provident girls took a supply of olive oil with them in case the lamps went out. As the evening wore on and the bridegroom still not come, one after another dropped off to sleep. However, their lamps were lit, ready for the warning shout. Suddenly the shout came: "Here he is!" They set off to join his party, but as they trimmed the wicks of their lamps, five of them found that their lamps were going out, and they had no extra oil. The others could not lend them any of theirs, for then there would not be enough to last the journey. So the improvident girls had to go and buy some, and that would not be too easy at midnight; yet by persistence they managed at last to get some. But by that time they were too late to join the procession, and when they reached the house, they could not get in. They hammered on the door and shouted to the doorkeeper, "O sir! O sir! please let us in." But all the answer they received was "No; I don't know you." So they had to go back home in the dark, tired and disappointed, because they had not been ready.

The oil was good oil, while it lasted; but the oil that was used yesterday will not keep today's lamps alight. So perhaps we may learn not to depend exclusively on past experiences; they will not be sufficient for the needs of the present. Daily grace must be obtained for daily need. The explicit lesson attached to the parable is "keep awake, then, for you do not know the day or the hour" (Mt 25:13 NEB). Later forms of the text (represented by the KJV) add the words "when the Son of Man comes." Certainly in the context of the parable those words are implied, but the fact that the Evangelist did not include them suggests that the parable has a more general application. Keep awake, because a time of testing may come without warning. Be ready to resist this temptation (whatever form it may take); be ready to meet this crisis; be ready to grasp this opportunity. Somebody needs help; be ready to give it, "for you do not know the day or the hour" when the call may come.

See also comment on LUKE 18:8.

25:26 Salvation by Works?

See comment on JOHN 5:28-29.

26:26-28 This Is My Body and Blood?

See comment on MARK 14:22-24.

26:63-64 You Will See the Son of Man?

See comment on MARK 14:61-62.

27:5 How Did Judas Die?

See comment on ACTS 1:18.

27:9-10 Wrong Prophet?

While commenting on what happened to Judas Iscariot and his blood money, Matthew introduces a reference to the prophets as part of his favorite theme of the fulfillment of Scripture. He clearly cites Jeremiah as the prophet who gave the saying, but the saying itself is from Zechariah 11:12-13. Did Matthew make a mistake?

The quotation is not entirely a quotation of Zechariah. The majority of the quotation does come from Zechariah 11:13, but there is a change from the first person singular ("I") to the third plural ("they"). Furthermore, there is no field mentioned in Zechariah (in fact, in Matthew the NRSV follows the Syriac translation and has "the treasury" instead of "the potter" because Matthew clearly is not quoting Zechariah about the location). Finally, Zechariah does not include the phrase "as the Lord commanded me."

Second, Jeremiah is also involved with potters (Jer 17:1-11; 19:1-13—in this second passage he purchases something from a potter). Furthermore, Jeremiah purchases a field (Jer 32:6-15), although the price is seventeen pieces of silver rather than thirty. Finally, Jeremiah 13:5 has the phrase "as the Lord commanded me" (RSV) (which also has to do with a purchase).

In the first century the Old Testament did not come as a bound volume with chapters and verses. Instead, the work was a series of scrolls. Shorter books were often put together on a single scroll. For example, Zechariah would be part of "The Book of the Twelve," a single scroll containing all twelve minor prophets. There were paragraph divisions, but they were not numbered. It would be after A.D. 1500 before chapter and verse divisions and numbering were introduced. That means that Jesus in Matthew would have cited an Old Testament passage simply by the name of the author.

When it came to interpreting the Old Testament, it was common to bring passages together based on words they had in common (this is the second of Hillel the Elder's seven rules of interpretation). In this case, it is clear that Jeremiah and Zechariah have several words in common, especially *potter* and *shekel.* Probably *potter* is the key term. As even the English reader might suspect from the information above, the quotation in Matthew is really Zechariah mixed with several phrases taken from Jeremiah. Again, we need to remember that while this may not be an acceptable way of citing Scripture today (although it is still done by accident!), it was a perfectly acceptable technique in the Palestine of Matthew's day. (Matthew was probably written in Syria or northern Palestine; he is certainly focused on the Jewish community. Thus he reflects the usage of Scripture in such communities.)

What we have, then, is Matthew pulling together at least two texts in Jeremiah with one text in Zechariah to show that there was a type of biblical prefiguring of Judas's actions, down to the amount of blood money and the fact that it was given to a potter and was used for the purchase of a field. While the logic of this type of exegesis is strange to the modern Western way of thinking, it would have been viewed as quite normal in Matthew's time. Likewise it was normal for Matthew to cite the more important prophet, Jeremiah, despite the fact that most of his material came from Zechariah. Thus judged by first-century standards, Matthew is quite accurate and acceptable in what he does.

27:37 What Was the Crime?

See comment on JOHN 19:19.

27:46 Why Have You Forsaken Me?

See comment on PSALM 22:1; MARK 15:34.

27:53 What Resurrection Happened at the Cross?

First, what does it mean that many holy people were raised to life? Is this a resurrection or simply the appearance of ghosts of some type? Second, why did they wait until after the resurrection to enter "the holy city" (Jerusalem)? Finally, what does this event mean? It sounds like a fantastic detail, a legend which has slipped into the text.

Matthew's version of the crucifixion has a far more triumphant ending than that in Mark. After underlining that Jesus was crucified as the king of the Jews and fulfilled Scripture in his death (so it was part of God's plan), Matthew includes four unique incidents after Jesus' death: (1) the earthquake, (2) the resurrection of the holy people, (3) the setting of the guard at the tomb and (4) the second earthquake before the women arrive at the tomb.

Earthquakes, of course, are relatively well known in Palestine (compare Amos 1:1). The Jordan Valley itself is the result of earthquake activity, and the country has fault lines not unlike those around San Francisco, another earthquake-prone locality. Earthquakes were also part of Jewish belief about the end times (Zech 14:4). The unusual thing in this passage is the timing of the earthquakes, their close association with both the death and the resurrection of Jesus. In each case the earthquakes appear to open tombs. That in itself is not surprising. The tombs of the wealthier people were generally natural caves suitably enlarged or else artificial caves carved into softer rock. Several hillsides around Jerusalem had many of them. The tombs were closed with a rock door which was like a cork worked into the small opening of the cave. An earthquake which moved the rock around it could pop such a door open. So far, however, we only have a natural event with unusual timing, a timing which indicates that God is behind it, but only for those who notice the coincidence.

But it is one thing for an earthquake to open tombs and quite another for the dead in them to come out! Matthew makes it clear that this is a resurrection, for he refers to the "bodies" as having been raised. This is also in line with a typical Jewish view of the afterlife, for they believed that any spirit departed from the dead when the body began to decay. Thus there would be no ghosts or spirits in tombs to come out, only corpses or their ultimate remains, skeletons (the bones of which were gathered and put into stone boxes called ossuaries). Thus Matthew obviously believed that this was a real resurrection, and for him the appearances of these people to others simply provide witnesses to the fact that the bodies were raised. The crucial thing for him is the resurrection of the "holy people" itself.

It was a belief of many of the Jews (and also later of Christians) that the dead would be raised.[1] For the Jews the stress was on the raising of the righteous dead (the "holy people"), for it is they who had a reward coming from God and thus must be raised to receive it. Furthermore, this resurrection was normally associated with the coming of Messiah. At some point in his setting things right and ushering in the age to come, the resurrection of the righteous would take place. The various Jewish groups disagreed on the details, but generally agreed on the overall outline.

Now we can see what Matthew is saying. The Messiah has come, although he was rejected and crucified at the request of the leaders of the people. Yet the King of the Jews died, not as simply some terrible miscarriage of justice, but as part of God's plan as laid down in the Old Testament Scripture. (This is why Matthew underlines the fulfillment of Scripture in the crucifixion narrative.) Now the Messiah is dead, yet God points out that this is not the end of his story, but the beginning of the end of the age, by sending an earthquake and along with the earthquake, a partial resurrection of "many" of the righteous dead buried in the Jerusalem area. It is as if the death of Jesus lets loose a wave of resurrection power that begins to ripple out, starting in Jerusalem.

Why were all of the righteous dead not raised? That is a tension endemic to the Gospels, especially the Synoptic Gospels. Teleologically it is expressed as the tension between the "already" and the "not yet." That is, many sick were healed when Jesus was in Palestine, but not all of the sick were healed. There are stories of Jesus' feeding the hungry, but that does not mean that all the hungry in Palestine were fed. Demons were cast out, but not every demon in Palestine was expelled. We could continue with every aspect of the ministry of Jesus (and later of his apostles and others). The coming age is characterized in both typical Jewish and Christian eschatology by "all." All of the righteous dead are raised, perfect justice reigns, no righteous person is sick, and so forth. When these things are experienced in part now we say that "already" we are experiencing a taste of what will eventually take place fully. When we notice that not everyone was blessed in this way (although we do not hear of Jesus ever turning anyone away), we note that that perfect state is "not yet" come. This is a tension not only of the Gospels, but also of the whole New Testament. Thus it does not surprise us to discover that many of the righteous dead in a certain area are raised, for "already" we experience a taste of the final resurrection, but that "not yet" are all of the dead raised, for Matthew still anticipates the making of disciples from "all nations" (Mt 28:19-20) before the end of this age fully comes.

Thus the righteous dead are raised through the power of the crucifixion, according to Matthew, but they do not go into the city yet. Why would they remain in the tombs? It would be inappropriate for them to precede their leader. (Matthew does not tell us if this is conscious or unconscious, if they knew why they remained in the tombs or if God simply did not empower them to leave.) They wait until his resurrection occurs and then leave the tombs. Of course no one would try to close the tombs again, for during a festival time Jews would avoid the tombs which would have made them ritually impure and thus unable to participate in the festival. Even if someone had noticed the open tombs, it was not something that needed to be done right away. Once Jesus appears in public, the resurrected dead are free to go into the city as a type of corroborating witness. We do not hear that they say anything about Jesus, or even that they know anything about him. Yet they are aware that God has raised them and when this happened, and such a resurrection is a sure sign of the presence of Messiah or, to put it another way, the beginning of the age to come.

The final obvious question is "What happened to these 'holy people' after they 'appeared to many'?" The answer is "We do not know." Since this appears to be the firstfruits of the eventual general resurrection of the righteous, it is unlikely that Matthew thought for a minute that they later returned to their tombs. It is possible that he believed that they were waiting around on earth for the return of Jesus, but it is far more likely that he believed that they went to heaven with Jesus (although Matthew does not have a story of the ascension). The fact is, once their witness function is finished, they are of no more interest to Matthew, for his Gospel is the story of Jesus, not of the righteous dead.

---

[1]Sadducees and perhaps other Jewish groups did not believe in the resurrection of the dead, but Pharisees and Essenes did, and this was probably the belief of the vast majority of the people of the land. All the same, their views of the resurrection varied. We are only giving one common version here.

28:1-8 What Really Happened at the Resurrection?

See comment on JOHN 20:1-8.

MARK

1:2 Wrong Prophet?

After the title verse of the Gospel of Mark we find a quotation that comes from Malachi 3:1, apparently introduced with the phrase "It is written in Isaiah the prophet." Mark seems to have confused his prophets, for the passage is obviously by Malachi, and no duplicate is found in Isaiah. Did Mark make a mistake?

To answer this question we first have to look at the text more carefully. The problem quotation reads, "I will send my messenger ahead of you, who will prepare your way." The next verse reads, "A voice of one calling in the desert, 'Prepare the way for the Lord, make straight paths for him' " (Mk 1:3).

Now we need to look at three Old Testament passages:

> See, I am sending an angel ahead of you to guard you along the way and to bring you to the place I have prepared. (Ex 23:20)
>
> See, I will send you the prophet Elijah before that great and dreadful day of the LORD comes. (Mal 4:5)
>
> A voice of one calling: "In the desert prepare the way for the LORD; make straight in the wilderness a highway for our God." (Is 40:3)

All three of these passages have elements in common. Each of them is preparing for something. The angel in Exodus is to lead the people to the Promised Land. Elijah is to prepare the people for the day of the Lord. The voice in the wilderness is to prepare a way for the coming of God.

Each of them is also a warning. The angel ("my messenger") in Exodus will bring blessing if obeyed, but will not pardon their sins if disobeyed. Elijah in Malachi (the name of the book means "my messenger") will set the families right so that the Lord does not come and "smite the land with a curse." The voice in Isaiah proclaims that every valley will be exalted and every mountain and hill be made low, probably indicating the exaltation of some people and the humbling of others.

Finally, two of the passages specifically mention a "way" for something, either preparing a way for the people or guarding the people in a certain way. "Way" in this case means "road."

What does all this information add up to? Here in the beginning of Mark we have not one passage from the Old Testament but three passages which are brought together because of common words or themes. The title of the person ("my messenger") comes from one Old Testament text, the general function ("I will send . . . who will prepare your way") from another, and the specific character and message ("in the desert" and "prepare the way for the Lord") from a third. When verses are brought together like this as proof texts for a particular point we refer to them as *testimonia* and to the fact that the verses are chained together as a *catena* (Latin for "chain"). Mark has probably not invented this particular *catena* of *testimonia,* for they were often used in the early church, but he has included in his Gospel *testimonia* known in the church.

Now we can see why he appears not to get the reference correct. We look at the nearest obvious quotation following Mark's reference to Isaiah and say, "It is from Malachi." That misses the fact that we have already skipped over a phrase from Exodus. More importantly, that misses the fact that Mark looked at the whole quotation as one unit and that it is the end of the *testimonia* that gives the most details about John the Baptist. This part is from Isaiah.

It is also true that the vast majority of people did not own any of the Scriptures, and most could not read, although literacy was more common among Jews than among the rest of the Greco-Roman world. The people might well recognize the phrases as being from the Scripture which was read in the synagogue, but would not be able to go to their Bibles to look it up. Since he does not expect people to look it up, Mark cites the longest of the two prophetic works in the *testimonia* chain, which is also the most important for his purposes.

Finally, it is also possible that the NIV has mistranslated the passage. In two other places where Mark uses "as it is written" (a more literal translation of the Greek behind the NIV's translation "it is written") the phrase *follows* what it refers to rather than introduces the next quotation. It may well be that Mark is saying that the gospel of Jesus Christ began (Mk 1:1) as it is written in Isaiah. By this he would mean to refer to the whole of the beginning part of the Gospel, Mark 1:1-15, indicating that this fulfilled Isaiah.

What is clear is that Mark had at least three good reasons for saying "Isaiah" rather than "Malachi." When we accuse him of inaccuracy, far from pointing out a reality in Mark, we are exposing our own lack of knowledge about how he and other ancient authors used Scripture. What is more, we are missing the point that Mark is making. The good news about Jesus continues the story of God's work with humans begun in the Old Testament. In fact, the opening of the Gospel fulfills parts of the Old Testament, as the narratives included after the Old Testament quotations show.

See also comment on MATTHEW 27:9-10.

1:4 What Was John's Baptism of Repentance?

The first event to appear in Mark's Gospel is the appearance of John the Baptist preaching "a baptism of repentance for the forgiveness of sins." What is intended by this phrase? How does baptism relate to the forgiveness of sins? Is this related to Christian baptism, or is it not?

There are three terms which are significant in this problem. The first is *baptism,* which simply means to dip or immerse. In Judaism one washed to remove certain types of ritual impurity. This was a repeated baptism. Later, and possibly during the period covered by the New Testament, converts to Judaism (proselytes) were cleansed of their past Gentile impurity and reborn as Jews by a once-for-all proselyte baptism. Finally, there is evidence of both repeated and initiatory baptisms in the Jewish sectarian group that wrote the Dead Sea Scrolls, which fits their character as a group that wanted to maintain the highest level of ritual purity. Mark's Gentile readers could understand these concepts, for in some pagan groups (for example, in the so-called mystery religions) there also were baptisms as initiatory or purificatory rites.

John was identified as "the Baptist" because baptism was so central to his message, and this baptism had the specific meaning of *repentance,* the second important term in this passage. In the Jewish world repentance meant not simply a change of mind (which is what the Greek term means in other contexts), but a change of life or a change of direction in life. Previously the person had not been living according to God's way (thought of as a direction to go in or a road to be walked), but now they have changed their direction and are going in that way. This involves a recognition that the way one is going is the wrong way, that God's way is the right way, and the decision to turn around and change direction. John does not tell us what specific sins or ways of life the people he preached to needed to repent of. Perhaps that is because it was individual to each person. Yet it is clear that he wanted them all going God's way as it was proclaimed by him.

Now one often cannot see immediately if a person's way of life has changed. Decisions do not register on the outside, nor is there an arrow on people showing which way their hearts and minds are headed in. When one makes a decision, however, one can pledge oneself to it by a symbolic act. Naturally such an act carried out before God falsely would bring condemnation, like an unfulfilled vow, so it was not something done lightly. The act which John called for was baptism, a baptism that would be meaningless if the person did not in fact repent inwardly and then bring "forth fruit of repentance" after the baptism.

The reason for changing one's way of life was that the Messiah was coming (Mk 1:7-8); in other words, God was drawing near to his people, which would mean both blessing for the righteous and condemnation for the unrighteous. This brings us to the third term, *forgiveness of sins.* There would be no impetus to baptism if the message were "It is too late. God is coming and all of your sins will be tallied up." One might as well "eat, drink and be merry, for tomorrow we die." Instead, John's message is "If you repent and pledge this through baptism, God will not hold your sins against you." This is also the theme of the Isaiah and Malachi passages quoted by Mark in the preceding verses. If the people repent, then God (or God's Spirit, which may be implied by the fact that Messiah baptizes with Holy Spirit) will remove their sin. That is the result of the baptism.

Thus we have a chain of events. The people accept John's message that God is drawing near and the Messiah is coming. They realize from this message that they need to "clean up their act" and be ready for God's coming. They understand that the way to do this is to decide to change their lives to accord to God's way (repent) and to make a pledge to do this by allowing John to baptize them. The result will be that their sins will be forgiven and they will be ready for the coming of God and his Messiah.

Mark must have realized that John's baptism was in continuity with Christian baptism. For example, in Acts 2:38 people are called to (1) believe that Jesus is the resurrected Messiah (which is what "in the name of Jesus Christ" implies), (2) change their minds to accord with this fact which will include conforming their lifestyles to his teaching (that is, repent) and (3) pledge themselves to this through baptism. The promise is that they will (1) have their sins forgiven and (2) receive the Holy Spirit. Thus we get a five-part sequence: repentance, faith in (that is, personal commitment to) Jesus, baptism, forgiveness of sins, reception of the Holy Spirit. This is exactly like John, except that, whereas John does not yet know who the Messiah is, only that he is coming, now the name of the Messiah is known.

In Acts 22:16 Saul, who has already had an encounter with Jesus and repented of what he was doing (persecuting Christians), is told to act on this inward change and be baptized, the result being that his sins will be washed away.

Thus whether we look at John's baptism or Christian baptism in Acts, baptism results in the forgiveness of sins. Baptism is not viewed as an automatic thing regardless of the state of one's heart, but as an effective act, because it expresses the person's inward disposition. The difference between John's baptism and Christian baptism is found in what is known about Jesus. John only knew that someone was coming and that that person would appear soon. In Acts the preachers know that Jesus was that person and that he is now resurrected and about to return. Yet whether the belief is in the coming One or the One who came and is coming again, the call is to turn from one's own way, align oneself with God's way, pledge oneself to this in baptism and so receive forgiveness of sins.

In the modern church this is often forgotten. Many modern churches connect baptism to forgiveness of sins, but do not seek repentance first. Others call for repentance and faith, but ask people to pledge themselves to it through praying a "sinner's prayer" or signing a "decision card." Baptism then becomes an "extra" and its connection to forgiveness of sins is forgotten. In this context John's message seems strange to many of us, but for those who first received the New Testament he was right in line with how they had become Christians.

See also comment on 1 PETER 3:21.

1:34, 44 Why the Secret?

Each of the Gospels is designed to proclaim who Jesus is, to present him to the world, so that people will commit themselves to him and become disciples. But within the Gospels, especially in Mark, is the curious phenomenon of Jesus' commanding people not to tell others who he is. If he wishes people to believe, why does he not allow the open confessions of those who really know him? In the case of demonized people, is this not one time that demons were telling the truth? Could this mean that Jesus had doubts about who he was? This is the problem of the so-called messianic secret in Mark.

In responding to such an issue we must look at the evidence. Jesus commands silence on three types of occasions. The first involves demons, who "knew who he was." The second involves people who have been healed, who may not understand who he is, but who do have a story to tell about what he has done. "See that you don't tell this to anyone," Jesus says to a leper he heals (Mk 1:44; compare Mk 5:43). The third occasion involves the disciples after they confess him as "the Christ" (Mk 8:30; 9:9). What is the purpose of all this secrecy? Each of these situations has a somewhat different explanation. We will discuss them in reverse order.

The disciples, whose confession Peter boldly states in Mark 8:29, had come to recognize Jesus over a period of time. They had followed him around, heard his teaching, observed his miracles and gone out to do the same at his command. Their faith had grown during that time. More important, Jesus had been able to define for them how he saw his own mission. Even though their understanding was far from perfect (the predictions of the cross still mystified them), their obedience made it relatively safe for them to think of him as "the Christ," or "the Messiah" ("Christ" is Greek for "Messiah"; both terms mean simply "the anointed one").

Unfortunately, Judaism did not have the same clarity about the Messiah and his mission. Some groups among the Jews were not looking for any Messiah. The golden age had come with the Maccabean victories in 164 B.C. As long as the temple functioned, deliverance was not needed. Others (for example, the people who wrote the Dead Sea Scrolls) believed in two Messiahs. One would be a descendant of David who would rule as king, while the other would be a descendant of Aaron who would purify temple worship as high priest. For both groups Scripture and the experience of Hasmonean priest-kings from 164 to 163 B.C. had proved that the roles of ruler and priest could not be combined. Still others were looking for a warrior-king who would deliver them from the Romans. In fact several people presented themselves as candidates for the office (Acts 5:36-37 has only a partial listing), and one, Simeon Ben Kosiba, would lead the Jews to a final defeat in A.D. 135.

Therefore the title "Christ," or "Messiah," was a dangerous one. It would immediately excite people's preconceived imaginations about what that figure was supposed to do. It would mark him out to the Romans as a rebel leader. And it would close people off to Jesus' own self-definition of his role. Because of this Jesus always referred to himself as the "Son of Man." In Ezekiel this phrase means "human being." In Palestinian Aramaic it could simply be a modest way of saying "I" (similar to Paul's modesty in 2 Cor 12:2-3). But it also appears in Daniel 7:13 for a being who receives power and authority from God. Therefore the phrase had three possible meanings, and only context could determine which was intended. Because of this ambiguity, people had to listen to Jesus to see how he used the term rather than attach to it their own preconceived meanings. This is precisely what Jesus wanted and needed until he had accomplished all he had to do. So he told his disciples not to say anything until he had "risen from the dead"; he did not need their semiunderstanding assistance in explaining who he is.

The people Jesus heals are another matter. Here the issue is in part modesty, for Jesus is not looking for a following as a wonder-worker, nor does he wish to "blow his own horn." This must be the case in Mark 5:43, for many individuals knew that the child had died, and they would recognize the miracle as soon as they saw her up and around the house. But Jesus was not looking for a string of requests to come to funerals! So he "gave strict orders not to let anyone know about this." This same motif can be seen in the "nonsecrecy" of the previous incident. Jesus tells the delivered Gerasene man to "tell [your family] how much the Lord has done for you" (Mk 5:19). While the man then tells "how much Jesus had done for him," Jesus had drawn the attention to God rather than to himself.

A second concern in keeping the healed quiet is the problem of publicity.

In the case of the Gerasenes Jesus was leaving the area, so publicity would be no problem. But the healed leper he tells to keep quiet (Mk 1:44) caused real problems when "he went out and began to talk freely, spreading the news. As a result, Jesus could no longer enter a town openly but stayed outside in lonely places" (Mk 1:45).[1] This popularity was bad in two ways. As we see in Mark 6:31, it made life difficult. The situation appeared so crazy to his relatives that they wanted to take him into protective custody (Mk 3:20-21)! In fact, it even made ministry difficult, for frequently crowds became a hindrance in people's attempts to get to Jesus (Mk 2:2-4). Furthermore the popularity attracted the attention of the authorities, which could be dangerous (Mk 6:14). So this problem reinforced Jesus' own humble modesty about his healing activities.

Finally, we turn to the demonized. The demons did indeed know who Jesus was. In fact, they knew who Jesus was far better than even his disciples did, for only they use the title "Son of God" until the very end of the Gospel (Mk 15:39). We are never told what their motives are for crying out; it could simply be a spontaneous astonished wail upon meeting their match, or it may have had a more sinister purpose. Jesus always silenced them, whatever their motives. While he also never says why he did so, we can see from the text that he would have had several reasons for wishing to keep them silent. First, "the teachers of the law" associated him with Beelzebub, "the prince of demons" (Mk 3:22). Any tendency to show that he accepted the demonic would have given extra evidence to these opponents.

Second, to accept the testimony of demons about himself would give a precedent to his followers to accept (or even seek) testimony of demons about other things. This would threaten to make Jesus' movement an occult movement. Here is also a parallel to the temptation narratives in Matthew and Luke: Jesus will not receive the kingdoms of this world from the devil (Mt 4:9-10), and neither will he receive help in his mission from the devil's agents.

Third, and most important, Jesus' whole mission was a call to faith based on evidence, not on authoritative testimony. Jesus proclaims the kingdom of God and acts according to kingdom values. Those who take the risk of faith and commit themselves become disciples and learn more, but others receive teaching only in obscure parables (Mk 4:11-12, 33-34). When John the Baptist requests more information, Jesus simply tells the messengers to report the events that they saw (Mt 11:4-6; Lk 7:21-23). Only in the account of his trial before the Sanhedrin does Jesus make a direct statement about himself. Therefore the demons were short-circuiting Jesus' whole methodology. His command to them was a sharp "Shut up!" His invitation to the crowd at their expulsion was "See and believe that the kingdom of God has come."

---

[1]B. Malina, *The New Testament World* (Atlanta: John Knox, 1981), p. 122, argues that this was because the healed man's report included the fact that Jesus had touched him and thereby had himself become unclean. Jesus is thus forced to stay outside villages, where unclean people were to stay. While this is a possible interpretation, the fact that the text of Mark 1:46 stresses that many gathered to him and implies that he went back to Capernaum as soon as the crowd dissipated makes this a less likely interpretation.

2:10 The Son of Man Forgives Sins?

When the four friends of the paralyzed man broke through the roof of the house in Capernaum where Jesus was teaching and lowered him on his pallet at Jesus' feet, Jesus appreciated their faith and determination and healed the man. But before he told the man to pick up his pallet and walk out with it, he said to him, "Son, your sins are forgiven" (Mk 2:5). Nothing is said of the cause of the man's paralysis, but Jesus evidently recognized that the first thing he needed was the assurance that his sins were forgiven. If this assurance were accepted, the physical cure would follow.

His words to the paralyzed man constituted a hard saying in the ears of some of the bystanders. Who was this to pronounce forgiveness of sins? To forgive injuries that one has received oneself is a religious duty, but sins are committed against God, and therefore God alone may forgive them. One may say to a sinner, "May God forgive you"; but by what authority can one say to him, "Your sins are forgiven"? Probably Jesus' critics would have agreed that a duly authorized spokesman of God might, in the words of the General Absolution, "declare and pronounce to his people, being penitent, the absolution and remission of their sins"; but they did not acknowledge Jesus as such a duly authorized spokesman, nor was there any evidence, so far as they could see, that repentance was forthcoming or that an appropriate sin offering had been presented to God. It was the note of authority in Jesus' voice as he pronounced forgiveness that gave chief offense to them: he imposed no conditions, called for no amendment of life, but spoke as though his bare word ensured the divine pardon. He was really arrogating to himself the prerogative of God, they thought.

How could Jesus give evidence of his authority to forgive sins? They could not see sins being forgiven, but they could see the effect of Jesus' further words in the man's response. It is easy to say, "Your sins are forgiven," because no one can ordinarily see whether sins are forgiven or not. But if one tells a paralyzed man to get up and walk, the words will quickly be shown to be empty words if nothing happens. "But," said Jesus to his critics, "that you may know that the Son of Man has authority on earth to forgive sins," and then, addressing himself to the paralytic, "get up, take your mat and go home." When the paralytic did just that, Jesus' power as a healer was confirmed—but more than that, it was the assurance that his sins were forgiven that enabled the man to do what a moment previously would have been impossible, so Jesus' authority to forgive sins was confirmed at the same time.

This is the first occurrence of the designation "the Son of Man" in Mark's Gospel, and one of the two occurrences in his Gospel to be located before Peter confessed Jesus to be the Christ at Caesarea Philippi (the other being the statement in Mk 2:28 that the Son of Man is lord of the sabbath). "The Son of Man" was apparently Jesus' favorite way of referring to himself. Sometimes the "one like a son of man" who receives supreme authority in Daniel's vision of the day of judgment (Dan 7:13-14) may provide the background to Jesus' use of the expression, but that son of man is authorized to execute judgment rather than to pronounce forgiveness (one may compare Jn 5:27, where the Father has given the Son "authority to judge, because he is the Son of Man"). Here, however, the expression more probably points to Jesus as the representative man—"the Proper Man, whom God himself hath bidden." This is how Matthew appears to have understood it. He concludes his account of the incident by saying that the crowds that saw it "praised God, who had given such authority to men"—that is, to human beings (Mt 9:8). The authority so given is exercised by Jesus as the representative man—or, as Paul was later to put it, the "last Adam" (1 Cor 15:45). To pronounce, and bestow, forgiveness of sins is the highest prerogative of God, and this he has shared with the Son of Man. *See also comment on* MARK 14:61-62.

2:17 Not the Righteous but Sinners?

Nineteen centuries and more of gospel preaching and New Testament reading have familiarized us with the idea that Jesus' ministry was specially directed to sinners—not simply to sinners in the sense in which most people will admit that "we are all sinners," but to sinners in the sense that their lives offended the accepted moral code of their community. "The saying is sure and worthy of full acceptance, that Christ Jesus came into the world to save sinners" (1 Tim 1:15 RSV); this is a great gospel text, and if the writer goes on to speak of himself as first and foremost among sinners, that serves to underline his claim on the saving grace of Christ. But during the ministry of Jesus it gave great offense to many respectable people that a religious teacher should have so little regard for what was expected of him as to consort with those who were no better than they should be. "If this man were a prophet," said Simon the Pharisee to himself, when Jesus allowed a woman of doubtful reputation to touch him, "he would know who is touching him and what kind of woman she is—that she is a sinner" (Lk 7:39). But Jesus knew perfectly well what sort of woman she was, and for that very reason would not prevent her from paying him such embarrassing attention (see comment on Lk 7:47).

Among all the traditional designations of Jesus, probably none is more heartwarming than "the friend of sinners." But this designation was first given to him by way of criticism: "a glutton and a drunkard," they said, "a friend of tax collectors and 'sinners' " (Lk 7:34)—tax collectors occupying the lowest rung on the ladder of respectability, matched only by harlots. It was not that he tolerated such people, as though he did them a favor by taking notice of them in a condescending way, but he gave the impression that he liked their company, that he even preferred it; he did not condemn them but encouraged them to feel at home with him. "This man welcomes sinners," the scribes said by way of complaint; and more than that, he actually "eats with them" (Lk 15:2). To accept invitations to a meal in the homes of such people, to enjoy table-fellowship with them—that was the most emphatic way of declaring his unity with them. No wonder this gave offense to those who, sometimes with considerable painstaking, had kept to the path of sound morality. If a man is known by the company he keeps, Jesus was simply asking to be known as the friend of the ne'er-do-wells, the dregs of society. And would not many religious people today react in exactly the same way?

On one occasion when Jesus had accepted a dinner invitation to the home of one of these disreputable people, his disciples were approached by the scribes. The disciples were included in the invitation, but some of them may have had misgivings. "Why does he eat with tax collectors and sinners?" they were asked. But Jesus interposed with the answer. "It is not the healthy who need a doctor, but the sick" he said. "I have not come to call the righteous, but sinners" (Mk 2:17). To call means to invite; he had accepted their invitation, but they received an invitation from him—to take and enjoy the love and mercy of the heavenly Father. It is inevitable that the "ninety-nine righteous persons who need no repentance" (Lk 15:7 RSV) should feel that too much fuss is made over sinners, but since the gospel is for sinners first and foremost—indeed for sinners only—it cannot be otherwise.

These words of Jesus are reproduced by the two other Synoptic Evangelists (Mt 9:13; Lk 5:32), but Luke adds a short explanatory gloss: "I have not come to call the righteous, but sinners *to repentance.*" Repentance figures more frequently in Luke's Gospel than in the other two (it does not figure at all in the Gospel of John). It has sometimes been suggested that Luke's addition betrays a misunderstanding on his part, but this is not really so. If repentance in the teaching of Jesus implies change of character rather than reformation of behavior,[1] then Jesus believed in dealing with the root of the disease and not merely with the symptoms. And the root could be dealt with effectively only by the practical assurance and demonstration of outgoing, self-giving love.

[1]As is pointed out by T. W. Manson in *The Teaching of Jesus*, 2nd ed. (Cambridge: Cambridge University Press, 1935), p. 308.

2:26 Who Was the High Priest?

In Mark we read that Jesus said that Abiathar was priest when David received and ate some of the bread of the Presence from the tabernacle. In terms of the point that Jesus is making it really does not matter who was priest, for the issue is the breaking of the rule about a layperson eating consecrated bread and its application to Jesus' disciples breaking the sabbath regulations. However, when we look up the incident in 1 Samuel 21:1-6, the text reads "Ahimelech" rather than "Abiathar." Was Jesus mistaken? Surely the Pharisees would have caught the error?

The first point to note is that Abiathar and Ahimelech are son and father. The son, Abiathar, first appears in 1 Samuel 22:20 as the one son of Ahimelech who escaped when Saul slaughtered the priests of Nob and their families for having helped David. Abiathar then remains with David and later serves as high priest during his reign. It looks like the son has been switched with the father.

The second thing we should look at is the textual tradition. There is no evidence that this switch is a textual error. It is true that the Western text does omit the priest's name, but none of the other textual traditions do, and the Western text does sometimes correct or add to the text in various books. When the Western text's reading remains unsupported by other textual traditions, it is not taken as very weighty. In fact, the Western text actually follows the other Synoptics, for Matthew 12:4 and Luke 6:4 both drop this offending name. Thus there appears to be solid evidence that Mark wrote "Abiathar."

There have been attempts to solve the problem by arguing that "in the days of Abiathar the high priest" should be understood to mean "In the section [of Samuel] entitled 'Abiathar,'" since this section explains how Abiathar joined David (and there were no chapter and verse numbers for citing Scripture in Jesus' day). However, if that is what it means, Mark found a most awkward way of expressing it. To mean this, the Greek phrase with "Abiathar" in it should have been placed in Mark 2:25 right after "Have you never read?"

Likewise some argue that the phrase means "when Abiathar who became high priest was alive." However, if this was what were intended (if Jesus had forgotten the name of Abiathar's father or thought his listeners would not recognize it), a phrase like "in the days of the father of Abiathar the high priest" or "in the childhood of Abiathar the high priest" would have expressed the thought clearly. The phrase as it stands would express such an idea so unclearly and awkwardly that it is unlikely that it means this.

What, then, are the possibilities? First, we can be fairly certain that Mark is not covering up the Pharisaic response to an error Jesus made. If Mark had been aware of such a problem, he would have omitted the whole story or changed the name rather than simply omitted the Pharisaic response. Mark probably did not see any other problem with this passage than the issue of Jesus' defending his disciples' breaking the sabbath regulations.

Second, if Mark did not see the problem, he did not see it for one of three reasons: (1) he actually wrote Ahimelech and the more familiar name crept into the text at a very early stage, perhaps as an error in the first copying (often texts were read aloud to scribes making copies, so an oral substitution of the more familiar name for the less familiar would be quite possible), or (2) he received the story as it is and did not himself realize that there was a problem with it (in the latter case, we do not know if Jesus actually said "Abiathar" or if he said "Ahimelech" and the more familiar Abiathar was substituted in the course of oral transmission), or (3) his view of historical accuracy was not bothered by such an issue, since the main point is not affected by it. Whatever the case, Mark apparently did not realize that there was a problem.

The truth is that this is one of the problems in Scripture for which we do not have a fully satisfactory solution. We do not have Mark's original edition to check which name was in it, nor do we have Mark here to question about his state of mind. We do not have a tape recording of the preaching of Peter (thought by many to be the source of Mark) to see if he was using the right or the wrong name. While many ancient historians would not have been bothered by such an innocuous slip, it did seem to bother Matthew and Luke, so we cannot be sure that it would not have bothered Mark. Thus we can either arbitrarily select one of the speculative solutions mentioned in the previous paragraph, perhaps choosing the one which pleases us the best, or we can say, "We honestly don't know what the answer is to this problem, nor are we likely to ever know." In that case, this verse makes plain that our knowledge is always partial so that our trust remains in God rather than in what we know.

2:27-28 The Sabbath for Man?

This is the second occurrence of the designation "the Son of Man" in Mark's Gospel—one of the two occurrences which he places before the Caesarea Philippi incident. The words were the conclusion of Jesus' reply to those who criticized his disciples for plucking ears of grain as they walked through the fields one sabbath and then (according to Lk 6:1) eating the grain when they had rubbed the ears in their hands to separate the kernel from the husk. Harmless enough actions, it might be supposed today (unless the owner of the crop complained that he was being robbed), but plucking the ears was technically regarded by the interpreters of the law as a form of reaping, and rubbing them to extract the kernel as a form of grinding, and reaping and grinding were two kinds of work that were forbidden on the sabbath. Probably, in addition to the expressed criticism of the disciples, there was an implied criticism of Jesus for allowing them to break the law in this way.

Jesus first invoked a precedent: in an emergency David had been permitted by the priest in charge of the sanctuary at Nob (perhaps on Mount Scopus; near Jerusalem) to have some of the holy bread (the "shewbread" or "bread of the [divine] presence") for himself and his followers to eat, although it was laid down in the law that none but priests should eat it (1 Sam 21:1-6). The point of Jesus' argument here seems to be that human need takes priority over ceremonial law; it is relevant to recall that in traditional interpretation (though not in the Old Testament text) the incident from the life of David took place on a sabbath (the day when, according to Lev 24:8-9, the old bread was to be removed, to be eaten by "Aaron and his sons . . . in a holy place," and replaced by new bread, "set in order before the Lord").

But Jesus went on to invoke an earlier and higher precedent. The sabbath was instituted by God; what was God's purpose in instituting it? If that can be discovered, then the sabbath law is best kept when God's purpose in giving it is best fulfilled. In Genesis 2:2-3, God is said to have "rested" on the seventh day when he had finished the creative work of the six preceding days, so he "blessed the seventh day and hallowed it." The Hebrew verb translated "rest" is *šāḇaṯ*, which is given here as the explanation of the word "sabbath" (Hebrew *šaḇbāṯ*). Neither Jesus nor his critics thought that God needed to rest on the seventh day because he was tired after a hard week's work. He "ceased" or "desisted" from his work. Why, then, did he "bless" the sabbath day and "hallow" it? Not for his own sake, but for the sake of his creatures, who, he knew, would certainly need to rest after a hard week's work. This is implied in the Genesis narrative itself. The fourth commandment, in the form which it is given in Exodus 20:8-11, bids the Israelites sanctify the seventh day by refraining from work, because God sanctified it by ceasing from his work after the six days of creation. But in the form which this commandment is given in Deuteronomy 5:12-15, it is made explicitly clear that the sabbath was given for the sake of those who need to rest after hard work: "that your manservant and your maidservant may rest as well as you" (RSV).

The sabbath day was instituted, then, to meet a human need, and the day is best sanctified when human need is met on it. Expositors regularly quote as a parallel the words of Rabbi Simeon ben Menasya preserved in a rabbinical commentary on Exodus 31:14: "The sabbath is delivered to you; you are not delivered to the sabbath."[1]

But the real problem of Jesus' saying is the significance of the "so" or "so that" introducing the next words: "the Son of Man is Lord even of the Sabbath." How does it follow from the fact that the sabbath was made for man that the Son of Man is Lord of the sabbath? In one way, this would not have been so much of a problem for those who first heard Jesus speak the words. Since "man" was regularly expressed in Aramaic by the idiom "son of man," the literal translation of the saying would have been "The sabbath was made for the son of man, not the son of man for the sabbath; so the son of man is lord even of the sabbath." The question that would rise in the hearers' minds was: "In what sense is the son of man lord of the sabbath? Does he mean that humanity in general is lord of the sabbath?" This question confronts us too, but we have a further question to think about: why did Mark use the simple noun "man" (human being, or the human race) in the first two clauses, but the locution "the son of man" in the third? He must have intended the subject of the third clause to mean something more than man in general. If so, what was that something more? Jesus probably meant that he who is Lord of the sabbath, he who has the sovereign authority to interpret the sabbath law in accordance with

the divine purpose in instituting it, is the representative man, and that is the role which he now discharges. Since the sabbath was made for man, he whom God has ordained to be man's representative before him is authorized to dispose of the sabbath at his own discretion.
See also comment on EXODUS 20:8-11.

[1]*Mekhilta* (rabbinical commentary) on Exodus 31:14.

3:28-29 An Unpardonable Sin?

The person who has committed the unpardonable sin figures powerfully in literature. There is, for example, Bunyan's man in the iron cage. There is the Welsh preacher Peter Williams, breaking the silence of night in George Borrow's *Lavengro* with his anguished cry: "Pechod Ysprydd Glan! O pechod Ysprydd Glan!" ("The sin against the Holy Spirit! Oh, the sin against the Holy Spirit!")—which he was persuaded he had committed. Or there is Mr. Paget, in Edmund Gosse's *Father and Son,* who

> had thrown up his cure of souls because he became convinced that he had committed the Sin against the Holy Ghost. . . . Mr. Paget was fond of talking, in private and in public, of his dreadful spiritual condition, and he would drop his voice while he spoke of having committed the Unpardonable Sin, with a sort of shuddering exultation, such as people sometimes feel in the possession of a very unusual disease. . . . Everybody longed to know what the exact nature had been of that sin against the Holy Ghost which had deprived Mr. Paget of every glimmer of hope for time or for eternity. It was whispered that even my Father himself was not precisely acquainted with the character of it.[1]

Of course not, because the "sin" existed only in Mr. Paget's imagination.

In real life there are few more distressing conditions calling for treatment by physicians of the soul than that of people who believe they have committed this sin. When they are offered the gospel assurance of forgiveness for every sin, when they are reminded that "the blood of Jesus . . . purifies us from all sin" (1 Jn 1:7), they have a ready answer: there is one sin that is an exception to this rule, and they have committed that sin; for it, in distinction from all other kinds of sin, there is no forgiveness. Did not our Lord himself say so? And they tend to become impatient when it is pointed out to them (quite truly) that the very fact of their concern over having committed it proves that they have not committed it.

What then did Jesus mean when he spoke in this way? His saying has been preserved in two forms. Luke records it as one of a series of sayings dealing with the Son of Man or the Holy Spirit (Lk 12:10), but Mark gives it a narrative context. (The Markan and Lukan forms are combined in Mt 12:31-32.)

According to Mark, scribes or experts in the Jewish law came from Jerusalem to Galilee to assess the work which, as they heard, Jesus was doing there, and especially his ministry of exorcism—expelling demons from the lives of those who suffered under their domination. (This language indicates a real and sad condition, even if it would commonly be described in different terms today.) The scribes came to a strange conclusion: "He is possessed by Beelzebul, and by the prince of demons he casts out the demons" (Mk 3:22 RSV). (Beelzebul had once been the name of a Canaanite divinity, "the lord of the high place," but by this time it was used by Jews to denote the ruler of the Abyss, the abode of demons.) When Jesus knew of this, he exposed the absurdity of supposing that Satan's power could be overthrown by

Satan's aid. Then he went on to charge those who had voiced this absurd conclusion with blaspheming against the Holy Spirit. Why? Because they deliberately ascribed the Holy Spirit's activity to demonic agency.

For every kind of sin, then, for every form of blasphemy or slander, it is implied that forgiveness is available—presumably when the sin is repented of. But what if one were to repent of blasphemy against the Holy Spirit? Is there no forgiveness for the person who repents of this sin?

The answer seems to be that the nature of this sin is such that one does not repent of it, because those who commit it and persist in it do not know that they are sinning. Mark tells his readers why Jesus charged those scribes with blaspheming against the Holy Spirit: it was because "they were saying, 'He has an evil spirit' " (Mk 3:30). Jesus was proclaiming the kingly rule of God, and his bringing relief to soul-sick, demon-possessed mortals was a token that the kingly rule of God was present and active in his ministry. "But if I drive out demons by the finger of God," he said, "then the kingdom of God has come to you" (Lk 11:20; in Mt 12:28, where these words also appear, "finger of God" is replaced by "Spirit of God"). If some people looked at the relief which he was bringing to the bodies and minds of men and women and maintained that he was doing so with the help of their great spiritual oppressor, the prince of the demons, then their eyes were so tightly closed to the light that for them light had become darkness and good had become evil. The light is there for those who will accept it, but if some refuse the light, where else can they hope to receive illumination?

Was Paul sinning against the Holy Spirit in the days when he persecuted Christians and even (according to Acts 26:11 RSV) "tried to make them blaspheme"? Evidently not, because (as it is put in 1 Tim 1:13 RSV) he "acted ignorantly in unbelief" and therefore received mercy. But if, when he had seen the light on the Damascus road and heard the call of the risen Lord, he had closed his eyes and ears and persevered on his persecuting course, that would have been the "eternal sin." But he would not have recognized it as a sin, and so would not have thought of seeking forgiveness for it; he would have gone on thinking that he was doing the work of God, and his conscience would have remained as unperturbed as ever.

Luke, as has been said, gives his form of the saying a different context. He does record the charge that Jesus cast out demons with Beelzebul's aid, but does so in the preceding chapter (Lk 11:14-26) and says nothing there about the sin against the Spirit. His report on Jesus' words about this sin comes in Luke 12:10, immediately after the statement "I tell you, whoever acknowledges me before men, the Son of Man will also acknowledge him before the angels of God. But he who disowns me before men will be disowned before the angels of God" (Lk 12:8-9). (The second half of this statement is paralleled in Mk 8:38, where it is located in the aftermath to Peter's confession near Caesarea Philippi.) Then, after the words about the sin against the Spirit, Luke quotes the injunction "When you are brought before synagogues, rulers and authorities, do not worry about how you will defend yourselves or what you will say, for the Holy Spirit will teach you at that time what you should say" (Lk 12:11-12). This injunction has a parallel in Mark in his version of the Olivet discourse (Mk 13:11); the parallel is taken over in Luke's version of the discourse, where, however, it is not the Spirit but Jesus who will give his disciples "words and wisdom" to reply to their inquisitors (Lk 21:15). Matthew has a parallel in his account of the sending out of the twelve apostles: "At that time you will be given what to say, for it will not be you speaking, but the Spirit of your Father speaking through you" (Mt 10:19-20).

Luke, then, places the saying about blaspheming the Holy Spirit between a saying about the Spirit's heavenly role as counsel for the defense of those who confess the Son of Man (that is, Jesus) and a saying about the Spirit's enabling confessors of Jesus before an earthly tribunal to say the right word at the right time. In this context a different emphasis is given to the matter of blasphemy against the Spirit from that given to it by Mark. It is suggested by Luke that the blaspheming of the Spirit involves a refusal of his powerful help when it is available to save the disciples of Jesus from denying him and so committing apostasy. If so, blasphemy against the Spirit in this context is tantamount to apostasy, the deliberate and decisive repudiation of Jesus as Lord. This is not the only New Testament passage which warns against the irremediable evil of apostasy: another well-known example is Hebrews 6:4-6, where it is said to be impossible to renew apostates to repentance, since they have repudiated the only way of salvation.

But Luke couples with the warning against the unpardonable sin of blasphemy against the Spirit the affirmation of Jesus that there is forgiveness for everyone who speaks a word against the Son of Man. On this there are two things to be said.

First, in Jesus' language (Aramaic), the phrase "the son of man" normally meant "the man"; only the context could indicate when he intended the phrase to have the special sense which is conveyed by the fuller translation "the Son of Man." Moreover, in the phrase "the man" the definite article could, on occasion, have generic force, referring not to a particular human being but to man in general (in English this generic force is best conveyed by using the noun without any article, as in "Man is born unto trouble, as the sparks fly upward"). So Jesus may have meant, "To speak against (a) man is pardonable, but to speak against the Spirit is not."

Second, if that is what Jesus meant, he included himself as a man, if not indeed as the representative man. Luke understands him to refer to himself in particular; otherwise he would have said "everyone who speaks a word against man" and not (as he does) "every one who speaks a word against the Son of Man." Why would it be so much more serious to slander the Holy Spirit than to slander the Son of Man? Perhaps because the identity of the Son of Man was veiled in his humility; people might easily fail to recognize him for who he was. There was nothing in the designation "the Son of Man" in itself to express a claim to authority. The Son of Man, at present operating in lowliness and liable to be rejected and ill-treated, might indeed be despised. But if those who had begun to follow him were afraid that, under stress, they might deny him, they were assured that the Spirit's aid was available. If, however, they resisted the Spirit and rejected his aid, then indeed their case would be desperate.

Peter, through fear, denied the Son of Man, but he found forgiveness and restoration; his lips had momentarily turned traitor but his heart did not apostatize. His repentance left him wide open to the Spirit's healing grace, and when he was restored, he was able to strengthen others (Lk 22:31-32). Why then, it might be asked, did he not strengthen Ananias and Sapphira when they came to him with part of the proceeds of the sale of their property, pretending that it was the whole amount? Presumably because, as he said, they had consented to the satanic suggestion that they should "[lie] to the Holy Spirit" and had "agree[d] to test the Spirit of the Lord" (Acts 5:3, 9). Thus, in Peter's reckoning, they had sinned beyond the point of no return. How Jesus would have regarded their offense is another question.

In Mark's context, then, the sin against the Holy Spirit involves deliberately shutting one's eyes to the light and consequently calling good evil; in Luke (that is, ultimately, in the sayings collection commonly labeled Q) it is irretrievable apostasy. Probably these are not really two conditions but one—not unlike the condition which Plato described as having the lie in the soul.[2]

See also comment on HEBREWS 6:4-6; 10:26; 1 JOHN 5:16-17.

---

[1]E. Gosse, *Father and Son* (London: W. Heineman, 1928), pp. 205-07.

[2]Plato *Republic* 2.382a-b.

4:11-12 Why in Parables?

In Mark's record this saying comes between the parable of the sower (or parable of the four soils, as some prefer to call it) and the explanation of that parable. The parable, the explanation and the saying quoted above are all ascribed to Jesus himself. But if the saying means what it seems to mean, then Jesus tells his disciples that the purpose of his use of parables is that his hearers in general (those who are not his followers) may hear him but not understand him; and it is difficult to believe that this was so.

Matthew alters the sense by using the conjunction *because* instead of *so that:* "This is why I speak to them in parables, because seeing they do not see, and hearing they do not hear, nor do they understand" (Mt 13:13 RSV). That is to say, because the general public was slow to grasp the sense of Jesus' teaching, he embodied it in parables to make it more immediately intelligible. The hardness of the saying is thus mitigated; it is readily accepted that

> Truth embodied in a tale
> Shall enter in at lowly doors.[1]

Luke 8:10 follows Mark's construction, with some abbreviation.

But what is the point of Mark's construction? One suggestion is that the saying was entirely Mark's creation. The parable, it is said, was told by Jesus; the explanation received its shape in the primitive church, but the hard saying is Mark's own contribution; it expresses his view (or the view of the school of thought to which he belonged) about the purpose of Jesus' parables. But is it out of the question that the saying represents something spoken by Jesus himself?

It is plain that the saying is an adaptation of an Old Testament text, Isaiah 6:9-10. When Isaiah received his call to the prophetic ministry, in the well-known vision that he saw in the temple "in the year that King Uzziah died," the voice of God said to him:

> Go, and tell this people: "Be ever hearing, but never understanding; be ever seeing, but never perceiving." Make the heart of this people calloused; make their ears dull and close their eyes. Otherwise they might see with their eyes, hear with their ears, understand with their hearts, and turn and be healed.

Should this commission be pressed to mean that Isaiah was ordered to go and tell the people to pay no heed to what they heard him say? Was it his prescribed duty to prevent them from hearing and understanding his message, and thus make it simple for them to repent and so escape the destruction that would otherwise overtake them? No indeed; if that impression is given, it is simply due to the Hebrew tendency to express a consequence as though it were a purpose. Isaiah volunteers to be God's messenger to his people, and God takes him at his word, but says to him in effect, "Go and deliver my message, but don't expect them to pay any attention to it. The effect of your preaching will be their persistent refusal to accept what you say, to the point where they will have rendered themselves incapable of accepting it." In the event, this is exactly what Isaiah was to experience for the next forty years. Isaiah's experience was reproduced in Jesus' ministry. For all the enthusiasm that greeted his ministry in its earlier phase, he had later on to lament the unbelief with which he met in the very places where most of his mighty works had been done. He might well have applied the words of Isaiah 6:9-10 to the effect (not, of course, to the purpose) of his own ministry. Certainly this text became one of the commonest Old Testament "testimonies" in the early church on the subject of Jewish resistance to the gospel. Apart from the allusion to it in the context of the parable of the sower in all three Synoptic Gospels, it is quoted in John 12:40 at the end of Jesus' Jerusalem ministry and in Acts 28:26-27 at Paul's meeting with the Jewish leaders in Rome, while there is an echo of it in Romans 11:8. Its pervasiveness in this sense could well be due to Jesus' application of it to his own experience. "As in its original setting in the Book of Isaiah, so here, it is most naturally taken as an arresting, hyperbolical, oriental way of saying, 'Alas! many will be obdurate.' "[2]

At the end of the Isaiah quotation the verb used is "be healed." It is so in the Hebrew text and it is so in the Greek version (the Septuagint). But in the corresponding position in Mark 4:12 the verb is "be forgiven." This might be set down as a free paraphrase on the Evangelist's part, were it not that the Aramaic Targum on the Prophets has "be forgiven." The date of the written Targum on the Prophets is considerably later than the date of Mark, but behind the written Targum lies an oral tradition: the Aramaic paraphrase of the Hebrew lesson was originally given in the synagogue by word of mouth. Perhaps, then, "be forgiven" is due not to Mark but to Jesus: speaking in Aramaic, he alluded to the Aramaic wording of the Isaiah passage.

Recognizing this, T. W. Manson went on to make a further suggestion.[3] If Jesus had the Aramaic version of the text in mind, then it is relevant to consider that in Aramaic one and the same form does duty for "so that" and "who," while the expression for "lest" may also mean "perhaps." The meaning of Jesus' saying would then be: "For those outside everything is in parables, (for those, namely) who see indeed but do not perceive, who hear indeed but do not understand; perhaps they may turn again and be forgiven."

This certainly removes most of the hardness from the saying, making it mean that Jesus imparted the "mystery" of the kingdom of God to the disciples but spoke in parables to those outside their circle in hope that they would grasp sufficient of his teaching to repent and receive forgiveness. But if this is what the saying meant, Mark (or his source of information) has misunderstood it and made it hard.

If we remember that in the idiom of Jesus and his contemporaries a result might be expressed as though it were a purpose, the saying remains hard, but not intolerably hard. It is helpful also to realize that in Hebrew and Aramaic the word for "parable" might also mean "riddle."

Jesus proclaimed the kingdom of God and made plain the far-reaching implications of its arrival. This was a "mystery" in the sense that it had not been disclosed in this form before: Jesus revealed it in his ministry. Among his hearers there were some whose minds were open to his teaching; they grasped its meaning and appreciated the point of his parables. There were others whose minds were closed. Even if at first they thought that he was the teacher and leader for whom they had been waiting, they soon changed their minds. His parables, luminous to those who had eyes to see and ears to hear, were but riddles to them. They could not take his message in, and so they could not profit by it. The more he spoke and acted among them the less responsive they became. And they were in the majority. Only a few, relatively speaking, embraced the good news of the kingdom, but for their sake it was worthwhile making it known.

If the saying is understood in this sense, its relevance to the context, immediately after the parable of the sower, should be clear. The sower scattered the good seed broadcast, but only a quarter of it yielded a crop, because of the poor soil on which the rest of it fell—the hard-beaten path, the thorn-infested ground, the shallow skin of earth on top of the rock. But the harvest that sprang up from the good and fertile ground meant that the labor of sowing was by no means in vain—quite the contrary. The gain derived from those "who hear the word and accept it" more than outweighs the loss incurred through those who turn away.

See also comment on EXODUS 9:12; ISAIAH 63:17.

[1]Tennyson, *In Memoriam,* xxvi.

[2]C. F. D. Moule, *The Birth of the New Testament,* 3rd ed. (San Francisco: Harper & Row, 1981), p. 117.

[3]T. W. Manson, *The Teaching of Jesus,* 2nd ed. (Cambridge: Cambridge University Press, 1935), pp. 75-80.

4:31 How Small Is a Mustard Seed?

See comment on MATTHEW 13:32.

5:1-20 Two Demoniacs or One?

See comment on MATTHEW 8:28-34.

5:11-13 Why No Concern for the Pigs?

See comment on MATTHEW 8:31-32.

5:34 How Much Faith Do We Need?

In the story of the woman with the flow of blood we find this verse (also found in Mt 9:22 and Lk 8:48) that indicates that her healing was due to her faith. A similar phrase appears in the healing stories in Mark 10:52, Luke 17:19 and Luke 18:42, and the forgiveness story in Luke 7:50. Does this mean that the answer to our prayers is determined by the amount of our faith?

Certainly faith is present somewhere in most of the healing stories in the Gospels. In the cases cited above, the faith is the faith of the person being healed, but such stories form only about one-third of the healing stories in the Gospels. In Mark 2:5 it is the faith of those bringing the person to Jesus which is cited. In Mark 6:6 (and Mt 13:58) it is the general climate of unbelief, that is, the lack of faith, in Nazareth that made Jesus unable to do anything more than heal a few sick people. In Mark 9:23-24 Jesus counters unbelief and stimulates faith in the father of a demonized boy. Yet in many cases of healing the only faith which appears to be present is that which Jesus has; for example, in the raising of the man in Nain (Lk 7:11-16) one searches in vain for faith in anyone but Jesus, as is also the case in John 11. How do we put all of this data together?

First, while Jesus can talk about "great faith" (in the case of the centurion whose servant was healed) or "little faith" (in the case of the disciples in Mark), normally it is not the amount of faith but whether or not it is present that counts. In Mark 11:23-24 we read,

> I tell you the truth, if anyone says to this mountain, "Go, throw yourself into the sea," and does not doubt in his heart but believes that what he says will happen, it will be done for him. Therefore I tell you, whatever you ask for in prayer, believe that you have received it, and it will be yours.

Yet the parallel in Luke 17:6 reads,

> If you have faith as small as a mustard seed, you can say to this mulberry tree, "Be uprooted and planted in the sea," and it will obey you. (compare Mt 17:20)

In other words, the key element in prayer is not the amount of faith, but whether faith is present at all.

The Scripture applies this to several different situations. First, there is faith which leads to salvation. Remember that in the New Testament the Greek term for faith *(pistis)* or believing *(pisteuō)* normally means trust in or commitment to some person. The woman in Luke 7:50 may have had all sorts of weird ideas about Jesus; she is not commended for her excellent theology. Yet whatever her ideas about Jesus she had something in her heart which pushed her to express trust in or commitment to Jesus. That faith, however rudimentary from a theological standpoint, brought about her "salvation" from her disease (the term translated "healed" is the same one often translated "saved"). Now the woman was not seeking deliverance from sin, yet the same principle holds throughout the New Testament, for it is not how much we understand about Jesus that saves us, but the mere fact that we trust in him. For example, we do not know what the Philippian jailer in Acts 16 knew about Jesus; surely it was very little. Most likely he had only just that night heard about him at all. Yet his willingness to trust in Jesus was enough to save him. Saving faith is commitment to Jesus and is not dependent on our understanding how he will save us or even that he will save us. Indeed, some people might be willing to obey Jesus as God's king (that is, confess "Jesus is Lord" as Paul says in Rom 10:9-10) and yet think that in the end Jesus would still send them to hell. Even in such a case their faith in Jesus (their commitment to him, their trust in him) saves them even though they are ignorant of the fact that God would never send someone to hell who repents and turns to him.[1] This is where Matthew 5:13 fits in, for we either have "flavor" (saltiness or faith) or do not. Minimal faith leads to salvation, while its lack leads to a far sadder result. Likewise in Mark 9:42-49 the issue is not one of the amount of faith, but that of leaving the faith altogether (which is the sense of the Greek word translated "causes to sin" in the NIV). It would be better to be maimed for life rather than to leave faith; a miserable death would be better than turning another person from faith. Again, the issue is whether people trust in or are committed to Jesus, not which theological ideas they have about him. Is Jesus or is he not one's Lord and King, however imperfectly that is understood? Thus salvation is said to be a product of faith, and in the case of salvation the mustard seed of trust (or faith) appears to reside in the individual.

When it comes to praying for healing, the locus of faith is more widespread. We noticed in the Gospels that only in about one-third of the cases is faith found in the person who is sick. After all, illness often sucks faith and other forms of willing out of a person. Thus the gifts of healing in 1 Corinthians 12:9 are normally given through someone other than the person who is ill. In

James 5:14-15 there may be little or no faith in the sick person, for we do not know whether he or she calls the elders of the church out of a spark of faith, or only because the church said to do it, covering all the bases before they die. Whatever the case of the sick person, the only faith actually said to be present is in the elders, for it is they who pray and their "prayer offered in faith" which makes the sick person well. The fact is that people who do not believe that God wants to heal a sick person normally do not see those they pray for healed; conversely, those with even a mustard-seed-sized belief in their hearts often do.[2]

This perspective fits with Mark 11:23-24 and Luke 17:6. In those cases the context is that of a miracle, which is also a gift of God. Again, not the amount of faith but the presence of faith is the quality which leads to prayer being answered. Does something in our hearts say that God will do this, or is there no expectation in us? It is this spark of faith which is the mark of the person who prays and sees miracles happen.

Finally, we should note in all of these cases that faith is also a gift of God. We saw that about the gift of faith in 1 Corinthians 12:9, but Jesus says the same about saving faith (for example, Jn 6:64-65). And whether one talks in Pauline terms about gifts of healing or whether with James one talks in terms of a prayer of faith (which surely comes because the elders have heard the heart of God), the source is God. So even faith is not a work of ours; it is a gift of God. Our only action is to respond appropriately to the faith in our heart.

Therefore we should not get worried about whether we have enough faith or not. What Christian are called to do is to look into the face of the Father and pray what they do have faith for. If they lack faith, they should honestly say, "Help my unbelief!" Trying to work up "faith" within us will not result in faith at all, but in emotional persuasion or mere positive thinking. Spending time in the presence of God (as Jesus did) will result in a spark of faith, perhaps so small we do not even notice it, which trusts God and receives the request that God in giving that faith has already put into our heart. *See also comment on* MARK 11:23; JAMES 5:14-15.

---

[1]This author has actually known some such troubled souls, who recognized Jesus as their Lord and committed themselves to serve him the rest of their lives and yet believed that they had done something that could not be forgiven. They lived with unnecessary pain, but this misbelief did not mean that God had not fully accepted them. Of course they were far happier when someone helped them get rid of their bad theology.

[2]Ken Blue in *Authority to Heal* (Downers Grove, Ill.: InterVarsity Press, 1987) points out that those who pray successfully for healing in whatever tradition have three characteristics in common: (1) the conviction that God is willing to heal (faith), (2) compassion for the sick person (also a characteristic of Jesus) and (3) the willingness to risk (faith must be put into action; the prayer of faith must be prayed).

5:39 Not Dead but Sleeping?

The statement that Jairus's twelve-year-old daughter was "not dead, but sleeping" appears in all three Synoptic narratives (see Mt 9:24; Lk 8:52 RSV). But what did Jesus mean when he said this? The girl's death had certainly been reported. As Jesus was on the way to the house where she lived, in response to her father's anguished plea to him to come and lay his healing hands on her, a messenger came to say that she had died; therefore, "why trouble the Teacher any further?" (RSV). But Jesus encouraged her father: "Do not fear; only believe" (RSV), and went on with him to the house. It was then that he rebuked the crowd for the noise they were making. Did he mean that she was not dead (as had been reported) but only sleeping in the literal sense of the word? The crowd took him to mean that, but it was perfectly evident to them that she was dead: "they laughed at him," say all three Evangelists; "knowing that she was dead," Luke adds (and the fact that he says "knowing" rather than "supposing" suggests that he believed that she had died). Or did Jesus mean that her state of death, though real, was not to be permanent—that it would prove to be nothing more than a temporary sleep? Did he, in other words, use the word *sleep* figuratively, as he did when he reported the death of Lazarus to his disciples by saying, "Our friend Lazarus has fallen asleep, but I go to awake him out of sleep" (Jn 11:11 RSV)? It is beside the point to say that two different Greek words for "sleep" are used—one in the story of Jairus's daughter and the other in the Lazarus narrative. Both of them can be used figuratively for death in appropriate contexts.

Which way, then, should our Lord's words be taken? We cannot be sure, in the absence of the confirmation which a medical certificate would supply. To the modern reader his words are ambiguous. To the child he used the kind of language which might be used by anyone waking a child up from sleep: *Talitha cumi* is the Aramaic for "Little girl, get up!" But the mere waking of a child from sleep is not the kind of action which would call for special commemoration: the fact that the Evangelists record the incident, coupled with the way in which they record it, implies their belief that she was really (if only temporarily) dead.

5:43 Why the Secret?

See comment on MARK 1:34, 44.

6:8 Were the Twelve to Take a Staff?

When we read Mark 6:8-9, Jesus' instructions seem clear enough: the only item that the Twelve are to take with them on their missionary journey is a staff. Yet then we read Matthew 10:9-10 and Luke 9:3, which prohibit the taking of a staff.

The first piece of information that we notice is that although Matthew seems to know Mark quite well in other places, here only his mention of copper is in common with Mark (the word for "money" in Mark means "copper," while the word in Luke means "silver"). The rest of Matthew's version has more in common with Luke. Since Matthew has many other passages in common with Luke which Mark does not have at all (commonly called Q passages from the German word for "source," *Quelle*), the lack of common vocabulary with Mark looks like here Matthew is drawing on his common source with Luke more than on Mark. We also notice that Matthew says "no sandals," although Mark tells them to wear sandals. Thus we conclude that in this case Matthew and Luke follow a common source rather than Mark.

The second thing that we notice is that despite the differences there is general agreement among the accounts. The Twelve are not to take money, bread, a bag (in which to carry their provisions and into which to put anything they were given) or a second tunic (this was the inner garment, so it indicates a change of clothing). Thus all of the accounts agree that either the trip was so urgent or their dependence on God was to be so radical that the disciples were not to take the normal necessities for a journey with them. Luke's absolute "Take nothing for the journey" is certainly how the Twelve felt. They were setting out on a trip totally unprepared, without even food or money to buy food. They were also setting out quite differently from the wandering Cynic and Stoic philosophers of Greece, who traveled simply but were permitted to carry food with them and to take up collections in their begging bag. By way of contrast, if Jesus' followers had been given anything beyond what they could eat or put on there on the spot, they could not have carried it with them, for they had no bag to carry it in.

The third thing we notice is that these instructions were taken seriously by Christian missionaries throughout the New Testament period. The one place we find anyone shaking off the dust of their feet against a city is not in the Gospels but in Acts 13:51, where Paul and Barnabas do it outside Pisidian Antioch. Nor is there any indication in either Acts or his letters of Paul's carrying supplies of any type with him, although this is an argument from silence. We do note that when he comes to Corinth and needs to work he does not set up his own stall but joins in another man's workshop (Acts 18:3). The point is that these passages were put in the Gospels because they were relevant to missionaries throughout the New Testament period. The concern was not simply to record commands given to the Twelve that were irrelevant for later missions.

What, then, can we say about these three passages? It is possible that a corruption has crept into the text and that Mark originally read "no staff" (which was used for self-defense as well as an aid to walking), but that is unlikely. There is no solid manuscript evidence for that, nor would that explain the problem of the sandals as well. The sandals are mentioned twice in the Mark passage (once in Mk 6:9 and then later in shaking the dust off the sandals), while Matthew is consistent in saying no sandals and then telling them to shake the dust off their feet rather than off their sandals.

One solution is to suggest that it is possible that there were two such commands by Jesus and Mark has one and Matthew another. However, Luke, who agrees with Matthew, clearly identifies his account as the sending of the Twelve, not the Seventy, and there is no evidence that Jesus sent the Twelve out on more than one major trip of this type. This solution would be inventing trips simply to save us problems. It may have happened that way, but it is unlikely given the shortness of Jesus' ministry.

What seems more likely is that there were two traditions transmitting these instructions of Jesus. Both traditions have the same essence, that the disciples were to travel light, without the normal supplies needed for a journey, resulting in their total dependence on God, but they differed in their exact wording. Perhaps this was a difference in the understanding of Jesus' Aramaic (since the Gospels were written in Greek), or perhaps this was the result of an adaptation of the traditions to local missionary circumstances (in some areas one might need sandals or the assistance of a staff, while in others it might be more feasible to go without sandals and a staff). Whatever the reason for the differences in the traditions, Mark followed one (perhaps one he received directly from Peter) and Matthew and Luke followed the other (we have no idea who the source of their common tradition was).

These differences remind us that in the Gospels we have the meaning of Jesus, his voice, so to speak, transmitted to us, but not his exact words. None of the Gospels were written in the Aramaic he spoke and none of the Synoptic Gospels, with the possible exception of Mark, were written by eyewitnesses. Thus we are not surprised when the meaning and thrust of the words of Jesus is the same, but the exact wording is different. Only if one has a very legal mind is there a significant difference. Surely early missionaries reading Matthew's version would not feel guilty if while walking up a steep hill they picked up a stout stick to assist them on their way. They were traveling simply, not prepared for the normal problems of travel, and they just accepted assistance which was lying there to be taken, probably with thanksgiving to God. Jesus normally speaks in the hyperbole of a wisdom teacher, not the legal precision of a Pharisee.

These passages are also another reminder to us that we do not have all of the answers. There are issues which may have a perfectly good explanation if we could gather Mark and Matthew and Luke together, but for which we will not have an answer short of such a gathering.

Finally, these passages call us not to lose the forest for the trees. Jesus called his missionaries to travel simply, without the normal provisions for a journey. They had to depend on God for their support. What does that mean for us who call ourselves disciples of Jesus in our security-conscious age? When we would not think of setting off on any mission, ordered by God or not, without ten times the normal provision that Jesus prohibited (credit card as well as money; a suitcase of clothes, not just a change), the issue of whether or not sandals or a staff were or were not permitted to the Twelve fades into insignificance.

6:23-27 Inviolable Vow?

See comment on JUDGES 11:30-39.

7:27 The Children First?

This was Jesus' response to the plea of a Gentile woman that he cure her demon-possessed daughter. The woman was a Syrophoenician according to Mark, a Canaanite according to Matthew, who also records the incident (Mt 15:21-28). The incident took place during a brief visit paid by Jesus to the territory of Tyre and Sidon, north of Galilee.

The saying was a hard one in the first instance to the woman, yet not so hard that it put her off: if Jesus' healing ministry was for Jewish children and not for Gentile dogs, yet she reminded him that the dogs commonly get what the children leave over, and that was what she was asking him to give her and her daughter. To the modern reader it is hard because it seems so inconsistent with the character of Jesus. Its hardness is put in blunt terms by one writer: "Long familiarity with this story, together with the traditional picture of the gentleness of Jesus, tends to obscure the shocking intolerance of the saying."[1]

Jesus' Palestinian ministry was directed to the Jewish people; Matthew, in his account of the present incident, represents him as saying to the woman, "I was sent only to the lost sheep of the house of Israel" (Mt 15:24 RSV). There are suggestions here and there in the record of the ministry that, as a sequel to it, blessing would be available for Gentiles too, but very few instances of direct blessing to Gentiles appear within the context of the ministry itself.

Why did the woman not take offense at such an unpromising response? One obvious reason was that she was determined to get what she wanted for her daughter. In addition, what if there was a twinkle in his eye as he spoke, as much as to say, "You know what we Jews are supposed to think of you Gentiles; do you think it is right for you to come and ask for a share in the healing which I have come to impart to Jews?" The written record can preserve the spoken words; it cannot convey the tone of voice in which they were said. Maybe the tone of voice encouraged the woman to persevere.

Again, what are we to say of the term

"dogs"? That is a term of abuse, if ever there was one. The pariah dog was not an estimable animal in Near Eastern culture then, any more than he is today. But it is not the pariah dogs that are intended here, like those at the door of the rich man in the parable, whose attentions added to Lazarus's afflictions. It is the dogs beneath the table. That in itself might suggest that they are household pets, the children's playmates; and this is confirmed by the fact that the word for "dogs" used by both Jesus and the woman is a diminutive. Since the woman is said by Mark to have been a Greek (that is, one who spoke Greek), the Greek diminutive used by Mark may have been the word actually used in the conversation.

The woman was quick-witted enough to deduce from Jesus' words the kind of reply that would win the granting of her request: "Sir, even the little dogs under the table eat the children's leftovers!" The word *faith* is not mentioned in Mark's account of the incident (as it is mentioned in Mt 15:28), but the woman's reply expresses just the kind of faith that Jesus so greatly appreciated and that never failed to receive what it asked from him. Her daughter was healed immediately, and healed, as in the other instance of Gentile faith in the Synoptic Gospels (that of the Capernaum centurion and his sick servant), not by direct contact but at a distance.

See also comment on MATTHEW 10:5-6.

[1]S. G. F. Brandon, *Jesus and the Zealots* (Manchester: Manchester University Press, 1967), p. 172.

8:12 No Sign?

See comment on LUKE 11:29-30.

8:30 Why the Secret?

See comment on MARK 1:34, 44.

8:33 Get Behind Me, Satan!

Why did Jesus address Peter with such severity?

When, in the neighborhood of Caesarea Philippi, Peter confessed Jesus to be the Messiah, Jesus laid a strict charge on him and his fellow disciples not to mention it to a soul. Why? Probably because the title "Messiah" (the anointed king) was bound up in the minds of most people, and to some extent even yet in the disciples' minds, with ideas of political rule and military conquest, which were very far from Jesus' own understanding of his mission in the world. If the people of Galilee learned that his disciples considered him to be the Messiah, their own convictions about him, which he had done his best to dispel at the time of the feeding of the multitude, would be reinforced, and this might have disastrous results.

As for the disciples, they had to learn that, far from victory over the Romans and a royal throne awaiting him, Jesus faced suffering and violent death. If they believed that he was the Messiah, they must know what kind of Messiah he was; if they were still minded to follow him, they must realize clearly what kind of leader they were following, and what lay at the end of the road he was pursuing. The revelation shocked them; this was not what they expected. Their common sense of shock was voiced (as usual) by Peter, who in his concern took Jesus by the arm in a friendly gesture and began to expostulate with him: "Mercy on you, Master! Don't speak like that. This is never going to happen to *you!*" It was to this expostulation that Jesus made his severe reply.

The words of his reply recall those with which he repelled the tempter in the wilderness, and indeed they have much the same sense here as they had there. It should be understood that "Satan" is not primarily a proper name. It is a Hebrew common noun meaning "adversary." When it appears in the Old Testament preceded by the definite article, it means "the adversary." In the story of Job, for example, where Satan (better, "the satan") is said to have presented himself at a session of the heavenly court (Job 1:6), the expression means "the adversary" or, as we might say, "counsel for the prosecution." This is the regular function of this unpleasant character in the Old Testament. Every court must have a prosecutor, but this prosecutor enjoys his work so much that, when there are not sufficient candidates for prosecution, he goes out of his way to tempt people to go wrong so that he may have the pleasure of prosecuting them (see 1 Chron 21:1). His role as tempter is thus secondary to his role as prosecutor. The Greek word corresponding to Satan is *diabolos,* meaning "accuser" (it is the word from which our "devil" is derived). In Revelation 12:10, where the devil is thrown down from heaven (not at the beginning of time, as in Milton's *Paradise Lost,* but in consequence of the redemptive work of Christ), the holy ones in heaven rejoice because, they say, "the accuser of our brothers, who accuses them before our God day and night, has been hurled down."

In his character as tempter Satan encountered Jesus in the wilderness. Jesus had just been baptized by John the Baptist and had received the assurance from God that he was his Son, his beloved One in whom he found pleasure. The language addressed to him by the voice of God (Mk 1:11) bears a fairly close resemblance to the words of Isaiah 42:1 in which God introduces the one whom he calls his servant: "Behold my servant, whom I uphold; my chosen, in whom my soul delights." If Jesus learned from the heavenly voice that he was to fulfill his life mission in terms of the portrayal of the Servant of the Lord in Isaiah 42:1 and other passages of the same book (especially Is 52:13—53:12 [RSV], which similarly begins with "Behold my servant"), then it was clear to him that the common expectation of a conquering Messiah was not going to be realized through him. Humility, obedience, suffering and death marked the way of the Father's will for him. The temptations to which he was exposed in the wilderness were calculated by the adversary to weaken his trustful obedience to God, and included the temptation to fulfill his destiny along the line of common expectation and not in accordance with what he knew to be his Father's will. We recall in particular the temptation to accept world dominion on the adversary's terms. "It will all be yours," said he to Jesus, "if you will fall down and worship me." Many an ambitious man before then had yielded to that temptation, and many have yielded to it since. But Jesus repudiated the adversary's offer, and it was in his repudiation of this temptation, according to Matthew 4:10, that he said, "Begone, Satan!" (RSV) or, as many manuscripts have it, "Get behind me, Satan!"

And now, from the lips of Peter, Jesus heard what he recognized to be the same temptation again. Peter, in effect, was trying to dissuade him from obeying his Father's will. Peter had no idea that this was what he was doing; he was moved only by affectionate concern for his Master's well-being and did not like to hear him utter such ominous words: "The Son of Man must suffer many things and be rejected" (Mk 8:31). But he was, for the moment, playing the part of an adversary, however inadvertently, for as Jesus told him, "You are not on the side of God, but of men" (Mk 8:33 RSV).

In reproducing these words, Matthew inserts a clause not found in Mark: "Get behind me, Satan! *You are a hindrance to me,* for you are not on the side of God, but of men" (Mt 16:23 RSV). It is noteworthy that Matthew adds this reference to Peter's being a stumbling block, since it is he alone who, in the preceding paragraph, reports Jesus' words about the rock. There are two kinds of rock here: there is a kind of rock which provides a stable foundation, and there is the kind of rock which lies in the way and trips people up. Indeed, one and the same rock can sometimes fulfill both functions. There is an oracle in Isaiah 8:13-15 where God himself is a rock which offers safe sanctuary to those who seek refuge on it in times of flood, but which will become "a stone that causes men to stumble and a rock that makes them fall" to those who are swept against it by the swirling waters. Peter had it in him to be either a foundation stone or a stumbling block. Thanks to the intercession which his Master made for him in a critical hour, he strengthened his brethren (Lk 22:32) and became a rock of stability and a focus of unity.

8:34 Taking Up the Cross?

As commonly applied, this is not a very hard saying. As originally intended, it is very hard indeed; no saying could be harder.

As commonly applied, the expression is used of some bodily disability, some unwelcome experience, some uncongenial companion or relative that one is stuck with: "This is the cross I have to bear," people say. It can be used in this watered-down way because its literal sense is remote from our experience. In the West capital punishment is now rare or a thing of the past, and it is difficult even to paraphrase the saying in terms of ordinary experience.

There was a time when capital punishment was carried out publicly. The condemned criminal was led through the streets on foot or dragged on a cart to the place of execution, and the crowds who watched this grim procession knew what lay at the end of the road. A person on their way to public execution was compelled to abandon all earthly hopes and ambitions. At that time these words of Jesus might have been rendered thus: "If anyone wishes to come after me, let him be prepared to be led out to public execution, following my example."

In all three Synoptic Gospels these words follow the account of Peter's confession at Caesarea Philippi, Jesus' first warning about his impending passion, Peter's expostulation and the rebuke which it drew forth from Jesus. It is as though he said to them, "You still confess me to be the Messiah? You still wish to follow me? If so, you should realize quite clearly where I am going and understand that by following me you will be going there too." The Son of Man must suffer; were they prepared to suffer with him? The Son of Man faced the prospect of violent death; were they prepared to face it too? What if that violent death proved to be death on a cross? Were they prepared for that?

The sight of a man being taken to the place of public crucifixion was not unfamiliar in the Roman world of that day. Such a man was commonly made to carry the crossbeam, the *patibulum,* of his cross as he went to his death. That is the picture which Jesus' words would conjure up in the minds of his hearers. If they were not prepared for that outcome to their discipleship, let them change their minds while there was time—but let them first weigh the options in the balances of the kingdom of God: "for whoever wants to save his life will lose it; and whoever loses his life for me and for the gospel will save it" (Mk 8:35).

Many, perhaps most, of those who heard these words proved their truth. Not all of them were actually crucified.

This, we know, was Peter's lot; the first of those present to suffer death for Jesus' sake, James the son of Zebedee, was beheaded (Acts 12:2). But this is what is meant by "taking up the cross"—facing persecution and death for Jesus' sake.

When Luke reproduces this saying he amplifies it slightly: "he must deny himself and take up his cross *daily*" (Lk 9:23). A later disciple of Jesus, one who was not present to hear these words in person, entered fully into their meaning and emphasizes this aspect: "I die every day," Paul writes (1 Cor 15:31), meaning "I am exposed to the risk of death every day, and that for Jesus' sake." He says that he and his fellow apostles "always carry around in our body the death of Jesus" and explains himself by saying that "we who are alive are always being given over to death for Jesus' sake, so that his life may be revealed in our mortal body" (2 Cor 4:10-11). In another place he refers to "the surpassing greatness of knowing Christ Jesus my Lord" for whose sake he has suffered the loss of everything, and tells how his consuming ambition is "to know Christ and the power of his resurrection and the fellowship of sharing in his sufferings, becoming like him in his death" (Phil 3:8, 10). As a Roman citizen, Paul was not liable to be crucified, but he knew by experience what it meant to "take up his cross daily" and follow Jesus.

Jesus' words about the necessity of denying oneself if one wishes to be his disciple are to be understood in the same sense. Here too is a phrase that has become unconscionably weakened in pious phraseology. Denying oneself is not a matter of giving up something, whether for Lent or for the whole of life; it is a decisive saying no to oneself, to one's hopes and plans and ambitions, to one's likes and dislikes, to one's nearest and dearest, for the sake of Christ. It was so for the first disciples, and it is so for many disciples today. But if this is how it is to be taken—and this is how it was meant to be taken—it is a hard saying indeed.

Yet to some disciples it might be encouraging at the same time—to those actually being compelled to suffer for their Christian faith. The Gospel of Mark was probably written in the first instance for Christians in Rome who were enduring unforeseen and savage persecution under the Emperor Nero in the aftermath of the great fire of A.D. 64. For some of them this persecution involved literal crucifixion. It was reassuring for them to be reminded that their Lord himself had said that this kind of experience was only to be expected by his disciples. If they were suffering for his name's sake, this meant that they were sharers in his suffering; it meant also that they were truly his disciples and would be acknowledged as such by him in the presence of God.

See also comment on LUKE 14:26.

9:1 What Is the Coming of the Kingdom?

To say that some who are now present will not die before a certain event takes place is the same thing as saying that the event will take place within "this generation." What, then, is the event in question—the coming of the kingdom of God "with power"?

The kingdom of God, the new order which Jesus came to inaugurate, had drawn near when he began his public ministry in Galilee; this was the burden of his preaching at that time (Mk 1:14-15). Its presence was manifested by his works of mercy and power, especially by his healing of the demon-possessed: "If it is by the finger of God that I cast out demons," he said, "then the kingdom of God has come upon you" (Lk 11:20 RSV). But evidently it had not yet come "with power" as it would come one day in the foreseeable future. At present it was subject to limitations, but the time would come when those limitations would be removed and it would advance unchecked.

What, we may ask, had Jesus in mind when he made this prediction? And can we recognize its fulfillment in any event or development recorded in the New Testament? We can; but before we try to do so, let us think of a parallel set of sayings. Jesus sometimes spoke of the kingdom of God; he sometimes spoke of the Son of Man. He rarely used the two expressions together, but each implies the other. It is the Son of Man who introduces the kingdom of God, the Son of Man being Jesus himself. There are two sets of sayings about the Son of Man in the Gospels which stand in contrast to one another. In the one set the Son of Man is exposed to humiliation and suffering; in the other he is vindicated and glorified. His vindication is sometimes described pictorially as his being enthroned at the right hand of God. This expression is derived from Psalm 110:1, where the divine invitation is extended to a royal personage: "Sit at my right hand"—the right hand of God being the position of supreme honor and power. Thus, standing before his judges, on the point of receiving the death sentence from them, Jesus assures them that "from now on the Son of Man shall be seated at the right hand of the power of God."

His death marked the end of his humiliation and suffering and, with his resurrection, ushered in his vindication. As a later Christian confession put it, he "was manifested in the flesh, vindicated in the Spirit" (1 Tim 3:16 RSV). And this transition from the Son of Man's humiliation to his vindication corresponds exactly to the transition from the kingdom of God subject to temporary limitations to the kingdom of God now present "with power." The same phrase "with power" (or "in power") is used by Paul when he speaks of Jesus as "descended from David according to the flesh" but "designated Son of God in power according to the Spirit of holiness by his resurrection from the dead" (Rom 1:4 RSV).

With the death and exaltation of Jesus and the coming of the Spirit on the day of Pentecost following, some of those who were witnesses of his mighty works in Galilee and elsewhere saw the power of the kingdom of God manifested on a scale unmatched during his ministry. Within a few weeks, the number of his followers multiplied tenfold; his kingdom was visibly on the march.

This, at any rate, is an interpretation of his saying about the kingdom of God having come with power which makes it intelligible to us. Whether or not this interpretation coincides with his intention when he spoke in this way is a question to which it is best not to give a dogmatic answer.

The three Evangelists who record the saying (in varying terms) go on immediately to describe Jesus' transfiguration, as though that event bore some relation to the saying (Mt 17:1-8; Mk 9:2-8; Lk 9:28-36). It cannot be said that the transfiguration was the event which Jesus said would come within the lifetime of some of his hearers; one does not normally use such language to refer to something that is to take place in a week's time. But the three disciples who witnessed the transfiguration had a vision of the Son of Man vindicated and glorified; they saw in graphic anticipation the fulfillment of his words about the powerful advent of the kingdom of God. Matthew, strikingly, in his report of the words speaks of the Son of Man instead of the kingdom of God: "there are some standing here who will not taste death before they see the Son of Man coming in his kingdom" (Mt 16:28 RSV). This is an interpretation of the words, but a true interpretation. And Matthew follows Mark in saying that when the disciples had seen the vision, Jesus forbade them to speak about it to anyone "until the Son of man should have risen from the dead" (Mk 9:9 RSV). His rising from the dead would inaugurate the reality which they had seen in the vision on the mount of transfiguration, and would at the same time herald the coming of the kingdom "with power."

One final point: the coming of the kingdom of God is essentially the coming of God himself. In the Targum (the Arabic rendering of the Hebrew Bible used in synagogue services) the wording at the end of Isaiah 40:9 is changed from "Behold your God!" to "The kingdom of your God is revealed." The documentary evidence for this rendering is much later than the New Testament period, but it reflects rabbinical usage when the God of Israel overruled the course of events so as to bring his people home from exile, it might be said that his sovereign power (his "kingdom") was manifested, but what the prophet said was more direct: "Behold your God!" In the course of events which led to Israel's return from exile, God himself was to be seen. So again, when the new deliverance was fully accomplished by the death and triumph of Jesus, the sovereign power of God was manifested—God himself came with power.

See also comment on MATTHEW 10:23; MARK 13:30.

9:9 Why the Secret?

See comment on MARK 1:34, 44.

9:40 For or Against?

See comment on LUKE 11:23.

9:43-47 Plucking Out the Eye?

See comment on MATTHEW 5:29.

9:50 Saltless Salt?

One can use salt to season meat or bread, but if the salt that one was going to use loses its saltiness, what can be used to season it?

But how can salt lose its saltiness? If it is truly salt, of course, it must remain salt and retain its saltiness. But probably in the ordinary experience of Galilean life, salt was rarely found in a pure state; in practice it was mixed with other substances, various forms of earth. So long as the proportion of salt in the mixture was sufficiently high, the mixture would serve the purpose of true salt. But if, through exposure to damp or some other reason, all the salt in the mixture was leached out, what was left was good for nothing. As Luke, in his amplified version of the saying, puts it, "it is fit neither for the land nor for the dunghill" (Lk 14:35 RSV). It might have been thought that the dunghill was all that it was fit for, but Jesus may have used a word that meant "manure": "it is no good for the land, not even as manure." Matthew says, "It is no longer good for anything, except to be thrown out and trampled by men" (Mt 5:13), that is to say, people throw the useless stuff out into the street.

The figure of insipid salt appears in the words of the rabbis, with reference (it seems) to Israel's role as the salt or purifying agency among the nations of mankind. Matthew's version of Jesus' saying begins with the words "You are the salt of the earth" (Mt 5:13) addressed to his disciples. This implies that the disciples have a particular function to perform on earth, and if they fail to perform it, they might as well not exist, for all the good they will do. In what respect they are said to be salt is not specified, so the nature of their function has to be inferred from the context and from what is known of the effect of salt. They may be intended to have a preserving and purifying effect on their fellows, or to add zest to the life of the community, or to be a force for peace. The idea of an insipid Christian ought to be a contradiction in terms. One way in which the quality of saltiness can be manifested is in one's language. "Let your conversation be always full of grace, seasoned with salt," Paul writes to the Colossians (Col 4:6), where the "salt" seems to be that ready Christian wit or wisdom (specially apt in the answering of questions about the faith) which is far removed from the slanderous and unsavory talk deprecated earlier in the same letter (Col 3:8).

Since the disciples are spoken of as the salt of the earth in the same context of the Sermon on the Mount in which they are also spoken of as the light of the world and a city set on a hill (Mt 5:14), it is evidently their public life that is in view. They must be seen by others as living examples of the power and grace of God, examples which others are encouraged to follow.

Mark adds some other sayings in which salt figures. These "salt" sayings follow the warning that it is better to enter into life maimed than to be consigned with all one's limbs to the "Gehenna of fire" (Mk 9:43-48). A transition between that warning and the "salt" sayings is provided by the sentence "Everyone will be salted with fire" (Mk 9:49). The fires which burned continuously in the Gehenna or municipal garbage dump south of Jerusalem reduced the risk of disease, which might have arisen from the decomposing organic matter; fire had a purifying effect, as salt also had. The point of Jesus' words in this "transitional" sentence may be that the fire of persecution will have a purifying or refining effect in the disciples' lives (see 1 Pet 1:6-7). Some texts of Mark append here a quotation from Leviticus 2:13 (where the reference is more particularly to the cereal offering): "Season all your grain offerings with salt." This clause is probably not original in this context, but those who were responsible for inserting it (being moved to do so probably by the common theme of salt) may have intended it to mean "Every Christian, by enduring persecution, will be cleansed thereby and so become a more acceptable offering to God."

Then, after the saying about the salt that has lost its saltiness, Mark concludes this series of sayings with "Have salt in yourselves, and be at peace with one another." Again, we should understand this injunction better if we knew the situation in which it was originally spoken. "Have salt in yourselves" might mean "Have salt among yourselves" and might refer to the eating of salt together, an expression of fellowship at table and therefore of peaceful relations. If this is so, then "be at peace with one another" is a nonfigurative explanation of "have salt among yourselves." But we cannot be sure.

10:11-12 No Divorce and Remarriage?

This was felt to be a hard saying by the disciples who first heard it; it is no less a hard saying for many of their present-day successors.

Jesus was asked to give a ruling on a point of law which was debated in the Jewish schools. In Deuteronomy 24:1-4 there is a law which says in effect, "When a man divorces his wife because he has found 'some indecency' in her, and she is then married to someone else who divorces her in his turn, her former husband may not take her back to be his wife again." This, forbidding a man who has divorced his wife to marry her again after she has lived with a second husband, does not lay down the procedure for divorce; it assumes this procedure as already in being. Nowhere in the Old Testament law is there an explicit command about the divorce procedure, but in this context it is implied that to divorce a woman a man had to make a written declaration that she was no longer his wife: "he writes her a certificate of divorce, gives it to her and sends her from his house" (Deut 24:1). Elsewhere in the Old Testament divorce is disparaged as something unworthy: " 'I hate divorce,' says the LORD God of Israel," according to the prophet Malachi (Mal 2:16).

But in Deuteronomy 24 it is assumed that a man may divorce his wife, and that he may do so on account of "something indecent" or "something shameful" (NEB) that he has found in her. The interpreters of the law around the time of our Lord, who were concerned not only with deciding what it meant but with applying it to contemporary life, paid special attention to this phrase. What, they asked, might be indicated by this indecency or unseemliness which justified a man in divorcing his wife?

There were two main schools of thought: one which interpreted it stringently, another which interpreted it more broadly. The former school, which followed the direction of Shammai, a leading rabbi who lived a generation or so before Jesus, said that a man was authorized to divorce his wife if he married her on the understanding that she was a virgin and then discovered that she was not. There was, in fact, an enactment covering this eventuality in the law of Deuteronomy (Deut 22:13-21), and the consequences could be very serious for the bride if the evidence was interpreted to mean that she had had illicit sexual relations before marriage. This, then, was one school's understanding of "some indecency."

The other school, following the lead of Shammai's contemporary Hillel, held that "something indecent" might include more or less anything which her husband found offensive. She could cease to "find favor in his eyes" for a variety of reasons—if she served up badly cooked food, for example, or even (one rabbi said) because he found her less beautiful than some other woman. It should be emphasized that the rabbis who gave these literal interpretations were not moved by a desire to make divorce easy; they were concerned to state what they believed to be the meaning of a particular Scripture.

It was against this background that Jesus was invited to say what he thought. The Pharisees who put the question to him were themselves divided over the matter. In Matthew's account of the incident, they asked him, "Is it lawful to divorce one's wife for any cause?" (Mt 19:3 RSV). If his answer was yes, they would want to know for what cause or causes, in his judgment, divorce was permissible. He gave them his answer and then, in private, expanded it for the benefit of his disciples who had heard it.

As usual, he bypassed the traditional interpretation of the rabbinical schools and appealed to the Scriptures. "What did Moses command you?" he asked. "Moses," they replied (referring to Deut 24:1 RSV), "allowed a man to write a certificate of divorce, and to put her away." They rightly said "Moses allowed," not "Moses commanded"; the enactment to which they referred, as we have seen, took for granted the existing divorce procedure and wove it into a commandment relating to a further contingency. But Jesus told them that it was "because your hearts were hard that Moses wrote you this law." Then, as with the sabbath law, so with the marriage law, he went back to first principles. "At the beginning of creation," he said, "God 'made them male and female.' 'For this reason a man will leave his father and mother and be united to his wife, and the two will become one flesh.' So they are no longer two but one. Therefore what God has joined together, let man not separate" (Mk 10:2-9).

Jesus reminds them of the biblical account of the institution of marriage. The marriage law must conform with the purpose for which marriage was instituted by God. It was instituted to create a new unity of two persons, and no provision was made for the dissolving of that unity. Jesus does not idealize marriage. He does not say that every marriage is made in heaven; he says that marriage itself is made in heaven—that is, instituted by God. To the question "Is it lawful for a man to divorce his wife?" his answer, in effect, is "No; not for any cause."

There is a feature of Jesus' answer to the Pharisees that could easily be overlooked. The stringent interpretation of the school of Shammai and the "liberal" interpretation of the school of Hillel were both given from the husband's point of view. In the stringent interpretation it was the bride's virginity that had to be above suspicion; the bridegroom's chastity before marriage did not enter into the picture. As for the "liberal" interpretation, it was liberal in the husband's interest, in that it permitted him to divorce his wife for a variety of reasons; so far as the wife's interest was concerned, it was most illiberal, for she had little opportunity of redress if her husband decided to divorce her within the meaning of the law as "liberally" interpreted. What was true of these interpretations was true of the original legislation which they undertook to expound: it was because of the hardness of *men's* hearts that divorce was conceded. The law was unequally balanced to the disadvantage of women, and Jesus' ruling, with its appeal to the Creator's intention, had the effect of redressing this unequal balance. It is not surprising that women regularly recognized in Jesus one who was their friend and champion.

We may observe in passing that, in referring to the creation ordinance, Jesus combined a text from the creation narrative of Genesis 1 with one from the narrative of Genesis 2. In Genesis 1:27, when "God created man in his own image," the "man" whom he so created was humanity, comprising both sexes: "male and female he created them." And in Genesis 2:24, after the story of the formation of Eve from Adam's side, the narrator adds: "For this reason a man will leave his father and mother and be united to his wife, and they will become one flesh." That may be the narrator's comment on the story, but Jesus quotes it as the word of God. It is by God's ordinance that the two become one; men are given no authority to modify that ordinance.

When the disciples asked Jesus to clarify his ruling, he reworded it in the two statements quoted at the head of this section. The second of the two statements refers to a situation not contemplated in the Old Testament law, which made no provision for a wife to divorce her husband and marry another man. It has therefore been thought that this second statement is a corollary added to Jesus' original ruling when Christianity had made its way into the Gentile world. In a number of Gentile law codes it was possible for a wife to initiate divorce proceedings, as it was not under Jewish law. But at the time when Jesus spoke there was a recent cause célèbre in his own country, to which he could well have referred.

Less than ten years before, Herodias, a granddaughter of Herod the Great, who had been married to her uncle Herod Philip and lived with him in

Rome, fell in love with another uncle, Herod Antipas, tetrarch of Galilee and Perea, when he paid a visit to Rome. In order to marry Antipas (as Antipas also desired), she divorced her first husband. She did so under Roman law, since she was a Roman citizen (like all members of the Herod family). For a woman to marry her uncle was not a breach of Jewish law, as it was commonly interpreted at that time, but it was certainly a breach of Jewish law for her to marry her husband's brother. John the Baptist was imprisoned by Herod Antipas for insisting that it was unlawful for him to be married to his brother's wife. Jesus named no names, but any reference at that time, either in Galilee or in Perea, to a woman divorcing her husband and marrying someone else was bound to make hearers think of Herodias. If the suggestion that she was living in adultery came to her ears, Jesus would incur her mortal resentment as surely as John the Baptist had done.

But it was his words about divorce and remarriage on a man's part that his disciples found hard to take. Could a man not get rid of his wife for *any* cause? It seemed not, according to the plain understanding of what Jesus said. No wonder then that in the course of time the hardness of men's hearts modified his ruling, as earlier it had modified the Creator's original intention.

In Matthew's version of this interchange, Jesus' ruling is amplified by the addition of a few words: "anyone who divorces his wife, *except for marital unfaithfulness,* and marries another woman commits adultery" (Mt 19:9). The same exception appears in another occurrence of his ruling in this Gospel, in the Sermon on the Mount: "Anyone who divorces his wife, *except for marital unfaithfulness,* causes her to become an adulteress, and anyone who marries the divorced woman commits adultery" (Mt 5:32). The ruling in this latter form appears also in Luke 16:18, but without the exceptive clause; the exceptive clause is found in Matthew's Gospel only, and found twice over.

What is to be made of the exceptive clause? Is it an addition reflecting the hardness of men's hearts? Or is it an expansion stating the obvious—that if something is done which by its very nature dissolves the marriage bond, then the bond is dissolved? Is it an attempt to conform Jesus' ruling to Shammai's interpretation—that if the bride is found to have had an illicit sexual relation before her marriage, her husband is entitled to put her away? All these suggestions have been ventilated. Most probable is the view that the exceptive clause is designed to adapt the ruling to the circumstances of the Gentile mission. If this is so, the term "marital unfaithfulness" or "unchastity" (RSV) has a technical sense, referring to sexual unions that, while they might be sanctioned by use and wont in some parts of the Gentile world, were forbidden by the marriage law of Israel. It is a matter of history that the church's traditional marriage law, with its list of relationships within which marriage might not take place, was based on that of Israel. What was to be done if two people, married within such forbidden degrees, were converted from paganism to Christianity? In this situation the marriage might be dissolved.

Certainly the Gentile mission introduced problems that were not present in the context of Jesus' ministry. One of these problems cropped up in Paul's mission field, and Paul introduced his own "exceptive clause" to take care of it, although in general he took over Jesus' prohibition of divorce among his followers. Some of Paul's converts put to him the case of a man or woman, converted from paganism to Christianity, whose wife or husband walked out because of the partner's conversion and refused to continue the marriage relationship. In such a situation, said Paul, let the non-Christian partner go; do not have recourse to law or any other means to compel him or her to return. The deserted spouse is no longer bound by the marriage tie which has been broken in this way. Otherwise, he said, "To the married I give this command (not I but the Lord): A wife must not separate from her husband. But if she does, she must remain unmarried or else be reconciled to her husband. And a husband must not divorce his wife" (1 Cor 7:10-11).

Plainly Paul, a considerable time before Mark's Gospel was written, knew what Jesus had laid down on the subject of marriage and divorce, and knew it in the same sense as Mark's account. Like his Master, Paul treated women as persons and not as part of their husbands' property. But the disciples who first heard Jesus' ruling on the subject found it revolutionary, and not altogether welcome; it took them some time to reconcile themselves to it.

Is it wise to take Jesus' rulings on this or other practical issues and give them legislative force? Perhaps not. The trouble is that, if they are given legislative force, exceptive clauses are bound to be added to cover special cases, and arguments will be prolonged about the various situations which are, or are not, included in the terms of those exceptive clauses. It is better, probably, to let his words stand in their uncompromising rigor as the ideal at which his followers ought to aim. Legislation has to make provision for the hardness of men's hearts, but Jesus showed a more excellent way than the way of legislation and supplies the power to change the human heart and make his ideal a practical possibility.

10:18 Why Do You Call Me Good?

This is not a very hard saying. Schmiedel, however, included it in his list of pillar texts, arguing (quite cogently) that it is most likely to come from Jesus himself, since no one else was likely to put into his mouth words which seemed to cast doubt on his goodness. A would-be disciple (a rich man, as the sequel shows, but that is irrelevant at this point) ran up to Jesus once and said, "Good Teacher, what must I do to inherit eternal life?" Before answering his question, Jesus took him up on his use of the epithet "good." A word that in its proper sense belonged to God alone should not be used lightly as a mere expression of courtesy, and Jesus suspected that it was simply as a polite form of address that the man used it. He himself did not refuse to describe people as good when he really meant "good." If it be asked how such language squares with his assertion here that "No one is good but God alone," the answer is plain: no one is altogether good, as God is, but men and women are good insofar as they reflect the goodness of God.

It appears, indeed, that the form in which Mark (followed by Luke) preserves these words of Jesus was felt to present a difficulty at quite an early stage in the formation of the Gospels. In the parallel passage in Matthew 19:16-17 the weight of the textual evidence favors the recasting of the man's question as "Teacher, what good deed must I do, to have eternal life?"—to which Jesus replies, "Why do you ask me about what is good? One there is who is good" (RSV). This recasting of the question and answer, however, was not perpetuated. Whereas normally, in the process of transmitting the Gospel text, the tendency is for the wording of the other Evangelists to be conformed to that of Matthew, here the Matthean wording has been conformed to that of Mark and Luke in the majority of later manuscripts, followed by the KJV: " 'Good Master, what shall I do, that I may have eternal life?' . . . 'Why callest thou me good? there is none good but one, that is, God.' " If the saying had been felt to be insuperably hard, the Matthean form would have prevailed throughout the Synoptic record of the incident.

10:21 Sell Everything You Have?

The man to whom these words were spoken certainly found them hard. He was the rich man who came to Jesus and asked what he should do to inherit eternal life. Jesus said, "Well, you know the commandments," and mentioned those which sum up one's duty to a neighbor. That keeping the commandments was the way to life is stated in the law itself: "Keep my decrees and laws, for the man who obeys them will live by them. I am the LORD" (Lev 18:5). The man answered that he had kept all these from early days—presumably ever since the age of thirteen, when he became *bar mitzvah,* personally responsible to keep the commandments.

But he plainly expected Jesus to say something more; he did not come to him just to learn that keeping the commandments was a way to life. And the something more that he waited for came quickly: "There is one thing you haven't done," Jesus said, "and you can do it now: sell your property, give the poor the money you get for it, and come and join my disciples. You will get rid of the burden of material goods, and you will be laying up treasure in heaven." But the man, an honest and attractive character evidently, found this counsel too hard to accept. It is sometimes called a counsel of perfection, from the way in which another Evangelist phrases it: "If you want to be perfect, go, sell your possessions and give to the poor" (Mt 19:21).

But this does not mean that keeping the commandments is the duty of all, whereas giving all their goods to feed the poor is the privilege of those who would attain a higher level of devotion. Paul reminds us that even giving all our goods to feed the poor is worthless without love in the heart (1 Cor 13:3). Matthew's wording might be rendered: "If you want to go the whole way in fulfilling the will of God, this is what you must do."

For those who wish to treat the teaching of Jesus seriously and make it, as far as possible, their rule of life, this is still a hard saying. It is easy to say, "This is how he tested one man's devotion, but he did not ask all his hearers to give away their property in the same way." It is true that those who joined his company and went around with him as his disciples appear to have left all to follow him. But what of those friends by whose generosity they were maintained—those well-to-do women who, as Luke tells us, "were helping to support them out of their own means" (Lk 8:3)? They were not asked to make the sacrifice that this rich man was asked to make; it might be said, of course, that they were doing something of the same kind by supplying Jesus and the Twelve out of their resources. When Jesus invited himself to a meal in the house of the chief tax collector of Jericho, no pressure apparently was put on Zacchaeus to make his spontaneous announcement: "Behold, Lord, the half of my goods I give to the poor" (Lk 19:8 RSV). It is usually inferred that this was to be his practice from that time on; it is just possible, however, that he meant that this was what he regularly did. Either way, Jesus recognized him as a "son of Abraham" in the true sense, a man of faith. But he did not tell him to get rid of the other half of his goods as well, nor did he suggest that he should quit his tax collecting and join his company, as another tax collector had done in Capernaum at an earlier date.

Even so, Jesus' advice to the rich man is by no means isolated; it is a regular feature of his teaching. The same note is struck in words appearing without a narrative context in Luke 12:33-34: "Sell your possessions and give to the poor. Provide purses for yourselves that will not wear out, a treasure in heaven that will not be exhausted, where no thief comes near and no moth destroys. For where your treasure is, there your heart will be also." And Matthew includes the same message in his version of the Sermon on the Mount (Mt 6:19-21).

This teaching was not given to one special individual; it was intended for Jesus' followers in general. He urged them to have the right priorities, to seek God's kingdom and righteousness above all else (Mt 6:33). But it is very difficult to do this, he maintained, if one's attention is preoccupied by material wealth. Experience shows that some wealthy men and women have promoted the kingdom of God above their worldly concerns—that they have, indeed, used their worldly concerns for the promotion of his kingdom. But experience also shows that their number is very small. There is something about concentration on material gain that not only encroaches on time and energy that might otherwise be devoted to the interests of the kingdom of God; it makes one less concerned about those interests, less disposed to pay attention to them. Naturally so: Jesus was stating a law of life when he said that where one's treasure is, there the heart will be also. He would clearly have liked to enroll the rich man among his disciples, and up to a point the rich man was not unwilling to become one of them. But the sticking point came when he was asked to unburden himself of his property.

Fulness to such a burden is
That go on pilgrimage.[1]

But he decided that he would sooner go on bearing his burden than become a pilgrim. Jesus' words to him were not intended for him alone; they remain as a challenge, a challenge not to be evaded, for all who wish to be his disciples.

See also comment on MATTHEW 6:24; MARK 10:25; ACTS 4:32; JAMES 5:1.

---

[1]John Bunyan, *The Pilgrim's Progress,* Part 2.

10:25 Easier for a Camel?

In all three Synoptic Gospels this saying follows the incident of the rich man who was anxious to know how to inherit eternal life—and, in the idiom of the Gospels, inheriting eternal life is synonymous with entering the kingdom of God. His record in keeping the commandments was unimpeachable—he assured Jesus that he had kept them all ever since he came to years of discretion, and Jesus said nothing to suggest that his claim was exaggerated. But, to test the strength of his commitment, Jesus bade him sell his property and distribute the proceeds among the poor. "And," he said, "you will have treasure in heaven; and come, follow me" (RSV). At that the rich man's face fell: this sacrifice was more than he was prepared to make. The incident brings out the real nature of the discipleship to which Jesus called people.

Then, to illustrate "how hard it is for the rich to enter the kingdom of God" he used this striking figure of speech. His hearers recognized it immediately to be a hard saying. It is not merely difficult, it is impossible for a rich man to get into the kingdom of God, just as it is not merely difficult but impossible for a camel to pass through the eye of a needle—even a needle of the largest size. The listeners were dismayed: "Who then can be saved?" they asked. ("Being saved" in the Gospels is a further synonym for entering the kingdom of God and inheriting eternal life.) The disciples themselves were not affluent. Peter spoke for the others when he said, "We have left everything to follow you" (Mk 10:28). But they had not realized, perhaps, just how stringent the terms of entry into the kingdom were—and are.

Not only those who heard the words when they were first spoken, but many others since have found the saying to be a hard one. Attempts have been made to soften it somewhat. The eye of a needle, we are sometimes assured, is a metaphor; the reference is to a small opening giving independent access or egress through a much larger city gate. Visitors are sometimes shown such a small entrance in one of the city gates of Jerusalem or another Eastern city and are told that this is what Jesus had in mind. If a man approaches the city gate on camelback when it is closed, he can dismount and get through the small entrance on foot, but there is no way for a camel to do so, especially if it is loaded; it must wait for the main gate to be opened to let it through. Even if a small camel, unloaded, tried to get through the small entrance, it would be in danger of sticking halfway. It is ordinarily impossible for a camel to get through such a narrow opening, but not so ludicrously impossible as for anyone to try to get it through the eye of a needle. But this charming explanation is of relatively recent date; there is no evidence that such a subsidiary entrance was called the eye of a needle in biblical times.

Others point out that there is a Greek word *(kamilos)* meaning "cable" very similar in appearance and sound to the word *(kamēlos)* meaning "camel." In fact the word meaning "cable" appears in a few late witnesses to the Gospel text. Their reading is reflected in a version of the English New Testament entitled *The Book of Books,* issued in 1938 to mark the quartercentenary of Henry VIII's injunction requiring a copy of the English Bible to be placed in every parish church in England: "It is easier for a rope to go through the eye of a needle than for a rich man to enter the kingdom of God." The editors of *The Book of Books* did not commit themselves to the view that the word meaning "rope" or "cable" stood in the original text; they simply remarked that while the familiar form with "camel" would "doubtless be preferred by Eastern readers," their own chosen reading "makes a more vivid appeal to the West." This is doubtful. In any case, the substitution of "cable" or "rope" for "camel" should probably be recognized as "an attempt to soften the rigor of the statement."[1] "To contrast the largest beast of burden known in Palestine with the smallest of artificial apertures is quite in the manner of Christ's proverbial sayings."[2] In Jewish rabbinical literature an *elephant* passing through the eye of a needle is a figure of speech for sheer impossibility.[3]

No doubt Jesus was using the language of hyperbole, as when he spoke of the man with a whole plank sticking out of his eye offering to remove the splinter or speck of sawdust from his neighbor's eye (Mt 7:3-5; Lk 6:41). But the language of hyperbole was intended to drive the lesson home: it is impossible for a rich man to enter the kingdom of God—humanly impossible, Jesus concedes, for God, with whom nothing is impossible, can even save a rich man. But if so, then the rich man's heart must be changed, by having its attachment to material riches replaced by attachment to the true riches, "treasure in heaven."

It is not easy for anyone to enter the kingdom of God—"the gate is narrow and the way is hard" (Mt 7:14 RSV)—but it is most difficult of all for the rich. Jesus' absolute statement in Mark 10:24, "how hard it is to enter the kingdom of God!" has been expanded in later witnesses to the text so as to read: "how hard it is *for those who trust in riches* to enter the kingdom of God!" This could be another attempt to soften the hardness of his words, making it possible for a reader to comfort himself with the thought "I have riches, indeed, but I do not trust in them: I am all right." But, according to Jesus' teaching, it was very difficult for people who had riches not to trust in them. They would show whether they trusted in riches or not by their readiness to part with them. But the inserted words "for those who trust in riches" are not so wide of the mark. What was it about riches that made Jesus regard them as an obstacle to entrance into the kingdom? Simply the fact that those who had them relied on them, like the rich farmer in the parable (Lk 12:16-21), who encouraged himself with the thought of the great wealth which he had stored up for a long time to come, or his counterpart today whose investments are bringing in a comfortable, inflation-proof income.

There is probably no saying of Jesus which is harder in the Western mind today than the saying about the camel and the needle's eye, none which carries with it such a strong temptation to tone it down.

See also comment on MATTHEW 6:24; MARK 10:21; JAMES 5:1.

---

[1]B. M. Metzger, *A Textual Commentary on the Greek New Testament* (New York: United Bible Societies, 1971), p. 169.

[2]H. B. Swete, *The Gospel According to St. Mark,* 3rd ed. (London: MacMillan, 1909), p. 229.

[3]Babylonian Talmud, tractate *Berakot* 55b.

10:31 The First Will Be Last?

The saying about the first being last and the last first is not peculiar to the teaching of Jesus; it is a piece of general folk wisdom, which finds memorable expression in Aesop's fable of the hare and the tortoise. But in the Gospels it is applied to the living situation during Jesus' ministry.

The saying occurs in two contexts in the Gospels. The first context (in Mk 10:31 and the parallel in Mt 19:30) is the sequel to the incident of the rich man who could not bring himself to sell his property and give the proceeds to the poor. Jesus commented on the difficulty experienced by any rich man who tried to get into the kingdom of God, and Peter spoke up: "Well, we at least are not rich; we have given up everything to be your followers." To this Jesus replied that, even in this age, those who had given up anything for him would receive more than ample compensation, over and above the persecutions which would inevitably fall to the lot of his followers, while in the age to come they would receive eternal life. Then he added, "But many who are first will be last, and the last first."

What is the point of the saying in this context? It seems to be directed to the disciples, and perhaps the point is that those who have given up most to follow Jesus must not suppose that the chief place in the kingdom of God is thereby guaranteed to them. It is possible to take pride in one's self-denial and suppose that by it one has established a special claim on God. "No amount of exertion, not even self-denial or asceticism, can make one a disciple. Discipleship is purely a gift of God."[1] Even those who have made great sacrifices for God are not justified in his sight for that reason; and even Peter and his companions, who gave up all to follow Jesus, may get a surprise on the day of review and reward by seeing others receiving preference over them.

In Luke 13:30 the words (but in the

reverse order) "there are those who are last who will be first, and first who will be last") are added to Jesus' affirmation that "people will come from east and west and north and south, and will take their places at the feast in the kingdom of God" (in Mt 8:11 this affirmation is attached to the incident of the centurion's servant). Those who come from the four points of the compass are plainly Gentiles, whereas some of Jesus' Jewish hearers, who looked forward confidently to a place in the kingdom along with "Abraham, Isaac and Jacob and all the prophets," would find themselves shut out. The free offer of the gospel might be extended "to the Jew first" (Rom 1:16 RSV), but if those to whom it was first extended paid no heed to it, then the Gentiles, late starters though they were, would receive its blessings first.

In Matthew 20:16 the parable of the laborers in the vineyard is rounded off with these words: "So the last will be first, and the first will be last." In the parable the last-hired workmen received the same wage at the end of the day as those who were hired at dawn. It might be said indeed that in that situation there was neither first nor last: all were treated equally. But the words had a wider fulfillment in Jesus' ministry. Those who were far ahead in understanding and practice of the law found themselves falling behind those whom they despised in receiving the good things of the kingdom of God. The son who said "I will" to his father's command but did nothing about it naturally yielded precedence to the son who, having first said "I will not," later repented and did it. "Truly, I say to you," said Jesus to the chief priests and elders in Jerusalem, "the tax collectors and the harlots go into the kingdom of God before you" (Mt 21:28-32 RSV). This was a hard saying to those who heard it, who must indeed have regarded it as an insult—as many of their present-day counterparts equally would. But the work of Jesus brings about many reversals, and the day of judgment will be full of surprises.

[1]Eduard Schweizer, *The Good News According to Mark* (London: S.P.C.K., 1971), p. 215.

10:35 Who Asked for the Seats of Honor?

In Mark it clearly states that James and John themselves came to Jesus to ask him for the places of honor in his kingdom. Yet when we turn to Matthew 20:20 we find: "Then the mother of Zebedee's sons came to Jesus with her sons and, kneeling down, asked a favor of him."

What actually happened? Did the mother come or did the sons come?

The first thing that is clear is that if the mother did come, James and John were very much part of the request. In Matthew 20:22 Jesus responds "to them," indicating that the sons are there. In fact, from that point on he ignores the mother and speaks only to the two men. In 1 Kings 2:13-24 we have a roughly analogous incident in which Adonijah gets Bathsheba, Solomon's mother, to make a request for him. David is impressed neither by the request nor by the means Adonijah used; he quickly sees that the request came from Adonijah himself. Thus the account in Matthew agrees with Mark that the real issue was with the two men rather than with their mother.

The second thing that is clear is that Mark is harder on the Twelve than Matthew. Where, for example, Mark will have Jesus asking, "Do you still have no faith?" (Mk 4:40), implying that there is none, Matthew will have "You of little faith" (Mt 14:31), which seems a bit more generous. Matthew is more generous toward the Twelve throughout the Gospel. If Peter is the source of Mark, does this fact indicate that he is harder on himself and his companions than other writers tended to be?

Thus we are left with two possibilities. Either Matthew, trying to be gentler on the two apostles, added the mother to make the question less direct, or else Mark left her out to cut to the heart of the matter. It seems more likely that the latter is the truth, for Mark's is a far briefer, stripped-down account, and he would have had more than one reason to leave out the mother, who is actually extraneous to the story. It is not that she was trying to push her two sons forward to get herself a better position, but that she was the spokeswoman for her sons, a way of making the request less direct and stark.

Ancient historians did not feel compelled to tell us exactly what actually happened, but rather to give us the right impression from history. They were more interested with the meaning of history than the bare bones of the facts. Thus Mark would have had no problem feeling that he was perfectly accurate in putting the question on the lips of James and John, for they were in fact behind the question, even if they did not actually speak the words. Matthew, wanting to be a bit gentler on the men or perhaps wanting them to appear more polite, notes the role of the mother, but also reveals that Jesus quickly saw through it and turns to the men to give his answer. In either case we get the accurate impression.

The irony of these two version is that in our society we might prefer the way the question is put in Mark to the way it is done in Matthew, since we, unlike the ancient Palestinians, tend to value directness and speaking for oneself. Many ancient cultures, however, valued the use of a respected sponsor or intermediary to make a personal request, feeling that speaking for oneself was too crass and thus impolite. Going through an intermediary allowed the person receiving the request to say no without having to say it directly to you, thus preserving everyone's honor. This observation reminds us again that we need to read ancient documents like the New Testament through the eyes of the original authors and their culture and not impose our cultural values and norms upon them.

Finally, the story itself reminds us of the cost of discipleship: honor in the kingdom of God will be bought through costly discipleship, not through influence; we cannot even evaluate our own place, for it is the Father who grants us our role, but often with accompanying suffering that will feel like anything but honor.

10:46 Two Blind Men or One?

See comment on MATTHEW 8:28-34.

10:52 How Much Faith Do We Need?

See comment on MARK 5:34.

11:2 How Many Mounts for Jesus?

See comment on LUKE 19:30.

11:14 Why Was the Fig Tree Cursed?

This incident is related by Mark and, in a more compressed form, by Matthew. According to Mark, Jesus and his disciples spent the night following his entry into Jerusalem in Bethany. Next morning they returned to Jerusalem. On the way he felt hungry, and "seeing in the distance a fig tree in leaf, he went to find out if it had any fruit. When he reached it, he found nothing but leaves, because it was not the season for figs." Then Jesus cursed the tree: "May no one ever eat fruit from you again." They continued on their way into Jerusalem, where that day he cleansed the temple;

in the evening they returned to Bethany. Next morning, as they passed the same place, they saw the fig tree withered away to its roots. And Peter remembered and said to him, "Rabbi, look! The fig tree you cursed has withered!" (Mk 11:20-21).

Was it not unreasonable to curse the tree for being fruitless when, as Mark expressly says, "it was not the season for figs"? The problem is most satisfactorily cleared up in a discussion called "The Barren Fig Tree" published many years ago by W. M. Christie, a Church of Scotland minister in Palestine under the British mandatory regime. He pointed out first the time of year at which the incident is said to have occurred (if, as is probable, Jesus was crucified on April 6th, A.D. 30, the incident occurred during the first days of April). "Now," wrote Christie, "the facts connected with the fig tree are these. Toward the end of March the leaves begin to appear, and in about a week the foliage coating is complete. Coincident with [this], and sometimes even before, there appears quite a crop of small knobs, not the real figs, but a kind of early forerunner. They grow to the size of green almonds, in which condition they are eaten by peasants and others when hungry. When they come to their own indefinite maturity they drop off." These precursors of the true fig are called *taqsh* in Palestinian Arabic. Their appearance is a harbinger of the fully formed appearance of the true fig some six weeks later. So, as Mark says, the time for figs had not yet come. But if the leaves appear without any *taqsh,* that is a sign that there will be no figs. Since Jesus found "nothing but leaves"—leaves without any *taqsh*—he knew that "it was an absolutely hopeless, fruitless fig tree" and said as much.

But if that is the true explanation of his words, why should anyone trouble to record the incident as though it had some special significance? Because it did have some special significance. As recorded by Mark, it is an acted parable with the same lesson as the spoken parable of the fruitless fig tree in Luke 13:6-9. In that spoken parable a landowner came three years in succession expecting fruit from a fig tree on his property, and when year by year it proved to be fruitless, he told the man in charge of his vineyard to cut it down because it was using up the ground to no good purpose. In both the acted parable and the spoken parable it is difficult to avoid the conclusion that the fig tree represents the city of Jerusalem, unresponsive to Jesus as he came to it with the message of God, and thereby incurring destruction. Elsewhere Luke records how Jesus wept over the city's blindness to its true well-being and foretold its ruin "because you did not know the time of your visitation" (Lk 19:41-44 RSV). It is because the incident of the cursing of the fig tree was seen to convey the same lesson that Mark, followed by Matthew, recorded it.

11:23 Faith Moves Mountains?

Of these sayings, or varieties of an original saying, emphasizing the limitless possibilities open to faith, Mark's form (followed in Mt 21:21) has a life setting in the neighborhood of Jerusalem, during Holy Week; Luke's form may be from the Q collection, in which case the form in Matthew 17:20 (an amplification of Jesus' words to the disciples after the healing of the epileptic boy at the foot of the mountain of transfiguration) combines features from Mark and Q.

In any case, Jesus illustrates the power of faith by analogies from the natural world. If faith is present at all, even if it is no bigger than a mustard seed, it can accomplish wonders: think what a large plant springs from something as tiny as a mustard seed. "We are not afraid when the earth heaves and the mountains are hurled into the sea"—so Psalm 46:2 (NEB) describes a convulsion of nature that leaves men and women of God unshaken because he is their refuge and strength. It may be that Jesus is using such a form of words figuratively to describe the incalculable effects of prevailing faith.

But in Mark's account there may be some more explicit point in the form of words. In that account the words are addressed to the disciples after the incident of the cursing of the fig tree. There may not seem to be much to connect that incident with a lesson on the power of faith. The connection, however, may be provided by the place where, according to Mark, the words were spoken. They were spoken in the morning, as Jesus and his disciples made their way from Bethany to Jerusalem, crossing the Mount of Olives. So, in Mark's account, "this mountain" in the saying would be the Mount of Olives.

Now, in current expectation regarding the time of the end, the Mount of Olives played a special part. It would be the scene of a violent earthquake on the day of the Lord. "On that day," said one of the prophets (referring to the day when the God of Israel would take final action against the enemies of his people), "his feet will stand on the Mount of Olives, east of Jerusalem, and the Mount of Olives will be split in two from east to west, forming a great valley, with half of the mountain moving north and half moving south" (Zech 14:4). If Jesus had this and related Old Testament prophecies in mind on his way across the Mount of Olives, his meaning might have been, "If you have sufficient faith in God, the day of the Lord will come sooner than you think."[1]

See also comment on MARK 5:34.

[1]For this suggestion I am indebted to William Manson, *Jesus the Messiah* (London: Hodder & Stoughton, 1943), pp. 29-30, 39-40.

11:33 Neither Will I Tell You?

See comment on LUKE 20:8.

12:17 Render to Caesar?

For many readers of the Gospels this does not seem to be a particularly hard saying. They pay their taxes to the state and give financial support to the church and various forms of religious and charitable action, and consider that this is very much in line with the intention of Jesus' words. There are others, however, who find in these words material for debate, arguing that their meaning is not at all clear, or else, if it is clear, that it is quite different from what it is usually taken to be. Our first business must be to consider the setting in which the words were spoken. When we have done that, we may realize that some of those who heard them felt that here was a hard saying indeed.

Mark, followed by Matthew (Mt 22:15-22) and Luke (Lk 20:19-26), tells how a deputation of Pharisees and Herodians came to Jesus while he was teaching in the temple precincts during his last visit to Jerusalem and, expressing their confidence that he would give them a straight answer, without fear or favor, asked him if it was lawful to pay taxes to Caesar or not. By "lawful" they meant "in accordance with the law of God, the basis of Israel's corporate life." Mark says that the questioners planned "to entrap him in his talk" (Mk 12:13 RSV); Luke spells this out more explicitly: their purpose, he says, was to "take hold of what he said, so as to deliver him up to the authority and jurisdiction of the governor" (Lk 20:20 RSV). The governor or prefect of Judea was the representative of Caesar, and any discouragement of the payment of taxes to Caesar would incur sharp retribution from him.

It was, indeed, a very delicate question. After Herod the Great, king of the Jews, died in 4 B.C., the Romans divided his kingdom into three parts, giving each to one of his sons. Galilee, where Jesus lived for most of his life, was ruled by Herod Antipas until A.D. 39. Judea, the southern part, with Jerusalem as its capital, was given to Archelaus (compare Mt 2:22). The sons of Herod received taxes from their subjects, as their father Herod had done. The Herods were not popular, but religiously they were Jews, so no religious difficulties stood in the way of paying taxes to them. But Archelaus's rule in Judea proved to be so oppressive that, after nine years, the Roman emperor removed him to forestall a revolt and reorganized Judea as a Roman province, to be governed by a prefect appointed by himself. From now on the people of Judea were required to pay their taxes to the Roman emperor, Caesar. A census was held in A.D. 6 to determine the amount of tribute the new province was to yield.

The Jews had been subject to Gentile overlords for long periods in their history, but no prophet or religious teacher had ever taught in earlier days that there was anything wrong in paying tribute to those overlords. On the contrary, the prophets taught them that if they fell under Gentile domination, this was by God's permission, and they should acknowledge the divine will by paying tribute to their foreign rulers. But around the time of the census in A.D. 6 a new teaching was spread abroad, to the effect that God alone was Israel's king, and therefore it was high treason against him for his people to recognize any Gentile ruler by paying him tribute. The principal teacher of this new doctrine was Judas the Galilean, who led a revolt against the Romans (see Acts 5:37). The revolt was crushed, but its ideals lived on, and the propriety of paying taxes to Caesar continued to be a subject for theological debate. It would be generally agreed that Jews in the lands of the Dispersion, living on Gentile territory, should pay taxes in accordance with the laws of the areas where they lived. But the land of Israel was God's land; this was recognized by its inhabitants when they handed over one-tenth of its produce to the maintenance of his temple in Jerusalem. But the taxes that the Roman emperor demanded were also derived from the produce of God's land. Was it right for God's people, living on God's land, to give a proportion of its produce to a pagan ruler? When the question was framed in those terms, the obvious answer for many was no.

What would Jesus say? While he stayed in Galilee the question did not arise; taxes in that region were paid to a Jewish tetrarch. But when he visited Judea, he came to a place where it was a burning question. However he answered it, it would be almost impossible to avoid giving offense. If he said that it was unlawful to pay taxes to Caesar, the Roman governor would get to hear of it and he could be charged with sedition. If he said that it was lawful, he would offend those who maintained the ideals of Judas the Galilean, and many would think him unpatriotic. This would lose him much of his following in Judea.

"Bring me a denarius," said Jesus; "let me look at it." The denarius was a Roman silver coin; Roman taxes had to be paid in Roman coinage. When a denarius was forthcoming, Jesus asked, "Whose face is this? Whose name is this?" The answer, of course, was "Caesar's." Well, said Jesus, the coin which bears Caesar's face and name is obviously Caesar's coin; let Caesar have it back. The verb translated "render" has the sense of giving back to someone that which belongs to him.

Did he imply that the use of Caesar's coinage was a tacit acknowledgment of Caesar's sovereignty? Perhaps he did. There were some Jews whose orthodoxy was such that they would not look at, let alone handle, a coin which bore a human face. Why? Because it was said to infringe the second commandment of the Decalogue, which forbade the making of "any likeness of anything that is in heaven above, or that is in the earth beneath, or that is in the water under the earth" (Ex 20:4 RSV). Jesus did not necessarily share this attitude—money of any kind was held in little enough regard by him—but there may have been an implication in his words that the Pharisees among his questioners might have appreciated: such coins were unfit for use by people who were so scrupulous about keeping the law of God, and should go back where they came from. Caesar's coins were best used for paying Caesar's tribute. If that was what Caesar wanted, let him have it; the claims of God were not transgressed by such use of Caesar's money. What was really important was to discover what God's claims were, and see to it that they were met. Once again, he laid primary emphasis on seeking God's kingdom and righteousness.

Some interpreters have discerned more subtle ambiguities in Jesus' answer, as though, for example, he included in "the things that are God's" the produce of God's land and meant that none of it should go to Caesar, not even when it was converted into Roman coinage. But this kind of interpretation would render the whole business about producing a denarius pointless. Certainly his answer would not satisfy those who believed that for Judeans to pay tribute to Caesar was wrong. If some of the bystanders had been led by the manner of his entry into Jerusalem a few days before to expect a declaration of independence from him, they must have been disappointed. And indeed, there seems to have been less enthusiasm for him in Jerusalem at the end of Holy Week than there had been at the beginning. On the other hand, if his questioners hoped that he would compromise himself by his reply, they too were disappointed. He not only avoided the dilemma on the horns of which they wished to impale him, but turned it so as to insist afresh on the central theme of his ministry.

13:30 This Generation Will Not Pass Away?

This has been regarded as a hard saying by those who take it to refer to Christ's Second Advent, his coming in glory. If Jesus really affirmed that this event would take place within a generation from the time of speaking (which was only a few days before his arrest and execution), then, it is felt, he was mistaken, and this is for many an unacceptable conclusion.

The genuineness of this saying is argued on the ground that no one would have invented an unfulfilled prophecy and put it on Jesus' lips. If an unfulfilled prophecy is ascribed to him in the Gospel tradition, that can only be (it is argued) because he actually uttered it. In more recent times, however, the utterance has been widely ascribed not to the historical Jesus but to some prophet in the early church speaking in Jesus' name. Rudolf Bultmann regarded the discourse of Mark 13:5-27 as "a Jewish apocalypse with a Christian editing," and thought that this utterance would have made a suitable conclusion to such an apocalypse.[1]

Some students of the New Testament who do not concede that Jesus might have been mistaken are nevertheless convinced that the reference is indeed to his glorious Advent. If "all these things" must denote the events leading up to the Advent and the Advent itself, then some other interpretation, they say, will have to be placed on "this generation." Other meanings which the Greek noun *genea* (here translated "generation") bears in certain contexts are canvassed. The word is sometimes used in the sense of "race," so perhaps, it is suggested, the point is that the Jewish race, or even the human race, will not pass away before the Second Advent. Plainly the idea that the human race is meant cannot be entertained; every description of that event implies that human beings will be around to witness it, for otherwise it would have no context to give it any significance. Nor is there much more to be said for the idea that the Jewish race is meant; there is no hint anywhere in the New Testament that the Jewish race will cease to exist before the end of the world. In any case, what point would there be in such a vague prediction? It would be as much as to say, "At some time in the indefinite future all these things will take place."

"This generation" is a recurring phrase in the Bible, and each time it is used it bears the ordinary sense of the people belonging to one fairly comprehensive age group. One desperate attempt to combine the recognition of this fact with a reference to the Second Advent and yet exonerate Jesus from being mistaken in his forecast is to take "this generation" to mean not "this generation now alive" but "the generation which will be alive at the time about which I am speaking." The meaning would then be: "The generation on earth when these things begin to take place will still be on earth when they are all completed; all these things will take place within the span of one generation."[2]

Is this at all probable? I think not. When we are faced with the problem of understanding a hard saying, it is always a safe procedure to ask, "What would it have meant to the people who first heard it?" And there can be but one answer to this question in relation to the present hard saying. Jesus' hearers could have understood him to mean only that "all these things" would take place within *their* generation. Not only does *generation* in the phrase "this generation" always mean the people alive at one particular time; the phrase itself always means "the generation now living." Jesus spoke of "this generation" in this sense several times, and generally in no flattering terms. In fact, his use of the phrase echoes its use in the Old Testament records of the Israelites' wilderness wanderings. The generation of Israelites that left Egypt did not survive to enter Canaan; it died out in the wilderness—all the adults, that is to say (with two named exceptions). And why? Because it refused to accept the word of God communicated through Moses. Hence it is called "this evil generation" (Deut 1:35), "a warped and crooked generation" (Deut 32:5).

Similarly the generation to which Jesus ministered is called "a wicked generation" (Lk 11:29), "this adulterous and sinful generation" (Mk 8:38), because of its unbelief and unresponsiveness. "The men of Nineveh," said Jesus, "will stand up at the judgment with this generation and condemn it; for they repented at the preaching of Jonah, and now one greater than Jonah is here" (Lk 11:32). In fact, "this generation" has so capped the unhappy record of its predecessors that all their misdeeds will be visited on it: "Yes, I tell you, this generation will be held responsible for it all" (Lk 11:51). The phrase "this generation" is found too often on Jesus' lips in this literal sense for us to suppose that it suddenly takes on a different meaning in the saying which we are now examining. Moreover, if the generation of the end time had been intended, "*that* generation" would have been a more natural way of referring to it than "this generation."

But what are "all these things" that are due to take place before "this generation" passes away? Jesus was speaking in response to a question put to him by four of his disciples. They were visiting Jerusalem for the Passover, and the disciples were impressed by the architectural grandeur of the temple, so recently restored and enlarged by Herod. "Look, Teacher," said one of them. "What massive stones! What magnificent buildings!" Jesus replied, "Do you see all these great buildings? Not one stone here will be left on another; every one will be thrown down." This aroused their curiosity, and seizing an opportunity when they were with him on the Mount of Olives looking across to the temple area, four of them asked, "Tell us, when will these things happen? And what will be the sign that they are all about to be fulfilled?" (Mk 13:1-4).

In the disciples' question, "all these things" are the destruction of the temple and attendant events. It seems reasonable to regard the hard saying as summing up the answer to their question. If so, then "all these things" will have the same meaning in question and answer. The hard saying will then mean that "this generation will not pass away before" the temple is totally destroyed. It is well known that the temple was actually destroyed by the Romans under the crown prince Titus in August of A.D. 70, not more than forty years after Jesus spoke. Forty years is not too long a period to be called a generation; in fact, forty years is the conventional length of a generation in the biblical vocabulary. It was certainly so with the "evil generation" of the wilderness wanderings: "Forty years long was I grieved with this generation," said God (Ps 95:10 Prayer Book version).

But if that is what the saying means, why should it have been thought to predict the last Advent within that generation? Because, in the discourse which intervenes between Mark 13:4 and Mark 13:30, other subject matter is interwoven with the forecast of the time of trouble leading up to the disaster of A.D. 70. In particular, there is the prediction of "the Son of Man coming in clouds with great power and glory" and sending out his angels to "gather his elect from the four winds, from the ends of the earth to the ends of the heavens" (Mk 13:26-27). Some interpreters have taken this to be a highly figurative description of the divine judgment that many Christians, and not only Christians, saw enacted in the Roman siege and destruction of Jerusalem; but it is difficult to agree with them.

Mark probably wrote his Gospel four or five years before A.D. 70. When he wrote, the fall of the temple and the coming of the Son of Man lay alike in the future, and he had no means of knowing whether or not there would be a substantial lapse of time between these two events. Even so, he preserves in the same context another saying of Jesus relating to the time of a future event: "No one knows about that day or hour, not even the angels in heaven, nor the Son, but only the Father" (Mk 13:32). What is the day or hour to which this refers? Certainly not the day or hour of the destruction of the temple: what the whole context, and not only the hard saying of Mark 13:30, emphasizes about that event is its nearness and certainty. The event whose timing is known to none but the Father cannot be anything other than the coming of the Son of Man, described in Mark 13:26.

Luke, as he reproduces the substance of the discourse of Mark 13:5-30, lays more emphasis on the fate of Jerusalem, the city as well as the temple: "Jerusalem will be trampled on by the Gentiles until the times of the Gentiles are fulfilled" (Lk 21:24). When "the times of the Gentiles" (the period of Gentile domination of the holy city) will be fulfilled is not indicated. But this saying, though peculiar to Luke in the Gospel record, is not Luke's invention: it turns up again in the Apocalypse, and in a part of it which is probably earlier than that work as a whole and was subsequently incorporated into it. The outer court of the temple, John is told, "has been given to the Gentiles. They will trample on the holy city for 42 months" (Rev 11:2). This is a prophetic utterance communicated to John by a voice from heaven, but it has the same origin as the words recorded in Luke 21:24.

Matthew, writing his Gospel probably a short time after the destruction of the temple, could see, as Mark naturally could not, the separation in time between that event and the coming of the Son of Man. For Matthew, the one event had taken place, while the other was still future. He rewords the disciples' question to Jesus so that it refers to both events distinctly and explicitly. Jesus, as in Mark, foretells how not one stone of the temple will be left standing on another, and the disciples say, "Tell us, (a) when will this happen, and (b) what will be the sign of your coming and of the end of the age?" (Mt 24:3). Then, at the end of the following discourse, Jesus answers their twofold question by saying that (a) "this generation will certainly not pass away until all these things have happened" (Mt 24:34), while (b) with regard to his coming and "the end of the age," he tells them that "no one knows about that day or hour, not even the angels of heaven, nor the Son, but only the Father" (Mt 24:36). The distinction between the two predictions is clear in Matthew, for whom the earlier of the two predicted events now lay in the past; but it was already implicit, though not so clear, in Mark.

[1]Rudolf Bultmann, *The History of the Synoptic Tradition* (Oxford: Oxford University Press, 1963), p. 125.
[2]Compare G. H. Lang, *The Revelation of Jesus Christ* (London: Garden City, 1945), p. 387.

14:22-24 This Is My Body and Blood?

The words of institution, spoken by Jesus at the Last Supper, were not intended by him to be hard sayings; but they may be included among his hard sayings if regard is had to the disputes and divisions to which their interpretation has given rise.

Mark's version of the words, quoted above, is not the earliest record of them in the New Testament. Paul reproduces them in 1 Corinthians 11:23-25, written in A.D. 55. He reminds his converts in Corinth that he "delivered" this record to them by word of mouth (presumably when he came to their city to preach the gospel in A.D. 50) and says that he himself "received" it "from the Lord" even earlier (presumably soon after his conversion); he had received it, that is to say, through a (no doubt short) chain of transmission that went back to Jesus himself and derived its authority from him. There are differences in wording between Paul's version and Mark's, perhaps reflecting variations in usage among the churches of the first Christian generation, but we are not concerned here with those differences; it is more important to consider the meaning of what the two versions have in common.

The Last Supper was most probably a Passover meal. It may be that Jesus and his disciples kept the Passover (on this occasion, if not on others) a day earlier than the official date of the feast fixed by the temple authorities in Jerusalem. At the Passover meal, which commemorated the deliverance of the Israelites from Egypt many centuries before, there was unleavened bread and red wine on the table, as well as food of other kinds. In the explanatory narrative which preceded the meal, the bread was said to be "the bread of affliction which our fathers ate when they left Egypt" (see Deut 16:3). A literal-minded person might say that the bread on the table was not the bread which the exodus generation ate: that bread was no longer available. But to the faith of the eaters it was the same bread: they were encouraged to identify themselves with the exodus generation, for "in each generation," the prescription ran, "it is a duty to regard oneself as though one had oneself been brought up out of Egypt."

At the outset of the meal the head of the family, having broken bread, gave thanks for it in time-honored language: "Blessed art thou, O Lord our God, King of the universe, who bringest forth bread from the earth." But at the Last Supper Jesus, as head of his "family," having given thanks for the bread, added words which gave the bread a new significance: "Take it," he said to the disciples, "this is my body." The Pauline version continues, ". . . which is for you; do this as my memorial." The Passover meal was a memorial of the great deliverance at the time of the exodus; now a new memorial was being instituted in view of a new and greater deliverance about to be accomplished. And if any literal-minded person were to say, "But the bread which he took from the table could not be his body; the disciples could see his living body there before their eyes," once again the answer would be that it is to the faith of the eaters that the bread is the Lord's body; it is by faith that, in the eating of the memorial bread, they participate in his life.

At the end of the meal, when the closing blessing or "grace after meat" had been said, a cup of wine was shared by the family. This cup, called the "cup of blessing," was the third of four cups which stood on the table. When Jesus had said the blessing and given this cup to his companions, without drinking from it himself, he said to them, "This is my covenant blood, which is poured out for many." (The Pauline version says, "This is the new covenant in my blood, which is poured out for you; do this as my memorial, every time you drink it.")

When Moses, at the foot of Mount Sinai, read the law of God to the Israelites who had come out of Egypt and they had undertaken to keep it, the blood of sacrificed animals was sprinkled partly on the altar (representing the presence of God) and partly on the people, and Moses spoke of it as "the blood of the covenant which the Lord has made with you in accordance with all these words" (Ex 24:8). To the disciples, who had the passover and exodus narratives vividly in their minds at that time, Jesus' words must have meant that a new covenant was about to be instituted in place of that into which their ancestors were brought in Moses' day—to be instituted, moreover, by Jesus' death for his people. If, then, when they take the memorial bread they participate by faith in the life of him who died and rose again, so when they take the cup they declare and appropriate by faith their "interest in the Savior's blood." In doing so, they enter by experience into the meaning of his words of institution and know that through him they are members of God's covenant community.

Matthew (Mt 26:26-29) reproduces Mark's version of the words, his main amplification of them being the explanatory phrase "for the forgiveness of sins" after "poured out for many." In Luke 22:17-20 we find (according to the information in the margin or footnotes) both a longer and a shorter version; the longer version has close affinities with Paul's.

Luke's account is specially important because he is the only Evangelist who reports Jesus as saying, "Do this in remembrance of me" (Lk 22:19). In his account these words are added to those spoken over the bread (in Paul's account they are attached both to the bread and to the cup). From Mark's account (and Matthew's) it might not have been gathered that this was anything other than a once-for-all eating and drinking; Luke makes it plain that the eating and drinking were meant to be repeated.

According to all three Synoptic Evangelists Jesus said, while giving his disciples the cup, "I shall not drink again of the fruit of the vine until that day when I drink it new in the kingdom of God"—or words to the same effect (Mk 14:25 RSV; see Mt 26:29; Lk 22:18). He would fast until the kingdom of God was established; then the heavenly banquet would begin. But when he rose from the dead, he made himself known to his disciples "in the breaking of the bread" (Lk 24:35 RSV); Peter in the house of Cornelius tells how he and his companions "ate and drank with him after he rose from the dead" (Acts 10:41). This suggests that the kingdom of which he spoke at the Last Supper has now come in some sense (it has "come with power," in the language of Mk 9:1): it has been inaugurated, even if its consummation lies in the future. Until that consummation his people continue to "do this"—to take the bread and wine—as his memorial, and as they do so, they consciously realize his presence with them.

See also comment on JOHN 6:53.

14:61-62 You Will See the Son of Man?

After his arrest in Gethsemane, Jesus was brought before a court of inquiry, presided over by the high priest. At first, according to Mark's narrative, an attempt was made to convict him of having spoken against the Jerusalem temple. Not only was violation of the sanctity of the temple, whether in deed or in word, a capital offense; it was the one type of offense for which the Roman government allowed the supreme Jewish court to pass and execute sentence at its own discretion. Two or three years later, when Stephen was successfully prosecuted before the supreme court on a similar charge, there was no need to refer the case to Pilate before execution could be carried out. On the present occasion, however, Jesus could not be convicted on this charge because the two witnesses for the prosecution gave conflicting evidence.

Then the high priest, apparently on his own initiative, asked Jesus to tell the court if he was the Messiah, the Son of God (using "the Blessed" as a substitute for the divine name). The Messiah was entitled to be described as the Son of God, if he was the person addressed by God in Psalm 2:7 with the words "You are my son," or the person who in Psalm 89:26 cries to God, "Thou art my Father" (RSV). Jesus was not in the way of spontaneously referring to himself as the Messiah. But to the high priest's question he answered, "I am." How Matthew and Luke understood this reply may be seen from their renderings of it: "You have said so" (Mt 26:64 RSV) or "You say that I am" (Lk 22:70 RSV). That is to say, if Jesus must give an answer to the high priest's question, the answer cannot be other than yes, but the choice of words is the high priest's, not his own. The words that followed, however, were his own choice. It is as though he said, "If 'Christ' (that is, 'Messiah' or 'Anointed One') is the term you insist on using, then I have no option but to say yes, but if I were to choose my own terms, I should say that you will see the Son of Man sitting at the right hand of the Almighty and coming with the clouds of heaven." (Here "power" on Jesus' lips, meaning much the same as we mean when we say "the Almighty" is, like "the Blessed" on the high priest's lips, a substitute for the divine name.)

What, then, does this saying mean, and why was it declared blasphemous by the high priest? It means, in brief, that while the Son of Man, Jesus himself, stood now before his judges friendless and humiliated, they would one day see him vindicated by God. He says this in symbolic language, but the source of this symbolic language is biblical. Mention has been made already of the Son of Man coming with the clouds of heaven (see comment on Mk 13:30); this language is drawn from Daniel 7:13-14, where "one like a son of man" is seen in a vision coming "with the clouds of heaven" to be presented before God ("the Ancient of Days") and to receive eternal world dominion from him. The "one like a son of man" is a human figure, displacing the succession of beastlike figures who had been exercising world dominion previously. The one whose claims received such scant courtesy from his judges would yet be acknowledged as sovereign Lord in the hearts of men and women throughout the world. His claims would, moreover, be acknowledged by God: the Son of Man would be seen seated "at the right hand of the Almighty." This wording is taken from Psalm 110:1, which records a divine oracle addressed certainly to the ruler of David's line: "Sit at my right hand, until I make your enemies a footstool for your feet." The present prisoner at the bar would be seen to be, by divine appointment, Lord of the universe—and that not in the distant future, but forthwith. "*From now on,*" in Luke's version, "the Son of Man will be seated at the right hand of the mighty God" (Lk 22:69). (Luke omits the language about the clouds of heaven.) "*In the future,*" in Matthew's version, "you will see the Son of Man sitting at the right hand of the Mighty One and coming on the clouds of heaven" (Mt 26:64). The right hand of God was the place of supreme exaltation; the clouds were the vehicle of the divine glory.

The Servant of the Lord in the Old Testament, once despised and rejected by men, was hailed by God as "raised and lifted up and highly exalted" (Is 52:13); this role is filled in the New Testament by Jesus, obedient to the point of death, even death by crucifixion, being "highly exalted" by God and endowed with "the name which is above every name," in order to be confessed by every tongue as Lord (Phil 2:6-11 RSV). It is the same reversal of roles that is announced in Jesus' reply to the high priest.

Why was his reply judged to be blasphemous? Not because he agreed that he was the Messiah; that might be politically dangerous and could be interpreted as seditious by the Roman administration (as indeed it was), but it did not encroach on the prerogatives of God; neither did the claim to be Son of God in that sense. But the language which he went on to use by his own choice did appear to be an invasion of the glory that belongs to God alone. It was there that blasphemy was believed to lie. The historical sequel may be allowed to rule on the question whether it was blasphemy or an expression of faith in God which was justified in the event.

15:26 What Was the Crime?

See comment on JOHN 19:19.

15:34 Why Have You Forsaken Me?

This is the hardest of all the hard sayings. It is the last articulate utterance of the crucified Jesus reported by Mark and Matthew; soon afterward, they say, with a loud cry (the content of which is not specified) he breathed his last.

P. W. Schmiedel adduced this utterance as one of the few "absolutely credible" texts which might be used as "foundation pillars for a truly scientific life of Jesus," on the ground that it could not be a product of the worship of Jesus in the church. No one would have invented it; it was an uncompromising datum of tradition which an Evangelist had to either reproduce as it stood or else pass over without mention.

It would be wise not to make the utterance a basis for reconstructing the inner feelings which Jesus experienced on the cross. The question "Why?" was asked, but remained unanswered. There are some theologians and psychologists, nevertheless, who have undertaken to supply the answer which the record does not give. Their example is not to be followed. This at least must be said: if it is a hard saying for the reader of the Gospels, it was hardest of all for our Lord himself. The assurances on which men and women of God in Old Testament times rested in faith were not for him. "Many are the afflictions of the righteous, but the Lord delivers him out of them all," said a psalmist (Ps 34:19 RSV), but for Jesus no deliverance appeared.

It seems certain that the words are quoted from the beginning of Psalm 22. Arguments to the contrary are not convincing. The words are not quoted from the Hebrew text, but from an Aramaic paraphrase. (For the Aramaic form *Eloi,* "my God," in Mark, the Hebrew form *Eli* appears in Matthew. Any attempt to determine the precise pronunciation would have to reckon with the fact that some bystanders thought that Jesus was calling for Elijah to come and help him.) Psalm 22, while it begins with a cry of utter desolation, is really an expression of faith and thanksgiving; the help from God, so long awaited and even despaired of, comes at last. So it has sometimes been thought that, while Jesus is recorded as uttering only the opening cry of desolation, in fact he recited the whole psalm (although inaudibly) as an expression of faith.

This cannot be proved, but there is one New Testament writer who seems to have thought so—the author of the letter to the Hebrews. This writer more than once quotes other passages from Psalm 22 apart from the opening cry and ascribes them to Jesus. In particular, he says that Jesus "offered up prayers and petitions with loud cries and tears to the one who could save him from death, and he was heard because of his reverent submission. Although he was a son, he learned obedience from what he suffered and, once made perfect, he became the source of eternal salvation for all who obey him" (Heb 5:7-9).

In these words the writer to the Hebrews expounds, in terms of sufferings which Jesus endured, the acknowledgment of Psalm 22:24: God "has not despised or disdained the suffering of the afflicted one; he has not hidden his face from him but has listened to his cry for help." But when he says that Jesus' prayer "to the one who could save him from death" was answered, he does not mean that Jesus was delivered from dying; he means that, having died, he was "brought back from the dead" to live henceforth by "the power of an indestructible life" (Heb 13:20; 7:16).

The same writer presents Jesus in his death as being a willing and acceptable sacrifice to God. That martyrs in Israel should offer their lives to expiate the sins of others was not unprecedented. Instead of having his heart filled with bitter resentment against those who were treating him so abominably, Jesus in dying offered his life to God as an atonement for their sins, and for the sins of the world. Had he not said on one occasion that "the Son of Man [came] . . . to give his life as a ransom for many" (Mk 10:45)? But now he did so the more effectively by entering really into the desolation of that God-forsakenness which is the lot of sinners—by being "made . . . to be sin for us," as Paul puts it (2 Cor 5:21). "In His death everything was made His that sin had made ours—everything in sin except its sinfulness."[1]

Jesus "learned obedience from what he suffered," as the writer to the Hebrews says, in the sense that by his suffering he learned the cost of his wholehearted obedience to his Father. His acceptance of the cross crowned his obedience, and he was never more pleasing to the Father than in this act of total devotion; yet that does not diminish the reality of his experience of being God-forsaken. But this reality has made him the more effective as the deliverer and supporter of his people. He is no visitant from another world, avoiding too much involvement with this world of ours; he has totally involved himself in the human lot. There is no depth of dereliction known to human beings which he has not plumbed; by this means he has been "made perfect"—that is to say, completely qualified to be his people's sympathizing helper in their most extreme need. If they feel like crying to God, "Why hast thou forsaken me?" they can reflect that that is what he cried. When they call out of the depths to God, he who called out of the depths on Good Friday knows what it feels like. But there is this difference: he is with them now to strengthen them—no one was there to strengthen him.

See also comment on PSALM 22:1; HEBREWS 2:10; 5:7-9.

---

[1]James Denney, *The Death of Christ,* 6th ed. (London: Hodder & Stoughton, 1907), p. 160.

16:1-8 What Really Happened at the Resurrection?

See comment on JOHN 20:1-8.

LUKE

4:1-13 Order of the Temptations?

When we compare the account of the temptations (or better, testings) of Jesus in Luke 4:1-13 with that in Matthew 4:5-10, we quickly notice that their order is different. Both accounts agree that (1) the testing was initiated by the Spirit (although Matthew makes it clear that this was the purpose of the wilderness time, while Luke does not make it clear that this was the Spirit's purpose), (2) Jesus fasted during this period (Matthew adds the detail of forty days), (3) Jesus was hungry after his fast, (4) at the end of the fast Satan approached Jesus, (5) the tests involved Jesus' sense of identity, particularly his identity as Son of God, and (6) the first test was a demand for him on his own to make stones into bread. After this the two accounts diverge. While the two Evangelists agree on the content of the next two tests, they do not agree on the order. Luke ends with Jesus on the "the highest point of the temple," while Matthew ends with Jesus on "a very high mountain." Why are these accounts different, and doesn't this cast doubt on the accuracy of the Gospels?

To start with we will assume that the two authors are using the same source, a source that had the testings of Jesus in one of the two orders. We say this because there is plenty of evidence that Matthew and Luke had a source in common (although it was probably an oral source) and because these two accounts are so close that a common source seems probable. However, even if they were using separate sources we would still have the same problem, but just pushed back from Gospels we can examine to sources we will probably never see. Thus our assumption of a common source is helpful as well as logical.

Next we notice that none of the Gospel writers claims to be giving a careful chronology. It is true that in Luke 1:3 the author claims to be writing "an orderly account," yet this does not mean that the order he will set things down in is chronological. It was far more important to the ancient historian that we grasp the *meaning* of history than that we get the chronology straight. Thus Matthew groups the sayings of Jesus in five major "books" by topic: Sermon on the Mount (Mt 5—7), Mission Charge (Mt 10), Parables of the Kingdom (Mt 13), Church Discourse (Mt 18) and Eschatological Discourse (Mt 24—25). Luke has another way of grouping his material, so his Sermon on the Plain (Lk 6) does not contain everything in Matthew's Sermon on the Mount; instead, some of the material is found in Luke's section on God and Mammon (Lk 12) or on Prayer (Lk 11). In each case we get topical groupings, which give us an orderly account in that they order the material so we can better understand it. In neither case do we necessarily get the exact setting in which Jesus said all of the material. To do that would likely have made the material harder to understand, for it would have been split over large portions of the Gospel. Exact chronology is a relatively modern fixation; ancient writers were very happy to compromise chronology if by so doing readers got a better grasp on the inner meaning and real significance of the facts.

It is important, then, to try to see what significance the differing orders point to. Each of the Gospel writers is trying to bring out only some aspects of the character and significance of Jesus, so each of them will be different. Let us look at Matthew first. Matthew begins by noting "forty days and forty nights." Except for 1 Kings 19:8 and the flood account, every time this phrase is used in the Old Testament it refers to Moses on Sinai. Matthew notes this detail because he is quite aware of the parallel. Notice also that all of the responses Jesus gives come from Deuteronomy 6—8, where Moses is exhorting the Hebrews after narrating the story of Israel in the wilderness. So in Deuteronomy 8:3 we read, "He humbled you, causing you to hunger and then feeding you with manna, which neither you nor your fathers had known, to teach you that man does not live on bread alone but on every word that comes from the mouth of the LORD." The reference is to the manna, which was given when the people were hungry and did not trust God, but instead demanded food. Jesus trusts God and does not demand food. Deuteronomy 6:13, quoted in this passage, follows Deuteronomy 6:12, "Be careful that you do not forget the LORD, who brought you out of Egypt, out of the land of slavery." This verse reminds us of the golden calf at Sinai (the reason for Moses' second fast of forty days) when Israel got tired of waiting for Moses and instead made the calf, of which they said, "These are your gods, O Israel, who brought you up out of Egypt" (Ex 32:4). Again, we have a reference to the failure of Israel in the wilderness. Finally, look at the full context of Deuteronomy 6:16, "Do not test the LORD your God as you did at Massah." Again we have a reference to Israel's failure in the wilderness.

Matthew is very conscious of the parallel between Jesus and Israel. In Matthew 2:15 he cites Hosea 11:1, "Out of Egypt I called my son." The Old Testament refers to Israel as this son called out of Egypt. Matthew clearly applies it to Jesus. What, then, is Matthew saying in the testings of Jesus? Israel, God's son, was tested in the wilderness and ten times turned, refusing to trust God, and put him to the test (Num 14:22). They did not show themselves to be true as the collective son of God. Now Jesus comes. He is declared to be God's Son (Mt 3:17), but will he be a false son like Israel or a true son? Like Israel he is led into the wilderness in order to be tested (it is Matthew who stresses this purpose of the Spirit's action). Like Israel there is a forty-day fast (although in Israel's case only Moses is said to fast). Like Israel he is tested with hunger, with putting God's promises to the test (as in Massah, which means "testing"), and with false gods. Unlike Israel, Jesus passes the test every time. He is indeed the true Son, the heir of Israel's promises, able to represent his people. Notice that the test by false gods is the peak of the tests, just as in the Old Testament history the manna and Massah came before the golden calf at Sinai. And it would be false gods that would trip up Israel for centuries until the exile. Jesus conquers all of Israel's failures.

Luke is not writing to a Jewish audience who would see themselves as heirs to the Old Testament and appreciate the points we made above. He uses the same testings and the same responses by Jesus, but his main interest is not in Old Testament fulfillment. Luke's picture is more that of the kingdom of God invading the kingdom of Satan. For example, right after this event we find Jesus announcing the theme of his mission in Luke 4:18-19. We understand about the preaching of good news and the proclaiming "the year of the Lord's favor," and we know about "recovery of sight for the blind," but who are the prisoners who are freed or the oppressed who are released? The fact that the Nazareth incident is followed by the driving out of a demon in Luke 4:31-37 gives us one clue. Another comes in Luke 13:10-17 where the woman crippled by "a spirit" is said to have been "bound by Satan" and is now "loosed" (RSV). Throughout the Gospel we get a picture of Jesus entering the kingdom of Satan and releasing those who are "bound."

What does this have to do with the testing of Jesus? Luke is very directional in his story. It begins with Joseph and Mary traveling from Nazareth to Bethlehem (near Jerusalem), whereas Matthew simply mentions that the birth took place in Bethlehem. Luke has a central section from Luke 9:51—18:34 or perhaps to Luke 19:44 in which Jesus is traveling from Galilee to Jerusalem. Every so often during this narrative there is a notice about where Jesus is on his journey toward Jerusalem, although the section collects material from his whole ministry. Here is the Son of God, starting at the edge of Satan's kingdom, so to speak, and moving steadily toward the center where the final confrontation, the final drama of salvation history will be played out. (Acts, volume two of the story, will start the gospel in Jerusalem and move outward to Judea and Samaria and then on to Rome.) The testing story is this movement played out in miniature. Satan confronts him in the wilderness, then confronts him again on a high mountain (Jerusalem is up in the mountains) and finally confronts him in Jerusalem itself. Each time Satan loses until finally Satan leaves him "until an opportune time." The miniature confrontation is the parable for the larger confrontation of Jesus' ministry. At each juncture when Jesus meets an aspect of Satan's "kingdom" Satan loses, until the final confrontation in Jerusalem. There Satan seems to win, but in fact loses in the end. It is the one who trusts the Father in the testings who on the cross says, "Father, into your hands I commit my spirit." And it is the cross that he had to suffer before he could "enter his glory" (Lk 24:26).

What was the actual order of the testings of Jesus? We cannot be sure. We know which one was first, but do not know the order of the other two. I personally believe that Matthew had less reason to rearrange the testings than did Luke, so suspect that Matthew's order is the original order, but that is impossible to prove conclusively. Both the Gospel writers give what they promise, a truthful interpretation of the life of

Jesus that brings out the true meaning of the different events. Each of the authors sees a different aspect of this true meaning. Matthew focuses on Jesus as the fulfillment of the Old Testament and thus Jesus as the true Son that Israel failed to be. Luke focuses on Jesus moving toward Jerusalem as the Son of God invading Satan's kingdom and bringing God's salvation in history to those whom Satan has bound. Each orders the testings of Jesus and mentions details to bring out their picture. Both pictures are true, but neither is complete in itself. If we lacked either picture we would be poorer. This is why it is important to read each Gospel for itself and to get the distinctive message each author is proclaiming, to see the picture each author is painting. If we try to merge them together to get a homogenized harmony we lose these distinct contributions, moving from books Christians believe God inspired to an interest in mere history. If, instead of imposing our interests on the text, we listen to each author, we will profit as they proclaim to us that aspect of the good news about Jesus that was entrusted to each of them.

5:39 The Old Is Better?

The ancient authorities for the text read variously "The old is good" and "The old is better," but even if we accept the authority of those which read "The old is good," it makes no material difference: anyone who said, with reference to wine, "The old is good" meant that it was better than the new wine.

This is not so much a hard saying as a misunderstood saying. It is often treated as though it carried Jesus' authority and could be applied to a wide variety of situations in which the old is threatened by the new—an old version of the Bible, an old form of worship, an old method of evangelism, and in short everything that is popularly summed up in the traditional term "the old-time religion." But Jesus quotes the saying; he does not necessarily endorse it. The saying is preserved by Luke, who applies it to his version of Jesus' words about new wine and old wineskins. In those words, taken over from Mark 2:22, Jesus compares his message of the kingdom of God to new wine, which cannot be contained in old wineskins that have lost their elasticity. The old wineskins were the rules and forms of traditional religion, which were menaced, as many religious people thought, by Jesus' revolutionary teaching. If, in the saying appended by Luke, the new wine has the same meaning—Jesus' message of the kingdom—then the people who say "The old is good" or "The old is better" are expressing their preference for the old, established, familiar ways. New teaching is disturbing; it forces people to think, to revise their ideas and attitudes. Religious people tend to be conservative, to suspect innovations. Job's friends were like this: the wisdom to which they appealed had the sanction of antiquity, and Job's arguments tended to upset it. "What do you know that we do not know?" asked Eliphaz the Temanite. "What insights do you have that we do not have? The gray-haired and the aged are on our side, men even older than your father" (Job 15:9-10).

Jesus found that much resistance to accepting his message, on the part not of hostile but of well-intentioned and pious people, arose simply from this attachment to old ways and old ideas. They had stood the test of time; why should they be changed? This was a perfectly natural response, and one which was not totally regrettable: it could be a safeguard against the tendency to fall for anything new just because it was new—to embrace novelty for novelty's sake. But when God does a new thing or imparts a new revelation, as he did in the ministry of Jesus, then the instinctive preference for the old could be an obstacle to the progress of his cause. Ultimately, the question to ask about any teaching is not "Is it old?" or "Is it new?" but "Is it true?" Old wine has a goodness of its own and new wine has a goodness of its own. Personal preference there may be, but there is no room for the dogmatism which says, "No wine is fit to drink till it is old."

"The old is good" or "The old is better," then, far from expressing the mind of Jesus, could well express an attitude that he deplores because it hinders the advance of the kingdom of God.

6:24 Woe to the Rich?

See comment on JAMES 5:1.

6:29 Turn the Other Cheek?

See comment on MATTHEW 5:39.

6:35 Love Your Enemies?

See comment on MATTHEW 5:44.

7:6 Did the Centurion Come to Meet Jesus?

In the healing story of the centurion's servant in Luke, it is clear that the centurion does not meet Jesus. It is "some elders of the Jews" who first approach Jesus and request that he come to heal the servant (Lk 7:3). Then when Jesus is on his way the centurion sends "friends" to tell Jesus that the centurion does not feel that he is worthy of a personal visit by Jesus. However, when we turn to Matthew 8:5 we read, "When Jesus had entered Capernaum, a centurion came to him, asking for help."

Here the centurion comes to Jesus. The accounts do not seem the same. Who really did approach Jesus? Why are the accounts different?

First, let us see what is the same in the two accounts. In both a centurion has a servant who is seriously ill (although the word for "servant" differs between the two Gospels). In both Jesus is requested to heal the servant. In both Jesus says that he will come and heal the man. And in both the centurion requests that Jesus heal the servant but not come to the house, for he feels unworthy of Jesus' presence and understands that Jesus' authority does not require proximity. Jesus ends both accounts by marveling at the centurion's faith. So we see that the two versions are substantially the same. They make the same point about the faith of a Gentile centurion in comparison with the lack of faith in Israel, God's own people.

Second, let us see where the two accounts differ. We have noted that the Greek word for "servant" differs (the term in Luke could also be translated "child," but is probably correctly read "servant"). The details of the disease differ, for in Matthew he is "paralyzed and in terrible suffering" and in Luke he is "sick and about to die." In either case the accounts explain why the servant could not be brought to Jesus and why the healing was urgently needed. In fact, the expressions could focus on different aspects of the same situation. Finally, the nature of the mediating differs, for in Matthew the centurion himself comes on the servant's behalf and in Luke first the elders of the Jews and then friends of the centurion come on behalf of both the centurion and his servant. Yet there is also one other difference of significance, for Luke does not have an equivalent for Matthew 8:11-12, in which Jesus speaks of many Gentiles coming to the Messianic banquet while many Jews are thrown out.

Now we can see what is going on. Each Gospel devotes about the same amount of space to the story. In the case of Matthew, he leaves out all mention of the intermediaries, who are not significant in the narrative, because he wants to put in the two verses which draw a further specific point from the story. That point is aimed at Jews, the audience of Matthew's Gospel. In the case of Luke, even if his version of the story had those two verses in it (and we do not know that it did), they are irrelevant to him. His Gospel is not addressed to Jews at all. This gives him more space to describe the role of the intermediaries, whom Matthew left out, possibly in condensing the story. The presence of the elders and then the friends is quite realistic in that in the ancient world you normally sent an intermediary to a person from whom you wished a favor. This could have two purposes.

First, by avoiding the face-to-face contact you did not put the important person on the spot as much (which would not be polite) and you minimized shame for yourself if he turned you down. Second, by sending people more acceptable than yourself, you maximized the chances of receiving a favorable response. So the first set of intermediaries are Jewish elders who talk about this Gentile's goodness toward Israel. The centurion certainly knew that Jesus was a Jew and that he focused on ministry to Jews. He may have felt that a man whom some talked about as the Messiah would also be very nationalistic. Had he heard the story of the Syrophoenician woman (which he almost certainly had not), he would have been sure of this. So he sends important Jews to gain Jesus' favor for a Jew-friendly Gentile and his servant.

Now the second set of intermediaries, the friends, serves another role. It prevents Jesus from dishonoring himself by entering a Gentile's home (remember the issue that Peter has with Cornelius some years later), and it acknowledges the high honor of Jesus and the lower honor of the centurion (a servant had no honor at all, so the healing is viewed as a favor to the centurion, not to the servant). The friends could be Gentile associates or they might well also have been Jews. Now whether all this was necessary from Jesus' point of view is quite beside the point. The issue is that the centurion sees Jesus as a very important figure (far more than the Jews did) and treats him with the respect he would normally accord to such a figure. Luke gives us the full drama of the story so that the esteem in which the Gentile centurion holds Jesus (in contrast with the Jews in Nazareth in Lk 4:16-30) becomes clear. Here was a man of faith. In the people with the Scripture to inform them no faith was found, while in a Gentile we find not simply faith, but great faith. He is so impressed by Jesus that, centurion though he was, he humbles himself before him as if Jesus had been a lord like Caesar.

7:28 Who Is Greater Than John the Baptist?

With minor variations, this saying is reproduced by both Matthew and Luke in the same context. Matthew's wording is slightly fuller and, as usual, he has "kingdom of heaven" where his parallel has "kingdom of God." (The two expressions are completely synonymous; then as now there were some who used "heaven" as a substitute for the name of God.)

The saying is paradoxical: if John was not surpassed in greatness by any human being, how could anyone be greater than he? The paradox was certainly deliberate: we may wonder if any of Jesus' hearers grasped the point more readily than we do today.

In both Gospels the saying comes in the sequel to the account of the deputation of disciples that John, who was then imprisoned by Herod Antipas, tetrarch of Galilee and Perea, sent to Jesus. In his preaching in the lower Jordan valley

John had called on his hearers to amend their ways in preparation for the Coming One, who would carry out a judgment symbolized by wind and fire (Lk 3:17; Mt 3:12). Judgment involved the separation of the good from the worthless, the wheat from the chaff. The chaff, blown away by the wind, would be swept up and thrown into the fire.

After the baptism of Jesus, John recognized him as the Coming One of whom he spoke, but now he was not so sure. Jesus had begun his own ministry, but from the reports of it which reached John in prison, it bore little resemblance to the ministry of judgment that John had foretold for the Coming One. Hence he sent his disciples to ask Jesus, "Are you the one who was to come, or should we expect someone else?"

Jesus might have told the messengers to go back and say to John that the answer to his question was "Yes, I am the one who was to come; there is no need to look for anyone else." But that would not have been very satisfactory. John might have said, "Ah! but he might be mistaken himself." Instead, Jesus kept the messengers with him for some time, and they heard and saw what was actually happening in his ministry. Then, when he judged that they had heard and seen enough for his purpose, he sent them back to tell John all about it—how the blind had their sight restored, the lame were walking, the deaf were enabled to hear and so forth, and how the good news was being proclaimed to the poor. "Tell him this too," he added, "Blessed is the man who does not feel that I have let him down" (Mt 11:2; Lk 7:19-23).

Jesus knew what John would make of his disciples' report. Jesus was doing the very things that, according to the prophets, would mark the inbreaking of the new age: "Then will the eyes of the blind be opened and the ears of the deaf unstopped. Then will the lame leap like a deer, and the mute tongue shout for joy" (Is 35:5-6). Above all, he was fulfilling, and indeed embodying, the prophetic word that said, "The Spirit of the Sovereign LORD is on me, because the LORD has anointed me to preach good news to the poor" (Is 61:1). This should convince John that Jesus was indeed the Coming One: John had not been mistaken about him and need not feel that Jesus was letting him down by not doing the kind of thing John had said he would do.

When the messengers had departed, Jesus began to speak to the crowd about John in terms of unqualified commendation. John was nobody's yes-man, no weather-vane; he stood foursquare to every wind that blew and declared the message of God without fear or favor, to peasant and prince. And when Jesus asked them if they went out to the wilderness to see "a man dressed in fine clothes," they must have laughed, as they remembered John's rough coat of camel's hair. No, said Jesus, for people who wear fine clothes and eat more luxurious food than John's diet of locusts and wild honey you have to go to royal courts—and John was not at the royal court but in the royal jail. John was a prophet, as most people thought; yes, said Jesus, and more than a prophet; he was God's special messenger sent to prepare his way, foretold in Malachi 3:1; he was, in fact, unsurpassed by any other. "Among those born of women there is no one greater than John." John spoke of the Coming One as "one more powerful than I" (Lk 3:16), but here is the Coming One, himself born of a woman, paying a remarkable tribute to John. Then why did he add "yet he who is least in the kingdom of God is greater than he"?

I think we can ignore the suggestion that "the one who is least in the kingdom of God" was a reference to Jesus himself. The "least in the kingdom of God" is the most insignificant person who enjoys the blessings of the new age of salvation that Jesus was bringing in. John was like Moses, who viewed the Promised Land from the top of Mount Pisgah but did not enter it; he was the last of the heroes of Hebrews 11 who "were all commended for their faith, yet none of them received what had been promised." It is not in moral stature or devotion or service, but in privilege, that those who are least in the kingdom of God are greater than John—greater not for what they do for God (in this John was unsurpassed) but for what God does for them. On another occasion Jesus congratulated his disciples because they lived to see and hear what many prophets and kings had longed in vain to see and hear (Lk 10:23-24). It was not because of any superior merit of theirs that the disciples enjoyed these blessings; it was because they lived at the time when Jesus came and were called by him to share the life and service of the kingdom of God. Even to be his herald and forerunner, as John was, was not such a great privilege as to participate in the ministry of the Coming One, to be heirs of the kingdom which John, as the last of the prophets of old, foresaw and foretold.

7:47 Faith or Love?

When we read Luke 7:47, some of us become confused. We are familiar with the concept of "justification by faith" which was so important to Martin Luther, or if we do not use that terminology, we are aware that salvation is by faith. Then we read a passage in which salvation appears to be attributed to love. What is it that saves, faith or love or both?

First, it is easy to show that even in Luke faith is also connected to the forgiveness of sins. For example, when the paralyzed man is brought to Jesus by his friends, we read, "When Jesus saw their faith, he said, 'Friend, your sins are forgiven' " (Lk 5:20). In other places faith is connected to healing (Lk 7:9; 8:48; 17:19; 18:42). In fact, Luke refers to faith some twelve times in his Gospel. Faith does save and heal in Luke.

Second, it is also clear that love (used ten times in Luke) is a central religious attitude. The chief commandment, according to Jesus, is "Love the Lord your God with all your heart and with all your soul and with all your strength and with all your mind"; and "Love your neighbor as yourself" (Lk 10:27, quoting Deut 6:5 and Lev 19:18). Notice that it is love of God and love of neighbor, not faith in God, that is cited as central in the Old Testament text Jesus is quoting (compare Lk 16:13).

The question then arises, How shall we put these two together? The truth is, when we look closely at the two words, they turn out to be related to one another. For us, faith often means agreeing to some belief or concept. That would be the meaning in the New Testament in most places in which the text reads, "Believe that . . ." However, the most common use of "faith" or "believe" ("believe" or "have faith" is the verbal form of "faith") is to believe (in) a person. So we find "Believe God" or "Have faith in God" or "Believe in Jesus." When we read this the author is not asking us to have any particular belief about that person, but to trust in that person or entrust ourselves or commit ourselves to that person. Thus "trust" and "commit" are often better translations than "believe" or "have faith."

Turning to love, for us love usually means an emotion, especially when a person is its object. (Even "I love chocolate" is mostly an emotional expression, despite that fact that the object is not a person.) In the New Testament "love" rarely has any emotional content. It means something more like "seek the good of" or "care for." Thus for us it seems nonsense to say, "Love your enemies," for if they are really enemies how can one have positive emotions toward them? Can one command emotions? Yet the New Testament often instructs us to love: "Love the Lord your God," "Husbands love your wives," and so on. By this it means that we are to seek the good of or care for or even show devoted service to the other.

Now we can see how the two words are related. If we are committed to a person, we will indeed care for them and submit to their will. Loving God in the biblical sense is the flip side of believing in God. Thus it is not surprising that Paul would say, "For in Christ Jesus . . . the only thing that counts is faith expressing itself through love" (Gal 5:6).

Having looked at the two words, we can now turn back to the passage. The woman has come in while Jesus is at dinner, lying on a sofa at the table. She has washed his exposed feet with her tears, dried them with her hair (in loosing her hair in public she shamed herself), anointed them with perfumed ointment, and kissed them. It is clearly observable by all those in the room that she is loving Jesus, for she is seeking his good and caring for him. In that she is caring for his feet she is also expressing great self-abasement (only slaves cared for the feet of another, unless one were expressing great love) and submission to him.

Simon the Pharisee, who had invited Jesus, is concerned about the idea that the woman may have been ritually impure and that Jesus seems blithely unaware of that possibility. Jesus responds with a parable of two forgiven debtors and agrees with Simon that the one who is forgiven the greater debt will love the one who forgave the debt more. Comparing Simon, who had shown little care for Jesus, to the woman, who had shown a lot of care, Jesus notes in this verse that because she has been forgiven much she loves much. The NRSV catches this when it translates the verse "Therefore, I tell you, her sins, which were many, have been forgiven; hence she has shown great love. But the one to whom little is forgiven, loves little." Here the love is clearly the result of having been forgiven, which is certainly one possible meaning of the passage. Yet even if we accept the NIV translation, in which the woman's forgiveness is the result of her love, it is clear that normally without faith (that is, trust or commitment) one will not love, for if one is not committed to a person he or she will not express care for them. Going two verses further we see that this woman is, as we suspected, a woman of faith: "Jesus said to the woman, 'Your faith has saved you; go in peace' " (Lk 7:50).[1]

So what leads to forgiveness of sin? Is it faith or is it love? The fact is that one cannot see faith without love. Love is what faith looks like when it is put into action. As a result, one can look at the love and say, "That person is forgiven because they love much," because if they love much they are also very committed to the one they love, and commitment is another word for faith.

See also comment on MARK 5:34.

[1]The difference between the two translations is in how they understand a Greek conjunction, *hoti.* In most cases of a construction like this it would be translated "because," and thus one would get, "Her many sins are forgiven, because she loved much." This translation also fits well with the generalization "The one who is forgiven much loves much." Some grammarians argue, however, that this term can also express result. In that case one would translate, "Her many sins are forgiven, as a result she loved much." The problem is that the narrator does not speak of any earlier contact between Jesus and the woman and Jesus only tells the woman at

the end of the incident that her sins are forgiven. The general principle is still there (and applied to Simon, who loves little, apparently because he had experienced no forgiveness, nor, perhaps, thought he needed any). Yet the woman does not totally fit the principle in that she loves before she is pronounced forgiven. Did the woman know the rumor that Jesus received "sinful" women? Does she express trust in and devotion to such a man the only way she knew, perhaps not yet being sure he would receive her? We cannot be sure, yet this appears to be the picture, in which case the more difficult NIV translation fits best. Whatever the case, since faith and love are related and both have Jesus as their object, there is little difference between the two in the end.

8:10 Why in Parables?

See comment on MARK 4:11-12.

8:26-39 Two Demoniacs or One?

See comment on MATTHEW 8:28-34.

8:32-33 Why No Concern for the Pigs?

See comment on MATTHEW 8:31-32.

8:48 How Much Faith Do We Need?

See comment on MARK 5:34.

8:52 Not Dead but Sleeping?

See comment on MARK 5:39.

9:3 Were the Twelve to Take a Staff?

See comment on MARK 6:8.

9:27 The Coming of the Kingdom?

See comment on LUKE 9:27.

9:50 For or Against Christ?

See comment on LUKE 11:23.

9:60 Let the Dead Bury Their Dead?

These words belong to the second in the group of three incidents in which Jesus impresses on potential followers the absolute priority of the claims of the kingdom of God over everything else. Here he calls on a man to come along with him as his disciple. The man is not unwilling, but says, "Lord, first let me go and bury my father." A reasonable request, one might have thought. Burial took place very soon after death, so, if his father had just died, he would probably be buried the same day. The man would then be free to follow Jesus. If he was the eldest son, it was his responsibility to see to his father's burial. It may be, however, that he meant, "Let me stay at home until my father dies; when I have buried him, I shall be free of family obligations, and then I will come and follow you." This is not the most natural way to take his words, although it makes Jesus' response less peremptory. But an interpretation that makes Jesus' demands less peremptory than they seem to be at first blush is probably to be rejected for that very reason. His demands *were* peremptory.

Who then are "the dead" who are to be left to bury the dead? One suggestion is that Jesus' Aramaic words have been mistranslated into Greek—that he actually meant "Leave the dead to the burier of the dead." That is to say, there are people whose professional work it is to bury the dead; they can be left to look after this business, but there is more important work for you to do. But this again detracts from the rigorous peremptoriness of Jesus' words. They are best taken to mean "Leave the (spiritually) dead to bury the (physically) dead"—there are people who are quite insensitive to the claims of the kingdom of God, and they can deal with routine matters like the burial of the dead, but those who are alive to its claims must give them the first place. T. W. Manson thought that Jesus' reply was a vivid way of saying, "That business must look after itself; you have more important work to do."[1]

The burial even of dead strangers was regarded as a highly meritorious work of piety in Judaism; how much more the burial of one's own kith and kin! Attendance to the duty of burying one's parents was held to be implied in the fifth commandment: "Honor your father and mother." It took precedence over the most solemn religious obligations. But so important in Jesus' eyes was the business of following him and promoting the kingdom of God that it took precedence even over the burial of the dead.

The added words in Luke 9:60, "but you go and proclaim the kingdom of God," are absent from the parallel in Matthew 8:22. The proclamation that the kingdom of God had drawn near was part of the charge which Jesus laid on his disciples (Lk 9:2; 10:9). The direct sense of his injunction to this man is related to the circumstances of his Galilean ministry, but it retained its relevance after his death and resurrection, and a situation may arise in which it proves still to be strikingly relevant.

Job McNeill, a well-known Scottish preacher of a past generation, used to tell how he found this saying directly relevant to him. When his father died in Scotland, toward the end of the nineteenth century, he was in the English Midlands and was advertised to address an evangelistic meeting in a certain city on the very day of his father's funeral. People would have understood had he sent a message to say that he was compelled to cancel his engagement. "But I dared not send it," he said, "for this same Jesus stood by me, and seemed to say, 'Now, look, I have you. You go and preach the gospel to those people. Whether would you rather bury the dead or raise the dead?' And I went to preach."[2]

See also comment on LUKE 9:62; 14:26.

---

[1]T. W. Manson, *The Sayings of Jesus* (1933; reprint, Grand Rapids, Mich.: Eerdmans, 1979), p. 73. See M. Hengel, *The Charismatic Leader and His Followers* (Edinburgh: T & T Clark, 1981), pp. 1-20: in view of the urgent nearness of the kingdom of God there is no time to lose; all ordinary human considerations and ties must give way to this.

[2]A. Gammie, *Rev. John McNeill: His Life and Work* (London: Pickering & Inglis, 1933), p. 201.

9:62 No Looking Back?

This is the third response of Jesus to a would-be disciple: Luke has brought the three together into one context. There is no parallel to this response in Matthew's record, as there is to its two predecessors.

"I will follow you, Lord," said this man, "but let me first say farewell to those at my home" (RSV). The words "I will follow you, *but* . . ." have served as the text for many a powerful sermon, but in the present instance the "but" was not unreasonable and could indeed claim a venerable precedent. Over eight hundred years before, the prophet Elijah was divinely commanded to enlist Elisha the son of Shaphat to be his colleague and successor. As Elijah went to do so, he found Elisha plowing with oxen. He said nothing, but threw his cloak over the young man as he passed. The young man knew immediately what the prophet's gesture meant, ran after him and said, "Let me kiss my father and mother good-by; . . . and then I will come with you." "Go back," Elijah replied. "What have I done to you?" But Elisha would not be put off; he knew that Elijah had called him to go with him but did not wish to put any pressure on him; the response to his gesture must be Elisha's spontaneous choice. So Elisha went back and not only said goodby to his father and mother, but made a sumptuous farewell feast for all who lived or worked on their family farm; he killed two oxen, cooked their flesh on a fire made with the wood of their yoke, and after he had entertained the people in this way he "set out to follow Elijah and became his attendant" (1 Kings 19:19-21).

Elijah was a very important person, outstandingly engaged in the service of the God of Israel, but he offered no objection to Elisha's taking time to bid his family and friends farewell in a suitable manner. But the business of the kingdom of God, on which Jesus was engaged, was much more urgent than Elijah's business and brooked no such delay. Once again it is evident that, in Jesus' reckoning, family ties must take second place to the kingdom which he proclaimed.

Jesus' reply, like the story of Elisha's call, has a reference to plowing, but this is probably coincidental. In any agricultural society we might expect a proverbial saying about the importance of looking straight ahead when one's hand has been put to the plow: the plowman who looks back will not drive a straight furrow. Jesus may well have adapted such a saying: the plowman who looks back is unfit for the kingdom of God. Here the plowman who looks back is the would-be disciple whose mind is still partly on the life he left to follow Jesus. The work of the kingdom of God requires singleness of purpose.

Sometimes a reference has been detected here to Lot's wife, whose backward look as she and her family fled from the destruction of Sodom was her undoing (Gen 19:26). This reference is unlikely in the present context. On another occasion Jesus did say, "Remember Lot's wife" (Lk 17:32), but that was when he was warning his hearers to flee from a future destruction comparable with that which overtook Sodom.

See also comment on LUKE 9:60; 14:26.

10:18 What Is the Fall of Satan?

When we think of the fall of Satan, we tend to be more influenced by John Milton than by the Bible. In *Paradise Lost* Milton describes Satan and his angels being ejected from heaven and falling down to hell back in the primeval past, before the creation of the human race.

> Him the Almighty Power
> Hurl'd headlong flaming from th' Ethereal Skie
> With hideous ruin and combustion down
> To bottomless perdition, there to dwell
> In Adamantine Chains and penal Fire,
> Who durst defie th' Omnipotent to Arms.

It would be difficult to find biblical authority for this picture, however. The reader of the KJV may think of Isaiah 14:12, "How art thou fallen from heaven, O Lucifer, son of the morning!" And in truth the poetic imagery in which Lucifer's fall is depicted has been borrowed by the traditional concept of the fall of Satan. But Lucifer, son of the morning, is "Day Star, son of Dawn" (RSV). The prophet is proclaiming the downfall of the king of Babylon, who occupied such a high place in the firmament of imperial power that his overthrow can be compared to the morning star being toppled from heaven. In the Old Testament Satan, or rather "the satan" (the adversary), is chief prosecutor in the heavenly court, and when he fills this role he does so in the presence of God and his angels (Job 1:6-2:7; Zech 3:1-5).

So when Jesus speaks of seeing Satan's fall from heaven he is not thinking of an event in the remote past. He is thinking of the effect of his ministry at the time. He had sent out seventy of his disciples to spread the announcement that the kingdom of God had drawn near, and now they had come back from their mission in great excitement. "Why," they said, "even the demons are subject to us in your name!" To this Jesus replied, "I watched how Satan fell, like lightning, out of the sky" (NEB). It is implied that he was watching for this when suddenly, like a flash of lightning, it happened; Satan plummeted—whether to earth or down to the abyss is not said.

Jesus may be describing an actual vision that he experienced during the mission of the seventy—not unlike the vision seen by John of Patmos, when, as he says, war broke out in heaven and "the great dragon was hurled down—that ancient serpent called the devil, or Satan, who leads the whole world astray" (Rev 12:9). When Jesus' messengers found that the demons—malignant forces that held men and women in bondage—were compelled to obey them as they commanded them, in Jesus' name, to come out of those people in whose lives they had taken up residence, this was a sign that the kingdom of God was conquering the kingdom of evil. Many of the rabbis held that, at the end of the age, God or the Messiah would overthrow Satan. The report of the seventy showed that Satan's overthrow had already taken place, and Jesus' vision of his fall from heaven confirmed this. John's Patmos version of Satan being ejected similarly indicates that his downfall was the direct result of Jesus' ministry. So too, when Jesus says in John 12:31, "Now the prince of this world will be driven out," the adverb *now* refers to his impending passion, which crowned his ministry.

The downfall of Satan may be regarded as the decisive victory in the campaign; the campaign itself goes on. Hence Jesus' further words to the exultant disciples: "I have given you authority to trample on snakes and scorpions, and to overcome all the power of the enemy; nothing will harm you" (Lk 10:19). The "snakes and scorpions" represent the forces of evil; thanks to the work of Christ, his people can trample them underfoot and gain the victory over them. The imagery may be borrowed from Psalm 91:13, where those who trust in God are promised that they "will tread upon the lion and the cobra." Paul uses a similar expression when he tells the Christians in Rome that, if they are "wise about what is good, and innocent about what is evil," then the God of peace will soon crush Satan under their feet (Rom 16:19-20). The wording here harks back not so much to Psalm 91 as to the story of man's first disobedience, where the serpent of Eden is told that its offspring will have its head crushed by the offspring of the woman (Gen 3:15).

Finally, the seventy are directed not to exult in their spiritual achievements (that way lie pride and catastrophe) but to exult rather in what God has done for them. To have one's name "written in heaven" is to have received God's gift of eternal life.

See also comment on ISAIAH 14:12.

10:22 The Father and the Son

See comment on MATTHEW 11:27.

11:4 Lead Us Not into Temptation?

See comment on MATTHEW 6:13.

11:23 For or Against Christ?

There is no formal contradiction between this verse, "He who is not with me is against me," and Mark 9:40, "Whoever is not against us is for us" (or, as Lk 9:50 has it, "Whoever is not against you is for you"). In a situation where no neutrality is possible, people must be either on one side or on the other, so that those who are not for are against, and those who are not against are for. But there is a difference in emphasis between the two ways of expressing this.

The former saying comes in a context where Jesus is speaking of the conflict between the kingdom of God and the forces of evil. This is a conflict in which no one should be neutral. Since Jesus is the divinely appointed agent for leading the battle against the forces of evil, those who wish to see the triumph of God's cause must follow him. If they do not, then whatever they may think themselves, they are effectively on the enemy's side. As for the added words about gathering and scattering, gathering is the work of God, while scattering is the work of Satan. God is the God of peace; Satan is the author of strife. "The kingdom of God is the one constructive unifying redemptive power in a distracted world; and every man has to choose whether he will take sides with it or against it."

The latter saying is related to the same subject, although it comes in the course of a narrative, as the punch line in what is sometimes called a "pronouncement story." The story is told, that is to say, for the sake of the pronouncement to which it leads up. Here, then, we have such a punch line. John, one of the two "sons of thunder" (as Jesus called him and his brother James because of their stormy temperament), tells Jesus that he and his companions saw someone casting out demons in Jesus' name, "and we told him to stop, because he was not one of us" (Mk 9:38). In other words, he was not one of the regularly recognized disciples of Jesus. But he was showing clearly which side he was on in the spiritual warfare; moreover, he was acknowledging the authority of Jesus, because it was in his name that he was casting out demons. This was a far cry from the spirit that ascribed Jesus' demon-expelling power to the aid of Beelzebul. By his words and actions he was showing himself to be on Jesus' side.

John was no doubt concerned lest his Master's name might be taken in vain, if it was invoked by a man who had not been authorized by Jesus to speak or act in his name. But Jesus did not share his well-meant concern. John has always had his successors in the church, who feel unhappy when things are done in Jesus' name by people whose authority to do them they cannot recognize. But Jesus' reply remains sufficient to silence this attitude: "No one who does a miracle in my name can in the next moment say anything bad about me" (Mk 9:39).

11:29-30 No Sign?

This saying seems to contradict Mark 8:12 ("no sign will be given to [this generation]"): "no sign" does not seem to mean the same as "no sign except the sign of Jonah." Materially, however, there is little difference in sense between the two, as we shall see when we consider what the sign of Jonah was. In fact, we may be dealing not with two separate sayings but with two variant forms which the same original saying has acquired in the course of transmission. The form preserved by Luke was probably derived from the collection of sayings of Jesus which is conventionally labeled Q. Mark's form reappears in Matthew 16:4; the Q form is reproduced in Matthew 12:39. Both forms are amplified in Matthew's text and assimilated to one another.

According to Mark, the refusal to give a sign was Jesus' response to some Pharisees who, in the course of debate, asked him to supply "a sign from heaven." Jesus spoke and acted with evident authority; what was his authority for speaking and acting as he did? His practice on the sabbath day set at defiance the traditional interpretation of the sabbath law that had been built up over the generations;

what was his authority for refusing to accept the "tradition of the elders"? Whereas the great prophets of the past had prefaced their proclamation with "Thus says the Lord," Jesus was content to set over against what "was said to the men of old" his uncompromising "But I say to you." What was the basis for this claim to personal authority?

How can such authority be vindicated? When Moses approached Pharaoh as the spokesman of the God of Israel and demanded that his people be allowed to leave Egypt, he demonstrated the authority by which he spoke in a succession of signs, such as turning his rod into a serpent and changing Nile water into blood (Ex 7:8-24). No doubt Pharaoh was the sort of person who would be impressed by such signs, but Moses' enduring right to be recognized as a prophet of the living God rests on a firmer foundation than such signs. When Elijah entered the presence of Ahab to denounce his toleration of Baal-worship in Israel, he confirmed his denunciation with the announcement of three years' drought (1 Kings 17:1). Baal, the rain-giver, was to be hit in the one place where he could be hurt—in his reputation. This particular sign was thus highly relevant to Elijah's message. If Moses and Elijah, then, had confirmed their authority as messengers of God by signs such as these, why could not Jesus confirm his authority in a similar way?

First, what sort of sign would have convinced them? External signs might have been necessary to convince a heathen Egyptian or an apostate king of Israel, but why should they be necessary for custodians and teachers of the law of the true God? They should have been able to decide without the aid of signs whether Jesus' teaching was true or not, whether it was in line or not with the Law and the Prophets.

Second, would the kind of sign they had in mind really have validated the truth of Jesus' words? Matthew Arnold remarked, in the course of a nineteenth-century controversy, that his written statements were unlikely to carry greater conviction if he demonstrated his ability to turn his pen into a penwiper.[1] It may be suspected that it was some similarly extraordinary but essentially irrelevant sign that was being asked from Jesus. If, for example, he had thrown himself down in public from the pinnacle of the temple into the Kidron gorge and suffered no harm, that would have done nothing to confirm his teaching about the kingdom of God, even if it would have silenced the demand for a sign.

In the third place, what about the signs he actually performed? Why were they not sufficient to convince his questioners? One Pharisee, indeed, is reported as saying to him, "Rabbi, we know you are a teacher who has come from God. For no one could perform the miraculous signs you are doing if God were not with him" (Jn 3:2). Jesus himself affirmed that if it was by the power of God that he relieved those who were demon-possessed, that was a sign of the arrival of the kingdom of God (Lk 11:20). But some of those to whom these words were spoken chose to believe that it was not by the power of God but by the power of the prince of demons that he healed the demon-possessed. If the restoration of bodily and mental health could be dismissed as a work of Satan, no number of healing acts would have established the divine authority by which they were performed.

In his comments on the "pillar passages" for a scientific life of Jesus, P. W. Schmiedel included Mark 8:12 as the first of four such passages that had a special bearing on the miracles of Jesus. The saying "No sign shall be given to this generation" was an acutely authentic one, he maintained, and implied that the miracle stories of the Gospels were secondary constructions. To this it might be said that, while the healing miracles did serve as signs of the kingdom of God to those who had eyes to see, they did not *compel* belief in those who were prejudiced in the opposite direction. The Pharisees mentioned in this incident may have wanted a sign that would compel belief, but can genuine belief ever be compelled? While the miracles served as signs, they were not performed in order to be signs. They were as much part and parcel of Jesus' ministry as was his preaching—not, as it has been put, seals affixed to the document to certify its genuineness but an integral element in the very text of the document.[2] No sign would be given that was not already available in the ministry itself; to ask for more was a mark of unbelief.

What, now, of the sign of Jonah? Jonah, it is said, was "a sign to the men of Nineveh." How? By his one-sentence message of judgment. That was all the "sign" that the people of Nineveh had; it was sufficient to move them to belief and repentance. Schmiedel illustrates that there is no real contradiction between "no sign" absolutely and "no sign except the sign of Jonah" by the analogy of an aggressor who invades a neighboring country without provocation. When asked what justification he can give for his action, he replies, "I shall give you no other justification than that which my sword gives"—which is as much as to say "no justification." As Jonah's ministry in Nineveh was sign enough, so Jesus' ministry in Palestine is sign enough. No other sign would be given.

In the Q collection the refusal to give any sign but the sign of Jonah was followed by a comparison between the people to whom Jesus ministered and those to whom Jonah preached. Jesus' hearers shared the rich heritage of divine worship and revelation which had been enjoyed over the centuries by the people of Israel; Jonah preached to pagans. Yet Jonah's hearers made a swift and positive response to his message; the reaction on the part of the majority of Jesus' hearers was quite different. Therefore, he said, "The men of Nineveh will stand up at the judgment with this generation and condemn it; for they repented at the preaching of Jonah, and now one greater than Jonah is here" (Mt 12:41; Lk 11:32). The "something greater" was Jesus' proclamation of the kingdom of God, which was more important and far-reaching than Jonah and his preaching. Yet Jonah and his preaching were enough to bring the people of Nineveh to repentance; Jesus' proclamation of the kingdom made no such large-scale impact on his generation. On the day of judgment, therefore, the people of Nineveh would compare very favorably with the Galileans to whom Jesus preached; indeed, they would serve as tacit, if not as vocal, witnesses against them. Whether these words of Jesus were spoken on the same occasion as the saying about the sign or on another occasion, their relevance to it is unmistakable.

Matthew, for his part, adds a further analogy between Jonah's situation and that of Jesus: "For as Jonah was three days and three nights in the belly of a huge fish, so the Son of Man will be three days and three nights in the heart of the earth" (Mt 12:40). This is commonly supposed to be a later insertion among the Jonah sayings, but T. W. Manson has pointed out that no one after the resurrection of Jesus, which by common Christian consent took place on "the third day," would have represented him as being buried for a much longer period.[3] In any case, it would be unwise to press "three days and three nights" to mean seventy-two hours, neither more nor less. Jonah's experience in the Mediterranean was not a sign to the people of Nineveh, any more than Jesus' resurrection on Easter Day after his entombment on Good Friday was a public spectacle. In Matthew 12:40 we simply have an analogy traced between two servants of God, who were both brought up by God "from the Pit" (Jon 2:6; see Ps 16:10, quoted with reference to Jesus in Acts 2:27; 13:35).

See also comment on MATTHEW 12:40.

[1]M. Arnold, *Literature and Dogma* (New York: Macmillan, 1895), p. 95.

[2]D. S. Cairns, *The Faith That Rebels* (London: Student Christian Movement, 1928), p. 25.

[3]T. W. Manson, *The Sayings of Jesus* (1933; reprint, Grand Rapids, Mich.: Eerdmans, 1979), pp. 89-90.

12:4-5 Whom Should We Fear?

The first part of this saying presents no difficulty. Jesus faced violent death himself, and he warned his disciples more than once that they might expect no less. "Brother will betray brother to death," he said. "All men will hate you because of me" (Mt 10:21-22). In a counterpart to these words in the Fourth Gospel he tells them that "a time is coming when anyone who kills you will think he is offering a service to God" (Jn 16:2). But those who put them to death could do them no more harm. Stephen might be stoned to death, but his eyes were filled with the vision of the Son of Man standing to welcome him as his advocate and friend at the right hand of God (Acts 7:56). So too Paul, on the eve of execution, could say with confidence, "The Lord will rescue me from every evil attack and will bring me safely me to his heavenly kingdom" (2 Tim 4:18).

It is the second part of the saying that raises a question. Whereas in both Gospels "those who kill the body" are referred to in the plural, the person who is really to be feared is mentioned in the singular: it is he "who, after the killing of the body, has power to throw you into hell" or, as it is put in Matthew's version, "who can destroy both soul and body in hell" (Mt 10:28). Who is he?

There are those who "kill the body but cannot kill the soul," as it runs in Matthew; there are others who do serious damage to the souls of men, women and children by reducing them to obedient automata, by leading them into sin, or in other ways. Are such people to be feared more than ordinary murderers? Perhaps they are. The singular pronoun *him* in "fear him" could mean "that sort of person." But it is more probable that Jesus meant "Be more afraid of the condemnation of God than of the death sentence of human beings." This sense is not unparalleled in Jewish literature of the period. In a document from Jewish Alexandria, the fourth book of Maccabees (which quite certainly has not influenced the present saying of Jesus or been influenced by it), seven brothers about to be martyred because of the refusal to renounce their faith encourage one another in these words: "Let us not fear him who thinks he is killing us; for great conflict and danger to the soul is laid up in eternal torment for those who transgress the commandment of God" (4 Macc 13:14-15). If they are put to death for their fidelity to God, they have the sure hope of eternal life; if through fear of physical death they prove unfaithful to him, certain retribution awaits them. The sense is more or less the same in Jesus' present saying. The one who has power to cast into hell is not, as some have suggested, the devil; if he is resisted, he can do no real harm to the follower of Jesus. It is God who is to be feared:

Fear him, ye saints, and you will then
Have nothing else to fear.

The "hell" mentioned here is Gehenna, the place of eternal destruction after death. There are Jewish parallels for the belief, attested in Matthew's form of the saying, that soul and body alike are consumed in the fire of Gehenna.

It is noteworthy that in both Gospels, immediately after the warning that the condemnation of God is to be feared, comes the encouragement that the protecting love of God is to be trusted: the God who takes note of the fall of a single sparrow knows every hair of his children's heads (Lk 12:6-7; Mt 10:29-31).

See also comment on PROVERBS 1:7.

12:10 An Unpardonable Sin?

See comment on MARK 3:28-29.

12:33-34 Sell Your Possessions?

See comment on MARK 10:21.

12:49 Bringing Fire to Earth?

This saying is hard in the sense of being difficult to understand, mainly because it is not obviously related to the context in which it appears. It may be thought probable that it is somehow connected with the saying immediately following about the baptism that Jesus had to undergo before current restraints were removed, but this cannot be taken for granted. Each of the two sayings must first be examined by itself.

It is natural to link the "fire" in this saying with the "fire" mentioned in John the Baptist's description of the work to be accomplished by the one whose way he was preparing: "But one more powerful than I will come, the thongs of whose sandals I am not worthy to untie. He will baptize you with the Holy Spirit and with fire" (Lk 3:16). The fire is closely associated here with the Holy Spirit. A shorter form of John's words is found in Mark 1:8; there, however, there is no mention of fire: "He will baptize you with the Holy Spirit." Matthew, like Luke, adds the words "and with fire" (Mt 3:11), and both Matthew and Luke go on to report further words of John about the Coming One: "His winnowing fork is in his hand, and he will clear his threshing floor, gathering his wheat into the barn and burning up the chaff with unquenchable fire" (Mt 3:12; Lk 3:17). It is worth bearing in mind that the same word is used in Greek, the language of the Gospels, for "Spirit," "breath" and "wind"; similarly in the language normally spoken by John and Jesus, Aramaic, one and the same word did duty for all three concepts.

The picture John draws is of the grain and the chaff lying piled up on the threshing floor after the harvest. The mixture of grain and chaff is tossed up into the air with the winnowing fork or shovel; the light chaff is blown away by the wind and the heavier grain falls back on the floor, from which it is collected to be stored in the granary. The chaff is then swept up and burned. Both the wind and the fire are symbols of the Holy Spirit; they depict the work that the Coming One is to do by the power of the Spirit, separating the true children of the kingdom from those who were only nominally so. (The figure of chaff is an ancient one in this kind of context; according to Ps 1:4, "the wicked . . . are like chaff that the wind blows away.")

Jesus' ministry was not exactly the ministry of judgment that John envisaged, but a ministry of sifting and separating it certainly was. Yet Jesus plainly looked for something further when he said, "I came to set the earth on fire, and how I wish the fire had already broken out!"

One suggestion links these words with the hard saying that comes shortly afterward in Luke 12:51-53, where Jesus says that he did not come to give peace on earth but rather division. We shall have to consider this hard saying also, but the difficulty about understanding the fire in Luke 12:49 in the sense of the division and strife that Jesus foresaw as the effect of his ministry lies in his earnest wish that the fire "were already kindled." He foresaw the division and strife indeed as the effect of his ministry, but he did not desire it. It is more satisfactory to take these words as the expression of a longing for an outpouring of the Spirit in power the like of which had not yet been seen.

Jesus himself experienced a personal outpouring of the Spirit at his baptism in the Jordan. A pictorial account of this outpouring in terms of fire is preserved in the second-century Christian writer Justin Martyr: "When Jesus went down into the water a fire was kindled in the Jordan."[1] The same figure appears in a saying ascribed to Jesus in the *Gospel of Thomas* and elsewhere: "He who is near me is near the fire, and he who is far from me is far from the kingdom."[2] The fire was there in Jesus' ministry, but the earth had not yet caught fire. One day it would catch fire in earnest, with the descent of the Holy Spirit at Pentecost; but Jesus himself had to die before this consummation could be realized, and while his death is not explicitly mentioned in these words about the fire, it is probably implied as a prospect beneath their surface. Hence the note of poignancy which can be discerned.

[1]Justin *Dialogue with Trypho* 88.3.
[2]*Gospel of Thomas,* Saying 82; also in Origen *Homilies on Jeremiah* 20.3.

12:50 Distressed Until Baptism Completed?

There is nothing in the immediate context of this saying, which is found only in Luke's Gospel, to throw light on its meaning. It must be read in the wider context of Jesus' whole teaching and ministry. In form it resembles the saying which precedes it, in which Jesus longs that the fire which he came to start were already kindled, but in sense it has much in common with those sayings in which the kingdom of God is seen to be subject to temporary limitations until something happens to unleash its full power. Here it is Jesus himself who is subject to a temporary limitation. As the NEB renders the saying: "I have a baptism to undergo, and what constraint I am under until the ordeal is over!"

Two questions are raised by the saying: (1) What was the baptism Jesus had to undergo? (2) What was the constraint under which he had to work until this baptism had taken place?

First, there is little doubt that by his baptism Jesus meant his impending death. This is confirmed by the record of another occasion on which he used similar language. On Jesus' last journey to Jerusalem, Mark tells us, he was approached by James and John, the two sons of Zebedee, who asked that they might be given the two positions of chief honor when his kingdom was established—the one at his right hand and the other at his left. Their request betrayed an almost ludicrous misconception of the nature of the kingdom of which Jesus spoke, but he began to set them right by asking a question which at first did not seem to have much bearing on what they had said. "Tell me this," he replied: "Are you able to drink from my cup and be baptized with my baptism?" When they said, "We are," he replied, "You shall—but even so that will not guarantee you the two chief places for which you ask." When he asked, "Can you drink the cup I drink or be baptized with the baptism I am baptized with?" (Mk 10:38), he meant, simply, "Are you able to share my suffering and death?" In fact, they did not share his suffering and death—not, at least, at the time when he was crucified. If things had turned out otherwise, if the crosses which flanked the cross of Jesus had been occupied not by the two robbers but by James and John, would they not have secured there and then the two positions of chief honor—the one at his right hand and the other at his left? In all subsequent Christian memory this high glory would have been exclusively theirs.

For our present purpose, however, we note that Jesus spoke then of his impending suffering and death as his "baptism," and that supports the suggestion that the baptism to which he looked forward in the saying now under consideration bears the same meaning. If that is so, a further question arises: Why did he speak of his suffering and death as a baptism? He had undergone one baptism at the beginning of his ministry, his baptism in the Jordan. Was there some feature of that baptism, administered by John the Baptist, which lent itself to this figurative use?

John's baptism is said to have been "a baptism of repentance for the forgiveness of sins" (Mk 1:4). That is to say, people who were convicted of sin under John's preaching were invited to give public proof of their repentance by accepting baptism at his hands. Thus their sins would be forgiven and they would be "a people prepared for the Lord" (Lk 1:17), ready for the moment when he would begin to execute his judgment through the agency of a person whom John denoted as the "Coming One." Jesus recognized John's ministry to be a work of God and associated himself with it publicly by asking John to baptize him. True, Jesus at no time betrays any awareness of sin, any sense of repentance, any need for forgiveness. Yet he was never unwilling to associate with sinners; indeed, he was written off by some godly people as a "friend of sinners" (and therefore, by implication, no better than the company he kept). So his association with repentant sinners in receiving John's baptism was in keeping with his later practice.

Even so, some difficulty was felt about Jesus' undergoing a "baptism of repentance for the forgiveness of sins." Matthew in his account tells how John himself demurred at Jesus' request, saying, "It would be more fitting that I should be baptized by you; why do you come to me?" Jesus' response to John's protest is excellently rendered in the NEB: "Let it be so for the present; we do well to conform in this way with all that God requires" (Mt 3:15). These words are recorded by Matthew only, but they express perfectly the spirit in which Jesus sought and received John's baptism. That this is so is confirmed by his experience when he came up from the river: he saw heaven split in two and the Spirit of God descending on him in the form of a dove, while a voice addressed him from heaven: "You are my Son, whom I love; with you I am well pleased" (Mk 1:10-11). It was as though God said to him, "You dedicate yourself to the doing of my will? You conform in this way with all that I require? I tell you this, then: you are my Son, my chosen one, the one in whom I delight." Jesus' period of testing in the wilderness, which followed immediately after his baptism, reinforced the strength of his commitment to do the will of God without deviation.

But what did this have to do with the baptism to which he looked forward? He could, no doubt, have referred to his death, with the events leading up to it, as his baptism in the sense of a sea of troubles that threatened to overwhelm him. But in the light of the baptism which inaugurated his public ministry, we can see more in his language than that. His baptism in the Jordan gave visible expression to his resolution to fulfill the will of God, and it involved at least a token identification of himself with sinners. The ministry thus inaugurated manifested his constant devotion to the will of God and was marked by unaffected friendship with sinners. His death, which crowned that ministry, consummated his embracing of the will of God as the rule for his life, and it involved a real and personal identification of himself with sinners, on the part of One sinless himself. In this way he embodied the Old Testament picture of the obedient and suffering Servant of the Lord who "bore the sin of many, and made intercession for the transgressors" (Is 53:12).

It is not for nothing that one of the latest New Testament documents voices the Christian confession in these words: "This is the one who came by water and blood—Jesus Christ. He did not come by water only, but by water and blood" (1 Jn 5:6)—or, as we might say, not only with the baptism of water, but with the baptism of water and the baptism of death. The baptism of water, which inaugurated his ministry, was a faint anticipation of the baptism of death, which crowned his ministry.

What, then, was the constraint to which he was subject until he underwent this impending baptism? The answer to this part of our question is closely bound up with the meaning of another of Jesus' hard sayings—that about the kingdom of God coming with power (Mk 9:1). While Jesus was amply endowed with the Spirit of God for the messianic ministry that began at his baptism in the Jordan and continued until his death, his death and resurrection unleashed a power that was previously unparalleled. The limitation of which he was conscious during his ministry was due to the fact that, as it is put in the Fourth Gospel, "Up to that time the Spirit had not been given, since Jesus had not yet been glorified" (Jn 7:39).

I have spoken of Jesus' messianic ministry as lasting from his baptism in the Jordan to his death on the cross, but it would be more accurate to speak of that as the first phase of his ministry. His ministry did not come to an end with his death; he resumed it when he rose again, and continues it until now, no longer in visible presence on earth but by his Spirit in his followers. We should not think of the apostles as taking up the task which Jesus left unfinished at his death; we should think of them rather as called to share in his still very personal ongoing ministry. This is the perspective of the New Testament writers. Luke, for example, opens the second volume of his history of Christian beginnings—the volume we call the Acts of the Apostles—by referring back to the first volume as the record of "all that Jesus began to do and to teach until the day he was taken up" (Acts 1:1-2). The implication is that the new volume is going to tell of what Jesus *continued* to do and teach *from* the day in which he was taken up. To the same effect Paul, looking back on the major phase of his apostolic career, speaks of its very considerable achievements as "what Christ has accomplished through me in leading the Gentiles to obey God by what I have said and done—by the power of signs and miracles, through the power of the Spirit" (Rom 15:18-19).

The scale of the Christian achievement within a few years from the death and resurrection of Christ was out of all proportion to that of his personal achievement during his Palestinian ministry. The limitation was removed by the outpouring of the Spirit as the sequel to Christ's saving work. But without the Palestinian ministry, crowned by his death and resurrection, there would have been no such sequel, and the achievement that followed the outpouring of the Spirit was still Christ's personal achievement. He had undergone his baptism of death, and now worked on free of all restraint.

13:6-8 What Is the Fig Tree?

See comment on MARK 11:14.

13:27 Why Shut Out?

See comment on MATTHEW 25:11-12.

13:30 The First Will Be Last?

See comment on MARK 10:31.

14:26 Hate Your Parents?

This is a hard saying in more senses than one: it is hard to accept and it is hard to reconcile with the general teaching of Jesus. The attitude it seems to recommend goes against the grain of nature, and it also goes against the law of love to one's neighbor which Jesus emphasized to a radical extent. If the meaning of "neighbor" must be extended so as to include one's enemy, it must not be restricted so as to exclude one's nearest and dearest.

What does it mean, then? It means that, just as property can come between us and the kingdom of God, so can family ties. The interests of God's kingdom must be paramount with the followers of Jesus, and everything else must take second place to them, even family ties. We tend to agree that there is something sordid about the attitude that gives priority to money-making over the nobler and more humane issues of life. But a proper care for one's family is one of those nobler and more humane issues. Jesus himself censured those theologians who argued that people who had vowed to give God a sum of money that they later discovered was needed to help their parents were not free to divert the money from the religious purposes to which it had been vowed in order to meet a parental need. This, he said, was a violation of the commandment to honor one's father and mother (Mk 7:9-13).

Nevertheless, a man or woman might be so bound up by family ties as to have no time or interest for matters of even greater moment, and there could be no matter of greater moment than the kingdom of God. The husband and father was normally the head of the household, and he might look on his family as an extension of his own personality to the point where love for his family was little more than an extended form of self-love. Jesus strongly deprecated such an inward-looking attitude and used the strongest terms to express his disapproval of it. If "hating" one's relatives is felt to be a shocking idea, it was meant to be shocking, to shock the hearers into a sense of the imperious demands of the kingdom of God. We know that in biblical idiom *to hate* can mean to love less. When, for example, regulations are laid down in the Old Testament law for a man who has two wives, "one beloved, and another hated" (Deut 21:15 KJV), it is not necessary to suppose that he positively hates the latter wife; all that need be meant is that he loves her less than the other and must be prevented from showing favoritism to the other's son when he allocates his property among his heirs. The RSV indicates that positive hatred is not intended by speaking of the one wife as "the loved" and the other as "the disliked," but the Hebrew word used is that which regularly means "hated," as in the KJV.

That "hating" in this saying of Jesus means loving less is shown by the parallel saying in Matthew 10:37: "Anyone who loves his father or mother more than me is not worthy of me; anyone who loves his son or daughter more than me is not worthy of me." In Matthew's Gospel these words are followed by the saying about taking up the cross and following Jesus; the implication of this sequence is that giving one's family second place to the kingdom of God is one way of taking up the cross.

We can perhaps understand more easily the action of those who choose a celibate life to devote themselves unreservedly to the service of God, those who, as Jesus said on another occasion, "have made themselves eunuchs for the sake of the kingdom of heaven" (Mt 19:12 RSV; see comment on Mt 19:12). But the saying with which we are at present concerned refers to those who are already married and have children, not to speak of dependent parents. That Jesus' followers included some who had dependents like these and had left them to follow him is plain from his own words: "No one who has left home or brothers or sisters or mother or father or children or fields for me and the gospel will fail to receive a hundred times as much in this present age . . . and in the age to come, eternal life" (Mk 10:29-30). Might this not involve the abandonment of natural responsibilities? Who, for example, looked after Peter's family when he took to the road as a disciple of Jesus? We are not told. Clearly his wife survived the experience, and her affections apparently survived it also, for twenty-five years later Peter was accustomed to take her along with him on his missionary journeys (1 Cor 9:5).

Later in the New Testament period, when family life was acknowledged as the norm for Christians, it is laid down that "if anyone does not provide for his relatives, and especially for his immediate family, he has denied the faith and is worse than an unbeliever" (1 Tim 5:8). There is no evidence in the Gospels that this conflicts with the teaching of Jesus. But this needed no emphasizing from him: it is natural for men and women to make what provision they can for their nearest and dearest. Jesus' emphasis lay rather on the necessity of treating the kingdom of God as nearer and dearer still. Because of the natural resistance on the part of his hearers to accepting this necessity with literal seriousness, he insisted on it in the most arresting and challenging language at his command.

See also comment on MATTHEW 19:12; LUKE 9:60; 9:62.

14:34 Saltless Salt?

See comment on MARK 9:50.

15:25-28 Is the Elder Brother Unreasonable?

The prodigal's elder brother deserves our sympathy. He had never given his father a moment's anxiety, but no fuss was ever made over him. Of course not; no one makes a fuss over people who are always at hand and always dependable. The tendency is rather to take them for granted, and those who are always being taken for granted become aware of the fact and do not like it.

How different it was with the younger son! His original request was reasonable: for the two sons to share the family smallholding would probably not have worked. It was better that he should get his share of the inheritance in cash and seek his living elsewhere. His was in any case the smaller share; the elder son would get his double portion in land.

The trouble arose when the younger son squandered his money instead of investing it wisely. The day of reckoning was bound to come for him. For a Jew to be reduced to looking after a Gentile's pigs was degradation indeed; yet he would gladly have joined the pigs at the feeding trough for a share in the carob-bean pods which they munched, so hungry was he. To go back and beg for employment as a casual laborer on his father's land was humiliating, but he could think of nothing better. Casual laborers might earn but a denarius a day, but that was probably more than he was getting from the pig owner; and while they were at their duties, they could eat as much as they wanted. So he swallowed his pride and went back.

The father might have said, "That's all very well, young man; we have heard fine speeches before. Now you buckle down and get to work as you have never worked before, and if we see that you really mean what you say, we may let you work your passage. But you can never make good the damage you have done to the family's good name and property." That in itself would have been an act of grace; it might have done the young man a world of good, and his elder brother would probably not have objected. But—and this is the point of the parable—that is not how God treats sinners. He does not put them on probation first, to see how they will turn out. He welcomes them with overflowing love and generosity. And Jesus, in befriending such undesirable types as he did, was displaying the generous love of God.

Those who entered into theological controversy with Jesus would not have denied that God was like that. In a later rabbinical work God is represented as saying to the Israelites, "Open to me a gateway of repentance only as wide as the eye of a needle, and I will drive chariots and horses through it."[1] But it is not always easy to put theological theory into practice. They might magnify the grace of God, as we may do, but does it not seem prudent to put repentant sinners on probation first? Can they be admitted to the holy table, not to speak of our own tables at home, without more ado?

That is how the prodigal's elder brother felt. He had stayed at home all the time, led a blameless life, worked on the farm, carried out his father's direction. It had not occurred to him to expect much in the way of appreciation until the black sheep of the family turned up with his hard-luck story and the occasion was celebrated with an evening's feasting and jollification—the fatted calf killed, the neighbors invited in, music and dancing and no expense spared!

But life is like that. As the parables of the lost sheep and the lost coin showed, more fuss is made over the recovery of something that was lost than over the safe keeping of what has been there all the time, and where human beings are concerned, this is even more so.

There are young people who have come up through Sunday school and Bible class, who join the church and are present week by week at all the meetings—perhaps notice is taken of them, perhaps not. But here is a rank outsider—a youth out on probation, maybe—who has been dragged along to a Billy Graham meeting and has gone forward when the appeal was made; and what a fuss is made of him! He is billed at every youth rally and invited to give his testimony at every opportunity (and it must be admitted that his testimony is rather more colorful than that of someone who has never strayed from the straight and narrow). One can understand the jaundiced point of view of some of the others!

No blame is attached to the elder brother; he remains sole heir to all his father's property. He simply does not feel the way his father does about the prodigal's return. A human father feels that way, and the heavenly Father feels that way. "There will be more rejoicing in heaven over one sinner who repents than over ninety-nine righteous persons who do not need to repent" (Lk 15:7). No blame attaches to the ninety-nine; of course not. But they were never lost; that is what makes the difference.

---

[1]*Shir ha-Shirim Rabba* 5:2.

16:9 Use Money to Make Friends?

This is the "moral" of the parable of the

dishonest steward, a story which presents problems of its own. The steward looked after his master's estate, dealt with the other employees and tenants, and in general should have relieved his master of all concern about the day-to-day running of his affairs. But he mismanaged the estate, and not simply (it appears) through incompetence or negligence, until the time came when his master discovered that his affairs were in bad shape and ordered the steward to turn in his books, since his employment was terminated.

Before he turned in his books, the steward took some hasty measures with an eye to his future interests. In particular, he summoned his master's debtors and reduced their debts substantially, altering the entries accordingly. Perhaps we are to understand that he made good the difference out of his own pocket; if he did, his money was well invested. He wanted to be sure of bed and board when he was dismissed from his employment with no severance benefit. No one would take him on as steward (his master was not likely to give him the kind of testimonial that would encourage any other landowner to employ him); the alternatives were casual labor (digging, for example) or begging. He did not feel strong enough for the former, and to be a beggar would be insufferably disgraceful. But if he made some friends now by a judicious expenditure of his means, they might give him shelter when he was evicted from his tied cottage.

His master got to know of his action and called him a clever rascal. No more than this need be understood of Jesus' remark that "the master commended the dishonest manager because he had acted shrewdly" (Lk 16:8). The master may well have recognized some analogy between the steward's conduct and the methods by which his own wealth had been amassed. "You see," said Jesus, "worldly people, with no thoughts beyond this present life, will sometimes behave more sensibly and providently than other-worldly people, 'the children of light.' *They* will use material wealth to prepare for their earthly future; why cannot the children of light use it to prepare for their eternal future? Use the 'unrighteous mammon' to win yourselves friends in the world to come." It is called "unrighteous mammon" because it is too often acquired unjustly and used for unjust ends. It is ethically neutral in itself; it is people's attitudes to it and ways of dealing with it that are reprehensible. As has often been pointed out, it is not money as such but "the love of money" which Scripture affirms to be "the root of all evils" (1 Tim 6:10 RSV).

But how can material wealth be used to procure friends who will receive one "into eternal dwellings" when it is no longer accessible? This parable is followed by a collection of isolated sayings, several of which are concerned with the subject of wealth, and then comes another story—the story of the rich man and Lazarus. In it we meet a man who had plenty of the "unrighteous mammon" and used it all to secure comfort and good cheer for himself in this life, giving no thought to the life to come. The time came when he would have been very glad to have even one friend to welcome him into the "eternal habitations," but he found none. Yet he had every opportunity of securing such a friend. There at his gate lay Lazarus, destitute and covered with sores, only too glad to catch and eat the pieces of bread which the rich man and his guests used to wipe their fingers at table and then threw to the dogs outside. If the rich man had used a little of his wealth to help Lazarus, he would have had a friend to speak up for him on the other side. "This man," Lazarus might have said to Abraham, "showed me the kindness of God on earth." But Lazarus had been given no ground to say any such thing. The rich man in Hades found himself without a friend when he needed one most—and he had no one to blame but himself.

16:13 You Cannot Serve Both God and Mammon?

See comment on MATTHEW 6:24.

16:16 Forcefully into the Kingdom?

Matthew (Mt 11:12) and Luke (Lk 16:16) appear to present us here with two versions of one and the same original saying. We have to try to determine what each of the two versions means in the context in which either Evangelist has placed it; then, if possible, we have to determine what the original saying meant in the context of Jesus' ministry.

Both versions agree on this: the ministry of John the Baptist was an epoch marking the end of one age and the approach of a new. "All the prophets and the law prophesied until John" (Mt 11:13 RSV). John himself belonged rather to the old age than to the new. He is viewed as being the last and greatest of the "goodly fellowship of the prophets"; while he was the herald of the new order he did not actually participate in it. When his public ministry was forcibly ended by his imprisonment, that was the signal for Jesus to embark on *his* ministry in Galilee, with the proclamation that the kingdom of God had drawn near.

"Since that time," says Jesus in Luke's version of his words, "the good news of the kingdom of God is being preached." That was a statement of fact, which his hearers must have recognized. But in what sense is everyone forcing his way into it, or "enter[ing] it violently" (RSV)?

Luke includes his version in a series of sayings inserted between the story of the dishonest steward and the story of the rich man and Lazarus and linked together by the general theme of law. "Everyone forces his way in," says the NEB; the TEV has the same wording. This might suggest something like a universal gate-crashing, which does not tally too well with some other sayings of Jesus on the relative few who will enter the kingdom, such as "Make every effort to enter through the narrow door; because many, I tell you, will try to enter and will not be able to" (Lk 13:24; Mt 7:13-14). But perhaps the meaning is "Everyone who enters must force his way in," which implies the same kind of determined and vigorous action as "Make every effort to enter" or "Strive to enter" (RSV). So far as the Lukan version of the saying goes, this could well be its meaning. It was no doubt this interpretation of it that moved an eighteenth-century hymn-writer to say, in language which probably sounded less strange in his contemporaries' ears than it does in ours:

> O may thy mighty word
> Inspire each feeble worm
> To rush into thy kingdom, Lord,
> And take it as by storm!

But Matthew's version now demands our attention. Where Luke says, "The good news of the kingdom of God is being preached," Matthew says, "The kingdom of heaven has suffered violence." But there is an ambiguity in the particular form of the Greek verb in this clause; it may have passive force, meaning "has been treated with violence" or "has been suffering violence," or it may have intransitive force, meaning "has been acting violently" or "has been forcing its way in." It could be said in favor of this last interpretation that in the ministry of Jesus the kingdom of heaven was on the march, taking the field against the forces of evil that held the souls and bodies of men and women in bondage. The mighty works that were an essential part of his ministry were the "powers of the age to come" invading the present age and establishing a beach-head on its territory that was destined to expand until nothing of the old order was left.

If the passive force of the verb be preferred, then Jesus says that from the time of John the Baptist the kingdom of heaven has been violently attacked. This meaning too could fit the setting of the words. Matthew records them among several of Jesus' sayings about John (including the description of him as unsurpassed among those born of women), which he appends to the incident of John's messengers who were sent to question Jesus. It could be said that the imprisonment of John the Baptist (with his ensuing execution) was one instance of a violent attack on the kingdom of heaven by forces opposed to it—whether one thinks of human forces or demonic forces using men as their instruments. Further attacks were to be experienced until they reached their climax in the arrest and crucifixion of Jesus himself. The same meaning could be attached to the following clause: "and men of violence take it by force" or "men of violence seize it." In that case, the two clauses say very much the same thing.

But the "men of violence" need not be those who violently attacked the kingdom which Jesus proclaimed. There were other "men of violence" around at the time—those who came to be known as the party of the Zealots. They were passionately devoted to the bringing in of the kingdom of God, but their methods were clearly contrary to those which Jesus practiced and recommended. The kingdom of God, as they understood it, was a new order in which the Jewish people would live in freedom from Gentile rule, subject to no king but the God of their fathers. This new order could be introduced only by the forcible expulsion of the occupying Roman power from Judea. Many of Jesus' hearers could remember the revolt of one such "man of violence," Judas the Galilean, in A.D. 6. That revolt was crushed by the Romans, but the spirit which inspired it lived on. It could be said that men of this outlook were trying to take the kingdom of God by force, and on the whole it seems most probable that Jesus was referring to them.

Matthew's wording, then, seems to mean that, despite the setback which the cause of God might have seemed to suffer by the imprisonment of John the Baptist, his kingdom has in reality been advancing irresistibly ever since. Men of violence may attempt to speed its progress by armed force, but that is not the way in which its triumph will be assured.

When Luke's account and Matthew's are compared, it appears that Matthew's wording is more relevant to the immediate circumstances of Jesus' ministry, while Luke's wording generalizes the application of the saying, showing how its principle continued to work itself out in the worldwide proclamation and progress of the gospel. The good news was still being made known, and it still called for courage and resolution to enter the kingdom of God.

16:17 Eternal Law?

See comment on MATTHEW 5:17-20.

16:18 No Divorce and Remarriage?

See comment on MARK 10:11-12.

16:25 Woe to the Rich?

See comment on JAMES 5:1.

16:26 What Is the Great Gulf?

This verse is part of Abraham's reply to

the rich man, explaining why Lazarus could not go and cool his tongue with a drop of water and so relieve his anguish.

Even if the rich man had used some of his wealth to help Lazarus on earth (see article on Lk 16:9), and Lazarus had therefore been willing to do something for him in the afterworld, how could Lazarus have crossed the great gulf or chasm that lay between them? But the chasm is not a geographical one, whose width and depth could be measured. When the story is read in the KJV, a wrong impression may be given by the statement that, when the rich man died and was buried, "in hell he lifted up his eyes, being in torments" (Lk 16:23 KJV). As more recent versions indicate, "hell" means Hades, the undifferentiated abode of the dead. It was not because he was in Hades that the rich man was in pain, but because of his past life. Had he made a friend of Lazarus by helping him in his wretchedness, there would not have been the impassable gulf that prevented Lazarus from coming to help him. The impassable gulf, in fact, was of the rich man's own creating. This may mean more or less what C. S. Lewis expressed by a different metaphor when he suggested that "the doors of hell" (and he meant the abode of the damned, not just the abode of the dead) "are locked on the *inside.*"[1]

The story of the rich man and Lazarus appears to have a literary and oral prehistory, and it is interesting to explore this. But such exploration will not help us much to understand it in the context which Luke has given it (and Luke is the only Evangelist to record it).

The rich man, hearing that it is impossible for Lazarus to come and help him, turns his mind to something else. Let Lazarus be sent back to earth to warn the rich man's five brothers to mend their ways, lest they find themselves after death sharing his own sad lot. Perhaps there is the implication here: "If only someone had come back to warn me, I should not have found myself in this plight." But Abraham replies that they have all the warning they need: "They have Moses and the Prophets," that is, the Bible. If the rich man himself had paid heed to what Moses and the Prophets say about the blessedness of those who consider the poor—a theme so pervasive that it cannot well be overlooked—it would have been better for him.

But Moses and the Prophets are not enough, argued the rich man. Let them have an exceptional sign that will compel their repentance. Abraham's response has special relevance to what was happening in the course of Jesus' ministry. People asked him to validate his claim that the kingdom of God had approached them in his ministry by showing them a sign from heaven—something spectacular that would compel them to acknowledge his authority to speak and act as he did. He refused to grant their request: if his works and words were not self-authenticating, then no external sign, however impressive, could be any more persuasive. Moses and the prophets, pleads the rich man, are not persuasive enough, "but if someone from the dead goes to them, they will repent." But Abraham has the last word: "If they do not listen to Moses and the Prophets, they will not be convinced even if someone rises from the dead" (Lk 16:31). Or, as James Denney paraphrased it, "If they can be inhuman with the Bible in their hands and Lazarus at their gate, no revelation of the splendours of heaven or the anguish of hell will ever make them anything else."[2]

Is it a pure coincidence that another of the Evangelists tells of a Lazarus who did come back from the dead? His restoration to life was certainly a very impressive sign, which strengthened the faith of those who already believed in Jesus or were disposed to believe in him, but according to John it strengthened the determination of those who were convinced that the safety of the nation demanded Jesus' death—indeed, they "made plans to kill Lazarus as well, for on account of him many of the Jews were going over to Jesus and putting their faith in him" (Jn 12:10-11).

But by the time Luke wrote his Gospel one greater than Lazarus had risen from the dead. The proclamation that Christ had been raised "according to the Scriptures" (1 Cor 15:4) led many to believe in him, but it did not compel belief; even his resurrection did not convince those who had made up their minds not to believe.

---

[1]C. S. Lewis, *The Problem of Pain* (London: Fount, 1940), p. 115.

[1]James Denney, *The Way Everlasting* (New York: Hodder & Stoughton, 1911), p. 171.

17:6 How Much Faith Do We Need?

See comment on MATTHEW 13:32; MARK 5:34; 11:23.

17:19 How Much Faith Do We Need?

See comment on MARK 5:34.

17:37 There the Eagles?

There is a slight difference between the two forms of this saying which does not appear in the English of the RSV: in Matthew 24:28 the Greek word translated "body" means specifically a dead body, whereas Luke uses the more general word for "body," alive or dead, although in the present context a dead body is implied.

The saying gives the impression of being a proverbial utterance, applied (as proverbial utterances regularly are) to some appropriate situation. But are the birds of prey mentioned in the saying really eagles? Might we not have expected a reference to vultures? Yes indeed; but there are two points to be made.

First the Hebrew word normally translated "eagle" in the Old Testament appears occasionally to denote the vulture. "Make yourselves as bald as the eagle," the people of Judah are told in Micah 1:16 (RSV); but it is the vulture, not the eagle, that is bald (as translated in NIV). In those places where the Hebrew word for "eagle" seems to have the meaning "vulture," it is the Greek word for "eagle" that is used in the Greek version of the Old Testament; so that for Matthew and Luke there was this precedent for the occasional use of the Greek word for "eagle" in the sense of "vulture."

Next, even if (as is probable) the proverbial utterance referred originally to vultures, the change to "eagles" may have been made deliberately, if not in the Aramaic that Jesus spoke, then in the Greek version of his words on which the Gospels of Matthew and Luke drew. "Where there is a dead body, there the vultures will gather" means in effect "Where there is a situation ripe for judgment, there the judgment will fall." But the situation in view in the context is the city of Jerusalem, doomed to destruction because of its unwillingness to pay heed to the message of peace that Jesus brought. The executioners of this particular judgment were Roman legionary forces. The eagle was the standard of a Roman legion, and this may explain the choice of the word "eagles" here.

T. W. Manson, who prefers the rendering "vultures" here and sees no reference to the Roman military eagles, thinks the point of the saying is the swiftness with which vultures discover the presence of carrion and flock to feast on it.[1] So swiftly will the judgment fall "on the day the Son of Man is revealed" (Lk 17:30).

In Luke's account, but not in Matthew's, the saying is Jesus' reply to a question asked by the disciples. He has just told them how, on that day, the judgment will seize on one person and pass over another, separating two people asleep in the same bed or two women grinding at one mill (one of them turning the upper stone and the other pouring in the grain). "Where, Lord?" say the disciples—possibly meaning "Where will this judgment take place?" To this his answer is "Wherever there is a situation which calls for it."

Among several instances of the kind of proverbial utterance illustrated by this saying special mention may be made of Job 39:27-30:

> Is it at your command that the eagle
> mounts up
> and makes his nest on high?
> On the rock he dwells and makes
> his home
> in the fastness of the rocky crag.
> Thence he spies out the prey;
> his eyes behold it afar off.
> His young ones suck up blood;
> and where the slain are,
> there is he. (KJV)

[1]T. W. Manson, *The Sayings of Jesus* (1933; reprint, Grand Rapids, Mich.: Eerdmans, 1979), p. 147.

18:8 Will the Son of Man Find Faith on Earth?

This is a hard saying in the sense that no one can be quite sure what it means, especially in relation to its context. When a question is asked in Greek, it is often possible to determine, from the presence of one particle or another, whether the answer expected is yes or no. But no such help is given with this one. Many commentators assume that the answer implied here is no, but in form at least it is a completely open question.

Luke is the only Evangelist who records the question, and he places it at the end of the parable of the persistent widow—the widow who refused to take no for an answer. Jesus told this parable, says Luke, to teach his disciples that "they should always pray and not give up" (Lk 18:1). But what has this purpose to do with the Son of Man finding faith on earth when he comes?

The widow in the parable showed faith of an unusually persevering quality—not personal faith in the unjust judge whom she pestered until he granted her petition to keep her quiet, but faith in the efficacy of persistent "prayer." The point of the story seems to be this: if even a conscienceless judge, who "neither feared God nor cared about men," saw to it that a widow got her rights, not for the sake of seeing justice done but to get rest from her importunity, how much more will God, who is no unjust judge but a loving Father, listen to his children's plea for vindication! It is vindication that they seek, just as the widow insisted on getting her rights, of which someone was trying to deprive her.

Then comes the question: "When the Son of Man comes, will he find faith on earth?" It is possible indeed that it is Luke who attaches the question to the parable, and that in Jesus' teaching it had some other context which is no longer recoverable. T. W. Manson leant to the view that "the Son of Man" does not bear its special meaning here—that the sense is "Men and women ought to have implicit faith that God will vindicate his elect people, that righteousness will triumph over evil. But when one comes and looks for such faith—when, for example, I come and look for it—is it anywhere to be found?" The answer implied by this interpretation is no—people in general, it is suggested, do not really expect God to vindicate his chosen ones, nor do they at heart desire the triumph of righteousness over evil.[1]

But perhaps we should look at a wider context than this one parable. The coming of the Son of Man is a major theme in the preceding section of Luke's record, in the discourse of Jesus about "the day when the Son of Man is revealed" (Lk 17:22-37). The lesson impressed by this discourse on the hearers is that they must keep on the alert and be ready for that day when it comes. When it comes, God will vindicate his righteous cause and therewith the cause of his people who trust him. But they must trust him and not lose heart; they must here and now continue faithfully in the work assigned to them. (This is the lesson also of the parable of the pounds in Lk 19:11-27.) The Son of Man, whose revelation will be like the lightning, illuminating "the sky from one end to the other" (Lk 17:24), will be able to survey the earth to see if there is any faith on it, any "faithful and wise steward" whom his master when he comes will find loyally fulfilling his service (Lk 12:42-44 RSV).

So the question "Will he find faith on earth?" remains open in fact as in form: its answer depends on the faithfulness of those who wait to render account of their stewardship when he calls for it.

---

[1]T. W. Manson, *The Sayings of Jesus* (1933; reprint, Grand Rapids, Mich.: Eerdmans, 1979), p. 308.

18:19 Why Do You Call Me Good?

See comment on MARK 10:18.

18:25 Easier for a Camel?

See comment on MARK 10:25.

18:42 How Much Faith Do We Need?

See comment on MARK 5:34.

19:30 How Many Mounts?

When we read the story about Palm Sunday in Luke (or in Mk 11:2), it is clear that the disciples are to find one animal, a donkey colt, and then bring it to Jesus to ride on. However, when we turn to Matthew we read, "Go to the village ahead of you, and at once you will find a donkey tied there, with her colt by her. Untie them and bring them to me" (Mt 21:2). This sounds like more than one animal. How many animals were there, and why does Matthew have two while Luke has one?

First, it is clear that we have understood Matthew correctly. Not only does the text say "bring *them*" in Matthew 21:2, but it also says "the Lord needs *them*" in Matthew 21:3. And Matthew 21:7 reads, "They brought the donkey and the colt, placed their cloaks on *them*, and Jesus sat on *them*." So Matthew clearly has two animals with Jesus sitting on both.

Second, it is clear that in Luke's and Mark's stories the text consistently reads *it* rather than *them*. Both of the stories indicate throughout that only one animal is involved.

Third, it is clear why Matthew includes the donkey as well as the colt. Only Matthew has the quotation from Zechariah 9:9:

> This took place to fulfill what was spoken through the prophet:
> "Say to the Daughter of Zion,
> 'See, your king comes to you,
> gentle and riding on a donkey,
> on a colt, the foal of a donkey.' "
> (Mt 21:4-5)

Both the donkey and the colt are mentioned in the Zechariah text, so Matthew includes the two animals to make the fulfillment of prophecy clear.

When we ask what actually happened, we are asking a question which would not concern the Gospel writers as much as it does us. They are sure they have conveyed the right interpretation of the event, which is more their interest than the bare facts. We tend to be interested in history, so we come up with the following.

On the one hand, all three Gospel writers agree that Jesus rode on the colt, for they either name the colt (Matthew) or indicate that the animal had not yet been ridden (Mark and Luke), which could be the case with a colt but would hardly be the case with a mature donkey. On the other hand, it is clear that Matthew is allowing the prophetic passage to influence his story. The text in Matthew says that Jesus sat on "them" (that is, the two animals). It is unlikely that Matthew wants us to take him literally, for how would one man sit on two animals? If he tried he would not look like a king, even a humble king, but like a clown. Matthew is underlining the fulfillment of prophecy by how he tells the story, allowing his reader's good sense to fill in the exact form of the details.

Thus two answers to our question are possible. One answer would be that Matthew mentions the donkey, although she was not there, because clearly the colt was the foal of a donkey and by including the donkey the reference to the prophecy is brought out. Another answer would be that given that the colt was young enough to have not been ridden, the donkey was in all likelihood there with it, perhaps still nursing it on occasion. If Mark and Luke know this, they are not interested in the fact. What they are interested in is the fact that Jesus actually wanted to ride the colt (perhaps showing the submission of an unbroken animal to the true Master). If the donkey was trailing along, it is no concern of theirs. Matthew because of his interest in prophecy does mention the donkey, even if it makes the story read more awkwardly.

Whichever explanation one accepts, it is important not to miss the point that the three authors are making. Jesus, who owns no mount, has to borrow an animal to make his final self-presentation to Jerusalem. That the untried mount submits to him (Mark and Luke) and that prophecy is fulfilled (Matthew) are part of the picture that each author paints. Yet the focus is on the cries of "Hosanna" and the acclamation of Jesus as the one "coming in the name of the Lord," phrases which the authors clearly interpret as a royal acclamation. We must be careful not to miss the king in the details of his entourage.

20:8 Neither Will I Tell You?

Why did Jesus refuse to give a straight answer to those who asked him why he acted as he did?

It was during Holy Week, while he was walking in the temple precincts in Jerusalem, that some representatives of the Sanhedrin, Israel's supreme court (comprising chief priests, scribes, or teachers of the law, and elders, as we are told in Mk 11:27), came to Jesus and asked him, "By what authority are you doing these things? Who gave you this authority?" By "these things" they meant not so much his teaching in the outer court but his cleansing of the temple, which had taken place the previous day. What right had he to put a stop to buying and selling within the bounds of the temple, or to forbid anyone to carry anything through the temple—to use the outer court as a short cut on their business errands? Many religious people might have agreed with him that the sacred area should not be turned into a bazaar, but a temple police force was stationed to protect its sanctity. Who authorized Jesus to act as he did?

His cleansing of the temple was what would have been recognized in Old Testament times as a prophetic action—the kind of action by which a prophet would occasionally confirm his spoken message and bring it home to the people around him. Jesus protested that the temple was being prevented from fulfilling its purpose as "a house of prayer for all nations" (see Is 56:7). Gentiles were not allowed to enter the inner courts, but in the outer court they might draw near to the true and living God and worship him, like those "Greeks" who, according to John 12:20, went up to worship at Passover. Because of this the outer court was sometimes called "the court of the Gentiles." But Gentiles were hindered in using it for its proper purpose if space within it was taken up by market stalls and the like. One of the latest Old Testament prophets had foretold how, when representatives of all the nations were to go up to Jerusalem to worship, "there shall no longer be a trader in the house of the Lord of hosts on that day" (Zech 14:21 RSV). Jesus' prophetic action was designed to enforce this lesson.

But by what authority did he perform such a prophetic action? By what authority did any of the ancient prophets perform prophetic actions? By the authority of God, in whose name they spoke to the people. So, when Jesus was asked, "Who gave you this authority?" the true answer was "God." Why then did he not say so? Because his questioners would not have believed him. He tested them first with another question, to see if they were capable of recognizing divine authority when they saw it. Reminding them of John the Baptist's ministry, he asked them whether John's authority was derived "from heaven [that is, from God] or from men." This put them on the spot: they argued with one another, "If we say, 'From heaven,' he will ask, 'Why didn't you believe him?' But if we say, 'From men?' all the people will stone us, because they are persuaded that John was a prophet" (Lk 20:6). Could they recognize divine authority when it was expressed in the actions and teaching of John? If so, they might be expected to recognize it when it was manifested in the deeds and words of Jesus. But they professed themselves unable to say what the source of John's authority was. So Jesus said to them in effect, "If you cannot recognize divine authority when you see it in action, no amount of argument will convince you of its presence. If you cannot tell me by what authority John baptized, I will not tell you by what authority I do these things." There are some people who will demand authority for truth itself, forgetting that truth *is* the highest authority.

20:25 Render to Caesar?

See comment on MARK 12:17.

21:32 This Generation Will Not Pass Away?

See comment on MARK 13:30.

22:19-20 This Is My Body and Blood?

See comment on MARK 14:22-24.

22:36 Buy a Sword?

This is a hard saying in the sense that it is difficult to reconcile it with Jesus' general teaching on violence: violence was not the course for his followers to take. It is widely held that this saying was not meant to be taken literally, but if not, how *was* it meant to be taken?

It occurs in Luke's Gospel only. Luke reports it as part of a conversation between Jesus and his disciples at the Last Supper. Jesus reminds them of an earlier occasion when he sent them out on a missionary tour and told them not to take a purse (for money) or bag (for provisions) or sandals. Presumably, they could expect their needs to be supplied by well-disposed people along their route (Lk 10:4-7). But now things were going to be different: people would be reluctant to show them hospitality, for they might get into trouble for doing so. On that earlier occasion, as the disciples now agreed, they had lacked nothing. "But now," said Jesus, "if you have a purse, take it, and also a bag"—they would have to fend for themselves. More than that, "if you don't have a sword, sell your cloak and buy one." If that is surprising, more surprising still is the reason he gives for this change of policy: "It is written: 'And he was numbered with the transgressors'; and I tell you that this must be fulfilled in me."

It is doubtful if the disciples followed his reasoning here, but they thought they had got the point about the sword. No need to worry about that: "See, Lord," they said, "here are two swords." To which he replied, "That is enough" or, perhaps, "Enough of this."

Luke certainly does not intend his readers to understand the words literally. He goes on to tell how, a few hours later, when Jesus was arrested, one of the disciples let fly with a sword—probably one of the two which they had produced at the supper table—and cut off an ear of the high priest's slave. But Jesus said, "No more of this!" and healed the man's ear with a touch (Lk 22:49-51).

So what did he mean by his reference to selling one's cloak to buy a sword? He himself was about to be condemned as a criminal, "numbered with the transgressors," to use language applied to the Servant of the Lord in Isaiah 53:12. Those who until now had been his associates would find themselves treated as outlaws; they could no longer count on the charity of sympathetic fellow Israelites. Purse and bag would now be necessary. Josephus tells us that when Essenes went on a journey they had no need to take supplies with them, for they knew that their needs would be met by fellow members of their order; they did, however, carry arms to protect themselves against bandits.[1]

But Jesus does not envisage bandits as the kind of people against whom his disciples would require protection; they themselves would be lumped together with bandits by the authorities, and they might as well act the part properly and carry arms, as bandits did. Taking him literally, the disciples revealed that they had anticipated his advice: they already had two swords. This incidentally shows how far they were from resembling a band of Zealot insurgents: such a band would have been much more adequately equipped. And the words with which Jesus concluded the conversation did not mean that two swords would be enough; they would have been ludicrously insufficient against the band that came to arrest him, armed with swords and clubs. He meant "Enough of this!"—they had misunderstood his sad irony, and it was time to drop the subject. T. W. Manson rendered the words "Well, well." In contrast to the days when they had shared their Master's popularity, "they are now surrounded by enemies so ruthless that the possession of two swords will not help the situation."[2]

> This text . . . has nothing to say directly on the question whether armed resistance to injustice and evil is ever justifiable. It is simply a vivid pictorial way of describing the complete change which has come about in the temper and attitude of the Jewish people since the days of the disciples' mission. The disciples understood the saying literally and so missed the point; but that is no reason why we should follow their example.[3]

[1]Josephus *Jewish War* 2.125.
[2]T. W. Manson, *Ethics and the Gospel* (London: SPCK, 1960), p. 90.

[3]T. W. Manson, *The Sayings of Jesus* (1933; reprint, Grand Rapids, Mich.: Eerdmans, 1979), p. 341.

22:67-70 You Will See the Son of Man?

See comment on MARK 14:61-62.

23:38 What Was the Crime?

See comment on JOHN 19:19.

23:43 Today in Paradise?

Jesus tells the thief on the cross, who has asked to be remembered by Jesus when Jesus receives his kingdom, that he would be in paradise with Jesus that very day. Yet was not Jesus in the tomb for three days? And does not the Bible teach that he went to Hades between his death and resurrection? Didn't he ascend to paradise only after the resurrection? If this is true, how could he make such a promise to the dying thief?

This question presupposes the answers to a number of questions. The first of these is, Where was Jesus between his death and resurrection? It is clear that his body was in the tomb. That is why all three Synoptic Gospels mention the witness to the burial (Mt 27:61; Mk 15:47; Lk 23:55). Matthew adds the story of the sealing of the tomb (Mt 27:62-65), letting us know that until the resurrection the tomb remained shut with the body inside. However, this says nothing about Jesus' spirit. When Paul contemplates death in Philippians 1 or 2 Corinthians 5, he speaks of his immediate presence after death before Christ (for Paul the important thing is not being in heaven, but being with Jesus, so that is where he puts his stress). He witnesses to the Christian and late Jewish belief that the spirit or soul of a person has conscious existence somewhere between the person's death and their resurrection. Thus what Jesus is talking about is where his spirit and the spirit of the thief were to be.

Some Christian traditions have believed that Jesus' spirit was in Hades (or hell) between his death and resurrection. This idea is based on 1 Peter 3:19 (and possibly 1 Pet 4:6) and Ephesians 4:4. However, such an interpretation is not supported by these texts. While the Ephesians 4:9 text in the KJV seemed to say that Jesus descended into the lower regions of the earth (which could be Hades), in the NIV we read the better translation: "the lower, earthly regions." That is, this passage speaks of Jesus' descent from heaven to earth, his incarnation, not his location after death. The 1 Peter passage does speak of something happening after Jesus was executed, but it does not tell us (1) what the spirits are which are in prison, (2) where the prison is, (3) when this event took place (other than after his death) or (4) how long it took. Let it suffice here to indicate that (1) in my view the spirits are not the spiritual part of dead humans, but the fallen angels of Genesis 6 (contrary to comment on Gen 6:4), (2) the prison could be located below the earth, but there is also a Jewish tradition that locates it in the second heaven, (3) the event may have taken place before his resurrection or it may have been part of Jesus' ascension, and (4) we have no idea if it took more time than a single trumpeting announcement of his triumph, which could have taken a minute or less. Assigning any length of time to this event is pure speculation. (The preaching of the gospel to those now dead, 1 Pet 4:6, probably does not indicate an action of Jesus, but the preaching of the gospel to people who believed and then died, but who still have the same hope as the living Christians Peter is writing to.) My conclusion is that there is no reason to believe that Jesus actually spent any significant length of time in Hades or hell or wherever the "prison" was. If it was a preresurrection trip, it did not necessarily take a lot of time.

The second of the assumptions is that paradise is another name for heaven and Jesus was not in heaven until his ascension. The first part of this assumption is probably true. While "paradise" is actually a Persian term adopted by the Jews to indicate the Garden of Genesis 2, in the New Testament it means something more than this. In 2 Corinthians 12:2-4 it indicates a place that Paul was "caught up" to, also identified as the "third heaven" (which is the abode of God, the first two being the place of the birds and the place of the stars). This impression is confirmed by Revelation 2:7. So we are on firm ground in that part of the assumption. Jesus is promising to be in heaven with the thief on that day.

The second part of this assumption is not true. The only verse that could indicate that Jesus was not in heaven until after the resurrection is John 20:17, but there the issue is one of not holding on to Jesus physically because he has not yet ascended to the Father. His physical absence from the earth was necessary for the sending of the Spirit (Jn 16:7). He is now physically present, and Mary must not hold on to him to keep him from leaving. This passage says nothing about where the spirit of Jesus was between his death and resurrection.

My conclusion, then, is that there is only one passage that tells us whether or not Jesus was in heaven at some point between his death and resurrection, and that is the passage we are discussing. Jesus promised that both he and the thief would be together in paradise, which is heaven, on the day they died ("day" probably indicating "when we die" rather than the precise Jewish or Roman period of time, although all of the traditions place both of their deaths before the end of the Jewish day on which they were crucified). If Jesus was correct, he may have made a proclamation in a "prison" on the way (or that proclamation may have taken place later, at his ascension), but that would be where he apparently spent most of the time between his death and resurrection. If he was correct, it also explains his final words in Luke, "Father, into your hands I commit my spirit," (Lk 23:46) for he was going to his Father at his death. His work was complete; he did not have any major work to do between his death and resurrection. Of course, if Jesus was not correct, we have only theological speculation to rely on for where Jesus was during this period of time, for there is no way to test this claim without investigating the place itself. What is certain is that the Gospel writers assume that he was correct about such matters.

When Jesus makes this promise to the thief, it does more than simply comfort the dying man and promise him the reward of faith. What it does is to announce the completion of salvation. Salvation was completed at the cross. There were no more battles for Jesus to fight. Satan had met his match at the cross. The victor, Jesus, could proceed to heaven and there await the resurrection, when his triumph would be made known to the whole world.

See also comment on 1 PETER 3:19.

24:10 What Happened at the Resurrection?

See comment on JOHN 20:1-8.

JOHN

1:1 One God or Three?

How can there be a Trinity when the Old Testament insists there is only one God? If the Old Testament is right, how can John assert that the Word (later identified with Jesus) is God? Does this mean that the one God became a human being and so all of God was on earth? Does it imply there are two (or, with the Holy Spirit, three) Gods? Or are the Jehovah's Witnesses correct that Jesus really is not God? What does the teaching of the Trinity imply anyway?

This question calls for such a profound answer that books have been written on the topic. We can attempt to look only briefly at what the Bible says on this topic.

First, the question is quite right in implying that the Old Testament teaches that there is only one God or, better, that God is one. We need only look at Deuteronomy 6:4, "Hear, O Israel: The LORD our God, the LORD is one." What is more, the New Testament also affirms the same doctrine. For example, James 2:19 reads, "You believe that there is one God. Good!" As in Deuteronomy, an even better translation would be, "You believe that God is one." The unity of God and the fact that there are no other gods besides him are foundational doctrines of the Bible (See Mk 12:29; Jn 5:44; Rom 3:30; 1 Cor 8:4, 6; Gal 3:20; Eph 4:6).

Second, the New Testament also teaches that Jesus was divine. This verse is only one of several verses indicating this fact (see also Phil 2:6; Tit 2:13; Heb 1:3 for a few examples of other verses pointing in this direction). Naturally, groups like the Jehovah's Witnesses dispute such verses. For example, they point out that a literal translation of the last phrase of John 1:1 reads, "God was the Word." There is no definite article *(the)* with God, and in such cases this sometimes implies an indefinite article *(a)*, and so they translate "The Word was a god." This translation, however, is itself problematic. First, God often functions as a proper name, and when a proper name has been used once in a context (so that one knows which Peter or John or whoever one is talking about), it can be used other times without the definite article. Second, sentences with the verb "to be" in them (in this case, "was") do not have a subject and an object, but a subject and a predicate noun or predicate adjective. In English subject and object are differentiated by word order. "Jim hit John" means Jim is the subject and John the object. Reverse the word order and Jim and John would reverse roles. In Greek you do this by special endings on the words. In that way you can, for example, place the object first if you want to emphasize it. Now if you have a sentence with a predicate noun, your endings will be the same. Yet you can indicate which is which by using the definite article with the subject and omitting it with the predicate noun. Thus the sentence would read, "The Word was *God,*" with God being emphasized.

Finally, another reason to omit the article is if the noun is functioning as a predicate adjective, giving a quality of the subject. That is probably John's main reason for not including it here (although all three reasons may be true). That is, John is quite aware that the Word was not all of God. The Father still existed separately after the Word became flesh (Jn 1:14). Thus, "The Word was God" could be misleading; it could imply that all of God had become incarnate in Jesus. The omission of the article makes this verse mean "The Word was divine" or "What God was the Word was." In other words, the text is indicating that the Word had all of the qualities of God, but this text is also indicating that not all of God was in the Word. The Jehovah's Witnesses ignore all of these three reasons, and instead use simplistic grammatical explanations to try to make the sentence mean what they wish it to mean.

We are left with the question as to whether there are not three Gods. The answer is that the New Testament does not give us an explanation, but does give us the data which was later used to make an explanation of how there can be three beings but not more than one God. As we pointed out above, the New Testament makes clear that there is only one God. "God is one" is "bottom line" New Testament teaching, just as it is also true in the Old Testament. The New Testament also makes clear that Jesus (and also the Holy Spirit) is God. Well, then, perhaps all of God became incarnate in Jesus? This teaching, later called patripassionism, would solve our problem, but will not fit the New Testament data. Jesus is constantly distinguishing himself from the Father. For example, in John 11:41-43, he thanks the Father that he has heard him and then goes on to speak of the Father's sending him. This is part of an ongoing dialogue between the Father and the Son. There is a constant discussion about the Son and the Father which makes them equal, but at the same time distinguishes them (see Jn 5:16-23). Thus the Father did not become incarnate in Jesus. This is the data which the New Testament gives us (and we can find it outside of John as well), but it does not tell us how to explain this data. It offers facts, not a theory to explain the facts.

The church fathers and mothers had to deal with these facts: God is one; Jesus is God; Jesus and the Father are not the same (and then that the Holy Spirit is also God and he is not the same as either the Father or the Son). The way that they put these truths together was through the doctrine of the Trinity. The actual word appears to have been coined about A.D. 200 by Tertullian, but it would take more than another 150 years to fully define the doctrine. This explanation depended on the ability of Greek philosophy to separate being (substance) from person. Thus they argued that there were three persons and yet only one being, one substance. The closest analogy which we might find in human existence would be instances of true multiple personality, except that because they all have to use the same limited human body only one personality can appear to the world at any given time.

One does not need to hold the explanation with its Greek philosophical assumptions to hold the truth of Scripture, although we know of no better explanation. The fact is that the Scripture asserts that God is one, Jesus is God, and that Jesus and the Father are separate conscious centers. The Father can send the Son and the two of them can dialogue together. At its core this teaching is a mystery, so all human explanations (including the doctrine of the Trinity) are only more or less crude human attempts to come to terms with a divine reality that is beyond us. The doctrine points to a transcendent God who could yet simultaneously become a human being and then after the resurrection also indwell other human beings (that is, the Holy Spirit). He is a God great enough to rule the universe, caring enough to live a fully human life and intimate enough to live in each believer. This is the reality that the doctrine points to. This is the truth that John teaches. Try as we like, we will never understand this divine depth, yet we can still enjoy the reality of God being with us that the doctrine points to.

See also comment on ISAIAH 63:10-11.

1:18 No One Has Ever Seen God?

This verse is clearly saying that no one has ever seen God, but in Exodus 33:20 we read, "You cannot see my face . . . and live," and in Exodus 24:11, "They saw God, and they ate and drank." How can John claim that no one has ever seen God when the Old Testament text indicates that people did see God on at least two occasions?

First, notice that even the Old Testament indicates that no one has seen the face of God: "You cannot see my face, for no one may see me and live" (Ex 33:20). It is in this context that the two theophanies occur. In the earlier theophany it appears that what the elders see is "a pavement made of sapphire" (which will appear again in the early chapters of Ezekiel as the floor of the divine chariot). No form is seen, although they may have had some awareness of a Being above the pavement. In this sense they "saw God" but apparently did not see his "face." In the later theophany Moses asks to see God's "glory" (Ex 33:18). In the view of the author of Exodus, he is asking for more than what he saw along with the elders of Israel. God grants more, but not all that Moses asks for. The only experience God will allow is for Moses to be hidden while God passes by and declares his character audibly; then Moses will get to see God's "back," which some commentators identify with an "afterglow," but which could mean the back side of a retreating form (in Near Eastern fashion this would be shrouded with clothing so only an outline would be visible). Even this experience is so powerful that Moses' face glows afterward (Ex 34:29).

John is clearly contrasting Jesus with Moses (Jn 1:17; Moses' theophany was at the giving of the law), but even later theophanies in the Old Testament do not contradict our observation. Isaiah has some awareness of a throne and a being on it, but the only things that he can describe are the hem of God's "robe" and the seraphim who are associated with him (Is 6:1-5). Ezekiel in a vision sees a form on a throne (Ezek

1:26-28), but there is no face and no features, only burning fire in a vaguely human shape. The face of God is never seen.

Now we can understand what John is saying. The Word is with God (Jn 1:1), and the image implied in the preposition is the face-to-face position of equals. What is more, the Word is what God is (as we noted in the previous chapter). Now the Word becomes a human being ("flesh," Jn 1:14), and he has a "glory" or character or reputation which is that of one who is exactly like his Father, full of grace and truth (which are Greek equivalents of "love and faithfulness" of Ex 34:6). So Moses brought law from God (Jn 1:17), but Jesus brought the very character of the Father to us. Thus while no one has ever seen God, Jesus makes him known with an accuracy brought about by his being in the most intimate contact with him ("at the Father's side" in the NIV or, better, "in the bosom of the Father" [RSV]). They may have seen a form or outline in the Old Testament, but Jesus, the Word incarnate, has not only seen the Father face to face, but has also looked into his soul and contains within himself his very character.

This is an important theological point. Ever since Marcion in the second century there have been those who contrast the distant and harsh Father with the gracious and kind Son. The Father seems to be law and the Son grace. The Father seems to be difficult or impossible to relate to, apparently existing without feeling, and the Son seems to be caring and even warm and friendly. This contrast is entirely false. What John is saying is that if we want to find out what the Father is like, we only have to look at the Son. The "love and faithfulness" we see in Jesus is the "love and faithfulness" of the Father. The kindness we see in Jesus is the kindness of the Father. The healing we seen in Jesus is his doing the works of the Father (Jn 5:19). In sum, Jesus is the place where we get our best view of the face of the Father; in Jesus we can see what the Father's heart is really like. When this truth sinks into our heart, many of us will receive a renewed vision of the Father and thus develop a new love for and intimacy with God.

See also comment on EXODUS 24:9-11; 33:18-23; JOHN 1:1.

1:25 What Was John's Baptism?

See comment on MARK 1:4.

1:51 Angels Ascending and Descending?

What is meant by the angels "ascending and descending on the Son of Man"? Nathanael was not talking about angels, although he had been convinced by Jesus' prophetic insight into his life that Jesus was indeed the Messiah. Now Jesus responds to him, saying in effect, "You haven't seen anything yet!" He goes on to describe the experience we find in this verse. What does it mean to see heaven open? And why would it be significant to see angels of God "ascending and descending" on Jesus? In fact, does it not seem strange to talk about such beings coming down on top of a human being like Jesus?

It is obvious that there is a change of audience in John 1:51. Up until this time Jesus has been addressing Nathanael, and the pronoun *you* is singular. In this verse Jesus speaks "to him" (singular) and says, "I tell you (plural) . . . you (plural) shall see . . ." In other words, within the verse the focus shifts from Nathanael to the whole group of disciples. Jesus is broadening his audience. It is not just Nathanael who will have this experience, but the whole group of at least four of them.

What is it that the whole group will

experience? The reference to angels of God ascending and descending is probably a reference to Genesis 28:12: "He had a dream in which he saw a stairway resting on the earth, with its top reaching to heaven, and the angels of God were ascending and descending on it." The difference between "on it" and "on him" (underlying John's "on the Son of Man") is not significant in that the Hebrew could be translated both ways. In fact, in later Jewish literature there is a discussion between Rabbi Hiyya and Rabbi Yannai on this very point (*Genesis Rabbah* 69.3 on Gen 28:12).

John's reference is wider than simply Genesis 28, for he also uses the phrase "you shall see heaven open," which suggests the descent of the Spirit at Jesus' baptism (Mk 1:10).

So what we have here is a complex picture. Heaven is open; there is a way from heaven, the presence of the Father, to earth. That way ends in or on the Son of Man, or Jesus. As Jacob comments in Genesis 28:17, "This is the gate of heaven." All of this is said in a context of seeing greater things than simply a prophetic word from Jesus, which is what Nathanael had already received.

There is no place in John in which the disciples see literal angels moving between heaven and earth, or heaven and Jesus. However, angels are those who bring the divine presence and so are the divine intermediaries. So the question becomes, "Where in the Gospel of John do we see the divine presence revealed to the disciples?" The answer comes quite quickly: in the next chapter.

In John 2:11 we read, "This, the first of his miraculous signs, Jesus performed at Cana in Galilee. He thus revealed his glory, and his disciples put their faith in him." In the miracle of turning the water into wine the disciples saw Jesus' "glory" revealed. This resulted in faith. What was Jesus' glory? John has already answered that question in John 1:14-18: "The Word became flesh and made his dwelling among us. We have seen his glory, the glory of the One and Only, who came from the Father, full of grace and truth. . . . No one has ever seen God, but God the One and Only, who is at the Father's side, has made him known." John is saying that the "glory" or reputation that belongs to the Father is seen in Jesus. We could put it that Jesus is the window through which one sees the Father.

Jacob at Bethel sees a stairway to heaven and experiences the presence of God. The disciples during Jesus' life did not literally see a stairway to heaven, but they did experience the presence of God and commerce between heaven and earth. They had this experience when they observed the signs which Jesus performed and saw his "glory," which was the "glory" of the Father. Nathanael had believed because of a prophetic word given by Jesus. Both he and the other disciples would experience more than this: they would experience Jesus as the "gate of heaven," the place where the presence of the Father in heaven was expressed on earth. They saw this in the signs which Jesus worked, and they responded with commitment (faith).

John picks up this theme in John 14:12, when he indicates that the presence of the Spirit in the believer will make him or her into one who can be even more of a window into heaven, the topic of another chapter. At this point what we notice is that Jesus is the point of contact between God and the world. In him there is traffic between heaven and earth. That traffic is seen in his signs in which the presence of the glory of the Father in him shines through. This, John is saying, calls for belief. Nathanael committed himself to Jesus on the basis of what he had; we have far more basis for committing ourselves than he did.

3:5 Born of Water and the Spirit?

What does it mean to be born of "water and the Spirit"? When Jesus speaks to Nicodemus, he first speaks about being "born again." Nicodemus does not understand, so Jesus explains the issue to him in this verse. However, the meaning of this verse is obscure to us. There have been several attempts to explain it, and the most common are these:

1. Water means natural birth and Spirit indicates spiritual birth.
2. Water and Spirit together indicate a cleansing and spiritual renewal.
3. Water is the baptism of John and Spirit is what comes with Jesus.
4. Water indicates the outward part of Christian baptism and Spirit the inward part.

In order to decide among these interpretations and understand this verse, we need to drop back to John 3:3, where Jesus told Nicodemus that no one could "see the kingdom of God" without being "born again." The Greek term translated "again" has two possible meanings: "from above" and "again." In John 3:4 Nicodemus assumed the "again" meaning and found it incomprehensible. He pictured himself as a grown man trying to get back into his mother. In this verse Jesus restates himself, making it clear that what he meant was not "again" but "born from above." He does this by paralleling "born from above/again" with "born of water and Spirit/spirit." (We will use "Spirit/spirit" because the Greek word could mean the Holy Spirit or spirit in some other sense, such as the human spirit.) Both "born from above" and "born of water and Spirit/spirit" lead to the kingdom of God and therefore they are two ways of saying the same thing. Notice that "water and Spirit/spirit" in this verse is not two items but one, for in Greek one article governs the two words, indicating that only one concept is being thought about. What does Jesus mean by this one concept?

The first interpretation is that Jesus means physical birth (born of water) and spiritual birth (born of Spirit), the water image for physical birth coming from the amniotic fluid surrounding the baby. However, it is clear that Jesus expects Nicodemus to understand this image and also clear that Jewish sources do not use water as an image for birth, at least not until centuries later than Jesus. Furthermore, we noted above that the grammar indicates that these two are thought of as one item, not two. Therefore it could not be two separate births that Jesus is speaking about. We must reject this interpretation.

Moving on to the second proposal, Jesus certainly knew that Nicodemus was quite knowledgeable about the Old Testament. Thus this interpretation is more likely because it sees in this verse an allusion to Ezekiel 36:25-27. We see that in the Ezekiel passage the cleansing image of water is combined with the giving of God's Spirit for the renewal of the people. Of course, there are other passages in the Old Testament which also refer to the Spirit using water imagery, such as the Spirit being "poured out" upon people. We are not depending on a single reference for our argument, but Ezekiel gives us the most explicit association of Spirit and water. Furthermore, the association of Spirit with birth is clear enough in that it is when God's Spirit or breath (in Hebrew the same word means "spirit," "wind" and "breath"; in Greek "spirit" and "wind" are two meanings of the same word) comes into Adam that he becomes a living being (Gen 2:7). This is not literally a birth (no woman was involved), but the parallel is close enough, for it is when the man came alive.

What we understand Jesus to be saying, then, is that one must receive the cleansing and spiritual renewal that comes from God. At this stage he may be alluding to the later coming of the Holy Spirit, but Nicodemus would know nothing about that. What Nicodemus is being instructed about is the cleansing from sin and spiritual renewal that come through Jesus, the One from above.

What, then, about the interpretations which refer the phrase to baptism? In John 3:25-30 there is a discussion about baptism. We discover that Jesus was baptizing people as John the Baptist had done, although he did not do this personally. Could there be a reference to John's baptism or Christian baptism here? The answer to this is that while such a reference is unlikely if baptism and Spirit are thought of as separate (remember, the grammar indicates that water and Spirit are one item), there may be a reference to the baptism that John and (later) Jesus and his disciples were doing if it is thought of as one with Jesus. That is, if the repentance and cleansing from sin were thought of as one with spiritual renewal rather than as a first step. It is possible that Nicodemus might have understood this, but it would be secondary to the scriptural image from Ezekiel. What was going on in John's baptism was Ezekiel "put into action" when combined with Jesus, the One to whom John pointed.

What about Christian baptism? In writing his Gospel John is surely aware of Christian baptismal practice. In those days if one wanted to become a Christian, what one was instructed to do was not to say a "sinner's prayer" or sign a "decision card" but to be baptized. It was in baptism that one took the vow to turn from sin and follow Jesus. It was also likely that at baptism the newly baptized person was prayed for to receive the Spirit. At the least, baptism signified a new life, a life from above, and thus a new birth. But of course Nicodemus would have no way of knowing this, so this would not have been what Jesus was trying to tell him. Yet John, knowing the practice of the church as he did, surely saw this as a further meaning in the words of Jesus.

5:28-29 Salvation by Works?

In John 5:28-29 Jesus is in a debate with the Judean Jews, talking about the authority of the Son of Man to command the resurrection of the dead. He then adds a comment that refers to the two classes of resurrected people, not as believers and unbelievers, but as "those who have done good" and "those who have done evil." Does not this indicate that eternal life is given on the basis of one's deeds? Is this not the very salvation by works that Luther and the other Reformers were so much against?

The first point that we should notice about this verse is that Jesus is indeed in a debate with a group of Jews, who were questioning his authority to heal a person on the sabbath. His central point is that his authority is far greater than that needed to set aside the sabbath. The healing was simply a sign of a more significant authority than they had yet seen: it is Jesus they will meet on the final judgment day! We must keep that point in mind, for the issues of faith and works are here actually peripheral to the main point Jesus is making.

Second, in saying what he says, Jesus is saying the same thing as any good rabbi of his time would say. Some of the dead were called righteous, for they had done good, and some of the dead were called unrighteous, for they had done evil. The resurrection was a time when God would set right the accounts, rewarding the righteous with "the age to come" (to use the rabbinic phrase) and barring the unrighteous from that happy kingdom. Thus what Jesus said would not have raised an eyebrow among the Jews. They knew that those who truly loved God obeyed the law and thus did good, while those who rejected God disobeyed the law and thus did evil.

However, third, Jesus is saying something much more profound than this. In John 5 Jesus has made it clear that the resurrection to life at the end of time is simply the logical conclusion of what Jesus is doing now, for after telling them that the Father has given him authority to raise the dead, Jesus adds, "I tell you the truth, whoever hears my word and believes him who sent me has eternal life and will not be condemned; he has crossed over from death to life" (Jn 5:24). In other words, Jesus is able to grant eternal life now, so his resurrecting people at the end of the age is simply an extension into the physical world of what he has already done in the present in the spiritual world. Notice that the only criteria for gaining eternal life now is "hears my word and believes him who sent me." Of course, this "hearing" means not simply to listen to, but also to accept and submit to the teaching of Jesus. One who does this is in fact believing "on him who sent me," for Jesus makes it clear that to reject him is to reject his Father.

What is said here about how one gains eternal life has already been said in John 3:17-21. In that section we discover that those whose deeds are evil reject Jesus, while those whose deeds are good "come into the light." Yet what leads to condemnation or salvation is whether or not one "believes in" him ("believes in" could better be translated "entrusts oneself to" or "commits oneself to," for it is not mental assent to certain doctrines that is being talked about). In John 6:28-29 Jesus amplifies what he has said on the other two occasions. The works of God are defined as a single work: to believe in Jesus. If we accept this definition, we see that those whose deeds were evil would be those who rejected Jesus and those whose deeds were good would be those who accepted Jesus. One's attitude toward Jesus becomes the central criterion of whether one is good or evil.

Yet this is not to say that behavior is totally separated from salvation. Jesus is also the one who said, "If you love me, keep my commandments" (Jn 14:15 KJV). In other words, saying that one is committed to Jesus (or believes in Jesus, to use the traditional language) without actually obeying Jesus is so much useless hot air. It is the heart that counts, and the heart is seen in one's actions. This is why 1 John will say that those who love Jesus will not continue to sin (see 1 Jn 3:6, 9). Real love, real faith leads to a life that shows it. Yet the life is the result of commitment, the result of eternal life residing in the person, not the cause of it.

So is John teaching salvation by works? The answer is no. That is, not unless committing oneself to Jesus is the work that one is talking about. Those who do good are those who believe on Jesus (and probably also, in Jesus' mind, those who accepted God's previous revelation and died before Jesus came); those who do evil are those who reject Jesus. This underlines that Jesus is the source of eternal life now, as well as the Judge at the end of time. Indeed, we could picture judgment day as Jesus calling out for all the dead to rise. Some rise and come toward him, drawn by their previous commitment to him. Others rise and turn away, for they have rejected that voice and in that sense are judged already. The one group comes to him who is life itself. The others reject life and thus choose death. What makes all of the difference is not whether one has sinned this or that sin, but whether

one has committed oneself to Jesus.
See also comment on JAMES 2:24; 1 JOHN 3:9; 3 JOHN 11.

6:53 Eating the Flesh, Drinking the Blood?

This was the original hard saying: as John reports, "On hearing it, many of his disciples said, 'This is a hard teaching; who can accept it?' " (Jn 6:60). The implication is that they not only found it difficult to understand, but suspected that, if they did understand it, they would find it unacceptable. The NEB expresses a different nuance with its rendering: "This is more than we can stomach! Why listen to such talk?" That implies that they thought Jesus was talking nonsense, and that it was a waste of time listening to it; but that is probably not what John means.

The feeding of the five thousand is one of the few incidents in the ministry of Jesus recorded by all four Evangelists. The narrative of Mark 6:31-52 (including the sequel in which Jesus came walking to his disciples across the water) is reproduced substantially in Matthew 14:13-33 and (without the walking on the water) in Luke 9:10-17. John tells the story independently (together with the walking on the water) in John 6:1-21.

In the Synoptic Gospels we get the impression that there was more in the feeding of the multitude than met the eye at the time or meets the reader's eye today. Mark in particular makes it plain that the feeding was intended to teach the disciples a lesson which they failed to learn, and that Jesus was surprised at their failure. When Jesus had joined them in the boat on their way back to the other side of the lake of Galilee, and the strong head wind which had made progress so difficult for them stopped blowing, then, says Mark, "they were completely amazed, for they had not understood about the loaves; their hearts were hardened" (Mk 6:51-52). "Their hearts were hardened" means "their minds were closed," as the NEB puts it: they were too obtuse to take the lesson in, and the lesson evidently had something to do with the person of their Master.

But the further meaning which lies beneath the surface of the Synoptic record is brought up above the surface by John and spelled out in detail. He does this in the form of an address given by Jesus shortly afterward in the synagogue at Capernaum. The subject of the discourse is the bread of life. It has been suggested that on that sabbath day one of the Scripture lessons in the synagogue was Exodus 16:13-36 or Numbers 11:4-9, which tell of the manna, the bread from heaven with which the Israelites were fed during their wilderness wanderings. At any rate, this is the subject with which the address begins.

The manna that their ancestors ate in the wilderness, Jesus tells his hearers, was not the food of immortality: those who ate it died nevertheless—some sooner, some later. Similarly, the bread with which he had recently fed the multitude was but material bread. They wished to make him their leader because he had given them that bread, but really he had come to give them better bread than that. Just as he had offered the Samaritan woman at Jacob's well better water than that in the well, the eternally satisfying water of life, so now he offers these Galileans better bread than the loaves with which the five thousand had been fed, better bread even than the manna which their forefathers had eaten, "food that endures to eternal life" (Jn 6:27). The manna might be called bread from heaven, even the bread of God; but the true "bread of God is he who comes down from heaven and gives life to the world" (Jn 6:33).

Not only so, but God has one authorized and certified agent to bestow this life-giving bread—the Son of Man, Jesus himself. So far, so good; as the Samaritan woman, hearing of the water of life, said, "Sir, give me this water so that I won't get thirsty" (Jn 4:15), so now Jesus' present hearers say, "Sir, from now on give us this bread."

This sets the stage for the next step of the lesson. Jesus not only *gives* the bread of life; he *is* the bread of life. True life, eternal life, is to be had in him alone: "he who comes to me will never go hungry, and he who believes in me will never be thirsty" (Jn 6:35). Indeed, not only will those who come to him in faith find in him perpetual sustenance and refreshment for their souls' hunger and thirst; they will never die. "I am the living bread that came down from heaven. If anyone eats of this bread, he will live forever. This bread is my flesh, which I will give for the life of the world" (Jn 6:51).

Now the lesson really begins to be hard. Anyone who has the advantage of reading these words in the context of the whole Gospel of John knows what their purport is. To believe in Christ is not only to give credence to what he says: it is to be united to him by faith, to participate in his life. Up to a point, his words about giving his flesh for the life of the world are paralleled in Mark 10:45, where he speaks of the Son of Man as coming "to give his life as a ransom for many." In the language Jesus spoke "my flesh" could be another way of saying "myself": he himself is the bread given for the life of the world. But the saying in Mark 10:45 makes no reference to the Son of Man as food for the souls of the "many"; this is an additional emphasis, and one which leaves the synagogue congregation out of its depth.

On the lips of people who felt out of their depth, the question "How can this man give us his flesh to eat?" (Jn 6:52) was a natural one. But it is John's practice when recording Jesus' discourses or conversations to quote words which have a spiritual meaning and then make the hearers show by their response that they have failed to grasp that meaning; Jesus is thus given an opportunity to repeat his words more fully. So here he repeats himself more fully in reply to the congregation's bewilderment: "Whoever eats my flesh and drinks my blood has eternal life, and I will raise him up at the last day. For my flesh is real food, and my blood is real drink. Whoever eats my flesh and drinks my blood remains in me, and I in him" (Jn 6:54-56).

What could he mean? Plainly his language was not to be taken literally: he was not advocating cannibalism. But how was it to be taken? It was not only obscure, they thought: it was offensive. For Jews the drinking of any blood, even the eating of flesh from which the blood had not been completely drained, was taboo. But drinking the blood of a human being was an idea which ought not even to be mentioned. This was a hard saying in more senses than one.

Jesus answered their protest by pointing out that his words were to be understood spiritually. "It is the spirit that gives life, the flesh is of no avail" (Jn 6:63 RSV). The physical or literal meaning of the words was plainly ruled out. But what was the spiritual meaning?

Again the reader of this Gospel, viewing these words in the context of the whole work, has an advantage over the first hearers, who had no such explanatory context. What we have in Jesus' strange language is a powerful metaphor stating that a share in the life of God, eternal life, is granted to those who in faith come to Jesus, appropriate him, enter into union with him. Let us hear two doctors of the church: Augustine of Hippo (at the end of the fourth century) and

Bernard of Clairvaux (twelfth century).

The hard saying cannot be taken literally, says Augustine, since it would seem to be enjoining a crime or a vice: "it is therefore a figure, bidding us communicate in the sufferings of our Lord, and secretly and profitably treasure in our hearts the fact that his flesh was crucified and pierced for us."[1] Elsewhere he sums the matter up in an epigram: *Crede et manducasti,* "Believe, and thou hast eaten."[2]

Bernard expounds the words "he who eats my flesh and drinks my blood has eternal life" as meaning "he who reflects on my death, and after my example mortifies his members which are on earth, has eternal life—in other words, 'If you suffer with me, you will also reign with me.' "[3]

The question is naturally raised: What relation do these words of Jesus bear to the Communion service, in which believers receive bread and wine as tokens of the body and blood of the Lord? Since John, unlike the other Evangelists, does not record the institution of the Lord's Supper, it could be said that this discourse represents his counterpart to their accounts of what Jesus did and said in the upper room when he gave his disciples the bread and the cup (see comment on Mk 14:22-24). In the discourse of John 6 Jesus is not making a direct reference to Holy Communion, but this discourse conveys the same truth in words as Holy Communion conveys in action. This truth is summed up in the invitation extended to the communicant in the Book of Common Prayer: "Take and eat this in remembrance that Christ died for thee, and feed on him in thy heart by faith with thanksgiving." To feed on Christ in one's heart by faith with thanksgiving is to "eat the flesh of the Son of Man and drink his blood" and so have eternal life.

---

[1]Augustine *On Christian Doctrine* 3.16.
[2]Augustine *Homilies on John* 26.1.
[3]Bernard *The Love of God* 4.11.

10:34-35 You Are Gods?

See comment on PSALM 82:1.

12:39-40 God Blinded Their Eyes?

See comment on MARK 4:11-12.

14:6 No One Saved Without Jesus?

When we read John 14:6, it sounds like a very exclusive statement. "No one comes to the Father except through me." Does this statement mean what it seems to imply, that no one can be saved without Jesus? What about those who lived before Jesus? Are they all damned? This verse appears so out of place in our tolerant society in which we have learned to respect the beliefs of others.

John 14:6 is one of those verses that are difficult not because we do not understand them but because we understand them all too well. It is the central verse of the whole section, John 14:1-11. It builds on the question of Thomas in the previous verse: "Lord, we don't know where you are going, so how can we know the way?" Jesus has told his disciples that he is going to his Father's house to prepare a place for them. Thomas is concerned about how they will get there to be with Jesus. This verse is Jesus' answer. It is followed by a discussion of who the Father is.

In this verse Jesus speaks of himself as "the way, the truth and the life" (KJV). The emphasis is clearly on "the way," for that is the question that Thomas was asking. Jesus does not show or teach about the way; he *is* the way to the Father's house. He is the way, of course, because he is also the truth (a term found twenty-one times in John, beginning with the Logos passage [Jn 1:14, 17]) and the life (found thirty-nine times in John, beginning with Jn 1:4, but especially important in Jn 5:21-29 with reference to raising the dead). The concept of truth is what will lead us forward into the next section of the chapter, for it is his being full of grace and truth (Jn 1:14) that is connected to his being the full revelation of the Father on earth.

Why did John, who admits that he had much more material than he included in his Gospel, put this material into his book? First, John includes a lot of discussion between Jesus and the Jews. The issue is whether Jesus is the fulfillment of the Old Testament hopes or not. Jesus in the Gospel consistently indicates that he is that fulfillment and that he supersedes Jewish expressions of worship (for example, Jn 2:13-22, in which it is his body which is the true temple, and Jn 4:21-26, in which the presence of the Messiah, Jesus, makes both Jerusalem and Gerazim irrelevant). Thus John surely interprets this saying as indicating that the old ways of Jewish worship, good as they were ("salvation is from the Jews") will no longer do. A new era has dawned in Jesus and the way of salvation and life is through him.

Second, this Gospel was written in a Gentile-dominated world. In that world there were many cults offering salvation and many saviors associated with those cults. Also part of that world was the idea that one need not be totally committed to any one cult. One "worshiped" the Roman deities, of course, for it was one's patriotic duty, much as Americans honor the American flag. And then there were the deities of one's city, trade guild (if one were an artisan) and clan. The various mystery religions and exotic cults (many of them with Eastern roots) were on top of all of this. In the Greco-Roman world there were many "ways," and while one selected what one felt was the best way, one also tried to keep all of the deities happy. It is obvious that Jesus' words in such a world are quite exclusive. There are no other ways to the Father, there is no other source of real life, there is no alternative source of truth. Jesus is the Logos incarnate. Thus he is the final revelation from God. He is the one to whom the Father has committed the resurrection of the dead (see John 11 as well as John 5). No one comes to the Father who does not come through him, for he is the way.

John is certainly aware of this exclusive claim, for it repeats in different forms over and over again in the Gospel. It is also clear that the Gospel was written for people who do not yet believe, for that is clearly stated in the author's purpose statement: "But these are written that you may believe [the best manuscripts imply 'come to believe'] that Jesus is the Christ, the Son of God, and that by believing you may have life in his name" (Jn 20:31). These people are probably not Jews, for otherwise he would not have presented "the Jews" in such a negative light. What John appears to be doing is telling his Gentile readers that none of their former ways to life will do. Jesus is the only way.

John's Jesus may in fact be offensive to us, but this is part of the offense of classic Christianity. The belief that Jesus is the way to God is also presented in Acts 2 and 3 (to Jews) and Acts 17 (to Gentiles). First Peter, written to Gentiles, claims that the whole world will appear before God to be judged according to the standards Jesus gave (for example, 1 Pet 4). The author of Hebrews does not believe that there is any salvation for those who turn back to Judaism from Jesus. The whole New Testament teaches that Jesus is the exclusive way to God or eternal life (it uses a variety of terms for these concepts).

The issue, then, is not whether or not we like this claim, but whether or not it is true. The usual smokescreen is to say, "What about those who have never heard of Jesus?" The response to this is twofold: (1) there is a missionary imperative in the New Testament to minimize this problem (that is why, for example, Paul dedicates his life to preaching Jesus where he has not yet been preached) and (2) how God may choose to reveal himself or deal with those who have no human messenger is his business. If we know God's character, we can trust him to do his business well. Our problem is that we do know about Jesus and are living in a culture in which Jesus is all too well known. Furthermore, the missionary imperative falls to those of us who believe.

If, then, this claim is true, two conclusions follow. First, we are deceiving ourselves if we think that we can come to God any other way than through Jesus. What is more, no other way will supplement or add to Jesus as *the* way. Second, if we are already following Jesus, we are called, in John's terms, to be witnesses to the truth and life found in Jesus.

14:12 What Greater Things?

In John 14:12 Jesus says that those who have faith in him will do "greater things than these." What are these "greater things" that he is talking about? Surely he could not be talking about greater miracles? How can any person do greater things than the Son of God?

In the discussion of John 1:51 we saw that Jesus spoke of his miraculous works as "see[ing] heaven open." He was the gate between God and human beings, so to speak, and through him the powers of heaven were opened to those on earth. He continues this theme in John 5:19-20.

What Jesus is saying is that he does not act on his own but participates in the works of his Father. He is indeed a window into heaven, and while his listeners see Jesus in the flesh, the one actually doing the deeds is the Father.

With this background we now turn to John 14. The request that began the discussion was "Show us the Father" (Jn 14:9). Jesus' response was "You have seen the Father in me." He explains this by noting that the Father was the one actually doing the works. Thus the disciples should believe that he was in the Father and the Father in him because of the works. What are these works? We know that they are not his teachings, for he refers to his words as evidence for believing his teachings. Thus they must be "the miracles" (as the NIV correctly translates), for those are the works which in John are connected with people believing. It is immediately after this that Jesus says that "anyone who has faith in" him will do "greater works" than these. Given the context, the greater things can only be greater miracles.

This brings us to the other part of the problem: how can believers do greater miracles than Jesus? (The greater works are not preaching the gospel, for Jesus has distinguished between believing his claims about himself, that is, his preaching, and believing his works, which in context are clearly his miracles; in this text it is greater works than his that people will do, not greater preaching than his.) For Jesus this is no problem. He will be with his Father and he promises to do whatever believers ask. Presumably this is conditioned by their being in harmony with him, for that seems to be the purpose of John 14:15.

The next section in the chapter adds to this picture, for it describes the work of the Holy Spirit. The Spirit is viewed as another of the same type as Jesus. He will "be in you" (Jn 14:17). This is amplified as "I will come to you" (Jn 14:18 RSV). Finally, Jesus notes in John 14:23

with reference to his Father, "We will come to him [the one who loves Jesus and keeps his commandments] and make our home with him." Thus through the Spirit there is a unity produced: "On that day you will realize that I am in my Father, and you are in me, and I am in you" (Jn 14:20). Thus there is no problem with believers doing the works, for they will not be doing the works on their own at all. Through the Spirit the believer will have God inside of him or her. Just as the Father did the works which people saw Jesus doing, so he (or Jesus or the Spirit—the text refers to all as inside the believer) will do the miracles that the believers will do.

This point of view would not be strange to the rest of the New Testament. Acts reports miracles done by the apostles which are fully as impressive as any done by Jesus. Are they greater miracles? We must respond, By what standard? They are at least equal in kind and could be viewed as greater in the sense that they are done over a wider area and thus on a scale that Jesus could not do while on earth but can do as glorified in heaven. Galatians 3:5 refers offhandedly to God's having worked miracles through the Galatians (the issue there is not whether they worked miracles, but how they did, by faith or by following Jewish practices). First Corinthians 12 refers to a gift of miracles as if it were a known example of spiritual gifts. James 5:14-16 mentions effective prayers for healing in an end-of-the-letter context where one would expect to be reminded of old teaching, not introduced to new. Hebrews 6:4-5 indicates that that community had experienced the "powers of the age to come" (RSV), probably meaning miracles. In other words, wherever we turn in the New Testament, we find a miracle-working community of faith. John 14:12 would not have caused any of them problems. They knew their own limitations, but they also knew what God could do through them.

So the deeper difficulty for the modern reader, once they understand that it is God doing the works through them and not their own having to produce the works, is why they may not be experiencing such events. At least part of the response John might make would be to point us to "If you love me you will obey what I command" (Jn 14:15). This is amplified in John 14:21, "Whoever has my commands and obeys them, he is the one who loves me. He who loves me will be loved by my Father, and I too will love him and show myself to him." This is not a legal statement but a relational one: if you are in harmony with me, then you will receive. The fact is that two cannot walk together unless they are agreed. Jesus lived in harmony with the Father, listened to the Father and did his works. The believer lives in harmony with Jesus (which includes obedience), experiences the presence of Jesus and his Father and does their works. Of course, we also remember that one of the works the Father had in store for Jesus was the cross, which is a form of following Christ that this section of John does not leave out (Jn 13:36).

There are, then, two further responses to our question: maybe our naturalistic worldview keeps us back from hearing the voice of the Father calling us to do such works as these, and maybe also, having read the whole book, we shrink back from following Jesus to glory because we fear that (to use Johannine terms) our ladder to glory like his may turn out to be a cross.

14:28 The Father Is Greater?

In the context of John we realize that Jesus' "going away" has to do with his death, resurrection and ascension, for they are a single entity in John, and his "coming back" refers first to his resurrection and then more importantly to his coming to his disciples in the Spirit, for that is the context of this chapter. Yet it is puzzling to read that "the Father is greater than I." How can God be greater than God? Or does this mean that Jesus is not in fact God? In what sense is the Father greater than Jesus?

Any response to this question must take into account all of what John says about Jesus. For example, there are a number of passages in which the writer or Jesus claims Jesus' equality with the Father (Jn 1:1, 18; 5:16-18; 10:30; 20:28). Thus we can assume that the author is not denying these statements. Along with this there are passages we have already noted in which Jesus claims dependence on the Father (Jn 4:34; 5:19-30; 8:29; 12:48-49). Thus we have two major themes in the Gospel: equality and yet dependence.

To understand what John means in this passage, we should notice that the meaning is something which Jesus believes should make the disciples glad, if they love him. Also, the meaning should take the wider context into account.

One possible meaning would be that Jesus is a lesser being than the Father, a demigod or a lesser god (given that Jn 1:1 indicates his divine character). Not only has this solution been rejected by the church throughout the ages (it was known as the Arian heresy), but it does not make sense within John. First, it does not make sense in the context of Jewish monotheism within which John and all of the Gospels are set. If you have multiple gods, whether of the same rank or of higher and lower rank, you have polytheism, against which Judaism cried out, "God is one." There is no indication that John is trying to enter such a dispute with Judaism. Second, it does not make sense in terms of John, for the author has gone through some trouble to establish the unity and essential equality of the Father and Jesus. Furthermore, one can hardly see how this would make the disciples glad.

Another possible explanation is that the Father exists in heaven in complete power and glory, while Jesus was then living on earth in relative humility and obscurity. People who really loved Jesus would want him to return to the greater state of the Father. Not only would his return to glory be pleasant for him, but it would also be good for them since their leader would have his full power and glory. This is certainly an interpretation that does justice to the context and to Johannine theology and its context in Judaism. The only problem with such an interpretation is that this verse seems a rather awkward way to express this sentiment.

Finally, Jesus may be expressing the idea that there is organization in the Godhead and thus the disciples' having their personal master directly in front of the Father would be advantageous for them. If this is what is intended, then we are taking the language of Father and Son quite seriously. In an ancient family with a father and an adult son, the two men would be the same in being. Both are adult human males, fully educated in the particular culture in which they exist. Yet the one designated "father" has greater authority in the household, including authority over the one designated "son." (This is different from Western culture in which adult sons are viewed as independent of or emancipated from their fathers and thus as totally equal adults.) If this is what Jesus means, then we understand that his going to the Father not only puts him back with his own Father (about which those who love him should be glad), but also puts him with the one in whom the family (divine, in this case) authority is vested. He represents his disciples directly to the highest authority. That should also make his disciples glad. This interpretation fits with the context in which Jesus' going to the Father brings the release of the Spirit and greater authority and access to God in prayer to the disciples.

In my view, this latter perspective makes the most sense of the passage and the culture and context in which the passage was written. However, the second position is also acceptable, although it does not seem to make as much sense out of the context. If we accept the second position, it reminds us to be glad of the good things which happened to Jesus in his ascension, rather than mourning over our personal loss that he is not present (although we saw before that this is only an apparent loss, for he is in fact present through the Spirit). If we accept the second position, we will not only enter into the joy of the divine family being together, but will also rejoice that the one who represents us stands directly before the throne of the universe (see 1 Jn 2:1).

See also comment on MATTHEW 11:27.

19:19 What Was the Crime?

It was Roman custom to post on the cross the crime of the one being executed. When we read John 19:19, it seems very clear what was written on the cross: "Jesus of Nazareth, the King of the Jews." However, then we read the other Gospels:

Mt 27:37: This is Jesus, the king of the Jews.

Mk 15:26: The king of the Jews.

Lk 23:38: This is the king of the Jews.

What was the crime that was posted over Jesus?

It is clear that the Gospels agree on the charge: "king of the Jews." That is, officially he was being executed as one who had proclaimed himself a king, specifically, king of the Jews, and so was being executed for rebellion against Caesar. This charge is consistent with the trial accounts and consistent with what we know of the concerns of the Roman government of the day about any popular Jewish movement. It is further reinforced by the fact that those executed with Jesus are called "thieves," for the Jewish historian Josephus uses the same term to describe revolutionaries. In fact, Jesus may well have replaced Barabbas, who is clearly described as a revolutionary and could have been the leader of the other two.

What about the rest of the charge? Did it identify Jesus by name? How much of his name did it use? In all probability it did identify Jesus by name. A crucified person was not easy to recognize, given how brutally he or she had been treated. Furthermore, the purpose of crucifixion was not simply execution, but terror, for by crucifying a person in a public place (usually along a road leading into the city), the dying (and usually afterward, rotting) person would be a warning to anyone contemplating doing what the victim had done. Obviously identifying the victim would serve as more of a warning than leaving them unidentified.

Why, then, the differences in the Gospel accounts? First, each of the Gospel writers knows that words are precious. Papyrus only came in certain lengths, and three of our four Gospels fill the longest papyrus scrolls of the day. Mark, of course, could have bought a longer scroll, but by the time he came to this point in the story the scroll was already purchased and mostly used. The readers of the Gospels have no doubt about who is on the cross, so the only reason to include the name is for effect, if one has space. John includes the full name for he is going to make a comment on the accusation and the reaction it caused among the Jews (Jn 19:20-22). The other Gospels have not chosen to discuss the charge, so they can use a shortened form.

Second, while the accusation, according to John, was written in Aramaic (or Hebrew), Greek and Latin, we do not know in what form it passed into the Gospel tradition. Did one person remember the Aramaic and another the Greek? Or was the Aramaic the only form in which the charge was remembered? There is plenty of room here for various versions to be passed on, especially since only the charge itself was the essential part of what was written.

Thus this passage reminds us again of the process of writing the Gospels. The early oral accounts probably circulated in Aramaic and were then translated into Greek as needed. The significant point is that despite their history of transmission they agree on the central issue. This reminds us to focus on the core point, that Jesus was crucified as a revolutionary, and not on the details, which did not bother the writers of the Gospels.

20:1-8 What Happened at the Resurrection?

The story of the resurrection in John is quite exciting and seemingly straightforward. One woman shows up at the tomb, discovers it is open, informs the disciples, who investigate, and then meets first an angel and afterward Jesus. This straightforwardness is true enough so long as we look only at one Gospel. When we examine Matthew 28:1-8 or Mark 16:1-8 or Luke 24:1-10 we discover differing pictures. Can these pictures be put together? If they cannot, what does this mean for the truth of the accounts?

In responding to this issue, it would be helpful to look at the events in the four accounts (see chart).

When we examine these four accounts, we notice some similarities. First, all agree that the events happened around dawn, although they disagree about whether it was already light. Given that the events happened over a period of time, this difference is hardly significant. Second, all agree that Mary Magdalene was at least one of the ones discovering that the body had disappeared. The purposes of the individual narratives seems to determine how many other women are mentioned (with Luke, who has a special interest in women, noting the most women). Third, all agree that the women find an open, corpseless tomb. Matthew seems to imply that they also saw the opening of the tomb, although he may narrate the opening of the tomb as something that happened while the women were traveling and before they arrived at the tomb. None of the other Gospels mentions the guards, so how the tomb gets opened is less of a problem for them. Fourth, all agree that the women saw one or more angels (only Luke has two). However, the angel in John's account appears to be functioning in a different narrative role than the ones in the other accounts. It is, perhaps, more accurate to say that John does not inform us if Mary saw anyone at the tomb *before* going to tell the disciples. What the angels say also differs, although in all cases the women are informed that Jesus is not there. In the various accounts they are told not to fear (and that they were afraid anyway), to report to the disciples and to meet Jesus in Galilee. Finally, all agree that the women left the tomb, and three of the four accounts note that they did inform the disciples. (Mark breaks off with verse 8, the longer ending probably not being part of the original text; it is debated whether an original ending of Mark has been lost or whether he intended to break off with the women in fear and the question of whether they would follow Jesus into Galilee hanging in the air.)

Furthermore, two of the accounts agree that the woman or women met

Event	Mt 28:1-8	Mk 16:1-8	Lk 24:1-10	Jn 20:1-8
When?	at dawn	just after sunrise	very early in the morning	while it was still dark
Who comes first?	Mary Magdalene and the other Mary	Mary Magdalene, Mary the mother of James, and Salome	Mary Magdalene, Joanna, Mary the mother of James, and the others	Mary Magdalene
What do they find?	earthquake with angel who rolls back the stone	stone rolled away	stone rolled away	stone removed from the entrance
Whom do they see?	angel sitting on the stone	young man in white robe, sitting on the right	two men in clothes that gleamed like lightning	no one
What do they do?	ran to tell his disciples	fled from the tomb, afraid to say anything	told what had happened to the Eleven and others	ran to tell Peter and the disciple, the one Jesus loved
What happens next?	Jesus met them		Peter goes to the tomb to investigate	Peter and the other disciple investigate
What is the third scene?	guards report to chief priests and are bribed		story of two disciples on the Emmaus road	Mary sees two angels in white, seated where Jesus' body had been

Jesus, that they tried to hold on to him, and that he sent them on their way. However, John appears to put this meeting after Peter and the beloved disciple investigate, and Matthew puts it before the women report to the disciples.

What can we conclude from this data? First, it is possible to make this data into a coherent story. If we assume that the pre- or postdawn timing depends on whether one gives the time of the women starting their trip or their arrival at the tomb, if we assume that the earthquake and angelic descent happened before the women arrived at the tomb, if we merge what the angels say into one account, if we assume that the angels moved around, and if we assume that Mary Magdalene remained behind at the tomb while the others went and reported (and thus had a separate meeting with Jesus), one can make a single coherent account out of the various stories. Obviously, if there were two angels, one writer could report only one. Not every writer has to report all of the details another mentions. In other words, these are different stories but not necessarily conflicting stories. All could be true at the same time.

Second, while it is possible to make the data fit into a coherent story, we cannot be sure that we have the right coherent story. We have a jigsaw puzzle of information and cannot be sure that we have all of the pieces. Thus, since the Scripture has not given us a single unified story, we must be careful or else we will end up believing that our reconstruction is the truth. A reconstruction may be the truth or it may distort the truth. Perhaps if we had some other critical pieces of information we would make quite a different reconstruction.

Third, these stories are exactly what one would expect to discover after a significant event like the resurrection. The chancellor of this author's university died at the end of an address to the student body. Within an hour of the event a sociology professor had his thirty students each write down their own account of what had happened. Each was instructed to write as honest and detailed account as they could, given the limited time of the class period. When the accounts were later compared, there were numerous differences in detail, although all agreed that the chancellor had died at the end of his address. Presumably each Gospel writer had a series of stories about the resurrection to sort through. For example, we know that Matthew knows and values Mark's account, but in the resurrection story he obviously has some independent information as well. The Evangelists selected and combined data to get the accounts that they give us. But even the beloved disciple in John is not an eyewitness of most of the events, so we are not surprised to find a lot of differences in their reporting what happened.

Finally, when we try to put the stories together, we miss the point of the authors. The church accepted into its canon four separate Gospels, viewing each as inspired by God. It did not put into the canon a harmony of these Gospels (although such existed). The fact is that each writer is trying to bring out his unique perspective and theological insights by the details he includes or leaves out (although, unless Matthew and Luke are differing from Mark, which we know that they knew, we often cannot be sure that the author actually knows a detail and so purposely leaves it out). Matthew wants to underline the miraculous and also explain a rumor that the body of Jesus was stolen. Luke stresses the fulfillment of the words of Jesus and yet the disbelief of the apostles. John, by focusing on a single character and her intimate discussion with Jesus, points out that in the resurrection and ascension of Jesus the promises of John 13—16 are fulfilled. Jesus cannot be held, for it is better for him to go to the one who is not only his Father but is now also our Father. It is when we look at the resurrection through such eyes, informed by the perspective of each Gospel writer, that we see not simply a miracle, nor even the fact of the resurrection, but the message the church has believed that God wanted to communicate in and through the resurrection of Jesus Christ.

20:22 Receive the Holy Spirit?

Did the disciples receive the Holy Spirit before the ascension or at Pentecost? In John 20:22 Jesus breathes on the disciples and indicates that he is granting them the Holy Spirit, which fulfills a promise repeatedly made in John 14—16. However, in Acts 2:4 we learn that later, after the ascension of Jesus, the 120 disciples gathered in the upper room had an experience, and "all of them were filled with the Holy Spirit and began to speak in other tongues as the Spirit enabled them." When was the

Holy Spirit actually received by the disciples?

In John 20:21 we have the commissioning of the disciples: "As the Father has sent me, I am sending you." The sending of the Son in John is a sending into the world to save the world. The sending of the disciples is thus a continuation of this sending of Jesus as they go out into the world to preach the gospel. At this point Jesus grants them the power for mission with the words "receive the Holy Spirit." Along with this empowering comes the authority to forgive sins (which, of course, is part of preaching the gospel, for in it one indicates whose sins are forgiven and whose are not). In other words, the three verses, John 20:21-23, fit together.

There have been three approaches to these verses. The first notes that this linking of empowering with the Spirit and the preaching of the gospel also appears in Acts, where the disciples wait until the Spirit comes at Pentecost and then begin to preach the gospel. Therefore, it is argued, this must be John's version of the Acts event. John, of course, never mentions the ascension. Jesus comes and disappears repeatedly right to the end of the book. This is appropriate, for in John Jesus is said to come in the Holy Spirit to the disciples (Jn 14:18). Here, according to this argument, we have a symbolic presentation of what Acts speaks of as a later event. Symbolism is the way of John.

This is certainly a possible approach. In its best form it takes both John and its style seriously and Luke-Acts and its style just as seriously. It notes real parallels in the two accounts. Yet the approach also has its problems. First, the disciples do not go out and witness after receiving the Spirit. In fact, they cannot even convince Thomas (Jn 20:24-25). What is more, Thomas would then appear never to receive the Spirit. Second, this solution really says that the two accounts are not reconcilable. One is historical and the other symbolic. While it is clear that we do not always know how accounts fit together, and thus there is some truth to such solutions, it is also clear that when John reports events he thinks of them as events, not symbols of events. The events may symbolize something (as the raising of Lazarus symbolizes the final resurrection), but they are viewed in themselves as historical. Thus this solution does not fit John's normal methodology.

A second approach views John as one type of giving of the Spirit and Acts as another. John is the impersonal breath of God and Acts is the personal Holy Spirit. John is a sprinkling with the grace of the Spirit and Acts is full empowerment, saturation with the Spirit. John is the Spirit as new life and Acts is the Spirit as empowerment for ministry. The list of how these two givings are to be distinguished could be extended much further. Now this solution takes both of the events as quite historical and tries to distinguish why there should be two events. The problem with it is that neither John nor Acts seems to know about two receptions of the Spirit. Reading through John 13—16 one does not notice two receptions but rather one Holy Spirit or "paraclete" (a transliteration of the word sometimes translated as "comforter" or "advocate"). In Acts the reception of the Spirit they are awaiting is not distinguished from any previous reception, despite Luke's interest in the topic of the Spirit. Thus this approach seems to be an explanation imposed on the texts by people who read both Acts and John rather than something that either Luke or John thought of.

A third approach looks at John 20:22 as Jesus' symbolic giving or promising the Spirit, which was experientially received on Pentecost. The breathing (not necessarily on the disciples, for there is no "on" in the text) symbolizes what the words say, namely the Holy Spirit. Yet nothing seems to happen. It is a promise. For John it is all that is needed, for those who experienced the power of the Spirit in the church knew that the disciples really did receive the Spirit. There is no need to mention that it did not occur until later, for John is not going to carry on the story that long. For Luke there is no need to mention any previous symbolic giving, for Jesus refers to the promise of the Spirit before his ascension (Acts 1:4-5). Luke is concerned with the reality of the power and how it directs the mission of the church. Thus both writers have their reasons for not needing to mention what the other includes (assuming that they knew of both stories). Naturally, it would not be surprising to think of Jesus as wanting to act out the giving of the Spirit personally, especially if he is aware that his physical presence with the disciples is coming to an end and he will not be physically present at Pentecost. In other words, John 20:22 may be John's version of Acts 1:4-5 rather than John's version of Pentecost.

It will remain for the reader to decide which of these approaches is the most satisfying in that it best fits the data of the texts in question. What is more important than harmonizing the texts is recognizing that both John and Acts do indeed insist that the Holy Spirit is needed for the mission of the church. Mere human power and authority cannot carry out the mission Jesus received from the Father. It takes the Spirit in the believer to produce the results the Father intends, the forgiveness of sins.

ACTS

1:18 How Did Judas Die?

While Luke's description of Judas's death is rather gory, Acts 1:18 would not be a problem were it not that Matthew seemingly has a different story. In Matthew's account, "Judas threw the money into the temple and left. Then he went away and hanged himself" (Mt 27:5). Matthew also reports that the chief priests used the money "to buy the potter's field as a burial place for foreigners." Aren't the two accounts contradictory?

It is clear that Matthew and Luke have different concerns in mentioning the incident. Matthew is more interested in the purchase of the field, which he sees as a fulfillment of Scripture. He combines Zechariah 11:12-13 (the thirty pieces of silver and the potter) and Jeremiah 32:6-12 (buying a field), perhaps with overtones of Jeremiah 18:1-4 (going to the potter's house), and links them all under Jeremiah's name (see comment on Mt 27:9-10).

Luke has another concern, which is that Judas got what he deserved, a horrible death. (A similar situation is reported in Acts 12:21-24, where the author narrates the story of Herod Agrippa I's death.) The focus is not on the purchase of the field (which would have appeared a reward, especially to Jews for whom landowning in Palestine was important), but on his death in the field (which was ghastly).

Both authors want to point out that the field was called "The Field of Blood," thus memorializing the deed. Acts appears to connect the title to Judas's blood in his death, while Matthew ties it to the fact that the blood money paid for the field. It is hardly surprising that the same name might mean different things to different people.

A closer look at the two stories highlights gaps in the narrative that raise questions about the events. But the accounts are not necessarily contradictory. Acts is concerned that Judas's money and name were connected to a field. Whether or not the chief priests actually purchased it, perhaps some time after Judas's death, would not be a detail of concern to the author. His point was the general knowledge that Judas's money went to the purchase, which resulted in the title "Field of Blood" being attached to the field. Another possible reason for the name, also a concern of Acts, was that Judas split open and his intestines poured out. Such a defacing of the body, probably with the concomitant result of the corpse being at least partially eaten by vultures and dogs, was horrible in the view of the Jews, for whom proper burial was important. In fact, they even valued forms of execution that did not deface the outside of the body (such as strangulation) over forms that defaced the body (such as stoning, the worst form in their eyes).

Matthew points out that it was a guilt-motivated suicide, accomplished by the most common means, hanging. Suicide in Jewish literature is most often connected to shame or failure. (So 2 Sam 17:23; compare the other accounts of suicide in Old Testament history, which were normally to avoid a more shameful death.) However, since suicide by hanging was usually accomplished (at least by poorer people) by jumping out of a tree with a rope around one's neck, it was not unusual (nor is it uncommon in India today) for the body to be ripped open in the process.[1] I hesitate to say that this was exactly what happened, but it is certainly a plausible explanation.

Therefore, we will never be fully certain about what happened at the death of Judas. What I have shown is that there are certainly credible explanations as to how the two accounts fit together. I have shown how it may well have happened, not how it must have happened. In doing so we see that there is no necessary contradiction. Yet what is important in reading these narratives is to focus on the points they are making, not on the horrible death. With Matthew we see that Scripture is fulfilled even while those fulfilling it are driven by guilt and shame to their own self-destruction. And with Acts we see that sin does have consequences: Judas not only lost his office through his treachery, but came to a shameful end as well, an end memorialized in the place near Jerusalem named "Field of Blood."

---

[1]I owe this information to an Indian pastor well acquainted with such tragic events. There is, however, another translation of the passage: "Swelling up, he burst open, pouring out his intestines." While "falling headlong" is a more likely translation than "swelling up," which is first encountered in Papias's reported comments on the event, there is still no conflict, for a corpse left hanging would swell up and often eventually break open, resulting in the same defaced body to which Acts wishes to point us.

1:26 Casting Lots?

The eleven apostles, together with many other disciples, were gathered in the upper room after the ascension. At Simon Peter's suggestion the decision was made to replace Judas, who had forfeited his office by his betrayal of Jesus. Unfortunately, the group of disciples contained not one but two qualified candidates, Matthias and Joseph Barsabbas. A decision has to be made. They pray. Someone brings out some dice. The dice are thrown and Matthias wins. He is from then on counted as an apostle, one chosen and sent by the Lord. This scenario is difficult for two reasons. First, if this procedure was of God, why isn't church business conducted in this way now? Second, if this method is not to be used now, how could it have been legitimate then? Did Matthias really become the twelfth apostle, or was this the first major postascension failure of the church, a use of worldly methods?

The Eleven certainly had a legitimate concern. Jesus had promised that the Twelve would "sit on thrones, judging the twelve tribes of Israel" (Lk 22:30). The situation that confronts them in

Acts 1:26 is that now, as they await the inauguration of the mission to the world (Luke explains Pentecost more as empowering for mission than as the beginning of the church), there is a vacant spot. The issue was not that Judas had died. James son of Zebedee would also die, but he would not be replaced (Acts 12:2). The apostles believed in the resurrection of the dead, so in their eyes James was still available to take his place on his throne. Instead, the issue with Judas was that by betraying Jesus he had forfeited his place.

Some have suggested that Paul was God's choice as a replacement and that the decision here was premature. That can hardly be the case. First, one qualification was that the person had been with Jesus during his whole earthly ministry (Acts 1:21-22). While many disciples other than the Twelve often followed Jesus, Paul was certainly not one of them. Second, the Twelve were oriented toward the "twelve tribes of Israel"; that is, their focus was and remained the Jewish-Christian mission. Paul was the great apostle to the Gentiles. Third, in his letters Paul never groups himself with the Twelve but rather maintains the uniqueness of his own apostleship (for example, 1 Cor 15:8-9; Gal 1:12, 15). Finally, Paul knows several other apostles, such as James (Gal 1:19) and Andronicus and Junia (Rom 16:7). Thus, while all of the Twelve were apostles, not all apostles belonged to the Twelve. The Eleven correctly realized that unique qualifications were needed to fill that twelfth spot.

Throughout the Old Testament the lot was the normal means of discerning the divine will when a prophet was not available. It was the means of decision on the Day of Atonement (Lev 16:8) and was how the land had been divided (Josh 18:10). Centuries later, when the returning exiles wanted to know God's mind, they still used it (Neh 10:34; 11:1). More important than the historical examples are the instructions of Proverbs, which were understood as divine teaching. How could harmony be preserved when there were two contenders? "Casting the lot settles disputes and keeps strong opponents apart" (Prov 18:18). Could the dice really give God's answer? "The lot is cast into the lap, but its every decision is from the Lord" (Prov 16:33). In other words, since the decision in Acts was not automatic (two men were fully qualified), those gathered in the upper room had every reason in terms of both biblical precedent and biblical teaching to believe that God would make his will known through the lot. There was nothing incorrect in their procedure.

Why, then, is this the last time that we read about the early church using dice? In the next chapter, with the gathering fully organized (all twelve apostles in place), the Holy Spirit falls. The Spirit was also the Spirit of prophecy, whose departure from Israel had left them with only dice as a means through which God might communicate his will. But now in the wake of the coming of Jesus the Spirit is back, not resting only on a few prophets, but on the whole people of God. Many of them received the gift of prophecy. From this point on Acts records prophetic words that explain decisions (for example, "the Spirit told me," Acts 11:12), indicate people chosen for special roles (Acts 13:2) and apparently lead to consensus (Acts 15:28). In the church empowered by the Spirit, God speaks through that Spirit. It is therefore no wonder that in such a context the lot and similar indirect means of discerning the divine will (such as seeking omens from God like Gideon's fleece) were relegated to history. We who live in a church still filled with that Spirit can continue to be thankful that due to our direct connection with God we no longer have to copy the means that were necessary for the first ten days of the church after Jesus left.

See also comment on JONAH 1:4-5, 7.

2:38 Baptism for the Forgiveness of Sins?

Peter in his sermon at Pentecost connects baptism to the forgiveness of sins. Does baptism really forgive sins? If so, what about the unbaptized?

The connection of baptism with the forgiveness of sins has already occurred in Luke-Acts, for in Luke 3:3 the author has already mentioned "a baptism of repentance for the forgiveness of sins" (so also Mt 3:6, 11; Mk 1:4). What is more, baptism is connected to salvation in 1 Peter 3:21. Thus what we are looking at is not an isolated text, but the function of baptism, not only in Acts, but also in other New Testament documents. In effect, we are asking about the process of Christian initiation in the New Testament: how does one come into the Christian faith?

In Acts Peter outlines the process in logical steps. First, there is repentance. That is, (if a person acts in logical order) one first realizes that he or she is in a bad position. In Acts this repentance is a turning from their identification with the crucifixion of Christ (brought about by their leaders) and the judgment that that was a just act. In Luke and the other Gospels this is defined as a turning from specific sinful acts, specific ways one has lived life independent of God. Repentance in general is turning from one's own way because now he or she knows that it is not God's way.

The second step could be broken into two parts. Peter expresses it as being "baptized . . . in the name of Jesus Christ." If repentance is a turning from, this is a turning to. It is not enough to simply reject one's former way of life as not being God's way; a person must turn to go God's way. What constitutes God's way is Jesus Christ. The early Christian confession was "Jesus is Lord" (Rom 10:9, 10). "Faith in Jesus" could also be translated "commitment to Jesus" or "trust in Jesus." In other words, the person acknowledges and Jesus is indeed God's Anointed One (or Messiah or Christ), God's designated ruler (not a criminal justly condemned), and Jesus is living (for one cannot follow a dead man) and worthy of obedience and worship.

If that is the commitment, how does one make it? The answer given by Peter is baptism. It is in baptism that the early Christian (and in many places, the Christian today) made his or her official pledge of allegiance to Jesus. That is why 1 Peter 3:21 refers to a "pledge of a good conscience," that is, the pledge to God to follow Jesus made, not deceptively, but in good conscience. It is no wonder, then, that baptism is connected to the forgiveness of sins, for without commitment to Jesus there is no forgiveness of sin, and this is the normal way in the New Testament to make that commitment. In other words, baptism is viewed in Acts something like a marriage ceremony: it is the time when one takes the pledge of identity with Jesus. It is how one expresses faith.

The third step in the process is not one which the person does, although on at least some occasions in Acts the leaders of the church do function as vehicles for it (Acts 8:17; 9:17; 19:6). In this step God grants the gift of the Holy Spirit. Paul will argue that a person can know that they are truly a Christian by the fact that they have received the Spirit (Rom 8:9), and Acts agrees. With this response of God, the process of Christian initiation is complete. The person is a full part of the church, equipped for all that God has called him or her to do, although there will certainly be a process of learning and maturing to go through as they begin to live out the new life.

The reason that Peter's statement in Acts seems so strange to us is that in the modern church we sometimes do things differently. Because so many different understandings of baptism exist, evangelists who work across denominational lines generally avoid talking about it. Even those working within a single denomination often separate baptism from the conversion process. Thus in some Baptist groups one "prays a sinner's prayer" and/or signs a "decision card" at the point of conversion and then may be baptized as part of "joining the church" or "giving a public testimony" to one's faith. Yet the individual is recognized as a full Christian even without baptism. On the other hand, some (but by no means all) people baptized in mainline denominations may have grown up in families that rarely attended church. They come to adulthood with a baptismal certificate and no conscious faith. Then they hear an evangelist and make a conscious commitment to Christ. They too pray a prayer and/or sign a card. But unless they decide to leave their old denomination, they will not be baptized. They will perhaps say, "I have finally personally actualized those vows that my parents spoke over me." In either case the prayer and decision card substitute for the role of baptism in Peter's speech.

So what of the unbaptized believer? The critical issue is the making of a pledge in good conscience. God looks on the heart.

See also comment on 1 PETER 3:21.

4:12 Salvation in No One Else?

This verse is the climax of Peter's defense to the Sanhedrin in Jerusalem. The author of Acts explicitly states that Peter was "filled with the Holy Spirit" when he made this statement (Acts 4:8, fulfilling the promise of Lk 12:11-12). Peter claims that "Jesus Christ of Nazareth," the one raised from the dead and powerful enough to have healed a lame beggar, is the sole bringer of salvation to Israel.

The first issue to address is the meaning of *salvation.* Salvation is a special interest of the author of Luke-Acts. It can mean deliverance from everything from sickness to sin, from political oppression to divine judgment. The lame man in Acts 3—4 had been saved by being healed, while Zechariah speaks of salvation in terms of deliverance from the political enemies of Israel (Lk 1:71). Acts 27:31 refers to rescue from a storm at sea as salvation. But a further issue is one of escaping divine judgment (Acts 2:21, 40). This escape not only is a rescue, but also has a positive side, namely, "that times of refreshment may come from the Lord" (Acts 3:19). This last meaning dominates the speeches in Acts. Thus while the author certainly knows many meanings for salvation (for example, that Jesus is the one through whom physical healing comes), the stress in this passage is on what he believes is the most significant meaning, salvation in its fullest sense: deliverance from divine judgment and the release of the blessings of God. This type of salvation, he states, comes only through Jesus Christ.

It is significant that Peter makes this statement in front of Jewish leaders. Their Judaism could not save them. They needed the one "name," the name of Jesus. This theme of the exclusiveness of salvation through Christ is repeated a number of times in Acts, but perhaps Paul puts it most starkly over against Athenian Greek religion and philosophy when he states, "In the past God overlooked such ignorance, but now he commands all people everywhere to repent. For he has set a day when he will judge the world with justice by the man [Jesus] he has appointed" (Acts 17:30-31). In other words, the teaching throughout Acts (and the rest of the New Testament, for that matter) is that there is only one way to escape God's judgment and receive his favor, and that is through Jesus. This exclusivity is a consistent claim of the early church.

Obviously, this teaching goes against the grain of our age. We would like to think that salvation might also be found in Krishna or Buddha or Muhammad or simply in belief in God without specific Christian faith.[1] This position, however popular it may be and however tolerant it may seem, both contradicts the teaching of this passage (and many others in the New Testament, such as Jn 14:6) and is logically problematic. If the scriptural claim that God sent Christ to die for us is in any way true, and provided God himself were not confused, then none of the other existing ways is possible. Furthermore, if God sent his Son to death when other ways of salvation already existed (such as through Buddha or Judaism) or would come into existence but not involve death (such as Islam), then God is either a masochist (due to the pain it caused him) or a sadist. In other words, the exclusivity of Christianity is rooted in the logic of the faith, as well as in the teaching of Scripture. It may be offensive to the modern mind, but, like the offensiveness of being carried in a fireman's dirty, smelly arms from a burning building, it may be necessary. The cross has always been a scandal.

Given salvation's exclusive nature, what does Peter mean by stating that salvation is in a "name"? Again, we return to Peter's first sermon, where he states, "Everyone who calls on the name of the Lord will be saved" (Acts 2:21). Peter is quoting Joel 2:32, which in its Old Testament context meant calling on Yahweh ("the Lord" is the Greek term substituted for "Yahweh" to avoid saying the divine name) for deliverance (rather than calling on Baal or some other god). The "name" stands for the person himself; but Peter in Acts 2 does not intend that one call on Yahweh. Instead he argues in the next few verses that Jesus of Nazareth is precisely the one God has made "both Lord and Christ" (Acts 2:36) and therefore is the one to whom any appeal for salvation should be addressed.[2] This is also the meaning in Acts 4:12. We appeal to Jesus, doing so by name. No other name is appropriate, not in the sense that another of the names for Jesus of Nazareth would be inappropriate, but in the sense that calling upon any other person, religious leader or deity will not work. It will take us to the wrong address, to someone or something which cannot save.

Therefore there is no mystical meaning in the name Jesus. Nor is simply knowing or using that name what is intended. Rather, Peter is calling for a commitment to a person, which is what believing, or faith, means in the New Testament sense. We must cry out to him in repentance (which means turning from living one's life independent of the authority of Christ) and turn to him in obedience as Lord. The statement "Jesus is Lord" (and therefore the lord or "boss" of the person making the statement) was the basic confession of the early church (see, for example, Acts 17:7; Rom 10:9-10). This commitment to that person, the one named Jesus Christ, is what will bring salvation, whether in its broader or narrower sense. No other appeal, no other name, will do.

See also comment on JOHN 14:6.

---

[1]Since I am Canadian, I note that in the Canadian context, with its multicultural ideal of cultural preservation and toleration (versus the United States's

melting-pot ideal of cultural assimilation), this Bible verse appears positively racist. The Native American, the Jew, the Sikh and others all have their own forms of salvation. Isn't it racist to suggest that they will not find salvation in the way that their own culture dictates?

[2]Peter can make the shift from Yahweh to Jesus easily because in reading the Hebrew scriptures, 'ădōnāy, "lord," was traditionally substituted for every place the consonants for "Yahweh" appeared. In the Greek version of the Old Testament the consonants for "Yahweh" were therefore translated by *kyrios,* "lord." This Greek term is used every time Jesus is called "Lord." So the term used in the Old Testament is the same as that which the church was commonly using to refer to Jesus, making the identification of the two easy, especially since, according to the Gospel stories, God designated Jesus as his Anointed One or Christ (Lk 2:11; 4:18; 9:20; Acts 4:27; 10:38). Furthermore, Psalm 110:1, a favorite text of the New Testament church, used "lord" in two senses in one verse, giving Old Testament precedent to the New Testament usage.

4:19 Submitting to Government?

See comment on ROMANS 13:1-7.

4:32 They Shared Everything?

Does this verse describe an idealized behavior of the church, later abandoned? Could it be called "primitive communism"? Is this practice the reason the Jerusalem church became poor? What is its relevance for today?

To understand the two passages that describe the behavior of the early church (Acts 2:42-47; 4:32-35), we need to understand the methodology of Acts, the context of the passages and their meaning. First, we note the methodology. The author is writing in an environment in which writing space is limited. Both Luke (the first volume in the two-part work) and Acts fill what would be the longest scrolls available in that day. Thus, the author must compress the text in his effort to fit a massive history within a limited scroll. Any word of Jesus that appears in Luke does not appear in Acts. Conversely, the saying that appears in Acts 20:35 does not appear in the Gospel. Another way the author shortens the text is by describing a topic once and then abbreviating it in succeeding references. The gospel messages in Acts are given in their fullest form the first time they appear and after that only in abbreviated form. New material, however, is given in full. Pentecost is the fullest description of filling with the Spirit; only variations are mentioned later. Acts 2 and 4—5 describe what the experience of the early church is supposed to be like. New details are added later, but the basic description of the church is not repeated. We expect, then, that these passages show how the author believed church life should be lived.

Second, both Acts 2 and Acts 4 fall within a context of the filling of the Spirit. Acts 2 includes Pentecost and the initial evangelistic thrust of the church. In the general description of life in the Spirit-filled church (Acts 2:42-47) we discover three elements: (1) signs and wonders, (2) evangelistic outreach and (3) sharing (teaching, food, possessions, prayer). In Acts 4 the believers respond to persecution with prayer for boldness (Acts 4:29-30). Again the church is filled with the Spirit. Again the three elements appear: (1) signs and wonders (Acts 5:12-16), (2) evangelistic outreach (Acts 4:33; 5:14) and (3) sharing (Acts 4:32—5:11). In this last passage the author chooses to expand upon the sharing aspect, first describing it and then giving two examples. For the author of Acts, sharing (often translated "fellowship") is a key mark of the Spirit-filled church. It is not a historical curiosity.

Third, what does the author intend by these passages? We can immediately lay to rest the idea of a "primitive communism" in which everyone turned all of their goods over to the community upon conversion. That has been a viable way of life for some Christian communities, but it is not what was happening in Acts. The description of selling one's goods in Acts 2:45 is expanded in Acts 4:34. In both cases the verb tense indicates an ongoing process.[1] Whenever a need came to light, those having goods sold them and brought the money to provide for the need. As if these descriptions were not clear enough, in Acts 5:3-4 the author makes it plain that such generosity was not a legal requirement; it was the lie, not the failure to give, for which Ananias and Sapphira are condemned.

What was happening in the Jerusalem church, then, was simply that "they shared everything they had" (Acts 4:32). What had been an ideal to some of the Greek philosophers has been realized by the power of the Spirit in the church. Because they were "one in heart and mind" all thought of possessiveness vanished. They shared freely with one another. This resulted in powerful evangelism and an experience of grace, perhaps indicated by the signs and wonders (Acts 4:33). Consequently, they realized the goal of Deuteronomy 15:4 ("There should be no poor among you"): "There were no needy persons among them" (Acts 4:34). Why was that? To hear of a need was to search one's heart to see if one could meet the need. As soon as a need was announced those with possessions would want to share (since the Spirit had removed their possessiveness and joined them in heart to their poorer fellow Christians). They shared by bringing the money to the apostles, probably because (1) the apostles would know if the need had been met already and (2) the apostles would guard the anonymity of the donor. Later Jewish charity rules valued the anonymity of both donor and recipient. Joseph Barnabas is viewed as a good example of this practice. Ananias and Sapphira appear as negative examples, trying to fake the impulse of the Spirit and by deceit get the apostles to think of them as more Spirit-filled than they are. But, as someone observed, "in the church in which the lame walk liars die." The same Spirit that is present for signs and wonders is also present for judgment.

We should not imagine, however, that this practice is what impoverished the Jerusalem church. On the one hand, there were plenty of reasons for that church to become poor. Jerusalem was not in a good economic position, being off trade routes and not in the best agricultural area. Its main business was government and the temple, but the Christians were probably given only limited access to the revenues from either of these sources. Also, evidence in James indicates that the church experienced economic persecution, both in terms of legal oppression and in terms of "last hired—first fired" discrimination. The church had a large group of apostles to support (unlike the tentmaker Paul, a fisherman like Peter could not support himself on a mountain), many visiting Christians to feed and care for, and probably a large proportion of older believers, since many older Jews moved to Palestine to die and be buried in its soil (such pious dislocated people would be especially open to the gospel). To add to its problems Jerusalem experienced more than one severe famine during the 40s. We can read reports of Queen Helena of Adiabene sending relief to Judea, as well as rabbinic references to famine and poverty in Jerusalem. All of these would conspire to make it difficult to maintain the church in Jerusalem. But for the early Christians it was important for symbolic reasons that a large Christian presence remain in that city. It is no wonder that Paul took up a collection to support this church (Rom 15:26; 1 Cor 16:1; 2 Cor 8—9).

Acts, of course, is giving us historical precedents, not a pattern to be slavishly imitated. It shows what happened when the Spirit was present in power, not necessarily how the church must live today. However, we have already noticed that there is no other pattern for church life in Acts. The frequency of meetings may have dropped to once a week as the church moved into the Gentile world (because the church was no longer located in one small city where meeting was easy and because the large group of slaves in the church made frequent meetings more difficult), but the author mentions nothing about a change in the charitable spirit. In fact Paul in 2 Thessalonians 3:6-15 deals with an abuse of church charity that assumes some system of sharing was in place. He tells the abusers to "shape up or ship out," but, far from changing the system, he turns to the church and says, "Never tire of doing what is right" (2 Thess 3:13). If this were not enough, we discover the same Spirit is poured out on the Macedonian churches (2 Cor 8). They lived in "extreme poverty," but had given themselves so freely to God that they begged to be allowed to share with the poor in Jerusalem. The principle, Paul argues, true even across continental boundaries, is "that there might be equality" (2 Cor 8:13; the context makes it plain that economic equality is in view). This equality due to Spirit-directed sharing is precisely the situation we observed in practice in Jerusalem in Acts.

The modern church is concerned about the power of the Spirit. Evangelism is desired; signs and wonders are called for. Given that Paul turns the third part of the precedent of Acts into principle, we should take seriously the practice of the church in Acts, expecting that a full outpouring of the Spirit in any period of history would have all three effects. While it may not take the identical form it took in Jerusalem, the presence of the Spirit will open the wallets of anyone whose heart is truly open to his presence.

---

[1]That is, the verb is in the imperfect tense, indicating a habitual or repeated action, not the aorist, which would have indicated a one-time action.

5:9 Testing the Holy Spirit?

The story of Ananias and Sapphira is an uncomfortable one that contains a number of difficult issues. What did this couple do that was so wrong? Why weren't they simply exposed and then called to repentance? Why did they die, and why don't we see the same penalty happening in the church today?

The church after Pentecost was "filled with the Holy Spirit" (Acts 4:31), which was manifested in three ways: through (1) bold proclamation or evangelism, (2) signs and wonders, and (3) great generosity. The Spirit of God freed people from the spirit of Mammon so that they gave whenever they saw a need, selling property and belongings if necessary. There was no compulsion, no requirement. It was simply a natural response to the presence of the Spirit of the generous God within them.

Immediately before this story is that of Barnabas, who, moved by the Spirit, sold his property and gave the money to the church. Obviously, the church approved of this generosity. Ananias and Sapphira apparently wanted this same approval but did not have the same Spirit-caused generosity within their hearts. As a result they chose to sell their property but to give only part of the proceeds to the church. At the same time they agreed to claim that they were giving the whole amount. The text makes it very clear that the sin was not that they gave only part of the money (Acts 5:4), but that they lied (Acts 5:3). If they gave and how much they gave was a matter between them and God. It was not a major issue. That they lied about what they were doing *was* a major issue—in fact, it is the issue of the rest of the story.

Before addressing Sapphira, Peter speaks to Ananias: "Satan has so filled your heart that you have lied to the Holy Spirit" (Acts 5:3). In other words, not being open to the Spirit of God, but instead living in their need for security in owning money or property, they had allowed themselves to be directed by Satan into deception. They, members of the church, had been to some extent demonized. This was a natural conclusion for Peter, for Satan is pictured as a deceiver and "the father of lies" (Jn 8:44) from Genesis 3 on. When they turned from the truth (perhaps only the uncomfortable truth that they were not secure enough to give as generously as others), they opened themselves to the archliar. Such a situation does not differ from that of today, for people who reject the impulses of the Holy Spirit or turn from God's truth are likewise often caught in the web of deception and falsehood that seems to descend upon them.[1] Ananias and Sapphira apparently were aware that they were telling a lie before the church, although they were themselves deceived in failing to recognize that the Spirit would reveal the truth to Peter. Peter calls this attempt at deception "test[ing] the Spirit of the Lord."

In saying the sin is that of testing God's Spirit, Peter recalls the Old Testament testing tradition and in particular Israel's experience in the wilderness. Even before coming into the wilderness and during their years there Israel had good evidence of the reality and presence of God. He had divided the sea and defeated Pharaoh. He had provided food and water for them. But he also announced his intention to test them (Ex 15:25). He let them come into hard places to see if they responded with trust or with mistrust. In Exodus 17 they came to a place named "Testing" (Massah). Again there was no water. Again the people responded with mistrust: "Is the LORD among us or not?" (Ex 17:7). This mistrust and the demand that God act or they will not believe that he is among them is termed "testing God." In fact, God later says that Israel "tested me ten times" (Num 14:22). It is no wonder that Deuteronomy 6:16 says, "Do not test the LORD your God as you did at Massah." The same theme is repeated later (Ps 78:18, 41, 56; 95:9; 106:14). The Jews were quite aware of this tradition, for it was picked up quite often in their literature.

Peter, then, is saying to Sapphira that in spite of the evident presence in the church of the Spirit of the Lord ("the Lord" here refers to Jesus) she and her husband had chosen to attempt to "pull a fast one" on him. Their lie contained within it the assumption that the Spirit would do nothing; conscious or not, it was a challenge as to whether God was really present in the church. Will he respond, or will he turn a blind eye to their deception? As noted later in the New Testament (Acts 15:10; 1 Cor 10:9), that is a dangerous challenge. God responds, and they die.

Their immediate death without a chance to repent probably had two reasons. First, it was the first time that believers had issued such a challenge to God, so it was important for God to act clearly and decisively to prevent any misunderstanding about the reality of his presence and his willingness to hear and judge. Second, it was a time of intense spiritual presence, and where the evidence of God's presence is greater the sin of challenging that presence is more serious. There also may be mercy involved in such a judgment. While death is an ultimate penalty from the human perspective, from the divine perspective it is far less serious than a continued movement into sin and deception; the quick divine judgment prevents full apostasy (1 Cor 11:32).

The teaching of the story, then, is twofold. First, Christians are not to put God to the test. Jesus gave the proper example of endurance under testing in Matthew 4:7. Christians are to follow suit and trust God in hard places. Second, the presence of the Spirit in the church is not without its dangers. Some died for ignoring the presence of the Lord (1 Cor 11:30; the sin is a rubbing of salt in the wounds of social divisions in the church). The church was given the authority to make declarations that may have the same effect as Peter's (although perhaps not with such an immediate result; 1 Cor 5:3-5; compare 2 Cor 13:10). I have observed similar incidents in the church today, some of which were reasonably dramatic and others of which took place over a longer period of time. God is a God of holiness, and those who will not treat him as holy will experience the consequences.

The church today often prays for revival. Perhaps it should ask if it really wants what it is praying for. Obviously we would welcome the power of God in evangelism and signs among us. We might even welcome a growing presence of the Spirit in prophecy. But reading this passage in the context of Acts should remind us that "in the church where the lame walked liars died." With the power of God comes his holiness, and those who are not prepared to live in his holiness will do well to fear rather than to seek his power.

[1]The most obvious parallels are the numerous pastoral leaders who have been deceived into thinking that their sin, whether sexual or not, somehow would not be discovered and that they could still go on ministering. Their public humiliation has not always broken through this deception, but it has paralleled the humiliation of Ananias and Sapphira when their sin is revealed to Peter.

7:14-15 How Many Went to Egypt?

Our verse says that seventy-five members of Jacob's family went down to Egypt, but upon reading Genesis 46:27, Exodus 1:5 or Deuteronomy 10:22 we are told that only seventy people went down to Egypt, and this smaller number includes Joseph and his children.[1] Which of these texts is correct?

As in the previous chapter, we have here a problem with text. All English versions are translated from the Hebrew Masoretic text of the Old Testament. However, one of the Hebrew texts found at Qumran has seventy-five in Exodus 1:5 (4QEx[a]). The Septuagint (Greek translation) of both Genesis 46:27 and Exodus 1:5 also has the number seventy-five (and omits Jacob and Joseph in the number). The Jewish writer Philo knows about the problem, but does not solve it for us (*De Migratione Abrahami* 199-200). In other words, Stephen's (or Luke's) Bible probably had the number seventy-five rather than seventy.

When we ask which of these numbers is correct, we notice that counting the names listed in the Old Testament stories we come out with seventy. This appears to be the more firmly established tradition. However, we say that from the point of view of modern textual criticism. Stephen and Luke, assuming that they read the Septuagint, would not have known that Hebrew Scriptures had a different number. It would be like a person reading a King James Bible and not knowing that 1 John 5:7 is based on poor textual authority and so is not found in most modern translations. That person would claim that 1 John 5:7 is in the Bible; the others would just as rightly claim that it is not. A scholar would say that both were right in terms of their own English Bible, but that the original version of 1 John came without that verse.

If Stephen knew the Septuagint (and as a Greek-speaking Jew that was probably true), then he surely said seventy-five.

Stephen was honest to his Bible and Luke was honest about what Stephen said (or perhaps did not even notice the problem for his Bible said the same thing). We see that Stephen was off by five persons. It is not an issue of scriptural accuracy, for neither Stephen nor Luke is teaching about Jacob's genealogy or the size of his family; they are teaching about how God was with Joseph in Egypt and then brought the whole nation out of Egypt. The point is that God deals with Israel outside of the Promised Land.

That is also why in the following verse the speech combines the burial of Joseph at Shechem (Josh 24:32) with the burial of Jacob at Hebron in the cave of Machpelah (Gen 23:17; 49:29-32; 50:13). The point is not accuracy of historical detail (any learned Jew would have known that this was a summary combining two accounts), but God's action and human (especially Jewish) resistance to him. The fact that Shechem was in Samaritan territory may be deliberate, for it places the burial of the patriarchs (and this was quite accurate for Joseph, the one God used) outside of Jewish land and into the territory of the hated Samaritans.

What we have to remember is that in speeches like these the speaker does not intend to give a history lesson. Before he started, he would know good and well that his audience knew the history as well as he did, if not better. What he is trying to do is to *make a point from* the history. Therefore he can streamline it to fit his purposes. What we have to focus on is the point that the author is making about God (and human resistance) rather than losing our focus through fixating on numbers and chronology.

[1]All of the texts count only males, for the Hebrews were patrilineal and the purpose of such genealogical texts was to trace the male line. It is also clear that none of the texts give any indication that the numbers are anything other than literal head counts, for no special meaning is attached to either 70 or 75.

8:1 All Were Scattered?

The persecution in Acts 8:1 raises some questions. Didn't a major Jewish leader call for tolerance in Acts 5? And isn't it strange that when the church was persecuted the leaders of the church would be allowed to remain?

More is going on in this passage than meets the eye. Returning to Acts 2:42 and 3:1, we note that the apostles (and the church in general) had been born within Judaism and lived their lives as pious Jews. They attended the temple at the three times of prayer (morning and afternoon sacrifices and again at dusk) and followed the other pious practices of good Jews, such as generous charity. What distinguished them was their belonging to a fellowship that believed that Jesus of Nazareth was the promised Messiah, or deliverer, of the people, a fellowship that ate meals together and followed the living direction of this Jesus through the Spirit.

Because they were a growing popular religious movement, they threatened the temple hierarchy (who were not in any way popular). The priestly leaders of this hierarchy in turn arrested and persecuted the apostles (Acts 4:1; 5:17, both of which name the Sadducees as the source of persecution). But in order to convict them before the high court, the Great Sanhedrin, the Sadducees had to convince the Pharisees, who were also part of the court, that the apostles were guilty of some major crime, such as blasphemy. The Pharisees certainly rejected the beliefs of the church, for they were a fellowship still awaiting the appearance of the Messiah, believing that Jesus had been rightly executed for blasphemy. Gamaliel's defense of the apostles in Acts 5:34-39 shows a typical Pharisaic attitude: as long as the Christians are living like pious Jews, there is no need to attack them. Orthopraxis (right practice) rather than orthodoxy (right teaching) was the Pharisees' main issue. As they saw it, the church was not doing anything wrong; it was just wrong-headed. The apostles were beaten (perhaps "just for good measure"), but nothing else happened.

In Acts 6 we discover two groups in the church, the original Aramaic-speaking group, among whom were the apostles, and a new group of Greek-speaking Jewish-Christians. This group perhaps began with some of those converted at Pentecost and grew as other pilgrims were converted when they visited the city. Due to their linguistic differences such Jews went to separate synagogues in Jerusalem. Within the church they probably met in separate house churches. Stephen belonged to this Greek-speaking group.

Stephen was arrested for "speaking against [the] holy place and against the law" (Acts 6:13). In his defense he argued that Israel had at every turn rejected God and his messengers, including Moses and especially Jesus. He also argued that the temple was not where God lived, but was another example of Jewish disobedience (Acts 7:48-50). This was enough to unite the Pharisees with the Sadducees in lynching Stephen, for they saw in this statement the implication that temple worship, one of the pillars of Judaism, was not important. (In fact, another Greek-speaking Jewish-Christian, the author of Hebrews, later argued that the Pharisees' worst fears were in fact true. Jesus had superseded the old system.) Thus Christians do not need to follow Jewish customs. To the Pharisees, this was teaching Jewish-Christians to do something wrong and would lead to the defiling of the nation and the delay of the coming of Messiah; it was far worse than being wrong-headed. One of the leaders in this execution was Saul, a Pharisee (Acts 7:58; 8:1).

This background explains the persecution. In the eyes of the authorities the Greek-speaking Christians (already suspect because they came from outside Palestine and spoke only Greek) were the problem. They were persecuted and scattered, pursued as far as Damascus (Acts 8:1; 9:1-2). But the Aramaic-speaking Christians, including the apostles, were not suspect. Were they not known to be people of exemplary piety, frequently in the temple? The persecutors, principally the Pharisees, did not consider them in the same category as their Greek-speaking brothers and sisters.

Persecution would come to the Aramaic-speaking Christians about a decade later (Acts 12), but even then it would come from Herod, not from the Sanhedrin, and would not be enough to drive them all out of Jerusalem. They would remain until the Romans began to surround the city in the war of A.D. 66-70. In the providence of God, then, the Greek-speakers, linguistically and culturally equipped to fit into other areas from which many of them had originally come, were scattered to bring the gospel to the Roman world. At the same time the core of the church remained in Jerusalem to carry on the Jewish-Christian mission in the very heart of Judaism.

8:16 Baptized but Without the Holy Spirit?

Mention "baptism in the Holy Spirit" in a group of assorted evangelicals and you are likely to have a fight on your hands. For one group it happens at conversion with no outward experience, and to insist on a later experience is to attempt to suggest that the work of Christ was incomplete. For another group it is a necessary second work of grace after conversion that empowers one for ministry. Both groups struggle in their own way with Acts. Why didn't God give a single unitary pattern for the church to follow? How was the Holy Spirit received in the early church? What type of a historical precedent occurs in Acts 8:17? Should we be doing this today? These are just some of the issues we struggle with as we consider this topic.

The story in Acts 8 is that of the first missionary outreach of the church. The Greek-speaking Jewish-Christians were forced to flee Jerusalem, and as they traveled to safety they "preached the word wherever they went" (Acts 8:4). The author of Acts chooses to follow one of them, Philip, who goes first to Samaria, announcing the good news about Jesus and the kingdom of God and demonstrating through signs and wonders the reality of the message. This was a typical early Christian evangelistic pattern, and typical results followed: many believed. At this point the story takes an interesting twist. As we would expect, the new believers were "baptized, both men and women" (Acts 8:12). But none of these believers received the Holy Spirit until Peter and John arrived and placed their hands on them. This raises two questions. First, why was it necessary for the apostles to take this action? Second, how could one be a Christian believer and not have received the Holy Spirit?

It is clear that these people were true believers, the one exception being Simon Magus, around whom the story revolves. He sees the normal effects of the Spirit, recognizes that it surpasses his magic, and wishes to purchase the power (as he has all of his magical powers). Although Simon had believed (Acts 8:13), he had failed to repent and abandon his former way of life and so had not come to true faith (Acts 8:21-23). He had believed in his head the story of Jesus and confessed it in baptism, but without repentance Jesus had not yet become his Lord. He was still lost. But Simon is the exception. The apostles appear satisfied with the rest and lay their hands upon them. They were fully Christian, but had not received the Spirit.

Clearly Luke considers this failure to receive the Spirit at baptism an exception. He feels it necessary to explain to his readers that "the Holy Spirit had not yet come upon any of them; they had simply been baptized into the name of the Lord Jesus" (Acts 8:16). Normally repentance, faith and baptism were followed by just such a laying on of hands and reception of the Spirit.[1] After all, the experience of the Spirit was the promise of the first preaching (Acts 2:38; 3:19). Paul also assumes that a believer can say, "I know I have experienced the Spirit so I know I am a Christian" (the assumption of Rom 8:9). But this experience of the Spirit is something different from the regenerating work of the Spirit (which Paul, not Luke, talks about), although the two acts of the Spirit (along with baptism) were normally joined so closely together in practice as to be distinguishable only in theory. This is so much the case that in Romans 8 Paul goes on to question the regeneration of a believer who has not had an experience of the Spirit.

A parallel situation occurs in Acts 1:8, where Jesus describes the Pentecost experience in terms of empowering for mission. Here again was a group of baptized believers (at least 120 of them). But they lacked one thing before they could be sent out on their mission: the Holy Spirit. There was no one to lay hands on them, so rather than wait for a human visit they wait for a divine visitation. In Acts 8 the order of events is the same, as are the results of the coming of the Spirit, although the waiting is for human agents.

So it is obvious from this story that it is possible to be regenerate and not to have received the Spirit's empowering presence. Since it was not the normal experience of the church, it had to be explained, but it was a possible experience. We note in this connection that Acts and Paul use the phrase "baptized in the Holy Spirit" differently as well.[2] For Acts it indicates precisely this experiential reception of the Spirit as empowerment for mission. For Paul (1 Cor 12:13) it describes the action of the Spirit in making a person part of the body of Christ, something closer to regeneration. This difference in the use of the same terminology is, of course, what one expects in the New Testament, for such phrases had not yet become technical terms but were living metaphors to describe experience. The modern discussions and controversies were not even remotely in the minds of the authors.

The discussion to this point, however, does not answer the question of the delay. If the normal experience of the early church was to join both baptism in water and the laying on of hands for the reception of the Spirit to a person's confession of faith, why was there a delay in this case? There are several possible reasons for this. First, we do not have any evidence that Philip normally laid hands on new believers. It is quite possible that while the church was concentrated in Jerusalem many people took part in evangelism and baptism, but only the apostles laid hands on people to receive the Spirit. It was unique to be doing evangelism away from the apostles, for this is the first reported Christian mission outside of Jerusalem.

Second, Philip was a Greek-speaking Jewish-Christian, perhaps originally from outside of the Jerusalem area. There were some suspicions between the Greek-speaking and Aramaic-speaking groups, as Acts 6 shows. Philip may have waited for the apostles to come as a gesture of church unity. They could then approve his mission. This was no schismatic enterprise.

Third, the Samaritans were not fully Jewish. They accepted the Pentateuch and were circumcised, but they did not accept the rest of the Old Testament, and they worshiped on Mount Gerazim, not in Jerusalem. Nor were their bloodlines purely Jewish. Furthermore, a lot of hostility existed between Samaritans and Jews. It would be no wonder, then, if Philip himself did not desire apostolic approval to see if his new church was fully "kosher." Obviously the apostles did approve, and they took the appropriate action.

Thus, while we cannot know the exact reason for the delay of the laying on of hands and reception of the Spirit, there were a number of logical reasons for it. In the end, however, these baptized believers (except Simon Magus) were initiated fully, just as the believers in Jerusalem. In the process they illustrate to the modern reader the elements of the initiation process as practiced in that era. They give us historical precedent for the possibility of a delay between conversion and the experience of the Spirit, but the author has no intention of teaching that such a two-stage process is necessary. Instead, he shows that the Spirit did not guide the mission by giving a unitary pattern or set of rules, but instead personally led those under his direction into adapting the practices of the church to the needs of the local cultural and historical situation, operating relationally rather than according to a handbook.

---

[1]David Pawson, *The Normal Christian Birth* (London: Hodder & Stoughton, 1989) is the best source for a full discussion of this process.

[2]One good discussion of this difference is in Clark Pinnock, "The New Pentecostalism: Reflections of an Evangelical Observer," in Russell P. Spittler, ed., *Perspectives on the New Pentecostalism* (Grand Rapids, Mich.: Baker, 1976), pp. 182-92.

12:15 His Angel?

Rhoda was a slave in the house of Mary, the mother of John Mark, and was assigned to door-keeping duty. Inside the house a group of Christians were gathered in prayer for Peter, who was chained in Herod Agrippa's most secure dungeon and slated for execution the next morning. They had prayed and fasted for days, but Herod had not changed his mind. The situation looked similar to that of James son of Zebedee, who had been beheaded earlier that year. Then in the middle of the night someone knocked on the door. Rhoda went to the door and may have opened a peephole to see a man she did not recognize in the darkness. He spoke a greeting. She recognized the voice of Peter. Not bothering to unbar the door, she rushed away to the room where the others were praying and breathlessly announced that Peter was standing at the door. Acts 12:15 is the response she received. It is hardly surprising under the circumstances (given that they apparently did not believe their prayers for deliverance would be answered and perhaps were already praying that Peter would be faithful and calm in his execution). But it is a surprise that when Rhoda insisted that there was a man at the door and that he did sound like Peter, they responded, "It must be his angel." What does this phrase mean? If they meant "ghost" or "disembodied spirit," why didn't they say "his ghost" or "his spirit"?

If they meant that Peter's disembodied spirit were appearing at the door, which is what some commentators assume, they could have used other terms. For example, in Mark 6:49 (Mt 14:26) the disciples saw Jesus walking on the water at night and cried out in fear because "they thought he was a ghost" (*phantasma*, "apparition"). In Luke 24:37 the disciples in the upper room were similarly terrified by the risen Christ, "thinking they saw a ghost" (*pneuma*, usually translated "spirit"). But here under similar conditions they use the term "angel" *(angelos)*, which just a few verses earlier was used for "the angel of the Lord" (as it is five times in Acts 12:7-11). It is likely, then, that they meant something different from a ghost or a disembodied spirit.

According to Matthew 18:10 children (and presumably everyone) have angels that have direct access to God himself. They are usually called "guardian" angels, although we do not know if they guard anyone, just that they represent them before God. This "guarding" (if there is any) may be similar to what Jacob described as "the Angel who has delivered me from all harm" (Gen 48:16)—if this expresses a belief in a given angel accompanying him and caring for him. Protection through an angel also appears in Daniel 3:28 and Daniel 6:22, although it seems that these angels come for momentary deliverance rather than for continuous protection as in the Genesis account. Whatever the exact meaning of these passages, Jewish angelology developed far beyond them. While no two Jewish groups would likely have agreed in full on the topic, some Jews did believe that angels were capable of taking human form and representing particular individuals, as we can see in the Apocrypha. In Tobit 5 the archangel Raphael appears to Tobias as a human being and accompanies him on a journey, protecting and rewarding him. He has impersonated "Azarias the son of the great Ananias, one of your relatives" (Tobit 5:12 RSV), although there is no indication that Tobias or Tobit had ever met Azarias. So convincing is this angel that only toward the end of the book does Raphael find it advisable to reveal who he really is. A similar belief in angels taking human form appears in Hebrews 13:2, although there they appear as strangers, seeming to be simple Christian travelers.

This information makes the passage in Acts clear. Since Peter was known to be in prison, when a person sounding like Peter arrived the believers in the house concluded that it must be his "guardian" angel, whom they naturally assumed would act like Peter. This situation differs from those involving Jesus, where there was some reason for the apostles to believe that they might be seeing an apparition (it was a dark and stormy night, Mk 6:49) or a spirit or ghost (it was after his death, Lk 24:37). But as far as these Christians knew Peter was not yet dead, although he was surely in prison; nor would they have expected an apparition to knock before entering a prayer meeting. From their point of view Rhoda's experience could only mean that Peter's "guardian" angel had come, either to inform them of his death or in some other way to guide their prayers. Only when the door is flung open and the figure stands in the light are they convinced they are not welcoming an angel, but Peter himself—perhaps due to his having the marks and smells of a person fresh out of prison.

Interesting as this passage is, it simply witnesses to the beliefs of the Christians in that house. The author of Acts reports rather than endorses their views. Only from Hebrews and similar passages can we gather what evidence there is in the New Testament for angels in human form. And Matthew makes the only clear reference to "guardian" angels. Yet, taking into consideration these passages and their evidence for the real existence of angels in human form, within this context in Acts the only thing that appears to have been lacking in the worldview of the Christians in Mary's home is the belief that God, who specializes in eleventh-hour deliverances, might just release Peter and that it could be him, not his angel, at the door.

15:29 How Kosher Should Christians Live?

While I was living in Germany, a group of German-speaking Christians from Russia moved into our community. When they attended our church, there was an immediate cultural clash because some of their customs were strange to us, while some of ours, especially women's dress, were totally offensive to them. They wondered how people such as us could really be Christians. We could have adopted their cultural patterns, but would that not have imposed a rigid legalism upon us that would have stifled church growth? Yet their consciences struggled with our way of life. How could we live together in one church without on the one hand compromising the grace of Christ in legalism or on the other offending the sense of decency of some good Christian brothers and sisters? That is precisely the issue that the early church is struggling with in Acts 15:29.

The cultural issue according to Acts was whether circumcision (that is, becoming a Jew) was necessary for salvation (Acts 15:1). Peter voiced the eventual solution: "We believe it is through the grace of our Lord Jesus that we are saved, just as they are" (Acts 15:11). James agreed, referring to "all the Gentiles who bear my name" (Acts 15:17, quoting Amos 9:12 in a form somewhat different from the Hebrew Old Testament). In other words, the Gentiles might remain Gentiles and still be saved. Circumcision was not necessary. From this it seems that Paul and the Gentile mission have been victorious. But in spite of his apparent agreement, James added the stipulations of this verse both in his advice to the council and in the letter to the Gentile believers. What is more, he prefaced them with "It seemed good to the Holy Spirit and to us," which makes them sound rather binding. Is this a case, then, in which Paul won the first round but was knocked out in the end? Does this not contradict all that Paul stood for? And if it does not, is it binding today? Must the Germans give up Blutwurst and the English black pudding? All of these questions press in on us in the reading of this verse.

First, we must be clear about what the council did not do. It did not require circumcision or the keeping of the sabbath or tithing or (in their full form) the kosher regulations (the Jewish dietary laws). These rules marked out a Jew from a Gentile and, in the end, were not enforced upon Gentile Christians, although James adds, perhaps as a concession to the Pharisaic party in the church, that since the Mosaic books were being read in every synagogue their teaching was available to any Gentile to whom it might commend itself. Paul surely would have been satisfied with such a situation, for his concern with "works" and "law" in Romans and Galatians is not with moral rules, but with those practices that marked out Jew from Gentile. That they were not necessary for salvation is a point of agreement between Paul and the council.

Second, we need to be clear about the nature of a worship service in the first two centuries of the church. Typically the Christians would gather in the home of one of the members, perhaps the person with the largest house. A city church would have many such cells, each with an absolute maximum of perhaps sixty people, given the size of even large rooms in those days. The central feature of the service was a meal to which every member contributed what they could. At the beginning a loaf of bread was ritually broken and shared, and at the end a cup of wine was likewise shared. But between the two a full meal was eaten.[1] This means that if they were in the same church Jews and Gentiles would eat together and share each other's food in the context of worship. Therefore the Pauline discussions of food in 1 Corinthians 8—10 and Romans 14 were not to regulate one's private behavior at home, but to assist a church in living together.

Third, while Paul never refers to the decree of the council (nor would it have been advisable for him to have done so, since he was often accused of being secondary to Jerusalem), all of the regulations are explicitly or implicitly contained in his letters. The issue of meat in Romans 14, for example, is mainly an issue over whether the animal had been properly slaughtered, that is, whether it had been strangled and whether the blood had been properly drained. The discussion in 1 Corinthians 8—10 revolves around the issue of meat that had been offered to idols. In 1 Corinthians 5 Paul discusses sexual immorality. None of these issues was foreign to Paul and on none of them does he take a position different from that of the council.

Finally, what do these rules mean in their context in Acts? All of them have to do with the Mosaic law and are drawn from Leviticus 17—18. The first issue in those chapters is the sacrificing of an animal to anything other than Yahweh—or even sacrificing it to him outside of the appointed place. Thus a Jew would find it impossible to eat meat that came from a sacrifice to a god other than Yahweh. Most meat found in pagan markets was in some way associated with sacrifices to idols. Paul does not believe that this contaminates the meat (1 Cor 8—10), although he rules out actually going to a meal in an idol temple. But in 1 Corinthians 8 he states clearly that love would make one refuse to offend a "weaker brother" (that is, a Jew) on this issue.

The second issue of Leviticus 17—18 is that of blood. Here both this regulation and the previous one are applied not only to Israelites but also to aliens, the Gentiles who might live among the Jews. There were two ways in which blood might be eaten. On the one hand, it was common in many cultures for blood to be eaten directly (as in the examples of Blutwurst [blood sausage] and black pudding mentioned above). On the other hand, in some cultures the manner of slaughter might lead to the retention of blood in the meat, perhaps as a deliberate means of keeping it tenderer or juicier. But neither the direct eating of blood nor retaining the blood in the meat through strangling the animal were acceptable to the Jew. The blood must be poured out.

All of these regulations have to do with meat, not with vegetables, grain or fruit. The reason for this is simple. Meat was at the core of Israelite sacrificial rites, as well as the rites of other religions. Furthermore, Jewish kosher practices had virtually nothing to say about vegetables. So one could share bread or vegetables freely between Jews and Gentiles. It was when meat was served at the Lord's Supper (as it normally was) that the issues arose, as we see clearly in Romans 14.

The third issue of Leviticus 17—18 is that of sexual relations with inappropriate women, mostly with women who were too closely related, although the same group of regulations also prohibits adultery (defined in the Old Testament as a man having sexual relations with a married woman who was not his wife), bestiality and homosexuality. Again the regulations are applied to both Israelites and aliens. This, then, is what Acts means by "sexual immorality." It would be highly disturbing to a Jew to have table fellowship at the Lord's Supper with a person and his partner if the relationship was one that God had labeled an abomination. Paul opposes just such a relationship in 1 Corinthians 5, ending with a general prohibition of sexual immorality (1 Cor 5:11). In the specific case in Corinth, Paul believed that even the Gentile world would disapprove of the relationship. However, many of these types of relationships would be approved of in Gentile cultures but would make table fellowship in the church difficult.

What we are talking about, then, is Paul's rule of love in Romans 14, summed up in the principle "The kingdom of God is not a matter of eating and drinking, but of righteousness, peace and joy in the Holy Spirit" (Romans 14:17). If the Gentile Christians would keep the minimal food standards, not so much in what they did privately at home but in what they brought to church or served Jewish believers, and if they would observe minimal rules of sexual decency, then Jews and Gentiles could live and function together in the church. As long as the principles were based on love and unity, Paul had no problem. It was only when the legal rituals became a means of salvation that he put his foot down.

Are these principles binding today? It is true that we find a similar rule in Revelation 2:14, 20, which may have been written later than Acts. And there are examples of Christians in the late second and early third centuries who feel bound by the rules. But at the same time there is often an observing of the rules and an ignoring of the reasons for them. In a context in which people of differing cultures must relate in the church these or analogous rules (depending on the sensitivities of the cultures) would be applicable. But as permanent principles we should let Paul be our guide. He clearly prohibits sexual immorality for all Christians everywhere, leaving the dietary rules to our own conscience before God and our love for our fellow Christians.

[1]Perhaps the best available description of such a meeting is that of Robert Banks in *Going to Church in the First Century* (Auburn, Maine: Message Ministry, 1990).

16:3 Why Did Paul Circumcise Timothy?

Inconsistency confuses us, and arguing for one point of view and then turning around and acting contrary to that point of view appears inconsistent. Of course, we sometimes misunderstand the actions of others, and an inner consistency can exist behind apparently contradictory deeds. Yet when we see truly inconsistent actions we at best call the doer fickle, at worst hypocritical, even deceiving. This is the issue that appears to face us in Acts 16:3. No sooner does Acts report the Jerusalem council's decision that it is not necessary for one to be circumcised or keep the Mosaic law to be saved (Acts 15) than it mentions Paul's circumcising Timothy in order to take him along as a coworker. Doesn't this contradict Paul's principles in Acts 15? And doesn't Galatians 2:3 state, "Yet not even Titus, who was with me, was compelled to be circumcised, even though he was a Greek"? How could the Paul who in Galatians 2:5 writes, "We did not give in to [those who wanted to circumcise Titus] for a moment, so that the truth of the gospel might remain with you," have Timothy circumcised? Was Paul himself two-faced, or is one of the accounts historically inaccurate?[1]

The resolution of this issue turns on a very important point. In Jewish eyes Titus was clearly a Gentile, for his parentage was Gentile, but Timothy was considered a Jew, because his mother was a Jew. The Mishnah, the Jewish legal tradition, makes it clear that children of Jewish mothers are really Jews, regardless of the race of their fathers.[2] Acts states that Timothy's father was a Gentile. It is also clear from the verb tense used that his father was dead by the time Paul selected Timothy as a coworker. Timothy's mother and grandmother (according to 2 Tim 1:5) were Jews, which fits with what we know about the laxity in the Jewish community in Asia Minor, for allowing a Jewish woman to marry a Gentile was not orthodox Jewish practice. Paul presumably converted the family during his first missionary journey, but even before that Timothy was probably steeped in Scripture and observed the religion of his mother, although she may have practiced it in secret. When his father died and what his father had felt about his religious practice is not known. He may have been a God-fearer, on the fringes of the synagogue. But neither the father himself nor his son had been circumcised. The father had not allowed his son to be fully Jewish (circumcision in the days of public baths was a public mark that would have identified Timothy as a member of a different race, the Jews).

Normally, Paul's missionary practice was to go to the local synagogue first. How could he do so with Timothy, who would have been viewed as a type of renegade Jew? And how could Timothy participate fully in the mission while being only half-Jew? With Titus a principle was involved: Gentiles do not need to become Jews. But with Timothy the question was whether a half-Jew could or should fully actualize his Jewish heritage. Paul's decision is to regularize Timothy's status, perhaps to facilitate mission ("To the Jews I became like a Jew, to win the Jews," 1 Cor 9:20) or perhaps to allay suspicions ("They have been informed that you teach all the

Jews who live among the Gentiles to turn away from Moses, telling them not to circumcise their children or live according to our customs," Acts 21:21). For Paul, Gentiles had no need to become Jews to improve their spiritual status, but it was not wrong for a Jew to live his Jewish culture to the fullest.

It might have appeared more consistent if Paul had not taken this step, especially in light of the issues discussed in Galatians and the fact that Timothy lived in the Galatian area. Some have suggested that troubles stemming from this action led to the writing of Galatians and the citing of the counterexample of Titus. However, it is more likely that Galatians was written before the second missionary journey and that this incident clarified Paul's stance. When seen as a cultural rather than a religious issue, circumcision was an indifferent practice. Where it could be used for the advantage of the gospel, it was good. Where it hindered the gospel, it was to be avoided. In no case did it make the person more or less spiritual. Analogous cultural practices can be found today. Likewise today slavish consistency may hinder mission, while apparent inconsistency may point to a deeper underlying consistency and meet the requirements of a nuanced cultural situation. Until this is understood, it is unwise to criticize the apparent surface vacillation.

[1]Many scholars view this text as an indication of historical inaccuracy in Luke-Acts, that is, as an unhistorical attempt to reconcile the Jewish-Christian and Gentile-Christian positions on circumcision. Yet this is in reality a surface reading of the text, for while it may save Paul from the charge of being inconsistent, it means that the author of Luke-Acts has Paul argue against circumcision in Acts 15 and then act contrary to this in Acts 16. If he were making up the story, he could have made it more consistent than that. Instead, this shows that the author is reporting history and probably understands the reasons for Paul's action, although he reports them cryptically.

[2]The references in *m. Bikkurim* 1:4-5 show that this applied to both men and women. If one were brought up in a Gentile family, one could not become fully Jewish unless one's mother was a Jew. But there would then be no difference between this person and a person whose mother and father were Jews. The same basis is recognized today in Israel's Law of Return: One is a Jew and may have automatic citizenship if one's mother was a Jew.

19:2 Did You Receive the Holy Spirit?

Paul has just arrived in Ephesus to begin a major evangelistic effort. Priscilla and Aquila have perhaps already established a house church and laid the groundwork, but Paul's arrival will trigger the major thrust. As he proclaims repentance in the face of the kingdom of God, much as Jesus did before him, he is informed that there are other "disciples" like him in the area. On meeting them he apparently senses something different among them, so he asks the diagnostic question of Acts 19:2. This is certainly not the question we would expect to ask today. Their response, however, might not be untypical of what many modern churchgoers might give: No, we have not even heard that there is a Holy Spirit. Paul then takes a step backward and asks a second diagnostic question about their baptism, another question that sounds strange today. They had been baptized with John's baptism. Proclaiming that John's baptism pointed forward to Jesus, Paul rebaptizes them into Jesus, places his hands on them, and they receive the Spirit, prophesying and speaking in tongues. Why, we ask, did Paul rebaptize them? This is not what happened in Acts 8 when there was a separation between baptism and receiving the Spirit. Were these disciples Christians before they received the Spirit? Why this strange (to us) evangelistic procedure? What does it tell us of the role of the Spirit in the church today?

The messages of John the Baptist and Jesus were very similar. Both announced the coming of the kingdom of God and demanded repentance. Both called for baptism as the outward step of repentance (Mk 1:4, 14-15). They differed, however, because John stated that One who was coming was stronger than he, while Jesus indicated that the kingdom had come in his person (Lk 17:21). It is not until after Pentecost, however, that the mark of John's Coming One is seen in Jesus. That is, John predicted that the Coming One would baptize with "fire and the Holy Spirit" in contrast to his own baptizing with water, which does not happen in any of the Synoptic Gospels. All of this is significant to Acts, which begins with the prediction and fulfillment of the promise of the Holy Spirit.

Paul came to Ephesus, then, proclaiming the kingdom (Acts 20:25). The mark par excellence that the kingdom had come in Jesus was the presence of the Holy Spirit.[1] When Paul meets people who claim to be disciples but do not display any of the effects of the Spirit, he asks his question. Their negative answer indicates that at the least the instruction they had received was defective, for from Pentecost onward the promise of the Spirit was part of the gospel proclamation (see Acts 2:38), especially among Jews for whom the Spirit was the sign of the coming age, the kingdom. Throughout the early church Christian initiation consisted of four discernible steps: repentance, commitment to (faith in) Jesus, baptism into his name and reception of the Spirit.[2] Having discovered that these "disciples" were defective in the last step of initiation, Paul wonders how much of the whole process was defective. By moving backward one step Paul gets the information he needs. These folk were not Christians. They had gone through the first step, repentance, but they had yet to hear about Jesus. Their baptism was a sub-Christian baptism.[3] It was then natural for Paul to lead them through the final three steps of complete Christian initiation.

This situation differs from that in Acts 8 where there was no question about the adequacy of the preaching and belief. Philip, a trusted Christian leader, had done the preaching. The baptism was clearly "into the name of the Lord Jesus," so it in no way had to be repeated, for Christian baptism is once for all. The situation in Acts 19 also differs from Acts 10, in which Peter proclaims a proper gospel, but God sovereignly gives the Holy Spirit without the usual laying on of hands in order to convince Peter and the others to accept the Gentile Cornelius as a full disciple and therefore to baptize him. (One wonders if Peter would have dared to make such a step without the sign of God's acceptance in the Spirit.) Pentecost is different yet in that all of those in the upper room were believers in Christ and baptized. Only the empowering for mission in the Spirit was missing. In that situation, of course, no one could lay on hands.

The situation in Acts 19, then, is similar to the others in that the Holy Spirit is seen as the experience of normal Christian life. Furthermore, as in all Scripture, Old or New Testament, when the Holy Spirit comes something happens. The most frequent manifestation in Acts is speaking in tongues (Acts 2, 10, 19), with prophecy second (Acts 19; in Acts 8 something observable happens but we are not told what it is). In his letters Paul does not mention any particular gift as being characteristic of receiving the Spirit, but he does indicate that the Spirit is a concrete experience, a down-payment on the full experience of Christ in heaven. Thus we can safely say that Acts gives us historical precedence for the initial experience of the Spirit as evidenced in tongues or prophecy. These gifts are, of course, easy to observe. Presumably any of the gifts in 1 Corinthians 12 or Romans 12 might be similarly produced, although, for instance, a gift of healing would be difficult to manifest if there was no one around who was ill. (In Gal 3:5 Paul associates the Galatians' reception of the Spirit with their working miracles, which may be another example of gifting.) The important issue for Paul, which Acts illustrates, is not how the Spirit manifests (according to 1 Cor 12 that is under the sovereign control of God), but that believers know that they have the Holy Spirit (see Rom 8:9).

Thus it was natural for Paul, given his theology of conversion, to ask if people claiming to be "followers of the Way" or "disciples" (as the early Christians were often called) had received the Spirit. This experience, however it was manifested, was the indication that Christian initiation was complete. It was equally natural for him to lead those who had not had a full Christian experience (for instance, had not yet committed themselves to Jesus as Lord) into that experience and then to baptize them and pray that they might receive the Holy Spirit. He was simply completing the preevangelism that John the Baptist had begun. What would be quite unnatural would be for Christians to rebaptize individuals who had already committed themselves to and been baptized into Christ, even if their doctrine were somewhat faulty. Likewise it would be incorrect to take the historical precedent of Acts and turn it into an invariable rule of how conversion and Spirit-filling must take place. Still, "Have you received the Holy Spirit?" is as appropriate a question today as it was then, for it is not only a historical question in Acts, but an underlying question in Paul's letters and 1 John as well.

---

[1]See, for example, J. D. G. Dunn, *Jesus and the Spirit* (Philadelphia: Westminster, 1975), or *Baptism in the Holy Spirit* (London: SCM, 1970), for an exhaustive treatment of this theme.

[2]For a full explanation, see David Pawson, *The Normal Christian Birth* (London: Hodder & Stoughton, 1989). This book is about the process of Christian initiation and its implications for the church today.

[3]In Acts 18:24-26 Aquila and Priscilla meet Apollos, who "had been instructed in the way of the Lord" and "taught about Jesus," but "knew only the baptism of John." While it may be that this account is very compressed, we do not hear of them rebaptizing Apollos, only of their "explain[ing] to him the way of God more adequately." If the basic commitment to Jesus is already there, even if somewhat defective, only further instruction, not rebaptism, appears to be necessary.

20:23 Ignoring Prophetic Warnings?

It is not easy to deal with prophetic words. When someone says, "Thus says the Lord," it puts the hearer in a difficult situation, especially since the meaning of the prophetic message may not be self-evident. How does one handle prophecy? That is the issue raised by the statement in Acts 20:23, which Paul made in Ephesus on the way to Jerusalem. Even earlier Paul had some concerns about his safety in Jerusalem, for in a letter written from Corinth he asked the Romans to pray for him (Rom 15:30-32). By the time he traveled around through Macedonia to Ephesus he could cite frequent warnings by "the Holy Spirit." Since they happened "in every city" they were probably prophetic oracles given to Paul by believers in each city. These warnings continued. When he arrived at Tyre on the Palestinian coast the believers "through the Spirit . . . urged Paul not to go on to Jerusalem" (Acts 21:4). Again we must assume some type of prophetic word or divine insight.

While we may wonder what, if anything, Philip's prophesying daughters said in Caesarea (and if they said nothing, why did the author mention that they prophesied?), another event that happened there overshadows everything else. Agabus arrived. His accurate prophecy had previously guided Paul into timely famine relief in Jerusalem (Acts 11:27-30). Now he walks over to Paul's group, takes Paul's belt, ties himself up, and states, "The Holy Spirit says, 'In this way the Jews of Jerusalem will bind the owner of this belt and will hand him over to the Gentiles' " (Acts 21:11). Paul's friends were sure that this prophecy meant that Paul ought not to go to Jerusalem. Paul, however, ignored the pleas of his companions, traveled on to Jerusalem and was in fact arrested, remaining a prisoner for at least the next three years.

How are we to evaluate this response to prophecy? Was Paul disobedient, receiving in his imprisonment the results of such disobedience? Were his companions, including the author of Acts (who includes himself among the "we" who wanted Paul to avoid Jerusalem), misinterpreting the prophecy? What does it all mean for both this passage and the interpretation of prophecy today?

We note first of all that the whole series of prophetic words, beginning with Paul's own inner "knowledge" in Romans, indicates trouble in Jerusalem. The messages appear to become increasingly clear the nearer he gets to Jerusalem. All warn Paul, but none contains a directive. A warning can be taken in one of two ways. It can point out a danger to avoid, or it can point out a danger to walk into with one's eyes open. In itself a warning does not tell a person what to do, unless one assumes that God's will is always to keep his people out of danger. One prophecy, however, gave something more than a warning. In Tyre Paul was urged "through the Spirit" not to continue his trip. He obviously chose to ignore this message.

Second, while all the prophecies are accurate in indicating danger, they are not unequivocally clear. Agabus's is the only detailed one, but it was not fulfilled in every particular. It is true that the result of Paul's visit to Jerusalem was that he was bound and ended up in the hands of the Gentiles, that is, the Romans. It is also true that this happened because of the Jews. But it certainly was not the Jewish plan to "bind" Paul and "hand him over to the Gentiles." In fact, they were trying to lynch Paul when the Romans arrived and bound him with chains (Acts 21:31-33). An exacting historian would be correct in saying that Agabus was at least in part wrong in his prophecy. At the same time, if we did not have the story in Acts, the prophecy would have given us an accurate impression, although not in detail. Prophecy by nature is "dark speech" (RSV) or "riddles" (Num 12:6-8) and partial (1 Cor 13:9, 12). Even Old Testament prophecies did not mean what they seemed to mean (Dan 9:2, 24), and both Jeremiah (Jer 17:14-15) and Jonah complained that their prophecies were not fulfilled. In what form did Agabus receive the prophecy? Was it a vision, perhaps of Paul bound, standing between Roman soldiers with Jewish accusers facing him (see Acts 21:40; 22:30)? Or did he receive words or impressions from God? Whatever he experienced, his expression of it shows some fuzziness.

Third, all prophecy needs discernment or testing. The church through the ages has already passed its judgment on the prophecies recorded in Scripture, but Paul himself taught that new prophecy has to be "weighed carefully" (1 Cor 14:29). This is not simply to determine whether it is true or false, but also to discover what it means. Paul also indicates that during this process a further revelation might clarify the meaning of the first one (1 Cor 14:30). This instructional passage explains Paul's response to the prophetic words he receives in Acts. He apparently understood the words to be a warning about what would happen, preparing him for the problems facing him, rather than telling him not to go to Jerusalem. In coming to this conclusion he obviously stood against the judgment of his companions. Furthermore, he must have believed that the speakers in Tyre had gone beyond the message God was trying to communicate and had added their own interpretation, for he certainly does not obey it. In other words, he shows that in responding to a prophetic word the responsibility for discernment and decision remained on his own shoulders. In the end he would answer to God for his actions.

Was Paul wrong in his interpretation? Different Christians may come to different conclusions on that matter. For some his three-year imprisonment indicates a failure to heed God's warnings. For others the prophecies are to be seen as preparation to endure just such a trial. God was bringing Paul to Rome in his own way. Apparently his companions concluded from their inability to persuade him that Paul had a strong inner conviction that what he was doing was right and that he ought to interpret the prophecy accordingly. They fall silent and say, "The Lord's will be done." The same principles of personal testing of a prophecy one receives, of personal decision as to its meaning and of personal responsibility for that decision hold true today. We cannot tell others what to do, although we may mediate to them messages from God or give them good advice. If we hold to these principles, we will clear up some of the confusion surrounding prophecy today.[1]

[1]Several recent works discuss the gift of prophecy. The best and most practical is Clifford Hill, *Prophecy Past and Present* (Crowborough, U.K.: Highland Books, 1989). Also good are Wayne Grudem, *The Gift of Prophecy in the New Testament and Today* (Westchester, Ill.: Crossway Books, 1988) and Graham Houston, *Prophecy: A Gift for Today?* (Downers Grove, Ill.: InterVarsity Press, 1989).

20:35 Missing Words of Jesus?

How complete are our Gospels? Have the authors missed anything? That is the issue raised by Acts 20:35. In this context Paul is defending his ministry to the Ephesian elders. They do not doubt his ministry, but Paul knows that after he leaves false teachers will come in and will (1) seek to discredit him and (2) attempt to establish a new pattern of ministry. Paul's own example of self-giving in ministry will help them distinguish the true from the false. Having noted his faithfulness in teaching and pastoring (Acts 20:18-21), Paul points out that he supported himself and his companions in ministry; he took no offerings from them nor raised money elsewhere. This was in part to teach them to "help the weak," to support poorer Christians financially. But then Paul quotes "the words of the Lord Jesus himself." The problem here is that we know of no Gospel context where these words appear. Where do they come from? What does this say about the nature and formation of the Gospels?

Jesus left no literature behind him. He taught his disciples as a rabbi would teach his students. They were expected to memorize the words and deeds of the teacher. That is why the earliest rabbinic writings come from the third century, although they contain some oral traditions going back to the first century. That was, of course, a time when memory was well developed. Any scribe in Palestine would have memorized the whole Old Testament.

The author of Luke-Acts tells us in the prologue to Luke (Lk 1:1-4) that in the years after Jesus' ascension "many" collected the words and deeds of Jesus into Gospels of one type or another. He distinguishes these writers from the "eyewitnesses," probably because the eyewitnesses themselves (such as the twelve apostles) felt no need to write, for they had seen and heard enough to last them a lifetime. Furthermore, he states that he himself used careful research to sort through these accounts in writing his own Gospel. Most scholars believe that one of the written sources he used was Mark's Gospel.

In any such process of research and writing some material is discarded for one reason or another. The author of the Fourth Gospel tells us that there was a vast amount of material that he could not include in his work (Jn 20:30; 21:25). Each Gospel author had the goal of providing certain information to the church and painting a portrait of Jesus from a particular angle; what did not fit into this plan had to be dropped. Scrolls only came in limited sizes.

The fact that such material was not included in this or that Gospel, however, does not mean that the stories or sayings were not genuine or were immediately forgotten. Many of them circulated in the oral tradition of the church for the first generation or two as the eyewitnesses and their first hearers told stories about Jesus. Some were later distorted and recorded in Gnostic Gospels such as the *Gospel of Thomas.* Such second-century or later works, dug up by archaeologists or found in the recesses of ancient libraries, have been heralded by some scholars as "secret sayings" of Jesus. These later heterodox Gospels contain such distorted versions of Jesus' sayings that they add nothing to our knowledge of him. In the first century, however, before there was a lot of distortion, some of these sayings found their way into orthodox and even canonical works, even though they were rejected by (or unknown to) the Gospel writers. For example, James 5:12 quotes a saying of Jesus which appears in a longer form in Matthew 5:33-37. Other short sayings in James also may well be sayings of Jesus (see Jas 1:27; 2:13; 3:18; 4:11-12, 17), but since James never tells us if he is quoting Jesus, we will never know which come from Jesus and which are his own coinage. But his readers probably knew, for in the first century when few could read the church memorized the teachings of Jesus and would have recognized them in print.

In Acts 20:35, then, Paul indicates that he knows a saying of Jesus that was not included in any of the canonical Gospels. We appreciate the fact that he tells us that it comes from Jesus, for that enables us to identify it. The author of Luke-Acts, who obviously knows the saying since he cites Paul as using it, does not include it in his Gospel, perhaps because it did not fit into his scheme or perhaps because he knew he would cite it later. His method appears to be not to repeat material if he can avoid it. So words of Jesus found in the Gospel do not appear in Acts and this one in Acts does not appear in the Gospel.

While we in the present age may lament the loss of a wealth of sayings and stories after the first century (especially given our own drive to preserve as much of the past as possible in museums, archives, libraries and on computer disks), we need to remember two things. First, orthodox Christianity believes in the Holy Spirit who oversaw getting what was necessary into the canon. What was not included might have been nice but was not necessary for us to have in written form. Second, believers in the first century had no New Testament to help them distinguish between accurate and distorted traditions. They had to rely on the personal interpretations of eyewitnesses. As the church grew and the eyewitnesses died, getting such a judgment became more and more difficult. Those first-century Christians who knew a major eyewitness would have had access to far more information about Jesus than we have today, but most Christians never met a single eyewitness and so actually had far less trustworthy information available than is contained in the New Testament.

We can be thankful for having what we do today in a form that all Christians everywhere can consult at the same time, assuming it has been translated into their language. We have sufficient fully trustworthy information about Jesus for the needs of the church, although we do not have exhaustive information or even enough to answer all of our questions or direct us in our personal lives. Yet what is needed in personal direction beyond Scripture Jesus is still quite capable of providing through his Holy Spirit in the hearts of believers, even if that does not come in canonical form and so cannot be imposed upon others.

---

[1]Some scholars, such as Birger Gerhardsson, *Memory and Manuscript* (Uppsala, 1961), believe that some of Jesus' disciples (such as Levi/Matthew) were literate and may have taken a type of shorthand notes. But even if some of the sayings were recorded in writing, Gerhardsson admits that memory was the major means of preserving Jesus' teaching and that such notes were at best partial.

[2]Matthew, Luke and John fill the longest scrolls available in that day. Each of them would have needed a second volume if he had wanted to include more information.

21:21 Should Christian Jews Live like Jews?

A fascinating phenomenon has occurred in the Christian world in the last few decades. The Messianic Jewish movement consists of Jews who have committed themselves to Jesus as their Messiah and thus are completed, not converted. This movement is both welcomed and questioned by Gentile Christians. It is welcomed because it enriches the Christian church with Jewish tradition and provides a culturally relevant path for Jews to come to Christ. It is questioned because it is a form of church to which Gentile Christians can never fully belong and perhaps because of the fear that it contains overtones of superiority. The statement in Acts 21:21 raises this same question: Is it legitimate for Jews upon conversion to maintain their Jewish culture? Or did Paul declare that any such attempt is illegitimate from the start?

The context of the passage is Paul's arrival in Jerusalem for the last time. James receives him warmly but is concerned for the unity of the church. The Jewish-Christian mission has been very successful. "Many thousands" of Jews have believed, but upon committing themselves to Christ they expressed their faith in a very Jewish way; they have become "zealous for the law." The rumor in Jerusalem is that Paul is turning Jews away from the law, which could cause a split in the church. James reaffirms the decision of the Jerusalem council concerning Gentile believers (Acts 15), but he assumes that Paul himself as a Jew keeps the law of Moses. He suggests that Paul join some of the church members who are finishing a Nazirite vow and pay their expenses, demonstrating to all that he is in favor of such observance. Paul does this, but before the process is complete is arrested by non-Christian Jews. Why did Paul offer sacrifice in the temple and take part in Jewish rites? Did he really want Christian Jews to live according to the law? Doesn't this contradict faith as a basis for salvation? What would Paul have said to today's Messianic Jews?

Paul clearly had no place for the observance of Jewish ceremonies by Gentile believers. He states in the strongest terms in Galatians and Romans that circumcision, sabbath observance and Jewish dietary laws are not binding on Christians.[1] In fact, he writes, "If you let yourselves be circumcised, Christ will be of no value to you at all" (Gal 5:2).

It is also clear that Paul believed that God's promises to Israel were still in effect. Therefore he expected not just a remnant of Israel to be saved in the present, but "all Israel" to be saved in the end (Rom 11:26). He could therefore also write about a separate Jewish-Christian mission with a methodology different from his Gentile-Christian mission (Gal 2:7-10).

Finally, Paul states that even though he was free he became "all things to all men," which included becoming a Jew and living under the law while among Jews, for the sake of the gospel (1 Cor 9:19-23). This means that Paul personally could take part in Jewish ritual, if for no other reason than to forward the gospel. For him this would not be the same sort of compromise as the circumcision of Titus would have been (Gal 2:3), for Titus was a Gentile by birth and Paul was already a Jew when he was converted. Thus Jewish behavior would not have been adding anything to his Christianity, but saying that he did not have to abandon his Jewish culture to become a Christian.

The evidence of Acts along with Paul's letters confirms that James was correct about Paul: Paul did keep the law, although probably imperfectly, given what Gentile Christians must have served at the Lord's Supper (which was a communal meal for the first two centuries of the church's life). Paul, after all, was very conscious of being a Jew (Rom 11:1). Rituals such as circumcision, sabbath observance, dietary laws and tithing were part of his national and cultural identity as a Jew. If Israel as a people was still important to God, then it was fitting that those who belonged to Israel racially live out their cultural identity. On the other hand, it was not fitting for Gentile believers to observe Jewish customs, for they would gain no advantage in becoming Jews, since they already had Christ. What is more, such actions would put a barrier in the way of the Gentile mission.

The observance of his Jewish identity must have been more than simple cultural custom for Paul. In Acts 18:18 we read that he shaved his head due to a vow. This probably indicated the start of a Nazirite vow (see Num 6) that was fulfilled when he reached Jerusalem. At the least this indicates that Paul had a place in his own personal piety for such observance, which was voluntary in Judaism.[2] It was a cultural expression of worship and submission to God that was meaningful to him, and thus there was no reason for him to have refused James's suggestion. Very likely there were many other similar private practices as well.

Thus for Paul there was no theological reason why Jews could not observe Jewish customs, as long as they were seen as signs of national identity or cultural expressions of piety, not a way of making themselves more holy than Gentile Christians. At the same time it was improper for Gentile Christians to follow such observances, for they were not Jews and becoming Jews would be no advantage to them. Instead, such observances would indicate that Christ was not enough for them. Finally, he insisted that Jewish and Gentile Christians remain in table fellowship with one another (Gal 2:11-21; Rom 14), which meant principally the observance of the Lord's Supper together. However difficult this may have been due to Jewish dietary rules and Gentile freedom from them, the rule of love was to prevail in maintaining their unity in Christ.

Within such constraints Paul felt personally free to live as a Jew whenever possible. For him returning to the temple as a worshiper was a meaningful experience in continuity with his early zeal for God that, although misdirected, had now been brought to its proper fulfillment in Christ. Likewise he would surely bless today's Messianic Jews who also find their Jewish culture meaningful in continuity with their Christian belief. What he would discourage is any tendency to separatism or elitism, for love and the unity of the faith must be preserved across cultural and ethnic barriers.

[1]Also significant is Paul's resounding silence on the matter of tithe, a fourth major mark of Jewish practice, especially since he does discuss giving extensively in 2 Corinthians 8—9. As law it can no longer be binding on Christians.

[2]It is significant that this is a voluntary practice, which means that there was no reason for Paul to do this simply to maintain his acceptance in the Jewish community. The only reason to observe such a vow was because it was a meaningful part of personal devotion.

22:16 Baptism to Wash Away Sins?

Does baptism really wash away sins? Is it not the death of Christ (or, to use the biblical metaphor, the blood of Christ) the cleanses us from sin? Does this not introduce a deed of ours into the salvation process?

Paul is standing on the steps of the Fortress Antonia in Jerusalem, defending his activities. He has just recounted how he met Jesus on the Damascus road and has been told to go into Damascus to await further instructions. He is already a believer of sorts, but the Christians do not know it yet. Ananias comes to Paul, heals him, mentions the fact that Paul had met Jesus and that God was commissioning him to be a witness. Then comes Acts 22:16, which gives him his further instructions, telling him what to do next.

This verse pictures baptism as a washing (in that period it was probably a complete immersion, although Didache 7 indicates that the church did not delay baptism if they lacked enough water to immerse). This aspect is similar to the washings for purification in the Old Testament (Lev 14:8-9; 15:5-13, 21-22, 27; 16:26, 28; 17:15-16; Num 19:19; Deut 23:11). When one was ritually impure, it was often necessary to wash oneself (and in other cases just to wash one's clothing) in order to be rid of the impurity. The difference between these Old Testament washings and baptism is that when one turns to Christ he or she gets rid of objective guilt and not simply ritual impurity. Previously the person being baptized has lived without being submitted to Christ as Lord. Thus they were guilty of ignoring the wishes of the King of kings. Now the person is repenting and in the act of baptism officially turning from that way of life to one which recognizes Jesus as exalted Lord.

Of course, it is not the water itself that cleanses a person from sin, but the sincere pledge of oneself to Christ. This point is made in 1 Peter 3:21. A person could drown in an ocean of baptismal water and not wash away sin if they were not sincerely turning to Christ. Ananias makes this same point when he says, "Calling on his [Jesus'] name." It is this commitment to Christ that is the critical part of baptism.

So does baptism wash away sins? We could answer this with another question, "Does turning to Christ wash away sins?" The answer is clearly yes. Then, since baptism is where one officially turns to Christ, it can be said to wash away sins. In fact, that is one aspect of the symbolism of the water. Paul has had an encounter with Jesus; Ananias is inviting him to make his private commitment official. The means God ordained for this is baptism, and so Paul is invited to be baptized.

See also comment on MARK 1:4; JOHN 3:5; ACTS 2:38; 1 PETER 3:21.

ROMANS

1:16 First for the Jew?

See comment on MATTHEW 10:5-6.

1:18 Is God Wrathful?

God's wrath is difficult both to understand and to believe. For some, the idea of a wrathful God has been a roadblock to faith. For others, who have experienced the transforming grace and love of God in their lives, the idea of God's wrath has seemed to contradict their experience of God. Can we believe that the God whose unconditional love is revealed "in this: While we were yet sinners, Christ died for us" (Rom 5:8) is at the same time a God of wrath?

Before we tackle the main issues here, we need to discuss the biblical use of anthropomorphisms—the use of analogies from human experience to describe God. The Bible speaks about God's nature, work and purposes in terms analogous to what we know and experience as human beings. This is by necessity. God's absolute nature is not open to finite creatures. We can only approximate what God is like by comparing him to us. Indeed, the Incarnation, God's coming into our midst in the Word become flesh (Jn 1:14), gives legitimacy and authority to anthropomorphic speech about God.

In traditional theological language, this necessary and legitimate use of anthropomorphisms has been recognized, but it also has its limitations. Thus, while knowledge and power are aspects of human experience, God is said to possess these in an absolute, infinite sense: he is *omniscient* (all-knowing) and *omnipotent* (all-powerful). Generally, those aspects of human nature and experience which we have identified as the highest and the best have been ascribed to God. We see God as the one who is or possesses truth, grace, beauty, love, righteousness, faithfulness in their most complete or absolute forms. But a corollary of this way of speaking about God is the resistance to ascribe to God human attributes or feelings which we perceive as negative: hate, anger, a vindictive spirit, ugliness and so forth. Wrath is clearly one of these.

There is some biblical warrant for this

resistance. For example, in Hosea 11, the reason for God's refusal to give up on Israel—though it clearly deserved destruction on the basis of human standards of justice—is the fact that "I am God and not man" (Hos 11:9). However, the major reason for our difficulty in accepting such negative human attributes for God is an idealistic, romantic notion of God, born from philosophical speculation. The Bible does not have such a notion of God, for it takes both God and the world more seriously than abstract philosophical speculation.

The Lord of the Bible enters into relationship with his creation in Jesus of Nazareth, in whom "all the fullness of God was pleased to dwell" (Col 1:19 RSV). It is this Jesus who is, at the same time, in all respects like us (Heb 2:17). The Bible also takes the relationship between Creator and creation with utmost seriousness. Because the creation is God's, it is responsible to God. Within such a relationship of accountability, romantic, idealistic, sentimental concepts of God are out of place. Against this larger background the concept of God's wrath must be understood.

It is instructive that Paul speaks of the revelation of God's wrath within the context of a theology of creation. The biblical story of creation and alienation contained in the opening chapters of Genesis clearly forms the backdrop of Romans 1:18-23. Romans 1:21-22 especially is a poignant reminder of the refusal of humankind (Adam) to live as creature in relationship with God and instead to grasp for likeness with God (see Gen 3:1-7).

In the Genesis narrative, the temptation is to deny our creatureliness, our limitations, our dependence on the Creator in order to become "like God" (Gen 3:5). The result of that denial is that we become debased, less than authentically human. According to the narrative of Genesis 3—11, the denial of dependence on and accountability to God results in a wide variety of distortions within various spheres of human community. Paul, in Romans 1:25, sums up this situation with these words: "They exchanged the truth of God for a lie, and worshiped and served created things rather than the Creator." It is within this assessment of God's purposes for creation and its refusal to be accountable within those purposes that the idea of God's wrath needs to be heard.

Paul speaks of the wrath of God in two ways. Mostly, the expression refers to a future event in which God's judgment is executed on the world's sinfulness (Rom 2:5, 8; 5:9; Eph 5:6; 1 Thess 1:10; 5:9). In these contexts, God's wrath (or its synonym, God's judgment) is clearly perceived as an activity of God, his decided action against sin. It is important to note here that wrath is God's personal response to sin, though unlike that of the various divinities of Greco-Roman religions and myths, God's wrath is never capricious, vindictive or malicious.

In Romans 1:18 Paul does not say that God's wrath *will be* revealed at the last day (that is, judgment day) but rather, "The wrath of God is being revealed from heaven" now. It is not only the divine response to the creation's unfaithfulness in the future judgment; it is already a present reality. This sense of a present manifestation of God's wrath is confirmed in several other passages from Paul (Rom 3:5; 4:15; 9:22; 1 Thess 2:16), as well as in other New Testament writings (see Jn 3:36).

As the passage which follows shows, the present manifestation of God's wrath is *indirect* rather than *direct;* it is an expression of God's permissive will, not God's active will. God is not depicted here as doing something in response to human sin. In some sense, God's wrath is built into the very structure of created reality. In rejecting God's structure and establishing our own, in violating God's intention for the creation and substituting our own intentions, we cause our own disintegration.

The human condition, which Paul describes in Romans 1:18-32, is not something caused by God. The phrase "revealed from heaven" (where "heaven" is a typical Jewish substitute word for "God") does not depict some kind of divine intervention, but rather the *inevitability of human debasement* which results when God's will, built into the created order, is violated. Since the created order has its origin in God, Paul can say that the wrath of God is now (constantly) being revealed "from heaven." It is revealed in the fact that the rejection of God's truth (Rom 1:18-20), that is, the truth about God's nature and will, leads to futile thinking (Rom 1:21-22), idolatry (Rom 1:23), perversion of God-intended sexuality (Rom 1:24-27) and relational-moral brokenness (Rom 1:28-32).

The expression "God gave them over" (or "handed them over"), which appears three times in this passage (Rom 1:24, 26, 28), supports the idea that the sinful perversion of human existence, though resulting from human decisions, is to be understood ultimately as God's punishment which we, in freedom, bring upon ourselves.

In light of these reflections, the common notion that God punishes or blesses in direct proportion to our sinful or good deeds cannot be maintained. God's relationship with us is not on a reciprocal basis. God's radical, unconditional love has been demonstrated in that, while we were sinners, Christ died for us. God loves us with an everlasting love. But the rejection of that love separates us from its life-giving power. The result is disintegration and death. Against such a perverted creation, God's wrath is revealed.

See also comment on PSALMS 5:5; 11:5.

1:24-28 God Gave Them Over to Sin?

See comment on ROMANS 11:32.

1:27 Homosexuality Condemned?

Romans 1:27 appears to speak of homosexual relations as sinful. Is this actually the case? Would the Bible really condemn people for such acts, or is it speaking about something quite different from what we understand as homosexuality?

In our day speaking negatively of homosexuality is often declared to be evil. Several factors have led to this. First, postmodern society believes that all personal options are equally good. Thus one should take pride in one's ethnic background or religion or sexual preference. None is better than another and no one should judge another. This postmodern view may express a truth about our relative human judgments, but does it give God's view? What if God really does exist and has a view by which he will judge the world in the end? Furthermore, there are limits to our tolerance of cultural diversity, for we are not very accepting of Nazi culture, for example.

Second, genital sexual expression is viewed as a right and even as a necessity for emotional health. This is a new view, which ignores the fact that many who cannot function sexually (such as impotent males) can and do live full and meaningful lives. Unlike food and water and shelter, sexual expression is not a need. Nor is it a right. Many people, whatever their sexual inclinations, are deprived of opportunities for full sexual expression (think of those heterosexuals who want to be married but cannot find an appropriate spouse) and, while it may not be a desirable situation for them, it is not that they are being wronged.

Third, homosexuality has found increasing acceptance in our society. However, acceptance does not make something right. Nor does the evidence that homosexuality may be inborn make it right. Some types of personality are apparently inborn, and we think of these varieties of personality types as equally good, but alcoholism, schizophrenia and a tendency to violence may also be linked to genes, and we look at these as genetic defects. We view them as bad and try to control their expression.

Fourth, there have been attempts to label any rejection of homosexuality as "homophobic" and thus make a rejection of this lifestyle appear wrong. Such labeling begs the question. Is one "kleptophobic" if he or she calls theft wrong? It is not always an issue of fear (phobia) at all, but one of sober judgment about what is right and wrong based on a given standard. For Christians the standard has been the Bible, so that is why looking at this passage is so critical.

There are several passages in the New Testament that refer to homosexual genital sexuality: Romans 1:26-27, 1 Corinthians 6:9, 1 Timothy 1:10 and Jude 7. These build on the Old Testament attitude toward homosexuality found in Leviticus 18:22 and 20:13. What conclusions can we draw from these texts?

First, all of these passages condemn particular sexual acts. None of them speak of homosexual desires. In the Scriptures it is not homosexual temptation that is wrong, but the actual acts themselves. This is an important distinction, for it reminds us that the Scriptures honor people successfully struggling with temptation rather than condemning them for their temptations. The man who has never been tempted to commit adultery is not more virtuous than the man who has successfully resisted repeated significant temptations. The first man is only untested in that area.

Second, we recognize that while homosexual practice does not appear to have been common in Palestine, it was a significant feature of the Greek culture. It is not that Greeks were exclusively homosexual, for in fact the general practice was bisexuality, with wives being necessary for procreation, but the use of prostitutes and boys also being more or less accepted. It is also not true that all Greeks equally accepted homosexuality. One form of it, pederasty, was debated by Greek thinkers.

Third, we notice that the explicit rejection of homosexuality is found mostly in Paul's letters, for he was the Christian writer most in contact with the Greek world. Romans was probably written from Corinth and 1 Corinthians was, of course, written to Corinth. It is sometimes argued, then, that Paul's concern was only with pederasty, that he was entering one side of the discussion which was common in the Greek world. However, his language in this passage is not a description of pederasty. A case can be made for making 1 Corinthians 6:9 refer to that vice, but such a case is not totally convincing to scholars in this field. What it looks like is going on in 1 Corinthians 6:9 is that Paul, living in the Greek world, needing an example of vice to use in his letter, used the vice that he found close at hand, homosexual practice, which included, but was not limited to, pederasty.

In other words, homosexual practice was not a major problem within the church. It was a problem in the Gentile world around the church. Why was this the case? Probably the reason is that the church taught fidelity to one's wife. For example, look at the teaching of Jesus in Matthew 19. When in Matthew 19:9 Jesus prohibits divorce, the disciples respond in shock that it would be better not to marry than to be stuck forever with a single woman. Rather than softening his statement, Jesus comments that it might be good not to marry and distinguishes those who cannot marry due to sexual dysfunction from those who choose not to marry because of "the kingdom of heaven." In other words, he gave people only two alternatives: faithful marriage (and he has already made it clear in Mt 5:27-28 what he means by faithfulness) or celibacy. While Jesus does not appear to have been married, Simon Peter was. It would be Paul who would follow the route of celibacy.

Turning to Paul, we find the same alternatives offered. In 1 Corinthians 6:9-20 he rules out "sexual immorality" by which he means sexual intercourse with a person who is not one's spouse, especially a prostitute. He makes the alternative clear in 1 Corinthians 7:9: if one does not have the gift of celibacy, then one should marry. For the same reason married couples should practice regular sexual intercourse (1 Cor 7:2-5). One can read through the whole of the rest of 1 Corinthians 7 and find only two options: celibacy or faithful marriage. These same two options are offered to the widow and to the never-married, to the old and to the young.

As we noted above, in the Greek world as in the world today there were very few who were exclusively homosexual. Most men married out of duty to their family, if for no other reason. The church had only one instruction to such men and women: your wife or husband is to be your exclusive sexual focus. Satisfy one another. There is no option of a homosexual relationship on the side. For the few who were not married the church had two options: remain celibate or marry. Again homosexual sexual intercourse is not an option. By stressing these two positive options (rather than ranting against homosexuality) the early church appears to have had little problem with the practice of homosexuality, despite its being in the world around them.

Does the Bible really condemn homosexuality? The answer is yes, it does. In every place it mentions any homosexual practice it roundly condemns the practice. In no place does it speak positively of homosexuality. Does the Bible dwell on the issue, especially since parts of it were written in a world full of bisexuality? No, it does not. Instead the Bible focuses on its alternative. It encourages sexual expression in the context of a faithful marriage, and it exalts celibacy for those who cannot or choose not to marry. Both are honorable lifestyles. There is no third way.

2:5 Is God Wrathful?

See comment on ROMANS 1:18.

2:7 Salvation by Works?

See comment on JOHN 5:28-29.

2:12 Is God Fair to Condemn Those Who Have Never Heard?

The Bible seems to be teaching that those who have not heard the gospel will be condemned. This does not seem fair—after all, they have not heard that they could believe and live.

Obviously the standard of judgment for those who have not heard the message of the Bible is a truly thorny issue, one which Christians have discussed for ages. No short answer to this question is going to be fully satisfactory. However, we can discuss the particular aspects of this issue which are brought up in this verse.

First, Paul's purpose in writing this verse is not to discuss the issue of the judgment on pagans. He is writing to the church in Rome in order to address the issue in his teaching which caused the most controversy, his insistence that both Jews and Gentiles could come to God on the same basis, that of the grace of Jesus. At this point in his argument he is pointing out that Jews who hear and understand the law but do not actually obey it are under the judgment of God. Jewish religious practice will not make one any better off before God if one lives sinfully. Romans 2:13 states, "For it is not those who hear the law who are righteous in God's sight, but it is those who obey the law who will be declared righteous."

This was an important point for Paul to make. The Jews assumed that the pagans were under God's judgment, for they did not observe the commands of God as stated in the law. Paul is arguing that Jews who did not obey all of the law (as none of them could hope to) were also under the judgment of God. Both were equally in need of salvation through Jesus, and thus the Jews' Judaism did not give them any advantage in this respect (later, in chapters 9—11, he will mention some advantages Jews do have). The outcome of this argument is that Gentiles who have come to believe in Jesus will not be any better off if they become Jewish Christians, for they are already in the same state of salvation that Jews have when they believe in Jesus.

Thus we conclude that Paul is not arguing that Gentiles will be judged on the basis of commands that they have never heard about. He is arguing that both Jews and Gentiles will be judged on the basis of their deeds, whether or not they have ever read the Mosaic law.

Second, Paul does know of a source of revelation for all Gentiles, as we read in Romans 2:14-16.

Paul's point is that even the Gentile cultures he knew of taught the main virtues and condemned the main vices mentioned in the Mosaic law. Roman and Greek law condemned murder and theft and adultery just as the Mosaic law did. Likewise care of one's parents, loyalty to one's fellow compatriots and other virtues were commended in both sets of law. Where did these pagans get such ideas, since it is quite unlikely that any of the ancient Greeks or Romans had read the Hebrew Scriptures? Paul's answer is that such principles were written on their hearts. God had revealed such principles to them, making them the standard of their consciences. Of course this does not mean that every regulation in the Mosaic code can be found in all pagan legal institutions. The point is that the main virtues of the Mosaic law can be found in most pagan legal traditions.

Thus, third, Paul is teaching that people will be judged according to the standards that they know, not according to the standards that they do not know. Now this does not mean that it is not important to know the Bible if one can know it. There are two reasons for this conclusion. On the one hand, the law showed one how to live well, so people suffer when they ignore it, whether or not they know about it. Ancient societies would have been a lot less violent and a lot better places to live had the Mosaic law been in force in them. In the end it does not matter whether one knows a cliff is there and purposefully jumps or does not know it is there and accidentally falls.

On the other hand, Paul will go on to point out that only the revelation found in Jesus can deal with the problem of sin, whether one is Jew or Gentile. The problem is not that the Gentiles are not living up to the Mosaic law that they are ignorant of. The problem is that they are not living up to their own laws which they know very well. About 150 years later than Paul the church father Tertullian would point out as part of a defense of the faith that Christians were living the virtues that Greco-Roman pagans taught but did not live up to.

Thus, returning to our question: How fair is God? Paul's answer would be, "Perfectly fair!" Pagans will not be judged on the basis of a law of which they are ignorant. They may suffer the natural consequences of their ignorance, but this is not the basis of guilt before God. Pagans will be judged on the basis of their obedience to the law that they find written in their own hearts, their violations of their own consciences. They will be judged on the basis of their obedience to what they know. And not only pagans will be judged on this basis, but also the Jews. They know the Mosaic law, so they will be judged, not on their knowledge, but on their obedience.

Naturally, there is an extension of this principle for the readers of this volume. God is also fair toward us. We will not be judged on the basis of how much Bible we know or how many theological exams we can pass. The orthodoxy of our minds will not excuse us. We will be judged on how much of that Bible which we know we actually obey. Indeed, if we ignore the rich knowledge that we have, a pagan who obeys the little knowledge that he or she has may be better off than we. *See also comment on* JOHN 14:6; ACTS 4:12.

4:9-12 Is the Church Israel?

See comment on GALATIANS 6:16.

5:3 Rejoice in Suffering?

See comment on JAMES 1:2.

5:9-10 Salvation: Past, Present or Future?

See comment on 1 PETER 1:9.

5:12 One Man's Sin Means My Death?

Why should the sin of the first human being become the downfall of the entire race? Why should all subsequent human beings stand under God's judgment against a basic sinfulness for which none of us is ultimately responsible? How, in the face of such claims, are we to believe that God is just?

This text has provided the basis for commonly held doctrines about the nature of the human predicament. Many of the questions and problems that arise from it are in fact the result of improper interpretations or misunderstandings of the text itself.

The word *sin* (and its synonym, *trespass*) is the key word in Romans 5:12, just as it is in Paul's description of the human condition in the first three chapters of this epistle. How are we to understand what Paul means by that term? What is his understanding of the origin of the human situation which he describes with this term?

Paul's understanding of human sinfulness is expressed in two phrases: (1) "they did not think it worthwhile to retain the knowledge of God" (Rom 1:28) and (2) "you rely on the law and brag about your relationship to God" (2:17). Sin is seen as refusal to accept our creatureliness, to acknowledge our dependence on our Maker, to recognize our limitations. "We are sinners" does not mean, primarily, that we have moral problems, but that in the deepest and final sense we are severed from relationship with God because of refusal or bragging.

Sin is not a *genetic defect.* The idea that sin is passed on genetically and thereby becomes the property of each individual through heredity ultimately led to a low view of sex. Sex came to be seen as the prime locus of human sinfulness—tolerated for the purpose of procreation, but not celebrated as a part of God's economy for human wholeness and fulfillment.

Nor is sin a *perverted inner nature.* The problem with this understanding of sin is that it divides the individual into a number of separate boxes. It arises from the idea that the Fall resulted in the perversion of one essential part of ourselves. A number of candidates for this part have been proposed. For some, the perverted part is the will. For others, it is the emotions or passions. For still others, it is reason. The pervasive mood of anti-intellectualism in some Christian circles is traceable to such an understanding. Since the mind was affected by the Fall, our reasoning capacity is perverted and depraved and the quest of the mind cannot be trusted. But such a view does not do justice to all the biblical data. As total persons we are fallen and stand under the judgment of God. Both our heads *and* hearts stand under the signature of death. Both are dust.

From the biblical point of view, the term *sin* designates a particular kind of relationship between the creature and the Creator. And a relationship cannot be inherited; it can only be established or destroyed, affirmed or denied. Sin is thus a *relational reality.*

We are sinners insofar as we are unrelated to God. The questions raised by that statement are: *Why* are we that? *Why* is that our condition? *Why* do we find ourselves in such a dilemma? Paul's answer to such questions is found in Romans 5:12-13.

This text has traditionally been seen as the biblical foundation for the Christian doctrine of original sin: "We all stand under the Fall of first man; that is why we are in the mess we are in!" But this view is inadequate. For Paul does not say that we sin *because* Adam sinned. He does not say that we die *because* Adam sinned. What he does say is this: Sin (alienation from God) entered the stage of history in the first man's rebellion ("sin entered the world through one man"). The result of that separation is disintegration and death. But the universal penetration of that condition is due to the fact that all persons have sinned; all persons have become revolutionaries against God ("because all sinned").

There is a two-sided perspective here in Paul that must be taken seriously if we wish to understand him adequately. On the one side of this dual perspective is the Hebrew idea of *human solidarity,* the recognition that each individual shares in a common humanity. On the other side is the recognition of *individual responsibility.* By virtue of the former, we are in bondage; by virtue of the latter, we become responsible for participation in that bondage.

Human solidarity. Paul was heir to a tradition concerning the human condition that was deeply rooted in Jewish beliefs. That tradition recognized the intimate interdependence of individuals and the effect that such solidarity could have, both positively and negatively. The Old Testament concept that the sins of parents would have their effect down through several generations reflects the Hebrew idea of corporate solidarity. The immediate background for Paul's statements concerning the relation between first man and the rest of humankind (Rom 5:12-21) can be clearly seen in a Jewish work of the first century A.D.:

> [Adam] transgressed. . . . Thou didst appoint death for him and for his descendants. . . .
>
> For the first Adam, burdened with an evil heart, transgressed and was overcome, as were also all who were descended from him. Thus the disease became permanent. (2 Esdras 3:7, 21-22)
>
> O Adam, what have you done? For though it was you who sinned, the fall was not yours alone, but ours also

> who are your descendants. (2 Esdras 7:118)

Paul clearly reflects this Jewish understanding in Romans 5:12-13. Adam, the typical representative and first human being, yields to the temptation to determine his own existence and his own destiny (that is, he sins). The result of that self-determination is death. Death is the condition of separateness, since the creature apart from the Creator does not have life. Physical death is clearly a part of this picture in the Hebrew-Pauline understanding. Separation from the source of life results in decay and disintegration.

But both for the Old Testament and for Paul, death is also an existential reality, a real condition of life. Thus Ezekiel receives a vision of "dry bones" that are representative of the failure of Israel to be and remain God's people (Ezek 37). Hosea can speak of the resurrection of Israel from the grave of its national downfall (Hos 6:2). And Paul can speak of Christians as those "who have been brought from death to life" (Rom 6:13). The uniform affirmation of this biblical tradition is that there exists a mysterious relationship between human self-determination and death and between the first man's self-determination and our own death. We belong to one another, and the condition of one has inevitable consequences for others.

Sociological and psychological studies have confirmed that scriptural understanding of human solidarity. We have been shown how heredity, upbringing and environment play major roles in the formation of our personalities. I am, to a large degree, the product of my world. What I am in the present is a continuation of all that I have assumed—consciously and unconsciously—from my past. Thus the child raised in an environment with violent models is more likely to be involved in violent behavior than those not raised with such models. The child of psychologically disturbed parents is more likely to become neurotic than the child of mentally healthy parents. The child who grows up in a broken home is less likely to become a whole, healthy person than one raised in a home with genuine love and caring from both parents in a consistent and stable relationship.

All of us are born into a human community that is overshadowed by the cumulative weight of human sinfulness, oppressive structures, prejudices and injustices. We are, all of us, more or less affected by the shadows that these clouds cast over our motives and orientations, our attitudes and priorities.

Individual Responsibility. In Romans 5:12-21, Paul not only reflects Jewish religious thought that we share a common humanity and that we are affected by that interdependence, but also reflects the Jewish belief that as individuals we are responsible and held accountable for the way we relate to that common humanity.

At the time of Ezekiel a protest was raised against the ancient Hebrew idea that the sins of parents will be visited upon the children and that the children will be held accountable for their parents' transgressions. In Ezekiel 18 the prophet speaks the decisive word of God for individual responsibility:

> Yet you ask, "Why does the son not share the guilt of his father?" Since the son has done what is just and right, . . . he will surely live. The soul who sins is the one who will die. The son will not share the guilt of the father. (Ezek 18:19-20)

This concept of individual responsibility made itself increasingly felt and is clearly enunciated in Jewish writings close to the time of Paul. In the Wisdom of Solomon, which dates from the first century B.C., the author discusses the presence of evil in the world in clear allusion to Genesis 2:

> Do not invite death by the error of your life, nor bring on destruction by the works of your hands; because God did not make death. . . . But ungodly men by their words and deeds summoned death. (1:12-13, 16 RSV)

The parallel between this understanding of individual responsibility and Paul's statement in Romans 5:12 is unmistakable. The same idea is voiced in a Jewish book of the first century A.D., the Apocalypse of Baruch:

> Adam is therefore not the cause, save only of his own soul, But each of us has been the Adam of his own soul. (2 Baruch 54:19)

Paul also affirms that each person continues the rebellion and self-determination of Adam in his or her own life. It is in that sense that each of us becomes a part of that fateful history that stands under the signature of death. Each individual participates in the Adamic humanity and becomes accountable for that participation. Death marches across the pages of human history because humans in their own individuality have sinned. They do what Adam did. And the attempt to determine our own existence, however that may work itself out in everyday living, leads to separation from God.

Paul, in this text, affirms both parts of Jewish teaching about the origin and nature of sin: we stand in mysterious solidarity with *Adam* (Eve and Adam) in sin; we are also individually responsible. There is a sense in which we are determined; there is another sense in which we are absolutely free. But since we are both, neither the one nor the other is the final word.

This Pauline understanding of sin as dynamic, relational reality leads directly to what is his final word; namely, that this paradoxical reality of our bondage to, and freedom from, sin is overcome in a new relationship—one with Jesus Christ. Through that relationship, we are reconciled to God, and in Christ we become members of a new humanity.

5:20 The Law Increases Sin?

On first reading, Romans 5:20 seems to suggest that the purpose of the law of God, given to Moses for the people of Israel, was to increase human sinfulness. But is it possible that the God revealed in our Lord Jesus Christ deliberately acted in such a way that sin increased? Doesn't the revelation of God, from beginning to end of redemptive history as recorded in the Bible, tell about a God who seeks to bring his lost and fallen creation back into restored relationship with himself?

In order to hear Paul accurately, the context of this passage needs to be considered, as well as several other statements about the purpose of the law.

In Romans 5:12-21 Paul presents the contrast between the devastating consequences of human sinfulness and the magnificence of God's gift of salvation in Jesus Christ. Sin entered the human sphere through Adam's decision to reject God's purposes, and it gained universal dominance through continuing human disobedience (Rom 5:12). Having established this, Paul recognizes immediately that though sin has been here from the start, the law was given much later (Rom 5:13). The point is this: Even though individuals could not be held accountable for a standard that did not yet exist, they are part of a humanity alienated from God and his good purposes (Rom 5:13-14).

Within this understanding of the corporate solidarity of human sin and individual responsibility, Romans 5:20 must be understood. "The law was added so that the trespass might increase" cannot mean that God intended to increase sin.

Paul has already shown both sin and its consequence, death, to be a universal reality. It cannot increase beyond this. What sin can be greater than that which separates the whole creation from its Creator?

Thus the meaning of the passage must be that the law was given to "increase the awareness, the consciousness, of sin." Its destructive, devastating nature is revealed for what it really is when the good intentions of God, expressed in the law, are violated.

Throughout the Old Testament, and in rabbinic interpretations of the narratives that tell of the giving of the law to Israel, it is clear that the law was actually understood as a gift from God. Paul shared this view (see Rom 7:10). But in disobeying the law humankind revealed the magnitude of its brokenness.

This understanding of Romans 5:20 is confirmed in several similar statements made by Paul elsewhere. In Romans 3:20 he says that "through the law we become conscious of sin." In Romans 7:7-8 he clearly exonerates the law. It is not the law that leads to sin. Rather, it simply shows what sin looks like and how it expresses itself: "I would not have known what sin was except through the law." Finally, in Galatians 3:19, Paul asks the question "What, then, was the purpose of the law?" and then supplies the answer: "It was added because of transgressions."

When all of these insights are taken together, it becomes clear that "increasing sin" does not refer to the accumulation of sins or to greater sins (as opposed to lesser sins). Rather, in light of both the law and God's grace in Christ (Rom 5:20-21), human sin is exposed and revealed to our consciousness in all its magnitude.

See also comment on EZEKIEL 20:25; MATTHEW 5:17-20; ROMANS 10:4.

6:2, 7 Dead to Sin?

The basic dilemma expressed in this question and answer is the relationship between our new life in Christ—a life freed from sin—and our actual day-to-day living, where sin in fact is all too often present. In order to grasp Paul in this matter, we must first attempt to understand his language about the nature of the believer's relationship to Christ.

The theme of Romans 6 is the contrast between an existence characterized by death and one characterized by life. The former is in view when Christians permit their new life in Christ to be infiltrated by the forces of sin, by their former life "in Adam." The latter is in view when Christians increasingly yield to the claims that Christ has upon them.

The way of belonging to the new humanity, established in Christ, is expressed by Paul in very mystical language. He speaks of believers as those who have been "crucified" and "buried" with Christ; as having "died" and been "raised" with him. These phrases suggest an intense union between the believer and Christ that we, who have been thoroughly conditioned by rationalistic, scientific and technological thinking, have difficulty grasping. Perhaps Eastern mysticism and various cults with their meditation and inwardness prove so attractive because our civilized, acculturated form of Christianity fails to provide people with a sense of the mysterious, a sense of the "otherness" of the divine.

Paul's idea of being in Christ, or *being united with Christ,* has often been referred to as "Pauline mysticism," where "mysticism" designates a particularly intense relationship between the human and the divine. What was Paul's understanding of the nature of the mystical relationship between the believer and the Lord?

In Romans 6:1-10, Paul tells us that

entrance into the new humanity is by means of an intense union with Christ that he presents by use of baptismal imagery of immersion: going into the waters of baptism and emerging from them symbolizes one's dying and rising with Christ. Further, the way of belonging to the new humanity is expressed in two ways:

1. By way of negation: we are dead to sin (Rom 6:2), no longer enslaved by sin (Rom 6:6), freed from sin (Rom 6:7) because the old self was crucified (Rom 6:6).

2. By way of affirmation: there is newness of life (Rom 6:4), union with Christ (Rom 6:5) and life with him (Rom 6:8) because a new self emerged in our being raised with him (Rom 6:4).

Now in these images what is extremely interesting, as well as puzzling, is that Paul presents them as statements of both *fact* and *possibility.* In the Greek language the indicative mood is employed to make factual assertions. In the context of this passage, Paul uses the indicative mood to assert without equivocation the *fact* that believers are dead to sin, freed from sin, crucified with Christ and so forth. Side by side with these assertions, Paul uses the subjunctive mood, which in Greek is used to express possibility, to express the *hope* that believers, as a result of being crucified and risen with Christ, might no longer be enslaved by sin (Rom 6:6) and might walk in newness of life (Rom 6:4).

There is a real tension between the affirmation that we died to sin and are therefore free from its bondage, and the assertion that such freedom is always and only present as a possibility that must be actualized.

How are we to understand this paradoxical juxtaposition of both fact and possibility? Perhaps another look at the baptismal imagery can help us, since Paul clearly associates baptism with the death and resurrection of Christ and with our dying to sin and rising to newness of life.

Baptism has been understood in the various Christian traditions as sacramental or mystical-spiritual or symbolic. In the first, the event is seen as actually mediating the saving qualities of the death and resurrection of Christ. In the second, the event is understood to signal the real presence of the crucified and risen Christ and an inner, spiritual union between Christ and the baptized person. In the third, the event is seen as an external symbol of movement from death to life, resulting from personal decision, commitment and faith.

This is not the place to argue the merits or demerits of these major positions and their variations. All of them have been supported with weighty theological arguments. But it may be possible to combine the deepest truths expressed in these various understandings in a way which also sheds new light on the paradox between fact and possibility in the life of the believer.

In Romans, Paul teaches that the work of God, accomplished in Christ and received by faith, leads to our justification or restored relationship with God. Since the sign of that transaction or restoration is baptism, it may be possible to view baptism in *relational terms.* In baptism we affirm that the life of the one who is baptized is henceforth to be determined by the fact that Christ died and was raised, that *in relationship with him* as justified persons, we are delivered from the dominion of sin and freed for life.

The dynamic of such a relational understanding allows us to deal with the paradoxical nature of new life in Christ, expressed so strongly in the indicative "He who has died is freed from sin" (Rom 6:7 RSV) and the imperative "Let not sin therefore reign . . ." (Rom 6:12 RSV).

New life, says Paul, has become both a reality and a possibility. How do we know that? Paul's answer is given in Romans 6:9-10. Christ is alive; death no longer has dominion over him. Therefore, according to Romans 6:11, we affirm that in relationship with him we are dead to sin and alive to God. The following passage (Rom 6:12-23) then speaks about the practical outworking of this life-giving relationship.

Let me illustrate this point from ordinary human experience. The relationship between a man and a woman in the covenant of marriage exists on two levels. There is that reality which exists on the basis of their mutual commitment in love and interdependence. On the second level is the practical incarnation of that reality, that commitment in concrete acts in everyday living.

Now it is clear that the relational reality, existing on the level of commitment, does not translate automatically or inevitably into the incarnational reality of everyday life. As C. S. Lewis put it, "[There is the possibility] of disappointment . . . on the threshold of every human endeavor. . . . It occurs when lovers get married and begin the real task of learning to live together. . . . [There is] the transition from dreaming aspiration to laborious doing."

In every relationship, there must constantly be movement from *affirmation* to *incarnation,* or else it is in difficulty. There are all sorts of threats and temptations that must be rejected again and again. To be married means that our lives are governed by the continual affirmation and incarnation of the commitments in that covenant. To be "in Christ," to be united with him in death and resurrection, means that our lives are determined by the continual affirmation and incarnation of the commitments in that relationship. In our relationship with Christ we are free from the *bondage to sin;* yet it is possible even for the Christian to "let sin reign" (Rom 6:12).

What does our life look like when affirmation is not translated into incarnation? When our relationship with Christ does not impinge on our everyday living, then other relationships will certainly fill this vacuum. If it is not the Lord Christ whose mind is being brought to bear upon our human relationships, then other lords will most certainly bring their minds to bear upon them.

Parents are models for their children, whether they like it or not. Our children sense very quickly who we are and what gods we serve. So the questions for me as a father are these: Do my children sense that my life is ruled by a higher kind of authority than tomorrow's paycheck, the expectations of my neighbors, the priority of things over persons? Do they sense, as they observe my relations with their mother, that we share a real love, that we are truly there for one another, that we keep pace, in that relationship, with a "different drummer"? To the extent that they sense these things, my life is an incarnation of my relationship with Christ. To the extent that they do not observe these, my life is an incarnation of other relationships.

Christian life is lived between the *indicative* ("you are raised with Christ") and the *imperative* ("let not sin reign in your mortal body"). Only by the empowering presence of God's Spirit can the imperative find realization in our living. *See also comment on* 2 CORINTHIANS 5:17; PHILIPPIANS 2:12-13; 1 JOHN 3:6, 9.

7:4 Freed from the Law?

See comment on ROMANS 10:4.

7:14-19 A Slave to Sin?

On plain reading, what we have in this text is the candid confession of a basic split within the person, of an inner division that leads to utter weakness. Paul's final word about this condition is in Romans 7:24: "Wretched man that I am! Who will deliver me from this body of death?"

If this passage and the verses that surround it are a description of what the Christian life is all about, then they stand in stark contrast to the joy and freedom and newness Paul describes in Romans 5, 6 and 8. Indeed, it would seem that the "good news" of the gospel, expressed with such exuberance in Romans 5:1 and 11, has become the "bad news." For how can Paul say, in Romans 6:6, that "our old self was crucified with him" so that "we should no longer be slaves to sin," and then go on to say, in Romans 7:25, that "in the sinful nature [I am] a slave to the law of sin"?

Yet, despite these difficulties, the most common understanding of this text is that Paul is here speaking about an internal tension between the Christian's higher and lower selves. Some have even used this text as a biblical warrant for sinful behavior, as a cop-out from Christian responsibility.

As so often, it is important that both the immediate and the wider context of this text be grasped if we are properly to understand Paul's meaning. When we do that, it becomes difficult to maintain the usual understanding of the text.

Paul's discussion of justification on the basis of God's work in Christ (Rom 1—6) shows that the whole person is reconciled to God—body, soul and spirit. Justification does not create a new moral or spiritual core within us which then has to fight it out with the rest of our being, our "baser instincts," our "flesh" with its passions and desires. That idea rests on both a misunderstanding of certain words Paul uses and an inadequate hearing of Paul's intention, revealed in the structure of his argument.

The troublesome word in Romans 7:5-25 is *flesh,* a word used several times in association with the dominion of sin and death (Rom 7:5, 18, 25). It is the contrast between "flesh" and the "I" with its higher aspirations which is largely responsible for the view that Romans 7 talks about a divided self in which constant warfare is raging.

When Paul speaks about "being in the flesh" throughout his writings, he is not talking about our physical nature as such, about physical passions and desires, but about a way of life, an orientation of life, a life lived apart from God's purposes for us. The Ephesians are told that they have been made alive, released from "the passions of [the] flesh." The passage then goes on to define "passions of [the] flesh" as "desires of body and mind" (Eph 2:1-3 RSV). This then defines the religious use of the term *flesh,* which for Paul included what in Greek thought was understood as the highest part of the human being, the mind.

A similar use of *flesh* is found in Romans 8. In drawing a contrast between two ways of life, Paul speaks of one way as "liv[ing] according to the flesh," "set[ting] the mind on the flesh," "[being] in the flesh" (Rom 8:5-8 RSV). Then he says, "But you are not in the flesh." Obviously, *flesh* is used here not with any physical, biological connotations. Rather, the religious use of the word *flesh* makes it possible for Paul to say that there *was* a time when "we were living in the flesh" (Rom 7:5 RSV) with the full recognition that Christians *continue* to be physical creatures.

When Paul, therefore, contrasts a "fleshly" with a "spiritual" way of living, he is not speaking about two distinct parts of the total self, but about two possible life-orientations of that total self. In the contrast between the "I" and "my flesh" (7:18 RSV), the "I" represents the total self insofar as it affirms the good, the will of God as expressed in the law; "my flesh" represents the total self insofar as it is powerless, dominated by sin, unrelated to God.

Beside these considerations of Paul's terminology, the structure of the argument supports the thesis that Romans 7:7-25 is not a description of "life in Christ." In Romans 7:5-6, Paul contrasts the former life ("while we were living in the flesh") with the new life ("but now" RSV). These verses serve as topical sentences for what follows: Romans 7:7-25 provides the interpretation of 7:5, while Romans 8 interprets 7:6. The former describes existence unto death; the latter, existence unto life.

Let us briefly trace the argument in Romans 7:7-25. Since the law exposes our sinfulness, is the law therefore sin? By no means! For the law is holy and spiritual, just and good (Rom 7:7-14). The reason we are in bondage to sin is because we are "fleshly" (Rom 7:14 RSV—remember the discussion above about this term). Now Paul goes on in Romans 7:15-24 to explain what it means to be "fleshly, sold under sin." It means that we fail to accomplish God's will, even though we acknowledge the goodness of God's law, even though we intend to live our lives accordingly (Rom 7:15-16). The self is so thoroughly in bondage to sin that one can indeed speak of a life in which the "I," which acknowledges God's law, is not in control (Rom 7:17-23). The result of such bondage is "wretchedness" (Rom 7:24). But now there is a new way: Through Jesus Christ our Lord, we are freed from this desperate condition in which, though we serve the law of God with our mind, our concrete, actual living is "fleshly," dominated by sin (Rom 7:25 RSV). In the next verse (Rom 8:1), Paul begins the description of this new life in Christ, this new life of the Spirit.

What Paul has given us is a description of the ultimate futility of life lived in external conformity to law, even though that law is God's law. Clearly, Paul's encounter with Christ caused him to see his former life "under the law" as bondage from this new vantage point. Now, he wants his readers in Rome, as well as us, to understand that legalistic religion leads to death. Only the grace of God revealed and enacted in Jesus sets us free from bondage to sin to experience the "glorious liberty of the children of God" (Rom 8:21 RSV).

8:28 All Things for Good?

The apparent discrepancy between this profound affirmation of faith and our human experience makes Romans 8:28 one of the difficult sayings of Paul. For how can we see the hand of God at work in the killing of a young child by a drunken driver? Where are God's loving purposes revealed in the agony of a cancer victim's last weeks? What measure of good can be discerned in the massacre of a Christian congregation by guerrillas? All these kinds of experiences and events seem to contradict Paul's affirmation. It is therefore imperative that we understand what it is that Paul is saying and how, in light of his own experience, he was able to say it.

Apart from anything else which might be said about this text, it is clear from the context that it expresses Paul's deep faith and trust in the loving purposes of God. We must remember that this affirmation is not the result of abstract rationalization or theologizing. It is, furthermore, not a word that emerges from the lips of one whose life coasted along in serenity, uninterrupted by the stresses and strains, the pains and perplexities, the turmoil and tragedies that most human beings experience to one degree or another.

No, this word of confidence and hope is written by one who, according to his own testimony in an earlier correspondence, was "under great pressure" and "despaired even of life" (2 Cor 1:8); he was "hard pressed on every side" and "perplexed," "persecuted" and "struck down" (2 Cor 4:8-9); he experienced "beatings," "imprisonments," "riots" and "hunger" (2 Cor 6:4-5). It seems clear that we have in Romans 8:28 no "armchair theory," but a profound affirmation of faith that emerges out of experiences which, on the surface at least, would not seem to support that affirmation.

What then is the "good" toward which God works? I believe we can only discover that when we take the whole context of the passage seriously. In Romans 8:1-18, Paul shows that Christians are people who are "in Christ" (Rom 8:1), whose existence is determined and empowered by the Spirit of Christ who dwells within (Rom 8:9-11). On the basis of this reality, we are "children of God" and "heirs with Christ" (Rom 8:16-17 RSV). We are therefore no longer in bondage to "the law of sin and death" (Rom 8:2).

But to be free from the enslaving realities of sin and death does not mean that we can live our lives unaffected by the continuing presence of sin and death in this world. And it is precisely this dual reality of "freedom from" as well as "continuing experience of" that Paul deals with in the second part of the chapter.

Paul concludes his description of "life in Christ" or "life in the Spirit" by affirming in Romans 8:17 that this new life is lived in the tension between present suffering and final glorification. That is to say, freedom from bondage to sin and death does not mean the absence of either the reality of sin and death or the experience of this reality in the present.

The present reality of "peace with God" and "justification" (Rom 5:1) is but the first installment of God's gracious, redemptive action in Christ. There is much more yet to come. The "not-yet" dimension is already anticipated in Romans 5: beyond the present experience of being at "peace with God," there is the "hope of [sharing] the glory of God" (Rom 5:2) and the expectation of being "saved through his life" in the final judgment (Rom 5:9-10). This "not-yet" aspect of God's redemptive purpose is taken up again: in Romans 8:11 Paul points to the future resurrection of our "mortal bodies," which in Romans 8:17 he refers to as our "glorification." Then he goes on to show "our present sufferings" need to be placed in proper perspective in light of "the glory that will be revealed" (Rom 8:18).

In these verses our experiences, which do not seem "good" at all, are placed in the context of the totality of God's creation, which "in eager expectation" (Rom 8:19) and which is presently "subjected to frustration" (Rom 8:20) and in "bondage to decay" (Rom 8:21). It is a creation which "has been groaning as in the pains of childbirth" (Rom 8:22) just as we human beings "groan" inwardly (Rom 8:22). And just as the total creation "will be liberated from its bondage to decay and brought into the glorious freedom of the children of God" (Rom 8:21), so we can anticipate "the redemption of our bodies" (Rom 8:23).

The proper attitude for our living between the first installment of our redemption and its final culmination is hope and patience (Rom 8:24-25). Our present situation, says Paul, is a situation of "weakness" (Rom 8:26). If it were not so, patience and hope would not be necessary. Yet it is precisely in the midst of our weakness that the Spirit of God is present and working (Rom 8:26-27).

Thus Romans 8:28 must be seen within the context of the redemptive purposes of God. In all things—in our suffering, groaning, hoping, waiting; in "trouble or hardship or persecution or famine or nakedness or danger or sword" (Rom 8:35)—in all things God is working "for the good of those who love him." That "good" is the final and complete realization of God's love for creation, incarnated in Christ, from which nothing can separate us (Rom 8:39).

"In all these things," Paul is convinced, we can be "more than conquerors" (Rom 8:37). Not on the basis of our efforts, nor on the basis of blind faith, nor through a kind of stoic resignation, but rather "through him who loved us" (Rom 8:37) and called us "according to his purpose" (Rom 8:28). That good and loving purpose finds its completion when the whole creation, including our bodies, is freed from bondage to decay.

Prior to this final act in God's redemptive work, it is God's love in Christ that sustains us and empowers us—even in the midst of our experiences of sin and death—"to be conformed to the likeness of his Son" (Rom 8:29). God works in all things toward that good purpose. But only "those who love him" know that, because they are participants "with him" in the outworking of that purpose.

8:29 Predestination?

Our verse appears to say that God predestined some people. Does this mean that God predestined who will be saved? Does it then also mean that he predestined who will go to hell?

The passage in question comes in Paul's letter to the Romans that deals with the relationship of Jewish and Gentile believers. The Jews viewed themselves as the elect of God, and they viewed Gentiles as those who could not possibly be chosen of God unless they became Jews (that is, became proselytes). Because of that attitude, some Jewish Christians argued that Gentile Christians needed to become Jews and keep the law if they really wanted to be saved, while others felt that while salvation was not at stake, without keeping the law one could not be fully pleasing to God. Paul opposes this teaching in Romans. In the first section of the book he has argued that Jews are just as lost as Gentiles, for it is not having the law that blesses one, but living the law. His main points are that both Jews and Gentiles needed Jesus' death and that if one is committed to Jesus he has all of God's salvation. Now in Romans 6—8 he is making three further points: (1) dispensing with the Mosaic law does not lead to more sinful living, for in Christ Christians die to sin as well as to the law, (2) the Mosaic law was not a solution for sin anyway, for it resulted in transforming innocent wrong into conscious sin, and (3) the Holy Spirit received through Christ is the solution to human sin, for while we have to cooperate with him, he is the one who makes us children of God. In the climax of his argument in Romans 9—11, Paul will conclude by showing the purpose of the Jewish nation and its relationship to the preaching of the gospel to the Gentiles. We are, then, in the middle of these three sections.

In the first part of chapter 8 Paul has discussed the role of the Spirit in overcoming sin in Christians, ending with a description of the believer's exalted status in Christ:

> The Spirit himself testifies with our spirit that we are God's children. Now if we are children, then we are heirs—heirs of God and co-heirs with Christ, if indeed we share in his sufferings in order that we may also share in his glory. (Rom 8:16-17)

As is often the case in Paul's writing, he points not only to believers' exalted status, but also to their present reality of suffering. Identification with Christ is not simply identification with the exalted Christ, but also with the suffering Christ. Since living Christians have not yet died, they tend to experience more of the suffering than the exaltation. This observation leads into a meditation on the meaning of Christian suffering (Rom 8:18-25) and how the Spirit helps believers in the middle of their suffering (Rom 8:26-27).

Now we come to Paul's point, made in part in this verse. Despite the present reality of suffering (although God through his Spirit is in it with us), God will work history for good for everyone who loves God. These "who love God" are those who are the "called," for it is not just the Jewish people who are called, but everyone who hears and responds to the gospel. Christians are not simply called and then dropped or forgotten about, but called in accordance with God's purpose, which is God's plan in history. Paul has already referred to this grand purpose in Romans 8:18-25: God has a future hope for Christians, and not only for Christians, but also for the whole of the creation. However painful the present may be, it is part of God's grand plan to redeem human beings from sin, to spread the gospel throughout the earth and to bring his redemption to those human beings who turn to him and to the creation itself.

Another way of putting this is that those whom God foreknew he predestined to be like his Son. The idea of knowing a person in Hebraic thought (in which Paul was immersed) is that of coming into relationship with a person (Gen 18:19; Ps 1:6; Jer 1:3; Hos 13:5; Amos 3:2; or, negatively, Mt 7:23). Now we find out that it is not simply the physical children of Abraham with whom God has come into a relationship, but all of those who love God. Therefore the idea of "foreknew" is to come into a relationship with someone before some point in time. This "coming-into-relationship-before" can mean one of two things: (1) God chose this relationship with believers before they ever existed, for he has worked through the whole course of history for the salvation of such people and (2) God chose them *as a group* before they existed, for he also formed them and sent the gospel to them. Yet, whichever of the two is the focus of Paul's concern, it is not only that God chose them, but that he also has a plan for them, which is to be like his Son. Unfortunately for their comfort, this includes not only the glory of his Son, but also the sufferings of his Son. Thus Christians' present sufferings for Jesus have a purpose: to make them like Jesus. In the next verse Paul will mention other benefits: how those who love God were called through the gospel, justified through the death of Christ and are certainly to be glorified when Christ returns.

Thus Paul is not answering our question about predestination at all. He is writing in a book addressed to the church in Rome. This means the letter is addressed to people who were already Christians. He is in the middle of a section where he has been talking about the sufferings of the Christian life. Now he is telling them the purpose of these sufferings. However unpleasant they may be (and given what non-Christians thought about Christians in the culture, they may have been very unpleasant indeed), these sufferings do not mean that God has forgotten them. "On the contrary," Paul says, "when you were called in the gospel, it was part of a plan of God. That plan was not to leave you as you were. No, God, according to his plan, entered into relationship with you in order to make you like Jesus. Part of that, of course, is suffering, but the other part is glory. So when the plan is complete you will stand before God fully justified and gloried, in the very image of his Son." That is why in Romans 8:31-39 we get the exclamations of praise to God. Christians have not fallen out of his hand; even when they do not see him, he is bringing them on toward his glorious purpose for them.

So what is God saying about predestination? All those who love God are predestined. God has a previously thought-out plan for them. And that plan is to make them like Jesus. In this security every lover of God can rest, even if their present life seems full of pain and chaos.

9:13-15 Is God Unjust?

Is God fair? Does he treat us unjustly? These natural human questions are only magnified when we read passages like "Jacob I loved, but Esau I hated" (Rom 9:13). Yet Paul himself wrestled with precisely this question as he reflected on Judaism's rejection of Christ in light of Old Testament passages. What these Old Testament passages, appealed to by Paul, seem to reveal is a sovereign arbitrariness in God's dealing with human beings. Statements like "Jacob I loved, but Esau I hated" provoke from us the question: But why? What did they do to deserve either God's love or his hate? Our sense regarding some injustice here increases when we read in 9:11 that decisions about Jacob and Esau were made "before the twins were born or had done anything good or bad."

The "hardness" of this text arises at least in part both from assumptions which we tend to bring to it and from our neglect regarding the flow and content of the surrounding text.

Paul anticipates the reader's response to the apparent injustice of God. In words reminiscent of those put to Job (Job 9:12; 40:2), he begins by questioning the appropriateness of even raising such questions (Rom 9:20). Then he drives home the point by citing Isaiah 29:16 and 45:9: "Shall what is formed say to him who formed it, 'Why did you make me like this?' " (Rom 9:20-21).

Paul's point is, of course, that the question "Is God unjust?" arises from our human propensity to measure and critique God's ways on our terms. To even raise the question of unfairness assumes that we know what *fairness* in its final, absolute sense looks like. That is the creature's presumptuousness. Since we do not know the mind of God nor can we fathom his ways (Rom 11:33-34), we are not in a very good position to judge God's purposes. We see and experience only pieces; we see but poor reflections in a mirror and know only partially (1 Cor 13:12); we perceive God's revelation in the context of our earthen vessels (2 Cor 4:7). Only God sees the whole, and from that perspective what may seem "unjust" to us will finally be revealed as God's saving grace.

We bring another assumption to this text which skews our hearing of it in a particular direction. Because of certain inherited theological traditions, we tend to hear this text in terms of predestination and eternal destiny. This theological tradition holds that our eternal destiny has been predetermined. The inevitable question to such a view is the one which Paul's hypothetical reader asks: "Then why does God still blame us? For who resists his will?" (Rom 9:19).

This question has validity only if Paul is in fact concerned here with the matter of individuals' eternal destiny. On close reading of the passage, however, it becomes clear that he is not speaking about salvation and eternal destiny, but about God's calling of individuals and peoples to service, and God's use of events and persons in the accomplishment of his redemptive purposes, namely the salvation of both Jews and Gentiles.

Let us attempt to hear Paul's argument clearly. He begins his consideration of the fate of his own people by recalling all that God had done for them and given them (Rom 9:1-5). The purpose of Israel's calling is to be a vehicle for the realization of "the promise" (Rom 9:4, 8-9)—the promise made to Abraham that through his descendants "all peoples on earth will be blessed" (Gen 12:1-3). Paul saw this promise as finding fulfillment in Christ (see Gal 3:15-18), through whose death both Jew and Gentile would be brought into God's family (Gal 3:28-29).

Yet the reality which Paul, and with him all Jewish Christians, faced was the rejection of Jesus by the people of Israel as a whole. Had God's word failed? (Rom 9:6). In answering this question, Paul shows, by reciting Old Testament events, that God chooses ways and means for accomplishing his redemptive purposes, and that even the present rejection of the Messiah by Israel is used by God toward that end. Not all the children of Abraham are part of the line which leads to the Christ. Isaac, the son promised to Sarah, becomes the vehicle (Rom 9:6-9). Jacob not Esau, is used by God for moving toward the fulfillment of the promise (Rom 9:10-13). God's choices have nothing to do with human merit or status or achievement (Rom 9:11-12). Isaac was not better than his brother Ishmael; Jacob not better than his brother Esau. In other words, they were not "more deserving." In fact, on purely human terms, Jacob's deception should have made him less deserving (Gen 25, 27).

At this point, Paul cites the prophetic word regarding Rebekah's unborn twins: "The older will serve the younger" (Gen 25:23). This is not a statement so much of predestination as of prophetic foreknowledge. The historical record reveals that Edom frequently was dominated by Israel and forced to pay tribute (2 Sam 8:13; 1 Kings 11:14-22). For Paul, confirmation for this prophecy regarding the future of Jacob and Esau (and their offspring) is found in Malachi 1:2-3, which he quotes in Romans 9:13.

In the use of this word from Malachi about God's love for Jacob and hate for Esau, two things are to be noted. First, it is the prophet's concern to demonstrate God's love for Israel (Jacob's descendants), in order to go on to show that her unfaithfulness deserves God's judgment. The Edomites (Mal 1:4) are the descendants of Esau, who stand in a relationship of enmity with Israel. According to Malachi 1:3-4, they have apparently suffered military defeat, and the prophet sees this as evidence of God's judgment (1:4-5). Since God is using Israel to accomplish his purposes—despite her frequent rebellions—Edom's enmity sets it squarely against the purposes of God.

The expression "Jacob I loved, but Esau I hated" must be understood in this historical context. In contrast with God's obvious love for Israel, the situation of Edom could only be interpreted as evidence of God's lesser regard for it. The strong expression "Esau I hated" must be seen as a typical example of Eastern hyperbole, which expresses things in terms of extremes. Further, in the Hebrew language "to love" often means "to favor," and "to hate" can mean "to favor or to love less." Note, for example, that in Genesis 29:31, 33, the RSV renders the Hebrew word *hate* literally, while the NIV renders the word with "not loved." That rendering recognizes, in light of Genesis 29:30, that Jacob loved Leah less than Rachel; he did not "hate" her. (See also Deut 21:15-17, where the Hebrew word for *hated* is rendered "not loved" in the NIV and "disliked" in the RSV.)

Neither in Malachi nor in Paul's use of it is there then any warrant for the idea that God has determined in advance the eternal destinies of either the people of Israel or the people of Edom. The historical situations of the two nations, their "election" or "rejection," are but temporary evidences of God's sovereign freedom with which he moves history toward his redemptive purposes. "God so loved the world" (Jn 3:16), including Jacob and Esau, Israel and Edom, Jew and Gentile.

This redemptive purpose is strongly underlined by Paul's citation of Exodus 33:19 in Romans 9:15. God's mercy and compassion are absolutely free and at his sovereign disposal. No one can earn them; no one deserves them. Even the hardening of Pharaoh's heart, to which Paul refers in Romans 9:17-18, is to be subsumed under the activity of God's mercy and compassion for his broken creation. For its purpose is that God's name "might be proclaimed in all the earth" (Rom 9:17). Thus, what from the limited vantage point of our human observation seems "unjust" is in fact only a misunderstanding of the mysterious workings of God's mercy.

See also comment on MALACHI 1:2-3; ROMANS 8:29; 9:18.

9:18 God Hardens Whom He Wants to Harden?

We have no trouble reading that God has mercy on whom he wishes. We like to think of God as a God of mercy. Yet it is quite troubling to hear that he hardens whom he wants to harden. Does that mean that some people do not have a chance and that the mercy of God is less than universal?

In order to understand this passage, we first have to understand the context. Paul is writing to the Romans defending his position that Gentiles do not have to become Jews in order to become full Christians. That is, he is defending a Christianity that is free from the Jewish law insofar as it marked out people as Jews. At this point in the argument he has just answered the objection that such an approach would lead to immoral behavior (Rom 6—8). Now he is completing his argument by showing that there is a place in the heart of God for the Jewish people. In other words, he is arguing that Old Testament history is not simply a plan that did not work out or a way of producing Jesus, but instead has value in its own right.

Paul begins the chapter by asserting that he does care very much for Israel or the Jewish people (he returns to this theme in Rom 10:1). He cares so much that he would go to hell himself if by so doing he could save the Jewish people from hell. He then lists some of the good things that God has given the Jewish nation in the past. Having said this, he addresses a problem: do these facts imply that God's plan has failed? His full explanation will take from Romans 9:6 to Romans 11:36. His main point is that the plan of God was to send the gospel to the Gentiles and thus stir Israel to jealousy, resulting in the salvation of Israel in the end. In the middle of this argument he makes it clear that he is talking about the Jews (or Israel) as a whole, not every individual within the nation, for on the individual level there are Jewish people (including himself) who have believed in Jesus.

Our verse comes in the first part of the argument. Paul is establishing the ability of God to work his plan, not only by getting people to cooperate with what he is doing, but also by getting them to oppose what he is doing. Paul's point is that God is absolutely sovereign in his choices.

The Jewish people prided themselves

in the fact that God had chosen Israel and had not chosen the Gentiles. Part of this theme is picked up in the argument in Romans 9:7-13. While Abraham had more than one son, God chose Isaac as the one through whom the promise would be passed down. Isaac also has more than one son, but God chose Jacob and not Esau. Any Jewish reader would nod affirmingly, especially if he or she had not read the opening verse (Rom 9:6): "For not all who are descended from Israel belong to Israel" (RSV). Paul's reason for arguing this is not to prove that God could choose the Hebrew people for his purposes and reject others. All Jews knew this. Paul is pointing out that if this is the case, God can also choose some *Jews* and reject others. Paul is using the Jews' own teaching against their national complacency.

The Jewish people also prided themselves on their adherence to the Mosaic law. Surely God would reward their careful observance with salvation; surely he would not select Gentiles for salvation when the Jews were so much more righteous. Paul argues that this is not the case. In the opening parts of the book he has argued that there is no one who is righteous, so no one has a claim on God's salvation. Any salvation which people get is mercy and grace, not just deserts. Now in this chapter he goes out of his way to point out that God's choice in the case of Isaac and Jacob was not based on their character. It was made before they developed their character. It does not help to argue that God knew what sort of people they would become, for that would be to deny what Paul is arguing. He is arguing that God simply chose. To underline this point he cites God's words to Pharaoh in Exodus 9:16: "But I have raised you up for this very purpose, that I might show you my power and that my name might be proclaimed in all the earth." Pharaoh did not arise by chance or by his own power, but God had raised him up. Why would God raise up such an obstinate ruler? So that God's power could be clearly seen when he brought about the exodus. Pharaoh's hardening was part of God's plan for God's own purposes.

If we have any doubt about this interpretation, in the next section (Rom 9:19-24) Paul argues for the right of God to make anything that he wishes out of human beings. In Romans 9:24-33 he is making the point that God has chosen, but he has chosen *Gentiles* for salvation, *not just Jews*, nor have the Jews as a whole been chosen for salvation at the present time. The point is that God would have had just as much right to have chosen Pharaoh for salvation and the Jews to oppose him as otherwise. In fact, something like that has happened in the case of Jesus.

We should not act, however, as if this were Paul's only word on predestination and the hardening of people. Here he is making a point about how God has worked with broad groups of people, the Jews as a whole and the Gentiles as a whole. He is also pointing out that Jewish prophets knew about this plan of God long before it took place. Yet Paul goes on to underline in the following chapter that all of this happened through human choices. God chose to make his salvation available, not on the basis of the Jewish law, but on the basis of the grace of Christ. This was proclaimed to Jew as well as Gentile, so God did not coerce the Jews into hardening themselves. Yet, as God predicted, this good news was largely rejected by the Jews and often accepted by the Gentiles.

So here are two sides of the same reality. On the one hand, people hear the gospel and reject it, just as Pharaoh heard the command of God through Moses and rejected it. There is a true moral choice made by the individual in each case. On the other hand, the sovereign God tells us that he had raised up such a Pharaoh precisely so that he could make that choice. It is no surprise to God when Pharaoh chooses to oppose him, nor is it a surprise to God when many of the Jewish people reject the gospel.

So, does God harden some people? Paul's answer is yes. Does God have mercy on everyone? Paul's answer is no. Yet do people freely choose to reject God? Paul's answer is also yes. And does God have mercy on everyone who believes the gospel? Again Paul's answer is yes. How do these two things fit together? Paul never tells us. He knows on the one hand that God is the sovereign ruler of history, shaping it for his own purposes. There is no power that can resist God. He knows on the other hand that people make choices for or against the gospel and all who come to God are accepted by him. He never tries to explain how these two fit together.

The point he is making is that we must never presume on our status with God ("God, of course, will always choose people like us") or be proud that we are chosen ("God must have seen something great in us"). Each attitude fails to recognize the sovereignty of God. Paul warns us that the Jewish nation fell into the first assumption and thus missed Jesus, and in chapter 11 he warns Gentile believers not to fall into the second assumption. Instead he counsels us to thankfulness, based on knowing that we are where we are, not because we deserved it, but because God chose to extend his mercy to people like us, a mercy that we did not deserve.

See also comment on EXODUS 9:12; ROMANS 8:29.

9:22 Is God Wrathful?

See comment on ROMANS 1:18.

10:4 The End of the Law?

Romans 10:4, though not the only place where Paul deals with the law, raises more strongly than any other the question of the place of the law and its continuing validity for the Christian. This radical word about Christ as the end of the law—and similar expressions in other letters of Paul—has been the object of intense discussion throughout the history of the church, even beginning as early as Paul's missionary journeys themselves.

On the face of it, we are confronted with the affirmation that the law no longer determines our relationship with God. To the thinking of many, this has been a hard saying, which is open to the charge of antinomianism, the rejection of any and all laws and regulations, especially absolute norms, for the moral life.

Since the early church used the Jewish Scriptures as their Bible and included them in the canon together with the Gospels and other apostolic writings, the question of the relation between the law of God and Christian faith is an extremely important one.

In attempting to understand this text and its implications, we need to consider three things. First, Paul's understanding and experience of the law; second, his Damascus road experience as encounter with the Messiah of Jewish expectation; third, his new understanding of the law on the basis of the Christ event. Before we consider these three matters as a background for interpreting this text, a few words about Paul's use of the term *law* are in order.

Paul uses the term in both the figurative and the literal sense. When he speaks of "another law at work in the members of my body waging war against the law of my mind" (Rom 7:23) or "the law of the Spirit of life" (Rom 8:2), he is using the term figuratively to denote realities that are determinative for pagan or Christian life, like the Torah is determinative in the life of Israel. Apart from such usage, Paul only has the Mosaic law in view, that religious system with its cultic, ritualistic and moral obligations under which Israel lived its life since Moses. In this latter, literal sense, the term *law* in Romans 10:4 must be understood.

1. Paul's understanding and experience of the law. For Paul—"a Hebrew of Hebrews, in regard to the law, a Pharisee, . . . as for legalistic righteousness, faultless" (Phil 3:5-6)—the law was God's law; it expressed God's will and purposes for God's people. To obey the law was to be obedient to the will of God. "The law is holy, and the commandment is holy, righteous and good" (Rom 7:12). It is "spiritual" (Rom 7:14) because it comes from God (Rom 7:22), and its intent is to lead human beings to real life (Rom 7:10).

As a rabbi, Paul knew very well that the law, as a gift of God's grace, was a privilege to possess (Rom 3:1-2; 9:4). But he also knew that this gift contained within it accountability. To "know [God's] will," to "approve of what is superior," to be "instructed by the law" (Rom 2:17-18)—and therefore to qualify as "a guide for the blind, a light for those who are in the dark" (Rom 2:19)—also meant that one was obligated to keep the law (Rom 2:17-24).

According to his own testimony, Paul believed that the keeping of the law was possible. With regard to its obligation, he was "faultless" (Phil 3:6). But that conviction was obliterated by his experience of Christ.

2. Paul's encounter with Christ. Beginning with the Damascus road experience—which Paul describes variously as that turning point where God "was pleased to reveal his Son in me" (Gal 1:16) or that event where "Christ Jesus took hold of me" (Phil 3:12)—Paul's understanding of the place and function of the law underwent significant transformation. It had been his passionate commitment to the law and the resultant zeal to uphold and defend it which led him to persecute the early followers of Jesus. There can be no doubt that he believed deeply that he was carrying out the will of God. But his encounter with the risen Lord opened his eyes to see him as the Messiah of God. In his zeal for the law he had actually opposed the purposes of God. He had resisted the inbreaking of the messianic age (1 Cor 10:11) in the very act of trying to keep the law.

This realization takes on particular force when it is seen against the background of rabbinic views of history with which Paul was likely familiar. Within that tradition some rabbis held that human history was divided into three periods: (1) the period of "chaos," lasting from Adam to Moses, when the law had not been given; (2) the period of "Torah," lasting from Moses till the Messiah, when the law would reign; (3) the period of the Messiah. Now regarding this last period there was considerable discussion among the rabbis about the place of the law. According to some, the Torah was expected to cease in the messianic age; others held that the Messiah would perfect the law by giving it a new interpretation or that he would promulgate a new Torah.

Though the dominant thrust of the rabbinic tradition was that Torah would continue in and through the messianic age, that it was eternally valid, there are also many who thought there would be modifications, that some teachings would cease to be applicable, that others would acquire a new relevance, that the sacrificial system and the festivals would cease, and that ceremonial distinctions between "clean" and "unclean" would no longer hold. Thus, a rabbinic tradition which both affirmed the continuance of the law in the messianic age and recognized some form of cessation and/or modification forms the backdrop for Paul's experience and new understanding. The messianic age had dawned. The Torah could no longer be seen as before.

In addition to this rabbinic tradition, the attitude of Jesus himself to the law must have had some impact on Paul's thinking. Though we cannot know to what extent Paul was informed about the precise content of Jesus' teaching and actions, the general stance of Jesus with regard to the law was surely part of the traditions Paul received from his predecessors in the faith. And that stance contains elements which provide both continuity and discontinuity with common Jewish perceptions about the law.

According to Matthew 5:17, Jesus did not come to abolish the law. Throughout the couplets which follow ("You have heard that it was said, . . . but I tell you") it is clear that Jesus affirms the eternal validity of God's will as expressed in the law, but that he also drives his hearers to the deepest and most comprehensive meaning of that will by transcending traditional and often limiting interpretations of the law. As Messiah he provides authoritative interpretation.

Further, according to Matthew 5:17-18, the witness of the Gospels and the earliest Christian preaching, Jesus "fulfilled the law" in his life, death and resurrection. He is declared as the fulfillment of Scripture. In him, the purposes of God are accomplished. This general conviction is undergirded by the authoritative, sovereign way in which Jesus deals with specific and limiting dimensions of the law and sets his mission on a level of significance above the law. Thus, laws of separation between clean and unclean, of ceremonial defilement, of sabbath observance are set aside in the pursuit of his ministry to sinners and ritually (ceremonially) "unclean" persons. "For all the Prophets and the Law prophesied until John," he said (Mt 11:13; Lk 16:16), indicating that a new reality, the messianic kingship, had entered the scene and was replacing the old order (Mk 1:15).

With this background in focus, it is perhaps easier to grasp both the continuity and the discontinuity between Paul's thinking about the law and that of his rabbinic contemporaries.

3. Paul's new understanding of the law. Paul reflects acquaintance with the rabbinic discussion about the three periods of human history. But on the basis of his own experience of Christ and Jesus' own stance toward the law, Paul intensifies and explicates particularly that strand of the tradition which envisaged either a cessation of the law or at least its transformation in the third or messianic period. He saw Jesus as "abolishing in his flesh the law with its commandments and regulations" (Eph 2:15). Through him "we have been released from the law" which once "bound us" (Rom 7:6).

Serving "in the old way of the written code" (Rom 7:6) and seeking to establish his own righteousness (Rom 10:3) had only brought Paul into opposition to the very purpose of God rather than into peace with God. In Romans 7 he shows that the law as expression of God's will remains; that it reveals, as ever, human sin and rebellion against God. But he also shows that the law is powerless to bring about obedience. It is an external norm; it does not provide the power with which to achieve the norm. Therefore the attempt to achieve righteousness based on the law (Rom 10:5) invariably ends in the experience of failure. Paul's summation of this experience is caught up in the words "What a wretched man I am! Who will rescue me?" (Rom 7:24).

His answer to that question is "Jesus Christ our Lord" (Rom 7:25). Why? Because "Christ is the end of the law." The word "end" *(telos)* can designate either the "goal," "outcome," "purpose" toward which something is directed, or the "end," "cessation." Many interpreters believe that both meanings are caught up in this text. For Paul, the law "was our custodian until Christ came" (Gal 3:24 RSV). Its temporary function has now been accomplished; and Christ is therefore also the terminus, the cessation of the law.

But Paul is saying much more here than simply repeating the conviction of one aspect of his tradition and the witness of the early church that there is a cessation of the law in the messianic period. He qualifies the conviction that the Mosaic law has been completed and abrogated in Christ with the phrase "unto righteousness." English translations have not served us well here, for they have generally blunted the connection between the statement "Christ is the end of the law" and the qualifying phrase "unto righteousness."

The preposition *unto* expresses purpose or goal. Christ is not the end of the law in an absolute sense. He does not abolish the will of God as expressed in the law. Rather his coming signals its end with regard to the attainment of righteousness (that is, right relationship with God). He is the revelation of God's righteousness (Rom 1:17). His life is an incarnation of God's relation-restoring action, God's way of setting us right (Rom 10:3). Therefore, the law as a means of approach to God, as that which determines relationship with God, as that which was perceived in Paul's Jewish tradition to lead to life on the basis of conformity, has been abolished.

A third phrase in this text adds a further qualifier to the assertion that Christ is the end of the law. Namely, he is the end of the law "for everyone who believes." For it is only in the response of faith to Christ, in the humble submission to God's righteousness (Rom 10:3) that the bondage of the law—consisting of its revelation of sin and its inability to help us beyond it—can come to its end. *See also comment on* MATTHEW 5:17-20; ROMANS 5:20.

11:26 All Israel Will Be Saved?

Does this mean every single Jew, or Israel as a national entity? Didn't Judaism on the whole reject Christ and thus refuse God's saving act? How then can "all Israel" be saved? And didn't Jesus, before Paul, say that the kingdom of God would be taken away from the Jewish people and given to a new people (Mt 21:43)?

Romans 11:26 has been at the heart of much Christian reflection about eschatology or doctrines about end times. I remember well the interpretation given this text by one of my college teachers. According to his eschatological timeline, the establishment of the state of Israel in 1948, which ended an almost two-thousand-year period without nationhood, inaugurated the final days of "the time of the Gentiles," namely that period when the land of Israel was occupied by Gentiles. (Compare Lk 21:24, where Jesus predicts the destruction of Jerusalem and a subsequent period of its being "trampled on by the Gentiles until the times of the Gentiles are fulfilled.")

But our teacher said there was one piece of the eschatological puzzle still missing: the Old City of Jerusalem was still being held by the Arabs. A barbed-wire fence separated Jews from their ancient city, including the temple mount. When that fence comes down and Israel regains control over the Old City, so our teacher confidently predicted, Jerusalem will no longer be "trodden down by the Gentiles." Thus "the times of the Gentiles will be fulfilled," and the conversion of Israel to its Messiah will be inaugurated. Many of us who took this and other very specific eschatological views seriously waited expectantly when, during the 1967 Arab-Israeli War, the fence did come down and Israel regained control over its ancient city. Over twenty years have passed, but Israel has remained a thoroughly secular state.

This rather recent historical experience illustrates the precarious nature of all eschatological theories which tie particular biblical texts to very specific historical events. It also reveals the difficulty of understanding the precise meaning of Paul's words "all Israel will be saved." In order to gain a clearer perspective on this matter, we will examine Paul's extended discussion with regard to Israel in Romans 9—11 with particular focus on the immediate context of Romans 11:11-27.

After showing that God's redemptive action in and through Christ (Rom 1—4) has brought freedom from condemnation (Rom 5), sin (Rom 6), law (Rom 7) and death (Rom 8), Paul brings this part of his letter to a climax with a magnificent description of God's love in Christ from which nothing can separate us. This glorious doxology is abruptly overshadowed in Romans 9:1-2 by an expression of Paul's deep pain over the fact that Israel, the people of God, had rejected their Messiah.

The question of Israel's fate, in light of its rejection of the early Christian proclamation that Jesus of Nazareth was the fulfillment of Israel's prophetic hope, was very much in the consciousness of Jewish followers of the risen Christ. A sense of perplexity and incredulity regarding Jewish unbelief is reflected throughout the New Testament, beginning with the Gospels. But for Paul, it must have been particularly intense. Had not he, a leader of the opposition to this messianic faith, been grasped from the darkness of unbelief to the light and freedom of faith in Christ? But beyond this personal dimension, were not his people those who had been the objects of God's gracious activity through the calling of father Abraham, the creation of a nation, the deliverance of the exodus, the giving of law and covenant? Had not they been the objects of God's steadfast love and faithfulness from which "nothing can separate," as he had just confessed in Romans 8:35? If the word of God does not fail (Rom 9:6), why is Israel stuck in the failure of disobedience? That is the agonizing question which Paul addresses in Romans 9—11.

After the opening lament over Israel (Rom 9:1-5), Paul proceeds to show in a variety of ways that God's redemptive purposes, inaugurated with the call of Abraham and brought to a climax in Christ, have in fact not failed, even with regard to the people of Israel.

He begins by demonstrating that from the very beginning belonging to the people of God was not a matter of birthright (Rom 9:7-8) or of human achievement (Rom 9:11, 16). Rather, membership in God's family is determined solely by the promise (Rom 9:8), calling (Rom 9:11) and mercy (Rom 9:16) of God. In this context, Paul introduces a different use of the term *Israel,* which he has already indicated earlier in this epistle (see Rom 2:28-29; see also Gal 3:7; 6:16); namely, there is an Israel "of the flesh" and an Israel "of the promise." Both are determined by the gracious action of God, but the latter transcends the boundaries of the former. That "the children of God" (Rom 9:8 RSV) have their existence purely on the basis of God's calling and mercy is underlined by the analogy of the potter and the clay in Romans 9:19-23. The potter is sovereign over the clay. And, in that sovereignty, he has called into peoplehood a remnant both from the people of Israel and from the Gentiles. The citation of prophetic words from Hosea and Isaiah (Rom 9:25-26) underlines this fact.

In the following section (Rom 9:30—10:4), Paul goes on to state why the redemptive purposes of God are being received and realized among the Gentiles and why Israel as a whole is rejecting them. Israel rejected the righteousness of God—his relation-restoring action that culminated in the servant-ministry of Jesus—because it sought to establish its own righteousness by external conformity to the law. This attempt to secure one's own worth and standing with God—which, according to Paul's earlier discussion (Rom 2:17-29), invariably results in boasting and self-righteousness—leads to refusal to submit to God's way (Rom 10:3). And God's way is that as creatures we respond to the love and faithfulness of the Creator with faith, that we believe his Word, that we respond in trust (Rom 10:5-13).

The opportunity to respond to God in this way has been there throughout Israel's history, as Paul demonstrates by reference to Old Testament texts (Rom 10:14-21). And throughout that history, including the coming of God's righteousness in the Messiah, Israel has been "a disobedient and obstinate people" (Rom 10:21).

Does this history of rejection and disobedience mean that God has finally given up on his people Israel? That is the question which occupies Paul in the next section of the epistle (Rom 11:1-10). The answer to the question is no. For just as God called out a remnant from a disobedient nation in the past (Rom 9:2-4), so too there is a remnant in the present that has responded in faith to God's grace (Rom 11:5). Paul himself is evidence of the existence of such a remnant within Judaism (Rom 11:1).

But the fact remains that the vast majority of Israel has refused to submit to God's way of salvation and has rejected his Messiah. True enough. But God is not yet done with his people. Though Paul has been very adamant throughout the epistle that faith and belonging to Christ are the only criteria for what it means to be "of the seed of Abraham" (Rom 2:20; 9:6-8), Paul also decidedly rejects the idea that this truth means the exclusion of the nation of Israel from God's redemptive purposes (the analogy of the olive tree in Rom 11:17-24 underlines that). For him, such a conclusion would have been inconsistent with the historical election of Israel (see Rom 11:29).

Thus Paul acknowledges Israel's failure and rejection (Rom 11:7), but he proceeds to argue that within God's overarching purposes this reality is temporally limited. Indeed, God uses the present rejection for his purposes. This activity of God is underscored by the Scripture citations from Isaiah 29 and Psalm 69 about the hardening of Israel (Rom 11:8-10), for since Israel's disobedience is placed in the service of God's purpose, God can be spoken of as "hardening" Israel. But the goal of disobedience and hardening is not their ultimate rejection and destruction; it is, rather, twofold: (1) the salvation of the Gentiles (the world) and (2) the ultimate salvation of Israel (Rom 11:11-15).

Paul is convinced that through the proclamation of the gospel to the Gentiles and its acceptance by them, the promise to Abraham—that all the people of the earth shall be blessed in him—is being fulfilled (see Rom 4). He is also convinced, on the basis of Deuteronomy 32:21, which he cites in Romans 10:19, that the salvation of the Gentiles will provoke Israel to jealousy and open them to the gospel (Rom 11:11, 14).

Within the context of this argument, Paul anticipates the "mystery" regarding the nation of Israel's ultimate destiny, which he will articulate in Romans 11:25-26. If the failure of Israel is leading to the salvation of the Gentiles, the manifestation of God's grace and blessing will be much greater with "their full inclusion" (Rom 9:12 RSV). What does he mean by this expression?

The term translated "full inclusion" is the Greek word *plērōma.* The ASV renders this term by "fulfillment" or "fullness." In Romans 11:25 the same expression is used again, but this time in connection with the Gentiles. Here the RSV renders it as "full number of the Gentiles," while the ASV renders "fullness of the Gentiles." I am persuaded that the idea of a divinely predetermined number, which has to be made up of both Gentiles and Jews, is not within Paul's purview here. When noncanonical Jewish apocalyptic literature speaks of a "full number" of Israelites in relation to end events, the word used is not *plērōma* but *arithmos.* In Revelation 7:4 we read of "the number of the sealed" (RSV). The word used is again not *plērōma* but *arithmos,* and the number is generally regarded as symbolic rather than indicative of numerical extent. Thus we do better to seek the meaning for Paul's use of *plērōma* in his use of the term elsewhere in his writings.

With but one exception (Rom 13:10), the most natural rendering of Paul's use of *plērōma* is "fullness" or "completeness" (Rom 15:29; Gal 4:4; Eph 1:23; 3:19; 4:13; Col 1:19; 2:9). What then do the expressions "[Israel's] fullness" (Rom 11:12) and "the fullness of the Gentiles" (Rom 11:25 KJV) mean? Light may be shed on this problem by Paul's use of verbal cognates of *plērōma* in three texts where his mission to the Gentiles is in focus. In Romans 15:18-22 he speaks of having "fully proclaimed" the gospel of Christ to the Gentiles and now being desirous of expanding this mission to Spain. In Colossians 1:25-27 he speaks of having made the "word of God fully known" (RSV) among the Gentiles. And in 2 Timothy 4:17 he confesses God's empowerment "so that through me the message might be fully proclaimed and all the Gentiles might hear it."

In light of these usages, Johannes Munck argues convincingly, in his book *Christ and Israel,* that Paul's commitment to the full dissemination of the gospel to the Gentiles must provide the interpretive key to his use of *plērōma* in Romans 11. The expression "the fullness [or completion] of the Gentiles" in 11:25 (KJV) then denotes the final result of Paul's proclamation of the gospel to the Gentiles. God's purpose through that preaching is their salvation, their completion (as children of God in Christ; see Col 2:10).

The completion of the mission to the Gentiles will result in, or lead to, Israel's "fullness" or "completion" (Rom 11:12), her "acceptance" (Rom 11:15). These phrases anticipate the affirmation that "all Israel will be saved." The way from the anticipation of this conviction to this climactic expression is paved by the analogy of the olive tree (Rom 11:17-24) and its astounding claim that God will indeed graft the broken-off branches of unbelieving Israel back into the olive tree to join the branches of "remnant Jews" and believing Gentiles who have already been grafted to the olive tree.

Paul proclaims this future realization of God's intention as "a mystery" (Rom

11:25). He is not referring here to a special revelation he had received, some esoteric secret communicated to him directly in a vision or dream. Rather, he is referring to God's redemptive action and purpose, revealed in the life, death and resurrection of Christ which he proclaims (Rom 16:25; 1 Cor 2:1-2; Col 2:2, where "God's mystery" is simply identified as "Christ"). Sometimes, as in this text, the term is used more specifically for God's plan of salvation. The most instructive parallel to this text—which envisions the grafting of both Gentile and Jew into the same olive tree—is Ephesians 3:3-6, where Paul says that the content of the "mystery of Christ" is the inclusion of the Gentiles as fellow heirs of the promise with Jews in the new community of Christ's body.

Within this overarching content of the mystery Paul proclaims is a more specific component, namely, that the "hardening [which] has come upon part of Israel" (Rom 11:25) is limited not only in extent, but also with regard to time: its rejection will last only "until the fullness of the Gentiles" comes (KJV). This completion of God's purpose among the Gentiles leads then to the completion of that same redemptive purpose for Israel, in that "all Israel will be saved" (11:26). Commentators are agreed that "all Israel" means Israel "as a whole," as a historical people who have a unique and particular identity, not necessarily including every individual Israelite. Support for this way of understanding the phrase "all Israel" comes from a rabbinic tract (Sanhedrin X, 1), where the statement "all Israelites have a share in the world to come" is immediately qualified by a list of exceptions, such as the Sadducees, heretics, magicians and so on. The salvation of Israel is comprehensive, but not all-inclusive. In this text, just as "the fullness of the Gentiles" does not mean that each individual Gentile will believe in his heart and confess with his lips (Rom 10:10), so the "fullness of Israel" cannot mean every individual Jew.

While in Romans 11:25-26 the present "part of Israel" which is hardened is contrasted with "all Israel" which will be saved in the future, it is clear that "all Israel" denotes both the already-saved remnant and the yet-to-be-saved "others" or "rest" (Rom 11:7). What is also clear from the whole thrust of the discussion in Romans 9—11 is that God's purposes for the salvation of Israel will be realized in no other way and by no other means than through the preaching of the gospel and the response of faith. It is that preaching and that response which will lead to "life from the dead" (Rom 11:15), clearly a reference to the eschatological event of the resurrection which will be preceded by the "completion of Israel" (Rom 11:26) as the last stage in the process initiated by the death and resurrection of Jesus.

There is no indication anywhere in these chapters of Romans that Paul has in view the conversion of Israel as a nation-state, located on a particular piece of real estate. Already in Paul's time, there were more Jews living outside Palestine than within. What Paul does envision is a time when the gospel will be heard and accepted by his people as a whole, scattered throughout the world but, nonetheless, a unique, identifiable people whose identity is rooted in the great historical events of redemptive history and whose future is guaranteed by the God who has saved his people and will again save them by "banish[ing] ungodliness" and "tak[ing] away their sins" (Rom 11:26-27 RSV).

See also comment on ISAIAH 63:17; GALATIANS 6:16.

11:32 God Has Bound All to Disobedience?

If God has bound all human beings to

disobedience (or, as the RSV translates, "consigned all men to disobedience"), where does human responsibility lie? How can God hold us responsible for disobedience when he caused it? The text seems clearly to indicate that the disobedience of both Jews and Gentiles (Rom 11:30-31) is in some sense the activity of God so that his mercy can be demonstrated. An analogy will highlight the "hardness" of this text. In order to demonstrate my heroic nature, I push a nonswimmer into a swift current. As he is about to drown, I jump in and save him. Is such a view of God's ways a valid understanding of Paul's words?

An answer to this problem depends largely on the meaning of the Greek word rendered "bound over to disobedience" and our understanding of Paul's general view of God's relation to human sinfulness or disobedience.

That the Greek word used by Paul is open to a range of meanings and nuances is clear from the following list of a representative sample of English versions:

NIV	has bound over to disobedience
ASV	has shut up unto disobedience
KJV	hath concluded them in unbelief
NEB	making all prisoners to disobedience
Berkeley	confined under the power of disobedience
JB	imprisoned in their own disobedience
TEV	has made prisoners to disobedience

The Greek word reflected in these translations is *synkleiō.* In the Greek-English Lexicon by Bauer/Arndt/Gingrich, both literal and figurative meanings are given. The literal meaning of the verb is "close up together," "hem in," "enclose." That meaning is clearly present in Luke 5:6, where a catch of fish is "enclosed" in a net. The figurative meaning is given as "confine, imprison," and illustrated from Romans 11:32. The word's possible meanings in this text are then given as *"he has imprisoned them all in disobedience,"* that is, put them under compulsion to be disobedient or given them over to disobedience." The sense of "compulsion" by God is reflected strongly in the renderings of TEV, ASV and NEB. The alternative meaning, "given them over," is reflected in the translation of the JB.

In the New Testament, apart from its literal use in Luke 5:6 and here in 11:32, *synkleiō* is used in only one other Pauline text, Galatians 3:22-23. Here Paul affirms that "Scripture declares that the whole world is a prisoner of sin." That statement of bondage to sin is paralleled by the statement that "we were held prisoners by the law." The meaning of *synkleiō* in this text is certainly that of confinement (or restraint, as in RSV). Yet God is not seen as determining that bondage in any direct way. The meaning seems to be that Scripture shows—by virtue of the history of human disobedience since the Fall—that all are in the grip of sin. The reference to confinement under the law in Galatians 3:23 must be interpreted in light of Galatians 3:24-25, where the function of the law is put in very positive terms: it is the custodial caretaker, leading us to Christ. What is confirmed in this passage's use of *synkleiō* is the reality of bondage to sin or disobedience, as expressed in Romans 11:32. But the possibility of God as determiner of human disobedience does not seem to be in view.

Help for grasping Paul's meaning may be found in the Old Testament as well as in Romans 1. The Hebrew Scriptures had been translated into Greek in the centuries before Jesus' coming, and Paul made frequent use of this translation when he cited, or referred to, those Scriptures.

The Hebrew word *sāgar,* which means "to deliver up," "to surrender," "to give over," is translated in the Greek Old

Testament by two different words. In Psalm 31:8 and 78:50 the translators used *synkleiō*. In Psalm 78:48 and Deuteronomy 32:30, the same Hebrew word was represented by the Greek *paradidōmi.*

It is clear from this and many other examples which could be given that for the Greek translators these Greek words were both valid equivalents for the Hebrew *sāgar,* if not synonymous. Kittel's *Theological Dictionary of the New Testament* states that *synkleiō,* as a translation of *sāgar,* means "to deliver up" or "to surrender," and that it is parallel to *paradidōmi.*

It is this latter word which Paul uses in Romans 1:24, 26, 28. In Romans 1:18-32, as in Romans 11:32, Paul stresses the pervasiveness and depth of human sin. Its origin is the human refusal to acknowledge God as God (Rom 1:18-23). Paul then goes on to show that in the context of this rejection of God, human life deteriorates and degenerates (Rom 1:24-32). This depiction of human sinfulness is accompanied by the threefold refrain "therefore, God gave them over to" (RSV "gave them up"). The meaning is clearly that God allowed his creation to sink into the quicksand of its own disobedience. He neither forced its obedience nor determined its disobedience.

Thus Paul's use of the word *synkleiō* in Romans 11:32 can best be understood in keeping with its usage in the Greek Old Testament where, in translation of the Hebrew *sāgar,* it means "to deliver up," "to surrender." This sense of the term is confirmed, as we have seen, by the use of the parallel word in Romans 1:24-28. The meaning of Romans 11:32 would then be "God has given up all people to their disobedience." What we have here then is an expression of God's permissive will. By permitting the creation to become absorbed in and by its sinfulness, God has acted in such a way that the result is their bondage in disobedience. It is from that bondage that God in his grace brings liberation.

See also comment on EXODUS 9:12; 1 SAMUEL 2:25; ISAIAH 63:17; ROMANS 9:18.

12:20 Burning Coals?

The image of pouring burning coals on another's head—even though we realize that it is a figure of speech—conjures up negative connotations. It sounds like vengeance or retribution. Surely that is not the result to be achieved by acts of kindness. Could Paul be saying that doing good to one's enemies is an indirect way of punishing them?

These negative assessments disappear rather quickly when we see this passage in its larger context (both in Rom 12 and in Prov 25:21-22, from where it is cited) and properly grasp the meaning of this figure of speech in its ancient Near Eastern setting.

The entire context argues against the possibility of interpreting this figure in a negative sense. As a whole, Romans 12 begins the final section of the epistle in which Paul, on the basis of his theology of justification by faith and the empowering of Christian life by the Spirit, works out some of the practical implications of this theology for everyday Christian existence. He begins by speaking of the transformation of life in such a way that God's good will is accomplished in and through Christians (Rom 12:1-2). He continues by showing that as Christians we do not stand alone in this task, but are one body, gifted by God's grace to empower each other in mutual loving service (Rom 12:3-13). Then he focuses on Christians' existence in the larger world, a world which, for the early believers, was often hostile toward the followers of Christ (Rom 12:14-21).

In such a world, it would have been very natural and easy to build resentment, to lash out, to resort to even violent means in order to protect oneself against hostility and persecution. But Paul knew, on the basis of Jesus' "suffering servant" messiahship, that the way of bitterness, resentment and violence was not to be the way of Jesus' followers in this world. God's love, demonstrated in Jesus' death on the cross and poured into believers' hearts (Rom 5:5), was stronger than hate. He had experienced its grasp on his life while he was a persecutor of Christians (see Phil 3:4-12).

The proper response to those who persecute is to bless, not curse, them (Rom 12:14). The evil done to you should not be repaid by evil (Rom 12:17). In situations of conflict, Christians ought to be about the search for peace (Rom 12:18). Where the world's values would call for retribution and vengeance when evil is done to us, we are, on the contrary, to respond in love and kindness, going as far as giving food and drink to enemies who are hungry and thirsty (Rom 12:19-20). Why? Because God is the one who judges and holds evildoers responsible in the final judgment (Rom 12:19). When we respond to evil in the radically unexpected form of goodness, we are in effect pouring "burning coals" on the head of the perpetrator of evil (Rom 12:20). Paul drives home this radical Christian response to evil, urging that we refuse to "overcome by evil," but instead "overcome evil with good" (Rom 12:21).

Romans 12:21, in confirmation of the entire context of the passage, demonstrates that the figure of "pouring burning coals" is to be understood as an act of goodness, as something which "overcomes evil with good." This meaning of the figure is confirmed even by the context in Proverbs 25:21-22, which closes with the words "and the Lord will reward you." And in the Old Testament, God's rewards are always seen as response to human acts of kindness.

This analysis of the context shows that the image of burning coals must have a positive meaning. It does not tell us precisely what that meaning is, what "pouring burning coals" on an enemy's head is to accomplish. To that question we now turn.

Romans 12:2 implies that the "burning coals" image refers to an "overcoming" of evil. How is the evil of the enemy overcome? Help in answering this question comes from both biblical (internal) and nonbiblical (external) sources. In the narrative of the prophet Isaiah's call (Is 6), the recognition of his sinfulness receives a divine response of purging and purification. A burning coal is taken from the altar and applied to his mouth, with the assurance that "your guilt is taken away, and your sin forgiven" (Is 6:7 RSV). This connection between burning coals and repentance and cleansing is also present (though not as directly) in Malachi's picture of God as one who is "like a refiner's fire" (Mal 3:2). As fire refines silver and gold to purify it, so God will "purify the sons of Levi . . . till they present right offerings to the LORD" (Mal 3:3 RSV). The point of this passage is that Israel's sin and disobedience shall be separated out through the refining process of God's judgment.

A possible cultural background, outside the Bible, for the connection between burning coals/fire and the purging of sin/evil is to be seen in the ancient Egyptian custom in which a penitent demonstrated his repentance of a wrong committed by carrying a dish of burning coals on his head. Some commentators see this as the immediate background of the proverb which Paul cites (Prov 25:21-22).

In light of the above discussion, the purpose of "pouring burning coals" seems to be that, by means of responding to evil with good, the doer of the evil may be brought to repentance. It is the enemy's benefit which is intended. When the adversary is treated with kindness, when good is returned for evil, then evil may be overcome; the antagonist may be transformed by a renewal of mind, a change of orientation from darkness to light.

13:1-7 Submitting to Government?

How do Christians deal with the tension created by their presence in a society in which the need to preserve their integrity as individuals and to be faithful to their understanding of the lordship of Christ may conflict with the demands of that society?

In Romans 13 Paul focuses on the tension between the individual and society at large in terms of the problem of civil obedience or disobedience. The question which is raised concerns the individual's responsibility toward the social order, insofar as that social order is regulated by laws that are upheld and enforced by government authorities.

Individual Christian responsibility has often been compromised on the basis of a one-sided use of biblical injunctions. Thus Romans 13 and 1 Peter 2:13-14 are often cited as proof that the state always demands and deserves our total and unquestioning obedience. But Revelation 13 and 18 are neglected. The former pictures the state as a beast opposed to God's purposes; the latter speaks of the downfall of any nation that becomes a modern Babylon, corrupted by wealth, materialism and injustice.

Some Christians are quick to condemn any person who upsets or threatens to upset social norms and regulations. But those same Christians tend to disregard Acts 17:6-7, where the apostles are described as "men who have turned the world upside down" and who "are all acting against the decrees of Caesar, saying that there is another king, Jesus" (RSV).

The Gospel accounts also make clear that Jesus did not accept all legal and governing authorities as ultimate dispensers of God's will. Wherever he went, he bucked the system, upset the status quo and challenged the authorities' claim to the right and the truth. And in the context of a life of discipleship, countless martyrs have given their lives because they resisted the decrees of the authorities.

Thus a serious look at the scriptural material will prevent us from viewing the demands of society and its rulers with uncritical acceptance and automatic approval. Are there conditions when the demands of the social order must be resisted and the worth of the individual as a responsible being before God must be affirmed and defended?

If we cannot give uncritical and unquestioning allegiance to the demands of society and its governing authorities, we must also be careful not to go to the other extreme, that of concluding that government is inevitably an evil institution which should be resisted, disobeyed, distrusted or ignored. For we are instructed to honor and pray for those in authority. The Bible makes clear that government has a positive role to play in God's plans for human community. According to the New Testament, all authority is ultimately under the rule and judgment of Christ.

In light of this double perspective, how are we to understand Romans 13, which seems to come down on one side of this double perspective? First, we need to read Romans 13 more carefully than it has often been read. Second, we need to read these admonitions in light of the context of Paul's missionary activity, which took place in a world in which Roman law and rule had created relative peace and order, conducive to the rapid spread of the gospel.

Let us carefully follow, in outline form, Paul's argument:

Statement:	"Everyone must submit himself to the governing authorities" (Rom 13:1).
Hypothetical Question:	Why?
Answer:	Because all authority exists ultimately by God's design, including the authority of the state (Rom 13:1).
Conclusion:	Therefore, to resist the authorities is to resist God's intent (Rom 13:2).
Hypothetical Question:	But what is God's intent?
Answer:	It is God's intent that through his "servants" (governing authorities) evil acts are punished (Rom 13:4); bad works are restrained through fear of punishment (Rom 13:3); and the good is promoted and encouraged (Rom 13:3).

In summary, Paul's argument is this: It is God's intent that human life in the context of community will be life in harmony and peace and order (see Rom 12:10, 18). Since life in community becomes chaotic and anarchistic without the presence of regulatory laws enforced by authorities, the presence of these are part of God's overall intent for human existence. Therefore, insofar as the state and its rulers exercise their authority in keeping with God's intent, they act as God's ministers for the common good of society.

If, however, the authority of the state runs counter to this divine intent, then that authority should not be understood as God-given. In fact, it becomes quite clear from Revelation 13 and 18, as well as other places in the New Testament, that the state which persecutes Christians, which dispenses injustice instead of justice, which supports moral decay, which tramples on the weak and powerless, has been usurped by demonic powers and forces diametrically opposed to God's intents and purposes.

The passage that follows Paul's discussion about the relationship between the individual and the demands of the social order (Rom 13:8-10) is very instructive for a proper understanding of that relationship. Most commentators feel that Paul has completed the considerations about obedience to the state and is now speaking about morality and ethics in general. It seems to me, however, that such an understanding of the thrust of the argument overlooks Paul's specific intent at this point.

Indeed, the admonitions concerning love for others (Rom 13:8-10) are not a departure from the previous topic but are rather a climax of the entire discussion. Romans 13:8 picks up very pointedly from Romans 13:7. There the argument for obedience to the state and for responsible existence within the social order is driven home in terms of specific things that we owe: taxes, respect, honor. But beyond these specifics, Paul goes on to argue (Romans 13:8-9) that what we really owe is to love others even as we love ourselves.

According to Paul's Jewish heritage, government authorities are intended to be guardians of the commandments which make community life possible. The commandments "do not kill," "do not steal," "do not commit adultery" and so forth, if violated, lead to the destruction and fragmentation of community. Since the law is summed up in the command "You shall love your neighbor as yourself" (Rom 13:9 RSV), the loving of one's fellow human beings—not doing any wrong to them—"is the fulfilling of the law" (Rom 13:10 RSV). It is responsibility for both the protection and the enforcing of this law which is given to human authorities by God's design.

What if, in our expression of love to our fellow human beings, we run smack into the laws of the society in which we live? What if the rulers act in opposition to their intended purpose as stated in

Romans 13:3? What if they become "a terror for those who do right"? What if the demands of the social order require us to be molded into a lifestyle that is contrary to the implicit and explicit demands of the gospel?

There are no pat answers to these questions. Anyone who suggests easy solutions or indeed *the* Christian response fails to take seriously the complexities of the world in which we find ourselves. Nonetheless, we must be sensitive to the issues raised by these questions and must respond in keeping with our understanding of the call of Christ. And that call is decisively a call to be there for others in love. If we fail at this point, even the most carefully woven cloth of orthodox belief and pious practice will finally become nothing but a tattered rag.

14:15 To Eat or Not to Eat?

Romans 14:15, together with the related texts in 1 Corinthians 8 and 10, contains what has often been called the "stumbling block" principle. It is the principle of Christian life and conduct that whatever we do or say should not become a hindrance to the faith and life of a Christian brother or sister.

The difficulty this principle has created for many Christians is related to understanding not so much its import, but rather its implementation. What guidance does the apostle give in this regard? How can we know whether what we eat (or drink or wear or participate in) merely offends fellow Christians and is rejected as inappropriate by them, or causes fellow Christians to stumble and fall in their faith-pilgrimage and perhaps even reject the faith?

These are precisely the issues with which Paul deals in Romans 14. We shall carefully trace his argument, completing that investigation with insights from 1 Corinthians, where Paul struggles with similar concerns.

In the previous chapters of this epistle (Romans 12—13), Paul has laid down central principles for Christian conduct, both within the community of the church and in the larger world of human relationships. Within the fellowship, we are to be more concerned with others than with ourselves (Rom 12:3, 10). In the larger human society, we are to respond to evil with good (Rom 12:14) and thus overcome the evil (Rom 12:21). Both of these "principles" for Christian conduct are undergirded by the most central principle: "Love does no harm to the neighbor. Therefore love is the fulfillment of the law" (Rom 13:10).

It is this principle with which Paul now confronts a problem that was very acute in several of the young churches. For Gentile Christians, the issue was whether they could eat meat that was sold in the open marketplace but had come from animals sacrificed in heathen temples. It was a very concrete problem in the context of their continuing social relationships with heathen neighbors and friends. For Jewish Christians, in the context of fellowship with Gentile Christians, there was the tension between Jewish ceremonial laws regarding "clean" and "unclean" foods and the freedom of Gentile believers from those regulations. We see early Jewish Christians struggling with that issue in the Acts accounts of Peter's vision (Acts 10) and of the Jerusalem Council (Acts 15).

Most likely Paul wrote Romans from Corinth. Thus his views about the issues facing believers in Rome would surely have been informed by the way he treated this matter in the church in Corinth. There (1 Cor 8, 10) he talks about the "weak," those who are young in the faith, whose consciences are tender, who are still prone, due to their heathen background, to make the link between the idol and the meat sacrificed to the idol. The "strong" are those who know, who are clearly convinced that idols (and the gods they represent) have no real existence. For them, therefore, meat offered to these gods in sacrifice is neutral. One cannot be defiled by it. The "strong" are clearly "correct" in their theology; the "weak" are definitely "wrong." And yet, Paul argues, those who have correct knowledge should take care that their knowledge does not lead to the ruin of a brother or sister (1 Cor 8:7-9). For the freedom of the "strong" with regard to this matter may lead the "weak" to return to the sphere of idolatry (1 Cor 8:10-13; 10:23-32).

We must recognize that Paul is not concerned here about simply offending others by doing something with which they disagree, or which they deem inappropriate or unacceptable for Christians. Rather, he is concerned about the eternal welfare of these "weak" Christians, about acts which cause them to fall in their spiritual journey, leading to the destruction of their young faith (1 Cor 8:9, 11-13; 10:32).

The principles which Paul lays down are identical to those given in Romans 12—13: Do nothing that causes fellow believers to come to ruin (1 Cor 8:13; 10:32); rather, build them up in love (1 Cor 8:1); seek the good of others (1 Cor 10:24, 33).

With this background from the Corinthian situation, we are now ready to follow Paul's similar argument in Romans 14. There the "weak" seem to be Jewish Christians, who have not yet been able to become free from the ritual and ceremonial laws concerning clean or unclean foods (Rom 14:1-6) or the observance of special days (probably a reference to sabbath observance—Rom 14:5). The majority who stand in tension with the weak are most likely Gentile Christians, for whom there is no such thing as "unclean foods" or special days to be observed.

Their conflict with each other apparently manifested itself in an attitude of haughtiness or spiritual superiority by the Gentile believers and a condemning, judgmental spirit toward them by Jewish believers. Paul comes down hard on both for three reasons: (1) God has already accepted both (Rom 14:3); (2) we are ultimately accountable in these matters to God and not subject to each other's limited perspectives (Rom 14:4, 10-12); and (3) since participation in the kingdom of God is not determined by what we eat or drink, neither abstaining nor partaking is a cause for judgmentalism (Rom 14:13, 17).

Having shown that both the strong and the weak are to be faulted for their attitude toward each other (Rom 14:10), Paul nonetheless surfaces a special concern for the weak ones (Rom 14:15-16). In this he is clearly in keeping with the special divine concern for "the weak ones" throughout the Old and New Testaments. A strong faith is less vulnerable than a weak faith. In the race of faith toward the finish line (see Phil 3:13-14), the strong are less likely to stumble over some obstacle than the weak. Therefore, the eating of foods which the weak believe to be unclean is an act that is potentially dangerous for those of young faith (Rom 14:13-14). It is an unloving act by the strong if a fellow Christian "is distressed because of what you eat" (Rom 14:15). In light of the rest of the verse ("Do not by your eating destroy your brother for whom Christ died") the NIV rendering "distressed" is probably too mild. The Greek word *lypeō,* in addition to "grieve," "pain," "distress," can also mean "to injure," "damage" (as in RSV). Injuring another's faith may lead to its ultimate destruction.

As in 1 Corinthians, so here also Paul is deeply concerned about Christians' growth toward mature faith and their eternal well-being. The imperative of love (Rom 14:15) means that Christians are to act in ways that build each other up rather than in ways that tear each other down (Rom 14:19-20), in ways that hold each other up and help each other along rather than in ways that cause others "to stumble" and "to fall" (Rom 14:20-21).

The basis for this kind of Christian conduct is the principle that "each of us should please his neighbor for his good, to build him up," which Paul articulates at the conclusion of the discussion (Rom 15:2) and grounds in the life of Jesus: "For even Christ did not please himself" (Rom 15:3). In the final analysis Christian conduct is grounded in Christ's self-giving, sacrificial love (Rom 15:8).

Paul does not tell us how to discern, specifically, when our conduct will bring injury to a fellow believer's spiritual life and possibly to a falling into sin's sphere of domination. What he does seem to believe deeply is that when life is lived in fellowship with Christ, driven by his love, seeking to imitate his life, then we will have the kind of sensitivity to each other which will prevent us from harmful acts.

1 CORINTHIANS

1:18 Salvation: Past, Present or Future?

See comment on 1 PETER 1:9.

3:17 Destroying God's Temple?

The difficulty of 1 Corinthians 3:17 has to do both with the meaning of the important terms used and with the implications of it for our living as Christians. Who, or what, is God's temple? By what actions or lifestyle or words can this "temple of God" be destroyed? Are the words or deeds which destroy this temple of God like the "unforgivable sin" of Matthew 12:31-32, since they bring down the judgment of God ("God will destroy him")?

The most common understanding of the text is that Paul is here talking about our individual bodies as temples or dwellings of God's Spirit. If we destroy these "temples"—through the way we live (for example, through sexual impurity) or by what we put into them (for example, alcohol, drugs, tobacco, excess food) or by what we do to them (for example, suicide)—we become the objects of God's final, destructive judgment. For, since our bodies are both created by God and the objects of God's redemptive work, they are sacred and should not be destroyed by us in these ways.

These are all significant insights, and Paul specifically addresses the issue of the proper use of our physical bodies with regard to sexuality later in this epistle (1 Cor 6). But Paul is not speaking to these important issues in this text. Our physical, individual bodies are not what he is here concerned about. For both grammatical and contextual reasons, this understanding must be set aside in order to truly hear God's word for the Corinthians and for us in this text.

First Corinthians 3:16-17 forms one unit of thought and must be treated as such. This is recognized by most English translations, which set verses 16-17 apart in a distinct paragraph, and it is clear from the fact that both verses speak of God's temple.

The question "Who or what is God's temple?" is answered when we understand Paul's use of the personal pronoun "you" here. In Greek there are different words for singular "you" and plural "you" (that is, "you all"). Further, verbs have distinct endings that show whether the subject of the verb is singular or plural, first person ("I," "we"), second person ("you," "you all") or third person ("he," "she," "it" or "they"). Thus the Greek text of 1 Corinthians 3:16-17 is unambiguous regarding the number of the "you" addressed; the verb endings and pronouns all reflect the plural.

Among modern translations, only the NIV and TEV make a partial attempt at accurately rendering the Greek. In 1 Corinthians 3:16 the NIV reads, "Don't you know that you yourselves are God's temple?" And in 1 Corinthians 3:17 TEV reads, "and you yourselves are his temple." Yet even these do not bring out the meaning as clearly as the Greek. The following annotated rendering is an attempt to catch the precision of the Greek: "Do you (the many) not know that you (the many) are God's temple and that God's Spirit lives in (among) you (the many)? Anyone who destroys God's temple will be destroyed by God; for God's temple is sacred, and you (the many) are that temple."

This recognition of the nuances of Paul's Greek shows that he is not here thinking of individual Christians as temples inhabited by God, but of the church, the fellowship of believers in Corinth, among whom the Spirit of God dwells and is operative. Paul expresses this same sense in 2 Corinthians 6:16 where he says that "we are the temple of the living God." If he had wished to address individual Christians in their physical bodies, Paul would have had to say, "Don't you know that you are temples of God?" and "You are those temples." (And in 2 Corinthians 6:16, "We are the temple of the living God.")

In many ways, 1 Corinthians 3:16-17 reveals Paul's foundational understanding of the church and is a key to the meaning of the entire letter. Namely, the church, the people of God among whom God's Spirit dwells, is God's option, God's alternative to the fragmentation and brokenness of human society. The Christian congregation gathered in Corinth was called to model that alternative in the midst of the brokenness of Corinthian society. But their divisiveness, their immorality, their enthusiastic spirituality which disregarded concrete, bodily dimensions of life—all these were destroying the viability of God's option, God's temple in Corinth. And it is that destruction which stands under God's judgment.

This corporate understanding of God's temple is confirmed by the context. Paul is occupied in the first four chapters of this epistle with divisions which are threatening the very life of the church (1 Cor 1:10-17; 3:3-4). These schisms apparently centered around loyalty to certain teachings that the Corinthian Christians had received from their founder (Paul) or from leaders who worked among them after Paul's departure (Apollos, Peter, see 1 Cor 1:12).

In this section (1 Cor 3:10-15), Paul shows that those called to leadership in the church, and perhaps all Christians, are accountable to God for the way in which they participate, through life and work, in the growth of God's building. It is possible to build with materials that endure (gold, silver) or with materials that are of inferior quality (hay, stubble). The end-time judgment ("the day"), pictured here and elsewhere in Scripture as a fiery ordeal, will reveal with what materials individuals have built. It may be, as some commentators have suggested, that Paul has the followers of Peter and Apollos in mind. The former may be attempting to build their own legalistic Jewish practices into the structure of the church; the latter may be building with eloquent (worldly) wisdom and superspirituality. These "building materials," as Paul shows throughout his writings (particularly Gal and 1 Cor), are ultimately useless. Though Christians who build with these materials are not excluded from God's salvation, their passage through God's judgment into eternity will be accompanied by the experience of failure and loss.

But beyond the danger of using worthless building materials in the growth of God's people, there is the greater danger of acting and living in such a way that "God's building" will in fact be destroyed. It is that danger which Paul addresses in 1 Corinthians 3:17.

The congregation of people composing the church at Corinth was in danger of destroying itself. As the entire catalog of problems with which Paul deals in this epistle reveals, the possibility of this church's destruction was real: their haughtiness regarding the presence of flagrant immorality (1 Cor 5); their use of pagan courts for settling internal disputes and the continuing participation of certain members in pagan rites of cultic prostitution (1 Cor 6); the use of Christian freedom and knowledge in such a way that the "weak in faith" would fall back into sin and be destroyed (1 Cor 8, 10); the rejection of Paul's teaching on the resurrection of the body in favor of an emphasis on purely "spiritual redemption" (1 Cor 15), which led the Corinthians to a total disregard for the concrete, practical dimensions of life within the fellowship and the larger society.

To destroy the church, this temple of God, is to destroy God's alternative to the brokenness of human society; it is to make it impossible for God's redemptive presence and work, through his "temple" in Corinth, to redeem Corinthian society. Those who thus oppose the very redemptive purposes of God—by factious and contentious, acrimonious behavior; by false doctrines which reject the message of the cross as scandalous and foolish; by perverting the freedom of the gospel into unrestrained libertinism; by replacing salvation by grace through faith with legalistic dependence on works—are liable to God's destroying power. Their destruction, however, is not to be seen as an act of vindictive retribution, but rather as the inevitable result that comes to those who reject God's way of salvation.

It is in this sense that the one who "destroys the temple of God" belongs to the category of those who, according to Jesus in Matthew 12:31-32, commit the unpardonable sin. There, it is the rejection of the redemptive presence of God's Spirit in the life and ministry of Jesus. To reject that work of God is to refuse God's forgiveness. For Paul, it is the destruction of God's way of salvation through the church, in which the Spirit of God is operative (1 Cor 3:16), that leads to destruction. For to destroy this work of God (see Rom 14:20) is, in the final analysis, the rejection of God.

5:5 Hand Him Over to Satan?

This instruction of Paul to the Christians in Corinth, part of his call for the excommunication of a member because of serious immorality, needs careful interpretation, or considerable distortion of his meaning is possible.

Questions such as the following are often asked: What does "handing over to Satan" really mean? Why would the apostle want anyone to be handed over to Satan? Though the man committed a grievous sin, is there no room for discipline and forgiveness within the Christian community? What is envisioned in the idea "destruction of his sinful nature" (literally "flesh")? And how can that possibly be a means toward the salvation of his spirit?

In the preceding discussion of 1 Corinthians 3:17 it was suggested that Paul understood the church in its local manifestation in Corinth (and any other place) to be God's alternative to the fragmentation and brokenness of human society. The viability of that alternative was being undermined in a number of ways in the church at Corinth. First Corinthians 5, where this hard saying is located, deals in its entirety with one of these ways.

The specific problem is the sexually immoral life being led by one of the members. The larger problem is an attitude about physical life among the Corinthian Christians which allows them not merely to be tolerant of the immoral behavior of a brother, but to exhibit a certain pride, even arrogance, about the matter.

Paul lays the matter clearly before them in 1 Corinthians 5:1. The word rendered "sexual immorality" (NIV), or simply "immorality" (RSV), is the Greek word *porneia* (from which we derive "pornography"). Literally, it means "prostitution," but Paul uses it, as normally throughout the New Testament, in its broader meaning of sexual impurity of various kinds. The following sentence, "A man has his father's wife," points out the nature of the immorality. The verb *has* is in the present infinitive form, indicating that the situation is not a single occurrence, but a continuing immoral affair. It is not defined as incest, so the woman is likely his stepmother. Nor does Paul speak of adultery; thus, her husband is either dead or she is divorced from him.

From Paul's Jewish perspective, such a relationship is a serious break of divine law. Leviticus 18:8 clearly forbids it, and according to rabbinic tradition, the offender was liable to stoning. What makes the situation even more grave is the recognition that such a sexual relationship is "of a kind that does not occur even among pagans." By this Paul is probably not claiming that this kind of immorality never occurs among pagans; rather, he must be referring to the fact that even Roman law (as stated in the Institutes of Gaius) forbade such a practice (that is, "Even in the pagan world this is unheard of as acceptable behavior!"). It was clearly detrimental to the moral fiber of the entire congregation, as well as to the viability of its witness in the pagan world.

The seriousness of this matter, which elicits Paul's rather harsh judgment and direction for congregational action, is undergirded by his assessment of the congregation's attitude, which apparently not only tolerated this illicit union, but found in it an occasion of prideful boasting. Indeed, Paul may have seen, behind their attitude, a view of Christian faith and life which promoted and nurtured the kind of sexual immorality addressed (both here in 1 Corinthians 5 and another form of it in 1 Corinthians 6).

"The man is having sexual relations with his father's wife—intolerable in both Jewish religious and Roman civil law—and you are proud" (see 1 Cor 5:2). This judgment on their attitude is anticipated already in 1 Corinthians 4. Here, Paul throws a series of sarcastic barbs at their lofty pride: "already you have become rich!" "you have become kings" (1 Cor 4:8); "you are so wise in Christ!" "you are strong!" (1 Cor 4:10). Then he sums it up with the words "Some of you have become arrogant" (1 Cor 4:18). After his instruction about the excommunication of the offender, he points again to their attitude: "your boasting is not good" (1 Cor 5:6).

What is the ground for this lofty arrogance? It has long been recognized that many of the problems Paul addresses in the church at Corinth seem to be grounded in a religious mindset that devalued physical life and emphasized spiritual liberation. This view developed out of Hellenistic syncretism, with contributions from both philosophy and mystical cults that spread across the Roman Empire from the East.

Plato had taught that the body was the tomb of the soul; that death brought liberation from physical captivity; that already in this life one could transcend the negative arena of matter by a higher knowledge of ultimate reality. Various Hellenistic cults offered immortality via union with the god or gods, sometimes symbolized or achieved through cultic prostitution. Within such a religious philosophical climate, Paul's teaching regarding freedom "in Christ" and life "in the Spirit" was all too often, and particularly at Corinth, perverted into an enthusiastic libertinism that rejected moral restraints, particularly in the realm of the physical. Since the physical realm is by definition of no account—so they seem to have argued—it does not really matter what we do with our bodies. Indeed, their arrogant pride regarding sexual immorality in their midst indicates that they may have seen this matter as the very proof of their spiritual perfection. Theirs was a religion of enthusiastic intoxication without moral enthusiasm!

The proper response, both to the intolerable case of sexual immorality, as well as to their imagined superior spirituality, should have been mourning, not pride. And a repentant attitude would inevitably lead to the removal of the offender from the fellowship.

That some form of excommunication is intended is clear not only from 1 Corinthians 5:2, but from the Passover analogy in 1 Corinthians 5:6-8 ("Get rid of the old yeast") and the citation of Deuteronomy 17:7 ("Expel the wicked man from among you"—1 Cor 5:13). The nature of the removal is expressed in the ambiguous phrase "hand this man over to Satan." Its purpose is twofold: (1) that his "sinful nature" or "flesh" would be destroyed and (2) that his "spirit" would be saved (1 Cor 5:5).

The phrase "hand over to Satan" must be recognized in some figurative, metaphorical sense, since a person literally abandoned to Satan would seem to be lost irrevocably. Yet here such an end is not envisioned.

Some have seen behind the expression the Jewish practice of excommunication, imposed particularly for infringement against marriage laws. In banning an offender, it was believed that separation from the people of God, and therefore from God's special care, would lead to premature death. (Yet, within Jewish practice, the hand of God was understood to execute this punishment, not Satan.) Premature death, in this view, could be referred to by "destruction of the flesh." How this premature death would affect a final salvation is not clear.

It seems best to find an explanation within the larger background of apocalyptic Jewish thought which Paul shared. According to that thought, Satan was understood as the "prince of this world" (see Jn 12:31), as the "prince of darkness" with sovereignty over "this present evil age" and the realm of death. According to the Gospels, Jesus' teachings and deeds are the reign of God breaking into the realm of Satan's dominion (see Lk 11:14-22). For Paul, Jesus' death and resurrection were the decisive events: the evil powers had been robbed of their control (Col 2:15); the "end of the ages" had broken into this present evil age (1 Cor 10:11 RSV); the "new creation" had dawned (2 Cor 5:17); Christians were people who had been delivered "from the dominion of darkness" and transferred into the kingdom of God's beloved Son (Col 1:13).

Within this larger understanding of Paul's view the expression "hand him over to Satan" must be interpreted. The new creation had begun, but had not yet been consummated; the dominion of evil had been invaded, but had not yet ended; the new age had superimposed itself on this present evil age, but had not yet replaced it. Thus the church was the arena of Christ's presence and continuing work; it was the community of God's Spirit. To be excommunicated was therefore to be transferred out of the kingdom of God's Son into the dominion of darkness (a reversal of Col 1:13!). Such a transaction is aptly described as a "handing over to Satan," that is, into the world, the sphere of his continuing domain.

If that is the proper sense of the phrase, then how are we to understand the stated purposes of this transaction?

A literal reading of the phrase "for the destruction of the flesh" leads to several possible meanings: (1) abandonment of the man's physical existence to the powers of destruction; (2) premature death, in keeping with Jewish ideas; (3) physical sufferings. Two difficulties arise: (1) How do any of these lead to the stated purpose of the excommunication, namely, salvation? (2) In light of Paul's teaching regarding bodily resurrection and his rejection of Corinthian libertinism (with its antiphysical thrust), would he be promoting the dichotomy: destruction of the flesh versus salvation of the spirit?

These difficulties disappear when we take seriously the way in which Paul generally uses the terms *flesh* and *spirit* when speaking about human life. Paul clearly rejected the dichotomy between the physical and the spiritual so prevalent in Greek thought. When he contrasts "flesh" with "spirit" in human existence, being "in the flesh" with being "in the spirit," he is contrasting two means of existence, two orientations of life. "Flesh" represents the total being (including the human spirit) in its opposition to God; "spirit" designates the total being (including the physical) as redeemed by God, in relation with Christ. (See the discussion on Romans 7:14, 19.)

The Greek says literally, "for destruction of the flesh"; the NIV rendering "so that the sinful nature may be destroyed" rightly catches Paul's "religious" use of the word *flesh.* The aim of the excommunication would then have been the destruction of the offender's "way of life." Surely he had grasped something of God's grace, experienced dimensions of Christ's love in the fellowship, witnessed the Spirit's transforming power in the lives of his brothers and sisters. Excluded from this sphere, might he not come to his senses (like the prodigal son)? Might he not come to the recognition that his immorality would only lead to death, but that the death of his immorality would lead to life?

Only in such an understanding is the concept "destruction of the flesh" an appropriate preliminary step to "salvation of his spirit." In this last phrase, "spirit" denotes the human being as regenerated by the Spirit of God, living "in the Spirit" or "according to the Spirit" (see Rom 8:5-11 RSV). As such, the one who had once again been claimed from the dominion of darkness, through the destruction of his "fleshly" orientation, would be saved "on the day of the Lord."

6:9-10 Who Inherits the Kingdom?

After reading 1 Corinthians 6:9-10, some people breathe a sigh of relief. They see that they are not included in this list of vices that disqualify from membership in the kingdom of God. Others read this list and even though they are not guilty of the major sexual sins and criminal activities listed, they recognize that they are sometimes dishonest, or want more things than they need, or have said things which hurt other people, or have an alcohol problem. Are they excluded from the kingdom? Still others reading this text who have misused the gift of sexual intimacy outside the boundaries of the covenant of marriage, or who find themselves overpowered by a homosexual orientation and its expression, hear in this text a harsh word of judgment and condemnation.

The question "Who inherits the kingdom?" becomes even more acute when we recognize that the list of sins enumerated here is only representative and not exhaustive. Paul catalogs several other vices that exclude people from kingdom membership. In Galatians 5:19-21, in addition to sexual immorality, idolatry and drunkenness (which are in the 1 Cor text), Paul lists the following: impurity, debauchery, witchcraft, hatred, discord, jealousy, fits of rage, selfish ambition, dissensions, factions, envy, orgies. He closes the list with these words: "Those who live like this will not inherit the kingdom of God."

The lists in Ephesians 5:3-5 and Colossians 3:5-9 share some of those already in the other two and add a few more: obscenity, foolish talk, coarse joking, evil desire, anger, malice, lying. The Ephesians list also speaks of disqualification from kingdom membership (Eph 5:5). In Colossians, Paul assigns these sins to the "earthly nature" (Col 3:5), the "old self" (Col 3:9), "the life you once lived" (Col 3:7), and tells them they must rid themselves of these (Col 3:8), for they have no place in the "new self" (Col 3:10) which "will appear with [Christ] in glory" (Col 3:4).

Once we have read all of Paul's lists, we become painfully aware that even those among us who breathed a sigh of relief after reading 1 Corinthians 6:9-10 are also tainted and, as such, disqualified from kingdom membership. And so we are tempted to ask, with Jesus' disciples, "Who then can be saved?" (Lk 18:26). We shall see that Paul's answer to this question is surely the same as Jesus' response to his disciples: "What is impossible with men is possible with God" (Lk 18:27).

In 1 Corinthians 5, Paul has addressed the presence of a particularly scandalous case of sexual immorality. After calling for action that could lead to the offender's salvation, Paul speaks about the nature of the Christian fellowship via elements from the Jewish Passover (1 Cor 5:6-8). The church is like the dough used for the Passover bread. Yeast, which in the Old Testament symbolizes evil, is to be removed so the dough can become uncontaminated, unleavened bread. So in the church a little yeast (for example, sexual immorality, a haughty spirit) contaminates the whole batch of dough (the church, 1 Cor 5:6). The church must remove the yeast so it can be a new batch without yeast, which, in a real sense, it already is (1 Cor 5:7).

We have here a typical example of Paul's understanding of both the church and individual believers as living in the tension between the "already" and the "not yet." The church is the present expression of the reign of God, the kingdom of God in the midst of the world; but it is still on the way, not yet identical with the kingdom of God at the end of history. Christians have been set free from the bondage to sin; yet they must appropriate that freedom in specific decisions to continually resist the encroachments of evil (see Rom 6).

In 1 Corinthians 6:8 Paul exposes another fragment of "yeast" that needs to be dealt with. The spectacle of church members taking each other to civil court underlines the "not-yet" dimension of the church. They cheat and wrong each other!

These evidences of unrighteousness among the Corinthian believers lead Paul to denounce all forms of evil as incompatible with the kingdom of God: "Do you not know that the wicked will not inherit the kingdom of God?" (1 Cor 6:9). Why not? Because by definition, the future kingdom of God is one of absolute righteousness, since the forces of evil have been overcome (see 1 Cor 15:24-28). In such a kingdom, the unrighteous will have no part.

As we saw in the discussion of 1 Corinthians 5:5, not only was Paul concerned about specific acts of immorality or conduct incompatible with our status as the community of the Spirit. He was also concerned with a religious view that disregarded practical morality and thus encouraged, perhaps even affirmed, immoral and unethical behavior. Toward that stance, Paul is emphatic: "Do not be deceived" (1 Cor 6:9 RSV). The Corinthians were deluding themselves into believing that God's moral demands did not need to be taken seriously. But to reject God's moral imperatives is to reject membership in God's kingdom (1 Cor 6:9-10).

Having laid the cards on the table so there could be no misunderstanding about the lofty goal of Christian life and faith (that is, a kingdom of perfect righteousness), Paul now reminds them of God's transforming intervention in their former lives of unrighteousness. "That is what some of you were" (1 Cor 6:11). Paul had founded the church several years earlier (1 Cor 4:15), and the faces of his converts, including the lives they had lived, may have flashed across his mind as he was penning the list of representative vices. "But you were washed, you were sanctified, you were justified in the name of the Lord Jesus Christ and by the Spirit of our God" (1 Cor 6:11).

Paul reminds them of what is possible when the broken and sin-scarred wrecks of human lives are yielded to God in faith and touched by his grace. They were the result of a miracle, redeemed sinners won from destructive ways of life by God's power. The image of having been "washed" surely recalled their baptism and reminded them of what the ritual symbolized: an inward cleansing brought about by God's forgiving love in Christ. Further, they were "sanctified." In this context the term does not have the more technical meaning, namely, that of moral-ethical growth toward perfection. Rather, it reminds them that through baptism they became part of the people of God, whom Paul called "saints." Finally, they are reminded that they were justified, called back into right relationship with God, on the basis of God's relation-restoring love in Christ.

On the ground of this action of God and their faith response in the past, Paul can speak of them in analogy to the Passover dough as really unleavened, free from evil. Yet, on the basis of their present reality, marred by acts and lifestyles of unrighteousness, he can call them to become what they are, to remove from their fellowship and their individual lives "the yeast of malice and wickedness" (1 Cor 5:8), to "flee from sexual immorality" (1 Cor 6:18), to honor God with their bodies (1 Cor 6:20). How is that possible? It is possible because their bodies are the dwelling places of the Spirit of God (1 Cor 6:19), who can continue to transform them toward conformity with the image of their creator (see also Col 3:10).

Who inherits the kingdom? All those whose lives have been scarred by one or more of the sins in the Pauline lists with which we began, whose scarred lives have been healed and cleansed by the grace of God, and who reject the continuing encroachments of sin, moving in the power of the Spirit toward the coming kingdom of the Lord.

Paul's words to the Christians in Ephesus, in the context of one of his catalogs of vices, are an apt summary for this chapter: "For you were once darkness, but now you are light in the Lord. Live as children of light. . . . Have nothing to do with the fruitless deeds of darkness" (Eph 5:8, 11).

See also comment on ROMANS 1:27.

7:1 Is It Good to Marry?

Paul's statement that "it is good for a man not to marry," at the beginning of a chapter in which he deals with issues of singleness, celibacy and marriage, as well as the appropriate place for the expression of sexuality, has raised numerous questions. This is so especially for those who take the Bible seriously as the ultimate authority for Christian life and faith.

If Paul is teaching that singleness and celibacy are superior expressions of Christian spirituality, then are all Christians who are married and choose to marry opting for an inferior lifestyle? How are Christian young people, in the process of making vocational and relational decisions about their future, to respond to Paul's words? Are they deciding against "the best" God has for them and for "the lesser good," namely, their physical-psychological needs, the passions of their flesh, if they decide to marry?

Yes would seem to be the obvious answer in light of both this text and others, such as in 1 Corinthians 7:7 ("I wish that all men were as I am"), 1 Corinthians 7:8 ("It is good for [the unmarried and widows] to stay unmarried, as I am") and 1 Corinthians 7:26 ("It is good for [virgins] to remain as you are").

Even if we are not to take Paul's apparent preference for celibacy as an expression of God's optimum will, the value and expression of physical, sexual intimacy seems to be viewed somewhat negatively, in light of statements such as 1 Corinthians 7:2 ("But since there is so much immorality, each man should have his own wife"), 1 Corinthians 7:5 ("Come together again so that Satan will not tempt you because of your lack of self-control") and 1 Corinthians 7:9 ("But if [the unmarried] cannot control themselves, they should marry").

If we are to deal fairly with this hard saying and the way in which Paul explores its implications in the rest of chapter 7, we need to take seriously some important principles for the interpretation of the Epistles. One of these is the recognition that the Epistles (and 1 Cor more so than perhaps any of the others) are occasional documents, written for specific situations in the life of Christian congregations. Thus, in the case of 1 Corinthians, in chapters 1—4 Paul is responding to concerns and problems that have been communicated to him orally, apparently by a church delegation. In chapter 7 he begins his response to matters that had been laid before him in a letter: "Now for the matters you wrote about" (1 Cor 7:1; see also 1 Cor 8:1; 12:1; 16:1). Though Paul does not explicitly tell us what they wrote, we have a good general idea about what the issues were for which they sought his advice or counsel.

A second principle of importance is the recognition of the particular historical or cultural or church context within which the needs or questions addressed by the apostle are located. Thus the pervasive sexual immorality in Corinthian society, which even spilled over into the church (Paul deals with it in 1 Cor 5—6), needs to be kept in mind when we read 1 Corinthians 7:1-24. Also to be remembered is the Corinthian Christians' view regarding the dichotomy between the spiritual and the physical, which led to various responses regarding human sexuality and resulted in a libertine view of sex ("anything goes!"). In 1 Corinthians 7, Paul seems to be responding to the "ascetic" implications of their negative views regarding the physical.

A third principle of significance for understanding this saying (as well as many other sayings dealt with in the following chapters of this book) is to recognize that the inspired, authoritative word of the apostle may be either *normative* for Christian life and faith generally, transcending all times and situations, or it may be *corrective,* intended to address a particular issue in a particular context, without necessarily intending to have universal application.

With these perspectives in mind, the issues Paul raises for us in 1 Corinthians 7:1 and several other hard sayings in 1 Corinthians 7:10, 12, 20 and 29 can be more easily understood.

The Greek sentence translated "It is good for a man not to marry" in the NIV and TEV is more literally translated "It is well for a man not to touch a woman," as in the NASB and RSV. The NIV gives this alternative reading in a footnote: "It is good for a man not to have sexual relations with a woman." That rendering recognizes that the term "to touch" is a biblical euphemism for sexual intimacy (see Gen 20:6; Prov 6:29). Since for Paul sexual intimacy and the covenant of marriage clearly belong together, the term "to touch a woman" can legitimately refer to marrying. The verses which follow strongly support such a meaning.

On the basis of the introductory phrase, "Now for the matters you wrote about," and several other places in the letter where Paul seems to be quoting slogans that the Corinthians waved in his face in support of their position (see 1 Cor 6:12-13 and 1 Cor 10:23), several modern translations suggest an alternative reading for 1 Corinthians 7:1: "A man does well not to marry" (TEV; see also the footnote rendering in the NEB, "It is a good thing for a man to have nothing to do with women"). Attributing the hard saying to the Corinthian position might lessen the problems raised at the outset, except for the fact that, if it is their slogan, Paul seems to cite it with at least restrained approval and certainly personalizes the sentiment in the same chapter (1 Cor 7:7, 8, 26).

What the slogan—whether a citation from the Corinthians' letter to Paul or Paul's summary of their views—clearly reveals is an attitude about marriage and sexual expression within it that advocates asceticism. The lofty (and haughty) spirituality of some believers in Corinth expressed itself—in relation to concrete, physical things—in the attitude "everything is permissible" (1 Cor 6:12). That same spirituality could also express itself in an ascetic attitude, the rejection of all physical, sensual aspects of life. That is apparently the view with which Paul does battle in most of chapter 7. Not only did some reject marriage as such as unworthy of "true spirituality"; some even rejected the expression of sexual desire within marriage. And for still others, divorce seemed to be desirable as a means for developing their spirituality apart from the sexual intimacy of marriage.

Within this larger context, then, Paul's personal preference for celibacy, and his equally strong affirmation of the goodness of marriage and of sexual intimacy within it, needs to be understood.

The affirmation "It is good for a man *not* to marry" does not necessarily or logically lead to the conclusion "It is *not* good for a man to marry." Paul affirms the value of singleness and the celibate state, but he does not devalue marriage and sex within it. This is shown in what follows, where he strongly qualifies the statement "It is good not to marry" and lifts up the purposes of marriage.

In 1 Corinthians 7:2-7, he affirms one of these good purposes: "Since there is so much immorality," normally people should marry. This conviction is grounded in Paul's view of created design and order, based on Genesis 1—2. God created the human species as male and female (Gen 1:26-27), with and for each other, in complementary polarity. Aloneness "is not good"; God creates the woman "corresponding to him" (Gen 2:18). Therefore the man and the woman are united in the covenant of marriage and become "one flesh" (Gen 2:24).

Paul recognizes this divinely created and ordained context for human intimacy and the expression of the sexual drive. In light of the pervasive sexual immorality (that is, sex outside the male-female covenant of marriage) in Corinth and even in the church (1 Cor 5—6), Paul affirms that one of the purposes of marriage is the legitimate expression of the God-given drive toward physical union. Sex in marriage is not to be rejected. Setting it aside should only be by mutual decision and for a limited period of time (1 Cor 7:5), not (by implication) because it is of no value or hurtful. God-given sexuality is a strong force. If it is not given its proper context for expression, it is in danger of spilling over into sexual immorality (1 Cor 7:5).

For Paul, the temporary setting aside of sexual intimacy in marriage is "a concession, not a command" (1 Cor 7:6). The norm in marriage is the mutual right of the partners to each other in physical union. The concession (a limited time of abstinence for the purpose of prayer) seems to be for the sake of the Corinthian ascetics, who probably wanted to abstain totally.

Paul concludes this carefully balanced discussion by affirming that his own celibacy, which he has experienced as a great good and therefore wished for others also, is a gift from God (1 Cor 7:7). This gift provides singleness of purpose in the service of Christ (1 Cor 7:8-9, 32-35). Those who are not gifted in this way have other gifts which they should exercise.

The latter part of the chapter (1 Cor 7:25-35) makes clear that Paul's preference for celibacy and his wish that others follow his example is strongly grounded in the early church's expectation that the reign of God—which had broken into this present age in Jesus' life, death and resurrection—would soon be consummated, perhaps even in their lifetime (1 Cor 7:26, "because of the present crisis"; 1 Cor 7:29, "the time is short"; 1 Cor 7:31, "this world in its present form is passing away"). In light of this brevity of time, Paul is concerned that Christians who have the opportunity—because they are not yet, or no longer, married—be involved in the work of the Lord, spreading the good news (1 Cor 7:32, 35). This eschatological urgency helps to explain Paul's passionate commitment regarding the value of celibacy, while at the same time strongly arguing against the Corinthian ascetics in behalf of marriage and the expression of God-intended sexual intimacy within it.

See also comment on MATTHEW 19:12.

7:10, 12 Not I, but the Lord?

The distinction which Paul makes here between a command which has its origin in the Lord and instruction which he gives to the church has raised questions for many readers. If, in terms of authority, there is no proper distinction between a word from the Lord and Paul's opinion, why does Paul seem to distinguish so clearly between what the

Lord commands and what he himself has to say? If Paul intends to make a distinction between levels of authority, what are the implications of that distinction for the authority of the Gospels relative to Paul's letters? Do we need to scrutinize all of Paul's writings in light of Jesus' teaching in the Gospels and elevate those parts of his letters which are clearly corroborated by Jesus' teaching above those which are clearly the product of Paul's thought?

Beyond these questions regarding the authority of what Paul wrote is the more basic issue of Paul's apostolic authority. In several documents from his hand (including the Corinthian correspondence), his apostolic authority is a key concern. His sometimes harsh words to the schismatics at Corinth, as well as to the hyperspiritualists (1 Cor) and his opponents (2 Cor), seem to be grounded in a clear sense of apostolic authority, which he asserts and defends vigorously. What then does he mean to communicate by saying, "I say this (I, not the Lord)"?

Paul's understanding of his apostolic authority must be seen against the background of his Jewish heritage and in light of his experience of the risen Lord and his sense of divinely ordained vocation.

Within Judaism, rabbinic authority was grounded in the God-given Torah. Those learned in the law received, interpreted and passed on the authoritative tradition because they sat "in Moses' seat" (Mt 23:2). Their authority as teachers of the law was a derived authority, but it was nonetheless binding because it was understood to be in continuity with the primary authority.

Just as Paul once was a student of the rabbis and was "extremely zealous for the traditions" of his fathers (Gal 1:14)—who derived their authority from Moses, and therefore from the God who gave his law to Moses—so he now could pronounce a curse on anyone who preached any gospel other than the one he preached and the Galatians had accepted (Gal 1:8-9). Why? Because the gospel which he preached was not of human origin; rather it had its origin in the Lord (Gal 1:11-12). Thus not only Paul's gospel, but the teaching derived from it, is rooted in the authority of Christ. Therefore Paul's instruction to churches and individuals is to be received, not as merely human words, but as the word of God (1 Thess 2:13).

Further, Paul stands within the chain of "receiving" and "passing on" the authoritative tradition (see 1 Cor 11:2, 23; 15:1-3). He knows that he has been grasped by Christ (Phil 3:12), that he is a recipient of Christ's authoritative revelation (1 Cor 15:9-11) and that he is called to be an apostle not through human instrumentality, but by direct divine intervention (Gal 1:1). Though it is doubtful that the word *apostolos* had in this early period the later technical sense of "office" (occupied by the Twelve plus Paul), its primary meaning, "one sent," certainly involved for Paul the authority of the Sender (see Rom 1:1; 1 Cor 1:1).

Paul is endowed with the authority of the Sender, and his message and preaching are a demonstration of the power of God's Spirit (1 Cor 2:4). He is God's Sent One *(apostolos),* and his instruction to excommunicate an offender is accompanied by "the power of our Lord Jesus" (1 Cor 5:4).

In light of his self-understanding of apostolic authority, it is very improbable that Paul's words in 1 Corinthians 7:10 and 12 indicate a lessening of that sense of authority.

Throughout this chapter Paul frequently adopts a pastoral role, giving advice and counsel. He expresses the wish that others were as he is (1 Cor 7:7). He lays options before them and calls on them to make responsible choices (1 Cor 7:8-9, 28, 36-38). He gives instruction for a course of action in light of his concern for them (1 Cor 7:32-35). When Paul speaks in this mode, it is quite clear that he is not demanding obedience; yet he makes it also quite clear that he does not simply express neutral human opinion. His opinion does have behind it "the Spirit of God" (1 Cor 7:40), and he does want them to know that he is trustworthy as one guided by the Lord's mercy (1 Cor 7:25).

However, the instruction which follows the words "I say this (I, not the Lord)" is surely an application—in a new situation—of the instruction which follows the words "I give this command (not I, but the Lord)." The distinction Paul makes is simply this: in the matter of divorce and remarriage, Paul is in possession of a direct command of the Lord. It can hardly be doubted that his instruction in 1 Corinthians 7:10-11 is based on the teaching of Jesus preserved for us in Mark 10:2-12. But for the question of what is to be done when a believer is married to a nonbeliever, Paul was not in possession of a direct teaching from Jesus. Jesus did not address this issue during his ministry. Thus, after appealing to the direct teaching of Jesus regarding the sanctity and permanence of marriage as intended by the Creator, Paul goes on, after simply acknowledging that he does not have another direct word from the Lord, to apply the implications of that divine intention to the complex situation of marriages between believers and unbelievers. The thrust of the passage makes it difficult, if not impossible, to assume that Paul intended his words to convey a lessened sense of authority.

7:17, 20 Remain in Slavery?

The difficulty with which 1 Corinthians 7:17 and 20 present us arises primarily from the surrounding verses in the paragraph (1 Cor 7:17-24). In 1 Corinthians 7:21 the situation chosen as an illustration is that of slavery. In 1 Corinthians 7:17 the various situations in which persons found themselves when they were called to faith in Christ are understood as assigned or apportioned by the Lord, and they are told to remain in those situations. That instruction is given further weight in the sentence "This is the rule I lay down in all the churches" (1 Cor 7:17).

In light of these statements, Paul has often been charged not only with failure to condemn the evil system of slavery, but indeed with abetting the status quo. These charges can be demonstrated to be invalid when the paragraph which contains this text is seen within the total context of 1 Corinthians 7 and in light of the historical situation as Paul perceived it.

In 1 Corinthians 7 Paul is dealing with questions about marriage, the appropriate place for sexual expression, the issue of divorce and remarriage, all in response to a pervasive view in the church which rejected or demeaned the physical dimension of male-female relationships. In the immediately preceding paragraph (1 Cor 7:12-16), Paul's counsel to believers who are married to unbelievers is twofold: (1) If the unbelieving partner is willing to remain in the marriage, the believer should not divorce (and thus reject) the unbelieving partner; for that person's willingness to live with the believer may open him or her to the sanctifying power of God's grace through the believing partner (1 Cor 7:12-14). (2) If the unbeliever does not want to remain in the union, he or she should be released from the marriage. Though the partner may be sanctified through the life and witness of the believer, there is no certainty, especially when the unbeliever desires separation (1 Cor 7:15-16).

Having recognized the possibility, and perhaps desirability, of this exception to his general counsel against divorce, Paul reaffirms what he considers to be the norm ("the rule I lay down in all the churches"): that one should remain in the life situation the Lord has assigned and in which one has been called to faith (1 Cor 7:17). In light of exceptions to general norms throughout this chapter, it is probably unwise to take the phrase "the place in life that the Lord has assigned" too literally and legalistically, as if each person's social or economic or marital status had been predetermined by God. Rather, Paul's view seems to be similar to the one Jesus takes with regard to the situation of the blind man in John 9. His disciples inquire after causes: Is the man blind because he sinned or because his parents sinned (Jn 9:2)? Jesus' response is essentially that the man's blindness is, within the overall purposes of God, an occasion for the work of God to be displayed (Jn 9:3).

For Paul, the life situations in which persons are encountered by God's grace and come to faith are situations which, in God's providence, can be transformed and through which the gospel can influence others (such as unbelieving partners).

The principle "remain in the situation" is now given broader application to human realities and situations beyond marriage. The one addressed first is that of Jews and Gentiles (1 Cor 7:18-19). The outward circumstances, Paul argues, are of little or no significance ("Circumcision is nothing and uncircumcision is nothing"). They neither add to nor detract from one's calling into a relationship with God, and therefore one's status as Jew or Gentile should not be altered. (It should be noted here that under the pressure of Hellenization, some Jews in the Greek world sought to undo their circumcision [1 Maccabees 1:15]. And we know from both Acts and Galatians that Jewish Christians called for the circumcision of Gentile Christians.)

Once again, it is clear that the general norm, "remain in the situation," is not an absolute law. Thus we read in Acts 16:3 that Paul, in light of missionary needs and strategy, had Timothy circumcised even though Timothy was already a believer. Paul's practice in this case would be a direct violation of the rule which he laid down for all the churches (1 Cor 7:17-18), but only if that rule had been *intended as an absolute.*

Paul now repeats the rule "Each one should remain in the situation which he was in when God called him" (1 Cor 7:20), and applies it to yet another situation, namely, that of the slave. Paul does not simply grab a hypothetical situation, for the early church drew a significant number of persons from the lower strata of society (see 1 Cor 1:26-27). So Paul addresses individuals in the congregation who were of the large class of slaves existing throughout the ancient world: "Were you a slave when you were called?" (that is, when you became a Christian). The next words, "Do not let it trouble you," affirm that the authenticity of the person's new life and new status as the Lord's "freedman" (1 Cor 7:21-22) cannot be demeaned and devalued by external circumstances such as social status.

As in the previous applications of the norm ("remain in the situation"), Paul immediately allows for a breaking of the norm; indeed, he seems to encourage it: "although if you can gain your freedom, do so" (1 Cor 7:21; note the RSV rendering: "avail yourself of the opportunity"). As footnotes in some contemporary translations indicate (TEV, RSV), it is possible to translate the Greek of verse 21 as "make use of your present condition instead," meaning that the slave should not take advantage of this opportunity, but rather live as a transformed person within the context of continuing slavery. Some scholars support this rendering, since it would clearly illustrate the norm laid down in the previous verse. However, we have already noted that Paul provides contingencies for much of his instruction in chapter 7, and there is no good reason to doubt that Paul supported the various means for emancipation of individual slaves that were available in the Greco-Roman world.

And yet, Paul's emphasis in the entire chapter, as in the present passage, is his conviction that the most critical issue in human life and relations and institutions is the transformation of persons' lives by God's calling. External circumstances can neither take away from, nor add to, this reality. The instruction to remain in the situation in which one is called to faith (which Paul repeats several more times, in 1 Cor 7:24, 26, 40, and for which he also grants contingencies, in 1 Cor 7:28, 36, 38) can be understood as a missiological principle. To remain in the various situations addressed by Paul provides opportunity for unhindered devotion and service to the Lord (1 Cor 7:32-35), or transforming witness toward an unbelieving marriage partner (1 Cor 7:12-16), or a new way of being present in the context of slavery as one who is free in Christ (1 Cor 7:22-23).

The transforming possibilities of this latter situation are hinted at elsewhere in Paul's writings. Masters who have become believers are called on to deal with their slaves in kindness and to remember that the Master who is over them both sees both as equals (Eph 6:9). The seeds of the liberating gospel are gently sown into the tough soil of slavery. They bore fruit in the lives of Onesimus, the runaway slave, and Philemon, his master. The slave returns to the master, no longer slave but "brother in the Lord" (Philem 15-16).

Note too that the three relational spheres which Paul addresses in 1 Corinthians 7—male-female, Jew-Gentile (Greek), slave-free—are brought together in that high-water mark of Paul's understanding of the transforming reality of being in Christ: "There is neither Jew nor Greek, slave nor free, male nor female, for you are all one in Christ Jesus" (Gal 3:28). As a rabbi, Paul had given thanks daily, as part of the eighteen benedictions to God, that he had not been born as a Gentile, a slave or a woman. It was his experience of Christ that led him to recognize that these distinctions of superior and inferior were abolished in the new order of things inaugurated in Christ. Surely in this vision the seeds were sown for the ultimate destruction of slavery and all other forms of bondage.

Finally, Paul's understanding of the historical situation in which he and the church found themselves provides another key for his instruction that believers should remain where they are. He, together with most other Christians, was convinced that the eschaton, the climax of God's redemptive intervention, was very near. Statements in 1 Cor 7:26 ("because of the present crisis") and 1 Cor 7:29 ("the time is short") underline that conviction. This belief created a tremendous missionary urgency. The good news had to get out so that as many as possible could yet be saved (see 1 Cor 10:33). This expectation of the imminent end was surely an important factor for the Pauline norm "remain where you are."

See also comment on EXODUS 21:2-11; EPHESIANS 6:5-8.

7:29 Live as Though You Had No Spouse?

What does Paul mean? How can one live

with one's spouse "as if" one had none? And why should we have to or want to? How and why is "shortness of time" a factor in favor of living "as if"?

In the preceding paragraph (1 Cor 7:25-28), Paul has just counseled single persons, in view of "the present crisis," to remain single (1 Cor 7:26). Should they, however, decide to marry, they would not be sinning. Yet, as married persons, they would "face many troubles in this life," and he wants to spare them this difficult time (1 Cor 7:28).

This reference to difficult experiences is most likely connected with the earlier mention of a "present crisis" (1 Cor 7:26), as well as with the reference to "the time is short" (1 Cor 7:29). An understanding of the image-world behind these cryptic phrases is imperative if we are to follow Paul's reasoning.

Early Christianity, in continuity with Jesus' teaching about the inbreaking of the kingdom of God and its future consummation, was heir to Jewish understandings of the present and expectations about the future. Their understanding is known as apocalyptic eschatology. The word *eschatology* comes from the Greek words for "last" and "word," and means "teaching about the end." The word *apocalyptic* comes from the Greek word *apokalyptō,* which means "to reveal." Its noun form is *apokalypsis* ("revelation").

Apocalyptic eschatology, as a particular way of understanding the present and envisioning the future, arose in Judaism during the last three centries B.C. The canonical book of Daniel is its earliest literary expression, which was followed by a host of apocalypses, literary works published in the names of worthy figures in Israel's past, which sought to "reveal" the meaning of Israel's present experience of bondage, deprivation and evil in light of God's purposes. Some of these apocalyptic works were part of the Greek translation of the Hebrew Scriptures, read by Diaspora Jews (that is, Jews living outside Palestine) and later Gentile and Jewish Christians.

The main features of the worldview of these visionaries within Israel are the following: (1) the belief that this present age was largely under the control of evil powers; (2) the conviction that the suffering of God's faithful people in this present evil age was a necessary part of the outworking of a divine plan; (3) the certainty that history was quickly moving toward its climax and that the time immediately prior to the cataclysmic destruction of this world and the creation of a new one would be a time of intense tribulation and crisis; (4) the participation, in the outworking of God's purposes, of a transcendent figure seen as one like a man, or the Son of Man; (5) the belief that the day of the Lord, the day of his victory over the powers of evil, would be accompanied by the resurrection of the dead (or at least of the righteous dead).

It is clear from the Gospels that Jesus taught and carried on his ministry in light of this Jewish apocalyptic understanding. The battle with evil powers was signaled in his exorcism of demons and interpreted in parables, such as the one about the strong man, whose realm is invaded by one stronger than he (Lk 11:17-22). Satan's power over this present age is breaking (Lk 10:18); the "prince of this world" shall now be cast out (Jn 12:31). Jesus is the apocalyptic Son of Man in whom the reign of God is already breaking into this age, and who will come again to gather his righteous ones (Lk 13:27), raise the dead (Jn 5:28-29) and exercise judgment (Mt 25:31-32). The Olivet discourse, Jesus' teaching about the crisis of the present and the judgment to come (Mk 13; Mt 24—25; Lk 21), conveys a sense of urgency and imminence. And Matthew's account of the signs accompanying Jesus' crucifixion (darkness, earthquake, raisings of the dead—Mt 27:45, 51-53) surely communicates the conviction that this event signaled the coming of the last days.

On the basis of Jesus' life and teaching, his death and resurrection, and the experience of the outpouring of the Spirit at Pentecost (which was perceived as an evidence that the last days had come—Acts 2:14-21), the early church lived under the intense conviction that the final chapter of the scroll of history was being unrolled.

Paul shared this conviction. In his correspondence with the Christians in Thessalonica, he expresses his hope regarding the nearness of the Lord's return (1 Thess 4:13-14) but also reminds them that his return will be preceded by a time of tribulation, the evidence of evil's last struggle to retain control of the world (2 Thess 2). In the cross, the principalities and powers are defeated (Col 2:15). Jesus' resurrection is the downpayment, the first fruits, of the resurrection to come (1 Cor 15:2-23). And because the era of resurrection has already been inaugurated, believers are those who have been transferred from the dominion of darkness into the kingdom of his beloved Son (Col 1:13); they are those on whom the end of the ages has come (1 Cor 10:11). At the same time, believers are participants in the final end-time struggle against the powers of evil (Eph 6:10-18).

Against the background of this worldview and within the context of these convictions about living in the last days, Paul's language about "the present crisis" and "the time is short" must be understood. His counsel to the various groups addressed in 1 Corinthians 7 "to remain" in their present relational and institutional contexts, and in those contexts to "live in a right way in undivided devotion to the Lord" (1 Cor 7:35), is eminently appropriate. Life can no longer be lived in its normal, ordinary way, "for this world in its present form is passing away" (1 Cor 7:31).

This conviction about the transitional nature of the present determines Paul's thinking about the various arenas of life in 1 Corinthians 7:29-31. Christians are "new creations" (2 Cor 5:17), and even though they are still living in this world they are no longer of this world (see Jn 17:15-16), but already part of a new order ("the old has gone, the new has come," 2 Cor 5:17). Therefore, "from now on those who have wives should live as if they had none." This statement is followed by four more "as if" contrasts, representative of various areas of life and work and relationships. The point Paul makes is simply that all of life—in light of the fact that Christians are already people of the new creation and that the old order is therefore no longer determinative—must be lived in a new key.

In contrast to the Corinthian spiritualists who wanted to reject marriage, Paul affirms it, but the values and priorities of persons living in this and other human institutions must be kingdom values. There is a higher loyalty than even that to one another in the covenant of marriage. The ordinary structures and expectations which are part of this present order of things—such as the use of power and status to subject others, whether in marriage or social arrangements like slavery—are no longer valid and determinative. Christians are members of a new order while still living in the final days of the old order. And so they should live "as if" the new order had already arrived. And in that new order, even divinely ordained institutions like marriage will be radically transformed.

8:5-6 Many Gods and Lords?

Paul expresses a number of ideas in

1 Corinthians 8:5-6 which, at least on the surface, create some inner tension or dissonance. Though he clearly states that "there is but one God," a phrase that reaffirms what he has already said in the previous verse ("we know . . . that there is no God but one"), that conviction seems to be qualified by the phrase "for us." Is Paul admitting the existence of divine beings "for others"? A second, corresponding problem is created by Paul's concessive statement "even if there are so-called gods" and the apparent qualification which follows: "as indeed there are many 'gods' and 'lords.' "

These difficulties can be solved once we understand the problem which Paul addresses, the situation in Corinth and Paul's general Jewish-Christian worldview.

In 1 Corinthians 8—10 Paul is apparently addressing a second problem the church had laid before him in their letter (the first one was addressed in chapter 7; see discussions on that chapter). The question was: Is it permissible for Christians to eat food that has been offered to idols (1 Cor 8:1, 4, 7, 10; 10:14-30)? In light of practices in the pagan world, that question arose in at least three settings. Animals which were sacrificed to pagan divinities at the various temples and shrines were not wholly consumed in the sacrificial flames; often only certain organs were actually offered. The meat not consumed was sold by the priests to merchants, who resold it to the populace in the meat markets (1 Cor 10:25). The heathen called such meat "sacrificed for sacred purposes" (see 1 Cor 10:28), while Jews and Christians, recognizing idols as the work of human hands (Is 40:18-20), called it "idol-meat" (see 1 Cor 8:1, 4; 10:19).

In addition to public sacrifices in the temples, there were also sacrificial rituals performed in private homes. Food remaining from such events was then consumed at regular meals. Would Christians invited by their pagan friends or neighbors be contaminated by such food (1 Cor 10:27-28)? Sometimes banquets were held by individuals or associations in temple courts, and Christians could be invited (1 Cor 8:10). Since such meals were associated with the god or gods worshiped in these temples, the question of pagan defilement was very acute, not only for Jewish Christians, but for Gentile Christians who were "still so accustomed to idols that when they eat such food they think of it as having been sacrificed to an idol" (1 Cor 8:7).

Within this context the words of Paul in 1 Corinthians 8:5-6 are to be understood. He affirms, in concert with those believers in Corinth who had arrived at true knowledge, a deeply held and central belief of his Jewish heritage: "There is no God but one"; and because this is the ultimate truth (see Deut 6:4; Is 44:8; 45:5), "an idol is nothing at all in the world" (1 Cor 8:4). From the perspective of both Jewish and Christian convictions (Deut 4:15-19; Is 40:18-19; Acts 17:29; Rom 1:18-19), idols represent no god; they represent nothing at all. That means therefore (at least on the level of true knowledge) that food offered to idols is in essence neutral.

Paul also recognizes, however, that human actions and thoughts and habits are often shaped and determined more by "perceived reality" than by "true reality," more by humanly created superstitions than by divine revelations. It is this recognition which stands behind the words about "so-called gods" and "gods and lords."

The words "so-called gods" appear one other time in the New Testament (in 2 Thess 2:4, though "god" is in the singular here), where Paul speaks of "the man of lawlessness" who "will exalt himself over everything that is called God or is worshiped," prior to the coming of the Lord. In both cases, Paul simply recognizes that the pagan world is involved in the belief in, and worship of, gods. Temples to the various Roman and Greek gods in Corinth were ample testimony to this reality. In neighboring Athens, according to Acts 17, Paul addressed the Athenians as "very religious," for he found there many "objects of worship," including an altar "to an unknown god."

Yet, while recognizing this pervasive reality in the pagan world, Paul emphatically qualifies it by claiming that these are only "called" gods. In other words, whatever the degree of reality or unreality assigned to these "objects of worship," what Christians mean by "God" when they speak of the God of Israel and the Father of our Lord Jesus Christ cannot be claimed for these pagan idols.

Having acknowledged the pagan perception concerning the terrestrial and heavenly worlds as peopled by a host of divinities, and having qualified these as "so-called gods," Paul goes on to acknowledge that even though what pagans worship cannot be called "God," there is a reality that claims pagan allegiance and dominates their lives. The statement "there are [indeed] many 'gods' and many 'lords,' " (1 Cor 8:5) could be interpreted as a further acknowledgment of the spurious character of all those supposed beings whom the pagans defined as both "gods" and "lords." That interpretation would certainly seem to be confirmed by the next sentence, where the claim "yet for us there is but one God . . . and but one Lord" represents the direct Christian counterclaim.

Without setting this view aside, it is also possible that we see in the phrase "as indeed there are many 'gods' and many 'lords,' " a reflection of the Jewish and early Christian view of the world as populated by superterrestrial (not divine!) powers, angels, demons, largely opposed to God's purposes, enslaving humans and leading them into idolatry. In 2 Corinthians 4:4 Paul speaks of the head of this host of spiritual powers as "the god of this world [who] has blinded the minds of unbelievers." In Colossians 1:16 and Ephesians 1:21 Christ is pictured as above all "authority," and in Ephesians 6:10-11 Christians are seen as those who are engaged in spiritual struggle with powers that are clearly superterrestrial. It is also clear that Paul acknowledged the existence of angelic beings (1 Cor 4:9; 6:3), but just as clearly denounced the worship of such beings (Col 2:18).

In light of this larger view of reality, we can understand why Paul, in the continuation of the discussion about "meat offered to idols" in 1 Corinthians 10, maintains that though idols are not real (1 Cor 10:19), what pagans sacrifice to them they are actually, unwittingly, offering to demons. The point seems to be that the evil spirit-powers called demons use the pagans' idolatrous practices to separate the creature from the Creator.

For Paul, there is but one God, the Father, and one Lord, Jesus Christ (1 Cor 8:6). The designations "gods" and "lords" for the objects of pagan worship are false and inappropriate. What Christians are to be concerned about, however, are forces and powers of evil against which they must stand "strong in the Lord and in his mighty power" (Eph 6:10).

8:1-13 To Eat or Not to Eat?

See comment on ROMANS 14:15.

10:8 Twenty-three Thousand or Twenty-four Thousand?

In the warning of 1 Corinthians 10:8 we notice that the main point is that Christians should not commit immorality. Yet the number surprises us when we look at Numbers 25:9: "But those who died in the plague numbered 24,000." Which text is correct? Why did Paul use one number if the book of Numbers has another?

In some situations of this type the solution is easy: the New Testament is citing the Greek version of the Old Testament, while the Hebrew version, the basis of English Bibles, reads differently. In this case that is not the solution. All of the various versions of the Old Testament and all known Jewish traditions agree that 24,000 is the correct number. How could Paul have gotten a different number?

Some apologists have resorted to speculation. One theory says that while the total number who died was 24,000, the number that died "in one day" was only 23,000. Another theory argues that the true number was 23,500, and while Numbers rounded it up, Paul rounded it down. The truth is that both of these ideas are pure speculation. No Jewish tradition contains either of these ideas, nor does Paul give any explanation in this verse that would lead us to believe that he is doing one of these things. While either of these theories *could* be true, only special divine revelation could have revealed them as truth to Paul, and Paul does not claim such special revelation in this passage.

It is difficult to explain exactly what happened. The one place where 23,000 appears in the Old Testament is Numbers 26:62 (the number of the male Levites a month old or more). It is possible that Paul, citing the Old Testament from memory as he wrote to the Corinthians, referred to the incident in Numbers 25:9, but his mind slipped a chapter later in picking up the number. Paul dictated his letters, and if he had written copies of the Old Testament to check, which he often did not, they would have been scrolls and thus awkward to use. It is unlikely that he would unroll one to check a number in a passage. It is certainly not because 23,000 was meaningful that Paul chose it, for it is 24,000 that is a multiple of 12 and which appears in other places in the Old Testament (for example, multiple times in 1 Chron 27). Of course we cannot rule out the possibility that there was some reference to 23 or 23,000 in his local environment as he was writing and that caused a slip in his mind, although given that he was thinking about the Old Testament the explanation from Numbers 26:62 is the more likely.

What does this mean? In this passage in Corinthians Paul was not attempting to instruct people on Old Testament history and certainly not on the details of Old Testament history. What Paul is doing is using a known Old Testament text as an illustration. He assumes that his readers know the Old Testament text and will recognize the incident. Their knowledge that the Old Testament incident happened should then warn them that God might do something like it again, if they behave like Israel did. In regard to the point that Paul is making, there is no difference whether 10 individuals or 1,000 or 20,000 or 24,000 died. The point is that they committed immorality and they died, as the Corinthians may also die if they commit immorality.

Thus here we have a case in which Paul apparently makes a slip of the mind for some reason (unless he has special revelation he does not inform us about), but the mental error does not affect the teaching. How often have we heard preachers with written Bibles before them make similar errors of detail that in no way affected their message? If we notice it (and few usually do), we (hopefully) simply smile and focus on the real point being made. As noted above, Paul probably did not have a written Bible to check (although at times he apparently had access to scrolls of the Old Testament), but in the full swing of dictation he cited an example from memory and got a detail wrong. Since he is not writing an Old Testament commentary, the issue is not that he slipped, but whether or not we will take warning from his teaching and not presume on our baptism and participation in the Lord's Supper to save us from judgment should we fall into immorality like the ancient Israelites did. The issue is not the missing 1,000 from the Old Testament, but whether we will be counted among those judged by God in the New.

10:14-33 To Eat or Not to Eat?

See comment on ROMANS 14:15.

11:3 Head of Woman Is Man?

These words in 1 Corinthians 11:3 are easily part of one of the most difficult and debated passages in all of Paul's epistles. What, precisely, does he mean when he says that "man is the head of woman"? How are we to understand the assertion of 1 Corinthians 11:7, which follows the "head" passage, that man "is the image and glory of God; but the woman is the glory of man"? And finally, who are "the angels" in 11:10, due to whom "the woman ought to have a sign of authority on her head"?

These sayings, because they appear in the same immediate context (1 Cor 11:2-16) are closely tied to one another; thus in my interpretation I shall occasionally need to refer to matter treated in one or both of the other sayings.

In 1 Corinthians 11:3 the often-heated debate centers on the meaning of the word *head* (a literal rendering of the Greek *kephalē*). For most English readers of the text, the common figurative sense of "head" as ruler, leader, chief, boss, director suggests itself almost immediately. Such an understanding of "head" as connoting "authority over" leads to an interpretation of this text (and of Eph 5:22-23) as Paul's teaching about hierarchical order in the relation between men and women. Some who stand within this interpretive tradition go so far as to posit a "chain of command," where authority is passed along: from God to Christ to man to woman.

While the NIV, RSV, NASB and NEB are cautious in their translation, rendering the Greek *kephalē* with its literal English equivalent "head," other contemporary versions opt for a figurative meaning. Thus the TEV renders *kephalē* with "supreme over." The LB's paraphrase becomes even more interpretive when it renders the text: "a wife is responsible to her husband, her husband is responsible to Christ, and Christ is responsible to God."

Even when such explicit interpretations of the term *kephalē* are not employed, the literal "head," as in the NIV, implicitly suggests an interpretation along the same lines because of the common understanding of "head" in English when applied to persons in relationships such as marriage or other institutions. Common phrases like "she is head of the division" or "he is the head of his family" illustrate this everyday metaphorical meaning of "head" in our language.

Apart from the question whether this common English meaning is also the common Greek meaning of "head" when used figuratively, serious issues are raised by such an interpretation. How are we to see the relation between Christ and God? If God occupies a rank superior to Christ, then we have here a revival of the ancient heresy of "subordinationism" and a challenge to the classical doctrine of the Trinity.

Further, if husbands (or men; the Greek word is the same) are under the authority of Christ, and wives (or women; the same Greek word) are under the authority of husbands/men, do we then not have a situation where women stand only in indirect relation to Christ, via their husbands? Such a conclusion is in fact reached by some when they understand the series (God - Christ - Man - Woman) as indicating a "growing distance from God," or by others who extend the "chain of command" to children (on the basis of Eph 5:21—6:4) and maintain that the woman's authority over her children is a "derived" authority; that is, she exercises that authority "on behalf of" her husband.

The core issue in our attempt to grasp Paul's instruction is this: what meaning, or meanings, did the word *kephalē* have in the common Greek language of the New Testament period? How would Greek-speaking Christians in Corinth have heard Paul when he used *kephalē?* And how did this help them understand Paul's instructions concerning appropriate decorum in their public worship (1 Cor 11:4-16)? To answer these questions attention will be given to linguistic data, Paul's use of *kephalē* elsewhere in his epistles, and the thrust of his argument in 1 Corinthians 11:2-16.

The linguistic evidence points strongly, if not overwhelmingly, away from the common reading of *head* as "chief," "ruler," "authority over," though there are many conservative scholars who would challenge this. The most exhaustive Greek-English Lexicon covering Greek literature from about 900 B.C. to A.D. 600, among numerous metaphorical meanings for *kephalē* does not give a single definition to indicate that in ordinary Greek usage it included the meaning "superior rank" or "supreme over" or "leader" or "authority."

What is especially interesting in this lexicographic evidence is that in the 1897 eighth revised edition of this lexicon, the final entry under "metaphorical" meanings is "of persons, a chief."[1] But not a single citation from the literature is given to support or illustrate such a definition. Therefore, in light of the lack of evidence, that definition is not included in the later editions. However, among the range of meanings which *kephalē* had in ordinary Greek were "origin" or "source" or "starting point" and "crown" or "completion" or "consummation." As we shall see below, these meanings do far greater justice to the Pauline usages of *kephalē* than the "authority" nuances conveyed by the English "head."

Strong support for the linguistic evidence (that is, that the metaphorical range of meanings of *kephalē* did not normally include the ideas of "authority over" or "superior rank") comes from the Greek translation of the Hebrew Scriptures (commonly called the Septuagint) made between approximately 250-150 B.C. by a large group of Jewish scholars for the Jews living outside Palestine whose first, and sometimes only, language was Greek.

Like the English word "head" and the Greek word *kephalē*, the Hebrew word *rōʾš* has first of all the literal meaning "head of man or beast." But like English and Greek, it also has numerous figurative meanings. In an exhaustive study of how the Septuagint translators rendered the Hebrew word *rōʾš*,[2] the following data emerged. In the more than 200 times when it refers to a physical head, the translators almost always used *kephalē*. About 180 times, *rōʾš* clearly has the figurative meaning of "leader" or "chief" or "authority figure" of a group. There is thus a close similarity between the English "head" and the Hebrew *rōʾš*; figuratively, both frequently designate an authority figure.

When the translators, however, sought the appropriate Greek word to render this figurative meaning, they used not *kephalē* but *archōn* (and its derivatives) in the great majority of cases (138 times). *Archōn* means "ruler," "commander," "leader." Its derivatives include meanings such as "authority," "chief," "captain," "prince," "chief of tribe," "head of family." Most of the remaining occurrences of *rōʾš* (when it designates an authority figure) are translated by several other specific Greek words (such as *hegeomai,* "to have dominion over"). In only eight out of 180 cases was *kephalē* used to translate *rōʾš* when it designated the leader or ruler of a group. It is very possible that one of the figurative meanings of *kephalē* (namely, "top" or "crown") allowed the translator to use it in describing a prominent individual. It may also be that in these few cases one of the Septuagint translators simply used the literal equivalent for *rōʾš,* namely *kephalē* (since both mean "head"). This is in fact what happens all too frequently in any translation when it is too literal. The exact equivalent may, in fact, distort the meaning conveyed by the original in its own context.

It is clear from this data that the Greek translators were keenly aware that *kephalē* did not normally have a metaphorical meaning equivalent to that of *rōʾš.*

This linguistic evidence, which suggests that the idea of "authority over" was not native to the Greek *kephalē,* has led numerous scholars to see behind Paul's use of "head" either the meaning "source, origin" or "top, crown, completion."[3]

Another factor to take into consideration is that nowhere else in the New Testament is *kephalē* used to designate a figure of authority. If that had been a prominent meaning, it could have served well in numerous places in the Gospels where the head or master of a household appears; yet it is never used to convey this meaning (see, for example, Mt 10:25; 13:52; Lk 13:25; 14:21).

If the readers of Paul's Greek did not hear our "headship" concept in the word *kephalē,* but rather the idea of "source, origin," what did it convey to them, and how did that meaning in 11:3 lay the foundation for Paul's admonitions about appropriate hair length and decorum in public worship? Cyril of Alexandria, an important Greek-speaking leader of the church in the fourth century, commenting on this text wrote: "Thus we say that the *kephalē* of every man is Christ, because he was excellently made through him. And the *kephalē* of woman is man, because she was taken from his flesh. Likewise, the *kephalē* of Christ is God, because he is from him according to nature."[4]

This interpretation meets all the requirements of the passage and its context, and at the same time sheds light on several other of Paul's statements where both Christ and the man are designated as "head" of something or someone (Eph 1:15; 5:23; Col 1:15-20; 2:19). Paul, as other New Testament writers, affirms Christ as the one by whom all things were created (Jn 1:3; 1 Cor 8:6; Col 1:16). Thus Paul can say that Christ, as God's agent of creation, gave the first man, and thus every man, life ("Christ is the source of man's life"). Such a meaning is confirmed by the fact that in the same passage (1 Cor 11:7-9) he clearly has the creation narrative of Genesis 1—2 in mind. Though it is obvious that, in a final sense, Christ/God is also the source of the woman's life (1 Cor 11:12), Paul is here considering the sequence of creation of the human species in Genesis 2.

This temporal, sequential thought continues in the sentence "And the head of the woman is man" (that is, "the man is the source of woman's life"). According to Genesis 2:21-23 Adam is the origin of Eve's being. And it is precisely this Old Testament text which Paul has in mind (1 Cor 11:8, 12). That "source" is the appropriate meaning of *kephalē* in 1 Corinthians 11:3 is confirmed by Paul's "source" language in his appeal to Genesis 2.

Behind this temporal sequence stands God ("everything comes from God"; that is, God is the source of everything; see 1 Cor 8:6). Therefore, "the head of Christ is God" (that is, the source of Christ's being is God). Cyril of Alexandria said, "the *kephalē* of Christ is God because he is from him according to nature" (emphasis mine). Though Cyril's language reflects the later trinitarian discussion, his affirmation is solidly grounded in the New Testament. According to John 1:1-14, the Word, which was God and was with God, came forth and became flesh in the Incarnation. In John 8:42, 13:3 and 16:27 Jesus is said to have come from God.

It would therefore seem best to translate 1 Corinthians 11:3 as "I want you to understand that Christ is the source of man's being; the man is the source of woman's being; and God is the source of Christ's being." When read like this, it lays a solid foundation for, and sheds light on, the rest of the passage (1 Cor 11:4-16), in which the next two hard sayings are located.

See also comment on GENESIS 2:18; 1 CORINTHIANS 11:7; 11:10.

[1]Henry George Liddell and Robert Scott, *A Greek-English Lexicon,* 2 vols., rev. H. S. Jones and R. McKenzie (Oxford: Clarendon Press, 1940), 1:944-45.

[2]Berkeley and Alvera Mickelsen, "What Does *Kephalē* Mean in the New Testament?" in *Women, Authority and the Bible,* ed. Alvera Mickelsen (Downers Grove, Ill.: InterVarsity Press, 1986), pp. 97-110.

[3]See, for example, Stephen Bedale, "The Meaning of *Kephalē* in the Pauline Epistles," *Journal of Theological Studies* n.s. 5 (1954): 211-15; C. K. Barrett, *The First Epistle to the Corinthians* (New York: Harper & Row, 1968); H. N. Ridderbos, *Paul: An Outline of Theology,* trans. J. Richard deWitt (Grand Rapids, Mich.: Eerdmans, 1975), pp. 379-82; S. Scott Bartchy, "Power, Submission, and Sexual Identity Among the Early Christians," in *Essays on New Testament Christianity,* ed. C. R. Wetzel (Cincinnati: Standard Publishing, 1978), pp. 50-80.

[4]G. W. Lampe, *A Patristic Greek Lexicon* (Oxford: Oxford University Press, 1968), p. 749.

11:7 Woman the Glory of Man?

Once again Paul seems to put women one step further removed from God than men. Why is man said to be the glory of God, while woman is the glory of man? Why are women not also said to be the glory of God? And does the fact that God's image is affirmed for man, but not for woman, mean that only the male half of the species is made in God's image? And what does covering of one's head (with a veil or one's hair) have to do with being or reflecting someone's glory?

In 1 Corinthians 8—10, Paul has been dealing with the issue of Christian liberty in light of true knowledge ("correct beliefs"), caring love for one's fellow believers, and concern for living and acting in ways which "build up" others or the church. That is, Christian freedom with respect to externals—to rules and regulations, to forms of ritual and ceremony—is not an absolute freedom. Christian freedom, based on the liberating grace of God, is freedom for the other, for the other's good, for the growth of the fellowship in love and faith and hope.

Paul sums up this discussion with these words: "whatever you do, do it all for the glory of God" (1 Cor 10:31). How do we live and act for the glory of God? By not causing "anyone to stumble, whether Jews, Greeks or the church of God. . . . For I am not seeking my own good but the good of many, so that they may be saved" (10:32-33). Both with respect to the outside world and the fellowship, this principle of Christian behavior is the source for Paul's specific instructions which follow.

Concerns about propriety with regard to appearance in the context of public worship are addressed first (1 Cor 11:2-16). This is followed by a severe criticism of their misunderstanding of the nature of the Lord's Supper and its consequence in their actions (1 Cor 11:17-34). Finally, Paul addresses the use and misuse of the gifts of the Spirit (1 Cor 12:1—14:40). In each of these situations, the principle for Christian action laid down in 1 Corinthians 10:31-33 must be kept in mind.

What precisely is the problem regarding proper appearance for worship in 1 Corinthians 11:2-16? As frequently is the case in this "occasional" letter, we must make deductions from Paul's answers. From 1 Corinthians 11:4-5 we may assume that social, cultural or ritual norms were being ignored or deliberately set aside in the context of worship. It is possible that their libertine enthusiasm, which had led them to a demeaning or total rejection of male-female sexuality and distinctions (see 1 Cor 7), had also led them to reject other cultural and religious norms. Thus, perhaps in a deliberate attempt to wipe out distinctions, some men may have worn a head covering in worship (1 Cor 11:4), while some women rejected the covering prescribed for them by cultural or religious conventions (1 Cor 11:5).

Though the Greek word for "veil" does not appear in this text (and therefore some commentators have argued that Paul is here speaking only of hair as a covering), it is best to understand the phrase "having [something] down from the head" (1 Cor 11:4) to refer to a head covering that concealed the hair and shoulders. First Corinthians 11:6 seems to confirm this sense, where "not covering the head" is likened to shaving or cutting the hair short. The sense seems to be that "if you are not going to cover (veil) your head, you might as well cut off your hair; it amounts to the same thing!"

Why does a man who prays and prophesies with his head *covered* dishonor his head (1 Cor 11:4), while a woman who prays and prophesies with her head *uncovered* dishonor her head (1 Cor 11:5-6)? The answer to this question is cryptically given in the hard saying in 1 Corinthians 11:7. But in order to understand that answer, the problem of honoring and dishonoring the head needs some unraveling.

The first uses of "head" in these sentences ("with his head covered" and "with her head uncovered") are obviously references to their physical heads. Does "head" in the phrases "dishonor his/her head" refer also to their physical heads or to their figurative heads given in 1 Corinthians 11:3 (Christ, of the man; the man, of the woman)? Commentators are fairly divided, with some holding that both meanings may be intended.

In either or both cases, dishonor is the result. When a man wears a covering on his head, it is as if he wore long hair; but long hair on men is against "nature" (1 Cor 11:14). For Paul, as in popular Greek philosophy, cultural customs were perceived as extensions of natural law (and for Paul, more specifically God's created order of things). Therefore, wearing a covering was against God's purposes. It demeans God's design and thus dishonors both God and man. Woman's long hair—also designed "by nature" (that is, God)—is her glory (1 Cor 11:15). To uncover it is the same as cutting it off. That disgraces her, since her very being is demeaned. It may also disgrace her "figurative" head (that is, her husband), since appearing in public without a covering brings reproach on him from the society (especially if, as some have argued, it was the practice of prostitutes and other libertines in Corinth to move in public without a covering).

In light of Paul's principle for Christian life—to act in ways that lead to the good, the salvation of as many as possible (1 Cor 10:32-33)—he is concerned that Christians maintain the kind of public worship which does not bring disgrace through unacceptable, shameful practices. The church was God's alternative to broken Corinthian society (see discussion of 1 Corinthians 11:3). Its flouting of contemporary cultural conventions could bring social criticism and hinder the gospel.

Yet Paul is much more than a pragmatist. He grounds his reasoning in an understanding of God's revealed intention. This intention is focused in 11:7, though its foundation is already laid in 11:3. If, as we have argued in the previous chapter, Paul's use of the Greek word *kephalē* ("head") is to be understood not in terms of our idea of "headship" (that is, authority over), but rather in terms of "source/origin," then a central, unifying theme in his argument emerges.

Paul's guiding principle for Christian conduct (1 Cor 10:32-33) is grounded in the even higher principle: "whatever you do, do it all for the glory of God" (1 Cor 10:31). Since the word *glory* appears three more times in the passage which follows (1 Cor 11:7, 15), we can assume that the manifestation of God's glory and human participation in that glory is a central purpose of community worship.

In biblical thought, that which is made, or emerges out of another, manifests or reflects the glory of its maker or origin. Thus, "the heavens are telling the glory of God; and the firmament proclaims his handiwork" (Ps 19:1 RSV). The worshiper is exhorted to declare God's glory (Ps 96:3-8) and stands under judgment when God's glory is perverted in false worship and distorted human living (Rom 1:22-32). According to both John and Paul, Jesus' life reflected God's glory (Jn 1:14; 13:31-32; 17:4; Col 1:27). Since in Christ the fullness of God expressed itself (Col 1:19), Paul could say that "the light of the knowledge of the glory of God [was revealed] in the face of Christ" (2 Cor 4:6). Not only that, but Christ is the very "image of God" (2 Cor 4:4).

This complex of ideas seems to stand behind the language and ideas here. Insofar as the man is the result of God's creative work (Gen 1:26; 2:7) and has his existence out of Christ (1 Cor 11:3), who is the glory and image of God, "he is the image and glory of God." And insofar as the woman has her existence out of the man (Gen 2:21-23; 1 Cor 11:3), she "is the glory of man."

What Paul does not say in this context is important. He does not say that woman is the image of man; she is only his glory. For Paul knew that, according to Genesis 1:26-27, human beings as male and female were created in God's image. He is also clear that both the man and the woman have their being ultimately out of God's being as a result of God's creative act (1 Cor 11:12). Thus the woman as man's glory is only a recognition of the temporal sequence of God's creative activity, since her being is derived from the being of Adam. But no less than man, woman is the glory and image of God since she too is "from God" (1 Cor 11:12).

The purpose of worship is to glorify God. In contexts where cultural-religious norms and customs for proper attire and length of hair were understood as reflecting, at least to some extent, the order of "nature" (1 Cor 11:14-15),[1] the rejection of those customs in the worship of the church in Corinth undermined the purpose of worship. A "covered" man or an "uncovered" woman would bring dishonor rather than glory. It is this concern which motivates Paul's thought in this difficult passage.

[1]See the discussion of this matter in C. K. Barrett, *The First Epistle to the Corinthians* (New York: Harper & Row, 1968), pp. 256-57.

11:10 What Is the Sign of Authority?

Who are "the angels," because of whom women are "to have a sign of authority" on their heads when praying and prophesying? Why should they be interested in women's appearance in worship? What is the "sign of authority" on a woman's head, and whose authority does it signify?

In the discussion of 1 Corinthians 11:3 and 1 Corinthians 11:7 we saw that Paul argued for the appropriateness of women praying and prophesying in public worship with a head covering for both practical evangelistic reasons and biblical-theological considerations. Now he adds yet another dimension to the discussion. The opening words of the sentence, "For this reason," are most naturally a reference to the preceding discussion and the reasons already given for the propriety of a woman's head covering. Some see this statement as pointing forward to the phrase "on account of the angels." A good example is the TEV, which reads, "on account of the angels, then, a woman should have a covering." To take it in that way would make the whole prior discussion, with its various reasons for a head covering, meaningless.

Why is "because of the angels" another reason for the observance of the custom? What do angels have to do with the situation? Because of the obscurity of this statement, various interpretations have been offered throughout the church's history.

Among early church fathers the interpretation of the "angels" as priests or bishops was prominent. The Greek word *angelos* literally means "messenger" and could refer to a human messenger in the sense of an envoy, one who is sent. Thus the "angel of the church in Ephesus" (as well as the other "angels" of the churches addressed in Revelation 2—3) were held to be the bishops of those churches. From this the conclusion was drawn that the "angels" in 1 Corinthians 11:10 referred to visiting leaders from other churches, who would be offended by women's inappropriate appearance in worship.

This interpretation is unsatisfactory because nowhere in Paul's epistles, or the rest of the Epistles, is the word *angelos* ever used as designation of a church leader. In all but one case, Paul uses the word exclusively for supernatural, spiritual beings, the servants of God. The one exception is Galatians 4:14, where it is a self-designation: "You welcomed me as if I were an angel of God." Since it is used as an analogy, it really belongs to the category of Paul's normal usage.

A second line of interpretation sees these "angels" as a threat to women, against which the head covering in worship protects them. On the basis of Genesis 6:2-4, where it is said that the "sons of God" were attracted by the beauty of human females and impregnated them, Jewish traditions arose which interpreted these "sons of God" as angelic beings, who, as fallen angels, lusted after women. There are numerous passages in the noncanonical intertestamental literature that build on the Genesis narrative and speculate on the danger to humanity from these fallen angels.[1] This linkage of 1 Corinthians 11:10 with Genesis 6 and subsequent speculation is at best problematic. There is no indication whatever in this text that

Paul is concerned about women's protection from evil angelic beings. And how would the veil, while the women were praying or prophesying, protect against their lustful advances?

A third interpretation, which seems more fruitful as a context for Paul's cryptic allusion, sees behind the reference "because of the angels" the common Jewish belief that God's servants, the angels, are present especially in the worship of God's people. In Psalm 138:1 the worshiper exclaims, "I will praise you, O LORD, with all my heart; before the 'gods' I will sing your praise." These "gods" were understood as heavenly beings, servants in the divine court and guardians of the created order. Hebrews reflects these ideas when it envisions the ultimate context of worship, the heavenly Jerusalem where God and "thousands of angels in joyful assembly" are present (12:22). Paul elsewhere posits angels as observers of human conduct as well (1 Cor 4:9).

A more specific background for this text from Judaism is to be found in the Qumran writings, commonly known as the Dead Sea Scrolls. J. A. Fitzmyer has shown that these Jewish sectarians believed that angels were present when the community assembled for worship, and that they would be offended by any acts which transgrssed created order.[2] Paul confirms the presence of such a belief in a word addressed to Timothy: "In the presence of God and of Christ and of the elect angels I charge you to keep these rules" (1 Tim 5:21 RSV). We have here, as in 1 Corinthians 11:3, the connection between worship, congregational norms and angels who are present.

If, in light of this background, the angels of 1 Corinthians 11:10 are to be understood as guardians of those orders which are according to "the very nature of things" (1 Cor 11:14), then women's uncovered heads would be an infringement on that order. Thus, "because of the angels, the woman ought to have a sign of authority on her head."

What, then, constitutes the "sign of authority"? Why "authority"? Whose authority?

The text reads literally, "The woman ought to have authority on the head." Because of the emphasis on a head covering in the context, one would have expected Paul to say, "The woman ought to have a head covering." This expectation in fact caused some early church fathers to replace the word *authority* with the word *veil.* The identification between the head covering and "authority on the head" seems certain (note the RSV decision to translate, "That is why a woman ought to have a veil on her head, because of the angels"). By using the word "authority" (the Greek *exousia,* "authority," "power," "right"), Paul apparently intends to interpret the significance of the covering for the woman's participation in the prayer life and prophetic ministry of the congregation.

Since the head covering cannot by itself possess authority, some commentators and translations have opted for "a sign of authority" (that is, the veil is a sign for something else); examples are the NIV and NEB (NASB renders "symbol of authority"). Such a rendering leaves open the questions "Authority for what?" and "Whose authority?" In my judgment, both TEV and the LB go significantly beyond both the textual and contextual evidence. The TEV translates, "A woman should have a covering over her head to show that she is under her husband's authority." That translation decision answers the questions posed above by giving the husband authority over the wife. The LB interprets essentially the same way, except that it generalizes the concept of authority: not only is the wife to be under the authority of her husband, but "woman . . . is under man's authority."

These readings of the text presuppose two things and then import them into the text: (1) They assume that the relationship between man/husband and woman/wife as posited in 1 Corinthians 11:3 is a relationship of "authority over," and that this "principle of headship" determines all aspects of the rest of the passage (1 Cor 11:4-16). I have attempted to show (see discussion on 1 Cor 11:3) that such a reading is likely incorrect. (2) They assume that the head covering is in fact a symbol of the husband's authority over his wife. Yet no convincing proof of this assumption exists. A parallel has been sought in the Greek word *basileia,* which usually means "kingship" or "kingdom," but also can have the meaning "royal crown"; and the crown was a "sign of royal power/authority." This supposed parallel breaks down when we recognize that here the power and authority of the wearer is meant, and not that of another person.

In view of these problems, the text needs to be read much more literally. What really does Paul say? The text reads: "the woman should have *exousia* ['power,' 'right,' 'authority'] on the head." By choosing the word *exousia* rather than "head covering," Paul seems to suggest that by wearing the covering—and thus conforming her outward appearance with "nature/custom"—the woman has authority. Such an understanding of the text is strongly supported by recent studies.[3]

Authority for what? is the final question. We have seen that the ultimate purpose of worship is to give glory to God. A part of the way by which the glory of God is reflected is through the prayers of the worshipers and the proclamation of the gospel. Now since the woman has her origin in the man and thus reflects his glory, she ought to wear a head covering in worship in order to conceal "man's glory" and therefore be in a position to reflect the glory of God in praying and prophesying. By being veiled, women would not distract attention from the worship of God and avoid accusations of disgraceful behavior.

At the same time, the covering also represents her God-given right to bring glory to God through praying and prophesying, a gift of the Spirit (see Acts 2:17-18) which transcends former religious and cultural limitations imposed on women in public worship. As Walter Liefeld has shown, Paul used the word *exousia* ("authority") five times within the larger context of 1 Corinthians 8—14, always in the sense of Christian freedom from externals for the sake of others and the progress of the gospel.[4] By linking this same concept with the woman's covering Paul is, at one and the same time, affirming the need for restraint regarding externals and her right (authority) to participate in that which is essential; namely, the expression of her direct relation to God in prayer and the exercise of the gift of prophetic proclamation for the edification of the church and the glory of God.

This understanding of the text leads naturally to the next two verses. The statement that "in the Lord" man and woman are interdependent and complementary (1 Cor 11:11-12) has often been taken to represent a halfhearted concession by Paul. In light of the interpretation of the previous verses which has been offered, these verses are a ringing affirmation that in the new era which has been inaugurated (that is, "in the Lord"), despite the need for temporal limitations, man and woman have their being in God ("everything comes from God") and are called to do everything "for the glory of God" (1 Cor 10:31).

See also comment on 1 CORINTHIANS 11:3; 11:7.

---

[1]See the passages in the following books of the Pseudepigrapha: Enoch 6-7, 67-78; Testament of Reuben 5; Jubilees 5; Apocalypse of Baruch 56:8-13.
[2]See Joseph A. Fitzmyer, "A Feature of Qumran Angelology and the Angels of 1 Corinthians 11:10," *New Testament Studies* 4 (1957-1958): 45-58.
[3]M. D. Hooker, "Authority on Her Head: An Examination of 1 Corinthians 11:10," *New Testament Studies* 10 (1963-1964): 410-16. Walter L. Liefeld, "Women, Submission and Ministry in 1 Corinthians," in *Women, Authority and the Bible,* ed. Alvera Mickelsen (Downers Grove, Ill.: InterVarsity Press, 1986), pp. 145-46. C. K. Barrett, *A Commentary on the First Epistle to the Corinthians* (New York: Harper & Row, 1968), pp. 254-55; William F. Orr and James Arthur Walther, *1 Corinthians,* The Anchor Bible, vol. 32 (New York: Doubleday, 1976), pp. 260-64.
[4]Liefeld, "Women, Submission and Ministry," pp. 145-46.

11:29 Discerning the Body?

The ominous words of 1 Corinthians 11:29 are written by Paul right after he reminds his readers of the tradition about the institution of the Lord's Supper (or Eucharist) and the words of interpretation Jesus gave as he broke bread and passed the cup on the night before the crucifixion (1 Cor 11:23-26). These words were usually spoken before the celebration of the Lord's Supper in the churches where I grew up. The emotions they called forth from me were not only a sense of seriousness and awe, but also, and perhaps overwhelmingly, a sense of fear. What if I did not properly discern or recognize "the body of the Lord"? How would, or could, I make sure that in my eating of the bread and drinking of the cup I would not sin "against the body and blood of the Lord"? (1 Cor 11:27; this warning comes just before the hard saying we are looking at and is followed by the admonition "a man ought to examine himself . . .")

The fear of "sinning against" and "not discerning" at times caused me to avoid participation in the Lord's Supper or to stay away from worship altogether on those Sundays when Communion was celebrated. In some Christian traditions, these warnings and admonitions have been used to exclude persons from the celebration who are identified as having committed particular sins and are thus "unworthy" to partake of the elements.

The criterion of "worthiness," whether self-imposed or imposed by others, is really the crux of this passage. What makes one worthy and thus not subject to judgment? And if one's worthiness is related to moral-ethical perfection or spiritual maturity, can anyone ever qualify to participate at the Lord's table? These questions are particularly troublesome since they arise from a text related to the celebration of that event—the passion of our Lord—where God's unconditional love for sinners is revealed (see Rom 5:8, "While we were still sinners, Christ died for us").

For me it was amazingly liberating to discover, after giving greater attention to the problem that Paul was addressing in Corinth and the special terms he used, that my fears were not warranted; that the celebration was indeed a powerful reminder that Christ gave his life to save sinners like me; that it was a challenge to discern, again and again, the significance of his death for my own life.

The larger context for our saying begins at 1 Corinthians 11:17, and it is clear from Paul's introductory words ("In the following directives . . .") that he is moving away from a discussion of women's decorum at worship (1 Cor 11:3-16) to deal with a second problem in their life as a gathered congregation. What is that problem? Paul shoots rather straight: "Your meetings do more harm than good" (1 Cor 11:17). Then he proceeds to articulate the nature of the harm that results when they "come together as a church." He has heard that "there are divisions" among them and that these divisions manifest themselves precisely at the point where they "come together" (1 Cor 11:18, 20).

What a paradox! Were they not, as a gathered fellowship, the temple of God's Spirit (1 Cor 3:16)? And wasn't the Spirit the one who had incorporated them, as diverse a group as they were, "into one body . . . so that there should be no division in the body, but that its parts should have equal concern for each other" (1 Cor 12:13, 25)? Paul's vision for the fellowship of God's people in Corinth was far from being realized. Indeed, at the very occasion where one would have expected the greatest realization of that vision for mutuality and caring—at their common meals they manifested a haughty, individualistic disregard for others.

In the verses which follow the introductory charge (1 Cor 11:20-26), it is apparent that the occasion at which their divisions manifest themselves is an ordinary meal that includes symbolic actions and the recital of significant words. These festal occasions came to be known as love feasts (see 2 Pet 2:13; Jude 12). What was to be central—a caring love for one another grounded in Christ's sacrificial death—was manifestly absent: "When you come together, it is not the Lord's Supper you eat" (1 Cor 11:20). Rather, they were eating and drinking in an individualistic, selfish manner (1 Cor 11:21). Some, apparently the more affluent among them, had brought their food and, without waiting for others, had gone ahead and eaten their meals. There was even excessive drinking of the wine. All of this took place while the poorer members of the fellowship, who were able to bring little or nothing, were humiliated (1 Cor 11:22). Rather than sharing out of their abundance (as the Jerusalem Christians had done; Acts 4:32), those of means acted as if they were in their own homes. It was not the Lord's Supper they were eating, but their own!

Having laid bare the irregularity at their love feasts, which he describes as a "despising of the church of God" (1 Cor 11:22), Paul reminds them of the words which Jesus spoke at his last meal with the disciples (1 Cor 11:23-25). In those words, symbolically represented in broken bread and poured-out wine, Jesus interpreted the significance of his life and death: it was for them (1 Cor 11:24); a new covenant had been inaugurated through the sacrifice of his shed blood (1 Cor 11:25); they had become participants in that new covenant community, as Paul had already reminded them earlier ("Because there is one loaf, we who are many are one body" 1 Cor 10:17). When they ate and drank, and heard the words of the Lord, they were to "remember" him. Their eating and drinking was to be a declaration and proclamation of the Lord's self-sacrifice (1 Cor 11:26).

Some commentators understand the emphasis on "remembering" the Lord and "proclaiming" his suffering servanthood on our behalf as a special call to discipleship and the imitation of Jesus. In light of Paul's teachings elsewhere (for example, "Be imitators of God as beloved children and walk in love, as Christ loved us and gave himself up for us," Eph 5:1), this is surely what Paul wanted believers in Corinth to be doing. Instead, they were eating the bread of the Lord and drinking the cup of the Lord "in an unworthy manner" (1 Cor 11:27).

Thus the issue for Paul is not the "worthiness" of individuals. If that were the case, none would ever be "worthy." Rather, they were participating in the Lord's Supper in an unworthy manner by demonstrating contempt for the community as a whole, by actions that were not controlled by love for the needy brothers and sisters. In this they are "guilty of sinning against the body and blood of the Lord" (1 Cor 11:27).

The phrase "guilty of sinning against" (NIV) translates the Greek word *enochos.* It is used mostly as a legal term, meaning "liable for," "answerable for" or "guilty." The thrust of Paul is then that those who eat and drink unworthily (in the sense indicated above) are guilty of Christ's sacrificial death. They oppose and contradict in their loveless behavior the purpose of Christ's death, namely, to create a new covenant community which will model, in the midst of a fragmented, broken world, a new way of servanthood which seeks the good of others.

It is within the context of these concerns of Paul and this understanding of the meaning of their love feasts that the admonition to "self-examination" (see 1 Cor 11:28) and properly "recognizing the body of the Lord" (1 Cor 11:29) must be heard. The Corinthians are to examine themselves with regard to the spirit in which they approach their participation: Is it other-directed or self-centered?

Some of the earliest and best Greek manuscripts do not have the phrase "of the Lord." It is therefore quite probable that Paul's original letter simply read, "recognize the body." But in either case, the context indicates that Paul is speaking about that reality which elsewhere he designates "body" or "one body" or "the body of Christ" (see 1 Cor 10:17; 12:12-13, 27; Eph 2:16; 3:6; 4:4; Col 1:18). Not discerning the body (or the body of the Lord) is to fundamentally misunderstand the nature of Christian community and act in ways which undermine its vitality, its life and witness. It is that which stands under God's judgment, for to do harm to Christ's body is to oppose the purposes of God for which the Lord's body was broken and his life's blood was poured out.

See also comment on MARK 14:22-24.

11:31-32 Believers Judged by the Lord?

See comment on 1 PETER 4:17.

14:5 Should All Speak in Tongues?

Paul's words in 1 Corinthians 14:5 and the surrounding discussion of the presence and function of spiritual gifts in individual believers and the church have raised numerous questions: What is the place of "speaking in tongues" in the church? Are those who have experienced this gift more spiritual Christians, more open to the Spirit's working, than those who have not? Is Paul's point that all Christians should have this gift? Or is it rather that all should participate in prophetic work, assigning a negligible place to "speaking in tongues"?

Some Christians, on the basis of this and other texts, have come to feel superior, or more complete, because they have the gift of tongues, and wish with Paul that their brothers and sisters could have this same rich experience. Other Christians, on the basis of the same texts, consider glossolalia (from the Greek *glossai,* "tongues") a manifestation of primitive, immature faith, and they believe that the absence of this gift or experience is a mark of greater maturity. Still others, seeing the lively, enthusiastic faith and witness of some who have the gift of tongues, feel somehow not quite in tune with God's Spirit and earnestly desire or seek an experience of the Spirit that would bring vitality into an otherwise static faith.

These concerns and positions which have been present in parts of the church to some degree throughout church history have come to the fore again more recently in what has become known as the charismatic movement (from the Greek *charisma,* "gift"). Since this movement has crossed denominational boundaries and influenced believers in virtually all Christian traditions, it is particularly important that we come to understand this hard saying.

A brief definition of Paul's terms will help. The two activities that are being contrasted are "speaking in tongues" and "prophesying." The phenomenon of "tongues," which Paul identifies as a gift of the Spirit (in 1 Cor 12—14), must be clearly distinguished from the phenomenon which accompanied the outpouring of the Spirit at Pentecost (in Acts 2:1-12).

In Acts, the Spirit enabled Jesus' disciples to "speak in other tongues" (*glossai,* Acts 2:4, 11) in such a way that the audience, made up of peoples from various language groups throughout the Greco-Roman world, "heard them speak in their own languages [*dialekton,* "dialect/language"] the good news of Jesus" (see Acts 2:6, 8). Here it is clear that a miraculous speaking and hearing is indicated in which intelligible meaning is articulated and perceived. Peter's interpretation of this phenomenon also shows that it is to be taken as intelligible proclamation of the wonders of God. He cites the prophecy of Joel 2:28-32, where the outpouring of the Spirit leads to prophetic proclamation (Acts 2:17-18).

In Corinth, on the other hand, the phenomenon of tongues with which Paul is concerned is identified as "unintelligible utterance": no one understands it (1 Cor 14:2); it needs to be interpreted if it is to benefit the church (1 Cor 14:5); it is contrasted with "intelligible words" (1 Cor 14:9, 19) and "all sorts of languages . . . none of them without meaning" (1 Cor 14:10); it does not involve the mind (1 Cor 14:14); others won't know what is being said (1 Cor 14:16).

With this gift of "tongues" Paul contrasts the gift of "prophecy." This word does not mean simply "predicting the future." Prophesying sometimes included this predictive element (among both Old Testament and Christian prophets), but this aspect is neither exclusive nor primary. The prophets of Israel primarily addressed the word of God to their people's present reality. This is also the primary aspect of prophetic proclamation in early Christianity.

In Acts, Joel's prophecy (that "your sons and daughters will prophesy," Acts 2:17-18) is fulfilled in the declaration of what God has done in Jesus Christ (Acts 2:22-36). In 1 Corinthians 11, praying and prophesying are spoken about as two characteristic aspects of Christians in communal worship. Prayer is addressing the Lord; prophecy is addressing the word of the Lord to worshipers. In 1 Corinthians 14:29-33 the activity of Christian prophets is defined as addressing the content of divine revelation to the church for its instruction and encouragement. This purpose of prophetic speech is central in Paul's contrast of prophesying with speaking in tongues: strengthening, encouraging, comforting (1 Cor 14:3).

Thus Paul understood "tongues" as inspired, ecstatic utterance that in itself is unintelligible. Its native, proper place is the arena of prayer (1 Cor 14:2, 16). He understands "prophesying" as inspired utterance of revelation (probably including both the gospel, that is, God's act in Christ, and further revelation of God's purposes based on that event), which is addressed to the church in intelligible speech for its continuing growth.

The larger context is provided by the preceding chapters, where Paul addresses problems in the church's corporate life, specifically in the setting of worship. A primary and central principle for Christian action is the principle of edification. All Christian life and action is to be governed by the questions: Does it benefit others? Does it lead to their salvation and/or growth in faith? Is it for their good? (1 Cor 8:1, 9, 13; 9:12, 19-22; 10:23-24, 31-33; 11:21, 33). This principle continues as a guiding trajectory in Paul's discussion of the place and function of spiritual gifts in 1 Corinthians 12—14.

The focus of that discussion in 1 Corinthians 14 is on the relative merits of "tongues" and "prophesying." But Paul uses "prophesying" in order to deal with what seems to be the core of the issue in Corinth: a glorification of the gift of speaking in tongues in such a way that the other gifts, as well as those who possessed them, were minimized. Those who spoke in tongues apparently saw this gift as a sign of their superior spirituality. Such a view would naturally emerge among a faction of the believers in Corinth who believed themselves to have been freed from all responsible relationships and practical ethical concerns.

In the context of worship, these superspiritualists gloried in an obviously inspired phenomenon as the ultimate validation that they were free from earthbound existence, including rational, intelligible speech. Paul's question to them here, as earlier in connection with other problems, is: How does this gift contribute to the salvation or strengthening of others, rather than just the edification of the self (1 Cor 14:4)?

The foundations for tackling the issue are carefully laid in 1 Corinthians 12—13. In summary, Paul's thought develops as follows. There are diverse gifts available for believers, but they all have their origin in God's Spirit (1 Cor 12:4-6). The implication is that no one has any ground for pride! The manifestation of this one Spirit in the diverse gifts is for the good of all (1 Cor 12:7). Thus, the possession of a particular gift is not for one's own benefit. It is the Spirit who determines how the gifts are distributed (1 Cor 12:11). Therefore, the possessor of one gift has no basis for feeling especially favored or in any sense elevated over one who does not have the same gift.

This series of thoughts is now buttressed by the picture of the church as the body of Christ, compared to the living organism of the human body (1 Cor 12:12-27). The main purpose is to affirm that, despite all the variety of persons and their gifts in the church, there should be no division; all parts should be concerned about all others (1 Cor 12:25).

Having stressed the importance and validity of all members of the body, and with them their diverse gifts, Paul now goes on to show that with regard to the guiding principles of Christian life and action—namely, that others may be saved and built up—some callings and gifts take priority, are more foundational than others, and contribute more directly and substantially to that purpose.

Though he begins the list of callings and gifts by enumerating ("first of all apostles, second prophets, third teachers," 1 Cor 12:28), he does not continue that enumeration through the remaining list of gifts. The threefold ministry of the word—namely foundational apostolic witness to the gospel, prophetic proclamation of the gospel to the church and instruction in the meaning and practical implications of the gospel—is clearly primary, while the other activities designated by the gifts (1 Cor 12:28) are dependent on, and secondary to, the "word" ministries. The fact that the gift of tongues is named last does not necessarily mean that it is "least" in a hierarchical order (since the five gifts are not numbered). It is more probable that Paul names it last because for the

Corinthian enthusiasts it had top billing. It is, however, eminently clear that "tongues" belongs to a group of gifts which stand on a level below that of the ministries of the word. That is confirmed by Paul's summary sentence in 1 Corinthians 12:31, "But eagerly desire the greater gifts." It may be assumed from what follows in 1 Corinthians 14 that prophetic proclamation (preaching) and teaching are those "greater gifts."

The injunction to desire the greater gifts is followed by a call to an even greater preoccupation, "And now I will show you the most excellent way" (1 Cor 12:31—"a still more excellent way," RSV). Even better than seeking the greater gifts, Paul argues, is following the way of love (1 Cor 13:1). For, as he so eloquently shows, both the lesser and the greater gifts will someday cease. But love is eternal. Paul may have introduced this magnificent call to love because he knew that love is purely other-directed and would be the motivating power for seeking those gifts that build up others.

The stage is now set for the specific discussion of the nature, function and relative merit of tongues and prophecy (in which this hard saying is located). "Tongues" is the language of the heart, addressed to God (1 Cor 14:2). "Prophecy" is God's word addressed to people for their encouragement and comfort (1 Cor 14:3). "Tongues" are primarily a private matter; they edify the self. "Prophecy" is a public matter; it edifies the church (1 Cor 14:4).

Paul affirms the importance of both the personal and the public dimension of the contrasting gifts when he expresses his wish that they all had the gift of tongues, and then immediately qualifies that wish with his even greater wish: "but I would rather have you prophesy" (1 Cor 14:5). Private, ecstatic experience, especially in the intimacy of one's prayer relationship with God, is not to be rejected ("Do not forbid speaking in tongues," 1 Cor 14:39). Paul knows its value from personal experience (1 Cor 14:18). Even in the context of public worship, it can have a place if it is made intelligible through interpretation (1 Cor 14:5) so that others can be "edified" (1 Cor 14:16-17).

Since "tongues" is recognized as a gift of the Spirit and is at the disposal of the Spirit, Paul can say, "I wish you all had it." It would be an evidence that the Spirit was at work in them. And yet, his operative principle (the good of others) leads him unqualifiedly toward preference for prophetic proclamation: "But in the church I would rather speak five intelligible words to instruct others than ten thousand words in a tongue" (1 Cor 14:19).

This analysis leads to these concluding, summary observations: None of the spiritual gifts is an absolute; only the way of love is. Therefore, neither the possession nor the exercise of any of them is a mark of spiritual superiority. Believers are to be open to the Spirit's gifts and when they receive them to exercise them gracefully and humbly. Any earnest seeking for particular gifts ought to be guided by the desire to be involved in strengthening the church so that the whole people of God may truly be the divinely ordered alternative to the brokenness of human society.

14:33-34 Women to Keep Silence?

Several acute problems are raised by 1 Corinthians 14:33-34 for the Bible reader who seeks to be a faithful interpreter of the whole counsel of God revealed in Scripture as well as an obedient follower of Christ.

First, a series of questions is forced on us by the text itself and the verses which follow: Does the New Testament as a whole show that women were routinely excluded from verbal participation in Christian worship? Why are they not allowed to speak? Which "Law" is referred to in 1 Corinthians 14:34? How are "submission" and "silence" related?

A second series of questions is raised by the relation between this hard saying and the immediate and wider biblical context. How can Paul say earlier in this epistle that women are to have a head covering on while praying and proclaiming the gospel (1 Cor 11:3-16) and now in the same letter forbid verbal participation? Further, how are we to take the apparent discrepancy between this blanket prohibition and the fact that there are numerous examples of women's active participation in the worship life of early Christianity?

The text we are looking at is located at the conclusion of a lengthy section (1 Cor 11—14) in which Paul deals with problem situations in the context of worship. He has dealt with proper decorum of men and women while praying and prophesying (1 Cor 11:2-16); with irregularities at the Lord's Supper (1 Cor 11:17-34); and finally with the nature, function, use and abuse of spiritual gifts (1 Cor 12—14), with special consideration of the ecstatic phenomenon "speaking in tongues" and "prophecy" (1 Cor 14:1-25).

It is apparent in the immediately surrounding context (1 Cor 14:26-40) of this saying that the elevation and glorification of ecstatic, unintelligible utterance by some faction in the congregation created disorder and confusion in worship (see comment on 1 Cor 14:5). Thus in addressing those who speak in tongues (1 Cor 14:27-28), he calls for order: they should speak "one at a time." The utterances should be interpreted (1 Cor 14:27), since without interpretation it would confound the hearers and cause them to wonder whether there is madness here (1 Cor 14:23). Without an interpreter, "the speaker should keep quiet in the church" (1 Cor 14:28). In addressing those who have the gift for prophetic proclamation of the gospel (1 Cor 14:29-33), the concern for order in worship is also evident. Their speaking is to be "in turn," that is, not all at the same time. The purpose of all verbal communication is "the strengthening of the church" (1 Cor 14:26) through the instruction and encouragement of everyone (1 Cor 14:31). That purpose, as Paul sees it, can only be accomplished when there is order in worship, "for God is not a God of disorder, but of peace" (1 Cor 14:33; see also 1 Cor 14:40).

All of the above shows that Paul is dealing with abuses and actions in worship which disrupt God's purposes and which therefore need correction. Within such a setting, the text seems clearly to belong to the category of "corrective texts" whose purpose is focused toward a local situation. Paul's word that "women should remain silent in the churches" would therefore seem, at least primarily, to have authoritative import ("What I am writing to you is the Lord's command," 1 Cor 14:37) for the particular situation in Corinth (as well as similar situations; for example, the one addressed in 1 Tim 2:11-12). One must be careful therefore not to immediately jump to the conclusion that Paul's injunction has implications for all women in all churches.

Support for restraint in this area comes from both other things Paul writes and practices in the early churches which show that women's vocal participation in worship and in other instructional or leadership roles was accepted and affirmed. Paul himself acknowledges in this same letter the validity and appropriateness of women as full participants in public prayer and the proclamation of the gospel (1 Cor 11:5, 13). What he finds invalid and unacceptable is that they engage in this activity without a head covering, since that rejection of cultural/religious custom creates a potential stumbling block. Paul even affirms in that context that "the churches of God" recognize no other practice (1 Cor 11:16), namely, the appropriateness of a head covering for women who are praying and prophesying in the church.

If Paul believed that women should be silent in the churches in a comprehensive, universal sense, he would not have spent so much time instructing women what to do with their heads; he would have simply forbidden their practice of praying and prophesying in the assembled congregation.

Paul's larger view—which acknowledged and validated the vocal participation of women in the churches—is supported in other New Testament writings. Thus the proclamation of the "wonders of God" (namely, his redemptive work in and through Jesus of Nazareth—Acts 2:11, 22-36) is interpreted in Peter's Pentecost sermon as the fulfillment of the prophecy of Joel 2:28-29 that in the last days, under the inspiration of God's outpoured Spirit, "your sons and daughters will prophesy. . . . Even on my servants, both men and women, I will pour out my Spirit in those days, and they will prophesy" (Acts 2:17-18, emphasis mine). In keeping with this prophetic word and the commencement of its fulfillment at Pentecost, Luke mentions matter-of-factly that the evangelist Philip had four daughters who were engaged in the prophetic ministry of the good news (Acts 21:8-9).

In light of this evidence that women in the early churches were moved by the Spirit to engage in ministries of the Word side by side with men, it is difficult, if not impossible, to understand Paul's injunction as a categorical imperative intended for all churches in all places in all times. Rather, the injunction must be understood within its own context as addressing a problem in Corinth which needed correcting.

We have already seen above that the particular problem was disorder and confusion in public worship. This situation was apparently caused by the inappropriate expression of both the gift of prophecy and speaking in tongues (1 Cor 14:26-31). It is thus probable that the admonition to silence is in some way related to women's participation in the inappropriate use of these gifts. It is possible that women in the Corinthian congregation, due to the liberating experience of the gospel from all sorts of cultural and religious bondage, may have been at the forefront of noninterpreted, unintelligible utterance (glossolalia) and enthusiastic prophetic proclamation which did not yield the "congregational floor" to others. Some may have continued to speak at the same time another was prophesying, creating noisy confusion in which no one could be "instructed and encouraged."

That such a connection existed between the women who are asked to be silent and the disorderly expression of tongues and prophetic speech receives support from two sets of parallel phrases in these texts. In addressing those speaking in tongues without the benefit of interpretation, Paul says, "The speaker should keep quiet in the church" (1 Cor 14:28). Then, in 1 Corinthians 14:34, he uses the same words: "the women should keep quiet in the churches." The NIV variation in translation does not reflect the fact that the Greek verb *(sigaō)* is the same in both.

Second, in addressing the issues of disorderly prophetic speaking (1 Cor 14:29-32), Paul again urges silence on some so that others can speak. The NIV's "the first speaker should stop" (1 Cor 14:30) again does not reflect the fact that the verb *sigaō* ("remain silent") is also used here. But more important, in calling on the prophets in the congregation to recognize that they are mutually accountable to each other, Paul says, "The spirits of prophets are subject to the control of prophets" (1 Cor 14:32). The Greek word rendered "subject to the control of" is *hypotassō*. That is the same word Paul uses in 1 Corinthians 14:34, where he follows the admonition to silence (according to the NIV) with the words "[they] must be in submission." In other words, prophets must be in submission to other prophets (and thus to each other) in the church.

If, as seems likely, women were prominently in that group of prophets who were disposed to be "disorderly," Paul may be addressing them specifically with regard to this matter of submission to other prophets for the sake of order and peace (1 Cor 14:32-33). These parallelisms in the imperatives to "keep quiet" and "to be in submission" strongly suggest that the problem of disorderly participation in prophetic proclamation and tongues was particularly prominent among women believers in Corinth, and that it is with respect to this context that Paul's admonitions must be understood.

A final problem needs brief attention. What is the "Law" on which the injunction to submit is based (1 Cor 14:34)? Assuming that the submission envisioned is to the men/husbands in the congregation, some have sought Old Testament texts to ground such an injunction. The most common text cited from "the Law" is Genesis 3:16. Two factors militate against it. Wherever Paul deals with the relation between men and women, he never appeals to this passage. Further, it is clear from the context of Genesis 2—3 that 3:16, "Your desire will be for your husband, and he will rule over you," does not announce God's created design for "male leadership" but is the statement of a cursed existence because of sin. Surely Paul knew that Christ's redemptive work freed human beings from the curse of Eden.

Others see in Paul's term ("as the Law says") a reference to both Jewish and Gentile norms which restricted women's public participation, and these restrictions existed within the context of male-dominant cultures. Yet Paul uses the word "be submissive" without saying "to whom." Thus the assumption that it is to men/husbands may not be warranted. It is more likely that he is referring back to the statement that "prophets are to be submissive to (other) prophets" (see 1 Cor 14:32). The question "Submissive to whom or what?" would then have an answer in the immediate context: either to other prophets or to the principle of order which has its origin in God (1 Cor 14:33).

Paul's operative principle for congregational life and worship is constant. Whatever hinders the movement of the gospel, causes confusion rather than growth, offends rather than encourages or strengthens, builds up the self at the expense of others—all this is contrary to God's intention. And insofar as the women in Corinth and elsewhere in the young churches used their gifts contrary to God's intention, the injunction to silence is an appropriate, authoritative word. The principle which underlies the injunction is authoritative for both men and women in all churches.

See also comment on 1 TIMOTHY 2:11-12.

15:2 Salvation: Past, Present or Future?

See comment on 1 PETER 1:9.

15:29 Baptism for the Dead?

From the rather straightforward way in

which Paul discusses baptism for the dead, it appears that both for him and for his readers the rite or practice of "being baptized for [literally, 'on behalf of'] the dead" was as obvious and clear as it is puzzling and obscure for us. What is Paul's point in referring to such a practice? What is the meaning and purpose of the practice? Did Paul approve or disapprove it?

First a word about the context in which this text appears. In 1 Corinthians 15, Paul gives an elaborate apologetic for both the resurrection of Christ and the future resurrection of the dead. This apologetic assumes that among the Corinthian Christians were some who denied the very concept of resurrection. Such a denial seems to have emerged out of a view of reality which rejected the goodness of physical life and held that only the human spirit or soul (the immaterial aspect) was the object of redemption. Thus among the superspiritualists in Corinth there were the "libertines" for whom concrete, bodily realities, including sexual relations, had no ultimate significance; for them, anything was possible. Paul's discussion of the resurrection responds to questions raised in the congregation by the views of these hyperspiritualists.

Paul's apologetic is expressed in a series of "if/then" arguments: If there is no resurrection, then Christ has not been raised (1 Cor 15:13). If Christ has not been raised, then our preaching and your faith are futile (1 Cor 15:14, 17) and those Christians who have already died are lost (1 Cor 15:18). If the dead are not raised, then "let us eat and drink, for tomorrow we die" and that's the end of it (1 Cor 15:32).

Our text is part of this series of arguments. Though the Greek of the first part of 1 Corinthians 15:29 does not contain the phrase "no resurrection" (as in NIV; compare NASB, RSV), the preposition *epei* ("now if" or "otherwise") clearly carries this sense from the previous "if/then" series, as well as from the latter part of verse 29, "If the dead are not raised, why then . . . ?"

Apart from the question of the nature and meaning of the practice and Paul's attitude toward it, the force of the argument is unambiguous: If there is no resurrection, if the dead are not raised, what is the point of the rite in which people are baptized on their behalf? Will not those who undergo this ritual look like fools if in fact there is no resurrection? No matter what efficacy is believed to come from such vicarious baptism, the whole enterprise is a total waste of effort and time! The core of this apologetic is of course the contradiction between their belief and their practice. They believe that there is no resurrection; yet their practice belies that belief.

What was the practice and its purpose? This reference to baptism on behalf of the dead is unique in the New Testament. Its mention here indicates that it was practiced by some Christians in Corinth (if not generally by the congregation as a whole). Its absence from the rest of the New Testament, as well as from the apostolic fathers, probably indicates that it was not a common practice. Practices with some affinity to it show up in some second- and third-century heretical groups and may be developments from the practice mentioned by Paul. But these later practices are of no help in determining what the Corinthian believers intended in this ritual.

The scantiness of the evidence has given rise to scores of interpretations, some of which are fanciful and highly speculative (for example, that it was a practice of being baptized on the tombs of the dead). However, the plain reading of the text probably allows for no more than two possibilities: (1) some Christians in Corinth (presumably persons who had already undergone their own baptism) were undergoing the rite on behalf of dead relatives or friends; (2) the rite was being practiced on behalf of persons who were Christians, but who had died before baptism was administered. This latter possibility would certainly fit a time in the history of the church when those who professed faith in Christ went through an extended "probationary" period of as much as a year before they were baptized and became full members of the Christian fellowship.

Baptism on their behalf would be a visible demonstration that these departed had appropriated Christ's atoning death and, therefore, would be raised by God. What argues against this second possibility is the New Testament evidence that in the early decades, baptism was generally administered almost immediately after persons came to faith in Christ (for example, Acts 2:37-41; 8:34-38; 10:44-48; 16:29-33). Yet it is quite possible that even in this early period, due to circumstances or illness or large-scale epidemics, numerous believers died before baptism had been administered.

As to the meaning and purpose of the practice, the wording suggests some "vicarious" significance. Those who underwent the rite "on behalf of" a deceased person must have held to a belief that by this act their resurrection could be secured. If the second view mentioned above is adopted, baptism on behalf of dead—but unbaptized—believers could have been understood as a visible sign and celebration that these departed ones had appropriated Christ's atoning death for themselves in faith and would therefore participate in the resurrection. In this sense, the practice would certainly not have violated Paul's own understanding of the significance of baptism, and he would probably not have rejected the practice. According to Romans 6, baptism was for Paul a dramatic reenactment of death and resurrection: first of all, death to sin and resurrection to new life, but also participation, by faith, in Christ's death and resurrection; and finally, a powerful proclamation of victory over death in the final resurrection.

If, however, this vicarious baptism was on behalf of nonbelievers, then a view of the nature and efficacy of baptism beyond Paul's own view must have been held by these Christians. Such a view (some would call it highly sacramental; others magical) would have understood the baptismal ritual as so effective that its benefits would accrue to the one for whom it was enacted. The departed person would have been seen to be included in the sphere of the saving faith of those who enacted the ritual.

Underlying such a view, and leading to it, is no doubt a deep concern, present among believers from the beginning, about all those who died before the event of Christ in history. Were those who died before the Incarnation, or those who died before the gospel was preached in their communities, deprived of the opportunity to be redeemed and join the community of the resurrected ones? The practice of baptism on behalf of the dead may have been an early response to such concerns. That same concern also lies behind the idea that Christ entered the realm of the dead after his death and before his resurrection in order to offer salvation to all those who died before the Incarnation (1 Pet 3:18-20).

2 CORINTHIANS

1:21-22 What Is the Anointing?

See comment on 1 JOHN 2:27.

3:14 A Veil over Their Minds?

These words are written by Paul about his own people Israel, who, in respect to a knowledge of God and his purposes, have been and continue to be in a twilight zone. The questions raised by this statement are, Why is that so? How were their minds made dull? Who or what caused this? What is the veil that covers them when the Law is read?

This text is part of a section in which Paul contrasts the old covenant and its results with the new covenant and its results. The old covenant—though that was not its intention—leads to death (2 Cor 3:6, 9), as the history of Israel's disobedience and her rejection of the Messiah clearly demonstrates for Paul. The new covenant, inaugurated in Christ, leads to life, as Paul's experience and his understanding of the Incarnation also clearly demonstrates. Behind this contrast stands Paul's deep conviction that the old covenant, focused in the giving of the law, reveals the nature and purposes of God indirectly (Gal 3:19-20), while the new covenant, focused in Christ, reveals God directly and fully. Christ is the very image of God (2 Cor 4:4); he is the incarnation of God's "fullness" (Col 1:19; 2:9).

Within the context of this overall view, Paul's discussion, which leads to this text, develops as follows. He sees his ministry of proclaiming the gospel as resulting in a new covenant community in which the revelation of God is not present on inscribed tablets but engraved on hearts by the Spirit of God (2 Cor 3:3-6). In the use of this imagery, Paul is clearly reflecting the prophecy of Jeremiah 31:31-34 about the promise of a new covenant where the will of God will be written on people's hearts. Paul understands the church as the fulfillment of this prophetic vision. The contrast between "indirect" and "direct" contact with the living God is here implicitly given.

Paul continues the contrast by reflecting on the experience of Moses and Israel when the Ten Commandments were given. According to Exodus 34:29-35, when Moses brought the tablets from Mount Sinai, his face was radiant because he had been in the presence of the glory of the Lord (see Ex 33:18, 22), and the people were afraid to come near. Then Moses veiled his face, thus covering the reflection of God's glory in his face. Paul contrasts this indirect and muted mediation and reflection of God's glory at the time of the establishing of the old covenant with the greater glory of the new covenant, established by the presence of the Spirit (2 Cor 3:7-11). That Spirit is the "Spirit of the Lord" (2 Cor 3:17), and it is that Lord in whose face "the light of the knowledge of the glory of God" is fully revealed (2 Cor 4:6).

Having established this contrast, Paul now uses the veil—which covered Moses' face to conceal the reflected radiance of God's glory (2 Cor 3:13)—to symbolize Israel's past and present blindness "when the old covenant is read" (2 Cor 3:14).

Paul knew, on the basis of the history of his people and his own experience, that the words of Scripture with regard to Israel's "dullness of mind" (2 Cor 3:14) and blindness of sight are true. What causes this lack of full comprehension and unobstructed vision?

According to Deuteronomy 29, in the context of a covenant renewal ceremony, Moses tells the people that even though they have seen and experienced the mighty deeds of the Lord on their behalf, they have not really grasped its full significance, for "to this day the LORD has not given you a mind that understands or eyes that see or ears that hear" (Deut 29:4). The context shows that Israel's breaking of God's covenant with them stands in the background. With their own eyes and ears and minds they failed to grasp God's truth for them. The statement "the LORD has not given you . . ." does not mean that the Lord caused their disobedience, but rather that if their eyes and ears and minds were really in tune with the Lord, the mighty works of God on their behalf would have been seen for what they were—namely, evidences of God's steadfast love and faithfulness (Ex 34:6). By not "giving them minds that understand," God allowed their minds to dull.

That same mysterious relation between human decision and divine action is expressed in the context of the prophet Isaiah's call, where he is told that the word of the Lord that he will address to the people of Israel will make their heart calloused, their ears dull and their eyes closed (Is 6:10). This is a prophetic anticipation of what in fact happened as a result of Isaiah's preaching: the nation continued on its way of disobedience toward national collapse and exile. Because this was the result of the word of the Lord that Isaiah proclaimed, it could be said that the Lord "closed their eyes." What is reflected here is the lack of precise distinction in Hebraic thought between primary and secondary causes. Since God is sovereign, human will and freedom to decide for or against God were often subsumed under divine sovereignty.

An increasing sense of individual and corporate responsibility before God is reflected in the Greek translation of the Hebrew Scriptures. There the Hebrew of Isaiah 6:10—"Make the heart of this people calloused"—is rendered "This people's heart has become calloused, they hardly hear with their ears, and they have closed their eyes." The translators understood the Isaiah passage to mean that Israel's disobedience led to their lack of understanding.

It is this background in the Old Testament which is reflected in Paul's statement that "their minds were made dull." And the rejection of the Messiah shows that "to this day" their rebellion against God continues. That is the veil which remains. Whenever "Moses is read" (that is, the Law, 2 Cor 3:15), the veil remains. For, as Paul shows elsewhere, the Law was only able to reveal human sin; it could not save (Rom 3:20). But, when one turns to the Lord, so Paul concludes, the veil is taken away (2 Cor 3:16).

That conclusion surely emerged from Paul's own experience. In the very attempt to obey the Law, he found himself opposing the true purposes of God. In Christ, those true purposes have been revealed; not indirectly, but directly. Therefore, we can "reflect the Lord's glory" (2 Cor 3:18). The veil of disobedience and dullness has been removed.

4:4 Who Is "the God of This Age"?

It is clear that Scripture (including the parts that Paul wrote) teaches that there is only one God (e.g., Rom 3:30; 1 Cor 8:6; Eph 4:6; 1 Tim 2:5; Jas 2:19). Who then is "the god of this age"? Why would Paul refer to another god if he believed that there is only one God?

As a Jew, Paul divided world history into two "ages": "this age" and "the age to come" (Eph 1:21). This age is a period when Satan has significant sway in the world, but in the age to come God's kingdom will be fully revealed and he will right all the wrongs from this age. When Paul submitted to Jesus as his Messiah, he gained a new perspective on this division of time. In Jesus the age to come has already arrived. Christians have already entered under the control of God and already experience the kingdom in the fruit of the Spirit (Rom 14:17) and the Spirit's power (1 Cor 4:20). This does not mean that the kingdom is *fully* present, for the full experience of the kingdom is in the future, when it will rule the earth (1 Cor 15:24). Thus Christians both experience the kingdom now and are yet to inherit the kingdom (Col 1:12).

Everyone, however, is not a Christian. This evil age is still very much present (Gal 1:4). In this age there is a "dominion of darkness" (Col 1:13) in which people are controlled by "the ruler of the kingdom of the air" (Eph 2:2). Paul refers to the human rulers of "this age" (1 Cor 2:8), the philosophers of "this age" (1 Cor 1:20) and the standards of "this age" (1 Cor 3:18). In this passage he refers to the being that controls "this age" as "the god of this age," rather than using one of his other titles, such as Satan (2 Cor 11:14). Paul refers to Satan by such a title, not because he is a god in the sense of being an ultimate being, but because he is the being who controls the lives of unbelievers (including blinding their minds) and the one whom they serve (even if they think that they are serving their own self-interest or money or some particular deity).

Therefore, for Paul there only is one true God. The true God is the ultimate God, the one ultimate being, for in the end Christ will put down all other dominions and authorities, including that of Satan, and "deliver the kingdom to the Father." Satan is not God; he is a being who will in the end bow the knee before God. Yet for now Satan holds sway over this age everywhere that people have not turned to Christ and thus been transferred from "the dominion of darkness" into "the kingdom of God's dear Son." Satan is not the ultimate God, but for those who have not turned to Christ, the dark lord is all the god that they know. That terrible reality is what Paul is recognizing in this verse.

See also comment on 1 CORINTHIANS 8:5-6.

5:17 All the Old Has Gone?

Paul's joyful proclamation in 2 Corinthians 5:17 expresses a conviction that seems all too frequently contradicted by our experience. We affirm that life in Christ produces a new kind of living and are embarrassed to find so little difference between our actual living and the lives of those who make no such claims. We rejoice in the forgiveness of God for our sinfulness and then recognize how our living often fails to convey this reality to others. We worship the Christ who gave his life for others, yet devote so much time and energy to promoting ourselves. We proclaim allegiance to Christ as Lord while living by priorities and values which indicate that there are indeed "many gods and lords" by which we really live.

Like us, the early Christians to whom Paul addressed those words recognized that in many ways the "old" remained with them and the "new" life of faith in Christ needed to be appropriated again and again. These early Christians saw that Rome and its oppressive power continued. Injustice and immorality prevailed in their world. They experienced continuing bondage in their personal lives, bitter strife within communal Christian life, the continuing reality of personal failure, anxiety, frustration and sin. Why the old when the new is come? Why are these things still with us, if it is true that "the old has gone" and "the new has come"?

How are we to understand this tension between Christian affirmation and Christian experience? There have been two main ways by which Christians have sought to deal with this problem. Both ways have arisen out of an understanding of human nature which sees us as consisting of essentially two parts: the physical (flesh) and the spiritual (soul), which are opposed to each other.

One way manifested itself as early as A.D. 50 in the Christian community at Corinth. It was the "spiritualizing" of Christian faith. The argument went something like this: "Since the body, the flesh, the physical aspect is at best weak, at worst corrupt, what we need to do is to concentrate on the spiritual side, on the soul. And since, through Christ, our souls have been redeemed, it really does not matter what we do with our bodies." It does not take much imagination to see where this way of splitting the human personality leads. In Corinth, it led to libertinism, which manifested itself in a complete disregard for the moral-ethical life and a haughty disdain for the brother or sister who had not attained to such a "liberated spirituality."

A second response to such a dualistic view of human nature manifested itself during Paul's missionary activity in Asia Minor. It was the *legalizing* of the Christian faith. The argument here went as follows: "The flesh really interferes with the attempt of the human spirit to be in perfect communion with God. Therefore, 'the flesh,' with all its passions and desires, must be made subservient to the spirit. We must impose—by means of codes of conduct—such close strictures on our lives that the inner purity of the spirit is not somehow defiled by the flesh." The extreme form of this response was a rigorous asceticism and monastic isolation from entanglements with the world.

Much of contemporary Christian thinking continues to be influenced by such dualism. Sometimes it becomes an escape hatch from the demands of Christian discipleship. At other times it forms the basis of a disregard for bodily, concrete things and an elevation of the spiritual or a suppression of the physical with a view to the purification of the soul.

If the above ways of dealing with the basic tension in Christian existence are inadequate, how then are we to understand the presence of that tension, how are we to account for it, and how are we to come to grips with it?

There were Greek thinkers, prior to and contemporary with the birth of Christianity, who saw the human body as the prisonhouse or tomb of the soul. They believed that salvation consisted of the liberation of a person's higher self, the spirit or soul, from its entrapment with the body. This understanding of human nature, which has influenced much Christian thought, must be decidedly rejected as contrary to the biblical point of view. In the witness of the Bible, the *total being* is the object of God's redemptive purposes. As physical-spiritual beings we are the objects of God's forgiving act in Christ. In our *wholeness* we stand under the constraining love of Christ by which we become new creations. In our concrete existence we can be transformed into the image of Christ. The human person—in the context of relationship to others—is the locus of God's intervention. To affirm less than that is to limit God!

If a dividing of the human personality into antagonistic physical and spiritual components cannot account for the tension between the "old" and the "new," what can? What, we must ask, is Paul expressing in our text? In what sense are Christians "new creations"?

An instructive perspective comes to light when Paul's word is seen against the backdrop of Israel's prophetic hope. One of the main features of that hope was the belief that the *end of time* was going to be like the *beginning of time.* When the prophets spoke about the expectation of God's final coming and reign in human history, they frequently described that time in imagery associated in the Old Testament with paradise and the original creation. A new creation was going to replace the fallen old creation. Isaiah's picture of the return of paradise is a striking example of this prophetic expectation: "The wolf will live with the lamb, the leopard will lie down with the goat, the calf and the lion and the yearling together; and a little child will lead them" (Is 11:6).

Now, for Paul, the end of time had dawned on a broken world. The end of the ages had broken into the old age (see 1 Cor 10:11). The world was a new world insofar as it had encountered the Creator in the Christ. The person "in Christ" was part of a new humanity, created in Christ Jesus for a new existence. As Adam and Eve, the typical representative human beings, stood before the Creator in radical freedom, so the new person in Christ stands before the Creator in radical freedom. In some sense, the situation before the Fall has been re-created for the Christian. In that sense the Christian is a "new creation." As Adam and Eve were faced with the decision to give allegiance to God the Creator or to create their own gods and give allegiance to them (see Rom 1:20-23), so the new-creation person has been freed from the Fall's bondage for the same decision. As they lived with the possibility of either dependence on the Creator or independence from him, so the new-creation person exists within that possibility. As they could either exist in fellowship with their Maker or hide from God among the trees, so the new-creation person can live in trust before God or make jungles in which to hide from God.

God's redeeming love in Christ has reclaimed us for relationship with our Creator. In this relationship we are free from the *bondage to sin* which characterized us while alienated from God. But this relationship *does not automatically remove us* from the influence of sin's reality which surrounds us in all arenas of life.

For Paul, "the old" which has gone is the condition of alienation from God and its bondage to sin. "The new" which has come is our relationship with God in Christ, a relationship which empowers us for a kind of living in which the continuing reality of sin can be overcome again and again. To be a "new creation" is not to be perfect or faultless, or immune from anger and pain, or insulated from the tough experiences of life. Rather, to be a "new creation" is to live life turned toward the God whose grace has reclaimed us in Christ.

6:14 Yoked with Unbelievers?

There are two ways in which 2 Corinthians 6:14 may be viewed as a hard saying. It may be hard because we don't like the rigorous implications it seems to have for our everyday relationships with persons who are not believers. If it is hard for this reason it should not be made easier, for that would be to obscure its meaning. The saying may, however, be hard because (1) it seems to present the incompatibility between believer and unbeliever more narrowly than other New Testament texts, and (2) it is not clear what being "yoked together" means precisely and how it is to be put into practice. A careful look at the text and its context should help.

One of the major themes in 2 Corinthians is the defense of the integrity of Paul's apostolic ministry, the authenticity of the gospel which he preached and the implications that gospel had for the life of Christians. It is clear from statements in both canonical letters that Paul's relationship with Corinth was a tumultuous one, giving rise to several visits and as many as four letters. There were elements in the church who opposed Paul and his teachings, and because of that opposition (often arising out of misunderstandings of what Paul had said or written earlier), the church at Corinth was in danger of self-destructing again and again.

In the discussion of 2 Corinthians 5:17 we saw that central to Paul's thought was the conviction that "in Christ" believers were "new creatures," their old allegiances had been replaced by a new relationship with God, "who reconciled us to himself" (2 Cor 5:17-18). On the basis of that truth, Paul knew that God had called him into the "ministry of reconciliation." Recognizing that reconciliation in the divine-human relationship had far-reaching implications for human relationships, Paul was grieved by those who opposed him and the gospel (2 Cor 2:1-4) and was concerned about their salvation. So he pleads earnestly with them: "We implore you on Christ's behalf: Be reconciled to God" (2 Cor 5:20) and "We urge you not to receive God's grace in vain" (2 Cor 6:1).

From his earlier letter (1 Cor) it is clear that there were several areas in their life as a congregation and as individual believers where God's grace seemed to be in vain (for example, continuing participation in pagan cultic rituals, 1 Cor 6; 10; taking disagreements into pagan courts, 1 Cor 6). How can "receiving God's grace in vain" be avoided? Second Corinthians 6:14 is a response to that question.

The Greek word for "yoked together" is found only here in the New Testament. In the Greek Old Testament, the word is used in the prohibition against breeding cattle with a different species of animal (Lev 19:19). From this use of the Greek word comes the meaning "mismating," which several translations employ for this text (RSV; NEB, "Do not unite yourselves with unbelievers; they are no fit mates for you"). From this rendering of the word has emerged what is probably the commonest understanding of this text; namely, that Paul warns against marriage between believers and nonbelievers.

Though this understanding may be a

valid application of the idea, the context of the passage suggests that marriage was not what Paul had in mind here. He seems to use the term in its more general meaning of "unevenly yoked," such as placing animals of a different species in the same harness. Paul may have used the prohibition against such yoking in Deuteronomy 22:10 as a metaphor:[1] there is a decided difference between the Christian and the non-Christian. There is a basic incompatibility which must be recognized and which has implications for life in an environment of unbelief. What is the nature of that incompatibility? And what are its implications?

The statement "Do not be yoked together with unbelievers" is followed by a series of five antithetical questions which define the nature of incompatibility between believers and unbelievers. The questions are rhetorical; thus the answers are obvious. What do righteousness and wickedness, light and darkness, Christ and Belial,[2] believer and unbeliever, the temple of God and idols, have in common? Absolutely nothing! "For we are the temple of the living God" (2 Cor 6:16).

The idea of Christians being, collectively, the temple of God was already laid before the Corinthians in Paul's earlier epistle (1 Cor 3:16). There they were also reminded that God's temple was sacred (holy), and they were that temple (1 Cor 3:17). They were to "flee from sexual immortality" (1 Cor 6:18) and "from idolatry" (1 Cor 10:14), for all forms of wickedness are incompatible with the kingdom of God (1 Cor 6:9-10). In 2 Corinthians 6:14-18 the reminder that they are God's temple is followed, via a series of Old Testament texts, by the call to really be God's holy people among whom he is present as in a temple. This exploration of the temple imagery as applied to the Christian community in the world closes with a final exhortation: "Let us purify ourselves from everything that contaminates body and spirit, perfecting holiness out of reverence for God" (2 Cor 7:1).

The whole passage from 2 Corinthians 6:14 on seems to drive toward this climax. Here is the key to what "not being yoked with unbelievers" means. It means that the Christian is in process, moving toward holiness. The concept of holiness, as applied to both the temple and the people of God, is grounded in the Old Testament. The Hebrew word meaning "separated" always has a double meaning: separated from evil and *dedicated to* the service of God. Separation from evil is demonstrated by a distinctive way of life which evidences moral behavior of the highest order. Dedication to God's service is demonstrated by the rejection of all idolatrous contamination (1 Cor 10:14; 2 Cor 6:16), whether in its ancient or modern forms (for "idolatry" is giving ultimate allegiance to beings or powers or things or values, rather than to God).

What are the implications for today? Not monastic isolation from the world. In 1 Corinthians 5:10 Paul recognizes that disassociation from immoral, worldly persons is impossible, since that would mean that one "would have to leave this world" (see also Jesus' prayer in Jn 17:15, "not that you take them out of the world but that you protect them from the evil one"). In 1 Corinthians 7:12-16, he recognizes that the marriage of a believer and unbeliever may lead to the sanctification of the unbelieving spouse. And in 1 Corinthians 10:27, he recognizes the possibility of believers at dinner parties in the homes of unbelieving friends or neighbors.

Separatist movements in church history, in the attempt to be faithful to the radical nature of Paul's call for holiness, have often interpreted that call in terms of external associations or contacts or affiliations. Such a focus has often missed what seems to be the core of Paul's concern; namely, that while living in the world and in contact with unbelievers, Christians have nothing in common with the darkness and evil and unrighteousness and immorality that claims the loyalties of those who are as yet not reconciled with God.

Thus to be "yoked with unbelievers" is to be of one heart and mind with them, co-opted by the values that guide them, seduced by their commitments to various "gods and lords" (1 Cor 8:5), conformed to a view of things which dismisses absolute truth and moral absolutes. Christians, according to Paul, are new creations living in the midst of the old order. As such, they are to "live as children of light," bearing "the fruit of the light" which is "goodness, righteousness and truth" (Eph 5:8-9).

---

[1]In light of the fact that both Leviticus 19:19 and Deuteronomy 22:9-10 forbid various unequal combinations, such as sowing different seeds in the same soil and garments made from different materials, it is apparent that the metaphor "unevenly yoked" speaks of incompatibility, such as the common expression "oil and water don't mix."

[2]Paul uses the name Belial only here as the opponent of Christ; his usual term is Satan. Belial (or Beliar; the spellings vary) is the name given to the head of evil forces opposed to God in the noncanonical literature of Judaism (for example, Jubilees 1:20; 15:33; Martyrdom of Isaiah 1:9; 2:4; 3:11).

12:2 Caught Up to the Third Heaven?

In 2 Corinthians 12:2 Paul refers to "a man" (probably himself) who is "caught up to the third heaven." Isn't there only one heaven? What is this third heaven?

Of the 231 times that the word *heaven* occurs in the New Testament, the vast majority are absolute uses: voices come from heaven, Christ ascends to heaven, there is a kingdom of heaven. Heaven in these verses stands for either the dwelling place of God or the place the rain comes from. The context provides the information needed to decide which is meant.

In this passage, however, Paul is talking about a journey somewhere. The man he is referring to is almost certainly himself. It was considered proud or boastful to directly refer to great honor or great shame coming to oneself. If you wanted to make such a reference, the proper way to do so was in the third person: "Such and such happened to a man." This is the convention that Paul is using here. He has felt forced by the apparent claims of his opponents in Corinth to visions to refer to his own visionary experiences. Rather than roll out a list of experiences, starting with the Damascus road incident, he cites the one vision that he knows will top any of theirs, a vision in which his experience of heaven was so real that he is not sure if it was a vision or a physical rapture to heaven. This vivid experience took place fourteen years before Paul wrote 2 Corinthians, or about A.D. 44. This places the event in the period between Paul's departure from Jerusalem after his conversion (Acts 9:30) and his commissioning for his first missionary journey (Acts 13:1-3). During this period he was very active in ministry in Syria and Cilicia, eventually being recruited by Barnabas to minister in Antioch. Into this period we must put many of the experiences he refers to in 2 Corinthians 11.

Where, then, is the third heaven to which Paul was caught up? In the Old Testament there seems to be a threefold division of heaven into the heaven in which the birds fly, the heaven where the stars exist (often thought of as a "firmament"), and above that the heaven where God resides, referred to as "the highest heavens" (1 Kings 8:27; 2 Chron 2:6; 6:18; Neh 9:6; Ps 148:4).

Unfortunately, this information is derived from occasional references in the Old Testament and not clearly taught in it. There is no Old Testament discourse on the nature of heaven. In the time of Paul some Jews made a finer distinction than that made in the Old Testament, dividing the heavens into five (*3 Apocalypse of Baruch* 11:1), into seven spheres (*Testament of Levi* 3:1; *Ascension of Isaiah* 9; in the Talmud *b. Hagigah* 11b), and into ten (*2 Enoch* 20:3b; 22:1). Paul does not indicate to which of these schemes he subscribes until he gets to 2 Corinthians 12:4 and says that he was "caught up to paradise." The term "paradise" is a Persian loan word referring to a walled garden, which came to indicate the abode of God (even when located in the seventh heaven, *Ascension of Isaiah* 9:7; *b. Hagigah* 12b). In the New Testament it is identified as the place where Jesus was with the blessed dead (Lk 23:43) and the location of the tree of life (Rev 2:7; compare Rev 22:1-5 for a fuller identification of where this tree is). Thus Paul is indicating that he was caught up to the very presence of God, the highest of the heavens.

The New Testament does not encourage speculation about the structure of heaven. In fact, while we can discover the various patterns that this or that biblical author apparently believed in, none of them teach on the divisions of the heavens. When Paul says "the third heaven" we cannot be sure that he himself firmly believed that heaven was divided into three and only three parts, or only that he realized that his readers would understand that he meant the highest of the heavens. The point is that for Christians the divisions of heaven are relatively meaningless. They know that they are on earth now and that where they long to be is in the presence of their Lord, whether that be the third, fifth, seventh or tenth level of heaven. Wherever Jesus is, all of the intermediate levels are relatively meaningless, for the Christian goal is Christ more than heaven. Paul is indicating, then, that he received a foretaste of what it will be like to be in the very presence of the Lord.

12:7 What Is the Thorn in the Flesh?

Paul refers to "a thorn in my flesh" as a disciplinary measure to keep him from becoming too proud due to his experience in heaven. What exactly was this "thorn"? Was it some type of a disease, or was it something else?

The identification of this "thorn" has eluded scholars for centuries. At the end of the second century Tertullian identified it as a pain in the ear or head (*De Pudicitia* 13.17). In the early Byzantine period the great Chrysostom (*Homilies* 26) argued that it was opponents (based on the meaning of "Satan" as "adversary"). In the medieval period it was understood to be sexual temptation, while the reformers viewed it as a spiritual temptation. Some modern commentators opt for a physical disease, especially a severe form of ophthalmia (based on Gal 4:13-15) or malarial fever (so William M. Ramsay, *St. Paul the Traveler and Roman Citizen* [Grand Rapids, Mich.: Baker Books, 1962], pp. 94-97). Others have pointed to nervous disorders (including epilepsy), agony over the Jewish rejection of the gospel, or a speech impediment.

There are some things that we can definitely say about the "thorn." First, it was evil. It is described as a "messenger of Satan," not as an angel of God. This means that it comes from the Evil One with evil intent. Whether adversaries or disease, the "thorn" was evil (and in the Scripture both adversaries and disease come from evil). Second, God was allowing this thing. This is what appears to be indicated by "there was given me." It is certainly what is intended in the next verse, when Paul prays three times for the removal of the problem and gets a no in reply. Third, the "thorn" caused some type of weakness. In fact, after coming to accept that God would not remove it, Paul says, "That is why, for Christ's sake, I delight in weaknesses, in insults, in hardships, in persecutions, in difficulties. For when I am weak, then I am strong" (2 Cor 12:10). In this weakness Paul knew that God's strength could be shown.

None of the suggestions made above is entirely without merit, but in my view Chrysostom was probably right in general. First, in the Old Testament adversaries are sometimes referred to as "thorns in your sides" (Num 33:55; Judg 2:3; compare Ezek 2:6; 28:24; Micah 7:4) or "thorns in your eyes" (Josh 23:13). There is no metaphorical use of "thorn" in the Old Testament for illness or temptation. Most of the other uses of "thorn" in the Old Testament are images drawn from farming or the awareness that briars and thorns grew among the rubble of cities which were destroyed. Second, the term "messenger" (Greek *angelos*) in Paul's writings always refers to a person. Third, in 2 Corinthians 10—13 the basic topic is Paul's opponents. The whole section refers to the interlopers who are oppressing his beloved Corinthian church and at the same time criticizing Paul for not having had the courage to be equally oppressive. Fourth, Paul parallels this "thorn" with a "weakness" in which he will glory. While the term "weakness" (Greek *astheneia*) can refer to illness (Gal 4:13; 1 Tim 5:23), in its seven occurrences in the Corinthian letters (and in both its occurrences in Romans) it refers to moral, spiritual or social weakness. In 2 Corinthians 11:30 it refers to Paul's shame at having to flee from Damascus rather than face his enemies (in a culture in which an honorable death was better than fearful flight). Another weakness-strength contrast comes in 2 Corinthians 13:3-4 in which Jesus was weak in his crucifixion, unable to withstand his adversaries, but was raised in strength; so Paul who was socially weak when present in Corinth will return with Christ's power, for Christ will defeat his adversaries. Furthermore, in 2 Corinthians 12:10 he lists weakness in a list which includes "insults, hardships, persecutions, difficulties," but no terms for illness. Thus I conclude that the evidence from both the Old Testament background and the actual use of the term in Paul points to the "thorn" as being the opponents who dogged Paul's tracks throughout his mission, confusing churches every time he left one church to plant another. If Paul was tempted to feel proud, how proud would he feel when even his strongest churches and best converts proved to be subvertable by newcomers?

This is not to say that Paul never became ill. In fact, in Galatians 4:13-15 he is probably referring to illness, an unknown illness that brought him to preach in the Galatian region, perhaps because of its climate or perhaps because he could go no further. What we are talking about is not whether Paul ever became ill, but what is the exact interpretation of this one passage.

What is clear is that even something sent by Satan himself can be used by God. Paul apparently did not impress people. He frequently speaks of himself as weak and his speech as unrefined. Yet people who met him were forced to contrast that weakness with the evident power of the Spirit working through Paul. It was clear that the power he exhibited was not Paul's power. Something greater was at work in him. Weakness and poor speech does not glorify God;

he puts no value on it. Yet when it becomes an occasion for contrasting us with him, he can use it for his glory. In Paul's case the results spoke for themselves. Paul by himself could not have accomplished what he did; he himself was satisfied that the results of his ministry showed the hand of God, even if he wished that the process of so displaying God were more comfortable.

See also comment on JOB 2:1-6.

GALATIANS

1:9 Condemning Opponents?

Paul's curse in Galatians 1:9 is a hard saying for two reasons: it does not seem to be in agreement with some other statements of Paul, and it seems diametrically opposed to the teaching of Jesus with regard to our attitudes and actions toward those who are opposed to us.

In Romans 2:1-4 Paul lays down the principle that judgment passed on others is in some sense "reflexive"; that is, when we pass judgment on others, we condemn ourselves at the same time. For only God knows the truth about us, and only he is able therefore to pass judgment. We are mere creatures, limited with respect to both the truth about others and the truth about ourselves. We, like all others, are sinners (Rom 3:23); that is the ultimate reason we ought not to pass judgment.

This same sentiment is expressed again in a context where there is mutual judging going on within the congregation (Rom 14:1-13). Here the admonition not to judge others in respect to certain practices and beliefs considered inappropriate or wrong is based on the assertion that each disciple is accountable ultimately to the Lord (Rom 14:4), and all will equally "stand before God's judgment seat" (Rom 14:10). The larger perspective which ought to guide Christians' attitudes toward opponents is derived by Paul from the teaching of Jesus. Thus, echoing Matthew 5:44, Paul says, "Bless those who persecute you; bless and do not curse" (Rom 12:14). Our task as Christians is to "overcome evil with good" (Rom 12:21).

The overall teaching, attitude and life of Jesus stand also in apparent conflict with Paul's word of condemnation. Jesus' radical imperative on the matter is "Do not judge, or you too will be judged. For in the same way you judge others, you will be judged" (Mt 7:1-2). The reason given for this imperative is that our own vision may be so impaired that it is sheer hypocrisy to try to remove the sawdust particle in the other's eye (Mt 7:3, 5). The proper response to those who are opposed to us is to love them and pray for them (Mt 5:44). Beyond these words, Jesus' entire life is a demonstration of his words' validity. He did not come into a world opposed to God to condemn it but to save it (Jn 3:17). Because of his deep compassion he weeps over Jerusalem (Lk 19:41), the city that kills the prophets and those (like Jesus) sent to it (Lk 13:34). To the adulteress he speaks the word of forgiveness rather than judgment (Jn 8:10-11); to the criminal hanging on a cross next to him he speaks the word of grace (Lk 23:39-43).

As Paul's words against judging seem to stand in conflict with his harsh words in Galatians 1:9, so the larger picture of Jesus' teaching and life, characterized by love and compassion, by humility and forgiveness, stands in apparent conflict with another dimension of his life. Jesus' words and actions could be uncompromisingly harsh toward those who opposed him and his ministry and whose "piety" excluded the redemptive work of God. He calls the religious leaders of his own people "sons of the devil," whose desire they carry out (Jn 8:44). Those who oppose his ministry of releasing the possessed from bondage are called "an evil generation" (Lk 11:29 RSV), who will be judged and condemned (Lk 11:31-32). Those who oppose the work of the Spirit of God in and through his life (Mt 12:28) will be condemned eternally; for them there is no forgiveness (Mt 12:31-32). Words of bitter denunciation are spoken against the teachers of the law and Pharisees, whom he calls "child[ren] of hell" (Mt 23:15 RSV), "blind fools" (Mt 23:17), "whitewashed tombs" (Mt 23:27), "snakes" and a "brood of vipers" who cannot "escape being condemned to hell" (Mt 23:33).

When we carefully compare this radically harsh tone in Jesus' teaching with that strand in his life which exudes compassion and forgiveness, we recognize where the essential difference lies. He came as the incarnation of God's redemptive love, and wherever there is openness to it, forgiveness is given, grace is experienced, sin is overcome. But where there is absolute rejection of that redemptive love, where the work of God is identified as demonic, where truth is trampled underfoot, there condemnation is pronounced. It is within this latter context of the rejection of God's redemptive love that this hard saying must be understood.

In Paul's epistle to the Galatians, the central issue addressed is this: the core of the gospel which Paul had preached and on which their faith was based is that we are justified, brought into a right relationship with God, solely by his grace and through faith, not by gaining a standing before God on the basis of obedience to the law (Gal 2:15-21). That gospel was being challenged by the so-called Judaizers; namely, Jewish Christians who demanded that Gentile Christians observe the Mosaic law, including ritual observances such as special days, kosher foods and circumcision (Gal 3:1-7; 4:8-11, 17, 21-22). Those who respond to their teaching, who are led away from the truth (Gal 5:7), who now seek "to be justified by law, have been alienated from Christ" and have "fallen away from grace" (Gal 5:4).

For Paul the conflict between the gospel which he preached and the teaching of the Judaizers is a life-and-death struggle. Why? Because legalistic obedience, life before God based on religious achievement, does not bring one into right relationship with God (Gal 2:16; 3:3) but to alienation from him (Gal 5:4), to rejection of God's grace (Gal 2:21), to a life of legalistic bondage (Gal 4:9, 21; 5:1), to the curse of death (Gal 3:10-13).

Those who teach this way are "false brothers" (Gal 2:4) who oppose the "truth of the gospel" (Gal 2:5, 14), confuse the believers (Gal 1:7), "pervert the gospel of Christ" (Gal 1:7), bewitch the saints (Gal 3:1). Therefore, let anyone who does this "be eternally condemned" (Gal 1:8-9). This strong language shows how serious the matter was for Paul. George Duncan puts it well when he calls these words "an imprecation such as we cannot imagine him using had it been merely his personal prestige . . . anything, in fact, but the gospel of Christ which was at stake."[1]

It is clear then that Paul is not calling for the condemnation of his opponents (that is, the Judaizers) because they are opposed to him, but rather because they are *enemies of the gospel.* That gospel is of divine origin, not of Paul's invention (Gal 1:11-12). Therefore, those who pervert it subvert God's redemptive purpose. On those who thus act and teach, the judgment of God is justly pronounced. Thus there is here no real conflict between Paul's general call for a nonjudgmental spirit and his strong word of judgment here, just as there is no real conflict between Jesus' teaching on love for one's opponents and his words of judgment. In both cases, where the work and truth of God is at stake, those who reject it stand under judgment.

See also comment on PSALMS 137:8-9; 139:20.

[1]George S. Duncan, *The Epistle of Paul to the Galatians* (London: Hodder & Stoughton, 1934), pp. 18-19.

3:23-25 The End of the Law?

See comment on ROMANS 10:4.

3:24-26 Is the Church Israel?

See comment on GALATIANS 6:16.

5:2 Christ of No Value?

Galatians 5:2 seems to express a limitation in the work of Christ. Doesn't this verse devalue the extent and efficacy of Christ's life and death? Can the submission to something as external as the rite of circumcision blunt the effectiveness of his sacrificial death?

The central theme of Galatians is that salvation is by faith and not by works; that justification (that is, a right relationship with God) is the result of the gracious gift of God's Son, not human achievement; that freedom from the bondage to sin does not come by even the most meticulous obedience to the law, but through the atoning death of Christ on the cross. This gospel was being undermined and perverted by the so-called Judaizers.

These Jewish Christians opposed the Pauline gospel as antinomian ("against law"), apparently believing that in addition to God's work in Christ, both Jewish and Gentile Christians needed to observe the law, including particularly ceremonial and cultic observances, such as special days, kosher foods and circumcision (Gal 3:1-7; 4:8-11, 17, 21-22). Paul calls them the "circumcision group" (Gal 2:12), because their demand for obedience to the Mosaic law from the followers of the Messiah expressed itself most specifically and radically in the demand that Gentiles, in order to become full members in the new covenant community, be circumcised (Gal 6:12).

That demand of the Judaizers Paul rejects uncompromisingly, because it sets up a criterion for salvation—namely, human achievement (Gal 3:3)—which lies outside God's way of salvation. To seek righteousness—which in this context does not refer to moral-ethical goodness, but conveys Paul's technical sense of "right relationship with God"—through observance of the law would be to "set aside the grace of God" (Gal 2:21).

Why is Paul so opposed to any intrusion of legal observance? One reason is worked out in the opening three chapters of Romans. While as a rabbi Paul seems clearly to have believed that complete obedience to the Mosaic law was possible (Phil 3:4-6), he was just as clearly convinced that such a path toward relationship with God led inevitably to self-righteousness, to pride in one's religious achievements, to boasting before others and God, and therefore to an implicit rejection of a stance of humility before the Creator. A second and perhaps more fundamental reason for rejecting the way of external, legalistic obedience was Paul's conviction that from the very beginning of redemptive history, the divinely established way toward saving relationship with God was by faith, not by works of the law (Gal 3:6-25; see also Rom 3—4).

On the basis of these convictions, Paul argues that if a system of law, even the Mosaic law, could impart life, then a right relationship with God "would certainly have come by the law" (Gal 3:21); but the only power the law has is to reveal our standing as sinners before a holy God and to show that we are finally dependent on his grace, receiving it in faith (Gal 3:18, 22-25).

That understanding of God's way of salvation, in contrast to the way of the Judaizers, elicits from Paul the charge that submission to circumcision [as a means toward right standing before and with God] means that Christ "is of no value" to them whatsoever (Gal 5:2). The bracketed phrase seeks to interpret Paul's meaning, in light of a parallel statement he makes in Galatians 2:21; namely, "if righteousness could be gained through the law, Christ died for nothing." The center of Paul's concern is of course that circumcision—which for Paul is "shorthand" for life lived in relation to the Mosaic law—understood and practiced *as a means to righteousness,* excludes the operation of God's grace. It is in fact the assertion that one can make it through personal achievement; as such it negates the necessity of the atonement.

For those who choose that way "Christ will be of no value," for the attempt "to be justified by law" leads to alienation from Christ and departure from grace. If we live "by the law," Christ and his atoning work have no value for us. But if we are "in Christ Jesus, neither circumcision nor uncircumcision has any value. The only thing that counts is faith expressing itself through love" (Gal 5:6).

See also comment on ACTS 16:3; 21:21; PHILIPPIANS 2:12-13; 3:4-6.

5:12 Hate Your Enemies?

See comment on PSALM 139:20.

5:19-21 Who Inherits the Kingdom?

See comment on 1 CORINTHIANS 6:9-10.

6:16 Who Is the Israel of God?

Galatians 6:16 is part of Paul's benediction with which he closes the letter. Who is included among "the Israel of God"? What is "this rule"? The answer to the last question emerges quite naturally from the context. Based on differing understandings of both the structure of the sentence and Paul's terminology, opinions vary widely concerning the answer to the first.

Let us begin with the context. Paul has argued throughout this letter that God's way of salvation consists of his grace, offered in the atoning death of Jesus Christ through which persons are freed from the bondage of sin and legalistic religion. This redemptive work of God in Christ is appropriated in the response and life of faith. That thesis is worked out over against what can be called a Judaizing faction among the Galatian Christians who believed and taught that right standing before God (that is, justification) is achieved, for Jews and Gentiles alike, only through adherence to the ritual of circumcision (and other parts of the ceremonial-ritual law).

This discussion is brought to a conclusion in the verses immediately preceding our saying (Gal 6:12-15). Those who insist on circumcision (which for Paul is here shorthand for religion under the law) are really seeking to establish an external measuring stick for human achievement before God on the basis of which one can boast (Gal 6:12-13). But, counters Paul, the only ground for "boasting" is outside us, namely, the cross of Christ (Gal 6:14).

In such a case, boasting really becomes the praise of God for his unspeakable gift! That leads Paul to the sum of the matter: "Neither circumcision nor uncircumcision means anything; what counts is a new creation" (Gal 6:15). That is, in the new creation inaugurated in Christ "there is neither Jew nor Greek" (Gal 3:28; see also 2 Cor 5:17). Neither the practice of external ritual or ceremony nor its absence is a basis for redemptive relationship with God. The only basis is the new creature, established by grace and through faith. That is the "rule" (or principle) to which Paul refers in this saying.

An understanding of the structure of the sentence, as well as the unique term "the Israel of God," is our second order of business. Notice first that the sentence punctuations in our English version, as well as in the Greek texts behind them, are the work of interpretation. Thus there are often a number of ways in which the text can be punctuated. And how one punctuates can determine the meaning or nuances of a text. In Galatians 6:16 there are basically two options, and slight variations within each of these:

1. The text used in this book (NIV), as well as most other modern English versions, places the essential comma between two sentence parts: one contains the words "peace" and "mercy," the other contains the term "the Israel of God." This reading, based on the punctuation of the commonly accepted Greek text,[1] can be understood in at least two ways: (a) The benediction "peace and mercy" is pronounced on one group. "All who follow this rule," in part one of the sentence, are identified as "the Israel of God" in the second part of the sentence. Such a meaning is implied in the NIV reading of "even to the Israel of God," and the RSV's "upon the Israel of God." (b) The benediction is pronounced on *two groups,* those "who follow this rule" and the Israel of God. However, the term "Israel of God" is seen as a comprehensive term, *including* those in Galatia "who follow this rule." Among modern versions, the TEV ("may peace and mercy be with them—with them and with all of God's people") and NEB ("and upon the whole Israel of God") support this understanding of the text.

2. Some commentators punctuate the Greek text differently.[2] It is grammatically possible to place the decisive comma so that the terms "peace" and "mercy" are separated as belonging to two distinct parts of the sentence. In that case it would read: "Peace to all who follow this rule, as well as [or, 'and'] mercy upon the Israel of God." On this reading, the benediction is divided and addresses two very distinct groups. "Peace" is pronounced upon believers in Christ ("those who follow this rule"); "mercy" is pronounced upon Israelites who are not yet, but may become, participants in the redeemed community of God's people.

The first option assumes that the term "Israel of God" is used by Paul for all those who are "in Christ," whether they are Jews or Gentiles. Since Paul uses the term only here, and it is found nowhere else in the entire New Testament, the use of it as synonymous with "Christian" must be derived from the broader Pauline context.

As in Galatians, so in Romans Paul argues that righteousness (right standing before God) comes by faith, not by works of the law. In Romans 4 he shows that way to have been God's way from the start. Proof is given in the example of Abraham, who believed God and thus came into right relationship with him before the external sign of circumcision was given (Rom 4:9-11). From this Paul draws the conclusion that Abraham "is the father of all who believe," both the uncircumcised (that is, Gentile believers, Rom 4:11) and the circumcised (that is, Jewish believers, Rom 4:12). Since Abraham (the father of historical Israel) is also the father of all who believe, the designation of this company as the "Israel of God" would surely be appropriate (see also Rom 9:6-8).

Further support for such a correlation comes from Philippians, where Paul pointedly calls all those who put their faith in Christ Jesus "the circumcision," in contrast to those "who put [their] confidence in the flesh" (Phil 3:3), that is, who depend on their circumcision (Phil 3:4-6). In Galatians, too, "those who believe" are called "children of Abraham" (Gal 3:7), including Gentiles who respond in faith (Gal 3:8). This strand in Paul's thought is brought to a focal point in Galatians 3:26-29. Addressing the company of believers, consisting of both Jewish and Gentile believers, Paul says to them, "You are all sons of God through faith in Christ Jesus" (Gal 3:26). This designation is grounded in the Old Testament, where Israelites are called "sons of the living God" (Hos 1:10) or, collectively, "Son [of God]" (Hos 11:1). Here emerges the equation: Israel = son/sons of God = believers in Christ. Paul concludes the thought by affirming that those who are in Christ, both Jew and Gentile, are Abraham's offspring (Gal 3:27-29).

It would be difficult to deny that the designation of the Christian fellowship as "Israel of God" could have emerged out of Paul's thought-development. Thus there is a high degree of probability in this line of interpretation. Yet the second option outlined—which assigns to the term "Israel of God" a more limited scope—has merit and should be given serious consideration.

In addition to seeing Abraham as "the father of all who believe" (Rom 4:11), Paul distinguished *two groups* within historic Israel. In Romans 2:28-29, he argues that there are two kinds of Jews: those who meet only the external requirements (circumcision and physical descent) and those who, in addition, are authentic Jews inwardly, whose circumcision is not only external but also of the heart, worked "by the Spirit." To this idea of a "true" Israel within the historical, physical Israel may be assigned Paul's concept of the "remnant," which he explores in Romans 11. By God's grace, there are those within Israel who, like Paul, will yet respond in faith to God's work in Christ (Rom 11:1, 5). Is it possible, in light of this distinction between the whole people and the remnant, that Paul coined the term "Israel of God" to distinguish the remnant from simply "Israel"? If so, this text would receive a unique meaning. Paul's benediction of "peace" would be addressing "those who follow the rule," that is, those who already belong to Christ. The benediction of "mercy" would be addressed to the faithful remnant within Israel, all those who had not yet grasped God's revelation in Jesus the Christ, but who by God's mercy would yet come to faith.

A final support for such an interpretation comes from the fact that the normal Pauline sequence in benediction and greetings is "grace and peace" (or "mercy and peace"), while here it is "peace and mercy." Since, according to Paul, God's mercy is that which leads to the condition of peace (with God, self and others), logical consistency would assign "peace" to those who are already in Christ, and "mercy" to those who are "not yet." That is plausible, with the reservation that greetings and benedictions are not always or necessarily logical formulations.

Whichever interpretation is accepted, one fact is clear; namely, Paul's overall view saw the church, the fellowship of God's people, as a new covenant community in which Jew and Greek, Israelite and Gentile, become one new people. And this people is the fulfillment of God's promise to Abraham at the beginning of redemptive history: "All peoples on earth will be blessed through you" (Gen 12:3; Gal 3:29).

See also comment on ROMANS 11:26; REVELATION 7:4.

---

[1]The standard New Testament Greek text editions are those by Eberhard Nestlé and the United Bible Societies text (edited by Aland, Black, Metzger, Wikgren). It must be remembered that the punctuation is a result of the editors' decisions.

[2]For example, E. Burton, *The Epistle to the Galatians*, International Critical Commentary (New York: Scribner's Sons, 1970), pp. 357-58; also George Simpson Duncan, *The Epistle of Paul to the Galatians* (London: Hodder & Stoughton, 1934), p. 192.

EPHESIANS

1:10 Universalism?

See comment on COLOSSIANS 1:19.

1:11 Predestination?

See comment on ROMANS 8:29

2:15 Abolishing the Law?

See comment on ROMANS 10:4.

4:9-10 Christ Ascending and Descending?

The section of the epistle in which Ephesians 4:9-10 is located makes clear that the subject of the action referred to is Christ. But what does the language of "ascending" and "descending" refer to? What are the "lower earthly regions"? Are there various "heavens"? With what does he "fill the whole universe"?

These questions literally tumble out of the text at us. That is particularly remarkable because the thrust of Paul's thought in the total context of this passage is crystal clear. The obscurity of this hard saying is at least partially due to the fact that the question in Ephesians 4:10 ("What does 'he ascended' mean?") is in reference to an Old Testament text cited in Ephesians 4:8. Hoping to get a clue to Paul's purpose in citing the text of Psalm 68:18, we read the text in its own setting. That, rather than helping, confuses even more when we realize that Paul cites the text with a significant alteration, apparently to make it fit his own purpose.

The central theological theme in the first four chapters of Ephesians is that the church of Jesus Christ is a creation of God in which a divided, fragmented humanity can be reconciled into one unified organism (Eph 1:22-23). The dividing wall between Jew and Gentile has been broken down (Eph 2:14-16). Those who were once "far away" (that is, Gentiles) have become part of God's "household," which is being shaped into a "holy temple" in which God is present by his Spirit (Eph 2:17-22).

It is the unity and life and ministry of this "temple," this body of Christ, which is the subject matter of Ephesians 4. After expressing the unity of the church in eloquent terms, grounding that unity in the fact that there is one Spirit, one Lord, one God and Father of all (Eph 4:1-6), Paul moves on to acknowledge the body's diversity. Christ has given grace to the members of this body (Eph 4:7) for one purpose: that there would be apostles, prophets, evangelists, pastors and teachers (Eph 4:11) who would prepare all of God's people for service, so that the whole body would grow toward maturity, expressing in this world "the fullness of Christ" (Eph 4:12-13). It is the gifting of the church for its task which is the context for understanding Paul's reference to Psalm 68:18 and its application to Christ.

Paul moves from consideration of the unity of the church toward its diversity by stating that "to each one of us grace has been given as Christ has apportioned it" (or, more literally, "according to the measure of Christ's *gift,*" Eph 4:7 RSV, emphasis mine). Paul knew that the ascended, exalted Christ had poured out the gift of the Spirit at Pentecost (Acts 2:32-38) and that by this Spirit the church had been endowed with a variety of gifts (1 Cor 12:4-11).

As often in Paul's writings, a word or phrase or concept he is using recalls for him a word from Scripture, which he then proceeds to quote: "When he ascended on high, he led captives in his train and gave gifts to men." It is apparent that the point of contact between what he has just written and the text from Psalm 68:18 is that this text speaks of an exalted, victorious one who gave gifts to his people. However, when we read the Psalm verse in the Old Testament, we note that the victorious one *"received gifts from men."* What is at first either disturbing or puzzling is the impression that Paul alters the Old Testament text to suit his purpose.

The Psalm quoted celebrates the victory of God over Israel's enemies and pictures that victory in terms of a triumphal procession to the sanctuary on Mount Zion, where the vanquished bring their gifts of tribute to the victorious king, who receives their gifts (Ps 68:17-18). This depiction of the triumph of God may have struck Paul as expressing well the triumph of the messianic king in cross, resurrection and exaltation. But since he thought about the gifting of the church by the exalted Christ, and the Psalm speaks of the exalted One receiving gifts from men, does Paul simply alter the text? One answer has been that Paul may neither have intended to quote exactly nor to interpret, "but in familiar Jewish fashion adapts the passage to his own use, knowing that his readers . . . would recognize the alteration and see the purpose of it."[1] That is possible. But there is another, and likely better, explanation.

In Paul's time most Jews no longer understood Hebrew, Aramaic being their everyday language. In the synagogue, when the Hebrew text was read, a translator would freely render the text in a paraphrased form, often clarifying difficulties and making contemporary applications. These "interpretative translations" were handed down in oral form and later written down in what were called Targums. Now the Aramaic Targum text of Psalm 68:18 has precisely the change from "receiving gifts" to "giving gifts" that we find in Paul's quotation. It is quite possible that Paul simply makes use of the rabbinic interpretation of the Psalm passage. That interpretation may have arisen from the recognition that though the Psalm celebrates God's victory in analogy to the victory procession of earthly monarchs who receive gifts of homage and tribute from their conquered subjects, the exalted God of Israel is the one who bestows salvation on his people.

Having quoted the Psalm text, in keeping with its Targumic restatement,

Paul now continues in typical rabbinic fashion to explore an aspect of the Psalm text in relation to the action of Christ, the messianic king who came and triumphed over death and was exalted to lordship (Eph 1:20-21; see also Phil 2:5-11). Thus the words "he ascended" (from the Psalm), when applied to Christ, presuppose (or imply) "that he also descended to the lower, earthly regions" (Eph 4:9). What "descent" is in view here? And what are "the lower, earthly regions" (or, as in the NIV notes, "the depths of the earth")?

One view holds that Paul has in mind the Incarnation, the descent of the Son of Man from heaven to earth (see Jn 3:13). Within this view, there are two ways in which "the lower, earthly regions" can be understood: (1) It could be seen as a reference to the lowest parts of the earth, namely, the underworld—the world of the dead, Hades. That could refer simply to the fact that the descent of Christ climaxed in death and burial. Or it could be a reference to the idea found in the New Testament only in 1 Peter 3:18-20 that before his resurrection, Christ entered the world of the dead and preached to the departed spirits. (2) It could be taken to mean "the lower, that is, earthly regions," in contrast to the height of heaven to which the Christ ascended (Eph 4:10).

An alternate view holds that the "ascent" precedes the "descent." In light of everything said previously in this epistle, Paul had no need to prove the Incarnation; that could be presupposed. Since the immediate context (Eph 4:7, 11) speaks about the giving of gifts to the church by the ascended, triumphant Lord, what Paul needed to show was that a descent was necessary in order for the exalted one to give these gifts. That descent is identified with the coming of Christ in the Spirit.

Paul's concept of the indwelling Christ (Eph 3:17) and John's teaching about the coming of Christ to the believers in the Spirit, subsequent to Jesus' "exaltation" (Jn 14:23-24), would support the possibility of such an understanding of the text.

However, since Paul nowhere speaks of the gift of the Spirit or the indwelling presence of Christ as a result of a "descent," it seems more probable that the well-established Pauline concept of Christ's humiliation and exaltation (Phil 2:5-11), in that order, stands behind the sequence here. This would admirably fit the context of the giving of Christ's gifts to the church. The one who emptied himself of divine glory and humbled himself even to death has been highly exalted "in order to fill the whole universe. It was he who gave . . ."

With what does he, literally, "fill the whole"? The TEV interprets the text to mean "fill the whole universe with his presence." The RSV simply translates, "fill all things." Some have understood this "filling" in direct connection with the giving of the gifts, that is, he fills everything (or all) with his gifts.

Perhaps it is better to take the other common sense of the Greek word *plēroō* ("fill"), which is to "fulfill" or "bring to completion." That meaning would correspond well with a similar statement made earlier in the letter (Eph 1:23), where Paul speaks of the completion of the work of Christ. In that case, Paul speaks of Christ's descent (Incarnation) and ascent (ascension, exaltation) as having one purpose: to bring the mysterious purposes of God for humanity (Eph 1:8-10) to their completeness, to "fulfill" them. And the giving of gifts to the church is part of that "bringing all things to completion," since it is to lead to the church's perfection as expressing "the fullness of Christ" in the world.

---

[1]T. K. Abbott, *Epistles to the Ephesians and Colossians,*

International Critical Commentary (New York: Charles Scribner's Sons, 1897), p. 112.

5:3-5 Who Inherits the Kingdom?

See comment on 1 CORINTHIANS 6:9-10.

5:22 Wives, Submit?

The difficulty of Ephesians 5:22 is not in understanding the rather straightforward language, but its meaning. Since the patriarchal norms of the Greco-Roman world, built into the rules and regulations for everyday life and relationships, clearly demanded a wife's submission to the authority of the husband, is Paul simply advocating the continuance of conventional norms? If so, why would that be necessary? Does the qualifying phrase "as unto the Lord" introduce a radically new dimension into the nature and form of submission (or subordination)?

Of utmost importance for a proper grasp of Paul's intention are (1) the part this saying plays in the larger argument and (2) the specific meaning of terms and phrases in this saying and the surrounding text.

The larger context of this saying deals with Paul's concern that the believers, as a community and as individuals, would be strengthened by the Spirit of Christ (Eph 3:16-17) so that they would grow toward maturity (Eph 4:11-16). Such maturity comes as they are "kind and compassionate to one another" (Eph 4:32), living a life of love in imitation of God, as modeled in Christ's self-giving, sacrificial servant ministry (Eph 5:1-2).

How does this "imitation of Christ" work itself out concretely in the fellowship and common human relationships? That is the subject matter of Ephesians 5—6, and Ephesians 5:22 is part of that.

A general discussion of Christian behavior under the admonition "Have nothing to do with the fruitless deeds of darkness" (Eph 5:3-16) is followed by more specific instructions regarding relationships in the fellowship and other social contexts, like the family. This section is introduced by the admonition "understand what the will of the Lord is. . . . Be filled with the Spirit" (5:17-18 RSV). Then, by means of four closely related participial phrases (5:19-21), he shows how the Spirit-filled and guided life, in tune with God's will, expresses itself: (1) "speaking to each other," (2) "singing and making music," (3) "giving thanks" and (4) "submitting to one another."[1] It is this last participial phrase which is critical for our understanding of Ephesians 5:22.

Paul has clearly shown throughout the epistle that Christians are a new social order created to express the fullness of Christ in the midst of the old, fallen order. What he is saying in Ephesians 5:21 is that the Spirit empowers Christians to exist in relationship with each other in a radical, culturally transforming way, namely, through mutual self-submission. The ground for this radically new approach to human relationships is "out of reverence for Christ." The reason for that reverence (or, perhaps better, awe) is the radical nature of Christ's earthly life, the total, free submission of himself as God's suffering servant, climaxed in his self-giving on the cross (Eph 5:2, 25). It is reverence and awe toward that self-giving love that is to motivate our mutual self-submission to each other.

This understanding of Ephesians 5:21 ("Submit to one another") sheds critical light on Ephesians 5:22 ("Wives, submit . . ."). Both the English translations and commentators often fail us at this point, printing the participial clause of Ephesians 5:21 as an isolated paragraph, separating it from both the preceding clauses and what follows (for example, NIV, NEB) or assigning it either to the preceding paragraphs (NASB) or to head a new paragraph (RSV, TEV). None of these do justice to the structure of the whole passage and to the grammar.

The participle of Ephesians 5:21 is the last of a series of four, as shown above, and clearly belongs to what precedes it. This verse also supplies the verb "to submit" for this hard saying, without which Ephesians 5:22 would be grammatically incomplete and without meaning. The verse in Greek reads literally: "Wives, to your husbands as to the Lord." The verb "to submit" is absent and can only be read into the sentence because of the intimate connection between the two verses. Ephesians 5:21 is therefore transitional, both belonging to what precedes and setting the agenda for what follows. Thus the kind of radical self-submission to one another which evidences the fullness of the Spirit is now explored in terms of its implications for husbands and wives. That is, what does this self-submission, modeled in Jesus, look like in marriage?

The submission of the wife to the husband is to be "as to the Lord." It is no longer to be the kind expected as a matter of course by cultural norms and forced upon women—who were seen as inferior to males in both Jewish and Gentile cultures. No, her submission is to be freely chosen, being there for her partner "as to the Lord," that is, as a disciple of the Lord, as one who followed in his servant footsteps, motivated by self-giving love. This kind of submission is not a reinforcement of the traditional norms; it is rather a fundamental challenge to them.

From much of Paul's correspondence we can see that the new freedom from restrictive and often enslaving cultural norms brought by the gospel led at times to rejection of the very relationships in which these norms had been operative, such as marriage itself. It is that danger which Paul may be addressing in Ephesians 5:23. Appealing to the creation account in Genesis 2, where the woman is created out of the being of the male (Gen 2:21-23), Paul says, "For the husband [man] is the head of the wife [woman]."

As discussed in the chapter on 1 Corinthians 11:3, in common Greek the idea of "authority over" was not normally conveyed by the word "head" *(kephalē)*. Besides its literal, physical meaning ("head of man or beast"), *kephalē* had numerous metaphorical meanings, including that of "source." It is this meaning that seems most suited to the texts (1 Cor 11:3 and Eph 5:23) in which the relationship of husband and wife (or man and woman) is addressed.[2]

In both texts appeal is made to Genesis 2, where the woman is created from the man. Thus Paul, in arguing against those who would reject the marriage relationship because of a new freedom in Christ (see Gal 3:28), reminds them that, according to God's design, the man is the source of the woman's being; they were created for each other and belong together, as Ephesians 5:31, citing Genesis 2:24, underlines. Similarly (and here begins the analogy between husband/wife and Christ/church), Christ is the *kephalē* ("source") of the church's life (Eph 5:23). His relation to the church is not expressed in "authority" language, but in "source" language. Christ is the church's savior because he laid down his life for her.

A final argument for the validity of a radically new self-submission of wife to husband is now given: "As the church submits to Christ, so also wives should submit to their husbands in everything" (Eph 5:24). What is the nature of the church's submission to Christ? It is freely assumed in humble response to his self-giving, sacrificial servanthood and his continuing empowering and nurturing presence. The church's submission to Christ has nothing to do with external control or coercion. For the life and ministry of Jesus demonstrates uncompromisingly his rejection of "power over others" as valid in the new creation which he is inaugurating (Lk 22:24-27).[3] Christ stands in relation to the church, his bride, not as one who uses his power to control and demand, but rather to invite and serve.

Having radically challenged the nature of the culturally expected and demanded submission of the wife to the husband, Paul now goes on (Eph 5:25-32) to show what self-submission by the husband to the wife looks like in practice. The husband's self-submission (Eph 5:21) is to express itself in the kind of radical self-giving love that Christ demonstrated when "he gave himself up for" the life of the church (Eph 5:25). Husbands were of course expected to have erotic regard for their wives. But within a culture in which women were often not more than doormats on which male supremacy could wipe its feet, and in a religious setting where Jewish males thanked God daily that he had not made them a Gentile, a slave or a woman—in such a context erotic regard for the wife more often than not became a means of self-gratification and control over the wife. That position of superiority is daringly challenged by Paul's call upon husbands to love *(agapaō)* their wives, that is, to be there for them and with them in self-giving, nurturing, serving love. For that is the way Christ loved the church, and husbands, like their wives, are to be imitators of Christ (Eph 5:2).

See also comment on GENESIS 2:18; 3:16; 1 CORINTHIANS 11:3; 11:7; 1 PETER 3:6.

[1]For an excellent discussion of the meaning of these four participial phrases, see Markus Barth, *Epistle to the Ephesians,* The Anchor Bible, 2 vols. (New York: Doubleday, 1974), 2:583-85.

[2]In Ephesians 4:15-16 the Greek word *kephalē* ("head") is also used with the metaphorical meaning of "source." Christ is the "head" (that is, source) from whom the whole body grows and upbuilds itself in love. In the physiology of the period, the physical head was understood to give life to the rest of the body.

[3]See also Mark 8:31-38; 9:30-37; 10:32-45; John 13:12-17; Philippians 2:5-11.

6:5-8 Did Paul Approve of Slavery?

When addressing slaves in Ephesians, Paul tells them to obey their masters. There is not a hint of a suggestion that slavery is wrong. Does this mean that Paul approved of slavery? Does the Bible teach that slavery is morally acceptable?

We could add to this passage the parallel passage in Colossians 3:22-25, the whole book of Philemon, and 1 Peter 2:18-25, for in none of them is there any criticism of the institution of slavery, and in two of the three there is an exhortation to the slave to obey his or her master. In other words, in the New Testament there is no clear critique of slavery. This passage is a good example of a general New Testament attitude.

Having said the above, we see in this passage the general strategy that Paul took toward social reform. In Ephesians 5—6 there are three pairs of social relationships mentioned (wives and husbands; children and fathers; slaves and masters). In each of the three Paul addresses the subordinate first. He calls them to the traditional virtue of submission (which any pagan moralist would also have called for). Yet Paul adds a new twist in that in one form or another he reframes the traditional duty in terms of a relationship to Christ. In other words, he takes it out of the earthly context and puts it in the context of something that the Lord will reward. In doing this he qualifies the absoluteness of the duty, for obviously one cannot do something "as unto the Lord" or "like slaves of Christ" if it is something that the Lord has made it perfectly clear that he hates. This may seem like a small point to us, but in that world the obedience of wives to husbands, children to parents and slaves to masters was understood to be absolute. These three classes of people were thought to have no right (or even in some cases no ability) of moral decision beyond simple obedience. But Paul addresses them as full moral beings and puts their obedience, demanded by their culture, into a wider theological context. Obedience now has a higher meaning, and they must make decisions regarding it and set limits to it (although in setting limits they will probably face suffering). Paul has raised the status of the subordinate to that of a full human being before God, yet he has done this without calling for rebellion. Paul teaches this partially because Christ also gave up his rights and suffered, so rebellion does not express the spirit of Christ, but even more because social status does not matter to him. The important issue is that one is serving Christ. Social status is simply the context for that service (compare 1 Cor 7:17-24).

Yet in each pair of relationships Paul also addresses the social superior and points out that he (in all cases he is addressing males) has responsibilities toward his subordinate. The husband is to lay down his life for his wife; the father is not to exasperate his child. The father also has a duty of moral instruction. The master is to treat slaves appropriately in the light of knowing that in reality both he and they are slaves of the same heavenly Master (Eph 6:9). After all, even Paul calls himself a slave of Jesus Christ. This part of Paul's teaching is revolutionary. It was unheard of to call a social superior to respect and respond to a call to duty toward social inferiors. In fact, one could say that Paul brings the masters down to the level of their slaves and makes them treat their slave as a brother or sister. This implication in Ephesians becomes quite explicit in Philemon. Paul's strategy, then, is to elevate the inferior and to abase the superior by pointing to their relationship to Jesus Christ as the context for all other relationships in their lives.

Having looked at Paul's general strategy, let us look at slavery in particular. In the social world of Paul's day slavery was an accepted institution. There was also a genuine fear of slaves. In Rome slaves were prohibited from wearing distinctive clothing for fear that they would discover how numerous they were and start a revolt. Slaves all over the Roman world were under the total control of their masters. If a master wished, he could have a slave executed (or kill the slave himself). While this was frowned on if there was no reason for it, it was not outside of the master's rights. It was just as today a person can demolish their house if they wish, even though their neighbors may think it a stupid and wasteful act. A slave in the first century was property.

Given this context, what would it look like if Christianity were believed to be calling slaves to disobedience? Christianity was already viewed as a subversive form of thought. It rejected the traditional gods (which made it seem treasonous to city and country, for worship of the traditional gods was a major expression of patriotism) and did not allow any compromises in this matter. It rejected many of the "normal" forms of recreation (drinking bouts, use of prostitutes and the like). It formed its members into "secret societies" (at least in the eyes of pagan observers), and in those societies it was rumored master and slave ate the same food at the same table and that wives were present along with their husbands. In other words, first-century social decorum was not observed in the church. Notice that in the New Testament there is no separation of religious duty according to social status. Every member is spiritually gifted, whatever their social status. Any person can become an elder, not just freeborn males. Every member of the church is called to the same obedience to Christ, slave or free, male or female.

So Paul (and other New Testament writers) calls the social inferiors, including slaves, to obedience. This both reassured the Roman society and made the real reason for persecution clear. Christian slaves should be more obedient slaves than other slaves, for they knew that the "pay" in heaven would be good. If their masters persecuted them, it should be for their faith and nothing else. Christianity was not subversive in the sense of stirring up rebellion. At the same time, it raised the slave to a new status of an equal human being before Christ. After all, in the eyes of the church slavery was just a job, and what job or social status one had on earth did not matter (Jesus did not have a great social status at any time in his life either, and he died a most shameful death, an executed slave's death). If the job was done "as a slave of Christ" the reward was equal, whether one was a human slave or a human master. Paul's strategy was thus that of producing an expression of the kingdom of God in the church, not that of trying to change society.

What was the result of this strategy? The church never adopted a rule that converts had to give up their slaves. Christians were not under law but under grace. Yet we read in the literature of the second century and later of many masters who upon their conversion freed their slaves. The reality stands that it is difficult to call a person a slave during the week and treat them like a brother or sister in the church. Sooner or later the implications of the kingdom they experienced in church seeped into the behavior of the masters during the week. Paul did in the end create a revolution, not one from without, but one from within, in which a changed heart produced changed behavior and through that in the end brought about social change. This change happened wherever the kingdom of God was expressed through the church, so the world could see that faith in Christ really was a transformation of the whole person.

Did Paul believe in slavery? Yes, indeed. He believed that all Christians are all equally slaves of Jesus Christ and that that is the one social relationship that has permanent value.

See also comment on EXODUS 21:2-11; 1 CORINTHIANS 7:17, 20.

6:12 Many Gods and Lords?

See comment on 1 CORINTHIANS 8:5-6.

PHILIPPIANS

2:6 Is Jesus God?

See comment on JOHN 1:1.

2:10-11 Universalism?

See comment on COLOSSIANS 1:19.

2:12-13 Work Out Your Salvation?

Philippians 2:12-13 is difficult only when we do not hear it within the context of everything else Paul says about God's work of redemption and our involvement in that work. Certainly since the Reformation, when the essence of Paul's gospel was captured in the joyful proclamation *sola gratia, sola fide* ("by grace alone, by faith alone"), anything which even hints at "works righteousness" or "salvation by works" is suspect. And that is the concern which often emerges when believers read these verses.

A careful look at Paul's teaching on all aspects of God's redemptive work in Christ reveals that salvation is not based on the accumulated merits of our piety and good deeds. No, salvation is God's business from beginning to end. It is inaugurated, maintained and completed by him. Yet we human beings, the objects of that divine activity, are not robots manipulated by the divine button pusher. We are creatures created in God's image (Gen 1:26-27), called to respond in faith and love to the Creator and to give ourselves in active participation to God's purposes. It is this dual perspective of divine action and human response and participation which is in view in this text.

The center of Paul's proclamation, repeated in numerous ways throughout his writings, is most concisely and eloquently stated in Ephesians 2:8-9: "For it is by grace you have been saved, through faith—and this not from yourselves, it is the gift of God—not by works, so that no one can boast." The meaning is without ambiguity; there are no conditions imposed (such as "if . . . then"). God's reaching toward us in unconditional love (Rom 5:8) is all grace. We neither deserve it nor earn it, and therefore we cannot take credit for it ("so that no one can boast"). The verb "you have been saved" is in the perfect tense and the passive voice, which means that the action comes from outside ourselves and that it is something which is both an accomplished act and a reality which continues in its effectiveness through the present and into the future.

Now this strong affirmation is immediately followed in Ephesians 2:10 by the words "For we are God's workmanship, created in Christ Jesus to do good works." Here, as throughout his letters, Paul is very clear about the fact that restored relationship with God is the condition within which our lives are being transformed in such a way that God's purposes for our lives are brought about. A few examples will make this abundantly clear.

In Romans 6 believers are defined as those who have been baptized into Christ, buried with him and raised with him so that we "might walk in newness of life" (Rom 6:3-4 RSV). Here the transaction of being saved is pictured as accomplished fact; the "walking in newness of life" as a possibility yet to be realized. Then Paul goes on to say that our sinful self has been "crucified with" Christ, that we are no longer "slaves to sin" (Rom 6:5-11).

The affirmation of this accomplished fact is then immediately followed by the imperative: "Therefore do not let sin reign. . . . Do not offer [yourselves] to sin as instruments of wickedness . . . but rather to God . . . as instruments of righteousness" (Rom 6:12-13).

In Galatians, where salvation by faith in Christ is particularly stressed (for example, in Gal 2:16, "a man is not justified by observing the law but by faith in Jesus Christ"), Paul can also stress that "in Christ," that is, in our relationship to God in Christ, what really matters is "faith expressing itself through love" (Gal 5:6). Therefore, "serve one another in love" (Gal 5:13).

The seeming tension between affirmations of accomplished salvation and a life in which a new reality is expressed and put to work is partially due to the fact that Paul's use of particular words or expressions is somewhat flexible. In this Philippians text, salvation is a reality still in process and yet to be accomplished. In Romans 1:16 and Ephesians 1:13 the term *salvation* is used in a general, comprehensive sense and as a synonym for *gospel* (that is, the good news of, and power for, salvation). In 2 Corinthians 7:10, repentance is said to lead to salvation. There are other texts in which salvation is depicted as the final stage or event in the redemptive activity of God. The Thessalonians are told that they were chosen "to be saved through the sanctifying work of the Spirit" (2 Thess 2:13) and that one piece of the Christian's armor against the darkness was "the hope of salvation" (1 Thess 5:8). The clearest example of the futuristic use of the term is in Romans 13:11, where we hear that "salvation is nearer now than when we first believed."

When we take all these aspects together, we see that Paul thought of salvation as the totality of God's redemptive work; yet he freely used the term also to denote various parts of the whole. The best illustration of Paul's understanding of salvation in its totality, described in terms of its various stages, is found in Romans 5. We "have been justified through faith" (Rom 5:1). To be justified—Paul's most usual term for what happens to us when we respond in faith to God's love in Christ—is to be brought into right relationship with God, a condition he describes as "peace with God" (Rom 5:1). The culmination of that which has thus begun is sharing "the glory of God" (Rom 5:2). Between these two poles, Christian life is characterized by joy in the midst of adversity, hope in the midst of suffering (Rom 5:3-5), because, having been justified by Christ's sacrificial death (Rom 5:9), the continuing work of the resurrected Lord in the life of the believer will lead to final salvation (Rom 5:10).

The larger context for this saying, as worked out above, consists of three elements: (1) the duality of "already" and "not yet"; (2) the actuality of restored relation with God and the necessity of living in newness of life; (3) the understanding of salvation as the comprehensive work of God in which we participate through faith, hope and love. Within this context, Philippians 2:12-13 is best understood.

Paul calls his readers to unity in their common life, to be achieved through humble other-directedness (Phil 2:1-4), motivated by the example of Christ's humiliation and utter self-giving (Phil 2:5-11). It is this work of Christ which for Paul is the basis ("therefore") of the imperative "work out your salvation with fear and trembling" (Phil 2:12). The salvation which comes to us through Christ's "obedience to death" (Phil 2:8) is to be "incarnated," implemented and worked out, within the context of our relationships with each other. The motivation for this "outworking" is "fear and trembling," not in the sense of "being afraid of," but rather in the sense of "awe," namely, the "awe" which comes when we contemplate God's work of "amazing grace" in Christ.

But this "outworking of salvation" in our human contexts—in Philippi toward unity within the congregation—is not "human achievement" on the basis of which we can "boast." No, for this outworking of salvation is empowered by the continuing operation of God's grace, for God is at work "in you" (or "among you").

Salvation is not something we possess. It is rather a relationship in which we stand. And within that relationship, we become partakers of God's Spirit. Thus Christian action is never "our work"; it is always the outgrowth of a dynamic relationship, whose author and completer is God.

See also comment on ROMANS 6:2, 7; 2 CORINTHIANS 5:17; JAMES 2:24; 1 PETER 1:9.

3:3 Is the Church Israel?

See comment on GALATIANS 6:16.

3:4-6 Faultless Before the Law?

What strikes us immediately about Philippians 3:4-6 is the sense of superiority it seems to convey along with the lofty claim about moral and religious perfection. The tone of this statement seems somehow unbecoming the "apostle to the Gentiles." Did Paul not say, earlier in this same letter, that a Christlike spirit leads one to consider others better than oneself (Phil 2:3)? And isn't this the same apostle who invested much of his energy showing that boasting on the basis of human achievement—even in religious practice and moral righteousness—was a hindrance to relationship with God? As to the claim to faultlessness regarding the Mosaic law, did he not also spend a great deal of energy showing that perfection under the law was impossible, that "all have sinned and fall short of the glory of God" (Rom 3:23)?

The situation addressed in this text, as well as in two other letters where a similar tone emerges (2 Cor 10—12; Gal 1—3), shows that Paul is involved in a polemical situation where he carries on a debate with opponents whose teachings or responses to Paul's apostolic authority threaten congregational life or the integrity of his gospel. What often characterizes polemical rhetoric is irony or hyperbole or both. One side of the argument is overstated in order to reveal the absurdity or error of the other side.

Or the opponents and their position are pilloried in the worst possible light in order to drive home the main point of the argument.

These rhetorical, literary devices account for the tone of superiority conveyed in this text. Paul is arguing either against the Judaizers—those Jewish Christians who continued to demand that both Jewish and Gentile Christians adhere to the rite of circumcision and the ritual law—or against representatives of the synagogue—who opposed Paul's proclamation in Macedonia from the very beginning (see Acts 16:1—17:15).[1] He calls his opponents in Philippi "dogs," an epithet of derision commonly used by Jews against Gentiles, now turned against his own people. In a caustic wordplay in reference to the rite of circumcision *(peritomē),* he labels them "mutilators of the flesh" *(katatomē,* Phil 3:2). That this is polemical rhetoric is clear in light of the fact that these are the same people for whom Paul has deep compassion and in exchange for whose salvation he is willing to be "cursed and cut off from Christ" (Rom 9:3).

Within this polemic Paul now, in a twist of irony, assumes their point of view and argues on their terms to show that even at its best, the way of achievement under the law does not lead to authentic relationship with God. To insist on the accumulation of merit before God by adhering to the meticulous precepts of the ritual law of Judaism is "to put confidence in the flesh" (Phil 3:3). The term *flesh* here denotes human ability, the capacity apart from dependence on God to live life in such a way that God is pleased. If that is the standard by which one is ultimately measured, says Paul, then I have as much reason as anyone, perhaps more, to be confident (Phil 3:4).

The list of qualifying credentials which follows—"circumcised on the eighth day, of the people of Israel, of the tribe of Benjamin, a Hebrew of Hebrews; in regard to the law, a Pharisee; as for zeal, persecuting the church" (Phil 3:5-6)—emphasizes his natural credentials, the ritualistic accuracy of acts performed ("on the eighth day" as required by Levitical law) and his personal achievements. This latter is expressed first of all in the phrase "in regard to the law, a Pharisee."

Though we have come virtually to equate "Pharisee" with "hypocrite" (largely by generalizing Jesus' denunciation of those Pharisees who opposed his ministry, see Mt 23:13), to be a member of the religious party of the Pharisees was a badge of honor. Jewish sources tell us that these religious leaders were extremely meticulous about the observance of the Mosaic law and its traditional interpretations.[2] It was the Pharisees who believed that if all Jews would keep the law perfectly for just one day, the kingdom of God would come. Thus it was their lofty goal to lead Israel to perfect obedience. Many were deeply pious and earnest about the accomplishment of God's will as they understood it. For many others that same effort became a source of pride and self-righteousness (see Rom 10:2-3). I, says Paul, was one of these Pharisees.

In addition, his zeal for the law as a Pharisee expressed itself in his persecution of those who claimed that the one who had been rejected by the Pharisees was the expected Messiah (Phil 3:6; see also Gal 1:13-14). For him this new faith threatened the inherited tradition, and he saw himself as the defender of that tradition.

The ultimate claim on which "confidence in the flesh" could be based is now made—namely, legalistic perfection. Paul the Pharisee, schooled by the rabbis in the traditions of the law, was convinced that in all respects he had adhered to the letter of the law; he had kept the myriad rules and regulations that had been established in order to keep the faithful from disobeying the law of Moses. Paul echoes here the words of the young man who, in response to Jesus' question about the commandments, says in absolute confidence, "All these I have kept since I was a boy" (Lk 18:20-21).

Paul shared the conviction of his fellow rabbis that it was possible to keep the law and that he had, in fact, mastered it.[3] Though this affirmation may at first sight appear to contradict other statements Paul makes (see Rom 2:17-24; 7:7-20), it is quite consistent with his belief that even if one were able to keep the entire law, one would not be justified (that is, come into right relationship with God) on that basis (Gal 2:16-17; 3:21). Surely Paul's experience of being grasped by Christ on the Damascus road led to this assessment. In the ultimate act of zealousness for the law—namely, the persecution of Jesus' followers—he found himself to be opposing the very purposes of God. He discovered that confidence in one's ability to prove oneself worthy in God's sight has the effect of separating one from God. Why? Because it implicitly rejects humble dependence on God. Only in faith—in dependence on God—can one be open, both to an understanding of God's purposes and to God's empowerment for participating in those purposes.

---

[1]For example, F. W. Beare, *A Commentary on the Epistle to the Philippians,* Harper's New Testament Commentaries (New York: Harper & Brothers, 1959), pp. 103-5.

[2]For one of the best treatments of Judaism in the New Testament period and a comprehensive understanding of the religious sects and their beliefs, see G. F. Moore, *Judaism in the First Centuries of the Christian Era,* 2 vols. (Cambridge, Mass.: Harvard University Press, 1927).

[3]E. P. Sanders, *Paul and Palestinian Judaism* (Philadelphia: Fortress Press, 1977).

3:10 Somehow Attain the Resurrection?

In Philippians 3:10 we have no real problem with Paul's wanting to know Christ, but when he concludes with "somehow to attain to the resurrection from the dead" some of us are surprised. Is Paul talking about "works righteousness"? Did he believe that we earn resurrection through our becoming like Christ? Is he unsure of his salvation?

There is no doubt that this is a difficult passage in that commentators disagree about the details of its interpretation. However, we can affirm first of all that Paul is not thinking of something that does not come by faith, for in the previous verse he said, ". . . and be found in him, not having a righteousness of my own that comes from the law, but that which is through faith in Christ—the righteousness that comes from God and is by faith." This is not the language of a person trying to earn his own salvation.

Yet this righteousness has a goal. Paul did not want to be righteous simply for his own sake. For Paul, everything was for the sake of a greater intimacy with Christ. He did not so much want to go to heaven as to be with Christ; his desire for heaven was simply because Christ was there. Thus he expresses his goal: "that I may know Christ." By this he is talking about personal, experiential knowledge. His one goal above all others was closeness with Jesus.

Closeness with Jesus is made up of two parts. One part is experiencing "the power of his resurrection." He started off his Christian life that way when he encountered the risen Christ on the Damascus road. He continued his life having experiences of the risen Christ. And he also experienced the resurrection power of Christ flowing through him in various signs and wonders. Yet there is also another part of knowing Christ, "sharing in his sufferings." As with Christ's resurrection, this is first and foremost an appropriation of and identification with Jesus' own sufferings. Yet as one identifies with Christ, he or she will in fact enter into the sufferings of Christ in this life. "Becoming like him in his death" may refer to baptism, when one identifies with the death of Christ, and the inward dying to self that results from confessing that Jesus is one's Lord, but it also implies an outward way of the cross in this life. Jesus' resurrection came after suffering, so also his followers experience resurrection power, but often in the middle of suffering.

Paul wants to make it clear that resurrection power is not only present identification or inward spiritual experience or even outward signs and wonders done by the power of the resurrected Christ working through a person. All of this would make the Christian life temporal, lasting only for this lifetime. Paul's deepest expectation was that present intimacy and identification with Jesus would lead to future resurrection life with him. Perhaps some in Philippi believed that the resurrection was only inward and thus that no future resurrection was needed. Paul states emphatically that his hope is "to attain to the resurrection from the dead." The expression states pointedly that the ultimate Christian hope is indeed resurrection from among the dead, not merely a hope for something inward and spiritual that one can have in this life.

What is this language "somehow, to attain"? That is the language of humility and of hope. Paul knew he had not yet attained the resurrection, for he had not yet died. His physical resurrection was still a future hope. It is not that he is unsure of it, for Christ is already risen so the eventual resurrection is sure. The point he is making is that he is not there yet. He is still "pressing on."

Paul is not unsure of his salvation, for he will say in the very next verse that he knows that "Christ Jesus took hold of me." Yet he wants to attain to everything for which Christ did this. Paul knew he was not yet perfect. He knew that he did not yet know Jesus fully. He knew that he had not yet gained all of the prize that Jesus offered him. Paul was not a man to be content with less than all that was possible in Jesus.

So far from finding a man unsure of his salvation and trying to earn it, we find a man gripped by Christ Jesus, knowing that his salvation is by faith. Yet we also find a man who because of this relationship will not be satisfied with less than experiencing the fullness of Christ, including both his resurrection power and his sufferings, so that having reached every goal that Christ has set for him he will finally arrive at the resurrection goal having fulfilled all that to which he was called by grace through faith.

The challenge of this passage, then, is not about whether we as Christians will make it to the resurrection. The challenge is whether we as Christians have caught enough of a vision of Christ that we will not be satisfied unless we know him more fully. And in knowing him more fully, are we just as ready to embrace his sufferings as we are his resurrection? Or do we want to try to get to glory without a cross?

See also comment on PHILIPPIANS 2:12-13; 1 PETER 1:9; 2 PETER 1:10.

4:4 Joy in All Circumstances?

See comment on HABAKKUK 3:16-18; JAMES 1:2.

COLOSSIANS

1:15 Christ the Firstborn?

We read in Colossians that Christ is "the firstborn over all creation." What does this mean? If Christ is eternal, how can he be first*born?* Does this mean that he was simply the first thing that God created?

The term "firstborn" appears 107 times in the NIV, but only two passages create difficulties, this one and Hebrews 1:6: "And again, when God brings his firstborn into the world, he says, 'Let all God's angels worship him.' " Most of the other passages are in the Old Testament and refer to firstborn children of human beings. Two passages refer to Jesus as Mary's firstborn (Lk 2:7, 23), which is like the normal Old Testament use. Two refer to Christ as the firstborn from the dead (Rev 1:5) or the firstborn of many siblings (Rom 8:29).

Colossians 1:15-20 is a poem (or at least poetic prose) about Christ, which many scholars believe to be a hymn of the early church. This poem appears to revolve around the first word of the Hebrew Bible, "in the beginning" (one word in Hebrew), which contains within it the words for "first" and "head." The poem divides into two sections. In the first (Col 1:15-17) Christ is presented as the source of creation. In the second section (Col 1:18-20) he is presented as the source of new creation or redemption. Even a quick reading will reveal that the two sections are rough parallels of each other, like two stanzas of a hymn.

In the first stanza Christ is presented as the visible presence ("image") of the invisible God and the agent of the whole of creation. What is more, he sustains creation. Likewise in the second stanza he is presented as the One through whom reconciliation came to humankind. He is therefore the source of the church, the One who brought it into being. In both cases Christ stands apart. He is not part of the creation, but the One who made it. He is not part of the church, but the One who brought her into being. It is clear in this passage that Christ is being viewed as God (Col 1:15, 19), exercising the creative and redemptive prerogatives of God.

How, then, can Paul use "firstborn" language? Generally in the Old Testament "firstborn" means the son who was born first (daughters were not counted if there was a son born after them). That child had a leading place in the family and normally took over as head of the family upon his father's death. However, even in the Old Testament this is more a right conferred by the father than a place in the birth order. For example, in Genesis 25:29-34 Esau can sell his birthright, his place as the firstborn, to Jacob, although this sale was apparently not recognized by their father, for Jacob later has to trick Isaac into giving him Esau's blessing as the firstborn (Gen 27:19). A generation later Jacob makes it clear that it is not the son born first (Reuben) whom he considers to have the rights of the firstborn, but Joseph, the one born to his favorite wife. He demonstrates this by having a special garment made for his heir designate (Gen 37:3-4). In this case a younger son is designated as firstborn, arousing the jealousy of the others, especially when he exercises his designated leadership. Even later Joseph brings his own sons to Jacob, who puts the one born second before the one born first (Gen 48:13-20). Again "firstborn" will not mean the one born first, but the one who will be the leader or the greatest. Even when talking about literal families, then, "firstborn" can indicate a favorite son rather than the one born first. So in Micah 6:7 and Zechariah 12:10 the "firstborn" is the most loved child, the one the parent is most loath to give up.

In Exodus 4:22 we find another meaning of "firstborn" when God calls Israel his "firstborn son." This is taken up in Jeremiah 31:9. In neither of these passages (nor anywhere else in the Old Testament) is there even a hint that God in some way gave birth to Israel. What he is saying is that he has designated this nation as his number one nation, the one closest to his heart. To injure this nation is to injure God and to feel the consequences. The symbolic consequence in Exodus is that Pharaoh loses his own literal firstborn son. Thus we see that a nation put in the number one place can also be called a "firstborn."

Finally, in Psalm 89:27 we discover that the Davidic king will be appointed God's "firstborn." Again there is no hint that God actually has a hand in this man's procreation. What is meant is that God symbolically adopts him and places him in the number one position in his family. "Firstborn" is thus the place of honor and leadership which the Davidic king is said to occupy.

Now we see why a poetic person steeped in the Old Testament might use the term "firstborn." He was already thinking in terms of "heads" and "beginnings" or, in other words, of the number one place in the universe and in redemption. Drawing on the language of Psalm 89:27, he points to Christ as the one who is number one in God's family, God's designated "heir" and the ruler next to God. Of course it is also true, as the poem points out, that Christ was before any other parts of creation, although the use is still metaphorical, for a firstborn son does not procreate the rest of the family, while Jesus is said to create all that is created.

The term "firstborn" is flexible enough that it can also be used of Christ as the firstborn from the dead, for he is the first to rise to unending life (although others before him were raised from the dead to temporal life) and also the chief or leader of all those who will rise from the dead.

So Paul is using the language about a firstborn son metaphorically, as the Old Testament does. Jesus is not presented as a creation of God or as a child of God born through some goddess (as was common in pagan mythology), but as the chief of God's family, whether the old family of creation or the new family of redemption. He is before it. He is the cause of the family. He is the leader of the whole family. In every way he is first. Yet he is not part of the creation, nor even one of the redeemed, for he is the image of God and the One in whom all the fullness of God dwelt.

1:19 Universalism?

Does Colossians 1:19 mean that all people will be saved (universalism)? Does it teach that even the fallen angels, even Satan himself, will be reconciled to God?

In reading Colossians, we must remember that much of the book parallels Ephesians. We do find a parallel idea to this hard saying in Ephesians 1:10: "to be put into effect when the times will have reached their fulfillment—to bring all things in heaven and on earth together under one head, even Christ." This, however, does not answer our question. In what way will "all things" be brought under Christ?

Philippians 2:10-11 also has everything brought under Christ:

> that at the name of Jesus every knee should bow, in heaven and on earth and under the earth, and every tongue confess that Jesus Christ is Lord, to the glory of God the Father.

What we notice is that this "bowing" and "confessing" is not necessarily that of loving subjects. Remember that Psalm 110 was a favorite text of the early church and is frequently quoted in the New Testament. Psalm 110:1 reads:

> The LORD says to my Lord:
> "Sit at my right hand
> until I make your enemies
> a footstool for your feet."

The psalm pictures the king (understood in the New Testament to be Christ) functioning indeed as the ruler and his enemies confessing that he is their lord, but it is not a willing submission nor a salvation. It is the confession of defeated enemies.

In the Ephesians passage the focus is on the redeemed. It is "us" who have been chosen and redeemed and who understand the mystery (Paul's term for God's plan) of what God is going to do in the future, namely reveal Christ as the "one head." If we continue to the end of the sentence (the Greek sentence ends at Eph 1:14) or to the end of the chapter, we find numerous promises, but all of the promises are made to people who have believed on Christ. Thus we are told that God is going to make Christ the one head (especially head of the people of God, unifying Jew and Gentile in the church), yet there does not seem to be any thought of this bringing benefits to people who are not part of the church. In fact, in Ephesians 2:1-13 it is clear that those who do not believe in Christ are in a bad place: "objects of wrath . . . without hope and without God."

Does the same perspective hold true in Colossians? As we read on beyond this passage, we find that before the Colossians became Christians they did not have hope of reconciliation. "Once you were alienated from God and were enemies in your minds" (Col 1:21). What made the change for them was that "now he has reconciled you by Christ's physical body through death" (Col 1:22). It is clear that the cause of this is not simply God's declaration without any response on the Colossians' part; God's provision had been appropriated through faith: "If you continue in your faith, established and firm, not moved from the hope held out in the gospel" (Col 1:23). So the perspective of Colossians is that God is indeed reconciling all things to himself, but the means of this reconciliation is the death of Christ and its appropriation by human beings through faith. Outside of the gospel and commitment to it, people are, according to Paul, "dead" (Col 2:13).

When it comes to the state of spiritual beings, Colossians has something to say. In Colossians 2:15 we read, "And having disarmed the powers and authorities, he made a public spectacle of them, triumphing over them by the cross." Here there is also a type of "reconciliation," in that these powers and authorities (spiritual beings) will no longer be in rebellion against God. Yet it is the "reconciliation" of a defeated enemy. It is a picture of a Roman conqueror leading a parade in which the leaders of his enemies are dragged along in chains (which is what making a "public spectacle" of an enemy meant in those days).

All of this teaching fits with Scripture as a whole. God has appointed Christ the head of all things. There are two ways to relate to this king. One can accept the gospel and submit to him now, receiving his forgiveness for past rebellion and entering a state not simply of reconciliation, but exaltation alongside Christ. This exaltation is not apparent in this age, but it will be fully revealed in the coming age. The other way to relate to this king is to continue in one's rebellion and so refuse to accept the gospel. In that case the person will be forced to submit to Christ when his rule is fully revealed, but this submission will be a prelude to receiving the punishment of a conquered enemy. As for fallen angels, demons, Satan and other spiritual powers presently in rebellion against God, no hope is held out for them. Whatever they believe leads only to their "shuddering" (Jas 2:19). According to Jude and 2 Peter, some of them are already in chains. According to Revelation, their end is the lake of fire.

It is clear, then, that Paul is not teaching universalism and that in this he agrees with the rest of the New Testament. He is certain that Christ will rule over the whole world and all beings in it, human or spiritual. He is certain that in Christ God has made possible the reconciliation of humanity to himself. He is just as certain that only those who by faith commit themselves to Christ will participate in this reconciliation in ways other than as conquered foes. The deciding question for Paul is how each person he comes across will relate to this reconciliation offered in Christ. The choice is theirs.

1:24 Lacking in Christ's Afflictions?

The phrases "what is still lacking" and "Christ's afflictions" from Colossians 1:24 confront us with several difficulties. On the surface they seem to imply that there is some sort of deficiency in Christ's sufferings, that the effectiveness of our Lord's suffering is somehow limited and that its redemptive purpose must be supplemented or completed by Paul's suffering. In addition to this central problem, there is the question of how Paul's suffering can be "for the sake of" the church, especially since the church at Colossae was not established by Paul, nor had he visited it (Col 1:3-8).

In light of everything else which Paul affirms about the redemptive significance of Christ's life, death and resurrection, it is virtually impossible to attribute to him the idea that this redemptive work is in some way incomplete. Even within the immediate context, Paul clearly articulates the finality of God's saving action in Christ. In the cross, Christ triumphed over all those powers of sin and bondage and death which separate us from God and his purposes (Col 2:13-15). As a result of the proclamation of the gospel, Christians are those who have been rescued from the dominion of darkness and brought into the kingdom of God's Son (Col 1:13), through whom redemption and forgiveness of sins has been bestowed (Col 1:14). Though once alienated from God, they have been reconciled to God by Christ's death (Col 1:22).

This sense of the finality, absolute completeness and all-sufficiency of Christ's vicarious suffering is confirmed both by other key texts from Paul's hand and by the terms which he normally uses when he speaks of Christ's atoning work. Among the many passages which could be cited is Romans 5:1, 10, where justification and reconciliation, as results of Christ's death, are described as accomplished facts (see also Gal 4:1-7; 1 Cor 1:21-30; Eph 1:7, 13-14). In addition to this larger evidence from his epistles, Paul's normal way of speaking about Christ's redemptive work is in terms of his death, his blood, his cross or a combination of these terms (see Rom 5:8-9; Col 1:20). The expression "Christ's afflictions" is nowhere else attested as a reference to his saving work.

What then can be the meaning of this enigmatic expression? In what sense are "Christ's afflictions" incomplete? How do Paul's sufferings "fill up" that incompleteness? Several interpretations have been proposed.[1] One holds that the word "afflictions" is a reference to Paul's sufferings and that the genitive "of Christ" is to be taken in an objective sense, that is, meaning "for the sake of Christ." The sentence would then read: "I rejoice in what was suffered for you, and I fill up in my flesh what is still lacking in [my] afflictions for the sake of Christ." This idea that Paul saw his own sufferings as being endured for the sake of Christ is certainly present in his experience (see Acts 9:16; 2 Cor 4:10-11). The attractiveness of this interpretation is hindered by the fact that the term "of the afflictions" goes most naturally with "of Christ" in the grammatical construction, and thus means "the afflictions of Christ." The proposed interpretation also does not adequately explain how what is yet to be filled up in Paul's afflictions is for the benefit of the church.

An alternative to the above way of dealing with the problem is to understand the genitive, "of Christ," as a reference to the nature of Christ's suffering. Paul's sufferings are "like those of Christ." But how the model of Christ's sufferings, now experienced by Paul, is deficient and is to be "filled up" is not answered by this explanation.

A more satisfactory understanding of this passage has been suggested by recent studies which seek to take seriously the background of Paul's terminology in the Old Testament and in the apocalyptic literature[2] of intertestamental Judaism. Within that background, there are several related concepts which parallel those in Colossians: (1) Israel's experience of affliction throughout its history—particularly Egyptian slavery, Babylonian exile and subsequent oppression under the Syrians and Romans—is understood as part and parcel of God's redemptive purposes. Within this larger frame, the sufferings of God's righteous ones, God's special servants (Ps 34:19; 37:39; 50:15), were often taken as representative and vicarious (for example, Is 53). (2) In the apocalyptic literature, beginning with Daniel 12:1, the time prior to the culmination of God's redemptive work and the inauguration of the reign of God in the messianic age was depicted as a period of great affliction. These afflictions were known as "the woes of the Messiah," not referring to sufferings to be endured by the Messiah, but to afflictions out of which the messianic age would be born. (3) Finally the apocalyptic seers announced that this present age of suffering was limited, that the "age to come" would soon dawn and that God had determined a definite measure for the afflictions that had to be experienced.[3]

These elements of Paul's Jewish background help us to understand this hard saying. Paul was certainly convinced that the final days had dawned (1 Cor 7:29) and that the present time was one of difficulty and crisis (1 Cor 7:26). Christians are those "upon whom the end of the ages has come" (1 Cor 10:11 RSV) and who are therefore participants with Christ (the Messiah) in his sufferings as a prelude to sharing in the glory of his reign (Rom 8:17-18). Within this larger view, the difficult concepts of the passage can be understood.

The "afflictions of Christ" may be a reference to the "woes of the Messiah"; namely, the sufferings experienced by God's people in the last days. Paul's own sufferings, experienced in his missionary work (see 2 Cor 1:3-6), would then be seen as a part of this suffering of Christ's followers. The phrase "fill up what is still lacking" may be in direct correspondence to the apocalyptic notion that a definite limit has been set by God to the sufferings to be endured. Paul could be expressing the conviction that his sufferings, alongside the sufferings of God's people generally (see 2 Cor 1:6), contribute to the total measure of afflictions determined by God. Thus his sufferings are "for the sake of the church," since they hasten the day when the church's present affliction will be replaced by glory.

Though understanding the text within the larger apocalyptic view of "the afflictions of the Messiah" solves the various difficulties identified at the outset of this chapter, a more direct explanation may suggest itself from within Paul's own thought.

As shown above, there can be no question that Christ's sufferings, climaxed in the cross, are all-sufficient. Peace, reconciliation, right standing with God are their results. At the same time Paul is also convinced that this gospel must be proclaimed, received in faith and implemented in everyday life in order for God's redemptive purposes to be achieved. Thus, within the immediate context of the passage, the good news of Christ's death which the Colossian Christians heard (Col 1:22-23) is intended to bear fruit in their lives (Col 1:6) and to lead to a life pleasing to the Lord (Col 1:10) that is characterized by endurance and patience (Col 1:11), continuing faith (Col 1:23) and unity in love (Col 2:2). The ultimate purpose of Christ's atoning death is to present holy and without blemish to God those who have received redemption (Col 1:14, 22). Paul's work as a servant of the gospel of Christ is part of God's means to accomplish that purpose (Col 1:23).

Elsewhere Paul affirms that the good news of Christ's saving death can only be heard and believed if it is proclaimed (Rom 10:14-17), and he knows himself to be a proclaimer of that good news (1 Cor 1:17-23), as well as one whose life is an imitation of Christ's self-giving love on behalf of others (1 Cor 10:33—11:1; Eph 5:1-2). All of this does not mean that there is something lacking in Christ's redemptive work, but rather that Paul's servant ministry, which includes suffering, is an integral part of bringing redemption to all. Such a sense for Colossians 1:24 is supported by a very similar text, 2 Corinthians 1:5-6.

In 2 Corinthians 1:5-6 Paul affirms that Christ's sufferings are extended in his own and that this suffering is "for the sake of" the Corinthian believers' salvation. Paul's suffering in the service of Christ and his gospel do not add anything to the perfection of Christ's atonement. They are, however, one of God's instruments to extend that atonement into the lives of others. Only in that sense can it be said that Paul's sufferings fill up what is lacking in regard to

Christ's afflictions.

---

[1]Extensive discussions of various interpretations can be found in commentaries on this epistle. A good example is Peter T. O'Brien, *Colossians, Philemon,* Word Biblical Commentary 44 (Waco, Tex.: Word, 1987), pp. 77-78.

[2]From approximately 200 B.C. to A.D. 100 there appeared an extensive religious literature which, like the canonical Daniel, sought to give hope to an oppressed, persecuted and suffering people. Various concepts of this literature, which revealed *(apokalyptō)* the purposes of God, were very much a part of Jesus' understanding of his person and mission, as well as Paul's interpretation of Christ's work and its significance for Christian living. O'Brien, *Colossians, Philemon,* pp. 78-81, gives a detailed analysis of this literature's concepts relating to this passage.

[3]As examples of this element in Jewish apocalyptic writings, see 1 Enoch 47:1-4, Baruch 30:2 and 4 Ezra 4:36-37 in R. H. Charles, ed., *The Apocrypha and Pseudepigrapha of the Old Testament,* vol. 2 (Oxford: Clarendon Press, 1976 77).

2:18 The Worship of Angels?

In Colossians 2:18 Paul warns Christians against the worship of angels. What does this mean? Why would anyone worship angels?

Angels are spiritual beings who can be quite impressive. Not only do we have the witness of the Old Testament in which a number of people show reverence for the angel of the Lord, but even late in the New Testament period the prophet John is tempted to fall down and worship an angel, not just once, but twice (Rev 19:10; 22:8-9). So we see that the writers of the New Testament themselves could feel the power of such a temptation.

We do not know the full context of what was going on in Colossae, for Paul never explains it. Whatever was happening there, the Colossians obviously already knew about it, and Paul does not know that his letter will be read centuries later by Christians who will have no knowledge of the Colossian situation. Yet while we do not know the full extent of the practices being urged on the Colossians, some of the elements are clear in this passage.

First, the people promoting angel worship had experienced visions. That is the point of the reference to "what he has seen" (the NRSV refers to this correctly as "visions"). Visionary experiences were well known in the early church and, indeed, throughout the history of Christianity. However, not every vision is for public consumption. Paul notes in 2 Corinthians 12:4 that what he had seen in heaven he was not permitted to report. John in Revelation is permitted to report much, but not all, of what he saw and heard. A person without maturity or who fell prey to temptation might easily report on a vision that was not supposed to be told (assuming that the vision was from God in the first place).

Second, the person or persons engaging in this activity is puffing himself up. This indicates that the person considered himself to be someone special because of the revelation he had received. This is in fact a significant temptation. He had heard information that others must have. It is clear to all that he is the person who has been chosen to mediate this revelation to the community. If this process is successful, such a person receives special status, this status hooks him, and he becomes proud.

Third, the focus of the vision is on two things. On the one hand, it is on some type of false humility. That could be the particular practice of fasting or devotion that the recipient of the vision was engaging in when the vision came. It could be some practice he believed that the angelic messenger revealed to him. Whatever it is, it is a practice through which a person humbles himself or herself. It is a rule or law through which a person can "get more holy," more perfect (Col 2:20-23). Such a position ignores the fact in Christ Christians have received all the status and holiness they will ever receive. One does not earn a higher status with God; it has all come in Christ (Col 2:9-10).

On the other hand, the vision (or the report that the people gave of it) focused on angels. "If you get to know these angels as we do, then you will get inside information too." In some systems of Jewish and Christian thought the angels were named. In others they were ranked, and the goal was to get to know the more highly ranked angels. Or it may be that these people in Colossae only thought that special honor should be paid to a particular revealing angel. All of this does one thing: it takes the focus off Christ. Paul points out that "he [the person teaching on angels] has lost connection with the Head" (Col 2:19). If one knows Christ, one does not need to know the angels, their ranks or their names. They are all servants of the One the Christian already knows. The Bible does incidentally reveal the names of a few angels, but it always keeps its focus on Christ or God. If the names of the angels or even their presence were removed, but the revelation were retained, nothing of great significance would be lost. To focus on the angels is to detract from Christ and thus to lose a grip on the "Head."

That is probably why John reports his two attempts to worship angels in Revelation. Perhaps some reader would be tempted to give honor to the various angels who mediated such a great revelation. John is crystal clear: don't even think of it. If honor is given to Christ and God, the angels will be quite pleased, for then they have done their job as servants.

Religious experience is great. God grants it because it is good for us. Yet it is also dangerous. True experiences can be distorted. The temptation is always there to focus on our experience or to use our experience as a lever to gain personal status or power. This does not invalidate the experience (while there are demonic visionary experiences, Paul gives no hint here that these visions were not true visions from God), but it does distort it. Instead of leading the person to a greater devotion to Christ (that type of devotion that faces martyrdom fearlessly), such a use of visionary experiences turns the person from his or her focus on Christ, and can shift a whole group as well. The person becomes the "mediator" between Christians and some angel or angels, using rites about which God does not care a snap, however pious they may seem.

In Revelation there is a role for angels. They stand along with the redeemed before the throne of God and of the Lamb. That is the image to keep in mind: redeemed human beings and angels stand side by side looking at one and the same focus, God. Once this is grasped, both angels and visionary experiences will be kept in their proper perspective.

3:22-25 Did Paul Approve of Slavery?

See comment on EPHESIANS 6:5-8.

4:6 Seasoned with Salt?

See comment on MARK 9:50.

1 THESSALONIANS

2:14-15 Anti-Semitism?

Throughout the history of Jewish-Christian relations, 1 Thessalonians 2:14-15 and several other passages in the New Testament, like John 8:44, have been used all too frequently as a justification for inappropriate attitudes and actions toward Jewish people. Those actions and attitudes are called anti-Semitic. A dictionary definition of anti-Semitism includes such terms as "prejudice against Jews; dislike or fear of Jews; discrimination against or persecution of Jews."[1] Such anti-Semitism on the part of Christians has led to the charge that the New Testament, or at least certain writers of New Testament Gospels or Epistles, is anti-Semitic. Can the use of 1 Thessalonians 2:14-15 (and others) for anti-Semitic attitudes and actions, or the charge that these texts are in themselves anti-Semitic, be justified?

First, it should be noted that the statements in question come from persons who were themselves Semites. They were not uttered by Gentiles hostile to Jews or to Jewish customs or beliefs. Their Jewishness and their commitment to the sacred writings which give to Judaism its uniqueness and identity are affirmed. Thus Jesus points to the Jewish Scriptures as bearing witness to him (Jn 5:39); and throughout John's Gospel, Jesus' identity as Messiah, as the royal Son of God, is prominent. In the same vein, Paul repeatedly underlines his Jewishness, his belonging to the people who trace their ancestry to Abraham (Rom 11:1; Gal 1:13-14; Phil 3:4-6).

Not only do we have an affirmation of Jewish identity, but that identity is expressed in powerfully positive ways. Throughout the Gospel record, Jesus' love and compassion for his own people is amply demonstrated. A particularly tender expression of it is found in Jesus' lament over Jerusalem: "How often I have longed to gather your children together, as a hen gathers her chicks under her wings" (Lk 13:34). Paul parallels this deep yearning for the wholeness and salvation of his own people when he expresses his deep sorrow over Israel's rejection of Christ and his willingness even to be cursed for their sake (Rom 9:2-3). In addition, Paul sees the rejection of the Messiah by his own people as but a temporary reality. He knows that God has not rejected his own people (Rom 11:1) and envisions a time when they will be grafted back into God's olive tree (Rom 11:17-24).

Paul's strong words in this text are elicited by a situation in Thessalonica in which Christians (probably Gentile Christians) are suffering at the hands of their own countrymen (1 Thess 2:14). The new faith, based on the gospel of Jesus Christ, is being opposed in Thessalonica, just as it was being opposed in the Judean churches by their countrymen, namely, their fellow Jews (1 Thess 2:14). To this point in the text, Paul has not singled out any national group. The gospel is opposed by both Greeks and Jews, and those committed to it are liable to persecution. It is the following verse (1 Thess 2:15) which singles out "the Jews" for special denunciation: "They displease God and are hostile to all men."

This statement has the same anti-Semitic flavor as the rather slanderous remarks made against Jews in the ancient world. Tacitus says that they nurtured a hatred against all non-Jews that one would normally reserve only for one's enemies; and the Egyptian Apion, a contemporary of Paul, is quoted by the Jewish historian Josephus as saying that the Jews swear by their Creator to show no good will toward the Gentiles.[2]

Though in external form Paul's statement is similar to these, the specific context of Paul's words should caution us against viewing them as an indiscriminate anti-Jewish polemic and using them as grounds for collective prejudice and discrimination. For just as the Gospel of John uses the term "the Jews" to designate the Pharisaic-Sadducean leadership that opposed Jesus, so Paul has in mind those Jews who opposed his mission (1 Thess 2:16). Thus we see that Paul's denunciation of "the Jews" takes place with a specific historical context, and it should in no way be generalized. Only when such statements are used indiscriminately in the service of generalized prejudice—as they often have been in the past—can they be called anti-Semitic.

[1]*Webster's New World Dictionary* (New York: The World Publishing Co., 1967).

[2]Cited by F. F. Bruce, *1 & 2 Thessalonians,* Word Biblical Commentary 45 (Waco, Tex.: Word, 1987), p. 47.

2 THESSALONIANS

2:3 Who Is the Man of Lawlessness?

Paul does not tell us who "the man of lawlessness" is, but he apparently expects his readers in the church at Thessalonica to recognize him.

We must remember that Paul's letters are "occasional" documents, sometimes written in response to issues or questions brought to Paul by his churches. They are thus fragments of a conversation. And since we are not privy to that larger conversation, we do not have the same body of information at our disposal which helped the Thessalonian Christians to "decode" Paul's terms. To them Paul could write: "When I was with you I used to tell you these things" (2 Thess 2:5). That was enough to refresh their memory. For us, the meaning of Paul's terms must be discerned, if possible, by giving attention to (1) the issue he addresses and (2) the beliefs of both Judaism and early Christianity behind that issue.

Both of Paul's letters to the Thessalonians are in response to questions about the return of Christ. In the first few decades the faith of these earliest Christians was energized by the lively hope and expectation of the imminent return of the Lord. The new era, announced by Israel's prophets and inspired seers, had dawned in Jesus' life and ministry (1 Cor 10:11). His resurrection was a sign that the power of death was defeated (Acts 2:24), and that these "last days" (Acts 2:17), inaugurated by his life, death and resurrection, would soon come to their culmination (1 Cor 7:29) in the glorious Second Coming of Christ (Acts 3:20). Paul shared with others the belief that this culmination might happen within their lifetime (1 Thess 4:15).

In light of these convictions, certain experiences and events raised troubling questions for the Christians in Thessalonica. From what Paul says in 1 Thessalonians 4:13-14, we can assume that members of their fellowship had died. Would they be excluded from the glorious event of Christ's Second Advent? Paul's answer to that concern is that at

Christ's coming those who belong to him, even though they have died ("the dead in Christ"), will be raised from the dead and gathered in one fellowship with those who are still living and will meet the returning, exalted Lord (1 Thess 4:16-17).

In the second letter we hear about fears stirred up among believers by some voices within the church who claimed that the "day of the Lord" had already come (2 Thess 2:2). Such a claim was unsettling and alarming, for it implied that they had been excluded from the event of Christ's return and "shut out from the presence of the Lord and from the majesty of his power" (2 Thess 1:9). Paul calls that claim "deceitful" (2 Thess 2:3), asserting that certain events which precede Christ's coming have yet to occur.

In describing these events (2 Thess 2:3-10) Paul first mentions "the man of lawlessness." He is apparently the key figure in a general rebellion (2 Thess 2:3) who exalts himself above the so-called gods of heathen worship and "sets himself up in God's temple, proclaiming himself to be God" (2 Thess 2:4). His coming "will be in accordance with the work of Satan" and accompanied by "all kinds of counterfeit miracles, signs and wonders" (2 Thess 2:9), as well as "every sort of evil" (2 Thess 2:10). He is "doomed to destruction" (2 Thess 2:3) at the hands of the Lord Jesus (2 Thess 2:8).

This depiction of "the lawless one" within the context of a rebellion against God has affinities with related concepts in Judaism and early Christianity. The "lawless one" is anticipated in the vision of Daniel 11, where a future ruler is said to exalt himself above all gods (Dan 11:36-37) and to desecrate the temple (Dan 11:31). Jewish Christians would also have remembered that the celebrated Maccabean revolt against the Syrian overlords in 167-164 B.C. was provoked by the Syrian monarch Antiochus IV, who claimed that he was "God manifest" and defiled the temple. Other adversaries of Israel and its God had earlier been depicted as exalting themselves and seeking divine status (see Ezek 28:2 and Is 14:13-14).

About a decade before Paul wrote to Thessalonica, the emperor Caligula had attempted to erect a statue of himself in the Jerusalem temple. His claim to divine honor, underscored by this attempt, showed the absolute rejection of God concentrated in an individual and provided a foreshadowing of what could be expected from "the man of lawlessness" in the future.

The more immediate parallel to this figure in early Christian thought is that of the antichrist in John's epistles, a figure associated with the culmination of history ("the last hour"), who denies both God and Christ (1 Jn 2:18-22). Like the lawless one in Paul's letter, the antichrist is a deceiver (2 John 7). And just as "lawlessness" is already at work prior to the historical revealing of "the man of lawlessness," so the "spirit of antichrist" is already at work prior to the personal, incarnate form of that spirit (1 Jn 4:3).

Paul's word that the coming of the lawless one "will be in accordance with the work of Satan" (2 Thess 2:9) is paralleled by an assertion in the intertestamental apocalyptic work *The Martyrdom of Isaiah.* In this work, Beliar, the "ruler of this world," is called "the angel of lawlessness" (2 Thess 2:4).

In light of this religious and historical background, Paul's words about the appearing of "the man of lawlessness" prior to the Second Advent of Christ express the belief that demonic opposition to God, already present in the world, though in a restrained way, will ultimately reach a peak and become incarnated in a historical person who will lead a massive anti-Christ movement.

For Paul and his Thessalonian disciples, the appearing of this figure lay in the future. For Christians in subsequent decades who endured persecution at the hands of Rome and its emperors, the spirit of antichrist, if not the antichrist himself, was seen as personified in the persecuting Caesars. Frequently, throughout subsequent church history, both secular and religious leaders have been identified as this "man of lawlessness," or "antichrist."[1]

These attempts to discover the lawless one along the stream of history have clearly not been successful, revealing that such undertakings are likely presumptuous and futile. When he is *revealed,* believers will recognize this final incarnation of evil. In the meantime, they are called to be present in the world in such a way that the spirit of lawlessness is resisted and the strongholds of evil's dominion challenged.

[1]See the concise study of the figure of the antichrist in the New Testament and subsequent Christian history by F. F. Bruce, *1 & 2 Thessalonians,* Word Biblical Commentary 45 (Waco, Tex.: Word, 1982), pp. 179-88.

2:7 Who Is the One Who Holds Back Lawlessness?

The figure of "one who holds back lawlessness" appears in a text where Paul speaks about events and experiences which precede and accompany the Second Coming of Christ (2 Thess 2:1-12). One event is the appearance of "the man of lawlessness" (2 Thess 2:3), a final personal incarnation of evil who will be overthrown "with the breath" of the Lord Jesus at his coming (2 Thess 2:8). That event is still to come, contends Paul. Yet, the reality and power of lawlessness is already presents though not as obviously as it will be when it reaches its climax in "the man of lawlessness."

The context of this passage shows that "lawlessness" is to be understood as opposition to God, as everything that violates the purposes of God for the creation. "Lawlessness" is at work wherever human beings "refuse to love the truth" (2 Thess 2:10) and "delight in wickedness" (2 Thess 2:12).

This lawlessness is a present reality, but it is being restrained, held in check, by a figure whom Paul vaguely refers to as "one who now holds it back." Who is this?

As with "the man of lawlessness," so with this enigmatic "restrainer," Paul assumes that the Thessalonian believers are aware of whom he speaks. "During my visit with you," he reminds them, "I used to tell you these things" (2 Thess 2:5). But since we were not there, Paul's veiled reference leaves us groping for that figure's identity. In that task we are not alone. As early as the fifth century, the church father Augustine admitted that the meaning of this hard saying completely escaped him, and as eminent an exegete as F. F. Bruce is sure with Augustine that the best we can do is "guess at its meaning."[1] Such guessing, however, is not totally subjective, for we have enough of Paul's view of things from his extensive writings to provide at least some clues.

In the history of this text's interpretation, two interpretations of the "restrainer of lawlessness" have commended themselves as most probable. One view sees in this enigmatic figure a reference to the power of the Roman Empire, represented in the person of the emperor. The state exists, Paul held, for the purpose of restraining wickedness (Rom 13:1-5). In the execution of this purpose the state is an instrument in the hands of God. When it violates that mandate, promoting evil and suppressing the good, it is demonic and the instrument of Satan (see Rev 13).

At the time of his missionary work in Macedonia, not long before he wrote his epistles to Thessalonica, Paul had experienced the protecting benefits of Roman citizenship (Acts 16:35-39). Later the progress of the gospel in Corinth was shielded from the power of lawlessness by a Roman magistrate (Acts 18:12-17), and Paul's life was saved from certain death at the hands of an angry mob and for several more years of missionary work by Roman authorities in Palestine (Acts 22—23). These experiences of the apostle no doubt confirmed the conviction that, within the sovereign purposes of God, the Roman state, with its laws and extensive power, acted as a restraint against a full manifestation of the powers of lawlessness and evil. He knew that this restraining power would not last forever. Caesar would one day be "taken out of the way" (2 Thess 2:7). But that day was not yet (2 Thess 2:3, 8).

A second interpretation of the "restraining power" (2 Thess 2:6) and the "restrainer" (2 Thess 2:7) takes its clues from another very important dimension of Paul's teaching. In the epistle to the Christians in Rome—written several years after the Thessalonian correspondence and from the same city, Corinth—Paul shares his belief that the proclamation of the gospel to the Gentiles was God's plan and that its rejection by the Jews was temporary (Rom 11:13-32). That belief is in keeping with Jesus' word that the gospel would be preached to all nations before the end would come (Mt 24:14; Mk 13:10). Within this understanding, the proclamation of the good news and its operation in the lives of believers would act as a restraint against evil in the world. Paul, as the apostle to the Gentiles, would be "the one who holds evil back" by his evangelistic ministry.

Both of these interpretations are possible within Paul's overall thought. Two considerations make the latter one somewhat less probable. First, since Paul speaks quite clearly about his Gentile mission and purposes elsewhere, the somewhat oblique reference to the something and someone who holds back evil in the present is difficult to understand. On the other hand, his reticence to name this reality explicitly, if Paul has Rome in mind, makes sense. For to say openly that Rome would be "taken out of the way" could cause unnecessary difficulty. Second, it is clear that the one who removes the restraining reality is God. But would Paul speak about his missionary work and the proclamation of the gospel—which he saw as mandated by the Lord—as being taken out of the way by God? It is thus more probable that "the one who holds back lawlessness" is a reference to the state—in the first instance, Rome, but in a larger sense all civil authority which, when properly fulfilling its mandate, acts as a restraint against anarchy.

---

[1]F. F. Bruce, *1 & 2 Thessalonians,* Word Biblical Commentary 45 (Waco, Tex.: Word, 1982), p. 175.

1-2 TIMOTHY

1 Timothy

1:17 Invisible God?

See comment on EXODUS 33:18-23; JOHN 1:18.

2:11-12 No Women Teachers?

The language here is seemingly straightforward and clear. But does Paul really mean what we think he means? And if he does mean it, is this an instruction he intended for universal application, regardless of historical context and circumstances?

This passage and 1 Timothy 2:13-15 are at the heart of the ongoing discussion of the place and role of women in church, home and society. Answers to the above questions are critical in that discussion.

This passage is a difficult one for yet another reason, namely, an emotional/experiential one. As a male, I am sure I cannot fully grasp the impact this apostolic word must have on women. But given that limitation, I can nonetheless understand something of the damage to one's self-worth and sense of giftedness this restrictive word must evoke. We are living at a point in history in which women and men are recognized as equally gifted in intellectual ability and communication skills. In such a climate, the apostolic prohibition seems particularly difficult to understand and accept. For what is it about gender which militates against the full expression of the Creator's gifts of heart and mind and spirit?

This question has often been answered with the assertion that clearly defined roles for men and women are divinely ordained and that Paul's restrictive instruction is evidence of such a universal norm. That response, however, is problematic. The account of the creation of male and female in Genesis 1—2—which we take as a foundational theological statement of the Creator's design and intention—affirms male and female as equal and complementary. Both are bearers, together, of God's image (Gen 1:26-27). Both are given the mandate to responsible sovereignty over the created order (Gen 1:28). The creation of the woman is intended to rescue the man from his aloneness and to provide him with a complement (Gen 2:18).[1]

Over against an ancient view that the gods played a trick on man by creating woman of inferior material, the creation account of Genesis affirms the woman to be of the same essence as man ("bone of my bones and flesh of my flesh," Gen 2:23). Thus the view that God intended the woman for a restricted role in home, church and society cannot be grounded in the order of creation.

A restricted status for woman has been traditionally grounded in the account of the Fall (Gen 3) in both Jewish and Christian thought and practice. But it is clear from the context of Genesis 2—3 that the words of 3:16—"Your desire will be for your husband, and he will rule over you"—do not announce God's created design for a male hierarchy. Rather these words announce a cursed existence because of a broken relationship between the human creation and the Creator. A restricted place for woman, and male-over-female dominance, is thus not divine purpose but an expression of human sin.

For Paul, the purpose of Christ's redemptive work was to set God's creation free from the curse of Eden. Those "in Christ" were new creations (2 Cor 5:17), freed from the bondage of sin and its expression in human relationships (Rom 6:5-7). In the new humanity created in Christ, the culturally and religiously ingrained view that some human beings, on the basis of gender or race or social status, were in some sense inferior could no longer be maintained (Gal 3:26-28). That was surely one of Paul's central theological convictions.

In discussing the passage in 1 Corinthians 14:33-40, where Paul instructs women in the church to "remain silent," we saw that this restriction was not universally applied either by Paul or by other early congregations. Women functioned in prominent leadership positions (Phoebe, Lydia, Euodia, Syntyche, Priscilla, Junia), designated as ministers (or deacons, Rom 16:1), fellow workers (Rom 16:3), colaborers in the gospel (Phil 4:2-9), apostles (or messengers, Rom 16:7). The Spirit of God empowered both men and women to be proclaimers of God's redemptive work in Christ (Acts 2:14-18). Women's participation in the edifying presentation of the gospel and vocal prayer in the congregation were a normal part of early church life (1 Cor 11).

In light of the above considerations, reasons for the particular restriction imposed on women in Timothy's congregation must be discovered from within the text and the situation in the church which Paul addresses. If, as we have seen, a curtailed role for women was neither a part of the divine intention in creation nor a normative aspect of the redeemed order, then the curtailment of their speaking and teaching and leading—in 1 Corinthians 14 and 1 Timothy 2—must be in response to critical, local situations. Investigation of 1 Corinthians 14 revealed such a crisis setting in Corinth. A critical situation in the life and faith of Timothy's congregation seems likewise the reason for Paul's instruction here.[2]

Upon reading 1 Timothy, one becomes immediately aware that the integrity of the Christian faith is at stake. There are some in the church who teach false doctrines and are occupied with myths and other speculative ideas which militate against sound and sincere faith (1 Tim 1:3-4). Some have wandered into vain debates, seeking to be teachers without understanding and discernment (1 Tim 1:6-7). There is throughout a concern for maintaining and guarding the truth of the faith (1 Tim 1:19; 2:4-7; 3:14-16; 4:1-3, 6-7, 16; 6:1-5, 12).

We do not know the identity of the false teachers or the full content of their teaching. From the instructions given, we can conclude that the false teaching led to a disregard for proper decorum and practices in the church (1 Tim 2:8-15) as well as to a rejection of the institution of marriage (1 Tim 4:3). In light of this last aspect of the heretical teaching, it is noteworthy that particular attention is directed to young widows (in 1 Tim 5:9-15), who are urged to marry, have children and manage their homes (1 Tim 5:14). When these normal, socially prescribed roles and functions are neglected or rejected, these women are prone to "gossiping" and being "busybodies, saying things they ought not to" (1 Tim 5:13).

On the basis of this data, at least two reconstructions of the situation in Timothy's congregation at Ephesus are possible: (1) the women in the church at Ephesus were the primary advocates and promoters of the heretical teachings which were upsetting accepted patterns of congregational and home life; (2) the women in the church had been particularly influenced by the heretical teachers. Such a situation in the Ephesian church is addressed in 2 Timothy 3:6-9, where women, the special targets of those "who oppose the truth" (2 Tim 3:8), become "unable to acknowledge the truth" (2 Tim 3:7).

In either case, Paul's restrictive word in 1 Timothy 2:11-12 must be understood within a context where false teaching is at issue. The general prohibition against all those who "teach false doctrines" (1 Tim 1:3) is now focused specifically on the women who have fallen prey to such false teaching or who are involved in its promulgation.

The admonition of 1 Timothy 2:11—"learn in quietness and full submission"—is thus directed at the women who, on the basis of the heretical teaching, have become loud voices, strident advocates of ideas that are upsetting the ordered contexts of congregational and home life. The "submission" enjoined on them is most likely a submission to the elders in the church, who are guardians of the truth and ordered worship. The prohibition against their teaching is occasioned by their involvement in false teachings. Finally, the prohibition against "authority over a man" (1 Tim 2:12) must be understood within the context of their rejection of the authority of others, probably the male leaders in Ephesus whose orthodox, authoritative teaching is being undermined by their heretical views. The unusual Greek word used carries primarily the negative sense of "grasping for" or "usurping authority." Thus, the restriction of women's place and participation in the life and ministry of the church at Ephesus is most probably "directed against women involved in false teaching who have abused proper exercise of authority in the church (not denied by Paul elsewhere to women) by usurpation and domination of the male leaders and teachers in the church at Ephesus."[3] Paul goes on to ground this instruction in reflections on selected passages from Genesis.

See also comment on GENESIS 2:18; 3:16; 1 CORINTHIANS 11:3; 11:7; 14:33-34.

[1]The Hebrew word translated "helper" (in Genesis 2:18 and 2:20), as a designation for the woman, is used only 16 more times in the Hebrew Bible. In those cases, it is always a designation of God as the One who saves, upholds and sustains his people (as in Ps 46:1). There is no sense in which this word connotes a position of inferiority or subordinate status. The word translated "suitable for" literally means "in front of," signifying one who stands "face to face" with another, qualitatively the same, his essential equal, and therefore his "correspondent."

[2]See Gordon D. Fee, *1 and 2 Timothy, Titus,* Good News Commentary (San Francisco: Harper & Row, 1984), who makes a persuasive case for 1 Timothy as an occasional letter addressing specific heretical teachings.

[3]David M. Scholer, "1 Timothy 2:9-15 and the Place of Women in the Church's Ministry," in Alvera Mickelsen, ed., *Women, Authority & the Bible* (Downers Grove, Ill.: InterVarsity Press, 1986), p. 205. This essay, and several others in this volume, present an excellent study of the exegetical, historical-cultural and linguistic issues in this hard saying and related biblical texts.

2:13-15 Salvation Through Childbirth?

When the writer of 2 Peter claims that there are some passages in Paul's writings which "are hard to understand" (2 Pet 3:16), it is easy to imagine that he had 1 Timothy 2:13-15 in mind. The passage has been more intensely debated and analyzed than almost any other single text in the Bible.[1] Rather than exploring all the suggestions and possibilities, I will seek to focus on the central issues and attempt to understand the main point of the passage within the situation Paul is addressing.

Since 1 Timothy 2:13 begins with the connective particle "for . . . ," it is clear that the following sentences are a continuation of what precedes. Thus this text gives Paul's biblical reflections that provide a rationale for his prohibition against women's teaching and usurping authority in the church (1 Tim 2:11-12), discussed in the previous chapter.

The conclusion of that discussion was that Paul was addressing problems of heresy in the church at Ephesus and that the women in this congregation were strongly captivated by these false doctrines or were vocal proponents. Their teaching led to the questioning and rejection of culturally accepted norms and roles for men and women, causing difficulties for this young congregation within its social context. Paul is concerned that their witness to the truth of the gospel is thereby undermined. He is concerned with "propriety" (1 Tim 2:9, 15), that is, socially acceptable behavior; with the possibility of being "disgraced" in the sight of outsiders (1 Tim 3:7); and with giving "the enemy no opportunity for slander" (1 Tim 5:14; 6:1).

Paul's restrictive admonitions regarding women must be understood within this particular historical situation. They are therefore not to be understood as divine imperatives, applicable universally to all women in all cultural contexts and historical circumstances. Rather, they are authoritative apostolic counsel, given for the correction of abuses in a particular situation that threatened the truth of the gospel and the viability of a young church in an antagonistic environment. The transcendent principle standing behind Paul's particular instructions is the imperative of the gospel (applicable in *all* cultural contexts), namely, God's intention that "all be saved" (1 Tim 2:4; see also 1 Cor 10:33).

Insofar as specific expressions of their new freedom in Christ resulted in the undermining of social conventions (as in rejection of marriage and domestic responsibilities), the undermining of truth (as in teaching of false doctrines) and a domineering presence (as in usurping authority from the designated leaders of the church), women were threatening the church's credibility and therefore its missionary effectiveness. That is the reason Paul imposes limits.

But why does Paul ground all this in Scripture? Why argue for priority for the male on the basis of Genesis 2? Why does he reason from the woman's participation in the Fall (Gen 3) to a restricted role for her in the church? And finally, what is the point about women being saved through childbearing?

Answers to those questions begin to emerge when we recognize an essential truth of Paul's life: He was a rabbi who had been transformed into a follower of Christ. As a trained rabbi he became a disciple of Jesus and an apostle to the Gentiles. His training as a rabbi—gained as a student of Gamaliel, one of the great rabbinic teachers in first-century Palestine (Acts 22:3)—was placed at the service of the interpretation and articulation of the gospel. Thus Paul's writings are thoroughly pervaded by scriptural citations or allusions.

One of the chief functions of the rabbinic tradition was to respond to the broad range of concerns within the community of faith, from the most minute aspects of everyday life to the deepest theological issues. Over hundreds of years of such rabbinic reflection on the biblical text (our Old Testament), a massive body of biblical interpretations accumulated. Some of this material is reflected in the Jewish intertestamental literature, including the Apocrypha, a group of writings that was part of the Greek Old Testament read by the early church. Paul was heir to that tradition.

At critical points, where the essence and integrity of the gospel was at stake, Paul uncompromisingly broke with that tradition, as his Lord had done during his earthly life.[2] But in matters that were not at the heart of the gospel, or when he gave instructions for particular situations, he sometimes used interpretations of Old Testament texts that were familiar to him from that tradition.

When we read 1 Timothy 2:13-14, we realize two things immediately. First, Paul does not quote the biblical passages directly. He gives us rather a particular and partial understanding of the meaning of those passages. Second, the situation which he is addressing is a limited, local situation that calls for a limited, partial use of the biblical material.

The reason he instructs women to be silent, not to teach and not to usurp authority over men (1 Tim 2:12) is because Adam was formed before Eve (1 Tim 2:13). The Genesis 2 creation narrative is of course referred to here. Within the synagogue, which provided a model for early church life and structure, male dominance was traditionally certified by a reading of the *chronological sequence* of Genesis 2 in terms of male *priority*.

It is clear that Paul does not intend this interpretation of Genesis 2—which he uses here to give authority to his instructions—to be applied universally. For in 1 Corinthians 11, where Paul argues for women's head covering, also on the basis of the chronological sequence in Genesis 2 (1 Cor 11:8-9), he then goes on to admonish his readers that the origin of *both* male and female is in God, and that since the creation every male emerges from, and is therefore preceded by, a female (1 Cor 11:12). In this argument, Paul goes beyond the traditional rabbinic interpretation based on chronological priority to the heart of the Genesis 2 narrative. For its focus is on the fact that the male, in his chronological priority, is pronounced as "not good" (Gen 2:18). It is the creation of the female as one "corresponding to him" that saves the male from his aloneness.[3]

Thus a traditional interpretation of Genesis 2 is addressed to a specific, limited situation. And it is authoritative primarily for that situation. If women were creating havoc in the congregation by rejecting socially accepted roles and were grasping for authority, especially those who were peddling heretical teachings, then it was natural for Paul to emphasize biblical texts and interpretations that affirmed culturally and religiously accepted views of female roles.

A further argument for women's restricted place, given in 1 Timothy 2:14, is that Eve was deceived and became a sinner, while Adam was not deceived.

Here, as in the appeal to Genesis 2 above, Paul refers to a truth expressed in Genesis, this time in the story of the Fall in Genesis 3. In Genesis 3:13, Eve says that "the serpent deceived me, and I ate." From this the rabbinic tradition reasoned that women were by nature more vulnerable to deception than men. That view of womanhood was widespread in Judaism. Philo, the important Alexandrian Jewish scholar who was a contemporary of Paul, expressed the view that since woman "is more accustomed to be deceived than man" and "gives way and is taken in by plausible falsehoods which resemble the truth," the proper relation of a wife to a husband is epitomized in the verb "to serve as a slave."[4] In the apocryphal work *The Wisdom of Ben Sirach* (25:24), the author concludes that "from a woman sin had its beginning and because of her we all die."

Yet, side by side with this emphasis in Jewish tradition was the acknowledgment of Adam's full responsibility. In 2 Esdras 7:118 there is the lament "O Adam, what have you done? For though it was you who sinned, the fall was not yours alone." Paul also knew this part of the tradition, for in Romans 5:12-14 and 1 Corinthians 15:21-22 he makes Adam, rather than Eve, responsible for the entrance of sin. The basis for this emphasis in the interpretation is of course material from Genesis 3, where Adam is with Eve at the fateful moment (Gen 3:6), where God holds him responsible for reaching beyond his limits (Gen 3:11), and where he was deceived, just like Eve, into transgressing God's command (Gen 3:17).

In light of the above data from both Genesis 3 and other Pauline texts, the phrase in 1 Timothy 2:14 "Adam was not deceived" is particularly problematic. For it is clear that *he was in fact deceived,* just like Eve. Some interpreters have concluded that Paul has here simply reverted to the dominant rabbinic interpretation that focuses on the woman's deception, letting man off the hook. But that is pitting Paul the rabbi against Paul the Christian; I do not think this is either legitimate or necessary.

Paul is *always* the rabbi who has been baptized into Christ. And in his fellowship with Christ his rabbinic learning is also baptized. As such, it is placed into the service of his missionary work. And this work of the gospel determines the use he makes of rabbinic interpretations of Old Testament material.

His interpretive method and its application in the particular situation at Ephesus *does not mean* that he shared with his rabbinic tradition the view that women were *inherently* more deceivable. This is confirmed by the fact that Paul uses Eve's deception in 2 Corinthians 11:3-4 as an *illustration* of the possibility that *all* believers in Corinth, both men and women, may be deceived and led away from faith in Christ. Thus we see that Paul uses the Eve tradition variously, depending on the problem being addressed.

Once again, it is apparent that the needs of the situation in Ephesus dictated Paul's use of various aspects of the scriptural tradition which, on the whole, was considered authoritative. Since women in Timothy's congregation seem to have been prominent among those who "have wandered away" from the faith and its appropriate expression in life (1 Tim 1:3-7), or those who "have in fact already turned away to follow Satan" (1 Tim 5:15), or those "who are loaded down with sins and swayed by all kinds of evil desires" (2 Tim 3:6), Paul's partial use of the Genesis material and its application to this particular situation is quite understandable.

A final difficulty of this text is the statement that "women will be saved through childbearing" (1 Tim 2:15).[5] What is the meaning of this statement, and how does it function in the context of the whole passage?

First, if there is one truth which Paul spent his entire ministry driving home to his listeners and readers, it is this: that salvation is not gained by the performance of functions and duties or the exercise of specific roles, but by faith in Jesus Christ. It is therefore impossible to conclude that Paul is speaking about personal salvation. That is, women are not saved by any other means than men.

Second, 1 Timothy 2:15 is the conclusion to the entire paragraph. In 1 Timothy 2:9-14 the specific instructions to women are restrictive and negative. Verse 15 begins with the word "but" (or, better, "yet"), and what is said is apparently intended as a positive affirmation. The various restrictions imposed on women are now qualified. They are not absolute norms, essential conditions determined by gender. Rather, they are necessary adjustments in light of the historical situation in which the missionary effectiveness of the young churches was at stake.

In Timothy's situation, heretical teaching undermined the validity of marriage. We are not told why. But on the basis of 1 Corinthians 7, where marriage seems to be rejected by the superspiritualists who despise physical, bodily reality, we can conclude that the heretical teaching viewed marriage, and its specific expression in the bearing of children, as negative, or as unworthy of those who were truly spiritual and members of a new community of "saved" persons. Over against that heretical teaching, Paul may be affirming that the bearing of children, which is a woman's natural procreative, life-giving function, does in fact not keep her from full participation in the community of the saved.

Thus women are and will be saved, even as they perform those domestic and maternal roles expected of women in the social-historical context, but rejected by the heretical teachers. It is possible that the heretical teachers and the women who had been deceived by them saw a rejection of normal domestic and maternal roles as evidence that they were truly saved and spiritual. Such a situation makes Paul's strong and difficult restrictive injunctions to the women in Ephesus absolutely necessary, for the heretical teaching and its consequences represented a comprehensive misunderstanding and denial of the gospel.

---

[1]For further information on the literature dealing with 1 Timothy 2:11-15 and related biblical texts, see Alvera Mickelsen, ed., *Women, Authority & the Bible* (Downers Grove, Ill.: InterVarsity Press, 1986).

[2]Examples are (1) Jesus' rejection of rabbinic regulations regarding sabbath observance—which were based on the fourth commandment (Ex 20:8-11)—by focusing on the heart of God's compassion for broken humanity (Mk 3:1-6; Jn 5:2-18) and (2) Paul's rejection of Jewish Christians' attempt to impose ritual requirements, such as circumcision, on Gentile converts, by affirming that salvation is purely by God's grace and the response of faith (Gal 2:11-16).

[3]See note 1 in comment on 1 TIMOTHY 2:11-12, where the meanings of the significant Hebrew words in this verse are discussed.

[4]Philo *Questions on Genesis* 1.33 (Loeb Classical Library).

[5]The NIV correctly indicates in a footnote that the Greek text reads: "She will be saved through childbearing." In the previous verse the subject is Eve, the singular, representative of womanhood. That singular subject determines the personal pronoun of 1 Timothy 2:15, "but she will be saved." However, the sentence goes on in the plural, "if they continue in faith." It is thus clear that Paul sees Eve as representing all women.

5:8 Worse Than an Unbeliever?

The point of 1 Timothy 5:8 is rather clear. Failure to care for the needs of particular individuals is tantamount to rejection of one's faith. And a person of faith who acts in such a way as to deny that faith in practice is worse than those who never profess faith in the first place.

What creates difficulties for us is the rigorous tone of this instruction and the finality that seems to be attached to one's failure in following the instruction. A related difficulty—in light of Paul's insistence that salvation is by faith and not by works—is the close connection in this text between a very particular action and one's faith, and therefore one's salvation.

A careful look at Paul's argument in its larger context and within his thinking about faith and its fruits should alleviate the difficulties.

Our verse is part of a longer passage (1 Tim 5:3-16) in which Paul is concerned about the place and care of widows in the church. In the ancient world, partially due to patriarchal family and social structures, widows were often among the most weak and vulnerable members of society. It is clear from the Old Testament that God has a special concern for the least, the little ones, the oppressed, the powerless. And that concern includes widows (Deut 10:18; 24:17; Ps 68:5; Is 1:17). From Luke's account of the ministry of Jesus and the early church (Lk 7:11-15; 18:2-8; 21:1-4; Acts 6:1; 9:39), we see that concern for widows naturally continued in the "new Israel," that the Christian community saw care for widows as a special responsibility, and that groups of widows in the churches were particularly involved in good deeds of charity for others in need.

The larger passage, of which this text is a part, reveals this abiding concern for widows. It also shows that particular circumstances called for greater clarity regarding the church's responsibility in this area. Paul distinguishes between "widows who are really in need" (1 Tim 5:3) and those who have family able to care for them (1 Tim 5:4). Given the fact that the early churches, on the whole, were constituted of people who were from the lower socioeconomic strata (see 1 Cor 1:26-28), their economic resources cannot have been extensive. Thus the need arose to channel limited resources to meet the most urgent situations of deprivation. It may even be that the church's compassion for widows was expressed so consistently that charity became something to be expected, even when there was no real need.

In any case, Paul's instruction is that the primary responsibility for the care of widows rests on members of the immediate family (children or grandchildren, 1 Tim 5:4). Only when that assistance is not available, when the widow is "left all alone" (1 Tim 5:5), does the larger community become responsible.

Paul grounds that instruction in two ways. Such action is, first of all, "pleasing to God" (1 Tim 5:4). The imperative to care for parents was derived in Judaism from the fifth commandment ("Honor your father and your mother," Ex 20:12), and obedience to the commandment was understood to bring with it God's blessing. Second, Paul grounds his instruction in a truth stated over and over in the Word of God; namely, that one's faith, one's beliefs, must find expression in concrete action and relationships. Thus, following a harsh rebuke against the emptiness and shallowness of Israel's worship (Is 1:10-16), Isaiah calls on the people to "seek justice, encourage the oppressed. Defend the cause of the fatherless, plead the case for the widow" (Is 1:17). A right relationship with God is expressed in the doing of justice, the loving of kindness (Mic 6:6) and the demonstration of steadfast love (Hos 6:6). The truest expression of the worship of God is when God's people are involved in letting "justice roll on like a river, righteousness like a never-failing stream!" (Amos 5:24).

This central Old Testament conviction is also at the heart of the message of Jesus and his followers. We shall be known by the fruit we bear (Mt 7:16, 20) and thus bring glory to God (Jn 15:8). The world will know that we are Jesus' disciples if we genuinely love one another (Jn 13:35). If God's forgiving, reconciling work does not find expression in our relationships, then our worship of God is empty (Mt 5:23-24). The fruit of the Spirit in us, says Paul, expresses itself in kindness and the practice of goodness (Gal 5:22). New life in Christ (Col 3:1-3) is to express itself in a life clothed with compassion and kindness (Col 3:12). Faith that is not evidenced in deeds is judged to be dead, inauthentic faith (Jas 2:14-17). Religion that is "pure and faultless is this: to look after orphans and widows in their distress" (Jas 1:27).

Within this larger New Testament perspective, Paul's directive for the care of widowed mothers or grandmothers by children or grandchildren must be understood. They should "learn first of all to put their religion into practice by caring for their own family" (1 Tim 5:4). The reality of our relationship with God most naturally flows over into our human relationships. And the members of our immediate families are the first ones to feel the impact of our relationship with God. The expression "Charity begins at home" is rooted in the conviction that if love of neighbor does not express itself concretely in our closest relationships, then our claim to love God ("our religion") is a lie (1 Jn 4:19-21).

This is why Paul judges a person who does not provide for family members to have "denied the faith" and to be "worse than an unbeliever" (1 Tim 5:8). Though this judgment seems harsh in relation to this particular failure in practical Christian behavior, Paul's concern throughout the letter that Christian life be above reproach from outsiders (1 Tim 2:2; 3:1-7; 5:14; 6:1) helps us to understand his strong word. The phrase "to be worse than an unbeliever" implies that even unbelievers are expected to care for those of their own households. Believers who neglect this responsibility are thus acting "worse than" unbelievers. Whenever that happens (see also 1 Cor 5:1-2), the church is not being God's alternative community in a broken, fragmented world. And such a life in the world represents a denial of the faith.

See also comment on JAMES 2:24; 2 PETER 2:20.

5:23 Wine for the Stomach?

In the context of a society in which the abuse of alcohol is such a serious problem, this piece of personal advice from Paul to Timothy raises for many the question of the legitimacy of the use of alcohol. Since alcohol is so easily abused, and since its abuse leads to the enslavement of people to addiction, should not Christians be encouraged to abstain from any use of it? This latter, prohibitionist view is expressed in a somewhat humorous anecdote from a discussion of this issue among a group of deacons. To the factual affirmation by one deacon that Jesus had turned water into wine at the wedding at Cana (Jn 2), another deacon replied, "Yes, he did, but he shouldn't have!" When the basic premise is the conviction that any use of alcohol is wrong, then Jesus' action and Paul's admonition become problematic.

Paul's word must be understood in the context of other advice in the correspondence with Timothy and Titus. It also must be seen as a sound piece of advice in the cultural context and as an expression of a central biblical principle for Christian living.

Earlier in 1 Timothy, Paul had listed among the characteristics of those who would be leaders in the church that they be "not given to drunkenness" (1 Tim 3:3) or "not indulging in much wine" (1 Tim 3:8). In advice to Titus, elders need to be examples who are "not given to drunkenness" (Tit 1:7), and the elder women in the church are to be taught not to be "addicted to much wine" (literally, "slaves to wine," Tit 2:3). In all these injunctions, the emphasis is clearly on moderation; namely, a responsible use of alcohol that does not lead to its control of one's life.[1] This is in keeping with a central principle of Christian life stated by Paul in Ephesians 5:18: "Do not get drunk on wine, which leads to debauchery. Instead, be filled with the Spirit." The only legitimate controlling reality in the believer's life is to be God's Spirit. All other controlling realities are, in fact, idolatrous.

In light of these prohibitions against the excessive use of alcohol, Paul's advice to Timothy, "Stop drinking only water and use a *little* wine" (emphasis mine), implies that Timothy may have concluded, from the warnings against excessive use, that total abstinence was called for. It may even be that the false teachers, in their prohibition against certain foods (1 Tim 4:3), had argued for total abstinence.[2]

In any case, Timothy's total rejection of alcohol seems to have had harmful consequences for his health. So Paul, in keeping with his warnings against abusive use, counsels for the use of "a little wine." In this, he is simply reflecting the common use of wine, especially for medicinal purposes, in the ancient world. Its beneficial effects "against dyspeptic complaints, as a tonic, and as counteracting the effects of impure water, were widely recognized in antiquity"[3] and are confirmed by modern medicine. Paul's view on this matter may have been backed by the advice of his fellow worker Luke, the beloved physician.

See also comment on PROVERBS 31:6-7.

---

[1]Gordon Fee understands these warnings as "negative reflections on first-century culture itself, which often admired heavy drinkers" (*1 and 2 Timothy, Titus,* Good News Commentary [San Francisco: Harper & Row, 1984], p. 140).

[2]Whether these teachings were grounded in Jewish regulations regarding clean and unclean foods, we do not know. But in the advocacy of an ascetic style of life, the Stoic philosopher Epictetus (A.D. 55-135) taught that one should "drink water only." (Cited by A. J. Hultgren, *1 Timothy, 2 Timothy, Titus, 2 Thessalonians,* Augsburg Commentary on the New Testament [Minneapolis: Augsburg, 1984], p. 93.)

[3]J. N. D. Kelly, *A Commentary on the Pastoral Epistles* (New York: Harper, 1964), p. 129, cites several Jewish and Hellenistic sources, including Hippocrates, who recommended moderate amounts of wine for a patient for whose stomach water alone is dangerous.

6:16 Whom No One Has Seen?

See comment on EXODUS 33:18-23; JOHN 1:18.

2 Timothy

4:14 A Call for Revenge?

See comment on PSALMS 137:8-9; 139:20.

TITUS, PHILEMON

Titus

1:12-13 Cretans Are Always Liars?

These sentences strike us at best as extreme, at worst as untrue. The people thus categorized are inhabitants of the island of Crete in the eastern Mediterranean, where Titus is a leader among the churches. Presumably most members of these churches, and especially the elders in those churches, whom Paul expects to be blameless, self-controlled, upright, holy and disciplined (Tit 1:8), would not qualify as "liars, evil brutes, lazy gluttons." Even among the general Cretan population there were surely many who led good and upright lives. Thus the definition of Cretans as "always liars" is hardly justified. Though Paul is clearly citing from "one of their own prophets," he supports the generalization by concluding that "this testimony is true." How are we to understand this harsh language? A closer look at the situation addressed in the Cretan churches, as well as the citation's origin and history, should ameliorate, if not eliminate, the difficulty.

The situation addressed is one in which heretical teachers are abroad in the churches, opposing "the knowledge of the truth" (Tit 1:1), the promises of God "who does not lie" (Tit 1:2), "the trustworthy message" and "sound doctrine" (Tit 1:9). They are "deceivers" (Tit 1:10), "teaching things they ought not to teach" (Tit 1:11), rejecting "the truth" (Tit 1:14).

It is this focus on the untruthfulness of the opponents of the gospel and the untruthfulness of their teaching that brings to Paul's mind a line from a revered Cretan, Epimenides, a religious teacher and wonderworker from around 600 B.C. Paul's designation of him as a "prophet" is probably based on the description of Epimenides as an inspired, prophetic man by Plato, Aristotle and other ancient writers. The ground for Epimenides' unsavory characterization of his fellow Cretans was apparently their popular claim that the tomb of Zeus, the head of the Greek pantheon of gods, was located on their island. This claim was considered false, since Zeus, as a god, could not be dead. By Paul's time, Epimenides' words had become a popular slogan, expressing the widespread reputation of Cretans as untruthful. The verb "to Cretize" became slang for lying or cheating, just as the city of Corinth's reputation for sexual immorality led to the slang verb "to Corinthianize."

As we have seen, the context in which Paul appeals to Epimenides' words is one of crisis. In such a situation of polemical confrontation, exaggerations are common. Paul is obviously angry at the enemies of the truth in the Cretan churches, and he responds to their deceptions by using the typical device of overstatement. What Paul intends to communicate forcefully is clear; namely, in the case of these teachers who peddle false teaching, Epimenides' dictum is in fact shown to be true.

That Paul's words are not to be understood in an absolute sense (that is, that every Cretan is a liar!) is confirmed by the fact that his appeal to Epimenides would otherwise involve a contradiction. For since Epimenides is a Cretan, his statement that "Cretans are always liars" would include him. And that would lead to the conclusion that he *always* lies and that his statement is therefore false. It is clear then that neither Paul nor Epimenides intended the statement to be understood in an all-inclusive general sense.

3:5 Salvation: Past, Present or Future?

See comment on 1 PETER 1:9.

Philemon

12 Did Paul Approve of Slavery?

See comment on EPHESIANS 6:5-8.

HEBREWS

1:3 What Is the Trinity?

See comment on JOHN 1:1.

2:10 Make the Author of Their Salvation Perfect?

If Jesus was the Son of God, how could he become perfect through experiences on earth? Was there some imperfection in him that had to be worked out through ordeal? Doesn't this challenge an orthodox view of Christ?

The author of Hebrews implies that Jesus, as the preincarnate Son of God, was indeed perfect (Heb 1:2-3). He is greater than the prophets, heir of all things and maker of the universe. But in the passage under consideration he is not in that preincarnate role. His role here is that of "the author of [the Christians'] salvation." The preincarnate Son of God was not yet perfect *in relation to that role.* In fact, he could not fulfill that role at all until he became incarnate and died for the sins of humanity.

Perfection is an important concept in Hebrews (Heb 5:9, 14; 6:1; 7:11, 19, 28; 9:9, 11; 10:1, 14; 11:40; 12:2, 23). The Greek term means "to bring to maturity, perfection or fulfillment."[1] The fulfillment aspect is the most important in Hebrews. The theme of the whole book is the fulfillment of the reality behind Mosaic ritual, but there is also a fulfillment coming to the lives of Christians as they go on to complete that to which they were called at their conversion. Even though Christ has done everything for them on the cross and they receive this upon committing themselves to him, there is a promise involved in this reception that is not fulfilled until they live out that to which they were called.

This same concept of fulfillment appears in Christ. At birth he is designated as Savior, but he has at that time done nothing to deserve such a title. It is a promise, a hope, but not yet a reality. He goes through life obeying the will of God and therefore experiencing suffering (Heb 2:18). The question remains: Will he keep on until the end? At Gethsemane, facing the time of fulfillment, he cries out, "Not my will but yours be done" (Heb 5:7 reflects this

Gospel cry). He continues on his way to the cross and fulfills everything that is needed to be "founder" (the Greek term means "author," "founder" or "leader" in most contexts) of salvation for his followers. Before that point he was not yet perfect, for death was a requirement to bring life to his people. After his death and resurrection he was the total fulfillment of all that was needed to bring salvation.

Therefore the perfection of Christ referred to here is a functional perfection, not a moral perfection, for he was never anything less than sinless. It is an earned perfection that will show up in its other aspects three more times in Hebrews (Heb 2:18; 4:15; 5:7-9), but at this point the function is salvation, earned only through death. Thus in talking about the perfecting of Christ the author underlines the fact that it was only through death that the world could gain a Savior.

See also comment on HEBREWS 5:7-9.

---

[1]The Greek terms are the verb *teleioō* and the adjective *teleios.*

4:15 Tempted in Every Way?

How could God be tempted? Hebrews states twice that Jesus was tempted, for the author first writes, "Because he himself suffered when he was tempted, he is able to help those who are being tempted" (Heb 2:18), and now he states that Jesus "has been tempted in every way, just as we are" (Heb 4:15). Yet many Christians argue that Christ really could not have been tempted "just as we are." After all, he was the sinless Son of God. Would not his very existence as God mean that his experience of temptation was at most that of watching a strong enemy smash himself on an impregnable castle? Was there ever any feeling of the desirability of sin that makes temptation so difficult for us?

Actually, these verses are difficult because they involve two issues, the nature of temptation and the nature of Christ. The first we have experience with; with the second we as human beings have no experience, and we must rely on the simple statements of Scripture.

The Greek term for "temptation" could also be translated "test." Human beings are tested to see if we will obey God when the chips are down (see Gen 22:1, the classic example of passing a test). We are tested to see if we will remain faithful when there is nothing to win (for example, Job 1—2). We are tested to see if our hearts are truly for God or whether we are trying to serve two masters (Jas 1:14-15; compare Jas 4:3-4). Jesus experienced all of these things. In Matthew 4 Jesus faces three tests, parallel to the tests of Israel in the wilderness: (1) When he appears to be starving will he, like Israel, demand that God feed him? He passes the test and refuses, being willing to trust God to the point of death if necessary. As long as God has said, "Fast," he will fast. (2) Could he be certain that God would care for him? Why not test God to be sure that he would come through? Jesus passes this test because his trust in God is unshakable. He will not put God to the test, for he has genuine faith. (3) Will God really give him the kingdoms of this world? Does that not look impossible, since Satan controls them? Is not God's way an unlikely and difficult one? One little compromise is all it will take to bring the kingdom without pain. Jesus again passes the test because he refuses to compromise with evil, however enticing or even spiritual it may seem. Thus Jesus demonstrates he is God's true Son, as Israel in the wilderness proved to be a false son. These three examples are precisely the same types of tests that we as human beings face.

But what makes us fail the test? James

(Jas 1:14) and Paul (Rom 7:17) trace the cause to a principle within us that James calls "desire" and the Jews called the "evil impulse," or *yēṣer*. None of the writers believe that this is guilt-producing in the sense that simply to have it made one guilty. Rather it was just "desire"—or what a psychologist might call a "drive." Food is desirable because I am hungry; shelter is desirable because I am cold. But hunger also makes my neighbors' food desirable. Likewise their house or clothing might be desirable if I were cold. As we see in observing a baby, drive or desire has no moral boundaries. Part of becoming godly is to learn when to say yes to desire and when to say no. Err on the side of saying no too often and one might become an ascetic, refusing God's good gifts, or possibly even die. Err on the side of saying yes too much and one becomes a libertine, breaking God's boundaries in some way or another. Satan's destructive purposes are served by either error.

Did Jesus have desire? The answer, found in Hebrews, is that he "has been tempted in every way, just as we are." Matthew 4:2 states that he was hungry. The drive or desire was present. Likewise we assume that all other normal human drives were present. He felt thirst, weariness, sexual desire, loneliness and all else that we feel. Some of these he felt to the extreme. Think of the loneliness that he felt when he cried out from the cross, "My God, my God, why have you forsaken me?" Jesus was, according to this text and the witness of the New Testament in general, fully human.

The one exception to human experience we find in Jesus is that he did not sin. In Matthew 4 he never gives in, but passes each of the tests. In Gethsemane he struggles mightily, but in the end says, "Not my will, but yours." At the cross he surely felt the impulse of pain and anger as he was stripped naked and nailed to the crossbar, but his response is "Father, forgive them." To each situation, Hebrews asserts, he gave the proper response in the sight of God. He was without sin. Could he have sinned? Scripture never enters into such philosophical speculation. But it certainly implies that there was virtue in not sinning and that the test was real, which seems to imply the possibility of failing. One point, however, Hebrews makes crystal clear: whether Jesus could sin or not, the issue in the end is academic. He did not sin.

Although the church through the ages often practically has denied the humanity of Christ, picturing him as more divine than human, it has refused to allow that distortion doctrinally. The creeds assert that there were not two natures, as if the human nature would feel something and the divine nature would give the right response. There was also no attenuation of the human nature so that he experienced human feelings in some less intense manner than other human beings. He was, the creeds assert, fully incarnate, everything that we as human beings are, except that he never sinned. While the creeds are not Scripture, they safeguard what the author of Hebrews is attempting to express: Jesus experienced testing just as all of us do.

The reason for this dogmatic statement is important. According to Hebrews 4:15, Jesus can "sympathize with our weaknesses." He can do this, the argument runs, because he has experienced the same type of weaknesses. He may be exalted at God's right hand now, but he fully and experientially understands all that human beings are going through.[1] "Because he himself suffered when he was tempted, he is able to help those who are being tempted" (Heb 2:18). One must have experience with a situation to be helpful in the situation, but even then one will not be helpful unless the experience is successful. A person who failed a test is hardly the one to coach another on how to prepare for the test. Jesus took the very same test as we do, indeed, a more intense form of the very same test. But he passed. He "was without sin." He did not fail in any way. As a result he can in fact respond with true sympathy to human beings now suffering under testing, for he truly "feels with," having himself felt the same pain and impulses. He can also show by example the successful way through the test.

The Incarnation is a mystery, but the witness of Hebrews is that it was real. There is no way Jesus was not like us, except in our sinning. Offensive as this may be to the mind, which prefers a Greek view of a God untouched by real human feelings and testings, it is comforting to the heart, which is precisely why the author of Hebrews taught it.

---

[1]One might object that a major part of human experience is that of guilt, which Jesus could not share because he did not sin. Such a response would be correct when one considers Jesus' life, but it breaks down at the cross. There Jesus did take sin upon himself—even if it was not his own—experiencing fully what it means to be guilty before God. In fact, because he knew God so well, it is likely that he experienced our guilt far more keenly than we do. Therefore there is truly no human experience other than the act of sinning with which Jesus cannot identify.

5:7-9 Jesus Learned Obedience?

When we read Hebrews 5:7-9, we are keenly aware of Jesus' emotions, his "loud cries and tears," and we appreciate this look into Jesus' humanity. But then the passage grates against our sensitivities when we read that Jesus "learned obedience." Wasn't Christ already obedient in becoming incarnate? Was there anything that the Son of God had to learn? Can God learn? Can we hold an orthodox view of the divinity of Christ and still accept this Scripture?

The context of this passage is that of the high priesthood of Jesus. Immediately after describing the exalted nature of this call, the author turns to the qualifications of Christ. The main qualification of a true priest is that he must obey God. Jesus was obedient to God. The author then makes it clear that obedience was learned in the context of suffering.

The example of suffering given here appears to be that of Gethsemane; it is the only occasion we know of when Jesus prayed intensely while facing death. The author does not describe a serene Jesus calmly facing the cross, but rather a deeply distressed Jesus wailing out loud prayers to his Father. This in itself shows a genuinely distraught human being, not an individual who minimizes the cross because he knows it will turn out all right. What is interesting, however, is that God saved him from death, not because of the intensity of the prayer, but because of his reverence or piety (what the NIV translates as "reverent submission"[1]). That is, even in the most intensely trying situation Jesus maintained reverential submission toward God. And his prayers were heard, not in the sense that he did not die, for Hebrews is very aware of the death of Christ, but in the sense that he was "delivered out of death" (an overliteral translation that makes the intended point) or raised from the dead.

This information, then, instructs us about what it means to learn obedience and be made perfect. The obedience Jesus learned was the obedience of suffering. It is one thing to obey when there is no resistance; it is another thing to obey when that very obedience will bring you pain. Before the Incarnation who resisted the Son? Only in his life on earth did he suffer for his obedience. In other words, there are some things that even God can experience only by becoming a human being with all of our human limitations.[2] Obedience in the face of suffering is one of them. This in turn brought Jesus to perfection, which has the sense of "maturity" or "fulfillment." That is, through obedience in the face of intense suffering, Jesus was able to complete or fulfill his mission, namely to become the source or basis of eternal salvation (versus a temporal deliverance) to those who in turn obey him. This completed mission is the basis for his present high priesthood.

This whole passage, then, turns on obedience in the face of suffering. Jesus was the Son, heir of all and exalted above the angels (Heb 1). But as a good Son Jesus submitted to the will of the Father. God's will for him included intense suffering, and yet he obeyed to the end. The result was that he was eternally delivered from death and so is now a high priest forever. The believers Hebrews is addressing are experiencing suffering, although so far no one has died (Heb 12:4). They, like Jesus, will also obtain eternal salvation by obedience to the end, obedience to Christ.

Thus, Jesus does learn, although it is not a theoretical learning but an experiential learning of what it is to obey in the face of intense suffering. He also experiences a perfecting through this obedience, a perfection in the sense of a completion of his work as Savior, making him in reality what he was by God's declaration. Any Christology that has a place for genuine humanity must also have a place for such a learning (with "loud cries and tears") and such a perfection. Furthermore, it is just such a Christ that is worthy of trust when we are ourselves facing suffering.

See also comment on HEBREWS 2:10.

[1]Some translations prefer "he was heard [delivered, set free] from his fear." This has a good basis in the use of the Greek term in the Greek Old Testament, but given that (1) the author of Hebrews is a literate person and (2) classical Greek literature uses the Greek term used here for "piety" and (3) the context of this verse, the meaning used here is more likely.

[2]This is similar to the difference between our experiencing a hurricane by means of a computer model and living through a real hurricane. The first might give one a tremendous understanding of a hurricane, perhaps a far better one than could be obtained by the person in the middle of the storm, but it is the second type of experience that makes it possible to empathize with the terror of those living through the storm.

6:4-6 Is Repentance Ever Impossible?

Most Christians know of individuals who for one reason or another have left the faith. They may not have actually denied the faith, but they are certainly not practicing the faith. For such people this is a very troubling passage. Is there anyone who cannot be brought to repentance? Can a person have shared the Holy Spirit and then be lost? And are these people really eternally lost? Is this really a description of a Christian?

First, this passage is not unique but rather is part of a group of passages concerning people who cannot be forgiven or brought to repentance. Mark 3:28-29 refers to blasphemy against the Holy Spirit, which will never be forgiven. The context is that of people observing the work of the Spirit through Jesus and calling it the work of the devil. In 1 John 5:16 the author speaks of a "sin unto death" (KJV) about which, the elder implies, prayer is useless. Finally, the verse under consideration here refers to a class of people who cannot "be brought back to repentance." The issue is not whether God would forgive them if they repented, but whether there is any way to bring them to repent at all. The answer is no. They are like farmland that produces nothing useful; "in the end it will be burned." People can so harden themselves against God that nothing will keep them from hell.

Second, the people under discussion are fully initiated Christians. In the preceding passage, the author contemplates whether he should discuss Melchizedek, a difficult teaching, or return to the basic teachings of the faith. He lists these foundational experiences as repentance, faith and teaching on (a) baptism (differentiating the Christian baptism from other types of cleansing rituals), (b) reception of the Spirit (laying on of hands), (c) resurrection of the dead and (d) eternal judgment. If the instruction they received had been defective, there would be some reason to go over it again. But he will not return to these teachings, for he knows these readers. They are fully initiated Christians. There was nothing defective in how they were brought to Christ, so there is no use in going back over the basics.

These individuals are "enlightened" (often a reference to baptism, but at the least meaning that they have received accurate teaching about God), "have tasted the heavenly gift" (often a reference to participating in the Lord's Supper, but at the least meaning salvation or reception of the Spirit), "have shared in the Holy Spirit" (who except Christians receives this?), and "have tasted the goodness of the word of God and the powers of the coming age" (probably indicating their experience of prophetic words and miracles, seen as a present experience of what would be fully realized in the coming age; see Gal 3:1-5). These are people with a full Christian experience, defective in no way. In fact, this is one of the clearest descriptions of Christian initiation in the New Testament.

Third, what is the author's concern about these people? Hebrews 6 is an excursus the author inserted into the argument because he is afraid that when he gets to the difficult subject of Melchizedek the readers will "turn him off." He is not afraid that they will not understand or go to sleep while this section of the book is read, but that they will reject the teaching and with it their commitment to Christ. Throughout the book he is concerned that they will leave their Christian faith and return to Judaism. The concept of an order of priests after Melchizedek (namely Jesus, the only one he cites as being in that order) contrasts with, and is an implicit criticism of, the Aaronic order that served in Jerusalem, which is something the readers may not have wanted to hear. The author is warning them before he brings the difficult teaching not to apostatize, because the consequence of such an action is damnation.

His warning comes as a description of what it would mean to apostatize. That he is talking about full-blown apostasy is clear, for he uses the phrase "they are crucifying the Son of God all over again and subjecting him to public disgrace" (Heb 6:6). That is, they once confessed that Jesus was Lord and Messiah, which means they repented of the injustice of the crucifixion. Now in rejecting the faith they are declaring that the crucifixion was correct after all—Jesus was a blasphemer and not Messiah. Such a public recantation exposes Jesus to public disgrace.

Is it possible that the author is simply writing about a hypothetical situation? If so, there are two possible ways to understand it. The first is that both the author and his readers know that this cannot happen, so it is hypothetical for all of them. In that case one wonders why the author wasted his ink. His purpose clearly is to exhort them not to return to Judaism. If his warnings are only hypothetical, how would they keep people from apostatizing? The second possibility is that the author knows this is hypothetical, but he believes his readers will take it seriously. In that case it would serve as a warning, but it would be deceptive. Is the author of Hebrews likely to defend the truth with deception? Would he scare his readers with a situation he knows could never happen?

What, then, is the author of Hebrews saying? He is refusing to return to basics on the grounds that there is no use in doing so for people who have been accurately initiated into the Christian faith. His arguments to keep them in the faith must come from deeper truth, not from a clarification of the foundational truth. He then points out by way of warning that if fully initiated Christians turn their backs on Christ, they will so harden themselves that nothing anyone can do will bring them back to repentance. Their end result will be eternal damnation. But, he concludes, while this is a real possibility for some, "we are confident of better things in your case" (Heb 6:9). If he were not, at least for some of them, there would have been no use in writing the letter at all. They may be on the verge of apostasy, but they have not made the decision and crossed the line.

In so writing the author strikes the balance found throughout the New Testament. The New Testament authors write out of an experience of the grace of Christ and a firm conviction that they are on their way to a greater inheritance in heaven. At the same time, they write with a concern that they or their readers could apostatize and thus lose what they already have. So long as people are following Christ they are supremely confident about them. If their readers turn back to the world, rejecting the rule of Christ, then the New Testament authors never express any hope that without repentance such people will enter heaven. This is a sobering, but not a fear-producing, type of tension seen in Paul (1 Cor 9:27; Gal 5:2, 7-10; Phil 3:12; 2 Tim 4:7, sometimes speaking of the tension in his own life and sometimes speaking of his concern for others), James (Jas 5:20, the purpose of the letter being to "save [a sinner, meaning a believer who has turned to the world] from death"), Jude (Jude 23) and John (1 Jn 5:16-17 KJV, the emphasis being on praying for people before they commit the "sin unto death"). The call to the modern reader is to pay attention to the warning and "to imitate those who through faith and patience inherit what has been promised" (Heb 6:12) so that the author would say of us as well, "We are confident of better things in your case—things that accompany salvation."

See also comment on MARK 3:28-29; HEBREWS 10:26; 2 PETER 1:10; 1 JOHN 5:16-17.

7:1 Who Was Melchizedek?

The historical Melchizedek and his deeds occupy three verses of the Old Testament, Genesis 14:18-20. The comparison of Jesus with this figure occupies a whole chapter of Hebrews, beginning with Hebrews 7:1. What is more, the author of Hebrews has some strange things to say about King Melchizedek: "First, his name means 'king of righteousness'; then also, 'king of Salem' means 'king of peace.' Without father or mother, without genealogy, without beginning of days or end of life, like the Son of God he remains a priest forever" (Heb 7:2-3). Who was the historical character Melchizedek? How is Hebrews using the Old Testament? Is this use legitimate? Was it legitimate only for the author of Hebrews, or is it still legitimate today?

Palestine in the Middle Bronze Age (the period before 1500 B.C.) was divided into numerous city-states. Melchizedek is identified as the priest-king of Salem, which many scholars identify with Jerusalem. There they worshiped *El Elyôn,* or God Most High. While this term is frequently used in the Psalms for Yahweh, it is not recorded as a name by which the patriarchs knew God. Still, Abraham must have recognized an identity between this One and the God he worshiped, for he later takes an oath by God Most High (Gen 14:22). Perhaps he had previous contact with Melchizedek or he and his allies had paused to pray and worship in Salem on their way north. But Melchizedek remains one of the shadowy non-Israelite figures of the Old Testament, including Balaam, which show that God apparently was known to people other than to Israel.

Melchizedek fades from view after this incident, presumably returning to Salem and living out his days. Some scholars point to the sudden appearance of the Zadokite line of priests after David captures Jerusalem, suggesting that they descended from Melchizedek (the *ZDK* in Zadok and Melchizedek are forms of the same root) and merged with the Aaronic line. Whatever the case, later Judaism did speculate on Melchizedek. There is some evidence that the Hasmonean priest-kings of Judah (164 B.C.—63 B.C.), from which the Sadducees probably came, looked to Melchizedek for a precedent of a person who was both a priest and a king. In response, rabbinic Judaism (and presumably Pharisaic Judaism earlier) named Melchizedek as one who would "not inherit the age to come" because he blessed Abraham first before he blessed God! A third Jewish view is found in the Dead Sea Scroll 11Q Melchizedek, in which he appears as an archangel warrior. None of this speculation is taken up by the author of Hebrews, although his caution in speaking about Melchizedek may be related to the low view taken of him in Pharisaic circles.

What the author does is look at what the text does and does not say and draw historical correspondences to Christ. He first looks at his name. *Melek* is the standard Hebrew for "king," and *zedek* comes from the same root as "righteous" or "righteousness." Originally the name probably meant "my king [= god] is righteous" or "my king is *Zedek,*" but the author reads it as one might normally read what is called a Hebrew construct state, "king of righteousness." He then looks at his being king of Salem and notes that Salem comes from the same root as *šalōm,* the Hebrew for "peace" or "well-being." Thus he derives the meaning "king of peace." It is clear that he wants the readers to draw a parallel between Melchizedek and Jesus, whom he has argued is without sin and therefore righteous (Heb 4:15), in contrast to the Aaronic priests. He also has called Jesus the bringer of God's true rest (Heb 4:1-11), which might be comparable to peace. But the author never makes either of the comparisons explicit. Nor do we discover if calling Melchizedek "king of righteousness" has any implications for the low view we presume was taken by Pharisaic Judaism. Presumably the author knows the background of his readers and expects them to draw the proper conclusions.[1]

Then the author notes that Melchizedek is not called "son of" anyone. That several other individuals in the Abraham stories are also named without their parents (such as Abimelek) is immaterial, for he is only interested in the parallel with Melchizedek. He is not talking about history. He then points out that Melchizedek also has no descendants named in the text, nor is there any mention of his birth or death. Historically we expect none of this for a figure who makes only a cameo appearance in the narrative. But for the author they are a parallel with Jesus. He has already indicated that Jesus existed before his birth (Heb 1:2-3), but his real interest is that Jesus exercises his priesthood in heaven as a resurrected being. Thus it literally has no end, just as no end is reported of Melchizedek's life. This contrasts with the repeated changes of ministry, even under ideal circumstances,[2] in the Aaronic priesthood due to the deaths of the high priests.

The author of Hebrews, then, demonstrates a way of interpreting the text that is foreign to modern methods of exegesis. That is, he sees Melchizedek and each detail of the Genesis text as a "type" or historical precedent for Jesus, the "antitype." This form of exegesis is frowned upon today, but such a typological interpretation was quite moderate according to the standards of the author's age. We argue that neither etymology (explaining the meaning of the names) nor typology (noting the correspondences in history in what the text does and does not say) bring out the meaning that the original author (the author of Genesis) had in mind when he wrote the text, and therefore that they are not appropriate means of interpretation if we are interested in *biblical* authority being behind our interpretation.[3] This was not the point of view of the New Testament writers, who believed that there were deeper meanings than the historical to be discovered in texts, a view that they shared with their contemporaries. Furthermore, they believed that they were under the inspiration of the Spirit and had in Jesus the key to the deeper meaning of the Old Testament. The surprising thing is not how they interpreted Scripture, but how conservative they were in doing it.[4]

How can the modern reader evaluate this? Orthodox Christians believe that the writers of Scripture did have the inspiration of the Spirit. Therefore it would be the prerogative of the Spirit to give whatever message he wanted through his Scripture, even if it might not be the historical message. But can the same be done today? Certainly the New Testament expects that the Spirit will remain in the church, but any speaking under the inspiration of the Spirit, according to Paul, cannot be a claim to absolute truth but must be "weighed carefully" (1 Cor 14:29). Scripture, of course, has already been weighed carefully by the church as a whole and found fully of the Spirit. No present speaker can claim such credentials. Thus, exegesis such as we find in Hebrews could be appropriate and helpful for the church so long as the speaker (1) did not claim the authority of the scriptural text for it and (2) did not expect his words to be accepted without careful sifting and weighing (and perhaps correcting and revising). The only exegesis that can claim a higher level of authority is that in which the speaker points his or her finger to the text and is aligned with its message clearly enough for all to see.

[1]For a fuller study of the interpretation of this passage, see Bruce Demarest, *A History of Interpretation of Hebrews 7:1-10 from the Reformation to the Present* (Tübingen: J. C. B. Mohr, 1976).

[2]The circumstances in the first century were not ideal, for since 170 B.C., when the Seleucid king had deposed the last Zadokite high priest, Onias III, rulers of Palestine had frequently stepped in and changed high priests, except during the relative independence of 164-63 B.C. Under the Romans the high priest was often changed every year or two as a deliberate policy to limit their power. The author of Hebrews quietly ignores these facts, for he wants to look at ideal Judaism, not the actual situation.

[3]See, for example, Walter Kaiser, *Toward an Exegetical Theology* (Grand Rapids, Mich.: Baker, 1981).

[4]For further information, see Richard N. Longenecker, *Biblical Exegesis in the Apostolic Period* (Grand Rapids, Mich.: Eerdmans, 1975).

8:5 A Copy of What Is in Heaven?

In a college philosophy course I learned

that Plato believed that what we call realities on this earth are really only shadows of the eternal ideals, which are not physical at all. Likewise Buddhist thought looks on the phenomenal world as unreal. If we read Hebrews 8:5 with this in mind, we are quite likely to be somewhat confused. The verse quite clearly refers to the tabernacle in the wilderness, which it claims was a copy of something in heaven, as the rest of the verse points out: "This is why Moses was warned when he was about to build the tabernacle: 'See to it that you make everything according to the pattern shown you on the mountain.' " In what way was this a copy? Is there a sanctuary in heaven? And if so, could it be made out of goats-hair cloth and sea-cow skins? If not, has the author been influenced by Plato (since it is unlikely that he had ever met a Buddhist)?

Hebrews does have a great concern with the tabernacle. In fact, the author never once mentions the temple, either Solomon's temple or the second temple (later enlarged and beautified as Herod's temple), which Jesus knew. Some see this as an indication that the temple was destroyed before Hebrews was written, while others note that if this were true, the author could have pointed the fact out, strengthening his case for the inadequacy of Judaism by showing that sacrifices were no longer being offered. Therefore it is more likely that the author views the temple as irrelevant, whether or not it was standing. God never commanded the building of the temple (2 Sam 7:5-7); he never gave a blueprint for it. He certainly did not say anything about Herod's version of the temple. But he did command the building of the tabernacle in the wilderness. The author, who shares with Stephen (Acts 7) a rather negative evaluation of the temple, therefore points to the ideal, to the tabernacle. In fact, in every way he points to Judaism at its ideal, as if it were actually running the way the Old Testament said it should. In this way he can clearly point beyond reform (cleaning up the present wrongs) to replacement (Jesus as the end of the old system).

There was probably a variety of beliefs in Judaism concerning the tabernacle itself, but clear evidence exists that at least some Jews believed that it corresponded to a heavenly sanctuary. For example, 2 Baruch 4:5 states, "And again I showed [this building . . . that was already prepared from the moment that I decided to create Paradise] also to Moses on Mount Sinai when I showed him the likeness of the tabernacle and all its vessels" (compare Josephus *Antiquities* 3.123; *Wars* 5:212-13; *Martyrdom and Ascension of Isaiah* 7:10). We do not know how far back this tradition goes, but it was a common idea in the ancient Near East that the temples on earth were models of the homes of the gods.

But we need to contrast this belief with the Platonic Judaism of Philo. Philo also used the language of "shadow," but for him what was in heaven was not a structure, but ideas and principles. These were metaphorically expressed in the physical structure on earth. The real is the world of ideas. This is not the position of Hebrews. In quoting Exodus 25:40 the author's stress is on "the pattern shown you," something that Moses saw (a more literal translation of the Hebrew reads, "that you were caused to see"). There is a correspondence between heaven and earth, but it is that of two physical realities in different spheres, not that of the ideal and the material. Heaven may be a better form of the material, a spiritual material, so to speak, for the New Testament, but it is viewed as real and solid, unlike Platonic and Buddhist thought.[1]

The belief in a heavenly sanctuary is

also found in Revelation. The altar in heaven (perhaps the altar of sacrifice) is mentioned (Rev 6:9), as well as the altar of incense (Rev 8:3). Both the temple and the altar are mentioned in Revelation 14:17-18. That the temple contains "the ark of his covenant" is noted in Revelation 11:19. Finally, the temple is called "the tent of witness" in Revelation 15:5 [RSV] (in the context of the singing of the "song of Moses the servant of God"). In other words, in the prophet John's vision there exists in heaven a temple that is the original of the tabernacle. To the extent that it is described, its furniture corresponds to that of the Mosaic tabernacle. While Revelation is an apocalyptic vision, there is no indication that the author did not believe that what he saw was real, as real as God, the Lamb and the events he saw on earth. Hebrews, then, is far from alone in this belief in a heavenly sanctuary.

What this means for the author is that Moses saw the heavenly tabernacle while on Mount Sinai. He copied the pattern by divine command—not that he used the same materials (after all, he had to make a portable earthly shrine), but that he translated the plan into the available materials of the wilderness. That this was a tabernacle and not a temple was probably deliberate, since a tent or tabernacle is a temporary dwelling, while a house or temple is a permanent dwelling. The permanent was in heaven; the temporary (or as Hebrews puts it, the "copy and shadow") was on earth.

The point the author is making is twofold. First, just as the copy is inferior to the original, so also all the features of the earthly tabernacle and its worship are inferior to the heavenly. Jesus' ministry is in the heavenly tabernacle, not the earthly. Second, just as the earthly tabernacle was set apart as holy by sacrifice, so must the heavenly be cleansed. But its sacrifice must be superior to earthly sacrifices. "It was necessary, then, for the copies of the heavenly things to be purified with these sacrifices, but the heavenly things themselves with better sacrifices than these" (Heb 9:23). This better sacrifice was none other than the blood of Christ, brought into the Holy of Holies, not of the earthly tabernacle, but of the heavenly.

In other words, the presentation of the earthly tabernacle as a copy is not a downgrading of the material world, but an exaltation of the work of Christ. His work is complete and final, superior to anything that could have been done on earth, because it was done in the very dwelling of God, in the heavenly tabernacle itself.

---

[1]This fits with the belief in the resurrection of the dead, which is repugnant to the Platonist and something from which the Buddhist would attempt to escape. Throughout the New Testament the resurrected dead have bodies. They are not just spirit. So while Paul in 1 Corinthians 15 can speak of a transformed body, a spiritual substance, he is clearly talking of something other than mere spirit (otherwise there would be no need for a resurrection at all). The Gospel narratives also speak of the physical properties of the resurrected body of Jesus, even though some of his abilities appear to transcend normal physical activities.

10:14 Made Perfect?

The men who wrote the Dead Sea Scrolls used to call themselves "the perfect of way," but Christians have not wanted to call any human being (other than Jesus) perfect. In fact, when people intimate that they are in any way perfect, we call them proud and believe that they are self-deceived. Thus it does not surprise us that Hebrews glorifies the work of Christ, but it does surprise us when we read in this passage that Jesus has "made perfect forever" a group of human beings. How could living human beings be perfect? Furthermore, how can they be perfect if they are still "being made holy"? Aren't the two expressions contradictory?

The meaning of the first part of the verse is clear in context. Hebrews 10:11-12 contrasts the daily offerings of the Aaronic priests, "which can never take away sins," with the completed once-for-all sacrifice of Christ. The Aaronic priests still stand, working at a job that will never be finished, while Christ sits "at the right hand of God," his work completed. From this perspective he has made all who believe in him "perfect forever." The author then quotes Jeremiah 31:34, a passage about a new covenant, arguing that according to this new covenant in Christ, "their sins and lawless acts I [God] will remember no more" (Heb 10:17). He then adds, "And where these have been forgiven, there is no longer any sacrifice for sin" (Heb 10:18). In other words, perfection here does not mean that people are free from moral error, but that they are completely forgiven for their moral error. This sense is possible because the Greek term for "perfect" can mean "complete" or "fulfilled" or "brought to a conclusion." For the author of Hebrews, Jesus has brought the work of forgiving sins to a conclusion or to completion. He has fulfilled the new covenant. Those who commit themselves to him are perfect in that there is nothing remaining in them that God has to forgive.

How does this fit with the concept of "those who are being made holy"? In Hebrews 10:10 the author uses the same Greek term (for making something holy) in another tense. There he refers to a work completed in the death of Christ, a holiness given to the believer on the basis of what Jesus has done. "And by that will [of God in establishing the new covenant], we have been made holy through the sacrifice of the body of Jesus Christ once for all." Four verses later he changes the tense, using the same one as in Hebrews 2:11, which refers to a process.

We can interpret this in two ways. The first is that individuals are made holy as they commit themselves to Christ. Thus this verse would indicate that the work of Christ is once-for-all, but as individuals repent and commit themselves to Jesus they enter into this completed work, being made holy, that is, fit to enter the presence of God—forgiven of their sins. The progressiveness of making people holy is in this interpretation that of spreading the gospel so more and more people enter into the holiness available in Christ.

The second way of interpreting the phrase is that there is a tension in the Christian life. On the one hand, we have been forgiven. Nothing else is needed. No further work of Christ is necessary. On the other hand, sanctification is a progressive action in the Christian life. We are not yet completely free from sin. Our past sins may have been forgiven; the power of sin in our lives may have been broken; but we keep sinning and God must continue to confront us and bring us to repentance over and over again. We are in the process of being made truly holy, not just forgiven for our failure to be holy.

While both explanations are possible, I personally prefer the second, because it appears most fully to take into account the change in tense in the verb and reflects the fact that the spread of the gospel is not a topic in this chapter. Furthermore, it expresses a tension that is frequently found in the New Testament. Christians are not to walk around feeling guilty, but forgiven. They stand before God in an attitude of gratitude for forgiveness, not cringing because of guilt. Yet the more they appreciate the sacrifice of Christ, the more they become aware that they are not yet holy; indeed, that which they might not have viewed as sin before they now see as sinful. God is producing holiness in each believer, but it is a process that takes discipline (as Heb 12 will argue). Losing sight of either side of this tension is disastrous. On the one hand, we might so focus on the perfection accomplished on the cross that we neglect to cooperate with God in growing in holiness. On the other hand, we might so focus on the process of becoming holy that we lose the relief of knowing that Christ has done all that is necessary, and so wallow in guilt and feel alienated from God. Both sides of the balance are necessary, and both are found in this verse.

See also comment on 2 CORINTHIANS 5:17; 1 JOHN 3:6, 9.

10:26 No Forgiveness for Deliberate Sin?

All who examine their lives according to Jesus' standards discover sin; it may not be a frequent event or a flagrant sin, but none of us has lived up to what Jesus has revealed of the Father's character. We are also forced to admit that some of our sin is deliberate. That is, we do not deliberately set out to sin, but we know in ourselves that some deed or activity is wrong (at least for us, if not for everyone), yet we stifle our consciences and do it anyway. At times we may even recognize that we planned our sin quite carefully, or at least planned to walk into temptation, knowing full well (in our hearts, if not in our minds) that we would give in. If this is an accurate description of the human condition, then Hebrews 10:26 is very disturbing. Is this verse making the distinction that the Old Testament does between deliberate and accidental sins? Is it saying that there is forgiveness for accidental or unknowing sins, but not for the other type? And if this is the case, are all of us who have knowingly sinned after our conversion lost? If that is in fact the meaning, this verse should cause terror and despair rather than mere concern.

The Old Testament makes a clear distinction between willful or deliberate sin and inadvertent sins.[1] After discussing the procedure for obtaining forgiveness for inadvertent sins in Numbers 15:22-29, the author adds, "But anyone who sins defiantly, . . . that person must be cut off from his people" (Num 15:30). The example that follows this passage tells of a person who gathered wood on the sabbath, presumably because his fire was going out and he had neglected to gather enough wood the previous day. Surely this was a small act, unlike murder or even theft. But it was also clear that he had consciously gone out to do work on the sabbath and was not ignorant of the law against work on that day. It was a deliberate sin. He was stoned to death at the command of the Lord. A deliberate sin is not to be taken lightly.

Although the Old Testament makes a distinction between deliberate and accidental sin, that does not appear to be the point being made in Hebrews, which looks at life from a perspective of Jesus' already having come and died for sin. If Jesus understands human weakness and helps those who are tempted (Heb 2:17-18; 4:15), he is hardly going to fail to understand our failure. Similarly, Paul's response to failure was to restore the person (Gal 6:1), even when the sin was quite serious (2 Cor 2:5-11).[2] Hebrews is not a Pauline writing, but it comes out of the same circle of acquaintances (Heb 13:23). We would therefore expect similar attitudes toward forgiveness of sin.

The point Hebrews is making can best be seen by following the author's progression of thought. Having noted the adequacy of Christ's sacrifice in Hebrews 10:1-18, he urges the readers to draw near to God with confidence (Heb 10:19-22). This is expressed in (1) holding on to the hope that we have in Christ, (2) encouraging each other to live the faith in practice and (3) gathering together (Heb 10:23-25). The opposite of these would be to withdraw from the Christian gatherings, to stop doing public expressions of faith, and to give up commitment to Christ and hope in him. In other words, the opposite would be apostasy.

That this is the point of the passage is clearly seen in Hebrews 10:29, where the "deliberate" sinners are described as those who have "trampled the Son of God under foot," treated the "blood of the covenant" as something common (in other words, looked upon Jesus' death as just any common criminal's death) and "insulted the Spirit of grace." This is deliberate sin, but deliberate in the sense that a person willfully is renouncing Christianity and rejecting Jesus, his death and the personal experience of the Spirit (which is the slander against the Holy Spirit condemned in Mk 3:28-29).

It is not that such deliberate sinners (or apostates) did not know the truth. The author is clear on that point. Only "after we have received the knowledge of the truth" is such an action so serious. Like those mentioned in Hebrews 6:4-8, they have been fully initiated into Christianity, for the phrase "knowledge of the truth" is common in the later New Testament writings for having come to full Christian conversion (Jn 8:32; 1 Tim 2:4; 4:3; 2 Tim 2:25; Tit 1:1; 1 Jn 2:21; 2 Jn 1). But they have chosen to reject their experience of Christ. Had they received a distorted picture of Christianity there might have been hope, for one could correct the distortion. But they have developed a "sinful, unbelieving heart that turns away from the living God" (Heb 3:12). For such people there is no sacrifice for sin remaining; they have rejected the only one that exists. What remains is the judgment of God.

This does not mean that the early church took sin lightly, deliberate or accidental. Any sin called for rebuke and restoration or, if unrepented of, discipline (see Mt 18:15-20; 1 Cor 5:1-5). And sinning could lead to sickness (Jas 5:15) or death (1 Cor 11:30). Furthermore, deliberately hardening one's conscience and disobeying God could start one on the way to this outright rejection of the faith. It might also indicate that the person remains outside the faith, for Jesus is not yet Lord to the one who disobeys him (1 Cor 6:9-10; Gal 5:19-21). Yet serious as their condition is, the possibility remains that all such people can be brought to repentance in one way or another. There are still arguments to be put forward and evidence to be shown. For the people the author is talking about, however, nothing of the kind is possible. They knew the truth fully, but have deliberately renounced what they once embraced. There is no new evidence or arguments to present. We can only tremble at the thought of the judgment awaiting them and take care that we stay far away from the slope that leads down into that pit.

See also comment on HEBREWS 6:4-6; 2 PETER 2:20; 1 JOHN 5:16-17.

---

[1]With the possible exception of the Day of Atonement, the Old Testament required no sacrifices for what we call sin. The unintentional sins mentioned there are situations in which a person or the community does not know the law. Only after doing something do they discover that God has prohibited it. Other types of sin and guilt offerings that were required were for such things as the healing of leprosy (restoring the former leper to the community) and the blood of childbirth, neither of which involves any moral failure. Old Testament offerings were primarily for ritual impurity and had almost nothing to do with what we call sin.

[2]The sinner here is probably not the person mentioned in 1 Corinthians 5, but a leader who had

opposed Paul and forced him to withdraw from the church during the "painful visit" (2 Cor 2:1). Paul wrote his "letter of tears" after this, and the church responded by disciplining the rebel leader (2 Cor 2:3-4). So the sin was rebellion against God's apostle, perhaps even expelling the apostle from the church he had founded.

11:30 Did Jericho's Walls Really Collapse?

See comment on JOSHUA 6:20.

11:31 Was Rahab Right to Lie?

See comment on JOSHUA 2:4-6.

12:15 What Is the Bitter Root?

We all know the truth that "suffering produces perseverance" and other Christian virtues (Rom 5:3), but at the same time we know people who have experienced suffering or sickness (which are treated as quite different categories in Scripture)[1] and have become bitter rather than better due to the experience. Bitterness, to be sure, is no Christian virtue, even if it is at times overlooked in people of faith (see Ruth 1:20-21 for the example of Naomi). It is not addressed directly in Scripture, except possibly in this one verse, Hebrews 12:15. Yet this text still raises a number of issues. What is a "bitter root"? Does it have anything to do with the vice of bitterness? Why is it connected to missing "the grace of God"? And how does it "defile many"?

A frequent interpretation of this verse is that it simply warns against bitterness or "bitter root judgments." Since the term "bitter" appears in the verse and all of us know individuals who have for one reason or another become bitter, such an interpretation sounds reasonable. The verse, then, would rightly point out that such attitudes (and the judgments of others that flow from them, like poison seeping out of a festering wound) can injure those who hold them, blocking these people from the many good things God has for them. In addition, it can injure the whole Christian community, infecting it with a fractious negativity and smearing the character of its leaders. Such observations have been made by most pastoral leaders. The question is whether the author has these observations in mind.

The answer to that question must be no. The context of the passage in Hebrews 12 is that of holding on to the faith despite difficulties. Where commitment has grown weak, it is to be strengthened; the "lame" in the community are to be healed; "level paths" are to be made for their feet (Heb 12:12-13). The "level paths" (from Prov 4:26) are the ways of holiness without which no one will see God (Heb 12:14). Having called for a firm commitment, the author continues with a series of warnings. Esau, an irreligious man,[2] had an inheritance and lost it, being unable afterward to regain what he had so lightly sold. Israel was disciplined severely at Mount Sinai for their disobedience, but the Christians to whom Hebrews is addressed have come to an even more glorious place and therefore will be so much more severely disciplined if they reject God. What might they be in danger of rejecting? They might reject the message of the author, who is calling for them to hold fast to Christ and not abandon him in apostasy.

The phrase "bitter root" is an Old Testament allusion, for it is very similar to a phrase in the Greek version of the Old Testament, the version normally quoted by the author of Hebrews. In Deuteronomy 29:18 we read, "Make sure there is no [person] among you today whose heart turns away from the LORD our God to go and worship the gods of those nations; make sure there is no root among you that produces such bitter poison." By comparing the two contexts, we see the point the author is making. To miss or fall short of the "grace of God" is the equivalent of turning away from the Lord in the Old Testament. Simply put, it means apostasy, a failure to commit oneself to God's grace. Such an apostate is a "bitter root" or, to use the Old Testament phrase, a "root that produces bitter poison." Just as one apostate in Israel could influence many neighbors to serve gods other than Yahweh, so one apostate among these Christians could lead others to forsake their faith. This, then, is the meaning of the text within its context.

Bitterness is not good. It is, in fact, a form of anger (that is, a nursed anger that has been allowed to smolder within), a topic about which the New Testament has much to say (see Gal 5:20; Jas 1:19). It can also be a characteristic of jealousy, which is condemned in James 3:14. Thus, if bitterness is broken down into its root vices, one will discover that Scripture has a lot to say about it. But this passage is not about bitterness; it is about apostasy. If bitterness is not good, apostasy is devastating. It means missing the grace of God and coming into judgment before the God who is "a consuming fire" (Heb 12:29).

---

[1]See Peter H. Davids, "Sickness and Suffering in the New Testament," in C. Peter Wagner and F. Douglas Pennoyer, eds., *Wrestling with Dark Angels* (Ventura, Calif.: Regal, 1990), pp. 215-37.

[2]While the biblical Esau was not, strictly speaking, a fornicator, he did marry Hittite wives (Gen 26:34-35), which is commented upon negatively. Both intermarriage with non-Hebrew people and the use of temple prostitutes connected fornication to apostasy, the serving of other gods. In extrabiblical traditions both Esau and his wives are viewed as sexually immoral: see Jubilees 25:1, 8; Palestinian Targum on Genesis 25:29; *Genesis Rabba* 70d, 72a; *Exodus Rabba* 116a. Whatever the connection (or lack of it) to Esau, the author is clearly against all sexual misconduct (Heb 13:4).

JAMES

1:2 Are Christians Masochists?

The term *trials* used in this verse means a "test," and it is often translated "temptation" in other contexts. The trials in this case are the tests of faith that come from low-grade persecution from outside the church and from conflict within it. This is hardly a situation in which one would expect to have joy. How then can James argue that we should consider it "pure joy"? Is he some type of masochist? Is it necessary for Christians to deny pain and smile all the time? Our humanity cries out for an honest explanation of such questions, for to deny the reality of pain is a denial of our being human.

James 1:2-4 does not stand alone. It parallels similar sayings in Romans 5:3-5 ("we also rejoice in our sufferings") and 1 Peter 1:6-7, all of which are "chain sayings" that link together virtues, one leading to the next. The situation pictured in all three of these passages is that of persecution. James and 1 Peter picture the persecution as a test of faith, a trial or temptation (the two authors use the identical phrase). Romans simply calls it "suffering" or "affliction" or "tribulation" (the term, like all terms for suffering, indicates persecution or hardship endured because of the faith, not illness). We know something about the type of persecutions that Paul endured; James's community appears to be experiencing low-level economic persecution; Peter's readers have apparently been ostracized from their society and subjected to some violence (although not death). None of these are pleasant situations.

The call to rejoice, however, is not masochistic. Masochism is taking pleasure in pain. The masochist wants to experience pain because it is the pain that gives this person pleasure. In these passages, however, we are not to rejoice in the pain, but in the future reward beyond the pain. James believes we should rejoice because trials give us an opportunity to develop the virtue of perseverance, which will in turn lead to a mature Christian character. We rejoice like an athlete in a practice session. Athletes may run or lift weights to the point of pain, but all the time their eyes are set on the big race or game. They rejoice not in the enjoyment of the stress but in the knowledge that their muscles are growing stronger and therefore they will do better when it counts. James is probably dependent upon Jesus: "Blessed are you when people insult you, persecute you and falsely say all kinds of evil against you because of me. Rejoice and be glad, because great is your reward in heaven" (Mt 5:11-12). Here we see why character is important: it will be rewarded in heaven. In other words, faithfulness under pressure today earns eternal reward tomorrow. This is seen in the life of Jesus, who "for the joy set before him endured the cross, scorning its shame" (Heb 12:2). This is how Christians are to live. As one writer puts it, James is talking about "eschatological anticipated joy."[1] It is joy not in the present feelings but in the anticipation of praise when one finally stands face to face before Jesus. The joy of that day is tasted in part already in the painful present. Thus Paul and Silas sing in the Philippian jail, not because they enjoyed the beating (although it may have been one reason why they were awake) but because they knew their Lord would more than adequately reward their suffering (Acts 16:25). It is a privilege to suffer for Jesus (Acts 5:41).

This is not to say that we cannot call pain, pain. Paul makes it very clear that he could recognize pain, call it what it is, and experience it with the full depth of human anguish (1 Cor 4:9-13; 2 Cor 4:3-12; 11:23-29). He also left us the example of fleeing from persecution when it was appropriate (Acts 17:10, 13-14). Yet even in such situations he, with James, could look beyond them to "an eternal glory that far outweighs them all" (2 Cor 4:17). We may know less of James's life, but from the passion in his letter there is no reason to believe that on this point he would have disagreed with Paul. His is a real humanity and depth of feeling, but at the same time he looks beyond the present experience to a transcendent reward.

James, then, is no masochist, but he points to an important truth. Only those who are heavenly minded will suffer for their faith in the present. Those who do not have this anticipated joy invest themselves in the present and avoid disgrace and suffering for Christ, for it could cost them all they have invested themselves in. Those who do have James's perspective can be reckless in their obedience to Christ, for any price they may pay today will be paid back with interest by their Lord. And it is that smile of pleasure on his face when he greets them that they rejoice in, for they already see it dimly down the halls of time as the Spirit makes it real in their hearts.

---

[1]J. J. Thomas, "Anfechtung und Vorfreude," *Kerygma und Dogma* 14 (1968): 183-206. I have translated the term *eschatologische Vorfreude* as "eschatological anticipated joy."

1:13 God Does Not Tempt Anyone?

When a person is suffering, it is always a temptation to blame God. After all, is God not sovereign? Doesn't everything in some sense come from him? Thus James 1:13 pictures a situation in which a person is suffering (being persecuted or experiencing disadvantage due to a commitment to Christ), and this suffering is testing the commitment to God. The question is, Will this person remain faithful to God or disobey him? (The Greek term that is translated "tempted" also can be translated "tested," so I will use the two terms interchangeably.) Precisely in such a situation the person might want to blame God. "God, you sent this situation, and it is too hard for me. It is your fault if I give in."

Paul speaks to just such a concern in 1 Corinthians 10:13. Yet the problem for modern readers is not the situation, but James's response. How can he say God does not tempt anyone when Genesis 22:1 says, "Some time later God tested [or tempted] Abraham"? Furthermore, if God cannot be tempted, how could the Scripture speak of Jesus' being tempted, assuming that the writers believed that he was God? Isn't this a clear situation of one scriptural author contradicting another?

These problems are related, for both the issue of whether God tests (tempts) anyone and the issue of whether God can be tested call upon the Old Testament testing (tempting) tradition. This tradition begins with Abraham, who is presented as one who is tested and passes the test, God concluding, "Now I know that you fear God, because you have not withheld from me your son, your only son" (Gen 22:12). Later in the Pentateuch, however, Israel is presented as the group that when tested "disobeyed me and tested me ten times" (Num 14:22). This means that their response to the testing of God in the wilderness (Ex 15:25) was not that of trusting obedience, but that of blaming and demanding (this is what happened at Massah, a name that means "testing" or "tempting"; Ex 17:2, 7). This resulted in commands such as that in Deuteronomy 6:16, "Do not test the LORD your God as you did at Massah." (Ps 78, 95 and 106 reflect on this tradition.)

James sees the testing situation occurring in his community in these Old Testament terms. His concern is that the believers should be trusting like Abraham; they are not to be as Israel and fail the test by blaming God. James gives two reasons for not blaming God. We can translate the first reason "God ought not to be tested by sinful people," instead of the traditional translation "God cannot be tempted by evil." The Greek word *apeirastos,* translated "ought not to be tested" (or "cannot be tempted"), is found only once in the New Testament and nowhere else previously in Greek. Later it is found only a very few times in the church fathers. In those later contexts my translation fits as well as or better than the traditional translation. Furthermore, my translation makes better sense in the context in James. It would be hard to see why the fact that God cannot be tempted would make it wrong to claim that he is behind a test, but it is easy to see that "God ought not to be tested" meets the situation, for then the phrase paraphrases Deuteronomy 6:16 and tells them not to blame God as Israel did at Massah, which is the very thing James pictures them doing. This also solves the problem of Jesus' testing (or temptation), for he was in fact tested by an evil being, which this translation allows to be possible, even if it is a sinful act.

But what about "God does not tempt [test] anyone"? To deal with this problem we must consider the development of doctrine within and between the testaments. Old Testament Hebrews, at least in their earlier period, traced all events directly back to God. Whatever happened, God caused it. This level of revelation was quite appropriate, since God's first task with Israel was to convince them that there was only one God for them to worship. Beginning late in the Old Testament, however, and continuing into the intertestamental period, it became clear that other beings often actually caused the test. While God, since he is sovereign, could have prevented a given situation,[1] he did not instigate every event. This development is seen clearly in Scripture by comparing preexilic (or early exilic) 2 Samuel 24:1, which reads,

"[God] incited David against them," with the postexilic 1 Chronicles 21:1, which says, "Satan . . . incited David." The later book shows a more complex picture. It does not deny the previous model, but it admits that the model that traces all events directly to God leaves out details and complexities that later revelation fills in.

The Jews took their clue from such examples of development in Scripture and understood many other Old Testament Scriptures in this same way. For example, in Jubilees 17:15—18:16 the story of Abraham is retold in terms similar to Job. (Job is a later book that, with Chronicles, fits into the period when Judaism knew more about Satan than it did before the exile.) In Jubilees the Prince Mastema (Satan) comes to God and demands that he test Abraham (whom God knows has already proved faithful in many tests). The test, then, does not originate with God, but with Satan.

This appears to be James's position. In his concluding call to remain faithful to God under pressure, James says, "Resist the devil" (Jas 4:7). Satan is the one who is behind the test. This belief is simply stated, not argued. Even in his earlier passage (Jas 1:13) James does not have to explain this to his readers, for they share with him the same theology. So he can simply remind them of the fact in one line, "God does not test [or tempt] anyone." It is not God who wills ill to people and tries to make them fall; it is Satan. It was not God who wished to do evil to Abraham, but the devil. Therefore rather than blame God (who gives only good gifts, Jas 1:17), Christians should look within at their own desires, which make them vulnerable to the Satanic test and lure them to fall (Jas 1:14). Having seen this, they should stand firm, thus resisting the devil, the ultimate mastermind behind all temptation. Not only is this position good for James's day, but it warns against the same danger of blaming God and gives the same strategy for standing in the test that is appropriate for today.

[1]The Scripture never asks why God does not prevent certain situations, except in statements such as 2 Peter 3:9, which suggests that his desire for the salvation of as many as possible keeps him from intervening in a drastic way. We human beings, of course, do not know which events God does not prevent because he has some hidden purpose in them and which he does not prevent because to do so would mean to bring the end of the age prematurely. We can speculate on this, but Scripture does not enter into our speculation.

1:17 Does God Change?

See comment on GENESIS 6:6; 1 SAMUEL 15:29; JONAH 4:1-2.

2:5-7 God Chose the Poor?

See comment on JAMES 5:1.

2:24 Justified by What You Do?

Ever since Martin Luther, Christians have struggled with putting James 2:24 together with such statements of Paul's as "we maintain that a man is justified by faith apart from observing the law" (Rom 3:28). It appears at first glance that James is advocating a justification through works and Paul one through faith. This impression grows when we realize that each cites the example of Abraham to support his argument. Are these two authors opposed to one another? Must we choose between the two for our theology? Was Luther correct that James is an "epistle of straw" that contradicts Paul's essential insight into the gospel?

The answer to all of these questions is no. A surface reading of James and Paul is apt to miss what both authors were saying. Therefore, we must examine each of the critical terms in the verse in James: *faith, works* and *justified.*

The first term James and Paul have in

common is *faith.* In James 2:19, the author gives a clear definition of what he means by "faith alone": "Do you believe that God is one?" This is not only the basic creed of Judaism (Deut 6:4) but also a truth about God that Jews believed Abraham discovered. It is orthodoxy, but in James it is an orthodoxy totally separated from obedience ("You have faith; I have deeds," Jas 2:18), an orthodoxy that demons have as well. Elsewhere James gives a different definition of faith. The faith of James 1:6 and 2:1 is that of personal commitment, which includes trust and obedience; in contrast, the faith that James sees his opponents claiming in James 2:14-26 is orthodoxy without action.

Paul also has a definition of faith, which he gives in Romans 10:9-10. Faith means a commitment to a living Lord Jesus and a confession that "Jesus is Lord." This is similar to the relational trust type of faith that James refers to in chapter 1. In Galatians 5:6, Paul goes on to state that in Christ the issue is not one of Jewish rituals (circumcision), but of "faith working through love" (RSV). This faith-love pairing is not accidental, for it occurs repeatedly in Paul (see 1 Cor 13:13; 1 Thess 1:3; 3:6). Love, of course, is not a feeling or emotion, but loving action, that is, deeds or works. For Paul, then, faith is a commitment to Jesus as Lord that results in a life of love. If the love is lacking (as "the deeds to the flesh" or "unrighteousness" show), then such a person is no heir of God's kingdom (1 Cor 6:9-10).

Since James (in Jas 2:14-26) and Paul are using different definitions of faith, it is not surprising that they use the example of Abraham differently. For Paul (in Rom 4 and Gal 3), the critical issue is that Abraham was declared righteous in Genesis 15:6, which comes chronologically before the institution of circumcision in Genesis 17. Since ritual law is the issue for Paul, as we will see below, the fact that Genesis 15 comes after significant acts of obedience by Abraham (such as leaving Haran to journey to Palestine) is no problem. For James, on the other hand, the critical issue is that the declaration of actual righteousness in Genesis 22:12 shows that the faith referred to in Genesis 15:6 is not mere orthodoxy but a trust leading to actual righteous deeds, so that "[his] faith worked together with his deed and the faith was completed by the deeds" (Jas 2:22). In other words, the two men come at the Abraham narrative from different directions, using different definitions of faith, and as a result argue for complementary rather than contradictory conclusions.

The second term James and Paul share is "works" or "deeds," the Greek word *ergōn.* In the verse cited above (seen against the wider context of Jas 2:14-26), James is clearly arguing for *certain* works. The two deeds he cites are (1) Abraham's offering of Isaac and (2) Rahab's hospitality to the spies. Within the epistle he mentions other acts of charity and the control of language. These fit well with Abraham's act, for in Jewish eyes this offering was the culmination of a lifetime of obedience to God and charity toward others. The fact that Isaac was not sacrificed was seen as a declaration of Abraham's righteousness.[1] Furthermore, Rahab's hospitality, like some of Abraham's actions, was viewed as an act of charity. We are not surprised, then, to discover that charity is the issue that begins the argument leading to James 2:14-17. Thus the works James is arguing for are good deeds (charitable acts, generosity).

Paul is clearly against certain works as a means of becoming righteous, but the works he is against are "the works of the law," a phrase also found in the Dead Sea Scrolls, but never used by James.

The "of the law" is always present, at least in the near context, when Paul speaks negatively of works. What are these deeds? The principal one Paul mentions is circumcision, although he also speaks of the observance of (Jewish) holy days and (Jewish) dietary laws. In other words, while Paul never mentions charity and other good deeds in these negative contexts, he is against those cultic acts of the Mosaic law that set apart a Jew from a Gentile. This fits the context of the Pauline letters, for the issue he is facing is that some Jewish Christians are demanding that the Gentile believers become proselytes to Judaism to be saved. Paul denies there is any such need to become Jewish, although there is a need to become godly.[2]

There is, then, no real conflict between James and Paul on the issue of works. Just as his use of "faith" is different from James's, so is Paul's use of "works" different. Not only does Paul always use a phrase James never uses, but in places such as Galatians 5:19-21 he can list evil deeds (similar to James's list in 3:14-16) and then say, "I warn you [now] as I did [earlier] that those who live like this will not inherit the kingdom of God." Paul will not separate moral righteousness from eternal salvation.

Perhaps the most misunderstood of the three terms used in common by James and Paul is the Greek word group including *dikaiosynē* ("righteousness"), *dikaiōsis* ("justification") and *dikaioō* ("declare righteous," or "justify"). The usual meaning of these words in the Septuagint is actual righteousness or a declaration of such righteousness (for example, Rom 1:17; 2:13). James invariably uses these traditional meanings (he never uses *dikaiōsis*). Paul, on the other hand, often writes of God's making a sinner righteous (justifying a sinner, Rom 3:24) or of a righteousness obtained by Christ's being given to the sinner (Rom 5:17) or of the resulting state (justification, Rom 4:25; 5:18).

The Pauline meaning (of which James may well have been ignorant) has dominated Protestant thinking since the Reformation and has been read into James by many translations (as the KJV, RSV and NIV all do in Jas 2). This creates an artificial conflict between James and Paul. James, on the one hand, is asking how God knew Abraham was righteous when he made the statement in Genesis 22:12 and how the reader can know that the faith in Genesis 15:6 was a trust that actually made Abraham righteous. The answer is—from his deeds. And without such deeds any claim of righteousness or of faith is empty. Paul, on the other hand, is pointing out that both Jews and Gentiles are equally short of God's standard of righteous judgment, and thus the issue is how God will make the unrighteous righteous. The answer is—not through cultic ritual but through commitment to (faith in) Jesus Christ. The two authors use their terms in different ways because they address different issues.

It is clear, then, that James and Paul are moving in two different worlds. In James's world Jewish ritual is not an issue (perhaps because all of those in his church are Jews), but ethics is. His problems are with those who claim to be right with God on the basis of their orthodoxy although they are ignoring obedience issues, especially charity. Abraham and Rahab, in contrast to the demons, demonstrate that saving faith is seen in its deeds. Paul, on the other hand, is concerned about the relationship of Jews and Gentiles in the church. His concern is that commitment to Jesus as Lord is all that is necessary for salvation. A Gentile does not have to become a Jew to enter the kingdom; those ritual deeds that marked the Jew are unnecessary. In the places where Paul does address the issue of whether a person can enter the kingdom while living in sin, he emphatically denies this is possible, agreeing with James.

Paul himself realized that he was at times misunderstood. Some misinterpreted his denial that legal ritual was needed for salvation, making it into an argument that ethical issues were irrelevant to salvation (Rom 3:8; 6:1; 1 Cor 6:12). Paul strongly repudiated these people. It is unclear whether James was contending with an orthodoxy-without-deeds rooted in Judaism (such as rabbis would later attack) or a misunderstood Paulinism (such as Paul himself attacked). Both are possible backgrounds. It is clear that James is not attacking any actual belief of Paul's, but that Paul could endorse everything James wrote, although given his differing use of vocabulary, Paul would not have said it the same way.

This verse, then, remains hard, but it is hard because its teaching is uncomfortable. God is concerned with our deeds, and they are related to whether or not we enter the kingdom. It is not hard because there is any conflict between this teaching and Paul's. The two merely *sound* contradictory rather than *are* contradictory. In fact, a lot of the apparent contradiction is due to the misunderstanding of Paul found in Luther and perpetuated by those who fail to put Paul into his proper Jewish background.

If James is dealing with a misunderstood Paulinism, then, it is probable that the sermon in James 2:14-26 comes from a period before he met Paul, for it is likely that once they discussed the gospel together James would have cited Paul's own words against anyone who claimed Paul as an authority for such a twisted doctrine as James is countering.

The James-Paul issue, then, is partially a misunderstanding of Paul (stemming from the fact that Luther was concerned with earning his salvation through penance and pious deeds rather than with Jewish ritual, thus a reading of Luther into Paul) and partially a problem of reading Paul into James. In reality, the writings of James and Paul demonstrate a relative harmony, combined with differing spheres of ministry and thus differing perspectives (which are apparent in Galatians and Acts).

---

[1]For further information on this, see R. B. Ward, "The Works of Abraham: James 2:14-26," *Harvard Theological Review* 61 (1968): 238-90, and Peter H. Davids, *Commentary on James,* New International Greek Testament Commentary (Grand Rapids, Mich.: Eerdmans, 1982), pp. 126-32.

[2]See further J. D. G. Dunn, "The New Perspective on Paul," *Bulletin of the John Rylands University Library of Manchester* 65 (1983): 96-122, or the discussion of the relevant passages in J. D. G. Dunn, *Romans 1—8,* Word Biblical Commentary (Dallas: Word, 1988).

2:25 Was Rahab Right to Lie?

See comment on JOSHUA 2:4-6.

4:4 Friendship with the World Is Hatred Toward God?

James seems to argue in James 4:4 that one cannot love God and at the same time, for example, have a career. Is this advocating some type of otherworldly Christianity? Does not the Scripture teach that God loves the world? Should not we also?

The language of this verse is very direct. James literally calls his readers "adulteresses" (a fact obscured by the NIV translation). This does not mean that he is addressing only women, but that he wants us to see that he is borrowing language from the Old Testament. The Old Testament pictures Israel as God's bride, who at the same time wanted to enjoy other "lovers," finding security in other gods and imperial powers (see Is 1:21; Jer 3; Hos 1—3). Given the New Testament bride-of-Christ language (2 Cor 11:2; Eph 5:22-24; Rev 19;

21), borrowing this language for the New Testament is quite appropriate. The "other lover" in this case is "the world"; that is, the values and goals of their culture.

The Christians whom James is addressing wanted to be successful and gain status in the world's eyes, while at the same time they were followers of Jesus. This parallels what Israel did in trying to serve both Yahweh and Baal. Israel, and especially the kingdom of Judah, never planned to give up the worship of Yahweh. All of his feasts were duly celebrated, his sacrifices made. The priests were employed to ensure this. But at the same time the people served Baal (and other gods), even erecting their altars in the courts of Yahweh's temple. Likewise these Christians were struggling for worldly status even within the church (Jas 4:1-2; compare Jas 2:2-4).

Jesus pictured a similar situation when he said, "No one can serve two masters. . . . You cannot serve both God and Money" (Mt 6:24). The issue is not *how well* one can serve this or that master, but that one *cannot* serve them both. It is impossible. It is impossible first of all because one has only so much emotional energy. If you are deeply invested in the values of your culture, you cannot have enough energy left over to have a similar investment in God and his values. If you are invested in God,[1] you do not at the same time have the energy left to value what the surrounding culture values. We display what we value in our use of time, energy and money. All are in limited supply. All are placed at the disposal of what one is emotionally invested in. If these treasures go to one place, they cannot go to another.

Second, it is impossible to serve two because both are jealous lovers. Throughout the Old Testament, God presents himself as the one who demands exclusive loyalty. He is a husband who will not share his wife with anyone else, even if the sharing only happens when he is off at work! Likewise Baal (or whatever other god) demands more and more. What begins as a both-and arrangement slowly erodes into a Baal-only arrangement as Baal takes so much energy that the worship of Yahweh begins to be neglected. In the New Testament Jesus points to God's exclusive demand when he speaks about taking up one's cross and following him (see Mt 10:38). The person going out to execution on the cross has invested all—wealth, reputation, even life itself—in the cause for which he is dying; there is no future separate from that cause. It is this same total commitment to which Jesus calls all of his followers. For this reason the New Testament does not talk about a tithe—God wants it all (see 2 Cor 8:2-5).

James is doing nothing more than calling his readers to a similar total commitment. In the preceding verses we discover that the readers have been using two means to get what they want. First, they struggle with each other, perhaps including vying for power within the Christian community. Second, they pray. But, adds James, they receive no answers to their prayers. This is because they are trying to use God to gain their own ends. God becomes the "sugar daddy" to fulfill their desires, but it is desire, not God, that they are really serving. Both strategies, that of struggle and that of manipulative prayer, show that they are invested in the world. The one is clearly a direct and open struggle, while the other sounds very pious; the underlying commitments and results are the same. When push comes to shove they are committed to their cultural values, not to God.

Our verse, then, is a warning. They have become God's enemies by their commitment to the world. Is there any hope? The next verse tells us that God is indeed jealous, but then James goes on to point out that God gives grace to the humble. Yes, there is hope if they will humble themselves and repent. God is ready to give them grace.

Can one have a career and serve God? James's answer is no. The career or vocation of every Christian is to serve God. One might serve God *within* a given career, but the career must not be where one's heart is invested if the person is indeed serving God (and not God's enemy). How can we tell the difference? Watch what happens when there is a conflict of values. (The conflict can come over issues of personal morality, but more often comes over issues of corporate morality and goals or over the issue of commitment to the job, such as whether one will agree to a transfer.) Does the person compromise and do what is expected by the corporate (or academic or professional) culture? Or does the person lose status on the job by refusing to compromise? This decision shows clearly whom they are really serving. Is this, then, an otherworldly lifestyle? James's answer is yes. By this he would not mean that one does not have a very down-to-earth practical effect on this world (especially since caring for the poor is a very important part of his message), but that all of one's life and lifestyle is determined by a commitment to Christ. The only reward that really counts is that which comes from Christ. The values that a person values are Christ's values. For James this is not a special level of Christianity; it is Christianity pure and simple.

This saying in James is hard, but not because it is that difficult to understand. It means just what it says. The problem is that we with our divided hearts find what it means very uncomfortable. Here, however, James is just as uncompromising and just as realistic as his master, Jesus.

See also comment on MATTHEW 6:24; JAMES 5:1; 1 JOHN 2:15.

---

[1]Being invested in God does not necessarily mean being busy in church work. It would mean spending enough time in the presence of God to learn from him what priorities he has for one's life. See Joyce Huggett, *The Joy of Listening to God* (Downers Grove, Ill.: InterVarsity Press, 1986) and Peter Lord, *Hearing God* (Grand Rapids, Mich.: Baker, 1988). Church work itself often can be simply more worldly business, a way to gain status or one's personal ends in another sphere.

[2]For further reading, see John White, *Magnificent Obsession* (Downers Grove, Ill.: InterVarsity Press, 1976, 1990), especially chap. 2.

5:1 Woe to the Rich?

Picture a person walking into an exclusive restaurant near Bay Street or Wall Street where the corporate elite dine and crying out, "Hey, you rich folk, weep and wail because of your misery!" This is the incongruity that appears in James 5:1, which begins a six-verse condemnation of the rich. Such a condemnation immediately raises the question "Why are these rich people condemned?" Does not God love the wealthy people as well as the poor ones? Are not many wealthy folk just as good Christians as their poorer brothers and sisters?

James already has mentioned the rich, referring to them specifically in James 1:10-11, 2:5-7, and in general terms (without using the word "rich") in James 2:2-3, 4:13. In none of the references does he say anything good about them. Interestingly, in these latter passages the individuals are members of the Christian community; in the passages where he uses the term "rich," the people are not Christians. James apparently finds the terms "rich" and "Christian" mutually exclusive.

Why does James not connect the term "rich" to Christians? He is certainly free in calling Christians "the poor" (Jas 1:9;

2:2-3, 5-6). The reason is probably that James is following the teaching of Jesus, who said, "Blessed are you who are poor," and also, "But woe to you who are rich" (Lk 6:20, 24). In fact, Jesus indicated that wealth was a stumbling block to entering the kingdom of God—it is only God's ability to do the impossible that gets wealthy people in (Mk 10:23-27). It is incorrect to try to soften this by saying, "It is impossible for anyone to enter, poor as well as rich. All enter through a miracle of God," for Jesus does not say this. He notes that he came especially to preach the gospel to the poor (Lk 4:18), and he tells the poor whom he blesses, "Yours is the kingdom of God" (Lk 6:20). He never says anything like this to the rich.

The key to this distinction is found at the end of his major discourse on wealth in Luke 12:34, "For where your treasure is, there your heart will be also." Given that human beings have only a limited amount of emotional energy to invest in anything, to the degree that one is earth-invested, one's heart is not set on heaven or the love of God. To have a heart set on heaven will mean placing one's "treasure" or investments there as well, which normally means giving earthly wealth in charity. Thus when we see God's miracle in the saving of a rich man, Zacchaeus announces his new-found freedom from wealth before Jesus announces his salvation (Lk 19:1-10).[1] Likewise, when the Spirit comes in Acts, the Christians begin to share their possessions with the poor. James is very aware of this gospel tradition and bases his teaching on that of his older brother Jesus.

So the people James is referring to as "the rich" are not believers. That, of course, would be enough to condemn them to hell. But there is another reason that he singles out these particular rich people for such strong condemnation, and that is their treatment of the poor.

There is a progression in the argument in James 5:1-6. First, it notes the uselessness of wealth, described in terms of garments and money. Stored goods deteriorate, as Jesus pointed out (Mt 6:19-20). Since James's church knows the words of Jesus, James is implying that these people could have had lasting investments had they shared their goods with the poor and thus obtained wealth in heaven. But of course they do not do this, for they are not followers of Jesus and so do not have his values. (Although the wealthy in James's day would have included the political and religious leaders of the Jewish people, who should have had spiritual values similar to those of Jesus.)

Second, their failure to obey the gospel (the teaching of Jesus) will witness against them in the last judgment. Here we find the parable of the rich man and Lazarus (Lk 16:19-31) condensed into two clauses. The rich man was probably an observant Jew, but he failed to submit to God in that he had plenty and yet did not help the poor beggar lying at his very gate. So these rich have stored up goods, but it is the "last days," or end of the age, and the final judgment is coming. Their failure to use their goods for God's purposes will "eat [their] flesh like fire," the fire of hell.

Third, they have practiced injustice. The other charges were bad enough, but now we discover that these absentee landlords (a typical rich person in first-century Palestine) have withheld the pay of the reapers. Leviticus 19:13 states, "Do not hold back the wages of a hired man overnight" (compare Deut 24:14-15). The reason for this law was that the poor laborer would immediately spend his wages for food for himself and his family. No pay meant no food. But even though they were reaping and therefore had a harvest to sell, these wealthy people found some reason not to pay their workers, perhaps arguing that they could not afford to sell the crop and pay them until the price was higher. They surely had a "legal" reason, justified by the "rabbinic" interpretations of their day. But God condemned such people in Isaiah 5 (especially Is 5:9-10), and he continues to do so. (Contrast Job in Job 7:1-2; 24:10; 31:13, 38-40.)

Fourth, the rich have been self-indulgent. Feasting is fine if there is enough to go around, but self-indulgence when there are those without is a horrible crime before God. Again we think of the parable of the rich man and Lazarus, but we should also note that in the laws for the feasts of the Lord (Deut 16) no one was to appear empty-handed; the typical poor (Levite, widow, orphan, alien) were to feast with those who had means. In his condemnation of indulgence, James sounds like Amos.

Indulgence, of course, was viewed more seriously in James's world than in ours of the recent past. The first-century Mediterranean cultures believed that there was only a limited amount of goods in the world, so if someone collected more, someone else would have less or go without altogether.[2] The Western world has behaved as if goods or wealth were limitless and all could be rich if they worked hard enough or were smart enough. Only recently has Western society begun to face limitations and to see that on a global scale, especially when the environment and future generations are taken into account, the first-century view is probably more realistic than ours.

Fifth, these people have oppressed the righteous ("innocent men" in the NIV). In the phrase "condemned and murdered," James probably does not mean that they carried out an illegal activity, but rather that they used the courts to kill. Probably even this killing was not done directly, but through taking away the means of support of the poor through fines or giving judgments in favor of the rich. A peasant who loses his farm or is thrown out of work will soon starve if no other force intervenes. It is all the same to God whether the death is direct or indirect, whether the proceeding is legal or illegal in human terms. In his book it is all murder. That these people were poor Christians (the most likely ones being referred to) makes his judgment that much more certain.

Therefore, James is hardly arbitrary in his condemnation of the rich. Not only are they not Christian, but he has a number of charges against them. Furthermore, prophetic warnings like this one call people to repentance (although the repentance of wealthy people is less likely than that of the poor, according to Scripture), so these people, like those of Nineveh whom Jonah warned, are not outside of God's love. Yet, before we shake our heads sadly about the rich, we must remember that any one of the five charges is serious enough to bring God's condemnation. It is not enough to avoid judicial murder and legal oppression if we are living in self-indulgence and storing up what might have been shared. The Christian response to such a condemnation should not be to continue to point the finger, but to "stand firm" in obedience to Christ (Jas 5:8) and pray to be so filled with the Spirit that we will joyfully join with those in Acts who laid up treasures in heaven by sharing with their poorer brothers and sisters. This will provide a model of the virtue that God desires in a world that still practices (and even extols) the vices he condemns.

See also comment on MATTHEW 6:24; MARK 10:21; 10:25; JAMES 4:4.

---

[1]This matches John the Baptist's call to repentance

in Luke 3:7-14, which also has an economic focus and also demands repentance before acceptance by God, in his case symbolized by baptism.

[2]See B. Malina, *The New Testament World* (Atlanta: John Knox, 1984). Not all of his arguments are equally convincing, but his demonstration of the concept of "limited goods" is well founded.

5:12 Do Not Swear?

See comment on MATTHEW 5:34.

5:14-16 Prayer Makes the Sick Well?

"Faith healing" has a bad reputation in much of the church. Many of us have known people who have been mishandled by others who believed in healing. I personally can remember a widow who was told that the only reason her husband had died was that he had failed to have enough faith or he had sinned. Others who have not been abused to that extent have been confidently promised healing but have not in fact been healed. With this background, James 5:14-16 concerns us, for it appears to many to give support to these very "faith healers" who have abused or misled us or our friends.

James has given us the picture of a person sick in bed. The proper response to this situation, he instructs us, is to call for the elders of the church; they will pray over the person, anointing him or her with oil in the name of the Lord. But how can James say so matter-of-factly that "the prayer offered in faith will make the sick person well"? Did he not have failures in prayer? Does he really mean that elders will have no such failures? And why does he bring in the issue of sin? Did not Jesus deny that sin had anything to do with sickness (Jn 9:1-3)? Isn't James giving people a basis to load guilt for supposed sin on top of the illness that is already afflicting the person? This passage looks more dangerous than it does pastoral.

Prayer for healing is mentioned frequently in the New Testament. Jesus, of course, healed many (although we never hear him using prayer as a means), and he sent his disciples to do the same. It is they, not Jesus, who anoint with oil (Mk 6:13). Acts continues the acts of Jesus (now being done through the Holy Spirit) and notes numerous healings, beginning just after Pentecost (Acts 3) and continuing to the end of the book (Acts 28:7-10). Paul's mission and preaching were characterized by miracles (Rom 15:18-19; Paul's miracles appear to have been mainly healing miracles and demon expulsions), and his converts experienced the same (Gal 3:5). Furthermore, he mentions "gifts of healing" among the gifts of the Spirit (1 Cor 12:9). It is not surprising, then, to find James writing about healing prayer in the close of his letter where a pagan writer would have put in a health wish. (A normal Greek letter of this type characteristically ended with a summary, an oath, a health wish and a purpose statement; Christian versions of all of these occur in James 5.) He is not introducing something unfamiliar to his readers (one did not do that in the closing), but underlining a practice they knew about and shared in common with others in the early church.

While anointing with oil is mentioned in the context of this passage (Jas 5:14), probably as a type of acted prayer,[1] it is clear that the operant force in healing is God's activity in response to prayer: "the prayer offered in faith will make the sick person well." But this prayer is to be a "prayer offered in faith." Of course, we would expect the elders to be able to pray in faith, for they were supposed to be the most mature spiritual leaders of the church and should have the most faith. Notice that it is the elders' faith, not the person's faith, that is mentioned; there is absolutely no basis in this verse for blaming continuing sickness on a person's own lack of faith. If anyone is to be blamed, it is the elders, the people who prayed. Faith itself is a commitment or trust in God, like the asking in faith of James 1:6.[2] It is a personal relationship, not simply an intellectual conviction. It is also a gift of the Spirit (1 Cor 12:9).

So we are not talking about prayer based on an intellectual conviction that God heals; we are talking about praying out of a relationship with God in which the conviction has grown that God will heal, not in the sense that this is the general will of God (which it always is),[3] but in the sense that it is the specific desire of God now. George Müller, famous for his prayers for funds for his orphanages but also known in his day for his prayers for the sick, noted that while he always had faith (in the sense discussed here) for funds, only until 1836 did he have faith for healing the sick.[4] He still continued to pray for the sick and people were often healed, but apparently he no longer did so with the certainty and success that he continued to experience in praying for funds. It was no longer the prayer of faith in that sense. James, like Jesus (Mk 11:22-24), promises that a prayer of faith will be answered. His statement is a straightforward expectation, which must have been the experience of his community.

This prayer does not appear to be of the five-minute variety, for not only is it likely that such prayer would take time, especially time for listening to God, but there appears to have been some discussion of the person's sins. James is clear that sin is not always the cause of illness. He says, "*If* he has sinned." Like Jesus in John 9:1-2, he apparently knows of situations, perhaps many situations, in which sin was not involved. But like Paul in 1 Corinthians 11:30, he knows of other situations in which it was involved. If James 5:16 is any guide to the practice of his community, an opportunity was given under the wise guidance of the elders for self-examination and confession, with prayer for forgiveness (if needed) being included in the prayer for healing.

Most modern people who pray regularly for the sick can give many illustrations of times when resentment or anger or bitterness or other sins were at the root of an illness. It is important to James to promise that the sin will be forgiven, not just the sickness healed, for without knowing that the sin (which could not be seen directly) was also removed, the person might fear that it would reappear in yet a worse illness. In fact, the experience of forgiveness itself has been known to lead to healing without any further prayer about the disease. Conversely there are examples of healing that was short-lived because the person returned to the root sin.

Finally, James notes, "Confess your sins to each other and pray for each other so that you may be healed." Nowhere in his discussion has James mentioned a gift of healing. Perhaps he expects such gifts of the Spirit to show up when needed in people filled with the Spirit. The focus of his interest is different from Paul's. But up to this point he has been discussing the activity of the elders called to the bedside of a person who is ill, probably too ill to go to church.

Now he broadens the scope of his teaching. Before a person becomes so ill that the elders must be called, Christians should confess their sins and pray for one another. Confession of sin keeps the slate clear and prevents sin from being able to cause illness. Confession to another Christian (presumably one who has some spiritual wisdom and does not gossip) makes the repentance and confession concrete. It also makes it much harder to rationalize the sin. And it makes the prayer for forgiveness just as concrete. James does not mention these reasons; he just states the command.

Likewise, prayer for each other before the illness becomes serious is in order. Why wait until the elders must be called? Why should the elders do all of the pastoral ministry? And how else will Christians gain the experience in prayer and the faith that will make them good elders? In case the believer says, "I'm not an elder and so God would hardly listen to me," James adds, "The prayer of a righteous man is powerful and effective" (Jas 5:16). All that is needed is to be in harmony with God (righteous), and any Christian can pray with the effects of Elijah.

James is not giving a full treatise on prayer for the sick. There was no need to do so in the early church, for such prayer was their practice. It could be observed everywhere; they had not yet learned not to do it. James is just giving a reminder, encouraging them when the Greek letter form gave him opportunity. In doing so he presents a challenge to the modern church to learn what it is to pray the prayer of faith and so to pray effectively in such a way that people are healed, not abused.[5]

---

[1]The oil is certainly not a medicine, for (1) ancient peoples knew of more types of medicine than oil and would not prescribe a single medication for all ailments, and (2) there was a perfectly good term for "medicine" in Greek, so there was no need to use "oil" to substitute for a more general term. It is also not sacramental if this term implies virtue in the oil itself, for it is the prayer, not the oil, which heals, although the oil may be part of the praying.

[2]The point in James 1:6 is that one is to ask in childlike trust in God, confident of his character as the God who gives generously. The doubter or "double-minded" person is the person who prays but at the same time has their real confidence in their own skills or ability to manipulate others. They pray more to "make sure" or to "get God's blessing on our plans" or because it is the pious thing to do than because they really trust God. In James 4:1-5 James points out that these people are really friends of the world and even such prayers are motivated, not by a call of God, but by an attempt to manipulate God to fulfill their own desires.

[3]See Peter H. Davids, "Suffering and Sickness in the New Testament," in C. Peter Wagner and F. Douglas Pennoyer, eds., *Wrestling with Dark Angels* (Ventura, Calif.: Regal Books, 1990), pp. 215-37.

[4]The reason for this appears to have been a conflict within the Christian Brethren movement, of which he was one of the leaders, over the place of spiritual gifts. Until the late 1830s the Brethren actively sought and expected spiritual gifts. However, around 1836, after J. N. Darby (another leader) reacted negatively to Edward Irving (a pastor who was what we might call a "proto-charismatic"), they abandoned this expectation. Darby then developed the concept of the cessation of spiritual gifts, which has characterized later dispensationalism.

[5]Perhaps the best contemporary book on prayer for healing is Ken Blue, *Authority to Heal* (Downers Grove, Ill.: InterVarsity Press, 1987).

5:20 Saved from Death?

Instead of ending his epistle with a greeting or blessing, James ends with a strange statement. Who is the "sinner" to whom James is referring? And is it the sinner who will be saved from death, or the one saving him or her? And from what type of death will the person be saved? Are we still in danger of eternal death if we sin, or is James saying that sin can lead to physical death?

The verse is in fact very significant. James is written in a typical Greek letter form. It was customary to end such a letter with a summary (Jas 5:7-11), an oath (Jas 5:12), a health wish (Jas 5:13-18) and a purpose statement (Jas 5:19-20). This verse, then, should be part of the statement of the purpose of the whole letter. That in itself is reason enough to assign it great importance.

The condition this verse speaks to is described in James 5:19. A Christian ("one of you") has erred. James gives us plenty of illustrations of this in the letter. The errors he addresses are those of partiality and greed, of anger and jealousy. All of them are found within the church. Such error calls for another Christian ("someone") to point it out so that the person can repent and be restored ("bring him back"). That, of course, is what the entire letter is about, bringing the Christians he addresses back to proper Christian behavior. This is indeed the purpose statement of James. Therefore the sinner in this verse is a Christian who has fallen into sin, such as greed or criticism of others.

This Christian brother or sister has erred or gone the wrong way—the text is not talking about an individual sin, however "serious" we may consider it, from which the believer quickly repents. As Jesus points out in Matthew 7:13-14 (which may be the word of Jesus that James is applying here), there are two ways. The way that leads to life is narrow and difficult, while the one leading to death is broad and easy. Unfortunately there are many ways to get from the narrow to the broad way. This Christian (the sinner) has taken one of them and is observed by another, whom we shall call the rescuer. The question is, Who is saved from death—the sinner or the rescuer? Ezekiel 3:18-21 is a discourse on the responsibility of the rescuer. If someone sees a person fall into sin and sits by and does nothing, the sinner will indeed receive the results of the sin, but the potential rescuer will be held guilty of the sinner's blood. In the Old Testament such guilt usually cost the person his life. On the other hand, the rescuer who tries to warn the sinner is free of any guilt, whatever decision the sinner makes. This is certainly the message of Ezekiel (Ezek 33:9; compare 1 Tim 4:16), but is it the message of James?

It seems to me that James's message is that the sinner is the one rescued from death by the rescuer's efforts. There are four reasons for this. First, the fact that sins are covered (an adaptation of Prov 10:12: "Love covers all wrongs") seems to refer to the sinner's sins, not the potential sin of the rescuer. Only the sinner has erred in the context. Second, the word order in the Greek text makes it more likely that it is the sinner who is delivered from death. Third, the very picture of turning a person from his wandering way (a rather woodenly literal translation that brings out James's imagery) suggests that it is the error that is putting the individual in danger of death. The rescuer is presumably safe (although potentially in error, if he or she fails to help the erring Christian).

What, then, is the death that the person is saved from? Certainly sin can lead to physical death in the New Testament, as shown by the deaths of Ananias and Sapphira (Acts 5:1-11), as well as by Paul's statement in 1 Corinthians 11:30 (compare 1 Cor 5:5). Moreover, in James 5:15-16 we discover that sin may be involved in the illnesses of Christians. Could this be what James is referring to? By turning a sinner from their error a person is saved from physical death, their sins being forgiven?

Attractive as this solution is, it is not the most likely interpretation of the passage. The fact that each of the units of James 5:7-20 is separate and dictated by the letter form means that we should look to the body of the letter (and the call to repentance in Jas 4:1-10) rather than to the "health wish" (Jas 5:13-18) for the meaning of "death" in this verse. Both testaments view death as the end result of sin, usually referring to death in terms of eternal death or condemnation at the last judgment (Deut 30:19; Job 8:13; Ps 1:6; 2:12; Jer 23:12; Jude 23; Rev 20:14). James has already mentioned this in James 1:15: desire gives birth to sin, which results in death. That death is contrasted with the life that God gives (Jas 1:18). Since death and life are parallel ideas, it is likely that they are not physical but eternal (or eschatological, to use the more technical term). This parallel, plus the seriousness of the tone in James 5, indicates that it is this sort of death, the ultimate death that sin brings about, which is in view. What James is saying, then, is that a Christian may err from the way of life.[1] When another Christian attempts to rescue him or her, it is not a hopeless action. Such a rescue effort, if successful, will deliver that erring person from eternal death. That is because the sins will be covered (the language is that of the Old Testament sacrifice; when atonement was made the sin was said to be covered as if literally covered by the blood). It may be one simple action of rescue, but it can lead to the covering of "a multitude of sins." In stating this, James shows his own pastor's heart and encourages all Christians to follow in his footsteps, turning their erring brothers and sisters back from the way of death.

[1]Neither James nor the rest of the New Testament is concerned to answer the speculative question "How could a Christian who had eternal life lose it?" All of the theological answers given are based on various theological assumptions and either deny the meaning of the various texts (such as "The Christian does not really die eternally, but simply loses his or her reward") or explain the texts according to their theological beliefs (such as the Calvinist "They appeared to be Christian, but their lack of perseverance shows that they were not really regenerate," or the Arminian "Yes, people can fall away from the faith and be lost"). James, like all New Testament writers, is not interested in theological neatness, but in pastoral concern. He simply sees the situation (a Christian on the wrong way), recognizes the danger (death) and goes to the rescue, rather than asks how it fits into his theology. So while theological responses are appropriate in their place, we ought not to expect a New Testament writer to select among them.

1 PETER

1:9 Salvation: Past, Present or Future?

Evangelical Christians frequently speak of being "saved." In other words, it is easy for them to speak of having received salvation at some point in the past, when they committed themselves to Jesus as Lord. But does this language fit with that of 1 Peter? Peter appears to be speaking of salvation as a goal, an end result, not as something already possessed. Does this mean that salvation is uncertain?

Peter uses the term *salvation* four times in his first epistle (1 Pet 1:5, 9-10; 2:2); he refers to being saved three more times (1 Pet 3:20-21; 4:18). One of these references is to a present process of salvation (1 Pet 3:21, the subject of a later chapter), and the rest refer to a future salvation (except 1 Pet 3:20, which refers to Noah's salvation). In 1 Peter salvation will not be revealed until the last time (1 Pet 1:5). It comes after the end of the present process of suffering for Jesus (1 Pet 4:19). Therefore it is something that one can grow up into (1 Pet 2:2; not "in" as NIV). In other words, Peter is relatively consistent in viewing salvation as something future.

It is true that the New Testament sometimes speaks of salvation in the past tense. Jude 3, for example, speaks about "the salvation we share," and Titus 3:5 states, "He saved us through the washing of rebirth." Acts 15:11; Romans 8:24; Ephesians 2:5, 8; and 2 Timothy 1:9 also speak of salvation in the past tense. But these are a minority of the references to the term in the New Testament. It is far more common to speak of salvation as a present process (1 Cor 1:18; 2 Cor 2:15) or a future event (Rom 5:9-10; 10:9; 11:26; 13:11; 1 Cor 3:15; 15:2; 2 Cor 7:10; Phil 1:28; 1 Thess 5:8-9; 1 Tim 4:16; Heb 1:14; 9:28; 10:39). While some may argue with the categorization of this or that verse, the general trend is evident in these lists of passages. Salvation may be thought of in terms of a past event, but normally it is viewed as a future event.

This focus on the future has to do with the very nature of salvation. All of the verses that speak of salvation as past focus on *the basis* for salvation, which is Jesus' death appropriated by commitment to him (faith), not human rituals, even those in the Old Testament. But most of the verses speak of *the reality* of salvation, and that is future. Salvation means deliverance from some danger. When the term is used theologically, it means the danger of condemnation in the final judgment (Rom 5:8-9). Since that is the nature of the danger, then the salvation cannot become actual until the final judgment happens. Until that point the Christian has hope of salvation (1 Pet 1:3), but not the salvation itself. By "hope," of course, Peter does not mean an "I hope so" type of hope, but a confident expectation that something will happen. It is the type of hope one has for graduation when the registrar of the school has already indicated that the requirements have been met and one's place in the graduating party reserved.

Salvation, then, is a goal. It is what Christians are moving toward. According to 1 Peter it begins with baptism (1 Pet 3:21), but it is finally revealed only in "the last time" (1 Pet 1:5). The mark of those who are "being saved" is their remaining firm in the faith under pressure.

Should evangelical language be revised? It would not be a bad idea to regain the balance of Scripture. In speaking of salvation almost exclusively as a past event there is a loss of two things. First, there is the loss of a sense of the last judgment. That creates a lack of seriousness about judgment, which no New Testament author had. Second, there is a loss of the sense of tentativeness. It is not those who "make a decision for Christ" (which is not a New Testament term), but those who "stand firm to the end" (Mt 10:22; 24:13; Mk 13:13) who will be saved. Historically, theologians have expressed this in two ways. In the Wesleyan tradition, salvation is truly tentative and may be lost, while in the Reformed tradition, God assures that those whom he has truly regenerated will in fact endure (persevere) But both traditions accurately reflect the biblical stress that it is not a one-time decision, even if long ignored, that brings salvation, but a commitment to Christ lived out through obedience to the end of life. Salvation is fully certain, but only for those who are now living life in obedience to Christ. While we must not forget the basis for our salvation and totally stop referring to our having been saved (past) by the death of Christ on the cross, it would be helpful for language about salvation to reflect the tentativeness and sense of the final judgment observed in the New Testament. Then, with 1 Peter, people will look forward to salvation more as a goal than as a past event.

See also comment on PHILIPPIANS 2:12-13; 3:10-11; 2 PETER 1:10; 2:20.

2:13-14 Submitting to Government?

See comment on ROMANS 13:1-7.

2:18 Slavery Approved?

See comment on EPHESIANS 6:5-8.

3:6 Call Your Husband Master?

Is Peter teaching that women should refer to their husbands as if the women were the slaves and the men were their owners? Isn't the expression "master" offensive and demeaning to the woman? And what does not giving way to fear have to do with such a situation? Is Peter setting women up for second-class status and abuse?

The passage in 1 Peter is referring to Genesis 18;12, in which Sarah laughs and says to herself, "After I am worn out and my master is old, will I now have this pleasure [of having a child]?" The point is that Sarah (perhaps even in her thoughts) refers to her husband as "my lord" (not "my master"),[1] showing a proper respect toward him. The irony is that in the context, while appearing to respect Abraham, she is laughing at the words of Yahweh himself; Peter, however, like most New Testament authors, is not concerned with the context, only with the single use of the term.

But what is the context in 1 Peter? The passage is addressed to upper-class Christian women with unbelieving husbands (a far more common situation in that culture than that of Christian husbands with unbelieving wives). These women are advised to be subject to their husbands, for it is their virtuous behavior that will convert them, not their arguments for Christianity or their fancy dress (the fact that fancy dress was possible points to their being upper-class women; peasant women typically had one decent set of clothing and virtually no expensive jewelry). Such submission was also the mark of "the holy women," that is, the Old Testament women, of whom Sarah is the chief. This submission will mark these Christian women out as being themselves holy (Sarah's children).

Notice what is not said. First, it is not being implied that this submission extends to giving up the practice of the Christian faith or compromising the standards of holy living laid down by Jesus. These women are to continue to "hope in God" and "do what is right." Their husbands, being unconverted, may in fact threaten them with punishment or divorce, demanding that they not go to the church gatherings or that they practice something Christ has forbidden, but these women are not to "give way to fear." Suffering for the name of Christ is honored in 1 Peter. Yet like all of those to whom 1 Peter is written, they should suffer because they are committed to Christ, not because they have broken cultural standards of which Christ would approve.

In other words, what we see here is that the submission of these women is not to be absolute. They have submitted to Christ first of all. That is the one absolute submission. Now they follow him and submit to their husbands. Their culture demanded absolute submission to their husbands, including in matters of religion. This epistle is calling for them to take an independent stand on religion and morality, but to be model wives in every other way, which means that Christ would not be blamed for what was not truly the result of obedience to him.

Second, this pattern is not presented as the ideal for Christian marriage. Only in 1 Peter 3:7, as we shall see in the next chapter, does the author get around to discussing Christian marriage. Given that he has so little to say about it, it is likely that either such marriages were not a problem or that they were relatively rare in the communities he is addressing. In a Christian marriage the wife is an heir with her husband "of the gracious gift of life." In other words, she is an equal partner in the gospel. The husband is to give her honor and treat her with consideration, "so that nothing will hinder your prayers."

In 1 Peter 3:1 Peter is doing three things. First, he is presenting an evangelistic strategy. People are won to Christ not by words alone and certainly not by rebellion, but by living to the fullest pagan virtue (when it is consistent with Christian virtue), so that the non-Christian will see that the effect of Christ in one's life is to make one able to live the ideals that pagans could write about but rarely live.

Second, he is noting that the normal Christian position is the way of submission. No New Testament writer has a problem with submission, for it is what Jesus practiced, as Peter points out in 1 Peter 2:23. Liberation in the New Testament comes from the powerful giving up power, the wealthy sharing their wealth, not by the oppressed demanding their rights or the poor their share of the pie. The effect of the Spirit is seen in the act of giving up, not that of demanding. Thus Sarah's action shows an attitude consistent with New Testament virtue. This was especially important, given the role possibilities for women in that day.

Third, he is following the pattern Paul described in 1 Corinthians 5:12-13 (and illustrates in 1 Cor 7:12-16), that Christians should not try to impose their standards on non-Christians. After all, such people do not have the power of the Spirit to follow Christian standards. Thus this passage does not address the behavior of the unbelieving husband, only that of the wife. She alone can show Christian virtue. She can hope that her husband will in fact come to faith and, filled with the Spirit, in turn begin to treat her as an equal, as instructed in 1 Peter 3:7.

This passage illustrates the fact that the concept of marriage as an intimate relationship between husband and wife is a relatively modern concept. The Mediterranean culture did not expect emotional intimacy between husband and wife. A man was closest to his mother and siblings; he might also have male friends (the father-son relationship generally was not an emotionally close one). A woman was closest to her children and her siblings, perhaps having other women friends (although women were generally expected to stay at home). The emotional distance between husband and wife in this passage (which the term "lord" certainly indicates) would not have bothered Peter, for while there are a very few examples in Scripture of marital emotional intimacy, it was not a cultural expectation. Likewise, although it may be culturally desirable today, it cannot on biblical grounds be made the essence of marriage. The essence is the publicly sanctioned covenant or commitment of each spouse to the relationship.[2]

See also comment on EPHESIANS 5:22; 1 PETER 3:7.

---

[1]The translation "my master" in the NIV is unfortunate in that it implies that Peter is thinking about women as slaves. In fact, he is following the Greek translation of the Old Testament in using *kyrios,* or "lord," which may mean simply the respectful "sir" or could imply superior status such as "my lord" would imply in traditional British usage. When Peter refers to the master of a slave, however, he uses a different term, *despotēs* (1 Pet 2:18).

[2]See B. Malina, *The New Testament Word* (Atlanta: John Knox, 1984), for a description of Mediterranean culture, and R. Paul Stevens, *Married for Good* (Downers Grove, Ill.: InterVarsity Press, 1986), especially the first four chapters, on the concept of what marriage is (the rest of the book works out these and other issues in the context of the marriage pattern of the Western world).

3:7 The Weaker Partner?

This passage raises some of the same questions as 1 Peter 3:6, but it is addressed to Christian husbands. In what way is the wife "the weaker partner"? Isn't this a condescending term? Doesn't it imply the inferiority of women? And what does being "considerate" mean? Is this the consideration of a master taking a slave's desires into account? Finally, why would a failure here hinder people's prayers? The interesting thing about questions based on this verse is that several translations have interpreted the Greek term in different ways. What is translated "weaker partner" in the NIV in a more literal translation of the Greek would be "weaker vessel" (as KJV; compare RSV: "weaker sex"). The translation "weaker vessel" is almost as confusing as the use of the term "vessel" in 1 Thessalonians 4:4. A study of this vocabulary reveals that most likely the author is thinking of the person either as a body that is the vessel for the Spirit (a meaning found in the apostolic fathers) or as a creature created by God (a meaning coming from the parable in Jer 18:1-11). Either of the two meanings declares that the man and the woman are both creatures, but one of them, the woman, is weaker and more vulnerable.

Unlike the later church fathers, Peter is not thinking of the woman as being weaker morally (Rom 5:6 says that all human beings are weak this way, and 1 Peter is close to Paul in its thought) or weak in conscience (Rom 14:1, something Paul never links to sex), for neither of these applies to woman as "vessel" or "creature," and neither of these applies to woman as over against man. Instead, Peter's idea must be that the man experiences the woman in the context of most cultures as weaker both physically (and therefore we hear so much of the abuse of women by men) and socially. Physical weakness is clear in that males are on average larger and stronger than women. Social weakness is illustrated in 2 Corinthians 10—13, in which Paul repeatedly speaks of being socially weak because he was neither imposing to look at nor spoke good Greek (due to his foreign origin); this put him at a social disadvantage and often required that he have a local sponsor. A woman is likewise often disadvantaged the moment people realize that they are dealing with a woman rather than a man, a fact even more true in first-century culture than today.

It is obvious that this weakness, whether physical or social, gave (and still gives) the husband a great advantage in the marriage; he could abuse his wife's vulnerability. But the topic of this section in 1 Peter, understood from 1 Peter 2:13, is that of submission. The husband, argues Peter, shows his proper submission by not taking advantage of his wife's weakness. Instead he is to "live with" her "considerately" or "according to knowledge." The knowledge referred to is not theoretical knowing about her but personal knowledge, which could form the basis either for exploiting her or for considerate care. The latter is what the Christian husband is to exhibit. This considerate care based upon personal knowledge of one's wife is to extend to the whole marital realm, for "live with" includes the sexual as well as other areas of the marriage.

Another way Peter expresses this idea is to say that the husband is to treat his wife with "respect" or "honor," which means that even if the culture does not honor women, he will honor his woman. His honoring her gives her the advantage of his strength in a culture that may be physically abusive and of his status in a culture that might look down on women. Like Christ, he takes (and even gives up) what he has and bestows it upon the one who lacks it.

The culture may look at the woman as "weaker" or inferior—in fact, that low view of women was very true of the Mediterranean culture of Peter's day—but 1 Peter says that she is a "joint heir" (the "heirs with you" translation in the NIV may disguise the strength of the phrase). In other words, in the realm that counts, the spiritual, she is an equal. The New Testament perspective is that marriage itself and sexual differences in particular are temporal and will not continue in heaven (see Mt 22:30). Thus from the heavenly perspective it is not the weakness of the woman that is ultimate, but her equality. Since this is the reality of the future, the Christian husband is to recognize this in the present in the way he respects or honors his wife. There is, as Paul argued in Galatians 3:28, no real (in the sense of ultimate or lasting) difference between male and female. Fully Christian marriage lives this out, being more determined by the fuller reality of the future (the eschatological reality) than by the legal and social givens of a culture.

Therefore, we can now see why this would affect prayers. Several New Testament passages (Mt 5:23; 6:12, 14-15; 1 Cor 11:33-34; Jas 4:3) indicate that relational differences with others will hinder one's prayer life. How much more would this be the case if one's wife were complaining to God of her husband's mistreatment of her? Even if she did not complain, would not God see her tears? Isn't he a God of compassion and justice? Doesn't he stand up for the weaker and the oppressed? On the one hand, then, we have the promise implied in Matthew 18:19-20 that husband and wife make the smallest church, a place in which Christ can be present; therefore prayers made in unity with him will be heard. On the other hand, when they are estranged and especially when the more powerful is oppressing the weaker, no prayer will be heard, for God will put the relationship and living like Christ in self-giving ahead of any request—except that of repentance.[1]

Is Peter then condescending to women? No, he is not condescending; he is realistic. He recognizes that in the cultures with which he was dealing (and to a large extent today as well), the wife was disadvantaged in the relationship, almost always physically and often legally and socially as well. He therefore counsels the husband to live like Jesus and to take his physical and social advantage and use it to make his wife the equal she really is in God's eyes. This type of relationship, 1 Peter argues, will lead to the situation in which prayer can be answered. Any exploitation of one's wife, however, blocks the way between the husband and his God.

[1]It is unclear whether the "your" (plural) in "your prayers" refers to the husbands' prayers only (since husbands are addressed as a group) or both the husbands' and the wives' prayers. Probably the former is meant, but we must remember that bitterness and resentment in the wife will also block prayers as surely as the husband's oppressiveness.

3:19 Who Are the Spirits in Prison?

It is unclear what Peter means when he says that Christ preached to the spirits in prison. Could it be that Christ is giving a second chance to people who have died? What does it mean that these beings are in prison? Could there be some type of purgatory after death where people are given a second chance?

The first step to understanding this passage is to look at it in context. The passage is speaking to Christians faced with the possibility of persecution. Peter is giving the example of Christ, who was also persecuted. This fact is important, for the Christians he is addressing are being encouraged to identify with the experience of Christ. Jesus also suffered. In fact, he was "put to death in the body" (NIV) or "in the flesh" (RSV), but "made alive by the Spirit" or "in the spirit." While admittedly difficult, it appears that two different spheres of life are being described. In the human sphere of life ("the flesh"—the NIV translation is unfortunate in that it does not make this clear) Jesus was put to death. As far as the world was concerned, he was dead forever, executed as a criminal. Yet the church knew that on Easter he came alive, not in the merely human sphere, but in the spiritual sphere. So his body was raised, but it was not raised as only a natural human body (as was Lazarus's body), but as an immortal body. Therefore we find stories about the risen Christ being able to do things that he could not do before his death, such as appear and disappear and enter locked rooms.

It was in this spiritual sphere of life (a better translation than the NIV's "through whom" would be the NRSV's "in which") that Jesus went to the "spirits in prison." We learn in the next verse that these spirits "disobeyed in the days of Noah." Who, then, could they be? There are two possibilities. In the days of Noah the earth was full of violence because people were very wicked (see Gen 6:3-6, 11). These people all died in the flood. Could they be these spirits? When we look at the use of the term *spirit* in the New Testament, we notice that it is almost never used of dead people. When it is used of dead people, it is always qualified in some way to make it clear that it is people who are being written about (for example, Heb 12:23). Normally dead human beings are referred to as "souls." Since there is nothing in this passage to make it clear that it is human beings who are being written about, it is unlikely that these are dead people.

The other possibility is that they are the "sons of God" of Genesis 6:2, or perhaps their offspring. The term "sons of God" refers to spiritual beings from the divine council. The New Testament refers to them as angels who "abandoned their own home" (Jude 6) or who "sinned" (2 Pet 2:4). Here, then, we have truly rebellious, disobedient spirits. Furthermore, there is a long tradition, both in the New Testament and in other Jewish writings, that these fallen angels were kept in a prison (see 1 Enoch 10-16; 21 for a discussion of the punishment of these "Watchers," as he calls them). This, then, appears to be the mostly likely identification of these "spirits in prison." Not only are we talking about beings usually referred to as "spirits," but we are also talking about beings who were known to Jews as being in a "prison."

Was Jesus proclaiming the gospel to these "spirits"? Was he giving them a "second chance"? The term for "preach" is normally used in the New Testament for preaching the gospel, but it can also mean to "announce" or "proclaim" (Lk 12:3; Rom 2:21; Rev 5:2). Therefore it does not necessarily mean to proclaim the gospel. Are there other passages in Jewish or Christian literature in which something is proclaimed or preached to these spirits? Again we turn back to 1 Enoch (which was known to the early church, for it is cited in Jude) and discover that Enoch proclaims to these spirits their doom.

Does such an interpretation fit this passage? The passage ends on a note of triumph with the submission of all "angels, authorities and powers" to the exalted Jesus. While the New Testament does not speak anywhere of preaching the gospel to spirits, it does speak of the victory of Christ over the spiritual world (for example, 2 Cor 2:14; Eph 6:11-12; Col 2:15; Rev 12:7-11). Thus a reference in this passage to the proclamation of that victory fits right in with the tone of both the passage and the New Testament in general.

We can now summarize what the passage is saying. The Christians in Asia Minor were facing persecution and possible martyrdom. Peter calls them to look at the example of Jesus. He was, from the human point of view, killed. Yet, in fact, he rose, not simply to renewed natural life, but to transformed life in the spiritual world, and in that world he proclaimed his victory to the fallen angels who were disobedient in Noah's day. This may have been during his ascension, for while this text does not tell us where this prison was, some Jews located it in the "second heaven" and thus on the way between earth and the heaven where God dwells. Whatever the case, in the end of this section in 1 Peter Christ is in heaven with all spiritual beings subject to him.

Peter's point is that Christians through baptism have identified with Christ and so will be saved in the final judgment and share his triumph. They too will live with Christ in exaltation, no matter how human beings persecute or condemn them. As for their persecutors, unless they repent, what hope do they have, living as they do in the purely human sphere? Christ triumphed over his foes and proclaimed his victory. The Christians in Asia Minor (and today) will do the same if they remain faithful to this Christ.

3:21 Baptism Saves You?

Most Christians have been baptized, but they disagree about how to baptize, when to baptize, and what baptism means. This passage speaks to this latter issue (and perhaps by implication to the others), but for many Christians it complicates the problem rather than solves it. In fact, the whole paragraph of 1 Peter 3:18-22 is difficult. However, the problem on which we are going to focus is only that of baptism, for while several statements in the paragraph may be confusing, this appears to have major doctrinal issues at stake. If baptism saves a person, how does it do this? Isn't it salvation by grace through faith? This seems to add a ceremonial work, much like circumcision. And what, then, is the state of people who are not baptized? Should our opening statement be modified to say that "all Christians have been baptized" and that those who believe themselves to be Christians but are not baptized have not in fact been saved?

The point of this paragraph (1 Pet 3:18-22) is to give a reason for suffering for doing good. The reason is found in the example of Christ. "For Christ died for sins once for all, the righteous for the unrighteous, to bring you to God. He was put to death in the body but made alive by the Spirit" (1 Pet 3:18). Christ also was righteous, but he still suffered. He was condemned to death in the arena of the world (better than "in the body" of the NIV). Yet this was not the end of him. Instead God raised him from the dead, no longer in the arena of this world, for death and evil can no longer touch him. Jesus was raised in the arena of the spirit, just as Paul taught in 1 Corinthians 15:42-49. And he has been exalted so that all beings in the universe are subject to him. Since he is an example for the Christians to whom Peter is writing, the implication (brought out clearly in the next chapter) is that for them also suffering for righteousness is not ultimately an evil, but the door to a resurrected life in which they too will be beyond the grasp of all evil and will reign with Christ.

In mentioning the triumph of Jesus at the resurrection (1 Pet 3:18-19), Peter is reminded that Noah built the ark and that "in it only a few people, eight in all, were saved through water" (1 Pet 3:20). Why would this fact be important to Peter and his readers? The believers in Asia Minor to whom he is writing were once pagans, very much part of their culture, fully accepted in their cities and villages. Now they are being ostracized and slandered because they are Christians. The whole world appears to be against them. True enough, Peter reminds them, but the world was also against Noah. He looked a fool building the ark, but the majority were wrong and drowned in the flood. The minority of eight people (Noah, his three sons and their wives) were the only ones saved, although they were saved through water, and it must have been a rough voyage at that.

This has set the stage for 1 Peter's drawing an analogy to the Christian experience. The concept that an Old Testament event symbolized a New Testament one is common in Scripture. It is found in Paul (Rom 5:14; 1 Cor 10:6, 11) and in Hebrews (Heb 8:5; 9:24).[1] This is not surprising, since the same God operates in both Testaments and his character is consistent. One would expect corresponding actions. There are, however, some differences; Paul sees a correspondence between baptism and the crossing of the Red Sea and the covering cloud in Exodus (1 Cor 10:2), while Peter draws his parallel with Noah. Neither interpretation is wrong since we are moving in the world of analogy, not of literal meaning.

As Noah was saved through water, so is the Christian: "Baptism now saves you." How does baptism save a person? The answer is "by the resurrection of Jesus Christ." In other words, baptism is a union with Christ, and, united with Christ, we are carried with him to resurrection life. Paul has similarly used baptism as the point of union with Christ (Rom 6:4-11; Col 2:12). The key is that, as in 1 Peter 1:3, it is being joined to Jesus that saves. Without Jesus and his resurrection, baptism would be useless.

Peter goes on to argue this when he explains his point in more detail. Christian baptism consists of being immersed in water (in fact, at least in the third and fourth centuries it was done naked to be sure that one came in full contact with the water). The amount and type of water is never mentioned, although by the second century cold running water was preferred. (See *Didache* 7:1-4 in the apostolic fathers for the order of preferred types of water in Asia Minor between A.D. 100 and 150.) The point in 1 Peter is that the outward washing is not the important part. That is simply "the removal of dirt from the body." Without something more one would go into the water a dirty sinner and come out a clean sinner. The water has no magic properties, nor does the ritual itself save. If it did, baptism would be like circumcision was for the Jew, and Christians would indeed be saved by works (which in Paul means ritual acts), although not works of the Old Testament law.

What does save in the baptismal experience is the "pledge" or "answer" to God from "a good conscience." For some scholars this means a request made to God for a good conscience; in other words, it is a request made in baptism that God would purify one and forgive one's sins (see Heb 10:22). This certainly is a possible interpretation, for it makes the expressed commitment to Christ, not the ritual act, the point of salvation. More likely, however, is the interpretation based on parallels with Jewish rites and the use of the term "pledge" in other literature. This sees the candidate for baptism being asked a series of questions, such as "Do you pledge yourself to follow Jesus as Lord?" (perhaps reflected in Acts 8:37 and 1 Tim 6:12). The response of commitment to God and identification with Christ is what saves, if it comes from a good conscience. In other words, a hypocritical response will have no effect. An honest pledge of commitment, however, will result in salvation, for it joins the person to the resurrection of Christ.

However, this leaves many questions open for us, such as "What about people who are never baptized and yet make a commitment to Christ in another setting?" For Peter this would be a strange question, though, for after adequate instruction in the faith, baptism in the name of Jesus was the first thing done to all converts in the New Testament period. The idea that a person would confess Christ and yet would not be baptized would be absurd to Peter. Therefore he does not consider it a question needing an answer. He would surely have admitted that the thief on the cross had been saved without being baptized (Lk 23:43), but why should that be the norm for people who are not on crosses or otherwise inhibited from baptism? Are they trying to avoid a command of Christ? If so, have they ever committed themselves to Christ at all? These are the type of questions Peter would have wanted to ask had the question been put to him. In short, rather than ask such a question (unless we are concerned about a thief-on-the-cross type we know), why not simply get baptized? Yet all of this is unstated, an assumed part of New Testament teaching.

What Peter does say is clear enough, however. Christians are saved through their being joined to Christ and his resurrection. This should make them unafraid of what any human persecutor can do to them, for Christ has triumphed over all that sphere of life and the spirit world that operates behind it. The normal point of salvation for Christians in the early church was baptism. Even here it is not the ritual itself or the water that saves, but the commitment that one makes to Jesus as Lord. (Or the forgiveness one asks from Jesus the Lord, taking the alternative interpretation.) As in Paul, salvation is a relationship. Baptism in Christianity, just as a wedding in marriage, is simply the way of entering into that relationship.

See also comment on ACTS 2:38; 22:16.

For more on this type of interpretation, see Leonhard Goppelt, *Typos: The Typological Interpretation of the Old Testament in the New* (Grand Rapids, Mich.: Eerdmans, 1982).

4:1 Done with Sin?

At first glance 1 Peter 4:1 does not appear difficult. That Christ has suffered in his body is a given of the Christian faith, for how else would one describe the cross? Likewise it is a very common idea in the New Testament that Christians should be prepared to follow Christ, including following his example of suffering. One need only read Philippians 2:5-11 to get an example, or 1 Peter 2:21. But in this passage something else is added, namely the idea that "he who has suffered in his body is done with sin." Does this mean the same as Romans 6:7, "Anyone who has died has been freed from sin"? Or does it have another meaning, especially since it uses "suffered" rather than "died" and "is done with" rather than "has been freed from"? If "done with sin" means "stopped sinning," why am I still sinning? Does it mean that I have not suffered enough?

There are five different explanations of this passage. First, it might refer only to Christ (the "he" is Christ and no one else). Second, it may refer to a Christian's identification with Christ at his or her conversion-initiation (especially baptism). That is, when one identifies with Christ's death, sin has no more power over that person (Rom 6:1-12; 1 Jn 5:18-19). Third, it may mean that when a Christian decides to suffer for Christ, that believer has chosen decisively to break with sin and its compromises. Fourth, it may mean that when Christians suffer, they break the power of sin over their life. Finally, it may mean that when Christians die, they will be freed from sin as Christ was.

In choosing among these we notice, first, that Peter, unlike Paul, never uses "sin" as an abstract principle or power. Peter is always thinking of concrete acts of sin. This makes the second and third options unlikely. Furthermore Peter speaks of the suffering as a completed action, which also makes the concept of identification or decision (both of which are ongoing) unlikely.

Second, when we consider the remaining options, we see that while 1 Peter is about persecution, it is not about martyrdom. Naturally, one can hardly say that the prospect of dying for one's faith was totally absent from Peter's consciousness, yet the types of suffering that he mentions are those of social ostracism and abuse, not the official proceedings that could lead to execution. This makes the last option unlikely.

That leaves two options remaining, and both are probably in Peter's mind. The source of the saying is Christ, who is preeminently the one who "suffered in the body"—or better, "suffered in this physical world"—right up to the point of death (which is more than these Christians have been called to do yet). The result was not a loss for Jesus, but rather a freedom that he has from the whole realm of sin and death. He is no longer subject to those things which he endured while living on earth. So likewise the Christian who has suffered has made a decisive break with sin. This happens totally when the Christian goes to the extent of Christ and dies; but it happens in part when the Christian suffers in any way. The act of suffering for Christ makes the attractiveness of sin hollow. The believer has put all his eggs in one basket, that of Christ, and has paid too great a price to turn back now.

This explains why it is an attitude with which believers are to arm themselves. It is the attitude seen in Christ and expressed in the saying "He who has suffered in his body [or flesh] is done with sin." If Peter's readers have this attitude their own suffering will result in their "not liv[ing] the rest of [their] earthly life for evil human desires, but rather for the will of God." That is, if Christ is really the one they are following, their great example, then suffering will separate them more and more from sinful acts, making them increasingly invested in heaven, until they come to that point when they die like Christ, and, like him, are totally finished with sin and all its effects in this world.[1]

We may in fact still be sinning because we have not chosen to suffer and thereby have done with sin. Perhaps when we come to the point of choice, we choose compromise and then wonder why we cannot overcome temptation. On the other hand, we may still be sinning because we have not suffered enough. While we have chosen Christ and against sin and are making good progress in the battle, we have not yet died. We may be longing for a perfection that will only be ours in resurrection, not that very real maturity that is possible in this world.

See also comment on ROMANS 6:2, 7; HEBREWS 10:14; 1 JOHN 3:6, 9.

[1]For further explanation, see the comment on this verse in Peter H. Davids, *The First Epistle of Peter*, New International Commentary on the New Testament (Grand Rapids, Mich.: Eerdmans, 1990).

4:14 The Spirit of Glory and of God?

No one likes being insulted. It is certainly not the time in life when a person usually experiences either God or glory, yet 1 Peter seems to associate the two. In 1 Peter 4:12-18, Peter encourages his readers to be faithful under persecution and not to think of it as something foreign to their Christian experience. In the middle of that section is 1 Peter 4:14. It seems strange because it makes us wonder if the Spirit "of glory" in any way differs from the Spirit "of God." Also, why should the Spirit rest on people just because they are insulted?

This phrase in 1 Peter is unusual. In fact, it is so grammatically difficult that some of the scribes tried to "clean it up" by making various "corrections" to the text. Yet the context is clear, and it is this context that enables us to understand what Peter is getting at.

Immediately before this verse the author has called the sufferings that these Christians are experiencing a participation in the sufferings of Christ (1 Pet 4:13). They have identified with Jesus and are experiencing sufferings (such as persecution) on earth parallel to those he received. But this participation in his sufferings will lead to participation in his glory. Suffering is not virtuous in itself, but when it is endured because of one's faithfulness to Christ it is the path to glory.

Now Peter makes the nature of some of those sufferings clear; they are being "insulted because of the name of Christ." These Christians claim to be serving Christ, and their neighbors are making fun of them or perhaps slandering them (with all types of rumors about what Christians *really* did in their services). That enduring such rejection brings a blessing is something Jesus made clear when he said, "Blessed are you when people insult you, persecute you and falsely say all kinds of evil against you because of me" (Mt 5:11; compare Lk 6:22). The world around them is rejecting them, but Jesus is accepting them. He has called them blessed.

It is also clear that the only persecution that will result in this blessing is that which results from their faithfulness to Christ. In the next verse Peter notes that suffering as a criminal or a meddler in the affairs of others will not bring a blessing (unless, of course, the accusation is false, an excuse for punishing them for being Christians). Sometimes Christians are persecuted because they are obnoxious, not because they are faithful!

When genuine persecution happens, 1 Peter promises that the Holy Spirit will rest upon them. This may recall Jesus' promise "When they arrest you, do not worry . . . for it will not be you speaking, but the Spirit of your Father speaking through you" (Mt 10:19-20; compare Mk 13:11; Lk 12:11-12). At times this glory could be visible to the Christian (Acts 7:55) or to others (Acts 6:15; compare Stephen's term for God in Acts 7:2). Yet note that this "glory" did not always get the person out of trouble; it was the vision of glory that led to Stephen's being stoned! In other words, through the Spirit of God, the Christians undergoing persecution for Christ will experience in the present a taste of the glory they will have in its fullness later (1 Pet 1:7; 5:4 refer to the coming glory).

There is another reason for the dual name for the Spirit. The people insult the Christians; God causes his Spirit of glory to rest on them. Instead of insult they receive glory in the eyes of God. The people persecute because of the name of Christ; it is the Spirit of God himself that rests upon them. They have been faithful to Christ, so God is happy to let his name be identified with them. The balance in this passage is impressive.

What, then, is Peter saying? The call to Christ is a call to come and die. Part of the dying with Christ includes persecution for Christ. But the Christian is not alone in persecution. While the world is heaping up insult and shame, God is placing his Spirit of glory upon them. It is no surprise that this is the reported experience of many of the martyrs of the first centuries of the church. And because they have identified with the name of Christ, God identifies with them through his Spirit. Thus Peter can say, "Praise God that you bear that name [for which you are suffering]" (1 Pet 4:16). Rejection is never pleasant, nor is it to be sought, but when it comes out of faithfulness to Christ it brings with it the presence of the Spirit. It is this idea that our strange expression brings out. And it is in this, not in the suffering itself, that a Christian can truly rejoice and praise God.

See also comment on HABAKKUK 3:16-18; JAMES 1:2.

4:17 Judgment to Begin with the Family of God?

I do not enjoy thinking about the judgment of anyone; I especially dislike considering my own possible judgment. Thus, it bothers me when the author of this epistle suddenly begins to refer to the persecution of Christians (the context of this passage) as judgment. But did not Christ take the judgment of believers? How can Peter take such a gloomy perspective, if he really believes in grace? Does that mean that if I am persecuted I am a sinful Christian in need of judgment? Wouldn't that perspective add guilt to my suffering, rather than allow me to rejoice in suffering for Christ?

The answer to our questions is relatively easy, although it is not comfortable to contemplate. The topic of the passage is "the judgment" (the Greek text has the definite article). What judgment could this be? Peter has already referred to judgment (1 Pet 1:17; 2:23; 4:5-6), and in every case it is God's judgment and therefore probably the final judgment. Given the use of the same phrase in other New Testament passages (Acts 24:25; Rom 2:2-3; Heb 6:2; 2 Pet 3:7; Jude 4; Rev 17:1; 18:20), this conclusion becomes firm. Thus 1 Peter is saying that the final judgment is beginning not with the pagans or the unbelieving Jews, but with the family of God, the church. The persecution they are experiencing is a phase of that final judgment.

How this is the case becomes clear when we examine God's judging in Jewish tradition. In an Old Testament tradition, judgment begins at God's house. For example, Ezekiel 9:5-6 reads, "Follow him through the city and kill. . . . Begin at my sanctuary." Jeremiah, in speaking to the nations, says, "See, I am beginning to bring disaster on the city that bears my Name, and will you indeed go unpunished?" (Jer 25:29). The nations will not go unpunished, for judgment has begun with God's own people. Likewise, at the end of the Old Testament period, Malachi 3:1-6 speaks of the Lord coming to his temple and purifying the Levites. He concludes, "So I will come near to you for judgment." Does the Lord judge his people? The answer of the Old Testament is yes, and if so, how much more severely will he judge the pagan nations.

In Malachi and continuing in the intertestamental period, this judgment is interpreted as a purifying judgment, which will bring God's people to repentance. "Therefore, he did not spare his own sons first. . . . Therefore they were once punished that they might be forgiven" (2 Baruch 13:9-10).1 The New Testament shares this position. Not only is the story of Ananias and Sapphira (Acts 5) a graphic example, but Paul clearly states this teaching. Speaking to Christians who were ill because of their sin, Paul writes, "If we judged ourselves, we would not come under judgment. When we are judged by the Lord, we are being disciplined so that we will not be condemned with the world" (1 Cor 11:31-32). Hebrews 12:7-11 also speaks of the suffering of Christians as discipline, although discipline can come for two reasons. Soldiers go through the discipline of training programs to harden themselves so that they may stand in battle; children are disciplined when they have done wrong. Both appear to be in the mind of the author of Hebrews, although the latter is foremost for Paul.

There is, then, a New Testament teaching that God will judge his church, his people. This judgment is a discipline to harden them so that they will not sin or to turn them from the sin into which they have already fallen. It is therefore grace, for God disciplines so that he will not have to condemn Christians in the concluding phase of the final judgment (that is also the hope of church discipline; 1 Cor 5:5). It is based on grace, for we never hear of God judging Christians for sins that they have repented of. Yet, gracious as it is, such a judgment is very real and very painful, a point upon which all of the New Testament authors agree.

Part of the graciousness of God's act is seen in Peter's question "What will the outcome be for those who do not obey the gospel?" If the beginning of the final judgment, the purifying action of God within his church, is so severe, despite the fact that they are God's own family and have obeyed the gospel, what will the conclusion of the final judgment be like when he turns his attention to those who have refused to obey him? It is a mercy that God turns his church to repentance and spares it from the fate of the unbeliever. That is precisely what Peter concludes, citing the Greek form of Proverbs 11:31, "If it is hard for the righteous to be saved, what will become of the ungodly and the sinner?" (1 Pet 4:18). Faith will be tested (1 Pet 1:6; 4:12), for Jesus said that the way to life was narrow (Lk 13:23-24), but for the unbelievers, "It is a dreadful thing to fall into the hands of the living God" (Heb 10:31).

In this passage, then, Peter has three ways of looking at persecution. First, it is a test of faith, showing if the commitment of the professed Christian is genuine or not (1 Pet 4:12). Second, it is an identification with the sufferings of Christ, which will not only result in glory in the future, but leads to the Spirit of glory resting upon them now (1 Pet 4:13-14). Finally, it is a discipline or judgment, which shows that they are in fact God's family and purifies them to live more in the character of the family. The final judgment has begun, but it has begun with the purification of God's church, God's people, just as happened in the Old Testament. It will be consummated, however, not in condemnation for his people—they are his family and will be saved after being purified—but in terrible conclusive judgments upon unbelievers, which Jesus described so graphically (for example, Mt 24—25) and Revelation pictures in visions (Rev 15—16; 20).

I still do not like the idea of judgment, but my suffering does not necessarily mean that I am specially sinful. Since I am committed to Christ, the persecution I suffer is a sign that I am part of the household of God. He, as a good father, is purifying his family for our good. It is a sign of belonging. I may not enjoy the experience, but I can rejoice that I am among those facing judgment now, being purified in preparation for heaven, rather than among those who will face the full force of divine judgment later.

---

[1]The same teaching is in 2 Baruch 13:1-12; *Testament of Benjamin* 100:8-9; and the Dead Sea Scrolls 1QS 4:18-21; 1Qh 8:30-31; 9:10; 11:8-10, all of which are Jewish writings that are available in English.

2 PETER

1:4 Participate in the Divine Nature?

Can a human being participate in the nature of God? This sounds like something written by a New Age guru!

There is a clear progression in Peter's thought in this passage. First, he presents Christ's divine power (his first use of the adjective "divine") as providing Christians with everything needed for a godly life (2 Pet 1:3). Christ mediates this power to us human beings through personal knowledge of (not simply theological knowledge about) God, who is the one who has called believers to Christ. Therefore the movement in this passage is from a call to Christ through the power and glory of the Father to a life of godliness through Christ's divine power revealing the Father to human hearts.

This glorious power of God forms the basis of his promises. What are these promises? They are surely the promises, found in many New Testament presentations of the gospel, of a place in Christ's eternal kingdom (2 Pet 1:11) and the rewards that go along with it (such as those described in 1 Pet 1:3-5). Then why were these promises given? So that Christians might become "partakers in the divine nature." The phrase "divine nature" itself is well known from Greek philosophical literature, but it is also found in the Jewish-Hellenistic literature of the New Testament period. In this first-century literature, to "participate in the divine nature" does not mean merging into God or union with deity (which is the sense equivalent language has in true New Age thought). In other words, neither the Greeks (for the most part) nor the Jews, even the most Greek of them, were pantheists. They all expected a continuing personal existence beyond death, not a uniting with the Eternal or a becoming part of the One. What "partaking of the divine nature" does mean for Greek and Jewish authors is to take part in the immortality and incorruption of God (or "the gods" in pagan Greek literature). One who has so participated will, like God, live in the immortal sphere and like him will not be tainted with any corruption. Certainly

Peter means at least this much. And if this is all that he means, then he is indicating what will happen at death (or the return of Christ). That is, the promises of God lead us on and direct our life until we obtain the inheritance of what they promise, the divine nature, at death.

This presentation of the goal of the Christian life contrasts with the lifestyle of the false teachers against whom 2 Peter is written. God's goal is that we set our eyes on his promises and head toward heaven, thereby escaping "the corruption in the world caused by evil desires." The false teachers, on the other hand, are involved in these evil desires. In fact, it is their lifestyle, not their doctrine, that shows them to be corrupt. Desire, of course, can be good. We desire food so as not to be hungry, for example. But desire needs to be controlled by God's goals and principles. When desire itself rules us, it is indeed evil (for it desires the bad as well as the good), and it leads us to corruption. Those whose goal is really the divine nature will not be turned aside or controlled by such evil desires.

It is possible that Peter means more than this. Paul, for example, speaks of the Holy Spirit being within Christians. Therefore the divine nature (a term Paul does not use, but could have) is within, giving life (Rom 8:11; compare 2 Cor 3:18). James (Jas 1:18) and John (Jn 3:5-6) speak of being born of God and therefore having something of God's nature. In fact, 1 John 3:9 describes new birth so literally that it says God's "sperm" (usually translated "seed," but the same word is used for the sperm or semen of a male) remains in the child of God. According to 1 John, because this or that person is born of God he or she does not sin. This is because the nature of the Father is in them.

What can we say, then, about this passage? The author boldly uses the terminology of Greek philosophy and culture and redefines it in a Christian sense. He points to the Christian's supply of all that is needed for a holy life in the divine power of Christ. He also points to the goal of the Christian life as a participation in the divine nature, at least at death, when—like Christ—the Christian will live immortally in the incorruptible heavenly realm. He may be indicating that this participation is an experience that the Holy Spirit mediates to Christians in the present life, although his language is not clear enough to be certain of this. In saying what he does, Peter actually says less than some of the other New Testament writers about the joining of human beings to God, even if his language is more striking. At the same time he clearly calls Christians to use the provision of Christ and fix their eyes on the promises of God so that they will in fact escape the corruption in the world and in the end receive the promised divine nature. It is this drawing on Christ's power and focus on the future, which includes allowing that future to determine present lifestyle, which is all the Christian need do to receive the glorious hope of participating in the nature of God.

1:10 Make Your Calling and Election Sure?

Because Christians take salvation seriously, we are often plagued with doubts about it. Even if the problem does not afflict us, most Christians have had friends who were fearful that their salvation might be in doubt. Therefore the exhortation to ethical duty in 2 Peter 1 is not in itself an issue, for similar exhortations occur throughout the New Testament. But what does the author mean in 2 Peter 1:10 in exhorting us to make our "calling and election sure"?

Does this mean that if we do not live the type of lifestyle that he is suggesting, we may not be elect? Does it mean that we might not be saved? Or does it mean that we might lose the salvation that we already have?

The passage is certainly calling for moral effort. The call for zeal in the phrase "be all the more eager" tips us off to that fact. If that were not enough, this verse comes right after another exhortation to moral living. In 2 Peter 1:5-7 we discover a chain of virtues that Christians are strongly encouraged (using a phrase similar to "be all the more eager") to develop. Developing them will make us effective and productive in our relationship to Christ, while the failure to develop them means that we are blind and have forgotten the cleansing from past sins that we have experienced. We are not surprised at this encouragement to moral effort, for the false teachers in 2 Peter are false precisely in that they are not living morally (false teaching in 2 Peter and in many other New Testament writings is false because it sets a wrong moral example, not just because it teaches wrong doctrine). They apparently claim to see, but in Peter's eyes they are blind.

To make one's "calling and election sure," then, is to guarantee or confirm or ratify (the term has those meanings in various contexts) the calling one has received. The calling, of course, is the calling to Christ referred to in 1 Peter 1:3. The ideas of calling and election are closely associated. Paul in Romans 8:30 puts election before calling, which is a logical order (God would decide and make a choice, or elect, before he called the person to Christ, or so it would seem to us), but other New Testament writers, including Paul himself, often pair the two concepts as virtual synonyms (see 1 Cor 1:26-27; 1 Pet 2:9; Rev 17:14). The point is that this word pair (and Peter is fond of word pairs) indicates God's action in bringing a person to Christ. This is what needs to be confirmed or ratified by the ethical obedience of the Christian. However, the author is not saying that moral effort can produce election to Christ's kingdom. The calling and election are first (the grace of God appears in 1 Pet 1:3), just as faith comes first in his list of virtues in 1 Peter 1:5. Everything else is to be a fruit of faith. What Peter does believe is that without moral living one will not enter the kingdom, which is precisely what Paul also believed (1 Cor 6:9-10; Gal 5:21).

Peter makes his point clear in the second half of the verse. To confirm one's calling is not to "stumble." This term can mean to sin, as in James 2:10, 3:2. But if this were all Peter had in mind, the sentence would be so obvious as to be meaningless: If you live ethically (do these things), you will not sin (fall). Therefore Peter is using the term as it is used in Romans 11:11, to "fall" in the sense of "come to grief" or "fall disastrously." In Jude 24 a related term refers to God's grace in keeping people from falling in this way, meaning "leaving the faith." The opposite of falling, then, is to "receive a rich welcome into the eternal kingdom of our Lord and Savior Jesus Christ" (2 Pet 1:11). In other words, the author pictures Christians on a journey begun with the calling and election of God. If they fall on the way, they will never reach the goal of the kingdom (salvation). But if they do not stumble, and instead develop the virtues he has already listed, they will in the end arrive at the kingdom and be warmly welcomed into it.

This teaching is important within the context of 2 Peter. As noted above, the false teachers in the church were not living according to Christian standards, yet they were claiming to be elect and on their way to Christ's kingdom. The author is denying this claim. While the whole New Testament witnesses to forgiveness of sin for all who repent, and acknowledges that Christians do sin from time to time, no author in the New Testament, whether Paul or James or Peter or John, believed that a person could be living in disregard of Christian standards and still be "saved" (or still inherit the kingdom). As Jesus said, a good tree bears good fruit (Mt 7:17). You cannot consistently get "unsaved" fruit from a "saved" tree.

The call in 2 Peter, then, is to move onward. There is no attempt to solve the question as to whether one can be "lost" after being "saved." Peter's concerns are much more practical. "Make sure that you are in fact saved!" That is, if you have experienced the call of God, you are to ratify it by your obedience to him, your moral submission. If you do this, there will be no doubt of your salvation nor of your eventual welcome into the kingdom. What about those who are concerned that they might not be truly elect? Their lifestyle of obedience to Christ, which flows from trust in him, should be convincing proof of their state of grace; if they lack this evidence, they would do well to repent and to make their "calling and election sure."

See also comment on HEBREWS 6:4-6; 10:26; PHILIPPIANS 3:10; 1 JOHN 3:6, 9.

1:19 The Word of the Prophets Made More Certain?

How can Scripture be "made more certain"? Is there some of Scripture that is not certain or is less certain? If it is not certain, or not fully certain, can Scripture be trusted? Even if it applies only to the Old Testament, the passage raises the question of how this scriptural author understands his Bible.

The teaching that 2 Peter sees to be at issue (and which therefore triggers this whole discussion) is the doctrine of the Second Coming of Christ (or the *parousia*),[1] "the power and coming of our Lord Jesus Christ" (2 Pet 1:16). This is precisely the doctrine denied by the false teachers (2 Pet 3:3-10), which may be the basis for their loose living (especially if it included a denial of final judgment). In 2 Peter 1 the author argues first that the apostles have in the transfiguration actually seen a foretaste of the return of Christ (2 Pet 1:16-18). At this point he brings in Scripture to strengthen his case.

The NIV translation that we have quoted (along with the RSV and NEB) appears to state that the eyewitness report of the apostles confirms and thus makes more certain what the Old Testament says about the Second Coming of Christ. But that probably is not the best translation of the text. The Greek idiom Peter uses normally meant "to have a firm hold on something." If that is the case, then we should translate it "We place very firm (or firmer) reliance on the prophetic word."[2] What Peter is saying, then, is that, yes, the apostolic eyewitness report is certain and reliable, but that Christians (including himself) place even more reliance on what the Scriptures say about the return of Christ.

That he is talking about Scripture when he speaks of "the word of the prophets" is virtually certain, for with one minor exception in the apostolic fathers, all other occurrences of this phrase refer to the Old Testament. For the early Christians the whole Old Testament was viewed as messianic prophecy, speaking about Christ, even if they normally used only certain passages. The concept that "the word of prophecy" equals the Old Testament is reinforced in the next verse, in which Peter discusses the origin of the "prophecy of Scripture." Unlike the false teachers who are presenting their own ideas, the Old Testament writers (while 2 Pet 3:15-

16 refers to Paul's writings, it is doubtful that the author thought of them as "prophecy" like the Old Testament) spoke from God. That is, they spoke God's ideas taught to them by the Holy Spirit.

Peter, then, is calling on his readers to hold on to Scripture and its meaning until "the day dawns and the morning star rises in your hearts." The morning star is Jesus (Rev 22:16) and the dawning of the day is his coming. The dawning is "in your hearts," for the context is speaking about revelation, not about government or judgment or other aspects of Christ's return. When Christ returns the full revelation of God will be revealed in the hearts of the believers. Until then they need to hold on to the confident expectation of his return on the basis of the apostolic witness and especially the word of Scripture. These, of course, are partial, "a light shining in a dark place," but they are accurate and true—they are light. The dawn will come and the full light of the sun will overwhelm the small light of the lamp, but it does this by giving more light, not by giving something other than light.

Thus, Peter is not implying that Scripture is at all uncertain. What he is saying is that there are two bases on which one can know that Jesus will return. The first is the apostolic witness of the transfiguration, when the glory of Christ was revealed in part. The second is the word of Scripture. More reliance is put on this second basis than on the first. Yet both are true. Therefore for Peter Scripture is the firmest basis on which to establish one's faith. Nothing more certain can be found until the presence of Christ himself at his Second Coming makes the limited light of Scripture unnecessary.

For Christians this is a helpful reminder. We are to value Scripture, depend on Scripture and support our faith through Scripture. Yet Scripture is not eternal nor what our faith is placed in (in contrast to the teaching of some of the rabbinic writings that the Law or Torah was before the world and was in fact the reason for the creation of the world). We worship our Lord and his Father, not Scripture. Scripture simply points us to them. It is a true light shining in the darkness. What we ultimately long for is not a fuller knowledge of the book, but the blazing brightness of the presence of the One of whom the book speaks and whom even now the book directs us to experience in our hearts.

---

[1]*Parousia* is the Greek word for "presence," translated "coming" in the NIV in 2 Peter 1:16, and it has become the technical term in New Testament scholarship for what Christians refer to as the Second Coming of Christ.

[2]See R. J. Bauckham, *Jude, 2 Peter,* Word Biblical Commentary (Waco, Tex.: Word, 1983), pp. 223-24.

2:1-22 Condemning Opponents?

See comment on GALATIANS 1:9.

2:10-11 Which Celestial Beings?

In 2 Peter the author is condemning false teachers, and specifically their pride and presumption. We would understand it if he then aimed some verses against their slandering angels in some way, but suddenly he refers to "celestial beings" that are not angels, for the angels are presented over against them in the very next clause. Who could these celestial beings be? Have we in fact entered some science-fiction world of dark monsters? Are these simply mythological, or a figment of Peter's imagination? And if they are real, what is their significance for Christians today?

The false teachers of 2 Peter were known for their immorality. The author says they will be condemned, for they "despise authority" or, better, "despise the authority of the Lord" (2 Pet 2:10). Not surprisingly, then, these people have nothing but contempt for other beings too.

The concept of celestial beings of one type or another has already been mentioned in 2 Peter. In 2 Peter 2:4 the author mentions the sinning angels of Genesis 6:1-4. Jude 6 refers to them as "the angels who did not keep their positions of authority." They are kept in prison, waiting for the final judgment, a picture we also see in 1 Peter 3:19-20. Now in the passage under consideration, Peter refers to "glorious ones" (a more literal translation than "celestial beings"). While some commentators believe that these are church leaders, the language appears too exalted for that. They could, of course, be good angels, but a natural reading of the passage shows a contrast between these "glorious ones" and the angels mentioned in the next clause. Also, the parallel passage in Jude 9 refers to the archangel Michael's dispute with Satan, which Peter has generalized into the behavior of angels in general over against that of evil angels (perhaps because he did not think his readers would know the story to which Jude refers). Therefore we conclude that by "glorious ones" or "celestial beings" Peter is referring to evil angelic beings of some description.

That such beings exist is clear elsewhere in the New Testament. Paul refers to "rule and authority, power and dominion" (Eph 1:21) and "thrones or powers or rulers or authorities" (Col 1:16). He also mentions that Christians fight against "the authorities, against the powers of this dark world and against the spiritual forces of evil in the heavenly realms" (Eph 6:12). Furthermore, Revelation 12 and Daniel 10 refer to battles among spiritual forces in the unseen world. In other words, there is plenty of evidence in the New Testament for the existence of evil celestial beings, in terms of either fallen angels or other types of celestial beings. Nowhere is this terminology explained to the church nor is detailed information about these realms offered (perhaps to prevent our entering into the speculation and fascination evident in some intertestamental Jewish writings), but it is everywhere assumed that they exist.

The false teachers 2 Peter opposes, then, speak disrespectfully, even slanderously, of such beings, even though they are far weaker than these spiritual beings. But the angels, who are more powerful than these beings (our author may be thinking of archangels, since an archangel is mentioned in Jude) would not make such an accusation against them before the Lord. The contrast shows the magnitude of the foolishness of the false teachers.

Why would they slander celestial beings? We do not know. Perhaps they had been warned that if they continued in their licentious ways they would fall under the power of such beings. (We do not call them demons, for we do not know if demons are the same as or different from such beings; they may be far more powerful than demons, who appear in the New Testament to attack or control single individuals and so may be low-level evil spiritual beings.) They may have scoffed at their existence or boasted of being able to control them. All such presumption is dangerous.

What does this mean for the church? The church is called to take the existence of an infernal hierarchy seriously. Spiritual powers do rule in this world. But the church is not called to spend time learning a lot about such powers or to speak against them, although the Lord could, of course, give a person a prophetic word to speak to that realm. Paul lists the means of spiritual warfare in Ephesians 6, and although they include prayer, they do not include direct confrontation with celestial beings. Unfortunately, in our fascination with such powers we may be tempted to speak against them (without a direct command of the Lord, but simply to try to demonstrate "our authority") or to live in fear of them. Peter expects them to be taken seriously, but the way they are taken seriously is by living a holy life free from the desires and pride to which they appear to be related (and which pastoral experience reveals to be the principal means by which they control a person). This means that the New Testament does take such celestial beings seriously, but wants Christians to focus on Christ, not on the dark powers. If Christians live in intimacy with and obedience to Christ (unlike these false teachers), then such beings can do nothing ultimate to them.[1]

[1]For further information on this area, see C. Peter Wagner and F. Douglas Pennoyer, eds., *Wrestling with Dark Angels* (Ventura, Calif.: Regal Books, 1990).

2:20 Worse Off at the End?

Christians recognize that before people know Christ they are in bad shape, for they live under the judgment of God, who has commanded all people everywhere to repent and believe the gospel. It is therefore not hard to see how Christ enables people to escape from the corruption of the world, since this corruption is tied up with their pre-Christian life. Nor do most of us lack for examples of people who have again been "entangled" in the world after they knew Christ; we may even know some who after initially turning to Christ have later totally rejected the gospel in word as well as in action (although most of our "backslidden" brothers and sisters would still confess to the truth of the gospel, even if it is playing no active role in their lives). Yet 2 Peter 2:20 does more than make these common (if sad) observations. It states that such people are "worse off" than before their initial conversion. How can this be the case? Aren't they still Christian even if they are backslidden? Will they not go to heaven despite their sinful life? And isn't this "better" than their original state? Isn't salvation by faith, not works? What 2 Peter says appears incompatible with our concept of a God of grace and mercy.

When we read this verse in context, we recognize that the people being discussed are the false teachers whom Peter opposes. They were once orthodox Christians who were "cleansed from [their] past sins" (2 Pet 1:9), or "washed" (2 Pet 2:22). They had come to know Jesus Christ, and this was a personal knowledge that released them from "the corruption of the world," or, in Pauline language, the power of sin over them had been broken. And they had come to know "the way of righteousness" (meaning a righteous lifestyle; 2 Pet 2:21). It is not that in some way they had been taught poorly or had not experienced the power of God freeing them from the world and its desires. They had experienced all of this. They were in every way righteous and orthodox.

But now they have done exactly what they are enticing others to do (2 Pet 2:18-19). They have claimed freedom, but their freedom is a freedom to live according to their desires. These desires have mastered them. They have rejected "the way of righteousness" or "the sacred command" (perhaps the teaching of Jesus or even the Old Testament standard of righteousness). They are back doing what they did before they were converted, but now they are claiming Christian justification for it.

Peter says that such people are worse off than before they were converted. He takes his words from the story in Matthew 12:45 and Luke 11:26 about the person cleansed from a demon who ends up in a worse state because the demon returns with seven others. The implication is that the person is in more bondage than before. Yet although verbally 2 Peter is closer to the statement about the demonized person, we are reminded even more of Luke 12:47-48, in which Jesus says that the person who does not know his master's will is beaten with few blows, while the one knowing it and still disobeying is beaten with many blows. Applied to the people in 2 Peter this indicates that the knowingly disobedient people he refers to will get a worse punishment than they would have received had they never been converted. They had been introduced to Jesus and experienced the power and freedom of his lordship, but now they have turned their backs on his teaching and are walking in willful disobedience.

This, then, is the state of the apostate, including the moral apostate who still tries to rationalize his or her sin with Christian theology. As Hebrews 10:26-27 says, "If we deliberately keep on sinning after we have received the knowledge of the truth, no sacrifice for sins is left, but only a fearful expectation of judgment and of raging fire that will consume the enemies of God." These people knew the truth and had been freed from their sin, coming under the rule of Christ. Now because of their web of rationalizations Christ is no longer Lord and they "deliberately keep on sinning." Peter has already told us of their end: "Blackest darkness is reserved for them" (2 Pet 2:17). God will still forgive them if they repent, but people who have rejected truth they once knew fully and have woven a fabric of doctrine to justify their sin will be most unlikely ever to repent. This letter, then, appears to be more aimed at those people the false teachers are beginning to deceive (see 2 Pet 2:18) than at the teachers themselves, for while the teachers are not beyond grace, they are certainly not listening to the ideas of the author.

The teaching of this passage (and of the New Testament in general), then, is that people are responsible for what they know. To reject truth one has once appropriated is far more serious than never to have known it. Furthermore, only those who follow the way of righteousness, who are really following Jesus as Lord and have therefore been freed from the corruption in the world, are on the way to the kingdom. To claim to be "saved" while living in sin is self-deception of the worst type. It not only blinds one to one's own state, but it may deceive those who were getting along well in the faith, dragging them back into the quicksand in which those living in sin are themselves trapped.

This verse, then, is not implying that righteous living saves a person, but that salvation means repenting from a sinful lifestyle, turning to Christ as Lord, and living under his kingship. Where the results of this process (such as a freedom from the power of sin) are lacking—even if they once were present—we have no right to think for a moment that such people are in the kingdom, especially if they show no grief for their sin and are not attempting to forsake it. Furthermore it is dangerous to imply that such people are headed to heaven (even if without "reward"), for it cheapens the grace of God and implies to others that they too can take the "low road" to heaven and get in without truly submitting their lives to Christ. Such an implication could effect the same result that the false teachers were trying to produce in Peter's day, that is, entice a believer who is in the process of escaping the "corruption in the world" back into the entrapment.

See also comment on HEBREWS 6:4-6; 10:26; 1 JOHN 5:16-17.

3:10, 12 The Earth Renewed or Destroyed?

See comment on REVELATION 21:1.

3:11-12 Speeding Up Its Coming?

It is surprising to read in 2 Peter 3:12 that the coming of the day of judgment can be speeded up. Can it be true that the behavior of Christians can speed up (or delay) the day of God? In what way can they do this? And what does this mean for the idea of the sovereignty of God? Does he not decide about the "times and seasons" without any input from us and our behavior?

The whole of 2 Peter 3 concerns the return of Christ. Two terms are used: "coming" (sometimes left untranslated as "parousia," 2 Pet 3:4) and "day" (2 Pet 3:10). The "day" here is the "day of God" rather than the usual "day of the Lord." "Day of God" also appears in Revelation 16:14. It probably appears here because "the day of the Lord" occurs three times in the previous verses and so a change in terminology is demanded by good style.[1]

This "day of God" will be marked by the destruction of "the heavens" by fire, including the melting of the "elements." We are not told exactly what will be the mechanism of this process, but it is clear that it is caused by the "day of God" and therefore not a natural catastrophe or something touched off by human carelessness. God will remove the old heaven and earth, says Revelation 21:1, preparing the way for a new heaven and new earth (which 2 Pet 3:13 mentions). Peter refers to this event not to scare Christians, but to remind them that everything done or built on this earth is temporal. Therefore living in radical obedience to God pays the only lasting dividends, and this "day" is the time when they will receive those rewards.

Christians are to "look forward to" or "watch expectantly for" this day. This means keeping it in their awareness, and living in the light of it. For the New Testament writers eschatology determined ethics. That is, what one believed about the return of Christ would determine how one lived. If people have the lively expectation that Peter wants them to have, then they would live a holy life, whatever the immediate consequences, for they would be so expectant of ultimate reward that temporal losses would make no difference.

Yet Christians are also to "speed" the coming of that day. Jesus himself told his followers to pray for that day, for the Lord's Prayer contains the line "Your kingdom come." Furthermore, the church prayed *"Marana tha"* (1 Cor 16:22), translated in Revelation 22:20 as "Come, Lord Jesus." But Peter probably is referring to something more than prayer. There was a strong Jewish tradition based on Isaiah 60:22 (which in the Septuagint uses the same word for "speed" used here) that the coming of Messiah was held back by the sins of the people and that repentance would hasten this day. Peter appears to agree with this. He has talked throughout the letter about holiness. In the verse immediately before this one he has exhorted the people to "holy and godly lives" (2 Pet 3:11), and two verses later he summarizes with "Make every effort to be found spotless, blameless and at peace with him" (2 Pet 3:14). Therefore what is said here is that the holiness of Christians both expresses their expectation of that day and hastens its coming.

If Christians have this much influence over the timing of the coming of Christ, what does that mean for God's sovereignty? Peter has already explained that. In 2 Peter 3:8-9 he stated that God is patient; time in our terms is not an issue to him. What is his issue is that he does not want "anyone to perish, but everyone to come to repentance." The special focus of this concern in 2 Peter is the Christian community, which is being polluted by sin. God is sovereign, and in his sovereignty he has determined to bring as many people to repentance and obedience as possible. (Peter does not explain what factors will make God call a final end to his efforts.) He has chosen to take human choices into account in setting the time of the return of Christ. What this means for Christians is that if they really desire the coming of the kingdom they had best get on with repentance and holy living so that they cooperate with God in preparing for the end.

Peter has taken our breath away. On the one hand, the vision of the earth that we know dissolving into a fireball along with all of the accomplishments and monuments of human culture shakes our security to the extent to which we are invested in this age. On the other hand, the idea that our lives, to the degree they are holy, may speed the coming of Christ and thus the whole timetable of the universe produces a sense of awesome humbling privilege. Peter hopes that together these images will prod Christians to that expectancy of Christ's return and the holy living that will in fact speed it along, for this is God's holy sovereign will.

---

[1]This is seen also in the use of "God" and "Lord": 2 Peter 3:3-7 uses "God," 2 Peter 3:8-10 uses "Lord," 2 Peter 3:11-13 uses "God," and 2 Peter 3:14-16 uses "Lord" first and then "God." There seems to be a deliberate switching back and forth between the synonymous terms.

1 JOHN

2:15 Love Either the World or the Father?

How can John say that we are not to love the world? Isn't John being too absolute in saying that if one loves the world, there is no love for God?

John uses the term *the world* six times in 1 John 2:15-17, but he also uses it seventeen more times in 1—3 John. The world in 1 John is not the planet, the people on it or the creation, but the human sphere in which we live. It is, then, the sum total of human culture and institutions, the collective living human community. This community is controlled by Satan (1 Jn 5:19; compare 1 Jn 4:4). It is therefore at root hostile to God and those who are committed to him (1 Jn 3:13). In fact, "the world" is where the false teachers go when they leave the church (1 Jn 4:1, 3, 5). This is different from the meaning of "the world" in John 3:16, where it refers to humanity. "The world" in 1 John focuses on this culture, which is at root hostile to God.

The Christian's relationship to such a world can hardly be a friendly one; they are to have a totally different orientation (Jn 17:15-18). To maintain this orientation they must have victory over the world, not in the sense that the world is conquered and becomes Christian, but in the sense that the world does not conquer them or force them back into its own lifestyle and way of thinking. Rather, Christians live within the world as Christ would (1 Jn 5:4-5; 4:17).

This makes it clear why a believer cannot love the world. To love is to be emotionally invested in something; in Scripture this investment includes caring for or serving the object of love. Those things which characterize the world are "the cravings of sinful man" or, better, "the desires of the body," "the lust [better, "desire"] of his eyes" and "the boasting of what he has and does." Obviously the Christian has bodily desires and also looks at things and desires them (the English words *cravings* and *lusts* are too strongly negative to carry John's meaning accurately), but the issue is whether the Christian is emotionally invested in these desires. Many people have only these desires to live for, but Christians have someone beyond the world to live for, namely Jesus. Thus although they experience the same desires they sort them out according to the principles and priorities seen in Jesus.

We cannot be totally emotionally invested in two contradictory directions. We choose either God and his values or the world and its values. If Jesus is truly Lord (and John has written extensively of obedience to Christ as being the essence of loving him), then it will be his values that will determine our emotional investments.

The natural human desire to be accepted and to "fit in" will not find these verses comfortable ones. The Christian will always live in tension with the world, suspicious of, if not rejecting, much of the product of human culture. The countercultural lifestyle of the Christian invites rejection, for living by different values suggests that the values of one's neighbors are inadequate. The tension is there. The pain is real. We cannot have it both ways. We cannot love both God and the world. At the same time God shows that he understands when John also writes, "You . . . are from God and have overcome them [those who are of the world], because the one who is in you [Jesus, through the Spirit] is greater than the one [Satan] who is in the world" (1 Jn 4:4).

See also comment on JAMES 4:4.

2:18-22 Who Is the Antichrist?

See comment on 2 THESSALONIANS 2:3.

2:27 What Is the Anointing?

What type of anointing is it that 1 John 2:27 claims the Christian receives? Is it anything like what was received in the Old Testament? Why does John then say that this means that "you do not need anyone to teach you"? How does an anointing teach us something? Can we now dispense with human teachers altogether?

This verse is a continuation of a thought first introduced in 1 John 2:20, "You have an anointing from the Holy One, and all of you know the truth." References to both anointing and knowing the truth appear in each of the two verses. In the Old Testament the anointing given kings and priests was with oil to consecrate them to ministry. There is clearly a consecration or initiation going on in this passage as well, but there is no mention of oil. By the time of Tertullian (A.D. 200) anointing with oil was practiced in the context of baptism, but there is no evidence that such a practice occurred as early as the New Testament period. In the New Testament oil is only connected with anointing the sick for healing (Mk 6:13; Jas 5:14-15). Yet the practice of the later church does give us a clue to the meaning here, for the oil meant the reception of the Spirit. Even in the Old Testament the anointing of kings (1 Sam 16:13) and prophets (Is 61:1) is connected with the Spirit coming upon them. Jesus at his baptism is said to be anointed with the Spirit (Acts 10:37-38; compare Acts 4:27; Heb 1:9), and in Luke 4:18 Jesus quotes, "The Spirit of the Sovereign LORD is on me, because the Lord has anointed me" (Is 61:1), which was the theme of his ministry. Jesus was never anointed with oil (other than perhaps the perfume poured over him at the end of his ministry in Bethany), but he was anointed with the Spirit, which came upon him at his baptism. It is quite appropriate (and probably a deliberate play on words) that Christians, who are followers of the Christ (which means Messiah, or "anointed one") should bear that same anointing (the root of "Christ" and "anointing" are the same in Greek).

Paul indicates that Christians have

been anointed with the Spirit when he says, "He anointed us, set his seal of ownership on us, and put his Spirit in our hearts as a deposit, guaranteeing what is to come" (2 Cor 1:21-22; the grammar indicates that this is one event, not several). The experience of the Spirit was a normative part of early Christian initiation. Paul explicitly denies the modern idea that one is not supposed to experience or feel anything at conversion when he argues that one knows if one is a Christian because of the presence of the Spirit within (Rom 8:9; see 1 Jn 3:24; 4:13). Acts also connects the reception of the Spirit to Christian initiation (Acts 2:38; 3:19; 8:15-17; 10:44-48; 19:5-6).

In the New Testament, then, baptism is normally associated with the experience of the Spirit, as are repentance from "dead works" and commitment to Christ. The four form a complex, but they are not interchangeable with each other. All need to be present for the complete initiatory experience. The data of Acts shows that at times the order of the events is different, and in some cases the various parts are separated by some time. But the assumption of the New Testament writers is that all four are present. Thus in 1 John 2:27 the anointing is something that has been received at a past point in time, the point of Christian initiation. However, John is not discussing baptism here, and therefore does not identify the anointing he is talking about with baptism.

John also does not identify the anointing with the Word, although he does not place Word and Spirit over against one another. In 1 John 2:24 we read, "See that what you have heard from the beginning remains in you. If it does, you also will remain in the Son and in the Father." The "what you have heard from the beginning" is the apostolic witness to Christ (1 Jn 1:1-3), which in the Gospel of John became Scripture. Those anointed are not the false teachers who have rejected this apostolic witness and left the orthodox Christian community, but precisely those who have accepted the witness, in which it remains. We see a similar continuity between the Spirit and Christ in John 14:26 and John 15:26. There is no conflict between the Spirit and the gospel tradition. Yet the two are not the same. The anointing is not "that which you have heard," but a complement to it, the Spirit within.

Those who have the Spirit (in whom it "remains," a continuing action), then, "do not need anyone to teach" them. This again parallels what we read in John 14:26 and John 15:26, not to mention the ongoing revelation of John 16:12-15. John has at least three reasons for writing this. First, the false teachers were probably claiming to have some secret knowledge into which they had been initiated and which the orthodox Christians did not have. Nonsense, says John, you yourself have the real, not the counterfeit. Unlike them you have Truth himself within.

Second, these people already have received the apostolic witness and remain in it, the anointing of the Spirit showing them that it is indeed true. There is no need for supplementary teaching, for they already have what is true. Third, the Spirit within will guide them into truth. While teachers may be helpful and an exhortation or teaching like 1 John useful, John trusts that the Spirit himself will be the real teacher, showing them the true and exposing the false, just as Paul trusts that the Spirit will lead Christians into righteous living (Gal 5:16, 18, 22-26) and James expects the "wisdom that comes from heaven" to bear the proper fruit (Jas 3:13-18). Christians who are listening to the Spirit should "smell a rat" when they see false versions of the faith or outright evil, and they should recognize the family likeness in that which is of God.

Unfortunately, Christians often do not listen to the Spirit, and when they do their perceptions can be warped, so the external guidelines of Scripture are always necessary. Furthermore, in the process of conversion the human teacher also instructs students in the truth, the apostolic witness, which they must accept and remain in to receive this anointing. Again John does not separate Word from Spirit or substitute one for the other, but he does recognize that the Spirit should be giving true discernment to the believer. Since he still has a place for the Word, John also has a place for human teachers, yet he recognizes that they may fall into error and it may be hard for Christians to sort out the true teacher from the impostor. It is the discernment taught by the Spirit that John believes will enable the believer who is committed to Christ to see correctly in this situation. The human remains important, but the divine Guide is the one in whom John places his ultimate confidence.

This passage is difficult, then, in two ways. First, it relies on our understanding the Jewish background of anointing so that we will connect it with the Spirit and Christian initiation. Second, it expects our experience of the Spirit to be real enough that we will understand that the Spirit himself does indeed teach us and lead us into truth. The challenge of the verse is to live in this experience, not in rejecting the role of the Word, for John never does that and in fact easily slips back and forth from Spirit to Word, but in so walking in obedience to the words of Christ in Scripture and the inner voice of the Spirit that we recognize immediately when the world tries to seduce us through that which claims to be Christian but is tainted in some way.

2:29 Everyone Who Does Right Is Born of God?

See comment on 3 JOHN 11.

3:9 No One Born of God Will Continue to Sin?

Most of use are quite conscious of sinning from time to time. Does this mean that we are not born of God? If we read three verses earlier, in 1 John 3:6 we find "No one who lives in him keeps on sinning. No one who continues to sin has either seen him or known him." This sounds even worse. Even stranger is the fact that in this very context the elder can write, "This then is how we know that we belong to the truth, and how we set our hearts at rest in his presence" (1 Jn 3:19). These passages are hardly likely to set our hearts at rest! Could they mean that if we sin after our conversion or baptism we are damned (as was thought by some in the period of the church fathers)? If not, what do these passages mean? How can we truly set our hearts at rest?

This passage, which includes the whole of 1 John 3:2-10, is quite difficult, and there have been a number of solutions suggested:

1. One group of commentators notes that the verbs for "sinning" in these verses are in the present tense, which in Greek is a continuous tense. The NIV stresses this continuous aspect by translating "keeps on sinning" and "continues to sin" and "go on sinning." The argument is that while true believers may sin on occasion (so 1 Jn 1:7-9), they will not habitually sin. The weakness of this position is that it depends on a grammatical subtlety which an interpreter cannot stress in other places in the New Testament where this tense is used. Furthermore, in 1 John 5:16 the same tense is used for a believer seen by a fellow believer "committing a sin." Here is a true believer who is doing the same

thing that is denied in 1 John 3:6, 9. Why doesn't the NIV translate consistently and so translate this passage "continuing to sin"?

2. Another group of commentators, noticing 1 John 5:16-17, suggests that "the elder" is thinking of two types of sin, a "sin that leads to death" and a "sin that does not lead to death." The true believer cannot sin a "sin that leads to death," but may sin the other type of sin. What these sins are is debated, some thinking that they are deliberate versus involuntary sins and others opting for other distinctions among sins (such as the difference between mortal and venial sins in the Roman Catholic tradition). Yet if this is what the elder means, why does he wait until 1 John 5:16 to mention this difference? His terms here appear rather absolute.

3. Still others suggest that John is pointing to an ideal or expressing a tension in the Christian life between the ability not to sin, expressed here, and the reality of sin, expressed in 1 John 1:7-9. That interpretation is also possible, yet does it adequately express the strength of the language used here?

4. Finally, there are commentators who suggest that this passage must be taken in the context of the whole of 1 John, which shows that John is arguing on two fronts. On the one hand, one group the elder opposes is arguing that they are beyond sin. He addresses them in 1 John 1:7-9. Another group is arguing that their sins do not matter, since they are enlightened within. He is addressing them here. The weakness of this position is that the author does not make any clear distinction between groups. He does not say, "Now addressing the other group," or make any similar transition.

How can we evaluate these positions? Any conclusion which we draw must be both exegetically and pastorally sound. On this basis, I believe that while none of the four solutions is impossible, it is the last of them which is the most likely.

The elder is addressing a church situation in which there are some people who hold that Jesus was not really incarnate, probably believing that he only seemed to be a human being. Such beliefs in their full-blown form (which happened in the second century) are the foundation of Gnosticism, a system of belief in which salvation is based in knowledge or enlightenment and in which the physical world is disparaged, while the spiritual world is held in honor.

With respect to sin there are two directions that Gnosticism took. One direction was to deny sin. On the basis of ascetic practices and inner enlightenment the Gnostics believed that they were beyond sin. Naturally such beliefs were underpinned by a good dose of denial. The author addresses such people in 1 John 1:7-9. Rather than think that we are beyond sin and deny that what we do is sinful, Christians should confess their sin and get it removed.

Another direction that Gnosticism took with respect to sin was to claim that sin was irrelevant. Sin was something done in the body, and the body, in their view, was (at best) simply the outside shell of a person. The real person was the spiritual being who through enlightenment was living in communion with God. So one's body might be sleeping with a prostitute, but one's spirit was not involved in the act. In this passage the elder is addressing such people in no uncertain terms.

Starting in 1 John 3:6 the author makes a series of contrasts: (1 Jn 3:6a) no one who lives in God sins, (1 Jn 3:6b) no one who sins knows God, (1 Jn 3:7) those who know God live righteously, (1 Jn 3:8) the one who sins belongs to the devil, (1 Jn 3:9) the one born of God cannot sin. Thus we have an A B A B A pattern, shifting back and forth between those who sin and those who do not sin. The person who is saying that it is fine to sin, since sins are only part of the body and thus irrelevant, is condemned in no uncertain terms.

So what is the elder saying? He is saying (1 Jn 3:6) that if believers remain in Christ (which the NIV translates "who lives in him"), which means to stay in intimate connection with Christ, they will not sin. Christ is not the one producing the carelessness about sin that could be seen in the semi-Gnostic opponents of the elder (we say semi-Gnostic or proto-Gnostic, because the full Gnostic systems did not develop until the second century). Far from it, the one who sins is showing that to that extent he or she does not know Christ. The next statement makes the point clear: it is the one who does right who is righteous, for that is what Christ is. If a person really knows Christ, they will live like him. On the other hand, sin shows a person's inheritance in the devil, so acceptance of sinful living shows where such people are from. It is these very works of the devil that Christ came to destroy.

Then the author makes it clear in the verse we started with that being born of God puts a new nature in a person and that new nature will not sin. John has already admitted that Christians do sin (1 Jn 1:7-9), but that sinning is not due to the new nature. The author draws from the Old Testament picture of God's putting a new "heart" into believers ("I will put my Spirit in you and move you to follow my decrees," Ezek 36:27). This was later picked up in intertestamental literature such as 1 Enoch 5:8 ("And then there shall be bestowed upon the elect wisdom, and they shall live and never again sin"; compare *Psalms of Solomon* 17:32; the *Rule of the Community* from the Dead Sea Scrolls, 1 QS 4:20-23; *Testament of Levi* 18:9). The elder, with a background in John 3, expresses this using a picture from typical first-century ideas about human procreation: the male's sperm (seed) determines what the child will be like. So God's spiritual "sperm" determines what his children will be like. Those born of God have a nonsinning nature. This is a far cry from the indifference to sin asserted by the opponents.

One way which a believer can see this difference practically is in the love of fellow Christians. The love of fellow Christians is what God has implanted in our heart, while neglect or hatred of fellow Christians shows that we are pseudo-Christians (not born of God, 1 Jn 3:10-18).

So how do believers set their hearts at rest? By noting the nature of God within them, giving them love for fellow Christians and leading them into other righteous deeds. Will "our hearts condemn us"? Yes, they will, for all people will sin from time to time. Yet the God who put his very nature in the believer is greater than "our hearts."

Is 1 John saying that a true Christian will never sin? No, for he has already admitted that true Christians do sin and will be liars if they deny this truth (1 Jn 1:7-9). What he is saying is that a true Christian has within him or her by virtue of their new birth a power not to sin. God within them is causing righteous living. He is not causing sin. In fact, the secret to not sinning is intimate fellowship with Christ, or "remaining in Christ," as John puts it. If a person does not experience this new life in them, if they can be indifferent to sin, then they are likely not born of God, as Paul also says (1 Cor 6:9-10; Gal 5:19-21). On the other hand, even if a person is struggling with temptation and at times falling prey to it—indeed because they are struggling and cannot be content with simply sinning—they can have the assurance that because they know the power of God within them impelling them away from sin and toward the love of their fellow believers, they are in fact one of his children and his new life in them will win out in the end.

Here, then, is the tension. We have the picture of a life totally free from sin which will be ours in the future. We have the reality of that new life already being within us. And we have the realization that that new life is not yet totally victorious, so that we must admit our sins, confess them, and appropriate that new life again each day.

See also comment on JOHN 5:28-29; ROMANS 6:2, 7; HEBREWS 10:14; 2 PETER 1:4.

4:2 Confessing Christ Come in the Flesh?

See comment on 2 JOHN 7.

4:7 Everyone Who Loves Has Been Born of God?

See comment on 3 JOHN 11.

5:6-8 By Water and Blood?

Christians have rightly written and sung about the blood of Jesus, for his atonement is central to the faith. But in 1 John 5:6-8 we discover that there is water as well as blood; we do not have songs about water. What does it mean to come by water and blood? Why are they placed alongside the Spirit as witnesses? And how do inanimate things bear witness?

Historically there have been three different types of answers to these questions. First, some of the church fathers linked the water and blood to the "blood and water" that came out of Jesus' side when he was pierced by a spear (Jn 19:34). Yet the essence of the cross was not that water flowed, but that blood was shed. In fact, no other New Testament text mentions water in connection with the cross. At the time of the spear-thrust Jesus was already dead; it only proved that he was in fact dead. Finally, the order of words in John 19 is different from that in John 5:6-8, which indicates that the author was not thinking of the Gospel passage when he wrote.

Second, others have seen a sacramental emphasis here. The blood stands for the Lord's Supper or Eucharist, the water for baptism, and the Spirit for the reception of the Spirit in Christian initiation. In that case part of the background would be John 3:5, being born of water (baptism) and the Spirit, and part would be John 6:53-56, the eating of the flesh and drinking of the blood of the Son of Man. This interpretation fits better with 1 John 5:8 than with 1 John 5:6, for the verb here indicates a completed act, not a repeating sacrament, while in 1 John 5:8 there is a present-time ongoing witnessing. Yet even there the order of the three terms is not the same as that in normal Christian initiation in which baptism (water) precedes both Eucharist (blood) and reception of the Spirit. Nor is the order the same as that in John 3:5. Finally, it would be unique to find the single term "blood" standing for the Eucharist. Even in John 6 both flesh and blood are mentioned. At the same time, since the Johannine writings are full of double meanings, it is quite possible that this is a secondary meaning implied by the author; namely, that in the Christian rites we reflect on the historical events in the life of Christ.

Third, and probably correctly, scholars have seen the water as standing for the baptism of Jesus and the blood for his death on the cross. The two events mark out respectively the beginning and end of his ministry. The context in 1 John argues that "Jesus is the Son of God" (1 Jn 5:5). What John is saying is that the human Jesus is in fact the divine, preexistent Son. This very Son is the one who had a real human existence marked by baptism and the cross. He is Jesus Christ; that is, both the human man and the divine Savior. This emphasis is reasonable in the face of the heresy John was refuting that denied that "Jesus Christ has come in the flesh" (1 Jn 4:2). He was really human, John states, for he was baptized, receiving the Spirit and entering upon a ministry open to all to see, and he died a real death marked by real blood. This whole life history of Jesus refutes the claims of the heretics.

How, then, do these inanimate elements bear witness? It is obvious that the Spirit is the central witness of the trio and the one most emphasized by John. His ongoing witness in the heart of the believers is clear throughout 1 John. The other two are historical events, but they stand as things that happened, a silent testimony to all who will accept their witness. To deny the reality of Jesus' humanity is to fly in the face of the historical data. They function as witnesses the same way that piles of stones and other inanimate objects could function in that way in the Old Testament (see Josh 22:27). Their importance is that the Spirit witnesses to something that is real—real historical events—not to something that happened only in the suprahistorical realm.

Readers of the Authorized or King James Version will notice that in the NIV and other modern translations 1 John 5:7 does not contain the three who "testify in heaven: the Father, the Word and the Holy Spirit." The reason for this omission is quite simple. The clause appears in late manuscripts of the Latin Vulgate, not in the early ones. And in the Greek manuscripts it does not appear before the sixteenth century. As a result, scholars universally conclude that the original text of 1 John lacked this statement, which was probably added by a pious scribe in the margin at some later time as a "Praise the Lord" and got copied into the text by a still later scribe (doubtless thinking that the first scribe was putting in the margin something that he had accidentally left out).

These verses, then, underline the importance of the real historical nature of the life and death of Jesus. Christians do not believe that salvation comes through actions that only took place in the realm of ideas or the spiritual world. Nor did Jesus come simply as a revealer of the truth, his deeds being incidental. Rather, Jesus came to do something as a real man in space and time and history. He lived a real life, accomplished a real ministry, and died a real death. The markers of the water of his baptism and the blood of his cross point to this reality. To this the Spirit bears witness. And, in a secondary sense, the celebration of the Christian sacraments point to this historical foundation.

5:14 Praying According to His Will?

All Christians believe in prayer, for the New Testament teaches us to pray; but some of the verses make us struggle with prayer. This is one of those verses. It forms part of the conclusion of 1 John and leads into a "health wish" (a standard part of the ending of Greek letters). It is not the place where we would expect radically new teaching on prayer, but a repetition of truths that the readers already know. Yet even what was a repetition for them may raise questions for us. What does it mean to ask "according to his will"? Does "he hears us" mean that he grants our request? If so, doesn't this fly in the face of the Christian experience of prayer? In other words, what is this "confidence" that John believes we should have? Is it something that makes sense in the light of the prayer experience of the church?

John has spoken of "confidence" three times before this in this letter. Twice it has to do with the return of Christ and the final judgment (1 Jn 2:28; 4:17). Once it has to do with prayer (1 Jn 3:21-22). In all three it is a confidence that we have before God; it is this relationship with God, not our relationship with the world, that is the issue.

The confidence here is that "if we ask anything according to his will, he hears us." John makes it plain in the next verse what "hears us" means: "We know that we have what we asked of him" (1 Jn 5:15). Therefore the hearing is not simply that God registers our request, that there is a heavenly "Ah, hum, I see; I heard that." Instead it is that God hears and answers the request, the same thing that the expression means in John's Gospel (Jn 9:31; 11:41-42).

This answered prayer is conditioned by "ask . . . according to his will." In the Johannine writings there are a series of conditions for prayer:

Passage	*Condition:*
John 14:13-14	Ask "in my [Jesus'] name"
John 15:7	Remain in Jesus/His words remain in you
John 15:16	Ask "in my [Jesus'] name"
John 16:23-27	Ask "in my [Jesus'] name"
1 John 3:21-22	We obey his [God's] commands
1 John 5:14	Ask according to his [God's] will

All of these conditions boil down to being in an intimate relationship with God/Jesus. To "remain in [Jesus]" or "ask in [his] name" is to be in such a relationship with him. To "obey his commands" or for "his words to remain in [us]" are expressions of this relationship as one lives in obedience to the declared will of God/Jesus. This, then, is what asking according to God's will means; it is to ask in submission to that will.

Such a condition does not surprise us, for in Matthew 6:10 we are taught to pray, "Your will be done." Yet what John is talking about is not a general prayer, for such general prayers get general answers. In fact, if the Lord's Prayer is an outline for prayer and not a prayer itself, it too is not expressing a general wish. Instead, John is talking about knowing and praying the specific will of God in a given instance. This is not always pleasant; nor does one come to know and submit to this will easily. Jesus in Gethsemane also prays, "Yet not what I will, but what you will" (Mk 14:36). He did not come to this submission without a struggle. He appears to have begun his prayer dreading what was coming and hoping that there might be a way in the will of God for it not to happen. In his struggle in those hours he apparently saw clearly that the Father had only one way, the cross. Therefore Jesus comes to the place of submission to that will. But it was not easy; it was not without groans and cries and sweat.

John, then, is suggesting to his readers a relationship with God in which they too will pray God's will back to him. It may be no easier for them than for Jesus, who, although he wrestled with bigger issues, did not have a background of sin and disobedience to fight against and had a more intimate relationship with the Father than believers experience. But the process is analogous. Believers live in obedience to God (having repented of sin); now they come in prayer, perhaps already knowing the divine will, but otherwise listening and praying until they know that they are in line with God. It is then that the confidence comes that this prayer will indeed be heard.

But why pray if one is only praying God's will back to him? Such a question, of course, tries to unravel the mystery of divine sovereignty and human responsibility. Yet without being able to solve that mystery, we can answer the real issue it poses. That answer is relatively straightforward. God in his sovereignty has chosen to work his will through human prayer. It appears to be his will not to do what he might like to do if human beings will not pray for it. On the one hand, this makes prayer a privilege. Christians are invited to work together with the Creator of the universe. He has chosen to make their freely willed prayers part of his plan. On the other hand, this gives prayer a security. If a believer does not correctly perceive the will of God, God is not bound to answer that prayer. We do not have to walk in fear that we will mess up the universe through ill-advised prayers.

This passage is often read as if it meant, "If we ask anything, according to his will he hears us." We do the asking, and then God decides if it is his will to hear us. This is not the relationship with God that John is presenting, for it is no confidence at all. Instead, he is presenting a relationship in which meditation on the words of Jesus (and obeying them as they are understood) and listening prayer are central.[1] Out of this struggle to hear and then, perhaps, to will that will oneself, the Christian prays. That prayer, says John, rising like incense to the Father (Rev 5:8), will certainly be heard, receiving whatever it is that is requested. This is not only the theory of John, but it is also the experience of the numerous people of prayer down the centuries who have taken the time to learn to pray in this manner.

[1]For more information on listening prayer, see Joyce Huggett, *The Joy of Listening to God* (Downers Grove, Ill.: InterVarsity Press, 1986).

5:16-17 A Sin That Leads to Death?

Is there a sin from which there is no recovery? There is certainly no problem with the concept that one should pray for a fellow Christian who sins. With John, Christians recognize that "all wrongdoing is sin" and that all of it separates individuals from God. Thus prayer and restorative counsel (Gal 6:1) appear to be in order when we observe a fellow believer who has sinned. Where John causes problems, however, is in mentioning "a sin that leads to death," for which prayer is not in order (not that it is necessarily wrong, but that it is useless). What type of sin is this? And what type of death is intended—physical or spiritual death? Since we ourselves fall into sin at times, the questions are of practical importance to each of us. This is no mere resolving an academic problem of Scripture.

This passage occurs at the end of 1 John, right after an encouragement to pray (1 Jn 5:13-15). According to John, it is because "we know that we have what we ask from him" that one should pray for the "brother" who sins. James has a similar structure in the conclusion of his letter. After talking about prayer for healing (Jas 5:13-16), he notes the encouragement to pray that Elijah's example gives (Jas 5:17-18) and then talks about turning a sinner from the error of his or her way and thus saving him or her from death (Jas 5:19-20), the purpose of his book. This structure of health wish plus purpose statement in the conclusion of a letter was typical of one form of Greek letters. Thus it is not surprising that in his conclusion John also has a modified health wish before reaching his final purpose statement (probably 1 Jn 5:20).

But what type of life and death is John talking about? This is a modern question; it was not one for John's readers, for the brevity of his reference assumes that they would know what he was talking about. We have to discover this from the rest of his letter. We note, then, that 1 John uses the term *life* thirteen times, seven of them in this chapter. Since he means spiritual life (eternal life) in every other case in which he uses the term, we would expect that this would also be the meaning here. Likewise the two other places where he uses *death* (both in 1 Jn 3:14) refer to spiritual death, not physical death. So even though in the New Testament sin can lead to physical death (1 Cor 11:30; compare Acts 5:1-11; 1 Cor 5:5) and physical sickness (Jas 5:15-16), it is unlikely that that is the meaning here. This is especially true in that in both his Gospel and epistle John sees physical death as something already transcended by the believer (Jn 8:51; 11:26; 1 Jn 3:14).

What, then, is the sin (not specific acts of sin, but a quality of sin) that leads to this spiritual death? In the Old Testament some sins carried the death penalty, while others did not (Num 18:22; Deut 22:26). In particular, deliberate or willful breaking of the commandments required death, while inadvertent sin did not (Lev 4:2, 13, 22, 27; 5:15, 17-18; Num 15:27-31; Deut 17:12). Both of these distinctions were common in first-century Jewish literature as well. While all of these Old Testament references are to the physical death of the offender, it would not be surprising for John to reinterpret the concept in terms of spiritual life and death, for that is his focus. In this he had help from Jesus, who referred to a category of sin that would not be forgiven (Mk 3:28 and parallels). What type of sin is this? For Jesus it was observing the activity of the Holy Spirit and calling it the devil's work. Similarly, John has been concerned with a group of apostates, people who were part of the Christian community and have left. What is their sin? They are continuing in (and therefore condoning) sin, they are hating and separating from their fellow Christians (thus not living out the command of love), they love the world and they even deny that Jesus has come "in the flesh" (probably a denial that Christ had a real human body). These are not casual errors or lapses into this or that sin, but a knowing and deliberate turning away from the truth they experienced in the Christian community. While they would probably still consider themselves Christians, John knows that their standards and their doctrines are quite different from those of his group.

Why, then, doesn't John say that one should pray for them? The answer is because such prayer is useless. It is not that it is absolutely wrong to pray. While John clearly does not intend Christians to pray for the forgiveness of such people, he words himself carefully so as not to forbid it. The issue is that these people are not repenting or about to repent. Like the people envisioned in Hebrews 6, they have known the truth and experienced the fullness of what God has, but have turned away. While God would surely forgive such people if they did repent, no argument will change their minds. They have left the true Christian community. They "know" they are right and John's group is wrong. Asking for their forgiveness is useless. Forgiveness comes to the repentant, not those willfully persisting in sin.

But that is not John's focus. His point is that Christians *should* pray for other members of the Christian community who sin. Why should they do this? First, God seems to prefer to grant forgiveness through confession to another and the other's praying (as in Jas 5:15-16). Psychologically this makes the repentance much more concrete and thus lasting. Second, sin is to be taken seriously. Today's slip, if persisted in, could turn into deception, and the brother or sister could slip farther and farther from God until they become part of the apostate group. The time to intervene is not when the person has become hardened in turning away from God, but when the first sin is observed. If one prays *then,* life will be granted and the individual will not slip further away from God.

John, then, is calling for two things that are often poorly practiced in the church today. The first is the taking of responsibility for the spiritual well-being of fellow Christians; that is, for observing errors (the point is that one "sees" the sin; it is observable), correcting the sinners (Gal 6:1-2) and praying for their forgiveness. The second is the taking of sin seriously, realizing that it can indeed lead to grave consequences if persisted in, and thus living in and calling others to live in a holy fear before God. John has no intention of our living in fear that we have sinned "the sin that leads to death," for the very fear is an indication of our repentance and thus that we have not sinned such a sin. John has every intention of calling us to lead lives open to each other so that we give and receive correction and thus not only keep each other from deliberate rebellion and its consequences, but also assist each other in walking in close fellowship with the God who is light (1 Jn 1:5).

See also comment on MARK 3:28-29; HEBREWS 6:4-6; 10:26.

2 JOHN

1 Who Is the Chosen Lady?

The little books of 2 and 3 John may well have served as cover letters to personalize the general letter 1 John. Whatever their purpose, they are addressed to individual people or groups. But what or who is this "lady" to whom 2 John is addressed? Why would the elder write such a letter to a lady? What was his relationship to her? Was she a real lady at all? And if this is a lady, what implications does that have for church leadership?

Three different views have been held on this topic. First, some of the earliest commentators on this text read the Greek as if "chosen" or "lady" were the personal names of the woman receiving the letter. In the first case her name would be Electa (as in Rom 16:13), and in the second Kyria (which would be the Greek equivalent of the Aramaic name Martha and does occur in Greek literature). But unfortunately there is no definite article with this Greek term, so it is unlikely that it is a proper name.

Second, another group of scholars have seen this as an honorable title for a certain woman leader in the church, although she remains anonymous (as does the author, who simply uses his title "the elder"). This would mean that a woman was serving at least as a house-church leader and possibly a city-church leader at the time 2 John was written. Such a situation is certainly possible, for women such as Phoebe (Rom 16:1-2), Euodia and Syntyche (Phil 4:2) probably served in such capacities. However, the decision on the meaning of the term (as well as that of "your chosen sister" in 2 John 13) depends on the context of this particular letter, not on historical possibility.

Third, and most likely, is the interpretation that the "lady" is a church. It is not that the second interpretation is impossible, but that the switch in Greek to the second person plural in 2 John 8, 10 and 12 (before returning to the second person singular in 2 John 13) appears to indicate that the elder has a group in mind, not an individual. Likewise the situation in 2 John 9-11 appears to fit best in a group of house churches, not with a single individual. In fact, 2 John 9-11 would be rather strong words to address to a person whom one "loves" and who has children "walking in the truth" (although not all the "children" are). Therefore, although it is possible to explain the plurals as references to the woman and her children, the letter fits better as a message to a church, which is in turn greeted by the church in which the elder is presently residing.

The background for this interpretation is clear. Jerusalem is often seen in both testaments as a mother (see Is 54:1-8; Gal 4:25; Rev 12:17; 21:2). Furthermore, the church is viewed as the bride of Christ (see 2 Cor 11:2; Eph 5:22-32). In fact, if she is his bride, the title here is especially apt, for she is certainly chosen in that she has heard and responded to the call of God, and she is therefore a "mistress" (the more archaic translation of the Greek term translated "lady"), which is the feminine form of "lord" ("lord" in Greek is *kyrios* and "lady" is *kyria*). She participates in the rule of her husband. As in the biblical passages in which a city's or a nation's citizens are her children (such as Mt 2:18 citing Jer 31:15), so the individual church members here are the children.

Why would the elder write so cryptically? One reason would be to bring out his theology of the church, making it meaningful by making it personal. Another reason would be to avoid naming names that would identify the church for Roman authorities. If this letter fell into the wrong hands it would look like a relatively innocent personal letter, while it was really a letter supporting a church. Even beyond its content, then, it gives us an example of supervisory support in the early church (when there were no offices of bishop or superintendent, which were later developments in the history of the church)[1] and of the warm mutual relationships among churches.

[1]Since none of the Johannine letters are "signed" except by the title "the elder," we do not really know who wrote them. Tradition has assigned them to the apostle John, but there are problems with this tradition and thus good reason to question whether any of the twelve apostles were associated with the Johannine literature. Thus this "elder" may well have had no formal office beyond that of "elder"—his supervision was informal, based upon his spiritual authority, not his formal position.

7 Who Are the Heretics?

We live in an age in which all sorts of people call themselves Christian, even if their continuity with historic Christianity is tenuous at best. This is not a new problem. All three of the Johannine letters deal with problems with schismatic groups, and in 1 and 2 John one of the characteristics of these groups is that they are heretical. But what are we to make of the heresy described in 2 John 7? In what way might a group call itself Christian and still "not acknowledge Jesus Christ as coming in the flesh"? Even the vast majority of our semi-Christian heresies acknowledge Jesus. What does it mean to "come in the flesh" anyway?

As I have noted, the Johannine community was struggling with heretical teaching. In 1 John 4:1 we read that "many" false prophets have left the church community for the world. In 2 John 4 we read that "some" of the Christians are walking in the truth, while in 2 John 7 we learn that there are "many deceivers." The impression is that the majority of the church is defecting and going "out into the world," probably to form their own groups based on their own doctrines.

The root of the heresy in both 1 John 4:2-3 and 2 John 7 is the denial of "Jesus Christ as coming in the flesh." There is a grammatical difference between the two passages that may indicate a shift in emphasis, but the root concept is the same in both. In Johannine terminology to confess something is not simply to agree that it is correct, but to acknowledge one's allegiance to it. So to confess Jesus Christ would be to state that one is committed to him as Lord. But why does John use the double title "Jesus Christ" and "in the flesh"?

This phrase in 2 John is designed to rule out christological heresy. Two types of heresy appeared in the second century, arising out of roots already apparent in the Johannine writings in the first century. The docetic heresy, on the one hand, argued that Jesus was not a real human being (not truly "in the flesh"), but only appeared to be human. He was truly Christ; the Christ was a spirit that appeared to materialize. Being a spirit, of course, he did not die on the cross, but in one way or another only appeared to suffer and die. (The term *docetic* comes from the Greek word meaning "to seem or appear.") The Cerinthian heresy, on the other hand, argued that Jesus was really a human being, but that at his baptism the Christ spirit came upon him, forsaking him at the crucifixion. Therefore the Christ did not die, although Jesus did. Although we do not know exactly what the heretics John is fighting believed (and some of them may have believed an early form of both of these heresies), the phrase in 2 John guards against both of them. According to John, a true Christian pledges allegiance to Jesus Christ, not just the Christ. And the believer acknowledges that this whole entity, "Jesus Christ," has come from God and is really human. The form of the phraseology in 1 John 4:2-3 stresses Jesus' having come from God and becoming truly incarnate. The form here in 2 John 7 stresses that Jesus remains incarnate and did not in some way "split apart" at death or the ascension. In John's view, an incarnate, truly human, truly divine Jesus Christ presently exists.

In 1 John 4 the heretics claim to be inspired by the Holy Spirit when they teach what they do about Jesus. This does not mean that they were under direct Spirit-control at the time of their speaking, but that they were claiming that this was what the Spirit had taught them. John says that one can tell the true Spirit of God by the doctrine he teaches. The true Spirit has the right doctrine; the spirit that does not lead people to pledge their allegiance to the orthodox Christ is in fact not the Holy Spirit, but the spirit of antichrist. This statement is not grounds for calling up spirits and trying to get them to speak through people and making them affirm or deny that Jesus Christ has come in the flesh, but it is grounds for examining the doctrine of the person who claims prophetic inspiration and seeing if it corresponds with the orthodox confession.

In 2 John we do not hear of the spirit-inspiration of the heretics, but they are themselves called deceivers and antichrist. It appears that they were trying to infiltrate the orthodox house churches and were actively recruiting people to their way of thinking. That is why they are deceivers and why the people need to "watch out" that they do not lose what they have in Christ (2 Jn 8).

The Christian church finds its unity not around this or that doctrine, but around Jesus Christ. To reject the real Jesus, either by denying his true humanity (being "in the flesh") or by denying his divinity (by denying that Jesus was really the Christ), is to break with the faith and to split from the church community. It is not that doctrine is the key issue, but that it expresses the distinguishing characteristics of the person to whom one is committed. The one not committed to the real Jesus Christ does not know either the Father or the Son, according to John. Unfortunately the church often has not kept this fact central. On the one hand, it has been willing to accept some who do deny its Lord, and, on the other hand, it has been willing to split over doctrinal differences that do not call into question real commitment to the true Jesus Christ. This letter reminds us of what is really central. It is Christ who unifies his church. Without him we have no unity. With him we have a unity that no human being dare try to destroy.

10 Do Not Practice Hospitality?

Schismatic or heretical teaching poses a big problem for any church. People begin to listen to the deceptive teaching and may soon end up slipping away to join the sectarian group. Yet 2 John 10 poses a problem for Scripture readers in that it appears to contradict an important Christian virtue, that of hospitality, not to mention the virtue of love. Is it love not to welcome a person into your house, even if you do not agree with his or her beliefs? Does not hospitality extend even to non-Christians, rather than just the Christians with whom we happen to agree? Furthermore, Christians struggle with knowing how far to take this verse. Does it mean that one may not invite inside the Jehovah's Witness (or the Mormon) who just knocked at the door? Does it mean that it was wrong to say a polite "good morning" to that person?

It is clear that 2 John is dealing with a serious problem in the church, not simply minor doctrinal differences or even significant differences over noncentral issues. A group of teachers who had left John's church did not "confess that Jesus Christ has come in the flesh." By this John probably means that these teachers argued that God was too holy to have become truly human, so Jesus only appeared to be a man. In fact, in one way or another his humanity was an illusion. This is a problem combated by the Gospel of John (Jn 1:14, "The Word became flesh," as well as many references to Jesus' emotions) and two of the three Johannine epistles. In other words, these heretics were denying a central part of the gospel rather than arguing over peripheral doctrines, important as some of these doctrines may be.

Second, we noted in a previous chapter that 2 John is addressed to a church (referred to as "the elect lady"). We need to understand what this church was like. It was normal until the mid-third century for Christians to meet in houses. (It was not until the mid-fourth century that house churches were outlawed and church buildings became the only legitimate place to gather as Christians.) Given the size of rooms in even a large house in those days (due to the limitations of building materials), it is unlikely that a house church would grow beyond about sixty people. In fact, there were many reasons to keep them smaller. Since most people had only their feet for transportation, several small groups conveniently located would be more accessible than a single large group. This also tended to make the churches take on the character of the neighborhood in which they were located. Furthermore, given that the meeting involved a meal (which developed into the symbolic meal presently celebrated in the Eucharist, or Lord's Supper), one would not want to crowd the room too much, for space was needed for tables and dishes of food. Finally, smaller groups enabled the church to attract less attention and thus avoid persecution as much as possible. Most house churches, then, probably served twenty to forty people.

Therefore we need to view the early church as a series of small house churches. While Paul, for example, might write a letter to the church in Rome or Corinth, that single church would in fact be made up of a group of such cells. For example, in Romans 16 Paul greets several house church leaders and their groups by name.

Third, hospitality was important to the early church. Christians would travel from place to place and need safe and wholesome places to stay. Some of these travelers were apostles, prophets or teachers. When such a person came to a church, they not only brought news of the situation of the church in other places, but they also brought a fresh stream of ministry. Lacking our easy access to books and other media, this was an important way for a congregation to increase its knowledge of the faith as it received insights and graces that initially had been given to another congregation and were now shared. We see the synagogue practice, which the early church copied, in Acts 13:15: "Brothers, if you have a message of encouragement for the people, please speak." Furthermore, the house-church services were relatively informal, so discussion and questions gave many people an opportunity to share their ideas.

Therefore what 2 John is referring to is the need to recognize that not every traveling Christian is to be received with such warmth. If in fact it was discovered that the visitor was carrying the serious christological heresy that John describes, the person was not to be greeted as a brother or sister in Christ (as would have been customary, often including in those days a kiss on both cheeks). Nor should the person be received into the house church and allowed to spread false teaching there. Otherwise the whole "cell" might become infected with the distorted ideas, and they might later spread them to other house churches, making the whole city church sick (or else splitting the church into two alternative structures, both of which claimed to be the true church).

This verse, then, is not intended to apply to individual Christians greeting people at the doors of their homes, but to churches and house groups. In such contexts it is wise for leaders to be assured of the orthodoxy of visitors before giving them a platform from which they can spread their views, even the platform of an official welcome as a visiting Christian leader. Christian hospitality stops where danger to the well-being of the church begins; love does not go to the extent of endangering one's fellow Christians nor of allowing those who deny the Lord one loves to peddle their wares in that Lord's church.

3 JOHN

7 Receiving No Help from Pagans?
Christianity, like first-century Judaism, is a missionary religion. In the first century, however, there were none of the organized societies and fundraising methods of our present age. The missionaries were assisted by voluntary giving from the people they met or else they were self-supporting, like Paul. But what does 3 John 7 mean in saying that the group of missionaries John is referring to received "no help from the pagans"? Is it that they did not accept any funds from non-Christians (the implication of the NIV translation), or is it that they did not accept any funds from Gentile Christians (one interpretation of the NASB and KJV translations)? And what implications does this practice have for our evangelistic methods today?

The Johannine letters mention two types of groups that "went out" from the Christian community. The first group is the heretics, who leave the church and go out into the world (2 John 7). The second group is the one mentioned here, which went out "for the sake of the Name." The Name is Jesus (Acts 5:41; Rom 1:5; Jas 2:7). They were "going out" on his behalf, probably as evangelists since they were among "Gentiles" or "pagans." The term "pagans" (more literally "nations" or "people-groups") could indicate a Jewish-Christian mission not willing to accept funds from Gentile Christians (perhaps to keep from being rejected by the Jews) and thus be translated "Gentiles" (as it often is in other contexts in the New Testament), but there is no other indication that the Johannine community was Jewish-Christian. Therefore the term is probably being used in the sense in which it is in Matthew 5:47, which distinguishes "brothers" from "pagans/Gentiles." In other words, it means "unbelievers."

Missionaries (this English term includes those called evangelists and apostles in the New Testament) had no regular means of support in the New Testament period. Paul notes that his mission was supported by the work of his own hands (Acts 18:1-4; 1 Thess 2:9). In rare cases he received funds from already established churches (Phil 4:14-19, which indicates that the Philippian church was alone in supporting him). Other missionaries (and at times perhaps Paul himself) may have had private family funds to draw on. But they held to the principle Jesus taught, "Freely you have received, freely give" (Mt 10:8). There was no fundraising, nor were collections received for the support of the missionary. While hospitality might be accepted from those who received the gospel (see Lk 10:5-7), Paul at times refused even this support (1 Cor 9:3-18).

What are the reasons for this behavior? First, of course, is the principle that the gospel is free. Even to appear to be charging for the gospel or to be making one's living by presenting it was viewed as contradicting this principle. Second, plenty of pagans were charging for their "gospels," such as Cynic and Stoic traveling philosopher-beggars (some of whom grew rich), and the devotees and priests of various cults. For example, a monument set up in Kefr-Haunar in Syria by a self-styled "slave" of the Syrian goddess boasts that when he went begging on behalf of his goddess "each journey brought in seventy bags" of money. For this reason Jesus forbade the taking of a "bag" (Mt 10:10), for then his disciples would not be able to carry anything with them when they left a town, making it obvious that they were not profiting by their mission. It is important not only to be honest, but also to appear to others to be honest.

Given this information, it is not difficult to understand what is going on in 3 John. These missionaries have left the security of their Christian community, not because they were uncomfortable there, but for the sake of their Lord. They are traveling through the area in which Gaius is located. The missionaries will need food (for they are not carrying anything with them) and a place to stay, perhaps even a short rest. To stop to earn money would detract from their travel. It is natural that Christians, especially Christian leaders, should provide them the needed hospitality along the way. John knows from experience that one of the major house-church leaders, Diotrephes, will not receive them because he is rejecting John's authority (which was spiritual authority, not "official" authority). Therefore John writes to Gaius, another house-church leader, requesting that he receive them, even though he may face rejection by Diotrephes because of it.

This has significant implications for Christian practice. This passage should not become an escape route for Christians who want an excuse not to support missions or their pastoral leadership. There is a clear principle that Christians should share material possessions with those giving them spiritual instruction (Rom 15:27; 1 Cor 9:11; Gal 6:6; 1 Tim 5:17-18). But, as we have seen, there is just as strong a principle that the gospel (including the healing and other ministries associated with it) should be free and that Christian workers, especially evangelistic ones, should not in any way appear to be profiting from those to whom they preach the gospel.

Given these facts and modern means of communication, it might be that the modern "Gaius" will wish to support evangelistic ministries even when they are at a distance from his home. It should at the least mean that the modern evangelist will want to do nothing that would make the unbeliever feel that the evangelist was trying to make his living from them. One would hope that an evangelist would rather pay his or her own way like Paul than give such an impression. Given the present scrutiny of the church and the feeling in the world that the church is out for money, other church workers as well should avoid even the hint that they are charging for ministry. Instead, church members should see to it that church workers are supported without their having to talk about money. Following such principles would not only be the application of 3 John's teaching to the modern era, but would also go a long way in avoiding the scandals that have accompanied the gospel in our present age.

11 Anyone Who Does Good Is from God?

Aren't there good people who make no claim to be Christians? For example, aren't there some Hindu individuals who do good? Have not kindness and even self-sacrifice been observed among many nations and religions? Are these people therefore from God? And what about the professing Christian who does evil? Have not Christians, for example, been convicted of crimes? Are they therefore not from God?

This particular verse is part of a whole series of Johannine statements, including 1 John 2:29 ("If you know that he is righteous, you know that everyone who does what is right has been born of him") and 1 John 4:7-8 ("Everyone who loves has been born of God and knows God. Whoever does not love does not know God, because God is love"). Each of these statements connects righteous living in some form (for example, love, doing good) to being a Christian (being born of God, being from God). Taken out of context any one of them would seem to imply that a person could deny Christ and yet qualify as being "from God." In fact, a guru who turned out to be genuinely caring and loving, but embraced Hindu theology, might on that basis find John endorsing his claim to be an incarnation of divinity! The key to this interpretive dilemma, however, is precisely the phrase "taken out of context," for within the context such a meaning is impossible.

In its proper context, the wider issue surrounding 3 John 7 is the behavior of Diotrephes. Diotrephes is a powerful church leader who may have the power to exclude Gaius and his house church from the wider Christian community if Gaius follows the elder's instructions and receives the traveling missionaries. The author is telling Gaius not to follow evil but good. The verse in question, then, suggests that Diotrephes is not from God or has not seen God, for he is doing evil, not good. This is an application of the principle that Jesus spoke concerning false prophets, "By their fruit you will recognize them" (Mt 7:16). If a person is truly a Christian, the proper lifestyle should be evident. If it is not, then, far from copying their behavior, one should doubt the reality of their new birth.

The same issue occurs in each of the other contexts. First John 2:29 begins a series of statements on righteousness (1 Jn 3:3, 6, 7, 9) that culminates in "This is how we know who the children of God are and who the children of the devil are: Anyone who does not do what is right is not a child of God; nor is anyone who does not love his brother" (1 Jn 3:10). The issue, then, is not whether those outside the church are or are not Christian (their status is known), but whether those *within* the church are truly born again. If people claim to believe orthodox theology and do not live righteously, John states, the regeneration of those people should be doubted, for their life shows that they are still a child of the devil.

The saying in 1 John 4:7-8 is in a similar context. This verse begins a series of sayings that culminates in 1 John 4:21, "Whoever loves God must also love his brother." The upshot of the discussion is that those claiming to love God and not loving their brothers are liars. They do not really love God. In other words, in each of these three cases the point of the saying is to distinguish genuine professing Christians from those who are not genuine. One way to do this is through looking at their behavior.

The author of the Johannine literature is quite clear. No one is born of God if that person is not committed to Jesus as Lord. That this commitment includes orthodox belief is clear in 2 John 9 and 1 John 2:22-23, 3:23, 4:3. But that the commitment includes living in obedience to Jesus is also clear. In fact, there are three tests of Christian faith in 1 John (and if 2 and 3 John are cover letters for 1 John, also implied in them). One is the experience of the Spirit. But how does one know it is the right Spirit a person is experiencing? The answer is, It must be the Spirit that leads one into commitment to Jesus as being the Christ and truly incarnate; in other words, right doctrine. But can one have right doctrine without being born again? Yes, one can. This is true. Therefore the third element comes in, which is a right character or a life that shows obedience to the Father and the Son. This fruit of the Spirit shows that the life of God is really within a person. To the extent to which any one of these three is missing, one should be uncertain about the reality of the new birth. Where all three are present, there should be no doubt but that one is truly a child of God. Therefore to isolate one of these elements and make it absolute (in this example, to isolate right character) is to violate the whole fabric of John's argument. It is not one element alone that proves that one is born of God, but three of them together.

Our verse, then, does not in any way argue that a non-Christian who shows the characteristics of Christian living is therefore born of God—such a person still lacks two of the three marks of a true child of God. What it does say is that those who claim to be Christians should be doubted, despite their orthodox theology, if they fail to live righteously.

See also comment on JOHN 5:28-29; 1 CORINTHIANS 6:9-10; HEBREWS 10:26; 2 PETER 1:10; 1 JOHN 3:9.

JUDE

3-16 Condemning Opponents?

See comment on GALATIANS 1:9.

7 Homosexuality Condemned?

See comment on ROMANS 1:27.

9, 14-15 Are the Pseudepigrapha Authoritative?

One can search the Old Testament from one end to the other and nowhere find a prophecy of Enoch. Likewise, the archangel Michael is mentioned in the Old Testament (Dan 10:13), but not in connection with Moses. Nor do we ever hear of a dispute with anybody about Moses' body. It is therefore obvious that Jude is using sources outside of the canonical Old Testament. What are these sources? Did Jude think of them as canonical? And what does Jude's use of them mean for our concept of the canon of Scripture?

The first question is easier to answer than the others. First, the reference to Michael is probably from a pseudepigraphal work known as the *Assumption of Moses* or the *Testament of Moses,* also used by Jude in verse 16. This first-century work is extant today, but the problem is that the ending, which should contain this passage, is missing. However, the church fathers agree that this was Jude's source, and a number of Jewish traditions that parallel it enable us to reconstruct the essence of this ending as follows: After the death of Moses the archangel Michael was sent to bury the body. Satan came and argued that Moses was not worthy of a decent burial, for he was a murderer, having killed an Egyptian and hidden him in the sand. Michael's response, "The LORD rebuke you" (a phrase from Zech 3:2), was here, as in Zechariah, a call for God's commanding word, which would assert his authority over Satan.

Second, the prophecy of Enoch is more easily identified, for it comes from *1 Enoch* 1:9. While 1 Enoch was probably not in its final form when Jude wrote his letter, it is clear from his citation that at least the first part of the book was finished. This first section also contains the tradition of the imprisonment of the "sons of God" (called "Watchers" in *1 Enoch*) from Genesis 6:1-4, which is referred to in Jude 6; 2 Peter 2:4, 9; and 1 Peter 3:19-20 (see also comment on Gen 6:1-4). It appears that these stories were favorites in the churches that 1 and 2 Peter and Jude represent.

The other questions are difficult because we find these few references to pseudepigraphal works in such short biblical books. Clearly Jude parallels the prophecy of Enoch with the words of the apostles (Jude 17); likewise the story of Michael and Satan is not differentiated from the biblical stories he cites in Jude 11. Jude (and probably 2 Peter, which refers to both of these topics but does not use direct references) obviously considers these stories true and authoritative. In fact, in labeling the 1 Enoch reference "prophecy," Jude appears to recognize it as divinely inspired, for he certainly would not cite a prophecy that he believed was not from God. This much is clear.

But did Jude recognize the books these stories come from as canonical, or did he just cite the stories themselves as authoritative? That question is impossible to answer. We have no evidence that anyone in the New Testament period, Jew or Christian, wanted to include these works within the Old Testament collection used in the synagogue (or church), although the Apocrypha was bound into biblical codices as early as the fourth century.[1] But the issue of what should or should not be in the canon of Scripture was not being asked in the church at the time Jude was writing. Even the Jewish debates about canon between A.D. 70 and 90 were not over issues that we would consider central to the canonical debate. This, of course, is the reason that Jude can make these citations so casually. He did not have to deal with our post-Reformation questions of canon.

What we can say is that Jude did consider the Old Testament authoritative. He also considered authoritative at least two pseudepigraphal writings and the tradition of the apostles (in whatever form he had it, written or oral). Even though he uses only two brief citations from these works, his failure to differentiate them from the Scripture he does cite indicates that in his mind there was probably no distinction to be made. Nor does he inform us that only these two passages are to be trusted, and the rest of the books rejected. However, all of this information we gain by "reading between the lines" in Jude. He does not say anything directly about the issue. While the later church did not believe that any of the pseudepigrapha were inspired Scripture, it did accept Jude with its use of them. In other words, it did not endorse whatever views Jude may have had about the works from which he took these citations, but it did endorse the explicit teaching in his letter.

This is not a clean and neat answer to our question, but no such answer is possible. First-century Jews used the Old Testament, but alongside it various Jewish groups read and valued a number of types of supplementary literature, ranging from the Apocrypha to the Dead Sea Scrolls to the pseudepigrapha. Early Christians likewise valued the Old Testament and gradually acquired collections of gospels and letters as they were produced and gathered. But they also read many of the works in the Apocrypha and other Christian literature such as the *Epistle of Barnabas* and the *Shepherd of Hermas,* binding many of these works into their Bibles as such codices began to replace scrolls. The situation was relatively fluid and imprecise. Only as the challenge of heresy forced the church to decide which books should be read in church and which should not were the lines begun to be drawn more clearly. Jude was written long before this time. It is therefore wrong to expect in him the precision of the later distinctions. It is also wrong to look at his casual use of what was being read in his church and assume that he meant to equate these works with Scripture in the sense that we use the term. Rather, we need to accept him on his own terms, but also to accept that the Holy Spirit through the church has given God's people increasingly clear direction about what bears his full imprimatur and what does not.

Finally, this brings us to an issue in biblical interpretation. What is considered authoritative or inspired in a biblical author is what they intended to communicate or teach, as that can be determined from the text. Often we can discover information that the author accidentally gives us about what he believed, the social class he came from, or the way his church assembled. While this is interesting information and may give us background that helps us understand what the author means by what he does intend to communicate, it is not in itself inspired. It may form a historical precedent for how a church or person might live or might believe, but it is not normative. If Jude accidentally reveals that he saw 1 Enoch on a par with Scripture, that is interesting, but since it is certainly not in the least his intention to give us that information (in fact, he was totally unaware it would even interest us), it does not form part of the teaching of Scripture. The same can be said about the meeting of churches in houses in Acts or the indication in 1 Corinthians 15:52 that Paul at that time believed he would be alive when Christ returned. As interesting as this is, it should not form the topic for a sermon or the basis for a doctrine. It does provide information about the history of the early church and examples of what might be legitimate today, but it is not normative. Once we master this distinction, we will realize that the incredible wealth of information that can be gathered from Scripture (which makes it come to life as we see the writers as real people in a real culture) must not obscure the message from God that these men wished to communicate to their generation and that we believe is still a message for us today.[2]

[1]The Apocrypha are the books and additions to books written during the intertestamental period that are found in the Roman Catholic canon but considered at best semicanonical in Protestant traditions. The pseudepigrapha are Jewish works, mostly from the period of 100 B.C. to A.D. 100, which no modern Christian group has included in their canon. Examples of Apocrypha include 1 and 2 Maccabees, Tobit, Judith, Wisdom of Solomon and Sirach, while *1 Enoch, Assumption of Moses, Testaments of the Twelve Patriarchs* and *Jubilees* are examples of pseudepigrapha.

[2]For more information on this distinction, see Gordon D. Fee and Douglas Stuart, *How to Read the Bible for All Its Worth* (Grand Rapids, Mich.: Zondervan, 1982), especially chapter six.

24 Possibility of Falling?

See comment on HEBREWS 6:4-6; 10:26; 12:15; 2 PETER 1:10.

REVELATION

2:6 Who Were the Nicolaitans?

See comment on REVELATION 2:15.

2:13 Where Does Satan Live?

This verse seems a little strange, for it mentions that Satan had his "throne" in the city of Pergamum in Asia Minor. We are accustomed to thinking about Satan as traveling everywhere in the world (Job 1:7; 2:2); is there really a locality in which Satan himself lives? Does he have an actual throne? And is it visible? Should this affect our own decisions on our place of residence? How did the church in Pergamum experience what John is writing about?

On the one hand, it is clear that Satan, as a finite being, must have a localized existence. Unlike God, he is not omnipresent, so he must be somewhere (and not be everywhere) at any given point in time. But Satan is also a spiritual being, probably the one identified in Ephesians 2:2 as the "ruler of the kingdom of the air." This means that he does not appear to be physically localized in our material sense, but rather lives in the spiritual world (or heavenlies) through which he has access to the physical world. Although we do not fully understand the relationship of the spiritual to the physical, we would be surprised to discover that Satan had limited himself to a specific physical locality by setting up his throne in a given city. Indeed, what we find elsewhere in Revelation is that when he rules on earth he does so through a human being whom he controls (see Rev 13:2).

On the other hand, Pergamum is a place known to us from history. It was an independent city until 133 B.C., when its last king willed it to Rome. It thereafter became the capital city of Roman Asia, the seat of the proconsul who as the senatorial governor of the province had an almost unlimited power for the period of his office. By 29 B.C. the city had become the center of the imperial cult with a temple erected to "the divine Augustus and the goddess Roma." The city also had a great temple to Zeus Soter (Savior Zeus), and its citizens worshiped the serpent god Asclepius, who was the god of healing. This history gives a rich background for identifying the city with Satan.[1]

Any of the images we have mentioned would have served Satan well. Asclepius as a serpent (found on the coat of arms of the city and used as a symbol of medicine today) would remind one of Satan as the serpent and dragon in Revelation. The altar of Zeus was said to have been thronelike, the temple dominating the city. He was, after all, the king of the Greek gods. But the central image in this passage appears to have been that of Roman rule.

The key to this identification is the reference to Antipas, a Christian martyr. Given that the proconsul did have the power to put people to death, this probably indicates official persecution (although it may have been localized). Where else but at the center of imperial rule would the church be more likely to come into direct conflict with Rome? Imperial rule was not separated from imperial cult. While educated people did not take the cult seriously—they looked on it as a patriotic ceremony, much as pledging allegiance to the flag is seen in the U.S.A. today—the church saw in it a clash between the call of Christians to worship God alone and the demand of the state to have one's ultimate allegiance. What is more, the state always kept a watchful eye on unsanctioned societies. The growth of the Christian community and its influence in the lower classes, especially among slaves (who had been known to revolt in Rome itself), was threatening. Here was a group who called Jesus, not Caesar, Lord, a group that could not be controlled. The clash was inevitable. Antipas had been martyred. And in the aftermath of his martyrdom the church must have lived in fear, for they were located in the very seat of Roman power and could hardly escape the notice of Rome.

This throne of Caesar, then, is the throne of Satan. Satan is not identified with Rome totally; he is independent of all of his tools. But in Revelation 13 it is Roman rulers through whom Satan works, and Roman power is in this sense the throne of Satan. It is the means through which Satan rules and controls that area, in this case Asia Minor. It is therefore also the means through which he persecutes the church of God.

The relevance of this passage to Christians today is obvious. While there may not be any recent martyrs in some Christian localities, many, if not most, Christians live under governments that claim absolute allegiance ("My country, right or wrong"). John reminds us that all such claims fly in the face of absolute obedience to Christ. They are satanic in origin. To the extent that the country decides to enforce its claim, either ceremonially or in action, a clash with a faithful church is inevitable. The closer one is to the center of government, the more certain the clash and the more inescapable the consequences. As Satan's throne appears behind whatever the architectural façade of our capital may be, the Christian will be forced to decide whom he or she serves. John lets us know that the decision is difficult, but he is encouraging us to be faithful, even if it means following in the footsteps of Antipas.[2]

A secondary application is also probable. Paul speaks eight times of "principalities and powers," which are part of the demonic hierarchy of Satan's kingdom (see Eph 6:12). Some such forces are on occasion identified with a particular people or land (see Dan 10:13). Thus, some demonic spirits appear to be localized, an idea that is confirmed by the experience of many Christian workers.[3] This means that some areas may be more directly under the control of such powerful beings than are others, or that the being that controls a given area may himself be more powerful than the one controlling another area.

Paul lists various articles of armor with which Christians are armed for battle with such beings (Eph 6:13-18). He does not mention direct prayer against them (such as "binding them" or "casting them out"), but rather exemplary Christian faith and conduct, such as the conduct that probably got Antipas in trouble and the faith that sustained him through his martyrdom.[4]

If this analysis is accurate, then some Christians should recognize that they live in very difficult territory. Such a recognition is not a call to move, but an acknowledgment that the situation they face is tougher than normal and therefore the virtues they must arm themselves with are more than normal. At the same time, this verse reminds us that Christ is in total control of these powers. Even our martyrdom is under his control. Although our area of the battle may be tough, there is no danger of losing. The important thing is that we, like the believers in Pergamum, hold out and remain faithful, even in the face of death itself.

---

[1]A. Deissmann, *Light from the Ancient East* (Grand Rapids, Mich.: Baker Book House, 1978), p. 109.

[2]An encouragement in this direction is found in John White's excellent *Magnificent Obsession* (Downers Grove, Ill.: InterVarsity Press, 1990).

[3]See C. Peter Wagner, "Territorial Spirits," in C. Peter Wagner and F. Douglas Pennoyer, eds., *Wrestling with Dark Angels* (Ventura, Calif.: Regal Books, 1990), pp. 73-100, for one description of this phenomenon.

[4]This does not imply that Christians are never called upon to pray directly against such beings, but that such activity is not their normal occupation; it should be engaged in only at the direct command of God.

2:15 Who Were the Nicolaitans?

Revelation has many strange symbols and images, but there are also unusual names. In Revelation 2:6, 15, the unfamiliar name blocks understanding. Here in two verses in letters written to two different churches (Ephesus and Pergamum) we discover the Nicolaitans. Presumably the author believed that the readers of the letters would know who they were, but we are not in their position. What were their practices, and why would God hate them?

The earliest identification of the Nicolaitans, found in the church fathers, was as followers of Nicolas of Antioch, a proselyte to Judaism, who was one of the Seven (Acts 6:5). Unfortunately, none of the writers seems to know much about the heresy, and one, in fact, argues that Nicolas himself was orthodox but had been misunderstood. While it is possible that some of this information is accurate (there have been Spirit-filled church leaders who have lapsed into heresy), this looks like an attempt to find some name in Scripture to use to identify this sect. Nicolas may have simply had the misfortune of bearing the wrong name. Still, even if the Nicolas of Acts had nothing to do with the movement, it is probable that some Nicolas was the leader of the group (after all, Nicolas was a reasonably common name).

A second identification common in some theological circles is to look at the Greek etymology of "Nicolaitan" (*nikan* and *laos* meaning respectively "conquer" and "people") and argue that this was a group that suppressed the laity in favor of the developing clergy. However, this explanation is determined more by modern concepts of clergy and laity than by any first-century information, for such terminology (such as the use of *laos* for only a section of the church) was unknown this early. Etymology is a notoriously dangerous way to discover the meaning of a term. Furthermore, there is nothing in the text to support this meaning.

The clue to the real meaning of this term is found in the identification of the

Nicolaitans with "the teaching of Balaam" in Revelation 2:14-15. Not only is it possible that "Nikolaitan" is a Greek form of "Balaam" (as understood by the rabbis), but, more important, this interpretation fits both the text and the first-century situation.

John identifies the teaching of Balaam with two problems: "eating food sacrificed to idols" and "sexual immorality." The early church constantly struggled with compromises with paganism, as we see in Paul's long discussion in 1 Corinthians 8—10, as well as in the conclusions reached in Acts 15:20, 29. Both of these center on food offered to idols, Paul's conclusion being that one could eat such food if purchased in the marketplace, but one should not go to a meal in a pagan temple. Following this Pauline rule, however, would cut one off from membership in trade guilds, patriotic celebrations (including ceremonies honoring the emperor, considered essential to good citizenship, although not taken seriously by the upper classes as religious events) and many family celebrations. We can easily see the pressure to rationalize and thereby develop a compromise.

The issue of sexual immorality is more difficult, for it is also mentioned in Revelation 2:20, 22, in the case of Jezebel (an Old Testament code word for a New Testament woman leader of the church in Thyatira, indicating her spirit and God's evaluation, rather than the woman's actual name). On the one hand, sexual immorality was a problem in the early church, as Paul's discussions show (1 Cor 5:1; 6:12-20; compare Heb 13:4). In the middle of a pagan society that accepted the use of prostitutes (although wives were expected to remain faithful), it was difficult to remain obedient on this point and relatively easy to compromise. On the other hand, "sexual immorality" was used in the Old Testament for involvement with pagan deities. For example, the Old Testament Jezebel was not to our knowledge physically immoral—she was likely faithful to Ahab all her life—but she did lead Israel into Baal worship. Since Israel was God's "bride," such involvement with other gods was called "adultery" or "sexual immorality."

Furthermore, the line between the two meanings of "immorality" was difficult to draw. Sexual immorality was involved in the Peor incident (connected to Balaam, Num 25:1-18), but the biggest issue was that the women were Moabites or Midianites, pagan women, and they led the men to eat feasts associated with their gods and then to worship the gods themselves. In other words, the sexual immorality was wrong because it was associated with the worship of other gods, a commonplace in the pagan world in which many temples had prostitutes in them through whom a man could become "joined" to the god.

If, then, John is taking the Old Testament examples as the basis for his discussion, the sexual immorality is figurative, standing for their worship of other deities, which was implied in their attending feasts in idol temples. If, on the other hand, he is using the Old Testament examples loosely, he may be indicating two related problems, attending feasts in idol temples and engaging in extramarital sexual intercourse, probably with prostitutes. The difference between the two explanations is narrow. Both types of problems are condemned elsewhere in the New Testament, however one may interpret this particular passage.

The Nicolaitans, then, appear to be a group that corrupted God's people by suggesting compromise with the culture of the day. Rather than worship God and him alone, they suggested that it was appropriate to engage in patriotic ceremonies (such as feasts associated with the worship of the emperor) and other cultural institutions (for example, trade guilds, something like our modern unions or professional associations, and their worship). It is possible that either as part of these ceremonies or as a separate area of compromise they also permitted the use of prostitutes (perhaps as an accepted part of the "business ethic" of their day). Jesus (who is speaking through John) was not impressed. In fact, he threatened judgment on the church.

While the exact issues are different, similar compromises face the church today. Each society has its own "idols" that it expects all its citizens to worship, whether those idols be the government itself or some values or practices of the society. These "idols" are the places at which the values of the society conflict with total allegiance to Christ. Furthermore, the Nicolaitans are still with us under a variety of names, for there are always people who in the name of being "realistic" or under any number of other theological justifications counsel compromise with the dominant culture. This passage warns us that Jesus will not "buy" these justifications. He demands nothing less than total loyalty to his own person and directions. Anything less than this will put those who compromise in danger of his judgment.

6:10 A Call for Revenge?

See comment on PSALMS 137:8-9; 139:20.

7:4 Who Are the 144,000?

The doorbell rings on a Saturday morning and two people stand on the porch offering literature about the return of Christ. If questioned, they might reveal that they are Jehovah's Witnesses. Their motives for their door-to-door activity are not simply to gain converts for the movement, but rather to gain merit for themselves through their exemplary zeal. Their hope (faint though it may be, given the number of Witnesses worldwide) might be to become one of the 144,000 who will reign with Christ. While there are certainly a number of more important places at which orthodox Christians would take issue with these Witnesses in terms of doctrine, what they say about the 144,000 remains troubling, not because it is believed, but because we ourselves do not know what this number means.

The problem with the number is that it is clearly symbolic, but the question is, Symbolic of what? Three major scholarly options have been given. The first is that this figure is symbolic of a group of Jews whom God will redeem at the end of the age. The second is that this is symbolic of a group of martyrs whom God preserves for martyrdom. The third is that this number is symbolic of the whole of the church, which God will protect through the tribulation at the end of the age. Only an examination of the data will show which of these is most likely to be correct.

John's picture draws on two Old Testament images. The first is that of Passover (Ex 12:12-13), during which the blood on the doorposts of the Hebrews' homes was a sign protecting them from the judgment that the Egyptians were receiving. The significant elements in Exodus are that the world around the Hebrews was experiencing judgment and a God-given sign protected the people of God from this judgment. The second Old Testament image is that of Ezekiel's man with an ink horn (Ezek 9). Again, the context is one of judgment. Again the people true to God are marked to be spared. In this case "a man clothed with linen who had a writing kit at his side" goes through the city and marks a Hebrew *tāw,* which in those days was an × or a +, on the forehead of each person faithful to God.

There may also be a New Testament background for John's picture. In 2 Corinthians 1:22, Ephesians 1:13 and Ephesians 4:30, Paul writes that Christians are sealed with the Holy Spirit. While the Spirit is not said to protect believers from anything, the image is one of security. Likewise, "the Lord knows those who are his" stands as a seal in 2 Timothy 2:19. While there is no evidence that John had read any of these books, the fact that Paul used sealing language implies that it was used around the church before John wrote.

In the picture in Revelation 7 the judgment of God announced in Revelation 6 is held back until the sealing is complete. The sealed are identified as "the servants of our God." The image is that of Ezekiel, both in the placement of the seal on the forehead and in the idea of only a remnant (in Ezekiel a remnant of Israel) being sealed from the judgment. This theme is picked up again in Revelation 9:4 in the fifth of the trumpet judgments, in which the "locusts" are to hurt only those "who did not have the seal of God on their foreheads." The sealed are protected in the midst of judgment all around them.

In Revelation 14 the 144,000 are "the 144,000 who had been redeemed from the earth." They are described as celibate virgins, which in Revelation means that they have not been seduced by the forces of evil nor made a compromise with idolatry. They are also totally truthful. "They were purchased from among men and offered as firstfruits to God and the Lamb" (Rev 14:4). The firstfuit picture appears in James 1:18 for all Christians in relation to the world and in Romans 11:16 for Gentile believers in relation to the full repentance of Israel.

Who are these 144,000, then? The theory that they are the martyrs of the last days is attractive, but in the end unconvincing because nothing is said in these passages of their being martyrs. Instead it appears that *all* of the "servants of God" are sealed. These "servants" are part of a larger group that is not serving God. That many of these folk might become martyrs is reasonable, given the persecution described in Revelation 13, but John says nothing to make us think that they are exclusively martyrs.

The theory that they are the Jewish believers of the end time is also attractive since the tribes of Israel are named. However, there are also problems here. Both the order of the tribal list and the names included are unusual. For example, both Manasseh and his father, Joseph, are included (Joseph apparently standing for Ephraim). Dan is missing, although he is present in Ezekiel's end-time list (Ezek 48). Thus John appears to indicate that the list stands for something other than any known form of Israel. Yet another problem is that most of "Israel" is not saved (that is, is not in the 144,000), while Paul's expectation (Rom 11:26) is that "all Israel will be saved." If both John and Paul have versions of Christian expectation about the Jews, there must have been two competing expectations in the early church. Finally, in Revelation 7 these folk are called simply the "servants of God," which is not a term unique to Jewish believers. Likewise the description of them in Revelation 14 could fit any believer who is faithful to God and does not compromise with the "beast" and the "false prophet." In Revelation 9 all who are not sealed are tormented. Does this mean that Gentile believers are tormented while Jewish ones are not? And doesn't a Jew-Gentile distinction *within the church* run counter to all of Paul's arguments about God's breaking down the walls between the races? These reasons persuade me that this cannot be the correct explanation.

The 144,000, then, stand for God's faithful people, Jew or Gentile. They are, just as the text says, "the servants of our God." The image of Israel is probably drawn from the picture in Ezekiel 9. Just as all of the tribes of Israel present in Jerusalem (the last stand of Judaism before the exile) were included then, so all of the tribes of humanity will be included in the end. The 12 × 12 × 1000 stresses the completeness of this number; all of God's servants from all of humanity are sealed. The purpose of their sealing is to protect them not from temptation or martyrdom, but from the judgment of God. This is God's church of the end times, when God's judgment is coming to a peak. Since they are faithful, there is no reason for judgment to fall upon them. In Revelation 7 the image of the 144,000 protected on earth is coupled with a parallel image of the church in heaven, an encouragement to persevere. In Revelation 14 the 144,000 are in heaven, for in the same chapter is the harvest of the earth. The final judgments, which will destroy everything and everyone in their path, are about to begin. No wonder that the church is withdrawn before that final curtain comes down.

What does this image say to the church today? On the assumption that we live in the last days (which in New Testament thought runs from the time of Christ to the end), our Jehovah's Witness friends are right to wish to be numbered in the 144,000. The sad thing is that they are going about it the wrong way. It is not a limited number to which one gains entrance by merit, but the complete number of God's faithful servants. One is counted in that number if he or she does not compromise the faith by going after the idols of the world and does not live in falsehood, but speaks and lives in truth. Another way of putting it is that "they follow the Lamb wherever he goes" (Rev 14:4). In the context of Revelation this means that they follow him in heaven (and perhaps in his conquest of earth in Rev 19), but they do so in heaven because they have already been his followers on earth, whatever the cost.

9:1 What Is the Abyss?

The term *Abyss* occurs nine times in five different passages in the New Testament. In Luke 8:31 it is the place to which demons do not wish to be sent. In Romans 10:7 it is translated "the deep" and is the opposite of heaven, the one being above the earth and the other below. In Revelation 9:1-2 the "shaft [or well or pit] of the Abyss" is opened. In Revelation 11:7 there is a "beast that comes up from the Abyss." And finally in Revelation 20:1-3 Satan is chained and thrown into the Abyss for one thousand years, the shaft being locked and sealed over him. This is the New Testament data that we have to work with.

The Greek translation of the Old Testament uses "Abyss" to translate "the deep" (Gen 1:2; Ps 42:7; 107:26) and "the depths of the earth" (Ps 71:20). In the first group of passages it refers to the deep seas or primeval deep from which solid ground is separated and which in some Hebrew cosmologies lie under the earth. In the second passage it refers to the place of the dead. These probably give us the background of Romans 10:7 (either the place of the dead into which no living person can go or the deep as opposed to the heights of heaven), but they do not help us with Revelation.

In the intertestamental literature we discover what a first-century Jew like the author of Revelation thought of when he wrote "the Abyss." In *1 Enoch* 10:4 a rebellious angel is bound and cast into darkness in a hole. This hole seems to be distinguished from the final place of judgment, a place of fire mentioned in

1 Enoch 18:11 and 21:7, although this is also a pit. Likewise in *Jubilees* 5:6-11 the fallen angels are bound in a pit. With this background we can now understand John's image.

The Abyss is apparently the prison of demons and fallen angelic beings (some Jews believed demons were fallen angels, while others distinguished them as being their offspring). This explains the fear of the demons in Luke 8:31. They wanted to remain free, not be placed in prison. Jesus apparently allows them freedom because the time of judgment has not yet arrived. Likewise it explains why Satan is imprisoned in the Abyss, for it is the standard place to imprison such beings.

Yet the Abyss can be opened. In Revelation 9 it is opened to let out what are apparently demonic beings to torment people. These beings are not unorganized, but have "as king over them the angel of the Abyss, whose name in Hebrew is Abaddon, and in Greek, Apollyon" (Rev 9:11). The name means "destroyer" in either language. The identity of this ruler is unclear. Is he an angel, perhaps the one who opens the pit and then is sent to control the host he allows out? John normally uses "angel" for one of those loyal to God; there is also plenty of evidence in Scripture to accept the idea of a destroying angel. Or is he one of the host allowed out, himself a fallen angel or demon? The evidence is fairly well balanced, but given John's use of the term "angel," we suspect that the first suggestion is correct.[1]

Not only do these demonic beings come up out of the Abyss, but "the beast" does as well. Revelation 11 does not explain this being, but given the connection of "the deep" with the sea, John identifies him as the beast "coming out of the sea" in Revelation 13:1, a world ruler who is inspired by Satan himself. This identification is repeated in Revelation 17:8, which combines elements of both the previous passages. In Revelation 11 he fights against God's witnesses, although they are protected by God until the time of their martyrdom.

The Abyss does not appear in the final two chapters of Revelation because it is no longer needed. After Revelation 20 there is no need for a prison. The time of the final judgment has arrived, and both the devil and those belonging to him are cast into their final place of torment, the lake of fire (Rev 20:10).

How should Christians relate to this information? Certainly the images in these passages are fearful. But other elements are at work as well. As previously noted, the witnesses in Revelation 11 are protected until such a time as God allows them to be injured. In all of the passages it is God and his angels who have the keys to the Abyss. Nothing comes out that God does not allow out. The beings that get out are not released to do their own will (although they may think that that is what they are doing), but to serve God's purposes. Finally, in Revelation 9:4 we read that the demonic beings from the Abyss are not allowed to touch those who have "the seal of God on their foreheads." Who are these? They are "the servants of our God" (Rev 7:3), who remain faithful to God and the Lamb (Rev 14:4-5). These people are not necessarily protected from martyrdom, but they are not able to be tormented or truly injured by the creatures of the pit. God remains in control even of the devil and his hosts. Thus, those who serve God should have no fear of the creatures of the Abyss, but instead should have a concern for others who do not walk under the protection of their Lord. This is an implied call to evangelism and to total faithfulness, even in the face of martyrdom.

---

[1]John uses "angel" in Revelation almost as many

times as it appears in the whole rest of the New Testament put together. While there is one time when it does refer to fallen angels (Rev 12:7, 9, the dragon's angels) and one time when it might do so (Rev 9:14-15), the vast majority of the time it refers to God's angels.

11:2-3 Symbolic Numbers?

In addition to its unusual personages and symbols, Revelation has some numbers that are difficult to decipher. Those in Revelation 11:2-3 are as confusing as anywhere. In fact, they are so confusing that commentators from all positions approach this particular passage with caution, admitting that in the end they are not certain of their identifications. What does it mean for the holy city to be trampled for 42 months? And who are these witnesses who prophesy for 1,260 days? How do these periods of time relate? We can only give tentative answers to these questions.

The context of Revelation 11:2-3 is the sixth of the series of trumpet judgments, the penultimate judgments of Revelation. This second "woe" (the last three of the seven trumpet judgments are called "woes") blew in Revelation 9:13; its judgment is finished in Revelation 11:14. This last part of the judgment contains both the numbers we mentioned above and the three and a half days that the witnesses (the main subjects of this last judgment scene) are to lie dead before their resurrection. Although the three and a half days are a separate issue, the other two numbers are the same, for it does not take much math skill to discover that 42 months equals three and a half years. Likewise the 1,260 days equals 42 months of 30 days each or three and a half years of 360 days each. Furthermore, in Revelation 12:14, the end of the next chapter, we discover that "the woman" will be protected for "a time, times, and half a time," or three and a half years. Therefore Revelation has three different ways of referring to the same length of time.

It is clear that this time period is symbolic. In Daniel 7:25 the fourth beast will oppress the saints of the Most High for "a time, times, and half a time." The same timing is mentioned in Daniel 12:7, although two other periods of 1,290 (43 months) and 1,335 days (44.5 months) respectively are mentioned in Daniel 12:11-12. Daniel 8:14 notes a period of 2,300 days (76.7 months or 6 years and 4.7 months) when the "little horn," Antiochus IV Epiphanes, would suppress Judaism. (This ruler, who deposed the last Zadokite high priest in 170 B.C. and suppressed sacrifice in Jerusalem from 167 to 164 B.C., is the model for much that happens in Revelation.) John does not use all of these numbers from Daniel. What he does use is the 3.5-year period, a period during which there will be oppression and the rule of "the beast," but also the protection of "the woman" and the activity of "the two witnesses."

When it comes to identifying this period and these individuals there are three basic schools of thought. One group sees the temple as a literal rebuilt temple in Jerusalem and the witnesses as two specific individuals. Given the nature of their miracles, they appear to be most like Moses and Elijah, the greatest of the Old Testament prophetic figures. The 3.5 years, then, is also a literal period at the end of the age during what John calls "the great tribulation," when the antichrist, who will be a world ruler, will oppress the temple worship. The problem with this view is that the oppression excludes the altar and inner court of the temple, which makes it appear to be more a symbolic temple than a literal one. Who would control the outer court of the temple and ignore the inner one?

A second interpretation sees the temple and Jerusalem (where the two witnesses are active) as symbols for the Jewish people. The antichrist oppresses the Jewish people as a whole in the end of the age for 3.5 years, but the faithful remnant (the worshipers in the inner court) will be protected (perhaps meaning the same thing as the protection of "the woman" in the next chapter). During this period of protection in the middle of the reign of evil, two eschatological personages will witness to the Jewish people (symbolized by Jerusalem), calling them to Christ. This interpretation has the advantage of retaining the sense of literality in the first interpretation, while avoiding the problems it faced in viewing the temple as a literal temple.

A third interpretation sees the temple and Jerusalem as symbols for the church and the world. The inner court is the true worshipers. The outer court is those members of the church who are corrupted by the world (the Nicolaitans and followers of Jezebel; see Rev 2). The holy city (Jerusalem) is the world outside the church. The church is oppressed by evil for a definite period (the 3.5 years normally are interpreted symbolically). Yet during this period witness will go on (the two witnesses being symbols for the witness of the church), although the witness will entail martyrdom. The strength of this position is that it takes seriously John's calling Judaism "the synagogue of Satan" (Rev 2:9; 3:9) and Jerusalem "Sodom and Egypt" (Rev 11:8), therefore assuming that John would not be interested in preserving either Judaism or Jewish institutions such as the temple. Furthermore, each of the pictures receives an interpretation from within Revelation. The problem is that in most apocalyptic scenarios (including intertestamental apocalyptic) there are real people and places with which the author is concerned, not simply symbolic groups. This interpretation appears to loose itself from history in any form.

Obviously, we cannot be sure of the interpretation of this passage. Too many good Christian scholars have taken too divergent positions to speak with any dogmatism. But from my point of view the second interpretation appears to fit John's perspective best. In his day the temple was gone and Judaism was oppressed. This, he says, will continue. There will be a period of intense persecution in the end of the age, when the embodiment of evil himself, the antichrist, will rule (at least in the Roman world). The Jews, symbolized by Jerusalem in Revelation 11, will be "trampled on" by this ruler, but a remnant that is faithful to God (the inner court of Revelation 11 and perhaps the woman of Revelation 12) will be protected. Just as there will be an embodiment of evil, so witness will be embodied in two individuals who will come in the spirit of Moses and Elijah. After 3.5 years they will be martyred, then raised to life. Yet this will lead to a turning of the Jews as a whole to Christ (Rev 11:13). It will also happen just before the final end of the age (which, if John is using Daniel's chronology, should happen within two or three months). This interpretation fits with Jesus' predictions about Judaism (Lk 21:24) and the temple (Mk 13:2 and parallels—there is no mention of its rebuilding) and takes the symbols as meaning something concrete.

This, then, is our understanding of what John anticipated in the end of the age. He appears to believe that it would happen within a short time. It did not happen that way during his lifetime, but perhaps we should look at the rapid spread of Christianity within the Roman Empire as a parallel to the repentance of Nineveh in Jonah. It led to the eventual repentance of Rome and perhaps, like in the case of Nineveh, to a putting of the judgment on hold. That is certainly in tune with the desire of God for repentance (rather than judgment) within Revelation. This may move the judgment picture to the end of the age, whenever this may happen to be. Yet will the judgment happen any less concretely or even any differently than John envisioned it 1900 years ago? Only our hindsight from heaven will reveal the truth—and the fully correct interpretation of this verse—which God alone knows.

12:1-3 Who Are the Woman and the Dragon?

The images presented in Revelation are vivid. The one in Revelation 12:1-3 is part of a set of pictures that serve as a prelude to the final end of the age, since the seventh trumpet, the penultimate judgment, has already blown. Yet what are we to make of this picture? Who is this woman? What is this dragon? How do we interpret such images, which remind us more of Greek mythology than of most Scripture?

John's images are intended to be meaningful, but at the same time he uses them because they can also be fluid. Both the woman and the dragon have a fluidity about them that allows them to be useful to the author.

First, we look at the woman. There are two women in this section of Revelation. The first is this woman, God's woman. The second is the woman of Revelation 17, a prostitute. The opposition reminds us of the two women of Proverbs 1—10, the one lady wisdom and the other the loose woman. Here the first woman is clothed with heavenly glory, the sun, with the moon being under her feet. The second woman is clothed in "purple and scarlet," colors of earthly emperors. The first woman has twelve stars for a crown. The second woman has gold and jewels. The first woman gives birth, but the second woman appears sterile. There is a contrast in every way.

We recognize that the second woman is Rome; is the first woman Jerusalem? There have been several answers to that question. Some scholars point to the twelve stars and argue the parallel to twelve patriarchs. Indeed, the whole picture, including the sun and the moon, reminds us of Joseph's dream (Gen 37:9). Other scholars look at the incident of the birth of the child and claim that the woman is Mary. Still others point out that the sign appears in heaven, so this must be some idealization of the people of God, God's true bride. I do not see that one must choose among these interpretations. Jewish thought often oscillates between the one and the many. For example, in the servant songs of the second part of Isaiah the servant is sometimes Israel (Is 49:3) and sometimes an individual (Is 49:5), and in Daniel the Son of Man (Dan 7:13-14) and "the saints of the Most High" (Dan 7:18) also alternate. So in our image the woman is God's people, the faithful of Israel. The woman is also Mary, who individualized that faithful group in giving birth to the Messiah.

In the second part of the chapter the image of the woman shifts, for she is persecuted. Is she still the faithful in Israel? Or is she now the wider people of God, Jew as well as Gentile? Certainly in her flight to the wilderness we are reminded of Jesus' words (Mk 13:14; Lk 21:21), which the Jewish-Christian church acted upon just before A.D. 70. Does it then mean that God will protect a Jewish-Christian group? Or should we remember his words in Matthew 16:18 that "the gates of Hades" would not overcome his church, therefore interpreting this as a reference to his whole church? Perhaps the correct answer is both. The image is that of the flight of Israel from Pharaoh into the wilderness and the flight of the church from Jerusalem in the A.D. 66-70 war. This shows that God will care for and protect his church, specifically during the time when the forces of evil reign apparently triumphant, the 1,260 days. All of the lies and demonic forces that the dragon can spit out cannot destroy this church. But at the same time the dragon makes war with the woman's children, the Christians. So while the church as a whole is protected and cannot be stamped out, Christians as individuals will experience the anger of Satan, even martyrdom.

Second, then, we have the dragon. This image is drawn from Old Testament pictures of Leviathan, the many-headed sea monster (Ps 74:13-14). The monster is sometimes mythological in the sense that he is not identified with any historical embodiment, and sometimes a specific enemy of God's people, such as Egypt (Ps 74:14; Ezek 29:3) or Assyria (Is 27:1). This picture was mediated to John via Daniel, who describes a fourth beast with ten horns (Dan 7:7). John, of course, makes very clear about whom he believes Daniel is talking (or in terms of whom he is reinterpreting Daniel), for he writes in Revelation 12:9, "The great dragon was hurled down—that ancient serpent called the devil, or Satan, who leads the whole world astray." Yet this dragon also has an earthly embodiment. The "beast coming out of the sea" (Rev 13:1) has seven heads and ten horns like the dragon, as does the beast the great prostitute rides (Rev 17:3). And as the prostitute parodied the woman clothed in the sun, so the dragon parodies someone else. Revelation 12:3 notes that he has seven crowns, while in Revelation 19:12 the "King of kings and Lord of lords" has many crowns on his head.

The dragon naturally tried to destroy Christ, the child in the story. John is not interested at this point in the life and death of Christ, but moves from his birth to his ascension. However, we must remember than in his Gospel the "lifting up" of the Son of Man is both cross and ascension, so this does not mean that the cross is absent from his thought.

John's concern is with the war of the dragon against God's people. The war has two phases, a heavenly and an earthly. The heavenly phase is fought by Michael, "the great prince who protects your [that is, Daniel's] people" (Dan 12:1), and his angels. The dragon has swept one-third of the angels with him in his fall, so he also has angels to fight with. But he is the loser. Even though God never appears on the scene, but fights through his angels, the victory is secured. Satan loses his access to heaven. When does John see this as happening? Although some scholars refer this to the original fall of Satan, it probably happens at the end of the age, for it happens after the child is caught up to heaven. Furthermore, there is plenty of Jewish testimony to the idea of Satan's having access to heaven during world history.

There is also a battle on earth. The human beings apparently do not see their foe. Yet they defeat the devil. In fact, the outcome of the war in heaven appears to be parallel to that on earth, just as Daniel's prayers in Daniel 10 appear to be parallel to a battle going on in the spiritual realm, a battle he knows nothing about until he is informed. In Revelation the human beings win, not because of their strength and wisdom, but because of their trust in "the blood of the Lamb" and their open confession of their faith in him. They were so firm in this trust and confession that "they did not love their lives so much as to shrink from death" (Rev 12:11). The devil could make martyrs, but each martyr was the devil's own defeat. The martyr was safe with God in heaven; the devil's power over the person had crumbled. In other words, the primary means of spiritual warfare is commitment to God and his redemption in Christ, a commitment so openly confessed and so radical that even death will not shake one from it.

This battle is fought throughout the Christian age, but it is most intense at the end of the age. In this period of 42 months the devil is fully aware that he has lost, both in heaven and on earth. Now he just wishes to destroy, to "make war" against "those who obey God's commandments and hold to the testimony of Jesus" (see Rev 12:17). The reason John is writing this picture is so that such people will hold on until martyrdom or the end of the age.

Like all of his apocalyptic pictures, this one is not intended to scare Christians. It does portray them as characters in an eschatological battle of gigantic proportions, but at the same time it portrays the limitations of the devil himself, not to mention his angels, and his final end. Furthermore, it portrays the protection of God over his saints, as well as his eventual victory. This is designed to encourage the Christian to stand fast, whether he or she is living in the ongoing struggle of the Christian age or in the intense struggle of the final phase of that time. Dragons may be the stuff of fantasy, but in this case the fantasy is real, even if hidden in the spiritual realm, and the stakes are high. Yet the outcome is sure for those who remain firm in their commitment to Christ.

12:7-8 Satan in Heaven?

See comment on JOB 1:6-12.

12:11 Overcame by the Blood of the Lamb?

Our acquaintance with video games and fantasy may prepare us for the use of some strange weapons in warfare, but Revelation 12:11 has some of the strangest ones, even given the context of fantasy. When we read about overcoming Satan by "the blood of the Lamb," don't we wonder how this is done? Blood is an exceedingly strange weapon. Furthermore, how does testimony function as a weapon? It isn't a type of curse or magic, is it? And while we may understand the usefulness of the courage implied in not loving one's life, how can these other things be weapons in a spiritual battle?

The context is that there has been a war in heaven between the devil and his angels and the archangel Michael and his angels. Michael, fighting in the name of God, has won. However, as the scene shifts to earth with the fall of the dragon, John inserts a hymn into the passage, which comments on the battle that has just taken place. First, the devil is called "the accuser of our brothers" and apparently had access to the presence of God to accuse Christians up until this point. Second, the battle itself is described, but we no longer hear of Michael and his angels. Instead we hear of the deeds of human beings.

It is clear from the setting that John is painting a picture of parallel scenes. One is a heavenly battle with angelic participants. The other is an earthly battle, with the devil on one side and the Christians on the other. Yet the two appear to be parallel. The casting down of Satan from heaven is attributed to the faithfulness of Christians on earth. The heavenly battle is apparently influenced by the earthly. It is analogous to Daniel 10, in which Daniel prays for twenty-one days. He is eventually told that his prayer had been answered the first day, but that there had been a heavenly battle preventing the answering angel from getting through to him until Michael came to take over the fight. All of this time Daniel is praying on earth, oblivious to the battle in the spiritual world. Is the author there implying that Daniel's struggles in prayer are part of what is affecting the outcome of the heavenly battle?

What, then, are the weapons of this earthly battle? The first is "the blood of the Lamb." John has already referred to the death of Christ, saying that the Lamb (Christ) appears "looking as if it had been slain" (Rev 5:6). Furthermore, John has confessed "to him who loves us and has freed us from our sins by his blood" (Rev 1:5). So this image of blood indicates what Christ has done for the Christian on the cross. It is a weapon, not in that it is flung in the teeth of Satan as a talisman, but in that the Christian is committed to it. It is this sacrifice in which the Christian trusts, and it does not fail him when the accuser roars out his accusations.

The second weapon is "the word of their testimony." Revelation 1:5 presents Jesus Christ as "the faithful witness." In Revelation 2:13 Antipas, "my faithful witness," has been put to death. The theme of witness or testimony (the same Greek word can be translated by either English word) flows from one end of the book to the other. This testimony, then, is the confession of obedience to Christ. It is not the story about what Christ has done for us (which is the common modern evangelical meaning of the term), but the statement that one is loyal to Christ and therefore will not compromise. Because it is something spoken, probably in the context of a demand for the explanation of one's behavior, it is a word.

The third item really is not a weapon, although it is in a parallel clause. Rather, it is an attitude of mind that underlies the other two: "they did not love their lives so much as to shrink from death." As Jesus said, "He who stands firm to the end will be saved" (Mk 13:13). If death remains a threat to a person, then there is a point at which they will compromise their commitment to the blood of Christ and certainly a point at which they will mute their word of testimony. The genuineness of commitment is seen when the heat is on. Those who pass the test are those who will not cling to life even under the threat of death, if it would mean compromising on their commitment to Christ.

In this context the devil has been presented as "the accuser of our brothers." This is the war that he wages against the people of God, for his weapons are lies and accusations. But these people have not believed the lie, for they have seen through Satan's deception to the reality of Christ. They know that life is not more precious than obedience to Jesus. And the accusations of Satan have no hold on them. Accuse as he will, he will only receive the response "I am trusting in the blood of Christ." And should he accuse them of being hypocrites, their faithful word of testimony even in the face of threatened death shows such an accusation to be completely false.

In other words, John is not saying that Christians win the battle against Satan by talking about the blood of Christ, telling Satan about that blood (he already knows about it all too well), or using it as a magic word in prayer ("by the power of the blood of Jesus"). Instead, Christians trust in the power of the death of Christ with a quiet confidence that is inwardly lived and outwardly confessed in word and deed (life matching speech), no matter what the threat. This radical commitment, John claims, is what defeats Satan.

John does not present this as super-Christianity, for martyrs only. Rather, it is normal Christianity. It is a Christianity that does not love Babylon (his image for the world and all it has to offer in power, wealth and advancement, as Rev 18 shows). It is a Christianity that is dedication to Christ, or, as he puts it, a faithful witness. This for him is spiritual warfare. No demons are necessarily seen,[1] just as Daniel saw no spiritual battle, but despite the lack of visible pyrotechnics, the devil is cast down. In such faithfulness the devil discovers that his time is short.

[1]This does not imply that John in any way rejects the expulsion of demons from the demonized, for this activity was universally part of the essence of spiritual warfare. Demon expulsion, evangelistic proclamation, healing the sick and caring for the poor are all part of the lifestyle of the gospel, but they flow out of the more basic trust in the blood of Christ and concomitant personal commitment to him, rather than replace it.

13:1 Who Is the Beast from the Sea?

John may well have drawn his basis for the picture of this beast from Daniel 7, which lists a series of four beasts. The first three are similar to recognizable animals, although with additions or modifications. The fourth is compared to no known animal, but is simply "terrifying and frightening and very powerful" (Dan 7:7). The only physical description is that it has iron teeth and ten horns. The beast in Revelation appears related to that one.

This beast is an embodiment of Satan. The seven heads and ten horns on the beast are copied from the picture of Satan in Revelation 12:3. And this is no wonder, for "the dragon [Satan] gave the beast his power and his throne and great authority." He represents the power of Satan on earth and is to Satan what Christ is to the Father. He is even more a pseudo-Christ in that he receives a mortal wound from which he is healed, a mimicked death and resurrection. Because of this event he is worshiped on earth.

The second place where this beast appears is in Revelation 17:3. This chapter explains (Rev 17:8-13) that the symbolism has more than one meaning. The ten horns are ten kings who rule along with a great ruler and support that ruler. The seven heads are both seven hills (a transparent symbol for Rome) and seven kings. Unlike the ten who rule simultaneously, these seven come one after another. John is living in the time when the sixth of them is ruling. The beast himself is an eighth. Yet, inspired by Satan as he is, his real origin is in "the Abyss," the place where Satanic spirits are imprisoned.

Because of the transparency of the symbolism in Revelation 17:9, it would seem that if we knew how John counted the rulers of Rome, it would be fairly easy to discover who the beast was. He should be the eighth emperor of Rome, John living in the age of the sixth. The fact that the Roman Senate declared several emperors to be divine and that some, especially Domitian, claimed divinity during their lifetimes, and one, Caligula, tried to have his statue erected in the temple in Jerusalem, adds to this impression (compare Rev 13:8, 14). Unfortunately we do not know either with whom John would start such a count or whether he would skip some of the emperors who reigned only a short time. Nor are we sure exactly when he lived, for a good case has been made for the time of Domitian (A.D. 91-96, the traditional date) as well as that of Galba (A.D. 68). Neither of these dates would meet the requirement of having an eighth emperor fitting the description of the beast.

Yet there is a further problem with the identification of this beast. As we have seen, the seven heads have two meanings, one of which is Rome (the seven hills) and the other seven kings. Some see these kings as literal rulers of Rome (as in the scheme above), and others see them as kingdoms or empires. In Daniel

7:17 the term translated "kingdoms" in the NIV is literally "kings" in Aramaic. That means that John could be shifting from a vision of literal Rome and its emperors to one of a succession of empires.

Finally, in apocalyptic scenarios there is often a place in which the writer "fades out" from the present historical circumstances and sees beyond them to future events. A good example of this is Daniel 12:1. Daniel 11 gives us a picture of the conflict between the Seleucid and Ptolemaic empires, culminating in the Seleucid ruler Antiochus IV Epiphanes (175-163 B.C.). If one reads 1 Maccabees or Josephus's histories, it is easy to identify everyone. But in Daniel 12 we are no longer in the realm of history. We are seeing beyond the period of Daniel 11 to the end of history. Since the beast "once was, now is not, and will come up out of the Abyss" (Rev 17:8), John appears to be suggesting that an evil force that had once been destroyed (or perhaps consigned to the Abyss) would reappear, not that a new emperor would appear. This would go beyond anything present in the Roman Empire.

What, then, can we say about the beast? John saw in his vision a personage coming at the end of time who would be the devil incarnate and demand worship. This personage would be accompanied by a second who would seem to be harmless enough ("two horns like a lamb," perhaps suggesting a likeness to Christ, the Lamb), but would speak for the devil ("he spoke like a dragon," Rev 13:11). The second personage will direct worship toward the first. The appearance of these two will be associated with the three-and-a-half-year period of intense persecution at the end of the age. John saw this in terms of the Rome that he knew, perhaps expecting in his own heart that it would happen in his lifetime. We have previously suggested that the vision of Revelation may have been delayed, like Jonah's, due to the widespread conversion to Christianity in the Roman Empire. Whether or not this is the case, all scenarios of the end (such as Paul's in 2 Thess 2) agree in seeing an embodiment of evil, like Antiochus IV Epiphanes was in his day, before the incarnation of good, Jesus Christ, appears.

What this means for the church is that its expectation of the end is not one of gradual improvement or Christianizing of the world until Christ appears, but one of evangelization in the face of persecution, a persecution that will become most severe just before the end. Certainly many Christians have felt they have lived in the times of the beast, such as those living under Napoleon or Hitler or Stalin. Yet they have been wrong in that the end has not come. But will those who live in the age of the real beast have any better insight? None of us evaluate our own times well. The important thing is that Christians respond appropriately to persecutors, whether a beastlike person (such as Hitler) or the genuine beast. John's picture shows that the beast is under the ultimate control of God. His time is limited. His coming and destruction are under the power of God. His persecution will be used by God for the perfection of God's church. The response expected, then, is firm commitment to God. That response will not be wrong in the face of any persecution, even if we are not sure whether or not it is the genuine beast.

13:18 His Number Is 666?

I can be described by a number of numbers. I have a Social Security number and a Canadian social insurance number. I am one number to the Society of Biblical Literature's computer and another to CompuServ Information Service. We expect this in our computer age, but we are surprised to find people in the Bible described in terms of a number and correctly suspect that the numbers are something more than identification for filing purposes. In the previous chapter I introduced the concept of the "beast coming out of the sea." His description was problematic, but the one thing about him that has caused more difficulty and speculation than any of the others is his enigmatic number noted in Revelation 13:18.

It is not surprising that numbers had meaning in the symbolic world of John's vision, for they had more than numerical meaning in his outer world as well. Numbers and letters were interchangeable. For example, many rabbinic scriptures to this day do not use Arabic numerals, but instead use Hebrew letters to stand for the various verse and chapter numbers. This led some rabbis to interpret Scripture via gematria, the turning of names into numbers and vice versa. For this reason many scholars believe that the fourteen generations counted three times in Matthew 1 are related to the name David, for DVD in Hebrew (the vowels were not written) would be 4 + 6 + 4, or 14.[1] The Greeks did a similar thing with their own alphabet. In the early Christian Sibylline Oracles Jesus is enumerated as 888. It was only with the spread first of Roman and then of Arabic numerals that this practice died out for most of the Western world.

We would expect, then, that the number 666 would stand for something, especially that it would stand for a name. One theory is that it stands for Nero Caesar. Nero is selected because he persecuted Christians and a legend arose after his suicide that he had not died, but had fled to the east and would return in triumph. Two false Neros tried to fulfill this legend and failed. Still, Nero Caesar in Greek totals 1,005, so one has to transliterate the Greek name into Hebrew to get the required 666. Did John, who wrote in Greek, expect his readers to know Hebrew or Hebrew letter values?

Two other methods to obtain the name of an emperor have been attempted. One added the values of the initial letters of the names of all of the Roman emperors up until a certain point (something that the *Sibylline Oracles* also does). Another used the abbreviation for the title of Domitian, another persecuting emperor. Unfortunately, for the first theory at least one of the emperors must be left out of the list to get an even 666 from the emperors' initials, and while we know of the abbreviations of Domitian's title, they do not appear together anywhere, which weakens the second theory.

Another solution has been via the observation that 666 is the triangular number of 36 (1 + 2 + 3 + 4 and on up to 36). The number 36 is the triangular number of 8 (1 + 2 + 3 + 4 + 5 + 6 + 7 + 8 = 36). The beast, of course, is the eighth king (Rev 17:11). Triangular numbers were seen as sinister in contrast to the square numbers, which are assigned to the martyrs (Rev 7:4) and the heavenly city (Rev 21:16). While this math is interesting and fits the Greek concern with geometry (because they did not have a mathematically useful system of numerals), it does not come up with a name. Nor can we be sure that such a complicated system was in John's mind. After all, there are other triangular numbers in Scripture that are not sinister at all, such as the 153 fish in John 21:11.

None of the solutions above has been found completely satisfactory. Perhaps the best observation is that 666 consistently (three times) falls short of the number of perfection, 7, and the number of Christ, 888. Rather than refer to a specific name, 666 may indicate that the person will be a parody of Christ. He will not come up to perfection, but as the prostitute of Revelation 17 mimics the faithful woman of Revelation 12 and the dragon in Revelation 12 mimics Christ in Revelation 19, so the beast mimics the incarnate Christ, being the embodiment of evil (the devil not being capable of true incarnation). Beyond this we can only observe that when such a personage appears, those who are wise in John's terms (which means first of all that they have divine insight) will recognize him and see that 666 does indeed fit.

[1]In transliteration the Hebrew alphabet runs ' B G D H V for the numbers 1-6.

16:15 Blessed Is He Who Keeps His Clothes?

What does it mean to stay awake? Does it mean that the blessed Christian will not be asleep in bed when Christ returns? How might a Christian be naked at such a time? Are we to fear this coming happening when we are in the bath? Particularly because the verse is an exhortation from Christ himself, we readers of Revelation want to be sure of what this means.

The context of this verse is the pouring out of the first six bowls of the final judgment of God. The previous verse mentioned that the way has now been prepared for the final battle of "the great day of God Almighty." The next verse describes the gathering of the nations for that battle, which will not take place until Revelation 19:11-21. Yet when that battle does take place the people of God are with their king, so they obviously have been gathered together, an event often referred to as "the rapture" (Mk 13:27; 1 Cor 15:51-52; 1 Thess 4:16-17).

The wider context of this verse is the sayings of Jesus that he would come "like a thief" (Mt 24:43; Lk 12:39; compare Mk 13:32-37). This image is picked up by Paul (1 Thess 5:2, 4; compare 2 Pet 3:10) and has already been mentioned once by John (Rev 3:3). The point of all of these sayings is that a thief does not announce his coming, but surprises the inhabitants of the house by coming when they are out or least likely to suspect his or her presence. Stealth and surprise are the chief weapons. To say that the day of the Lord is like this is to say that it too will come when least expected. As Jesus noted, no one knows the day or the hour (Mk 13:32); those who have claimed to have calculated it have always been proved wrong. But this does not mean that one cannot be prepared; instead it means that one must always be prepared, like servants waiting up through the night for their master to return from a party (Lk 12:35-40).

John has been writing about the gathering of the world's armies and the final battle between the beast and Christ. The alarming events in the world or even the expectation that this gathering must take place before Christ could return could distract his readers from their central focus, namely faithfulness to and expectation of Christ. He, not the armies of the antichrist, is to be their central concern. Therefore it is quite appropriate that the voice of Jesus himself interject a warning in the middle of the gathering storm, just as he previously interjected a blessing about the death of Christians to contrast with that of the destruction of "Babylon" (Rev 14:13).

The warning is to "stay awake" or "watch." The image is that of the watchmen at their posts, alert for any sign of their lord and expectant of his coming. As we saw above, this picture is drawn from the sayings of Jesus. This alertness, of course, implies that the Christian will be found doing what the master has commanded him or her to do, which includes sleep at appropriate times.[1] The wakefulness, then, is not the avoidance of physical sleep, but a moral wakefulness that does not allow the world to lull one into a laxity about the directions that Christ has given and the standards he has set.

The picture of the watching servant is connected to that for nakedness. When lying down to sleep, a person would take off the outer garment and use it as a blanket, or perhaps lay it aside altogether and sleep under a blanket or covered in straw (as rabbi Akiba and his wife were forced to do since they had only one outer garment for the two of them). A poor person's clothing was his or her most valuable possession; a thief would not miss the chance to steal it upon breaking into a house during the night (see Lk 10:30). Likewise if a person were asleep but would have to rush out in an emergency without taking the time to get clothed, he or she could lose the outer garment (see Mk 13:15-16). To be without that outer garment in public would be to be "naked" in terms of that culture (something like being in a shopping mall clothed only in underwear in our day). Jesus thus counsels keeping one's "clothes with him" or "guarding their clothing" to prevent the surprise of the moment finding them "shamefully exposed." The Mishnah reports that the captain of the temple would go around at night and, if he found temple police asleep at their posts, take their clothing and burn it, forcing them to leave the temple naked.[2] In this text the surprise of the moment finds the believer similarly "undressed."

The clothing of the Christian is mentioned several times in Revelation. Those in the church of Sardis whose deeds are not right have soiled clothes, while the worthy ones will be dressed in white (Rev 3:4). The church of Laodicea is naked and needs to purchase white clothing to wear (Rev 3:17-18). The martyrs under the altar are clothed in white (Rev 6:11), as is the multitude before the throne (Rev 7:9). The key to the image of clothing is found in Revelation 19:8, in which the bride of Christ is given "fine linen, bright and clean" to wear. Then comes the comment "Fine linen stands for the righteous acts of the saints." If one is not acting righteously, which means following the commands of Christ, he or she is naked before him, and his coming will leave such a person "shamefully exposed."

The two parts of the warning, then, fit together. The coming of Christ cannot be calculated. Certainly the last thing that John wishes is that his readers would try to calculate the time of that coming using the images in his book. That would be to put their focus on the world and the evil personages rather than on Christ. The goal of the whole of this book is that, given the ultimate end of all of the principalities and powers of this world and the final triumph of Christ, Christians will remain faithful whatever the cost. They are to be prepared for the coming of Christ at all times. This means not only expecting this coming verbally or doctrinally, but also living a life appropriate to that expectation. This means living in obedience to Jesus, however crazy such a lifestyle might appear in the light of the values of this world, and "clothing oneself" with righteous deeds. It is for such people that the coming of Christ will not be something for which they are unprepared. Instead, they will joyfully welcome it and, fully "clothed," join their Lord's throng as he completes his conquest of the world and ends this age.

---

[1]As one Christian teacher pointed out, so long as one is obeying Christ, whether sleeping or raising the dead, "the pay is the same"—both are simply obedient servants.

[2]So F. F. Bruce, "The Revelation to John," in

G. C. D. Howley et al., eds., *The New Layman's Bible Commentary* (Grand Rapids, Mich.: Zondervan, 1979), p. 1703.

19:10 The Testimony of Jesus Is the Spirit of Prophecy?

For a long period of time the church has relegated prophecy either to the classical prophets of the biblical period or to preaching (which is normally the gift of teaching, not prophecy). While the revival of interest in prophecy in the church began close to two hundred years ago, there has been a recent upsurge in interest in prophecy, both in scholarly circles and in church ministry. Revelation 19:10 appears to have something to say to this trend, especially since it comes from a Christian prophet. In the middle of a picture of "the wedding supper of the Lamb," when the hopes of the church will be consummated in union with her Lord, John is overwhelmed. He falls at the feet of the angel who is explaining everything to him, bowing his head to the pavement in worship. We are not surprised that the angel stops him (and will do so again in Rev 22:8-9), but the statement that "the testimony of Jesus is the spirit of prophecy" needs explanation. What does it mean? What is "the testimony of Jesus"? Just what is the "spirit of prophecy"? What might either of these have to do with prophecy today?

The New Testament mentions the gift of prophecy several times, most significantly in 1 Corinthians 12—14, although Acts mentions prophets several times as well. Yet we know very little concerning what New Testament prophets spoke about, other than the words of Agabus (Acts 11:27-28; 21:1), with the exception of Revelation.[1] This whole book is designated as prophecy (Rev 1:3; 22:7, 18-19) and is therefore our most extensive example of Christian prophecy. Within this context John says that "the testimony of Jesus" is "the spirit" of this prophecy.

Prophecy was not, of course, to be accepted without testing it to see if it were genuine or distorted in some way. Several New Testament passages address this issue. Colossians 2:18 suggests that some Christians had been led into the worship of angels, probably through prophetic speculation. The church is called to weigh prophecy (1 Cor 14:29), for, given our fallenness, prophetic words are normally more or less words from God, not the pure word. According to 1 John 4:1, Christians are not to trust every spirit, as not all are the Holy Spirit. Finally, in Revelation, "Jezebel" "calls herself a prophetess," functioning within the church (Rev 2:20), and the beast "out of the earth" (Rev 13:11), who persecutes the church, is called a false prophet (Rev 19:20). All of this shows the need for knowing the criteria for testing prophecy.

The angel in this verse notes that he and the Christians "hold to the testimony of Jesus" and that this same "testimony" is "the spirit of prophecy." That is, it is by this testimony or witness that one can discern the genuine prophetic Spirit. But what is "the testimony [or witness] of Jesus"? The phrase itself occurs several times in Revelation (Rev 1:2, 9; 12:17; 19:10; 20:4), while a related phrase occurs in Revelation 17:6. There are two interpretations of it. In the first, it is the testimony or witness that Jesus bore to God in his life and teaching, carrying that witness to the point of death and still bearing it from his exalted place in heaven. In support of this interpretation we see that Jesus is called the "faithful witness" (Rev 1:5; 3:14), and the whole book of Revelation is referred to as his testimony through his angel (Rev 22:16). The second interpretation is that this is a testimony about Jesus that one makes by conforming to his commands and confessing one's allegiance and his truth with one's mouth. In support of this we note those who are called witnesses or who give testimony, such as Antipas (Rev 2:13), the martyrs (Rev 6:9), the two witnesses (Rev 11:3) and the victors (Rev 12:11).

Given that both of the meanings are supported in the text, we may have created a false dichotomy between them, although the accent in the "testimony of Jesus" passages appears to fall on the latter rather than the former meaning. What Jesus witnessed to in his life and death is precisely what faithful Christians are to witness to in theirs. A true testimony to Jesus means obedience to his commands and faithfulness to his teaching. And, as Jesus openly confessed his allegiance to his Father, so the true Christian openly acknowledges faithfulness to Jesus. Life and word go together; the Christian who does not live like Jesus is a contradiction in terms, as is the idea of a secret Christian. Thus we see in Revelation 17:6 that the saints (not just the best of them) bore testimony to Jesus. In Revelation 12:17 to "obey God's commandments" is the equivalent of holding to "the testimony of Jesus." In Revelation 1:2, 9; 20:4 the "testimony of Jesus" is a parallel idea to "the word of God." The true Word of God, of course, was incarnate in Jesus (according to Jn 1), came through Jesus and is about Jesus.

That "the testimony of Jesus is the spirit of prophecy," then, means that true prophecy inspired of the Holy Spirit will be in conformity to the life and teaching of Jesus (who was himself in conformity with the rest of the Word of God) and will ultimately point to Jesus. By this standard one may evaluate both the life and the words of a prophet. Revelation itself, then, is on the one hand an attempt to uphold the standards that Jesus taught and lived (such as its call to watching; its rejection of compromise with the world; its demanding that God alone be worshiped; and its rejection of sexual immorality) and on the other hand a call to value the redemption by his blood, live in accordance with his faithfulness unto death, and expect his final victory as King of kings and Lord of lords. While addressed to human beings in seven churches, its ultimate focus is Jesus. It does indeed pass its own test.

In a time when the church is rediscovering the gift of prophecy, then, this verse is very relevant.[2] It is not the messenger who should be honored, but the giver of the message, Jesus himself. He becomes the standard by which all is measured. It is Jesus who clearly distinguishes between John and Jezebel, between the true spirit of prophecy and the spirit of the antichrist. Thus the true prophet is that prophet who lives like Jesus, teaches in harmony with Jesus and points others to Jesus as their Lord and King.

---

[1]Scholars also have believed that some of Paul's sayings and (more controversially) some of Jesus' sayings in the Gospels are the products of Christian prophets, but since none of these are actually called prophecy, even the most sure of them must be classed as disputed in terms of being prophecy. We will therefore keep our focus on what is actually called prophecy.

[2]Note, for example, Wayne Grudem, *The Gift of Prophecy in the New Testament and Today* (Westchester, Ill.: Crossway, 1988); Clifford Hill, *Prophecy Past and Present* (Crowborough, U.K.: Highland Books, 1989); and Graham Houston, *Prophecy: A Gift for Today?* (Downers Grove, Ill.: InterVarsity Press, 1989). Of the three, Hill's is the best, but all of them advocate a role for prophecy (meaning a direct word from God, not simply inspired exegetical preaching) today, and two of them have the imprimatur of no less than F. F. Bruce and I. Howard Marshall, indicating these scholars' positive evaluation of their solid exegetical basis.

20:2 Bound for a Thousand Years?

The setting is the end of the great period of persecution and the judgment of God. The war with the forces of evil has been fought and won by the rider on the white horse who is called "Faithful and True." Then comes the scene of which Revelation 20:2 is a part. What does it mean that the devil is bound for a thousand years? Why put him in prison rather than destroy him, and why for a mere thousand years? What does this time period have to do with "the millennium," and what does that term signify anyway?

This verse is another of those places in Revelation in which there appear to be two levels of conflict. In Revelation 12 we saw that there was a conflict in heaven between Michael and the dragon (Satan) and a parallel conflict on earth between the dragon and the saints. Here there is a conflict on earth in the physical realm between the exalted Christ, returning visibly as king, and the pseudo-Christ, "the beast," and his "unholy spirit," the "false prophet" (Rev 19:19-20). Both enemies have been summarily dealt with (they are tossed into the lake of fire, or hell) and their army has been destroyed by a word from Christ. All of that happens on a very physical level. But there is still the matter of the devil who inspired and embodied himself in "the beast" (Rev 13:1). Now we shift to the spiritual plane (although not to heaven, for the dragon was cast out of heaven in Rev 12).

In this prophecy Satan is taken captive by an angel, bound with a chain for one thousand years, tossed into the Abyss, the prison of evil spirits, and locked and sealed in. At the end of this period he is again released, again foments a rebellion among human beings on earth (although now in the tribes outside the Roman Empire), and in the end not only loses his army, but is himself tossed into the lake of fire, where he will remain forever (Rev 20:7-10).

"The millennium," then, refers to this thousand-year Satan-free period during which at least the martyrs are resurrected and reign with Christ on earth (Rev 20:4-6). The question that remains is how to interpret this information. There are three fundamentally different positions on the millennium. The first, the postmillennial view, interprets this passage as a look back on history. It sees the millennium as the period at the end of history that ushers in the reign of Christ. At times this is viewed as a spiritual rule of Christ through the triumph of the gospel and at times as a literal period of one thousand years characterized by the triumph of kingdom values at the end of time. The point is that the physical return of Christ comes at the end of the millennium.

The second, the amillennial view, does not really believe in no millennium (which is what "amillennial" should mean etymologically), but in a spiritual millennium. The binding of Satan has been accomplished during the lifetime of Jesus (see Mt 12:29; Lk 10:18; Jn 12:31; Col 2:15). During the age of the church Christ reigns in heaven and the power of Satan is limited in that he cannot stop the spread of the gospel. The first resurrection is the spiritual resurrection of the person's soul coming to life upon conversion. Therefore the millennial period (the thousand years being symbolic of a long time) overlaps the church age, the rebellion in Revelation 20:7-10 being essentially the same as that in Revelation 19:19-21.

The third position, the premillennial view, argues that the text should be taken at face value to indicate an actual period of time, during which Christ reigns and Satan is unable to deceive the nations. This fits with both the New Testament concept that Satan is alive and active on earth during the present age (see Lk 22:3; Acts 5:3; 2 Cor 4:3-4; 11:14; Eph 2:2; 1 Thess 2:18; 2 Tim 2:26;

1 Pet 5:8) and a common idea found in Jewish apocalyptic. For example, the pseudepigraphical book *2 Enoch* mentions the idea that there are seven thousand-year periods to world history, the last being a thousand-year sabbath when God returns (*2 Enoch* 32:2—33:2). A similar idea is found in a passage in the Talmud (*b. Sanhedrin* 97b) and in the early Christian *Epistle of Barnabas* (*Barnabas* 15). Other Jewish works reveal a belief in a shorter millennium (four hundred years or even just forty years) or mention no millennium. In the rest of the New Testament only one other passage (1 Cor 15:23-28) may indicate two stages in the overcoming of evil, but of course the interpretation of this passage is also disputed. At the same time, no New Testament passage excludes this view.

In John's view the millennium consists of several elements. First, Satan is bound so that he cannot deceive the nations (Rev 20:3). Second, the martyrs are resurrected and reign with Christ (Rev 20:4-7). This means that the armies destroyed in Revelation 19:21 are in fact armies, not all the people alive. The population of the earth not destroyed in the final series of judgments remains alive and is ruled by Christ and his martyrs. Third, the end of the period is marked by the release of the devil and his renewed deception of the nations, specifically Gog and Magog, which Ezekiel 38—39 locates in the far north (Asia Minor or beyond) and the Jewish historian Josephus identifies with the Scythians, a tribe outside the Roman Empire (*Antiquities* 1.6.1). All of the identifications appear to indicate that the nations outside of the Empire (now ruled by Christ) gather against the rightful King. Fourth, the rebellion is ended by the destruction of the opposing armies, the consignment of the devil to the lake of fire, the resurrection of all of the dead, and the final judgment (Rev 20:8-15). This is the end of the history of the earth, for the next chapter takes up the topic of the new heaven and new earth.

One might wonder why there should be a millennium. Several reasons can be given. First, it is a reward for the martyrs (or perhaps the martyrs and those who did not worship the beast, but Rev 13:15 seems to indicate that these would all be martyrs). In their faithfulness they lost their lives. Now they are rewarded with a long life, reigning with Christ. Second, it demonstrates the victory of Christ. That he holds power for a thousand years will vindicate the rule God has given him and which now is hidden in heaven. His triumph is complete. Third, it vindicates the righteous rule of God, redeeming history. Is it possible that God could not rule this earth any better than human beings (and Satan)? The millennium points to the idea that God can rule righteously and justly from within history. He does not have to simply end history. Presumably this would be when people would experience the just rulership that the world has been rejecting (and yet longing for) since the Fall.

We might further question why the antichrist and false prophet would be destroyed and Satan preserved. It is clearly not out of any love for or mercy toward Satan! The fact is that when the embodiments of satanic power have been exposed and lost their power, God has no more use for them. Their future on earth has come to an end. On the other hand, God appears to have a use for Satan, but not in the immediate future. He is used for the final probation of human beings after God has demonstrated his just rule. Thus Satan is not kept out of hell for his own sake, but is reserved for God's own good purposes (although in his own mind he surely rejects this idea). Even to the end God remains in control, including in control of Satan.

As we saw above, the millennium is symbolic for many people. But in calling it symbolic (or in calling it literal, my own preference) we must be careful to preserve the values that John expresses. The reign of Satan is doomed. He will be (or has been) chained. Christ will reign; his victory on the cross will be consummated. His martyrs will be rewarded. And rebellion against God will meet its end. These are the essence of the millennial teaching that must be preserved by any view. The test of a view is whether it best explains the data of Scripture and whether it preserves the values that John is trying to teach.

21:1 The Earth Renewed or Destroyed?

What does it mean to have a new heaven and earth? Why not simply renew or restore the present one? Why would there not be any sea in a new earth? What is the purpose of this change?

In this text we are in the period beyond the final rebellion and the final judgment. Satan is gone forever. Salvation history has totally run its course, for the King of kings has reigned over the world for one thousand years and each person has finally received his or her just reward. Now we are entering the eternal state beyond the struggles of human history.

Within this context there must be a renewal, a new setting for the now purified human race, an earth free from the scars of the rebellion that Satan inspired. This is a need sensed throughout the New Testament. Paul says that there is a new creation in human beings who are in Christ (2 Cor 5:17), which is in tension with the oldness of their own bodies and the rest of creation (Rom 8:19-22). Because of this he can say, "We fix our eyes not on what is seen, but on what is unseen. For what is seen is temporary, but what is unseen is eternal" (2 Cor 4:18). Peter expresses this as "looking forward to a new heaven and a new earth, the home of righteousness" (2 Pet 3:13). Now in Revelation we get a picture of that happening. As God says, "I am making everything new!" (Rev 21:5).

There are two opinions about the newness that is being described. Some scholars believe that John is only talking about a renewed heaven and earth. The old will be purified, but not destroyed. In fact, the real issue for John, they argue, is moral purification, not physical renewal, although physical restoration must also be included. This passage, then, describes a return to the goals left unrealized when humanity was driven out of Eden. To document their position, these scholars cite intertestamental literature such as *1 Enoch* 45:4-5 and 2 Esdras 7:75 (compare 2 Baruch 32:6; *1 Enoch* 72:1; 91:16), all of which speak of a renewal of creation as the expectation of the Jewish groups that the respective writers represented.

While all scholars must agree that the central issue for John is moral purification, the removal of all of the taint of sin and rebellion, some scholars look at such terms as "the first heaven and first earth had passed away" and argue that what we are talking about in this passage is a totally new creation. This appears to fit the language of Peter, who writes, "The heavens will disappear with a roar; the elements will be destroyed by fire, and the earth and everything in it will be laid bare. . . . That day will bring about the destruction of the heavens by fire, and the elements will melt in the heat" (2 Pet 3:10, 12). In other words, according to this view, the heavens and earth are so polluted that what is needed is something like the Genesis flood, a destruction and re-creation, but this time the destruction is done by fire, not water. This second position appears to fit the language of Revelation best. Thus while the goal is the moral purification of the world, the moral and the physical are so intertwined (which we are perhaps beginning to understand in our ecological consciousness) that this requires a major physical overhaul, one so extreme that it is called a new creation.

The heavens that are destroyed are not the abode of God (sometimes referred to as the third or seventh heaven) but the observable heavens. Genesis 1:1 describes the creation as "the heavens and the earth." Not just the planet, but all of creation has been polluted by sin. The whole will be remade. In this new creation there will be no sea. Having lived in Vancouver, Canada, I have a love for the sea, the scene of many happy holiday hours, a place of rest, but I must put aside such romantic feelings when I come to read Scripture, for that was not the Jewish view of the sea. In Scripture the sea is normally a negative image. For example, Isaiah 57:20 says, "The wicked are like the tossing sea, which cannot rest, whose waves cast up mire and mud." The sea is also the chaos of water out of which the heaven and earth were originally separated in Genesis 1:2, 6-10. While it is a creation of God (Ps 104:26), the sea is also the home of the sea monster Leviathan, whom God conquers and casts on dry land (Ps 74:13-14). It is no wonder that the pseudepigraphal Jewish work *The Testament of Moses* 10:6 states that when God comes at the end of the age the sea will retire into the Abyss. In Revelation the sea is the source of the beast and the throne of the great prostitute (Rev 13:1; 17:1). Such a symbol of chaos and the powers of evil could not exist in a new heaven and earth.

The new heavens and new earth likewise have a new city, the new Jerusalem. While this is not the place for detailed comment, it is true that here also there is something new. In Scripture the first cities are built by evil people (Gen 4:17; 10:10; 11:1-9). The old Jerusalem was the place in which God chose to put his name, but it was also an unfaithful city, which John could call "Sodom and Egypt" (Rev 11:8). Therefore there is now a need for a fulfillment of what sinful human beings could not produce, the true city with a God-centered community in which peace and justice are actually present.

This whole passage, then, speaks of the fulfillment of the hopes and dreams of humanity in the new creation. Human beings were created to live on earth, so a new earth will be their home. Human beings were created for fellowship with God, so he will dwell in their midst. Human beings were created for community, so a true city will be established. There is certainly a lot of symbolism in what is going on in this passage, yet the symbolism is symbolism of a new reality that straight prosaic description could not capture.

Whether or not the new heaven and earth are a renewal or a new creation, Revelation witnesses to the fact that the universe as we know it is temporal and "will all wear out like a garment" (Heb 1:11-12). Even should we interpret John as saying that the basic structure of the earth remains, he witnesses to a renewal so complete that human culture and creations have been wiped away. History as we know it has come to an end. God is beginning a new chapter in a new history, his eternal history. Yet at the same time human beings are not spirit. They are creatures with bodies, now resurrected and glorified. They do not live on clouds, but in a world and in a city. God provides for them what he designed them for in creation, a home on earth. It is not Eden, but a step beyond Eden, a more perfect development of what might have been, a new earth with a city with God in the midst. It answers an inner longing of the human heart, so it is fitting that John brings the narrative of his book to a close with this description of hope.

22:18-19 Protecting the Canon?

The canon of Scripture is both an emotional issue and a theological problem. It is a problem because the New Testament never speaks of such a canon (which is natural because while it was being written it was only in the process of becoming a canon). It is an emotional issue because, as the only authoritative document of the Christian faith (in Protestant eyes), anything that might add to or detract from Scripture is highly threatening. This emotion and this theology surrounds the end of Revelation. These verses come just before the close of the book. The question that they raise is, To what is John referring? Is "this book" a reference to the book of Revelation or to the Bible as a whole? Why did John write these words? What threat to "this book" would he have perceived?

The New Testament was written in a time before readily accessible libraries, communications media and printing presses. Virtually all of the teaching of that period was done orally, for few could read. For this reason John pronounces a blessing on "the one [singular] who reads" the book (out loud to the congregation) and "those [plural] who hear it and take to heart what is written in it" (Rev 1:3). This process of reading such books out loud in a house church (in which the reader might be the only one who could read) would make it very easy to leave out parts of a book being read or to add to it what one wished. It would be difficult for most church members to discover the differences.

John was not the only prophet during the New Testament period to be concerned with proper preservation of his message. Paul was concerned that his message might be falsified by people bringing another gospel (Gal 1:6-9) or a prophecy or a forged letter purporting to be from him (2 Thess 2:2). There was, then, the possibility that, besides the corruption that could be put into the text in reading it, people could deliberately add their own prophetic vision to the text or edit it according to their own perception of what the author should have said.

This type of problem was not unknown in the Old Testament. Deuteronomy 4:2 and 12:32 insist that the Law must be preserved without adding to it or subtracting from it. Later, according to the tradition in the Letter of Aristeas, when the Pentateuch was translated into Greek, those receiving the new translation pronounced a curse upon anyone making any alteration to the text. These verses in Revelation are also a curse, and in placing this curse John is similarly protecting the integrity of his writing and may in fact be thinking of it on a level with Scripture, although a similar curse was also reportedly used by Irenaeus in one of his writings.[1]

John, then, or perhaps Jesus speaking through John (since it is the revelation of Jesus Christ), places a curse to protect the document from well-intentioned or even sinister tampering. The curse itself has two parts. One protects the document from being added to on the threat of the person doing so receiving the plagues written about earlier in the book. The other protects the document from being subtracted from on the threat of the person losing his or her place in heaven, that is, their losing their place in the tree of life (the source of eternal life) and the holy city, the new Jerusalem. The curses are somewhat stylized and strong, as was the custom in the language of the day, so it would not be wise to draw theology from them (for example, as to whether one can or cannot lose one's place in the holy city). But the author intended them as real curses.

The question arises, then, as to whether these curses have to do with anything more than this one book. Do they include the whole New Testament or the whole Bible? Is this a notice closing the canon? We must answer these questions in the negative.

First, we are not certain that Revelation was the last book of the New Testament to be written. Some date Revelation as early as A.D. 68, placing other writings (such as 2 Peter, Jude, or the Gospel and Epistles of John) much later. It would be unwise to base an argument on an uncertain dating.

Second, at the time John wrote the Jews might not have been finished discussing their own canon issues. During the period between A.D. 70 and 90 some discussions about canon took place in the rabbinic center in Jamnia. While there is no evidence that the shape of the canon changed as a result of this discussion, it does show that even the Jews were in something of a state of flux on the matter and could discuss whether certain books (such as Esther) should be included.

Third, John wrote before there was any clear sense of a New Testament canon. There is no evidence that John had ever seen a written Gospel or a collection of Paul's letters. In fact, it would be at least two more centuries before a fixed selection of works would be considered the Christian canon. Some of the works that would be considered seriously and then rejected, such as the *Epistle of Barnabas* and the Didache, had not yet been written.

Finally, while in most modern versions of Scripture Revelation is the last book (even Luther had it last, although he and some of the early English translations put Hebrews, James and the Petrine literature just before it), that was not the case in the earliest period. There was a good deal of shifting in the first three centuries, some people rejecting Revelation, some putting works such as *1-2 Clement* after it, and some putting it earlier in their list of canonical books. There is no reason to think that this verse would have come almost at the end of the Bible for most Christians until the fourth century.

This does not mean that it is a good thing to add to or subtract from the Scripture. Certainly, even if the proverbial "lost letter of Paul" were found, not to mention some work of a more modern time that people thought might be inspired, it would take the universal consensus of the church that it were inspired to add it to the Scripture, a most unlikely event and thus a miracle in itself.[2] Nor should tampering with the present books themselves be done lightly. We do live in an age when some people wish to rewrite the Bible from their own ideological perspective. The only effect of this process is a distortion of Scripture and the production of a work that no one recognizes as canon. It would be better to write a separate work or a commentary selectively criticizing the existing Scripture, for either approach would be more honest. Even the scriptural authors themselves, when they wanted to reinterpret one another (as Daniel, for example, does to Jeremiah's seventy weeks), did not change the original but wrote their own book.

Therefore John's curse stands as a warning. Its true literal sense applies only to his own book, Revelation, but given that similar concerns were shared by Paul and others it is reasonable to argue that none of the writers of Scripture would have agreed to tampering with their works. Besides, such tampering would defeat the whole purpose of Scripture. The Scripture stands written as a witness to the revelation received in a given place and time. It is to be read, accepted (or, for some, rejected) and interpreted. To rewrite it, however, is to confuse one's own experience of God (or perhaps experience of something other than God) with that of the scriptural authors. It is to take the measuring line of Scripture (which is what *canon* means) and bend it to fit the wall that one is building in the present. In the end one has neither a measuring line nor a straight wall. It may not be the curse of John that one receives, but the resulting confusion will be curse enough and may in fact make one miss having a place in the holy city about which John wrote so glowingly.

---

[1]See Eusebius *Ecclesiastical History* 5.20.2 for a reference to this ending of a lost letter of Irenaeus.

[2]Universal consensus means just that. While we might argue about whether some Christian fringe groups (such as certain Christian groups in Africa or the remnants of ancient heretical groups) should be included in such a consensus, it must at least include the basic Protestant (that is, most Protestant denominations), Roman Catholic and Orthodox branches. Who could conceive of these groups agreeing on anything, let alone that a given book was inspired by God?

Subject Index

Scripture Index

Pages numbers in ***bold italic*** indicate where principal discussions of hard sayings may be found in the text.

Old Testament

Genesis

Who Wrote What

Walter C. Kaiser Jr. wrote all the articles on Old Testament hard sayings. He also wrote the following introductory articles: chapter four ("Why Don't Bible Genealogies Always Match Up?"), chapter five ("Aren't Many Old Testament Numbers Wrong?"), chapter six ("Do the Dates of the Old Testament Kings Fit Secular History?"), chapter seven ("Does Archaeology Support Bible History?"), chapter eight ("When the Prophets Say, 'The Word of the LORD Came to Me,' What Do They Mean?") and chapter nine ("Are Old Testament Prophecies Really Accurate?").

Peter H. Davids wrote all the articles on New Testament hard sayings that are not specifically attributed to F. F. Bruce or Manfred T. Brauch. He also wrote the following introductory articles: chapter one ("How Do We Know Who Wrote the Bible?"), chapter two ("Can We Believe in Miracles?"), chapter three ("Why Does God Seem So Angry in the Old Testament and Loving in the New?"), chapter ten ("Why Doesn't the New Testament Always Quote the Old Testament Accurately?"), chapter eleven ("Are the New Testament Accounts of Demons True?") and chapter twelve ("Why Are There Four Different Gospels?").

F. F. Bruce wrote the articles on the following Gospel verses: Matthew 5:17-20, 22, 28, 29, 34, 39, 44, 48; 6:13, 24; 7:6; 10:5-6, 23, 34; 11:27; 16:18-19; 18:35; 19:12; 20:14-15; 22:12, 14; 23:9, 33; 25:11-12; Mark 2:10, 17, 27-28; 3:28-29; 4:11-12; 5:39; 7:27; 8:33, 34; 9:1, 50; 10:11-12, 18, 21, 25, 31; 11:14, 23; 12:17; 13:30; 14:22-24, 61-62; 15:34; Luke 5:39; 7:28; 9:60, 62; 10:18; 11:23, 29-30; 12:4-5, 49, 50; 14:26; 15:25-28; 16:9, 16, 26; 17:37; 18:8; 20:8; 22:36; John 6:53.

Manfred T. Brauch wrote the articles on the following verses from Paul's letters: Romans 1:18; 5:12, 20; 6:2, 7; 7:14-19; 8:28; 9:13-15; 10:4; 11:26, 32; 12:20; 13:1-7; 14:15; 1 Corinthians 3:17; 5:5; 6:9-10; 7:1, 10, 12, 20, 29; 8:5-6; 11:3, 7, 10, 29; 14:5, 33-34; 15:29; 2 Corinthians 3:14; 5:17; 6:14; Galatians 1:9; 5:2; 6:16; Ephesians 4:9-10; 5:22; Philippians 2:12-13; 3:4-6; Colossians 1:15, 24; 1 Thessalonians 2:14-15; 2 Thessalonians 2:3, 7; 1 Timothy 2:11-12, 13-15; 5:8, 23; Titus 1:12-13.

About the Authors

Walter C. Kaiser Jr. is Colman M. Mockler Distinguished Professor of Old Testament at Gordon-Conwell Theological Seminary in South Hamilton, Massachusetts. For many years he served as professor of Old Testament and as dean and vice president for education at Trinity Evangelical Divinity School. A frequent speaker at churches, camps and conferences, he has written numerous books, including *Toward an Exegetical Theology, Toward an Old Testament Theology, Toward Old Testament Ethics* and *The Messiah in the Old Testament.*

Peter H. Davids is On-site Director of the Schloss Mittersill Study Center in Austria and has taught biblical studies at such institutions as Regent College in Vancouver and Canadian Theological Seminary in Regina, Saskatchewan. He is the author of commentaries on James and 1 Peter.

F. F. Bruce was for many years prior to his death the Rylands Professor of Biblical Criticism and Exegesis at the University of Manchester in England. He was the author of numerous biblical commentaries and other books, including *The Canon of Scripture, New Testament History, Paul: Apostle of the Heart Set Free* and *The New Testament Documents: Are They Reliable?*

Manfred T. Brauch is professor of biblical theology and president of Eastern Baptist Theological Seminary near Philadelphia.